American Foreign Policy in the Nuclear Age

Fourth Edition

Cecil V. Crabb, Jr.
Louisiana State University

HARPER & ROW, PUBLISHERS, New York
Cambridge, Philadelphia, San Francisco,
London, Mexico City, São Paulo, Sydney

1817

Sponsoring Editor: Ted C. Ricks
Project Coordinators: Betsy Feist Associates/A Good Thing Inc.
Production Manager: Marion A. Palen
Compositor: A Graphic Method, Inc.
Printer and Binder: R. R. Donnelley & Sons Company

**American
Foreign Policy
in the
Nuclear Age,**
Fourth Edition

Library of Congress Cataloging in Publication Data

Crabb, Cecil Van Meter, 1924–
     American foreign policy in the nuclear age.

     Bibliography: p.
     Includes index.
     1. United States—Foreign relations—1945–
2. United States—Foreign relations administration.
3. World politics—1945–   . I. Title.
JK1417.C695   1983   327.73   82-9384
ISBN 0-06-041391-3   AACR2

Contents

Preface

The fourth edition of this book entails the most complete revision of the work undertaken since the first edition was published in 1960. The success of previous editions has encouraged me to believe that the basic organizational format is sound, and with some modifications it has been retained here.

For this edition, all the chapters have been extensively rewritten with several goals in mind. A leading goal has been to take account of recent studies of international relations and American foreign relations and to incorporate relevant findings here. Another objective has been to make the discussion of American foreign policy as up to date as possible. Almost every chapter, for example, draws upon the diplomatic experience encountered by the Reagan Administration in its attempt to address problems in the foreign policy field. An additional goal has been to shorten the discussion: the number of chapters has been reduced, and in most instances the length of individual chapters has also been condensed.

As in earlier editions, the chapters are almost equally divided between those that focus upon the American foreign policy process and those that deal with substantive issues confronting the United States abroad. Our analysis of the foreign policy process (Chapters 1 through 8) begins with an examination of the setting, objectives, and means of American foreign policy. Here and in other chapters, considerable emphasis has been given to the impact of the Vietnam War upon American attitudes and behavior in foreign relations. At the same time, more recent developments—such as the impact of the Iranian Revolution and of the Soviet invasion of Afghanistan upon the diplomatic conduct of the United States—also receive detailed attention. Chapter 2 identifies and explains certain deep-seated ideas, traditions, and values shaping the viewpoints and behavior patterns of Americans in external affairs.

In Chapter 3, the presidency is identified as the "focal point" of the foreign policy process. The sweeping and decisive powers available to the chief executive for managing foreign relations are examined in detail. The concluding section of the chapter deals with the perennial question of whether, in the foreign policy realm, the presidential office has become "imperial" or "imperiled."

Two related issues provide the focus of Chapter 4: the "decline" of the State Department as the preeminent executive agency in foreign relations; and the emergence of a host of other executive agencies that sometimes eclipse State Department influence in the conduct of foreign affairs. The central theme of Chapter 5 is the concept of "national security," including a discussion of its meaning and of institutional mechanisms designed to achieve this goal. The paramount issue of Soviet-American military rivalry is analyzed here, along with the always controversial matter of intelligence activities carried out by a government founded upon democratic principles.

Chapter 6 calls attention to two important, but frequently neglected, aspects of American diplomacy: propaganda and informational activities abroad; and economic dimensions of foreign policy. Today, as in the past, Americans remain uncertain about the value and nature of propaganda as an instrument of foreign relations. Concurrently, to a degree unprecedented since World War II, economic questions have come to the forefront of America's relations with other countries. Accordingly, a dual dimension of that concern—the evolution and future of the foreign aid program, and the position of the United States in international trade—is treated in detail.

Chapters 7 and 8 deal with subjects whose importance was highlighted by the Vietnam War and by a number of developments in the American diplomatic record since that conflict: the roles of Congress and of public opinion, respectively, in the foreign policy process. In Chapter 7, the nature, scope, and importance of legislative prerogatives in foreign relations are analyzed; the forces producing growing congressional "activism" in foreign affairs are identified; and the overall impact of congressional initiatives upon recent and future American diplomacy is assessed. In Chapter 8, the major elements in the concept of public opinion are delineated, after which the growing influence of groups and lobbies in foreign policy decision making is evaluated. The interaction between public opinion and public policy is also examined.

The analysis of major substantive issues confronting the United States abroad begins with Chapter 9. Because of the importance of the issue—affecting, as it does, virtually every aspect of American diplomacy since World War II—two chapters are devoted to Soviet-American relations. That chapter is devoted to providing the background necessary to understand the Cold War and continuing tensions in relations between the United States and the Soviet Union. Then in Chapter 10, the central focus is upon the concept of detente between the super-powers. The significant connotations of this elusive concept—including diverse Soviet and American interpretations of it—are identified; and the factors likely to affect the future of detente in Soviet-American relations are analyzed in detail.

The chapters which follow are devoted to American foreign policy toward the major geographical regions, beginning with European-American relations in Chapter 11. The long-standing sources of disunity within the Western alliance are specified, and the future of NATO is assessed.

The subject matter of Chapter 12 is one of the most significant in the recent diplomatic experience of the United States: America's growing involvement in the affairs of the Middle East, including most recently its role as guarantor of Persian Gulf security. With the termination of the Vietnam War (if not earlier), the Middle East became perhaps the most volatile region on the globe. Responding successfully to developments in that crisis-prone area will provide a test of American diplomatic capability for many years in the future.

Sub-Saharan Africa as a problem area for American diplomacy is the dominant concern of Chapter 13. The specific issues of racial conflicts on the African continent and of Communist inroads within the region receive primary attention in this chapter.

Chapter 14 focuses on one of the most difficult and recurring problems in American foreign affairs: relations between the United States and Latin America. Ongoing revolutionary upheaval in Central America provides merely one well-publicized manifestation of that challenge. Three specific issues provide the framework of the chapter: the problem of maintaining hemispheric security; the challenge of Communism and revolutionary ferment south of the border; and the issue of military-dominated governments in Central and South America.

The final chapter is devoted to a question that was crucially affected by the Vietnam War experience and required numerous changes in the diplomacy of the United States thereafter: America's relations with Asia. Specific aspects of that general problem examined in the chapter are: the new era in Sino-American relations; recent developments in Southeast Asia; American relations with India and Pakistan; and efforts by the United States after the Vietnam conflict to serve as a "Pacific power."

A lengthy and up-to-date reading list has been included at the end of the book. It was designed specifically to assist students in compiling a bibliography for term papers and other research projects.

Finally, a portion of the concluding paragraphs from the third edition continues to be timely, and it is no less applicable to the fourth edition. Accordingly, it is reiterated here:

A conscious effort has been made in this book to present evidence and divergent points of view as objectively as possible, in full knowledge that total objectivity is unattainable (perhaps even undesirable). (Foreign policy discussions in the United States have not lacked polemical and doctrinaire utterances, slogans and simplistic formulas, distortions, emotionalism, and sometimes evident ignorance of pertinent background information.) Here, the basic goal has been to enhance student *understanding* of American foreign relations, not to reenforce prejudices, present fashionable points of view, or supply indictments of failures by public officials.

On the basis of experience in the classroom, I am convinced that greater student (and of course overall citizen) enlightenment with respect to the complexities of foreign policy decision making is an imperative need. I am no less convinced that it can be acquired only as the result of a willingness to examine the issues confronting policy makers calmly, rationally, and with a receptive mind. On controversial issues (like the origins and causes of the Cold War), I never ask students to "agree" with my interpretation or any other particular point of view. I do expect that they will familiarize themselves with diverse interpretations.

Acknowledgments

The author of any textbook is always greatly indebted to the contributions of others—none perhaps so much as the author of a comprehensive treatment of American foreign policy. While it is impossible to thank all those individually who have contributed directly or indirectly to this revision, a special debt is owed to a number of individuals without whose assistance this edition would not have been possible.

The countless scholars and informed observers who have written about various aspects of American foreign relations have provided a reservoir of data and insights from which I have drawn freely. In many instances, their contributions are acknowledged specifically in the documentation.

My colleagues at Louisiana State University and at other institutions have offered valuable ideas, suggestions, and criticisms, many of which were incorporated in this revision.

Among the hundreds of students who have used earlier editions of this book, a number have taken the time and trouble to communicate their reactions to it. They may be assured that their responses were seriously considered; and, in many instances, this edition reflects their viewpoints.

Under the supervision of the Director, George J. Guidry, Jr., and the Associate Director, D. W. Schneider, the staff of the Troy H. Middleton Library on the LSU campus has been unfailingly helpful and resourceful in responding to my requests for assistance. Special thanks are due to the staff of the Business Administration/Government Documents Department—Jimmie H. Hoover, Roberta A. Scull, and Milton Ternberg—for their endless patience and ingenuity in providing needed information and documentation; their efforts have gone far beyond the call of duty. The Assistant Director, Marion T. Reid, also rendered invaluable assistance in solving problems related to publication of the fourth edition.

Typing assistance was provided by a number of individuals. Characteristically, the able and experienced departmental secretary, Josephine Scurria, played an essential role in preparing th manuscript for publication. Several graduate students—notably, Wayne Guillory and Najoua Handal—assumed a major responsibility for preparing the extended bibliography included at the end of the book.

As in the past, my devoted and capable wife, Harriet, has endured the process of publishing "another book" with infinite patience and fortitude. Moreover, she has contributed to this edition in innumerable ways—most directly, perhaps, by reading and criticizing portions of the manuscript, and by skillfully reading galley and page proofs.

Indispensable as they are, the contributions of others cannot relieve an author of ultimate responsibility for errors of fact and judgment appearing in his work. These are mine alone, and I assume full responsibility for them.

Cecil V. Crabb, Jr.

Chapter 1

Foundations of American Foreign Policy

A meaningful discussion of American foreign policy must take account initially of the broad context within which the United States formulates its external goals and maintains a variety of relationships with other nations. This chapter and the one which follows attempt to provide that context. In this chapter, we shall examine America's role as a member of the contemporary international system. In Chapter 2, the focus is upon what is sometimes described as "national character" or "national style": those historical, ideological, and other influences which combine to produce a distinctively "American approach" to foreign relations. An implicit premise of Chapter 2 is that nearly all American attitudes and official polices toward the outside world are heavily conditioned by certain *unique influences*. If these are ignored or minimized, our understanding of international political relationships will inevitably be distorted and incomplete.

The United States in the International System

The Concept of the Global System

A useful starting point for our study of American foreign policy is recognition that the United States is (along with the Soviet Union) one of two superpowers belonging to an *international political system,* consisting of approximately 150 independent nations (or "national actors," as they are designated in systems theory). In recent years, students of international politics have devoted increasing attention to the concept of the international system and to the role of systemic influences upon the foreign policies of its members.[1]

Examples of systems are available on all sides. There is a planetary system to which the earth belongs. The human body is another system, consisting of several interacting and mutually supporting subsystems (e.g., the circulatory system, the nervous system, the skeletal system). What precisely is a "system"? Numerous, and sometimes elaborate and highly technical, definitions of the concept are available. In its most essential terms, however, a system may be defined as *a continuing interaction among a set of objects whose relationships are governed by some regulative principle (or principles).**

For a system to exist, three elements are thus essential to it. First, there must be *a set of objects or members* of the system. In the case of the international system (or its component subsystems), the members are usually nation-states (called, in the nomenclature of systems theory, "national actors"). But today, more than in any era in history perhaps, it is essential to recognize the existence of certain "non-state actors"—like guerrilla and terroristic organizations, and multinational business corporations—whose activities cut across national boundaries and which operate wholly, or in large part, independently of national governments.[2]

Second, the members of the system must *interact* and have *continuing relationships* with one another. According to its advocates, systems theory thus permits the student of international politics to focus upon the *regular and recurrent* interactions among its parts, rather than upon the isolated and nonrecurrent behavior of its members, as was characteristic of older and more traditional approaches to the subject. Members of the international system may interact regularly for innumerable reasons, such as promoting mutual security and well-being. Most fundamentally, perhaps, they engage in continuous interaction because they are increasingly aware of their *mutual interdependence* and their common destiny on the planet.

Third, this interaction *is dictated and regulated by certain principles or purposes.* A clock, for example, comprises a system of interdependent parts—all designed to function smoothly in order to provide an accurate indication of the time. The systems approach to international politics rests upon the assumption that the operation of the global system is governed by some comparable principle or purpose. Little unanimity exists among proponents of systems theory, however, concerning the nature of such regulative principles, beyond the idea of "systems maintenance" or the notion that the tendency of the system is to perpetuate itself and to resist impulses that would fundamentally alter its nature.† To assert, however, that the primary regulative principle governing the operation of the international system is systems maintenance leaves a number of unanswered questions and unre-

---

*An even simpler definition is the conception of the system offered by Legg and Morrison: "a system is any two or more phenomena (or objects) that interact over time." See Keith R. Legg and James F. Morrison, *Politics and the International System: An Introduction* (New York: Harper & Row, 1971), pp. 21–22. In Joseph Frankel, *Contemporary International Theory and Behaviour of States* (New York: Oxford University Press, 1973), p. 34, a "system" is defined as "anything formed of parts placed together or adjusted into a regular and connected whole ...." This same study cautions that systems theorists deal in "ideal types"—that is, "models" or conceptions of the international system which have no actual counterpart in real life—and it finds considerable variation among devotees of systems theory concerning the meaning of a "system."

†All systems are in a constant state of change and adaptation as a result of certain "variables" or influential forces operating within it. If the forces producing change are strong enough, there may be what is called "system transformation"—that is, either an existing system is replaced by another one, or the existing system may disintegrate completely. According to systems theory, the actors in any given system supposedly endeavor to preserve the system as it is or to engage in "systems maintenance." The problem again, however, is to avoid the kind of circular conclusion which says, in effect: a system is maintained until it is not maintained any longer; or actors prefer the existing system until their preferences for some reason change and they desire a different kind of system.

solved problems. For example, it may come dangerously close to the kind of circular reasoning which says: International systems exist to promote the existence of international systems! Alternatively, the concept of systems maintenance may translate into little more than the familiar human instinct for self-preservation. At any rate, the underlying purpose of the international system (and of its subsystems) is a question which generates continuing controversy both among members of the system and among students of international politics.

A key idea implicit in systems theory is that the relationship among the members of the international system is *continuous and ongoing*. On that assumption, the discrete and specific actions of states become meaningful because they fit into *patterns of regularized behavior,* which systems theory attempts to identify and evaluate.

These patterns have certain common ingredients. An important one is *memory,* whereby national actors obtain, sort, classify, store, and retrieve information required for effective decision making. (The concept of memory is useful to illustrate how the role of a particular agency—the Central Intelligence Agency—involved in the American foreign policy process might be analyzed from the viewpoint of systems theory vis-à-vis more traditional approaches. Proponents of systems theory view the CIA as but one among several agencies in the American government playing a key role in the "memory" stage of foreign policy decision making. We shall refer to this agency more fully in Chapter 5.)

Decision making—the series of steps involved in arriving at a decision leading to a particular action or policy—is another pivotal stage in systems theory. As some proponents of this approach see it, decision making is the common denominator or function of *all governments,* irrespective of their ideological or institutional differences; and all governments arrive at decisions by a sequence of comparable steps or stages. On this premise a vast literature exists in which the process of decision making is explained in all its complexity.[3]

Two other closely related concepts in systems theory are policy *inputs* and policy *outputs*. All systems experience inputs, defined as injection into the system of information, ideas, resources, and other factors influencing decisions reached. As is evident, the list of such inputs is virtually endless, which is one reason systems theory is sometimes characterized by a bewildering complexity. An analysis of post-World War II American policy from the systems theory perspective, for example, would regard the following as among the more influential inputs affecting the decision-making process: the American diplomatic tradition; the nature of the American constitutional system; the nature of the American two-party system and the impact of partisan controversies on foreign policy issues; the number and activities of innumerable interest groups in American society, which sometimes lobby intensively on foreign policy questions; the involvement of a growing number of executive departments in the foreign policy process; the nature of American public opinion and the forces shaping popular attitudes toward the outside world; the "perceptions" which policy makers have of the external world and the extent to which these perceptions accord (or do not accord) with reality.[4] This is in no sense an exhaustive list of the topics which must be included in any analysis of the principal inputs influencing the decision-making process in the United States. It is merely illustrative of the major influences determining American foreign policy.

Another problem with regard to policy inputs is posed by the determination of *their relative weight or influence* in the decision-making process. For example, it is easy to assert, and to document the contention, that public attitudes have been a significant element affecting postwar American foreign policy toward the Middle East (particularly toward Israel). It is an infinitely more difficult problem to determine the *relative* influence of public opinion on American Middle Eastern policy vis-à-vis a long list of other possible influences including: growing public and official recognition of the crucial importance of Middle East oil; concern in the United States about the growth of Communist influence in the region; Washington's desire to preserve regional stability. In some instances, even policy makers themselves would have difficulty explaining the relative weight that some of these factors have had on American diplomacy.

Some influential policy inputs are well-nigh incalculable and defy objective measurement. As an example, during World War II President Franklin D. Roosevelt (one of the most skilled political tacticians in American history) had unbounded confidence in his ability to "charm" and manipulate the Soviet dictator, Joseph Stalin. This personal behavior trait of FDR's crucially affected both the substance and style of American diplomacy during that period. Over two decades later, both Presidents Lyndon B. Johnson and Richard M. Nixon were personally convinced that the honor and prestige of the United States —along with their own "credibility" as chief executives—were at stake in the outcome of the Vietnam War. This was a highly influential factor in determining American policy toward Southeast Asia. In dealing with such intangible and personal policy inputs, the devotee of systems theory faces a difficult dilemma: Attempting to assign a mathematical weight to such inputs would be a highly subjective undertaking; but ignoring them would produce an incomplete and distorted understanding of the American foreign policy process.

Once policy inputs have been carefully considered by decision makers, the result is a policy *output,* or action taken as a result of decisions reached. Thus, as the result of a complex sequence of steps during the late 1940s, the Truman Administration decided to provide massive American assistance to promote Europe's recovery from the damage inflicted by World War II. The policy output was the European Recovery Program (or Marshall Plan).

Still another leading concept in systems theory is *feedback.* In theoretical terms, feedback may be defined as new information and responses received by decision makers which are the result of policy outputs. More concretely, if the United States arrives at a decision to reach a new arms-limitation agreement with the Soviet Union (and Soviet policy makers are similarly motivated), a new treaty designed to achieve that goal will be negotiated and ratified. As time passes, policy makers in both countries will receive *feedback,* which will in turn initiate a new cycle of decision making. For officials in Washington, such feedback might consist of: photographs from space satellites and other evidence indicating Moscow's compliance (or noncompliance) with the terms of the agreement; changes in military technology which may render certain provisions of the arms-control agreement inoperable or obsolete; and perceptions by Defense Department officials, and by the American public, concerning whether the agreement has strengthened or impaired the security of the United States. On the basis of such feedback, American officials may conclude that new decisions related to arms limitation are required, leading them to modify (or possibly abandon) the original agreement.

In systems theory, the sequence we have described is sometimes referred to as the *feedback loop:* Policy *inputs* lead to policy *outputs;* policy outputs generate *feedback,* which in turn give rise to new policy inputs, leading to a new output, producing an endless repetition of the cycle.

We need to be mindful of certain limitations and defects in systems theory as an approach to international politics. Systems theory is a relatively new and currently voguish mode of analysis. As with any new approach, its devotees are sometimes prone to romanticize its ability to supply insights not provided by more traditional approaches. Systems theory has also spawned a plethora of definitions, concepts, hypotheses, and principles, some of which are extremely abstract and appear to have minimal application to the actual behavior of nations. Another limitation in the approach is the lack of empirical evidence necessary to support propositions and theories advanced about the operation of the international system. Moreover, the concept of the international system contains an intrinsic bias or distortion. Inherently, it tends to ignore (or at least to minimize) those *unique factors and forces* influencing the foreign policy of the United States and all other members of the international system. American behavior toward the Soviet Union since World War II, for example, may well have been determined more *by influences distinctive to the American society and tradition*—such as its abhorrence of political tyranny and its devotion to a capitalistic economic system—than by influences arising out of, or dictated by, membership in a particular kind of international system.

It is essential to remember also that in our era, as in earlier historical periods, the international system *is continually evolving.* Almost all students of international politics today would agree that the contemporary global system (however it is described precisely) is a *dynamic,* not a static, one. For example, approximately 100 new nations have joined the international system since the end of World War II, and in the years ahead many more "ministates" will also become members of it. Changes in regional subsystems also proceed apace. Several years ago, some commentators were convinced that the Middle East constituted a cohesive regional subsystem. Today, the existence of such a subsystem could be seriously questioned.[5]

One final cautionary word about the limitations of systems theory is in order. In describing the international systems which may be identified throughout modern history, devotees of this approach focus upon *the concept of power* as the most relevant criterion for distinguishing types of systems. Thus, before World War II, the term *balance-of-power system* described the relationship existing among the nations of the world. After World War II, the concept of *polarity* was widely employed, the assumption being that the most crucial feature of the postwar system was the way power had become "polarized," or distributed throughout the world. For many years after the war, global power was believed to be *bipolarized,* or largely monopolized by the two superpowers, the United States and the Soviet Union. By around 1960, it was evident that the old bipolar configuration had become outmoded. There was less agreement about what kind of international system had superseded the old bipolar model. As a later portion of the chapter will explain, *the concept of power is itself changing, in some ways profoundly.* Inevitably, this fact raises questions about the utility of an approach in which the concept of national power is central.

Types of International Systems

Several types of international systems have existed throughout history. Before examining them, however, we must take note of the fact that, as many informed students of international politics see it, the dominant reality about the distribution of political power through the world is its essentially *anarchistic* nature. By definition, an anarchistic pattern means that no organized system can be discerned. According to this school of thought, since no systematic distribution or organization of power exists, there is accordingly no regulative principle governing or restraining the behavior of international actors beyond their own self-interest (or their "national interest"). The prevailing configuration of global power thus approximates a kind of Hobbesian "state of nature," where, in Hobbes' graphic phraseology, life was "nasty, brutish, and short," and where individuals (in our example, national actors) engaged in a war "of every man against every man."* If this Hobbesian description of the existing environment of international politics seems exaggerated, a number of informed commentators believe the essential point remains valid: The tendency since World War II has been toward a condition of *global anarchy,* or such a widespread diffusion of power among the members of the system that any "structure" or organized pattern in the distribution of global power is almost totally lacking. Thus in 1979, President Jimmy Carter's principal national security adviser said that "the real danger to today's world is that the conflicting aspirations of man will create massive global chaos and fragmentation" throughout the international system.[6] Still other commentators have called for the creation of an "international community" as a substitute for the anarchistic and ethnocentric pattern of relationships which has characterized international politics for many centuries.[7]

*Thomas Hobbes (1588–1679) was an English philosopher who was a spokesman for the concept of the "divine right of kings." In his major work *Leviathan* (or "the state"), Hobbes justified the existence and maintenance of strong central government within the state as a necessity for checking the egocentric and anarchistic impulses of human society. On the international level, the logical extension of Hobbes' ideas is a global political authority, or world government.

This point of view—that no international system in fact exists, and that the concept of the "global system" is, at best, a mental construct or methodological tool—is based upon considerable evidence. National compliance with international law (especially with regard to issues likely to engender violent conflicts among states) remains exceptional and largely voluntary. The post-World War II period has witnessed a resurgence of *nationalism* and of state behavior dictated by nationalistic goals and ambitions. The experience of the United Nations—and of various regional institutions like the Organization of American States (OAS) or the Organization of African Unity (OAU)—in preserving peace and security has not been impressive. The two superpowers continue to expand and improve their military arsenals, while expenditures for armaments by most of the other nations of the world continue to escalate. As we shall see, this problem—the apparent lack of structure or pattern in the relationship among states today—has clearly become progressively acute as the system has evolved from the era of bipolarity into an infinitely more complex nexus of global political relationships (sometimes called multipolarity).

According to systems theorists, several kinds of international systems may be identified (actually or theoretically).[8] We shall confine our attention here only to those which have existed in recent international politics and to those whose potential for future existence seems high. We begin with an analysis of the *classical balance-of-power system* which emerged in Europe during the eighteenth century and existed for almost two centuries until the First World War. Although a number of local and regional conflicts (today we would call them "limited wars") erupted during this period, the balance-of-power system successfully prevented a global war for a century after 1815.[9]

The classical balance-of-power system had several noteworthy characteristics enabling it to operate effectively. The system was confined *to Europe:* Its dominant actors or decision makers were European nation-states. (As in the Western colonial empires, other societies were the *objects* of decisions made by European states, but almost never decision makers themselves.) During the heyday of the balance-of-power system, the United States was devoted to an isolationist posture in foreign relations. China was extremely backward and immersed in internal political upheavals. Not until the late nineteenth century did Japan begin to emerge as an influential regional and global power.

The European actors in the balance-of-power system were also members *of Christendom:* They shared a common heritage of metaphysical and ethical values derived from the Judeo-Christian tradition. These actors were also united by ties of kinship among their ruling aristocracies, leading them to *support aristocratic political principles and institutions.*

Still another salient feature of the balance-of-power system was the fact that the number of influential members of it was *extremely limited.* A handful of nations—Great Britain, France, Prussia, Austria, Russia, and (for part of this period) Italy—constituted the effective decision makers within it. Decisions made by European actors (and the present-day boundaries of black Africa provide an example) determined the future of many non-Western societies for decades ahead.

Great Britain's role in the operation of the balance-of-power system was unique. Britain played the role of "balancer" in the system: Adhering to the policy of the "free hand," Britain customarily cast its power on the side of the weaker nation or coalition of nations in European disputes. London sought to preserve an equilibrium of power within the

system and to prevent a single member (or coalition) from dominating the Continent. Britain's approach exemplified a foreign policy dictated by the concept of "national interest" vis-à-vis one governed by ideological considerations, permanent loyalties to particular countries, or preferences for one system of government over another. As one of its statesmen described the principle actuating British policy: "Britain has no permanent friends, only permanent interests."[10] (Parenthetically, we should emphasize that in another realm—national competition in seapower—Great Britian did *not* adhere to the balance-of-power concept. In that sphere, London's goal was *naval supremacy,* as reflected in the strategic maxim that the British fleet should be stronger than any two fleets which might be combined against it.)

Among some students of international politics, the classical balance-of-power system is sometimes regarded as a kind of diplomatic golden age: The system is often cited as a model for policy makers in the United States and other influential nations today.[11] Other commentators are persuaded that the balance-of-power system was inherently unstable and inimical to the values and well-being of its members. A leading student of the First World War, for example, was convinced that the attachment of the European states to the balance-of-power principle played an influential role in producing the most violent and pervasive war in history up to that time.[12] In answer to those students of international politics who romanticize the balance-of-power era, James Chace has observed that what its practitioners gave to Europe before World War I "was not balance but extreme tension."[13]

Two general criticisms can be made of the classical balance-of-power concept. It belonged to *a unique historical era*—the age of aristocracy—in which monarchs could engage in the "sport of kings" (as the balance of power was widely called); where foreign policy decision making was confined to a small (nearly always appointed) governmental elite; where secret negotiations and secret treaties were the rule and where the desires of the masses of the people (who provided the bulk of the armed forces required to practice balance-of-power politics) could be ignored. The balance-of-power system has also been frequently criticized because of *its intrinsic ambiguity*. The term *balance of power* in fact possesses numerous and often conflicting interpretations. It can, for example, mean either "equilibrium" of power or "preponderance" of power (the United States may seek the former in its strategic relations with the Soviet Union, while it pursues the latter in the Western Hemisphere). More neutrally, the term may describe merely the *existing distribution* of global power; in this connotation, it has very little utility as a guide to national policy.[14]

Conditions since World War II are different, in some respects radically dissimilar, from those that existed during the nineteenth century. Almost none of the preconditions enabling the balance-of-power system to function earlier exist in the contemporary world. As a result of World War II, the principal European actors were devastated, and all except the Soviet Union disappeared from the ranks of the great powers. Great Britain's postwar decline was especially graphic. No longer a first-rank power, and preoccupied with acute internal economic problems, Britain was unable to play its traditional role as "balancer" in the international system.

Three other developments fundamentally altered the nature of the post-World War II international system. One was the emergence of the Soviet Union as one of two superpowers on the globe. While the Russian state had been an influential international actor for several centuries, its accession to the rank of superpower was significant for two

reasons. It was now in an unrivaled position to pursue certain *national goals,* many of which could be traced back to the Czarist period. And (until its leadership role was contested by Communist China around 1960), the Soviet Union was the acknowledged leader of an *ideological movement* whose principles caused anxiety in Washington and foreign capitals.

A second crucial development was the emergence of the United States as a superpower after World War II—in some respects, at least, the most influential nation in the history of the world. By the end of the war, American officials and public opinion alike realized that the old "isolationist" posture had become obsolete and could no longer serve the nation's diplomatic interests. As we shall see more fully in Chapters 2 and 8, "neo-isolationist" attitudes, especially prominent for several years after the Vietnam War, still characterize the American approach to foreign affairs. Yet by the end of the 1970s, officials in Washington—supported by American public opinion—had clearly returned to the idea that the United States was a global power with important international and regional commitments. After 1945, there was literally no region on the globe—and no major international issue—which was not affected by America's "presence" or influence. Future chapters give details of this phenomenon.

The third notable development in the postwar period rendering the old balance-of-power model of international politics inoperative was the emergence of the Third World (and its offshoot, the Fourth World). Since the end of World War II, some 100 new nations have joined the international system, the vast majority located in the Afro-Asian world. The creation of the Third World*—whose

*No uniformity exists with regard to membership of the Third World, and even influential members of it differ regarding the criteria for inclusion within it. The term

members are determined to preserve their political and diplomatic independence from both of the superpowers and to make the international system more responsive to their needs and goals—must be counted among the most far-reaching developments in modern history.

The Era of "Bipolarity"

Substantial unanimity exists among proponents of systems theory concerning the nature of the international system which emerged at the end of World War II and lasted until around 1960. It was a *bipolar system*. In the language of economics, the Soviet-American "duopoly" largely dominated the international system. Most crucial decisions affecting the system were made by Washington and Moscow, jointly or alone.

In this global political environment, the two superpowers functioned as the effective decision makers, and the conflict between them—popularly known as the Cold War— became the transcendent international issue, directly or indirectly affecting virtually every major global problem. The era of bipolarity was best symbolized perhaps by America's acquisition and use of the atomic bomb in 1945; by Moscow's successful development of a nuclear arsenal a few years later; and, thereafter, by the efforts of both superpowers to prevent other countries from joining the

"nuclear club." The possession of vast nuclear stockpiles by the superpowers nevertheless gave them a certain prestige and position in the international system which nonnuclear nations envied but could not match.

For some fifteen years after 1945, the era of bipolarity was characterized by extreme ideological tensions between the United States (the proclaimed leader of the "free world") and the Soviet Union (self-appointed spokesman for the Communist world). Each side was fearful of the other and built up its stockpile of increasingly sophisticated and expensive armaments for "defensive" purposes. During the period of bipolarity, the threat of global nuclear devastation seemed imminent and was of deep concern to societies from the Western Hemisphere to East Asia.

In contrast to the international system which superseded the bipolar era, the "rules of the game" or regulative principles, of the bipolar system seem relatively simple and clear. From the perspective of Washington and Moscow, it was a "zero sum game": A gain for one side was viewed as a loss for the other. A vast gulf separated the position of the two superpowers from the other members of the system—and Washington and Moscow alike showed no particular desire to change that reality. In dealing with weaker states within its orbit (like Yugoslavia and, later, Communist China), the Kremlin left no doubt concerning where final decision-making authority for the Communist bloc resided or whose version of Marxist orthodoxy should prevail. Similarly, the United States experienced restiveness among its allies. Several European countries (such as France) expressed disaffection because of America's nuclear monopoly and Washington's tendency to make strategic and diplomatic decisions in behalf of the Western alliance. Under bipolarity, the nations of Latin America became increasingly dissatisfied with what they viewed as their in-

---

Third World in fact has several connotations. It may designate the *non-Western societies* of the world, most of which were subjected to Western colonialism and have now become independent nations. (That definition would exclude the Latin American states.) It may refer to *those nations which profess "nonalignment" as their diplomatic credo:* They do not wish to participate in the Cold War or become "satellites" of one of the superpowers. Or it may describe *the developing or less developed nations:* those in which poverty, or a very low standard of living, is the rule, which are seeking above all to modernize their societies. Depending upon the definition accepted, the list of nations belonging to the Third World will vary significantly.

ferior position in the inter-American system. Initially skeptical of the concept of diplomatic "nonalignment," each superpower endeavored to draw states throughout the Third World into its diplomatic orbit.

The two superpowers almost invariably approached substantive issues arising during the period of bipolarity from the perspective of their own Cold War interests and goals. Arms-control agreements, for example, did little to change the relative military superiority of the United States and the Soviet Union vis-à-vis the rest of the world; nor did they halt the accelerating arms race. For Washington and Moscow alike, the United Nations served primarily as a mechanism for waging the Cold War (or preventing adversaries from waging it). While America and Russia dispensed billions of dollars in economic and military assistance to other countries, such aid was nearly always motivated by, or provided within a context of, Cold War objectives. As in the older balance-of-power system, after World War II those states not participating in the decision-making process became convinced that they served primarily as objects of decisions vitally affecting their future made in Washington and Moscow. Not surprisingly, except for the superpowers, few nations liked the bipolar system and most were determined to change it.

The Contemporary International System

Even before the 1960s, evidence began to accumulate that the international system was undergoing fundamental changes. By that period, it was apparent that a new distribution of global power was superseding bipolarity. No consensus exists among informed students of international politics concerning the precise nature of the contemporary global system. A bewildering variety of terms—a sampling of which includes *loose bipolar* and *tight bipolar,*

heterosymmetrical bipolar, bi-multipolar, bi-polycentric, tripolar, and *multipolar*—has been applied to the international system today.[15] This semantic confusion reflects the fact that the contemporary international system *is extremely complex,* that it possesses many novel features, and that it continues to evolve in the direction of greater complexity. This terminological disagreement also unquestionably reflects the fact that the concept serving as the foundation stone of the systems approach—the idea of *national power*—is also undergoing fundamental change.

Perhaps the most widely employed term to describe the existing international system is *multipolarity* (although it should be noted that many devotees of systems theory believe the term to be inappropriate and misleading). The central idea conveyed by the term *multipolarity* seems uncontestable: *Global power has become increasingly diffused throughout the international system.* In the military realm, the United States and the Soviet Union still lay claim to the designation of superpowers. Either superpower alone possesses the military might to devastate the planet. Yet neither is able to impose its will upon the Third World. New regional power centers have emerged; and membership in the "nuclear club" continues to expand (despite the objections of the superpowers). Or in another realm—economic power—the superpowers find their claims to dominance challenged by other states (like Japan) and groups of states (like the European Economic Community and the Organization of Petroleum Exporting Countries, OPEC).

What are the most noteworthy characteristics of the existing international system? We may most meaningfully approach that question by examining four categories, or levels of membership, in it. First, there are the two superpowers, the United States and the Soviet Union. For several reasons—most fundamentally, perhaps, their unrivaled military power—they occupy the highest level in the system, although their relative position within it has in many respects declined. The superpowers, for example, no longer exercise a duopoly in their control over nuclear weapons; nor have they been conspicuously successful in controlling the *use* of weapons which they have supplied to their allies and friends abroad.[16]

Economically, the United States and the Soviet Union remain at the forefront of the "advanced" nations of the world. The gap between their productivity levels and their standards of living vis-à-vis those throughout the Third World, for example, continues to widen. Yet both superpowers have become more dependent than ever upon other countries for their economic prosperity and the maintenance of their standards of living. After more than 60 years of Communism, for example, Soviet Russia is still unable to feed itself—and that prospect shows no sign of improvement. Similarly, the United States has become steadily more dependent upon foreign sources for most of its "strategic imports."*

The position of the superpowers has also been eroded in the ideological sphere. Communism is no longer a monolithic movement dominated by the Soviet Union, if indeed it ever was (to the degree imagined by American policy makers). Moscow now finds its claim to ideological leadership challenged by Western advocates of "Euro-Communism," by Communist China, by Yugoslavia, by Castro's

Cuba, and by other species of "national Communism." As for the United States, to use a term frequently employed by President John F. Kennedy, it has had to accommodate itself more and more to a "world of diversity" and to the reality of ideological pluralism throughout the international system.

Diplomatically, the once dominant positions of the superpowers has also deteriorated. Neither the United States nor the Soviet Union has been able to impose its ideological system upon the Third World or win converts widely among these states for its diplomatic position. In time, Washington and Moscow had to accommodate themselves to the existence of a diplomatically nonaligned Third World whose members represented the vast majority of the human race. In their relations with individual Third World states, the United States and the Soviet Union discovered that they were as likely to be "controlled" and manipulated by these countries as they were able to influence the behavior of these weaker nations.

In their relationships with each other (as we shall see more fully in Chapter 10), the superpowers had moved from a posture of overt Cold War tensions and rivalries into a new era of détente. Mystifying as that elusive concept often was, détente did signify a considerable lessening in Cold War hostilities, a reduction in the prospects for global devastation, a lower level of ideological conflict, a decline in overt Soviet-American competition in most areas of the Third World, and limited forms of Soviet-American cooperation in spheres like arms control, trade, and outer space. For both superpowers, détente also witnessed (and was perhaps in some measure produced by) growing preoccupation with domestic problems at the forefront of national concern.

The second level of membership within the contemporary international system con-

---

*By the end of the 1970s, the United States was dependent upon foreign sources for the following percentages of its domestic requirements: columbium, strontium, and mica, 100 percent; manganese and cobalt, 98 percent; bauxite and alumina, 90 percent; chromium, 89 percent; tin, 85 percent; nickel, 71 percent; mercury, 65 percent; zinc, 59 percent; petroleum, 41 percent; iron ore, 35 percent. See *Statistical Abstract of the United States: 1977* (Washington, D.C.: Bureau of the Census, 1977), p. 750.

sists of a small group of "Middle Powers"—or what, by the end of the 1970s, were sometimes referred to as "new influentials."[17] Occupying a position between the superpowers and the Third World, this group of nations possesses considerable power regionally or in selected realms of international politics. As always, the criteria for assignment of nations to this category are somewhat arbitrary and subjective. As a general characterization, however, the Middle Powers possess some combination of factors giving them the ability to influence the international system significantly; and several of them have a potential to become even more powerful than they are now. Leading members of this group are: those nations belonging to the European Economic Community,* embracing one of the largest market and productive networks on the globe;[18] Communist China, with the world's largest population, a nuclear arsenal, a unique Marxist system, and a determination to become more powerful regionally and globally; Japan, one of the world's most influential nations economically and financially (if its military and diplomatic power remain quite limited); India, with the world's second-largest population, a nuclear arsenal, one of the few democratic regimes among the Afro-Asian countries, and a strategic location in the Indian Ocean area; Iran, a major oil-producing state, a record of spectacular economic progress, and a dominant military position in the Persian Gulf area; and Brazil, the largest nation in the Western Hemisphere, possessing vast natural resources, and the potential power giant of Latin America.

*The European Economic Community (EEC) came into existence in 1957 and initially included: West Germany, France, Italy, the Netherlands, Belgium, and Luxembourg. In 1973, three other nations—Great Britain, Ireland, and Denmark—joined. Three other nations—Portugal, Spain, and Greece—have actively sought membership in the EEC in recent years.

Several other countries are potential candidates for inclusion among the Middle Powers.[19] Among these are Nigeria, potentially one of the wealthiest and most powerful states on the African continent; Saudi Arabia, the largest oil-producing state on the globe; and Mexico, already an influential state in Latin America and possessing vast unexploited oil wealth.

While each nation included among the Middle Powers has certain unique diplomatic objectives, they are also motivated by certain common aspirations. All seek to become more internally developed and externally powerful; to resist the hegemony of the superpowers; to gain recognition for their claim to regional leadership; to expand their military arsenals; and ultimately perhaps to be admitted to the ranks of the superpowers.

The third category of membership in the contemporary international system consists of those nations belonging to the Third World. Depending upon the criteria employed for determining membership in it (and, as we observed earlier, several different standards may be utilized), the Third World consists of from some 75 to more than 100 countries. (If the Third World is viewed as synonymous with the "nonaligned nations," for example, the number approximates the former figure. If the Third World designates all of the "developing" countries, then it is equal to the higher number.)

The emergence of the Third World is usually dated from the Afro-Asian Solidarity Conference held in Bandung, Indonesia, in 1955. The first Conference of Non-Aligned Nations was convened in Belgrade, Yugoslavia, in 1961; it was attended by some 25 neutralist nations (along with several "observer" countries). Since 1961, the number of nations attending the nonaligned conferences has more than tripled, and the members of the neutralist movement have created institutional machinery to promote its common goals and interests.

Even at the Bandung Conference in 1955, the degree of "solidity" uniting the nations of the Third World was exaggerated. As time passed, two issues which once imparted a high degree of cohesion to the Third World—common opposition to colonialism (nearly always Western) and the determination of the members to avoid involvement in the Cold War—have receded in importance. The era of traditional colonialism has largely come to an end (although members of the Third World from time to time express opposition to new forms of it, known as "neocolonialism"). Détente between the superpowers has superseded the Cold War era. Under these conditions, the Third World has been severely challenged to maintain its cohesion and to agree upon standards for its membership. Increasingly, the unity of the Third World has been impaired by a variety of conflicts and crises among its members: territorial disputes (as between Algeria and Morocco); ideological and political controversies (as between Syria and Iraq); ancient religious, ethnic, and tribal differences (as between India and Pakistan, or Ethiopia and Somalia); and disagreements over important policy issues like the Arab-Israeli conflict (as between Egypt and Libya, Syria and Iraq). By the end of the 1970s, the emergence of Cuban President Fidel Castro as a prominent leader of the Third World underscored the ambiguity and confusion governing membership in it!

The members of the Third World have gradually altered their diplomatic priorities. While they have in no sense abandoned a desire to remain diplomatically nonaligned —and to protect their independence from new encroachments by the superpowers—in the contemporary period their behavior has revealed two pervasive goals. First, the members of the Third World are interested in gaining a more influential role in the international decision-making process, to have their views considered by the superpowers, and to make the decision-making process more broadly representative of global opinion. In the language of systems theory, the Third World nations want their voices to become an influential *input* in major decisions affecting their interests and future. Efforts by the Third World to convert the United Nations into an organ reflecting their interests and views illustrate this phenomenon.

Second (in a reversal of roles vis-à-vis the earlier era of bipolarity), Third World nations often seek to enlist or involve the superpowers in their own external controversies and conflicts with other countries. Thus, during the late 1970s, Ethiopia sought massive Soviet assistance in its war with Somalia; Vietnam leaned heavily upon the Soviet Union in its conflict with Cambodia (supported by Communist China); and both Israel and Egypt actively sought American support for their respective positions in the Palestinian controversy.[20]

Economically, the members of the Third World seek more equitable access to and use of the world's raw materials (they are, for example, keenly interested in international agreements dealing with national access to raw materials to be found in the oceans). They also demand more favorable and stable conditions of trade, along with higher prices for their primary exports (in most instances, raw materials). An urgent need of Third World countries is larger infusions of governmental foreign assistance and private investment capital to promote their economic development.

Internally, nearly all nations belonging to the Third World confront two critical issues which absorb their energies and engage the attention of their policy makers. One of these issues is the necessity for successful *national development;* for most Third World societies, this challenge faces serious and continuing obstacles. The other issue—gravely jeopardizing the national cohesion of innumerable societies throughout the Third World—is *nation building:* the creation and maintenance of a strong sense of national cohesion and loyalty in the face of efforts by tribal groups, ethnic and religious minorities, and other dissident elements to destroy it. In contrast to the experience of the West, many of these Third World societies became independent *states* before they were in fact *nations.* For a number of them, the question of whether they really *are* viable nations (Lebanon provides a leading example) has not yet been decided.

By the 1970s, a pervasive conviction existed throughout the Third World that both superpowers—but particularly America— were losing interest in their problems and were indifferent toward their needs. Evidence to support this conviction was not lacking. The level of American foreign assistance, for example, had declined significantly since the 1950s; as a percentage of the Gross National Product, foreign aid by the United States ranked toward the bottom of assistance provided by all industrialized nations to poorer societies.* As the years passed, the United States had also clearly become less "UN-oriented" than in the early postwar era. The United Nations was largely under the control of the Third and Fourth worlds. As a result, its actions and resolutions were for the most part ignored by the superpowers; important agreements between them tended to be discussed and negotiated outside the United Nations. America's ultimate acceptance of the right of Third World countries to remain nonaligned diplomatically—combined with the reduction in Cold War tensions—perhaps inevitably meant that the United States felt a lessened sense of involvement in the problems of these nations. Another factor producing this frame of mind was of course the Vietnam War. Among the "lessons" of that traumatic experience for Americans was the realization that, even though it was a superpower, limits existed upon the power of the United States to achieve its goals abroad, especially in unfamiliar Third World settings.

On the bottom level of the international system are some 40 members of what is sometimes called the "Fourth World"—those societies where per capita income averages around $150 annually. Although there is not of course a perfect coincidence between economic and political power, the pervasive poverty existing in most Fourth World countries means that, as a group, they are usually inhibited from playing an influential regional or global role. For the vast majority of states in this category, endemic poverty is the norm; and (without some unexpected breakthrough in technology) most of them have little prospect for significant economic development for the future. With some of the highest rates of population growth found on the globe, a majority of nations in this group will be hard

---

*Foreign aid as an instrument of American foreign policy is discussed more fully in Chapter 6. Meanwhile, we may note that since the end of World War II the United States has provided well over $200 billion in various kinds of military and economic assistance to some 140 nations. This total has been divided into approximately two-thirds for economic assistance and one-third for military assistance. Among the less developed countries, those in the Far East and the Middle East have received the largest allocations, while Latin America and Africa rank considerably lower on the scale. In 1949, foreign aid constituted some 3.3 percent of America's total output of goods and services; by 1977, it had dropped to 6/10 of 1 percent of the Gross National Product. This decline placed the United States well below countries like Canada, France, West Germany, and Sweden as a source of foreign aid, expressed as a percentage of GNP. See Lyde H. Farnsworth, in *New York Times,* September 18, 1979; and *U.S. News and World Report,* **LXXXI** (November 1, 1976), 55–58.

pressed merely to *maintain* an already low standard of living. As a group—and the prototype in this regard is Bangladesh, with around 100 million people—many of these countries constitute economic "basket cases." They appear fated to continue their poverty-level existence based on primitive agriculture and nomadism, while "Malthusian" forces*—like rampant disease and malnutrition—weaken the existing population. For most societies within the Fourth World, a rapidly growing human population presses on already inadequate food supplies.

Collectively, the nations of the Fourth World presently contain around 1 billion people, approximately 25 percent of the human race. Projections of future population growth indicate that this percentage will almost certainly increase in the years ahead. Economically, the relative position of members of the Fourth World within the international system will probably continue to decline. With the passage of time, for example, there is likely to be a greater gap between the standards of living in the Fourth and Third worlds than currently exists between the Third World and the advanced industrialized societies (or the First and Second worlds).

The precarious struggle for existence leaves little time and energy for involvement by most Fourth World societies in affairs outside their own borders. Governments throughout the Fourth World are likely to encounter mounting popular unrest and political agitation, as incumbent leaders are unable to meet popular demands. Urgent as their requirements for outside assistance are, most Fourth World societies will be challenged to create an environment in which such outside funds can be attracted and effectively utilized. As the members of the Fourth World view the matter, the foreign aid provided by the superpowers and by some of the Middle Powers is "inadequate" for their needs—and by any objective standard, the allegation is probably correct. Yet there is no sign that either the United States or the Soviet Union is likely to increase significantly its assistance to this category of nations or that private investment capital will be massively attracted to what is viewed as an unpromising "investment climate."

Conditions existing throughout the Fourth World are of course unfavorable for the emergence of stable democratic regimes. But even Marxist, along with crypto-Marxist and various forms of socialist, regimes will experience great difficulty in solving the intractable problems endemic to Fourth World societies. With some exceptions, the inclination of the two superpowers will likely be to avoid involvement in, and responsibility for, the Fourth World's deteriorating problems, which Washington and Moscow have neither the available resources nor the insight to solve.

Foreign Policy Goals and Objectives

Our study of American foreign policy will proceed on an important implicit premise: that

*Thomas Robert Malthus (1766–1834) was an English clergyman who published a widely circulated essay entitled "A Summary View of the Principle of Population," which first appeared in 1824. Concerned with the improvement or happiness of human society, Malthus discussed the major impediments to it. In his view, the principal impediment was the tendency of population to outrun available food supplies. According to his formula, population increased geometrically (i.e., in the sequence 1, 2, 4, 8, 16 . . .), while food supplies increased arithmetically (1, 2, 3, 4 . . .). Meanwhile, Malthus believed that certain forces —disease, starvation, and war—served to reduce excessive population growth. Malthus' ideas may be legitimately criticized on many grounds, such as the fact that he overlooked the impact of modern science and technology in raising food output. But the basic problem with which he was concerned—the tendency of human population to expand faster than the means for satisfying its needs—has clear relevance throughout much of the world today.

the behavior of the United States in its relations with other states is *purposive*. Along with all other members of the international system, the American society has certain *goals and objectives* to which it is devoted; otherwise, it would not be a "society" (or community). This assumption, we should of course note, is sometimes contradicted by the evidence. At every level, the study of political behavior must take account of various "irrational," emotional, personal, and similar influences upon policy making. The fact, for example, that the Soviet dictator Joseph Stalin was almost certainly psychopathic had a profound influence upon postwar Soviet foreign policy. Similarly, America's continued involvement in the Vietnam War could be attributed in part to the personal convictions of Presidents Johnson and Nixon that the nation's honor—and perhaps their own credibility as chief executive—required an American "victory" in that conflict. These can be cited as examples of irrational influences upon the foreign policy process, and such influences are perhaps never totally absent. Despite this fact, the idea of a foreign *policy* postulates the existence of a set of conscious goals which the United States seeks to achieve outside its own borders.

We shall, therefore, define the foreign policy of the United States *as those external goals toward the achievement of which the nation is prepared to commit its resources.* Two elements are thus essential to the idea of a foreign policy: objectives and the means for attaining them (or the concept of "national power," with which we shall deal at a later stage).

It is, however, much easier to make generalizations about the existence of foreign policy goals than it is to obtain a satisfactory and unambiguous understanding of three interrelated aspects of the problem: a clear conception or "listing" of American foreign policy objectives; an understanding of how foreign policy goals are formulated (or reformulated); and the question of the "compatibility" among several (often conflicting) external objectives.[21] At this point, we shall concentrate on the first and third aspects of the problem, reserving a discussion of how foreign policy goals are formulated for future chapters.

Diplomatic Objectives of the United States

There is no dearth of lists setting forth the goals of the United States in global affairs. Nearly every presidential "State of the Union" message provides one, and each annual volume of the *Department of State Bulletin* is likely to contain several partial or detailed enumerations of them.*

Nearly always, the first objective listed (however it is formulated in particular statements) *is the security of the United States.* That has always been, and remains, the para-

---

*As merely one example, at the end of his first year in office, President Jimmy Carter cited the following major foreign policy goals of his Administration. A leading goal was to "connect our actions overseas with our essential character as a nation." The foreign policy of the United States must be "democratic" and attempt to use "power and influence . . . for humane purposes" abroad. The objective of American policy must be "constructive global involvement" with other countries. He listed five specific policy goals: his Administration's commitment to the promotion of international human rights; reenforcement of "the bonds among . . . democracies" throughout the world; a new arms-limitation agreement with the Soviet Union; the achievement of "lasting peace in the Middle East"; and new methods for curtailing the proliferation of nuclear weapons. In addition, he listed a number of other accomplishments and future goals—such as an improvement of America's relations with black Africa, closer collaboration among the NATO allies, a normalization in America's relations with Mainland China, and better understanding between the United States and Latin America—as high on the list of White House priorities. See "Carter Administration's First-Year Accomplishments," *Department of State Bulletin,* **78** (January, 1978), 15–16.

mount goal of American foreign policy. Any incumbent President and Congress operate upon the same premise which motivated much of President Lincoln's behavior during the Civil War. Lincoln repeatedly justified his actions by the assertion that "the Union must be preserved." Nearly any goal which might be listed for American diplomacy, by individuals and groups of varying political and philosophical orientation, *presupposes the continued existence of the United States as an independent nation.* For the overwhelming majority of Americans (Marxists and certain other dissident groups excepted), preserving the territorial and political integrity of the nation is both a transcendent goal in its own right and a necessary prerequisite for the attainment of a long list of subordinate objectives cherished by the American people.

The preeminence of national security as a foreign policy objective inevitably dictates a high level of priority for certain specific security-related goals. Leading ones are: the maintenance of adequate and well-equipped military forces to preserve national security under a variety of external conditions; the creation and maintenance of military alliances designed to strengthen the defensive position of the United States and its allies; the provision of arms aid to military allies and friendly countries, enabling them to play a more effective role in the common defense effort; and the operation of an intelligence network designed to provide national leaders with accurate information about the behavior and intentions of potential enemies.

Increasingly since World War II, the United States has become mindful of another set of security-related foreign policy goals which can be collectively designated as *crisis prevention.* Like the fire department—which believes it is better to engage in successful fire prevention than to extinguish conflagrations after they occur and perhaps get "out of control"—the United States is involved in a variety of "preventive" activities abroad. Such activities are numerous and diverse, ranging from the use of modern communications media, like the Washington-Moscow "Hot Line" and orbiting space satellites, to permit almost instantaneous communication of ideas; to support for the United Nations in its varied activities (many of which are designed to eliminate long-range causes of international tension); to the provision of economic and technical assistance to other countries, enabling them to solve critical internal problems.

Implicit in our discussion thus far is the idea that, in company with other nations, the United States has *a hierarchy of foreign policy objectives.* All goals pursued by a nation in its external affairs are not of equal importance or urgency. We have already emphasized the preeminence of national security. Next on the scale of diplomatic priorities is a variety of what might be called *secondary goals:* those objectives which the United States would like to accomplish in foreign affairs, provided there is no impairment of national security. Any listing of these secondary objectives is likely to be subjective and arbitrary (officials in the White House and Congress, or different citizens' organizations, for example, would almost certainly produce different lists). These goals are also subject to modification, as circumstances change at home and abroad. Important secondary goals, however, might well include: maintaining the internal economic well-being and prosperity of the United States; strengthening and promoting national compliance with international law; supporting the existence and programs of the United Nations; reducing the level of global armaments; resolving regional and international disputes peacefully; endeavoring to achieve a higher level of consensus among the nation's military allies in decision making; and encouraging and assisting the economic advancement of less developed countries.

At the bottom of the list of American foreign policy goals is a category of purposes and aspirations with which the United States is sometimes identified. Strictly speaking—when we remember that a *goal* of foreign policy is an objective to which the nation *is prepared to commit its resources*—most of these are not really "goals" at all. More accurately, they must be viewed as wishes, hopes, ideals, and aspects of "the American dream" which citizens and leaders would like to see achieved abroad. Such aspirations will almost invariably be sacrificed for goals in the first and second rank.

In this category are: the desire to see democracy become a universal philosophy or system of government; the "liberation" of Eastern Europe and other territories from Soviet control; global peace, permitting the dismantling (or massive reduction) of national military establishments; and realization of the old Wilsonian principle of "open covenants, openly arrived at"—or public and "democratic" diplomacy in which secrecy, intrigue, governmental deception, and disregard for public opinion no longer characterize the diplomatic behavior of nations.

The problem of conflicts among competing external goals is a challenge confronting policy makers in all states—but perhaps uniquely so for those in Washington. Several factors make it an unusually difficult and continuing problem for the United States. The United States is a superpower, with interests and responsibilities in every region of the globe. It has some kind of relations with approximately 150 countries, many of which complain about America's "neglect" of their welfare and endeavor to increase its involvement in their affairs. As the world's oldest democracy, the United States is a highly pluralistic society. Utilizing modern methods for communicating their opinions, literally thousands of citizen groups and organizations formulate goals which are conveyed to policy makers.

Another fundamental cause of the problem is the steady erosion which has occurred between "domestic" and "foreign" policy issues. Throughout American history, the distinction between these two realms was never as precise as was widely imagined. Yet since World War II—and especially during the past two decades—the line between these two categories of public issues has largely disappeared. "Domestic" policy often has the most profound implications for foreign policy. The American people's willingness, for example, to accept a particular level of taxation by the federal government directly affects American foreign policy—as in congressional willingness to support foreign aid programs or in determining the size and nature of the American military establishment. Conversely, foreign policy decisions impinge directly and crucially upon internal policies and problems as never before. The nation's prolonged involvement in the Vietnam War, for example, unquestionably contributed to an escalation in the rate of inflation for many years thereafter; it led to the neglect of certain domestic problems (like education, health, and welfare); and it crucially affected that intangible, but highly important, component of democratic government—public confidence in the nation's leaders. Although it may still be a matter of convenience to divide governmental decisions into "domestic" and "foreign" policies, it is essential to keep in mind that this distinction is increasingly artificial and tenuous.

The problem of foreign policy goal selection has also been compounded by other developments in the contemporary period. One of these—graphically highlighted by student protests and other forms of popular disaffection during the Vietnam War—is widespread uncertainty and perplexity within the American society concerning its norms, values, and goals. It is a truism to assert that traditional values are being widely questioned today and that many of them are in the process of rapid change. No doubt this has been true of every historical era, but seldom in American history have society's values and goals been as pervasively questioned and challenged as in the contemporary period. If it is often not clear what the United States seeks in its diplomatic relations, this lack of clarity may have its origins in deep confusion *within the American society with regard to its purposes and objectives.*

Still another development compounding the problem of goal selection requires brief mention. The Vietnam War was in some respects perhaps the most traumatic experience in the nation's diplomatic history. The "lessons" of the Vietnam War are likely to be discussed and analyzed endlessly. After that encounter, the foreign policy of the United States could be generally characterized by the term *diplomatic retrenchment*. The American people and their leaders agreed that two extreme positions in global affairs—the traditional "isolationist" posture which existed until World War II, and the kind of indiscriminate "interventionism" which motivated American policy during the 1950s and 1960s—must be avoided. Somewhere between these polar positions lay the proper course or posture for the United States in foreign relations.

That course might be characterized by the term *selective interventionism*. But many questions remain unanswered, even today. What are the *criteria* which ought to guide the United States in the application of its power abroad? If, as the Vietnam War demonstrated, America cannot achieve everything it undertakes outside its own borders—the United States is clearly not omnipotent—then what

can it undertake successfully? If the United States finds the external environment increasingly resistant to the application of American power, in what respects can its power be employed effectively and constructively throughout the international system? These and other questions require answers before the purposes of the United States in foreign affairs can be clarified.

Note must also be taken of another phenomenon which often renders the process of goal selection extremely difficult. This is the change that has occurred in the *nature and kinds of relationships* existing among the members of the international system today vis-à-vis earlier eras. Take the period of the classical balance of power to which we referred earlier. In that age, international relations revolved primarily around dynastic disputes and territorial changes or rivalries among leading European actors for colonies and "spheres of influence" abroad. While such issues have by no means disappeared as sources of international controversy and conflict, their importance has in large part been eclipsed by a variety of newer issues and problems, such as: the challenge of modernization and nation building throughout the Third and Fourth worlds; the desire of all members of the international system to escape global nuclear devastation; the necessity to solve numerous global environmental problems; concern about the "population explosion" and its attendant problems; and the urgent need to increase world food production.

Stated differently, during the past generation policy makers in the United States have become preoccupied with a variety of novel concerns, many of which involve attempts *to change traditional patterns of behavior by individuals and groups in foreign societies,* rather than merely to influence the actions of foreign governments. As exemplified by efforts to deal with the "population explosion," the United States and other governments involved in the problem are endeavoring ultimately to alter the age-old behavior of the Indian villager or the Egyptian peasant (and in some contexts, Washington must pursue this goal in the face of *active opposition* by established governments). This change in the concerns of the United States in its relations with other countries inevitably generates doubt and confusion both with regard to goal selection and, perhaps even more fundamentally, with respect to the choice of means best calculated to achieve the stated goal.

The Means of Foreign Policy

The Concept of National Power

Earlier we observed that there are two elements in the foreign policy of any nation: goals and the means for achieving them. Let us now look at the means which nations employ to attain their external objectives. This introduces us to one of the pivotal concepts in the study of international politics: *national power.*

The power of a nation may be defined variously. One study describes it simply as "influence and control exercised by one nation over others."[22] Another study envisions power as "man's control over the minds and actions of other men...."[23] Still another conception is that power "is the ability to influence the behavior of others in accordance with one's own ends."[24]

We shall define power *as the ability of a nation to achieve its foreign policy goals,* and this in turn necessarily implies its capacity to influence and control the behavior of other members of the international system. In this definition, national power is construed *as a means to a goal* (or goals), not as an end in itself. (It is recognized of course that sometimes, as in the case of Hitler's Third Reich, the possession and expansion of national power is an end in itself.)

For many years—particularly in the approach toward international relations known as *Realpolitik*—the concept of national power has served as the central or integrating idea for the study of global and regional political relationships. Global political relationships are frequently defined by terms like *power politics* or *power struggles* or exercises in the balance of power. Customarily, nations are ranked within the international hierarchy on the basis of the power they possess (or are thought to possess).

At the outset, we must take account of an aspect of the concept of power which is uniquely relevant for Americans. The people of the United States have not been conditioned by their ethos and history to view objectively the role of power in global political relationships. Concepts like power and power politics usually evoke a negative response from Americans, who regard them as part of the philosophical and political heritage of the Old World. They are among those ideas and practices which were deliberately *rejected* by the settlers of the New World. In perhaps the most famous state paper in American diplomatic history—the Monroe Doctrine (1823)—President James Monroe forcefully informed the nations of Europe that the political behavior of the United States was actuated by a different set of principles from those which had long governed political relationships in the Old World. Monroe's "doctrine"—admonishing the European powers to refrain from further colonization in the Western Hemisphere—was dictated in no small part by his determination to preserve that fundamental distinction.[25] The outspoken opposition expressed by many citizens and groups toward the Vietnam War reflected this old bias against the concept of power in the American society.

Yet it must also be noted that American attitudes toward power have also been ambivalent and contradictory. If Americans derogate the role of power in global political relationships, they extoll it in other activities —like lobbying and other methods of bringing pressure to bear upon political leaders, advertising, and the principles of effective salesmanship. Even toward international relations, the American people have usually reacted negatively to the idea that the military power of the United States was declining vis-à-vis the Soviet Union or to the notion that the nation was no longer self-sufficient in economic power. Even so, as a result of their ideological and historical conditioning, many Americans often *do not perceive the relationship between the possession and application of power and the achievement of a wide range of diplomatic objectives.*

The definitions of power cited above call attention to the fact that the concept embraces a wide range of means and instruments needed by nations to accomplish their external purposes. If national security is the paramount foreign policy objective, it follows that the ability of a nation to preserve its security —requiring the possession of an adequate military establishment and the willingness to employ it—is perhaps the most fundamental manifestation of national power. However power may be defined precisely, no nation possesses it if it is unable to maintain its independence.

Below the level of preserving national security, the concept of power has innumerable connotations and ramifications. For example, the power of the United States may be (and often is) defined *negatively*—as in America's ability to prevent military incursions against the NATO area by Communist forces or to counter moves designed to deny Western nations access to Middle East oil.

As never before in the history of international politics, however, power also has a *positive* connotation. From this perspective, power is *the ability of a nation to accomplish its constructive purposes.* In the contemporary international system this might, and usually does, mean working in collaboration with other members of the system to achieve common aims. Examples might include: working collaboratively with other countries to improve the global environment; creating new opportunities for trade and commerce, for exchange of scientific knowledge, and for other forms of "peaceful contacts" among nations; devising methods for solving the world food shortage and for achieving a more equitable system of food distribution; and promoting a higher degree of consensus among the nation's allies and friends in behalf of common diplomatic objectives.

In this connotation, power is likely to be synonymous with *influence,* exercised by such methods as leadership, persuasion, and—a technique which has always been a prominent idea in the American diplomatic heritage—the "power of example."* Under conditions of nuclear stalemate between the superpowers, this positive aspect of national power has become more important than ever. The ability of the United States to create and maintain a high level of support abroad for its foreign policy goals, or America's capacity to lead the industrialized nations in responding to the economic needs of the developing nations, or Washington's negotiating skill in persuading adversaries like Israel and the Arab states to make peace—in the contemporary period, these are likely to be viewed as key indicators of whether the United States is truly a superpower.

*During the isolationist era, for example, groups like the Progressive Movement around 1900 believed that America's "example" was the most influential tool available for influencing other countries. In the contemporary period, this same idea has been expressed by a group of liberal neo-isolationists, as exemplified in the views of ex-Senator J. William Fulbright. See his *Old Myths and New Realities* (New York: Random House, 1964), pp. 109–138; and *The Crippled Giant* (New York: Random House, 1972), passim.

The power of a nation is derived from many sources. These are customarily divided into the *tangible* and *intangible* elements of power, each of which in turn has several components. In the category of tangible elements, military force is of course a basic ingredient. The United States and the Soviet Union are regarded as superpowers in large part because of their unrivaled military strength and, above all, their nuclear arsenals. The Soviet Union, much more than the United States, also possesses impressive "conventional" (or nonnuclear) military forces which are available to the Kremlin for the pursuit of its foreign policy objectives.

The nineteenth-century Prussian General Carl von Clausewitz said that "war is the continuation of politics by other means."* By that dictum, Clausewitz meant that there is an integral relationship between diplomacy and the use of military force; each impinges upon the other. War, for example, usually erupts because of the failure of diplomatic techniques to resolve international disputes; in turn, the results of war directly affect the diplomatic negotiations which follow it. Paraphrasing Clausewitz, several years ago an American military leader said that no nation is likely to win at the conference table what it has lost on the battlefield. The diplomatic results of the Vietnam War clearly bear out that prediction. Thus, a nation's armed strength—and what may sometimes be even more crucial, *other*

nation's perception of its armed strength—is a crucial element in determining its power.†

Economic capability and potential constitute another tangible source of national power. No nation, for example, can be militarily strong without the requisite economic base to sustain its military efforts. Economic power encompasses a broad spectrum, ranging from a nation's total output of goods and services (its Gross National Product, or GNP); to its possession of (or unimpeded access to) a variety of raw materials needed to maintain a high level of industrial and agricultural production; to the ability to control inflation (an influential determinant of the value of a nation's currency in foreign markets). By these criteria, the United States can lay claim to being regarded as a superpower. By the end of the 1970s, its Gross National Product approximated *$2 trillion,* and its annual per capita income was around $7000, or close to $15,000 for each family unit in the United States.

In the contemporary international system, an unprecedented emphasis is placed upon the economic aspects of national power—so much so that many commentators today believe that it is the key element in determining a nation's ability to influence events outside its own borders. What is sometimes called "ecopolitics" has largely eclipsed traditional ideas (like "geopolitics" and military force) as the pivotal concept of international relations in the latter half of the twentieth century. While Soviet military superiority may

---

*General Carl Maria von Clausewitz (1780–1831) published a classic study entitled *On War,* focusing upon the relationship between military force and political goals. That these two concepts are integrally related is indicated by Clausewitz's principle that war is "an act of violence intended to compel our opponent to fulfil our will"—or, in other words, war is a manifestation of *national power.* For more detailed commentary on Clausewitz's thought, see Roger A. Leonard, *Clausewitz on War* (New York: Capricorn Books, 1967); and Anatol Rapoport, *Clausewitz on War* (Baltimore: Penguin Books, 1968).

†By the end of the 1970s, it had become evident that the United States was lagging seriously behind the Soviet Union in certain categories of armed strength; projections indicated that this disparity was likely to widen in the Kremlin's favor in the years ahead. Considerable anxiety existed among officials in Washington that the growing *perception* of America's relative military weakness might "invite aggression" by the Soviet Union. William Safire, in *New York Times,* January 11, 1979.

sometimes give the Kremlin an ability to intervene in areas (like East Africa) outside its borders, in any military competition between the superpowers, most advantages lie with the United States. Moreover, the ability of the United States to assist in the economic development of the Third World exceeds that of the Soviets.[26]

Geography is another tangible element in a nation's power. The geographical aspects of national power are numerous and varied, making generalization difficult. A leading consideration is the *geographic and strategic defensibility* of the country. Until World War II, the security of the United States was greatly enhanced (many Americans assumed that it was "guaranteed") by the existence of geographical barriers, like the Arctic ice cap and the Atlantic and Pacific "ocean moats," protecting it from potential enemies. In marked contrast to the Soviet Union and Poland—which have extremely vulnerable military frontiers—throughout most of its history, the United States has benefited from a highly favorable geographic location, a precondition for its successful adherence to an "isolationist" foreign policy position for nearly a century and a half.

Other geographical aspects of America's power position may be mentioned briefly. An important one is its extensive coastline, containing many good harbors which are essential for trade and commerce and for the operation of a vital defense component—naval strength. Another important dimension of a nation's geographical position is climate. The United States is located in the Temperate Zone—a key fact in accounting for the high level of its agricultural output (Soviet Russia, for example, has no geographic counterpart to America's "corn belt"). A related geographical feature is the rainfall pattern: except for isolated portions of the country, most regions of the United States receive sufficient rainfall to permit a high continuing level of agricultural production. Also indispensable to a high level of economic activity is the existence within the nation's borders of large areas of arable land. In contrast to perhaps the majority of the nations of the world, even today America has no land shortage and is not compelled increasingly to bring "marginal lands" under cultivation to feed its own people as well as millions of people outside its own borders.

Still another significant element in a nation's power is its *population*. Again, this component has several dimensions. The *size* of a nation's population is likely to be crucial in determining its power: While it is a somewhat arbitrary determination, to qualify as a powerful state, a nation must normally have 50 million people or more. America's population numbered just over 226 million people by the 1980s. Within the past two decades, the rate of population growth has slowed down appreciably (approaching Zero Population Growth, or ZPG). Yet a nation's power quite clearly is not a direct function of its population size. China and India have the largest populations of any countries on the globe, but their power to influence developments outside their own borders remains very limited. Conversely, Saudi Arabia has a very small population (estimated at 6 to 9 million people), while its power to determine world oil prices—and hence the economic prosperity and stability of both advanced and less developed societies—is vast.

Other significant aspects of population as an element in national power are such considerations as the *distribution* of the population among various age groups. Throughout the Third and Fourth worlds, for example, the extremely high percentage of young people within the society—who are as a rule economically nonproductive but who require expensive governmental services like health care and educational facilities—places a severe strain upon the resources of indigenous governments. Similarly, the age level of the population, particularly the proportion of older people within it, can affect a nation's economic as well as military capabilities. Since World War II, America's population has been "aging"; enhanced longevity has increased the proportion of elderly citizens within the society, and this fact has significant consequences for such specific problems as the nature of the labor force and the military manpower pool available to support foreign policy objectives. It is a no less influential development in shaping public attitudes toward internal and external policy issues—one of the "intangible" elements in any nation's power.

Every nation's power also consists of certain "intangible" elements affecting its ability to achieve diplomatic objectives. The condition of nuclear stalemate between the superpowers—along with such phenomena as the growing complexity of the international system and the changing nature of foreign policy goals—has greatly enhanced the importance of the intangible components of power.

One of the more important intangible ingredients of power is *public confidence* in the nation's political leadership. The importance of this element was underscored during the Vietnam War: Declining public confidence in the Johnson and Nixon administrations led to Washington's decision to terminate the war in Southeast Asia. Similarly, the effects of the Watergate scandal, which destroyed the Nixon Administration, upon the conduct of American foreign policy were far-reaching and sometimes momentous.[27] By contrast, throughout World War II, a high degree of public confidence supported the Roosevelt Administration's efforts to win the war; and for several years after 1945, public support for the Truman Administration's and later administrations' efforts to "contain" Communist expansionism was also outstanding.

What is the key to that elusive, but vital, condition of public trust in the policies and behavior of national leaders? The answer (if it is known at all) is far too difficult and complex to be discussed in detail here. It must suffice to say that in the realm of foreign affairs, its existence depends heavily upon the degree to which citizens are convinced their leaders are pursuing policies that are consonant with, and promote, the underlying values and goals of the society. In a word, the foreign policies of the government must possess "legitimacy" for a majority of the people: The external behavior of the nation must be—and must be widely *perceived* as being—conducive to the society's welfare and in harmony with its moral and ethical values. If it is not, then an essential ingredient of national power is likely to be lacking, thereby weakening the nation's diplomatic effectiveness.

A related intangible element of national power is the *stability of the government*. For the world's oldest democracy, this is perhaps not a crucial factor in America's ability to achieve its goals overseas. An outstanding consequence of the Watergate episode was the fact that it did *not* precipitate a prolonged constitutional crisis. The transition from the Nixon to the Ford Administration went smoothly, and the unity of the American society was not impaired fundamentally by the episode.

Still another intangible element of national power is the *diplomatic skill and acumen* of the nation's political leaders. The key question here is: Do they know how to *use* effectively the instruments of power which are at their disposal? Here again, we must take note of a unique characteristic of the American tradition and ethos. Throughout American history, both the practice of "diplomacy" and those officials who engage in it have enjoyed very low public esteem. Among all the executive departments, for example, the State Department probably has the poorest "image" among the American people; and since World War II, nearly every secretary of state has left office in the face of greater or lesser public criticism. Along with the concept of power, in the American mind diplomacy has long been associated with Old World political intrigue and conflict; Americans tend to view it as antithetical to New World values (like democracy and governmental decision making responsive to the popular will). During the isolationist era, for example, a major tenet of that approach to foreign affairs was the idea that active American involvement in diplomacy would corrupt the values of the American Republic. Diplomacy was not an activity in which Americans excelled, nor did they desire to acquire the talents needed to do it well!

Constraints on National Power

Within recent years, informed students of international politics have become more aware than ever of certain constraints upon the power of nations to achieve their foreign policy objectives. Early in the postwar era, a perceptive student of American life warned against "the illusion of American omnipotence"—or the expectation that every problem in international politics was susceptible to an "American solution." President John F. Kennedy told his countrymen:

> We must face the fact that the United States is neither omnipotent nor omniscient. . . . that we cannot impose our will upon the other 94 percent of mankind—that we cannot right every wrong or reverse each adversity—and that therefore there cannot be an American solution to every world problem.[28]

In some measure, America's failure to realize the limitations upon its own power was re-

sponsible for the "overextension" of the United States abroad before and during the Vietnam War; and it was perhaps an element in the disillusionment which in time characterized American attitudes toward the results achieved by the foreign aid program.

Initially, it must be recognized that national power is a relative concept. The answer to the question, "What is the power of the United States?" must always be given in terms of its ability *to accomplish some particular or concrete objective*. America's power to devastate the Soviet Union is obviously different from its power to preserve political stability in black Africa or to promote democracy throughout Latin America.

The power of the United States will also vary according to other factors. If it confronts Soviet countervailing power (as, for example, with regard to ideological influence throughout the Third World), the power of the United States will be less than if it does not. If American power is exercised in a familiar and congenial environment (like Western Europe), it will normally be more successful than when it is applied in an unfamiliar setting (like black Africa or the Middle East). And if the power of the United States is utilized to achieve goals which are widely shared by other countries, it will almost invariably yield more favorable results than under the opposite conditions.

Certain constraints exist upon the application of military power to achieve diplomatic objectives in the contemporary period which did not exist (or were not present in the same degree) in earlier eras of international politics. Here, we may think of two kinds of military power: nuclear and nonnuclear (or conventional) force. With the Soviet acquisition of nuclear weapons, a "nuclear balance of terror" came into existence. The superpowers are deterred from employing their nuclear arsenals out of fear of mutual annihilation; and by installing the Washington-Moscow Hot Line and other measures, they have taken steps to prevent an "accidental" nuclear holocaust. Meanwhile, neither the United States nor the Soviet Union has discovered a method of converting its unrivaled nuclear strength *into diplomatic leverage*. The Castro government of Cuba has no real apprehension that Washington is going to use nuclear weapons against it to liquidate massive Cuban involvement in the political affairs of black Africa or to terminate Cuban-sponsored revolutionary activities in Latin America.

Many of these same considerations also apply to nonnuclear weapons, although considerably more flexibility exists in this realm. Without resorting to nuclear weapons, the United States inflicted more destruction upon North Vietnam during the war in Southeast Asia than it inflicted upon Germany in World War II. Yet America still failed to accomplish its objectives in the region. Repeated Soviet military interventions in Eastern Europe since World War II have not guaranteed the loyalty of the peoples of the region, either to indigenous Marxist leaders or to the Soviet Union. In fact, it is possible to argue persuasively in both cases that massive reliance upon military force actually *reduced* the overall power or influence of the United States and the Soviet Union in global affairs by alienating many countries which were repelled by such behavior.

This of course is not to say that military force has totally lost is relevance as an element of national power. No less than in the past, under certain conditions nations must rely upon armed strength to achieve their external objectives. Faced with a steadily rising Soviet defense budget, for example, policy makers in Washington must at least accept the possibility that the Kremlin is planning some new aggressive move to the detriment of American security. On a more limited scale,

the military intervention of the United States in the Dominican Republic in 1965 did accomplish the *immediate* objective: successfully countering a threatened Communist takeover of the country. At the same time, this military intervention by the Johnson Administration also created and aggravated numerous problems in inter-American relations; and it alienated a considerable segment of opinion within the United States.

In more general terms, a major deterrent to reliance upon conventional force to support overseas objectives is that in many settings, the injection of American military power into the situation creates more problems than it solves. In the Third and Fourth worlds, much military intervention is invariably resented by the societies involved; and it often permits anti-American groups (like Communists) to claim that they are spearheading the struggle against colonialism and "Yankee interventionism." Even if it succeeds, the use of conventional force may also produce a kind of permanent or continuing American involvement in the affairs of the country concerned. In the process, the United States becomes (or is widely believed to be) "responsible" for the subsequent actions of the regime or groups which Washington has successfully supported. In the recent period, America's relations with several countries—South Korea, Thailand, Pakistan, and Iran—might be cited to illustrate the problems created by such interventionism.

Third, several commentators have pointed to the changing nature of the international system as another potent constraint upon the application of national power. So far-reaching are many of these changes—and so novel are many of the problems which are at the forefront of international politics today—that the traditional concept of national power may well be outmoded. In contrast to the situation which existed for several preceding centuries, one analysis contends, in the existing international system those nations

> with the most influence are likely to be those which are major constructive participants in the widest variety of coalitions and partnerships, since such countries would have the largest supply of usable political currency—in effect, promissory notes that say: "We will support you on this issue, if you support us on that issue."[29]

According to this interpretation, effective national power today is akin to successful "bargaining" ability, which in turn has at least two components: A nation must have something "to offer" other countries which they desire; and it must be prepared and ready to provide it, in return for concessions by the other countries. National power thus consists primarily of "constructive exchanges" of valued resources (such as an exchange of technological know-how for raw materials) rather than threats of physical devastation or other coercive measures.

Fourth, although it might be difficult to document convincingly, the experience of recent international politics indicates that more than ever, *certain moral-ethical constraints* regulate the application of national power today. In view of America's involvement in the Vietnam War, or the Soviet Union's reliance upon force in dealing with Afghanistan and Poland in more recent years, this might seem a strange and untenable conclusion. Nevertheless, as a generalization it seems warranted. The United States was compelled to *withdraw* its armed forces from Southeast Asia—in large part because of the moral opprobrium directed at its involvement by citizens at home and abroad. The Kremlin has not repeated its overt military intervention in the Eastern European satellite zone, despite evidence of independent diplomatic behavior by Poland, Rumania, and other countries. Nor

did the Kremlin rely upon force to maintain its position in Egypt after Sadat's government in 1972 ordered Moscow to liquidate its massive presence in the country.

For both of the superpowers, policy makers must ask the question: Is reliance upon military force really *worth* incurring the moral censure which is likely to be directed against it for seeking to impose its will upon weaker countries? And if such force is employed, will the net result be an enhancement or an impairment of the nation's power? The American Declaration of Independence called upon the government of Great Britain to exhibit "a decent respect for the opinions of mankind." Applications of national power which patently offend the moral-ethical sensibilities of citizens within the United States and abroad seldom achieve any constructive diplomatic purpose.

Fifth, what is sometimes referred to as the "new agenda" of international politics in the contemporary period imposes constraints upon the use of national power, as that idea has been traditionally construed. During the past two decades, a range of new problems has come to the center of the international stage. Challenges like preventing the proliferation of nuclear weapons and dealing with related issues (like disposal of nuclear waste materials); raising living standards and meeting age-old health and educational needs in less developed societies; strengthening regional institutions and cooperation; raising world food production and devising a more equitable global distribution system; agreeing upon international legal principles regulating national access to the oceans' raw materials—these are prominent items on the "new agenda" of international relations.

For several reasons, this transition has largely rendered traditional ideas about national power obsolete. In most cases—irrespective of whether it is nuclear arsenals or conventional military strength—military power possesses little or no utility in the solution of such problems. To the extent that military expenditures drain national resources, large military establishments may in fact be a real hindrance to their solution.

Moreover, most of these problems are novel challenges. Policy makers in America and other countries possess little or no applicable experience which may be brought to bear in resolving them. Precedents from the era of the classical balance of power are of little use in dealing with the global "population explosion" or ongoing political turmoil in black Africa.

This leads to what is surely one of the most serious constraints upon the power of the United States in the contemporary period. It is the existence of *a cognitive problem*. On the basis of their own experience as a nation—and their diplomatic posture of "isolationism" for some 150 years—Americans are ill-equipped to understand the origins and nature of many problems at the forefront of international concern today; and they are perhaps even less prepared to devise effective solutions for them. Nothing in the nation's past, for example, adequately prepares the American people or their leaders to comprehend why Latin Americans are unable to undertake the kind of internal reforms required for a new era of economic growth and political stability. Nor are Americans likely to understand why tribal, religious, and ethnic minorities in countries like India, Iraq, and Nigeria remain highly antagonistic, thereby impairing the national integrity of these states. For the most part, Americans have very little insight into the implications of curbing the rate of population expansion, or carrying out the "Green Revolution" in agriculture, for the villagers of Southeast Asia or the Nile Valley. Nearly all Americans agree that something "must be done" about such problems. But

specifically what must be done—and how the resources of the United States and other countries can be effectively used to do it—remains a complex and often highly debatable question.

Finally, we must take account of certain constraints upon the power of the United States imposed *by domestic considerations and forces*. Most governments today face intense pressure from their citizens to solve a variety of pressing internal problems. The dominant concerns of the American people revolve around domestic issues, like curbing the rate of inflation, reducing the overall burden of taxation, and doing something about "crime in the streets." (Policy makers in the U.S.S.R. have been under comparable pressures from Soviet citizens in the recent period.)

There has also been a related tendency reinforcing this emphasis upon internal problems. For the United States (and also for the Soviet Union), citizens have become widely disillusioned with the results achieved after nearly a generation of active American involvement in remote areas of the world. To cite a concrete example: The American taxpayers have made available over $200 billion in economic and military assistance to other countries since World War II. When they are confronted with new outbursts of anti-Yankee sentiment in Latin America, or with the fact of defeat in the Vietnam War, or with endless political turmoil in black Africa, or with the apparent impotence of the United Nations to deal with problems of global peace and security, Americans perhaps naturally wonder what this vast outlay of foreign aid has really accomplished. Whatever Americans may have expected their aid to achieve (and some of the goals of the foreign aid program may have always been Utopian), positive results are often difficult to identify. In some contexts (vast American military assistance to the Iranian monarchy is an example) such applications of national power may in the end have produced results *detrimental* to the security and diplomatic interests of the United States. After this experience, it is perhaps not difficult to understand why "neo-isolationist" currents are strong throughout the American society and why policy makers in Washington face public pressure to curtail overseas commitments.

NOTES

1. The literature on the concept of the international system, the subsystems within it, and the behavior of its members is voluminous, and becoming more so every year. A pioneering work using this approach was Morton A. Kaplan, *System and Process in International Politics* (New York: John Wiley, 1957). A convenient overview of the concept of systems theory, containing excerpts from leading proponents of this approach, is James N. Rosenau, *International Politics and Foreign Policy: A Reader in Research and Theory,* rev. ed. (New York: Macmillan, 1969). A sampling of other useful studies includes: Keith R. Legg and James F. Morrision, *Politics and the International System: An Introduction* (New York: Harper & Row, 1971); Karl W. Deutsch, *The Analysis of International Relations,* 2nd ed. (Englewood Cliffs, N.J.: Prentice-Hall, 1978); Raymond F. Hopkins and Richard W. Mansbach, *Structure and Process in International Politics* (New York: Harper & Row, 1973); C. W. Churchman, *The Systems Approach* (New York: Delacorte Press, 1968); E. Laszlo, *The System View of the World* (New York: Braziller, 1972); C. A. McClelland, *Theory and the International System* (New York: Macmillan, 1968); H. J. Spiro, *World Politics: The Global System* (Homewood, Ill.: Dorsey Press, 1966); J. S. Weltman, *Systems Theory in International Relations: A Study of Metaphoric Hypertrophy* (Boston: D. C. Heath, 1973). Nearly all of these studies contain additional bibliographic suggestions on systems theory.

2. For a detailed analysis of this phenomenon, see Richard W. Mansbach, Yale H. Ferguson, and Donald E. Lampert, *The Web of Politics: Non State Actors in the Global System* (Englewood Cliffs, N.J.: Prentice-Hall, 1976).

3. The literature on decision-making theory is voluminous. Among the more useful studies are Richard C. Snyder, H. W. Buck, and Burton Sapin, eds., *Foreign Policy Decision-Making* (New York: Macmillan, 1962); R. C. Snyder, "A Decision-Making Approach to the Study of Political Phenomena," in Roland Young, ed., *Approaches to the Study of Politics* (Evanston, Ill.: Northwestern University Press, 1958); John Golden, "System, Process and Decision-Making," in Morton A. Kaplan, ed., *New Approaches to International Relations* (New York: St. Martin's Press, 1968), pp. 54–83; and various excerpts from advocates of decision-making theory in James N. Rosenau, ed., *International Politics and Foreign Policy,* pp. 167–289.

4. For informative studies of the "perceptions" (and often pervasive misperceptions) which nations have of one another, see the works of John G. Stoessinger: *Why Nations Go to War,* 2nd ed. (New York: St. Martin's Press, 1978); and *Nations in Darkness: China, Russia, and America,* 2nd ed. (New York: Random House, 1975). An older, but useful, analysis of the Cold War is Peter G. Filene, ed., *American Views of Soviet Russia: 1917–1965* (Homewood, Ill.: Dorsey Press, 1968).

5. This concept is developed in detail in Leonard Binder, "The Middle East as a Subordinate International System," *World Politics,* **X** (April, 1958), 408–429. For a more recent exposition of that idea, see the chapter on "The Middle East: A Subordinate System in Global Politics," in Tareq Y. Ismael, ed., *The Middle East in World Politics: A Study in Contemporary International Relations* (Syracuse, N.Y.: Syracuse University Press, 1974), pp. 240–256. For an analysis of Asian political relationships from this perspective, see Michael Brecher, "The Subordinate State Sys-

tem of Southern Asia," *World Politics,* **XV** (January, 1963), 213–235.

6. See the interview by James Reston of Zbigniew Brzezinski, "The World According to Brzezinski," *New York Times Magazine,* December 31, 1978, p. 11.

7. Representative examples of such studies include Roger W. Cobb and Charles Elder, *International Community: A Regional and Global Study* (New York: Holt, Rinehart and Winston, 1970); and W. Andrew Axline and James A. Stegenga, *The Global Community: A Brief Introduction to International Relations* (New York: Dodd, Mead, 1972). See also the chapter on the concept of global community as an approach to American foreign policy in Cecil V. Crabb, Jr., *Policy-Makers and Critics: Conflicting Theories of American Foreign Policy* (New York: Praeger Publishers, 1976), pp. 128–165.

8. Thus Morton A. Kaplan, one of the earliest advocates of a systems approach to international politics, initially identified six kinds or "models" of global systems, only two of which had actually existed. He analyzed each according to five variables—the "rules of the game" obeyed by the members; the "transformation rules" (i.e., its response to factors tending to change the system or keep it from functioning); actors, such as nation-states, alliances, and international organizations; capability variables, such as the power of its members; and information variables—that is, the members' knowledge and perception of one another. See Kaplan, *System and Process in International Politics,* passim.

9. A detailed examination of the traditional balance of power is Edward V. Gulick, *Europe's Classical Balance of Power: A Case History of the Theory and Practice of One of the Great Concepts of European Statecraft* (New York: W. W. Norton, 1955). Briefer discussions of the theory and practice of balance of power may be found in Hans J. Morgenthau, *Politics Among Nations: The Struggle for Power and Peace,* 4th ed. (New York: Alfred A. Knopf, 1967), pp. 161–219; and Inis L. Claude, Jr., *Power and International Rela-*

tions (New York: Random House, 1962), pp. 11–94.

10. Britain's historic attachment to the balance of power was explained in a famous memorandum on the principles of British foreign policy written by Sir Eyre Crowe in 1907. For detailed excerpts from it, see Hans J. Morgenthau and Kenneth W. Thompson, eds., *Principles and Problems of International Politics: Selected Readings* (New York: Alfred A. Knopf, 1952), pp. 247–261. Prime Minister Winston Churchill repeatedly invoked balance-of-power considerations in explaining British foreign policy before and during World War II. See ibid., pp. 261–264.

11. Thus, as a result of his analysis of the Vietnam War and its long-term impact upon American foreign policy, Hans J. Morgenthau believed that threats to American security posed by "hegemonial powers in Europe and Asia" should be "countered by the traditional methods of balance of power. . . ." He also thought that the threat of nuclear destruction must be "countered by the novel methods of deterrence and arms control," while ideological challenges to national security should be "countered by the health and attractiveness of American society." See his *A New Foreign Policy for the United States* (New York: Frederick A. Praeger, 1969), p. 242.

12. One of the leading students of World War I identified attachment to the balance of power as a major cause of that destructive conflict. See the study by Sidney B. Fay, *The Origins of the World War* (New York: Macmillan, 1941), especially pp. 34–40.

13. James Chace, *A World Elsewhere: The New American Foreign Policy* (New York: Charles Scribner's Sons, 1973), p. 34.

14. For further discussion of the ambiguity of the term *balance of power,* see Inis L. Claude, Jr., *Power and International Relations,* pp. 11–40; and Ernest P. Haas, "The Balance of Power as a Guide to Policy-Making," *Journal of Politics* 15 (August, 1953), 370–398.

15. The problem of the nomenclature to be employed in describing the existing international system is analyzed in detail in Joseph L.

Nogee, "Polarity: An Ambiguous Concept," *Orbis,* **XVIII** (Winter, 1975), 1193–1224. See also the brief monograph by Wolfram F. Hanreider, "Foreign Policies and the International System: A Theoretical Introduction," published by the General Learning Press, New York, 1971.

16. Until 1974, five members of the international system—the United States, the Soviet Union, Britain, France, and Communist China—possessed nuclear arsenals. In that year, India also exploded its first nuclear weapon. Nearly 30 countries possess nuclear power plants, and among these several seem likely candidates for future membership in the "nuclear club." These include: Japan, West Germany, Argentina, Brazil, Pakistan, Israel, South Africa, Portugal, and Saudi Arabia—most of which have refused to sign an international agreement designed to halt the proliferation of nuclear weapons. See John W. Finney, in *New York Times,* July 5, 1974.

17. See Henry Bienen, in *New York Times,* January 15, 1979. This observer describes the "new influentials" as those members of the Third World "whose wealth, size, military and strategic importance give them a prominence in regional politics and in international forums."

18. The members of the European Economic Community have experienced considerable difficulty unifying their foreign policy positions on a variety of issues. For an illuminating discussion of the problem, see Robert S. Wood, "The Diplomacy of the Enlarged European Community," *World Affairs,* **137** (Summer, 1974), 3–23. For a discussion of the threat to European diplomatic cohesion presented by the "oil boycott" imposed by Middle Eastern producers in 1973, see John A. Cicco, Jr., "The Atlantic Alliance and the Arab Challenge: The European Perspective," *World Affairs,* **137** (Spring, 1975), 303–326. Within the EEC, by the late 1970s West Germany was seeking to establish its claim as an influential Middle Power based upon possession of perhaps the strongest economy in the region and its role as a "bridge" between East-

ern and Western Europe. See Karl Kaiser, in *New York Times,* January 21, 1979.

19. As always, in describing the present-day international system, the findings of informed commentators often vary widely. One recent study, for example, utilizes a different fourfold classification of members: the industrialized nations of the world (or "First World"); the "centrally planned" or Marxist nations (the "Second World"); the "middle-income developing countries" (the "Third World"); and the "low-income developing countries" (the "Fourth World"). Under this scheme, *economic* levels are the major criteria for determining a nation's place in the system. See Leslie Wolf-Phillips, "Why Third World?" *Third World Quarterly,* **1** (January, 1979), 103–114. One of the oddities of this system is that Yugoslavia—generally viewed as a leader of the Third World—is included in the Second World.

20. An illuminating case study of the tendency being described here—efforts by members of the Third World to involve the superpowers in controversies in which they are actively embroiled—is the recent analysis of Soviet-Egyptian relations by Alvin Z. Rubinstein, *Red Star on the Nile: The Soviet-Egyptian Influence Relationship Since the June War* (Princeton, N.J.: Princeton University Press, 1977).

21. For an informative discussion of the problem, see Bayless Manning, "Goals, Ideology and Foreign Policy," *Foreign Affairs,* **54** (January, 1976), 271–284. The author contends that "A list of generalized national foreign policy objectives proves to be of little or no assistance in working through . . . a typical matrix of questions, disputes and considerations" confronting the United States overseas. Ibid., p. 273.

22. See the definition of "power" in Jack C. Plano and Roy Olton, *The International Relations Dictionary* (New York: Holt, Rinehart and Winston, 1969), p. 133.

23. Morgenthau, *Politics Among Nations,* p. 26.

24. A. F. K. Organski, *World Politics,* 2nd ed. (New York: Alfred A. Knopf, 1968), p. 104.

25. The "Monroe Doctrine" was enunciated in President James Monroe's Seventh Annual Message to Congress, on December 2, 1823. For detailed excerpts, see Appendix No. 2, in Crabb, *Policy-makers and Critics,* pp. 302–304.

26. Flora Lewis, in *New York Times,* December 31, 1978.

27. For a discussion of the impact of the Watergate crisis upon American foreign diplomacy, see Leslie H. Gelb and Anthony Lake, "Watergate and Foreign Policy," *Foreign Policy,* **12** (Fall, 1973), 176–189.

28. See D. W. Brogan, "The Illusion of American Omnipotence," *Harper's,* **205** (December, 1952), 21–28; and for President Kennedy's views in this vein, see Theodore C. Sorensen, *Kennedy* (New York: Harper & Row, 1965), p. 511.

29. Seyom Brown, "The Changing Essence of Power," *Foreign Affairs,* **51** (January, 1973), 286–299. The quotation is found on p. 289.

Chapter 2

The American Ethos and Foreign Affairs

Every society is unified by certain ideas, ideals, and values, since otherwise it would not constitute an organized "society." These shared concepts are drawn from a wide variety of sources, the most important of which are the society's religious and moral codes, its cultural norms and values, and its history and experiences in responding to diverse internal and external challenges.

The commonly held ideas uniting a society are often described by such terms as its *national ethos* or its *national style* or its *national character*. The underlying idea is that every nation exhibits a reasonably predictable syndrome of attitudes and behavior characteristics which distinguish it in some measure from other nations.[1] If the concept of the "international system," discussed in Chapter 1, emphasized the uniformities and regularities in the behavior of the members of the international system, our examination of national ethos calls attention to the uniqueness of the American approach to foreign affairs. It highlights those characteristics of national diplomacy which are (in degree at least, if not always in kind) *distinctively American*. The head of the American bureau of the Soviet Foreign Office, for example, is amply aware that when the Kremlin negotiates an arms-limitation treaty with the United States, it may expect a different style of negotiating behavior and a different set of issue concerns than if it negotiates with Communist China, or with France, or with India. To no inconsiderable degree, these differences can be accounted for by reference to the distinctive traditions, character, and ethos of the American society.

The National Ethos: Pitfalls and Parameters

The concept of the national ethos or national character is an old idea. Before World War II, textbooks on international relations employed it extensively (and perhaps uncritically) to account for global political relationships. Today, the concept is often eclipsed by more quantitatively oriented approaches to the subject, although in recent years informed political commentators have rediscovered the concept and used it to explain the foreign policy behavior of particular nations.[2]

Admittedly, the idea of national character must be utilized with caution and with due regard for certain limitations and pitfalls surrounding it. Initially, it has to be acknowledged that the concept of national character tends to be *highly subjective*. The national ethos is not a concept which lends itself to scientific or quantitative analysis. The subjective nature of the idea does not mean, however, that it can be ignored by serious students of American diplomatic behavior. Instead, it may signify that in many instances a nation's conduct in foreign affairs must largely be accounted for by reference to certain "irrational" or nonquantifiable influences, which are sometimes as decisive as they are intangible and elusive.

In the second place, in employing the concept of national character there is perhaps an inherent tendency to lapse into stereotyped and prejudicial thinking about the behavior of the United States and other states. The Russians are "inherently aggressive"; or the Chinese (along with other Asians) are "inscrutable"; or the Latin Americans are "politically unstable"; or the Germans are incurably "militaristic"—such stereotyped ideas are commonplace, and their uncritical reiteration does little to promote genuine understanding of international political relationships.

In the case of the American society, a third admonition is in order. The principal elements in the American approach to foreign relations *do not comprise a harmonious, logically consistent set of national attitudes and behavior patterns*. To the contrary, collectively they form a congeries of disparate, sometimes rather antithetical, ideas and values which, when applied to the foreign policy

realm, tend to produce an *inconsistent* pattern of behavior toward other countries. Thus, throughout its diplomatic history the United States has sometimes been accused of acting "unilaterally" in foreign affairs (which was a major tenet of the old isolationist approach to foreign relations) and of seeking to create and strengthen a closer sense of "international community" (which was a conspicuous element of Wilsonian thought and of later Presidents, like Franklin D. Roosevelt). Alternatively, during any given period of time, Americans may find themselves accused of excessive "idealism" (of trying to "remake the world") and of unqualified "realism" or *Realpolitik* (or indiscriminately applying American power abroad to achieve national goals). Undeniably, such inconsistencies have been—and are likely to remain—a feature of American diplomacy; and they have their origins in no small measure in the incompatible and incongruous ideas deeply embedded in the American national ethos.

This is perhaps merely another way of calling attention to a singular characteristic of American foreign policy since the founding of the Republic. If any one label can legitimately be attached to American diplomacy (and that is of course a hazardous undertaking), it would be the word pragmatic. Insofar as the American society has a national philosophy or political credo, it is *pragmatism*.* If it can accu-

---

*Although European thought also contributed to the school of philosophy known as "pragmatism" (or "eclecticism"), it became uniquely identified with the American society. An early advocate of this approach was Benjamin Franklin; later nineteenth-century spokesmen for the movement were William James and John Dewey. Pragmatism was essentially a philosophical revolt against "universalist" and absolutist philosophies which depended upon *a priori* ideas incapable of scientific verification. Influenced by the English "Utilitarians" (who advocated "the greatest good for the greatest number") and by the scientific findings and theories of Charles Darwin, pragmatists emphasized such concepts as change, movement,

rately be called a philosophy (and informed students of modern political thought hold differing views on the question), pragmatism is synonymous with "the American way of life."[3] Judging "each case on its merits" and in the light of prevailing circumstances; solving "one problem at a time"; preferring a "middle-of-the-road" position on controversial public issues—these are all popular expressions of the American society's nondoctrinaire, eclectic orientation.

Pragmatists are seldom concerned with the consistency of their actions over time or with the long-range consequences of the kind of "incremental" decision making which led to American embroilment in the Vietnam War.[4] Since the circumstances facing the United States in East Asia may (and usually do) differ radically from those existing in the Middle East or Western Europe, American policies toward these diverse regions are likely to be different. For that reason, as many students of American diplomacy have complained, it is very difficult for the United States to adopt and pursue a general and totally consistent policy, applicable to all countries outside its borders. After World War II, the containment policy adopted by the Truman Administration, and supported by successive administrations for a generation or more after 1947, was interpreted and applied quite differently on the eastern frontier of non-Communist Europe, in the Middle East, in Asia, and in Latin America.

---

adaptation, and process. For pragmatists, *experience* was the most reliable test of truth. How well did a philosophical concept or system *actually work*? What were its *consequences* for human society? To what degree did it actually promote human well-being and betterment? How "practical" was it and to what degree did it conform to "common sense"? These were the guidelines which pragmatists believed should be applied to any search for truth. For more extended discussion, see John E. Bentley, *An Outline of American Philosophy* (Paterson, N.J.: Littlefield, Adams and Co., 1963), pp. 137–177.

Americans, most students of the society agree, are remarkably nonideological people. They evince little interest in philosophical questions and complex ideological systems. Indeed, they are perhaps *repelled* by such ideas, viewing them as contrary to "the American way of life." One reason for America's highly adverse reaction to Communism after World War II—and to Nazism before and during the war—was perhaps a deep-seated aversion to the idea that political behavior should be dictated by the requirements of a rigid ideological system.

It is, therefore, usually a mistake to characterize American foreign policy as solely "idealistic" or "realistic." Both elements can be identified in the nation's diplomatic tradition. During certain periods—and Dr. Henry Kissinger, who was an influential foreign policy adviser to Presidents Nixon and Ford, exemplified the point—American foreign policy is likely to contain both idealistic and realistic elements. While Dr. Kissinger was an avowed practitioner of *Realpolitik* diplomacy, he also recognized, and stated on several occasions, that the United States could never gain global support for its policies by relying upon narrowly conceived definitions of its "national interest" or by merely attempting to preserve the balance of power throughout the world.[5]

An intriguing question—and one which students of American diplomacy have thus far largely neglected—is why during any one period American policy makers are motivated to select the particular "mix" of idealism and realism which can be identified at any given time. In more general philosophical terms, the problem which consistently faces the pragmatist—as he seeks to solve "each problem on its merits"—is how to identify the salient "merits" of, let us say, America's relations with the Republic of South Africa. And how to decide that some "merits" are more important than other "merits" in terms of their impact upon the United States. Such questions are often extremely difficult to answer authoritatively, and the failure or inability to answer them sometimes leaves the student of American foreign policy to wonder what considerations are really uppermost in the minds of decision makers when they commit the United States to a particular course of action diplomatically.

Idealism, Morality, and Utopianism

In terms of its impact upon the conduct of diplomacy, few tenets of the American ethos can rival *idealism* as a conspicuous element in the nation's approach to foreign policy. Idealism is frequently (and in the author's view, not altogether correctly) regarded as the opposite of political "realism," whose tenets we shall examine at a later stage. By definition, idealism measures the acceptability of national policy by the degree to which it conforms with certain ideals, or values, or ethical principles identified with the American tradition. In contrast to the political realist (who is primarily interested in how nations *actually do* conduct their political relationships), the idealist is concerned chiefly with how nations *ought to* conduct their foreign affairs and with demanding that international politics promote human well-being.

In the postwar period, tangible expressions of American idealism include: Washington's attempts to promote political liberalization and human freedom behind the Iron Curtain; efforts to create and support democratic governments in Latin America and other regions; attempts to protect South Korea, South Vietnam, and other vulnerable countries from aggression or other foreign threats; programs designed to eliminate (or reduce) poverty throughout the Third World; efforts by the United States to limit the "proliferation" of nuclear weapons and to reduce the level of global armaments; and campaigns to promote international human rights. For two centuries, America's approach to external affairs has had what may be called a high "idealistic content," and there is no evidence that this characteristic of its diplomatic behavior is likely to change in the near future.[6] The concept—taken from the Declaration of Independence—that a nation's behavior should exhibit "a decent respect for the opinions of mankind"—perhaps epitomizes the idealist approach to foreign policy.

Two influential examples of American idealism may be cited from the nation's early history. One of these is the Constitution of the United States, particularly the first ten amendments (known collectively as the Bill of Rights). After its ratification, the Constitution influenced the political development of countless other countries. Ideas and provisions contained in it, for example, were widely adopted in the constitutions of the independent Latin American states. After World War II, newly independent nations throughout the Afro-Asian world also widely "borrowed" many of their constitutional principles from the American experience.

The other early example of the impact of idealistic principles on the conduct of foreign affairs was the Monroe Doctrine (1823)—in some respects, the most momentous development in the nation's diplomatic experience.[7] We shall discuss the specific provisions of this historic pronouncement more fully in Chapters 11 and 14, dealing with the United States' relations with Western Europe and Latin America, respectively. Here, our interest is confined to pointing out that in his celebrated speech, President James Monroe emphasized that the societies of the Old and New Worlds constituted *different political systems;* their political relations were actuated by dissimilar principles and goals. A major purpose of Monroe's doctrine, therefore, was *to preserve this fundamental distinction,* by keeping the American republics isolated from the contaminating political ideas and practices prevalent in the Old World.

Over the course of American diplomatic history, this idealistic propensity has had several different manifestations. Let us briefly examine a number of these. Initially, and perhaps most fundamentally, there is the American conception of the international political system. The basic premise underlying the nation's approach to external affairs has usually been that global political problems could be "solved," without recourse to war and violence, in a manner consonant with the American society's most cherished values. To the American mind, a peaceful and benign human society is the desirable and normal condition of mankind; wars and other forms of human conflict were, therefore, aberrations, which reflected the "failure" of human society to base its actions upon its highest ethical principles.[8] Thus, a leading student of modern international relations has contrasted the European with the American viewpoint toward war. For Europeans, wars were regarded as inevitable or as an integral part of international political relationships—in much the same way that "competition" is an intrinsic part of global business and commercial relationships. For Americans, wars are regarded as inherently "evil, senseless, and cruel." They are instigated by misguided or ambitious political elites, who ignore the pacific impulses of their own people; international conflicts are produced by "war criminals," who place the achievement of their egocentric goals ahead of the welfare of their own and other societies.[9] President Woodrow Wilson's characterization of World War I as "the war to end wars" clearly depicted this American attitude. The nation's attachment to isolationism stemmed in part from a conviction that this course would assure peace and stability for the Western Hemisphere and that ultimately it would contribute to global peace and stability. This same frame of mind underlay American efforts to "outlaw" war as an instrument of national policy (as in the Kellogg-Briand Pact of 1928).

Another conspicuous element in American idealism has been the society's long-standing opposition to "militarism," to the creation and maintenance of a large standing army in peacetime, to peacetime conscription of troops for the armed forces, and to undue military influence in national policy making. The concept of the all-volunteer army exemplifies this traditional American idea. From the colonial period (when British troops stationed in the colonies repeatedly infringed upon the rights of citizens), Americans have repeatedly expressed their deep-seated skepticism about the need for large military forces and about the dangers which they pose to internal liberties.[10] As we shall see more fully in Chapter 3, one of the most basic American constitutional principles is the idea that the President is the commander in chief of the armed forces. For over two centuries, the principle of "civilian supremacy" over the military establishment has been a cherished concept of the American democracy. When circumstances have compelled national leaders to resort to conscription (as during World Wars I and II), the American people accepted this necessity; but the "civilian army" which was raised during the Second World War, for example, was quickly demobilized once hostilities had ended, so that citizens could return to their normal civilian pursuits.

A corollary idea has been the belief—conspicuous in the American society since the end of the nineteenth century—that national military arsenals should be reduced and expenditures for new weapons drastically curtailed. Since around 1900, the United States has been at the forefront of nations calling for international agreements to limit armaments. From the first and second Hague conferences

(1899 and 1907), through the Washington Naval Armaments Conference during the early 1920s, to post-World War II efforts (like the "Baruch Plan") to limit nuclear weapons and thereafter to prevent "nuclear proliferation," to the more recent SALT I and SALT II proposals to curb the arms race between the United States and the Soviet Union in nuclear-armed missiles and bombers—in these and other instances, American officials have played a leading role in the quest for arms reduction. As with many other ideas forming part of the national ethos, this one is seldom adhered to with perfect consistency by the American people and their leaders. For example, in 1947, the Truman Administration committed the nation to the strategy of "containment," directed against expansive Communism—and for over a generation after that date implementation of the containment strategy required the creation and maintenance of a powerful military arsenal, particularly in airpower and seapower. By the early 1980s, Americans were deeply concerned about a growing military imbalance between the two superpowers. In certain categories of military strength, the Soviet Union already surpassed the United States, and (with Soviet military expenditures more than double the American rate of defense spending) this disparity was likely to widen in the years ahead. Consequently, the Reagan Administration advocated a substantial increase in American defense spending.

Another prominent feature of American idealism has been its emphasis upon *legalism* and *legal agreements* in its relations with other countries. It is a commonplace observation to say that America is perhaps the most "law-oriented" society in the modern world. (This is not the same as saying that Americans are an especially law-abiding people. The crime rate in the United States, for example, is higher than it is in most other Western soci-eties.) The American society has more lawyers per capita than any other society; and as the increasingly active role of the Supreme Court in dealing with contemporary social, economic, and racial issues illustrates, Americans rely heavily upon legal processes to solve urgent domestic problems.

This tendency has long characterized the American approach to foreign relations. George F. Kennan and countless other commentators have identified, and often deplored, America's penchant for "legalism" in dealing with diplomatic questions.[11] This propensity for legalism has taken several concrete forms. There is, for example, America's belief in the efficacy of treaty agreements as a method of resolving international tensions and promoting global security. Thus, President Wilson's secretary of state, William Jennings Bryan, advocated the novel idea of "cooling-off treaties": nations would promise to refrain from using armed force for a specified period of time in settling their disputes. At the end of the 1920s, the American people and their leaders were ecstatic about the Kellogg-Briand Pact to "outlaw war" among nations—another legal instrument, largely formulated at Washington's initiative. President Franklin D. Roosevelt thought (in most cases, erroneously) that, by reliance upon various written and verbal understandings with Soviet dictator Joseph Stalin, he had gained Soviet cooperation in achieving several American goals—like the preservation of international peace by reliance upon the United Nations, democracy in Eastern Europe, and the assurance of stability and democracy in China.[12] The expected result of course did not occur. The Kremlin showed no compunction about violating such agreements whenever its diplomatic purposes dictated this course. After 1945, American officials devoted untold time and energy to formulating "protests" about such violations and to other efforts designed to enforce the agreements in the face of Soviet intransigence. Yet such experiences have done little to diminish America's confidence in legal instruments and procedures for resolving international tensions.

For some 200 years, America's preference for legal instruments and procedures as effective diplomatic techniques has perhaps suffered from two major defects. The first is an underlying assumption that other societies accord the law the veneration it has traditionally received from Americans. The American approach is predicated upon certain ideas which do not enjoy universal acceptance in other societies: that *the law reflects the society's basic values and goals;* that it is just and equitable; that citizens enjoy "the equal protection of the laws"; and that (as President Richard Nixon discovered) no official or citizen is "above the law." In societies outside the United States, such conceptions of the law do not necessarily exist. In totalitarian or authoritarian states, for example, the law may often be viewed as an instrument of political oppression; in other societies, it may be regarded by some groups as a mechanism for perpetuating economic, social, and racial injustice.

The other defect in America's reliance upon legal instruments and processes to resolve international controversies is perhaps the failure to comprehend the implications of the fact that *a successful legal system reflects an underlying consensus within a society concerning basic values and goals.* With some exceptions, no such consensus exists throughout the international system. A single issue—continuing controversy between the Soviet Union and the United States over the existence of "democracy" in Eastern Europe—may be cited to illustrate the point. During and after World War II, officials in Washington thought they had obtained the consent of Moscow to create and maintain democratic political sys-

tems in that portion of East-Central Europe which was under Soviet military occupation. Yet as events proved, recurrent disagreement between the two superpowers over political developments in this zone proved to be a major factor causing and perpetuating the Cold War between them. A number of interrelated factors led to the breakdown of the Soviet-American agreements on Eastern Europe —none perhaps more crucial than differing interpretations in Washington and Moscow of the concept of "democracy." Inevitably perhaps, American leaders equated democracy with such fundamental concepts as freedom of speech, of religion, of assembly; with the right of dissent and political opposition; and with universal suffrage. The Soviet interpretation of democracy—exemplified by the concept of the "people's democracy"—was fundamentally different. To the American mind, it was the antithesis of true democracy, deriving perhaps primarily from two influences: the Marxist ideological credo and Lenin's notion of the "dictatorship of the proletariat"; and the centuries-old Russian authoritarian tradition.

American officials have confronted essentially the same problem in numerous other settings since World War II. In regions like black Africa and the Middle East, it is evident that leaders and masses view democracy in different terms from the way the concept is usually interpreted in the West. In these regions (as Egyptian President Gamal Abdel Nasser often explained), the concept of democracy is often tainted because of its association with Western colonialism. The British, for example, "imposed" democracy upon Egypt after World War I; but most Egyptians believe that real democracy did not exist in the country (if it exists even now) prior to the Egyptian revolution of 1952, which ultimately led to Nasser's accession to the presidency. In other Third World societies, democracy may be defined primarily as an effort *to improve living standards*. After the overthrow of the Iranian monarchy in 1979, the new government advocated a system called "Islamic democracy" based upon the principles of the Islamic (in Iran, the Shi'ite) religious faith. In other settings, concepts like "guided democracy" and "presidential democracy" have been added to the lexicon of political science since World War II. Successfully responding to such distinctive versions of democracy in Iran and other settings is likely to be a difficult and continuing challenge for American policy makers.

Still another prominent strain in American idealism *has been opposition to colonialism and imperialism*. Perhaps because of their own successful revolt against the British Empire, throughout their diplomatic history Americans have vocally, and sometimes materially, supported anticolonial causes. President James Monroe's celebrated doctrine was designed in part to protect the newly independent nations of Latin America from a reimposition of European colonialism. After the Spanish-American War, America's acquisition of the Philippines was reluctant; the step was taken only after the McKinley Administration became convinced that American acquisition was the only alternative to immediate German colonization of the country. During World War I, President Woodrow Wilson's concept of "self-determination" was perhaps the most subversive idea in modern history, in terms of its impact upon existing colonial empires. Ultimately this Wilsonian concept swept the Afro-Asian world and sustained the nationalist movements which finally destroyed the British, French, Dutch, Portuguese, and other European colonial systems after World War II. During the Second World War, in Gaddis Smith's words, "President Roosevelt and his advisers worried less about the possibility of conflict with Russia than about the continued existence of western, particularly British, imperialism."[13] A tangible expression of America's opposition to colonial rule was Washington's grant of independence to the Philippines in 1946. In some measure, America's adverse reaction to Soviet intervention in Eastern Europe since World War II stems from a conviction that Moscow has created a *de facto* colonial system in this region. To no inconsiderable extent, the opposition that developed within the United States to the Vietnam War reflected the nation's long-standing bias against colonialism. Many Americans believed, correctly or incorrectly, that by its intervention in Southeast Asia the United States was seeking to impose its own colonial regime upon the region, in the wake of the collapse of French colonialism.

After the liquidation of traditional European colonialism, a new term—*neocolonialism*—entered the vocabulary of international politics. Widely employed by political leaders throughout the Third World, the concept of neocolonialism purported to describe new forms of colonial dependency existing in the contemporary period. In reality, the term *neocolonialism* was a vague and imprecise concept encompassing a wide variety of political phenomena. It might denote the kind of "satellite" status which most Eastern European nations held in the Soviet European zone. It might equally well be applied to various forms of economic interdependence and dependency: Since the early eighteenth century, for example, Latin America has been dependent economically and commercially on the United States. It might also designate attempts by powerful countries to establish and maintain a "sphere of influence" or decisive political "presence" in particular regions, as the United States has preserved since 1947 in the Mediterranean area, or as the Soviet Union (joined by Castro's Cuba) created in the eastern horn of Africa in the late 1970s. In recent years, the United States has repeatedly confronted the accusation that its policies are motivated by a neocolonialist impulse. For several reasons, the accusation is perhaps inevitable and difficult to answer satisfactorily.

In the first place, the United States is a superpower, with global political and military responsibilities. In the second place, according to most criteria it also has one of the strongest economic systems on the globe —one whose continued prosperity increasingly requires dependence upon access to foreign raw materials and upon sales in foreign markets.

In the third place, in common with the Soviet Union, Japan, and most nations of Western Europe, the gap between the American standard of living and conditions in most Third World societies *continues to widen.* In the fourth place, Third World demands for a "new world economic order"—or, more specifically, for a more equitable distribution of the world's raw materials, for more favorable price levels for Third World exports, and for larger infusions of foreign aid by the developed countries—have thus far received what Third World governments view as inadequate support from officials in Washington and other Western capitals.

In the fifth place, charges of neocolonialism leveled against the United States, it may as well be acknowledged frankly, often serve useful purposes when employed by political leaders and movements in Third World societies. The old Chinese custom of blaming the evils of the society upon the activities of "foreign devils" has its counterpart in many other countries. As Voltaire once said about God: "If God didn't exist, it would be necessary to invent Him." The accusation that the United States is engaged in neocolonialism often serves useful purposes, such as diverting public attention from the lack of progress being made by incumbent political regimes or unifying domestic opinion by concentrating attention on a real or imagined foreign threat.

The accusation that American foreign policy is actuated by a neocolonialist impulse may be basically true or false, depending largely upon how the concept is defined. If neocolonialism means primarily that the United States is a more powerful nation than almost any other country with which it has relations—and that, therefore, the relationship is *an inherently unequal one*—the charge is basically true. If, however, neocolonialism means that in its relationships with weaker countries the United States consistently endeavors to dominate them politically, to control their decision-making processes, or to impose its own ideology and system of government upon them, the accusation is basically false. As we noted in Chapter 1, along with their Soviet counterparts, American officials have found their power to engage successfully in this kind of behavior increasingly limited; and there is no convincing evidence that this tendency will be reversed in the near future.

American Attitudes Toward Power

A strong American antipathy toward perhaps the most pivotal idea in international politics—the concept of "national power" and its variations (like "power politics," "power struggle," and "balance of power")—constitutes another element in the American approach to foreign affairs. Traditionally, Americans have viewed the concept of national power as part of the philosophical legacy of the Old World, having no place in the political ideology and relationships of the New World.

At the outset, we need to be aware of several anomalies with regard to traditional American attitudes toward power. Not infrequently throughout the nation's diplomatic history, Americans have deprecated the role of power in global political relationships—even while they were in the process of using it decisively! As all students of modern history are aware, American power tilted the scales in favor of the Allies in both the First and Second World wars. Since 1945 American power has been crucial in preserving the nuclear balance, in protecting the security of Western Europe, and in meeting the economic needs of societies throughout the Third World.

Moreover, no society in history perhaps is as well acquainted with the *reality* of power as the United States. Utilizing the land and other resources available to create one of the highest standards of living on the globe; having the highest per capita energy consumption of any society; relying upon modern advertising techniques to sell products; employing the techniques of successful salesmanship, lobbying, and the principles of "how to win friends and influence people"—these are all exercises in the use of power which have long been familiar to Americans.

We have already alluded to American attitudes with regard to reliance upon armed force to achieve national policy goals: Except where the security of the United States and its allies is in immediate danger, the United States has traditionally opposed such action. Few writers have stressed the American misunderstanding of the fundamental role of power in international politics as frequently, and as pointedly, as Walter Lippmann. Lippmann believed that our approach to foreign relations has been filled with "stereotyped prejudices and sacred cows and wishful conceptions," to the extent that we are often incapable of formulating workable policies. Our basic weakness is a failure to recognize, "to admit, to take as the premise of our thinking, the fact that rivalry and strife and conflict among states, communities, and factions are the normal condition of mankind."[14]

Such habits of thought stem from a variety of influences in the nation's history. From America's own internal experience, the people have taken the view that fundamental human conflicts did not exist, or if they did, that they could be quickly resolved, because down to the 1960s remarkably few such conflicts in fact did persist. Marxist ideology notwithstanding, the United States perhaps approximates more nearly than any other country the "classless society." Until recent years, conflicts of all kinds—economic, religious, ethnic, racial—produced relatively little enduring strife, compared with the Old World and the newer nations of Asia and Africa. America has never experienced prolonged and irreconcilable divisions among its people. Throughout most of their history, Americans somehow learned to channel existing differences into nonviolent avenues, to smooth them out, to make them seem secondary to the task of creating upon a continent the "American way of life." This has been done (or Americans *believed* it was being done) by providing unparalleled opportunities for material advancement; by steadily trying to offer equal opportunities for all in ever-widening spheres of national life; by de-emphasizing doctrinal and ideological differences in favor of immediate and attainable goals for human betterment; by listening to the demands of dissatisfied groups and, in time, meeting most of them; by insisting upon fair play in economic, social, and political life.

The consequences of America's attitude toward the role of power conflicts have been far-reaching and decisive. It has heavily colored the nation's appraisal of the basis of its security. From superficial examinations of their own history, Americans have believed that their security could be explained by a variety of factors, none of which had anything to do with power. There was first the evident fact of geographical separation from Europe and Asia which, before the air age, did provide a substantial degree of military protection. Then there was the fact that the United States had repeatedly warned other countries to stay out of the Western Hemisphere—and, with few exceptions, the warning had been heeded. From the time of the Monroe Doctrine in 1823 to World War II, the United States acted as though its security were a natural right; as though changes in the European balance of power could not affect it; and as though power played an inconsequential if not altogether negligible role in international relations. Walter Lippmann has written that for over a hundred years

> The idealistic objections to preparedness, to strategic precautions, and to alliances came to dominate American thinking. . . . The objections flourished, and became a national ideology, owing to the historical accident that in that period Asia was dormant, Europe divided, and Britain's command of the sea unchallenged. As a result, we never had to meet our obligations in this hemisphere and in the Pacific, and we enjoyed a security which in fact we took almost no measures to sustain.[15]

A corollary of the American failure to accept the role of power has been the failure to understand that, in the successful management of foreign affairs, assets must equal or exceed liabilities. While it is true that power cannot be calculated with great precision, a rough kind of equilibrium must be maintained between a nation's foreign commitments and its ability to protect them. Bankruptcy, Walter Lippmann argued, is the only word to describe American foreign policy at crucial intervals in history. American foreign policy was bankrupt for the same reason that we speak of a bankrupt business: Obligations were assumed greater than the nation's resources, at least greater than the resources available to

the nation's leaders at any given time. The art of conducting foreign policy successfully, Lippmann contended, "consists in bringing into balance, with a comfortable surplus of power in reserve, the nation's commitments and the nation's power."[16]

Lippmann's analysis suggests two kinds of problems or imbalances in American foreign policy which policy makers must seek to avoid. One is illustrated by the period before, and immediately after, World War II when the nation's diplomatic obligations exceeded its power capabilities. As the United States discovered painfully when the Korean War erupted in 1950, maintenance of the security of the non-Communist world demanded the existence of requisite military force—along with the willingness to use force when required—to defend vital diplomatic objectives.

The other imbalance was epitomized by the Vietnam War, when massive national power was employed in behalf of goals and objectives which were increasingly unclear and confused to citizens at home and abroad. Even without employing its nuclear arsenal, the United States possessed the power to devastate Southeast Asia—and it largely accomplished this. Yet the underlying *purposes* of the application of American power in this region—or the extent to which this massive reliance upon military force actually promoted the nation's diplomatic goals—were questions which successive administrations in Washington had difficulty in answering convincingly. To countless Americans and foreigners, the nation's military intervention in Vietnam seemed an undertaking unrelated to, and in some cases inimical to, the realization of the goals of United States foreign policy. The use of force in Southeast Asia, therefore, in time lost "legitimacy" and was repudiated by the American people. The Vietnam War experience reminded Americans painfully and perhaps indelibly of the limits of their nation's power.

After Vietnam, the pendulum swung in the opposite direction. America, many citizens believed, had become a "crippled giant" which was incapable of accomplishing *any* constructive purpose abroad. After several years of attempting to "police the world," throughout most of the 1970s the nation engaged in diplomatic retrenchment and exhibited a reluctance to assume international obligations. Then, by the end of the decade—following a series of diplomatic reverses in the Persian Gulf area, Latin America, and other settings—America found its diplomatic credibility seriously impaired. By the early 1980s, therefore, American officials were concerned about whether the nation possessed sufficient and applicable forms of power to protect the security and diplomatic interests of the United States.

The underlying American aversion to the concept of national power and *Realpolitik* diplomacy came most prominently to the fore perhaps in the growing public and congressional criticism directed at Secretary of State Henry Kissinger during the Nixon and Ford administrations. Kissinger was an avowed exponent and practitioner of *Realpolitik.** In the

post-Vietnam War era, Kissinger was convinced, what the international system needed most urgently was a new "structure" (or as President Nixon described it, "a new structure for peace").[17] Much of Kissinger's time and energy was devoted to creating this new structure, based upon balance of power and other *Realpolitik* principles. Yet Kissinger's efforts to function as a kind of American Bismarck encountered growing criticism and disaffection, particularly on Capitol Hill. His critics charged, and for the most part correctly, that *Realpolitik* diplomacy was not consonant with America's traditions and values. Yet as enamoured as he was of *Realpolitik* diplomatic techniques, even Kissinger recognized the limitations of this approach for the United States. "The best and most prideful expressions of American purposes," Kissinger declared on one occasion, were

those in which we acted in concert with others. Our influence in these situations has depended on achieving a reputation as a member of such a concert. To act consistently abroad we must be able to generate coalitions of shared purposes.[18]

Kissinger, in other words, recognized the evolution which has occurred in the concept of "national power," as emphasized in Chapter 1. As idealists have long contended, any operable concept of America's power in the modern era must include the nation's ideas and ideals. In the final analysis—in terms of accomplishing constructive goals abroad—the power of the United States depends heavily upon its ability *to lead and persuade others to support its goals*.

The negative American mind set toward the concept of national power also is clearly illustrated in another dimension: historic American skepticism toward "diplomacy" and the activities of the Department of State.[19]

---

*The concept of *Realpolitik,* or political "realism," describes an approach to international politics which emphasizes the role of power, particularly military power, in diplomacy. It draws from such classical political thinkers as Machiavelli and from such nineteenth-century political leaders as Austria's Prince Metternich and Germany's Prime Minister Bismarck. Devotees of this approach believe that foreign policy should be actuated by the concept of "national interest" and that global peace and security can best be preserved by maintenance of the balance of power. Leading American advocates of this approach have been Walter Lippmann, Hans J. Morgenthau, and (in some aspects of his thought) George F. Kennan. Among postwar secretaries of state, Dr. Henry Kissinger's approach most clearly reflected *Realpolitik* principles.

For citizens of the New World, diplomacy has always had an unsavory connotation, suggesting the political intrigues and machinations, the wars of territorial aggression, and the disregard for the rights and welfare of ordinary citizens characteristic of Old World political relationships. The isolationist approach to foreign affairs preferred by Americans down to World War II was supported in part by the pervasive apprehension that involvement in international politics would ultimately subvert and corrupt the American society, perhaps in time destroying its democratic system. Moreover, Americans were inexperienced in diplomatic affairs; in any diplomatic encounter with the European powers, they would almost certainly be "outsmarted" or otherwise defeated by the Old World masters of diplomatic intrigue. For centuries, the world's diplomats had been drawn from the aristocratic class, which neither understood the idea of democracy nor approved it. Hence, diplomats were prone to arrive at understandings which were often inimical to the welfare of ordinary citizens who were called upon to pay higher taxes or serve in the armed forces as a result.

Most Americans are familiar with the fact that for many years after 1789, the United States refused to follow customary diplomatic procedures and practices; Washington, for example, refused even to use the rank of ambassador until well into the nineteenth century. No less today than in the past, the Department of State enjoys very little prestige or esteem from most American citizens or from Congress. Since the end of World War II, the secretary of state has almost invariably left office under a cloud of criticism, irrespective of his particular personality or accomplishments. Among the major executive departments, the State Department continues to be one of the smallest, in terms of both its personnel and its operating budget. As in the past, in contrast to the Labor or Commerce departments, the State Department normally has no "domestic constituency" upon which it can rely to plead its case with Congress. (As often as not, the department has a "negative constituency"; that is, it has critics and citizens' groups which *object strongly and vocally* to prevailing American policy toward Israel, toward black Africa, or toward the Soviet Union.) Despite repeated "reorganizations" since World War II, morale in the State Department remains chronically low, and prominent State Department officials complain that their views are "ignored" (or, in some cases, not even solicited) by the White House and Congress.

This phenomenon of course has manifold causes, most of which we shall examine more fully in Chapter 4. At this point, our interest is confined to emphasizing that the American society's traditional bias against diplomacy and power politics creates an adverse domestic environment upon which to base a successful foreign policy. Even today, it may be doubted whether a majority of Americans are psychologically prepared to support the kind of diplomatic behavior often required of a superpower in the international system.

Isolationism—Old and New

No adequate understanding of postwar American foreign policy is possible without insight into the isolationist mentality which governed the diplomatic behavior of the United States from the founding of the Republic down to World War II. An understanding of the isolationist viewpoint is essential for two reasons. The first is that every nation's foreign policy is to a significant degree an outgrowth of its diplomatic history and experience. To cite merely two examples: It is impossible to comprehend modern United States–Latin American relations without at least a rudimentary awareness of the issuance and evolution of the Monroe

Doctrine; or, from the end of World War II until the termination of the Vietnam War, American foreign policy was massively influenced by "the lessons of the 1930s," when the United States (along with the Allied powers of Europe) failed to act decisively against German, Italian, Japanese, and other sources of aggression. Presidents Truman and Johnson, for example, repeatedly cited these lessons as justification for their staunch opposition to Communist expansionism after 1945.

The second reason why attention must be devoted to the isolationist viewpoint is that *many vestiges of the traditional isolationist mentality continue to influence public and official attitudes toward foreign affairs in the United States*. When the United States took the lead in establishing, and later joined, the United Nations in 1945, isolationism was officially repudiated as the guiding principle of American foreign policy. Two years later —when the Truman Administration enunciated the "Truman Doctrine" (or containment strategy) for resisting Communist expansionism, the United States committed itself to an "interventionist" foreign policy. Implementing this strategy required the nation to assume defense and diplomatic obligations throughout the world and led to active American involvement in every major region. Despite these developments, new forms of isolationist thought evolved after World War II. These species of neo-isolationism drew heavily from the more traditional isolationist approach; and many of the underlying assumptions made by devotees of the old and the new isolationism were identical or remarkably similar.

Isolationism has pervaded the American approach to foreign relations since the earliest days of the Republic. America's pattern of isolationist thought is well illustrated by its foreign policies during the 1920s and 1930s.

What is not so widely recognized is that isolationism goes much deeper than merely the desire to avoid foreign entanglements. It is above all a habit of mind, a cluster of national attitudes, a feeling of spiritual separation from other countries, especially Europe, with roots penetrating deeply into the nation's heritage and experience.[20]

Isolationism is more than a doctrine advanced to explain the objective facts of America's geographical relationship with the rest of the world. Instead, it is supposed to explain *what the American people believe to be the proper relationship between themselves and other countries*. Isolationist thinking permeates the American cultural experience, its philosophy, and what may be called more generally "the American way of life." It is basically a conviction that Americans are different from other people; that they do not look to foreigners for guidance but that foreigners should look to them; that their national destiny is to serve as a beacon to pilot all mankind into new paths of greatness—but that all this should be done primarily by precept and example.[21]

The influences that have contributed to isolationist thinking are many and complex. Here we can do no more than allude to some of the more important ones. The desire for separation from the vicissitudes of Europe brought settlers to the New World. The wish to begin life anew, to leave behind the turmoil, the hopelessness, the bigotry of the Old World—these ambitions brought the religious dissenter, the peasant, the adventuresome aristocrat, the skilled artisan, the speculator, and the felon to American shores. From all walks of life they came, and with one objective: to find a new birth, as it were, in a far-off continent.

The Revolution cut the political ties with England, and as the years passed, Americans came to believe more firmly than ever in their uniqueness. Presidents Washington and Jefferson both cautioned their countrymen that America and Europe had different interests and advised that America's best course was to concentrate on keeping these interests distinct.[22] Very early in the nation's history, isolationism became the underlying principle of foreign policy. One pretext after another, for example, was found to justify America's refusal to honor the French alliance during the Napoleonic wars. President Monroe in 1823 asserted that the United States had but one objective in its relations with the Old World. A free translation of Monroe's admonitions would be that America wanted the European countries to mind their own business and, if they must persist in power struggles, to keep them out of the Western Hemisphere. The United States, shielded by the British navy, experienced remarkably few challenges to the Monroe Doctrine during the course of almost a century.

From the Monroe Doctrine until World War II the American people were profoundly isolationist; isolationism may in fact still be the preferred foreign policy position of the American people. We must regard participation in World War I as an interlude. Its politico-strategic significance generally passed unnoticed within the United States. After the First World War, Americans looked forward to a return to "normalcy," or preoccupation with domestic affairs; they quickly became disillusioned with foreign affairs, preferring to "let Europe stew in its own juice" and to refrain from participation in the League of Nations. For example, the United States was prepared to do little more than reprimand Japan verbally for its aggression against Manchuria in the early 1930s; and it was unwilling to join with other countries in dealing decisively with numerous instances of Axis expansionism in the years which followed. Shaken by the impact of the Great Depression, the American society was overwhelmingly preoccupied with internal problems. Many leading isolationists remained convinced until Pearl Harbor in 1941 that America would escape involvement in another global conflict. Americans believed that creation of their "new society" demanded almost exclusive attention *to domestic problems and pursuits.* This fact prompted one of the nation's leading historians, and in time a prominent spokesman for the isolationist viewpoint, Charles A. Beard, to prefer the term *continentalism* to *isolationism* in describing the nation's foreign policy stance. A more recent observer, Max Lerner, has emphasized basically the same idea, but with the interesting thought that classical isolationism and post-World War II interventionism (or "internationalism") shared a common goal: Both were ultimately designed to enable the American society to devote itself chiefly to internal pursuits.*

*Lerner's comprehensive study, *America as a Civilization,* affords many insights into the American mentality toward foreign affairs. His discussion of isolationism is particularly illuminating. Lerner calls attention to the kinship existing between two seemingly antithetical schools of thought in foreign affairs, isolationism and interventionism. The isolationist wants to reduce the nation's foreign commitments and follow a go-it-alone philosophy in foreign relations. By contrast, the interventionist advocates greater reliance upon military power in dealing with threats to security, and urges the nation to undertake diplomatic offensives to achieve goals like the liberation of the Communist satellite countries or the defeat of Communism in Korea and Southeast Asia. Despite the marked dissimilarities in their methods, Lerner contends, their underlying goal is basically the same: to create conditions throughout the world that will permit the United States once again to focus its energies on domestic affairs, with minimum involvement in foreign affairs. Both schools operate on the assumpton that the nation's destiny continues to be, as in the past, preoccupation with the American way of life. Insistence by critics of the Vietnam War that the United States give first priority to internal problems is thus but a recent variation upon a very old theme. See Max Lerner, *America as a Civilization* (New York: Simon and Schuster, 1957).

The isolationist principle found concrete expression in several diplomatic behavior patterns and propensities. The best-known perhaps was America's traditional refusal to enter into military alliances with other countries; the concept of "no entangling alliances" was consistently adhered to until after World War II. Isolationism also dictated the nation's non-involvement in European political conflicts except (as President Monroe's message provided) when America's own security interests were directly affected. A position of "neutrality" toward Europe's wars—a stance which the United States tried to maintain in the early stages of both the First and Second World wars—was also a component of isolationism. Another element in the isolationist approach was what was sometimes called the doctrine of the "free hand": The United States would preserve maximum freedom of action diplomatically. Thus, the Monroe Doctrine (and, some 75 years later, the "Open Door Policy" toward Asia) was issued *unilaterally* by the United States; and Washington remained the sole interpreter of these policies. As explained more fully in Chapter 12, the Carter Doctrine issued early in 1980 was a recent example of another important unilateral foreign policy declaration by the United States, committing America to the defense of the Persian Gulf area.

The isolationist approach to external questions was marked by two conspicuous omissions. One of these was a clear American understanding of *the role of power,* particularly armed force, in global political relationships. Few Americans were aware (and many may still be unaware) that during most of the nineteenth century the British fleet largely provided whatever "enforcement" was needed to gain international compliance with the Monroe Doctrine. Not until after World War II did Americans accept the idea that an adequate and modern military establishment is essential for the preservation of national security and for the achievement of many major foreign policy goals.

The second fundamental defect in the isolationist viewpoint was the failure to comprehend, and to modify national policies in the light of, *significant changes in the nature of the international system.* Innumerable examples of this weakness might be cited. One was America's failure to comprehend the implications of the emergence of an increasingly powerful and assertive Japan after 1900. Another was the lack of awareness in the United States of the steady decline in British power in the twentieth century. After World War II, Great Britain no longer ranked among the more powerful members of the international system. Among its other consequences, this British decline meant that in instance after instance (and the issuance of the "Truman Doctrine" to protect the security of Greece was an example), the United States was compelled to assume international obligations once borne by Great Britain and its empire. Rapid and ongoing technological changes—like the invention of the telephone and the radio, the emergence of airpower, and the growing firepower of modern weapons—rendered all nations more vulnerable and largely canceled out many of the security advantages which geographical barriers (like the Atlantic Ocean or the Arctic icecap) had given the United States. Still another reality largely ignored by isolationists was *America's own growing dependence* upon a long list of "strategic" imports from abroad. Insofar as economic self-sufficiency had sustained the isolationist position throughout much of the nation's history, by the period of World War II this precondition of successful isolationism was rapidly being superseded by a new era, in which the prosperity and security of the United States depended as never before upon access to foreign raw materials and upon continuing sales of American goods in foreign markets.

As most informed citizens are aware, World War II ended the era of classical American isolationism. Nevertheless, many of the assumptions, habits of mind, prejudices, and in some cases misconceptions which had nourished the traditional isolationist approach continued to survive and to influence the nation's behavior in foreign affairs. Yet neither the historic isolationist nor the newer neo-isolationist viewpoint comprised a unified, logically consistent "system" of thought. In the isolationist approach, as in other points of view about the nation's proper diplomatic course, the American penchant for eclecticism could be discerned. Today, as in the past, isolationists often advocate incompatible ideas and favor mutually exclusive courses of action.

In the postwar period, however, two broad schools of isolationist thought could be identified. One of these could be labeled "liberal neo-isolationism" and was often espoused by liberal spokesmen in the Democratic and Republican parties, as well as by prominent citizens' organizations.[23] Contemporary liberal neo-isolationism draws freely from the old isolationist tradition. Prominent themes in liberal neo-isolationist thought are the ideas that the United States should avoid relying upon military force to achieve its diplomatic objectives (except perhaps to protect the nation itself from attack or to promote goals like racial equality in black Africa); that Washington should lean heavily upon the United Nations and upon international law to accomplish its external objectives; that it should respond generously (and more massively than American officials have done in recent years) to the economic needs of the Third World; that the United States should become identified with, and should support, "revolutionary" political movements abroad, which are directed at

abolishing the *status quo* and creating more equitable social, economic, and political systems in other societies; that American officials should directly encourage and support the emergence of democracy in other countries. Many contemporary liberal neo-isolationists believe that the most effective influence which America can exert upon the international system *is the power of its own example* in successfully eliminating racial conflicts, eradicating poverty, and providing equal opportunities for all citizens within its own borders.

The basic premise of the liberal neo-isolationist was that extensive American involvement in the affairs of other countries was objectionable for two reasons: More often than not (as in the case of Vietnam), it compounded the foreign society's problems and resulted ultimately in lessened American power and influence in the region; and it was also highly inimical to American domestic programs and goals, causing the nation to neglect pressing internal problems, producing a high level of internal dissension over foreign policy issues, and leading to the emergence of the "imperial presidency" over which Congress and the American people had little control.[24]

The conservative version of neo-isolationism shared the same basic goal—retrenchment in the nation's overseas commitments—but it supported this conclusion for different reasons.[25] Advocates of conservative neo-isolationism today share the view of traditional isolationists that the international environment is in the main *inimical to the achievement of American foreign policy goals*. Even more than in the late nineteenth century, or in the early postwar period, the external milieu is unfavorable for the beneficial application of American power. Soviet Russia's continuing military buildup (vis-à-vis a relative decline in American defense spending); Western Europe's apparent continued indifference to the problem of its own defense; continuing political upheaval and instability (often exploited by Communist and other anti-American groups) throughout the Third World; America's failure to use its military power to achieve "victory" in the Vietnam War; the nation's steadily worsening balance-of-payments deficit, created in large part by the policies of the Middle East oil-producing states—such developments have convinced conservative neo-isolationists that the "internationalism" practiced by the United States for some 25 years after World War II achieved few beneficial results.

One particular issue—American foreign aid spending—illustrates conservative discontent. According to some estimates, the United States had expended over $200 billion since World War II in various forms of military, economic, and technical assistance to other countries. What had this massive outlay of the American taxpayer's funds achieved for the United States? It had not "won friends" for the United States abroad. The Vietnam conflict demonstrated that America's "allies" were unreliable; and many did not hesitate to attack American foreign policy, while benefiting from American largess. Nor could it be said that America's commitment to internationalism had resulted in a more stable, peacefully inclined international system. By 1980, the Soviet threat, for example, appeared to be more ominous than ever. Nor had this vast outlay of American resources solved (or even substantially alleviated) the manifold problems of the Third World. A generation after World War II, the prospects for democracy abroad were less favorable perhaps than in the early postwar era. Meanwhile, at home the United States confronted a rising inflation rate, a steadily escalating federal budget, an energy crisis, and a deteriorating American position in world trade.

In view of these developments, the United States should engage in massive diplomatic retrenchment, limiting its international obligations to those *directly related to its own security and well-being.* It should abandon the attempt to "buy friends" or otherwise win the firm allegiance of countries throughout the Third World. American policy makers should assume the continued hostility and aggressive behavior of the Soviet Union (whose growing military power made the Soviet threat more ominous than ever). Far from cutting the defense budget, as liberal neo-isolationists advocated, the United States should *increase* defense expenditures to preserve (or regain) America's military superiority over any rivals.

Underlying these specific policy recommendations were two general principles which, in the view of conservative neo-isolationists, ought to govern American diplomacy. One was the idea that the nation's overseas commitments *should be limited to those directly promoting its security, economic well-being, or some vital interest.* The nation's resources should not be dissipated and wasted by indiscriminate involvement in the affairs of other countries and regions. The second principle was that the United States *should be prepared to carry out the commitments which it assumes.* In contrast to the Vietnam War, American officials should communicate unequivocally to the Soviet Union and other countries that it will *fulfill* the security obligations it has assumed, using whatever means are necessary to do so. For example, if continued access to Middle East oil is a vital interest of the United States, then officials in Washington should make it known that America intends to assure the availability of this crucial commodity by whatever means are necessary to do so. Successfully applying this principle of course implied that the United States *possessed* the requisite military power

Belief in Progress and the "American Mission"   **51**

to support its diplomatic efforts and that it was prepared *to use this power* in behalf of its foreign policy goals.

As was also true of liberal neo-isolationism, the conservative variety was far from monolithic.[26] Its proponents differed widely, for example, on the precise criteria which ought to govern American interventionism abroad and concerning the countries and regions whose security constituted a "vital interest" for the United States. An early version of conservative neo-isolationism—advocated by ex-President Herbert Hoover during the 1950s—was the "Fortress America" strategy. The United States should confine its diplomatic and military activities abroad largely to the Western Hemisphere. A more recent proposal in this vein urges the United States to concentrate its diplomatic and security efforts on the "Northern Hemisphere"—more specifically, Europe and Japan—where its vital interests supposedly lie. Implicit in this approach is the idea that most developments in the Third World are of marginal importance for the United States. A more recent alternative proposal, advocated by a former State and Defense Department official, calls for the United States to reformulate its diplomatic strategy around the concept of an "ocean alliance" to defend the freedom of the seas and a long list of countries (from Western Europe to East Asia) where American commercial interests lie.[27] As is evident, securing agreement upon the criteria which ought to be employed for defining America's "vital interests" poses as much difficulty for conservative neo-isolationism as for other approaches to American foreign policy.

During the 1970s, as we shall see more fully in Chapters 3 and 4, the foreign policy process in the United States tended to be highly disunified and fragmented—a phenomenon that was especially identified with the diplomacy of the Carter Administration. As many commentators pointed out, behind this fact lay the reality that the American people were themselves often confused and undecided about the underlying principles that ought to govern their relations with other countries. A majority of citizens, for example, desired to avoid two policy extremes. On the one hand, most Americans realized that as a superpower, the United States could not return to the classical principle of isolationism as its basic diplomatic strategy. On the other hand, in the light of the traumatic Vietnam War experience, few Americans favored indiscriminate interventionism as the guiding precept of American foreign policy. Exhibiting their typically pragmatic frame of mind, most Americans and their leaders advocated an approach to foreign affairs falling between these extremes—a strategy that might be described as "selective interventionism" or "pragmatic interventionism." Perhaps the most fundamental problem encountered with this approach—and it is one that will likely occupy the attention of thoughtful Americans for many years—is determining the criteria or guidelines that will determine the application of American power abroad. It would not perhaps be unwarranted to coin a new phrase—"neo-interventionism"—to describe the American approach to foreign relations in the decade of the 1980s.

Belief in Progress and the "American Mission"

In a speech in the spring of 1979, Secretary of State Cyrus Vance declared:

> From the first days of our nation, Americans have held a staunch optimism about the future. We have been a self-confident people,

certain about our ability to shape our destiny.... If we appreciate the extraordinary strengths we have, if we understand the nature of the changes taking place in the world, and if we act effectively to use our different kinds of power to shape different kinds of change, we have every reason to be confident about our future.... Because we and our allies are the engines of creative change in almost every field, because of the vitality of our political institutions and the strength of our military forces, we have a capacity for leadership—and an ability to thrive in a world of change—[that] is unsurpassed.[28]

Secretary Vance was reasserting one of the oldest and most distinctive themes in the national ethos, one which has profound implications for foreign affairs. These are two interrelated and mutually supporting ideas: the American society's belief *in progress and beneficial change* and its related conviction that *the American democracy has "a mission" to transform the nature of the international political system.*

As we noted in our earlier discussion of the Monroe Doctrine, a prominent theme in the American political and literary tradition is that the political values, institutions, and processes of the New World were fundamentally different from those of the Old World, or indeed from any previous society. Americans have long been convinced that the success of their "democratic experiment"—in the face of pervasive European expectations that it would ultimately fail—was a notable achievement, not only for themselves but for humanity at large. A penetrating foreign observer, D. W. Brogan, has written admiringly of Americans: "To have created a free government, over a continental area, without making a sacrifice of adequate efficiency or of liberty is the American achievement. It is a unique achievement in world history."[29] In "I Hear America Singing," one of the nation's most outstanding

poets, Walt Whitman, expressed this national conviction:

> Thou, too, sail on, O Ship of State!
> Sail on, O Union, strong and great!
> Humanity with all its fears,
> With all the hopes of future years,
> Is hanging breathless on thy fate!

The American belief in progress has impressed nearly every foreign visitor to the United States. One described America as "the land of perfectionism. The American knew that nothing was impossible, in his brave new world, and history confirmed his intuition. Progress was not, to him, a mere philosophical ideal but a commonplace of experience, and he could not understand why foreigners should see vulgar realities where he saw visions."[30] Lord Bryce found that, in America, "Men seem to live in the future rather than in the present. Not that they fail to work while it is called today, but that they see the country not merely as it *is* but as it *will be,* twenty, thirty, fifty, a hundred years hence, when the seedlings they have planted shall have grown to forest trees."[31] A more recent writer has stated that when he looked at America he saw "a people who, by everlastingly tugging at their own bootstraps, have raised themselves to a new peak of economic welfare."[32] Contrasting the attitude of Americans toward world affairs in the postwar period with that exhibited by Europeans, D. W. Brogan concluded: "Probably the only people in the world who now have the historical sense of inevitable victory are the Americans."[33]

Down to the period of the Vietnam War, the American society's belief in progress—reflected in the motto of the "Seabees" during World War II: "The difficult we do at once; the impossible takes a little longer"—conditioned its approach to innumerable internal and external problems. Within the nation's own borders, "the American way of life" was being translated into a steadily rising standard of living, available to an ever widening circle of citizens; into a society where its members were protected against unemployment, illness, and other threats; where educational opportunities were readily available; and, more recently, where intensive governmental efforts should be taken to guarantee equal opportunities for racial minorities, the handicapped, women, and other disadvantaged groups within the society.

For Americans, the New World and progress were largely synonymous ideas. But America's devotion to the idea of progress, it must be emphasized, is not one which is widely accepted throughout the world, particularly not in the Third World. There, one of the most difficult impediments to modernization and to "nation building" is the attachment of the Indian villagers or the Egyptian *fellahin* to traditional beliefs and behavior patterns—many of which have strong cultural or religious sanctions. To no inconsiderable degree, the most formidable challenge in these societies is convincing the masses that progress *is both possible and desirable*.

In foreign affairs, America's belief in progress has had a profound impact and has affected nearly every dimension of the nation's diplomacy. In general terms, the mission of the New World was not merely to create a new society at home; it was no less than *to transform the nature of the international system,* rendering it (as it had never been under the leadership of the Old World) benign, conducive to the promotion of human welfare, and consonant with mankind's highest ethical and spiritual values. The United States, said President Harry Truman with his customary candor in 1945, should "take the lead in running the world in the way that the world ought to be run." Two decades later, President Lyndon B. Johnson observed: "His-

tory and our own achievements have thrust upon us the principal responsibility for protecting freedom on earth...." President Gerald R. Ford declared that "America has had a unique role in the world...we have borne successfully a heavy responsibility for insuring a stable world order...." Writing early in 1979, one of the nation's most distinguished journalists recalled President Wilson's vision of a better world, emphasizing the continuity of this idea in American diplomacy:

> And still, it is the United States, more than any other nation these days, that is trying at the start of this new year to compose the differences between nations, to bring Israel and Egypt together in the Middle East, to control the military arms race with the Soviet Union, to avoid racial war in Africa, to compose the bitter struggles in Iran and to help bring China peacefully into the modern world.... There is, in this New Year's spirit, a kind of continuity of hope. Washington is determined to fuss and feud over the problems of the day, but somehow it never loses its Wilsonian vision of a better tomorrow.[34]

The history of American diplomacy is replete with tangible examples of this motif in the national ethos. For the purposes of brevity in treating a complex subject, we may say that the idea of "America's mission" to the world has taken three principal forms. First, there was the idea implicit in classical isolationism—and present also in contemporary liberal neo-isolationism—that *the power of America's own example* was perhaps its most potent influence upon the conduct of international relations. For 150 years after 1789, isolationists reiterated the idea that the principal contribution the United States could make to the political welfare of mankind was to demonstrate *by its own behavior* that democracy was possible, or that age-old problems of class, religious, and racial antagonisms could be solved, or that a nation could live peaceably with its neighbors. In the recent period, liberal neo-isolationists have expressed a variation on this old theme. In America's global competition with the Soviet Union, for example—sometimes described as a "battle for the minds of men"—it will be the American (or the Soviet) "model" which will ultimately prove decisive in influencing the thinking of East Asians, Arabs, or black Africans. It follows that the most decisive steps Americans can take to influence the course of global events is to resolve racial problems within the United States, to eliminate poverty for all citizens, or to assure all members of the society adequate health care.

A second manifestation of the idea of America's mission is supplied by numerous "interventionist" episodes in the nation's diplomatic history, ranging from early American support for the French Revolution and the effort by the Greeks (in the early 1820s) to achieve their freedom from Turkey, to the Greek-Turkish Aid Program of 1947, the Korean War, and the Vietnam War.[35] Throughout American history, the people of the United States and their leaders have seldom hesitated to identify themselves with, and to support verbally and sometimes materially, political movements abroad which advocated freedom and other goals favored by the American society. While isolationism largely governed official American policy down to World War II, the isolationist era was interrupted by periods of "interventionism" designed to change the nature of the global environment. The Monroe Doctrine (at least implying a threat to use force) was issued in part to assure the political independence of Latin America, whose governments had constitutional systems modeled in some measure after the United States Constitution. In 1848 (the "year of revolutions" in Europe), Americans were ecstatic about the prospects for the

emergence of democratic (or at least less autocratic) political systems in the Old World. The overthrow of the Czarist regime in Russia in 1917, and the installation of a democratic political system under Alexander Kerensky, was enthusiastically endorsed by President Woodrow Wilson, who unquestionably echoed the dominant American sentiment. America's "nonrecognition" of the Soviet regime until 1933 was largely dictated by official and public distaste for this setback for democracy in Russia. For some 50 years—from the issuance of the "Open Door Policy" in 1898–99 until World War II—American foreign policy toward China reflected this same thinking. Especially after the Chinese Revolution of 1911, when the Manchu Dynasty was overthrown and a new government led by Dr. Sun Yat-sen took power, the United States worked closely with the government of China to introduce reforms and to modernize its traditional political system. The operating assumption of American policy was that in time China was destined to join the ranks of the world's democracies and that it was incumbent upon the United States to assist the Chinese society toward that end.

The two most notable examples of American interventionism were of course the nation's participation in the First and Second World wars, following both of which Americans expected fundamental changes in the nature of the international system. During World War I, President Woodrow Wilson interpreted the struggle as "the war to end wars" and as an effort to "make the world safe for democracy." Largely as a result of American initiative, the first international organization in modern history—the League of Nations—was established to provide a mechanism for the peaceful resolution of international disputes. (America's own failure to join the League of Nations, and to take the lead in its activities, weakened the organization, perhaps fatally.)

Again, during and after World War II, the Roosevelt Administration took the lead in attempting to change the nature of the international system. These efforts took noteworthy forms. One of these was American initiative in formulating and establishing the United Nations, whose primary responsibility was the preservation of global peace and security. There were also innumerable attempts by President Roosevelt and his advisers to induce fundamental changes in Soviet diplomatic behavior, by bringing the U.S.S.R. into the UN, by getting Stalin to sign various agreements limiting Russia's freedom of action in Eastern Europe, and by seeking to conciliate Soviet leaders and to accept many of their "legitimate" demands. In addition, the Roosevelt (and later Truman) Administration insisted upon radical changes in the political systems of defeated Germany and Japan. The Western Allies (in the case of Japan, mainly the United States) imposed new democratic political systems on these leading Axis nations; and steps were taken, as in constitutional provisions against Japanese rearmament, to prevent their becoming a new threat to global peace.

The third approach illustrating American interventionism for the purpose of transforming the international system has involved efforts to create and to promote the concept of "international community." We have already alluded to America's traditionally active role in strengthening international law, in efforts to "outlaw" war as an instrument of national policy, and in planning and implementing the idea of international organization. Although popular and congressional support for the United Nations has unquestionably declined within the United States, America remains an active member of the organization; and ever since 1945, financial contributions by the United States have been essential for the UN's activities and survival. Throughout the postwar

period, as Chapter 11 will explain more fully, the United States has supported the concept of European political unity, or "integration." For Europe, as for other regions (as in Latin America), Washington has encouraged the emergence of viable *regional* institutions and mechanisms for the maintenance of regional security and the solution of other mutual problems. The common theme of these efforts has been the conviction of American policy makers that unrestrained "national sovereignty" is an outmoded, unproductive, and perhaps dangerous concept. In the late twentieth century, a host of global issues—from the preservation of international peace and security, to the maintenance of worldwide economic stability, to programs designed to improve the physical environment—can be solved only on a collaborative basis, as nations acknowledge a growing interdependence and common destiny among the members of the international system.

Perhaps no feature of American foreign policy has elicited more recurrent criticism than the idea that the United States possesses some kind of "mission" to transform the international system. Political realists view it as a form of Utopianism: Americans are incapable of comprehending the traditional rules of international political behavior, of understanding the central role of power in global political relationships, or of coming to terms with the centrality of concepts like "national interest" in the diplomatic behavior of all nations. This deficiency gives rise to expectations (such as "making the world safe for democracy") which are often followed, as was the case after World War I and the Vietnam War, by widespread disillusionment when such unrealistic goals are not achieved.

During and after the Vietnam War, another group of critics—sometimes called "revisionist" or "re-examinist" commentators on postwar American foreign policy—attacked the American sense of "mission" for essentially different reasons. It exemplified "the arrogance of American power"; or a thinly disguised impulse toward a worldwide American hegemony; or an ethnocentric compulsion to "remake the world" according to the American model. In brief, for many of these critics, little difference could be discerned between an American foreign policy actuated by such a sense of mission and the external behavior of the Roman Empire, the Napoleonic Empire, the Russian Empire, or other nation seeking to maintain an *imperium* beyond its own borders.[36] Many revisionists, therefore, blamed the United States and the Soviet Union equally for the existence of the Cold War. According to this interpretation, each superpower sought to dominate the international system, to impose its hegemony on weaker countries, and to get its ideological or economic model accepted as a universal norm.

That the historic concept of America's "mission" has posed problems and misunderstandings for the United States in its foreign relations, particularly since World War II, seems incontestable. The evidence that American foreign policy has reflected this idea is overwhelming. Whether it was the long-standing belief that international political relationships could be transformed by the influence of the American example, or the more contemporary idea that with American assistance and guidance Third World societies could be successfully "modernized," a sense of mission has always been a conspicuous element in the diplomatic behavior of the United States. The idea is perhaps intrinsic to the national ethos and is not, therefore, likely to be abandoned. As in the past, the American approach to foreign affairs can be expected to reflect a twofold assumption: that international political relationships both *can* be and *should* be changed to accord more fully with

mankind's highest ethical and spiritual aspirations.

Yet, as political realists continually point out, this belief can impart a Utopian quality to American diplomacy, leading other nations to believe that Washington's foreign policy proposals are naïve, simplistic, and have little utility for the "real world" of international politics. And, as idealistic critics emphasize, the concept of America's mission can also result in an approach to other countries which reflects arrogance, ethnocentricity, and an implicit premise that the American political or economic system constitutes the norm for mankind. In the post-Vietnam War era, redefining the nation's traditional sense of mission, and translating it into achievable foreign policy goals, will remain a continuing challenge for the American people and their leaders.

NOTES

1. For more detailed discussion of the concept of national character, see Henry S. Commager, ed., *America in Perspective* (New York: Random House, 1947), p. xi; and Ernest Barker, *National Character* (London: Methuen, 1948), p. xi.

2. A recent analysis emphasizing America's national character (or what the author calls its "national style") is Stanley Hoffmann, *Gulliver's Troubles, or the Setting of American Foreign Policy* (New York: McGraw-Hill Book Co., 1968).

3. For an illuminating and provocative discussion of the impact of America's pragamatic tendencies upon its foreign policy, see George W. Ball, *Diplomacy for a Crowded World: An American Foreign Policy* (Boston: Little, Brown and Co., 1976), pp. 302–312.

4. The process of "incremental" or pragmatic decision making whereby the United States became massively involved in the Vietnam War is analyzed in Roger Hilsman, *To Move a Nation: The Politics of Foreign Policy in the*

Administration of John F. Kennedy (Garden City, N.Y.: Doubleday and Co., 1967). See especially pp. 5 and 548.

5. See, for example, Henry A. Kissinger, *American Foreign Policy: Three Essays* (New York: W. W. Norton, 1969), p. 97.

6. The pervasive role of idealism in shaping the American approach to foreign affairs is the theme of Frank Tannenbaum, *The American Tradition in Foreign Policy* (Norman, Okla.: University of Oklahoma Press, 1955). A more recent assessment emphasizing this idea is Philip W. Quigg, *America the Dutiful: An Assessment of U.S. Foreign Policy* (New York: Simon and Schuster, 1971).

7. The "Monroe Doctrine" was enunciated in President James Monroe's message to Congress on December 2, 1823. For detailed excerpts from this speech, see Cecil V. Crabb, Jr., *Policy-Makers and Critics: Conflicting Theories of American Foreign Policy* (New York: Praeger Publishers, 1976), Appendix No. 2, pp. 302–304.

8. For a detailed analysis of traditional American attitudes toward power, and their consequences for the nation's foreign policy, see Walter Lippmann, "The Rivalry of Nations," *The Atlantic Monthly,* **181** (February, 1948), 19–26.

9. Anatol Rapoport, *The Big Two: Soviet-American Perceptions of Foreign Policy* (Indianapolis, Ind.: Bobbs-Merrill Co., 1971), pp. 48–49.

10. The Vietnam War era spawned many exposés and studies of the impact of militarism upon the American society. A typical one was Tristam Coffin, *The Armed Society: Militarism in Modern America* (Baltimore: Penguin Books, 1964). Another study—focusing on America's reliance upon its nuclear might to impose its will in other countries since World War II—is David Horowitz, *The Free World Colossus: A Critique of American Foreign Policy in the Cold War* (New York: Hill and Wang, 1971).

11. America's addiction to "legalism" in its approach to foreign policy is a major theme of George E. Kennan's *American Diplomacy: 1900–1950* (New York: New American Library, 1952). See especially his discussion of American policy toward Asia, pp. 41–56.

12. See Gaddis Smith, *American Diplomacy During the Second World War: 1941–1945* (New York: John Wiley and Sons, 1966), pp. 1–81.

13. Ibid., p. 81.

14. Walter Lippmann's views are quoted in D. W. Brogan, *The American Problem* (London: Hamish Hamilton, 1944), p. 18. His ideas are set forth more fully in Walter Lippmann, *U. S. Foreign Policy: Shield of the Republic* (Boston: Little, Brown and Co., 1943).

15. Lippmann, *U. S. Foreign Policy,* p. 49.

16. Ibid., p. 9.

17. See the White House document—which clearly bore Dr. Kissinger's imprint—titled "U.S. Foreign Policy for the 1970's: The Emerging Structure of Peace" (Washington, D. C., February 9, 1972). This publication provides an elaborate statement of the Nixon-Kissinger strategy for peace and stability in the post-Vietnam War era. For interpretive treatments of Kissinger's views, see David Landau, *Kissinger, the Uses of Power* (New York: Thomas Y. Crowell, 1974); and Harry M. Joiner, *American Foreign Policy: The Kissinger Era* (Huntsville, Ala.: The Strode Publishers, 1977).

18. Kissinger, *American Foreign Policy,* p. 97.

19. Evidence and numerous examples of the nation's antipathy toward the concept of "diplomacy" are provided in Warren F. Ilchman, *Professional Diplomacy in the United States, 1779–1939: A Study in Administrative History* (Chicago: University of Chicago Press, 1961), pp. 1–40. The gist of this discussion is that Americans viewed the art of diplomacy as contrary and inimical to democracy. See also Smith Simpson, *Anatomy of the State Department* (Boston: Houghton Mifflin Co., 1967), pp. 1–4, 152–183.

20. A succinct treatment of the principal tenets in traditional American isolationist thought may be found in Crabb, *Policy-Makers and Critics,* pp. 1–34. For informative discussions of the

nature and impact of isolationist thought during the 1930s, see Wayne S. Cole, *Senator Gerald P. Nye and American Foreign Relations* (Minneapolis: University of Minnesota Press, 1962); Marian C. McKenna, *Borah* (Ann Arbor: University of Michigan Press, 1961); and Raymond L. Buell, *Isolated America* (New York: Alfred A. Knopf, 1940).

21. Albert K. Weinberg, "The Historical Meaning of the American Doctrine of Isolation," *American Political Science Review,* 34 (April, 1940), 539.

22. One of the earliest expressions of American isolationist sentiment was President Washington's "Farewell Address" (September 19, 1796). For excerpts from it, see Crabb, *Policy-Makers and Critics,* Appendix No. 1, pp. 299–301.

23. Postwar "liberal neo-isolationism" is discussed more fully in ibid., pp. 253–299.

24. Among liberal neo-isolationists, none has perhaps been more influential than the former chairman of the Senate Foreign Relations Committee, Senator J. William Fulbright. His views on America's proper course in global affairs are set forth in *Old Myths and New Realities* (New York: Random House, 1964); *The Arrogance of Power* (New York: Random House, 1976); and *The Crippled Giant: American Foreign Policy and Its Domestic Consequences* (New York: Random House, 1972).

25. The conservative version of contemporary neo-isolationism is analyzed in detail in Crabb, *Policy-Makers and Critics,* pp. 214–252.

26. A leading spokesman for conservative neo-isolationism in the contemporary period has been Senator Barry F. Goldwater (Republican, Arizona). See his views on American foreign and defense policy, as contained in his *The Conscience of a Conservative* (New York: Macfadden, 1963). An earlier exponent of this approach was Edgar A. Mowrer, *The Nightmare of American Foreign Policy* (New York: Alfred A. Knopf, 1948).

27. Former President Hoover's "Fortress America" concept is explained more fully in Crabb, *Policy-Makers and Critics,* pp. 228–230. The idea that the United States should concentrate its diplomatic efforts on the "Northern Hemisphere" is the recommendation of the former high-level State Department official George W. Ball. See his *The Discipline of Power: Essentials of a Modern World Structure* (Boston: Little, Brown and Co., 1968), pp. 39–69 and 221–260. Another former State and Defense Department official, Ray C. Cline, has called for the formation of an "ocean alliance" between the United States and other (largely maritime) nations. See Drew Middleton, in *New York Times,* December 27, 1978.

28. The text of Secretary Vance's speech is reproduced in "Meeting the Challenges of a Changing World," Department of State, Bureau of Public Affairs, May 1, 1979, pp. 1–6.

29. Brogan, *The American Problem,* p. 101.

30. Commager, *America in Perspective,* p. xix.

31. Lord Bryce's views are quoted in Ernest L. Klein, *Our Appointment with Destiny* (New York: Farrar, Straus and Giroux, 1952), p. 97.

32. Quoted in ibid., pp. 8–9.

33. D. W. Brogan, "The Illusion of American Omnipotence," *Harper's,* 205 (December, 1952), 22.

34. These and other statements by American leaders in this vein are included in Charles W. Kegley, Jr., and Eugene R. Wittkopf, *American Foreign Policy: Pattern and Process* (New York: St. Martin's Press, 1979), p. 36. See also James Reston, in *New York Times,* January 7, 1979.

35. Our brief discussion of American interventionism draws heavily on the more detailed analysis in Crabb, *Policy-Makers and Critics,* pp. 34–81. For treatment of a related idea —American diplomatic leadership in behalf of the concept of "global community"—see ibid., pp. 128–165.

36. In addition to the works of former Senator J. William Fulbright and David Horowitz cited earlier, the following provide a representative

sampling of "revisionist" interpretations of American foreign policy: Richard J. Walton, *Cold War and Counter-Revolution: The Foreign Policy of John F. Kennedy* (Baltimore: Penguin Books, 1972); Stephen E. Ambrose, *Rise to Globalism: American Foreign Policy, 1938–1970* (Baltimore: Penguin Books, 1971); Joyce and Gabriel Kotko, *The Limits of Power: The World and United States Foreign Policy, 1945–1954* (New York: Harper & Row, 1972); and D. F. Flemming, *The Cold War and Its Origins,* 2 vols. (Garden City, N.Y.: Doubleday and Co., 1961).

Chapter 3

The Presidency:
Focal Point of the Policy Process

A leading student of governmental administration has identified the principle of "executive leadership" as one of the pivotal concepts of public administration in the twentieth century. As one analysis of the American foreign aid program concluded in 1962, "What the Department of State does in exercising leadership and coordination, it must do so as an agent of the President." A more recent study of the foreign policy decision-making process in the United States finds no "alternative" to a forceful executive branch under effective presidential leadership "around which foreign policy coherence can be built." In foreign affairs, "The Constitution and 180 years of tradition give foreign affairs primacy to the President."[1] One of the nation's most experienced diplomatic officials, former Secretary of State Dean Acheson, believed that all officials involved in policy making must recognize that "Politically, the President is the leader of the nation. Constitutionally, he is the director of American foreign policy."[2]

The Constitutional Setting

These statements underscore perhaps the central reality about foreign policy decision making in the United States: Ultimate responsibility for deciding external policy—and for determining the nature of America's relations with other members of the international system—*resides with the President.* The chief executive can call upon a variety of advisory and administrative agencies—such as the National Security Council, the Cabinet, the Department of State, the Department of Defense, the agencies comprising the "Intelligence Community," and numerous other sources—to assist him in the formulation of policy and the management of foreign relations. But these subordinate agencies, it must be emphasized, do not "make" American foreign policy. Constitutionally, that responsibility belongs to the President.

Our analysis of the President's key role in foreign affairs will focus upon three major aspects of the subject: constitutional sources of the President's powers; historical and traditional factors enhancing his leadership role; and an examination of the problem—which came sharply to the fore during and after the Vietnam War—posed by emergence of the "imperial presidency."

Constitutional Appearance and Reality

At the outset, students of American foreign relations must be cognizant of the distinction between constitutional *appearance* and *reality*. They must be mindful that constitutional theories, provisions, grants of power, and the like, must always be understood in terms of the context within which they were presented, the evolution in their meaning throughout American history, and the court decisions interpreting relevant principles of constitutional law. Chapter 7 calls attention to the fact, for example, that while the power of Congress to "declare war" (Art. I, Sec. 8) meant one thing to the Founding Fathers, conditions prevailing throughout American history and particularly since World War II have given this provision a very different meaning.

In any discussion of the powers of the national government in foreign relations, two constitutional principles are fundamental. One is the idea that the national government exercises only "delegated powers" or—in the light of the Supreme Court's classic decision in *McCulloch* v. *Maryland* (1819)[3]—those powers which may logically be *implied* to carry out its delegated powers. Whether granted outright or implied, the powers of the national government, according to this doctrine, are conferred upon it by the Constitution of the United States. This idea, the Supreme Court declared in *United States* v. *Curtiss-Wright Export Corporation* (1936), was subject to drastic modification when applied to foreign relations:

The broad statement that the Federal government can exercise no powers except those specifically enumerated in the Constitution and such implied powers as are necessary and proper to carry into effect the enumerated powers, is categorically true only in respect of our internal affairs.[4]

The powers of the national government in foreign affairs, the Court held, "did not depend upon the affirmative grants of the Constitution." If they had not been enumerated in the Constitution, they would have belonged to the national government "as necessary concomitants of nationality."[5] That is, they would have been among the prerogatives of the national government because the United States is a nation and a member of the family of nations.

Similarly, the constitutional doctrine of "separation of powers" is largely inapplicable to the sphere of foreign relations. In the same case of *United States* v. *Curtiss-Wright* the Supreme Court also dealt with this concept. Its judgment was that the participation by Congress and the courts in the control of foreign relations was "significantly limited," whereas the powers of the chief executive were vast. It concluded:

In this vast external realm, with its important, complicated, delicate and manifold problems, the President alone has the power to speak or listen as a representative of the nation. He *makes* treaties with the advice and consent of the Senate; but he alone negotiates. Into the field of negotiation the Senate cannot intrude and Congress itself is powerless to invade it. . . .

The Supreme Court referred to the "plenary and exclusive power of the President as the sole organ of the Federal government in the field of international relations. . . ."

The Supreme Court and Foreign Affairs

Applying such dicta to its own approach to constitutional and legal issues involving foreign affairs, the Supreme Court has been most reluctant to intrude into the conduct of foreign policy. We may dispose of the Supreme Court's role in American foreign relations by saying that in the vast majority of cases, its decisions have tended to follow one of two directions. In a number of important decisions the Court has, as we have seen, upheld the idea of broad discretionary power for the chief executive. Decisions of the Supreme Court, therefore, constitute a significant force adding to the President's powers in foreign relations.

In other cases, the Supreme Court has designated certain controversies in foreign affairs as "political questions," falling outside its jurisdiction. Does the President have the power to "recognize" another government, like Bolshevik Russia, Communist China, or some new regime among the developing nations? What are the recognized boundaries of Israel and the adjacent Arab states? Should the United States negotiate a new arms-limitation agreement with the Soviet Union? These and kindred questions arising in foreign affairs are political issues, not susceptible of resolution by the judicial branch of the government.* Time and again during the Vietnam War, citizens and groups attempted to have the Supreme Court or inferior courts declare America's participation in that conflict illegal

or unconstitutional—always without success. In dealing with all such cases, the Supreme Court in effect reiterated its traditional position: The nation's involvement in war was a question which had to be decided by the executive and legislative branches, and perhaps ultimately by the citizens as a result of the electoral process.[6]

The President's Constitutional Powers

The Treaty-Making Process

The Constitution provides that the President "shall have power, by and with the advice and consent of the Senate, to make treaties, provided two-thirds of the Senators present concur..." (Art. II, Sec. 2). It is worth noting that Article VI of the Constitution places "all Treaties made, or which shall be made, under the Authority of the United States" on the same level with the Constitution itself and "the Laws of the United States"; all three are to be regarded as "the supreme Law of the Land...." Article I, Section 10 of the Constitution alludes to another kind of international agreement or compact when it states that "No State shall, without the Consent of Congress,...enter into any Agreement or Compact with another State, or with a foreign Power...."

Implicitly, then, the Constitution of the United States recognizes two categories of international agreements. The first is *treaties*, in the making of which the President and the

---

*A landmark case in this connection is *Stewart* v. *Kahn,* 11 Wallace 493 (1871), in which Justice Swayne stated: "The measures to be taken in carrying on war and to suppress insurrection are not defined. The decision of all questions rests wholly in the discretion of those to whom the substantial powers involved are confided by the Constitution." Again, in the case of *United States* v. *Belmont,* 301 U.S. 324 (1937), the Court said that "who is the sovereign of a territory is not a judicial question, but one the

determination of which by the political departments conclusively binds the courts...."

In law, it needs to be observed, "political questions" do not denote issues which are politically controversial, although of course they may well be so. Rather, they are questions which are essentially *nonjudicable:* They are not capable of determination or resolution by legal processes.

Senate are given responsibilities. The second is *agreements or compacts,* the nature of which is undefined in the Constitution. Nor does the Constitution prescribe how they are made, as it does with treaties. Reference to this latter category, however, strongly suggests that the Founding Fathers were familiar with international agreements that were less formal and explicit than treaties, and that they expected the United States to engage in such agreements with other countries. We shall examine the nature of such agreements and the role they play in contemporary American foreign policy at a later stage.

Treaties are the most dramatic and legally binding agreements which nations engage in with one another. The process of treaty making involves two stages: *negotiation* of the agreement and its *ratification,* resulting in its promulgation as law. The Senate plays a key role in the process of treaty ratification: No treaty becomes law unless it has received a two-thirds affirmative vote of the Senate. Despite a widespread misconception, the Senate does not "ratify" treaties; the Senate gives its "advice and consent" to their ratification. Treaties are not officially ratified until (following Senate approval) they are signed by the President and promulgated. A President may "withdraw" a treaty from further consideration by the Senate; and he may also refuse to sign it after it has passed the Senate. Thus the chief executive has the final word in the ratification process.

The constitutional provision that the President "makes" (or negotiates) treaties has evoked controversy throughout American diplomatic history. Does the "advice and consent of the Senate" extend to the *negotiation* of agreements with other countries? Is the Senate entitled to be consulted as such negotiations proceed, and must it consent to provisions inserted in the treaty? Considerable evidence exists that the Founding Fathers envisioned a dynamic role by the Senate in the treaty-making process. In the beginning (with only 26 members) that body was perhaps intended to serve as a kind of Council of State to advise the President on important foreign policy questions. (Such questions, it should be remembered, were expected to be rare during the era of isolationism.)

But this conception of the Senate's role soon gave way to the now firmly established precedent that negotiations are under the control of the President. After a treaty has been negotiated, it is submitted to the Senate for approval. In the overwhelming majority of cases throughout American diplomatic history, the Senate has acted favorably on treaties submitted to it. When it has withheld approval—or (as in the case of the Treaty of Versailles after World War I) when it has attached "amendments" and "reservations" to it which are unacceptable to the White House*—the chief executive frequently has other means at his disposal for making his policy prevail.

Down to the late 1960s, as a rule the Senate's role in treaty making was what might be described as passive and "supportive" of

---

*"Amendments" to a treaty are changes in its provisions or terms which (for important issues) require that the treaty be renegotiated with the other signatories to it, since the amendments make the treaty a different agreement from the one initially signed by the parties to it. During Senate debate on the SALT II arms-control treaty with the Soviet Union in 1979, proposed amendments fell into two categories: Some amendments were designed to "perfect" the treaty, clarifying its terms and making it more acceptable to the Senate; other changes were known as "killer amendments," the evident purpose of which was to change the agreement radically, thereby compelling its renegotiation with (and probable rejection by) Moscow. In contrast, "reservations" are qualifications or understandings appended to the treaty by the Senate which do not as a rule require the treaty's renegotiation. Thus, a number of international agreements have been accepted by the Senate only with the understanding that they did not impair America's traditional rights under the Monroe Doctrine.

the President's leadership role. During the heyday of "bipartisanship" in postwar American foreign policy, for example (from the late 1940s until the mid-1950s), the Senate could usually be counted upon to approve agreements submitted to it by the White House. In many instances, as in the North Atlantic Defense Treaty, the idea had come initially from the Senate; legislative and executive officials had collaborated in formulating its major provisions. Even influential legislators, like Senator Arthur H. Vandenberg (Republican of Michigan), urged his colleagues to exercise restraint in construing the "advice and consent" clause broadly:

> I think the Senate is entitled, at any time it pleases, to use the advice clause of the Constitution to tell the Executive what it thinks concerning foreign affairs. But I think it would be a tragic and unfortunate thing if the habit ever became general or too contagious because I respectfully submit, ... only in those instances in which the Senate can be sure of a complete command of all the essential information prerequisite to an intelligent decision, should it take the terrific chance of muddying the international waters by some sort of premature and ill-advised expression of its advice to the Executive.[7]

During and after the Vietnam War, however, both houses of Congress demonstrated a new "assertiveness" and militancy in the foreign policy field. Correctly or not, many legislators and citizens blamed America's traumatic involvement in that conflict on unrestrained executive influence in foreign affairs. As part of the reaction against the "imperial presidency," legislators in both houses were determined to assert congressional prerogatives in foreign relations more militantly and effectively. As we shall see more fully in Chapter 7, the Senate utilized its role in the process of treaty making to express

legislative viewpoints and concerns. Under the Carter Administration, for example, the Senate insisted upon several changes in the new Panama Canal Treaty; debate on the treaty within the Senate was intense; and —only after one of the most extensive "public relations campaigns" by the executive branch in the nation's history—the Panama treaty won senatorial approval by a narrow margin.[8] In this instance, it must be emphasized, the forceful assertions of the Senate's prerogatives *set limits to the President's power* to make important foreign policy decisions. The Senate was still unable to dictate the terms of such agreements with other nations; and (as in the case of the Soviet-American SALT II arms-limitation accords) the chief executive publicly implied that senatorial opposition would not prevent the White House from using other methods to arrive at understandings with Moscow on arms control.[9]

The President's Use of Executive Agreements

Treaties, as we have noted, are only the most formal agreements reached among governments. The Constitution evidently contemplated that other kinds of agreements would be utilized in foreign affairs. In time, these came to be called "executive agreements"—formal and informal understandings among heads of state binding them to take a certain course of action. Such agreements may and do cover a great range of activities—from routine business like international mail delivery to diplomatic and political issues whose subject matter may be as important as a treaty.

The first executive agreement with another country, which provided for reciprocal mail delivery, was made during President Washington's Administration. Although other agreements were executed in the years which followed, President Franklin D. Roosevelt raised them to a new pinnacle of importance as an instrument for controlling foreign policy. As a result of his celebrated "Destroyer Deal" with Great Britain in 1940, and of numerous understandings arrived at with the Allied governments during World War II, FDR massively influenced the direction of American foreign policy for years to come. Executive agreements played a conspicuous role in two major issues of postwar American foreign policy: the nation's commitment to the security of South Vietnam and its escalating involvement in the Vietnam War; and the *de facto* commitment which the United States has assumed to protect the security of Israel from its hostile Arab neighbors. Today, the vast preponderance of all international commitments entered into by the United States is in the form of executive agreements.[10]

Few methods of presidential leadership in foreign affairs have been subjected to such critical legislative scrutiny in recent years as executive agreements. In terms of their *effects* upon America's relations with other countries—such as involving the United States in military hostilities abroad or committing the nation to expensive economic and military assistance programs—very little (if any) difference exists between executive agreements and treaties. Increasingly, Congress has insisted that understandings with other countries take the form of "statutory agreements"; that is, Congress must be informed of their existence, must be allowed to "veto" certain kinds of understandings to which it objects, and must either approve such agreements or require them to be resubmitted to the Senate in the form of a treaty. Yet it cannot be said that the emergence of "statutory agreements" has ended institutional conflict on the question within the government. For example, State Department and legislative officials often differ on what constitutes an "agreement" between the United States and another country and over precisely what forms of in-

ternational understandings must receive congressional approval.

Authority over the Military Establishment

During and since the Vietnam War, no issue related to the conduct of foreign affairs by the United States has perhaps evoked such heated controversy as the President's reliance upon the armed forces to achieve the nation's external objectives. In reality, the controversy has been escalating ever since the Administration of President Franklin D. Roosevelt. As the world was drawn ever closer to the brink of war, FDR became convinced that the security and diplomatic interests of the United States lay with Great Britain, France, and the other Allies; the United States must serve as "the arsenal of Democracy" to prevent an Axis victory. During the war, FDR made innumerable military decisions (such as his decision to accord the European theater priority over the Asian theater) which had profound implications for the postwar period. President Truman committed the United States to the defense of Greece and Turkey—and (under the "Truman Doctrine"), more broadly, to the defense of any "free peoples" whose independence was endangered by an external threat. In 1950 Truman ordered American forces in the Pacific to assure the defense of South Korea against Communist aggression (an action which he took without a "declaration of war" and which was often called by his critics "Mr. Truman's war"). President Eisenhower used armed force to intervene in Lebanon in 1957; and under his Administration, the United States assumed an obligation to defend South Vietnam. This latter commitment was honored and expanded by Presidents Kennedy, Johnson, Nixon, and Ford. In 1961, President Kennedy lent American support to the ill-fated "Bay of Pigs" invasion of Cuba. The following year, the "Cuban Missile

Crisis" was perhaps the most ominous Soviet-American confrontation in the postwar era. President Johnson directed the armed forces to invade the Dominican Republic in 1965 to protect that country from a threatened Communist takeover. President Nixon directed American forces to bomb Cambodia; and during the Arab-Israeli war of 1973, he placed the air force on full "alert" as a warning to the Kremlin against Soviet military intervention in the Middle East. Other examples could of course be cited, but these are enough to indicate the chief executive's reliance upon the armed forces in dealing with a variety of foreign policy issues.[11]

With the memory of the Vietnam conflict still vivid in their minds, many citizens today are perhaps insufficiently aware of the other side of this coin: the President's decision *not* to employ military force when external circumstances might induce him to do so. Since World War II chief executives have refrained from military intervention in the affairs of other countries much more frequently than they have engaged in it. On the basis of the evidence, Presidents have *not* been reckless or "adventuristic" in employing military force for foreign policy goals.[12]

Constitutionally, the President's power to utilize the armed forces for diplomatic ends is drawn from several sources. In the presidential oath of office, the chief executive swears to "preserve, protect and defend the Constitution of the United States." In Article II, Section 2, the President is designated commander in chief of the armed forces. Then in the same article (Section 3), the President is required to "take Care that the Laws be faithfully executed...." (In Article VI, it must always be remembered, the Constitution designates treaties as part of "the Supreme Law of the Land" which the President is obliged to enforce.)

Besides these specific grants of authority, many chief executives and students of the American constitutional system have contended, there is a more general residual responsibility which falls upon the President: to take whatever steps are necessary to defend the United States from threats to its security and diplomatic vital interests. As we shall see more fully in Chapter 8, the American people unquestioningly look to the White House —rather than to Congress or the Supreme Court—for forceful "leadership" in meeting internal and external challenges. At the same time, as Chapter 7 emphasizes, the President's reliance upon the armed forces to achieve foreign policy goals is crucially affected by the size and nature of the military establishment that Congress makes availiable for his use.

Among the constitutional sources of the President's power in this realm, none is more important than his role as commander in chief of the armed forces. The precise "intention" of the Founding Fathers in assigning this responsibility to the chief executive is not altogether clear. Throughout American history, two contending explanations of this provision have been given. One is that the Founders intended the President's designation as commander in chief to be a largely symbolic or honorific title (much perhaps like the British monarch's position in modern history). By implication, this interpretation necessarily means that someone else (presumably, Congress or the nation's military commanders) would actually determine military strategy. The other interpretation—and the one which has in fact largely prevailed throughout American diplomatic experience—is that the President's designation as commander in chief is among *his most important constitutional powers*, conferring upon him ample authority for using the armed forces to protect national security and for achieving diplomatic objectives under varying conditions abroad. Indeed, down to the period of the Vietnam War—as a result of one precedent after another involving the chief executive's use of the military establishment in behalf of external objectives—contemporary Presidents had perhaps become convinced that this power had few effective limits.[13]

Precedents were not lacking in American diplomatic history to support such a conception of executive power. Let us take note of merely a few selected ones. As we have already observed, the United States has been involved in approximately 125 "undeclared wars" in its 200-year history. These encompassed a highly varied group of major and minor military conflicts in which the President utilized the armed forces for foreign policy ends. (This list does not include innumerable instances in which a presidential statement or policy carried an *implicit threat* to rely upon military force, as in the issuance and reiteration of the Monroe Doctrine, or in repeated warnings by postwar Presidents that the United States intended to safeguard the security of Israel.) In the dispute with Mexico leading to the Mexican War (1847–1848), President James K. Polk ordered the army to occupy disputed territory along the Rio Grande River, although he knew that this action would lead to hostilities with Mexico. During the Civil War, President Abraham Lincoln took many steps—like ordering the armed forces to defend Fort Sumter, expanding the size of the military establishment once the war erupted and making important strategic decisions affecting the conduct of the war—in his role as commander in chief.*

In the early 1900s, Presidents Theodore Roosevelt, Taft, and Wilson carried out several military interventions in Latin America to enforce the Monroe Doctrine and for other purposes. On the eve of World War II, President Franklin D. Roosevelt proclaimed a 500-mile "security zone" to protect the Americas from the Axis threat; and he ordered the American Navy to "shoot on sight" Nazi submarines entering these waters. Such pre-World War II precedents were relied upon by successive occupants of the White House after the war to justify presidential decisions to defend South Korea and South Vietnam, to preserve the security of Lebanon and the Dominican Republic, to send armed forces to "rescue" Americans from the Congo and from Iran. Moreover, on countless occasions, the chief executive has implied that the armed forces of the United States would be employed if necessary to achieve foreign policy goals, as in President Carter's pledge early in 1980 to preserve the security of the Persian Gulf area.[14]

Such examples of executive behavior led to vocal concerns expressed on Capitol Hill and by many citizens' groups about the "imperial presidency" whose actions were not subject to *any* restraint. These apprehensions perhaps reached their apogee during the Nixon Administration. For many months the Nixon Administration seemed determined to prolong America's unpopular involvement in the Vietnam War—and even to expand that involvement by ordering military intervention

---

*In a landmark decision in 1863, the Supreme Court forcefully upheld President Lincoln's decision to blockade the Confederacy, although there had not been (and never was) a "declaration of war" between the Union and the Confederacy. The Court held that under long-standing international law wars may occur without a declaration of them and that President Lincoln was obliged to meet the threat to the integrity of the nation "in the shape it presented itself without waiting for Congress to baptize it with a name...." Subsequent congressional actions—such as financing the war and expanding the armed forces—gave *de facto* approval to Lincoln's actions. See *The Prize Cases,* 67 U.S. (2 Black) 635 (1863).

in Cambodia without the consent of Congress. These and other examples of executive reliance upon military power to achieve diplomatic goals led to mounting legislative concern about the powers of the presidency generally and, more specifically, about the unrestrained use of military force for foreign policy ends. Congressional anxieties on this issue were graphically expressed in the War Powers Resolution, passed by Congress over President Nixon's veto on November 7, 1973.[15] For many of its sponsors, the purpose of this resolution was to reverse the trend toward the "imperial presidency" and to reclaim Congress' rightful role in the foreign policy process.

The War Powers Resolution*

In effect, the War Powers Resolution recognized two kinds of situations requiring presidential reliance upon the armed forces which might confront the United States abroad. In the first place, there were sudden and acute foreign crises to which a President had to respond, such as North Korea's attack against South Korea in 1950, the discovery of the Soviet missile buildup in Cuba in 1962, or an impending Soviet intervention in the Middle East in 1973. The chief executive was largely left free to respond to such situations as he believed justified. The act required that he give a "report" to Congress on his actions and the reasons for them within 48 hours after employing the armed forces; and he was expected to consult Congress "if possible" before he intervened militarily in other countries.

In the second place (and the War Powers Act was directed primarily at this set of conditions), there were foreign crises which developed more slowly, were more predictable, and which proved to be prolonged and expensive American obligations. The prototype here was obviously the Vietnam War, and perhaps the Korean War earlier. For this category of conflicts, the War Powers Act attempted to set limits upon the President's prerogatives as commander in chief. He was obliged to comply with the requirements already identified for the first category of foreign crises. In addition, the President was directed to submit reports on his actions "periodically" to Congress. The heart of the act was the provision that the President must terminate the use of armed force within 60 days if during that period Congress either has not declared war or has not given the President a 30-day "extension" on the employment of armed forces abroad. At any time, Congress may by "concurrent resolution"† direct that the President withdraw American forces from a potential or active combat zone. The act also provided that the President could not (as Presidents Johnson and Nixon did during the Vietnam War) "infer" executive authority to send troops abroad from existing legislation, treaty provisions, or other sources unless Congress specifically passed legislation granting him such authority.

What are the implications of the War Powers Act for the conduct of American foreign relations? Initially, we may note that incumbent administrations since 1973 have

---

*Although its official title was the War Powers Resolution, it is also commonly referred to as the War Powers Act—which is perhaps a more accurate designation, since it was in fact an act or enactment of Congress having the force of law.

† A "concurrent resolution" of Congress is normally used to prescribe rules of legislative procedure or to express the opinion of the House and Senate on some issue. Such resolutions do not require the President's signature. By contrast, a "joint resolution" is an identical bill passed by the House and Senate which, after it is signed by the President, becomes law.

accommodated themselves to the existence of the act and have stated their intention of complying with its provisions whenever possible. The major purpose of the act, a spokesman for the Carter Administration said, was to insure "that the nation will not be committed to war without adequate deliberation and participation by both Congress and the executive." The State Department and other executive agencies have established procedures for providing the information to Congress which the act requires.[16]

How are the provisions of the War Powers Act likely to affect the balance of constitutional powers between the executive and legislative branches with respect to control over the military establishment? How will the act influence American foreign policy toward Latin America, Western Europe, and other regions? At the outset, it must be conceded that insufficient time has elapsed for the major implications of the act to be identified and understood clearly. In only a few instances since 1973 have presidential actions directly been subject to its provisions—and these involved relatively minor episodes in the nation's diplomacy. The popular mood of diplomatic retrenchment following the Vietnam War discouraged incumbent Presidents from relying overtly upon military power to achieve the nation's diplomatic objectives. By the early 1980s—with the United States once again concerned about Soviet expansionism in regions like East Africa, the Persian Gulf area, and possibly Latin America—it is likely that more cases will arise testing the legality and utility of provisions of the War Powers Resolution. Several aspects of the resolution are almost certain to engender controversy in the years ahead.

In vetoing the act, President Nixon asserted that it was unconstitutional, because Congress was attempting by legislation to deprive the President of powers conferred upon him *directly by the Constitution*. A number of constitutional authorities have agreed with Nixon's contention. (If this interpretation is correct, then the only acceptable means of limiting the President's constitutional powers is by constitutional amendment.) There is the further objection that a "concurrent resolution" of Congress requiring the President to withdraw the armed forces from a crisis zone abroad *has no legal force*. (Under the Constitution, laws can be enacted only with the President's signature; if he does not sign them, then he has in effect "vetoed" them.)

Constitutional and legal niceties aside, the importance of the War Powers Act is likely to be determined principally by a single criterion: How well does it serve the diplomatic and security interests of the United States in a rapidly changing, and often dangerous, global environment? Does it permit the nation to achieve its foreign policy goals more effectively, or does it seriously impede that process?

Imperfect as it may be in some respects, an analogy can perhaps be drawn between the War Powers Act and the "neutrality legislation" of the 1930s. In the latter case—reflecting deep-seated anxiety on Capitol Hill and in American public opinion about the prospect of the nation's involvement in another global war—Congress passed a series of measures designed to guarantee American "neutrality" in any future international conflict. The results were perhaps instructive for the American society today. In time, most provisions of the neutrality legislation were ignored or circumvented by executive policy makers. And as World War II approached, even most legislators came to recognize that the legislation was inimical to America's diplomatic and security interests. Rigid adherence to it would have led to a predictable and profoundly disturbing result: an Axis-dominated international system! Ultimately the American people and Congress accepted the Roosevelt Administration's contention that strict adherence to the requirements of the neutrality legislation courted diplomatic and military disaster for the United States. When that realization finally pervaded the American body politic, the neutrality legislation largely became a dead letter.

The "Recognition" Power

In 1979, after mainland China had been governed by a Communist system for a generation, the Carter Administration decided to "recognize" the People's Republic of China (Communist China). In this particular case, the Administration's decision involved a twofold change in American policy: officially recognizing the Communist regime as the legitimate government of the Chinese mainland; and withdrawing American recognition from the Republic of China (Taiwan) as the rightful government of China.

For centuries, the normal mode whereby one state communicates and maintains relations with another has been by the process of mutual "recognition," involving the exchange of diplomatic officials between them. Throughout the world, the American embassy (headed by an ambassador or minister) serves as the usual (although by no means the only) channel of communication between Washington and other foreign capitals. Conversely, the "nonrecognition" of another government by the United States indicates the presence of an abnormal situation—which may vary from the other country's having recently experienced (or still experiencing) political upheaval to the existence of tensions and fundamental policy disagreements between the two countries.

Should the United States "recognize" another government or withhold recognition? When a state (such as Nicaragua at the end of the 1970s) is experiencing political upheaval, at what stage does the government in power lose the "confidence" of the people, and among the contending factions, which one is entitled to American recognition? If a new regime desires recognition by the United States, what conditions must be fulfilled before such recognition is extended? What official in the United States decides such questions? American diplomatic experience leaves no doubt about the answer. As the Supreme Court declared in *United States* v. *Curtiss-Wright* (1936), the President is the "sole organ of the nation" in foreign relations. The recognition of another government is a purely presidential prerogative—and one of the chief executive's most influential tools in the management of foreign affairs.

The President's authority in this realm is derived from the Constitution (Art. II, Sec. 3), empowering him to "receive Ambassadors and other public Ministers. . . ." Ambassadors and other diplomatic officials from foreign countries are "accredited" to the President of the United States. Officially (although, as we shall see more fully in Chapters 7 and 8, not always actually), their contact with the United States government is through the executive branch. Until the post-World War II period, long-standing protocol prohibited foreign governments from having official contacts with other leaders or institutions within the American government, or from appealing to public groups over the head of the President.* Today, foreign governments routinely seek to influ-

---

*A colorful episode from President Washington's Administration involved the activities of "Citizen Genêt," the ambassador from the revolutionary government of France to the new American Republic. At the time of his

ence American policy by "appeals" to Congress and public opinion (the frequent visits to the United States by Israeli officials serve as a prominent example).

If part of the process of recognition of one government by another entails receiving ambassadors from abroad, the other involves sending America's own ambassadors, ministers, or lesser officials to foreign countries. Normal diplomatic intercourse assumes an exchange of officials between the countries. With regard to this latter process, the Constitution (Art. II, Sec. 2) stipulates that the President "shall nominate, and by and with the Advice and Consent of the Senate, shall appoint Ambassadors, and other public Ministers and Consuls...." Greater attention will be devoted to the Senate's prerogatives under this article in Chapter 7. At this point, it is sufficient to observe that, in contrast to the President's power to receive officials from abroad, the Senate must concur in the selection of diplo-

matic officials to represent the United States overseas or to serve in high diplomatic positions in Washington. Such positions as secretary of state, under secretary of state, assistant secretary of state, ambassador, and minister must receive senatorial confirmation.

Vigorous claims have been asserted periodically throughout American history that the Senate's power of confirmation gives that body the right to determine the substance of American foreign policy by specifying the duties that appointees are to carry out. Occasionally, the Senate will rely upon its power to confirm appointments to express its displeasure at the general direction of American foreign policy. For example, a number of senators endeavored to block President Carter's appointment of Leonard Woodcock as the new American ambassador to Communist China as an expression of their opposition to the Administration's recognition of Peking (and its concurrent withdrawal of recognition from Taiwan).[17] While the effort failed, the Carter Administration did make certain conciliatory concessions to its Senate critics in order to get the Woodcock appointment confirmed. As a general rule, however, in recent history the Senate has had minimum success in influencing the conduct of American foreign policy by reliance upon this power.

As with other legislative prerogatives in the foreign policy field, resourceful Presidents have discovered various techniques for circumventing restraints upon their action. They may, for example, and frequently do, appoint "personal representatives" to carry out important diplomatic assignments; these individuals may or may not already hold governmental positions. The chief spokesman for the Wilson Administration during and after World War I was often Colonel Edward M. House, one of Wilson's closest advisers. President Franklin D. Roosevelt leaned heavily on his personal

---

arrival in America, Britain and France were at war; and the Washington Administration had issued a proclamation of neutrality to prevent America's involvement in it. Landing in Charleston, South Carolina, early in 1793, Genêt leisurely made his way to the nation's capital (Philadelphia). *En route* he made numerous anti-Administration speeches and tried to rally public support for a pro-French policy by the United States. Increasingly aggravated by the ambassador's conduct, in time President Washington demanded his recall; Genêt left Philadelphia in disgrace. See Thomas A. Bailey, *A Diplomatic History of the American People,* 8th ed. (New York: Appleton-Century-Crofts, 1969), pp. 85–89.

With the passage of time, the line between permissible and impermissible activities by foreign diplomatic officials has become increasingly tenuous and difficult to draw sharply. Some students of modern diplomacy believe that influencing *public opinion* within the country to which he is assigned may be one of the most important functions of an ambassador and his staff. As we shall see in Chapter 6, routinely all governments today try to influence foreign opinion and to maintain contacts with foreign political leaders and movements.

adviser, Harry Hopkins, to carry out numerous diplomatic missions, including negotiations with Great Britian and Soviet Russia.[18] In the postwar period, one of the nation's most distinguished public servants, W. Averell Harriman, undertook numerous diplomatic assignments as the personal representative of successive Presidents.[19] Postwar chief executives have used the "First Lady" for such missions. And as we shall see more fully in Chapter 4, Cabinet officers (like the Secretary of Defense and the Secretary of the Treasury) frequently engage in diplomatic activities at the President's discretion.[20] Sometimes a President also may make an "interim appointment." Even if the Senate ultimately withholds confirmation, the individual so appointed may have carried out important diplomatic duties, as was the case with Philip Jessup, President Truman's appointee to the American delegation to the United Nations in 1951.[21]

If the recognition power must be counted among the influential techniques by which the President controls foreign policy, it may be asked, "What is the basis upon which a President normally decides to recognize another government?" In very general terms, the answer is when such recognition promotes the diplomatic interests of the United States, as the chief executive interprets them. Admittedly such an answer offers very little guidance for understanding presidential action or inaction. One factor which nearly always influences presidential decisions is *international law*. A leading authority has said this concerning the problem of recognition:

> Actually the subject of recognition is one of the most difficult branches of international law, not merely from the point of view of exposition of principles, but also intrinsically by reason of the many difficult questions which continually arise in practice.

The concept of recognition in international law, he adds, "can be presented less as a collection of clearly defined rules or principles than as a body of fluid, inconsistent, and unsystematic State practice."

It is neither possible nor necessary, in limited space, to enter into a discussion of the legal complexities involved in the matter of recognition of one state by another. Our purpose is served by observing that: (1) Certain criteria exist in international law which states must traditionally satisfy before they are entitled to recognition;* (2) even when nations invoke these criteria, considerable flexibility exists for them to interpret the extent to which particular states have met them; (3) some states give greater weight to certain criteria than to others in their recognition policy; and (4) as J. G. Starke notes, "there is an irresistible tendency in recognizing States to use legal principles as a convenient camouflage for political decisions."[22] While there exists an impressive corpus of international law dealing with recognition, nations are usually inclined to base their decisions in particular cases upon nonlegal or *political* considerations.

Such political considerations are likely to vary greatly from one case to another, making it difficult to generalize about why the United States many years ago recognized the Communist states of Eastern Europe but did not recognize Communist China until 1979, some 30 years after the end of the Chinese civil war; or why Washington accords recognition to some authoritarian regimes while

---

*Major international law criteria are: that the government seeking recognition *must in fact govern* without serious opposition to its rule; it must be reasonably stable and have a future beyond a few days or weeks; it must indicate its willingness to discharge its international obligations to other countries; and (if it applies for UN membership), it must theoretically be a "peace-loving nation."

withholding it from others; or how it determines that one political faction within a country can legitimately claim to represent the popular will while others cannot. No aspect of external affairs perhaps better exemplifies the American society's eclectic approach to foreign policy issues than the problem of recognition. Our purpose is served by emphasizing that the decision to grant, withhold, or withdraw recognition from a foreign government is a purely presidential prerogative.

Historical-Traditional Techniques of Presidential Leadership

Every informed student of the American governmental system is aware of certain practices, customs, and principles which form part of the "unwritten" Constitution. The second category of tools available to resourceful Presidents for controlling foreign policy—those historical and traditional techniques of executive leadership—may be so described.

The President's Control over Information

Wise decisions in foreign policy, as in any field, require the continuous collection and evaluation of information pertinent to the problems at hand. It follows, therefore, that executive leadership in foreign relations flows naturally from the ability of the executive branch to gather such information and, when national security demands it, to preserve its confidential character. In this realm, the chief executive has no effective rivals. As will be explained more fully in Chapters 4, 5, and 6, innumerable governmental agencies collect, evaluate, and transmit to the White House information which is essential to the decision-making process. For example, overseas diplomatic posts send hundreds of cablegrams daily to the State Department; reports come to the Defense Department from military attachés and other military officials stationed abroad; the Central Intelligence Agency and other members of the "Intelligence Community" within the government engage in a wide variety of activities—from "breaking" foreign codes and ciphers to monitoring foreign radio and other communications to securing secret information from agents in other countries—which expand the pool of information available to the President and his chief advisers.

Moreover, very early in the nation's history, Congress recognized the necessity to accord the chief executive and his advisers wide discretionary power to gather information and to preserve the confidential character of diplomatic decisions. Time and again, incumbent Presidents and their subordinates have invoked the principle of "executive privilege" in refusing to disclose information to Congress or other groups, the release of which might endanger national security or the nation's diplomatic interests. Down to the period of the Vietnam War, Congress was usually prone to accept the assertion of executive privilege without serious question, just as it acquiesced in other claims of executive primacy in the foreign policy field. Beginning with the Vietnam conflict, however, and extending through the "Watergate episode" involving the abuse of executive power by the Nixon Administration, Congress has been increasingly prone to challenge an unlimited right of executive privilege by the President and his subordinates. As the Watergate episode indicated, the claim could be invoked to shield the White House from legitimate inquiry into executive misdeeds and from public scrutiny. Yet despite the Watergate example both Congress and the federal courts recognize the concept of executive privilege and its importance in the foreign policy process.* The secretary of state or other high-level executive officials cannot be *required* to provide information to Congress, the press, or other sources if the President decides its disclosure would harm American security or diplomatic interests.

Realistically, of course, every incumbent President is mindful that successful American diplomacy usually has two prerequisites: constructive executive-legislative relations and public support for presidential actions in the foreign policy field. Neither of these preconditions is likely to exist if a chief executive regularly refuses to explain his policies and actions abroad to Congress and the American people. The old Wilsonian principle—"open covenants [or international agreements], openly arrived at"—is a cardinal tenet of the kind of "democratic" diplomacy with which the United States has been identified for a half-century or more. Perhaps more than ever in the light of the Vietnam War, Americans mistrust "secret diplomacy" or efforts by governmental officials to conceal their activities from public scrutiny. Yet after recognizing these constraints, it is no less true that when circumstances require it, the President and his

advisers may feel compelled to maintain the confidentiality of the foreign policy process. Under certain conditions—as during the early stages of the "Cuban Missile Crisis" of 1962,[23] or at a particularly delicate stage of the Egyptian-Israeli peace negotiations—premature disclosure of information could prove highly damaging to America's relations with foreign countries and deleterious to its own security interests.

This conflict between two contrary sets of principles—freedom of information, of the press, and "the public's right to know" versus the necessity for the President to maintain the confidential character of information and decisions in the foreign policy field—poses a recurring dilemma for the American democracy. As in the past, maintaining the proper balance between these principles will prove to be a difficult challenge for officials involved in the foreign policy process, for the press, and for the American people throughout the years ahead.

The President and Public Opinion

"The biggest problem facing any President," former President Truman once declared, "is to sell the American people on a policy. They have to be led forward. . . . That's the biggest challenge every President faces, and one which he cannot escape." In the same vein, early in 1919, President Wilson stated at the Paris Peace Conference: " . . . we are not representatives of governments, but representatives of people. It will not suffice to satisfy governmental circles anywhere. It is necessary that we should satisfy the opinion of mankind."[24] Early in the twentieth century, one of America's most forceful chief executives—President Theodore Roosevelt—gave his assessment of the relationship between presidential decision making and public opinion:

---

*The doctrine of executive privilege was invoked by President Richard M. Nixon and his principal advisers in defense of their refusal to provide the federal courts with records and other evidence bearing upon the Watergate episode. The Supreme Court held that in this case, the doctrine was inapplicable, since no evidence existed that disclosure of the information called for would damage the nation's security and diplomatic interests; and the concept could not be relied upon to cover up possible violations of the law by executive officials. Yet the Supreme Court also forcefully affirmed the validity of the concept of executive privilege, calling it "fundamental to the operation of government and inextricably rooted in the separation of powers under the Constitution." While the Nixon Administration's reliance upon the doctrine in this particular case had no legal sanction, when invoked *legitimately* the doctrine of executive privilege remained an important American constitutional principle. See *United States* v. *Nixon,* 418 U.S. 683 (1974).

People used to say to me that I was an astonishingly good politician and divined what the people are going to think. . . . I did not "divine" how the people were going to think; I simply made up my mind what they ought to think, and then did my best to get them to think it.[25]

These statements call attention to what has come to be one of the most crucial and complex dimensions of the American foreign policy process: *the interaction between decision makers and public opinion*. It is hardly necessary to underscore the organic relationship between democratic government and public opinion. Almost every definition of democracy (such as Lincoln's famous designation of it as "government of the people, by the people, and for the people") implicitly or explicitly recognizes that a democratic system must be responsive to the people's attitudes and needs. As President Lyndon B. Johnson discovered painfully during the Vietnam War, citizens expect that governmental policies and activities will be consonant with the society's goals and ideological values. In a word, the foreign policy of the United States must rest upon a foundation of "legitimacy."*

In his ability to influence public opinion, the President possesses certain advantages over Congress or other rivals to his position of leadership.[26] Modern technology has perhaps *strengthened* his position in this regard, mak-

---

*The concept of "legitimacy" (a synonym might be "effective authority") is one which has received increasing attention from political scientists in recent years. One study asserts: "We may speak of the legitimacy of a political administration in terms of the extent to which its actions are accepted as proper by its citizen subjects." This is indicated by public "agreement with the substance of behavior engaged in by political elites" and by "acceptance of the notion that coercion should be used to enforce the designated public policy if resistance is encountered." William A. Welsh, *Leaders and Elites* (New York: Holt, Rinehart and Winston, 1979), p. 16.

ing it very difficult for opponents of his policies to have a comparable impact upon public opinion. The President of the United States is the most "newsworthy" individual in the nation, if not in the world. Hardly a radio or television news program is presented which lacks some reference to the President's viewpoints or activities. When he wishes to address the nation, the President can preempt radio and TV time, at a period of his own selection, to present his views to the American people; when he travels within the United States or outside it, he is invariably accompanied by reporters and commentators representing all the major news media. With "live" TV coverage, the President's words—together with his expression and tone of voice in speaking them—can be communicated almost instantaneously throughout the world, where they are analyzed carefully by officials in nearly every government. A President's power over public opinion—together with another technique of presidential leadership we shall discuss presently, his power *to commit the nation* to a given course of action—gives the chief executive a formidable advantage over those seeking to contest his leadership.

A President possesses numerous methods for influencing public opinion. President Franklin D. Roosevelt, for example, utilized his highly effective speech-making ability: His radio "fireside chats" with the American people were employed repeatedly, and with telling effect, to rally public support behind his policies.[27] President Truman relied upon his numerous appointments—often as many as 95 weekly—to familiarize himself with public thinking. Beginning with FDR, Presidents have been routinely kept informed of the trend of opinion in mail received by the White House; occasionally, they read and answer some of the thousands of letters received weekly. Truman, Eisenhower, and other postwar Presidents have also from time to time sent their agents on trips to "take the pulse" of the public and report their findings. Conversations with legislators, together with reports submitted by executive officials who deal regularly with senators and representatives, also provide the President with viewpoints outside the circle of his immediate advisers. The Bureau of Public Affairs in the Department of State regularly prepares studies of public opinion, as expressed in newspapers, magazines, and other publications; in the results of public opinion polls; in the resolutions passed by various organizations within the United States; and in mail received by the State Department.[28] President John F. Kennedy excelled in keeping the presidency at the forefront of national consciousness.

Since World War II, American chief executives have been cognizant of a fact which must constantly be borne in mind: The President of the United States is an *international,* as well as a national, leader. At the end of World War I, President Wilson made a widely publicized "European tour," a major purpose of which was to influence public opinion on the Continent (and perhaps also in America) in behalf of his postwar politics and programs. More recent Presidents have attempted to influence public attitudes abroad—relying upon various techniques such as "state visits" to foreign countries by the President or his principal subordinates, interviews with foreign news reporters, maximum global publicity for presidential statements and foreign policy proposals, and other measures. These activities reflect perhaps one of the most significant changes in the nature of diplomacy in the twentieth century (discussed more fully in Chapter 6): The United States and most other governments now routinely endeavor *to affect the viewpoints of the people in foreign societies,* often in an evident attempt to influence the attitudes and behavior of their govern-

ments. In this process, the President of the United States has no peer—either within America or perhaps in the world.

The President as Legislative Leader

According to the principle of separation of powers, the President should not have anything to do with legislation. It is doubtful that even the Founding Fathers believed in rigid adherence to this principle, and it certainly has never been strictly observed in American governmental practice. In many ways, the President is the foremost legislator in the government.

Today, three-fourths or more of all bills enacted by Congress originate in the executive branch of the government. A former assistant to President Johnson has said (paraphrasing the President's own words): " . . . no person in his respective department could ever be any more important than the head of the congressional relations activity." In the view of this White House assistant, "Nothing has a greater priority in the President's view than the legislative program. . . ."[29] In the Kennedy Administration, some 40 officials in the executive branch dealt with what was called "legislative liaison. . . ."[80]

Nearly all of the great legislative enactments affecting American foreign relations in the postwar period—the Greek-Turkish Aid Program, the Marshall Plan, the China Aid Bill, the Point Four Program and the various programs of foreign assistance (like the Alliance for Progress) which followed it, the provision of military assistance to other nations, the support of American military involvement in the Korean and Vietnam wars, agreements with other countries for reciprocal tariff reductions, and America's cultural and informational programs—have had their origin in the executive branch. And after their initiation, executive officials have, at critical junctures, pressed for their adoption by

Congress. Conversely, executive officials engaged in "legislative liaison" have sought to *prevent* congressional enactment of bills deemed by the White House to be inimical to America's interests abroad. When such restrictions upon executive policy making could not be prevented, they could be (and often were) largely vitiated by inclusion of a provision permitting the President to waive the restriction when he believed circumstances warranted such action.

The scope of present-day global commitments of the United States has drawn Congress more than ever into the foreign policy process. But it has also drawn the executive as never before into the *legislative* process, requiring it, as in other spheres of foreign policy, to provide the direction and initiative needed for framing legislation bearing upon external affairs.

Chapter 7 will call attention to the fact that, as never before in modern history, in the contemporary period Congress is exerting its actual or claimed prerogatives in foreign relations. At the same time—in terms of its own internal cohesion, organizational structure, and ability to formulate unified national policies—Congress may be *less* prepared to undertake that task successfully than in any previous era. The effectiveness of the congressional role in foreign affairs, that is to say, will be determined in no small measure by the extent to which *presidential leadership* is exercised on Capitol Hill to produce consistent and constructive external policies. As the experience of the Carter Administration repeatedly demonstrated, in the absence of clear and forceful White House guidance in the foreign policy field, congressional activities are likely to be marked by piecemeal and inconsistent decision making, by disagreements and conflicts between the House and Senate, and by challenges from members of the President's own party on Capitol Hill to his foreign policy

proposals.[31] Much as they may favor forceful legislative influence in the foreign policy process, most legislators are well aware that Capitol Hill cannot supply diplomatic leadership and coherent direction in the foreign policy sphere. Without a clear sense of direction and unified efforts within the executive branch, Congress' own activities in foreign relations will tend to be diffuse, self-defeating, and sometimes inimical to the nation's external interests. As many legislators and commentators eventually demanded of the Carter Administration, Congress and the American people expect the President to serve as a forceful leader and articulator of American foreign policy. In many cases, this requires him to play the role of a successful legislative leader as well.

The President as Political Leader

Adequate discussion of the political role of the President would require a volume. The most we can do here is take for granted his preeminent political position and suggest some of the consequences of this position for foreign affairs. Historically, one of the President's most effective means for influencing the actions of legislators has been the patronage he has had to distribute to the party faithful, in the form of appointments to the federal service. No President in recent history has surpassed FDR in the skillful way he utilized this weapon.[32] Since the New Deal, the importance of patronage has declined, because more jobs have been placed under civil service regulations.

In addition, the President plays an influential role in national elections. Normally, a national candidate who is a member of the President's party desires to have his "endorsement" in a political campaign. The regularity with which candidates seek to "ride the President's coattails" is a well-known phenomenon in American political history. By contrast, in recent years candidates have sought to avoid close identification with an unpopular President, whose support might hurt their political prospects.

Among all the tools available to an incumbent President for managing foreign affairs, his position as a political leader may be the weakest. Several factors account for this development. Party lines in the United States are becoming increasingly blurred and meaningless as an index of an individual's ideological and public policy preferences. In recent years citizens have been less inclined than ever to identify themselves rigidly or consistently with a particular political party. Conversely, they are more disposed to view themselves as "independents" politically. On Capitol Hill, the party organizations in the House and Senate remain weak and, for the most part, ineffectual in terms of influencing legislative behavior. The Watergate episode (precipitated in part by President Nixon's advisers, who sought to gain a political advantage for the Republican Party) did not enhance the chief executive's public image as a political leader. And, as we have already noted, in the post-Vietnam era the lack of a national consensus about the nation's overall foreign policy role, and about the limits which ought to exist on its involvement in global affairs, made it difficult for a political party to formulate and gain support for the President's foreign policy proposals and programs.

The Power to "Commit the Nation"

On March 12, 1947, President Harry S Truman addressed a joint session of Congress to request legislative enactment of the Greek-Turkish Aid Program, inaugurating the "containment" strategy which the Truman Administration adopted to counter Soviet expansionism.[33] Truman's request initiated a series of congressional hearings and prolonged debate in the House and Senate. In the end, despite many misgivings, Congress approved the Greek-Turkish Aid Program—one of the landmark developments in American diplomatic history. Commenting on Congress' response, a leading American news journal observed:

> Congress may ponder and debate [the Greek-Turkish Aid bill] but the President's address has committed the nation to all-out diplomatic action just as a declaration of a shooting war must necessarily follow when the President asks for it.[34]

During the Vietnam War, many of President Johnson's and President Nixon's critics found themselves in the same dilemma. Much as they opposed America's growing involvement in that conflict—and disenchanted as they were becoming with White House policies toward Southeast Asia—they were often reluctant to vote against extension of the draft or against the Defense Department budget, thereby denying the executive branch the means to prosecute the war in Southeast Asia. Successive Presidents could (and did) say that, in effect, Congress had provided a "functional equivalent" to a declaration of war in the Vietnam conflict.

These are merely two examples of one of the most influential techniques available for use by the chief executive for controlling foreign policy: the President's power *to commit the nation* to a particular course of action abroad. Once he has done so, under certain circumstances it is extremely difficult—if not sometimes impossible—for critics in Congress and elsewhere to reverse the decision. As members of the House and Senate fully recognized, after President Truman publicly committed the United States to the defense of Greece and Turkey—and, more broadly, after he announced the "Truman

Doctrine" pledging America to defend the independence of "free peoples" throughout the world—Congress had little choice except to uphold the President's decision. To have done otherwise would have encouraged Soviet aggressiveness, would have provided evidence to foreign countries of a sharply divided American government, and would generally have given rise to implications and problems abroad which few legislators were prepared to face.

The number and nature of America's overseas "commitments" is a question which has been a source of deep concern to Congress in recent years. By various methods (and we shall examine some of them more fully in Chapter 7), Congress has endeavored to limit presidential discretion in assuming these commitments; and, in some cases, it has tried to limit their scope and duration. Time and again, congressional anxiety on this subject has been communicated to the White House; and since the end of the Vietnam War, there has perhaps been less of a tendency by the President and his advisers to assume such commitments than before.

Yet the point being emphasized here remains basically valid: If and when the chief executive commits the United States publicly to a given course of action in foreign affairs—particularly if it is a foreign policy issue involving *American security*—critics of his policy will find it extraordinarily difficult to reverse his policy.

The President's Emergency Powers

Immediately after the Civil War, the Supreme Court declared that "the government, within the Constitution, has all the powers granted to it which are necessary to preserve its existence. . . ."[35] This doctrine has been repeatedly affirmed, as in 1934 when the Court held that "the war power of the Federal Govern-

ment . . . *is a power to wage war successfully. . . .*"[36] From the Civil War onward, national crises have called for the exercise of sweeping governmental powers, powers which many students have thought were unknown to the original Constitution. The point of principal concern to us is that exercise of these powers has entailed a vast expansion in executive authority to deal with national crises.

The emergency powers of the President derive primarily from two constitutional sources: his designation as commander in chief (Art. II, Sec. 2); and his obligation to "take care that the laws be faithfully executed" (Art. II, Sec. 3). Together these two clauses constitute the so-called "war powers" of the executive. Besides this constitutional source, Congress within the last half-century has added to the President's power to deal with national emergencies. Relying both upon his authority as commander in chief and legislative authority given him for coping with emergency conditions, Franklin D. Roosevelt created numerous new governmental agencies during World War II and made them responsible solely to himself, often bypassing established executive departments. In an executive order issued on February 19, 1942, Roosevelt directed his military commanders to bar American citizens of Japanese ancestry from occupying designated areas on the West Coast; this order was subsequently incorporated into an act of Congress.[37] When President Truman, on December 16, 1950, proclaimed "the existence of a national emergency," according to the noted constitutional commentator Edward S. Corwin, he activated over 60 statutes or portions of statutes that become applicable during periods characterized as "a condition of emergency" or "in time of war or national emergency." In most cases, the President determines when such conditions prevail. His determination will, in turn, greatly enlarge his own powers, in part by removing limitations existing upon them during normal times.[38]

Lincoln was the first President to claim broad executive powers for dealing with a national crisis. During the spring and summer of 1861, Lincoln took many steps which, up to that time, had been thought to lie largely or exclusively within the domain of Congress, He ordered a blockade of Southern ports in the absence of a "declaration of war" and directed that ships violating the blockade be confiscated. He increased the size of the army and navy; called out the militia; closed the post office to treasonable correspondence; expended funds from the treasury without legislative authorization; and suspended the writ of habeas corpus. During the course of the Civil War, Lincoln also freed the slaves on his own authority and drew up plans for the "reconstruction" of the South that contemplated little, if any, active participation by Congress. Collectively, these actions asserted "for the President, for the first time in our history, an initiative of indefinite scope in meeting the domestic aspects of a war emergency."[39]

Lincoln's dynamic conception of presidential emergency power has become firmly incorporated into the nation's constitutional fabric. Speaking for the Supreme Court in the Neagle case, Justice Miller in 1890 asked whether the President was limited "to the enforcement of acts of Congress or of treaties of the United States according to their *express terms....*" He answered in the negative, holding that in the discharge of his constitutional obligation to take care that the laws be faithfully executed, the President also was required to include "the rights, duties and obligations growing out of the Constitution itself, our international relations, and all the protection implied by the nature of the government under the Constitution."[40] In the spirit of this idea, President Wilson armed American merchant shipping, in spite of the fact that Congress refused to pass a law giving him such authority. The power of Presidents to take such steps was justified by Solicitor General John W. Davis in 1914 by his assertion that "in ways short of making laws or disobeying them, the Executive may be under a grave constitutional duty to act for the national protection in situations not covered by the acts of Congress, and in which, even, it may not be said that his action is the direct expression of any particular one of the independent powers which are granted to him specifically by the Constitution."[41]

The Presidency—"Imperial" and "Imperiled"

The above identification and analysis of the chief executive's power in foreign relations perhaps inevitably raises apprehensions about the emergence of the "imperial presidency" and the implications of that fact for the American democratic system.[42] Two facts seem undeniable: By the second half of the twentieth century, the President of the United States was in a position to exercise vast and influential powers; and since the foundation of the American Republic, the enhancement of presidential powers has been especially noteworthy in the realm of foreign affairs. It is more than coincidence that most of the "strong Presidents" throughout American history—like Abraham Lincoln, Theodore Roosevelt, Woodrow Wilson, Franklin D. Roosevelt, and (to a greater or lesser degree) nearly all of the post-World War II chief executives —have faced threats to national security and major diplomatic challenges calling for forceful assertions of executive authority. Although the concept of dynamic executive leadership of course antedated World War II, the emergence of the United States as a superpower since that event has perhaps made the idea of the "strong President" a permanent feature of the American governmental system.

Moreover, we need to recall that in modern history (if not always earlier), the conduct of diplomacy has been almost exclusively *an executive function.** During the nineteenth and twentieth centuries—as most Western governments became increasingly democratized—national legislatures acquired new powers, and public opinion became an influential force in both internal and external decision making. Even so, in nearly all governments, irrespective of their type, the management of foreign relations has remained the province of executive officials. Indeed, it would probably be correct to say that throughout the modern world, national legislatures *have less real power* in the foreign policy field than they did a century or a half-century ago. The prototype in this regard is the British Parliament, whose role has largely been reduced to supporting policies formulated by the Cabinet.[43]

In accounting for this paradoxical result, two developments have been significant, particularly in the United States. As Congress and public opinion endeavored to impose new restraints upon the President's freedom of action, resourceful chief executives "answered" this challenge by devising new and often ingenious methods of circumvention. Increasingly, Presidents utilized executive agreements to bypass legislative restraints upon their actions; or they used the armed forces abroad under circumstances which left Congress very little choice except to acquiesce in their actions; or they announced major policy statements which Congress was extremely reluctant to repudiate.

The other development was that—despite growing involvement in the foreign policy process by Congress and public opinion—rivals to the President's dominant position in foreign affairs were still unable to make or manage foreign policy. Congress, for example, might specify what the White House *cannot* do in the nation's relations with other countries; almost never was it able to tell the President what he *must* do and then compel him to do it. Public opinion might set limits to presidential policy making in foreign relations; every chief executive became mindful of what the American people would not "tolerate" in external policy. Within these limits, however, public opinion was usually inclined to accord the President wide discretionary powers to manage foreign relations as he believed the national interest dictated.[44] Even in the second half of the twentieth century, Congress was neither inherently capable of seizing the wheel and navigating the ship of state, nor (as legislative behavior during the Vietnam War demonstrated) were the House and Senate normally willing to assume the *responsibility* for safeguarding the nation's security and promoting its diplomatic interests.

*A leading student of the history of diplomacy has said that, in many respects, modern diplomatic practice dates from the early seventeenth century, particularly from the era of Cardinal Richelieu in France. One of Richelieu's contributions was making certain that diplomatic agents "really represented the sovereign authority in his own country." Richelieu concentrated control over foreign affairs in his own hands; and he was in turn directly responsible to the French monarch. By this method, Richelieu assured that "the word of command in foreign affairs should be delivered by a single voice only, and not by a chorus of discordant voices." Harold Nicolson, *The Evolution of Diplomacy* (New York: Crowell-Collier, 1962), pp. 74–75. Generalizing the practice of modern governments, another student of diplomacy has said that the control of foreign affairs is "concentrated in all countries in the hands of one minister—placed under the control of the head of the government. . . . The relations between the ministers of foreign affairs and the heads of governments are the fundamental basis of foreign policy." Conversely, there is "no field where the collegial system is so dangerously inefficient" as in foreign relations. Jacques de Bourbon-Busset, "Decision-Making in Foreign Policy," in Stephen D. Kertesz and M. A. Fitzsimons, eds., *Diplomacy in a Changing World* (Notre Dame, Ind.: University of Notre Dame Press, 1959), pp. 79–80.

As the events associated with Watergate dramatically indicated, the American people and their legislative representatives are prepared to deal decisively with executive officials who abuse their vast power. Since colonial times, Americans have evinced a deep-seated apprehension about the misuse or usurpation of power by executive officials. A recent student of the presidential office has observed:

> Recurrently in American history, a latent fear of the presidency has risen to the surface, a fear that it would be transformed into a tyrant's throne. National independence came only after a war in which the personification of the enemy was the English king; the Declaration of Independence contained as justification for . . . rebellion a long list of grievances against that king. The Americans were not going to substitute a native tyrant for the one they had just cast off.

This commentator adds that the pervasive realization that George Washington would almost certainly become the nation's first President was a major factor in saving the Constitution from being rejected by the people, because it greatly strengthened executive power vis-à-vis the Articles of Confederation. During their incumbency, some of the nation's most outstanding Presidents—like Andrew Jackson, Abraham Lincoln, and Franklin D. Roosevelt—were accused of usurping power and of imposing a presidential "dictatorship."[45] Recent critics of postwar American foreign policy have focused upon the growth in the powers of the President in foreign relations—a phenomenon which produces great anxiety among some foreign observers. Thus, one commentator has written at length about America's gravitation toward "Caesarism," leading ultimately to a foreign policy of imperialism and the extinction of democracy in the United States. His contention is that "We must see in the President of the United States not merely the Chief Executive of one of the Western democracies, but one already endowed with powers of truly Caesarian magnitude."[46]

Grim predictions in this vein, however, overlook three fundamental considerations about the office of the presidency in the contemporary period and the future. One of these is that, as we have seen, the American people have always been apprehensive about the emergence of an "imperial" President; and as the history of the Nixon Administration proved, they are prepared to take the steps required to deal summarily with flagrant wrongdoing by the President and his subordinates.

Another consideration which must be borne in mind when evaluating the growth of presidential power—especially in the realm of foreign affairs—is the typically eclectic, and often contradictory, attitudes of the American people toward this phenomenon. A fine (sometimes almost imperceptible) line separates the idea of the "imperial" presidency—which the American people *oppose* as much as ever—from the "strong" presidency—which, during the past half-century, they have clearly *favored*. During the twentieth century particularly, Americans have supported—and in many cases demanded—dynamic presidential leadership capable of responding effectively to problems confronting the United States at home and abroad. They wanted a President (like Franklin D. Roosevelt) who was prepared to meet the twofold challenge of leading the nation out of the Great Depression and of preserving its security and diplomatic interests in the face of grave overseas threats. They gave overwhelming public endorsement to President Harry S Truman's decision (expressed in the "Truman Doctrine" enunciating the containment strategy) to "get tough" with the Soviet Union after World War II.[47]

Again, public opinion supported the Truman Administration's decision to defend South Korea from Communist aggression in 1950; Truman's critics were never able to muster significant public or congressional support for their positions. Similarly, public sentiment overwhelmingly endorsed President John F. Kennedy's decision to prevent the installation of Soviet missile bases in Cuba in 1962—even at the risk of possible war with the Soviet Union. Until very late in the conflict, public opinion also supported the actions of successive Presidents during the Vietnam War. Extreme "dovish" sentiment, for example, always reflected a small minority opinion in the United States.* Until it became evident to most Americans that the United States had no feasible options left in the conflict, public

*The Vietnam War provides a highly instructive and interesting case study of the relationship between presidential leadership and public opinion—yielding conclusions and hypotheses which often run counter to prevalent ideas on the subject. Little evidence can be found to support the contention, for example, that protests and demonstrations by critics of America's involvement in Vietnam altered majority public sentiment on the question or was responsible for changing the policies of the Johnson and Nixon administrations toward it. Throughout the war, the tendency of American public opinion was *to support the incumbent President's policies,* even when these changed radically from bombing North Vietnam to seeking peace negotiations. For example, at no time during the Nixon Administration—including his invasions of Cambodia and Laos, and his escalation of air attacks against North Vietnam—did the American people disapprove his conduct of the war. Conversely, riots, protests, and other demonstrations by antiwar critics usually had a negative impact on public opinion; a majority of Americans might have called for the nation's withdrawal from Southeast Asia *sooner* if the opposition had not been associated with riots, disruption, and other activities which alienated most citizens. Polls showed that even among Americans who thought that steps like invading Laos were a mistake, a significant majority of citizens still supported President Nixon in his decision to do so. See this and other evidence presented in Dorothy Buckton James, *The Contemporary Presidency* (Indianapolis, Ind.: Bobbs-Merrill Co., 1974), pp. 257–259.

opinion nearly always supported the policies of the incumbent administration.[48]

Conversely, by the end of the 1970s, the Carter Administration encountered a pervasive complaint that on a variety of internal and external issues it was failing to provide the nation with the leadership necessary in responding to existing challenges, like the "energy crisis" or Communist gains in Latin America. President Carter's "indecisiveness" was criticized at home and abroad; and it was a major element in his defeat at the hands of Republican candidate Ronald Reagan in 1980. As America's diplomatic credibility declined, it was significant that the people looked to the White House—and not to Congress—to supply the desired foreign policy leadership.[49]

Perhaps another way of expressing the ideas being emphasized here is to say that, as many commentators have pointed out since the Nixon Administration, the Watergate episode had a noteworthy result. While it discredited President Nixon and his principal advisers, it did *not* apparently diminish the American people's overall confidence in the presidency as an institution, nor did it reverse their long-standing tendency to look to the White House for leadership in responding to challenges at home and overseas. If Americans were still opposed to an "imperial presidency," they clearly wanted a dynamic, imaginative, and forceful chief executive who exhibited two outstanding qualifications: a capacity to *formulate effective policies* responsive to urgent problems at home and abroad, and *an ability to generate sufficient support for them in the executive and legislative branches* in behalf of unified policy measures promoting the American society's interests.[50]

That the prerogatives of the President, especially in the foreign policy sphere, are vast seems incontestable. Yet perhaps the transcendent lesson of the threatened impeachment and possible trial of President

Nixon is the realization that the American democratic system *does work* to prevent the emergence of the "imperial presidency"—a chief executive whose actions are unrestrained by law and are antithetical to the values of the American society. Specifically, what parameters keep executive power within proper constitutional and ethical bounds? One restraint, emphasized by the Supreme Court in a controversy arising out of the "steel seizure case" during the Truman Administration, is the requirement that when the chief executive is provided by Congress with methods for dealing with national emergencies, he is required to follow procedures specified by law.* Moreover, a President cannot take action that is plainly denied him by constitutional provisions. Furthermore, as the Supreme Court held in the "Nixon case" previously cited, a President cannot invoke the claim of national security or a national emergency to conceal wrongdoing or violations of the law by governmental officials. If he attempts to do so, as President Nixon discovered, he risks being impeached, fined, jailed, and almost certainly repudiated by the American people.

Then there are other restraints which are perhaps less tangible and coercive, but perhaps no less effective. Most Presidents (and Harry S Truman was a leading example) possess a sense of American history, venerate the office of President of the United States, and wish to be remembered as an incumbent who brought credit to the office they hold. Presidents, of course, are also political leaders: During their first terms at least, they normally desire to be reelected and are cognizant of the need to create and maintain a solid base

of political support for their policies and programs. Since World War II, most chief executives have been concerned about their "public image," as reflected in public opinion polls and other techniques for determining public attitudes. During the Carter Administration, for example, the President's chief aides (and sometimes even President Carter himself) were plainly apprehensive about his ratings in public opinion polls. One purpose of President Carter's "Summit Meeting" with Soviet Prime Minister Brezhnev in Vienna in mid-1979 was to improve Carter's standing as an effective chief executive in the eyes of the American people.[51] Since the tribulations experienced by the Johnson Administration during the Vietnam War—when public opposition to his policies in Southeast Asia compelled LBJ not to seek reelection—Presidents are unlikely to forget the necessity for *public support* for their actions at home and abroad. The concept we discussed earlier in the chapter—the idea of "legitimacy" or public acceptability of governmental actions and programs—must be regarded as among the more potent forces keeping executive power within prescribed bounds.† Expressed positively, every modern President is aware that, as never before in

---

*For a detailed analysis of the limits of presidential power in dealing with national emergencies, the student is referred to the Supreme Court's decision in *Youngstown Company* v. *Sawyer*, 343 U.S. 579 (1952).

† A contemporary student of the American presidency has highlighted the crucial role of the concept of legitimacy in discussing the differences between the fates of the Johnson and Nixon administrations. In one sense, of course, there was little or no difference: Both President Johnson and President Nixon suffered a severe erosion of popular support, brought on in large part by the existence of a widening "credibility gap" concerning their actions and policy statements. But in this commentator's view, there was a crucial distinction between these two cases. President Johnson's loss of public confidence stemmed primarily from a growing view that his Administration was guilty of "misjudgment, or misfortune, or mismanagement." His Vietnam policies were viewed as "dumb perhaps but not deliberately deceptive." Nixon, on the other hand, increasingly convinced Americans that he was "a deceiver," who engaged in "deception on a massive scale,

American history, constructive internal and external policies nearly always involve a *collaborative effort* by the executive and legislative branches, and they demand at least minimum acceptability by public opinion before they can be achieved. To obtain this result, presidential actions must be compatible with the American society's most deeply held values and attuned to its more urgent needs.

NOTES

1. These and other statements in this vein may be found in I. M. Destler, *Presidents, Bureaucrats and Foreign Policy* (Princeton, N.J.: Princeton University Press, 1972), pp. 83–90.
2. For former Secretary of State Dean Acheson's views, see Ronald J. Stupak, *The Shaping of Foreign Policy: The Role of the Secretary of State as Seen by Dean Acheson* (New York: Odyssey Press, 1969), pp. 81, 84.
3. See *McCulloch* v. *Maryland,* 4 Wheaton 316 (1819). The student is urged to become familiar with legal citations. After the name of the case, the first number refers to the *volume* number: Wheaton was one of the compilers of Supreme Court decisions in the nineteenth century. The next number is the *page number* on which the case begins. The date is of course the year the case was decided. After 1882, the name of the compiler was no longer used; the *United States Reports* (abbreviated in citations to U.S.) became the official compilation of Supreme Court decisions. Thus, after that date, a case would be cited as: *United States* v. *Belmont,* 301 U.S. 324 (1937).

4. See *United States* v. *Curtiss-Wright Export Corporation,* 299 U.S. 304 (1936).
5. Ibid.
6. For detailed discussion of the legal issues arising out of the Vietnam War, and of the decisions of the federal courts in dealing with them, see Anthony A. D'Amato and Robert M. O'Neil, *The Judiciary and Vietnam* (New York: St. Martin's Press, 1972).
7. Quoted in Cecil Crabb, Jr., *Bipartisan Foreign Policy: Myth or Reality?* (New York: Harper & Row, 1957), p. 16.
8. The new Panama Canal treaty as a case study in Congress' role in contemporary foreign relations is dealt with in detail in a study by Cecil V. Crabb, Jr., and Pat Holt, *Invitation to Struggle: Congress and American Foreign Policy* (Washington, D.C.: Congressional Quarterly, 1980). Briefer treatments may be found in *New York Times,* August 17, 1977, and May 18, 1979; and *Newsweek,* **XCI** (February 13, 1978), 18–20.
9. Thus, at his news conference on April 30, 1979, President Carter indicated that if the SALT II disarmament treaty failed to receive Senate approval, he would then "do all I could, monitoring very closely Soviet activities to comply with the basic agreements reached." Carter would *not* (as many Senate critics proposed) undertake a new American military buildup if the Senate rejected the treaty. See the text of President Carter's news conference in *New York Times,* May 1, 1979.
10. For an illuminating analysis of presidential reliance upon executive agreements in the recent period, and of Congress' efforts to limit that freedom, see Loch Johnson and James M. McCormick, "Foreign Policy by Executive Fiat," *Foreign Policy,* **28** (Fall, 1977), 117–139.
11. For more detailed discussion of these and other examples of reliance by postwar Presidents to achieve foreign policy goals, see Herbert K. Tillema, *Appeal to Force: American Military Intervention in the Era of Containment* (New York: Thomas Y. Crowell Co., 1973).
12. See, for example, Tillema's analysis on re-

substantial and sustained, directed at associates and citizens alike." Whereas Johnson simply ran out of policy options in Vietnam, Nixon and his advisers deliberately practiced deception and misuse of power for ends which had no relationship to the goals of the American society. The result was that the American people were relatively charitable in their verdict on the Johnson presidency, but were harsh in judging the Nixon record. See Richard E. Neustadt, *Presidential Power: The Politics of Leadership* (New York: John Wiley and Sons, 1976), pp. 6–8.

straints upon American military intervention, and his chapter "Where Military Intervention Has Not Occurred," in ibid., pp. 93–179.

13. A detailed examination of various constitutional theories related to the President's role as commander in chief is available in the commentary published by the Library of Congress, *The Constitution of the United States of America* (Washington, D.C.: Government Printing Office, 1973), pp. 449–472. A useful interpretive work is Ernest R. May, ed., *The Ultimate Decision—The President as Commander in Chief* (New York: G. Braziller, 1960).

14. See the citations of various precedents and constitutional authorities relied upon by the State Department to justify the President's use of the armed forces without congressional approval, in *The Constitution of the United States of America*, pp. 460–463. Discussing the Korean War, former Secretary of State Dean Acheson said that by that stage of American history, there was no doubt about the President's authority to use troops abroad for foreign policy ends, although doubts might exist about the wisdom of his doing so. Ibid., p. 460.

15. For the text of the "War Powers Act," see Public Law 93-148, 87 Statutes-at-Large 555 (November 7, 1973).

16. See Herbert J. Hansell, "Department Discusses War Powers Resolution," *Department of State Bulletin,* **LXXVII** (August 29, 1977), 291–293.

17. See the views expressed by several senators on the Carter Administration's recognition of Communist China, as contained in the *Congressional Quarterly Weekly Report,* **37** (January 20, 1979), 97.

18. FDR's reliance upon Harry Hopkins to carry out diplomatic assignments is described in Robert E. Sherwood, *Roosevelt and Hopkins,* Vol. 1 (New York: Bantam Books, 1948), pp. 283–285, 305, 328, 536.

19. For detailed examples of Harriman's role as a presidential envoy, see W. Averell Harriman and Eli Abel, *Special Envoy to Churchill and Stalin: 1941–1946* (New York: Random House, 1975).

20. For example, early in 1979, President Carter chose Treasury Secretary Michael Blumenthal to undertake diplomatic assignments in Communist China; in the same period, Secretary of Defense Harold Brown made military commitments to governments in the Middle East. See *New York Times,* February 13 and March 2, 1979.

21. *New York Times,* October 23, 1951.

22. J. G. Starke, *An Introduction to International Law,* 5th ed. (London: Butterworths, 1963), p. 120.

23. The Kennedy Administration's efforts to preserve secrecy in formulating the American response to the installation of Soviet missiles in Cuba—and of the necessity to do so—is a major theme in Robert F. Kennedy, *Thirteen Days: A Memoir of the Cuban Missile Crisis* (New York: New American Library, 1969).

24. President Truman's views are quoted in Sidney Warren, *The President as World Leader* (New York: McGraw-Hill, 1967), p. 97. President Wilson's views are cited in Louis W. Koenig, *The Chief Executive* (New York: Harcourt Brace Jovanovich, 1968), p. 184.

25. President Theodore Roosevelt's views are quoted in Warren, *The President as World Leader,* p. 23.

26. For fuller discussion of the President's unrivaled position, see Manfred Landecker, *The President and Public Opinion: Leadership in Foreign Affairs* (Washington, D.C.: Public Affairs Press, 1968); and James N. Rosenau, *National Leadership and Foreign Policy: A Case Study in the Mobilization of Public Support* (Princeton, N.J.: Princeton University Press, 1963).

27. Wilfred E. Binkley, *President and Congress* (New York: Alfred A. Knopf, 1947), p. 250.

28. The State Department's activities in this regard are described in Smith Simpson, *Anatomy of the State Department* (Boston: Houghton Mifflin Co., 1967), pp. 184–205.

29. See the views of Lawrence O'Brien, as cited in Sidney Warren, ed., *The American President* (Englewood Cliffs, N.J.: Prentice-Hall, 1967), p. 136.

30. Ibid., p. 135.

31. The end of the 1970s witnessed acute divi-

sions within Congress—and fundamental conflicts between executive and legislative policy makers—over three important diplomatic issues: United States recognition of the new government of Southern Rhodesia; the SALT II arms-limitation agreement with the Soviet Union; and continuing legislative dissatisfaction with the new Panama Canal Treaty, ratified in 1978. For further discussion see *New York Times,* April 13, June 5, and June 18, 1979; and *Newsweek,* **XCIII** (May 7, 1979), 44–46.

32. Binkley, *President and Congress,* p. 246.
33. For the text of President Truman's historic address to Congress on March 12, 1947, enunciating the "Truman Doctrine," or containment strategy, see *Public Papers of the Presidents of the United States: Harry S Truman, 1947* (Washington, D.C.: Government Printing Office, 1963), pp. 176–180.
34. See the editorial from the *St. Louis Post-Dispatch* on President Truman's speech, as quoted in Cecil V. Crabb, Jr., *Bipartisan Foreign Policy: Myth or Reality?* (New York: Harper & Row, 1957), p. 61. For a comparable reaction in this vein, see the views of Senator Arthur H. Vandenberg on Truman's speech, in Arthur H. Vandenberg, Jr., ed., *The Private Papers of Senator Vandenberg* (Boston: Houghton Mifflin Co., 1952), pp. 342–343. To Vandenberg's mind, Congress had no choice: If it failed to support the President, then it had to confront either "Communist encirclement" abroad or it could "get ready for World War No. Three." Ibid., p. 342.
35. *Ex parte Milligan,* 4 Wallace 2 (1886).
36. *Home Building and Loan Association* v. *Blaisdell,* 290 U.S. 398 (1934). Italics inserted.
37. For these and other examples of FDR's reliance upon "emergency" powers during World War II, see *Constitution of the United States of America,* pp. 453–459. In his message to Congress on September 7, 1942, President Roosevelt asked it to take several steps vital to the war effort. FDR frankly informed Congress that if it failed to act, then "I shall accept the responsibility, and I will act." His

view was that the President had ample powers "to avert a disaster" and to take steps necessary for "winning the war." FDR's views are cited in ibid., p. 453.

38. Edward S. Corwin, *The Constitution of the United States of America* (Washington, D.C.: Legislative Reference Service, Library of Congress, 1953), pp. 81–82.
39. Edward S. Corwin, *Total War and the Constitution* (New York: Alfred A. Knopf, 1947), p. 19.
40. See *In re Neagle,* 135 U.S. 1 (1890).
41. Corwin, *The Constitution of the United States of America,* p. 496.
42. A recent study of the subject—tracing the emergence of presidential power throughout the nation's 200-year history—is Arthur M. Schlesinger, Jr., *The Imperial Presidency* (Boston: Houghton Mifflin Co., 1973).
43. Thus one student of British foreign policy has asserted that "the Crown is responsible for British policy." In practice, this means that "responsibility is exercised by ministers of the Crown—the government" or the Cabinet, supported by its parliamentary majority. The management of foreign affairs is firmly exercised by the Cabinet and is "rarely subject to concessions necessary to retain . . . parliamentary confidence." In fact, a British prime minister "can make the crucial decisions, assisted by no more than a few inner Cabinet colleagues. . . ." Leon D. Epstein, "British Foreign Policy," in Roy C. Macridis, ed., *Foreign Policy in World Politics,* 3rd ed. (Englewood Cliffs, N.J.: Prentice-Hall, 1967), pp. 34–35.
44. The wide latitude accorded the President and his advisers by American public opinion in the management of foreign relations is a major finding of a detailed study by Bernard C. Cohen, *The Public's Impact on Foreign Policy* (Boston: Little, Brown and Co., 1973). For example, the "important publics" or proportion of public opinion motivated to threaten the President and his supporters with electoral defeat or other losses because of foreign policy decisions is very limited and rarely effective. Even the kind of "mobilized indignation" witnessed during the Vietnam War has "un-

certain power to constrain the policies of a President who has a strong sense of national interest and obligation." Ibid., p. 186.

45. Grant McConnell, *The Modern Presidency*, 2nd ed. (New York: St. Martin's Press, 1976), p. 2.

46. A detailed analysis of the emergence of strong presidential power in the United States and its implications, both for America and for the world, is provided in Amaury de Reincourt, *The Coming Caesars* (New York: Capricorn Books, 1957). The quotation is from p. 6.

47. For evidence of mounting public pressure upon the Truman Administration to "get tough" with Moscow in the early postwar period, see the public opinion polls and other data in Peter G. Filene, ed., *American Views of Soviet Russia* (Homewood, Ill.: Dorsey Press, 1968), p. 166; and Leonard S. Cottrell, Jr., and Sylvia Eberhart, *American Opinion on World Affairs* (Princeton, N.J.: Princeton University Press, 1948), pp. 48 ff.

48. See the informative analysis of the findings of numerous public opinion polls during the Vietnam War in Seymour M. Lipset, "The President, the Polls, and Vietnam," in Robert J. Lifton, ed., *America and the Asian Revolutions* (New York: Aldine Publishing Co., 1970), pp. 101–116.

49. By the late 1970s, President Carter faced recurrent complaints—often from individuals and groups who had previously supported him—because of his lack of leadership, especially in foreign relations. Thus, one report analyzed his poor "box score" in dealing with Congress; the Administration had demonstrated little effective follow-through in getting legislators to support the President's proposals. See Terence Smith, in *New York Times*, June 17, 1979. Another commentator referred to America as "a nation hungry for the sense that someone is in charge." But President Carter seemed to be "constantly temporizing" and exercising "questionable political leadership." Tom Wicker, in *New York Times*, March 2, 1979. Overseas, the International Institute for Strategic Studies also lamented the deterioration of America's diplomatic position under the Carter Administration. The President gave the appearance of lacking "a centralized means of translating difference of opinion into coherent policy." Recent congressional assertiveness in foreign relations only added to the sense of "fragmentation" which characterized American foreign policy. *New York Times,* May 16, 1979. Public opinion polls reinforced this conclusion among the American people. One national poll in the late spring of 1978, for example, found that only 29 percent of the people approved of Carter's management of foreign relations—the lowest percentage among five previous administrations in Washington! *New York Times,* June 30, 1978. Meanwhile, the American people continued to evince little confidence in Congress to provide the desired leadership. One poll showed that Congress ranked ninth on a list of ten institutions in the degree of public confidence shown toward them—well below churches, banks, and the military, and only slightly ahead of big business. See *Parade,* June 24, 1979, p. 19.

50. An analysis of public opinion polls dealing with the President's "popularity" or public reactions to his performance in office indicates that the main variable affecting public attitudes was the *results* a President achieved while in the White House. "If the news was good, the President's popularity rose; if bad, it fell." The principal conclusion from the study was that in judging the President, "people pay attention to *results*. Talk does not impress them much.... A popularity-maximizing President, then, would do well to produce good results." See Richard A. Brody and Benjamin I. Page, "The Impact of Events on Presidential Popularity: The Johnson and Nixon Administrations," in Aaron Wildavsky, ed., *Perspectives on the Presidency* (Boston: Little, Brown and Co., 1975), pp. 136–148.

51. See Hedrick Smith, in *New York Times,* June 18, 1979.

Chapter 4

The State Department and Other Executive Agencies

Reflecting upon his experience as secretary of state under the Truman Administration, Dean Acheson observed: "President Truman looked principally to the Department of State in determining foreign policy and—except where force was necessary—exclusively in executing it; he communicated with the Department and with the foreign nations through the Secretary [of State]."[1] Several years later, when he entered the White House, President John F. Kennedy expressed a similar view. According to one of his closest advisers, Kennedy made

> ... it very clear that he does not want a large separate organization between him and his Secretary of State. Neither does he wish any question to arise as to the clear authority and responsibility of the Secretary of State ... as the agent of coordination in all our major policies toward other nations.[2]

Routinely after assuming office, nearly every postwar President has made a comparable statement, designating the Department of State as the principal executive agency responsible for foreign affairs and naming the secretary of state as his "chief adviser" on foreign policy questions. Yet the Kennedy Administration's experience has not been untypical: Within a relatively brief period of time the President had "lost confidence" in the State Department and had begun to rely upon other agencies and individuals to assist him in making key foreign policy decisions. It is this interesting and by now rather predictable conflict—between the historic and theoretical role of the State Department in the foreign policy process, on the one hand, and its decline as an influential and effective agency in foreign policy decision making, on the other hand—which provides the central theme of this chapter.

The State Department and the Policy Process

Evolution of the Department

As a result of a difficult and frustrating experience under the Articles of Confederation—in which foreign affairs were managed (or, more accurately, *mismanaged*) by Congress—the Founding Fathers greatly strengthened the powers of the President in foreign relations. In 1789, three executive departments (foreign affairs, war, and treasury) were created. From the beginning, the secretary of state was recognized as the ranking Cabinet officer in the government and the President's chief policy adviser. Since, however, the new Republic's foreign relations were very limited, the Department of State was initially assigned such miscellaneous functions as serving as custodian for the Great Seal of the United States, issuing patents, receiving copyrights, and publishing census returns. Secretary of State Thomas Jefferson had a limited staff of five clerks, one translator, and two messengers; and (in company with many critics of the State Department in the contemporary era), Jefferson complained that the department was "overstaffed"!

As the United States grew in size and area—and as its contacts with other countries gradually expanded—the State Department grew apace. As long as the isolationist mentality continued to dominate the American approach to foreign affairs, the State Department's responsibilities were largely confined to reporting on conditions abroad, promoting foreign commerce, and ceremonial functions. As we observed in Chapter 2, throughout American history down to World War II, Americans remained suspicious of "diplomacy" and of the Foreign Service "elite" that conducted the nation's diplomatic business.

The Modern State Department

The modern State Department dates from the post-World War I era, with the passage of the Rogers Act (May 24, 1924). As a result of this act, for the first time the United States had a "professional" diplomatic corps—the Foreign Service of the United States—appointed on the basis of merit rather than political influence or social status.[3] Entry into the Foreign Service after that date was by competitive examination, designed to recruit the best qualified applicants from among those wishing to enter the diplomatic corps.* The Rogers Act provided for promotion on the basis of performance; and salaries and benefits for the members of the American diplomatic corps were substantially improved. The result, as one commentator concluded, was that the quality of the State Department's performance improved significantly in the years which followed, morale among the department's employees "soared ... and the Foreign Service rapidly increased in size and professional skill."

Even with the passage of the Rogers Act, however, the State Department remained ill-equipped to deal with the extent and kinds of international relationships in which the United States was involved after World War II. An experienced Foreign Service officer has referred to life in the State Department during the 1920s, for example, when messengers delivered communications within the department "at unhurried intervals." During that period:

> The coding apparatus belonged to another era; correspondence moved at the speed of molasses; nobody bothered to put the papers away or lock the safe at lunchtime; security-consciousness was nonexistent. Critics were to say that in 1914 the Department was about ready to cope with the Spanish-American War; that in 1939 it was prepared for World War I.[4]

---

*As intended, the Foreign Service entrance examination comprises a difficult battery of written and oral examinations. In 1974, for example, of 9300 applicants who took the written examination, 1300 passed; 400 applicants then took the oral examination; and 144 applicants were ultimately recruited into the Foreign Service of the United States.

The complaint has a familiar ring. Throughout the post-World War II period, critics have lamented that the State Department was "behind the times" and that it was endeavoring to manage American foreign policy on the basis of outdated concepts and administrative processes.

When the United States emerged as a superpower after World War II, the responsibilities of the State Department expanded greatly and steadily. By the late 1970s, for example, the department had nearly 29,000 employees in the United States and overseas (with about one-third of this total stationed in Washington). Some 134 American embassies, along with 132 other foreign posts, operated under the department's jurisdiction. In addition, the State Department supervises American activities in the United Nations and in regional organizations, like the Organization of American States (OAS).[5] As with all governmental agencies, the State Department's budget has steadily increased since World War II, reaching some $1.5 billion annually by the end of the 1970s. Even so, the Department of State is still one of the *smallest* executive departments. (The Department of Health and Human Services, for example, has nearly five times as many employees; the Defense Department's budget is some *70 times* larger than the State Department's; and the federal government spends three times as much on science and space technology as it does for the operations of the Department of State.)

The postwar period has witnessed fundamental changes in the nature of the State Department's concerns. Theoretically, the primary concern of the department is *political relations* between the United States and other countries. Since World War II, a noteworthy trend has been the extent to which new, nonpolitical aspects of diplomacy have been added to the State Department's traditional

responsibilities. These include: a greatly expanded involvement in international economic problems; policy supervision for the foreign aid program; promotion of cooperative State Department relations with Congress; involvement in international environmental and scientific issues; and, most recently, keen American interest in the problem of international human rights.

Basic Organizational Structure

The Department of State stands at the center of a continually expanding "complex" of executive agencies involved in the foreign policy process.* Its organizational structure conforms to the same hierarchical pattern found in most governmental agencies. At the top of the hierarchical pyramid is the secretary of state, who is responsible to the President. Directly under him is a deputy secretary of state, and at the next level there are three under secretaries of state, a deputy under secretary, and a counselor.

The organizational pattern of the State Department reflects its concern with four major functions. First, several units—such as the Executive Secretariat, the Protocol Office, and the Foreign Service Institute—are in-

---

*Several other agencies directly involved in the formulation and administration of American foreign policy will be considered more fully in future chapters. For example, the Arms Control and Disarmament Agency (ACDA) is a separate agency with responsibility for studying and making recommendations on the problem of arms control. The Agency for International Development (AID) has operating responsibility for the foreign economic aid program; it takes its policy directives from the State Department. The foreign aid program is discussed in Chapter 6. The United States International Communication Agency (USICA), formerly the United States Information Agency (USIA), is America's propaganda instrument. By 1982, Congress was seriously considering changing the agency's name again, reverting to the earlier designation (USIA). The agency's activities are described more fully in Chapter 6.

volved primarily with internal departmental administration and training programs. Second, other units are engaged in promoting the department's public relations (including relations with Congress) at home and abroad. Among these are the offices of Press Relations and of Congressional Relations, and the Bureau of Public Affairs.

Third, there are the "functional bureaus" of the State Department, which deal with a wide variety of international problems cutting across national and regional boundaries. These include the bureaus of Educational and Cultural Affairs and Economic and Business Affairs; and (reflecting one of the State Department's newest global concerns) the Bureau of Oceans and International Environmental and Scientific Affairs. Another office—the Bureau of Politico-Military Affairs—serves as the State Department's liaison unit with the Department of Defense to coordinate external policies involving the use (or possible use) of the armed forces abroad. The most recent addition to the list of functional bureaus is concerned with the problem of international human rights.

Fourth, the State Department contains five "geographical bureaus," corresponding to the major regions of the world, plus a sixth bureau for International Organization Affairs (dealing with the United Nations and other global organizations). Traditionally, the geographical bureaus have been viewed as the operating heart of the State Department for America's political relations with other countries. Within each bureau, a "country desk" staffed by one or more officers is responsible for American relations with each nation within the region. The "chain of command" for a country like Brazil, for example, extends upward from the American embassy and consulates within Brazil, to the "Brazilian desk" in the Bureau of Inter-American Affairs; important policy questions are referred upward

to the assistant secretary of state for Inter-American Affairs, to an under secretary (or a deputy under secretary), to the secretary of state himself, and possibly to the White House. Normally, policy directives move in reverse order, ultimately reaching American diplomatic and consular installations in the field. In general, a high level of expertise is available to the State Department among the officers assigned to the country desks, many of whom are Foreign Service officers who have had first-hand experience in the countries for which they are responsible.

As a result of the Hoover Commission's investigations and recommendations, the Office of Congressional Relations was established after World War II to facilitate the State Department's harmonious and continuous liaison with Congress. Working closely with legislative specialists in the White House, this office seeks to generate support on "the Hill" for legislation related to foreign affairs. In addition, it answers congressional inquiries on foreign policy and provides assistance in arranging trips abroad for legislative committees.

Special mention needs to be made of another bureau within the State Department, established after the creation of the United Nations in 1945: the Bureau of International Organization Affairs.* Its primary responsibility is to serve as a link between the State Department in Washington and the American

---

*The United Nations is not, however, the only international organization to which the United States sends a mission. Smaller ones include the mission to the UN Economic Committee for Europe (ECE), the International Labor Organization, the World Health Organization, and the UN Conference on Trade and Development (UNCTAD). Although it tends to exaggerate the extent to which the UN mission is free of State Department control, a recent study focuses upon the operation of the mission and upon the problems confronted in coordinating policy between it and the Department of State. See Ar-

mission to the United Nations in New York. Accredited to the United Nations, the American ambassador to the UN holds a position very different, in several fundamental respects, from those of ambassadors to nations with which the United States maintains relations. This difference is suggested by former UN Ambassador Stevenson's comment that "In a sense, a U.S. Ambassador to the U.N. is a U.N. Ambassador to the U.S." [6]

"Reorganizing" the State Department

Perhaps reflecting the existence of certain recurrent problems in American diplomacy, the post-World War II period has witnessed numerous major and minor "reorganizations" of the foreign policy machinery—so much so that "reorganizing" the State Department has become almost a national pastime! Alternatively, the impulse to change the diplomatic machinery may be a reflection of the American business ethic: From time to time, business corporations are "reorganized" in an effort to improve their profits and efficiency. As many Americans evaluate the matter, the nation's diplomatic ledger usually shows more losses than profits, and the usual remedy for this condition is to undertake a detailed study of the problem, followed by major changes in the appropriate organizational structure.

Not unexpectedly, the Department of State emerged from World War II ill-prepared to meet the challenges posed by the emergence of the United States as a superpower. In one instance after another, State Department officials were reluctant to assume novel postwar responsibilities; and the depart-ment was often not equipped to discharge them effectively. Guided chiefly by the State Department's own recommendations, in 1946 Congress enacted the Foreign Service Act, inaugurating the first of a series of major organizational changes within the department.

This new act did not contemplate sweeping changes in the Foreign Service. In the language of Congress, it attempted merely to "improve, strengthen, and expand" the existing corps. Salary scales for each officer grade were raised sharply; the number of grades was reduced; allowances, promotions, leaves, and retirement benefits were liberalized. The objective was to make the service a more attractive career, and give it a better competitive position among other governmental agencies and with private industry. The principle of "promotion-up, or selection-out" governed an officer's continuance in the service. A Foreign Service Institute was also established in Washington to train successful applicants for the service and to provide periodic in-service and language training for officers already on the job.

During the late 1940s and 1950s, the morale and efficiency of the Foreign Service were impaired by several developments. Instigated by Senator Joseph McCarthy (Republican of Wisconsin), attacks were widely made upon the loyalty and reliability of the Foreign Service, some of whose members were accused of what were tantamount to treasonable activities. The charges were almost never substantiated. Early in his tenure as secretary of state, John Foster Dulles made a speech to State Department officials in which he pointedly demanded "positive loyalty" from his subordinates; intentional or not, the implication was that American diplomatic officials were lacking in loyalty to their superiors or to the United States.[7] Along with declining morale, recruitment into the Foreign Service during this period dropped sharply.

nold Beichman, *The "Other" State Department* (New York: Basic Books, 1968); and John B. Martin, *Adlai Stevenson and the World: the Life of Adlai E. Stevenson* (Garden City, N.Y.: Doubleday and Co., 1977), pp. 579–781.

At length, the Eisenhower Administration appointed a Public Committee on Personnel, headed by Dr. Henry M. Wriston of Brown University, to investigate the Foreign Service and submit recommendations for its improvement. The process of "Wristonization" which followed brought far-reaching changes (if morale within the service did not notably improve).* As a result of the committee's findings, many State Department officials (who had hitherto been under Civil Service) were integrated into the Foreign Service.[8]

Late in 1964, President Johnson approved another modification in the Foreign Service, when he directed that officials of America's propaganda and informational agency, the United States Information Agency (USIA), be included in the Foreign Service of the United States. Some 900 USIA officials were immediately given Foreign Service officer status. Then in 1968, the Foreign Service (having grown to some 8,200 officers) undertook an experimental program to draw larger numbers of blacks, Spanish-Americans, and members of other minority groups into its ranks.[9]

---

*Several recommendations made by the Wriston Committee were not carried out. A leading one (also proposed by other groups and individuals from time to time) was for establishment of a Foreign Service Academy similar to the military academies, for training American diplomatic officials. This recommendation encountered opposition from a variety of sources. Many congressmen opposed it, both as a needless expenditure and because of a possible conflict between adherence to the principle of academic freedom at such an institution and the necessity to "support" the foreign policy of the United States. Former Secretary of State Dean Acheson also rejected the idea as "based on wholly false assumptions"; he urged that better use be made, in training future Foreign Service officers, of the existing Foreign Service Institute, the military war colleges, and private academic institutions. He also believed that a possible conflict between academic freedom and support for the policies of the United States would exist. See *New York Times* (June 3, 1963, and January 21, 1964).

Still another detailed study of the nation's foreign policy mechanism was undertaken in the mid 1970s. Headed by Robert D. Murphy, one of America's most experienced and distinguished former diplomats, the "Murphy Commission" engaged in an intensive investigation of the foreign policy process in the United States, centering upon the role of the State Department in it.[10] The Murphy Commission reiterated the long-standing idea that "The State Department will continue to be the central point in the U.S. government for the conduct of foreign affairs." In the commission's view, the State Department "should play a major part in the formulation of all U.S. policy having significant foreign implications...." The department should continue to have responsibility "for the actual conduct of relations with other government and international organizations." In an effort to enhance the State Department's role in the foreign policy process, the commission made a number of (relatively modest) recommendations for organizational reform within the agency. The commission believed, for example, that the department's influence in shaping national defense and international economic policies should be strengthened; that the State Department should bring foreign policy considerations to bear more directly on the formulation of national energy policy; that the department should improve its efforts to understand and inform American public opinion; and that the State Department should take more fully into account other new international concerns—like the global population problem, the growing world food shortage, and international environmental problems—which were engaging the attention of governments throughout the world. As in the past, the Murphy Commission's report elicited mixed responses (many legislators, for example, believed that it gave insufficient attention to Congress' increasingly assertive role in foreign relations). With the passage of time, it became evident that its findings and recommendations had done little to change the State Department's position fundamentally in the foreign policy process.

Continuing Problems and Prospects

Writing in 1969, an experienced State Department official observed:

> Recommendations for fundamental reforms in the organization and administration of foreign affairs have been made by high-level committees and task forces on the average of every two years since World War II. Despite the near unanimity of diagnosis, little has been done to deal with the serious problems uncovered; they are still with us, unsolved and debilitating.[11]

This verdict had lost none of its cogency as the United States entered the last two decades of the twentieth century. As had been true of administrations before it, for example, the Carter Administration experienced conflicts between the State Department and other executive agencies (like the National Security Council). Within a few weeks after it took office in 1981, the Reagan Administration began to experience similar conflicts revolving around the attempt by Secretary of State Alexander Haig to function as the President's chief and most influential foreign policy adviser.

During the Nixon Administration, one experienced American diplomat lamented, the State Department in reality had little more than "administrative authority" over foreign affairs. Despite innumerable studies and proposed reforms of the State Department since World War II, it had

> become, in essence, a collection of desk officers who answer the mail, compose and re-

ceive telegrams, and carry on relations with foreign governments at the level of the routine and pedestrian.[12]

Such complaints perhaps reached their zenith during the Vietnam War, when many informed citizens believed (correctly or not) that the State Department had largely defaulted to the Pentagon in the formulation of American policy toward Southeast Asia. Yet even in the post-Vietnam War era, the State Department found it difficult to gain acceptance for its historic claim as the executive agency with dominant responsibility in the foreign policy field.

What factors account for this phenomenon? The causes of the State Department's decline in the American foreign policy process are numerous and varied.[13] Some of them were perhaps inherent in the emergence of the United States as a superpower after World War II and in the changing nature of the international system. Other reasons can also be identified, some of them related to the State Department's own organizational structure, ingrained viewpoints and values, and the personalities of those who have served in the position of secretary of state during the past generation.

One cause of the State Department's decline has been the tendency of several modern Presidents to serve as their own secretary of state, often bypassing the State Department in the process. Among modern chief executives, Franklin D. Roosevelt was noteworthy in this respect. More often than not, his secretary of state—ex-Senator Cordell Hull—was excluded from foreign policy decision making and was left to concentrate on promoting cooperative relations with Congress. FDR was one of the most skillful political strategists known to American history. He believed that—as in relations with the Soviet Union during World War II—he could use his political genius and personal charm to attain American foreign policy goals. Consequently, innumerable diplomatic decisions during this period bore Roosevelt's personal imprint and they entailed little effective participation by State Department officials.[14]

Some two decades later, President John F. Kennedy exhibited the same tendency, although primarily for different reasons. In common with most new Presidents, Kennedy began his Administration by expressing confidence in the State Department and designating it as the premier executive agency in the foreign policy field. Within a few months, however—as a result primarily of the disastrous "Bay of Pigs" invasion of Cuba early in 1961—Kennedy had largely lost confidence in the State Department (along with several other executive agencies). After that episode, Kennedy was more and more inclined to take foreign policy decision making directly into his own hands and to depend for advice upon *ad hoc* committees established to deal with particular external issues.[15] Convinced that fundamental changes were needed in America's approach to several important external problems, Kennedy despaired of eliciting the required creativity and enthusiastic support from officials of the State Department.

President Richard Nixon continued this tradition. From the beginning of his Administration, it was clear that Nixon's White House adviser on national security, Dr. Henry Kissinger, was the *de facto* secretary of state. Dr. Kissinger was a recognized authority in the foreign policy field; he was an individual possessing creative ideas, enormous energy, and a determination to make his ideas prevail. By contrast, Secretary of State William Rogers had little or no applicable background in foreign affairs or other discernible talents for serving as the President's chief foreign policy adviser. As time passed, Rogers' standing with both the White House and Congress steadily declined—and in the process, the

Department of State appeared to become increasingly peripheral in making important foreign policy decisions. On September 22, 1973, Dr. Kissinger succeeded William Rogers as secretary of state; Dr. Kissinger also continued to hold the position as the President's chief White House adviser on national security affairs.[16]

As the experience of the Nixon Administration also indicated, the State Department has lost influence in the foreign policy process for another reason: Some modern secretaries of state *have largely ignored the department* in carrying out their responsibilities. Two postwar secretaries of state—John Foster Dulles in the Eisenhower Administration and Dr. Henry Kissinger in the Nixon and Ford administrations—exemplified this tendency. Secretary of State Dulles, it was often said, carried the State Department around "under his hat"! As Dulles saw it, he *was* the State Department, and he seldom bothered to consult his subordinates within it or to inform them of major impending decisions before they were announced. Perhaps more than any secretary of state in recent history, Dulles enjoyed the full confidence of the President, who relied upon Dulles heavily in making key foreign policy decisions. Possessing virtual *carte blanche* from the President—and mindful of his own extensive experience in the foreign policy field—Secretary Dulles seldom found it necessary to work closely with his State Department subordinates.[17]

Irrespective of whether the State Department has tended to be "ignored" by the President or the secretary of state (or both), to a substantial degree this phenomenon has resulted from certain problems existing within the department itself since World War II. At some stage during his administration, every postwar President has expressed disillusionment with the State Department; for 30 years or more, criticisms of the department have been endemic on Capitol Hill; and among all executive agencies in Washington, the State Department perhaps has the poorest "public image." Innumerable well-informed and objective studies have called attention to long-standing problems and behavior patterns which impede the State Department's effectiveness and often reinforce a President's tendency to "bypass" the department in decision making. During the closing months of World War II and in the early postwar era, for example, the State Department exhibited a marked reluctance to play a leadership role in responding to the new era confronting the United States abroad. In formulating policy for and administering occupied areas (Germany and Japan); in playing a leadership role in the reorganization of the nation's intelligence network; and in other areas the State Department showed little inclination to exert initiative in responding to postwar challenges.[18]

To many public officials and informed commentators, the State Department has become a synonym for bureaucratic "inertia," for lack of creativity and for resistance to change in its customary policies and practices. During the Kennedy and Johnson administrations, for example, Secretary of State Dean Rusk complained about the problem of "layering" within the department: Even the most routine diplomatic cable from an American embassy would have to pass through successive layers of the State Department bureaucracy before it could be answered.[19] Again, Rusk asserted that on the basis of his experience (confined almost entirely to service within the State Department), the tendency of the foreign policy bureaucracy was *to avoid taking responsibility whenever possible* for major foreign policy decisions—particularly those entailing innovations in American foreign relations.[20]

Certain internal organizational defects have also contributed to the deterioration of the relative position of the State Department in the foreign policy process. Nearly every study of the department undertaken since World War II has called for management and personnel policy reforms. The Foreign Service, for example, appears for too long to have rewarded "conformity," acceptance of the system, and quiescence on the part of younger officers seeking career advancement. Both in Washington and in overseas posts, the diplomatic corps has become inflated, in some cases seriously overstaffed, and bogged down in unnecessary paperwork—to the detriment of efficiency and high-level performance. Several American ambassadors in the postwar period have called for the drastic reduction in their embassy staffs, in an effort to enhance operations (although such entreaties have not always been received enthusiastically by their superiors in Washington). Also, within recent years a labor-management split has become evident within the Foreign Service, as younger officers have made numerous demands upon their superiors for a more influential role in the foreign policy process.[21]

During the "McCarthy era" of the late 1940s and 1950s,* the State Department was widely accused of harboring Communist and pro-Communist officials within its ranks. Although little reliable evidence was produced to substantiate such charges, their repetition was highly inimical to morale among State Department employees.[22]

Paradoxically, by the late 1960s State

---

*The "McCarthy era" is named for Senator Joseph McCarthy (Republican of Wisconsin). During the early postwar period, McCarthy gained public prominence for his frequent denunciations of Communist influence within the State Department. According to McCarthy's assessment, for example, pro-Communist elements in the department were responsible for "selling out" China to Communism and for other American diplomatic setbacks.

Department officials confronted the opposite criticism (expressed by opponents of the Vietnam War and certain "revisionist" interpreters of American diplomacy): that they formed an influential part of the governmental "establishment" in the United States which was responsible for America's involvement in the Vietnam conflict, for perpetuating the Cold War, and for the nation's opposition to revolutionary political movements throughout the Third World. Called by various terms (the "Military-Industrial Complex" or the "National Security Managers" were two frequently used ones), this elite presumably displayed an almost psychotic fear of Communism and was determined to rely upon military force to achieve the nation's diplomatic objectives.[23]

Still another frequently expressed criticism of the State Department was exemplified by President Eisenhower's complaint after word reached Washington that the Soviet dictator Joseph Stalin had died (March 5, 1953). As one account has explained it:

> The President said that since 1946 officials of the State Department and [other agencies] had been speculating on what would happen when the Soviet government changed hands. But now that it had occurred, he complained, he had looked in vain for any plans or studies that might have been worked out in advance so that the government would be ready to react.

Eisenhower regarded this "lack of planning" as a major State Department deficiency.[24]

President Eisenhower's lament has been echoed in one form or another by nearly every postwar chief executive. In 1979, for example, the Carter Administration was similarly caught unprepared for the overthrow of the Iranian monarchy, which had close ties with the United States. For several months, it was evident that American officials neither anticipated this event nor understood many of the causes of the Iranian revolution; nor were policy makers prepared to cope with many of the consequences of this traumatic event in the Middle East.[25]

To meet the complaint that the State Department's usual approach to developments abroad was to engage in *ad hoc* and improvised decision making, a Policy Planning Staff was created within the State Department in the early postwar period, headed by the distinguished expert on the Soviet Union, George F. Kennan. Yet almost from its inception, the Policy Planning Staff encountered great difficulty in carrying out its assigned task of formulating long-term diplomatic strategy, primarily because of two factors. First, many of the Policy Planning Staff's officers (frequently among the most competent in the department) found themselves increasingly drawn into the day-to-day administration of foreign policy. Second, and perhaps more fundamentally, the very concept of long-range diplomatic strategy—patterned after the strategic planning routinely engaged in by military establishments—may be an inherently faulty and largely unattainable goal.* In a global environment marked by rapid and often revolutionary change, events almost never occur at a

---

*See, for example, the views of a former State Department official, who is dubious that the model of military strategy is applicable to the conduct of foreign affairs. His belief is that "Few foreign policy futures can be defined as clearly as a U.S.-Soviet war." A major difference between the two realms is that the United States has only a handful of potential military enemies while it maintains relations with close to 140 independent nations. See Henry Owen, "Foreign Policy Planning," in *Commission on the Organization of the Government for Foreign Policy* (Washington, D.C.: Government Printing Office, 1975), Appendix, Vol. II, pp. 234–35. Another study estimates that around 80 percent of the time of Foreign Service officers must be devoted to "operational" duties, rather than to "analytic" functions like problem identification and formulation of foreign policy options. See James W. Clark, "Foreign Affairs Personnel Management," in ibid, Vol. VI, p. 199.

time, and in a form, anticipated by diplomatic planners; existing plans must nearly always be modified drastically—and sometimes altogether abandoned—because they do not reflect prevailing conditions.[26]

The effectiveness of the State Department also continues to be impaired by an old custom which is still engaged in today: the appointment of the nation's highest diplomatic representatives on the basis of their political affiliation and loyalty, their social standing, and other extraneous criteria. Despite continuing efforts to "professionalize" the Foreign Service, certain key ambassadorial appointments are still made by the President from among his political supporters, friends, and others who have no evident qualifications for the position. A classic case occurred during the Eisenhower Administration, when Mr. Maxwell H. Gluck was nominated by the President to serve as American ambassador to Ceylon (now Sri Lanka). When the Senate Foreign Relations Committee met to consider Mr. Gluck's nomination, the following dialogue occurred between him and Senator J. William Fulbright (Democrat of Arkansas):

Mr. Gluck: My qualifications generally are a varied business background. Ever since boyhood, I have had experience in industry, commerce, business, finance, and so forth.

I have never been in the diplomatic service before.

. . . . . .

Senator Fulbright: How much did you contribute to the Republican Party in the 1956 election?
Mr. Gluck: Well, I wouldn't know offhand, but I made a contribution.
Senator Fulbright: Well, how much?
Mr. Gluck: Let's see; I would say, all in all, twenty or thirty thousand dollars.

. . . . . .

Senator Fulbright: You don't think that is a pertinent reason for the appointment.

Mr. Gluck: I don't think it is the only reason.
Senator Fulbright: It is the principal reason, is it not?
Mr. Gluck: I don't think I want to admit that is the principal reason.

. . . . . .

Senator Fulbright: Why are you interested in Ceylon?
Mr. Gluck: I am not particularly interested only in Ceylon, but I am interested in a Government post where I can do some work and do some good at it.
Senator Fulbright: What makes you think you could do that in Ceylon?
Mr. Gluck: Unless I run into something that I am not aware of I think I ought to do a fairly good job in the job I have been nominated for.
Senator Fulbright: What are the problems in Ceylon you think you can deal with?
Mr. Gluck: One of the problems are the people there, not necessarily a problem, but the relationship of the United States with the people in Ceylon. I believe I can—I think I can establish, unless we—again, unless I run into something that I have not run into before—a good relationship and good feeling toward the United States.

. . . . . .

Senator Fulbright: Do you consider we are on friendly relations with India?
Mr. Gluck: Well, I think it is more—I think a lot depends on who is there, and what they do. I don't think we are on the friendliest relations with them, but I believe it can be strengthened a little more in one direction, or a little more in another direction, depending on what is done in that country.

. . . . . .

Senator Fulbright: Do you know who the Prime Minister in India is?
Mr. Gluck: Yes; but I can't pronounce his name.
Senator Fulbright: Do you know who the Prime Minister of Ceylon is?
Mr. Gluck: I have a list—
Senator Fulbright: Who is it?
Mr. Gluck: His name is a bit unfamiliar now.

I cannot call it off, but I have obtained from Ambassador Crowe a list of all the important people there and I went over them with him.

I have a synopsis of all the people, both Americans, ambassadors, and officials from other countries, and I have from him also a sort of little biography or history of them, with what his opinion of them is; and so—
Senator Fulbright: That's all, Mr. Chairman.

Alone among the members of the Senate Foreign Relations Committee, Senator Fulbright voted against Mr. Gluck's nomination. Fulbright lamented that "it is an old and evil custom that afflicts us."[27]

The "old and evil custom" about which Senator Fulbright complained continues to be a feature of the American foreign policy process. The *New York Times* lamented that other ambassadorial appointees by the Eisenhower Administration were "innocent of diplomatic experience." During the Nixon Administration, considerable evidence existed that a number of generous contributors to the Republican Party were "rewarded" by being given diplomatic assignments. President Jimmy Carter appointed an Advisory Board on ambassadorial nominations (consisting of 20 citizens, only one of whom had had diplomatic experience). The same complaint was heard about President Ronald Reagan's diplomatic appointments. According to Malcolm Toon (former American ambassador to the Soviet Union), Reagan was using the diplomatic service as a "dumping ground" for defeated politicians and contributors to the Republican Party. Toon lamented that an actor now headed the American embassy in Mexico City; and the ambassador to Great Britain had founded a "furniture-polish dynasty." Altogether, out of 100 people appointed to high-level diplomatic positions, nearly half had no discernible qualifications for the job.[28]

Several observations may be made about such appointments. It must be emphasized, for example, that the vast majority (around 75 percent) of the nation's ambassadors and ministers *is selected from the Foreign Service on the basis of merit*. As a rule, only a handful of ambassadorial positions are filled by individuals who have no apparent qualifications for them—and these posts are usually the larger and more prestigious American embassies in Europe (such as London, Paris, and Bonn). In many cases, a good reason exists for the continuance of this practice: Despite the complaints expressed by Senator Fulbright and other legislators about the custom, Congress has traditionally been unwilling to provide the funds necessary to operate the American embassy in such countries. (For example, the "Fourth of July Party," which is traditional in the more important American embassies abroad, and other forms of official entertainment may cost the American ambassador personally several thousand dollars!) The result has been that only individuals who have independent wealth, and are willing to spend it in effect to "subsidize" the operation of the embassy, are able to accept the position of ambassador to a number of countries.

A recent study of the State Department also calls attention to the distinction which should be made between "political appointments" and "presidential appointments" in the diplomatic field.[29] The former—whereby a chief executive "rewards" generous party contributors, or selects some socially prominent individual to serve in a diplomatic position—has little to recommend it, in terms of enhancing the performance of the State Department. Yet "presidential appointments" should be viewed in a different light. The American ambassador, we must remember, is the *personal representative* of the President of the United States to a foreign government. An incumbent President is entitled (both in domestic and foreign affairs) to choose advisers in whom he has confidence and who function cooperatively as members of his team. Moreover, a number of such presidential appointments to high-level diplomatic positions since World War II have been *outstanding,* resulting in the selection of individuals who performed their duties capably and who contributed positively to the achievement of American foreign policy goals.*

Another factor hindering the effectiveness of the State Department is its poor "image" with the American people and Congress—as indicated by the fact that, almost without exception, every postwar secretary of state has left office under a cloud of criticism! Some of them—like Secretary of State James M. Byrnes in the Truman Administration, Dean Rusk in the Johnson Administration, and William Rogers in the Nixon Administration—were accused of lacking the leadership qualities needed in the position. Others—like Secretary of State John Foster Dulles during the Eisenhower presidency, Dr. Henry Kissinger during the Nixon and Ford adminstrations, and Alexander Haig during the Reagan Administration—were denounced for attempting to dominate the foreign policy process to the point of excluding the President from it! Still others (and Truman's secretary of state, Dean G. Acheson, was a prime target)

*As examples of noteworthy presidential appointments to ambassadorial positions, several individual cases might be mentioned. Beginning with the Roosevelt Administration, Mr. Averell Harriman served successive Presidents in various diplomatic capacities; Mr. Chester Bowles (former governor of Connecticut) served the Kennedy Administration ably as American ambassador to India; Mr. Ellsworth Bunker was the principal negotiator of the new Panama Canal Treaty for the Carter Administration, and he held other diplomatic posts under earlier administrations; Mr. David Bruce also established an outstanding reputation as a diplomatic "troubleshooter" under several presidents. Yet none of these individuals was a "career diplomat" or had any significant experience in the foreign policy field.

were castigated for being "aloof," arrogant, and aristocratic in their approach to Congress and the American people. The salient point is that *nearly every postwar secretary of state has in time become unpopular with the American people and with Congress.* This fact indicates the presence of certain recurrent factors impairing the State Department's public image.

One of these has already been mentioned: the American society's traditional disdain for diplomacy and its belief that many of the skills required for effective diplomacy are inimical to democracy. Another factor was identified by Henry Adams late in the nineteenth century. As former Secretary Acheson summarized Adams' views,

> . . . the chief concern of the Secretary of State—the world beyond our boundaries—was to most members of the Congress only a troublesome intrusion into their chief interest—the internal affairs of the country, and especially of the particular parts of it they represented.

Acheson has added that, for Congress, "the principal consequence of foreign impact upon particular [congressional] districts is trouble. . . . The Secretary of State comes to Congress bearing word of troubles [abroad] about which Congress does not want to hear."[30] Or, as other commentators have pointed out, it is usually very difficult for most legislators to gain political capital from voting for proposals and programs—like paying adequate salaries to American diplomats, or foreign aid, or approval of agreements like an unpopular new Panama Canal treaty—advocated by the State Department. Since World War II, it has been very difficult for the State Department to demonstrate that because of its operations, the international system is becoming more peaceful, more stable, and more receptive to the achievement of American foreign policy goals. To the contrary, according to many criteria the ability of the United States to accomplish its purposes abroad appears to have declined sharply.

Since the end of the Vietnam War, another factor has detracted from the State Department's image with Congress and the people. Chapter 7 will call attention to Congress' increasingly assertive role in the foreign policy process, especially since the Vietnam War. To the congressional mind, the bureaucracy and activities of the State Department are often viewed with considerable skepticism. In contrast to nearly every other executive agency, the State Department has no influential, stable, and supportive "domestic constituency" to champion its cause among the American people and on Capitol Hill. The Agriculture Department can usually count on American farmers, and upon business interests dependent upon agriculture, to support its programs; the Labor Department has close ties with the American labor movement and routinely receives support for its programs from that segment of public opinion and from legislators sympathetic to labor's cause.[31] By contrast, the State Department's internal constituency (when it exists at all) tends to be fragmentary, ephemeral, and determined by the particular issues which are at the forefront of public attention at any given time. For several years after World War II, it was believed that the State Department had a solid base of public support among American intellectuals; but this base was severely eroded during the Vietnam War and shows no sign of being rebuilt.[32]

More often than not, perhaps, the State Department has "negative constituents": individual citizens and groups that are vocally *opposed* to existing policies toward the Arab countries, or toward Eastern Europe, or toward El Salvador. To cite a particular case:

Greek-Americans, for example, were incensed about the Ford Administration's apparent support of Turkey in the mid-1970s; and the influence of this group was potent enough to produce congressionally imposed restrictions upon American military aid programs and other ties with Turkey.[33] As we shall see more fully in Chapter 8, for a generation or more the pro-Israeli lobby in the United States could be counted upon to react strongly against the provision of American military assistance to Arab countries or other diplomatic moves deemed detrimental to Israel's interests and welfare. By the end of the 1970s, labor unions and American business interests alike joined forces in demanding changes in American trade policies toward Japan, in the interest of protecting the financially troubled American automobile industry. By contrast, almost never does the State Department encounter comparable outspoken and well-organized public sentiment *in favor* of its existing policies.

Finally, the State Department's image is tarnished by another factor, identified by the former diplomat, George W. Ball:

> The bad name the State Department has acquired in many quarters results, in part, from the fact that it has long been the scapegoat for every foreign policy failure, while Presidents have systematically claimed the successes. It is traditional for the White House to announce all happy foreign policy events, leaving the State Department to put out the bad tidings.[34]

Inevitably perhaps, State Department officials must accept the responsibility for what many citizens and legislators are convinced has been the decline of American influence throughout the world. Theoretically at least, the State Department is "in charge" of American foreign policy—and, on the basis of what many Americans perceive as a deterioration in the nation's global position since the early postwar era, the department's record has not been impressive. In fact, State Department officials are perhaps even more conscious than most citizens that the United States faces new and increasingly difficult constraints upon the successful application of its power abroad. Hence, spokesmen for the State Department are often unable to convince Congress, for example, that funds provided during the past 30 years to operate the Foreign Service, or for foreign aid, or for other diplomatic purposes have yielded a visible "return" for the United States, or have "won friends" for America abroad, or have otherwise enhanced the diplomatic position of the nation. Officials of the State Department are in the position of a physician called upon to treat a seriously ill patient who is brought to the Emergency Room of the hospital: He may be compelled to inform the family that the patient's condition remains serious, that it "could be worse," and that with continued treatment the patient "has a chance" to recover—but that the treatment will be long, costly, and difficult. For a society whose national credo has been the idea of progress and continual betterment, this was not the kind of prognosis calculated to win plaudits for the State Department among the American people and their representatives in Congress.

Other Executive Agencies and Foreign Affairs

Growing Diffusion in the Policy Process

A noteworthy trend in postwar American foreign relations has been the extent to which a steadily widening circle of executive departments and agencies has been drawn into the foreign policy process. Indeed, it would be no exaggeration to say that almost every agency within the executive branch today has respon-

sibilities impinging directly or indirectly upon foreign affairs. This development has created an increasingly serious problem for the President and his principal foreign policy advisers: *creating and maintaining unified policies within the executive branch* on major foreign policy issues.

The most conspicuous case perhaps has been the growing involvement of the Defense Department in the formulation and execution of key foreign policy decisions. As will be explained more fully in Chapter 5, the postwar era has witnessed an unprecedented concern among American officials with what is called "national security policy"—or the successful merger of political and military components of foreign affairs. The creation of a new agency in 1947—the National Security Council—symbolized this postwar emphasis. During some periods (as in the Nixon Administration), it appeared that the NSC, headed by presidential adviser Dr. Henry Kissinger, had largely supplanted the State Department as the dominant executive agency in the foreign policy field.

Among the more traditional Cabinet departments, nearly all of them are engaged in activities and programs involving other countries. The Agriculture Department, for example, has expanded its overseas operations dramatically in the postwar era. The "Food for Peace" Program and other projects involving the shipment of American agricultural commodities to needy societies come under its jurisdiction; and the department has sent hundreds of experts abroad to assist foreign societies in raising their agricultural productivity. More than in any earlier stage of American history perhaps, the prosperity of American agriculture depends upon massive and continuing sales in foreign markets—and the Agriculture Department plays a pivotal role in promoting such sales.[35]

The Labor Department has also added

an overseas dimension to its responsibilities. Since World War II, the American labor union movement has created close ties with labor organizations in many non-Communist countries; and it participates actively in international conferences and activities carried out by the United Nations and other organizations. During the height of the Cold War, the American labor union movement was regarded by officials in Washington as being in a key position to counteract Communist influence among labor organizations and workers in other countries; and foreign labor union leaders continue to be regarded as comprising part of the "opinion makers" in other countries whose attitudes the United States seeks to influence favorably.[36]

The interest of many American business and financial organizations in foreign markets is traditional. (In the nineteenth century, for example, it led the United States to proclaim the "Open Door" policy toward China.) This interest has been greatly intensified since World War II. American firms have led the way in establishing and operating the "multinational corporations" whose operations cut across national frontiers and whose activities often appear to be subject to little effective control by the United States and other national governments.[37] Encouraging and promoting American business and trade opportunities abroad has always been a major objective of the Commerce Department. Efforts by a number of Third World countries (and Egypt under President Sadat's regime was a conspicuous example) to encourage American and other Western investment in the country inevitably draw the Commerce Department more deeply into the foreign policy process.

Similarly, the Treasury Department's responsibilities impinge directly upon foreign affairs in several areas. As the department most centrally concerned with the stability of the monetary system and with the public credit of the United States, the Treasury Department is keenly interested in the "soundness" of the dollar in the world's currency markets; and its agents attempt to prevent counterfeiting and smuggling operations.

Two relatively new executive departments—the Department of Transportation (created in 1966) and the Department of Energy (created in 1977)—are concerned with external issues. The Transportation Department, for example, supervises the operation of the St. Lawrence Development Corporation; and it seeks to formulate a national transportation policy. The Energy Department is obviously immersed in foreign policy issues—particularly as these affect America's relations with oil-rich areas like the Middle East and Latin America. Over the years, even the Interior Department has acquired an interest in problems directly related to American foreign policy. Many of the flood control and water reclamation projects under its jurisdiction, for example, involve neighboring countries; as an example, a major source of controversy in Mexican-American relations has been allocation of the water resources of the Rio Grande River.

In addition to the Cabinet departments, a host of other executive agencies has become active in selected aspects of American foreign relations since World War II. The Civil Aeronautics Board (CAB) is responsible for imposing safety standards in air travel and for the development of air transportation. The Environmental Protection Agency (EPA) is directly involved in the solution of domestic and international environmental problems. The National Aeronautics and Space Administration (NASA) is in charge of space projects carried out by the United States government, many of which (like monitoring Soviet missile technology) are vitally related to national security.[38] Another influential participant in the foreign policy process is the Arms

Control and Disarmament Agency, created in 1961. Its responsibility is to study problems related to disarmament and arms limitation, and to prepare recommendations for the President on these problems.

Numerous other examples might be cited, but these are sufficient to illustrate the point: Increasingly, creating and maintaining a unified approach to major foreign policy issues by departments and agencies within the executive branch has become an urgent and recurrent problem in American foreign relations. The problem became particularly critical under the Carter Administration, when conflicts among executive officials over American trade policy,* the escalating price of oil imports, détente with the Soviet Union, normalization of relations with China, and several other major external issues were endemic. Observing this phenomenon, members of Congress and officials in foreign countries might be inclined to repeat the admonition which was given by Senator Arthur H. Vandenberg (Republican of Michigan) to the Truman Administration in the early postwar period. After witnessing a public disagreement between the President's major advisers on

America's proper strategy toward the U.S.S.R., Vandenberg bluntly informed the White House that Republicans wanted to work harmoniously with Democrats in behalf of a "bipartisan" foreign policy; but they could only cooperate with "one Secretary of State at a time"![39] The problem of which Vandenberg complained has become progressively more acute throughout the postwar period.

Centrifugal Forces and Tendencies

What are the causes of this phenomenon? One of them of course is the emergence of the United States as a superpower, with major and minor diplomatic interests throughout the world. Down to the early 1970s, it appeared that there were no regions (and very few countries) in which the United States was not actively, and sometimes massively, involved. After the Vietnam War a retrenchment occurred in the nation's diplomatic commitments. In the years which followed, for example, the United States played a marginal role in political developments in black Africa; and it showed no inclination to become em-

*Illustrative of the intra-executive branch conflicts over major foreign policy issues which characterized the Carter Administration was the dispute involving several agencies which erupted in 1979 over American trade policy. Led by the Commerce Department, a number of executive agencies called for a "reorganization" of administrative machinery dealing with the promotion of American trade abroad; not surprisingly, the Commerce Department sought to be recognized as the dominant agency in this field. Over a dozen executive agencies had major or minor responsibilities in the field of trade policy—and legislators had long complained that no central authority within the executive branch was responsible for formulating and overseeing a unified national policy on trade questions. Increasingly, agencies interested in environmental problems, human rights, and domestic employment had become drawn into the trade policy controversy—resulting in fragmented and disunified executive activities on trade questions. Yet two other powerful agencies—the

Treasury Department and State Department—were also centrally involved with trade issues. For some countries (as in Soviet-American relations), American officials viewed trade and commercial questions as directly related to *political* controversies, as in Moscow's treatment of dissidents or the problem of Jewish emigration from the Soviet Union. Commerce Department efforts to maximize American trade abroad had encountered opposition from President Carter's National Security Adviser, Zbigniew Brzezinski, who feared the implications for American security of expanding trade with the Soviet Union in products like oil drilling equipment and advanced computer systems. Meanwhile, Treasury Secretary Michael Blumenthal expressed his fear that if the Commerce Department became dominant in the formulation of trade policy, then American business interests would largely dictate American foreign policy. See Clyde H. Farnsworth, in *New York Times,* July 15, 1979.

broiled in new conflicts in Asia, such as those between North Vietnam and Laos or between North Vietnam and Communist China. Despite this diplomatic retrenchment, the United States remains a superpower; its overseas obligations are still extensive, and it continues to be an influential participant in efforts by members of the international community to solve a long list of global and regional problems.

Another factor producing disunity within the executive branch on foreign policy questions—and perhaps the most fundamental cause of this development—has been the changing nature of what is sometimes called "the foreign policy agenda." The frequently heard assertion that America confronts a revolutionary political environment overseas, or that the foremost challenge facing officials in Washington is to formulate policies geared to a condition of rapid change abroad, has many implications. A leading one, however, is the idea that *new concerns and policy issues* demand the attention of diplomatic officials, while many of the more traditional questions engaging the attention of diplomats throughout history have receded in importance. Solving (or attenuating) the world food shortage; curbing and dealing with the implications of the global "population explosion"; attempting to stabilize world trade and to assure fair prices for both importing and exporting nations; preventing the proliferation of nuclear weapons throughout the global community; endeavoring to promote "nation building" and to elevate living standards in most Third World societies; strengthening more successful regional cooperation in Asia or Latin America; revising international law to provide nations equitable access to the raw materials of the ocean—these are among the more conspicuous items on the new foreign policy agenda of the United States. With rare excep-

tions, such issues seldom engaged the attention of diplomats before World War II.[40]

Emphasis upon the new foreign policy agenda of course is not meant to imply that more traditional issues requiring diplomatic solutions have disappeared. Today, no less than in the past, officials in the United States and in other countries must still deal with such questions as boundary disputes in black Africa, the military balance of power between the United States and the Soviet Union, and rival national claims to disputed territories (like the Greek-Turkish controversy over Cyprus). During certain periods, age-old territorial disputes and conflicts arising out of clashing nationalist ambitions still come to the forefront of international concern. Yet to this list of older diplomatic questions must be added a wide variety of difficult problems comprising the new foreign policy agenda. Many of the latter are relatively new issues for which the United States has had little preparation. Inevitably perhaps, in grappling with such problems, new governmental agencies have had to be created; and considerable duplication of effort among them has characterized their activities.

This is perhaps merely an alternative way of observing that (if the distinction has ever been as defensible as widely supposed) the dichotomy between a nation's "domestic" and its "foreign" affairs has all but disappeared. Thus, a recent study of the future of American foreign policy has predicted that the effects of many diplomatic decisions will almost certainly be

increases in domestic price levels . . . increases in U.S. tax and public expenditure levels (to fund substantial foreign aid programs once again), and the ceding of elements of national sovereignty to international entities which alone will be able to make and monitor the necessary decisions concerning world allocation and control of population, food, non-renewable resources, oceans, and the like.

The emerging global environment, the study anticipates, is likely to be "a most unattractive one for responsible elected officials." It may be "even more unattractive for officials of foreign affairs-oriented agencies, forced steadily to advocate unpopular policies."[41] In a word, Americans have become conscious—and in the future they are likely to become even more mindful—of the *interdependence* of all members of the international system. This interdependence creates an increasingly acute problem in terms of achieving coherent and unified activities by agencies involved in the foreign policy process.

Innumerable examples might be cited from recent diplomatic experience to illustrate the point. A familiar one is the impact upon the American society internally of decisions by the Organization of Petroleum Exporting Countries (OPEC) to raise world oil proces. OPEC's decisions momentously affect such diverse problems as the inflation rate in the United States, the availability of gasoline, leisure activities, and consumer spending patterns. The opposite side of the coin of course is that important decisions *in domestic policy* can also momentously affect the nation's foreign relations. Assuming no increase in the level of federal taxation (and by the early 1980s, deteriorating business conditions could produce a *decrease* in tax revenues), massive continuing outlays for the Social Security program, welfare, education, and interest on the national debt placed severe constraints upon the Reagan Administration's efforts to restore the military balance with the Soviet Union, to increase foreign aid allocations, and to divert resources to other important foreign policy undertakings.

A third development which has contributed to, and aggravated, the problem of intra-executive disagreements and conflicts in foreign affairs has been the tendency of Americans, and societies generally throughout the world, since World War II *to look to government* to solve urgent internal and external problems. Beginning with the New Deal perhaps, Americans have expected the national government to take the initiative in solving a variety of problems—from the older ones, like unemployment and health questions, to the newer ones, like threats to the environment and the energy crisis—endangering the welfare of the society. Nearly all such issues today have an international dimension. The national government's efforts, for example, to reduce the hazards of nuclear radiation clearly demand that the problem be attacked on *an international basis* and that intensive efforts be made to enlist the cooperation of other countries. Similarly, in dealing with the progressively more acute energy crisis, events had made it clear that the "solution" to this problem must entail a series of interrelated steps—such as rapidly developing alternative fuel sources, equitably allocating available oil and gas supplies throughout the nation, and reducing the American society's overall energy consumption. As always, the American people looked to the President to take the lead in formulating a strategy designed to deal successfully with the energy crisis. Based upon experience since the New Deal, in the process new executive agencies would have to be created; and existing ones would assume new responsibilities involving internal and external aspects of the energy problem.[42]

Coordinating Executive Agencies

With the growing participation of an expanding number of executive agencies in the foreign policy process, a major challenge of American postwar foreign policy has been *coordinating executive activities in foreign affairs.* Several administrative devices and techniques have been utilized for this purpose, with varying degrees of success. One of the earliest of these mechanisms was of course *the President's Cabinet,* consisting of the heads of the executive departments. Down to World War II, this was the principal advisory organ for the chief executive. Recent years, however, have witnessed a steady deterioration in the Cabinet's role and prestige in the American system of government.* In recent years, the Cabinet's position has largely been displaced by the National Security Council, created in 1947. We shall discuss the NSC's establishment and evolution more fully in Chapter 5. Our interest here is confined to emphasizing two points about it. First, the National Security Council now rivals—and during some periods, as in the Nixon and Carter administrations perhaps has eclipsed —the State Department's once paramount position in the foreign policy process. Second, the establishment and growth of the National Security Council has not really "solved" the problem of intra-executive agency conflict in the foreign policy field. A generation after the NSC's creation, the problem was more acute than ever!

*When Ronald Reagan entered the White House in 1981, he stated his intention of reviving the Cabinet as an influential advisory agency. Within a few months, however, Reagan followed the practice of his predecessors in relegating the Cabinet to a relatively minor role in policy formulation and coordination. As time passed, Reagan's White House advisers assumed an increasingly influential role in both domestic and foreign policy. As one Reagan adviser explained, the main reason for the Cabinet's rapid decline perhaps was that "Cabinet officers become advocates for their constituencies—they always do...." Bickering and jockeying for influence among its members also detracted from the Cabinet's usefulness. See *U.S. News and World Report,* **92** (March 29, 1982), 28–29.

Another approach to the problem was adopted by the Kennedy Administration during the early 1960s; it was designed especially to resolve the problem of disunified and uncoordinated activities by executive agencies of the American government overseas. The Kennedy Administration's proposed solution was the concept of the "country team": In every foreign country in which the United States was represented, the American ambassador—the personal representative of the President, and the official in charge of the American embassy—was assigned responsibility for coordinating the activities of all American officials stationed within the country. Theoretically, this meant that all American officials operating within a particular foreign country carried out their assignments under the supervision of the American ambassador, who in turn received his policy directives from the State Department, and ultimately from the White House. The concept of the country team thus reflected three fundamental administrative principles: All American officials stationed abroad *were on the same team,* despite the fact that they might represent different governmental agencies; these officials should, therefore, be endeavoring to carry out a *unified and coherent American policy abroad;* and in their activities, all American officials stationed abroad should *acknowledge the dominant position of the State Department* as the agency charged with the management of American foreign affairs.

As the years passed, the concept of the country team produced mixed results.[43] Unquestionably, it alleviated the problem of intra-executive agency conflicts in many countries. As the later experience of the Vietnam War indicated, however, it could not be said that this approach disposed of the problem. During the period of peak American military involvement in Southeast Asia, uncoordinated and conflicting activities among the American

Embassy in Saigon, military officials in South Vietnam, American intelligence agents, and officials engaged in propaganda, in "counterinsurgency" activities, and in administering foreign aid programs were recurrent and widely publicized.

Yet two factors above all have perhaps limited the utility of the concept of the country team. From the beginning, the success of the concept depended heavily upon the personality and ability of the American ambassador appointed to represent the United States in a particular country. As we have seen, this condition varies widely; some ambassadors are appointed with little or no training or preparation for their assignments. The other conditioning factor was the continued deterioration of the State Department's relative position in the foreign policy hierarchy *in Washington*. As we have also seen, the department has been hard-pressed to preserve its traditional position of primacy within the executive branch. This fact alone perhaps guaranteed that the American ambassador in a foreign country would be similarly challenged to compel the kind of agency cooperation abroad —and to win acceptance for the idea that other agencies operating within the country were answerable to him—needed to make the country team idea a complete success.

Interagency committees within the executive branch have also been utilized by all postwar Presidents to achieve unity among participants in the foreign policy process. Such committees may be formed at various levels, from those embracing Cabinet officers, to those at the under secretary or assistant secretary levels. For foreign policy issues cutting across departmental and agency lines, the formation of such committees has come to be routine; and, as with the federal bureaucracy itself, such committees have proliferated as the United States has expanded its overseas commitments.

Every President since World War II has also from time to time utilized *ad hoc* executive committees and selected groups of his advisers with regard to particular foreign policy issues confronting his administration. President John F. Kennedy, for example, relied upon a selected group of senior executive officials to study and make recommendations during the "Cuban Missile Crisis" of 1962. This group operated secretly (most State Department officials did not know of its existence or its recommendations); and many observers credit it with highly effective results in responding to the threat posed by Soviet missile installations in Cuba.[44] President Lyndon B. Johnson had a different kind of senior advisory body—called the "Tuesday Group" (because it met for lunch on Tuesdays)—which provided advice on the conduct of the Vietnam War and other external problems.[45] When the Iranian monarchy was overthrown in 1979, President Jimmy Carter formed a special study group to undertake a policy review and evaluation of developments in that country; this group was headed by former Under Secretary of State George Ball (who had retired from government service). The committee's report to the President was highly critical of long-standing American policy toward that key Middle Eastern country.

Whether the problem posed by intra-executive disputes and conflicts on foreign policy questions is handled by highly institutionalized mechanisms (like the National Security Council), or by reliance upon *ad hoc* committees created to deal with specific diplomatic issues, experience has shown that two results can be expected. First the proliferation of such committees has made the foreign policy process in the United States *extremely intricate and time-consuming*. For a particular issue (like the energy crisis), the internal and external policy implications have become so complex—and the resulting agency involvement in the problem so extensive—as almost to defy description. Nearly every department and agency within the executive branch can legitimately claim that it is involved in, or its activities are affected by, policies and programs designed to alleviate the energy crisis. For these and a long list of other national policy issues, the resulting necessity to obtain the requisite "clearances" and agreements from participating agencies inevitably means that policy making in the United States has become inordinately diffuse, sluggish, and bureaucratized.

Second, and perhaps even more crucially, the expanding participation in foreign affairs by a host of executive agencies—and the necessity for coordinating their manifold activities—has had a *qualitative impact* upon American foreign policy. More often than not perhaps, the only kind of policy proposals likely to emerge from this labyrinth are those reflecting a kind of "least common denominator" of interagency compromise. To achieve the needed interagency consensus, compromises must be made, and policies must be "watered down" so that they are acceptable to (or, at a minimum, not objectionable to) the principal agencies involved in their formulation. As a result, policy innovations and imaginative ideas nearly always become casualties of bureaucratic in-fighting and rival agency interests that are frequently supported by influential pressure groups. Under these conditions, the dominant consideration becomes not whether the policy promotes America's interests abroad, but whether (perhaps because it contains few innovations) a consensus can be created within the executive branch for its adoption and implementation.

NOTES

1. Dean Acheson, *Present at the Creation: My Years in the State Department* (New York: W. W. Norton, 1969), p. 734.

2. See the views of McGeorge Bundy and President Kennedy's evaluation of the State Department in: I. M. Destler, *Presidents, Bureaucrats, and Foreign Policy: The Politics of Organizational Reform* (Princeton, N.J.: Princeton University Press, 1972), p. 97; and Arthur Schlesinger, Jr., *A Thousand Days: John F. Kennedy in the White House* (Boston: Houghton Mifflin Co., 1965), pp. 406–447.

3. The purposes and consequences of the Rogers Act are discussed more fully in Thomas H. Etzold, *The Conduct of American Foreign Relations: The Other Side of Diplomacy* (New York: Franklin Watts, 1977), pp. 31–61.

4. Henry S. Villard, *Affairs at State* (New York: Thomas Y. Crowell, 1965), p. 60.

5. See the State Department publication, "Foreign Policy and the Department of State" (Washington, D.C.: Government Printing Office, 1976).

6. A still useful (if somewhat dated) study of America's diplomatic representatives to the United Nations is Arnold Beichman, *The "Other" State Department* (New York: Basic Books, 1968). An informative discussion of the role of UN Ambassador Jeane J. Kirkpatrick and her staff in American foreign policy may be found in Bernard D. Nossiter, "Questioning the Value of the U.N.," *New York Times Magazine,* April 11, 1982, 16–20.

7. Richard Goold-Adams, *John Foster Dulles: A Reappraisal* (New York: Appleton-Century-Crofts, 1952), p. 57.

8. For the findings and recommendations of the Wriston Committee, see its report entitled *Toward a Stronger Foreign Service* (Washington, D.C.: Government Printing Office, 1954).

9. See *New York Times,* March 24, 1968.

10. The Murphy Commission's evaluation of the State Department and its recommendations are contained in its report entitled *Commission on the Organization of the Government for the Conduct of Foreign Policy* (Washington, D.C.: Government Printing Office, 1975). The three-volume Appendix to the report con-

tains a number of illuminating articles dealing with selected aspects of the foreign policy process in the United States.

11. Lannon Walker, "Our Foreign Affairs Machinery: Time for an Overhaul," *Foreign Affairs,* **47** (January, 1969), 309.

12. See the views of former Under Secretary of State George W. Ball in his *Diplomacy for a Crowded World: An American Foreign Policy* (Boston: Little, Brown and Co., 1976), p. 194.

13. For a recent critique of the State Department's loss of influence in the foreign policy process, see Robert Pringle, "Creeping Irrelevance at Foggy Bottom," *Foreign Policy,* **29** (Winter, 1977–78), 128–140.

14. According to one student of World War II, President Roosevelt "took crucial diplomatic negotiations more completely into his own hands than any president before or since." See the analysis of FDR's diplomacy in Gaddis Smith, *American Diplomacy During the Second World War: 1941–1945* (New York: John Wiley and Sons, 1965), pp. 1–19.

15. For discussions of the decision-making process in the Kennedy Administration's response to the Soviet challenge in Cuba, see Schlesinger, *A Thousand Days,* pp. 794–841; and Robert F. Kennedy, *Thirteen Days: A Memoir of the Cuban Missile Crisis* (New York: New American Library, 1969).

16. Fuller discussion of Dr. Henry Kissinger's dominant role in the Nixon Administration's foreign policy is provided in: David Landau, *Kissinger: the Uses of Power* (New York: Thomas Y. Crowell, 1974); and Marvin Kalb and Bernard Kalb, *Kissinger* (New York: Dell Publishing Co., 1975).

17. See President Eisenhower's account of his relations with Secretary of State Dulles in Dwight D. Eisenhower, *Waging Peace* (Garden City, N.Y.: Doubleday and Co., 1965), pp. 361–371; and Sherman Adams, *Firsthand Report: the Story of the Eisenhower Administration* (New York: Harper & Row, 1961), pp. 87–116.

18. See Etzold, *The Conduct of American Foreign Relations,* pp. 69–71.

19. Secretary of State Dean Rusk's views on the problems posed by the "layering" existing within the State Department are reported in *New York Times,* June 29, 1964. For a more recent discussion of the problem, indicating that it still exists in acute form, see "IDCA: Better Results and More Layering," *Foreign Service Journal,* **56** (May, 1979), 44–45.

20. Secretary of State Rusk's views on the tendency of the State Department bureaucracy to avoid decisions are contained in Roger Hilsman, *The Politics of Policy Making in Defense and Foreign Affairs* (New York: Harper & Row, 1971), p. 152.

21. These and other organizational and management problems existing within the State Department in recent years are summarized in Etzold, *The Conduct of American Foreign Relations,* pp. 43–63; and Destler, *Presidents, Bureaucrats, and Foreign Policy,* pp. 16–52, 154–191.

22. Detailed excerpts from Senator McCarthy's speeches, focusing upon Communist influence within the State Department, are contained in Morris H. Rubin, ed., *The McCarthy Record* (New York: Anglobooks, 1952); and for a discussion of the impact of McCarthyism upon the State Department, see Acheson, *Present at the Creation,* pp. 354–371.

23. The theme that officials of the State Department, together with those in other agencies centrally involved in foreign affairs, constitute an anti-Communist elite which has largely dictated postwar American policy is the theme of a number of "revisionist" interpreters on the origins and nature of the Cold War. For a sampling of such treatments, see: Richard J. Walton, *Cold War and Counter-Revolution: the Foreign Policy of John F. Kennedy* (Baltimore: Penguin Books, 1972); Richard J. Barnet, *Roots of War: the Men and Institutions Behind U.S. Foreign Policy* (Baltimore: Penguin Books, 1972); David Horowitz, *The Free World Colossus: A Critique of American Foreign Policy in the Cold War* (New York: Hill and Wang, 1971); Amaury de Riencourt, *The Coming Caesars* (New York: Capricorn Books, 1957); and Stephen E. Ambrose, *Rise to Globalism: American Foreign Policy,*

1938–1970 (Baltimore: Penguin Books, 1971).

24. Robert J. Donovan, *Eisenhower: the Inside Story* (New York: Harper & Row, 1956), p. 42.

25. For detailed discussion and analysis of the trauma created for the Carter Administration by the overthrow of the Iranian monarchy in 1979, see the symposium on "The United States and Iran's Revolution," *Foreign Policy,* **34** (Spring, 1979), 3–35.

26. The problem of long-term planning in the State Department is dealt with in Robert H. Puckett, "American Foreign Policy Planning," *Foreign Service Journal,* **49** (July, 1972), 12–14, 24–25.

27. These excerpts are taken from the hearings by the Senate Foreign Relations Committee on *The Nomination of Maxwell H. Gluck.* 85th Congress, 1st Session, July 2, 1957, pp. 1–4.

28. For a discussion of the filling of ambassadorships in more recent years, see Martin H. Herz, "Maxwell Gluck and All That," *Foreign Service Journal,* **55** (May, 1978), 19–22, 39–43; and *New York Times,* April 1, 1982.

29. See T. McAdams Deford, "Posts and Missions," in *Commission on the Organization of the Government for the Conduct of Foreign Policy,* Appendix VI, pp. 348–355.

30. See Henry Adams' views, and Secretary Acheson's assessment, in Acheson, *Present at the Creation,* p. 99.

31. For an illuminating discussion of the differences between the State and the Defense Department, in terms of the strength of their domestic constituencies, see Hilsman, *The Politics of Policy Making in Defense and Foreign Affairs,* pp. 46–48.

32. The degree to which the era of the Vietnam War witnessed a collapse of a long-standing American consensus in foreign affairs—and the alienation of the State Department's customary constituency—is emphasized in William Schneider, "The Beginning of Ideology?" *Foreign Policy,* **17** (Winter, 1974–75), 88–121. See also Lincoln P. Bloomfield,

"Foreign Policy for Disillusioned Liberals," ibid., **9** (Winter, 1972–73), 55–69.

33. For a detailed analysis of the activities of the pro-Israeli lobby in the United States, see *The Middle East,* 5th ed. (Washington, D.C.: Congressional Quarterly, 1981), pp. 63–68.

34. Ball, *Diplomacy for a Crowded World,* pp. 200–201.

35. For more detailed discussion of the Agriculture Department's role in postwar American foreign policy, see Donald F. McHenry and Kai Bird, "Food Bungle in Bangladesh," *Foreign Policy,* **27** (Summer, 1977), 72–89; and Raymond F. Hopkins, "How to Make Food Work," ibid., 89–109.

36. The American labor union movement's growing involvement in postwar American policy is analyzed in Ronald Radosch, *American Labor and United States Foreign Policy* (New York: Random House, 1969); and in Lane Kirkland, *et. al.,* "Labor's International Role," *Foreign Policy,* **26** (Spring, 1977), 204–248.

37. The problems posed by the operation of American-based multinational corporations abroad are analyzed in Raymond Vernon, "Multinationals: No Strings Attached," *Foreign Policy,* **33** (Winter, 1978–79), 121–135.

38. A recent discussion of the foreign policy implications of space exploration may be found in Michael A. G. Michaud, "Outer Space and Foreign Affairs," *Foreign Service Journal,* **56** (June, 1979), 10–13, 37–39.

39. Senator Vandenberg's criticism of the Truman Administration was made after Secretary of the Treasury Henry Wallace made a speech sharply at variance with its policies toward the Soviet Union. See Arthur H. Vandenberg, Jr., ed., *The Private Papers of Senator Vandenberg* (Boston: Houghton Mifflin Co., 1952), p. 301.

40. A general discussion of the new foreign policy agenda is provided in Joseph S. Nye, Jr., "Independence and Interdependence," *Foreign Policy,* **22** (Spring, 1976), 129–162. For other treatments of more selected aspects of the

subject, see Lester R. Brown, "Redefining National Security," *Foreign Service Journal,* **55** (May, 1978), 10–12; and Richard N. Cooper, "A New International Economic Order for Mutual Gain," *Foreign Policy,* **26** (Spring, 1977), 65–120.

41. Peter L. Szanton, "The Future World Environment: Near-Term Problems for U.S. Foreign Policy," in *Commission on the Organization of the Government for the Conduct of Foreign Policy,* Appendix I, p. 8.

42. For example, as part of his Administration's intensive effort to solve the nation's energy problems, in mid-1979 President Carter called for the creation of two new federal agencies, whose activities would have an impact upon foreign affairs. A new Energy Security Corporation would seek to develop alternative energy sources for petroleum; and an Energy Mobilization Board would attempt to expedite the development of synthetic fuels and would "coordinate" national, state, and local efforts in this field. See *Newsweek,* **XCIV** (July 23, 1979), 27–28.

43. A recent evaluation of the concept of the "country team" may be found in Raymond L. Thurston, "The Ambassador and the CIA," *Foreign Service Journal,* **56** (January, 1979), 22–23.

44. During the "Cuban Missile Crisis" of 1962, President John F. Kennedy formed an intra-executive branch committee called "Ex Comm," or the Executive Committee of the National Security Council, to analyze and formulate recommendations for dealing with the crisis. Leading members of Ex Comm were: Attorney General Robert Kennedy; Secretary of State Dean Rusk; Secretary of Defense Robert McNamara; CIA Director John McCone; Secretary of the Treasury Douglas Dillon; the President's adviser for national security affairs, McGeorge Bundy; and the chairman of the Joint Chiefs of Staff, General Maxwell Taylor. According to Secretary McNamara, largely because of the effective and unified deliberations of this group, the American government's response to the Cuban crisis was handled more successfully than any other foreign policy decision during his seven years of service in the government. See Kennedy, *Thirteen Days,* pp. 14, 30–31.

45. The "Tuesday Group" relied upon by President Johnson—primarily to deal with the problem of the Vietnam War—consisted of the President, the secretary of state, the secretary of defense, and the President's special assistant for national security affairs. Destler, *Presidents, Bureaucrats, and Foreign Policy,* p. 109.

Chapter 5

National Security Policy

A century and a half ago, a Prussian military leader—General Carl Maria von Clausewitz (1780–1831)—published one of the most influential books in modern history. Entitled *Vom Kriege (On War)*, Clausewitz's study endeavored to analyze the relationship between the use of military force and the political or diplomatic process in the achievement of national objectives. The dominant theme of Clausewitz's analysis was the idea that: "War . . . [is] only diplomacy somewhat intensified, a more vigorous way of negotiating, in which battles and sieges [are] substituted for diplomatic notes." Or, as Clausewitz expressed simply: War must be viewed as merely a "continuation of State policy [or politics] by other means."[1]

Although what is often referred to as "Clausewitz's rule" is not new, familiarity with and understanding of it by American policy makers is a relatively recent phenomenon, largely confined to the post-World War II period. Even today, it may be questioned whether a majority of Americans and their national leaders fully comprehends the nature and implications of Clausewitz's dictum for the conduct of foreign policy. The dominant theme of our discussion of "national security policy" is the effort by the United States since World War II to incorporate Clausewitz's teachings into the management of foreign relations.

The Concept of "National Security Policy"

Definitions and Elements

One of the most noteworthy developments in American foreign policy since World War II has been the emergence of "national security policy" as a major dimension of the foreign policy process. Events during and immediately after the war compelled American policy makers to "discover" Clausewitz, long after his ideas had been studied and accepted by policy makers in other countries.[2] In effect, the concept of national security policy represents an attempt to apply Clausewitz's principles to America's relationships with other countries; and on the basis of available evidence, national security policy is perhaps becoming an increasingly important aspect of the overall foreign policy process. President Jimmy Carter's promulgation of the Carter Doctrine in 1980, committing America to defend the Persian Gulf area, provides a recent example of this concept.

Let us begin our analysis of this phenomenon by asking a deceptively simple question: What *is* the concept of "national security"? Many definitions are available, but most of them highlight three ideas basic to the concept. First, there is the assumption that *the United States currently is, and is determined to remain, an independent nation.* As was emphasized in Chapter 1, preserving national security ranks above all other goals in the nation's foreign relations.

Second, the concept of national security policy presupposes that the United States *faces threats* to its continued independence; it presupposes that the international environment contains forces hostile to the interests and well-being of the American society. Since World War II, the most evident and ominous threat has been Soviet-supported Communism (which is discussed more fully in Chapters 9 and 10). Yet other major and minor threats of course endanger national survival and well-being. These can range from various forms of limited military encounters (like threats to military allies and Communist-instigated "wars of national liberation") to less dramatic, although no less serious, challenges like the global population explosion, or denial of American access to foreign oil supplies, or the pollution of the international environment.

Third, the concept of national security postulates the idea that in the future, as in the past, *military force will have to be used to preserve the safety of the American society.* This is not to suggest that the preservation of national security is *solely* a matter of military force; but the possession and use of appropri-

ate military force must be viewed as an indispensable prerequisite for the maintenance of national security.

For our purposes, national security policy will be defined as *the systematic and coordinated fusion of military, political, and other policy instruments to achieve the nation's external goals.* Several points about this definition require brief emphasis. National security policy explicitly recognizes the validity of Clausewitz's principles: Military and political or diplomatic aspects of national policy *are organically and inseparably related.* Each impinges directly upon the other. Military decisions can (and frequently do) affect the nature and outcome of diplomatic negotiations; and decisions made by political leaders frequently determine such military questions as if, when, and how American armed forces will be employed.

In thinking about this interrelationship, it is helpful to envision three separate (although connected) stages in international politics, as illustrated by the periods before, during, and after World War II. The *first stage* encompassed a decade or more of prewar diplomatic negotiations centering upon controversies created by Japan's ambitions and expansionist policies in Asia, by the determination of Hitler's Germany to become the dominant military power in Europe (and perhaps in the world), and by Fascist Italy's more limited ambitions to become an influential nation and to acquire an empire. During the 1930s, the world's political leaders engaged in intensive and ongoing diplomatic efforts to avert a new global war. In time, diplomatic negotiations collapsed—and on September 1, 1939, the world was plunged into global war when Nazi Germany attacked Poland.

The *second stage*—in which military decisions and calculations became uppermost—ensued, until the surrender of Japan (on August 14, 1945). During this phase of massive and worldwide violence, military questions were dominant. In the American mind at least (if not always in the Soviet mind), winning the war and achieving the "unconditional surrender" of the Axis powers were the paramount objectives. Time and again, President Franklin D. Roosevelt insisted that "political issues" be deferred until the end of the war; among other reasons, he feared that political controversies among the Allies (over questions like the future of Eastern Europe) might divide and weaken the Allied war effort.[3]

Innumerable military decisions made during World War II had a momentous impact upon the post-World War II political order. Most of the issues high on the list of the diplomatic agenda in the years which followed were an outgrowth of military decisions and developments during World War II. Perhaps the most contentious issue in Soviet-American relations in the postwar period—and, according to many authorities, the leading cause of the Cold War—was Moscow's dominant military and political position in East-Central Europe, as a result of which formerly independent nations in this region became "satellites" of the Soviet Union. This fact stemmed directly from the Red Army's military dominance of the area in the closing months of World War II and its continued presence there ever since. From this base, the Soviet Union was in a position to threaten the security of postwar Europe and adjacent areas. The continued division of the German nation today stems from the results of World War II, when east and much of central Germany were occupied by the Red Army, while the Western allies occupied western Germany. Wisely or not, President Franklin D. Roosevelt rejected the idea that Western forces try to reach Berlin ahead of the Red Army, thereby retaining Germany's capital under American, British, and French control in the postwar era.[4]

In Asia, two vexatious political issues derived from military decisions made during the war: the problems of Korea and of Indochina. To facilitate the surrender of Japanese troops at the war's end, Korea was "temporarily" divided along the 38th Parallel; ultimately, this military dividing line hardened into the boundary between South and North Korea. Basically the same phenomenon occurred with regard to Indochina, where the 17th Parallel was taken as the military line of demarcation for the purpose of facilitating the Japanese surrender. Yet this line also became the boundary between North and South Vietnam. In neither the Korean nor the Indochinese case were diplomats subsequently able to achieve the political reunification of these countries. As will be explained more fully in Chapter 15, this fact produced tension and conflict in Asia throughout the postwar period.

The *third stage* began at the end of World War II and extends to the present day. Once the war had ended *de facto* (although the usual peace treaties for countries like Germany have not yet really been negotiated), diplomacy once again was relied upon *in lieu* of military force to resolve postwar problems. Yet the problems confronting the world's diplomats—and in many cases, their ability to respond to these problems—were massively conditioned by military developments during and after the war.

The pervasive reality of the postwar era of course has been the Soviet-American confrontation known as the Cold War. That conflict was a direct result of World War II. It was produced by a variety of factors and developments, such as: the disappearance of Germany as a great power, creating a "power vacuum" in the heart of Europe which both superpowers feared the other would fill; the decline of Great Britain as a great power, leaving the United States to assume many of the regional and global commitments once borne by the British (as in the Mediterranean and the Middle East); the widespread devastation and political instability of Western Europe as a result of the war, requiring the United States to assume massive and ongoing responsibilities for the reconstruction and defense of the area in the postwar era; Soviet Russia's massive human and property losses during World War II, which left the country weak, insecure, and suspicious of the outside world; the collapse of European colonial empires in the postwar period, accelerated by Europe's own military and political weakness during and after the war; the resumption of the Chinese civil war, the eventual collapse of the Nationalist government of China, and the victory of Communism on the Chinese mainland; and, because of the devastation and the economic and social disruption accompanying the war, the creation of new opportunities throughout the world for revolution and intrigue by Marxist groups seeking to gain political ascendancy. As the Cold War crisis intensified, both superpowers resorted to military, political, ideological, economic, and other policy instruments to gain their objectives. During the Cold War, American policy makers learned something which Soviet officials had known for a long time. As Clausewitz taught, war "is the continuation of politics by other means," and the converse is equally true: Politics may be viewed as a (nonviolent) form of war or conflict by other means!*

*Certain qualifications must be recognized with the idea that politics is a form of war or nonviolent struggle. Political relationships *may*—and sometimes unquestionably *should*—be viewed in these terms. The Soviet-American Cold War is a primary example. It is no less true, however, that other forms of political relationships must be viewed differently. They can, and often do, entail an effort to achieve *common and constructive purposes* among nations. Unless language is grossly distorted, America's relations with Western Europe during the era of the Marshall Plan in the early postwar era can hardly be

National Security in the Nuclear Era

To assert that the dawn of the nuclear age has had momentous and unforeseen consequences for all nations of the world is to understate the matter. For the realm of national security, the implications of nuclear weapons have been numerous, varied, and in some cases still unclear. Unlike previous advances in military technology, the development of strategic and tactical nuclear weapons has introduced a new era in warfare by creating the possibility of mutual annihilation for nations employing nuclear arsenals, as well as for other societies on the planet. As some commentators and citizens view the matter, the existence of nuclear arsenals has largely outmoded Clausewitz's ideas about the relationship between military and political aspects of national policy. According to this view, nuclear weapons *have no political or diplomatic utility;* the risks inherent in relying upon any form of armed force to achieve political ends are incalculable and potentially disastrous. Several years ago, for example, Secretary of State Henry Kissinger expressed this frame of mind when he asked: "What in the name of God is strategic superiority?" And of what use to the United States and other countries was possession of a steadily expanding nuclear stockpile?[5] The logical corollary of Kissinger's question was that modern weapons make no contribution to the attainment of political goals. Indeed, as some commentators assess the matter, they make a *negative contribution,* by rendering the solution of global and regional political controversies infinitely more difficult!

Yet for several reasons, the notion that

described as a form of war or struggle. It entailed a highly successful cooperative effort to achieve a mutual goal—the reconstruction of a devastated and economically prostrate area. Similarly, for a century or more Anglo-American relations are not really understandable by reference to the converse of Clausewitz's rule.

in the nuclear age earlier principles governing the relationship between military force and diplomacy are now outmoded seems highly questionable and is, therefore, rejected in our analysis. One reason is that, as a result of the "nuclear balance of terror" between the superpowers, nations have perhaps been inclined as never before to rely upon *nonnuclear* (or "conventional") weapons to accomplish their foreign policy ends. Another reason is that in certain postwar political conflicts (such as the Soviet Union's suppression of Hungarian freedom in 1956 and its invasion of Czechoslovakia in 1968 or the "Cuban Missile Crisis" of 1962) the balance of nuclear forces in a particular time or region quite clearly *has* affected the political behavior of the superpowers. Insofar as the "Cuban Missile Crisis" resulted in a diplomatic victory for the United States, this fact was an outgrowth of America's *overall* nuclear superiority in the early 1960s and of its preponderant military power *in the Western Hemisphere.*[6]

Moreover, even in the nuclear age, Clausewitzian ideas both influence and are reflected in certain strategic concepts and diplomatic "ground rules" governing international politics. One commentator, for example, believes that, in answer to Dr. Kissinger's inquiry, today there is an inseparable connection between national military arsenals and political decision making in three key areas of national security policy. The first is found in the concept of *deterrence* subscribed to by both superpowers. The United States and the Soviet Union possess a sufficiently large and varied strategic arsenal to deter an attack by the other and to inflict a devastating (possibly fatal) "second strike" military retaliation against the other if deterrence fails. The behavior of both superpowers for the past two decades indicates mutual awareness of this fact and reflects a determination not to let political and other differences between

them escalate into a nuclear holocaust. Installation of the "Hot Line" between Washington and Moscow provides evidence that the superpowers desire to exercise caution in their relationships and to avoid nuclear war "by accident."

Second, the existence of massive nuclear firepower on both sides of the Iron Curtain has not prevented the United States, the Soviet Union, Communist China, and other countries from engaging in various forms of political interventionism abroad entailing the use (or potential use) of armed force. The United States has engaged in two major wars—the Korean and the Vietnam conflicts—to defend countries whose independence was threatened by external forces. In addition, it has engaged in a number of more limited military actions (such as the American landing in Lebanon in 1958, and the intervention in the Dominican Republic in 1965) to achieve diplomatic goals.[7]

A comparable tendency has existed in Soviet foreign policy. The reality of nuclear stalemate has not inhibited Moscow from relying upon force to impose its hegemony directly upon Poland and other countries in Eastern Europe; from supporting revolutionary movements in black Africa; or from seeking to subjugate Afghanistan. In more general terms, Soviet officials have said repeatedly that their acceptance of the idea of détente with the United States in no way inhibited the Kremlin from supporting "wars of national liberation" against capitalist or other non-Marxist systems throughout the Third World.[8]

Third, in the problem of the *disengagement of military forces* traditional principles governing the relationship between military and political components of national policy still apply. In the closing stage of the Vietnam War, for example, a number of separate American military actions were undertaken for a twofold purpose: to protect the scheduled American military withdrawal from Southeast Asia and to influence the course of the diplomatic negotiations accompanying the end of the war. Several years earlier (in 1954), Communist forces in Indochina had undertaken a massive and successful military campaign against the French, designed to influence the timing of the French military evacuation and to affect the outcome of the diplomatic settlement ending the "first" war in Vietnam.

Yet it is no less clear that the concept of national security today is subject to certain important qualifications and constraints. It is essential to remember that, for the United States as for all states, national security has always been—and it remains—*a relative or relational idea.* The question must be asked: Is the United States more or less "secure" with regard to what particular condition or challenge confronting it? One student of national security believes that the application of military power to achieve diplomatic goals is a much more complicated phenomenon than is widely supposed, involving four essential elements. There is the *operational problem:* devising effective strategy and tactics for bringing military power to bear upon specific conditions abroad. There is the *logistical problem* of continuously and successfully supplying military contingents beyond the nation's borders. There is the *technological problem* of achieving and maintaining superiority in various categories of offensive and defensive weapons. (Many Americans believe, mistakenly in this author's view, that this is the most important dimension of national security policy.) Then there is what is called the *social problem,* which, more than any other, impeded America's ability to attain its objectives in the Vietnam War. This encompasses a wide range of factors influencing national security: military morale, civilian morale and the degree of citizen support

given to the nation's leaders, and the effectiveness of the nation's political leadership —to name only the most important ones.[9]

To this list may be added another crucial dimension of national security policy: *formulation and communication of the nation's goals* by its political leaders. This too can involve a host of subproblems, such as lack of clarity about what the nation is *trying* to achieve abroad, the adoption of goals which are inherently incapable of realization, and the conflict among goals which may be totally or largely incompatible. In both the Korean and Vietnam conflicts, the United States experienced considerable difficulty with this dimension of national security policy. Goals were vague and unclear; some of them were incapable of attainment, given the resources at the nation's disposal; and the goals were often changed in the midst of the conflict, creating confusion at home and abroad about what the United States actually sought by its military intervention overseas. When the goals of the nation are confused or unintelligible, it becomes impossible to determine whether a given policy or action promotes or impedes the national security of the United States.

Other commentators have called attention to the *inherently subjective nature* of national security. Insofar as national security policy is directed at protecting America's "vital interests," Bernard Brodie reminds us,

> [vital interests] are not fixed by nature nor identifiable by any generally accepted standard of objective criteria. They are instead the products of fallible human judgment, on matters concerning which agreement within the nation is usually less than universal.[10]

The concept of "vital interests" is what Brodie calls an "expansible" idea: It is a very flexible term, which includes the requirement of national defense plus something more which is by no means obvious. Does sound national security, for example, require foreign military alliances? Does it demand military aid programs to endangered states? Does it dictate possible military intervention overseas in order to *prevent* a potential threat to American security from becoming an actual threat? Does it call for extensive activity abroad by the Central Intelligence Agency (CIA) in order to forewarn the nation's leaders about potential crises or to maintain a government in power which is friendly toward the United States? The list of such collateral questions is virtually endless.

This leads to another qualification of the concept of national security. As Paul Seabury has said, security is above all "a frame of mind and a mood, not a condition. . . . " Americans have been nurtured on the adage that "eternal vigilance is the price of liberty"; according to this precept, if the American society lapsed into a kind of indifference or apathy about threats to its existence, it might soon lose its freedom. The ancient Romans had a comparable mixim: *Si vis pacem, para bellum*—"If you want peace, prepare for war." Or in the post-World War II version, invoked by American officials on countless occasions in dealing with the Soviet Union, the United States must be in a position to "negotiate from strength" with its diplomatic adversaries. The central idea is that whether the citizens and leaders of a nation *feel secure* during any given period may or may not be determined by objective factors related to its military power.[11] For centuries, for example, Soviet Russia has exhibited a feeling of "insecurity" toward the outside world which appears to be minimally affected by the facts related to its military strength in any particular era.

There is of course another side to this coin. As illustrated by Soviet foreign policy since World War II, an intense preoccupation with achieving national security—expressed in a strong emphasis upon creating military superiority and in gaining and preserving "secure borders"—can produce feelings of profound *insecurity* for other countries and ultimately perhaps for one's own country.

In the final analysis, we must also bear in mind that national security policy rests on *perceptions* by the political leaders of the world of events, developments, and trends they identify in the international system. One author emphasizes that it is "*the perceived state of the strategic nuclear balance*" which will largely determine whether the United States and the Soviet Union are deterred from engaging in hostilities with each other.[12] As has often been true in history, what people *believe to be true* is often more important than what is objectively true; and this principle has special relevance for the subject of national security. Human perceptions are usually in some measure distorted, incomplete, and otherwise faulty. Not infrequently, they are heavily influenced by what the observer *wants to believe* or *hopes* he will find.[13] This problem was posed in a salient and troublesome form for Americans by the early 1980s. By that period, officials in Washington confronted a pervasive conviction at home and abroad that American power had declined while Soviet power was steadily growing. Although this might not be a correct assessment, some governments were unquestionably basing their policies upon this belief.

Implicit in our discussion of the qualifications surrounding the concept of national security is the idea that, while requisite military strength is necessary to preserve national security, armed strength alone does not guarantee national security. Former General of the Armies and President Dwight D. Eisenhower once observed:

No matter how much we spend for arms, there is no safety in arms alone. . . . I have had a varied experience over a lifetime, and if I have learned anything, it is that there is no way in which a country can satisfy the craving for absolute security—but it can bankrupt itself, morally and economically, in attempting to reach that illusory goal through arms alone.[14]

Postwar National Security Organization

As recently as World War II, American officials tended to view military and political decision making as separate realms having little or no connection with each other. For many years before the war, communication between officials concerned with military and diplomatic problems was minimal and sometimes nonexistent. Before the 1930s, for example, liaison among the secretaries of state, war (or army), and navy was more often than not by letter. The military disaster at Pearl Harbor at the end of 1941 could be attributed in part to a lack of coordination between the army and navy intelligence, as well as to a gulf separating political and military decision making in Washington.[15]

The traditional American mentality about the relationship between military and political components of national policy was illustrated by a number of developments during World War II. As we have already noted, President Franklin D. Roosevelt repeatedly insisted upon subordinating political considerations to military questions as long as the war was in progress. The war also highlighted the existence of another problem—the challenge of successfully coordinating military efforts by three separate service arms, the army, navy, and the air force (the last had gained unprecedented influence and prominence as a result of World War II)—which sometimes impeded America's ability to achieve its external goals. An illustration was provided by the proper strategy to be adopted toward Japan in the closing stage of the war. The army and the navy submitted sharply divergent assessments of Japan's military condition to President Roosevelt. At length, FDR accepted the army's evaluation (which turned out to be wrong)—and on the basis of it demanded rapid Soviet entry into the Pacific conflict. This decision was in some measure responsible for injecting the U.S.S.R. into postwar decision making affecting the future of such countries as China, Korea, and Japan.[16]

Down to the late 1940s, the long-standing American approach to national security issues was epitomized by the remarks of two of the nation's wartime military leaders. General George C. Marshall, chief of staff during World War II, frequently told President Roosevelt that he was giving the chief executive "purely military" advice, without reference to related political questions. General Omar Bradley, a troop commander in the European theater, wrote after the war: "As soldiers we looked naïvely on this British inclination to *complicate the war* with political foresight and nonmilitary objectives." (Italics added.) American military officials, General Bradley said on another occasion, "forgot that wars are fought for the resolution of political conflicts."[17]

As "Allied unity" evaporated in the tensions generated by the Cold War between Soviet Russia and the United States, traditional American indifference to the problem of national security policy gradually began to change. The Communist adversary, America finally became aware, had always placed a high premium upon the need to concert military and political moves; Marxist regimes in Eastern Europe, for example, were created by Moscow's skillful blending of military and political decisions during and after the war.

Although President Truman sent a plan for defense reorganization to Congress late in 1945, it was well over a year later that Congress finally passed the National Security

Act of 1947. Several times in the years that followed, this act was amended; the defense reorganization plan of 1958, for example, vastly increased the powers available to the Secretary of Defense to achieve a unified approach to national security. Without attempting a detailed chronological presentation of postwar defense reorganization, let us note certain major stages and developments.[18]

As is true of most questions of public policy, the National Security Act of 1947 emerged as a compromise. It was an attempt to accommodate and conciliate the viewpoints of a wide variety of official and public groups. Some of these (particularly military pressure groups like the Navy League and the Associations of the United States Army) wanted little or no change in existing arrangements. Ranged against them were extreme critics of the status quo, who pointed to catastrophes like Pearl Harbor as the price that could be paid for continuing provincialism and separatism within the military services. On Capitol Hill, a diversity of viewpoints also prevailed. Perhaps the most influential opinion, held by Representative Carl Vinson, powerful chairman of the House Armed Services Committee, was that America must resist creating anything resembling a "Prussian general staff," and must not concentrate too much power in the hands of even a civilian official, making him a kind of "defense Czar."[19]

The result of this interplay of conflicting forces was the National Security Act of 1947, which largely set the pattern for many years thereafter in American defense organization. Attempting to steer a middle course between too much and too little change, the act in effect created a kind of "federation" among the military services, leaving them substantial *de facto* autonomy within a newly established Department of Defense, headed by a civilian secretary of defense. This official's powers, however, remained circumscribed; possessing little authority and virtually no staff, vis-à-vis that of the separate services, the office was initially weak. Yet the principle of a single defense department, headed by a civilian secretary, was established in the months following World War II. Two decades later, as a result of continuing changes in defense organization, the secretary of defense had become one of the most powerful members of the President's Cabinet. Writing in the early 1970s, one commentator was convinced that the secretary of defense had now become "a rival" to both the secretary of state and the President's adviser for national security affairs for influence in the foreign policy process.[20]

Another major innovation introduced by the National Security Act of 1947 was the creation of a National Security Council. As its name implied, its function was to serve as the highest-level mechanism or committee in the government for recommending national security policy to the President. NSC was deliberately created as a *small* agency, to faciliate discussion and reasonably prompt decision making.

Membership on the National Security Council has changed over the years to reflect changes in the organizational structure of the American government. In the late 1970s, NSC's "statutory members" were: the President (as chairman), the vice president, the secretary of state, and the secretary of defense. Two points about NSC's structure and role require emphasis.

Our discussion of the President's powers in foreign relations (Chapter 3) called attention to the fact that the National Security Council, along with other executive agencies involved in the foreign policy process, serves *as an advisory organ* to the chief executive. In the last analysis, the President "makes" or determines the foreign policy of the United States. It should also be noted that—in conformity with America's long-standing and cherished tradition—the National Security Council is predominantly *a civilian agency.* The civilian secretary of defense represents the military viewpoint in NSC deliberations, although the chairman of the Joint Chiefs or other military officials may attend and participate in NSC meetings by invitation of the President. It must also be remembered that an incumbent President may (and nearly all of them do) receive advice from *any source* in which he has confidence—ranging from established governmental agencies like NSC and the executive departments, to *ad hoc* intra-executive committees, to private citizens.[21]

The postwar period has witnessed a steady expansion in the size of the National Security Council and in its importance as an influential agency in the foreign policy process. All Presidents since the late 1940s have viewed NSC as the highest coordinating mechanism within the government in formulating national security policy; and in some administrations, it has appeared that NSC had become the most influential agency in foreign affairs, displacing the State Department's historic role in the field. The zenith of NSC's influence was possibly reached during the Nixon and Ford administrations, when the agency was headed by presidential National Security Adviser Dr. Henry Kissinger (while the State Department was led by a relative unknown, Mr. William P. Rogers). Before he became chief White House aide for national security affairs, Dr. Kissinger had established a reputation as an authority in foreign relations. Kissinger was a very "strong" personality, who held firm views on many subjects—from the process of détente with the Soviet Union, to how to resolve the Arab-Israeli conflict, to what was wrong with the State Department. Kissinger enjoyed remarkable success in having his views accepted by the President. Conversely, the influence of the State Department under Secretary Rogers' direction reached a low ebb.[22]

While the influence of NSC under Kissinger may have been exceptional, in the Carter Administration the agency vied with the State Department for leadership in the foreign policy process. Carter's chief national security adviser was Dr. Zbigniew Brzezinski, who was also an authority on foreign affairs; the State Department was led by Mr. Cyrus Vance, an experienced and able diplomatic official. By the late 1970s, a better "balance" existed between NSC and the State Department for influence in the foreign policy field; and the State Department's fortunes had clearly improved via-à-vis the Kissinger era. On some issues (such as the desirability of détente with the Soviet Union and a new strategic arms-limitation agreement) the President clearly favored the views of his secretary of state; on other issues (such as endeavoring to limit Soviet intervention in black Africa and to protest Moscow's treatment of political dissidents behind the Iron Curtain), Carter was guided more by the recommendations of his national security adviser. Yet from time to time, press reports indicated the existence of major political divergencies between these two key foreign policy agencies. Such differences (often well publicized by the press and TV) made it difficult for the Administration to arrive at a unified foreign policy position. President Carter's own lack of experience in the diplomatic realm made it more than ordinarily hard for him to resolve such intra-executive differences.[23]

Another significant innovation made by the National Security Act of 1947 was the creation of the Joint Chiefs of Staff (JCS), to serve as a coordinating mechanism for the armed services. Consisting of the military heads of the army, navy, and air force, and headed by a chairman appointed by the president, JCS was expected to prepare unified strategic plans and to serve as the principal military advisory body to the secretary of defense and the President. The JCS mechanism, as we noted earlier, reflected Congress' determination to preserve the old pattern of *separate* military arms. Each member of JCS serves as the operational commander of his respective service. Collectively, the members of JCS are responsible for providing unified military advice to their civilian superiors and for assigning combat missions to the separate services to carry out agreed-upon national policy. Additional evidence of compromise in the postwar reorganization of the military establishment was the fact that each separate military department continued to be headed by a civilian secretary (for the army, navy, and air force), who reported to the secretary of defense. The essential "identity" of the separate military arms was, therefore, preserved and in some ways strengthened.*

For the most part, the organizational pattern established by the National Security Act of 1947 remained essentially unchanged in the

---

*That the existing military advice and command structure had serious defects was highlighted by General Edward C. Meyer, appointed by President Reagan to serve as Chairman of the Joint Chiefs of Staff in 1982. In General Meyer's view, the existing organizational pattern—in which the Joint Chiefs served both as military advisers and as service commanders—militated against "independent" and objective military advice to civilian policy makers. He advocated "decoupling" the members of JCS from command responsibilities, thereby enabling them to avoid the kind of inter-service "compromises" that had diluted and weakened their advice in the past. General Meyer's recommendations, it could be anticipated, would encounter intense opposition both in the Pentagon and in Congress. See the analysis by Drew Middleton in *New York Times*, March 31, 1982.

years that followed. Periodically, certain organizational changes were made in the Defense Department, as in 1953 and 1958. With varying degrees of success, most of these were undertaken with the objective of producing even more "unified" positions among the nation's military leaders and of strengthening the authority of the secretary of defense over the military establishment. Such steps by no means brought an end to intraservice rivalry, disagreements among national military leaders over issues like strategy and military procurement policies, or the tendency of spokesmen for the separate services to cultivate allies for their respective positions on Capitol Hill.[24] Yet some legislators and commentators believed that, within limits, such intraservice rivalries—a kind of "checks and balances" system within the military establishment —was an essentially healthy phenomenon for a democratic society.

Within the Department of Defense, one administrative unit deserves brief comment. This is the Office of International Security Affairs (ISA). As defined by a directive from the secretary of defense in 1961, ISA was given the responsibility of serving as the Defense Department's direct link with the Department of State, in order to blend military and political components of external policy into a coherent and harmonious whole. Staffed by civilian and military officials, ISA's organizational pattern resembles that of the State Department. The practice has also evolved of "exchanging" officials between the two departments so that officials from each will become familiar with the goals and procedures of the other.

The Soviet-American Military Balance

Our earlier discussion called attention to the fact that national security is a relative idea, conditioned by time and circumstances. Inescapably, therefore, the concept must be continually re-examined; and the machinery established to formulate and implement national security policy must periodically be adapted to new conditions. During the last two decades of the twentieth century, the American people and their leaders had become mindful of certain tendencies and problems directly affecting the security of the United States. One of these—America's growing dependence upon oil imports from the Middle East—is reserved for more extended discussion in Chapter 12. Here, we shall concentrate upon another problem, which by the early 1980s engendered deep concern on both ends of Pennsylvania Avenue and among informed students of American foreign policy: the growing imbalance between American and Soviet military power.

In order to illuminate what can be an extremely complex issue, let us look at three important aspects of the Soviet-American military equation: overall defense spending by Washington and Moscow, competition between the two superpowers in "strategic" (or nuclear) weapons, and American-Soviet competition in "conventional" (or nonnuclear) arsenals.

Soviet and American Defense Spending

Several factors accounted for the American people's selection of Ronald Reagan as President in 1980—one of which clearly was pervasive national concern about the deterioration of the nation's power during the 1970s. Determined to "make America great again," Reagan believed that achieving this goal required (among other steps) a significant increase in national defense spending, even at the price of a balanced budget. By mid-1982, the Reagan White House had submitted to Congress a recommended defense budget totaling some $216 billion. While the Adminis-

tration might not ultimately get all the funds it requested, on both ends of Pennsylvania Avenue a clear consensus existed that the American military position must be substantially strengthened vis-à-vis the Soviet Union and its Warsaw Pact allies. Even with these budget increases, defense expenditures by the United States approximated 7 percent of the nation's Gross National Product (which by this period had reached $3 trillion annually).

According to several estimates, for a decade or more the Soviet Union had been devoting an unusually high percentage of its national resources to military purposes. As a percentage of each nation's GNP, for example, even by the 1980s Moscow was still outspending Washington by a ratio of two to one. (Some 14 percent of the Soviet GNP was allocated to the military establishment.) In several categories of weapons—such as the number and size of certain missiles, modern tanks, and several forms of seapower —the Soviet Union had clearly overtaken the United States; and in some categories of armed force, its lead continued to widen. Policy makers in Washington, along with a number of private commentators and study groups, were convinced that the Kremlin was determined to achieve military *superiority* over the United States, rather than accept the idea of military "parity" that had governed Soviet-American relations for many years prior to the last decade. As Secretary of Defense Harold Brown asserted in 1979, during the past 15 years the U.S.S.R.'s overall rate of spending for military purposes had exceeded America's by from 25 to 45 percent. Soviet officials were committing from 11 to 13 percent of the Russian GNP (versus 5 percent for America) to their defense establishment. Moreover, the *rate* of growth in Soviet defense spending was also increasing (by about 3 or 4 percent annually in constant dollars), while the rate of military expenditures by the United States had been declining steadily since the Vietnam War.*

As our detailed analysis in Chapter 8 will emphasize, public opinion in the United States toward national security and foreign policy issues is nearly always incongruous and contradictory. (Since the end of World War II, for example, the American people have periodically wanted their national leaders to "stand up to the Russians," while denying them the military and other forms of power required to do so successfully.) These same qualities of public and congressional sentiment hampered the Reagan Administration's efforts to formulate a rational defense policy that enjoyed wide public and congressional support. As always, at the same time the American people were concerned about Soviet expansionist tendencies in Poland, Afghanistan, Latin America, and other settings, citizens also called upon the Administration to reduce taxes, cut governmental spending programs, and eliminate several expensive items in the proposed national defense budget! Despite this phenomenon, however, there appeared to be a consensus

among most Americans that the nation's military position had deteriorated since the Vietnam War and that substantial improvement in America's military posture was overdue (much as they might disagree over specific steps required).†

What specific forms does this present and future military competition between the United States and the Soviet Union take?[26] From the American perspective, several aspects of Soviet military and defense policy engendered deep concern. Since the mid-1960s, Moscow had used its increased military outlays to expand the total Soviet defense force by around 1 million men; it had added some 1000 new ground-based strategic missiles, along with 900 submarine-launched missiles, to its strategic arsenal; it had augmented Russian ground forces by an additional 25 divisions; some 1000 modern fighter aircraft had been added to the Soviet air force; and—in one of the most spectacular aspects of recent Russian military escalation—Soviet naval construction proceeded at a rapid pace, designed to give the Kremlin a "blue ocean navy" capable of operating globally.[27]

Executive and legislative officials alike, along with informed students of contemporary international politics, were puzzled and apprehensive about the meaning of these facts. As always, ascertaining the facts was considerably easier than interpreting their meaning and implications correctly. What did this (apparently widening) disparity in military expenditures by the superpowers portend for Soviet-American relations and for the stability of the international system as a whole? What was Moscow's *objective or intention* in em-

---

*The calculation of the relative military strengths of the United States and the Soviet Union (or any other countries) is always of course somewhat subjective and contingent. As we shall see more fully in the discussion of NATO (Chapter 11), for example, whether NATO is relatively weaker or stronger in the early 1980s than in the 1960s is a question that elicits widely varying answers. Unquestionably, a significant buildup of Communist (Warsaw Pact) forces has occurred in Europe during the past decade. Yet NATO has also made many qualitative improvements in its defense capabilities; and more were planned under the Reagan Administration. In Europe and other theaters, two variables always had to be calculated in the military equation. One was the *conditions* under which armed conflict might take place (to succeed, for example, an attacking force must always be stronger than a defending force). The other was the *objectives* for which armed forces were being employed. See, for example, the analysis by Leslie H. Gelb in *New York Times*, April 11, 1982.

†The strategic and national defense implications of the election of 1980 are assessed more fully in Ellis Sandoz and Cecil V. Crabb, Jr., *A Tide of Discontent: The 1980 Elections and Their Meaning* (Washington, D.C.: Congressional Quarterly Press, 1981); see specifically Chapter 7.

barking upon a prolonged and costly program of military expansion?

Kremlinologists and other authorities on Soviet behavior, it had to be acknowledged, gave conflicting answers to that key question. One group was persuaded, for example, that the Kremlin's attempt to achieve military superiority provided proof of its unaltered hostility toward the West and of its continued addiction to a foreign policy of gaining hegemony over weaker societies. According to this interpretation, détente was merely a tactic engaged in by Soviet authorities to lull the United States and its allies into a false sense of security—while the Russian military machine became more ominous than ever!

Other commentators advanced different interpretations for the phenomenon. In their view, it could be explained by reference to factors having nothing essentially to do with Soviet aggressiveness toward the United States; nor did it necessarily jeopardize détente between the superpowers. Russia's military escalation, for example, might be the result of the influence of powerful military groups upon Soviet policy making. The Soviet Union also had a "Military-Industrial Complex" whose interests and demands could not be ignored by the Communist Party hierarchy.[28] Alternatively, the Soviet military escalation could be mainly explicable by reference to growing tensions between the U.S.S.R. and its former ally, Communist China. The "thaw" in Sino-American relations which began under the Nixon Administration plainly worried Moscow, which feared the creation of a new Chinese-American axis at Russia's expense. The growth in the Soviet armed forces, therefore, might well be directed chiefly against rising Chinese military power and diplomatic assertiveness.* Other commentators were in-

clined to attribute growing Soviet military power to Russia's centuries-old concern about its "security." In this view, rising Soviet military might was primarily a response to America's own advances in many aspects of scientific and military technology.

Without access to the Kremlin's archives, it is extremely difficult for outsiders to be certain of the motivations that lay behind Soviet military expansionism. Conceivably of course, the Communist hierarchy might have *several* objectives in mind—not the least of which might be developing varied and powerful military forces for use in whatever possibilities were open to the Kremlin in the years ahead. If Soviet motives in embarking upon this course were certainly debatable, the fact of rapid Russian military progress on many fronts was much less so. More than at any time since World War II, Moscow was acquiring the *ability* to project Soviet power externally in behalf of political goals. This reality caused deep anxiety in Washington and in other foreign capitals.

Competition in Nuclear Armaments

By the early 1980s, officials of the Reagan Administration were convinced that the Soviet Union had acquired (or was rapidly achiev-

---

*Early in 1979, as part of the process of "normalization" in relations between the United States and Communist China, Peking communicated to Washington its apprehensions about a possible conflict with the Soviet Union. For several years, tensions between the two countries had been increasing. During the preceding months, Moscow had sent an additional 250,000 troops to the Chinese border zone. Chinese officials were plainly worried about a Soviet military strike—while China was still relatively weak militarily. During this period, Chinese officials indicated their desire to see an expansion in American naval forces in the Pacific and to have units of the fleet call at Chinese ports! See *Newsweek*, **XCIII** (February 5, 1979), 57–59. Yet the Central Intelligence Agency estimated that only a small part (some 15 percent) of Moscow's total military effort was directed at Communist China. See Drew Middleton, in *New York Times*, February 7, 1979.

ing) nuclear *superiority* over the United States. If this assessment was correct, it could of course have profound implications both for the strategic position of the United States and for the ability of the United States to achieve its diplomatic goals. (The reader is reminded of an aspect of national power emphasized in Chapter 1: existing *perceptions* about American power at home and abroad may be more crucial than the objective facts concerning it. Since the Vietnam War, officials in many foreign countries believed that American power had declined vis-à-vis Soviet power.)

Policy makers in Washington could point to considerable evidence underlying their apprehensions. Several criteria may be employed, for example, to compare the nuclear arsenals of the two superpowers; and by a number of them, it was clear that the military balance had tilted in favor of the Soviet Union.[29] Take the number of "strategic launchers" (missiles, submarines, and aircraft) possessed by both sides. The U.S.S.R. had 1398 missiles, 950 submarines, and 150 aircraft in this category; the United States had 1052 missiles, 576 submarines, and 316 aircraft. All told, Soviet officials had close to 2500 strategic launchers at their disposal, while American officials had less than 2000. By contrast, according to another index—"deliverable nuclear warheads" in their respective arsenals—the United States still had an advantage: 9480 for America versus 8040 for the Soviet Union.[30]

By another yardstick—the "payload" of nuclear delivery systems (providing an approximate index of destructive nuclear firepower)—the Soviet arsenal appeared to be from 15 to 20 percent stronger than its American counterpart. By a different calculation, the Soviet strategic arsenal had a total explosive power of 7.9 thousand megatons, while

the American nuclear stockpile measured 3.5 thousand megatons.*

At times, such comparisons could be misleading and could convey a distorted picture of the Soviet-American arms balance. In discussing Soviet and American military power, there was perhaps an inherent tendency for the discussion to degenerate into a meaningless "numbers game" that did little to clarify the basic issues involved. To cite merely one example of the kinds of qualifications that had to be kept in mind in such calculations: America's land-based missiles were more dispersed and better protected than their Soviet counterparts, thereby enabling a higher proportion of America's nuclear forces to survive a "first strike" attack. Conversely, most students of international politics would probably agree that Soviet strategists would gain many advantages if they launched a *suprise attack* against the United States and its NATO allies.

Although they recognized many such qualifications and contingencies, American officials believed that several aspects of the Soviet strategic buildup affected Western security directly and ominously. In the first place (in contrast to the views of American officials and students of nuclear strategy), Soviet policy makers did *not* accept the view that nuclear war was "unthinkable" or would result in mutual catastrophe for all nations engaged in it. As with most military conflicts throughout history, a "winner" would emerge from a nuclear holocaust; and the Kremlin was convinced it would be the Soviet Union. Current Soviet military doctrine was geared to the idea that nuclear war *was possible* and that in any military encounter between the United States and the Soviet Union (as in the

---

*One megaton is the equivalent of 1 million tons of TNT in explosive firepower.

NATO area), nuclear weapons would almost certainly *be used*. Under certain circumstances, a nuclear conflict might even be initiated by the United States. At any rate, the concept of "deterrence" was by no means foolproof: A nuclear exchange could occur between the superpowers, and if it happened Moscow was determined to emerge victorious.[31]

In the second place, Soviet strategists rejected the notion that the nuclear age had rendered obsolete classical principles governing the relationship between military force and political decision making. For many years, high-ranking Soviet officials had praised General Clausewitz's insights into this relationship; and they continued to apply his ideas to the realm of foreign policy. The possession of destructive nuclear arsenals on both sides of the Iron Curtain had not altered the fact that military force was still "an extension of policy."*

In the third place, the Soviet Union was rapidly acquiring a position of strategic superiority vis-à-vis the United States. This prospect threatened the reliability of America's nuclear deterrent and its ability to carry out a successful "second strike" attack against an aggressor. In the American view at least, the SALT I arms-limitation accord of 1973 assumed that a condition of approximate "nu-clear equivalence" (or "nuclear parity") would continue to exist between the superpowers. While their arsenals were different, each had sufficient power to deter the other and to launch a devastating "second strike" attack against the other if deterrence failed. American defense planners were willing to accept strategic parity with the Soviet Union; and, as we have seen, for almost a decade after 1973 the United States actually *reduced* its defense spending. Moreover, American officials decided not to proceed (or to proceed very slowly) with the development of several new weapons—such as the B-1 bomber, the neutron bomb, and the low-flying Cruise Missile. By contrast, the Kremlin moved rapidly ahead with permissible quantitative and qualitative improvements in its nuclear arsenal.

Even by the 1980s approximate nuclear equivalence still existed between the superpowers. As had been true for many years, the United States possessed over twice as many nuclear warheads (around 10,000) as the U.S.S.R. American missiles were reputed to be more accurate than their Soviet counterparts. And the nation's nuclear forces were widely dispersed among a defense "triad" consisting of land-based, sea-based, and air-borne missiles and bombers, making them less vulnerable than Soviet strategic forces. The new Cruise Missile (still to be produced in quantity) offered another modern component to the American strategic posture. Defense Department officials believed that the nation's strategic power remained awesome, that it was in no immediate jeopardy from the continuing Soviet military buildup, and that America's overall military position was in many respects superior or equal to that of any possible adversary.[32]

Yet Moscow's strategic power and potential were unquestionably impressive. The United States had only some three-fourths as

*Thus, one commentator quotes the following statement from a publication of the Soviet armed forces in 1975: "The premise of Marxism-Leninism on war as a continuation of policy by military means remains true in an atmosphere of fundamental changes in military matters. The attempt of certain bourgeois ideologists to prove that nuclear missile weapons leave war outside the framework of policy and that nuclear war . . . ceases to be an instrument of policy . . . is theoretically incorrect and politically reactionary." See Paul H. Nitze, "Nuclear Strategy: Détente and American Survival," in James Schlesinger, ed., *Defending America* (New York: Basic Books, 1977), pp. 98–99.

many strategic missiles (1700 versus over 2400) as the Soviet Union. Russia's missiles were larger and more powerful (giving them a higher "throw-weight" in nuclear firepower) than American missiles. In one of the most spectacular dimensions of Soviet military escalation, in recent years the Kremlin had acquired some 900 relatively new submarine-launched missiles; and it was adding to its sea-based nuclear fleet annually. While the U.S.S.R. had a relatively small number of strategic bombers (some 150), the United States had reduced its once commanding lead in this category, from 750 strategic bombers in the mid-1960s, to around 400 at the end of the 1970s.

Projections of future increases in Soviet military strength threatened to tilt the balance further in Moscow's favor. Since SALT I, the Kremlin had substantially improved the accuracy of its missile systems (largely canceling out an American advantage on this front). Old missiles (like the SS-9) were being replaced by the more accurate and powerful SS-18. In a move which was profoundly disturbing to the Pentagon, Soviet missiles were also being MIRVed,* thereby again offsetting another American advantage and greatly increasing the versatility of the Russian missile fleet. Moscow was also converting exposed missile sites to "hardened" underground silo sites, greatly reducing their vulnerability to a possible American second strike attack. The Kremlin was also producing a new ("Backfire")

strategic bomber, which compounded the problem of defending the NATO area. In contrast to America, the Soviet Union continued to construct civil defense shelters for its population in the event of nuclear war. In most categories of nuclear strength, the U.S.S.R. was rapidly nullifying earlier American advantages; and by the mid-1980s, it seemed likely that Soviet officials would achieve their goal of clear nuclear superiority.

This development would of course have extremely serious repercussions for American national security and for the stability of the international system. In one possible (although certainly not inevitable) scenario, relying upon its superior military position Moscow might be tempted to launch a preemptive strike against the United States, on the twofold premise that it could largely eliminate America's "deterrent" and its second strike nuclear force; and if the Soviet attack failed to do so, Russia would still be strong enough to win in any continuing nuclear exchange. While this might seem an unduly alarmist and "Strangelovian" prospect—and again, there is nothing preordained about it—even the *possibility* that the Kremlin could, at a minimum, wipe out most of the American strategic forces induced a searching re-examination of national defense by executive and legislative officials alike.

Much of the opposition within Congress, for example, to the second attempt to limit strategic armaments (SALT II) reflected this apprehension.[33] According to one interpretation, a dominant goal of the Carter Administration in supporting SALT II was to assure that the Soviet Union did not achieve a position of superiority in strategic weapons. Moreover, development of the proposed new MX missile system†—along with accelerated pro-

---

*The acronym MIRV stands for "Multiple Independent Reentry Vehicle"—a complicated idea which is simple in principle. Earlier missiles carried a single nuclear warhead, so that one missile could be fired at one target. A MIRVed missile has *several warheads,* each of which can be targeted and fired independently. A single MIRVed American missile, in other words, could deliver nuclear warheads against several Soviet military or civilian targets, thereby greatly compounding the problem of adequate defense against a missile attack.

†The new MX missile system being considered by American defense planners to offset rapid Soviet progress in

duction of the Cruise Missile and the production of a new bomber—would likely constitute America's "answer" to an ongoing and intensive Soviet strategic buildup.

Only two alternatives seemed possible: Superpower competition in nuclear weapons would be stabilized—and eventually, perhaps, arms reduction achieved—as the Reagan Administration advocated early in 1982; or, as had happened repeatedly in modern history, each side would continue to augment its military strength and to seek a commanding strategic advantage.

Rivalry in Conventional Weapons

Many of these same problems and difficult policy alternatives confront Americans in a third important dimension of the Soviet challenge to national security: the balance between the superpowers *in nonnuclear or "conventional" components of military strength.* At the outset, it is necessary to emphasize that in the contemporary world, any discussion of conventional military power is likely to be deceptive. The destructiveness of so-called conventional weapons has escalated sharply since World War II. Without using a single nuclear weapon, during the Vietnam War the

United States released more destructive firepower upon the enemy from conventional weapons than was inflicted upon Nazi Germany during World War II! Also in the realm of nonnuclear armaments, recent developments and projections of future trends indicate a shift in the balance of military power in favor of the Soviet Union and its Communist allies.

Throughout the greater part of American history—except for periods like the First and Second World Wars—American military strength has consisted primarily of *naval and air power.* The geographical position of the United States in large part dictates this reality. And (as we saw in Chapter 2) the American ethos has always opposed the idea of a "standing army" in peacetime. By contrast, for centuries the Russian state has depended upon *large and powerful ground forces* to form the core of its military strength. For over a half-century after 1900, Soviet officials showed little interest in naval power; and the Soviet air force consisted chiefly of aircraft designed primarily for defense.

At the end of the 1970s, the United States had a total of just over 1 million men and women in its military services—with about half this number stationed at sea or abroad (around 300,000 were in the NATO area). This total represented a decline of almost 50 percent in overall troop strength, from some 1.9 million in 1968. The United States Army consisted of 16 divisions. The navy had 464 ships in its active fleet (a little more than half the size of the fleet in 1960). The air force had 26 strategic air squadrons (down from 142 in 1960); and the total number of American aircraft was just over 10,000 (versus some 21,000 in 1960). After suspending the Selective Service (or "draft") System early in 1975, the United States depended upon the recruitment of volunteers for its military manpower needs. One result of this change was that steadily rising military pay

---

strategic weapons entailed a highly complex and costly land-based missile network, in which missiles might be placed in buried trenches (13 to 20 miles long) or widely dispersed in vertical shelters. Each missile would weigh some 192,000 pounds and carry an 8,000-pound nuclear payload; some 150 to 300 MX missiles would be deployed throughout the United States; and since they could be moved periodically, the Kremlin would be presented with upwards of 5000 "aim points" or targets if it tried to eliminate America's land-based nuclear arsenal. The MX missile complex would cost some $25 to $40 billion to construct over a 10-year period. On the basis of experience with new weapons systems, this estimate would almost certainly prove to be too low to complete the MX missile defense system. See Colin S. Gray, "The Strategic Forces Triad: End of the Road?" *Foreign Affairs,* **56** (July, 1978), 774.

scales and fringe benefits consumed an ever increasing proportion of the national defense budget. After several years' experience, it was also questionable whether the nation's military manpower requirements could continue to be met by relying upon volunteers.[34]

By 1980, the Soviet Union maintained a combined armed force numbering some 4 million men and women—four times as many as the United States. The expansion we have already described in Moscow's defense effort has been directed in part at giving the U.S.S.R. a qualitative and quantitative edge in conventional forces. For example, since 1964 the Kremlin has added 1 million troops to its military establishment; its ground forces have grown by 25 divisions; its air force has been expanded and modernized; and, as has already been emphasized, Moscow has moved ahead impressively with its campaign to acquire formidable naval power (such as in the continuing expansion of its nuclear submarine fleet, the addition of two light aircraft carriers, and the operation of the largest merchant marine fleet in the world). A particularly disturbing development for Western strategists was Moscow's decision during the early 1980s to install its new SS-20 missile system on the European continent, thereby significantly increasing the vulnerability of the NATO area. (The Reagan Administration's response was to add the Cruise Missile to the NATO defensive arsenal and to revive the possibility that the neutron bomb might be used to repel a Soviet military thrust across the Iron Curtain.)

As with strategic weapons, Soviet officials continually emphasize the role of the armed forces in realizing the nation's foreign policy objectives. Modern Soviet military doctrine emphasizes such concepts as the importance of surprise in employing the armed forces; the "suppression" of the adversary's defenses (by relying upon overwhelming artillery firepower and infantry strength); rapid maneuver and deployment of military units; and rapid exploitation of military gains. With regard to the NATO–Warsaw Pact front, American officials believe that Communist forces have steadily improved their capability of conducting either a nuclear or a nonnuclear war. If it were the latter, for example, America and its NATO allies would be placed in an excruciating dilemma: whether to contest superior Communist forces solely with *conventional weapons* (a contest the Communist side would most likely win in the end), or to employ *nuclear weapons* to defend the NATO area, thereby virtually guaranteeing regional, and possibly global, nuclear devastation.[35]

The Soviet Union's strength in conventional military power also has relevance for another crucial dimension of contemporary global politics: superpower influence and competition throughout the Third World. The era of Soviet-American détente has witnessed no diminution in Moscow's ability to "project" its power in this zone; nor was there any discernible evidence of a Soviet lack of interest in doing so. To the contrary, in the early 1980s, the Soviet Union was maintaining a continuing "presence" in key areas like North Vietnam, Afghanistan, and East Africa. It continued to support revolutionary and secessionist movements throughout black Africa. Cuba of course remained closely linked to the U.S.S.R. In 1979, as if to impress America and the world with its expanding military strength, the Soviet Union for the first time carried out large-scale naval exercises in the Caribbean Sea; and officials in Washington discovered evidence indicating the presence of a large contingent of Soviet ground forces in Cuba.

Constraints Upon the Superpowers

Each superpower confronted several constraints upon its ability to employ various kinds of military force for diplomatic ends.

For the United States, these limitations fell into three major categories. As we have emphasized, one was the relative decline in the nation's overall defense expenditures and the implications of this fact for many specific aspects of military power. A second limitation—still often crucial in the aftermath of the Vietnam War—was the American society's willingness to support reliance upon the armed forces for diplomatic purposes. After the Vietnam War, as Presidents Gerald Ford and Jimmy Carter discovered, public sentiment (as reflected, for example, in opinion on Capitol Hill) was often highly adverse to undertaking new military ventures abroad; and public support for existing commitments (such as the *de facto* alliance between the United States and Israel) appeared to be declining. A third constraint was familiar to every reader of the daily headlines: the nation's growing dependence upon foreign sources for key commodities like petroleum and a long list of strategic minerals. For the first time in American history, this development meant that the nation's defense effort was vulnerable to an "oil boycott" or any other impairment of its access to foreign oil and mineral supplies. (The implications of the rapid Soviet buildup of submarine strength had to be viewed in light of America's unprecedented dependence upon imports.).

Also, following the Vietnam War, the American society was, perhaps understandably, confused and ambivalent with regard to the role of military force in the foreign policy process. Very few Americans subscribed to the old idea, prominent in the thought of "isolationists" before World War II, that military strength was unimportant or played no role in successful diplomacy. Yet (as our more detailed analysis of public opinion in Chapter 8 will show), public sentiment in the United States was clearly uncertain and divided on *how and when* the United States ought to employ armed force in behalf of dip-

lomatic goals. If Americans wanted "no more Vietnams," this did not mean they were against *all* efforts to apply military power abroad. ("No more Vietnams" might mean primarily that the United States should intervene militarily in those foreign settings in which it was likely to do so successfully.) If many Americans approved a relative decline in overall defense expenditures, this did not necessarily signify a willingness to accept the indefinite deterioration of the nation's power and influence abroad. As Iran's seizure of American hostages late in 1979 dramatically illustrated, the people called upon their national leaders to protect the nation's interests abroad; and when the need was clearly demonstrated, they were prepared to support those defense measures required to achieve this objective. Although as usual, domestic economic concerns were the dominant issue of the 1980 presidential campaign, it would not be amiss to interpret the election of Ronald Reagan as at least a limited popular mandate to restore America's declining power and diplomatic credibility abroad.

Soviet Russia's military position was no less subject to certain vulnerabilities and constraints. Given the demands of Soviet citizens and the existence of several acute domestic problems, Western commentators wondered how long Moscow could sustain its extremely high level of military spending. Overall Soviet productivity remained low, and many Soviet-made goods were qualitatively inferior. The development of Siberia and other remote areas imposed enormous strains on the Russian economic system. With each passing year, the U.S.S.R. appeared to be more dependent than ever upon imports—such as massive American grain purchases and modern equipment and technology from the United States and other Western nations for computer development and oil exploration. Although it was a large oil producer—and in the past had supplied Eastern Europe with most of its oil needs, as well as exporting oil to Western Europe—the U.S.S.R. was on the verge of losing its self-sufficiency in this vital commodity. The Communist hierarchy also had to contend with continuing political dissent within the Soviet society; and in recent years, other ethnic and social conflicts impaired the cohesion of Soviet society.

Moreover, Moscow was required to deploy an ever larger number of military units to the troubled Sino-Soviet frontier. In any new global conflict, the U.S.S.R. would be compelled to fight a "two-front war," with its armed forces separated by several thousand miles. In this contingency, Soviet Russia's primitive internal transportation system would unquestionably weaken its military efforts. In addition, Soviet military strategists had to confront the same question which had been present since the end of World War II: How "reliable" were the military forces and populations of the Communist-ruled states of Eastern Europe? As the crisis in Poland during the early 1980s indicated, Soviet hegemony in the region had perhaps done little to win the enduring loyalty to Moscow of the peoples in that area; and in the event of regional or global war, some of them would almost certainly revolt against Soviet domination.[36]

The effort to project growing Soviet military power into the Third World also encountered numerous obstacles. Despite its active presence in areas like Southeast Asia, Afghanistan, and East Africa, the U.S.S.R. has also suffered a number of major reverses in the Third World—symbolized by the expulsion of several thousand Russian military advisers and officials from Egypt in 1972.[37] Most nations in the Third World sooner or later made it clear that, although they are willing to accept Moscow's assistance, they have little interest in becoming a Soviet "satellite" or entering Moscow's military orbit.

The Intelligence Function

Nature of the Intelligence Process

The remainder of this chapter will be devoted to a description and analysis of one of the most important—and for the American democracy, one of the most controversial—aspects of national security policy: the intelligence process. For reasons that will be identified at a later stage, any discussion of the activities of intelligence agencies in the American society is likely to evoke a spirited reaction from citizens and students of the nation's foreign policy. Moreover, because of the covert nature of many intelligence operations, it is often difficult for the observer to be certain that relevant and objective information is available about this aspect of national security affairs.[38]

Despite the fact that intelligence operations are often romantically depicted in "cloak-and-dagger" terms, in essence the concept of national intelligence is simple and unglamorous. The principal mission of intelligence agencies *is to provide policy makers with comprehensive and reliable information,* together with *an analysis or evaluation* of such information, as a basis for decision making. It is axiomatic that sound policy making must be based upon facts, rather than upon mere suppositions, subjective impressions, or other unreliable sources. In addition, intelligence involves certain other collateral and miscellaneous functions which are difficult to categorize. Throughout the postwar period, these have included: establishing and maintaining secret sources of information in foreign countries (particularly in unfriendly countries, such as the Soviet Union, Communist China, and Cuba); supporting friendly foreign governments against movements seeking their overthrow; endeavoring to raise sunken Soviet submarines, in order to acquire additional information about this aspect of Russian naval strength; endeavoring to win good-will for America (and to counteract Communist influence) in labor unions or youth movements at home and abroad; attempting to frustrate the operation of foreign intelligence networks within the United States and allied countries; and participating in "counterinsurgency" campaigns in Southeast Asia and other regions.[39]

Customarily, intelligence operations are divided into two categories: *overt* and *covert* operations. In terms of the time and resources devoted to them, overt or "open" intelligence activities by agencies of the United States government are by all odds the most important. The most valuable resources for American intelligence agencies may well be the Library of Congress! Despite the romantic mythology with which intelligence operations are often clothed in the popular mind, in reality they normally consist of painstaking examination of foreign newspapers, journals, governmental and technical reports, and other publications which are readily available. From such open sources, intelligence reports are prepared for the guidance of policy makers. What kind of progress is the Soviet Union making in solving its agricultural problems? To what extent does Israeli public opinion support the position of the Israeli government on the controversial issue of the future of the West Bank? What are the prospects for the continued political stability of the monarchy in Saudi Arabia? In the vast majority of cases, the Library of Congress and other public sources are apt to yield more reliable information needed to answer such questions than are the CIA's secret agents abroad.

The intelligence process has of course traditionally depended also upon covert sources of information. Cloak-and-dagger operations, secret agents, informers, and the like sometimes provide data needed by decision makers which is available from no other source. Totalitarian governments especially tend to be highly secretive about activities normally publicized widely in the American society. While the general public (misled often by popular novelists) tends to exaggerate the role of covert sources in intelligence operations, it remains true that information supplied by such sources does supply the missing pieces of the puzzle needed by intelligence officials to acquire a complete picture of the problem with which they are working. It is difficult to think, for example, of a substitute for the information provided to the Kennedy Administration by the U-2's and other reconnaissance aircraft which photographed Soviet missile installations in Cuba during the early 1960s. In the years which followed, as in the SALT I and SALT II arms-limitation agreements, Washington and Moscow took it for granted that each would "monitor" (or spy on) the other's progress in missile technology. Indeed, it is not an exaggeration to say that the stability of the international system depended in no small measure upon the expectation that intelligence operations by the superpowers *would go on continuously and effectively.*

Even more difficult than intelligence gathering, however, is the accurate *evaluation* of information collected. Facts, in the popular phrase, "speak for themselves"; but the task of the intelligence expert and of his administrative superiors is to ascertain what they are saying. More often than not, equally well-informed individuals can and do differ as to the *meaning* of intelligence data. A classic and very difficult case is the question posed earlier in this chapter: What interpretation should officials in Washington place upon the indisputable evidence of Soviet military escalation during the past decade or so? As we have seen, various alternative explanations of this phenomenon are available; and the explanation chosen will be crucial in determining America's response to the Soviet Union. As intelligence officials view the matter, their task is to supply the President and his advisers with intelligence information and with a set of alternative interpretations of it. Ultimately, the decision as to which interpretation is the "correct" or most accurate one is a determination to be made by the President or his advisory organs, like the National Security Council.

The Intelligence Community

The agencies of the United States government engaged in the intelligence function comprise a large and diverse "community"—widely referred to as "the intelligence community." Collectively, the members of the intelligence community spend upwards of $15 billion annually on intelligence operations, and they employ well over 50,000 people who are (or can be) engaged in performing some intelligence function.[40]

Although the United States has conducted intelligence activities since the period of the Revolutionary War, the modern intelligence community dates from the late 1940s. To the minds of many Americans, the military disaster at Pearl Harbor was viewed as stemming from an intelligence failure which could not be repeated. (More accurately perhaps, it was a *communications failure,* since certain intelligence units had acquired reliable information indicating an impending Japanese attack against American military bases in the Pacific, but this information did not reach Pearl Harbor until after Japanese warplanes struck the base.) Accordingly, one of the major innovations made by the National Security Act of 1947 was establishment of the Central Intelligence Agency (CIA). The CIA had two primary functions: to serve as an *operating intelligence agency,* carrying out missions assigned to it by the National Security Council and the President; and to serve as a *coordinating mechanism* for all intelligence operations within the American government.

As the years passed, successive Presidents strengthened this latter function of the CIA, by giving its director greater responsibility for unifying intelligence operations throughout the government. In view of the controversy which some of its activities have generated since its establishment, it is important to note that the CIA was created, and its overall mission was defined, *by act of Congress.* Ultimately, the CIA's operations continue to be governed by statutory authority. Yet such statutory provisions are, by their nature, extremely general and flexible.* One commentator on the American intelligence community is convinced that the "real operating constitution" of the CIA and the intelligence community as a whole is supplied by the more detailed, highly secret "intelligence directives" issued from time to time by the National Security Council, under the President's supervision.[41]

The CIA is believed to have around 18,000 employees and a budget of more than $1 billion annually to carry out its assigned missions. (Customarily, its budgetary allocation is concealed within the federal budget, by being included in the appropriations of several other governmental agencies.) The agency's basic mission is to collect and analyze foreign

---

*In the National Security Act of 1947 creating the CIA, Congress gave the agency a five-fold mission: to advise the National Security Council concerning intelligence activities by all governmental agencies; to make recommendations to NSC for the "coordination" of intelligence operations; to "correlate and evaluate" intelligence data and to disseminate it to policy makers; to perform "additional services" for governmental agencies, as assigned by NSC; and to undertake such "other functions and duties related to intelligence" as NSC may determine. This last provision—giving NSC power to assign the CIA "other functions and duties" in the intelligence field—has served as a mandate for many intelligence activities, some of which may be only marginally related to promoting national security. See the provisions of the National Security Act of 1947 (Public Law 80-253), 61 U.S. Statutes-at-Large 495.

intelligence, and to provide support for the work of other intelligence organs of the American government. In addition, the CIA has undertaken other assignments from time to time—such as supporting a coup which installed Shah Mohammed Reza Pahlevi on the throne of Iran in 1953; carrying out reconnaissance flights over the Soviet Union by U-2 aircraft during the late 1950s; aiding anti-Communist forces in Chile against the pro-Marxist regime of President Allende in 1964; and during the late 1960s, attempting to "infiltrate" student, religious, and political groups within the United States which were identified as "radical" or opposed to America's participation in the Vietnam War.

The Watergate episode during the Nixon Administration also provided evidence of CIA involvement in illegal activities directed against President Nixon's political opponents. For a period of several years thereafter, the CIA, the FBI, and other intelligence agencies were subjected to intense public and congressional criticism because of their deeds and misdeeds. The press, with innumerable exposés of its activities, depicted the CIA as an agency "out of control"; some of its activities threatened basic American liberties. Citizens and legislators alike were convinced that more stringent and effective controls had to be imposed upon the agency's operations. Accordingly, under both the Ford and Carter administrations, several widely publicized congressional investigations of CIA activities were conducted. Presidents Ford and Carter also issued executive orders reorganizing the intelligence community and imposing new restrictions upon its activities.

Under the Carter Administration, the CIA was headed by Admiral Stansfield Turner, whose dual title was director of Central Intelligence and director of the Central Intelligence Agency. More than at any time since 1947, the intelligence function was now "centralized" under the CIA. Admiral Turner was given the formidable challenge of supervising and coordinating the operations of a dozen or so separate members of the intelligence community.[42] For the first time, the head of the CIA had *budgetary control* over the entire intelligence community; it was now his responsibility to see that some kind of logical division of labor was adhered to by agencies in the intelligence field. The late 1970s was a highly traumatic period for the CIA. The agency's public image had been badly tarnished by the demise of the Nixon Administration and by its failure in late 1978 and early 1979 to forewarn the Carter Administration about the likely collapse of the Iranian monarchy. Morale within the CIA was low; the agency had difficulty recruiting new employees; and the reaction throughout the government to many of Admiral Turner's reforms was often highly adverse. The CIA was in a rebuilding stage—the most essential step of which perhaps was to regain the confidence of the American people and of Congress. As the months passed, the evidence indicated that it was slowly making progress toward accomplishing that goal.

The other members of the intelligence community may be identified briefly. Larger even than the CIA (in terms of both its budget and its personnel) is the National Security Agency (NSA). It is estimated that this supersecret organization expends well over $1 billion annually and has some 24,000 employees. Its principal mission is to "break" the codes and ciphers of other nations, to monitor foreign radio and radar transmissions, and to protect the security of the American government's communications systems.

Within the State Department, a Bureau of Intelligence and Research concentrates on the collection and analysis of overt information about foreign governments. This includes such questions as economic trends within

Country X, its prospects for political stability, and biographical information about its political elite and opposition groups.

The Department of Defense also maintains an elaborate intelligence system which contributes to the activities of the intelligence community. A Defense Intelligence Agency (DIA) is assigned the responsibility for providing unified intelligence reports to the secretary of defense and the Joint Chiefs of Staff. Each of the separate military services also operates its own intelligence network, to provide strategic and tactical intelligence reports adapted to its unique needs. Thus Army Intelligence (G-2) is engaged in intelligence operations geared to specific combat missions and requirements of the army. This pattern is duplicated for the other military arms.

The Federal Bureau of Investigation (FBI) also plays a role in intelligence operations. Its specific province is "counterintelligence"—thwarting the operations and gaining information about the activities of foreign intelligence networks within the United States. The Treasury Department carries out intelligence operations directed specifically at collecting and analyzing information related to United States foreign economic policies. The Energy Department contributes to the intelligence process by gathering and analyzing data on energy supplies and production overseas. One of its most urgent concerns is informing policy makers about the progress of other countries in nuclear technology and the extent to which nuclear proliferation is occurring throughout the international system. The Drug Enforcement Administration focuses upon gathering intelligence related to the foreign production of drugs and the drug traffic in the United States.

Intelligence Operations in a Democratic Setting

Every informed American is aware that for a decade or more the activities of the CIA and other members of the intelligence community have posed difficult questions, for which easy answers are not available even now. The problem created by the activities of agencies belonging to the intelligence community exemplify the classical dilemma sometimes confronting democratic societies which President Abraham Lincoln formulated over a century ago. Lincoln asked: Shall a government be *so strong* that its citizens find their liberties endangered, or shall it be *so weak* that it is unable to deal effectively with internal and external threats to its security? What we might call "Lincoln's dilemma" lies at the heart of efforts to define and to control the intelligence process in the United States. For purposes of analysis, we may conveniently examine the problem further by focusing upon three major questions with regard to intelligence operations by the American government. Does the United States need intelligence operations at all as an important component of national security policy? What are the desirable or permissible limits upon intelligence operations by governmental agencies? And how can the controls upon the activities of the intelligence community be made more effective? For all these questions, the search for answers must be *an ongoing process.*

The first question need detain us only briefly. For some (although by no means all) critics of the intelligence community's activities in recent years, there is an implicit assumption that the United States should abandon *all* intelligence operations. The logical corollary of this view of course is that the CIA and other intelligence units should be dismantled.[43] As these critics assess the matter, there exists a fundamental and irreconcilable conflict between democratic values and certain professed American foreign policy goals, on the one hand, and intelligence operations, on the other hand. According to this view, intelligence activities inherently jeopardize democratic freedoms and values: For example, the very idea of "secret" CIA operations affronts the concept of democracy and undermines the idea of democratic "accountability" for the conduct of governmental officials. Similarly, in foreign affairs there is a conflict between ongoing, increasingly more effective, American intelligence operations directed against the Soviet Union and the concept of détente between the superpowers. Nations cannot "distrust" and "trust" each other at the same time; and inevitably, actions stemming from distrust will counteract those directed at creating greater trust and goodwill between them. Even relations with friendly countries are imperiled, it is assumed, when the National Security Agency is engaged in breaking their codes and ciphers in an effort to discover their most closely guarded secrets.

Overdrawn as it often is, this point of view about the role of intelligence operations in a democratic setting cannot be dismissed lightly. Its central contention—that there *is* an intrinsic conflict between certain kinds of intelligence activities and the democratic ethos —can hardly be doubted. The hiatus exists, and it occurs and reoccurs in efforts to solve problems associated with national intelligence operations. By their very nature, for example, certain kinds of intelligence functions must be *clandestine;* otherwise, they would be self-defeating and possibly suicidal for the American (and foreign) agents involved in them. The premature disclosure of intelligence data, or of policy decisions based upon them, might have the most serious consequences for national security. To that extent, the public's "right to know" what the government is doing—and to debate whether officials ought to do it—is inherently compromised. For the United States, as for all other governments throughout the world, successful intelligence operations almost always demand the kind of "wall of secrecy" which many legislators, the press, and certain citizens' groups deplore as inimical to democracy.

Yet in 1947 and throughout the years which followed, Congress answered the fundamental question of whether the United States ought to be in the intelligence business unequivocally in the affirmative. After prolonged consideration of the matter, Congress established the CIA and assigned several major intelligence missions to it; and despite the numerous investigations of intelligence activities by House and Senate committees over the past generation, Congress has made no serious effort to disestablish the CIA and companion agencies. In effect, Congress has said repeatedly that the United States requires an extensive and effective intelligence network in the 1980s as much as it did in the early postwar period. In fact, as we have noted, détente with the Soviet Union appears to rest upon a tacit understanding that each superpower is monitoring the activities of the other successfully. Then by the early 1980s, as the Reagan Administration endeavored to restore America's power and diplomatic credibility, citizens and legislators alike were convinced that the intelligence community had an essential contribution to make to this process.

Whatever legitimate criticisms might be made of activities by intelligence agencies in recent years, Congress and the American people remained convinced that there is simply no alternative to an effective intelligence establishment. Without it, diplomatic failure would almost be guaranteed; and national security might in time be gravely jeopardized.

The second question—What *limits or constraints* ought to be imposed upon the activities of the intelligence community?—is also a necessary inquiry. In very general terms, the answer seems clear enough. The CIA and associated agencies are expected to carry out their missions in a manner which does not jeopardize the freedoms of citizens and which is consonant with the goals of the United States in foreign affairs. National security policy, intelligence agencies must always remember, is an aspect of American foreign policy; it should promote—and not hinder—the accomplishment of the nation's purposes abroad. The operations of the CIA, therefore, quite clearly should not embarrass the United States diplomatically, cause tensions in America's relations with other governments, or otherwise create the impression that in foreign affairs the nation is engaged in inconsistent and self-defeating actions abroad.

Such general caveats are of course easier to state than to apply to particular cases confronting the United States at home and overseas, where "Lincoln's dilemma" sometimes appears to be inescapable. Take the highly controversial matter of CIA or FBI efforts to penetrate, or "plant" agents in, citizens' groups within the United States. Ostensibly, such activities represent a threat to internal freedoms; they are the all too familiar tactics of police states which suppress political opposition movements. Yet there is clearly another side to this matter. From the evidence available during World War II, it became clear that Nazi agents had tried (in some cases successfully) to infiltrate and control citizens' organizations in the United States. In the postwar period, intelligence agents of the Soviet Union have utilized the same tactic. The period of Soviet-American détente has witnessed no discernible diminution in efforts by the Kremlin to conduct intelligence and espionage operations within the United States, the NATO area, and other regions. (During the late 1970s, several instances of Soviet efforts to recruit agents within European governments were reported in the press.)

Admittedly, all radical or political opposition groups within the United States are *not* Communist-directed. In the past, intelligence agencies perhaps have not always understood this fact. Yet ongoing Soviet, Cuban, and other foreign intelligence and espionage activities do occur in the United States.

Can the United States government safely ignore this reality? Can the American intelligence community *fail* to take appropriate countermeasures out of fear that the internal liberties of some citizens might be jeopardized, when failure to do so could ultimately endanger the freedoms of *all* citizens? For many concrete cases which arise in this category, it devolves upon the attorney general and courts to decide if and when intelligence operations potentially inimical to the liberties of citizens are legal and justified.

Or consider a different kind of case: CIA-sponsored "intervention " in the political affairs of foreign governments—such as has occurred in Iran, in Vietnam, in Cuba, in Chile, and in other countries since World War II. The circumstances of each case are different, so that generalizations about them are perhaps hazardous. Yet the complexities of the problem can be indicated briefly.

As we shall see in greater detail in Chapter 14, since the New Deal the United States has been identified with the principle of "nonintervention" in the internal political affairs of Latin America. CIA efforts to encourage and assist the overthrow of Communist regimes in Cuba, Chile, and other settings seem to be patently at variance with the nonintervention principle; and public disclosure of such activities unquestionably creates ill-will for the United States abroad. At the same time, it should also be noted that the United States is committed to other principles in hemispheric relations. Perhaps the oldest and best-known tenet of American foreign policy was enunciated in the Monroe Doctrine (1823) and reiterated at frequent intervals thereafter: The United States would resist the efforts of foreign powers to jeopardize the security of the Western Hemisphere. After World War II, this principle of the Monroe Doctrine was accepted and "universalized" as a concept supported by the Organization of

American States (OAS). Under prevailing conditions—the existence of the Cold War between the United States and the Soviet Union—no doubt existed that it was directed primarily at Soviet intervention in the hemisphere. After the communization of Cuba, indisputable evidence existed of Cuban (supported by Soviet) efforts to foment revolutionary activities in other Latin American countries.

Moreover, critics of CIA activities abroad often exhibit an ambivalent attitude toward interventionist behavior by the United States government. While CIA intervention against Cuba or Chile is deplored, such critics often *advocate* interventionist policies *toward right-wing regimes* in Latin America and other regions. Washington's alleged "failure," for example, to "do something about" the oppressive behavior of military-led governments in Brazil or Argentina has also been a matter of deep concern to some commentators on American foreign policy.

On the question of intervention versus nonintervention by the United States in Latin America and other regions, it is extremely difficult to formulate a satisfactory principle to guide American foreign policy. As Chapter 1 emphasized, the United States is one of the superpowers in the international system—and because of that fact, whatever course it takes, it is likely to be accused of "interventionism" in the affairs of other countries. According to some critics, even if it *does nothing* (in responding to the problem, for example, of internal oppression by a military-led government in Latin America) it faces the charge that its *failure* to act amounts to interventionism on the side of dictatorship and suppression of human rights!

Expressed differently, it is hard to formulate a rule of foreign policy which does not amount to saying something as vague and as unilluminating as: The United States should intervene in behalf of "good" causes (i.e., democratic or revolutionary) abroad, but should not intervene to support "bad" causes (like established governments or right-wing political movements).

The salient question really is: Under *what circumstances* is it permissible or desirable for the United States to intervene in political developments abroad? For each case, the consequences of several possible kinds of American action (or inaction) must be weighed carefully, and prospects for successfully achieving American objectives must be calculated. Little is to be gained from adhering to a doctrinaire approach to the problem or from an automatic invocation of the "noninterventionist" (or any other) foreign policy principle. Policy makers must recall that if criticism has been directed at the United States because it *did* intervene in several countries after World War II, the nation has also been denounced because it did *not* intervene to protect the rights of Jews in Germany during the 1930s, or to protect the freedom of Eastern Europe after World War II, or to safeguard the rights of political minorities in many Third World countries in the postwar era.[44]

When considering interventionist actions by intelligence agencies in recent years, note must also be taken of the fact that, in nearly all cases, these agencies *were acting under directives given them by the White House.* The CIA, in other words, was engaged in carrying out missions approved by the National Security Council and the President. In the overwhelming majority of cases, little or no evidence exists demonstrating that the CIA was "out of control" or was otherwise usurping power belonging to the President and his principal subordinates. Moreover, even after evidence of CIA involvement in questionable activities was publicized, the American people expressed no discernible objection to many of them. Direct and indirect efforts to displace the Castro regime in Cuba, for example, were perhaps criticized chiefly *because they failed,* rather than because they were undertaken. For the "Bay of Pigs" fiasco in 1961, the dominant complaint by President Kennedy himself and by many students of American diplomacy was that American intelligence operations *were faulty.* The CIA and other agencies badly misled the President concerning the prospects for a successful anti-Castro movement and underestimated seriously the extent and kind of military force needed to topple Castro's regime. The result was a dramatic diplomatic defeat for the United States.[45] (Admittedly, American foreign policy in Latin America would have been subjected to different, but no less intense, criticisms if the Bay of Pigs invasion of Cuba had succeeded!)

Paradoxically, with regard to the Iranian Revolution at the end of the 1970s, the opposite complaint was heard about American intelligence activities abroad. In that setting, the CIA was castigated because in effect its relations with the Iranian monarchy were "too correct": American intelligence agencies, critics asserted, failed to identify and establish contact with antimonarchial groups and individuals within Iran. The result was that the intelligence community gave the Carter Administration no advance warning of the collapse of the Iranian monarchy. Indeed, the CIA and its companion agencies insisted there was no prospect that a successful revolution against the monarchy could occur! The result was a kind of diplomatic Pearl Harbor for the United States: When rebel groups in Iran did topple the monarchy (much more easily than anyone had expected), officials in Washington were ill-prepared to deal with the resulting "Islamic Republic" or to respond to the broader consequences of the Iranian Revolution for American foreign policy in the Middle East.[46]

If it is almost universally conceded that limits must be placed upon the activities of intelligence agencies, a third fundamental question becomes: Who is to formulate these parameters and how are they to be made effective? Experience has shown that the problem of "controlling" the activities of the members of the intelligence community is not an easy one, in large part because the President and his high-level advisers, along with many senators and representatives, fail to exercise their responsibilities conscientiously in this realm.

When Congress established the Central Intelligence Agency in 1947, it was by no means indifferent to the problem of maintaining adequate controls over its activities. The CIA's mission was specified in the provisions of the National Security Act. According to its terms, CIA was responsible to the National Security Council, headed by the President; this body was expected to provide general guidance to intelligence agencies and to approve their more important missions and assignments. Since 1947, with a few possible exceptions, the evidence indicates that the controls originally envisioned by Congress *have operated as intended.* Whatever judgments may be made about their behavior, the members of the intelligence community have in nearly all instances received specific or general approval for their activities from the nation's highest civilian officials. Not infrequently, the White House has given overall approval to an intelligence mission (like conducting reconnaissance flights over Soviet territory), leaving it to the members of the intelligence community to determine when and how the mission was to be carried out. In addition, incumbent Presidents have also utilized committees of prominent citizens to provide advice and oversight on national intelligence operations. Under the Carter Administration, for example, an Intelligence Oversight Board, consisting of three private citizens appointed by the President, reviewed the activities of the members of the intelligence community; the board was empowered to report directly to the President if it believed these activities raised questions of illegal or improper conduct by intelligence agencies.[47]

Another set of controls over intelligence operations is provided by Congress. The CIA was created by act of Congress in 1947; and its five-fold mission was specified in the provisions of that act. Along with all governmental agencies, members of the intelligence community depend upon Congress for their operating funds. The House and Senate may also exercise their historic right to investigate activities of governmental agencies, in the process often subjecting the operations of those agencies to full public disclosure.

Legislative oversight of intelligence operations, it must be freely acknowledged, has been sporadic, feeble, and in general ineffectual. As a rule, details about the activities of the CIA and other members of the intelligence community have been known only to a handful of legislators (and even they sometimes were not privy to all covert operations). The vast majority of senators and representatives had to be content with the kind of statement regarding CIA operations in Laos made by Senator John Stennis (Democrat of Mississippi), who assured his colleagues: "I think we all know that if we are going to have a CIA, and we have to have a CIA, we cannot run it as a quilting society or something like that." Stennis asked other legislators to accept his assurance that in expending its funds, intelligence agencies were "in the clear and their forthrightness [in explaining their activities to legislative committees] is in the clear." Congress' usual readiness to accept such assurances has been interrupted from time to time, however, by often frenzied, well-publicized congressional investigations of "wrongdoing" by the CIA and other members of the intelligence community. For example, following revelations of CIA involvement in the Watergate episode, along with other evidence of illegal or ineffective intelligence operations, during the late 1970s no less than *eight committees* of the House and Senate were investigating national intelligence operations! Yet as always, Congress was responsive to American public opinion: Within a few months, public attention was diverted to new problems (like the collapse of the Iranian monarchy and the deepening energy crisis at home). Sustained congressional interest in intelligence operations waned rapidly. The Watergate affair aside, it was evident the American people wanted no "dismantling" of the CIA or other fundamental changes which might impair the nation's ability to engage in intelligence operations successfully.

According to one study, legislative control over national intelligence operations has been—and may always be—minimally effective for several basic reasons. As many legislators themselves are aware, Congress is "a well-known fountain of . . . leaks." If intelligence activities become known to a large body of legislators (and their increasingly large staffs), it is almost certain that in time they will become known to the world. In addition, committees of Congress seeking to exercise control over intelligence activities would have to be "bipartisan," consisting of both Democratic and Republican members. This fact would enable the minority party to acquire information about the President's foreign and national security policies which might be politically damaging to him and his supporters in Congress and the nation. Control of intelligence operations by Congress also poses a constitutional question. The CIA and other members of the intelligence community operate under the authority of the President, as head of the executive branch. If legislative committees, or groups of legislators, attempted to "decide" on what intelligence missions should or should not be undertaken, or how they ought to be carried out, Congress would be infringing upon the President's constitutional domain and diluting the responsibility of executive agencies.

Congressional control over intelligence operations has been minimal for another reason. Experience over a generation or so has shown that most senators and representatives *do not want to know* too much about the activities of the intelligence community, for a two-fold reason. If a particular intelligence mission is likely to be successful, legislators do not want to jeopardize its success by risking premature disclosure of information about it. If, on the other hand, the mission fails—and particularly if it results in highly adverse publicity for the CIA and other intelligence agencies—legislators do not want to be closely associated with it; they want to be left free to "expose" the failure of an undertaking which "Congress knew nothing about"![48]

Congressional failure to impose tight control over intelligence operations also stems from another factor, which we shall examine more fully in Chapter 7: the internal organization and procedures of Congress itself. Here we may note briefly that after the Vietnam War—perhaps more than in any era of recent American history—Congress was experiencing great difficulty in organizing its own activities coherently and in arriving at unified expressions of national policy. Political party organization was weak—and was perhaps becoming weaker every year. Committees and subcommittees of Congress have continued to proliferate; and their jurisdictions increasingly overlapped. Moreover, the 1970s witnessed a significant "turnover" in the House and Senate. A number of legislators with high seniority left Congress, and

their places were taken by new members, who were often disposed to defy long-standing legislative practices and to demonstrate their "independence" of the House and Senate leadership structures, as well as of the White House.

In addition, as always, congressional attitudes were heavily conditioned by prevailing popular sentiment. In the post-Vietnam War era, American public opinion was more than ordinarily confused and uncertain about the nation's proper foreign policy role. If most Americans did not want "another Vietnam," this did not mean that they favored a return to classical isolationism or that they were indifferent to challenges like the rapid growth in Soviet military power. If public opinion was now fully mindful of the problem of becoming "overextended" abroad, it was also conscious as never before of the nation's dependence upon access to foreign oil supplies, to the impact of expanding imports upon their own domestic prosperity, and to the overall fact of interdependency governing the behavior of all nations in the international system. If the American people approved attempts to reach new arms-control agreements with the Soviet Union, they no less favored efforts to preserve a defense posture "second to none," capable of protecting the security interests of the United States and friendly countries.

Several commentators on recent American foreign policy called attention to the fact that the old "anti-Communist consensus" which had supported American foreign policy for almost a generation after World War II had disintegrated (or was badly shattered). Yet a new national consensus on the proper goals and means of United States foreign policy had not emerged. Until it did, legislative efforts to impose clear and rigid guidelines upon intelligence activities would continue to be half-hearted and only partially successful.[49]

NOTES

1. Two convenient abridgments of General Clausewitz's thought are available. One is Roger A. Leonard, ed., *A Short Guide to Clausewitz on War* (New York: Capricorn Books, 1968); the quotations from Clausewitz are on pp. 11 and 13. The other is Anatol Rapoport, ed., *Clausewitz on War* (Baltimore, Md.: Penguin Books, 1968). An even briefer discussion is H. Rothfels, "Clausewitz," in Edward M. Earle, ed., *Makers of Modern Strategy: Military Thought from Machiavelli to Hitler* (New York: Atheneum, 1966), pp. 93–117.

2. Thus, Mao Tse-tung, the leader of the Chinese Communist movement until his death in 1976, once wrote: "...war is politics and war itself is a political action; there has not been a single war since ancient times that did not bear a political character....War is a special political technique for the realization of certain political objectives...." Quoted in Stuart R. Schram, *The Political Thought of Mao Tse-tung* (New York: Praeger Publishers, 1963), pp. 209–210.

3. See the illuminating discussion of the Roosevelt Administration's approach to controversial political issues (like the future of Poland and Germany) during the war in Gaddis Smith, *American Diplomacy During the Second World War: 1941–45* (New York: John Wiley and Sons, 1965), pp. 53–54. Smith emphasizes FDR's tendency to take "diplomacy more and more into his own hands at a time when his health, memory and powers of concentration were declining." His general conclusion is that, "Until 1944 military necessity gave orders to American diplomacy" (p. 119). A more general analysis of the subject—focusing upon several cases during World War II in which American officials failed to consider the relationship between military force and diplomacy—is Hanson W. Baldwin, *Great Mistakes of the War* (New York: Harper & Row, 1950).

4. A detailed analysis of American military strategy at the end of the war as it bore on Western versus Soviet occupation of Berlin and Germany is Stephen E. Ambrose, *Eisenhower and Berlin, 1945: the Decision to Halt at the Elbe* (New York: W. W. Norton, 1967).

5. For Kissinger's views, see Colin S. Gray, "The Strategic Forces Triad: End of the Road?" *Foreign Affairs,* **56** (July, 1978), 774.

6. Ibid., pp. 771–790.

7. These and other major examples of American military interventionism since World War II are analyzed in detail in Herbert K. Tillema, *Appeal to Force: American Military Intervention in the Era of Containment* (New York: Thomas Y. Crowell, 1973).

8. See, for example, the Soviet view of détente, which permits Kremlin support for revolutionary movements abroad, as presented in Coral Bell, *The Diplomacy of Détente: The Kissinger Era* (New York: St. Martin's Press, 1977), pp. 3–6.

9. Michael Howard, "The Forgotten Dimensions of Strategy," *Foreign Affairs,* **57** (Summer, 1979), 975–987.

10. Bernard Brodie, *War and Politics* (New York: Macmillan Co., 1973), pp. 343–344, 364. See also William W. Whitson, "The Global Security Environment of 1977: Security Concepts for National Leadership," in William W. Whitson, ed., *Foreign Policy and U. S. National Security: Major Postelection Issues* (New York: Praeger Publishers, 1976), p. 3.

11. Paul Seabury, "Beyond Détente," in James R. Schlesinger, ed., *Defending America: Toward a New Role in the Post-Détente World* (New York: Basic Books, 1977), pp. 242–243.

12. Gray, "The Strategic Forces Triad," p. 773. Italics in the original.

13. The importance of perceptions (and misperceptions) in shaping national policy is emphasized in the study by John G. Stoessinger, *Nations in Darkness: China, Russia, America* (New York: Random House, 1971).

14. Former President Eisenhower's views are quoted in *The Power of the Pentagon* (Wash-

ington, D.C.: Congressional Quarterly Inc., 1972), p. 2.

15. The relationship between military and political aspects of national policy in the United States before World War II is discussed in Ernest R. May, "The Development of Political-Military Consultation in the United States," *Political Science Quarterly,* **70** (June, 1955), 161–181.

16. See, for example, one former American diplomat's account of American indifference to political questions in the campaign in North Africa during the war, in Robert Murphy, *Diplomat Among Warriors* (New York: Pyramid Books, 1965), pp. 82–211. Military pressure upon President Roosevelt to gain a promise of Soviet entry into the war against Japan is described in James F. Byrnes, *Speaking Frankly* (New York: Harper & Row, 1947); and in Sidney Warren, *The President As World Leader* (New York: McGraw-Hill, 1964), pp. 252, 261–262.

17. For the views of General Marshall and General Bradley, see James Clotfelter, *The Military in American Politics* (New York: Harper & Row, 1973), p. 229; and General Omar N. Bradley, *A Soldier's Story* (New York: Holt, Rinehart and Winson, 1951), p. 536.

18. The ideas motivating American defense reorganization after World War II are discussed at length in Timothy W. Stanley, *American Defense and National Security* (Washington, D.C.: Public Affairs Press, 1956). Another useful account is William R. Kinter, *Forging a New Sword* (New York: Harper & Row, 1958).

19. The influence of congressional thinking upon postwar defense reorganization is highlighted in Russell Baker, "Again Vinson Mounts the Ramparts," *New York Times Magazine,* May 4, 1958, pp. 13, 78.

20. Clotfelter, *The Military in American Politics,* p. 199.

21. For more comprehensive discussion of the evolution of the National Security Council, illustrating how different presidents have used the agency, see Keith C. Clark and Laurence J. Legere, eds., *The President and the Management of National Security* (New York: Praeger Publishers, 1969). President Eisenhower's conception of NSC is depicted in Robert Cutler, "The Development of the National Security Council," *Foreign Affairs,* **34** (April, 1956), 441–458. How NSC's influence in policy making has expanded is brought out in John P. Leacacos, "Kissinger's Apparat," *Foreign Policy,* **5** (Winter, 1971–72), 3–28; and in Stephen D. Krasner, "Are Bureaucracies Important?" ibid., **7** (Summer, 1972), 159–182.

22. Dr. Kissinger's often crucial influence upon American foreign policy is brought out clearly in Marvin Kalb and Bernard Kalb, *Kissinger* (New York: Dell Books, 1975); and in David Landau, *Kissinger: the Uses of Power* (New York: Thomas Y. Crowell, 1974).

23. For a discussion of the influence of National Security Adviser Zbigniew Brzezinski upon the Carter Administration's foreign policy, see Richard Burt, in *New York Times,* July 20, 1979.

24. For a discussion of the pros and cons of the neutron bomb, emphasizing the military's interest in acquiring it, see Brigadier General Edwin F. Black, "The Neutron Bomb and the Defense of NATO," *Military Review,* **LVIII** (May, 1978), 53–62.

25. Data on comparative American and Soviet defense expenditures in recent years are drawn from several sources. An informative one is the annual report to Congress by the secretary of defense. See *Annual Report: Fiscal Year 1980* (Washington, D.C.: Government Printing Office, 1979) and other reports in this series. The annual volumes of *Statistical Abstract of the United States* (Washington, D.C.: Bureau of the Census) provide brief information on the subject. See also Richard Burt, "The Scope and Limits of SALT," *Foreign Affairs,* **56** (July, 1978), 751–771; and Gray, "The Strategic Forces Triad," pp. 771–790.

26. Detailed discussions and analyses of particular aspects of Soviet military escalation in the past decade or so are provided in: the secretary of defense's *Annual Report: Fiscal Year 1980,* pp. 49–63; Aaron L. Friedberg, "What SALT Can (and Cannot) Do," *Foreign Poli-*

cy, **33** (Winter, 1978–79), 92–101; Richard T. Ackley, "Strategic Arms Limitation: the Problem of Deterrence," in Whitson, ed., *Foreign Policy and U.S. National Security,* pp. 221–245; Major Tyrus W. Cobb, "Military Imbalance: Soviet Expansion During Détente," *Military Review,* **LVII** (March, 1977), 79–86; and Paul Nitze, "Nuclear Strategy: Détente and American Survival," in Schlesinger, ed., *Defending America,* pp. 97–109.

27. On Soviet-American competition in naval power, see Admiral Stansfield Turner, "The Naval Balance: Not Just a Numbers Game," *Foreign Affairs,* **55** (January, 1977), 339–355.

28. For alternative explanations of Soviet military expansion, see Johan J. Holst, "What Is Really Going on?" *Foreign Policy,* **19** (Summer, 1975), 155–163; Michael L. Nacht, "The Delicate Balance of Error," ibid., 163–178; and Alton Frye, "Strategic Restraint, Mutual and Assured," ibid., **27** (Summer, 1977), 3–27.

29. For the views of Joint Chiefs of Staff Chairman General David C. Jones on the growing Soviet-American military imbalance, and related data, see the Department of Defense's publication, *United States Military Posture for FY 1980* (Washington, D.C.: Government Printing Office, 1979), p. iv and *passim.*

30. See the data on the Soviet and American nuclear arsenals presented by Flora Lewis in *New York Times,* March 21, 1982; and in *Time,* **119** (April 12, 1982), 12-14.

31. Current Soviet military doctrines are discussed in: John Erickson, "Soviet Ground Forces and the Conventional Mode of Operations," *Military Review,* **LVII** (January, 1977), 49–57; Joseph C. Arnold, "Current Soviet Tactical Doctrine: A Reflection of the Past," ibid., **LVII** (July, 1977), 16–24; and Nitze, "Nuclear Strategy: Détente and American Survival," pp. 97–109.

32. In 1979, Defense Secretary Harold Brown said that in most components of military strength, the Soviet Union did not "have a comparative advantage over the United States." He and other American officials reiterated the idea that they would rather have America's military position over Soviet Russia's. See Department of Defense, *Annual Report: Fiscal Year 1980,* p. 4. A number of commentators concurred in this assessment. See Jan M. Lodal, "SALT II and American Security," *Foreign Affairs,* **57** (Winter, 1978/79), 245–269.

33. The implications of possible Soviet strategic superiority over the United States are discussed in: Nitze, "Nuclear Strategy: Détente and American Survival," pp. 102–103; and in Burt, "The Scope and Limits of SALT," 761–762.

34. Data on the nature and size of America's armed forces are contained in Department of Defense, *Annual Report for Fiscal Year 1980,* pp. 67–82, and in the Appendix, p. C-1. See also *United States Military Posture for FY 1980, passim.*

35. Information on the growth of conventional Soviet military power, and on how the Kremlin envisions its role, is contained in: Department of Defense, *Annual Report for Fiscal Year 1980,* pp. 4–8; 49–63; Cobb, "Military Imbalance: Soviet Expansion During Détente," 79–86; and see the analysis of the implications of the Soviet-American military balance by Secretary of State Alexander Haig in the State Department's publication, "Peace and Deterrence," *Current Policy,* **383** (April 6, 1982), 1–4.

36. Constraints upon Soviet military power are discussed in Department of Defense, *United States Military Posture for FY 1980,* p. iv.

37. The story of an expanding Soviet "presence" in Egypt after the 1967 war in the Middle East, followed by rising Egyptian resentment toward Russian behavior, is told in Alvin Z. Rubinstein, *Red Star On the Nile: the Soviet-Egyptian Influence Relationship Since the June War* (Princeton, N.J.: Princeton University Press, 1977). For a more general discussion of the constraints upon Soviet policy in the Middle East, many of which are broadly applicable to the Third World, see R. D. McLaurin, *The Middle East in Soviet Policy* (Lexington, Mass.: D. C. Heath, 1975), pp. 47–67.

38. Background on the emergence of the Ameri-

can intelligence community is provided in: Allan W. Dulles, *The Craft of Intelligence* (New York: Harper & Row, 1963); and Sherman Kent, *Strategic Intelligence* (Princeton, N.J.: Princeton University Press, 1949). More up-to-date information on the activities of the American intelligence community is available in: Lyman B. Kirkpatrick, Jr., *The U.S. Intelligence Community: Foreign Policy and Domestic Activities* (New York: Hill and Wang, 1973); David Wise and Thomas B. Ross, *The Espionage Establishment* (New York: Bantam Books, 1967), pp. 116–156; Wise and Ross, *The Invisible Government: the CIA and U.S. Intelligence* (New York: Random House, 1974); and Harry H. Ransom, *The Intelligence Establishment* (Cambridge, Mass.: Harvard University Press, 1970).

39. A summary of these and other well-publicized American intelligence activities during the postwar period is contained in Editorial Research Reports, *America's Changing World Role* (Washington, D.C.: Congressional Quarterly, Inc., 1974), p. 175.

40. An informative and objective discussion of the U.S. intelligence community as it had evolved down to 1980 is Tad Szulc, "Shaking Up the C. I. A.," *New York Times Magazine,* July 29, 1979, pp. 13–21, 33–46. See also the detailed article on American intelligence activities in *Time,* **111** (February 6, 1978), 10–18.

41. See the views of Harry H. Ransom, as cited in Editorial Research Reports, *America's Changing World Role,* p. 174.

42. Changes in the CIA and in the intelligence community generally under the Carter Administration are highlighted in Szulc, "Shaking Up the C. I. A.," *passim.*

43. The pivotal role of the CIA and other intelligence agencies in perpetrating the Cold War and in accounting for an antirevolutionary bias in postwar American foreign policy is emphasized in several studies. See, for example, Richard J. Walton, *Cold War and Counter-Revolution: the Foreign Policy of John F. Kennedy* (Baltimore: Penguin Books, 1972); Richard J. Barnet, *The Roots of War: the Men and Institutions Behind U.S. Foreign Policy* (Baltimore: Penguin Books, 1972); and Michael T. Klare, *War Without End: American Planning for the Next Vietnams* (New York: Random House, 1972).

44. For a general analysis of the dilemmas and constraints confronting American officials in deciding whether to intervene in the political affairs of other countries, see the concluding chapter in Tillema, *Appeal to Force,* pp. 179–200; and Marshall D. Shylman, "On Learning to Live with Authoritarian Regimes," *Foreign Affairs,* **55** (January, 1977), 325–339.

45. The intelligence failure involved in the 1961 "Bay of Pigs" invasion of Cuba is discussed more fully in Arthur Schlesinger, Jr., *A Thousand Days: John F. Kennedy in the White House* (Boston: Houghton Mifflin Co., 1965), pp. 250–297; and in Theodore C. Sorensen, *Kennedy* (New York: Harper & Row, 1965), pp. 294–309.

46. The failure of the American intelligence community to alert the White House to the possible overthrow of the Iranian monarchy in 1979 is analyzed fully in Szulc, "Shaking Up the C. I. A.," 16–17.

47. Ibid., 45.

48. A succinct summary of the reasons why legislative oversight of intelligence operations has been minimally effective may be found in Editorial Research Report, *America's Changing World Role,* pp. 182–184.

49. The problems involved in the continuing challenge of "controlling" intelligence activities in a democratic setting are analyzed more fully in Herbert Scoville, Jr., "Is Espionage Necessary for Our Security?" *Foreign Affairs,* **54** (April, 1976), 482–496; Peter Szunton and Graham Allison, "Intelligence: Seizing the Opportunity," *Foreign Policy,* **22** (Spring, 1976), 183–206; and William E. Colby, *et al.,* "Reorganizing the CIA: Who and How," ibid., **23** (Summer, 1976), 53–64.

Chapter 6

Propaganda and Economic Policy Instruments

One of the striking features of the contemporary international system, as we noted in Chapter 1, is the evolution which has occurred in the concept of national power. In this chapter, we shall examine two manifestations of this phenomenon: America's use of propaganda and informational programs, and its reliance upon economic instruments —principally, foreign aid and trade.

The Concept of "Psychological Warfare"

Psychological Dimensions of Diplomacy

Since the end of World War II, the United States and the Soviet Union have been engaged in a form of competition often described as "a battle for the minds of men." From another perspective, commentators on American foreign policy almost daily inform officials in Washington that the nation's "image" throughout the Third World is poor, and this fact detracted from the ability of the United States to influence developments in that zone. These are merely two examples

calling attention to the importance of *psychological* aspects of diplomacy in the modern period. As our earlier discussion of national power emphasized, the *perception* (or misperception) of America's power by foreign nations may often be more crucial than the objective facts about the power of the United States.

The concept widely employed today to describe this aspect of diplomacy—"psychological warfare"—can be traced back into ancient history.* When the Greeks failed to capture Troy by force of arms, they resorted to

*In common with many other general concepts, definitions of such terms as *psychological warfare* and *propaganda* often vary considerably; any definition offered is likely to reflect the emphases that the user thinks most basic or relevant to his discussion. Numerous definitions are thus available. Psychological warfare may be thought of as "the use of propaganda against an enemy, together with such other operational measures of a military, economic or political nature as may be required to supplement propaganda." Propaganda is a narrower concept, normally comprising only one element in psychological warfare. Propaganda may be conceived to be

skillful deception—the Trojan Horse—to bring them victory. In early American history, one purpose of the Declaration of Independence was to gain widespread support in England and Europe for the colonial cause by identifying it with the political aspirations of Western society as a whole. During World War I, tons of propaganda in the form of press releases, leaflets, posters, booklets, pictures, and the like, emanated from the Allied side. These were acknowledged by German military leaders as having been singularly effective in undermining the military and civilian morale of the Central Powers and in turning neutral opinion against their cause. One of the most brilliant Allied propaganda victories in the period was won through the proclamation of President Wilson's "Fourteen Points," which were of inestimable value in shortening the war by weakening the will to resist among populations in the enemy camp.[1]

No universally accepted definition of psychological warfare exists; and, indeed, it may be more difficult than ever in the contemporary period to formulate a satisfactory one. The earlier distinction which many Americans believed existed between peace and war is largely untenable today. Concepts like "cold war" or "protracted struggle" or "wars of national liberation," which may be applied to various categories of international crisis, suggest a close conjunction between traditionally peaceful and violent instruments of foreign policy. Even though it has moderated significantly since the 1950s, the Cold War between the United States and the Soviet Union still involves *a synthesis* of diplomatic techniques, ranging from preservation of a "credible" military establishment on each side to efforts by Washington and Moscow to win the goodwill of Afro-Asian societies.

Although they may often be difficult to differentiate in practice, two broad categories of psychological and informational activities in foreign relations may be identified. One of these is *psychological warfare*. As the term implies, it is a form of *conflict* among nations. It may be used either in *conjunction with* military force or as a *substitute for* it. Nearly all armed conflicts in the modern era have involved intensive propaganda campaigns against the enemy, as well as propaganda programs directed at the home front. Nations utilize psychological instruments during warfare to undermine the enemy's will to fight and to hasten his capitulation, to win victories as cheaply as possible, to convince the enemy that his defeat is certain, and generally to enhance the achievement of victory. Psychological techniques also sometimes can replace the need to apply force; a successful propaganda campaign, for example, can contribute to achieving certain goals (like the surrender of an enemy force, or the collapse of an unfriendly government, or the change in a government's policies) which might otherwise have to be effected by armed force.

The other category of psychological activity in foreign affairs which can be identified entails *normal informational and propaganda programs conducted in an overall atmosphere of relatively peaceful relationships*. Many relationships among nations are essentially peaceful and cooperative, although elements of conflict may sometimes be present in

---

"planned use of any form of public or mass-produced communication designed to affect the minds and emotions of a given group for a specific public purpose, whether military, economic, or political." Propaganda is concerned with *the written or spoken word* as an instrument of statecraft. These and other definitions are cited in Urban G. Whitaker, Jr., *Propaganda and International Relations* (San Francisco: Chandler, 1962), pp. 4–5; see also the views presented in Terence H. Qualter, *Propaganda and Psychological Warfare* (New York: Random House, 1962), pp. 15, 27.

them—as in America's relations with Great Britain or Japan in the contemporary period.

Even in this category of relationships, however, psychological instruments of foreign policy are routinely employed to achieve the nation's objectives. Thus, the United States has endeavored to create and preserve cohesion among the members of NATO; it has endeavored to eliminate sources of misunderstanding in American-Canadian relations; it has tried to promote a greater sense of common purpose and shared concerns among the nations of the Western Hemisphere; it has sought to convince the free nations of Africa that it respects their independence and will assist them in attaining their development goals.

As the concept of détente between the United States and the Soviet Union illustrated, in reality America's relations with other countries were, as often as not, likely to include both psychological warfare and more peaceful propaganda-informational elements. Détente between the superpowers, for example, entailed no diminution in competition between them on several fronts—such as military strength and technology, ideological rivalry, and efforts to influence the political behavior of the Third World. Soviet policy makers (more than their American counterparts) made it clear that détente was merely a new form of conflict or struggle between the superpowers. At the same time, détente also resulted in new forms of Soviet-American cooperation (as in certain aspects of the space program), in more extensive cultural and economic exchange between the two countries, and in an overall reduction in in tensions between them vis-à-vis the Cold War era.

Propaganda and American Foreign Policy

In this chapter, we shall concentrate on propaganda as a major technique of psycho-

logical warfare, defining it as the effort of one group or nation to influence the actions of another group or nation *by primary reliance upon methods of systematic persuasion, including methods of verbal coercion and inducement*. Propaganda is to be distinguished from other forms of psychological warfare by its utilization of the written and spoken word. Successful utilization of methods of persuasion depends in no small degree upon the effectiveness of other weapons in the arsenal of national power, such as economic strength and military force. Threats, unsupported by the requisite military power, are usually ineffectual; promises and inducements, without the willingness and capacity to make good on them, are equally worthless as diplomatic tools.

The successful propagandist is required to have a well-stocked and versatile arsenal and to be skilled in the use of these weapons. Among the variety of weapons available are radio broadcasts, television programs, speeches, films, public rallies and demonstrations, various symbols like armbands, flags, slogans, or buttons, posters, cartoons, comic books, newspapers, timely "leaks" of official information, libraries, lectures, seminars, clandestine radios, articles in magazines, news conferences, and a host of other techniques.[2] In successfully employing any or all of these techniques, the propagandist is continually conscious of a fact that is at the center of his operations. This is that propaganda is merely a *single instrument* of foreign policy; as such, it is intimately related to, and its success ultimately depends upon, the effective use and skillful coordination of other instruments to achieve diplomatic goals.

A high-ranking official in charge of America's postwar propaganda campaign once said that "Ninety percent of the impression which the United States makes abroad depends on our policies and not more than 10 percent . . . on how we explain [them]."[3] Or, as President Kennedy once expressed the idea: "It is a dangerous illusion to believe that the policies of the United States . . . can be encompassed in one slogan or adjective, hard or soft or otherwise." And referring to propaganda on another occasion, he asserted: "If we are strong, our strength will speak for itself. If we are weak, words will be of no help."[4] After recognizing that propaganda is always an *auxiliary instrument,* whose effectiveness is a function of the nation's overall foreign policy, it must be added that it can sometimes be a crucial policy component.

Several further points about propaganda require emphasis. A popular misconception is that propaganda is inherently false. This misconception explains in some measure why Americans have often been loath to support the propaganda activities of their government. Knowing that certain information is "propaganda" tells us nothing about the veracity or falsity of that information. The etymology of the word *propaganda* enables us to keep this point clearly in mind. Its root is the Latin verb *propagare,* meaning to propagate, to spread, to disseminate, to extend, to transmit. The term first came into historical currency after the establishment of the College of Propaganda by Pope Urban VIII (1623–1644), to promote the missionary activities of the Roman Catholic Church. Throughout the greater part of history, propaganda possessed none of the insidious connotations later associated with it in the Nazi or Communist periods. It meant merely the process of trying to gain converts to a particular cause, initially the Christian gospel as expounded by the Vatican. The process of propaganda, then, is the act of disseminating a belief; or propaganda may describe the belief so disseminated.[5]

Confusion can enter into any discussion

of propaganda, however, when we inquire: "What is good and bad propaganda?" In a *tactical* sense, good propaganda is that which attains its intended result—gaining converts for the belief in question—and bad propaganda is that which fails to attain this result. In an *ethical* sense, according to the Judeo-Christian tradition prevalent in the West, good propaganda is that which accords as nearly as possible with objective truth, and bad propaganda is that which relies heavily upon various forms of deception, falsehood, and chicanery. Whatever the ethical standards by which propaganda is judged, however, *any* propaganda, including of course American, is to be distinguished from an objective search for truth. The object of all propaganda is to utilize *carefully selected* data to induce the hearer to accept a predetermined point of view. The propagandist may *use* the truth—in fact, successful propaganda nearly always necessitates its use—but he is not *seeking* it objectively, nor is he prepared to follow where a dispassionate search for truth may lead.* This is the cardinal distinction between propaganda and education.

Propaganda, as we have suggested, often

---

*The relationship between truthfulness and propaganda may be highlighted by recalling the legal distinction between "the truth" and "the whole truth"; a fact or statement may of course be the former without necessarily being the latter. Effective propaganda must be grounded upon truth, if for no other reason than that falsehoods, when exposed, undermine the propagandist's credibility. Thus a study of American propaganda efforts by a House Foreign Affairs subcommittee in 1967 called for a new approach "based on telling the truth"; but it also demanded greater "selectivity" among the facts and ideas presented. USIA's goal ought to be an "attempt at persuasion . . . based on intelligent selection and emphasis"; fact should be used "with an objective in mind." Quoted in John W. Henderson, *The United States Information Agency* (New York: Praeger, 1969), p. 212.

arouses a feeling of revulsion among individuals steeped in the Western liberal or Judeo-Christian traditions, particularly if it is equated with outright falsehood. Yet, from another perspective, propaganda can properly be regarded as an alternative to military force in the conduct of international affairs. Wars occur when argumentation and negotiation *fail* to safeguard the vital interests of nations, leaving them no alternative but recourse to armaments. The ultimate objective of the United States therefore is not the elimination of propaganda per se as a permissible technique of international relations; rather, it is the substitution of words for bullets, so that propaganda and other nonviolent techniques may accomplish in the future what machine guns, howitzers, and, in the contemporary era, nuclear arsenals accomplish in safeguarding the nation's security interests and promoting its diplomatic objectives.

Americans, we may as well frankly acknowledge, usually have a highly negative mind set toward such concepts as psychological warfare and propaganda. Such techniques are perhaps associated in the American mind chiefly with the expansive and ruthless policies of Nazi Germany before and during World War II and, in the postwar era, with aggressive Soviet policies. The Third Reich's chief propagandist, Dr. Joseph Goebbels, was a skilled and unprincipled practitioner of the art.[6] From the beginning, the Communist regime in the U.S.S.R. has been guided by Lenin's contention that "Ideas are weapons." By the early 1980s, the Soviet Union was spending approximately $3 billion annually on propaganda activities—some six times America's expenditure for propaganda purposes.[7] Despite their own reliance upon propaganda during curcial states of their history, Americans have tended to derogate "mere talk" and to denigrate the role which propaganda plays in contemporary international politics. The level of appropriations provided by Congress for that purpose has reflected such deep-seated skepticism in the American mind.

Postwar Propaganda Activities

The United States was a comparative latecomer in recognizing the centrality of psychological warfare as an instrument of foreign policy. During World War I, the Creel Committee carried on an intensive campaign of propaganda which made a significant contribution to the Allied war effort. But from 1919 until the late 1930s, the United States conducted no noteworthy psychological warfare activities as a part of its foreign relations. Then in the late 1930s, several agencies within the government, particularly the Division of Cultural Relations in the State Department, began to undertake propaganda operations directed toward Latin America, where the threat of Axis penetration had become imminent.

Several civilian and military agencies with responsibilities in the propaganda field, such as the Office of Strategic Services and the Office of War Information, emerged during World War II. As a result of their contributions to the war effort, the United States acquired a backlog of experience and personnel trained in the propaganda field. After the war, many of the functions performed by these agencies were either eliminated or transferred helter-skelter to the Department of State. Yet until the Korean War, in 1950, postwar propaganda activities by the American government were fragmented and were accorded low priority by executive policy makers.

Disturbed by Communist gains in the early postwar era—and the Soviet Union's acquisition of nuclear weapons in 1949 was a noteworthy event—President Truman inaugurated a new and intensified American propaganda program, called the "Campaign of Truth." Its declared purpose was

> ...to present the truth to the millions of people who are uninformed or misinformed or unconvinced...to reach them in their daily lives, as they work and learn...to show them that freedom is the way to economic and social advancement, the way to political independence, the way to strength, happiness, and peace...[to] make ourselves known as we really are—not as Communist propaganda pictures us.[8]

Yet in time it became clear that these efforts by the Truman Administration to strengthen America's propaganda activities were only partially successful. After President Eisenhower took office in 1952, evidence mounted that the United States was lagging behind its ideological opponents in presenting its point of view to the outside world. Administratively, as one study concluded, the American propaganda campaign in this period consisted chiefly of a "patchwork of pieces." Organizational responsibility for conducting programs remained scattered, and the programs themselves were inadequate to meet the challenge. Consequently, upon the recommendation of President Eisenhower, the United States Information Agency (USIA), headed by a director appointed by the President, was established on August 1, 1953. The State Department was divested of operating responsibility for propaganda and informational programs, although USIA remained under the supervision of the State Department for overall policy guidance.

For some 25 years, the United States Information Agency functioned as the principal propaganda arm of the nation in foreign affairs.[9] Throughout its history, USIA had a "stormy" existence, characterized by frequent conflicts among executive and legislative officials concerning its proper "mission." Time and again, the question was raised concerning whether USIA's efforts were in fact promoting the foreign policy objectives of the United States. As had been true since the end of World War II, legislators were dubious about many of the agency's programs; and they were especially apprehensive about possible efforts to propagandize the American people and members of Congress.

On April 1, 1978, a new agency—the United States International Communication Agency (USICA)—was created to replace USIA; smaller administrative units having responsibilities in this field (such as the State Department's Bureau of Educational and Cultural Affairs) were merged into the new agency.[10] USICA is headed by a director, who reports to the President and to the secretary of state; and the agency advises the National Security Council on worldwide public opinion as it relates to American foreign policy. In common with the State Department, USICA is organized both functionally and geographically. Certain programs—like the broadcasting efforts of USICA's radio arm, the Voice of America (VOA)—are conducted across national and regional frontiers. The five regional bureaus of USICA endeavor to tailor America's propaganda and informational activities to specific audiences in Latin America, Africa, and other areas. Shortwave radio broadcasts by the Voice of America are transmitted in English and 39 foreign languages. In addition, USICA produces motion pictures and TV programs; publishes magazines and pamphlets; issues wireless bulletins and other forms of news releases; operates more than 250 libraries devoted to Americana in most countries of the world; sponsors educational and scientific exchange programs between the United States and foreign countries; provides services for foreign journalists working in the United States; and engages in numerous other activities designed to disseminate information about the United States abroad. By 1980, some 205 posts, in 125 foreign countries, operated under USICA's jurisdiction. The agency had close to 9000 employees and an annual budget of over $400 million.

When he established the agency, President Carter gave USICA a five-fold mission. Its objectives were: (1) to encourage, sponsor, and aid the broadest possible exchange of people and ideas between the United States and foreign countries; (2) to give peoples outside the United States a better understanding of America's policies and intentions; (3) to provide policy makers with information on, and understanding of, public opinion abroad; (4) to assist in the formulation of a national policy on international communications designed to promote the maximum flow of information and ideas among societies; and (5) to prepare for and participate in negotiations providing for cultural exchanges among nations.

Since USICA is a relatively new agency, there has been insufficient time in which to evaluate its performance adequately. One of the purposes of the reorganization undertaken in 1978 was to provide for greater *centralization* of the American government's efforts in the propaganda field; and the creation of USICA has unquestionably contributed to that goal. Yet for many years, American propaganda and informational efforts have been plagued by the existence of several recurrent problems and controversies, many of which, it is safe to predict, will pose obstacles to the nation's propaganda activities in the future. Let us focus upon five major questions central to American propaganda activities.

Continuing Challenges and Dilemmas

Early in 1982, major personnel changes were made by the Reagan Administration in the Voice of America, the nation's principal radio propaganda instrument. According to one report, the new director of VOA (John Hughes, a former reporter for the *Christian Science Monitor*) would be "caught in a tug of war" between the agency's "news and propaganda functions."[11] Such dilemmas were not new to American propaganda activities. Since the early post-World War II period, continuing and sometimes acrimonious controversy has surrounded discussion of the *precise mission* or goal of American propaganda efforts.

Two rather contradictory answers have been given to that question, and how the question is resolved will influence how USICA's performance is assessed. One point of view has long held that governmental agencies engaged in propaganda and informational activities should be frankly regarded *as instruments for the promotion of American foreign policy goals*. According to this conception, USICA has one paramount goal which ought to guide its activities: to facilitate in every possible way America's ability to *accomplish its diplomatic purposes*. Necessary corollaries of this idea are that the radio broadcasts by the Voice of America, the TV programs and news releases prepared by USICA, and all its other programs should be directed at conveying *as favorable an image as possible* of the United States. Toward the all-pervasive Cold War contest between the United States and the Soviet Union, America's propaganda program should have one paramount objective: to enable the United States to "win" the Cold War against its Soviet rival. As a former director of USIA said to President John F. Kennedy:

> any program established by government funds can only be justified to the extent that it assists in the achievement of the national objectives [of the United States] ... that *is* the purpose, sole purpose of USIA today.

Or as one observer formulated the Reagan Administration's conception of the proper role of American propaganda agencies: "President Reagan is intent on projecting an image of a more muscular America willing to safeguard its interests anywhere in the world." In addition, Washington sought "to counter a Soviet [propaganda] offensive that depicts America as a warmonger and Russia as a peacemaker."[12]

The other approach to USICA's proper mission is, in many respects, antithetical to the former conception. The key motif in this point of view is perhaps the idea of "credibility" as an essential element in successful propaganda operations.[13] To cite an outstanding example, by many criteria the most successful propaganda campaign waged during World War II was conducted by the British Broadcasting Corporation (BBC). The BBC acquired this reputation for one reason above all: Its broadcasts *were essentially truthful and factual, giving them credibility* to those who heard them. Even (as during the "Battle of Britain" early in the war) when objective broadcasting was not always favorable to Britain or the Allied war effort, the BBC preserved its factual approach. Then, as the tide of battle turned —and as the BBC told the peoples in Axis-dominated countries that the Allies were winning the war—the BBC's reputation for truthfulness greatly enhanced readiness on the enemy side to believe its messages. Unlike Nazi propaganda activities, the BBC's statements were not dismissed as "mere propaganda" by the hearer.

According to one interpretation, American propaganda programs ought to be guided by the same principle. As President Truman's "Campaign of Truth" implied, the dominant goal ought to be to portray American life and the policies of the United States government *truthfully,* in order to enhance receptivity for these activities by foreigners. This approach reflects the old principle that "honesty is the best policy" in informational and propaganda programs, since in the long run (in view of the existence of a resourceful and extensive free press) the truth about America is going to be told anyhow and disseminated around the world.* When that occurs, any fundamental discrepancy between information dispensed by government agencies and the facts will nearly always redound to the *discredit* of the United States, thereby impairing its diplomatic efforts. Propaganda agencies of the American government should never try to rival the efforts of Nazi Germany or Communist Russia in duplicitous, distorted, and unprincipled use of propaganda techniques.

This approach dictates that if the American society still experiences racial disputes and conflicts, then the USICA should say so and discuss the problem candidly. Or in foreign affairs, if the CIA has been "caught" intervening in the political affairs of a country like Chile, USICA should not attempt to hide or deny that fact. USICA should depict the American society *as it really is,* while providing objective and informative discussion of controversial features of the nation's domestic and foreign policy.

Organizational reform, like that resulting in the creation of USICA, has not eliminated the conflict between these two differing conceptions of the role of progaganda in American foreign policy. The conflict is perhaps *in-*

---

*Thus, one experienced official of the VOA has said that the credibility of America's propaganda campaign was greatly enhanced "by our candid reporting of the Watergate affair. After hearing us report on it for months, our listeners realized we were honestly reporting the dismantling of our government." A congressional charter for VOA programming, issued in 1976, emphasized that the maintenance of the agency's "credibility" was a high-ranking objective in the effort to depict American policies "clearly and effectively." See the views of VOA official Alan Baker in the dispatch by Peter Arnett, the Baton Rouge *Sunday Advocate,* November 16, 1980.

herent in the conduct of propaganda and informational programs by the world's oldest democracy. Moreover, the appeal of these two approaches has been dictated in no small measure by the overall atmosphere of international relations in any given period and by the specific issues confronting the United States abroad. The apparent waning of the Cold War during the 1970s, for example, perhaps inevitably and properly resulted in muting America's propaganda campaign against the Soviet Union and Communist groups abroad. By the early 1980s—with Cold War tensions again at the forefront of international concern—America's propaganda effort reflected this reality. Yet the conflict between these two schools of thought about the proper role of a propaganda agency in the foreign policy process will, as in the past, likely evoke controversy in the years ahead.

A second recurrent problem related to American propaganda activities has been the fact that, ever since World War II, policy makers in the State Department and the White House have often minimized or been indifferent toward psychological and propaganda dimensions of foreign policy, viewing them as relatively unimportant. On innumerable occasions throughout the postwar period, officials engaged in propaganda activities have complained that their viewpoints were "ignored" by their superiors in the stage of policy formulation. According to one former American official, in the early postwar period State Department officials resisted the assignment of propaganda functions to that agency, and Foreign Service officers were seldom prepared to acknowledge the importance of propaganda as an aspect of foreign policy.[14] A not untypical example was provided by the Kennedy Administration's plans for mounting the "Bay of Pigs" invasion of Cuba in 1961. Officials of the USIA were never informed by the White House that the undertaking was being planned; they had no time to prepare propaganda efforts supporting it, and yet they were compelled to explain this diplomatic fiasco to the world after it failed.[15]

We have already called attention to a third perennial problem besetting the operations of American propaganda agencies. This is long-standing congressional skepticism about the need for a propaganda program and about many of USICA's activities. For a generation or more, Congress has expressed apprehensions about the propaganda, informational, and "public relations" activities of governmental agencies.[16] The laws creating such agencies as USIA and USICA specifically prohibit them from engaging in internal propaganda activities. Congress is always apprehensive about campaigns by governmental agencies to influence American public opinion (and ultimately congressional opinion) on national policy issues. As both the Nazi and the Soviet Communist systems in recent history demonstrated, an extensive and skillfully managed internal propaganda network has been the hallmark of totalitarian regimes. For legislators, the line between impermissible "propaganda" activities and legitimate "informational" programs by governmental agencies is crucial—but often extremely difficult to draw in practice. In principle, agencies should *not* engage in the former; but they *should* provide maximum and accurate information to Congress and the American people about their activities. Yet Congress is seldom consistent in the application of this principle. For example, should the USICA be completely truthful to the world in disclosing the failure of the American intelligence community to predict the overthrow of the Iranian monarchy in 1979? Should it inform foreign societies candidly that American public opinion during the late 1970s rated the Carter Administration very low in terms of its "leadership," or that public opinion has consistently placed

Congress at the bottom of the scale among the three major branches of government, in terms of public confidence and esteem? Such "honest" reporting about the United States would almost certainly produce an outcry on Capitol Hill—and perhaps even from the American public at large.

Another problem engendering legislative disaffection with American propaganda efforts has been the always difficult question of *how to measure USICA's performance*. How is it possible to determine whether governmental agencies are making a positive contribution in the "battle for the minds of men"? Is USICA actually achieving its goals (however they are defined)? Are the radio programs broadcast by the Voice of America having an impact upon public attitudes in regions like Eastern Europe, the Arab World, or East Asia? Can the funds (close to one-half billion dollars annually) expended for USICA's operations be justified, could they be better spent in other dimensions of foreign policy, or should they perhaps be eliminated entirely? Ever since World War II, legislators have been troubled by such questions. To date, they have found few satisfactory answers to them.

A fourth problem, then, is the one we have just mentioned: devising satisfactory criteria for measuring the success (or failure) of propaganda campaigns. Over the years, officials of USIA and USICA have relied upon various criteria and evidence to support their claims that propaganda activities do in fact contribute positively to the nation's foreign policy objectives. Such criteria, however, tend to be highly selective, subjective, and questionable as reliable indicators of agency performance.[17]

Thus, officials engaged in radio broadcasting have employed several different techniques for measuring audience size for Voice of America broadcasts to regions such as Eastern Europe. Such estimates of audience size are, at best, crude approximations. Even if they were reasonably accurate, such studies can tell us little or nothing about the *effect* of Voice of America transmissions upon the viewpoints of citizens in Poland or Bulgaria. How have VOA transmissions, for example, influenced public attitudes behind the Iron Curtain toward the United States and toward the Soviet Union over a five-year period? Reliable data and criteria enabling such questions to be answered with assurance are almost impossible to obtain.

Or take another criterion sometimes employed by propaganda officials: the extent to which the Soviet Union endeavors to "jam" Voice of America broadcasts behind the Iron Curtain. Late in 1981, for example, during the Polish crisis, the Soviet Union was reported to be "heavily jamming" Voice of America broadcasts to countries behind the Iron Curtain. State Department officials interpreted this step as an effort by the Kremlin to prevent millions of people living within the Communist zone from learning the facts about Moscow's effort to suppress political dissent in Poland. Indirectly at least, it could be interpreted as an acknowledgment that Voice of America broadcasts had a large audience within the Communist orbit.[18] Yet quite clearly there may be many other reasons for Soviet efforts to counteract American propaganda activities, such as the traditional secretiveness and xenophobia of Russian society or the desire of the Communist hierarchy to allow no dissenting viewpoints to be disseminated behind the Iron Curtain. The magnitude of Soviet jamming activities may also be largely a function of overall Soviet-American relations at any given time. During the recent era of détente, for example, such activities largely ceased or were heavily curtailed.

Finally, in evaluating USICA's contribution to American foreign policy, we need to bear in mind a point emphasized earlier. Propaganda is *an auxiliary foreign policy instrument.* Even the most effective propaganda campaign cannot per se determine the success or failure of America's diplomatic efforts. The USICA's programs alone will not enhance America's "image" in black Africa, convince Arabs that Washington is sympathetic to their position in the dispute with Israel, or reassure the NATO allies that America's nuclear deterrent is "credible." Propaganda, in other words, nearly always serves *as a supportive policy instrument,* designed to be utilized in close conjunction with other instruments to achieve diplomatic objectives. Experienced propagandists are aware that in nearly all cases, the most effective propaganda is that which inclines groups and societies subjected to it to believe or to do *what they are already disposed to believe or do anyhow.* Propaganda thus strengthens or accelerates a preexisting tendency. For example, American propaganda programs will almost never turn a dedicated Communist or the leader of an anti-American movement abroad into a supporter of the United States. Skillful propaganda may, however, strengthen the preexisting pro-American sympathies of foreigners, or it may augment and reenforce anti-Soviet sentiments behind the Iron Curtain.

In the light of this reality, another constraint upon the conduct of successful propaganda programs by the United States must be noted. Perhaps more than any society in the history of the world, the United States is a "pluralistic" order, in which basic constitutional rights—like freedom of speech and of the press—are venerated. The Voice of America may be the American government's official broadcasting arm; but in reality, the American society has an almost infinite number of "voices" which speak to the outside world. There is the image of America conveyed by the news media and by the radio and TV industry; there are the products of Hollywood (by some criteria, perhaps, the single most influential force in shaping foreign attitudes toward the American society); there are the statements of officials in the executive and legislative branches of the government; there are the viewpoints and behavior of millions of American tourists who travel abroad; there are the activities of American business firms in foreign countries. Perhaps above all there is the impression of America conveyed by the policies of the United States government in distant parts of the world. More often than not, foreign attitudes toward the United States are likely to be determined more by these "voices" than by the programs conducted by USICA.

Foreign Aid and American Diplomacy

Postwar Patterns and Tendencies

We turn now to an examination of the second major diplomatic instrument discussed in this chapter: reliance upon foreign aid to achieve the foreign policy goals of the United States. Extensive and continuing reliance upon foreign aid as an instrument of foreign policy is one of the distinctive elements of international politics since World War II. By the early 1980s, the Reagan Administration's annual foreign aid budget was approximately $8.5 billion. Yet as we shall see (depending precisely upon how "foreign aid" is defined), overseas assistance by the United States has declined significantly in recent years—from some 23 percent of federal expenditures in the early post-World War II era to less than 3 percent of the national budget in the early 1980s. Even so, in the contemporary period some kind of foreign aid program has become an established feature of the diplomacy of nearly all advanced nations.

In this chapter, we shall briefly trace the emergence of the American postwar foreign aid program; after that, the principal kinds of postwar foreign aid—primarily economic and military aid—will be examined and evaluated; and the problems and prospects of foreign aid programs by the United States will be analyzed.

Some commentators would trace the beginning of the postwar foreign assistance program of the United States to the Lend-Lease program inaugurated by act of Congress early in 1941, several months before America entered World War II. During the war, under the Lend-Lease program the United States sent billions of dollars' worth of equipment, food, medicines, and other supplies to its allies.[19] American-supplied Lend-Lease assistance, for example, was crucial in the early months of the conflict in enabling Soviet Russia to defend itself against, and finally to defeat, the forces of Nazi Germany. One of the earliest causes of tension in Soviet-American relations after World War II was Washington's abrupt termination of Lend-Lease aid to Moscow once the European war was over.[20]

After the surrender of Japan (August 14, 1945), American foreign aid efforts were directed toward providing assistance for dealing with acute and urgent problems (particularly in Western Europe) which emerged in the early postwar era. Almost alone among the major participants in World War II, the United States escaped widespread physical and human damage; only America was in a position to provide aid to other societies which had sustained massive wartime destruction.

Events soon made it clear, however, that such *ad hoc* and emergency aid programs by the United States had little lasting impact upon the problems growing out of World War II. During the late 1940s, the countries of Western Europe continued to experience political unrest, economic dislocations, and social tensions. Such problems assumed unprec-

edented urgency for American policy makers in the light of the increasingly hostile Cold War between the United States and the Soviet Union. As officials in Washington viewed the matter, Europe and the Mediterranean area particularly were becoming a "power vacuum" which was in danger of being filled by Soviet hegemony. Debilitated by the war, Western Europe was defenseless against a possible Soviet military intrusion. World War II had also unleashed powerful nationalist currents throughout the Afro-Asian world. The emergence of the Third World of newly independent states provided a new incentive for America to expand and diversify its foreign aid activities. Problems like nation building, modernization, and the elimination of poverty became dominant concerns with societies throughout the Third World; and America's interest in their welfare was often measured by its willingness to provide tangible assistance in meeting such challenges.

The American foreign aid program has taken many specific forms, and has experienced a number of organizational changes, since World War II. Despite this fact, three principal forms of foreign aid have been utilized consistently by the United States for a generation or more. One of these—emergency aid—has already been mentioned. Throughout its history, the American society has been generous in responding to acute human needs in foreign countries, and this pattern has been continued in the postwar era. When famine conditions exist along the southern rim of the Sahara Desert in Africa, or when floods exact a high human and property toll in Bangladesh, or when hurricanes spread widespread devastation in the Caribbean region, the United States has nearly always responded generously to appeals by other countries.

Two other forms of foreign assistance merit more detailed examination. One of these is *economic assistance,* which the United

States has provided foreign societies since World War II and which continues to be an element in its diplomacy. The other is *military aid,* extended by the United States to allies and friendly nations requiring various kinds of outside assistance to bolster their defense efforts.

American Economic Assistance Programs

Since the end of World War II, the United States has provided a total of approximately $140 billion in several different categories of economic assistance to foreign countries.* In terms of regional beneficiaries, the largest proportion (some $35 billion) has gone to the Near East and South Asia, followed by the Far East and the Pacific (around $30 billion), and Western Europe ($27 billion). By the early 1980s, the total of American economic assistance was running over $7 billion annually.

America's consistent reliance upon foreign economic aid to achieve diplomatic objectives began in 1947, when, at President Harry Truman's urgent request, Congress passed the Greek-Turkish Aid Program, which marked the promulgation of the "con-

tainment" policy against the Soviet Union.† This program derived from a twofold realization by American policy makers. Vulnerable nations, like Greece and Turkey, had to be protected from external threats by the provision of military assistance to them. But in the long run, their security and independence perhaps depended even more upon their ability to solve urgent *internal* social and economic problems; and American economic assistance was a vital step toward that goal.[21]

By the spring of 1947, it had become apparent to officials in Washington that conditions in Western Europe were deteriorating rapidly. The emergency aid provided by the United States in the immediate postwar period had done little more than keep European societies from collapsing economically. Communist movements, particularly in France and Italy, were gaining strength; and by most criteria, European economic activity was declining. In this context, the Truman Administration committed the United States to the most ambitious and costly peacetime foreign aid program in American history. Known as the "Marshall Plan" (or, officially, as the European Recovery Program), this endeavor involved a five-year program, totaling some $11 billion in American aid, for the recovery and reconstruction of Western Europe.[22] By many criteria, the Marshall Plan has to be regarded as one of the most successful diplomatic ventures by the United States since World War II. Within a few years after its beginning in 1948, most of the countries of Western Europe had begun to recover their economic health. In time (particularly after the creation of the European Common Market in 1958), Western Europe emerged as one of the most prosperous and vibrant centers of economic

*Widespread variation is likely to be found in figures describing the extent and magnitude of both economic and military assistance programs by the United States. The total figures arrived at, for example, are a function of such questions of how foreign aid is defined (such as whether it includes all forms of *loans* to other countries); of whether it takes account of actual and scheduled *repayment* for assistance by other countries; and whether it includes the assistance made available by institutions like the Export-Import Bank and the World Bank, both of which are heavily supported by the United States. A succinct discussion of American foreign aid programs since World War II is available in the State Department's publication, "International Security and Economic Cooperation Program FY 1983" (Special Report No. 99), March, 1982, 1–17. Current information is also available in the *Statistical Abstract of the United States,* published by the Bureau of the Census.

†The doctrine of "containment" motivating American postwar policy toward the Soviet Union is explained and evaluated more fully in Chapter 11.

productivity and trade on the globe. For some 20 years, until the emergence of the movement known as "Euro-Communism" in the early 1970s, Communist influence in most European countries presented no threat to their stability or their ties with the United States. As Chapter 11 will explain in greater detail, the external threat to European security had significantly declined.

The Marshall Plan had a number of exceptional features which largely accounted for its phenomenal success. The impetus for the program—including a thorough study of the region's needs and its own resources for meeting them—came *from the European governments*. Moreover, the European recipients took the primary responsibility for administering the Marshall Plan successfully. No less crucial to the success of the enterprise was the fact that the European participants contributed upwards of 90 percent of the total funds required for its implementation. Vital as it was, American assistance was but a small part of the overall effort required to achieve the program's objectives. Essentially, the Marshall Plan was an outstanding example of European "self-help," supported by the United States. There was another notable aspect to this undertaking: The Marshall Plan (in contrast to later American foreign aid programs directed toward the Third World) was designed to promote the reconstruction of a once economically dynamic, highly industrialized region. As events proved during the years after 1948, this was a very different—and in most respects infinitely easier—challenge than achieving the "modernization" of Asian states or eliminating poverty and illiteracy throughout Latin America.

The next major stage in the evolution of postwar American economic assistance programs was the promulgation of the "Point Four" Program by the Truman Administration in 1950.* This program inaugurated America's continuing provision of aid to developing societies throughout the Third World—now the largest component of the foreign aid program. Sometimes called "developmental assistance," this aid was dispensed on a continuing basis to countries from East Asia to Latin America. One of the largest beneficiaries of American assistance to the Third World, for example, was India.† India was regarded by American officials as playing a key role in Asian stability and in providing experience with solving problems pervasive in other backward societies. Certain other smaller countries (like South Korea, the Republic of China on Taiwan, Turkey, and Iran) were also major beneficiaries of American economic aid. In time, these particular countries achieved an outstanding record of economic growth and productivity—a record which was not always, however, matched by comparable progress in political stability and respect for fundamental political liberties.

Another noteworthy development in the postwar foreign aid program was the Kennedy Administration's sponsorship of the Alliance for Progress in the early 1960s.[23] Responding to long-standing Latin American complaints that Uncle Sam had "neglected" their well-being, officials in Washington expressed their willingness to support a ten-year long-range development program for Latin America, initially entailing some $10 billion in aid by the

---

*The "Point Four" Program was named for the fourth point in President Harry Truman's State of the Union address on January 4, 1950, calling for American aid to underdeveloped countries. As time passed, this became one of the largest components of the American foreign assistance program. See Harry S Truman, *Years of Trial and Hope: 1946–1952* (Garden City, N.Y.: Doubleday and Co., 1956), pp. 234–239.

†America's postwar relations with India are discussed more fully in Chapter 15.

United States (in reality, over the years American aid to the region considerably exceeded this total). The details of the Alliance for Progress were worked out at a conference among the participants at Punta del Este, Uruguay (in August, 1961). The charter which was adopted at that session set forth the common goals of the program, the first of which was the promotion of democratic governments in the Western Hemisphere. From the beginning, the participating states accepted the idea that certain sweeping changes (such as tax and land reform, and the introduction of modern personnel systems in Latin American governments) were necessary if the Alliance for Progress were to succeed. We shall reserve detailed discussion of the major problems in United States relations with Latin America for treatment in Chapter 14. It suffices to observe here that the results achieved by the Alliance for Progress fell considerably short of the aims reflected in the charter of Punta del Este.

Still another significant development in the postwar foreign aid program has been the shift from "bilateral" (or government-to-government) assistance to "multilateral" (or aid from international and regional institutions to recipient governments) assistance by the United States. For many years, Washington extended economic assistance directly to a host of countries throughout the world. Then, beginning in the early 1970s, a high proportion of American assistance was channeled to multilateral and regional institutions—like the World Bank, the International Development Association, the Inter-American Development Bank, the Asian Development Bank, and the newer African Development Fund. Many American officials believed that greater reliance upon multilateral mechanisms avoided the abrasions and conflicts often accompanying debtor-creditor relationships; and it gave recipients a greater voice in the formulation of guidelines and policies governing the provision of foreign aid. By the early 1980s, however, the Reagan White House was moving back to the earlier pattern of American bilateral assistance, in which the United States provided aid *directly* to needy countries. To the minds of President Reagan and many of his supporters, foreign aid should be thought of—and it should be extended to other countries—as an overt instrument of American foreign policy. On that premise, no effort should be made to disguise the political aims of the foreign aid program, the paramount one being the achievement of America's diplomatic objectives.[24]

Under the Carter Administration, another prominent theme was evident in American foreign economic aid programs: Aid provided by the United States to other countries was often tied directly *to the enhancement of human rights abroad.*[25] Congress was especially active in demanding that aid to other countries be made contingent upon their efforts to safeguard and expand internal freedoms.

Since the late 1940s, various organizational mechanisms have been utilized to administer the American foreign aid program. In common with the State Department, the foreign aid program has been "reorganized" several times. In 1961, a major reorganization was undertaken by the Kennedy Administration. A new mechanism—the Agency for International Development (AID)—was created as a semiautonomous unit within the State Department to administer economic and technical assistance programs abroad. In concert with the Department of Agriculture, AID also administers the "Food for Peace" program, whereby the United States sends agricultural shipments to needy societies. Headed by an administrator, in 1980 AID had an operating budget of some $268 million annually and employed almost 6000 people.[26]

Just as the organizational machinery of the foreign aid program has changed, so too have the program's announced goals. Ever since 1947, every incumbent President has formulated the objectives of the foreign aid program in somewhat different terms, partly because conditions changed overseas and partly because evolution occurred in the goals of American foreign policy. Under the Carter Administration, for example, the goals of the foreign aid program were defined by Secretary of State Cyrus Vance as follows:

> Our foreign assistance efforts demonstrate America's humanitarian compassion for the world's poor, our willingness to invest in the social, economic, and technological development of poor countries and to foster a favorable atmosphere for our overall relations with these countries. And they do more:
>
> —They provide a means for peace by encouraging the economic stability that allows an atmosphere in which old quarrels, and potential new ones, can be dealt with;
>
> —They support, through selective military assistance, the security of our friends and allies, and thus the possibility for greater concentration on social and economic progress;
>
> —They encourage the movement toward a liberal world order based on an open economic system and on an international political structure accepted as fair and equitable by all participants;
>
> —They contribute to the long-term task of providing for the protection and advancement of human rights.[27]

As emphasized earlier, officials of the Reagan Administration were convinced that the overall purpose of the foreign aid program was clear enough and must be kept at the forefront of national consciousness. Foreign aid was but one among several techniques relied upon to enable the United States to achieve its foreign policy goals in an often unstable and hostile external environment.

Military Assistance Programs

The second major component of American foreign aid activities since World War II has been the provision of military assistance to nations endangered by threats to their national security. By 1980, the overall magnitude of this aid was estimated at some $73 billion. Close to $40 billion had been directed to countries in the Far East and the Pacific (with a high percentage of this total going to two countries—South Vietnam and South Korea); Western Europe received some $20 billion for the defense of the NATO area; and nations in the Near East and South Asia were granted over $10 billion in military aid.[28]

A major purpose of the Greek-Turkish Aid Program of 1947 was the extension of military assistance to these two countries, which were being subjected to internal and external Soviet-sponsored threats to their independence. By the end of the decade, in conjunction with the establishment of the North Atlantic Treaty Organization (NATO) in 1949, the United States undertook a large-scale program of military assistance to its Western allies. As a result of the Korean War, which erupted in 1950, and, in the years that followed, of the emerging Cold War contest in Indochina, massive American military aid commitments were made to Asian nations. In the Middle East, the major beneficiary of American military assistance has been Israel; on a smaller scale, countries like Iran and Jordan, and most recently Egypt, have had high priority. If military sales are regarded as military *aid* to a nation, then Saudi Arabia has also become a major beneficiary of American assistance. Since the early 1960s, American military aid has also been dispensed to the Latin American states. Throughout the postwar period, military aid has comprised approximately *one-third* of the overall American contribution to the economic and military needs of other countries.

As with economic assistance, the military aid program has also been subjected to administrative reorganization and changes in its principal aid categories. In general terms, however, this aid has been extended for a number of specific purposes, most of which have been centrally related to implementing America's containment strategy against the Soviet Union. Specific goals have been: strengthening and modernizing the armed forces of selected countries facing internal and external threats to their security; providing aid to countries, enabling them to expand their own defense-related industries; subsidizing training programs for the armed forces and police units of other countries; extending aid for the purpose of cushioning the economic impact and other consequences of high defense spending by certain nations; facilitating and often subsidizing the purchase of American arms by foreign governments; and promoting regional stability in key areas. While specific military aid programs assume many different forms, their purpose is to contribute to the overriding U.S. foreign policy and national security interest—to shape a more peaceful world.[29]

Brief note should also be taken of the special case of Israel in the American foreign aid program. Ever since its creation in 1948, Israel has been dependent upon massive private and governmental assistance from the United States. During the last half of the 1970s, for example, Israel received from $3 billion to $5 billion annually in various kinds of aid from the American government. At the end of the decade, the Carter Administration agreed to provide Israel an additional $3 billion grant (along with a regular $1.8 billion foreign aid allocation) as part of the Camp David peace accord with Egypt. As Israel entered the 1980s, many of its economic problems remained critical; and American aid would be as essential for its survival in the future as in the past. Along with Egypt, Israel continued to rank as a leading beneficiary of American foreign assistance.[30]

Economic and Military Aid in Perspective

How successful have the economic and military aid programs operated by the United States since World War II been in promoting national diplomatic objectives? Differing responses on that subject are likely to be given by the American people, their leaders, and informed students of the nation's foreign policy. In the popular mind, foreign aid is often described by such terms as "Operation Rathole," as a "boondoggle," and as a waste of the taxpayer's money which could better be spent solving domestic problems. Informed students of American diplomacy have singled out foreign aid as a major influence responsible for drawing the United States into the Vietnam War, as a force highly disruptive to the stability of foreign societies, and as an instrument enabling Washington to support anti-Communist dictatorships abroad.[31] In 1978, the chairman of the House Foreign Affairs Committee (for a brief period, called the International Relations Committee) said that getting congressional support for the President's foreign aid program would be "about as successful as selling ice cream freezers at the North Pole or furlined parkas in Africa."[32] In 1981, the Reagan Administration threatened to make massive cuts in the foreign aid budget as part of its campaign to reduce governmental spending.

The contribution of the foreign aid program to the postwar American diplomatic record must, of course, be assessed according to certain criteria. A major problem with the foreign aid program since the late 1940s has been that the criteria applied to it vary widely and are, in some cases, contradictory. Certain objectives and expectations about foreign aid, for example, have long shaped public and congressional attitudes toward the undertaking.

Unquestionably, a pervasive expectation in the public mind about foreign aid is that it will win friends and allies for the American diplomatic position abroad; and that major beneficiaries of Washington's foreign aid largess will show their "gratitude" tangibly by supporting its external political objectives. To the extent that the American people and many of their leaders have hoped that foreign aid would achieve such results, they have nearly always been disappointed. After more than 30 years of experience, there is no evidence to support the idea that granting assistance to other countries makes them dependable allies of the United States or, more generally, generates pro-American sentiment abroad.

Indeed, a case perhaps can be made for the existence of an *inverse correlation:* The greater the magnitude of American assistance to, let us say, the Third World, the more *anti-American sentiment* appears to exist among these nations, and the *less inclined* they are to follow Washington's diplomatic leadership! Frustrating and bewildering as many Americans have found this reality, it can be fairly easily explained. The creditor-debtor relationship inherent in the foreign aid program intrinsically generates tensions and conflicts.[33] Debtor nations seldom have warm feelings toward their creditors, particularly as in time (in recent years) the interest owed on foreign loans and the repayments of principal due become extremely burdensome. Not infrequently, governments in newly independent countries feel compelled to prove that they cannot be "bought" by countries furnishing them with foreign assistance. From time to time, foreign political elites are, therefore, motivated to demonstrate their independence of the United States by making flamboyant gestures and engaging in anti-American rhetoric designed to convey that fact dramatically.

Meanwhile, the American people and their representatives in Congress become increasingly impatient with the disappointing results achieved by consistent applications of foreign aid; they do not understand the lack of gratitude evident in the behavior of nations benefiting from American largess; and they begin to wonder whether the funds apparently "wasted" on many external aid projects cannot better be expended on needed domestic programs.

Such behavior patterns, it is necessary to emphasize, are not confined solely to America's relations with foreign aid recipients. The more limited Soviet foreign aid program (inaugurated in the mid-1950s) has been characterized by most of these same tendencies and problems. A dramatic illustration was provided by massive Soviet aid to Egypt following the 1967 war in the Middle East. Gradually, resentment against a growing Soviet presence in Egypt began to emerge, culminating in President Anwar Sadat's sudden "expulsion" of thousands of Russians from Egyptian soil in 1972.[34] The popular notion that foreign aid can be readily or easily translated into political capital, exchanged for support in the diplomatic marketplace, has always been a fanciful, although widely pervasive, idea. Comparable frustration has of course been experienced countless times by the United States. As will be explained more fully in Chapter 11, by the early 1980s many Americans had become deeply disillusioned because of the lack of "cooperation" exhibited by the NATO allies, for example, in supporting the American position in the Middle East or Central America.

A second pseudo-goal often identified with the foreign aid program is the promotion of democracy abroad. Sometimes (as in the Alliance for Progress), this is an explicit objective of a particular foreign aid program. For most aid programs conducted by the United States it is perhaps an implicit goal. The United States is the world's oldest democracy, and the encouragement of democracy abroad has been a longtime theme of American diplomacy.

Experience with foreign aid for more than three decades provides little convincing evidence that in fact it does promote democracy in foreign countries. With the exception of India—one of the very few functioning democracies in the Third World, and a major beneficiary of American aid—almost nowhere else in the Third World could a correlation between the provision of American aid and the emergence of democracy be demonstrated. For several reasons, any connection between these two phenomena is extremely tenuous. In the short run, at least, whatever forces and influences operate to promote democracy in most Third World societies have little relationship to American foreign assistance. Foreign aid by the United States may in fact under certain conditions hamper the quest for democratic values and institutions for several reasons. American foreign economic assistance can be (and not infrequently has been) misspent or wasted, producing widespread public resentment against a pro-American incumbent regime; only privileged classes within the society may really benefit from foreign aid, thereby widening the gap between advantaged and disadvantaged elements within the society; if foreign assistance stimulates economic growth, this fact may foster (and often has done so) growing discontents with the *pace* of change and popular demands by radical political movements that they be given control of the government.

But the most fundamental reason perhaps why foreign assistance by the United States is not likely to engender democracy throughout the Third World is that, even when it is successful, the process of economic and social "modernization" is likely to be a traumatic, difficult, and politically disruptive phenomenon characterized by intense social and political *conflicts and upheavals*. In one Third World country after another, as standards of living and productive levels begin to rise, this development has triggered widespread dissatisfactions with the rate of improvement and has engendered conflict among groups which believe that the benefits of modernization are not being shared equally among the elements within the society. Revolutionary political upheaval, most students of the modernization process are agreed, is most apt to occur when conditions *are improving,* not when societies remain attached to the status quo. Such a political environment is seldom congenial for stable democratic political institutions and processes.[35]

Briefly, we may allude to a third pseudo-goal related to the American foreign aid program: the belief that economic and military assistance by the United States *inherently strengthens the prospect for regional and international stability and peace.* Experience throughout the postwar era has also shown this to be an illusory expectation.[36] The same inverse correlation we noted above—the greater the overall magnitude of American foreign aid efforts, the greater the number of regional and local conflicts—can be detected here. The correlation may be (and most likely is) meaningless, but the fact remains that violent encounters throughout the Third World *have escalated sharply* during the past two decades. The injection of billions of dollars in foreign assistance by the United States and other countries into Third World societies has done nothing to reverse this tendency. To cite merely two examples: By the 1980s, the Middle East remained as volatile as it had been since late 1940s; and localized conflicts continued to erupt throughout black Africa.

A fourth goal of foreign aid—perhaps the most fundamental objective in the minds of millions of Americans—has been the "containment" of Communism globally. It would not be correct perhaps to list this among the pseudo-goals of foreign assistance. From the beginning, American economic and military aid has unquestionably had an anti-Communist dimension; it has been an important instrument for carrying out the containment strategy for over 30 years.

Moreover, it seems clear that in a number of significant cases since World War II, American economic and military aid *have* played a key role in the containment of Communism. Such aid was vital in preserving the independence of Greece in the late 1940s; it strengthened the independence of Turkey in the same period; and, as we have noted, the Marshall Plan was crucial in promoting the recovery of Western Europe and in enhancing the region's resistance to Communism. In the years which followed, American aid has contributed to preserving the security of South Korea. And in the early 1970s, Egypt's expectation that the United States would expand its economic and military assistance entered strongly into President Sadat's decision to expel Soviet personnel from that key Arab nation.

Yet after noting such cases, it remains true that as a generalization American economic and military aid has not overtly hindered the Soviet Union from successfully expanding its influence in many parts of the Third World. One of the largest beneficiaries of American economic and military assistance, of course, was South Vietnam, where the United States suffered a severe military and diplomatic defeat. Soviet influence

throughout the Middle East may, in some respects, be greater today than in the late 1940s; it is unquestionably greater in parts of black Africa than at any time in history.* Assistance provided by the United States to its Latin American neighbors has not impeded the emergence of revolutionary movements, many of which have ties with Moscow and Havana.

What, then, may be regarded as *legitimate* goals of the American foreign aid program? Quite clearly, the foreign aid program has some achievements to its credit—and several of them are noteworthy. First, external economic and military aid (but particularly the former) by the United States has served as a *tangible symbol of American concern* about other, less privileged societies in the international system. Implicitly, foreign aid signifies the American society's awareness that it is a rich and powerful member of the "family of

---

*On this point—the influence of the superpowers throughout the Third World, in part because of their foreign aid efforts—a subtle, but fundamental, distinction needs to be kept in mind. Both the United States and the Soviet Union are heavily *involved* in the Third World; they conduct ongoing programs of economic and military assistance to these countries; and, in many respects, the "dependency" of Third World societies upon the superpowers and other wealthier nations has *increased* during the past generation. Yet this is a different matter from American or Soviet *political and diplomatic influence* within the Third World. The result of both American and Soviet foreign aid programs has perhaps been *lessened political influence by both superpowers* over most nations in the Third World. With every passing year, the Third World demonstrates its imperviousness to outside political domination and its determination to preserve its diplomatic independence from Washington and Moscow alike. In brief, neither superpower has been able to "dominate" the Third World—which is one factor that may have contributed to a condition of détente between them. For example, during the late 1970s and early 1980s, the Soviet Union maintained a large "presence" in East Africa. Yet little evidence existed that in this region—or throughout Africa broadly—independent nations were politically and diplomatically subservient to Moscow.

nations," and that it is obliged to bear some responsibility for the welfare of the entire family. Just as within a society wealthy citizens are expected to demonstrate concern for disadvantaged citizens, so in international relations wealthy states must contribute to the solution of human problems outside their own borders.

Second, as a result of American aid efforts, some progress has been made abroad in achieving such goals as internal reform programs aimed at attaining economic, social, and political "modernization." While innumerable problems remain to be solved, the Alliance for Progress *has* stimulated reform efforts and other fundamental changes in many Latin American countries. Agricultural experts from the United States have fanned out through the Third World; and their contributions have been of immense value in changing ancient, and often highly unproductive, modes of agricultural cultivation and related activities. American doctors, nurses, and health specialists have assisted primitive societies in raising their sanitary, health, and dietary standards. Teachers and educational specialists from the United States have made a comparable contribution in efforts to wipe out illiteracy and expand educational resources abroad. Thanks in part to American foreign aid activities, scientific knowledge and modern technology have been disseminated throughout the world.

Third, economic assistance provided by the United States since World War II has been a key element in expanding overseas markets for American-produced goods and services. The leading examples of this phenomenon are Japan and Western Europe—two primary markets for American exports. At the end of World War II, Japan and Western Europe were prostrate; and American aid was essential to their recovery and subsequent economic progress. In later years, American trade with the developing countries similarly

began to expand, as they increased their economic output.* Other countries can pay for American goods and services only to the extent that they have purchasing power to do so, generated by a rising level of economic activity within the country.

Fourth, economic assistance by the United States is in some measure responsible for the fact that for most developing nations, overall levels of economic activity, of health, of education, of food production, and other important activities *have been rising, when measured in absolute terms.* Throughout the Third World, considerably more food is being produced now than 20 years ago; health and nutritional standards have unquestionably been elevated; new educational opportunities exist for millions of young people; the construction of new housing units has been impressive; cultural and recreational activities have been made available to citizens on an unprecedented scale.

Yet in nearly all cases, it must be emphasized, these are "absolute" or overall gains only. *Measured on a per capita basis,* there is less food today for the people of the Third World than in the late 1940s. The con-

*In justifying the foreign aid program for 1980, Secretary of State Cyrus Vance called attention to America's growing trade ties with the developing world. He noted, for example, that in 1977 the developing countries bought $42 billion worth of U.S. exports (one-third of total American exports). In the agricultural realm, developing societies purchased some 50 percent of the nation's foreign wheat sales, 60 percent of its cotton sales, and 70 percent of its rice sales. During the decade of the 1970s, American sales to developing countries grew by some 22 percent. During the five years prior to 1979, in turn, the developing nations supplied some 25 percent of the raw materials needed by the American economy. His conclusion was that: "We can enhance our own well-being by encouraging and assisting rapid and equitable growth in the developing world." See the statement by Secretary Vance in "U.S. Aid Programs, FY 80," in the series *The Secretary of State* (Washington, D.C.: Bureau of Public Affairs, Department of State), February 5, 1979, pp. 1–8.

struction of new educational facilities has been hard pressed to keep up with—and in many of these countries it has *not* kept pace with—the growth in the school-age population. In cities like Calcutta, Cairo, and Mexico City, slums are being created faster than new housing can be constructed—with the result that urban poverty in many countries is a much more serious problem today than it was a generation ago.* In a majority of Third World nations, unemployment and under-employment—especially among urban populations—is a critical problem and is becoming more acute every year. Quite possibly, for the masses of people in the Third World, there has been *no* discernible improvement in their standards of living after more than a generation of American (and other external) foreign aid programs.[37] This reality translates into an "explosive" political situation in India and Indonesia, in Egypt and Iraq, and in most Latin American states which can only engender ongoing local, regional, and possibly international instability. A major problem, of course, is the "population explosion" throughout the Third World, which has in many instances canceled out the absolute gains these societies have made in many

spheres of life, leaving individual citizens little better off than before.[38]

Aid programs by the United States have also served as a model for similar undertakings by other advanced nations. The Soviet foreign aid program, for example, was in large measure a response to America's efforts in this field; and the limited aid effort carried out by Communist China may be, in turn, a response to American and Soviet activities. Today, the nations of Western Europe supply most of the aid requirements of black Africa—a region in which American programs have always been limited. Even the wealthier oil-rich states of the Middle East are now providing foreign aid to needy recipients.

Finally, the foreign aid programs of the United States have unquestionably given impetus to and encouraged one of the most important tendencies in the international system today—the creation of viable regional institutions in nearly every area of the world. Back in the late 1940s, the Marshall Plan called for Western Europe to be treated as an "economic unit"—and out of that concept in time there came the European Common Market and the more comprehensive European Economic Community (EEC). (The trend toward European regionalism will be discussed more fully in Chapter 11.) More primitive regional institutions and mechanisms, however, have been established, and are functioning, in nearly every other area. In the Western Hemisphere, the Organization of American States (OAS) and the Central American Common Market involve collaborative efforts to solve common problems among their members. A number of regional bodies have been established in Asia for the same purpose. The Organization of African Unity (OAU) has achieved at least limited cooperation in dealing with regional problems among its members; and OAU may be expected to assume new functions in the years ahead.[39]

---

*A single example—the increasingly critical world food shortage—illustrates the pervasiveness and magnitude of the problem. During the two decades 1960 to 1980, the developing nations increased their overall grain production from some 250 million to around 350 million metric tons annually. Yet during that same period, their *per capita* output of grain held more or less constant (at 180 kilograms per person annually). Because of maldistribution of food and other resources, some groups within Third World societies perhaps had *less* food by 1980 than before. One study found that by the end of the 1970s, in 62 Third World countries, food production was failing to keep pace with the rate of population growth. This fact dictated intensified famine conditions and food shortages in the years ahead. See "World Population: Silent Explosion" (Washington, D.C.: Department of State, 1978), p. 15; and *New York Times*, July 19, 1978.

Trade and American Diplomacy

The Centrality of Trade Questions

By the early 1980s—when citizens had to cope with gasoline and fuel oil shortages—as never before in their history Americans were confronted graphically with the degree to which international trade affected their daily lives. Increasingly, the prosperity of the United States and the stability of its economic system depended upon world trade.

For several reasons, the informed student of American foreign policy needs to have least a rudimentary grasp of trade issues. First, the United States is more dependent upon other countries than ever before in its history for its economic welfare and its military security. As one study of America's position in international trade in 1982 concluded: "One thing is certain. Never again will the U.S. be as self-sufficient as it was in the years immediately after World War II, when it had most of the world's manufacturing plants, much of the advanced technology and the greatest amount of capital." By 1981, combined imports and exports were equal to 24 percent of America's total economic output. In that year, the American society was spending some $273 billion on imported goods and services; and the nation's sales in foreign markets totalled some $234 billion.[40]

Second, throughout history Americans have believed (correctly or not) that expanding trade ties among nations strengthen the prospects for global peace and security for all countries—an idea which has received renewed emphasis in the era of détente with the Soviet Union. Third, a relatively new development in American foreign policy has been the "linkage" of trade questions and political issues, notably the promotion of international human rights. Fourth, as well perhaps as any single issue which might be cited, global economic issues highlight the increasingly intimate relationship *between domestic and foreign policy problems*. Domestic considerations are often crucial in dictating the American position on trade issues, while international economic issues have the most profound consequences for internal policy and well-being.

At the outset, in order to understand the nature and problems of American foreign trade, some comprehension of basic concepts is indispensable. America's (or any nation's) *imports* consist of those goods and services it *buys* from other countries. Because they represent money *owed by* Americans to foreigners, imports are a drain upon, or a liability in, the nation's overall trading account. By contrast, of course, *exports* comprise those goods and services which Americans *sell* abroad. As purchases by foreigners, exports are, therefore, entered as credits or assets in the nation's trade account. As used traditionally, the term *balance of trade* refers to the difference between a nation's import and export accounts: If imports exceed exports, then the balance is negative or adverse, signifying that for a specified period (usually a year, or a quarter) a nation has incurred abroad more debts than credits. An excess of exports over imports of course signifies the opposite: A nation's trade balance is favorable or positive, in that its overall trade account shows a credit instead of a deficit.

The term *balance of payments* is a broad concept which shows the *totality* of a nation's international transactions during a particular time interval (normally, one year). In addition to imports and exports, the balance of payments will include other important entries—like spending by American tourists abroad and by foreign tourists in the United States; foreign aid extended by the United States to other countries and repayments to the United States by foreign aid recipients; expenditures to maintain the American armed forces abroad; loans granted by the United States to other governments; and foreign investments. In effect, the concept of balance of payments is a form of double-entry bookkeeping, showing *all* liabilities and credits for a nation in international trade. Since, by definition of the system, each side of the ledger must "balance" (or be equal to the other), it is misleading to talk about a "favorable" or an "unfavorable" balance of payments. When such nomenclature is used (as happens widely), it means that America, for example, is concerned about the imbalance between (or among) *particular items* in the overall balance of payments and desires some different pattern among them.

For example, as had occurred by the end of the 1970s, the United States was buying oil from the major oil-exporting states, and these imports totaled close to $50 billion annually—an enormous drain, or liability, in the nation's balance of payments. This drain, however, was partially offset by credits in the balance of payments generated by the sale of American exports to other countries. Still, with each passing year the United States was compelled to pay for its foreign oil purchases by some method—such as by sending dollars abroad, sending gold to other countries, allowing its creditors to build up large deposits in the United States, by borrowing, or by some other means. Ideally, of course, the U.S. would like to match (or even exceed) the volume of oil imports by the level of its own exports—thereby incurring a "favorable" trade balance, which requires foreign countries to remit payments in some form to the United States. There was, for example, clearly a limit upon the degree to which foreign oil purchases could be financed by such methods as gold transfers from America to its creditors, or by allowing its creditors in effect to lend America the money to meet its petroleum needs. En-

couraging the principal oil-producing states to "recycle" the dollars they receive—by reinvesting them in American businesses and government bonds—has been another approach Washington has taken to this problem.

Growing Dependence on International Trade

The increasing dependence of the United States upon international trade is not difficult to document. By the late 1970s, for example, America imported the following percentages of raw materials which were essential for a high level of industrial production and for national defense:[41]

Antimony	52%
Asbestos	85%
Bauxite	99%
Chrome	89%
Cobalt	97%
Diamonds	100%
Manganese ore	98%
Natural Rubber	100%
Nickel	70%
Petroleum	42%
Tin	86%
Zinc	58%

Other indexes call attention to the nation's growing dependency upon international trade. The United States has become the world's largest trader. It imports and exports some 13 percent of all goods and services exchanged in world commerce. During the decade of the 1970s, the United States almost doubled the volume of its exports. In certain industries—like heavy machinery, modern aircraft, fertilizers, pharmaceuticals, metal products, and milling equipment—as much as one-quarter or more of total domestic production is sold in foreign markets. The prosperity of American agriculture is increasingly linked to a large volume of foreign sales. Over 20 percent of the total production of major crops like wheat, soybeans, cotton, tobacco, rice, and corn is sold overseas. One out of every three acres of American cropland is devoted to commodities for sale to foreign customers. Overall, the jobs of 10 million American workers depend directly on exports, while one out of every three dollars in profits earned by American business firms is derived from sales in foreign markets.[42]

The importance of trade as an aspect of foreign policy became dramatically evident to Americans during and after the Arab "oil boycott" imposed upon the United States and other industrialized nations during the Middle East War of 1973. For a number of reasons which we shall reserve for discussion at a later stage,* the 1973 war had profound economic and political implications for the United States. The curtailment of oil shipments from the Middle East to the industrialized world underscored the degree to which the United States had become increasingly dependent upon foreign suppliers for this vital commodity. And the war demonstrated the extent to which the members of the Organization of Petroleum Exporting Countries (OPEC) were now prepared to use "oil power" to achieve (or support) their diplomatic objectives.

By the early 1980s, the level of American oil imports had declined from levels reached during the 1970s. A surplus of oil existed on the world market; and conservation measures taken by the American society had significantly reduced foreign oil consumption. Yet many commentators believed that this condition was unlikely to last, since major oil-producing nations were taking steps to lower production and since the global demand for oil and other energy sources would unques-

tionably climb in the years ahead. For an indefinite period in the future, therefore, the United States was likely to find oil imports a major item in its foreign trade deficit.

By 1982, oil imports constituted the largest single category of goods and commodities purchased abroad by the American society. In that year, some $78.5 billion was spent by the United States on oil purchases abroad—over three times as much as the United States earned from its major agricultural sales to other countries.[43] Although the level of oil imports might continue to decline moderately, this fact was unlikely to alter the reality that the United States had become —and for the foreseeable future it would remain—massively dependent upon foreign suppliers for its petroleum needs. Strategically and diplomatically, of course, this was a crucial reality. Economically, it meant that a substantial portion of America's export earnings would have to be used to pay for a high level of oil imports.[44]

Trade and Soviet-American Relations

A second reason why trade questions have come to the forefront of American diplomatic concern in recent years has been the emergence of détente between the United States and the Soviet Union. We shall discuss the meaning and implications of détente more fully in Chapter 10. Here, we are interested in its impact upon commercial relations between the superpowers. By the 1970s, although the reasons in both cases were different, Washington and Moscow alike were interested in expanded commercial relations between the two countries. In the American view at least, one reason often invoked for expanding trade across the Iron Curtain was the idea that it would break down ideological barriers and historic enmities between the United States and the Soviet Union; in the process of trad-

*The Middle East War of 1973, as a stage in the continuing Arab-Israeli conflict, is discussed more fully in Chapter 12.

ing, the two nations would "get to know each other better"—thereby enhancing the prospects for a more stable and peaceful international system. Business and commercial groups within the United States often became outspoken advocates of growing Soviet-American trade ties.[45]

For at least a century, George Ball has noted, many groups within Western society have adhered to the notion that "peace could best be promoted by encouraging the world-wide exchange of goods and commodities. The free flow of goods across national boundaries would, it was contended, erase misunderstandings and differences of opinion among the world's peoples." This was believed to be true because "merchants carried in their packs fresh ideas and new visions." Yet Ball doubts that modern history provides any reliable evidence to support such an expectation. The First World War, for example, cannot be made to fit such a theory of the relationship between an expanding volume of trade and world peace. Before World War II, which resulted in wholesale devastation for Germany and Soviet Russia, both countries had extensive trade relations. In more recent years, Communist China was the U.S.S.R.'s largest trading partner before the two countries "split" around 1960.[46] (It should also be noted that there is a contrary theory about the relationship between trade and peace. This is the idea—as exemplified by the notion that the "merchants of death" caused World War I—that commercial and trading interests *benefit from war* by reaping large profits from it. Some modern interpretations of American foreign policy endeavor to account for the nation's effort to establish massive political influence throughout the Third World by reference to the business and commercial incentives propelling American policy in that direction.)[47]

A more recent development in American foreign policy, highlighting the importance of trade questions, is the emphasis which officials in Washington have accorded to international human rights. The United States, for example, joined with other members of the international community in utilizing a trade embargo to alter the position of the government of Southern Rhodesia (or Zimbabwe) with regard to political participation by the country's black majority. For several years, Washington also expressed its opposition to the Castro regime in Cuba by attempting to impose trade sanctions upon that country.

Patterns in American Trade

Let us identify the principal patterns evident in recent American trade relations by focusing initially upon their direction, nature, and magnitude.

The largest single trading partner of the United States is its northern neighbor, Canada. Canada supplies almost 20 percent of the total imports entering the United States; and it buys approximately the same percentage of America's goods and services sold abroad.

Beginning with the postwar recovery of Western Europe in the early 1950s, that region in time emerged as one of the strongest trading centers on the globe and one of America's major trading partners. With both a population and a collective Gross National Product (GNP) larger than that of the United States, Western Europe is a primary market for American exports; and the region is in turn a leading supplier of imports into the United States. Those European states belonging to the European Economic Community (EEC)* comprise the largest single market for American foreign sales. For many years, the United States has shown a surplus in its trade

*For a fuller discussion of the European Economic Community, see Chapter 11.

balance with the EEC. Steady growth has characterized United States-EEC trade relations since the 1950s. Agricultural products comprise a large portion (upwards of 30 percent of total exports) of American sales in European markets.[48]

Japan is another important customer of the United States in international trade. Japanese-American commercial relations, as a difficult problem in American foreign policy, is dealt with more extensively in Chapter 15. Here, it suffices to say that, while the volume of Japanese imports to America has risen sharply, Japan is one of the largest purchasers of American agricultural commodities and other exports.[49]

Another striking development in postwar American trade policy has been the extent to which trade has grown steadily between the United States and the Third World. From 1970 to 1977, for example, exports by the United States to members of the Third World increased by some 400 percent; and projections by the World Bank indicate that continued growth can be anticipated. The United States depends heavily upon developing nations for purchases of raw materials and food imports. In turn, American exports to Third World countries comprise chiefly motor vehicles, industrial machinery, electrical equipment, aircraft, and agricultural products. By the late 1970s, nations throughout the Third World were buying some $40 billion annually in American goods and services—or over one-third of all sales by the United States abroad. The United States sold more manufactured goods to Third World nations than to Western Europe, Japan, and the Communist nations combined. Moreover, many Third World nations actively seek to increase private investments by American firms; earnings from overseas investments comprise another major category of assets in the nation's balance of international payments. Collectively (excluding the members of OPEC), the nations of the Third World still buy more from the United States than they sell to it.[50]

Another relatively new dimension of American trade policy is exchange with Communist countries, principally the Soviet Union and the People's Republic of China (PRC). In recent years, Soviet-American trade has become a widely debated aspect of foreign policy; Congress has been especially active in this sphere of foreign relations.

During the era of active Cold War hostilities, as much because of political as for economic reasons, trade between the superpowers was extremely limited. Stalin's death in 1953 marked a gradual change in both Soviet internal and external policy; and by the late 1960s, a condition of détente was beginning to supersede the Cold War. The Soviet hierarchy's ongoing program of modernization and industrialization compelled the U.S.S.R. to turn to the West for the purchase of a wide variety of imports. These included massive food (especially American wheat) purchases abroad; heavy machinery and industrial equipment; and advanced computer systems. Without such imports, the Soviet Union risked falling behind the United States and other advanced nations economically.

During the 1960s and 1970s, Soviet trade with the West rose sharply. Between 1970 and 1975, the volume of Soviet-American trade increased by around 1000 percent (from 161 million rubles to 1.6 billion rubles). From the United States, the Soviet state acquired large and ongoing grain shipments, along with oil drilling equipment and technology and modern computer systems. By contrast, few Soviet-made consumer goods were competitive in the American market; the problem of getting spare parts and necessary service impeded Soviet sales of items like industrial equipment. Another valuable commodity which the Soviet government had long sold in foreign markets—petroleum products —was of course desired by the United States; but extensive trade in this commodity presented numerous difficulties for both countries from the viewpoint of national defense and security. For obvious reasons, the United States could not risk becoming "dependent" upon the Soviet Union for a major portion of its foreign oil purchases.[51]

A continued (if slow) growth in Soviet-American trade may be anticipated in the future, provided the political climate does not impede this process. For both countries, the trade question is momentously influenced by political and strategic calculations. Since the Communist Revolution, Soviet officials have viewed trade as an instrument of their overall foreign policy. As illustrated by the Reagan Administration's attitude toward expanded trade with the U.S.S.R., during some periods American officials have been influenced by comparable calculations. During the early 1980s, for example—after Soviet efforts to subjugate Afghanistan, intervene in Poland, and support subversive activities in Central America—President Reagan and his advisers believed that the United States and its allies should curtail trade relations with the Soviet Union. As we shall see in Chapter 11, this proved to be a contentious issue in relations among the NATO allies.

An even more recent development in American trade policy is the prospect of expanding commercial relations with the People's Republic of China. More accurately, the emergence of this question represented a revival of one of the oldest themes in American diplomatic history. Trade relations between the United States and China were inaugurated in 1784, when the the Yankee trading ship *Empress of China* sailed to the Orient. In the mid-nineteenth century, American business interests were captivated by the thought of fortunes to be made in "the China trade,"

which (they erroneously thought) presented an unlimited market for American products.* Then, at the end of the nineteenth century, one of the most important principles of American diplomacy—the concept of the "Open Door policy" in China—was enunciated by the McKinley Administration. The Open Door concept was designed to guarantee free American commercial access to China.[52]

For a period of over 20 years after the Communist victory in 1948, relations between Communist China and the United States were extremely tense. Insofar as trade questions were important between them, the United States endeavored (with minimum success) to *prevent* trade by its friends and allies with the new Communist regime. By the early 1970s, the Nixon Administration concluded that the time had arrived to end the estrangement in Sino-American relations. After the President's historic visit to China in 1972, trade questions came to the fore rapidly. (The Chinese government was seeking alternative trade sources to replace its once heavy reliance upon the Soviet Union and to support its modernization program.) In that year, imports

---

*The prospect of seemingly unlimited profits to be made in the China market has lured American trading and commercial interests for almost two centuries. In the nineteenth century, Yankee traders were intrigued by the prospect of getting every Chinaman to lengthen his gown by an inch; if that occurred, the textile mills in New England would have a guaranteed market for many years in the future! Alternatively, if every Chinese male could be induced to wear a necktie, manufacturers in the United States would be prosperous for years ahead. A modern variation on this old idea is the notion that if every adult Chinese can be induced to buy one American-made soft drink annually, this would result in an annual market of close to half a billion sales! Today, as in the past, where the Chinese society would acquire the purchasing power for large-scale imports was not a question Americans tended to ask or be concerned about. For background on Sino-American trade, see John K. Fairbank, *The United States and China* (New York: Viking Press, 1962), especially pp. 106–128, 246–262.

and exports combined between the two countries totaled some $95 million; by 1978, this figure had grown to over $1.1 billion. By the latter date, China was importing goods and services from the United States valued at some $327 million annually, while its sales to America amounted to some $324 million annually. With each passing year, Chinese officials expressed interest in expanding their purchases in the American market. As in earlier eras, the lure of "the China market" exercised a potent attraction for some business firms. One projection, for example, anticipated that by the mid-1980s the United States would be selling goods and services valued at $2.5 billion annually to the Chinese.[53]

Many of the same problems confront a significant expansion in Sino-American trade as beset trade between the United States and the Soviet Union. No great demand for China's customary exports exists in the United States. As one authority has expressed it: "China needs United States food grains and technology more than the United States needs Chinese fireworks, bristles, down, and feathers...."[54] The Chinese viewpoint on trade is also heavily colored by political considerations, such as a desire to find sources of supply that are alternatives to the Soviet Union. Official American interest in trade with China is not, of course, lacking in political motivations, one of which is a desire to counterbalance Soviet influence in Asia by strengthening China's economic system and military potential. Expanded Sino-American trade also encounters the same problem (to this point, seldom raised directly between Washington and Peking) of the relationship between trade and Peking's readiness to observe certain human rights principles.

Then the old question remains unresolved: Where will one of the poorest societies on the globe find the money to finance a growing stream of American imports? Indica-

tions are, for example, that China possesses vast oil deposits—ultimately sufficient for its own needs and for export to foreign customers. Developing this important resource, however, is likely to take many years. Meanwhile, the cost of such development —entailing the importation of American and other foreign equipment and technology —is likely to be extremely expensive and to involve further drains on an already adverse Chinese balance of payments. For these reasons, Sino-American trade is likely to grow moderately in the years ahead and to be conditioned by China's ability to obtain foreign credits for its purchases from the United States and other countries.[55]

Trade Problems and Prospects

In this concluding section, let us examine three important questions affecting the future of American trade. The first is the evolution of American trade policy for almost a half-century after the New Deal. Throughout the history of the United States down to the mid-1930s, heated public debates erupted from time to time over the tariff question. During some periods (as in 1930, when Congress enacted the Hawley-Smoot Tariff, one of the highest tariff walls in American history), high tariffs have discouraged imports and have generally impeded the expansion of global trade. As part of its program to overcome the effects of the Great Depression, the Roosevelt Administration sponsored, and Congress enacted, the Reciprocal Trade Agreements Act in June 1934.[56] This act was a landmark in American trade policy: Throughout the years which followed, the United States was identified with the principle of "reciprocal," or liberalized, trade. According to the provisions of this act, the United States was prepared to grant tariff reductions on imports from Country X, if that country was prepared to grant the same concession on exports from the United States.

In the postwar period, the United States has repeatedly affirmed its adherence to the principle of liberalized trade, as in its efforts to encourage formation of the European Common Market (which in time became the European Economic Community). During the nearly half-century which elapsed between passage of the Reciprocal Trade Agreements Act and the late 1970s, the average tariff rate on imports into the United States declined sharply—from almost 60 percent of the value of the goods in 1934 to around 5 percent of their value in 1978. Conversely, in part because of its adherence to liberal trade principles, sales of American goods and commodities in foreign markets climbed to some $234 billion by the early 1980s. (The services performed by Americans for foreigners—as in banking, investment, and data processing—added another $140 billion as assets in the balance of payments.)

Since World War II, several major and minor revisions of the trade laws have been undertaken—all with the objective of maximizing opportunities for American commerce abroad and encouraging an expansion of international trade. Under the Kennedy Administration, for example, the Trade Expansion Act of 1962 gave the President the authority to grant further tariff reductions on a reciprocal basis with other countries and, over a period of years, to lift tariffs altogether on certain categories of imports. This act also contained certain "escape clause" provisions, whereby tariff relief could be granted to American industries which were particularly hard hit by a rising volume of imports; and it specified several steps which the government could take to assist domestic businesses and industries facing mounting foreign competition.[57] The Ford Administration sponsored, and Congress ultimately enacted, another significant revision of the nation's trade laws.

Significant changes in America's trade laws also received high priority from the Carter Administration.[58] After five years of discussion among the leading trading nations of the world, by early 1979 in the "Toyko Round" their representatives had virtually completed agreement upon a new set of principles which would govern trade among them. As in the past, the goal was to lower tariff rates; but in this period, an intensive effort was made to eliminate certain nontariff barriers to trade which restricted international commerce even more perhaps than high import duties.

As always on major public policy issues, executive officials were subjected to contrary forces and pressures. On the one hand—with petroleum imports escalating and the American balance of payments deficit rising—the President and his advisers had a strong inducement to *maximize trade opportunities abroad,* in order to stimulate exports. On the other hand—with imports into the United States continuing to rise and with an ever growing circle of domestic industries (often joined by labor unions) demanding protection from foreign competition—American officials were also subjected *to intense "protectionist" pressures* from the textile, steel, leather, rubber, automobile, and other industries, which believed their economic survival was at stake.

Congress was continually subjected to lobbying campaigns by domestic pressure groups seeking preferential treatment under the trade laws. By the early 1980s, for example, the Reagan Administration was under intense pressure from some American business concerns and labor unions to "protect" the American economy from the adverse effects of Japanese automobile and other imports.

Although Republicans have historically been less sympathetic to free trade than the Democrats, the Reagan White House hesitated to grant such requests, perhaps for two fundamental reasons. One was that, if Japanese imports to America were sharply restricted, in time Americans *sales* to Japan would inevitably decline, to the detriment of groups like American farmers. The other constraint was knowledge that protectionist measures did little in the long run to restore America's position in world trade. The fundamental problem—which the Reagan Administration sought to correct by a series of measures—was that America's *rate of economic productivity* was deteriorating vis-à-vis Japan and other foreign competitors. Until that reality was changed, the nation's competitive position in the world market would continue to decline.

The second major problem of deep concern to American officials by the late 1970s was the widening "trade gap," or balance of payments deficit, confronting the United States.[59] In its simplest terms, this meant Americans were buying more abroad than they were selling. This problem was in turn part of a larger phenomenon: the rapid growth in the debts which the United States owed to private institutions and governments abroad. America's external indebtedness rose from over $55 billion in 1972 to more than $130 billion by 1978.[60] Although Americans had reduced their purchases of foreign oil, by the early 1980s merchandise and commodity imports by the United States exceeded exports by some $7 billion dollars, giving the nation an adverse balance of trade. From Japan alone the United States bought almost $40 billion in imports, while selling only $22 billion in exports to the Japanese society. This disparity in Japanese-American trade had become a matter of deep concern to officials in Washington and to communities (like Detroit) whose prosperity was impaired by a massive influx of Japanese-made products.

In their campaign to reduce the nation's foreign indebtedness, American officials have proposed a variety of short-term and long-term remedies. In the short run, the most obvious step was to try to reduce the nation's reliance upon oil and natural gas imports—by all odds, the largest single item responsible for the trade imbalance. By encouraging energy conservation measures at home, the Carter and Reagan administrations were moderately successful in achieving this goal. Yet officials in Washington recognized that this was only a partial and expediential solution. In the long run, other steps—like developing alternative energy supplies for petroleum and natural gas, and increasing the nation's own output of oil and natural gas—were demanded.

As a solution to the trade deficit, even greater reliance was placed upon another approach—the promotion of American exports—to close the trade gap. Joining with other administrations before it, the Carter Administration took the position that this was a far more beneficial and promising step than for the American society to adopt "protectionist" measures drastically restricting imports.

This approach had several advantages. It involved expansion of economic activity for those industries and services in which the United States already enjoyed a comparative advantage.* It helped stimulate a growing worldwide demand for American products, technological know-how, and private investment—the last two being crucial perhaps for the economic advancement of many Third

---

*In its simplest terms, the concept of "comparative advantage"—a pivotal idea which is the basis of international trade—is that Country X can produce a unit of a particular commodity more cheaply than Country Y; and for some other commodity, the reverse may be true. Therefore, both societies benefit when the two countries exchange those goods and services each can produce more cheaply. Thus, both countries gain if America exchanges wheat for certain kinds of Japanese-made electronic equipment; or Third World societies gain by exchanging raw materials for American-produced industrial machinery.

World countries. If Japan's postwar experience served as a reliable guide, expanding export sales also generate a large volume of continuing American sales overseas. Nor would an expansion of exports call for the kind of radical readjustment in the life-styles and standard of living for millions of American citizens which would inevitably occur with a sharp cutback in imports.[61]

Late in 1978, President Carter announced a new campaign to stimulate American exports, in an effort to strengthen the nation's position in international trade. Carter emphasized three steps needed to expand American sales abroad. The first was governmental assistance to, and encouragement of, American business firms actively engaged in the export trade and desiring to increase their foreign sales. The second was an effort to remove domestic barriers (such as certain provisions of the tax law, export license requirements, and other governmental regulations) tending to inhibit exports. The third step entailed attempts by American officials to reduce foreign barriers to the sale of American products and services overseas. The outstanding example of this problem was Japan, which continued to place numerous restraints upon foreign sales and investments within its borders; but on a less publicized basis, such problems were duplicated in many other settings throughout the world. Eliminating or reducing these impediments would contribute significantly to encouraging higher levels of American sales in foreign markets.

Despite pervasive fears throughout the American society that the United States was unable to hold its own in international trade against countries employing "cheap labor," or having a primitive standard of living, as a rule this idea was erroneous. Admittedly, it was true of some categories of foreign-produced goods (such as textiles and certain consumer goods) involving a low level of industrial technology or in which labor costs were a high proportion of the overall costs of production. Yet, as Japan's experience clearly demonstrated, an industrialized society enjoying a high standard of living could remain competitive —and could even widen its competitive advantage over other countries—in certain categories of goods and services. For a number of American products—aircraft, advanced computer systems, oil exploration machinery and technology, certain chemicals, and agricultural products, to list the leading ones— few countries had a stronger competitive position in the world market than the United States. In 1979, for example, President Carter's Council of Economic Advisers (CEA) concluded that the global demand for American "services"—such as fees paid for technological planning and assistance (as in the oil industry), royalties, and the investment of American private capital abroad—was continuing to rise. The CEA's study found that in the years ahead, America would continue to have—and should be able to strengthen —its comparative advantage in this important segment of foreign commerce.[62]

Two other steps would also contribute significantly to reducing America's balance of payments deficit and to enhancing its position in world trade. One of these is the American society's ability *to control inflation*. Rapid increases in the prices of American goods and services did not improve the nation's competitive *status* in foreign trade. Among their other adverse effects, inflationary tendencies prompted the members of OPEC to promulgate new price increases for Middle East oil.

The other step—in the last analysis, perhaps the key to whether the United States could expand its foreign sales significantly —was *to increase domestic productivity*. In recent years, the rate of overall economic productivity in the United States has risen very slowly, in some years imperceptibly. Yet for many decades, rising productivity was the principal reason why (with fewer and fewer workers each year employed in this sector) American agricultural productivity in the United States had climbed steadily, owing in large part to the application of scientific methods and modern technology to food and crop production. The result was that today American agriculture is at the forefront in the production of commodities like wheat, corn, and soybeans. The American farmer could produce these and other crops at a lower unit cost than his counterpart in nearly any other country. As the Soviet state tacitly admitted by its constantly rising grain purchases in the American market, neither Communist nor other societies could usually match the productive levels achieved by American farmers.[63]

A third problem in American trade policy which had come to the fore by the late 1970s involved the use of trade as an instrument for the achievement of diplomatic objectives. The most widely publicized political issue in this regard was the matter of human rights violations in Soviet Russia. Prompted in part by keen congressional interest in the question, the Carter Administration committed the United States to an intensive campaign to promote and protect human rights globally.[64] Yet in practice, Washington's interest in human rights was *highly selective*. Evident concern, for example, was expressed about the Soviet Union's treatment of Jews and other minorities and dissidents; and the United States played an active role in supporting efforts by blacks to acquire equal rights from white-ruled governments, like Southern Rhodesia and South Africa, on the African continent. Conversely, American officials demonstrated much less concern about human rights violations by Communist China; about threats to human rights by black regimes in

Africa; or about widespread and systematic assaults upon such rights by several governments in Asia (such as the Philippines).

Toward the Soviet Union and Southern Rhodesia particularly, the United States government has relied upon trade sanctions to accomplish its diplomatic goals. In the case of the U.S.S.R., the impetus for restricting trade privileges for the purpose of compelling a more liberal Soviet policy toward Jewish citizens came largely from Congress, with little enthusiasm being displayed by the executive branch for this approach. The President and his advisers raised major questions about the wisdom of this course and about the tangible results which could be expected from it. Although congressionally imposed restrictions on Soviet-American trade perhaps achieved some temporary success, in the long run they failed to accomplish their basic purpose.[65] Predictably, Moscow objected strenuously to this infringement upon its sovereignty and repeatedly refused to revise its emigration laws to fit American demands; even critics of the Soviet regime often conceded that Congress' actions resulted in no discernible improvement in the treatment which Moscow accorded minorities and politically dissident groups within its borders. As time passed, Congress appeared to lose much of its ardor for relying upon trade sanctions to induce changes in Soviet behavior.

As will be explained more fully in Chapter 13, the other example of reliance upon trade policy to accomplish diplomatic goals is provided by the cases of Southern Rhodesia (Zimbabwe) and (at least potentially) the Republic of South Africa. For many years, both countries have had white-ruled governments; and South Africa epitomizes the concept of *apartheid,* or racial separateness, to which the vast majority of black Africans objects vehemently. Southern Rhodesia declared its independence from Great Britian in

1965—an act considered illegal by most members of the international community. Responding to censure resolutions by the United Nations, the United States joined other countries in imposing a trade boycott against Southern Rhodesia (a move it did not favor, except in arms sales, in relations with South Africa).

What impact did trade sanctions have upon developments in Southern Rhodesia? The verdict on that question clearly must be mixed. Under the Nixon and Ford administrations, Secretary of State Henry Kissinger engaged in a series of partially successful negotiations aimed at broadening the political base by granting blacks at least limited access to political power. By the late 1970s, a new government—led by a black prime minister, with several black cabinet officers, and a more representative legislature—was announced in Salisbury. It is reasonable to suppose that the trade embargo, and other evidence of international censure of the Rhodesian government's policies, contributed in some measure to this result.

Yet, too much emphasis should not be accorded American trade policy in explaining this outcome. In the first place, the trade boycott against Southern Rhodesia was never truly effective. Communist and black African nations violated it with impunity. The legislation requiring the United States to observe the boycott allowed for the importation of chrome ore from Southern Rhodesia when the President believed this step to be essential for national security (which the White House usually determined). In earlier cases—like those of Castro's Cuba and Communist China—America's reliance upon trade embargoes to achieve diplomatic goals had little noteworthy success in producing change in the behavior of the political systems of these countries. (The only evident result of the boycott was to inflame Cuban-American and Sino-American relations for many years thereafter.)

Moreover, as American officials repeatedly observed in discussing the case of South Africa, a trade embargo is a crude and indiscriminate political weapon. More often than not, when a boycott for diplomatic objectives can be made effective (which happens rarely), it penalizes most heavily *the disadvantaged groups* within the society concerned, or the black populations of Southern Rhodesia and South Africa. Unemployment and other forms of economic dislocation precipitated by the boycott are likely to injure low-income groups most seriously—or the very groups whose condition the boycott seeks to improve! In more theoretical terms, it is difficult to understand how precipitating economic dislocations within a society is likely to strengthen the prospects for democracy within it.[66]

No doubt, the United States will continue from time to time to utilize trade as a diplomatic instrument, perhaps chiefly because Congress demands it. The imposition of stringent terms of trade upon the Soviet Union in behalf of human rights or other goals, for example, appears to be a tempting and usually widely publicized blow for liberty! Whether such steps in fact actually enhance the cause of human rights or political freedoms abroad, however, remains a complex and highly debatable question.

NOTES

1. See Daniel Lerner, ed., *Propaganda in War and Crisis* (New York: Stewart, 1951), pp. 7–73, 84–85, 276.
2. For more detailed discussion of the weapons and techniques employed in psychological warfare, see Terrence H. Qualter, *Propaganda and Psychological Warfare* (New York: Random House, 1962), p. 74.
3. See the views of George V. Allen, as quoted in Thomas C. Sorensen, *The Word War: The*

Story of American Propaganda (New York: Harper & Row, 1968), p. 105.

4. President Kennedy's views are cited in ibid., pp. 127–128.

5. See Qualter, *Propaganda and Psychological Warfare,* p. 3.

6. For more detailed discussion and analysis of the Nazi propaganda machine, under its director Dr. Joseph Goebbels, see Alexander G. Hardy, *Hitler's Secret Weapon: the "Managed" Press and Propaganda Machine of Nazi Germany* (New York: Vantage Press, 1968).

7. For general treatments of Moscow's reliance upon propaganda to wage the Cold War, see: Frederick C. Barghoorn, *The Soviet Cultural Offensive* (Princeton, N.J.: Princeton University Press, 1960); and the same author's *Soviet Foreign Propaganda* (Princeton, N.J.: Princeton University Press, 1964). An illuminating study of Soviet propaganda directed at a particular region is Baruch A. Hazan, *Soviet Propaganda: A Case Study of the Middle East Conflict* (Jerusalem, Israel: Keter Publishing House, 1976). Current Soviet propaganda activities are described in greater detail in "The Great Propaganda War," *U.S. News and World Report,* **92** (January 11, 1982), 27–32.

8. Background studies of American propaganda activities during and immediately after World War II are provided in: John Henderson, *The United States Information Agency* (New York: Praeger Publishers, 1969), pp. 3–62; and Sorensen, *The Word War,* pp. 1–31.

9. For a detailed discussion of USIA's activities, see Robert E. Elder, *The United States Information Agency and American Foreign Policy* (Syracuse, N.Y.: Syracuse University Press, 1968).

10. For a discussion of the new United States International Communication Agency, see "International Communication Agency," *Department of State Bulletin,* **78** (May, 1978), pp. 32–33; and *United States Government Manual, 1979–1980* (Washington, D.C.: Office of the Federal Register, General Services Administration, 1979), pp. 583–588.

11. See the discussion by Barbara Crossette in *New York Times,* March 28, 1982. A more detailed treatment, providing background on the goals of American propaganda activities, is Robert E. Elder, *The Information Machine: The United States Information Agency and American Foreign Policy* (Syracuse, N. Y.: Syracuse University Press, 1968), pp. 178–333.

12. See the views of former USIA Director Edward R. Murrow, as quoted in Sorensen, *The Word War,* p. 144. Italics in the original. A detailed examination of the role of American propaganda agencies under the Reagan Administration is Chalmers M. Roberts, "New Image for Voice of America," *New York Times Magazine,* April 13, 1982, 107–114.

13. For one defense of this approach to American propaganda operations, see the views of former USIA Director George V. Allen, as quoted in Sorensen, *The Word War,* p. 208.

14. See I. M. Destler, *Presidents, Bureaucrats and Foreign Policy: the Politics of Organizational Reform* (Princeton, N.J.: Princeton University Press, 1972), p. 163; and Morton H. Halperin, *Bureaucratic Politics and Foreign Policy* (Washington, D.C.: The Brookings Institution, 1973), p. 37.

15. Halperin, *Bureaucratic Politics and Foreign Policy,* p. 126.

16. For detailed discussion and examples of congressional attitudes toward propaganda activities by executive agencies, see William O. Chittick, *State Department, Press and Pressure Groups: A Role Analysis* (New York: John Wiley and Sons, 1970), pp. 39–46. See also Henderson, *The United States Information Agency,* pp. 220–243.

17. See Henderson, *The United States Information Agency,* pp. 284–291; and Elder, *The Information Machine,* pp. 320–333.

18. See the report on Soviet jamming of VOA broadcasts in *U.S. News and World Report,* **LXXXIV** (June 12, 1978), 55–56; and the analysis by John F. Burns in *New York Times,* December 31, 1981.

19. America's Lend-Lease program before and

during World War II is discussed in detail in: Warren F. Kimball, *The Most Unsordid Act: Lend-Lease, 1939–1941* (Baltimore: The Johns Hopkins University Press, 1969); and Edward R. Stettinius, *Lend-Lease: Weapon for Victory* (New York: Macmillan and Co., 1944).

20. The decision by the Truman Administration to cancel the Lend-Lease program soon after the defeat of Germany is explained in the first volume of President Harry S Truman's memoirs, *Year of Decisions* (Garden City, N.Y.: Doubleday and Co., 1955), pp. 227–234.

21. The origins and purpose of the Greek-Turkish Aid Program are discussed in Arthur H. Vandenberg, Jr., ed., *The Private Papers of Senator Vandenberg* (Boston: Houghton Mifflin Co., 1952), pp. 337–373.

22. See ibid., pp. 373–399; and Dean Acheson, *Present at the Creation: My Years in the State Department* (New York: W. W. Norton, 1969), pp. 226–236.

23. The formulation of the Alliance for Progress, its goals, and early accomplishments are dealt with in J. Warren Nystrom and Nathan A. Haverstock, *The Alliance for Progress* (Princeton, N.J.: D. Van Nostrand Co., 1966). For more recent discussion, see Terence A. Todman, "Latin American Development in an Interdependent World," *Department of State Bulletin,* 77 (October 3, 1977), 440–445.

24. See "Department Urges Appropriation of Funds for International Financial Institutions," *Department of State Bulletin,* 76 (March 7, 1977), pp. 198–201. The Reagan Administration's viewpoint toward multilateral aid activities by the United States is analyzed by Jim Anderson in the Baton Rouge *Sunday Advocate,* April 25, 1982.

25. See, for example, "The Role of Human Rights Policy in Arms Transfers for Latin America," *Department of State Bulletin,* 78 (November, 1978), 51–53; and "Secretary [Vance] Testifies on Administration's Approach to Foreign Assistance," *Department of State Bulletin,* 76 (March 14, 1977), 236–240. Congress' interest in promoting human rights abroad is analyzed in a recent study by Cecil V. Crabb, Jr., and Pat Holt, *Invitation to Struggle: Congress, the President and Foreign Policy* (Washington, D.C.: Congressional Quarterly, Inc., 1980), Chapter 7.

26. See *United States Government Manual: 1979–80* (Washington, D.C.: General Services Administration, 1979), pp. 423–430.

27. "Secretary Vance Gives Overview of Foreign Assistance Programs," *Department of State Bulletin,* 76 (March 28, 1977), 284–291.

28. *Statistical Abstract of the United States: 1978* (Washington, D.C.: Bureau of the Census, 1978), p. 871.

29. Lucy W. Benson, "Security Assistance: FY 1980 Proposals," *Department of State Bulletin,* 79 (April, 1979), 42–48.

30. For a detailed discussion of Israel's critical economic problems, dictating continuing reliance upon public and private American aid, see Alon Ben-Meir, "Israel in the War's Long Aftermath," *Current History,* 80 (January, 1981), 23–27, 40; and *The Middle East,* 5th ed. (Washington, D. C.: Congressional Quarterly, Inc., 1981), pp. 129–131.

31. Indictments of the American economic and military aid programs have been numerous and sweeping since at least the mid-1950s. Many of them were popularized in the novel by William J. Lederer and Eugene Burdick, *The Ugly American* (New York: Fawcett World Library, 1958). Other telling charges against the foreign aid program have been brought by former Senator J. William Fulbright. See, particularly, his two books: *The Arrogance of Power* (New York: Random House, 1966), pp. 69–157; and *The Crippled Giant: American Foreign Policy and Its Domestic Consequences* (New York: Random House, 1972), pp. 72–102. America's reliance upon foreign aid as a means of imposing hegemony on other countries—and, in the process, creating hostile reactions to the United States throughout the Third World—is a major theme of "revisionist" interpreters of postwar American policy. See Richard H. Barnet, *Intervention and Revolution: America's Confrontation with Insurgent Movements Around the World* (New York: World Publishing Co., 1968).

32. See the views of Representative Clement J.

Zablocki (Democrat of Wisconsin) on the foreign aid program, as cited by Graham Hovey, in *New York Times,* July 30, 1978.

33. See, for example, the discussion of "The Aid Relationship," in C. R. Hensman, *Rich Against Poor: The Reality of Aid* (Baltimore: Penguin Books, 1975), pp. 189–233; and Theodore Geiger, *The Conflicted Relationship: the West and the Transformation of Asia, Africa and Latin America* (New York: McGraw-Hill, 1967). A concrete case in American policy is analyzed in Albert Fishlow, "Flying Down to Rio," *Foreign Affairs,* **57** (Winter, 1978–79), 387–405.

34. The story of massive Soviet involvement in Egypt after 1967, culminating in rising Egyptian resentment against the Soviet presence and the expulsion of Russian advisers in 1972, is told in Alvin Z. Rubinstein, *Red Star on the Nile: The Soviet-Egyptian Influence Relationship Since the June War* (Princeton, N.J.: Princeton University Press, 1977).

35. The politically disruptive effects of external aid upon Third World societies have been cogently analyzed by Robert L. Heilbroner, *The Great Ascent: the Struggle for Economic Development in Our Time* (New York: Harper & Row, 1963). See also Hensman, *Rich Against Poor,* pp. 63–162.

36. See, for example, the discussion of growing disparities and conflicts among Third World countries in: Leslie Wolf-Phillips, "Why Third World?" *Third World Quarterly,* **1** (January, 1979), 105–114; "Third World—Cockpit of Turmoil," *U.S. News and World Report,* **86** (June 25, 1979), 51–55; and discussions of disputes among Third World nations concerning Cuba's involvement in Africa, in *New York Times,* June 11, 1978.

37. See, for example, the interview with the Jamaican ambassador to the United Nations, Donald A. Mills, in *U.S. News and World Report,* **85** (July 31, 1978), 61–62. He observed that, while there had been considerable overall economic progress throughout the Third World, for millions of people "there was no progress. They are still abjectly poor—some even poorer than before." In that respect, the results of foreign aid for donor and recipient countries alike had been "disappointing"; few gains from foreign aid had in fact benefitted the masses of the people. This same disparity between overall gains and per capita gains throughout the Third World is highlighted in the detailed study "World Population: Silent Explosion" (Washington, D.C.: Department of State, 1978).

38. Thus, the Third World's share of the total world population grew from some 66% in 1950, to 70% in 1970, to 78% anticipated by the year 2000. While North America had a rate of population growth below .9% annually, Europe had .6%, and the Soviet Union had 1.0%. For the Third World, annual rates of population increase were: Africa, 2.6%; Latin America, 2.7%; China, 1.7%; India, 2.4%; and Asia, 2.4%. See "World Population: Silent Explosion," p. 4. A study by the World Bank indicated that in the period 1975–2000, the cities of the Third World would have to accommodate approximately 1 billion additional people. The study projected that some 600 million people throughout the Third World would still be living in "absolute poverty" by the end of the century. Graham Hovey, in *New York Times,* August 16, 1979.

39. Useful studies of the emergence and problems of regional organizations are: Paul A. Tharp, Jr., ed., *Regional International Organizations: Structures and Functions* (New York: St. Martin's Press, 1971); and J. S. Nye, *Peace in Parts: Integration and Conflict in Regional Organization* (Boston: Little, Brown and Co., 1971).

40. See the analysis of America's position in international trade in *U.S. News and World Report,* **92** (April 26, 1982), 56–57.

41. See the chart in "United States Trade and Foreign Policy," *Current History,* **76** (May/June, 1979), inside back cover.

42. See the data presented in: Ronald I. Meltzer, "United States Trade Policy: An Overview," ibid., 193–194; "Agenda of International Economic Issues," in the Department of State's *Current Policy* series (June, 1978), p. 1; and "Energy and Foreign Policy," in ibid. (June, 1979), p. 1.

43. Data on America's dependence upon oil im-

ports, primarily from the Middle East, are presented in: the State Department's publication, "Energy and Foreign Policy," pp. 1–3; *Newsweek,* **93** (February 19, 1979), 20–21; and the two articles by petroleum expert Walter J. Levy, in *New York Times,* January 4 and January 5, 1979. See also the discussion of the role of oil imports in the nation's balance of payments in *U.S. News and World Report,* **92** (April 26, 1982), 57.

44. See the views of Felix Rohatyn, projecting America's oil import needs in the years ahead, in *New York Times,* October 3, 1979.

45. Prospects and problems in Soviet-American trade are identified and discussed in: Raymond Vernon, "The Fragile Foundations of East-West Trade," *Foreign Affairs,* **57** (Summer, 1979), 1035–1051; Jack Brougher, "U.S. Exports Accelerating; Trade Support Reaffirmed," *Business America,* **2** (July 30, 1979), 22–23; and Robert C. Stuart, "United States-Soviet Trade," *Current History,* **76** (May/June, 1979), 206–209, 229.

46. George W. Ball, *Diplomacy for a Crowded World: An American Foreign Policy* (Boston: Little, Brown and Co., 1976), pp. 102–103.

47. The influence upon American diplomacy, both historically and in the postwar period, of powerful business and commercial interests is a major theme of several "revisionist" interpretations of external policy. See, for example, Stephen E. Ambrose, *Rise to Globalism: American Foreign Policy, 1938–1970* (Baltimore: Penguin Books, 1971); Richard J. Barnet, *Intervention and Revolution;* Melvin Gurtov, *The United States Against the Third World: Antinationalism and Intervention* (New York: Praeger Publishers, 1974); William A. Williams, *The Tragedy of American Diplomacy,* 2nd ed. (New York: Dell Publishing Co., 1972).

48. Detailed information on United States trade with Europe and projections for the future may be found in: "Western Europe: U.S. Exports Continue Upward," *Business America,* **2** (July 30, 1979), 10–21; Robert D. Hormats, "Managing Economic Problems in the Industrialized Democracies," *Department of State Bulletin,* **78** (December, 1978), 32–36; and Werner J. Feld, "Trade With West Europe and Japan," *Current History,* **76** (May/June, 1979), 201–206, 223.

49. A detailed examination of Japanese-American economic relations may be found in the State Department publication, "Japan and the United States: A Cooperative Relationship," *Current Policy,* **374** (March 1, 1982), 1–7. An informative analysis of problems in trade relations between the two countries—emphasizing the need to raise America's productivity to preserve its competitive position—is James C. Abegglen and Thomas M. Hout, "Facing Up to the Trade Gap With Japan," *Foreign Affairs,* **57** (Fall, 1978), 146–168.

50. America's trade with, and overall economic involvement in, the Third World is discussed in: David D. Newsom, "The U.S. and the Third World: Partners or Plaintiffs," *Department of State Bulletin,* **79** (January, 1979), 30–32; and Shams B. Fsraidoon, "United States Trade With the Developing World," *Current History,* **76** (May/June, 1979), 214–218, 226.

51. Recent data on Soviet-American trade is provided in Stuart, "United States-Soviet Trade," 206–207. For background on the development of Soviet-American trade, see Gerald L. Steibel, *Détente: Promises and Pitfalls* (New York: Crane, Russak and Co., 1975), pp. 34–46.

52. For detailed discussion of the evolution and application of America's "Open Door" policy in Asia before World War II, see Julius W. Pratt, *A History of United States Foreign Policy* (Englewood Cliffs, N.J.: Prentice-Hall, 1955), pp. 434–451, 576–591; and John K. Fairbank, *The United States and China* (New York: Viking Press, 1958), pp. 106–128, 246–278.

53. Data on recent and projected Sino-American trade are contained in: Jan S. Prybyla, "United States Trade With China," *Current History,* **76** (May/June, 1979), 209–214; Susanne S. Lotarski and Nai-ruenn Chen, "Visits, Agreements Improve Prospects for Trade with

China," *Business America,* **2** (July 30, 1979), 21–22; and *New York Times,* August 7, 1979.

54. Prybyla, "United States Trade With China," 211.

55. For a discussion of some of the problems facing expanded Sino-American trade, see "Entering the China Market," *Business America,* **2** (February 26, 1979), 3–8.

56. The Roosevelt Administration's prolonged campaign to gain congressional approval of the principle of reciprocal trade is described by FDR's secretary of state, in *The Memoirs of Cordell Hull,* I (New York: Macmillan and Co., 1948), pp. 352–378.

57. President John F. Kennedy's efforts to liberalize American trade, culiminating in enactment of the Trade Act of 1962, are discussed in: Theodore C. Sorensen, *Kennedy* (New York: Harper & Row, 1965), pp. 410–412; and Arthur Schlesinger, Jr., *A Thousand Days: John F. Kennedy in the White House* (Boston: Houghton Mifflin, 1965), pp. 844–848.

58. For recent affirmations of official American support for liberal trade principles, see: Secretary of State Cyrus Vance, "America's Stake in an Open International Trading System," *Department of State Bulletin,* **78** (April, 1978), 35–37; and his "America's Stake in the World Economy," ibid., **79** (April, 1979), 30–31.

59. Current information on the American balance of payments, highlighting the gap between imports and exports, can usually be found in the President's annual economic report to Congress, submitted early each year; and in the latest volume of the *Statistical Abstract of the United States,* published annually by the Commerce Department's Bureau of the Census. See, for example, "Economic Report of the President," *Department of State Bulletin,* **79** (April, 1979), 32.

60. Frank Vogl, in *New York Times,* February 18, 1979.

61. For further information on the Carter Administration's campaign to stimulate American exports, and the identification of the major problems this effort encountered, see the speech by President Carter on September 26, 1978, "Expanding U.S. Exports," in the Department of State's *Current Policy* series (September, 1978), pp. 1–4; and Robert Hormats, "U.S. Measures to Promote Exports—Part 1," *Department of State Bulletin,* **78** (July, 1978), 36–40. and "—Part 2," ibid. (August, 1978), 21–24.

62. *New York Times,* January 26, 1979.

63. The role of American agriculture in contemporary diplomacy is analyzed in the symposium on "Food for Aid and Diplomacy," in *Foreign Policy,* **27** (Summer, 1977), 72–109.

64. Human rights as an important dimension of recent American foreign policy, with emphasis upon congressional involvement in the question, is discussed fully in Crabb and Holt, *Invitation to Struggle,* Chapter 7.

65. The conclusion expressed in *idem* is that congressional efforts to promote human rights in Soviet Russia have had, at best, extremely limited results. The same basic conclusion is arrived at in Sandra Vogelgesang, "What Price Principle?—U.S. Policy on Human Rights," *Foreign Affairs,* **56** (July, 1978), 819–842. But for a contrary view of the effect of American diplomacy in behalf of human rights upon Soviet behavior toward its Jewish citizens, see William Korey, "The Future of Soviet Jewry: Emigration and Assimilation," ibid., **58** (Fall, 1979), 67–82.

66. See Crabb and Holt, *Invitation to Struggle,* Chapter 7. See also George W. Ball's assessment of American policy toward South Africa, in *The Discipline of Power: Essentials of a Modern World Structure* (Boston: Atlantic, Little, Brown and Co., 1968), pp. 243–259.

Chapter 7

Congress and the Foreign Policy Process

According to many criteria, the Congress of the United States is the most powerful legislative body in the modern world. Judged by one important standard—the influence of the legislative branch upon the nation's foreign policy process—the powers of Congress are unrivaled among the members of the contemporary international system. As a leading student of the American governmental system has observed: "No important policy, domestic or foreign, can be pursued for long by even the most forceful President unless Congress comes to his support with laws and money."[1] Another commentator has said that "The authority of Congress in foreign policy appears to be increasing as the boundaries of foreign and domestic policy become more and more obscure, and as the dollar cost of foreign policy programs requires congressional authorization."[2]

These generalizations have been illustrated at nearly every turn by congressional activity in the foreign policy field since the end of the Vietnam War. The period since the late

1960s has witnessed a pattern of congressional activism in foreign relations which has been, in many respects, unique in American diplomatic history. The post-Vietnam War stage has been distinctive in several key respects: in terms of the *extent* of legislative involvement in a wide variety of foreign policy issues; with regard to the *impact* which congressional action (or inaction) has had upon the course of American diplomacy; and in respect to the *problems* which have been created by the forceful intrusion of the House and Senate into the conduct of American foreign relations. As several legislators have expressed it in recent years, the goal has been to make Congress an "equal partner" with the President in the formulation and administration of American foreign policy—thereby reversing the long period of executive dominance in the diplomatic field.[3]

As advocates of enhanced congressional influence in foreign affairs see it, achieving this goal would produce a number of beneficial results. It would afford new safeguards against the emergence of the "imperial presidency." It would provide "legitimacy" to foreign policy decisions, by assuring that they reflect underlying American values and national goals. It would bring new perspectives to bear in foreign policy decision making which are (or are believed to be) lacking when such decisions are made solely by executive officials. In brief, a more influential role by Congress was expected to have a kind of purifying effect on the nation's foreign policy, guaranteeing that there would be "no more Vietnams" or other examples of major and minor political and military miscalculations which have marred America's recent diplomatic record and impaired its image abroad.

What has been the actual impact of congressional assertiveness upon American diplomacy? We shall deal with the major implications of an expanded legislative role in foreign relations in due course. Meanwhile, it is essential to understand more clearly the constitutional basis of Congress' involvement in foreign affairs and various informal, extraconstitutional powers available to Congress for influencing the course of American diplomacy.

Constitutional Powers of Congress in Foreign Affairs

The Senate's Role in Treaty Making

The Constitution (Art. II, Sec. 2) provides that the President "shall have Power, by and with the Advice and Consent of the Senate, to make Treaties, provided two thirds of the Senators present concur...." The Senate's power to ratify treaties is one of the upper chamber's prerogatives that is not shared with the House of Representatives.* From the

beginning of the Republic, therefore, the Senate was assigned an important role in the foreign policy process—a fact that even today gives that body a degree of prestige and a sense of involvement in foreign policy issues that differentiates it from the House.

One of the more interesting and important aspects of Congress' recent activism in the diplomatic field has involved efforts by the House of Representatives to end its "inequality" vis-à-vis the Senate in the foreign policy process. Innumerable times in recent years, representatives have complained about their exclusion from the treaty-making process—especially when (as frequently occurs) agreements between the United States and other countries subsequently require the expenditure of funds which must be appropriated by both houses of Congress. Attitudes in the House of Representatives on this point were conveyed dramatically, for example, during the negotiation and ratification of the new Panama Canal treaties by the Carter Administration during the late 1970s. In due course, the treaties were submitted to the Senate for its advice and consent. Time and again, members of the House of Representatives expressed their displeasure about having their viewpoints "ignored" (sentiment toward the new treaties in the House was in some respects highly adverse). The mood of many members of the House on this issue was conveyed by the remarks of one legislator early in

---

*Although it has become commonplace to refer to the power of the Senate to "ratify" treaties, it ought to be noted that such usage is incorrect. As required by the

Constitution, the Senate gives (or withholds) its advice and consent to treaties, as a crucial stage in the ratification process. The final stage in their ratification, however, is the signature of the President, who must also approve the treaty (often in modified form) after it has emerged from the Senate. A President can (and sometimes in American history did) refuse to sign a treaty after the Senate approved it, which meant the treaty was not ratified. Late in 1979, President Jimmy Carter "withdrew" the SALT II arms-limitation agreements from further Senate consideration, after Soviet forces invaded Afghanistan.

1979, who said regarding the new Panama Canal agreements:

> We in the House are tired of you people in the State Department going to your tea-sipping friends in the Senate. Now you good folks come up here and say you need legislation [to implement the Panama Canal treaty] after you ignored the House. If you expect me to vote for this travesty, you're sorely in error.[4]

Regarding House attempts to achieve equality with the Senate in this realm, Senator Frank Church, chairman of the Senate Foreign Relations Committee, retorted: "Their nibbles end up being big bites, and we [are] being bitten to death."[5]

In an earlier era (particularly when the United States was devoted to an "isolationist" policy), treaties were considered a vital dimension of the nation's relationships with foreign governments. It is significant that Article VI of the Constitution provides that the Constitution itself, laws made in pursuance of it, and "all Treaties made, or which shall be made, under the authority of the United States, shall be the supreme Law of the Land. . . ."

Today, however, the vast majority of understandings and accords between the United States and other governments takes the form of "executive agreements" (which will be discussed more fully at a later stage). In practice, there is little difference between treaties and executive agreements. While the relative importance of treaties has perhaps declined in recent years, it should be noted that many of the most *important* agreements between the United States and foreign governments—such as mutual defense commitments, understandings reached in the area of arms control and disarmament, and accords specifying mutual

rights (as in the new regime for the Panama Canal)—are embodied in treaty form.

The Impact of Senatorial Deliberations

In giving its "advice and consent" to treaties submitted to it by the President, the Senate has several alternatives which, at the risk of some oversimplification, may be reduced to three possible courses of action: (1) By a two-thirds vote, the Senate may *accept* a treaty without change, as submitted by the chief executive. (2) It may *modify* the treaty—by inserting amendments, reservations, "understandings," and the like, the result of which may be to make the treaty an essentially different instrument from the one submitted initially by the President. Or (3) the Senate may *reject* the treaty outright, by failing to give it the two-thirds affirmative vote required by the Constitution.

On the basis of over two centuries of American diplomatic experience, the odds are high that the Senate will approve without significant change treaties submitted to it by the President. One study found, for example, that in the period 1789–1963, the Senate approved without change 69 percent of those treaties which it considered.[6] From the end of World War II until around 1970, three potent considerations largely dictated this result. One of them was the fact that senators and executive officials shared a consensus (sometimes called the "anti-Communist consensus") about the principal threat facing the United States abroad and about America's proper course of action—the policy of "containment"—in responding to it. Another inducement for the Senate to approve most treaties was the fact that, in many instances, senators served as members of the American team which negotiated them.[7] Still another consideration inducing the Senate to approve treaties sent to it by the White House has been realization that failure to do so would risk a repudiation of presidential leadership in the eyes of the world—and that this would, in turn, impair American influence and prestige abroad.

During the 1970s, these three constraining factors were either significantly weakened or altogether absent as forces inhibiting the Senate's deliberations on treaties. As we shall see more fully in Chapter 8, the "anti-Communist consensus" underlying American foreign policy for some 25 years after World War II was largely absent for almost a decade after the Vietnam War. Pervasive uncertainty in the public mind concerning America's proper role in global affairs during the 1970s was reflected in disagreements among policy makers in Washington concerning this question.

As in the new Panama Canal treaties, successive Presidents continued to appoint senators to American negotiating teams, and this practice unquestionably enhanced support for the resulting treaty within the Senate.[8] Yet, in part because of demands by the House that its viewpoints also be considered and heeded in treaty making, there was less likelihood than in the past that the Senate would "automatically" consent to treaties submitted to it.

Another increasingly acute problem on Capitol Hill raised questions about the Senate's response to treaties: the tendency of a growing number of legislative committees and sub-committees to become involved in the foreign policy process, thereby encroaching upon the once largely exclusive domain of the Senate Foreign Relations Committee. As an example, late in 1979 this committee (by a narrow margin) voted to recommend *approval* of the SALT II strategic arms-limitation treaties between the United States and the Soviet Union by the full Senate; a few days later, the Senate Armed Services Committee (also by a narrow margin) voted to recommend that the Senate *disapprove* the SALT II agreements! Confronted with this division—and for several other reasons, like concern on Capitol Hill over the presence of Soviet combat forces in Cuba and Afghanistan—the Senate deferred consideration of the SALT II accords for a period of several months.[9]

On the basis of post-Vietnam War experience, we may say that the Senate has relied upon its treaty-making prerogatives to achieve two broad (and sometimes rather contradictory) goals. As illustrated by prolonged Senate deliberations on the new Panama Canal treaties, and on the SALT II strategic arms-limitation accord with the Soviet Union in the late 1970s, the Senate has insisted upon its right to examine international agreements *minutely,* to make numerous *changes in their terms,* and to accord them *full publicity.* (Legislators are aware that the United States became drawn into the Vietnam War because of a series of formal and informal understandings between the United States and South Vietnam largely arrived at by executive officials, with little congressional scrutiny.)

The other senatorial goal (clearly illustrated by the case of the new Panama Canal agreements) is to serve as the "protector" of American security and diplomatic interests. As a result of Senate deliberation, the Panama Canal accords were considerably "toughened" to allow American access to this vital waterway during periods of regional and global crisis. (In this approach, senators can, and did, "take credit" for defending American security interests, when the White House appeared to be oblivious to them.)

A second alternative available to the Senate in its consideration of treaties is to *modify them* both in important and minor respects. A number of often confusing and ambiguous terms have been used to describe specific steps available to the Senate in making such changes. Thus, the Senate may insist upon "amendments" in the provisions of a treaty, thereby altering its language and its meaning. Since they change the treaty's provisions, such amendments in turn require the concurrence (written or oral) of the other parties to the agreement before it can be ratified and is accepted as international law. Alternatively, the Senate sometimes attaches "reservations" to treaties; these are less formal modifications, usually spelling out or clarifying the meaning of a treaty's provisions as understood by the United States. As a rule, reservations do not require that the treaty be renegotiated with the other parties to it. The Senate also appends "understandings" to treaties which it considers. These are closely akin to reservations, and they normally set forth the Senate's perception or definition of certain provisions of the agreement or of procedures to be followed by the parties in the stage of treaty implementation. The distinction among these various changes, we need to reiterate, has become increasingly nebulous and of interest primarily to constitutional lawyers.

As a third alternative, the Senate may of course fail to give its advice and consent to a treaty, thereby *rejecting it* outright. This has seldom happened in American diplomatic history, and there is little reason to suppose that this tendency will be reversed in the future. As in the past, overt rejection by the Senate of a treaty submitted to it by the White House would provide dramatic evidence to the world of a serious internal division within the American government on major foreign policy issues; and it would constitute dramatic repudiation of the President's diplomatic leadership. Senators are also fully aware that, if the treaty is rejected, a resourceful President can (and perhaps will) resort to an executive agreement to arrive at understandings with foreign governments. At one stage in Senate deliberations on the SALT II arms-control agreements, in fact, President Jimmy Carter indicated publicly that he would follow this course if Senate opposition to the agreements prevailed.[10]

Legislative Scrutiny of Executive Agreements

Part of the discontent evident in the Senate, and throughout Congress as a whole, with the "decline" of legislative influence in foreign affairs can be attributed to a realization that the Senate's role in treaty making sometimes allows it minimal opportunity to affect the nature and extent of overseas commitments. Two developments in the postwar period have diminished the Senate's influence upon international agreements entered into by the United States. One has been the decline in importance of treaties per se. Although the Founding Fathers unquestionably viewed treaty commitments as a vital realm of foreign relations, modern diplomatic history has deemphasized their importance. Today, issues arising out of the nontreaty relationships of the United States are at least as crucial, and sometimes more so, than those related to the nation's treaty commitments. Not infrequently since World War II, as in the case of South Korea, America has protected its vital interests in a region and *after it has done so* formalized these interests by embodying them in a security treaty. In other cases (as in the long-standing *de facto* American commitment to the security of Israel), the nation's nontreaty obligations may often be more influential in shaping its foreign relations than those embodied in treaty form.

The second reason why the Senate has been unable to affect foreign policy decisively by giving its advice and consent to treaties is even more influential. This is the great enhancement of the power of the President in foreign relations over the course of American history. The President's dominant position in the foreign policy process was discussed at length in Chapter 3. There, it was pointed out that an influential instrument of presidential leadership is *the executive agreement.* Only in very rare instances would Senate refusal to consent to a treaty preclude a President from reaching some kind of *de facto* agreement with other heads of state. Especially in periods of external crisis, chief executives are largely unhindered in their freedom to arrive at understandings with other countries. This White House prerogative was illustrated, for example, by President Jimmy Carter's understandings regarding military and economic aid and other assistance for the governments of Pakistan and Communist China, following the Soviet invasion of Afghanistan late in 1979. In the same period, the Carter Administration sought to arrive at accords with governments in the Red Sea-Persian Gulf area concerning the use of naval facilities by American armed forces.[11]

Since the Vietnam War, Congress has been especially sensitive about the overseas commitments of the United States, particularly those made without its direct participation. More than at any time in American history, Congress has insisted that executive agreements with other governments *be made public;* and it has endeavored to inhibit the power of the President to enter into them without some form of legislative knowledge and approval.

Yet, as with many other aspects of congressional assertiveness in foreign relations, this effort has had mixed results. While the State Department and other executive agencies are now required to "report" the existence of such agreements to the House and Senate, Congress' subsequent evaluation and use of this voluminous information has been sporadic and often has had little apparent results.[12]

Senate Confirmation of Appointments

A second prerogative belonging to the Senate alone, as specified in Article II, Section 2, of the Constitution, is the power to "confirm" presidential appointments. Since our interest is confined to foreign affairs, this power entails Senate confirmation of ambassadors, ministers, and consuls; appointments to, and promotions within, the Foreign Service; and appointments to high policy positions (from the level of assistant secretary upward) in agencies like the State Department, the Defense Department, and comparable ranks in other executive agencies. During some periods (as in the mid-1960s), the Senate, through its Foreign Relations Committee, devoted considerable time and effort to scrutinizing the qualifications of appointees, such as candidates for appointment to the Foreign Service of the United States.[13] Again in 1981, some of President Ronald Reagan's appointees were subject to prolonged investigation before they received Senate confirmation.

In the early period of American history, the Senate was prone to use its powers of confirmation to pass upon the establishment of diplomatic missions abroad. This occurred, for example, in 1809, when the Senate refused to approve an exchange of ministers between the United States and Russia. The confirmation power has also been used to influence the treaty-making process, as when the Senate refused for some time to confirm negotiators who were to settle outstanding differences with Great Britain in Washington's Administration. Bitter and prolonged wrangling ensued between the President and Senate before the highly controversial Jay Treaty, signed in 1794, could even be negotiated.

In the postwar period, the Senate has occasionally relied upon its power to confirm presidential appointments in order to enhance legislative influence upon the course of American diplomacy. For example, when the United States joined the United Nations, the Senate insisted upon the right to confirm the appointments of American diplomatic personnel to existing and future UN agencies. During the Eisenhower Administration, the Senate clearly showed its displeasure about the tendency of earlier Democratic administrations to be conciliatory with the Soviet Union by questioning the appointment of Mr. Charles Bohlen to be the new American ambassador to the U.S.S.R.[14] Several years later, President Carter's designation of Leonard Woodcock as America's first ambassador to the People's Republic of China proved to be highly controversial in the Senate. Senate objections were directed not so much at Woodcock's qualifications for the position. Rather, opponents of his appointment used the occasion to express opposition to America's formal recognition of the PRC and to the inevitable weakening of the nation's long-standing political and military ties with Nationalist China (Taiwan). Despite such objections, Woodcock's appointment was eventually approved by the Senate.[15]

As a generalization, we may conclude that, even today, the Senate's power to confirm or reject presidential appointments does *not* rank among the more influential legislative prerogatives in the foreign policy field. With rare exceptions, senators accept and operate upon the premise that a chief executive is entitled to have advisers and subordinates of his own choosing, in whom he has confidence and who can be relied upon to carry out the goals of his administration.

As with other legislative restraints upon his powers in the foreign policy field, a resourceful President has techniques for circumventing senatorial control over his actions. Two such techniques may be identified briefly. One of these is the power to rely upon "personal representatives" for diplomatic missions (thereby also sometimes bypassing the State Department and regular diplomatic personnel abroad). Harry Hopkins served in such a capacity many times for President Franklin D. Roosevelt. In the postwar period, W. Averell Harriman was sent abroad as the personal representative of successive Presidents. Such agents (many of whom already hold government positions) do not require senatorial confirmation.

Increasingly, recent Presidents have relied upon Cabinet officers and other officials in the executive branch (such as the secretary of defense, the secretary of the treasury, and the President's national security adviser) to carry out important diplomatic missions. As an example, the Nixon Administration's "opening" to Communist China—preparing the way for a normalization between the United States and the People's Republic of China, under the Carter Administration—was carried out by Dr. Henry Kissinger, White House national security adviser (with little or no participation by the State Department in this crucial turnabout in American foreign policy).[16] Also in recent years, chief executives have used the vice president of the United States and the first lady for major and minor diplomatic missions.

Alternatively, if a President is concerned about possible Senate opposition to his candidate, he may make an "interim appointment," when Congress is not in session. The President is then required, however, to submit the candidate's name to the Senate within 40 days after the next session of Congress opens. A celebrated case of an "interim appointment" occurred in 1951, when President

Truman named Philip Jessup as a member of the U.S. delegation to the United Nations. Although the Senate refused to confirm his appointment, President Truman gave Jessup an "interim appointment" which permitted him to serve on the delegation for several months.[17]

Congressional Control over Appropriations

In the prolonged contest between the monarchy and Parliament in England—resulting ultimately in a victory by the legislature over the Crown—the "power of the purse" proved the decisive weapon in Parliament's triumph. Ever since this crucial encounter, legislative control over money has emerged as perhaps the most influential prerogative of national parliaments.

In the recent period, mounting congressional influence in the foreign policy process can perhaps be roughly correlated with the growth in total federal expenditures devoted (directly and indirectly) to external affairs.* Correctly or not (and differing interpretations existed among executive and legislative officials on the question), many legislators were convinced that Congress' termination of funds for the conduct of the Vietnam War was the crucial step in bringing involvement in that traumatic encounter to an end. Throughout the years that followed, in a number of key dimensions of foreign policy—ranging from American involvement in political crises on the African continent, to legislative attempts to promote respect for human rights abroad, to congressional determination of the size and

nature of the American defense establishment—the legislative branch has relied heavily upon its power to grant or withhold funds to influence the course of American diplomacy. In some cases—as in the possible extension of foreign aid to North Vietnam and other Southeast Asian states for reconstruction of the region after the Vietnam War—initial White House interest in the undertaking receded after it became evident that Congress was unwilling to appropriate the funds required for such projects.[18]

Today, there is hardly an activity or program in the foreign policy realm—from the creation of an adequate national defense establishment, to the extension of military and economic assistance to other countries, to the operation of the State Department in Washington and embassies and consular posts abroad, to America's contribution to the budgets of various United Nations agencies—that does not ultimately require expenditures by Congress. Moreover, to implement domestic policy decisions impinging upon foreign affairs—such as programs designed to solve the "energy crisis" or to maintain high employment in the face of a mounting volume of imports—substantial governmental outlays are needed.

Legislative reliance upon the "power of the purse" to influence foreign policy is important for another reason. Earlier, we called attention to the determination of the House of Representatives to play a more influential role in foreign affairs vis-à-vis the Senate. Traditionally, the "power of the purse" is uniquely identified with the House—the chamber which is in a special sense "the voice of the people" and is most directly responsive to their viewpoints. Article I, Section 7, of the Constitution provides that "All Bills for raising Revenue shall originate in the House of Representatives...." Although this provision specifically applies only to *revenue bills* (that

---

*In the early postwar era (in 1946), the total annual expenditures by the United States government were approximately $62 billion. By 1980, this total had expanded by some 900 percent. By the latter date, spending in one budgetary category alone—national defense—was some 50 percent greater than the *total* federal budget a generation earlier.

is, bills levying taxes and tariffs), long-standing custom within Congress has extended this constitutional requirement to *spending measures* (or *appropriations bills*) as well. Thus, the House of Representatives has acquired a special prerogative with regard to the "power of the purse" roughly analogous to the Senate's role in treaty making.

Stages in the Expenditures Process

The student of American foreign policy must be reminded of an elementary—but crucial—fact about the legislative process in the United States as it relates to policies and programs entailing expenditures. All bills requiring the expenditure of money must, in effect, go through Congress *twice*—once in the form of an "authorization" measure, and finally as an "appropriations" bill in which the required funds are actually provided by the House and Senate. Let us examine this complicated process in somewhat greater detail.

In the first, or "authorization," stage of a foreign policy expenditure, after a bill is introduced it is normally referred to the House Foreign Affairs Committee* and to the Senate Foreign Relations Committee for study and for a recommendation by these committees back to their respective chambers. Each chamber must in time "authorize" the program in question (like the provision of American economic assistance to various countries abroad). Theoretically, by doing so the House and Senate determine that the program is meritorious, that it is feasible, and that it makes some contribution to America's overall goals in foreign affairs. Differing House and Senate versions of an authorization bill must be reconciled by a conference committee and

ultimately accepted in identical form by both chambers. (The failure by either one of the houses to authorize the measure in question of course effectively kills it for that session of Congress.)

Next, programs requiring funds for their implementation must go through the "appropriations" stage, in which funds are actually provided. This is the province of the House and Senate Appropriations committees, with the former playing an extremely influential role in the outcome. Before funds are available to executive officials, each house must pass an identical appropriations bill for programs previously authorized by Congress. For certain diplomatic purposes and undertakings in the postwar era—and the foreign aid program serves as a leading example—the appropriations process has often been prolonged; has sometimes involved sharp conflicts between legislative and executive officials; and has had a profound impact upon the direction of American foreign relations.

This cumbersome process has evolved historically and, in common with other traditions and usages of the national government, its rationale has become increasingly confused and difficult to justify. In the authorization stage, as we have indicated, legislators are presumably concerned with such questions as: Is this a worthwhile program in foreign relations? Is there a high degree of probability that its goals can be achieved? Does it promote some American security or diplomatic interest abroad? Conversely, in the appropriations stage, legislators are attempting to decide: Are funds available from the anticipated revenues of the federal government to finance this program? Among the literally hundreds of budgetary claims presented to Congress in a given year, what priority ought to be given a program like foreign aid vis-à-vis poverty programs, support for education, or national defense (and the totality of such budgetary

*For a period of several years, this committee was called the House International Relations Committee; but in time the name was changed back to its historic title, the House Foreign Affairs Committee.

requests of course always *exceeds* estimates of anticipated revenues)?

With the passage of time, the line between the authorization and appropriations stages in dealing with expenditures has become ill-defined and impossible to delineate clearly. After all, how is it possible to separate the question of whether the United States *ought* to provide increased economic assistance to Egypt from the question of whether overall federal spending will exceed governmental income for the next fiscal year? Or, how can Congress really judge whether the United States should undertake an expanded program of economic assistance for Latin America without reference to the priority of certain domestic needs within the American society? Conversely, how can the House and Senate Appropriations committees arrive at intelligent judgments about various expenditures in the foreign policy field without at the same time evaluating the *results and implications* of these programs or deciding whether their *continuation* is still in the nation's diplomatic interest?

On the basis of postwar experience, it is possible to forecast a kind of cycle or rhythm when Congress acts on a program like foreign aid. Let us imagine a hypothetical case to illustrate the cycle as concretely as possible. After months of preparation by executive officials, in time the President's budget requests are formulated and submitted to Congress. Let us assume that they include an allocation of $2.5 billion for economic assistance to other countries. After the bill has been introduced in each chamber, the foreign aid "authorization" bill is considered by the Senate Foreign Relations Committee and the House Foreign Affairs Committee. In time, these committees will hold hearings and conduct studies of at least selected aspects of the foreign aid program. Eventually, each committee will authorize a given sum for foreign aid expenditures,

and in accordance with its usual practice, each chamber will in turn approve an authorized total very close to what its respective committee has recommended. As the result of a conference committee, both chambers in time approve an identical authorization measure. Experience has shown that the outcome is likely to be a slight reduction in the President's budget request—from a total of $2.5 billion to perhaps $2.2 billion, as finally authorized by Congress.

The $2.2 billion authorization for foreign aid must now be considered by Congress as an "appropriations" measure, in which funds are made available to finance the program. Invoking its constitutional and traditional prerogatives over revenue bills, the House takes the initiative in this process. After the bill is introduced in the House, it is referred to the House Appropriations Committee; the full committee in turn refers it to the proper subcommittee—in this case, the Subcommittee on Foreign Operations.* In due course, this

---

*Consideration of the foreign aid bill by the House Appropriations Committee (in practice by its Subcommittee on Foreign Operations) is often the crucial stage in determining the scope and nature of the foreign aid program in any given year. One commentator has asserted that the chairman of this powerful subcommittee (for many years Representative Otto E. Passman, Democrat of Louisiana) exercised more influence over the fate of the program than did the chairman of the House Foreign Affairs Committee. See Richard F. Fenno, Jr., "The Internal Distribution of Influence: The House," in David Truman, ed., *The Congress and America's Future* (Englewood Cliffs, N.J.: Prentice-Hall, 1965), p. 55.

What factors account for the vast power exercised by this committee? Several may be identified. The first is the unique position of the House in regard to *all* money bills (both raising and spending revenues). Historically, such bills have come to be regarded as the special province of the House vis-à-vis the Senate. With 435 members (versus only 100 in the Senate), the House is able to apportion work among its committees in a way that permits representatives to become greater "specialists" in their subject matter than senators; the latter often are compelled to rely upon their staffs for expert advice.

subcommittee "reports" its recommendations to the full Appropriations Committee, which nearly always endorses the report submitted to it. In turn, the Appropriations Committee "reports" the foreign aid appropriations bill to the House. Again, customarily the House of Representatives accepts this key committee's report with little or no change.

The House Appropriations Committee has some 50 members, making it the largest committee in the lower chamber. Assignment to the committee is highly coveted, since the committee is one of the most prestigious on Capitol Hill. More than most, this committee tends to be a "law unto itself." It meets in secret and almost never divulges its internal debates or votes; once agreement is reached within the committee (and its subcommittees), members unite to support its recommendations against critics, both within the House itself and outside it. Routinely, the full House accepts the committee's recommendations with little or no change.

Members of the House Appropriations Committee and its subcommittees view themselves as primarily "custodians" of the federal treasury against various claimants, whose demands (in the committee view, at least) are always inflated. One member of the committee likened budget requests submitted to it to the process of buying an automobile: Agencies had an "asking price" which the committee almost never accepted! Invariably, the committee "trims the fat" from budget recommendations it considers—and with some programs (like foreign aid) massive cuts are normal.

The House Appropriations Committee has consistently refused to accept any move—like making two- or three-year foreign aid appropriations—that would tend to weaken its control over spending or deny it an opportunity to review expenditures *annually*.

The role of the House Appropriations Committee in the legislative process is discussed in detail in Richard F. Fenno, Jr., "The House Appropriations Committee as a Political System," *American Political Science Review* **LVI** (June, 1962), 310–324; Nelson W. Polsby, *Congress and the Presidency* (Englewood Cliffs, N.J.: Prentice-Hall, 1964), pp. 91–96; Lewis A. Dexter, "Congressmen and the Making of Military Policy," in Robert L. Peabody and Nelson W. Polsby, eds., *New Perspectives on the House of Representatives* (Skokie, Ill.: Rand McNally, 1963), pp. 305–325; and Aaron Wildavsky, *The Politics of the Budgetary Process* (Boston: Little, Brown and Co. 1964), pp. 47–61.

Throughout the postwar period, this has been the stage at which foreign aid programs usually encountered massive legislative opposition. It is a safe prediction that substantial reductions will be made every year in the foreign aid programs by the Subcommittee on Foreign Operations and that these reductions will be accepted by the full committee and by the House itself. If $2.2 billion is initially authorized for foreign aid, we can reasonably predict that the House of Representatives will appropriate only $1.7 billion for the program.

Once the House has completed action on the appropriations for foreign aid (and characteristically this may be rather late in the legislative session), the Senate must act on the bill. Tradition, together with the nature of the Senate as a legislative body, decrees that the upper chamber's role in the appropriations process differ fundamentally from that of the House. In dealing with appropriations, the Senate—in practice, the Senate Appropriations Committee—serves as an "appeals" body, before which executive officials plead for a "restoration" of at least some of the budgetary items eliminated, or pared, by the House.

This dialogue, found in testimony before the Senate Appropriations Committee in 1967, illustrates the Senate's role. The witness was a State Department official, Mr. Joseph F. Friedkin, who was being interrogated by the chairman of the committee, Senator John McClellan (Democrat of Arkansas):

Senator McClellan: ... The 1968 estimate [submitted in the President's budget] is $2,760,000. The House allowed $2.5 million, a reduction of $260,000, and you are requesting that the full amount be restored.

You may proceed and tell us why it should be restored. ...

Mr. Friedkin: Yes, sir. Mr. Chairman and members of the committee, I do appreciate this opportunity to appear before you to appeal for the restoration of the House reduction of $260,000....[19]

Normally, the executive branch can count upon some "restoration" by the Senate of House-instigated reductions in the foreign aid budget. Because the Senate has historically been more involved in foreign policy than the House, or because in the postwar period senators have often cooperated closely with executive officials in foreign relations, or because their six-year terms give senators more political security than is true of representatives—for many such reasons, the Senate normally approves a higher foreign aid budget than was passed in the House. Let us assume that the Senate approved a foreign aid appropriation of $2.0 billion.

The differing appropriations bills voted by the House and Senate must be reconciled by a conference committee consisting of members from the two Appropriations committees. Since such conference committees meet in closed (or secret) session, little is actually known about the process whereby such agreement is reached. From the evidence available, however, it appears that the committee concentrates its attention upon disputed items in the bill in a search for a consensus. Ultimately, the conference committee will arrive at the necessary compromises and will report an identical bill to both the House and Senate. As a rule, this conference report tends to "split the difference" between the appropriations bills voted earlier by each chamber. Since conference reports are un-amendable, each chamber usually accepts the agreement worked out by the committee. (Rarely, however, one chamber may vote to send the report to the committee a second time for further changes.)

If the House approved an appropriation of $1.7 billion and the Senate $2.0 billion, the conference committee might arrive at the figure of $1.85 billion as a reasonable compromise. Thus, after many months of preparation in the executive branch, and several additional months of legislative deliberation, the President's foreign aid request of $2.5 billion for assistance to other countries has been reduced to a congressional appropriation of $1.85 billion.[20]

Congress and the Military Establishment

Among the most influential prerogatives of Congress in the field of external policy are several related to its control over the military establishment. A fundamental principle of the American constitutional system is the concept of "civilian supremacy" over the armed forces—implicit in which is the idea that civilian policy makers ought always to determine whether, when, and where the armed forces of the United States are employed. As we noted in Chapter 3, the Constitution designates the President as the commander in chief of the military establishment; and (with Senate confirmation), he appoints the nation's highest military leaders.

Yet Congress also possesses several important powers in this field. In Article I, Section 8, the Constitution empowers Congress to "provide for the common defense" of the United States; to "declare war"; to "raise and support armies"; "to provide and maintain" the navy; and to make rules and regulations governing the armed forces. Thus, a kind of constitutional division of labor governs the use of the American military establishment: The President commands (within recent years, sometimes under certain regulations enacted by Congress) the armed forces which Congress makes available for his use in behalf of national security and diplomatic objectives. Obviously, the President's position as commander in chief would be an empty one if he had no armed forces at his disposal. The effect upon American diplomacy of Congress' powers in this realm was forcefully conveyed during the late 1930s. For several years, even perhaps the most skillful political leader in the nation's history—President Franklin D. Roosevelt—failed to move Congress from its "isolationist" posture and persuade it to bolster national defense as the world drifted toward World War II.[21]

After the traumatic Vietnam conflict, for a period of several years intense debate on Capitol Hill followed on issues associated with the war—none perhaps more crucial and contentious than the question of the respective powers of the President and Congress in deploying the armed forces abroad. As advocates of a more influential legislative role in foreign affairs assessed it, for too many years Congress had failed to exercise its prerogatives in this critical realm of national policy. To the mind of many legislators, the "imperial presidency" had emerged, largely because of the chief executive's powers over the military establishment. Congress' deep concern about this development was exemplified by the War Powers Resolution, whose main provisions we shall examine at a later stage.

Congress and America's Military Needs

For convenience in discussing a complex subject in limited space, we shall focus upon the nature and importance of two specific legislative powers over the military establishment. These are Congress' right to determine the nature and size of the armed forces, and the congressional prerogative to "declare war."

The funds required for the national defense budget (over $220 billion by 1982) must be authorized and appropriated by Congress. In this twofold process, the House and Senate Armed Services committees, together with the two Appropriations committees, play pivotal roles. Congress' control over defense spending also allows it to determine the funds available to the separate military arms (the army, the navy, and the air force); to specify the level of military pay scales and other benefits (a crucial consideration, for example, in determining the success of military recruitment efforts); to allocate funds for the purchase of weapons and ancillary equipment; and to provide funds for the development of new weapons systems and other aspects of evolving military technology. In addition, Congress decides another crucial question: whether young people will be drafted into the armed services, or whether the military arms must depend upon voluntary enlistments to meet their manpower needs. The change from conscription (which existed during the Vietnam War) to the all-volunteer army, which Congress created early in 1973, had a momentous effect upon the size and capability of the American military establishment (particularly the United States Army).

For some 25 years—from the end of World War II until around 1970—for the most part, Congress accepted the President's assessments of the nation's military requirements; and with rare exceptions, it provided the kind of military establishment the White House requested. Now and again (as in the Truman Administration), the executive and legislative branches might differ over the nature of America's military needs (in this instance, the controversy involved the size of the air force). But one overriding reality—the realization on both ends of Pennsylvania Avenue that the United States and the Soviet Union were engaged in a Cold War, involving the possibility of limited and global hostilities—imparted a high degree of unity between the two branches on the size and nature of the nation's armed forces. Executive and legislative policy makers, for example, were agreed that American preeminence in at least certain categories of armed strength (like seapower and some aspects of airpower) had to be preserved; and Congress normally made the funds available for doing so.

Until the closing months of the Vietnam War, legislators seldom seriously questioned White House estimates of the nation's military requirements. For whatever reasons the United States failed to achieve its goals in Southeast Asia (and we shall not enter into that controversy here), it had little to do with Congress' failure to provide the military resources needed to win that conflict. As is of course usual during periods of external crisis, legislators were under considerable pressure to "support the President" in the Vietnam endeavor; and few members of Congress wanted to assume the responsibility for *failing* to provide the funds and other resources requested by the commander in chief.

For their part, successive chief executives tended to view Congress' willingness to support the Vietnam War effort with massive resources as evidence of legislative agreement with executive policies in Southeast Asia. President Lyndon B. Johnson regarded repeated and overwhelming congressional approval of the nation's military budget as what he called the "functional equivalent of a declaration of war," indicating solid legislative endorsement of American policies in Southeast Asia. Not until August 15, 1973, did Congress invoke the "power of the purse" to terminate America's participation in the conflict by cutting off funds needed to support that endeavor—but by that date, the Nixon Administration had already announced America's military evacuation from Vietnam.[22]

During the 1960s, many Americans became deeply concerned about the influence of what was sometimes described as the "Military-Industrial Complex" in American life—a danger described by President Dwight D. Eisenhower at the end of his Administration.[23]

While never very clearly defined, this nexus consisted of the armed services (including their rather large public and legislative relations staffs); the principal industries and business corporations in the United States which benefited from sizable defense contracts; labor unions whose members were heavily employed in defense-related industries; and even local communities whose prosperity was dependent upon defense industries and upon the presence of military installations nearby. This coalition of interest groups represented an impressive aggregation of financial and political power, and it was capable of exercising potent influence upon Congress and upon public opinion in behalf of high levels of defense spending.[24] Retired military officers not infrequently found employment with defense contractors and public relations firms and were used to lobby executive and legislative officials in behalf of a high level of military spending.[25] On Capitol Hill, critics of the Military-Industrial Complex often charged, a symbiotic relationship existed between the House and Senate Armed Services committees (but particularly the former) and the Pentagon; these key legislative committees were extremely sympathetic to the military point of view regarding the nation's defense needs. Even the President sometimes had difficulty preventing his subordinates from "appealing" over his head directly to Congress for increases in the national defense budget.

Although ample grounds existed for being concerned about the potential and actual power of the Military-Industrial Complex in American life, events during the 1970s indicated that its influence upon governmental decision making could be greatly exaggerated. For several years after the Vietnam War, Congress *rejected* costly defense projects— like the B-1 bomber, an expanded program of naval construction, and the new MX missile—advocated by proponents of higher defense spending. By the late 1970s, as a proportion of the total federal budget American defense expenditures were less than programs operated by the Department of Health, Education, and Welfare (HEW). Significant increases in American defense expenditures —initiated by the Carter Administration, and added to by the Reagan Administration—were engaged in because of incontestable evidence that the United States was falling behind the Soviet Union militarily. To no inconsiderable degree, defense spending was increased in response to an overwhelming public demand that this imbalance be restored.

In exercising the "power of the purse" with regard to national defense, Congress is responsive both to public opinion in the United States and to external developments. For several years after the Vietnam conflict, its approach to the military establishment reflected the "dovish" and antimilitary sentiments conspicuous in public opinion during the war and its aftermath. Inevitably perhaps, the climate of public sentiment within the United States and the conditions facing the United States abroad began to change. Three events in 1979—the crisis between the United States and Iran involving the holding of a large group of American hostages in that country, the belated discovery by American intelligence agencies of the presence of a large Soviet combat force in Cuba, and the Soviet invasion of Afghanistan—symbolized this transition and had a potent effect upon public and legislative opinion toward the military establishment. For example, many legislators now joined executive officials in calling for the creation and maintenance of a powerful and mobile Rapid Deployment Force (RDF) capable of projecting American power to vulnerable regions like the Persian Gulf area. By the early 1980s, in fact, congressional sentiment (reflecting American public opinion) had be-

come deeply concerned about the adequacy of the national defense effort. Less than a decade after the Vietnam War, many legislators were convinced that defense expenditures as proposed by the White House were inadequate to protect national security in the face of continuing Soviet interventionism in other countries.* After the Vietnam War, as in earlier eras, Congress was extremely reluctant to "take a chance with national security" during periods of threatened or actual global crises.

Congress' Power to "Declare War"

The domestic discontent over America's prolonged involvement in the Vietnam conflict often centered upon another legislative prerogative in the foreign policy field: the constitutional requirement that only Congress can "declare war." Along with the Korean conflict before it, the Vietnam War was never "declared" by Congress—a fact which, to many critics, meant that the United States was involved in an "illegal" military encounter.

The Constitution (Art. I, Sec. 8) gives Congress the power to declare war; and this is one among several indications that the Found-

*Thus, early in 1980 the House Armed Services Committee vocally criticized the Carter Administration's defense policies as being inadequate to safeguard the nation's security interests, at a time when Soviet defense spending remained at an extremely high level. Several members believed that the Administration's proposed increase of 5.4 percent in national defense spending was too low. As several members of the committee viewed it, American public opinion demanded that the defense establishment be strengthened—and legislators were determined to heed this rising public expectation. See Richard Halloran, in *New York Times,* January 30, 1980. See also the view of Senate Majority Leader Robert Byrd, that the Senate was "ahead" of the White House in proposing measures designed to strengthen national defense and the ability of the United States to respond to crises in the Middle East and other areas. Senator Byrd's views are contained in an interview in *U.S. News and World Report,* **88** (February 11, 1980), 45–46.

ing Fathers intended the legislative branch to participate directly and actively in decision making involving military hostilities.[26] Yet we must also take note of the historical context of this provision. During the eighteenth century, a "declaration of war" was normally given weeks or months before hostilities erupted between the belligerents. Congress, it was therefore anticipated, would debate and finally decide whether the United States ought to resort to arms in a particular crisis. Yet even before the Constitution was ratified, it was an established principle of international law that nations could in fact be engaged in war without a formal "declaration" of it by either side.[27]

In the post-World War II period, Congress' power to declare war has proved an increasingly weak instrument of legislative control. No longer do nations give notice of their intention of resorting to armed force. Warfare entered a new era, for example, during the 1930s—when Japan attacked Manchuria without warning in 1931 and when Nazi Germany used blitzkrieg tactics in its invasion of Poland in 1939. Today, Communist-supported "wars of national liberation" routinely depend upon stealth and deception for success. During the Cuban Missile Crisis late in 1962, President Kennedy informed the American people by national television that he had *already ordered* American naval forces to enforce a "quarantine" against Cuba and that he had directed the armed forces "to prepare for any eventualities." It is noteworthy that congressional leaders were informed of Kennedy's message approximately one hour before his broadcast (well after the Strategic Air Command and other military units had been placed on full "alert").[28] Similarly, when he issued the "Carter Doctrine" early in 1980—underscoring America's vital security involvement in the Persian Gulf area—President Carter in effect presented the Kremlin

with an ultimatum to use armed force if Moscow attempted to dominate this region.[29]

Another reason why the declaration of war is a relatively weak instrument of legislative control over foreign relations was identified by Senator Jacob Javits (Republican of New York) during the Vietnam conflict. Although he shared the views of some antiwar critics, Javits did *not* believe that Congress should have declared war in this encounter, since doing so would have greatly increased the risk of a Soviet-American (or possibly a Sino-American) global conflict, possibly involving the use of nuclear weapons.[30] The Vietnam War raised another question about the contemporary utility of a declaration of war, particularly as the United States confronts what are sometimes called "wars of national liberation" in the Third World. Against whom would an American declaration of war be directed in Southeast Asia, the government of North Vietnam, the elusive revolutionary group called the Viet Cong, the foreign supporters (such as the Soviet Union and Communist China) of the Communist war effort, or all of them collectively?

As we have already noted, postwar Presidents have regarded certain steps taken by Congress during periods of military hostilities as the "functional equivalent" of a declaration of war. President Johnson believed that Congress had taken several steps during the Vietnam conflict—such as providing funds requested by the White House for national defense, instituting and continuing the draft, and passing the Gulf of Tonkin Resolution in 1964—conferring ample legislative authority upon the chief executive to prosecute the war in Southeast Asia. The fact that Congress could at any time have used the "power of the purse" to terminate America's involvement in that conflict—and did not do so until after the President had announced his intention of withdrawing American troops from Southeast

Asia—was interpreted by the White House as at least tacit legislative acceptance of White House policies in Vietnam. Yet many legislators challenged this interpretation; they believed that Congress must act directly and positively to legitimatize the President's use of the armed forces overseas. This leads us to consider one of the more recent and important developments affecting the respective powers of the President and Congress in the foreign policy field: the War Powers Resolution, passed by Congress over President Richard Nixon's veto on November 7, 1973.

The War Powers Resolution

We may conveniently analyze the War Powers Resolution by giving attention to three aspects of it: the resolution's purpose, the context within which it was formulated and passed, and its principal provisions.[31] The purpose of the resolution can be stated simply: It was to make the commitment of American armed forces abroad, in actual or potential foreign danger zones, a *collective responsibility of the executive and legislative branches*. In effect, the measure gave to Congress final authority in deciding whether or not the armed forces of the United States should be engaged in prolonged military hostilities abroad.

In discussing the context within which the measure was passed, we may distinguish between the immediate circumstances and the long-range forces producing it. The immediate context of the resolution was of course the Vietnam War—in some respects, the most traumatic and internally divisive chapter in American diplomatic history. It was no coincidence that many of the sponsors of the War Powers Resolution were also numbered among the more outspoken critics of America's involvement in that agonizing contest. The resolution, its advocates hoped and expected, would prevent a recurrence of the Vietnam experience—in which successive Presidents committed the nation to a prolonged military engagement, with merely nominal (and sometimes no) participation in decision making by the House and Senate.

From a long-range perspective, the War Powers Resolution symbolized Congress' growing dissatisfaction with the steady accretion in the President's powers over the armed forces, particularly since World War II. During that conflict, President Franklin Roosevelt had made innumerable major and minor military decisions—a number of which had momentous political implications for the years ahead—without consulting Congress. This same pattern had largely been repeated during the Korean War (1950–1953), which was often referred to as "Mr. Truman's war." Again in 1962, President John F. Kennedy's forceful response to the Soviet Union during the Cuban Missile Crisis—the most dangerous Soviet-American encounter in the postwar period—was formulated by executive policy makers. Beginning in the mid-1950s, legislators believed (correctly or not) that the growing American military commitment to the defense of South Vietnam stemmed from a series of White House decisions, with no concurrence by Congress. For its advocates, therefore, the War Powers Resolution was intended to correct a long-standing constitutional imbalance between executive and legislative authority over the military establishment by giving Congress "the last word" in the disposition of the armed forces beyond America's borders.

The provisions of the War Powers Resolution are complex, and we do not need to become immersed in all of their intricacies here. In brief space, we may note that the measure envisions two different situations involving the use of American armed forces abroad. One is a *limited crisis overseas,* which perhaps arises suddenly and presents a threat to national security. The other (and the model here was clearly the Vietnam War) is a *prolonged and massive military engagement*—possibly entailing a regional or even a global conflict—involving the armed forces of the United States. Congress' role in these two situations differs rather fundamentally.

In effect, the War Powers Resolution recognizes the right—even the duty—of the commander in chief to respond promptly and decisively to threats to national security. In such cases, the President is required to "report" his actions to the House and Senate within 48 hours after committing military forces abroad; and, if possible, he is expected to consult Congress *before* doing so. By passing a "concurrent resolution,"* Congress may at any time require the withdrawal of American armed forces from combat zones abroad. The evidence since 1973 indicates that, for short-range crises of this kind, the War Powers Resolution has imposed no significant restraints upon a President's conduct of foreign relations, such as President Carter's attempt to rescue American hostages in Iran in 1980.

Different requirements exist for military conflicts of longer duration, in which the American commitment is much more extensive. For this category of conflicts, the President is also required to report his actions to Congress within 48 hours after American forces are committed overseas; and if possible, the chief executive is expected to consult with Congress prior to doing so. In addition, the President must submit reports periodically to the House and Senate on the conflict abroad, and he must estimate the duration of America's involvement in hostilities. Moreover, the resolution provides that America's participation in foreign conflicts is automatically terminated within 60 days unless: Congress declares war; or Congress extends this period of involvement for an additional 30 days; or Congress provides direct statutory authority for continuing America's involvement in hostilities. As with more limited military encounters, Congress may require the evacuation of American forces from foreign combat zones at any time by the passage of a concurrent resolution. The War Powers Resolution explicitly denies the President the right to "infer" authority to commit the nation's armed forces abroad from existing legislation, treaty provisions, or congressional resolutions which the White House might interpret as "functional equivalents" of a declaration of war or *de facto* legislative authority for its actions.

*A unique feature of the War Powers Resolution is the provision whereby Congress may terminate America's participation in military hostilities abroad by a "concurrent resolution" (rather than a "joint resolution," as is employed in the enactment of a law). A concurrent resolution requires a favorable vote of the House and Senate, but it does *not* require the President's signature. Consequently, a major legal and constitutional problem exists concerning whether such a concurrent resolution as envisioned by the War Powers Resolution is *legally binding* upon the chief executive, or whether it is merely an expression of legislative opinion. This is one reason why the constitutionality of the War Powers Resolution has been seriously questioned by some legal authorities. Thus far, the constitutional issues posed by these and other provisions of the resolution have not been tested in the federal courts.

The Future of the War Powers Resolution

Passage of the War Powers Resolution was clearly a victory for those advocating a more influential role by Congress in the conduct of American foreign relations. What has been the resolution's impact upon the nation's diplomacy? What contribution does the resolution make in assuring that there will be "no more Vietnams" to mar the nation's diplomatic record? Such questions are both legitimate and, for several reasons, very difficult to answer at this stage.

The War Powers Resolution is a relatively new measure. As such, insufficient time has elapsed in which to evaluate its implications fully. Moreover, its constitutionality has never been tested. In vetoing the resolution, President Nixon contended that it infringed upon the chief executive's constitutional prerogatives as commander in chief—a right which did not belong to Congress. In addition, some commentators believed that on balance, the War Powers Resolution actually *strengthened* the powers of the President in the foreign policy field, by allowing him considerable latitude to employ the armed forces in the absence of a declaration of war or other clear legislative authority.

The acid test of the contribution made by the War Powers Resolution, however, will most likely occur in the realm of American diplomatic experience. Does the resolution enhance or impede the ability of the United States to achieve its foreign policy goals? Insufficient evidence has been accumulated thus far to permit a definitive answer to that question. A few tentative conclusions, however, may be advanced. Since the passage of the War Powers Resolution, its existence has not seriously impeded the ability of chief executives to employ the armed forces in responding to a number of external crises. A conspicuous example was the *Mayaguez* incident in 1975, when President Gerald Ford employed the armed forces in an attempt to rescue American seamen who had been captured off the coast of Southeast Asia. In 1980, President Carter relied upon the armed forces in an unsuccessful effort to rescue Americans held hostage in Iran. Early in the year, he issued the "Carter Doctrine" (considered more fully in Chapter 12), committing the United States to preserve the security of the Persian Gulf area. Congress played no noteworthy role in the formulation and issuance of this foreign policy dictum.

By the early 1980s, the outlook of the American people and their legislative representatives had changed fundamentally from the early post-Vietnam War era. A succession of diplomatic defeats and setbacks—going back to America's defeat in the Vietnam War and the ensuing expansion of Communist power in Southeast Asia, followed by growing Soviet and Cuban influence on the African continent, by assaults on several American embassies abroad, by Iran's seizure of American hostages, and (early in 1980) by a massive Soviet incursion into Afghanistan—produced a discernible shift in popular and congressional attitudes. Throughout the American society, a mounting chorus of demands was heard calling upon President Carter to "take charge" of American foreign policy, and to exhibit vigorous "leadership" in responding to external challenges. A former White House adviser to the Kennedy Administration addressed a public "appeal" to President Carter, stating:

> Effective control over the conduct of foreign affairs is slipping away from Jimmy Carter. . . . a coherent and effective American foreign policy requires Presidential leadership. Not with unaccountable power. Not with an exclusive monopoly of power. But the Framers of the Constitution knew that decisive, unified initiative and implementation in foreign affairs were properly the prerogative of a single, nationally elected executive. . . .
>
> The President must seize initiative on every major international issue. . . . The President must define the terms of the foreign policy debate. . . . The President must be perceived to be in full command of his own forces. . . . Pray, sir, begin.[32]

Responding to such entreaties at home

and to threatened Soviet expansionism in the Middle East, on January 23, 1980—in perhaps the most forceful foreign policy statement of his Administration—President Jimmy Carter enunciated the "Carter Doctrine." Its key provision was the assertion that the United States regarded the Persian Gulf area as vital to its security and would respond decisively (with military force if necessary) to any Soviet attempt to dominate the region. As we shall see more fully in this chapter and in Chapter 12, the Carter Doctrine marked a major turning point in recent American foreign policy.

Two points about the doctrine are relevant for our discussion here. The first is that Carter's speech *evoked overwhelming public approval*. The doctrine seemed to exemplify the kind of presidential "leadership" Americans were demanding from the White House. The second remarkable fact about the doctrine—entailing the buildup of American armed strength in the Middle East and the clear risk of military intervention to block Soviet expansionism—was that almost nothing was heard on Capitol Hill about the War Powers Resolution and the limitations imposed upon the President's authority over the armed forces by its provisions. Instead, the Carter Doctrine was greeted with overwhelming *approval* on Capitol Hill—where the dominant sentiment seemed to be that the President should have issued his doctrine many months earlier![33] The utility of the War Powers Resolution, recent events have made clear, is likely to be determined in no small measure by the public mood during any given era and its impact upon Congress' activities in the foreign policy field.

General Legislative Authority in Foreign Affairs

Along with specific prerogatives bearing upon foreign relations, like the Senate's role in treaty making or the legislative power over appropri-

ations, Congress has general legislative authority over measures intimately related to foreign policy and domestic programs impinging upon external affairs. Indeed, as the line between "foreign" and "domestic" affairs has become more and more eroded, nearly every important legislative enactment, resolution, or investigation has some impact upon foreign affairs. Legislative enactments dealing with nuclear energy have inhibited America's ability to "share" atomic secrets with the NATO allies. Congressional authority is required to establish new executive agencies like the National Security Council and the International Communication Agency (ICA) or to reorganize the State and Defense departments. After the Vietnam War, Congress' authority over another group of governmental agencies—the members of the "intelligence community"—was repeatedly invoked in efforts to impose new guidelines upon their operations.

Theoretically, the principal duty of Congress is "law making." In practice, as we observed in Chapter 3, today the President plays a key role in the law-making process. Most major legislation originates in the executive branch of government; and throughout every stage in the law-making process, the President and his agents engage in "legislative liaison" designed to influence Congress' deliberations. So entrenched has this tradition become that (as President Jimmy Carter discovered during his Administration) a President's *failure* to exercise leadership on Capitol Hill is likely to weaken his public image significantly.[34] Today, even members of the House and Senate expect such White House leadership—and often complain vocally about its absence!

Even less than in the sphere of domestic policy, down to the period of the Vietnam War, Congress seldom took the initiative in enacting legislation dealing directly with foreign affairs. An exception was the Battle

Act (officially called the Mutual Defense Assistance Control Act) of 1951, passed during the Korean War. This act prohibited the extension of American foreign aid to countries trading with Communist nations or refusing to inform the United States government about the scope of such trade. Not untypically for such legislation, however, the Battle Act contained a provision allowing the President to disregard its terms when he believed the national interests of the United States justified doing so.[35] In the years that followed, and especially after the Vietnam conflict, Congress relied much more heavily upon its general legislative authority to enact measures affecting America's foreign relations. One sphere of keen congressional interest during the 1970s, for example, was the promotion of international human rights. In dealing with this issue, Congress enacted a range of measures designed to strengthen the observance of human rights abroad; and the State Department was required to file voluminous reports with the House and Senate on progress being made in attaining the goal.[36]

Extraconstitutional and Informal Techniques

The Power of Congress to Investigate

In recent years, few powers available to Congress for influencing the course of American diplomacy have been used with more telling effect than legislative investigations into the formulation and administration of foreign affairs. Although not mentioned explicitly in the Constitution, Congress' power to conduct investigations is a long-established prerogative incident to its general law-making function. In general terms, the House and Senate are empowered to conduct investigations centering upon two broad problems: the need for *new* laws (or changes in existing ones), in the light of existing conditions; and

the *administration* (or maladministration) of legislation already enacted by Congress. Since World War II, this "oversight" function has led Congress to investigate innumerable major and minor problems in the foreign policy field—ranging from why Communism engulfed China and the problem of European reconstruction in the early postwar period; to the conduct of the Vietnam War; the political activities of American business corporations; and, in more recent years, the problems associated with Soviet-American détente.[37]

On some occasions, Congress has employed its investigative powers in an evident attempt to take the initiative from the chief executive in the sphere of foreign and national defense policy. A celebrated example occurred during the Civil War, when the congressional Committee on the Conduct of the War sought to compel President Lincoln to accept the views of legislators on the conduct of the war. According to one commentator, the committee

> was encouraged ... by the public impatience at the slowness with which military operations against the Confederacy were proceeding.... They consistently urged a more vigorous prosecution of the war and less lenience toward the institution of slavery.... So far did the committee depart from its legitimate purpose that it became a veritable thorn in the flesh of the President. The members took over partial control of military operations. Their investigating missions to the front undermined army discipline and discouraged the more capable commanders .... Interrogating generals as if they were schoolboys and advising the President like military experts, they sought to intimidate Lincoln by threatening to arouse Congress against him.[38]

With certain modifications (at least as executive policy makers would assess the matter), this description might also apply to postwar congressional investigations of American foreign policy toward China, the conduct of the Vietnam War, and the activities of the Central Intelligence Agency and other members of the intelligence community at home and abroad. In many instances, it has been difficult for the informed citizen to detect any permanently beneficial results which have derived from several well-publicized congressional investigations in the foreign policy field.

By contrast, some investigations by Congress into foreign (and related domestic) policy problems have unquestionably been of value, and as a result of them, improvements have been made in the conduct of American foreign relations. A model of legislative inquiry, for example, was the investigation conducted by the Truman Committee during World War II.* Wilfred E. Binkley believes that the Truman Committee represented the "highest development of the congressional investigating committee," and that Senator Truman perhaps contributed more than any other civilian except the President to the winning of the war.[39] The committee grew out of Senator Truman's conviction that Congress ought to carry on investigations while waste could still be eliminated from the war effort and unsound practices could be corrected, instead of waiting until after the war when it could do no more than try to assess the blame for failures. By contrast, after World War I there had been over a hundred congressional investigations, most of them "motivated by partisan desires to fix blame on the opposition"; they had "raked over the coals for more than fifteen years after the war."[40]

Several congressional investigations after World War II also had a positive impact upon American foreign relations. Specific

mention can be made of the joint Senate Foreign Relations-Armed Services Committee investigation during the Korean War of President Harry S Truman's dismissal of the popular military commander General Douglas MacArthur. Truman's dismissal of General MacArthur precipitated what one commentator called "the gravest and most emotional [constitutional] crisis that the United States had known since the Great Depression."[41] As a result of its thorough investigation and impartial findings, the committee's activities went far toward calming the popular uproar over MacArthur's dismissal. Even more fundamentally, the committee reaffirmed the vital constitutional principle of civilian control over the military and largely restored public confidence in the Truman Administration's handling of the Korean War.[42]

Basically the same results have followed from a number of legislative investigations into the activities of the Central Intelligence Agency and other members of the intelligence community since the end of the Vietnam War. During the late 1960s and early 1970s, reports and sometimes sensationalized exposés of "wrongdoing" or questionable behavior abroad by the CIA and other intelligence units were daily fare in the news media. For a prolonged period during the 1970s, several congressional committees probed the organization and activities of the intelligence community. These committees uncovered ample evidence of abuses in the behavior of the CIA and other intelligence agencies; and these were usually given maximum publicity by the news media. Although these legislative investigations often tended to be uncoordinated (and sometimes actuated mainly by partisan or publicity considerations), in the end they made a number of positive contributions to the conduct of foreign affairs and to the protection of civil liberties within the United States.

In particular, these congressional inquiries achieved three positive results. First, they

---

*This committee, known as the Special Senate Committee Investigating the National Defense Program, was established in March 1941, and was named for its chairman, Senator Harry S Truman (Democrat of Missouri).

turned the spotlight of publicity upon the misuse of often vast, and sometimes largely unchecked, power by influential governmental agencies—a crucial step in bringing the CIA and other intelligence agencies under effective democratic control. Second, these investigations prompted the White House (particularly President Gerald Ford and President Jimmy Carter) to issue new "executive orders" reorganizing the intelligence operations of the executive branch and imposing more stringent controls over intelligence activities. Third, they were responsible for improving congressional oversight of intelligence operations by establishing new House and Senate Intelligence committees, whose missions were to provide *continuing legislative supervision* of intelligence activities and (when required) *congressional approval* for certain kinds of intelligence operations.[43]

Yet is should not be imagined that Congress has definitively "solved" the difficult and complex problems associated with the maintenance and operation of a vast intelligence apparatus in a democratic setting. Despite continuing legislative inquiry into the problem, the line between "permissible" and "impermissible" CIA activities abroad, for example, remains indistinct and difficult to draw satisfactorily. By 1980, approximately 200 legislators were still privy to information related to intelligence activities—meaning that there was a high risk of "leaks" about American intelligence operations, posing serious jeopardy to the security of particular intelligence missions and perhaps even to the lives of American and allied intelligence agents. Then as a series of political crises in the Middle East at the end of the 1970s caught the United States by surprise, it became clear that Congress had made more progress in imposing "controls" upon intelligence agencies than it had in correcting certain serious problems which impaired their performance and detracted from their ability to carry out legitimate intelligence missions successfully.[44]

Congressional Resolutions

Another technique available to legislators—sometimes used with telling effect to exert congressional influence upon the course of American diplomacy—is the power of one or both chambers to pass "resolutions" on foreign policy issues. Such resolutions, it must be emphasized, *are not law;* they are merely expressions of *legislative opinion* on particular questions. Yet under certain circumstances, they can have a potent impact upon American foreign relations.

A resolution expressing legislative opinion can take a variety of forms. If adopted by only one chamber, it is called a "sense of the House" or a "sense of the Senate" resolution. If both chambers join in passing it, it is a "concurrent resolution" of Congress. (It will be recalled from an earlier portion of the chapter that under the provisions of the War Powers Resolution,* Congress may by "concurrent resolution" direct the President to withdraw the armed forces of the United States from actual or potential combat zones.)

---

*Confusion is likely to be created by the title of the act given to the measure passed by Congress in 1973 limiting the President's powers over the armed forces. Although it is officially called by Congress the War Powers *Resolution,* it is nonetheless a *statutory enactment* having the force of law. Unlike other resolutions, its terms are thus binding upon the President and not merely an expression of congressional sentiment which he is free to follow or ignore. The question of whether Congress can *compel* the President to withdraw American forces abroad by passing a "concurrent resolution," which does not require his signature, has yet to be determined by the federal courts. Since it is deemed to have the force of law, the War Powers Resolution is sometimes referred to as the War Powers Act. See Gerald R. Ford, *A Time to Heal* (New York: Harper & Row, and The Reader's Digest Association, 1979), pp. 249–252.

For over 200 years, legislators have expressed their viewpoints on a wide variety of internal and external policy questions in the form of such resolutions. In any given session of Congress, several hundred are likely to be passed before Congress adjourns. Since such resolutions do not require the President's signature (and thus are not subject to his veto), they are not law and, therefore, have no binding force upon the executive branch or upon citizens.

Yet although such resolutions are not synonymous with law, sometimes they can be highly influential instruments whereby Congress has an impact upon the American foreign policy process. Neither the White House nor Congress operates in a vacuum. Each is highly sensitive to public opinion and to deep convictions held by officials in the other branch. Whenever possible, the President and Congress prefer to adopt policies that can command wide public support. Congressional resolutions on foreign policy issues are thus important barometers of opinion for the executive branch. They may reflect deep public concern about contemporary policy issues; they may call attention forcefully to widespread dissatisfaction with existing policies; and they may strengthen the President's hand in dealing with other countries by conveying the impression abroad of unanimity within the American government.

Two kinds of congressional resolutions in foreign affairs may be distinguished: those initiated by Congress itself, often in the face of presidential opposition; and those formulated by the executive branch (sometimes in concert with selected congressmen), which reflect viewpoints held by both executive and legislative policy makers. Throughout the postwar period, Congress has from time to time passed resolutions condemning Soviet policy in Eastern Europe, calling upon the President to use American influence to keep Communist China out of the United Nations, or asking for a reexamination of national policies in Southeast Asia.

Much more influential, however, is the other kind of resolution which is drafted in (or with the concurrence of) the executive branch. Its principal purpose is to provide a graphic display of governmental unity in dealing with a foreign crisis. Congress has passed several resolutions of this kind since World War II. Confronted with a threat by Communist China to invade Formosa and adjacent islands in 1955, President Eisenhower asked Congress to authorize the use of force to protect the area. Early in 1955, the Senate completed passage of a resolution granting the President the authority he requested.* In 1962, two similar resolutions were approved by Congress. One supported the President's determination to maintain the security of Berlin against Communist encroachments. The other expressed opposition to the Marxist regime in Cuba and reiterated America's determination to prevent Communist penetration of Latin America.[45]

The most celebrated and perhaps most controversial resolution of this type was the Tonkin Gulf Resolution of August 10, 1964. Requested by President Johnson, after North

*The Formosa Resolution of 1955, and those modeled after it later, involved a troublesome constitutional issue. When the President asked Congress to grant him "authority" to employ armed force in behalf of some foreign policy goal, did this mean that he *lacked* such authority if Congress withheld it? Successive Presidents have answered in the negative. Thus, President Eisenhower said in connection with the Formosa Resolution: "Authority for some of the actions which might be required would be inherent in the authority of the Commander-in-Chief." Nevertheless, he asked Congress for a "suitable resolution" in order to "clearly and publicly establish the authority of the President" to act and to "make clear the unified and serious intentions" of the American Congress. See Dwight D. Eisenhower, *Mandate for Change* (Garden City, N.Y.: Doubleday, 1963), p. 468.

Vietnamese naval vessels attacked American ships off the coast of Vietnam, this resolution put Congress on record as approving and supporting "the determination of the President as Commander-in-Chief, to take all necessary measures to repel any armed attack against the forces of the United States and to prevent further aggression." Adopted unanimously in the House of Representatives, and by a vote of 88 to 2 in the Senate, the Tonkin Gulf Resolution figured prominently in subsequent years, both as a basis for national policies in Southeast Asia and as a target for criticism by those who deplored America's involvement in Vietnam.[46]

The Tonkin Gulf Resolution illustrates some of the advantages and drawbacks of such executive-sponsored resolutions. Ostensibly, a resolution of this kind does reflect a high degree of unanimity between the executive and legislative branches on a particular foreign policy issue. Other than a declaration of war (rare as that is), it would be difficult to think of any step which more forcefully symbolizes the existence of a consensus within the American government than a resolution of this type.

Yet time has also revealed that such resolutions may, and not infrequently do, produce tensions, controversies, and intense personal antagonisms among policy makers in the executive and legislative branches. Nearly always, as in the case of the Tonkin Gulf Resolution, Congress deliberates in an atmosphere of crisis and urgency; little opportunity is afforded for legislative investigation and debate; legislators complain (later, if not at the time) that they were "pressured" into supporting the resolution or that the President and his agents did not reveal "all the facts" when the resolution was being considered. Also, with the passage of time it is not uncommon for legislators to disagree with the White House over the extent of authority granted to the President by Congress in such resolutions. The Tonkin Gulf Resolution, for example, was cited for several years after its adoption as one of the "functional equivalents" to a declaration of war, whereby Congress sanctioned American military intervention in Southeast Asia. When Congress passed the War Powers Resolution in 1973, therefore, its terms explicitly provided that the President could *not* derive authority to commit the military forces of the United States abroad from such measures as the Tonkin Gulf Resolution.[47]

Speeches and Activities of Individual Legislators

Unlike the British Parliament and most other legislative bodies in democratic governments, the Congress of the United States is characterized by very loose party lines and little or no "party discipline." If anything, centralizing forces within the House and Senate, like the power of party organizations and leaders, have become weaker in the post-Vietnam War era. A combination of forces—weakening party ties among the American electorate; the emergence of "single-issue politics" (whereby one question like gun control or abortion can dominate a political campaign); the appearance of a number of "caucuses" among like-minded legislators who are interested mainly in one overriding issue; attacks upon the "seniority" principle within the House and Senate, which for many years governed the selection of committee chairmen; the unchecked proliferation of legislative committees and subcommittees with jurisdiction in the foreign policy field—have tended now to provide greater freedom to individual legislators to express their views on national issues than in any previous period of American history. As one student of the legislative process in the United States has described these new tendencies on Capitol Hill:

No sooner is today's freshman [legislator] sworn in than he charges up to the nearest television camera to claim leadership in everything from sugar quotas to SALT II. Apprenticeship in the Senate is now as obsolete as the frock coat and string bow tie.... The result is a legislative "symphony" in which every performer is a soloist who plays for his own fans in the audience rather than acting in concert with the other players.

In this commentator's view, the result has been "an almost total lack of any discernible consensus" by Congress in dealing with national policy issues; and "a form of anarchy" routinely exists in the House and Senate.[48]

The impact of influential personalities within Congress upon external policy is of course no new phenomenon in American diplomatic history. Thus, Senator Henry Cabot Lodge (Republican of Massachusetts) emerged as the leading opponent to the League of Nations during and after World War I. During the 1930s, the isolationist viewpoint in Congress was vocally and influentially expressed by outspoken legislators like Senators Burton K. Wheeler (Democrat of Montana) and Gerald P. Nye (Republican of North Dakota).[49] Throughout his first two terms in the White House, President Franklin D. Roosevelt was nearly always unsuccessful in his conflicts with such defenders of isolationism.

In the early postwar period, a powerful voice on Capitol Hill belonged to Senator Arthur H. Vandenberg (Republican of Michigan). A former isolationist, Vandenberg became a spokesman for, and defender of, the "containment" strategy adopted by the Truman Administration as America's answer to Soviet expansionism. Time and again, in collaboration with officials in the executive branch, Vandenberg induced his colleagues on Capitol Hill to support such landmark undertakings as the Greek-Turkish Aid Program of 1947 and the Marshall Plan and North Atlantic Treaty of Western defense which followed.[50] Indeed, it would not be inaccurate to say that no single member of Congress since World War II has influenced the nature and direction of American foreign policy as momentously as Senator Vandenberg.

From a different perspective, during the Vietnam War the growing opposition to the Johnson Administration's policies in Southeast Asia—and, in time, in other settings —was embodied in the speeches and activities of Senator J. William Fulbright (Democrat of Arkansas), chairman of the Senate Foreign Relations Committee. For anti-Vietnam War critics, Fulbright actively and ably championed their point of view in his numerous speeches inside and outside Congress, in his voluminous writings, and in his direction of the activities of the Foreign Relations Committee. More than any other individual member of Congress, Fulbright was responsible for publicizing mounting criticisms of the Johnson Administration's diplomacy and, ultimately, for the Administration's loss of public credibility.[51]

A well-publicized case of independent diplomatic activities by legislators occurred late in 1979, after a group of Iranian students had invaded the American embassy in Tehran and seized some 50 Americans as hostages. After initial efforts by executive officials failed to obtain their release, Representative George Hansen (Republican of Idaho) decided to undertake his own negotiations with the captors of the American hostages. Hansen's mission, said the *New York Times,* risked "throwing matches" in a highly volatile situation and encouraged the "belief that the United States speaks with several voices" in foreign affairs. His self-appointed role as negotiator with Iran drew severe criticism even from other members of Congress, who accused Hansen of having few qualifications for the task, of creating the impression of American disunity abroad, and of arousing hopes which quickly turned to disillusionment when his mission failed.[52]

The coin of speeches and independent diplomatic initiatives by legislators, however, clearly has another side. In some instances, this tendency is unquestionably *encouraged* by the President and his foreign policy advisers, who believe members of Congress can make a useful contribution to American diplomacy under certain conditions. Thus, late in 1979 Senator Frank Church (Democrat of Idaho) delivered a widely publicized public speech condemning the buildup of Soviet military forces in Cuba. After American intelligence agencies had confirmed this Soviet military escalation in the Caribbean, executive officials gave the evidence to Senator Church, who released it publicly.[53] Among the other gains from this move (and improving Church's chances for reelection to the Senate was one of them), this speech by an influential legislator was designed to strengthen the Carter Administration's position on Capitol Hill and to convey a pointed warning to Moscow that the American government was *united* in its opposition to Soviet military incursions into the Western Hemisphere.

Congressional Travel and "Representation"

Among the techniques available to Congress to influence foreign relations in the modern period, none has perhaps become more publicized and more frequently utilized than *travel abroad* for a variety of purposes directly or indirectly related to legislative business. Before World War II, foreign travel by legislators was an almost unknown phenomenon (the first year in which legislators went abroad to inspect an American diplomatic mission was 1936). During 1978, 66 senators and 227 representatives—or over half the total membership of Congress—took trips abroad at the taxpayers' expense.

Today, it is an unimaginative member of Congress who cannot think of some reason why he needs to take a trip abroad at fairly frequent intervals.[54] In any given session of Congress, subcommittees or other groups of legislators find it necessary to make a first-hand inspection of NATO defenses; or observe the administration of American foreign assistance in South Korea, India, and other settings; or gather information about Communist movements in black Africa; or prepare a report on the economic progress of certain Latin American countries. The number of such overseas visits by members of the House and Senate has risen sharply since World War II, and no reversal of the trend seems likely in the future.

In some respects, foreign travel by legislators unquestionably enhances legislative understanding of foreign affairs and improves Congress' ability to influence American foreign policy. As the members of Congress see it, foreign trips provide them with firsthand and independent sources of information on important foreign policy issues, thereby reducing their dependence upon the executive branch for such information. In turn, a better and more accurately informed Congress is in a stronger position to serve as an enlightened critic of White House policies. (During the height of the Vietnam War, for example, the trips to Southeast Asia by a number of legislators provided them with data and insights which they used to challenge the White House position that the United States was "winning" the conflict in Vietnam.)

Foreign travel by legislators also serves to overcome a potent force on Capitol Hill which even today often shapes the foreign policy viewpoints reflected in the House and Senate: *provincialism and immersion in local issues.* The preoccupation of legislators with constituency-related business—generated by the pervasive involvement of the federal government in all spheres of American life—remains a powerful deterrent to informed congressional interest and participation in foreign policy decision making. Ironically, as Congress' participation in the foreign policy process has expanded significantly since World War II, the deliberations of Congress seem more than ever to be dominated by local and regional concerns.[55] Foreign travel thus plays some part in enabling legislators to acquire a sense of the "national interest" in dealing with international questions which they might not otherwise possess.

Congress and Diplomacy: the Road Ahead

Legislative "Activism" After Vietnam

One of President Lyndon B. Johnson's White House aides said that to LBJ's mind, "no person in his respective department could ever be any more important than the head of the Congressional relations activity."[56] During the decade from the late 1960s to the late 1970s, the State Department's "legislative liaison staff" increased by some 50 percent.[57] Former presidential adviser and Secretary of State Henry Kissinger has said: "That Congress should play a major role in the conduct of foreign policy [is] beyond argument."[58] A more recent analysis of executive-legislative relations in the foreign policy process concluded that an "enlarged role" by Congress in the foreign affairs of the United States "is here to stay."[59]

Among both officials directly involved in the foreign policy process and informed students of American foreign affairs, there is now recognition of a highly significant tendency in the evolution of American diplomacy. Since the period of the Vietnam War, Congress has established a forceful and influential "presence" in the foreign policy process—so much

so that at times Congress appears to have emerged as the *dominant organ* in the formulation and administration of American foreign policy. In contrast to earlier eras, one commentator has asserted, Congress is no longer willing to give a "passive majority" to support diplomatic decisions made in the executive branch.[60] Although he acknowledged a legitimate role for Congress in the foreign policy process, Dr. Kissinger was also convinced that during the 1970s "passion overwhelmed analysis," leading to a condition in which Congress preempted the President's position in foreign affairs and virtually dictated the foreign policy of the United States—often to the detriment of American diplomatic interests.[61]

Evidence to document the contention that Congress embarked upon a new course of diplomatic activism after the Vietnam War is available on all sides. At this point, we can do no more than allude to a portion of it (other examples will be supplied in Chapters 10 through 15, dealing with recent American foreign policy toward major regions and substantive international issues). As legislators viewed the matter, Congress played a crucial role in ending America's involvement in the Vietnam War and in preventing any new American participation in conflicts in Southeast Asia. Congressional opposition was also decisive in preventing the executive branch from extending American foreign assistance to North Vietnam and other countries in Southeast Asia. Under the Ford and Carter administrations, Congress adamantly opposed American military involvement in political upheavals on the African continent, although Soviet and Cuban intervention in them was evident. By passing the War Powers Resolution, Congress circumscribed the powers of the President to use the armed forces for diplomatic ends without the consent of the House and Senate.

As it had done consistently since the late

1940s, Congress insisted that the White House remain mindful of the security of Israel and that the President keep that goal at the forefront of efforts to resolve the Arab-Israeli conflict; measures to provide modern and extensive military assistance to Israel almost always received overwhelming legislative approval, even while sentiment toward the Arab position was becoming more favorable. Toward the Soviet Union, during the 1970s Congress favored White House efforts to promote détente with Moscow. At the same time, legislators insisted upon the right of Soviet Jews to emigrate from the U.S.S.R. and made the expansion of Soviet-American trade relations contingent upon Moscow's compliance with that demand. In approaching the Greek-Turkish dispute over Cyprus, largely because of domestic constituency pressure Congress sided overwhelmingly with Greece; imposed new restrictions upon American aid to Turkey; and played a key role in the rapid deterioration of Turkish-American relations.

During the 1970s also, several major congressional investigations were conducted of the activities of the Central Intelligence Agency and other members of the intelligence community—all with a view toward preventing CIA "misdeeds" and other instances of questionable behavior by intelligence agencies at home and abroad. By the end of the 1970s, Congress had made a major contribution to the reorganization of the intelligence community and the imposition of stricter controls upon the activities of its members. More perhaps than any other dimension of American foreign policy, Congress' new diplomatic activism was evident and had a profound impact in the area of international human rights. To a significant degree, because of congressional interest in this question, the promotion of human rights abroad was a high-priority goal of the Carter Administration. Congress took a variety of steps—from demanding that human rights be made a more central concern of State Department activities, to requiring executive officials to file voluminous reports on progress made by other countries in observing human rights abroad—designed to achieve this goal.

The Origins of Legislative Activism

What factors provided the impetus for a more forceful and independent role by Congress in American foreign relations after the Vietnam War? The phenomenon had a number of long-term and short-run causes.

From the perspective of American history and constitutional theory, a more active role by the House and Senate in foreign relations could be justified on several grounds. The Founding Fathers, for example, unquestionably believed that among the three branches of the American government, Congress uniquely embodied the concept of democracy; that it most accurately reflected the American people's will; and that it should function as the dominant branch in policy making. Conversely, the Founders were intensely suspicious of executive power, which they believed was (or could easily become) synonymous with autocratic government.[62]

Another historic force propelling Congress more actively into the foreign policy process has been the concept of "Wilsonianism." More than any occupant of the White House, President Woodrow Wilson believed in "open convenants, openly arrived at," in a more influential role for public opinion in foreign policy decision making, and in other steps designed to "democratize" the conduct of foreign relations. Wilsonianism had a potent impact upon the conduct of foreign relations by the United States. After World War I—and the process perhaps reached its high point during the Vietnam War—public opinion played an increasingly decisive role in foreign policy decision making. Viewing itself as the "voice of the people," Congress perhaps inevitably construed the democratization of American diplomacy as requiring enhanced legislative participation in all aspects of foreign relations.[63]

A third historic and deeply ingrained concept in the American ethos also contributed to the new era of legislative activism in foreign affairs. As explained more fully in Chapter 2, this was the American society's long-standing skepticism about "diplomacy" and the agencies and officials involved in it. To the American mind, diplomacy was an Old World concept, associated with ideas and practices (like balance of power) that were not congenial with New World values. For over a century and a half, America adhered (more or less consistently) to an "isolationist" foreign policy—which could be construed as *the avoidance of diplomacy*. In the post-World War II era, the State Department's customarily poor "image" with Congress could be attributed in some measure to these traditional ideas implicit in the American cultural ethos.[64] Not infrequently, the results achieved by the White House, the State Department, and other executive agencies in the Vietnam conflict seemed to confirm the worst fears of many Americans and their legislative representatives about diplomacy. In the light of these fears, it was perhaps natural for Congress to seek to "recover" control over the American foreign policy process.

By the period of the Vietnam War, several more immediate developments at home and abroad combined to inject Congress actively into the conduct of American foreign affairs. A leading one, of course, was the traumatic impact of the Vietnam conflict upon the American society. Its consequences and implications were manifold. For the first time since the War of 1812, the United States *lost* in a military confrontation with another country—and a small, economically backward one at that! The war created more internal dissension within the American society than perhaps any other event in the nation's diplomatic history. Rightly or wrongly, many legislators concluded that if Congress had exerted its powers in foreign relations earlier, the United States would have avoided a military and diplomatic defeat in Southeast Asia.

Then beginning in mid-1972, the credibility of the presidential office was further eroded by the Watergate scandal involving President Richard M. Nixon and his closest advisers. Facing almost certain impeachment, Nixon became the first chief executive in American history to resign his position. Thereafter, for a period of several years fears of the "imperial presidency" dominated public and congressional attitudes toward the executive branch; and not until the end of the decade did the American people once again call for vigorous White House leadership in solving urgent internal and external problems.

The Vietnam War had another result that created new opportunities for congressional influence in foreign relations: It raised fundamental questions about the *basic principles* which ought to guide American foreign policy in the years ahead. By the end of World War II, the American society had abandoned "isolationism" as its foreign policy credo—we may assume *permanently*. By the end of the Vietnam War, millions of Americans had also concluded that indiscriminate "interventionism" in Southeast Asia or other regions did not pay diplomatic dividends for the United States. For years to come, the slogan "No More Vietnams!" was likely to guide the deliberations of national policy makers. In the era of diplomatic retrenchment and reevaluation which followed the Vietnam War, many members of the House and Senate were convinced of two things: There must be a fundamental reformulation of the principles actuating the nation's diplomacy; and Congress should play a prominent role in this process.

In company with other experienced public servants and informed commentators, former Secretary of State Henry Kissinger has identified another force inducing Congress to play a dynamic role in the foreign policy process. Thus, Kissinger called attention to the consequences when the executive branch of government practiced the "separation of powers itself"![65] Progressive disunity and competing efforts *among executive agencies* involved in foreign relations—an evident tendency in recent years—offered Congress strong inducements to exert its prerogatives in external affairs. The problem reached a critical stage under the Carter Administration—when almost daily the question arose of "Who is really in charge of American foreign policy?" At least two major power centers—along with a host of minor ones—existed within the executive branch. There was the secretary of state and his subordinates in the State Department. Then there was the White House staff, headed (in the foreign policy field) by the President's national security adviser. Time and again during the Carter Administration, fundamental differences of opinion (as on the issue of détente with the Soviet Union) existed between these two power centers.[66] The tug-of-war between the White House and Capitol Hill for control over the foreign policy machinery could be traced in part to the President's own failure to produce a clear and unified approach to external problems within the executive branch.[67]

Such conditions invite and encourage congressional forays into the foreign policy sphere for three reasons. First, a disunified executive branch leaves a *policy vacuum* that Congress is almost certain to fill. Second, fundamental policy disagreements and bureaucratic infighting among executive agencies inevitably *weakens American foreign policy,*

impairing its success abroad and perhaps in some cases guaranteeing diplomatic failure. In these instances, Congress is irresistibly tempted to take remedial action. Third, differing viewpoints among executive agencies encourage fragmented and divided efforts *within Congress* in dealing with foreign policy issues. Not infrequently, executive agencies seek allies for their position on Capitol Hill (the symbiotic relationship, for example, between the Pentagon and the House and Senate Armed Services committees is legendary). Under these conditions, executive agencies are prone to "take their case" to Congress, where they often have sympathetic supporters for their point of view.

Finally, account must be taken of another development providing momentum for a dynamic role by Congress in the foreign policy process. This is *significant changes within the legislative branch* in recent years. As we have already observed, for example, Congress is getting "younger": Many new faces have appeared on Capitol Hill since the Vietnam War, and, while they may be legislative novices, these new members of the House and Senate are often not disposed to accept traditional principles and procedures governing Congress' role. They have demanded—and frequently won—changes in House and Senate rulings allowing them greater freedom of expression and action; and they have not been reluctant about exerting congressional prerogatives in the foreign policy field.[68]

The rapid growth in the congressional staff must also be viewed as a development which both permits Congress to play a more active foreign policy role and, in some instances, induces it to do so. During the 25-year period from 1955 to 1979, for example, the number of congressional employees increased almost 400 percent (from just over 5000 to some 20,000 staff members). The cost of maintaining the House and Senate staff rose from some $170 million in 1955 to almost $1.2 billion in 1980! One study found that five different agencies of government now have a major responsibility for providing information to members of Congress. Commenting on the impact of this change, one senator observed that today, the prestige and status of legislators tends to be measured by "how many whiz kids you have on the staff to get you mentioned in magazine articles, and get you headlines and get all those other things done."[69] In the foreign policy field, this staff escalation has meant that Congress "has developed a virtual counter-State Department composed of predominantly young, experienced and aggressive experts who are out to make their own marks on the foreign policy map."[70]

Along with the escalation in the legislative staff has gone another tendency that reenforces the impulse toward a more assertive congressional role in foreign relations. This is the *growing decentralization of Congress* and the increasingly difficult challenge of imparting cohesion and unity to its deliberations. For example, during the 20-year period from 1960 to 1980, the number of congressional subcommittees doubled (reaching 280 by the end of the period). By the opening of the 1980s, the House of Representatives alone had 83 committees and subcommittees dealing with some aspect of the energy problem! Even after extensive investigations of the intelligence community undertaken during the 1970s, the CIA was still required to report to eight separate committees on Capitol Hill (involving a total of some 200 legislators). Forces which had in an earlier period imparted some degree of unity and cohesion to Congress' deliberations—such as powerful committee chairmen and effective party leadership—had become progressively weaker and incapable of reversing the trend toward diffusion of power on Capitol Hill.

The continuing dispersion of power in the legislative branch was to no inconsiderable degree the result of two forces. One of these was the pressure of parochial and local interests on Capitol Hill, along with the growing involvement of legislators in constituency-related business. The proliferation of federal programs, and the increased involvement of the national government in local and state affairs since World War II, meant that the people's legislative representatives must now devote a disproportionate amount of time to local issues and concerns. The Speaker of the House, Representative Thomas "Tip" O'Neill, thus complained early in 1980 that "Members [of Congress] are dividing—many believing they are local rather than national leaders."

The other influential tendency producing decentralizaiton in Congress is the weakening of national political party ties and loyalties among citizens. By the end of the 1970s, for example, the number of Americans who regarded themselves as "independents" politically had risen from one-fourth to one-third of the electorate. In view of this trend, legislators were less disposed than ever to respect "party discipline"; as one report observed, they seemed primarily interested in "building their own power bases."[71] Or, as another commentary on legislative behavior found:

> ... more and more members [of Congress] are striking out on their own, banding together with like-minded colleagues to establish informal clubs and unofficial committees, such as the Democratic Study Group, the Black Caucus, the House Republican Study Committee.... The decentralization of Congress as a consequence has also encouraged fragmentation and factionalism.[72]

Let us take note of merely one important manifestation of this phenomenon in the foreign policy field: the decline in influence and cohesion of the once-powerful Senate Foreign Relations Committee. In the early postwar period, the voice of this committee—under the chairmanship of influential figures like Senator Arthur H. Vandenberg (Republican of Michigan) and Tom Connally (Democrat of Texas)—was usually *the voice of Congress* in foreign affairs. Agreements reached between President Truman and his principal advisers, on the one hand, and Senator Vandenberg, on the other hand, normally proved durable and were accepted by a majority in the House and Senate.

A generation later, the Senate Foreign Relations Committee was subjected to two forces impairing its influence and prestige on Capitol Hill: fragmentation within the committee on major foreign policy questions; and increasing competition from other Senate and House committees active in the foreign policy sphere. In recent years, internal disunity has beset the committee's deliberations. And other committees of the House and Senate have steadily intruded into its once almost exclusive foreign policy domain. As an example, late in 1979 the committee recommended that the Senate *approve* the SALT II strategic arms-limitation agreement with the Soviet Union. A few weeks later, however, after studying the agreement, the powerful Senate Armed Services Committee recommended that the Senate *disapprove* the accord. (Because of mounting tensions in Soviet-American relations, particularly after Soviet forces invaded Afghanistan late in 1979, President Carter ultimately withdrew the SALT II accord from further Senate deliberations.) By the late 1970s, one study found that 17 out of 22 committees in the House of Representatives, and 16 out of 19 committees in the Senate, had jurisdiction over some aspect of foreign relations.[73]

The diffusion of power evident on Capitol Hill has had a twofold effect upon Congress' foreign policy role. It has created *new opportunities and incentives* for the assertion of legislative prerogatives in the diplomatic field. And it has meant that, in recent years, the influence of Congress upon American foreign relations has more often than not been *divided, inconsistent, and ineffectual* in terms of accomplishing the nation's diplomatic objectives.

Contraints on Congress' Foreign Policy Role

If the House and Senate have played an increasingly active and independent role in the foreign policy process since the Vietnam War, certain powerful contrary forces may in time reverse that behavior pattern and reinvigorate the powers of the presidency in the diplomatic field. Several considerations point to that likely result.

Initially, there is the fact that, in the experience of modern governments throughout the world, the management of foreign relations has almost universally been viewed *as an executive function.* Historically, the conduct of foreign affairs was a prerogative of the chief executive (usually the monarch); diplomacy was the almost exclusive province of a small elite drawn from the aristocracy. Even today, in the United States and most other democracies the diplomatic corps constitutes an educational elite (which is one reason why legislators are often highly critical of the State Department).

In modern democratic governments, control over foreign affairs continues to be vested almost exclusively in executive officials. An independent legislative role (by, for example, the British Parliament or the French National Assembly) in foreign affairs is a highly exceptional phenomenon—and when it occurs, a governmental crisis, followed by new national elections, nearly always follows.

In other democratic systems, legislators must accept responsibility themselves with the electorate for their behavior and must be willing to submit their conduct to a popular verdict, entailing the risk that they will lose their legislative seats in the ensuing election. This realization serves as a powerful brake upon legislative tendencies to tie the hands of executive officials in the management of foreign affairs or to "deadlock" the government in responding to external challenges.[74]

As citizens of the New World, Americans of course have always prided themselves upon the uniqueness of their governmental institutions and many other features of the American way of life. Yet the experience of other democracies strongly suggests that the formulation and conduct of foreign policy is not a function suited to the talents, training, and primary interests of legislators. It is a not unwarranted conclusion that, from the experience of other democratic states, executive officials are charged with the management of foreign affairs primarily because this division of responsibilities *best promotes the nation's diplomatic interests and well-being.*

A second set of likely constraints upon an assertive and independent foreign policy role by Congress in the future is to be found in the existence of certain unique conditions in the post-Vietnam War period. The "agony of Vietnam" gave rise to consequences that would be felt in the conduct of American diplomacy for years, possibly decades, to come. Among these, six major implications seem directly pertinent to our discussion.

First, the American people and their leaders in Washington emerged from the Vietnam experience divided, disillusioned, and confused about the nation's proper foreign policy role. If the Vietnam encounter taught Americans that the United States could not serve as "the policeman of the world," did this mean that it should and could not successfully

serve as a "policeman" *anywhere* on the globe? Did the defeat signify (as President Richard M. Nixon warned) that the United States had become a "pitiful, helpless giant" in global affairs and that *any* exercise of the nation's power abroad reflected (in former Senator J. William Fulbright's words), the "arrogance of American power"? A number of Americans (possibly a minority) believed that such interpretations of the Vietnam experience were valid. Former members of Congress and informed students of American diplomacy wrote commentaries bearing such titles as *The Crippled Giant, Gulliver's Troubles,* and *Eagle Entangled,* suggesting that the United States faced insuperable obstacles in its efforts to influence political developments beyond its own borders.[75]

Second, in the aftermath of Vietnam the American society reverted to a familiar behavior pattern in its diplomatic experience (witnessed, for example, in the period following World War I): It became *massively preoccupied with internal issues.* Critics of the Vietnam War had argued (and in many instances, no doubt correctly) that the prolonged and massive military campaign in Southeast Asia had "diverted" the nation from the solution of pressing internal problems. By the end of the 1970s, the budget of the Department of Health, Education, and Welfare (HEW) exceeded the budget of the Defense Department. Throughout the 1970s, the American society came close to adopting the viewpoint identified with contemporary liberal "neo-isolationists": that ultimately, America's power and influence abroad would be determined by its success in *solving internal problems,* thereby influencing other countries by its exemplary behavior at home.[76]

In the third place, the years following the Vietnam experience were an era of *diplomatic retrenchment* by the United States. After Vietnam, contraction in many of the nation's existing overseas commitments—and a reluctance to assume new obligations abroad—was perhaps understandable and inevitable. During this period, Congress was extremely sensitive about the commitments of the United States abroad—particularly those which might entail the application of American military power. Toward a range of issues—from providing foreign assistance to the nations of Southeast Asia, to American military involvement in black Africa, to obligations undertaken for preserving peace in the Middle East—Congress usually insisted upon two points: The overseas obligations of the United States must have the *approval* of the House and Senate, and they must be *fully publicized.*

A fourth feature of the post-Vietnam era in American foreign policy was *the dissolution of the "anti-Communist" consensus* that had motivated the nation's diplomacy since the late 1940s. America's defeat in Southeast Asia; the emphasis upon détente in Soviet-American relations; the normalization in Sino-American relations, and Washington's subsequent readiness to play "the China card" in relations with Soviet Union; the failure of Communism to dominate the Third World; the emergence of several varieties of "national Communism," such as Euro-Communism in the West—these developments convinced many Americans that indiscriminate anti-Communism was no longer a viable foreign policy stance for the United States. After Vietnam, Americans were prepared to recognize many species of Communism abroad; and they understood that some species threatened the security and diplomatic interests of the United States more than others.[77]

What new principle would replace the anti-Communist consensus after the Vietnam War? A majority of Americans would perhaps agree that in the years ahead, two diplomatic extremes had to be avoided. On the one

hand, it was not possible for the United States to return to the traditional "isolationist" posture in external affairs, in the mistaken belief that foreign crises were none of its concern or did not affect its security. On the other hand, Vietnam had shown the futility of a policy of indiscriminate "interventionism" in the affairs of other countries in order to contain Communism or achieve other goals. After the defeat in Southeast Asia, Americans were neither attracted to that strategy nor believed that it was capable of being implemented successfully. Between these two polar positions lay numerous foreign policy options. In general terms, these alternatives might be described by terms like *selective interventionism* or *pragmatic interventionism.* In clarifying and formulating this new set of diplomatic guidelines, Congress was determined that its voice would be a key input in the foreign policy process.

A fifth characteristic of the post-Vietnam War era was *the dramatic decline in the prestige and credibility of the presidential office.* For many Americans, the administrations of two recent chief executives—Lyndon B. Johnson and Richard M. Nixon—epitomized the "imperial presidency." The Johnson presidency steadily lost credibility in the eyes of the American people because of the war in Southeast Asia. The Nixon Administration was of course totally discredited because of the Watergate episode, involving President Nixon directly, members of the White House staff, and agencies like the CIA. Nixon's threatened impeachment—and his unprecedented resignation as chief executive—perhaps brought the presidential office to its nadir in American history. As expressed by the title of President Gerald R. Ford's memoirs—*A Time to Heal*—the dominant objective of Nixon's successors was to restore public confidence and trust in the nation's political leadership and to improve the morale of a dispirited American society.[78] A major requirement for achieving this goal was avoidance of an "adventuristic" or interventionist foreign policy that might risk American involvement in "another Vietnam."

In the sixth place, the post-Vietnam era of American diplomacy was notable for another reason—which was perhaps the most crucial of all in inducing Congress to exert its prerogatives in foreign affairs. This was *the relative absence of external crises* directly involving the security and diplomatic vital interests of the United States. Once American forces were withdrawn from Southeast Asia, the United States played no active part in the subsequent conflict between North Vietnam and Cambodia, and between North Vietnam and Communist China, in the region. Beginning with Secretary of State Henry Kissinger's "shuttle diplomacy" in the Middle East during the Ford Administration, Washington attempted to ease Arab-Israeli tensions; and under the Carter Administration, Israel and Egypt finally arrived at a peace agreement (although most other Arab states refrained from joining in it).[79] During most of the 1970s, détente governed Soviet-American relations; and both countries attempted to reach a new arms-control agreement (SALT II) limiting nuclear weapons. (This attempt was aborted by the Soviet invasion of Afghanistan early in 1980.)[80] For almost a decade, then, after the Vietnam War, no serious external crisis confronted policy makers in Washington. Throughout American history, the existence of foreign crises has almost invariably *strengthened executive power.* In no small measure, the "imperial presidency" emerged as a result of America's response to foreign threats.

By the opening of the 1980s, it had become evident that the post-Vietnam War era contained a number of unusual and highly favorable elements conducive to an assertive

role by Congress in foreign affairs. A succession of events occurring at the end of the 1970s—the discovery of a large Soviet combat force in Cuba, Iran's seizure of American hostages, and Moscow's massive military invasion of Afghanistan—reminded Americans that the United States was still a superpower, with major and minor international responsibilities. Within a few brief months, a dramatic change occurred in American attitudes toward the outside world, as signified by the issuance of the Carter Doctrine early in 1980—in which President Carter proclaimed the Persian Gulf area vital to American security and forcefully affirmed the determination of the United States to defend it from threatened Soviet hegemony.*

Issuance of the Carter Doctrine took place against a background of mounting public and congressional demands that the chief executive exert dynamic leadership particularly in the foreign policy field. Its promulgation was a classic case in a familiar behavior syndrome in American diplomatic history. In a speech before a joint session of Congress (or perhaps on nationwide radio and TV), the President identifies an overt threat to the secu-

---

*Addressing a joint session of Congress on January 23, 1980, President Jimmy Carter devoted his speech chiefly to a description and analysis of the Soviet Union's recent invasion of Afghanistan and its implications for the United States. In what was quickly designated the "Carter Doctrine," the President declared that any Soviet attempt to dominate the Persian Gulf area would be considered dangerous to American security and would be resisted by the United States, by reliance upon armed force if necessary. For the text of Carter's speech, see *Weekly Compilation of Presidential Documents,* **16** (January 28, 1980), 194–200. In effect, President Carter's new foreign policy doctrine was merely a modification and extension of the Truman Doctrine enunciating America's strategy of containment of Communist expansionism. For the text of the Truman Doctrine, issued on March 12, 1947, see *Public Papers of the Presidents of the United States: Harry S Truman,* 1947 (Washington, D.C.: Government Printing Office, 1963), pp. 176–180.

rity of the United States; and he calls upon the American people and Congress to support him in responding to it. Nearly always, the people "close ranks" behind the President and give him overwhelming public support. And as "the voice of the people" (once it senses the public mood), Congress echoes the call for strong executive leadership and provides tangible evidence of support for the President's actions.

Typically, this syndrome was associated with the issuance of the Carter Doctrine. According to one report, President Carter's speech to the House and Senate was greeted by a

> thunderclap of applause in Congress ... to President Carter's sharp warning that he was ready to use force to protect vital American interests in the Persian Gulf.
>
> Reflecting the public mood, Capitol Hill is caught up in a wave of nationalistic fervor, angered, anxious, frustrated and feisty, above all, determined to react to the Soviet actions.

In order to implement his new doctrine, President Carter called upon Congress to enact a variety of measures—such as the creation of a new military Rapid Deployment Force capable of projecting effective American power rapidly to crisis zones abroad, and the easing of congressionally imposed restrictions upon the activities of intelligence agencies—designed to strengthen his hand and provide evidence of a unified governmental position toward Soviet expansionism. Liberals and conservatives alike agreed that President Carter's speech had brought the nation to a fork in the road in its recent diplomatic experience.

Reflecting upon the change which the eruption of foreign crises produced in American attitudes toward the presidency and Congress, one of the nation's most experienced political commentators asserted:

> The imperial Presidency may be gone but in a time of troubles overseas, the President remains the principal rallying symbol of our political life. He may be absent, inconsistent, even wrong in his estimate of the crisis [as many Americans judged President Carter's diplomacy toward the Soviet troop buildup in Cuba, the Iranian crisis, and the Soviet incursion into Afghanistan], but if he asks help in the name of the Republic, nothing is likely to prevail against him.[81]

Insofar as the 1980s would likely witness the eruption of new crises affecting American security and diplomatic interests abroad, the Carter Doctrine could well mark the beginning of a new (or a more normal) era of dynamic presidential leadership in the foreign policy field.

One final constraint upon a highly active and independent role by Congress in American foreign relations remains to be identified. This limitation was highlighted by the findings of a Gallup Poll in 1979, showing that only one American in five approved of the way national legislators were doing their jobs. Many informed students of the legislative process were concerned about Congress' "decline." As one report found:

> To many, the legislative branch seems rudderless, undisciplined and frequently unwilling or unable to grapple with pressing national issues. . . .

Even some of its own members viewed Congress as a "sick institution"; and informed students of the legislative branch believed that Congress "had no place to go but up." In the same period, another national poll showed that only 18 percent of those interviewed expressed a high degree of "confidence" in Congress as an institution. The deterioration in Congress' public image was noteworthy: Over twice that percentage (42 percent) of the people had expressed a high degree of confidence in the House and Senate in 1973.[82]

Congress' future foreign policy role is likely to be crucially affected by the existence of a dilemma growing out of two contrary conceptions of its institutional role and performance. On one side, there is the idea—deeply embedded in the American political tradition and ethos—that Congress serves as the "voice of the people" and as the truly "representative" branch of the American governmental system. Reflecting the Enlightenment philosophy of their age, most of the Founding Fathers believed that Congress should serve as the really dynamic organ of the American government; symbolically, its powers are listed first in the Constitution. Conversely, the Founders were highly suspicious of executive (and only slightly less suspicious of judicial) power—which they equated with actual or potential tyranny.

On the other side, throughout the nation's history Americans have traditionally been derogatory and skeptical about Congress as an institution. Based upon its performance (or nonperformance), popular attitudes toward Congress tend to be highly unfavorable. Surveys of public opinion since World War II, for example, nearly always reveal a higher degree of public confidence in the presidency than in Congress—a phenomenon that was not basically changed by the Vietnam War, the Watergate episode, and other developments arousing apprehensions about the "imperial presidency." Even when (as during the Carter Administration), the American people gave the chief executive low marks for failing to exercise leadership, they ranked Congress *even lower* in terms of its performance in dealing with urgent internal and external issues.[83] By the end of the 1970s, even former legislators themselves were expressing serious reservations about Congress' ability to produce unified and effective national policies —especially in the foreign policy realm.[84] Thus, one of the most outspoken critics of the "imperial presidency" a few years earlier, former Senator J. William Fulbright (Democrat of Arkansas) lamented:

> ... those of us who prodded what seemed to be a hopelessly immobile herd of cattle [Congress] a decade ago [to assert its powers in foreign affairs] now stand back in awe in the face of a stampede.[85]

Another legislator was even more candid in his appraisal of the congressional impact upon the nation's diplomacy. Asked what he thought Congress would achieve in external affairs, he replied that it would find a way to "foul up" American foreign policy! Still another experienced legislator expressed deep skepticism about the consequences of an assertive congressional role in foreign relations. Citing a number of examples of forceful legislative intrusion into the foreign policy process since the Vietnam War, he concluded that

> well-meaning congressional initiatives to promote specific and laudable policy goals failed, and serious challenges developed for diplomats in preserving our interests.

He warned his colleagues on Capitol Hill that "The instruments available to Congress to shape [foreign] policy are blunt"; and "effective foreign policy" called for the application of techniques often unavailable to legislators.[86]

Since the Vietnam War, Congress has demonstrated a determination to play a dynamic and sustained role in the foreign policy process unwitnessed in earlier eras of American diplomatic experience. During the 1970s, it would be difficult to cite a major area or problem of American diplomacy in which Congress did not leave its imprint. What Congress had *not* demonstrated, however, is recognition on Capitol Hill of the necessary implications of its demand to be treated as a "partner" with the executive branch in the conduct of foreign affairs. More specifically, it remains for Congress to exhibit the internal discipline and capacity for unified and coherent decision making required for the successful conduct of American diplomacy. Based upon experience since the Vietnam War, Congress has shown that it is capable of exerting its prerogatives frequently and influentially in the foreign policy field. It has yet to demonstrate that in many vital respects, an enhanced "congressional presence" in the formulation and management of foreign relations promotes the diplomatic interests of the United States.

NOTES

1. Clinton Rossiter, "President and Congress in the 1960s," in Cyril Roseman et al., *Dimensions of Political Analysis* (Englewood Cliffs, N.J.: Prentice-Hall, 1966), p. 34.
2. Bernard Cohen, *Foreign Policy in American Government* (Boston: Little, Brown and Co. 1965), p. 157.
3. For a detailed discussion of the era of congressional activism following the Vietnam War, see Cecil V. Crabb, Jr., and Pat Holt, *Invitation to Struggle: the President, Congress and American Foreign Policy* (Washington, D.C.: Congressional Quarterly, 1980).
4. See the views of Representative John D. Dingell in *U.S. News and World Report,* **86** (March 19, 1979), 46.
5. See the views of Senator Frank Church, as cited in Loch Johnson and James McCor-

mick, "Foreign Policy by Executive Fiat," *Foreign Policy,* **28** (Fall, 1977), 133.
6. For historical background, see W. Stull Holt, *Treaties Defeated by the Senate* (Baltimore: The Johns Hopkins University Press, 1933); and for evidence in the post-World War II period, see Johnson and McCormick, "Foreign Policy by Executive Fiat," 117–139; and the same authors' "The Making of International Agreements: A Reappraisal of Congressional Involvement," *Journal of Politics,* **40** (May, 1978), 468–478.
7. A detailed discussion of legislative participation in wartime and early postwar foreign policy is provided in Arthur H. Vandenberg, Jr., ed., *The Private Papers of Senator Vandenberg* (Boston: Houghton Mifflin Co., 1952); and see the case studies in Cecil V. Crabb, Jr., *Bipartisan Foreign Policy: Myth or Reality?* (New York: Harper & Row, 1957).
8. See Crabb and Holt, *Invitation to Struggle,* Chapter 3.
9. *New York Times,* November 20, 1979.
10. Early in 1979, White House spokesman Jody Powell announced that—even if the Senate did not consent to the SALT II strategic arms-limitation agreement with Moscow—the United States would "match" the Soviet Union in imposing restraints upon the expansion of its nuclear arsenal. The President, in other words, would observe the terms of SALT II even if the Senate failed to approve it. See Terence Smith, in *New York Times,* February 24, 1979.
11. Early in 1980, news dispatches indicated that executive officials were seeking to arrive at agreements whereby the United States would have access to naval stations and airfields in such countries as Oman, Kenya, and Somalia. Presidential envoys were also seeking agreements for expanding American military assistance to Pakistan. See *U.S. News and World Report,* **88** (January 28, 1980), 21–26; and *New York Times,* February 12, 1980.
12. See Johnson and McCormick, "Foreign Policy by Executive Fiat," 125.
13. Detailed information about the Senate's use of

this power in recent years is provided in U.S., Congress, Senate, Committee on Foreign Relations, *The Senate Role in Foreign Affairs Appointments*. 92nd Cong., 1st Sess., 1971, pp. 3–11.

14. Dwight D. Eisenhower, *Mandate for Change: 1953–1956* (Garden City, N.Y.: Doubleday and Co., 1963), pp. 212–213.

15. For a discussion of the controversy over Leonard Woodcock's appointment, see the Congressional Quarterly *Weekly Report*, **37** (January 29, 1979), 97.

16. Former White House adviser and Secretary of State Henry Kissinger's role in secret negotiations leading to the normalization of Sino-American relations is fully described in his memoirs, *White House Years* (Boston: Little, Brown, 1979), pp. 733–788.

17. *New York Times*, October 23, 1951.

18. For legislative restrictions upon the extension of American aid to North Vietnam, Cambodia, and other states in Southeast Asia, see Public Law 95–88.

19. U.S., Congress, Senate, Committee on Appropriations, *The Departments of State, Justice, and Commerce, the Judiciary and Related Agencies Appropriations for Fiscal Year 1968*. 90th Cong., 1st Sess., 1967, p. 117.

20. Our discussion of the appropriations process in Congress relies heavily upon Aaron Wildavsky, *The Politics of the Budgetary Process* (Boston: Little, Brown, 1964), pp. 47–61; Nelson W. Polsby, *Congress and the Presidency* (Englewood Cliffs, N.J.: Prentice-Hall, 1964), pp. 91–96; and Richard F. Fenno, Jr., "The House Appropriations Committee as a Political System," *American Political Science Review*, **56** (June, 1962), 310–324.

21. An illuminating study of the Roosevelt Administration's diplomacy is William L. Langer and S. Everett Gleason, *The Challenge to Isolation: 1937–1940* (New York: Harper & Row, 1952). See Walter Johnson, *The Battle Against Isolation* (Chicago: University of Chicago Press, 1944).

22. Congress' role in terminating America's involvement in the Vietnam War is related in detail in Kissinger, *White House Years*, pp. 968–1046. See the Congressional Quarterly *Weekly Report*, **31** (August 11, 1973), 2207–2210.

23. Dwight D. Eisenhower, *Waging Peace* (Garden City, N.Y.: Doubleday and Co., 1965), pp. 614–616.

24. See, for example, the data presented in *The Power of the Pentagon: the Creation, Control and Acceptance of Defense Policy in the U.S. Congress* (Washington, D.C.: Congressional Quarterly, 1972).

25. See the discussion of the military-industrial lobby, in *Legislators and the Lobbyists: Congress Under Pressure* (Washington, D.C.: Congressional Quarterly, 1968), 50–63.

26. For a discussion of various theories about the intentions of the Founders regarding Congress' power to "declare war," see the commentary by the Library of Congress, *The Constitution of the United States of America: Analysis and Interpretation* (Washington, D.C.: Government Printing Office, 1973), pp. 323–329.

27. See the Supreme Court's decision in *The Prize Cases*, 2 Black (67 U.S.) 635 (1863).

28. President Kennedy's reliance upon military force during the Cuban Missile Crisis of 1962 is discussed in Robert F. Kennedy, *Thirteen Days: A Memoir of the Cuban Missile Crisis* (New York: New American Library, 1969); and in Theodore Sorensen, *Kennedy* (New York: Harper & Row, 1965), pp. 667–719.

29. For the text of President Jimmy Carter's speech on January 23, 1980, enunciating the "Carter Doctrine," see *New York Times*, January 24, 1980.

30. See the views of Senator Jacob Javits regarding the contemporary utility of a declaration of war in his "The Congressional Presence in Foreign Relations," *Foreign Affairs*, **48** (January, 1970), 226.

31. Detailed analysis of the purposes and provisions of the War Powers Resolution may be found in Crabb and Holt, *Invitation to Struggle*, Chapter 5; and in Thomas M. Franck, "After the Fall: The New Procedural Frame-

work for Congressional Control Over the War Power," *American Journal of International Law,* **71** (October, 1977), 605–641.

32. See the views of Theodore C. Sorensen in *New York Times,* September 21, 1979.

33. Following issuance of the Carter Doctrine, one White House aide summarized the congressional reaction to it by saying: "It's almost as if they're giving [the President] a blank check" to protect American security abroad. See *Newsweek,* **95** (February 4, 1980), 23, and **95** (May 5, 1980), 41. As one commentator has observed, whenever the President determines that national security is endangered, and when he proposes to act decisively to defend it, neither public nor congressional opinion is likely to restrain his use of executive power under these conditions. See Sidney Warren, ed., *The American President* (Englewood Cliffs, N.J.: Prentice-Hall, 1967), p. 139.

34. See, for example, the opinions of George Gallup, Burns Roper, and other pollsters on the reasons for the loss of public confidence in President Carter's leadership capacity, in *U.S. News and World Report,* **87** (August 27, 1979), 20. See also the analysis of public opinion polls on the Carter presidency in the Congressional Quarterly *Weekly Report,* **37** (October 13, 1979), 2267–2274.

35. For provisions of the Battle Act, see 22 U.S. Code 1611.

36. More extensive discussion may be found in Crabb and Holt, *Invitation to Struggle,* Chapter 7.

37. A detailed history of legislative investigations is Arthur M. Schlesinger, Jr., and Roger Burns, eds., *Congress Investigates: A Documented History, 1792–1974* (New York: Chelsea House, 1975), five volumes.

38. Wilfred E. Binkley, *President and Congress* (New York: Alfred A. Knopf, 1947), p. 115.

39. Ibid.

40. Stephen K. Bailey and Howard D. Samuel, *Congress at Work* (New York: Holt, Rinehart and Winston, 1952), p. 296.

41. William S. White, *Citadel: The Story of the U.S. Senate* (New York: Harper & Row, 1957), p. 242.

42. Ibid., p. 250.

43. For a detailed description and analysis of congressional efforts to investigate and reform the intelligence community after the Vietnam War, see Crabb and Holt, *Invitation to Struggle,* Chapter 6.

44. The major problems related to intelligence operations requiring the continuing attention of both executive and legislative officials are identified in Roy Godson, ed., *Intelligence Requirements for the 1980's: Elements of Intelligence* (Washington, D.C.: National Strategy Information Center, 1979).

45. See Holbert N. Carroll, "The Congress and National Security," in David Truman, ed., *The Congress and America's Future* (Englewood Cliffs, N.J.: Prentice-Hall, 1965), pp. 155–156.

46. The text of the Gulf of Tonkin Resolution may be found in *Public Papers of the Presidents of the United States: Lyndon B. Johnson, 1963–64,* Vol. 2, (Washington, D.C.: Government Printing Office, 1965), pp. 927–932.

47. Criticisms of the Johnson Administration's formulation of, and reliance upon, the Gulf of Tonkin Resolution became widespread among opponents of the Vietnam War. See, for example, the detailed indictment in Joseph C. Goulden, *Truth is the First Casualty: The Gulf of Tonkin Affair—Illusion and Reality* (Chicago: Rand-McNally, 1969). Briefer treatments are J. William Fulbright, *The Arrogance of Power* (New York: Random House, 1966), pp. 50–63; and John M. Swomley, Jr., *American Empire: The Political Ethics of Twentieth Century Conquest* (New York: Macmillan Co., 1970), pp. 207–211.

48. See the views of Professor Ross K. Baker on recent tendencies in Congress in *New York Times,* November 13, 1979.

49. The viewpoints and influence of two powerful isolationist legislators are presented in Wayne S. Cole, *Senator Gerald P. Nye and American Foreign Relations* (Minneapolis: University of Minnesota Press, 1962); and Burton K.

Wheeler, *Yankee from the West* (Garden City, N.Y.: Doubleday and Co., 1962).

50. See Vandenberg, ed., *The Private Papers of Senator Vandenberg,* pp. 337–502.

51. See J. William Fulbright, *The Arrogance of Power; The Crippled Giant: American Foreign Policy and Its Domestic Implications* (New York: Random House, 1972) and *Old Myths and New Realities* (New York: Random House, 1964).

52. For accounts of Representative Hansen's self-appointed diplomatic mission to Iran, see John Kifner, in *New York Times,* September 26 and 27, 1979; and the editorial in *New York Times,* November 27, 1979.

53. See *New York Times,* September 10, 1979.

54. See the detailed report on overseas travel by legislators in "Congress Sets New Record for Foreign Travel," Congressional Quarterly *Weekly Report,* **37** (September 8, 1979), 1921–1946.

55. John Bibby and Roger Davidson, *On Capitol Hill: Studies in the Legislative Process* (New York: Holt, Rinehart and Winston, 1967), pp. 111–112; and James Reston, in *New York Times,* September 21, 1979.

56. See the views of President Johnson's White House adviser, Lawrence O'Brien, in Warren, ed., *The American President,* p. 136.

57. I. M. Destler, "Treaty Troubles: Versailles in Reverse," *Foreign Policy,* **33** (Winter, 1978–79), 53.

58. Kissinger, *White House Years,* p. 940.

59. Lee H. Hamilton and Michael H. Van Dusen, "Making the Separation of Powers Work," *Foreign Affairs,* **57** (Fall, 1978), p. 24.

60. Thomas L. Hughes, "Carter and the Management of Contradiction," *Foreign Policy,* **31** (Summer, 1978), pp. 48–49.

61. Kissinger, *White House Years,* pp. 940–949.

62. See Fulbright, *The Arrogance of Power,* pp. 44–46; and Javits, "The Congressional Presence in Foreign Relations," 221–223.

63. The impact of Wilsonian thought upon the conduct of American diplomacy is described and analyzed in Warren F. Ilchman, *Professional Diplomacy in the United States*

(Chicago: Universty of Chicago Press, 1961), pp. 132–244.

64. Ibid., pp. 1–40.

65. See Kissinger, *White House Years,* p. 548. For discussions of the general problem of growing disunity within the executive branch, see I. M. Destler, *Presidents, Bureaucrats and Foreign Policy: the Politics of Organizational Reform* (Princeton, N.J.: Princeton University Press, 1972); and Morton A. Halperin, *Bureaucratic Politics and Foreign Policy* (Washington, D.C.: Brookings Institution, 1974).

66. Stanley Hoffmann, "A View from at Home: the Perils of Incoherence," *Foreign Affairs* (Special Issue, 1978), 489.

67. Alton Frye and William D. Rogers, "Linkage Begins at Home," *Foreign Policy,* **35** (Summer, 1979), 49–50.

68. See "Congress is Getting Younger All the Time," Congressional Quarterly *Weekly Report,* **37** (January 27, 1979), 154.

69. See the data, and the views of Senator Ernest Hollings, in "Capitol Hill's Growing Army of Bureaucrats," *U.S. News and World Report,* **87** (December 24, 1979), 52–55.

70. See the views of Professors Thomas Franck and Edward Weisband in *New York Times,* November 29, 1976.

71. See the views of House Speaker O'Neill in *U.S. News and World Report,* **88** (February 4, 1980), 59; and the data on declining party loyalty in America in ibid., **87** (October 15, 1979), 70–71.

72. James McClellan, "The State of the American Congress," *Modern Age,* **21** (Summer, 1977), 234.

73. U.S. Congress, House Committee on International Relations, *Congress and Foreign Policy.* 94th Cong., 2nd Sess., 1977, p. 20.

74. For discussions of the legislative role in foreign policy in other democratic settings, see Kenneth N. Waltz, *Foreign Policy and Democratic Politics: the American and British Experience* (Boston: Little, Brown, 1967); and the treatment of individual countries in Joseph E. Black and Kenneth W. Thompson, eds.,

Foreign Policies in a World of Change (New York: Harper & Row, 1963).

75. See Fulbright, *The Crippled Giant;* Stanley Hoffmann, *Gulliver's Troubles, or the Setting of American Foreign Policy* (New York: McGraw-Hill, 1968); and Kenneth A. Oye, et al., eds., *Eagle Entangled: U.S. Foreign Policy in a Complex World* (New York: Longman, 1979).

76. An important variety of contemporary "neo-isolationism"—the liberal version—is analyzed in Cecil V. Crabb, Jr., *Policy-Makers and Critics: Conflicting Theories of American Foreign Policy* (New York: Praeger Publishers, 1976), pp. 253–299.

77. See James Chace, "Is a Foreign Policy Consensus Possible?" *Foreign Affairs,* **57** (Fall, 1978), 1–17.

78. Gerald R. Ford, *A Time to Heal* (New York: Harper & Row, and The Reader's Digest Association, 1979).

79. Kissinger's diplomatic initiatives in the Middle East are described in detail in *White House Years,* pp. 558–632; 1276–1301. The second volume of his memoirs carries the account throughout the remainder of the Ford Administration.

80. American efforts to strengthen and broaden the concept of détente with the Soviet Union after the Vietnam War is a major theme of Kissinger's *White House Years.* For an interpretive treatment, focusing upon differing American and Soviet conceptions of détente, see Coral Bell, *The Diplomacy of Détente* (New York: St. Martin's Press, 1977).

81. Hedrick Smith, in *New York Times,* January 27, 1980; *Newsweek,* **95** (February 4, 1980), 22–26; and James Reston, in *New York Times,* January 23, 1980.

82. See "As Troubles Pile Up for a 'Sick' Congress," *U.S. News and World Report,* **88** (February 18, 1980), 22; and see the CBS-*New York Times* national poll in *New York Times,* February 20, 1980.

83. Data on public attitudes toward Congress vis-à-vis the presidency are presented in Malcolm E. Jewell and Samuel C. Paterson, *The Legislative Process in the United States,* 3rd ed. (New York: Random House, 1977), pp. 315–317. See also Roger H. Davidson, et al., *Congress in Crisis: Politics and Congressional Reform* (Belmont, Calif.: Wadsworth Publishing Co., 1971), pp. 38–66.

84. See, for example, "What Congress Really Thinks of Itself," *U.S. News and World Report,* **88** (January 14, 1980), 39–42; and the survey data presented in *Time,* **114** (October 1, 1979), 25, and *U.S. News and World Report,* **87** (July 16, 1979), 21.

85. See the views of J. William Fulbright, "The Legislator as Educator," *Foreign Affairs,* **57** (Spring, 1979), 726.

86. Adam Clymer, in *New York Times,* July 3, 1977. See also the views of Representative Lee Hamilton, in *The Christian Science Monitor,* January 23, 1976.

Chapter 8

The Public
Context of Foreign Policy

Public Opinion and
the Democratic Process

An informed student of public opinion in the United States has said: "Probably the most widely held conception of democracy is that the government must serve its public."[1] Another commentator on public opinion has observed that—although conceptions and particular forms of "democracy" tend to vary widely throughout the contemporary world—the "key element" which unites them "is the notion that governments must take into account the wishes of the population and that the root of political power is the people themselves...."[2]

The Centrality of Public Opinion

Among the presuppositions underlying the concept of democratic government, none is perhaps more central than the notion that the most intimate and direct connection must exist between the wishes of the people and the policies adopted by their leaders. Few students of democratic government in the modern period would push this relationship to the point carried in the old Roman aphorism: *vox populi, vox dei* ("the voice of the people is the voice of God"). Yet in the writings of nearly every European or American philosopher who has contributed to the American political tradition, the responsiveness of the government to society's needs and demands has been viewed as an essential element in democracy. Classical philosophers like Montesquieu referred to the *esprit général;* the *volonté général* was a prominent theme in Rousseau's writings. The Declaration of Independence stressed the need for government to manifest a "decent respect for the opinions of mankind." The first words of the Constitution of the United States are: "We the People of the United States ... do ordain and establish this Constitution...." In President Lincoln's well-known characterization of the American system—as government of the people, by the people, and for the people—this relationship is again conspicuous.

Although such developments cannot of course be dated with exactitude, the role of public opinion as a crucial force in foreign policy seems to stem from World War I and the efforts to "democratize" diplomacy led by President Woodrow Wilson. Before that time, long after public opinion had begun to have an impact on domestic policy, foreign affairs were still regarded as largely outside public control or scrutiny. The "secret treaties" among the great powers during and after World War I illustrated this reality. By contrast, the first of Wilson's war aims, as set forth in his famous Fourteen Points (January 8, 1918), was "open covenants, openly arrived at." Not only should agreements among governments be publicized but, what was even more radical, Wilson advocated the idea that *the process of reaching agreements* should also be subject to public scrutiny.* Wilson had almost unlimited confidence in both the judgments of the people and his own ability to influence them. During World War I, he frequently differentiated between the views of the German *people* (who presumably desired peace and justice) and their misguided rulers (who had plunged the world into a bloody international conflict). On one occasion, Wilson asserted: "The real people I was speaking to were neither the Senate nor foreign governments, but the people of the countries now at war." And speaking to the Paris Peace Conference, Wilson declared that: "It is necessary that we should satisfy the opinion of mankind."[3]

Presidents after Wilson were no less concerned with the impact of public opinion upon national policies, foreign and domestic. President Harry Truman once commented: "The biggest problem facing any President is to sell the American people on a policy. They have had to be led forward. . . . That's the biggest challenge every President faces, and one which he cannot escape."[4] Secretary of State George C. Marshall was convinced that "no policy—foreign or domestic—can succeed without public support."[5] And a more recent student of the foreign policy process in the United States has concluded: "The Secretary of State must sell as well as negotiate American foreign policies today. He is a contender in the publicity marts of the world for support."[6]

In the more recent period, the student of American foreign policy has witnessed a number of influential examples of the role of public opinion in the nation's diplomacy. Perhaps the most outstanding episode was the impact of American public opinion in the termination of the Vietnam War. The failure of the Johnson and Nixon administrations to maintain public "credibility" in their policies toward Southeast Asia was quite possibly the most decisive element in Washington's decision to evacuate American military forces from Southeast Asia.[7] Similarly, the loss of public confidence in the Nixon Administration because of the Watergate scandal unquestionably contributed to the decline of American power and influence overseas. Throughout most of his Administration, President Jimmy Carter confronted the pervasive public belief that his leadership in the foreign policy field was weak and indecisive, and that for a variety of reasons (such as disunity among his advisers), his performance on the diplomatic

*It has not escaped the attention of modern students of diplomacy that even President Wilson, the champion of "open convenants, openly arrived at," found it virtually impossible to adhere to his own doctrine in negotiating the Treaty of Versailles. Commenting on the secrecy surrounding these negotiations, Thomas A. Bailey has written that some 150 American reporters went to Paris, but the "door was barred against these eager reporters; and at the end of the first day a secretary slipped out and read to them a dry five-line summary. The correspondents thereupon made a tremendous outcry." See Thomas A. Bailey, *A Diplomatic History of the American People,* 3rd ed. (New York: Appleton-Century-Crofts, 1947), p. 657.

front was ineffectual.[8] During such episodes as the Iranian crisis early in 1980, for example, this popular conception may in turn have been a major factor compelling the Carter Administration to take an increasingly firm position with the government of Iran.*

Since the end of World War II, the investigation of public opinion has forged ahead rapidly and on many fronts. Scholars have probably learned more about the nature and role of public opinion in the past generation than they knew for centuries before that time. If any generalization can be drawn from the innumerable studies made in the postwar era, it is that the concept of public opinion is a fascinatingly complex and variegated phenomenon. Simplistic ideas and assumptions have had to be totally discarded or seriously modified. For example, the conception implicit in the views of many classical writers on public opinion—the idea that a homogeneous "public" expressed a unified and unambiguous "opinion" to policy makers—possesses little or no validity. Even today, there remain many unanswered questions about the nature of public opinion, about how it is formed, how it is expressed, precisely how it enters into the conduct of national policy, and its effects upon the foreign policy of the United States. As in most other fields of knowledge, the more the concept of public opinion is studied rigorously and objectively, the more informed students of the subject become aware of its *inherent complexity* and of the difficulty of making doctrinaire statements about it.

---

*The Iranian crisis was precipitated by the seizure of some 50 American citizens who were taken prisoner and held as "hostages" by militants in Tehran. For several months, the Carter Administration sought to gain their release by relying upon diplomatic and other peaceful methods. Finally, at the end of April 1980, an abortive military effort was made to "rescue" the American hostages. To no inconsiderable degree, the President's hand was "forced" by the increasingly militant temper of American public opinion in responding to the crisis.

The Concept of "Public Opinion"

A logical starting point in our discussion is the question, "What exactly *is* public opinion?" What are the necessary components of a satisfactory definition?

A wide variety of definitions of public opinion is available (a fact which perhaps underscores the complexity inherent in the concept). In an earlier era, the eminent student of British government A. V. Dicey called public opinion a "body of beliefs, convictions, sentiments, accepted principles, or firmly-rooted prejudices, which, taken together, make up the public opinion of a particular era...." The sociologist Kimball Young conceived of it as the "beliefs, convictions, or views of individuals on matters or issues of widespread or public interest and concern."[9]

More recent students of public opinion, like Arthur Kornhauser, believe that public opinion

> ...may best be thought of...as the views and feelings current in a specified population at a particular time in regard to any issue of interest to the population.

Bernard Hennessy defines public opinion more simply as "the complex of beliefs expressed by a significant number of persons on an issue of public importance."[10]

The Components of Public Opinion

These and other definitions of public opinion that might be cited call attention to several ideas implicit in the concept. First, it refers to the viewpoints of a larger or smaller *group of individuals;* it is *collective,* rather than individual, opinion. The size of the group may vary from a few people to many thousands or perhaps millions. Without knowing precisely the line of demarcation, scholars customarily refer to the latter as *mass opinion* (the kind usually tested by public opinion polls), while the former is regarded as *group opinion* (as reflected in the resolutions of a labor or veterans' organization).

Second, the concept of public opinion logically suggests a fairly high degree of citizen *concern* about public issues; and this in turn requires citizen *awareness* of problems facing policy makers. Insofar as citizen concern about, and awareness of, important developments in American foreign policy constitutes an essential precondition for the existence of "public opinion," as we shall see more fully at a later stage, then the concept must often be restricted to a minority of the American people. In the absence of a foreign crisis, the usual attitude of the average American toward foreign policy questions is one of *apathy*. At the other end of the scale, there is that group often designated the "attentive public" or the "informed public"; constituting a small minority of the population (approximately 15 to 25 percent), this group is not only keenly interested in developments abroad but also reasonably knowledgeable about them.

Third, a group of people must not only be aware of, and concerned about, public issues; it must also hold, and in one way or another express, some kind of judgment or viewpoint about them. Here we encounter one of the most intricate questions associated with the analysis of public opinion. What precisely is an *opinion*? What kinds of reactions from or by the public qualify for inclusion as an "opinion"? Treatments of public opinion by traditional political theorists (especially those, like the Enlightenment philosophers, who stressed its central role) more often than not envisioned public opinion as a *highly rational force,* reflecting public awareness and *considered judgment* about matters requiring the attention of policymakers. One of the pillars supporting the case for democratic government in fact is the presupposition that citizens engage in *rational thought and discourse* when they consider major questions of public policy. In this conception, public opinion becomes synonymous with *reasoned deliberation* followed, at some point, by the formulation of *logical conclusions* by the citizenry.

On the basis of the evidence supplied by innumerable studies of public opinion since World War II, it is evident that this is a highly idealized and often extremely unrealistic depiction of "public opinion" in the United States toward foreign policy issues. The term *opinion* encompasses an extraordinarily wide range of possible responses by citizens on issues related to foreign affairs. It may, for example, include the viewpoints of highly informed and experienced citizens, like former governmental officials, commentators, and members of foreign policy study groups. Or it may describe merely the intuitive and emotional "feelings" and personal convictions of ordinary citizens that Communism ought to be opposed or that American influence has declined abroad. One student of the Roosevelt Administration has portrayed the public opinion context of foreign policy decision making in these terms:

> Outside Washington were the millions of voters who held the destinies of foreign policy makers in their hands. And here was the most unstable foundation of all on which to build a consistent program of foreign relations. Great numbers of these voters were colossally ignorant of affairs beyond the three-mile limit. . . . The American people, lacking stable attitudes built on long experience in foreign policy making, swung fitfully from one foreign policy mood to another, from isolation to neutralism to participation in world politics.[11]

Yet, however "irrational" or emotional citizens' reactions may be in dealing with foreign policy issues, it is no less true that their viewpoints often spring from *deep conviction;* that on some foreign policy questions, these viewpoints are held and communicated with *great intensity;* and that in many instances such informed judgments and emotional responses —collectively called "opinions"—have a profound impact upon the American foreign policy process.

Fourth, the concept of public opinion necessarily implies that the viewpoints of citizens *are in some way expressed to policy makers.* The communication of public attitudes may be essentially *passive,* as when pollsters ask the people their viewpoints on a variety of public issues. Or the public may communicate its opinions *actively,* as when citizens write to the White House or to their legislative representatives, or when interest groups lobby in behalf of their positions. We must also take note of the possibility that public opinion may be *latent and implicit:* In many cases, public officials believe (correctly or incorrectly) that they intuitively know what public opinion "demands" or will not accept, and such beliefs not infrequently influence the policy-making process.

As a rule, however, in the American democracy officials are seldom left in doubt about the sentiments and preferences of citizens. Instead, the opposite problem more often than not exists: In the midst of the cacophony of sounds emanating from the public, and from groups purporting to speak in its name, officials are challenged to obtain an accurate assessment of prevailing public attitudes and to "sort out" the extraneous from the authentic expressions of public opinion.

Finally, the concept of public opinion (at least in its democratic setting) suggests that the viewpoints of citizens are *carefully considered by policy makers* and that the wishes of the public are ultimately reflected in the activities and programs of the government. Every informed citizen of the United States is aware that "government by the people" does not mean that the mass of citizens actually formulates and carries out public policy. At a minimum, however, governmental policies and activities must not be consistently *disapproved* by the public or viewed by it as inimical to its interests and welfare.

The Properties of Public Opinion

As the tools of public opinion analysis have become more refined, scholars have shed new light upon many characteristics of society's viewpoints toward public policy questions. Public sentiment possesses several basic properties relevant to a more intelligent understanding of the foreign policy process.

The most familiar property of public opinion is the *direction* of citizen viewpoints. Is the public "for" or "against" a continuation of foreign aid? Does it "approve" or "disapprove" efforts to resolve cold war tensions? The customary tripartite division of public sentiment in measuring the direction of opinion is: affirmative, negative, and "no opinion" (a category whose importance should not be underestimated).

A somewhat more refined system for measuring the direction of mass opinion is to present the public with a series of policy alternatives, asking them to express their preferences for A, B, C, D, or E. On that basis, the proportion of public opinion favoring each alternative is tabulated. All measurements of the direction of public opinion, it should be pointed out, are to some degree a function of the questions to which the public is asked to respond. In the latter case, for example, some citizens may identify none of the alternatives listed as actually describing their preferences; nor will the list of choices always include the most attractive course of action recommending itself to policy makers.

Another fundamental property of public

opinion is its *intensity* or firmness. Policy makers may be just as interested in how strongly the public is attached to its views as in the direction of public sentiment. Some issues evoke public reactions of very low intensity; these are questions about which a majority of the public (in the popular phrase) "couldn't care less." Conversely, other foreign policy questions evoke public responses of extremely high intensity. On these issues the public reacts strongly and vocally; its viewpoints obviously stem from deep conviction and commitment. Postwar studies of public opinion have revealed time and again, for example, that high intensity usually accompanies issues affecting national security and perceived threats to the nation. As we shall see, the issue of America's relations with Israel also elicits high intensity from many individuals and groups in the United States.

From World War II until the Vietnam War, (real or imaginary) Communist threats to the security of the United States nearly always evoked an American response of very high intensity. For two decades or more, a pervasive "anti-Communist consensus" undergirded the policies of the United States government in foreign affairs: national policy makers could nearly always assume that a majority of citizens would oppose efforts by the Soviet Union and other Marxist nations to expand their hegemony or threaten the independence of weaker countries. After the Vietnam War, for a decade or more, however, the anti-Communist consensus characteristic of earlier American attitudes seemed to have disappeared; and it was not replaced by a high degree of national unity on some other diplomatic principle.[12] (This fact was in no small measure responsible for the phenomena we discussed in Chapters 3 and 7: the disunity evident within the executive and legislative branches in dealing with foreign policy issues during the 1970s.)

Another important characteristic of public opinion is the quality of *saliency*—or the degree to which citizens perceive their own or their family's interests and welfare as being directly involved in public policy questions. As a rule, for the majority of Americans external issues possess *very low saliency*. With some exceptions, for over 200 years foreign policy issues have been viewed by most citizens as indeed *foreign* or unrelated to their most immediate needs and concerns. To cite merely one example, even during a period when several external crises dominated the news media and engaged the attention of officials and citizens alike, a Gallup Poll taken early in 1980 found that a domestic problem (inflation) was still listed by 74 percent of the people as the "most important problem," with only 17 percent of those interviewed listing "international problems" as their primary concern. One student of American public opinion in the post-Vietnam War era believed that the people exhibited "abject contempt" for foreign policy issues, which usually ranked "at the very bottom" among issues at the forefront of their concern.[13]

Still another significant property of public opinion is its *concentration* or distribution among various segments of society. The properties of public opinion, as we have already suggested, tend to interact with one another. One group of people is likely to feel that a particular issue is more important to it than some others; when that situation occurs, we would expect a higher concentration, or greater homogeneity, of opinion within that group than is found throughout the population as a whole. Because their members already share certain common goals and values, group opinion is usually (although by no means always) more concentrated than mass opinion.

Policy makers are not interested only in what the public thinks and how strongly it feels about a given subject. Sometimes they are even more influenced by the pattern of opinion concentration. For obvious reasons, in formulating policies concerning foreign trade in agricultural commodities, officials are prone to listen more attentively to the viewpoints of farmers than to factory workers. A decisive majority opinion expressed by American scientists on nuclear disarmament is likely to carry more weight than the opinion of lawyers or ethnic minorities. Concentrated opinion among ethnic minorities, on the other hand, can be expected to have an impact upon American foreign policy toward Eastern Europe or toward the Arab-Israeli dispute. Not infrequently, highly concentrated opinion has an influence far out of proportion to its numerical strength. The leading example from post-World War II American diplomacy perhaps is the "Zionist lobby," whose nature and activities we shall examine more fully at a later stage.

Hierarchies and Categories in Public Opinion

Several schemes for classifying public opinion, and identifying hierarchies within it, are available. No single system has universal validity, however. Each system's usefulness and value depend heavily upon the purpose for which the classification is being made.

A former State Department official has written that this agency customarily conceives of three categories of public opinion. Each has its own unique role in the foreign policy process, and each presents a different challenge to officials seeking to understand public attitudes. First, there is the *general public* or what we have previously called mass opinion. Consisting of the views of citizens at large (or, in the popular phrase, "average" citizens), in a democratic system these attitudes form the foundation upon which public officials must erect their major policies at home and abroad. In the long run, such policies cannot succeed unless they are substantially accepted by the society as a whole. Perhaps the principal channel for the forceful expression of such mass opinion is the electoral process, as when the American people exhibited pervasive displeasure with President Jimmy Carter's management of foreign affairs by electing Ronald Reagan to the White House in 1980.

Yet one of the characteristics of mass opinion is that it has little sustained interest in, and is often poorly informed about, its government's activities overseas. Minimally concerned with most foreign policy questions, the general public may periodically become aroused by some crises abroad (as clearly occurred in 1980), as a result of which a groundswell of popular discontent may sweep the country. On the basis of experience, however, sustained public interest in foreign policy issues seldom lasts long, and the people soon become immersed once more in domestic concerns.

According to some students of public opinion, the proportion of the American people belonging to the general or mass public varies, depending in large part upon the nature of the particular foreign policy issue existing at any given time.[14] External issues related to the security of the United States, for example, elicit the highest degree of public interest and concern. Conversely, "diplomatic issues" (those external policy questions having little discernible relationship to the personal lives of citizens) exhibit the lowest degree of public interest and concern. One study contends that for the average foreign policy question, only about 20 percent of the American people are interested in it or exhibit any significant understanding of it. Other studies estimate the size of the "mass public" that is indifferent toward foreign policy issues and ignorant concerning them as comprising some 30 percent of the population.[15]

The individual citizen's involvement

with foriegn policy issues is depicted by this portrait:

> [The ordinary citizen lives in a society] where most newspapers usually apportion only 15 percent of news coverage to foreign items and where a scant 3 to 10 percent of their readers bother to look at that remnant anyway; where television customarily shrivels the world to a collage of 90-second summaries and photogenic symptoms.... After 35 years of world power and with far-flung interests and mounting vulnerability, we still give the rest of the planet only a distracted, fleeting glance.[16]

With rare exceptions, the foreign policy sentiments of the mass public are *passive opinion,* in that they are seldom communicated actively and directly to policy makers. These are the "opinions" normally revealed in public opinion polls and surveys. As one commentator has observed, the mass public probably has its greatest impact upon the policy process "at the voting booth" in national elections.[17]

At the other end of the spectrum is *elite opinion,* or what is sometimes referred to as the "informed public." Enormous qualitative differences, as we have already observed, characterize the "opinions" expressed by the public and its components. Although the State Department and White House cannot ignore mass opinion, policy makers are often more interested in the reactions of elite opinion to existing or proposed policies. Citizens whose viewpoints comprise elite opinion are usually keenly interested in America's relations with other countries; they possess background information and they endeavor to keep themselves currently and objectively informed about major developments in international relations. Policy makers look to this group of citizens to provide them with enlightened and informed judgments on diplomatic questions.

Depending upon the precise criteria employed to measure an individual's interest in, and knowledge of, foreign policy issues, this category of American public opinion usually constitutes a small proportion of the total population. Some estimates believe that the interested and informed stratum of the population is no more than 15 percent of the total, while other studies believe that it may encompass upwards of 40 percent of the American people. Within this category, some students of public opinion identify a very small, but sometimes highly influential, subcategory called the "mobilizers" of public sentiment. This group—normally comprising no more than 1 or 2 percent of the American people—is extremely interested in foreign policy questions; is well informed about them; and frequently devotes its time, energy, and money to communicating its viewpoints to national policy makers.[18]

The Vietnam War experience called attention to another subcategory of elite opinion in the United States: the attitudes toward American foreign policy exhibited by *intellectuals* in the American society. From the early post-World War II period until the Vietnam War, intellectual opinion usually supported the containment policy adopted by the Truman Administration to counter Communist expansionism. Even during the Korean War, for example, the group sided with President Truman against his critics (such as General Douglas MacArthur and his supporters). During the Vietnam War, however, many (perhaps a majority) of American intellectuals became "alienated" from the Johnson and Nixon administrations; and intellectuals often led the van of criticism demanding America's withdrawal from the conflict in Southeast Asia. After the war, such intellectuals were also often at the forefront of those Americans favoring a severely curtailed or "neo-isolationist" role for the United States in global affairs and a renewed preoccupation by governmental officials with domestic problems. Yet it also must be emphasized that, like other segments of public opinion, the viewpoints of intellectuals on international questions are not monolithic; within this category, considerable disagreement exists concerning what American foreign policy toward the Soviet Union, the Middle East, Western Europe, and other specific problem areas should be in the years ahead.[19]

A third category recognized by policy makers consists of *group opinion*. A distinctive characteristic of the American society is that it is "a nation of joiners." For over two centuries, Americans have formed and affiliated with organizations to promote their interests, and to express their viewpoints, on international, national, and local issues. Literally thousands of such organizations exist in contemporary American society, and most of them engage in lobbying activities designed to influence national policy favorably to their interests. Many informed commentators believe that (for reasons we shall discuss more fully in due course) lobbying activities by these organizations have become more intensive, more skillful, and more influential than in any previous era of American history.[20] Because of its unique importance in the American political and governmental system, and its often crucial impact upon the diplomacy of the United States, pressure group activity in the foreign policy field merits detailed examination.

Group Opinion and American Foreign Policy

The Group Basis of Political Action

Modern-day political scientists have increasingly devoted attention to the *group basis* of political activity. One recent study has asserted that "power to affect public policy rests mainly upon an individual's relationship to a major group or organization. Single individuals in this country, unless affiliated with some power group, seldom influence the course of government."[21]

Even before the American society achieved its political independence, the "Sons of Liberty" served as an organization championing the cause of freedom from Great Britain. Over the next two centuries, literally thousands of organizations emerged within American society—representing the interests of businessmen, workers, farmers, ethnic minorities, veterans, and countless other segments of public opinion. Almost every American belongs to a number of groups: the family, the neighborhood, religious organizations, business associations, labor unions, fraternal orders and lodges, recreational organizations, and numerous other groups. Perhaps the most crucial fact about most citizens is that they belong to *several* such groups, and this fact creates what some sociologists call "cross-pressures" in molding their opinions on contemporary issues. To express the matter in rather oversimplified terms: An individual citizen might be a black male (entailing his affiliation with certain ethnic groups); he may be a member of a labor union (whose national organization has a particular foreign policy orientation); and he may be a veteran (whose national policies on foreign policy issues might differ fundamentally from the ethnic and labor organizations to which he belongs). The existence of such cross-pressures may in no small measure account for one of the outstanding traits of American public opinion: the presence of fundamental *incongruities and ambiguities* in the public mind on a range of foreign policy questions. For example, on a question like American relations with black Africa, the viewpoints of this hypothetical individual might well be torn between the policies espoused by ethnic organizations to which he belongs and those of veterans' organizations of which he is also a member.

Today, it has become a commonplace phenomenon for *coalitions of groups* to cooperate in their lobbying and informational activities. Thus, on a specific issue (such as efforts to restrict the volume of Japanese imports into the United States), business organizations, labor unions, trade associations, regional and local constituency groups, and other organizations not infrequently collaborate in a campaign. By contrast, agricultural groups—together with business organizations and labor unions whose welfare is dependent upon the prosperity of agriculture—may oppose import restrictions, in order to maintain a high volume of American agricultural sales to Japan. On most foreign policy issues, such coalitions are *temporary alliances;* on other specific issues, different coalitions of interest groups will be formed to promote their common goal.

It is neither necessary nor possible to discuss all interest groups active in the foreign policy field. In limited space, let us concentrate upon certain of the more important and active ones.

Economic Interest Groups

By many criteria, the most important and influential interest groups in American society are those representing major *economic interests*—particularly the "big three": business, labor organizations, and farmers.

Since the earliest days of the Republic, American *business interests* have played a significant role in the diplomacy of the United States.[22] To cite merely a single example, American businessmen were an influential force persuading American officials to adopt the Open Door policy toward China at the end of the nineteenth century.* In the post-World

War II period, one study is convinced that business groups "were probably the single most powerful pressure force" affecting governmental policies; organizations representing the business point of view spent more on lobbying activities than any other interest group.[23] The two largest and most prominent business organizations are the Chamber of Commerce of the United States and the National Association of Manufacturing (NAM), the latter being oriented particularly toward business enterprises engaged in manufacturing.

Some interpreters of American diplomacy believe that the "expansionist" or "interventionist" impulse in American foreign policy can be accounted for primarily by the influence of business (sometimes supported by labor and agriculture organizations) upon national policy. Without subscribing to this oversimplified view of American diplomatic behavior, it is incontestably true that business interests have sometimes profoundly affected the foreign policy of the United States. They were undoubtedly a key element, for example, in America's commitment to an "internationalist" (vis-à-vis an "isolationist") foreign policy after World War II.

Perhaps better than most other segments of American opinion, businessmen have recognized two crucial facts about the nation's global position. One was that the United States had become *increasingly dependent*

---

*The Open Door policy toward China was promulgated early in 1899 by Secretary of State John Hay during the McKinley Administration. Initially, it sought merely to preserve an equal competitive position for the United States in the midst of an impending colonial struggle to wrest economic concessions from a weak Chinese government. In time, the policy became broadened into a more general American pledge to support the "territorial integrity" (or political independence) of China. America's adherence to this stated policy was perhaps the principal cause of tensions between the United States and Japan during the 1930s, leading to the Japanese attack against Pearl Harbor. For more detailed discussion, see Chapter 15.

upon the outside world for a long list of "strategic imports" and other raw materials needed to maintain a high level of domestic productivity and employment. As we observed in Chapter 6, that dependence has grown steadily since the end of World War II. The other fact is that (in order to pay for these needed imports), America must also rely heavily upon *access to foreign markets* for the sale of its own manufactured goods, commodities, and services. Today, for example, expanding American exports to regions like the European Economic Community and Japan constitute an extremely important asset in the balance of international payments, helping to offset the cost of oil shipments from the Middle East and other foreign sources. The maintenance of a high standard of living in the American society depends more than ever upon these two realities.

Yet, since business groups consist of individual citizens, they are usually subjected to the same cross-pressures affecting other citizens. As Barry Hughes cautions us, "There exists no single and identifiable 'business' view on all international issues."[24] On the foreign policy issues which are often of vital concern to business organizations—questions of tariff and trade policy—opinions within the business community are nearly always fragmented. Some groups advocate virtually unimpeded (or free) trade among nations; at the opposite end of the scale, other groups call for high tariffs and other stringent restrictions on trade designed to "protect" American business from foreign competition; still other business organizations take an intermediate position between these extremes. According to one study, the problem of "mixed interests" within the business community has made it increasingly difficult for business groups to take a unified position on international trade questions.[25] Yet during the past decade or so, there has been an overall increase in protectionist sentiment among the diverse organizations representing business viewpoints.

A recent problem in American foreign policy—eliciting extensive lobbying activities by business groups—has been the issue of Soviet-American trade. Ideologically, of course, American business interests are opposed to Communism; and presumably, they are also opposed to measures enabling it to succeed or become more powerful. Nevertheless, as we observed in Chapter 6, many American business organizations have favored a significant expansion in Soviet-American trade. (This same impulse was one factor instrumental in the decision of the Roosevelt Administration to "recognize" the Soviet Union in 1933.) Enticed by the prospective profits to be made on sales of everything from soft drinks to advanced computers behind the Iron Curtain, business groups have pressured the White House and Congress to expand Soviet-American commercial relations—even to the point of granting Moscow "credits" for the purchase of American goods. In return, some American business firms looked forward to expanding their purchases of petroleum products from the U.S.S.R.

As we have already indicated, many of these same considerations have long governed the attitudes of the American business community toward trade with China. For close to 200 years, lure of the "China market" has captivated American business and commercial enterprises. By the late 1970s, American business enterprises were once again attracted by the prospects of expanding Sino-American trade.[26]

Within recent years, some of the larger and more powerful American business corporations—sometimes called the multinational corporations (or MNCs)—have engaged in other activities affecting the course of American diplomacy. A celebrated case occurred in 1970, when the International Telephone and Telegraph Corporation overtly intervened in the political affairs of Chile, in an effort to topple the Marxist government of Dr. Salvador Allende.[27] In other cases, evidence exists that American corporations have engaged in the bribery of foreign officials in order to secure business contracts or for other reasons favorable to American commercial interests. Such activities quite clearly affect the political relations of the United States with other countries and influence the nation's overall image and influence abroad.

It should not be concluded, however, that all foreign policy activities of American corporations or business interests adversely affect the course of American diplomacy. On the positive side of the ledger, in recent years many Third World countries (Egypt is a leading example) have sought to encourage investments by American business corporations within their borders. After sometimes prolonged periods of suspicion and xenophobia toward foreign business enterprises, many Third World governments have in time concluded that American and other foreign business concerns have a vital role to play in achieving their goals of "modernization," national development, and increased productivity.

Interest group activities by the American business community are not of course confined solely to influential organizations like the Chamber of Commerce, the National Association of Manufacturing, and international corporations. Hundreds of American "trade associations" and specialized business organizations—ranging from those representing wholesale and retail merchants, to small businessmen, to the transportation industry, to banking, to a complex of industries involved in national defense—routinely lobby for their point of view. As in other spheres of American life, business activity has become more and more "specialized" and subdivided. As a result, the business community's approach to public policy issues has become increasingly disparate—with business groups not infrequently taking diametrically opposite positions on particular questions of internal and external policy.

Groups representing *organized labor* constitute a second important category among economic interest groups. Labor union activity became pervasive in the nineteenth century; and the American labor union movement received a strong impetus from the New Deal during the 1930s. Extensive and continuing lobbying campaigns by labor organizations, however, are largely a post-World War II phenomenon.[28]

The merger of the two most powerful national labor unions—the American Federation of Labor and the Congress of Industrial Organization into the AFL-CIO—in 1955 enhanced American labor's national (and increasingly, its international) influence. The Committee on Political Education (COPE) is the AFL-CIO's main mechanism for political activity. Smaller unions, not members of the AFL-CIO, have comparable organizations to represent their interests.

Besides the AFL-CIO, a great many smaller, independent unions exist in the United States, such as the Teamsters, the United Mine Workers, the United Automobile Workers, the International Ladies Garment Workers Union, and a host of others. Nearly all of these also engage in political and lobbying activities favorable to their cause.

The "leadership" of organized labor in the United States, one study asserts, "has traditionally been internationalist."[29] Labor organizations, for example, have generally favored an active role by the United States in global affairs since World War II, including such specific steps as American leadership in establishing and supporting the United Nations; the provision of American economic assistance initially to Western Europe and later to needy societies throughout the Third World; the maintenance of a strong defense establishment; and expanded cultural contacts between the United States and other countries (such as "exchange programs" and visits among labor unions in the non-Communist countries).

Three specific issues have been at the forefront of labor's concerns in the foreign policy field. One of them is the long-standing desire to protect the jobs of American workers from imported goods and services produced by "cheap" foreign labor. While labor organizations have generally endorsed the principle of free (or relatively unimpeded) trade between the United States and other countries, in recent years they have also often joined members of the business community in calling for the protection of domestic industries particularly vulnerable to foreign competition.

Since World War II, another theme in American labor's approach to international questions has been its pronounced *anti-Communist orientation*. The AFL-CIO and other labor organizations nearly always favor diplomatic policies and programs by the United States to counteract Communist influence abroad; and in some instances, labor leaders have collaborated closely with officials in Washington to achieve that goal. In recent years, spokesmen for the labor point of view have become highly critical of détente in Soviet-American relations, and they have questioned the value of the concept for the United States.

Routinely, the influence of the American labor movement in the postwar period has also nearly always been cast *on the side of Israel* in the Arab-Israeli conflict. The Zionist lobby (whose nature and influence we shall examine more fully below) can almost invariably rely upon the support of American labor unions in promoting Israel's interests and welfare.

Some commentators believe, however, that the influence of labor as a pressure group within the American political system has declined significantly within recent years. Several factors have contributed to this result: the tapering off of the growth in union membership, growing disagreements on public policy questions among spokesmen for the labor community, and the fact that Congress no longer "fears" labor's political influence. Perhaps even more than business and agricultural groups, the lobbying activities of the labor community have tended to be focused predominantly upon domestic issues affecting labor's welfare.[30]

The third component of the trio of influential economic interest groups in American society is what was traditionally called the "farm bloc," or *the agricultural community*. Since World War II, agricultural interest groups have often played a key role in the emergence of the U.S. Department of Agriculture as an agency having a decisive voice in the formulation and administration of American foreign policy. Measures like the "Food for Peace" program—entailing the shipment of surplus American agricultural commodities to needy societies—usually have the almost unanimous support of agricultural interest groups.[31]

Historically, when a majority of the American population lived in rural or semi-rural areas, the farm bloc was in some respects the most politically influential interest group in the American society. For many years, agricultural interests were overrepresented in the state legislatures and in Congress; and legislative bodies were closely attuned to their interests and needs. Since

World War II, however, changing population and economic patterns in the United States have altered this situation, greatly reducing the political influence of the so-called farm bloc. The American population is now predominantly urban and suburban; and the number of farmers within the society has declined to a small fraction of the total population of the United States. Legislative redistricting has enhanced the political power of cities and suburban areas; and as a result, Congress is strongly oriented toward their needs and viewpoints.

Three influential national organizations have long been active in representing the interests of farmers and farm-related enterprises in the United States. One of these—the best-known and the largest group—is the American Farm Bureau Federation, established in 1903. The Farm Bureau is especially strong in the South and in the Midwest. It also enjoys the unique distinction of having become a kind of "semigovernmental agency" because of the ties between it and the "county agents" (who are officials of the Department of Agriculture).

In its political orientation, the Farm Bureau generally takes a moderately conservative position on national policy issues. The Farm Bureau, for example, usually favors expanding American agricultural markets and exports abroad—such as to Japan and Western Europe—and it advocates government credits and other forms of assistance to farmers making this possible. On other issues—like the Vietnam War, America's participation in the United Nations, and the provision of foreign aid to other countries—the Farm Bureau's position has been rather markedly "nationalistic."

At the other end of the political spectrum is the National Farmers Union—an organization dating from the Populist era of American history and representing the "radical" agrarian viewpoint. The smallest of the na-

tional farm organizations, the Farmers Union is based in the wheat-growing area of the Great Plains and in the Northwest. With other agricultural groups, the Farmers Union has sought to protect the American farmer from the adverse effects of foreign competition and to expand market opportunities abroad for agricultural commodities produced in the United States. From an early date, however, the Farmers Union opposed America's participation in the Vietnam War; and in recent years, it has criticized the sale of American wheat to the Soviet Union because of the "windfall profits" supposedly reaped by speculators and business firms. The organization has been especially outspoken in opposing the global activities of multinational corporations deemed detrimental to the interests of American farmers.

The third influential group representing agricultural interests is the National Grange (or the Order of the Patrons of Husbandry). Particularly strong in the Mid-Atlantic area, New England, and the Northwest, politically the National Grange usually takes a position midway between its two rivals, the Farm Bureau and the National Farmers Union. For example, the National Grange normally supports the principle of relatively free trade; yet it also calls for tariff levels high enough to protect several segments of American agriculture from what it views as "unfair" or unreasonable foreign competition.[32]

The "Military-Industrial Complex"

At the end of his Administration, President Dwight D. Eisenhower—who had served during and after World War II as one of the nation's most distinguished military leaders —warned the American people about the emergence of what he called the "Military-Industrial Complex."[33] This was what the President identified as a vast and powerful aggregation of organizations and interest groups sharing the common purpose of maintaining an increasingly high level of American military expenditures (by implication, primarily to enhance their own economic well-being, rather than to protect the security of the United States).

What is the "Military-Industrial Complex"? What are the more important groups and institutions comprising it? And what is the nature and extent of its influence upon national policy? The answers to such questions, it should be candidly acknowledged, tend to be highly subjective and variable. No two informed students of the political process in the United States or of American defense policy would answer them in exactly the same way—for a very good reason. The very concept of the Military-Industrial Complex is amorphous and almost indefinable. Crucial to the definition, for example, is the question of whether all citizens and groups advocating a strong national defense program are to be included within it, or whether it comprises only those individuals and groups whose viewpoints on national defense issues are shaped primarily by their own self-interest, such as expanded profits and payrolls.

At any rate, as it is frequently defined, the Military-Industrial Complex has several large components. There are business corporations and organizations—numbering in the hundreds—directly and indirectly involved in defense production, whose continued prosperity depends upon obtaining "defense contracts." There are national and local labor unions representing workers whose livelihoods and wage scales depend upon the availability of jobs in defense-related industries. There are some segments of American agriculture producing commodities bought in large quantities by the armed forces. There are perhaps thousands of local communities and cities whose tax revenues and overall economic well-being are affected by the presence of nearby military installations and industries having defense contracts. Then there are agencies of the American government —chiefly the Department of Defense and influential legislative bodies such as the House and Senate Armed Services committees—that often express the view that national defense spending must be increased. In addition, individual members of Congress representing districts in which military installations or defense industries are located could also be included in the Military-Industrial Complex. Within the past two decades or so, retired military officers and ex-members of Congress have not infrequently taken positions in public relations firms and as lobbyists representing the Military-Industrial Complex. This practice has received widespread publicity in the news media and has been the subject of several congressional investigations. Moreover, organizations representing the separate armed forces —like the Association of the United States Army, the Navy League, and the Air Force Association—become active in campaigns to increase the defense budget and to maximize the funds allocated to the branch of the service with which they are identified.

By the early 1980s, the United States government expended some $220 billion in total defense spending. As we observed in Chapter 5, the proposed adoption of new defense projects (like expanded naval construction, the MX missile system, and the Cruise missile) would almost certainly guarantee substantial increases in defense outlays in the years ahead. This of course was an enormous budgetary outlay; and the livelihood of millions of American workers, and the profits of several thousand large and small business corporations, would be affected by it. The Military-Industrial Complex, therefore, had a direct stake not only in the total volume of national defense spending but in the precise allocation of these funds for various purposes (such as military pay scales, weapons' procurement, and research and development) related to the national defense program.[34]

What influence does this vast array of economic power, represented by the Military-Industrial Complex, exert in the formulation and administration of national policy? As with other forms of lobbying, this is an extremely difficult question to answer satisfactorily. It is much easier to identify the main groups comprising the Military-Industrial Complex —or to arrive at totals of the economic assets this pressure group complex collectively represents—than to determine its precise influence upon the policy-making process of the national government. To believe that the lobbying activities of the Military-Industrial Complex have *no* impact upon the thinking and decisions of officials in the executive and legislative branches would be naive and would ignore the political power that sometimes accompanies the possession of great economic and financial power. Yet it would be no less unrealistic to adopt another simplistic conclusion (prevalent among some Americans, for example, during the Vietnam War): that the Military-Industrial Complex somehow "dictates" national defense policy and, even more broadly, that it alone is responsible for America's diplomatic interventionism in distant parts of the world. That the Military-Industrial Complex represents an impressive array of wealth and of diverse pressure group interests in the American society cannot be denied. It is no less true, however, that its political influence can be (and often has been) highly exaggerated.

As in other areas of national policy, the level of defense spending must ultimately have a minimal basis of support in American public opinion. During some periods (as in the Vietnam War), the American people obviously approved of high defense outlays; and in other periods (as during most of the 1970s), they called for retrenchment in the national defense budget. Then by the early 1980s (in response to perceived external threats, like continued high levels of Soviet defense spending and the decline in the nation's influence abroad), the American people once again expressed approval for a new national defense buildup, dictated primarily by a conviction that American power had seriously declined. For a decade or so after the Vietnam War—for all of its presumed influence upon the national decision-making process—the Military-Industrial Complex was *not* able to prevent a massive redirection of governmental spending into welfare, education, and other domestic policies and programs. At best, the Military-Industrial Complex must be viewed as merely one pressure group active within the American political system; its views are often successfully contested by other groups and organizations interested in public policy questions, and certain other forces (like the strong antimilitary tradition in the American society and the principle of civilian dominance in decision making) often serve as potent deterrents to its influence upon national policy.

Ethnic Minorities

As every citizen is aware, the American society is a "melting pot" of diverse ethnic groups, many of whose ancestors arrived on the North American continent during the period of exploration and colonization. Although it reached its peak in the nineteenth century, the stream of immigration into the United States—particularly by those fleeing political oppression in their own countries—continues to the present day. In recent years, such groups as refugees from Southeast Asia, from Castro's Cuba, and from the Soviet Union and other Communist states in Europe have sought (and usually been granted) sanctuary in the United States.

The fact that the United States is "a nation of immigrants" has sometimes been crucial in affecting the course of American diplomacy. As a general rule, America's ethnic minorities have preserved close ties with, and interest in, the "old country"; and on matters of external policy affecting its interests, they sometimes express their viewpoints actively and intensely. German-Americans, for example, played a disproportionate role in shaping American attitudes toward Germany during the 1920s and 1930s.[35] Similarly, Italian-Americans often derived a sense of pride from Mussolini's accomplishments in Italy before World War II. After the war, they were keenly interested in lenient treatment of Italy by the Allies and in the country's postwar reconstruction.[36] Another ethnic group having a deep involvement in American diplomacy during and after World War II were the Polish-Americans. The diplomacy of the Roosevelt Administration toward Poland—especially the efforts of President Roosevelt to preserve Polish independence after the Soviet Red Army had occupied the country—was in some measure responsive to the desires of Polish-American citizens and organizations in the United States.[37]

Throughout American history, few ethnic minorities have surpassed the Irish-Americans in the vigor (and sometimes the violence) of their demands. There were many Irish

Who think that freedom must consist
In proving points, with sticks and fists.[38]

Traditionally, Irish-American sentiment in the United States has been profoundly and uncompromisingly anti-British. Irish-American groups are predictably suspicious of Britain's diplomatic intentions and of any scheme contemplating close Anglo-American cooperation. The opposition of this group (particularly strong in cities like Boston and Chicago), for example, contributed in some measure to America's rejection of the League of Nations after World War I (which Irish-Americans viewed as a scheme for perpetuating the British Empire).[39] Since World War II, many members of the Irish-American community have sought to involve the United States in the political upheaval in Ireland, on the side of Irish independence and freedom from British influence; and lobbying activities by these groups have sometimes been intense (although not discernibly successful).[40]

A relatively recent manifestation of ethnic influence upon American foreign policy has been the increasingly assertive role of black citizens and organizations in expressing their viewpoints on diplomatic issues affecting their interests. As one authority has noted, this phenomenon is an outgrowth of the civil rights movement in the United States. Many of the ideas and goals long associated with that movement are now being projected by blacks and other disadvantaged minorities into the foreign policy sphere. For these groups, the success of American diplomacy tends to be measured by how forcefully the United States promotes the cause of racial equality and human rights generally abroad—particularly in contexts such as the former British colony of Southern Rhodesia (now known as Zimbabwe) and South Africa, where racial conflicts remain acute. As one authority has expressed it:

American black intellectuals in particular are challenging the traditional method of separating domestic from foreign problems. They see American racial problems as a form of colonialism. This colonialism is perceived not only in discrimination and exploitation, but the entire American practice of assimilation is seen as analogous to the acculturation process of colonialism. Thus many young American black leaders . . . have internationalized the racial issue. . . . the struggle for equal rights in the United States has become, for many political as well as academic blacks, a global liberation movement.[41]

Yet the same admonition must be made about the foreign policy viewpoints and activities of black Americans as has been made about the business, labor, and other communities. The position of black Americans on foreign policy issues *is not monolithic.* Black Americans and other ethnic minorities are usually subject to cross-pressures and conflicting impulses characterizing the attitudes of other citizens. Sentiment among black Americans about the Vietnam War (in which many of their numbers participated), for example, did not differ fundamentally from overall American public opinion about it (during that episode, for example, there was no substantial "bloc" of unified black-American sentiment against the war). In 1979, when American citizens were taken as hostages by militant groups in Iran, the Iranian government engaged in a crude and transparent effort to divide American public opinion by attempting to win the support of black Americans for its cause. That effort patently failed and was abandoned by the Ayatollah Khomenei's revolutionary regime.[42] President Jimmy Carter's dismissal several months earlier of a prominent spokesman for the black community, Andrew Young, from his position as ambassador to the United Nations produced no pervasive "defection" or widespread alienation among black Americans toward the Administration's foreign policy.[43]

Lobbying by Foreign Governments

Early in 1979, Prime Minister Menachem Begin made one of his numerous trips to Washington, where he was to meet with President Jimmy Carter and President Anwar Sadat of Egypt in a renewed search for a resolution of the Arab-Israeli dispute. According to one report, Begin was ready to take the Israeli case in the controversy "directly to the American public," in an effort to swing the Carter Administration to a more pro-Israeli position. Instead of meeting at the presidential retreat at Camp David, Begin preferred that the meetings be held in Washington, where he "could go public at the first hint of 'pressure' from the U.S." An aide to President Carter said Israeli officials "love to have access to the press" in Washington, in contrast to Camp David, where it was "hard for them to have a public relations battle."[44]

This was merely one recent example of an increasingly important dimension of pressure group activity affecting contemporary American foreign policy: efforts *by foreign governments and political movements* to engage in lobbying activities designed to influence the policies of the United States government and American public opinion. The period since World War II has witnessed a significant upsurge in this aspect of lobbying activities. In the early 1960s, Deputy Attorney General Nicholas Katzenbach identified "a tremendous increase in the activities of Americans representing foreign governments and foreign interests." In view of the impact of American foreign aid programs, trade, and tariff measures upon these countries, foreign interests had developed

> . . . a major incentive . . . to engage in activities similar to those engaged in by domestic interests in the United States such as trade associations, labor unions, farmers . . . and

others whose economic welfare is directly and importantly affected by governmental decisions.

With the growing involvement of the United States in global affairs, this official anticipated that "the interest of these other countries in what we do will become ever more pervasive."[45]

Efforts by foreign interests to influence American diplomacy of course did not begin with World War II. Concern about the problem before 1941 had led Congress in 1938 to enact the Foreign Agents Registration Act, according to which paid agents of foreign principals were required to register with the Department of Justice and to disclose information about the nature of their interests and their finances. By 1960, some 500 such agents had registered as required. Even so, congressional and executive officials alike were convinced that many such agents active in promoting the cause of foreign interests had *not* registered; and, among those who did, some disclosed little useful information about the scope and nature of their activities in behalf of their clients. The chief cause of legislative concern about lobbying by foreign principals therefore was that frequently the activities of such groups remained shrouded in secrecy. In company with their counterparts in domestic affairs, pressure groups representing outside interests have cultivated the art of "indirect lobbying" into a highly ingenious, intricate, and surreptitious process. Primary reliance is placed upon "educational campaigns" to influence public opinion and prominent news media, in which the role of the lobbyist is often studiously concealed from the general public and from governmental officials. Occasionally, selected foreign policy issues elicit open and direct lobbying activities by individuals and organizations representing foreign interests. This occurred, for example, in 1962, with respect to congressional consideration of a bill proposing to eliminate the premium the United States has traditionally paid on foreign sugar imports. The records of the Senate Foreign Relations Committee reveal that

> . . . foreign governments and foreign sugar interests hired more than 20 lobbyists, to our knowledge, some of them on straight salary, some with contingent fees [i.e., the lobbyist's fee depended upon the success of his efforts in defeating the bill]. The final legislation contained both the global concept [i.e., elements of the Kennedy Administration's proposals] and the lobbyists' premium concept.[46]

In the years that followed, lobbying activities by foreign governments and political movements became, if anything, even more intensive, ambitious, and ingenious. A few brief examples will illustrate the point. Working closely with Greek-American organizations in the United States, the government of Greece mounted a highly successful campaign to win congressional support for its position in the controversy with Turkey over Cyprus. In 1974, despite strong White House objections, Congress voted to suspend American military aid and sales to Turkey as a means of expressing its sympathy for the Greek position on this issue. As a result, Turkish-American relations were tense for several years thereafter.[47]

For two reasons, this case of foreign lobbying in the United States is unusually interesting. First, it was a prominent example of a foreign lobby's *success* in persuading Congress to adopt a policy favorable to its objectives, in the face of vigorous White House objections. Second, the case illustrates how, in pressure group activities, it not infrequently happens that *a single interest group* largely dominates the lobbying process, because it has no effective "competition" from rival groups. In this instance, there was no comparably powerful Turkish-American lobby to present the opposite point of view to Congress and the American people.

During the 1970s, many other foreign governments endeavored to influence American foreign policy by engaging in lobbying activities. Representatives of the government of South Korea, for example, lavishly distributed gifts to legislative and executive officials in Washington, and utilized public relations campaigns and other techniques for the purpose of promoting the sale of Korean-made goods in the United States and of assuring American foreign aid to South Korea. Several Latin American governments undertook lobbying campaigns to influence legislative and executive officials in their behalf. The government of Southern Rhodesia (Zimbabwe) directed intense pressure upon Congress to lift or modify the trade boycott imposed by the White House against it because of its racist policies. After the "normalization" in Sino-American relations effected by the Nixon Administration, the People's Republic of China provided tours of the Chinese mainland for selected members of Congress. Under the Carter Administration, several Arab states carried out campaigns directed at officials in Washington and at the American people designed to improve the Arab image in the United States. For a brief period of time, even President Jimmy Carter's brother, Billy, participated in lobbying activities by pro-Arab groups.[48]

Lobbying by Governmental Agencies

President Lyndon B. Johnson (a former senator from the state of Texas) once said that nothing had higher priority in the White House than the efforts by his subordinates to engage in effective "legislation liaison"—or lobbying by executive officials on Capitol Hill on behalf of the President's program.[49] Johnson's interest in legislative liaison, and the skill displayed by his Administration in carrying out his directive, was one reason why the Johnson Administration had an outstanding record in gaining congressional support for its policies and program.

By contrast, the Carter Administration was subjected to recurrent criticisms because of its evident lack of interest in legislative liaison and its poor relations with Congress. One legislator complained in mid-1979 that "Carter couldn't get the Pledge of Allegiance through Congress"! Several months later an experienced reporter found that many of President Carter's problems stemmed not so much from members of the political opposition as from "his supporters in Congress" and members of his own White House staff. Meanwhile, public opinion polls revealed that the American people expected President Carter to "lead" Congress and believed that his Administration's performance in that respect had been inadequate.[50]

These examples highlight one of the more interesting aspects of lobbying in the contemporary American political system: efforts *by governmental departments and agencies* to gain congressional and public support for their policy proposals. Before World War II, lobbying activities were largely undertaken by private organizations; and they were *directed at* governmental agencies (primarily Congress). In the postwar era, however, governmental agencies themselves have increasingly engaged in legislative liaison activities, public relations campaigns, and other pursuits that are, in most fundamental respects, indistinguishable from lobbying by private groups. Nearly every executive department and agency, for example, has one or more organizational units whose function is to engage in legislative liaison and public relations in behalf of the department or agency. As we observed in Chapter 4, promoting collaborative relations with the House and Senate is the direct responsibility of the Bureau of Congressional Relations within the State Department; and for certain particularly controversial diplomatic issues, high-ranking officials within the department (not excluding the secretary of state himself) must devote a major portion of their schedules to this time-consuming assignment. As emphasized in Chapter 7, growing disunity within Congress has imposed a greater burden than ever upon State Department officials to produce a coherent and unified approach to American foreign policy.

From time to time, executive agencies form alliances with private organizations to undertake lobbying campaigns in behalf of common goals. This has been a commonplace phenomenon, for example, in the sphere of national trade policy—where business, labor, and agricultural organizations advocating liberal terms of trade cooperate with the Commerce Department, the Agriculture Department, the State Department, the White House, and other executive agencies to win public (and ultimately congressional) support for the President's trade bill. A dramatic case of such cooperation between governmental agencies and citizens' groups occurred in connection with Senate deliberations on the new Panama Canal treaties, negotiated by the Carter Administration. This coalition of pro-treaty forces had a significant impact in changing what initially appeared to be an adverse climate of American public and congressional sentiment toward the treaties into a climate of opinion that was ultimately favorable toward them.[51]

Congress' reaction toward lobbying campaigns by executive agencies has been highly ambivalent. On the one hand, legislators periodically denounce the practice, because they object in principle to one branch of the government exerting pressure against another; and they cannot justify the expenditure of taxpayers' money to finance lobbying campaigns. On the other hand, it is not unwarranted to say that (as Congress experiences increasing difficulty engaging in unified and rational decision making), legislators expect the President and his agents to exert "leadership" on Capitol Hill; and members of the House and Senate have been known to complain vocally when the White House fails to provide it! Ultimately, lobbying by governmental agencies could not take place without at least the tacit consent of Congress, which appropriates the funds making such activities possible. This fact may be an implicit admission that legislators themselves "need" or rely heavily upon such lobbying activities to guide their own deliberations on internal and external policy questions.

Our understanding of pressure group activity as it affects foreign policy will be enhanced by examining in some detail the nature and activities of a single lobby, believed by many commentators to have been the most consistently successful pressure group since World War II in affecting the policies of the United States government and the attitudes of the American people. This is the Zionist, or pro-Israeli, Lobby.

The Zionist Lobby: A Case Study

On December 9, 1974, 71 members of the Senate addressed a letter to President Gerald Ford. In the weeks that followed, the letter received widespread attention and circulation in the American news media. In their communication to the President, these senators emphasized their commitment to "the survival and integrity of the State of Israel"—a goal that, in their view, had served as "the bipartisan basis of American policy" for some 26 years previously. The letter identified various current threats to Israel's existence and well-being, and it called upon President Ford to "take the lead in organizing our friends and allies" abroad in enabling Israel to preserve its security and achieve its national goals.[52]

This letter provides merely one example of intensive and continuing efforts by pro-Israeli groups inside and outside the United States, often supported by the government of Israel, to influence the foreign policy of the United States. By many criteria, the Zionist lobby must be ranked among the most resourceful, skillful, and perhaps successful examples of pressure group activity witnessed in the annals of American diplomacy. A few months after the letter signed by 71 senators to which we have alluded, 76 members of the Senate sent President Ford another communication. Its purpose was to prevent a threatened "reassessment" of American foreign policy toward Israel (blamed by many of the President's advisers for obstructing efforts to achieve peace and stability in the Middle East). This forceful expression of senatorial opinion was widely interpreted as a sharp "rebuke" for Secretary of State Henry Kissinger and as at least a temporarily successful effort by the Zionist lobby to prevent an impending reorientation of American foreign policy toward a somewhat more sympathetic position for the Arab point of view on the Palestine question.

The Zionist lobby constitutes a complex network of domestic and foreign interest groups devoted to the welfare of the state of Israel. Its nucleus is the American Israel Public Affairs Committee (AIPAC), with headquarters in Washington, D.C. AIPAC draws its members and financial support largely from the American Jewish community and other friends of Israel in the United States. Its lobbying activities are also encouraged and (at least indirectly) supported by the government of Israel and pro-Israeli groups outside the

United States. AIPAC is an outgrowth of an earlier organization—the American Zionist Council—that was active in behalf of the Zionist cause before Israel was created in 1948.*

AIPAC is what is known as an "umbrella" organization, or spokesman for many different Zionist and Jewish organizations in the United States. For example, the presidents of most of the principal American Jewish organizations serve on AIPAC's executive

---

*At this point, the student of American foreign policy needs to bear in mind an important distinction: between Zionism and the Jewish religion, which are not identical. Zionism emerged as a movement at the end of the nineteenth century; it was founded by Theodor Herzl, who advocated the establishment of a Jewish state. In time, the location of this state was identified with the ancient land of Palestine—the site of the Jewish kingdom under Kings David and Solomon. The Zionist movement received a powerful impetus when on November 2, 1917, Great Britain issued the "Balfour Declaration," promising support for a Jewish "national home" in Palestine after World War I. Zionist groups continued their efforts to create a Jewish state in Palestine—and they finally achieved their goal when the state of Israel came into existence on May 14–15, 1948. Zionism is thus a *political movement,* seeking the creation and maintenance of a political entity, the state of Israel. Although Zionism is of course rooted in the Jewish religious tradition, all adherents of the Jewish religion are *not* Zionists. Conversely, many supporters of the Zionist movement in Israel, in the United States, and elsewhere are not members of the Jewish religious faith—such as President Harry S Truman and the late Senator Hubert H. Humphrey (Democrat of Minnesota), who were ardent supporters of Israel in the post-World War II period. Arab officials and spokesmen have repeatedly insisted upon the distinction between being *anti-Zionist*—or opposed to the state of Israel and its policies—which they are, and being *anti-Jewish*—or opposed to the Hebrew religion or culture—which they are not. For their part, supporters of the state of Israel sometimes equate criticisms of the state of Israel and its policies with a position of anti-Semitism or overall hostility toward the Jewish people and culture. The error in this reasoning is highlighted by the fact that many groups within Israel itself disagree with some of the government's policies (such as continued Israeli settlements in Arab-occupied territories).

committee. Although they occasionally undertake lobbying campaigns on their own, usually other Jewish organizations—like the American Jewish Committee, B'nai B'rith, the American Jewish Congress, the National Council of Jewish Women, and Hadassa—are usually content to let AIPAC represent Israel's interests in their behalf.

By the end of the 1970s, AIPAC had a staff of some 20 members and an annual budget of around $750,000—funds raised by contributions, ranging from $25 to $5000 annually, from over 15,000 members.

As with most pressure groups, AIPAC's lobbying activities may be divided into two broad categories: those aimed mainly at Congress and executive agencies of the American government; and "grass-roots campaigns" undertaken to influence the attitudes and political behavior of the American people. (In recent years, lobbies have often found the latter the most promising method of influencing governmental policies at the national level.) In its activities directed at legislative and executive officials, AIPAC employs familiar techniques. Spokesmen for the Zionist lobby endeavor to inform members of Congress and executive officials fully and frequently concerning Israel's policies and viewpoints on major regional and international issues; they attend congressional hearings and present statements in Israel's behalf; they arrange for officials of the Israeli government and other prominent citizens visiting in the United States to meet with legislative and executive officials; they collaborate with the Israeli government in planning the itineraries of members of Congress desiring to visit Israel; they provide information requested by members of Congress and their staff about Israel and its internal and external policies; and, on key congressional votes, they endeavor to persuade legislators in both houses to vote favorably on Israel's interests.

In their grass-roots lobbying activities, Zionist organizations seek to create an overall pro-Israeli public opinion climate in the United States—on the theory that, by successfully doing so, constituency pressure will compel officials in Washington to pursue policies beneficial to Israel.

Achieving the goal involves the lobby in a multiplicity of diverse activities: furnishing speakers to local community organizations interested in Israel or problems of the contemporary Middle East; working closely with Jewish organizations on college and university campuses to present lectures, discussion groups, and symposia in which the Israeli viewpoint is presented; developing contacts with other interest groups (such as labor unions and religious organizations) known to be favorable toward Israel and willing to cooperate in enhancing its image with Americans; writing or sponsoring "letters to the editor" in local and regional newspapers in which the Israeli point of view on particular issues is communicated; arranging for trips to Israel by interested citizens' groups; enlisting the support of prominent citizens on Israel's side. During national elections, the Zionist lobby is especially active in disseminating information at the grass-roots level about the voting records of legislators as they affect Israel's interests; in rallying popular support for those elected officials known to be favorable toward Israel; and in seeking to defeat those elected officials who have been identified with anti-Israeli or pro-Arab positions.

The Zionist lobby promotes Israel's interest in another crucial respect: eliciting voluntary contributions for Israel and supporting the purchase of Israeli government bonds by the American people. Massive external funds have been crucial in permitting the state of Israel to meet its internal and external needs since 1948—especially in carrying an extraordinarily heavy burden of national defense.

According to most criteria utilized to measure the results of pressure group activity (and none is perhaps totally reliable), the Zionist lobby must surely be regarded as one of the most effective in the post-World War II period. In terms of its dominant goal—maintaining official policies and public attitudes in the United States favorable to Israel—it has few peers in the arena of pressure group activities. For over a generation, congressional sentiment has remained consistently pro-Israel (even while some shift in attitudes in recent years has been discernible among executive officials). Routinely, measures beneficial to the state of Israel are approved by substantial House and Senate majorities, while those inimical to its interests are either defeated outright or substantially modified by Congress before they win legislative approval.

While pro-Israeli sentiment remains strong in Congress, two facts must be emphasized about it. First, national legislators are less prone today than formerly to support pro-Israeli measures *automatically and uncritically*. Although the Zionist lobby still regularly "appeals" decisions made by the President and other executive officials to a more sympathetic Congress, in the post-Vietnam War era members of the House and Senate have been somewhat more prepared to consider the Arab point of view and to realize that the United States has more than one foreign policy goal in the Middle East.

Second, after the Vietnam War, shifts have also occurred more broadly in American public opinion on questions related to the Middle East. Public opinion polls and other evidence have shown that, while it is still high, American public support for Israel has declined; and citizens have become more willing to consider and respond sympathetically to Arab viewpoints on Middle Eastern issues. Even Israeli officials have acknowledged, and

become concerned about, this erosion in support for Israel by the American people. Early in 1980, for example, both President Anwar Sadat of Egypt and Prime Minister Menachem Begin of Israel visited Washington. As spokesmen for their respective causes, Sadat's public image in America was unquestionably more favorable than that of Begin (regarded by many Americans as an ideologically "rigid" leader who was unwilling to compromise for the sake of peace in the Middle East).

In accounting for a more balanced attitude on Capitol Hill and throughout the American society on the Arab-Israeli controversy, two recent developments have had an important impact. One of these, which we shall consider more fully in Chapter 12, is America's massive and growing dependence upon oil imports from the Arab world—a reality that inevitably colored public and official attitudes toward Middle Eastern questions. The other change (symbolized by President Sadat of Egypt) was that Arab lobbying and propaganda efforts had unquestionably become more skillful and effective in influencing American attitudes than had been the case for many years before and after the creation of the state of Israel.

How can we explain the success that the Zionist lobby has achieved in preserving a high degree of support for Israel within the American society? At the outset, it must be understood that the interaction between lobbying activities and the formulation and administration of national policy is a highly complex process—so much so that in this and other cases, it is very difficult to establish a direct or simple causal relationship between lobbying efforts and governmental policies or public attitudes. It would be as unwarranted, for example, to say that postwar American policy toward the Middle East has been "dictated" by the pro-Israeli lobby as to assert that the lobby is totally without influence in the American political system.

Individuals and groups engaged in pro-Israeli lobbying in the United States *have* unquestionably been highly skillful, talented, and astute practitioners of their art. They clearly understand how to maximize support for Israel within the American society, and they have applied themselves conscientiously to that goal. Yet, as was emphasized in Chapter 6, students of lobbying and propaganda campaigns are aware of a pivotal fact that goes far toward explaining the success of the Zionist lobby in the American setting. The most effective propaganda is that which induces "the target" of it, or those toward whom it is directed, *to believe or act in a manner compatible with their preexisting inclinations,* rather than "converting" them to a point of view to which they are unsympathetic or antagonistic. This process (known as "reenforcement") has been skillfully utilized by the Zionist lobby in its activities toward the American government and people.

For a number of reasons, preexisting support for the Zionist cause has been pervasive throughout the American society for many years. In the first place, Americans are participants in the *Judeo-Christian tradition;* many of their most cherished religious and ethical principles are derived from the Jewish heritage. By contrast—as spokesmen for the Arab side have frequently complained—there is no comparable Islamic-Christian tradition. From the Middle Ages to the present day, Islam has had a "bad press" in Western culture—more so perhaps than any other major religious system in the world. To cite merely one example: In his celebrated work *The Inferno,* the Italian poet Dante placed Mohammed the Prophet in the next-to-last level of Hell, along with other "false pro-

phets"—lower than all other offenders against God's commands except the dissolute Popes! In the more recent period—as the United States was compelled to deal with what is sometimes called "resurgent Islam"—other commentators are convinced that Americans and other Westerners still are unable to comprehend the nature and appeal of the Islamic religious faith for its adherents.[53]

For many Americans (a majority of whom are not adherents of the Jewish religious faith), the creation of the state of Israel was the "fulfillment" of Old and New Testament prophecy. For other Americans, support for the Zionist cause stemmed from a conviction that—in view of Western indifference toward the plight of Europe's Jews in the face of Nazi Germany's systematic campaign to eliminate them during the 1930s—support for Israel was a powerful ethical and humanitarian obligation.

Moreover, the "pioneers" and early settlers of the state of Israel—and the political power structure that governed the country until the late 1970s—largely came from the West. Their ideologies and governmental principles were drawn from Western sources. In many cases, they had close friends and relatives in the United States and other Western countries. After 1948, in time hundreds of thousands of Americans visited Israel, where they saw firsthand evidence of Israeli talent, ingenuity, and hard work that "made the desert bloom" in the Negev and other regions. They felt "at home" in Israel in a way that was not possible if they visited other Middle Eastern countries. There was also the fact that Israel was a democracy in (as it was often described) "a sea of Arab totalitarianism (or authoritarianism)." Given their deep attachment to the democratic ideal, this fact unquestionably appealed to Americans. The Israelis had accomplished something no other people in the modern Middle East had achieved: They had successfully transplanted the Western democratic model to the region and made it operate successfully.

Unquestionably, the pro-Israeli policies of the United States since World War II (or earlier) also have been influenced by a political reality: the pivotal role of the "Jewish vote" in the American political system. Jewish citizens number just under 6 million in the United States, constituting less than 3 percent of the total population. Yet the *political influence* of this minority is sometimes greatly disproportionate to its numbers. One reason is that, traditionally, the Jewish peoples tend to be very "involved" in the political process. Jewish citizens, much more than the average American, are interested in questions of public policy and are informed about them; they contribute their time, energy, and money to political and pressure group campaigns; they express their convictions to policy makers and to other citizens vocally and persuasively. In addition, in certain states —like New York, New Jersey, Illinois, Florida, and California—the relatively large number of Jewish voters can decisively influence the outcome of key political contests such as congressional elections.[54] Yet even in states having relatively small numbers of Jewish citizens, officials from these states are often sympathetic to Israel's viewpoint, because these Jewish constituents involve themselves actively in political campaigns and communicate their ideas skillfully and forcefully to policy makers.

Finally, the pro-Zionist lobby in the United States has had an unusually high degree of success for another reason. Until the 1970s, there was the relative absence of effective competition or countervailing power provided by the "Arab lobby" in the United States.[55] Although the Arab states have maintained an organizational framework for presenting their viewpoints to the American people for many years, it was neither as well financed, as skillful, nor as effective as the Zionist lobby in influencing American opinion. As we have noted, the Arab lobby had many obstacles to overcome in its effort to influence American public opinion favorably— such as the American people's lack of knowledge of, and interest in, the Middle East; stereotypes in the American mind about Arab and other Middle Eastern cultures; and, as we have seen, strong residual sympathy in the United States for the Israeli point of view. Pro-Arab lobbying activities were also often inhibited and weakened by the *internal disunity* exhibited by the Arab states in their approach to the Palestine question. Americans were often left to wonder: *Which* Arab position on Middle Eastern questions is the correct one? Toward a single issue—such as the Lebanese civil war—there have been several conflicting Arab viewpoints. In addition, differing points of view—often dictated by rival national loyalties—have existed among pro-Arab organizations within the United States. Basic policy divergencies among them have often detracted from their ability to influence American opinion favorably.

Yet in recent years, the effectiveness of the Arab lobby as a vehicle for expressing Arab viewpoints in the United States, and for influencing national policy toward the Middle East, has unquestionably increased. Perhaps the dominant reason has been the realization of the American people that their economic, military, and diplomatic destiny depends upon unimpeded access to the oil fields of the Middle East. By relying upon "oil power," the Arab states have compelled Americans to become more interested in, and more receptive to, the Arab point of view. After the Arab states imposed an oil embargo on shipments to the West during the 1967 Middle Eastern conflict, executive officials exhibited a more balanced, less overtly pro-Israeli approach to Middle Eastern questions. During the 1970s, both official American policy statements and the sentiments expressed by American public opinion became more critical of many Israeli policies and more inclined to recognize the legitimacy of certain Arab contentions. Concurrently, Arab propaganda efforts in the United States became more skillful in presenting their point of view rationally and factually (rather than polemically and emotionally, as had often been true in the past).[56]

Although the Arab lobby still had many disadvantages to overcome vis-à-vis its Zionist counterpart, by 1980 this long-standing disparity was tending to disappear. One experienced observer of pressure group activities in the United States stated that

> Now, a pro-Arab lobby is beginning to emerge, and I believe that the interplay of lobbying by special interests, rather than merely by one side, may neutralize those interests and enable our national interests in the area [the Middle East] to emerge.[57]

Lobbying Activities in Perspective

Many informed students of the American governmental system are convinced that lobbying activities have become more extensive, more lavishly financed, and more ingenious and skillful than in any previous era of the nation's history. What factors account for this apparent escalation in lobbying activities in the United States? Several factors may be briefly identified as contributing to it.

One of them is the *expanding role of government* in all aspects of American life. In the contemporary period, there is hardly a major segment of national life in which decisions and programs of the national government do not have an important impact.

A related development has been the gradual extension of governmental activity

into *ever new dimensions of international relations.* Before World War II, for example (when the United States was not compelled to have a foreign policy at all), the nation's involvement in external affairs consisted chiefly of three functions: protecting the security of the United States; promoting foreign commerce; and operating American embassies and consulates abroad. After World War II, these traditional functions were broadened to include a wide range of new activities, involving an ever-expanding circle of governmental agencies and affecting the welfare of a correspondingly larger number of private citizens and organizations. Future chapters will provide concrete examples of these concerns. It suffices to note here that what is sometimes called the growing "foreign policy agenda" of the United States perhaps induces more intensive and novel forms of pressure group activity related to foreign affairs.[58]

For reasons we identified in Chapter 7, a number of developments within Congress have contributed to increased pressure group activity on Capitol Hill. Committee and subcommittee jurisdictions within the House and Senate have become increasingly blurred and overlapping. Nearly every major committee in both chambers has now acquired some responsibility for programs and activities in the foreign policy field. The influence of party organizations and party discipline on Capitol Hill has become progressively weaker (perhaps mirroring the weakening of party allegiances exhibited by the American voter generally). Another noteworthy tendency in the American political environment—the emergence of "single-issue politics"—has encouraged more intensive pressure group activity. Meanwhile, as a result of the Vietnam War and the Watergate scandal, throughout most of the 1970s executive power was highly suspect on Capitol Hill and in the minds of many American citizens, who feared the reemergence of the "imperial presidency." In this context, pressure groups found ample scope for their activities and discovered new opportunities for influencing the policies and programs of governmental agencies.[59]

If such developments supplied pressure groups with new incentives to expand their lobbying activities, technological advances provided them with improved *means* for doing so. Computers, for example, made possible the storage and almost instantaneous retrieval of information needed by pressure groups for their campaigns in Washington and throughout the nation at large. Photocopying and other electronic methods of printing enabled pressure groups to prepare and disseminate vast quantities of literature and other information rapidly and on a wide scale. Television and other modern techniques of communication gave them new opportunities to present their viewpoints to the American people.

Yet after acknowledging the intensification of pressure group activity in the United States, the relationship between lobbying and the formulation and administration of national policy remains a highly intricate and often subtle one. No more today than in the past can it be correctly asserted that national policy on major diplomatic issues is "made" or dictated solely by pressure group activity. Let us examine the interaction between lobbying and other manifestations of public opinion and national policy making more closely.

Policy and Opinion: The Interaction

Thus far in our discussion of the role of public opinion in the foreign policy process, we have devoted attention only indirectly to a central question: What is the impact of public opinion upon the formulation and administration of American foreign policy? Even today, it has to

be admitted, the question is a difficult one. Policy makers themselves may often be unaware of the degree to which public sentiment affects their approach to other countries. Moreover, much greater progress has been made in the postwar era in discerning *what* public opinion is on national policy issues than on how it is conveyed to policy makers or in determining its precise impact upon the foreign policy of the United States toward the Middle East, upon the issue of global trade policy, or upon the question of international human rights.

Official Efforts to Assess Public Opinion

Even in a democracy like the United States, the systematic study of public attitudes on external issues is a relatively recent phenomenon, dating from World War II. Officials before that time were not of course totally oblivious to public opinion. President Wilson's views on the subject were cited earlier in the chapter. Yet prior to World War II, policy makers usually conceived of public opinion as a force to be led or "educated" to support desired steps (like America's entry into the League of Nations); if national leaders were induced to influence public attitudes, they felt little inclination to study and analyze data informing them of society's viewpoints. The change that has occurred since World War II is highlighted by one commentator's remark that today, no government agency is more sensitive to public opinion than the Department of State.[60]

Several factors have played a part in this change. Foreign affairs were perhaps the last realm of governmental activity to become subjected to "democratization" (and many citizens perhaps believe that process has still not been carried far enough). The speed and global extent of modern communications have inevitably accelerated the interaction between the public and its leaders, greatly facilitating the exchange of ideas between them. Recent techniques for measuring and analyzing public opinion make possible the collection of data often unavailable in earlier periods. Above all, the vast change in the nature of America's overseas commitments since World War II dictated a new approach to public thinking about international problems. During the long era of isolationism, as one student has expressed it, American policies tended to be "mainly negative and hortatory."[61] Today, as one of the two superpowers in the international system, the United States is obliged to conduct a variety of programs—like foreign military and economic aid, the maintenance of a large and well-equipped defense establishment, and efforts to maintain economic stability at home and abroad—requiring the consent of the American people. Increasingly, the traditional distinction between "internal" and "external" policies has become indistinct and almost impossible to define clearly. As the "energy crisis" of recent years made dramatically evident, the internal well-being of millions of Americans depends as never before upon crucial developments and decisions in the foreign policy field.

During the early months of 1980, millions of Americans witnessed a familiar spectacle on daily TV newscasts. Assistant Secretary of State for Public Affairs Hodding Carter "briefed" the news media and the American people on the latest developments in Iran and other trouble spots around the world, after which he answered questions by reporters on major foreign policy issues. During the Iranian crisis, the State Department went to extraordinary lengths to inform the people of recent developments and to present the thinking of national officials concerning various proposed alternative strategies avail-

able to the United States in responding to them. At the same time, the White House and the State Department also made an intensive effort to keep abreast of public thinking on the Iranian situation; to adapt American policy to it; and to communicate the idea at home and abroad that public sentiment in the United States played a pivotal role in the diplomatic behavior of the American government.[62]

This example illustrates the twofold process that governs the relationship between public opinion and public policy in the American democratic system. On the one hand, as never before national officials are interested in public sentiment. They study and evaluate public opinion polls and other evidence of public attitudes on major policy issues; and ostensibly, they take public opinion "into account" in the formulation and administration of national policy. On the other hand, national policy makers also feel an obligation to "educate" public opinion, to explain the complexities and dilemmas nearly always accompanying any proposed national policy, and to provide leadership in shaping public attitudes on domestic and foreign policy questions.

Official concern with the public opinion context of American foreign policy largely dates from the Wilsonian period during and after World War I. Although the State Department created a Division of Information as early as 1909, World War I witnessed the first intensive effort by the department to inform the public about events overseas. Some 30 years elapsed, however, before the department formally conceived of public opinion as a two-way process involving "public relations" campaigns by government and efforts by officials to inform themselves more adequately of public attitudes.[63]

The public opinion dimension of American foreign policy is the specific domain of the

Public Affairs office within the Department of State. This office concentrates upon *domestic* opinion as it relates to American foreign policy.* Its mission may be divided into two broad categories: collecting data about public attitudes in the United States on external questions; and disseminating information and ideas to citizens and organizations within the American society about the foreign policy of the United States.

In its analysis of American opinion bearing upon foreign affairs, the office of Public Affairs relies upon a variety of sources—ranging from national and regional public opinion surveys, to petitions and mass-produced communications sent to national leaders by pressure groups, to viewpoints conveyed in letters to policy makers by individual citizens, to more subjective determinations of what American public opinion wants or will "not accept" in the realm of external policy. (Another important component in this process is the department's perception of *congressional opinion,* as determined by the Office of Congressional Relations and other agencies involved in legislative liaison.) The assistant secretary of state for public affairs and other State Department officials can also gain insight into public concerns from the questions directed at them by representatives of the news media in press conferences and interviews.

From a wide variety of sources, the office of Public Affairs prepares periodic reports on public sentiment, and these are circulated throughout the State Department, the White House, and other agencies involved in the

foreign policy process. Theoretically (if not always actually), the assistant secretary of state or his deputies are consulted in the stage of policy formulation, in order that public opinion is fully considered.

No less intensive and systematic efforts are made by the State Department's office of Public Affairs and other governmental agencies to familiarize Americans with the policies of the United States toward other countries, to explain the rationale of them, and to answer questions about external issues. In any given year, upwards of 1000 State Department officials give addresses and talks to citizens' groups throughout the country. The office answers questions from individual citizens and organizations about American foreign policy (many of which are relayed to it by members of Congress, who have received inquiries about the nation's foreign relations from their constituents). The State Department also publishes, and makes available to citizens at no (or small) cost, a range of pamphlets, booklets, brochures, and other publications dealing with United States foreign policy. The Historical Office arranges for use of the State Department's archives by scholars desiring to undertake research on various aspects of American diplomacy. The *Department of State Bulletin* provides up-to-date information, the text of official statements, and other informative materials on current American policy.[64]

The Role of Public Opinion in Policy Formulation

A recurrent complaint voiced by critics of America's involvement in the Vietnam War was that the Johnson and Nixon administrations did not heed American public sentiment or take it sufficiently into account in formulating policies toward Southeast Asia. Ulti-

---

*The reporting and analysis of public opinion abroad with regard to American foreign policy is the major responsibility of the United States International Communication Agency (USICA), whose role in the policy process was discussed at length in Chapter 6. The organizational structure of the State Department was discussed in Chapter 4.

mately, of course, adverse public sentiment toward America's continuing involvement in the Vietnam War compelled national officials to liquidate this draining and apparently fruitless commitment and, more generally, to rethink America's role in international affairs.

The criticism, nevertheless, highlights two fundamental problems about the role of public opinion in the foreign policy process. What role *should* public opinion play in policy formulation and execution? And how *does* public opinion influence American diplomacy? Experienced public officials and informed students of American foreign policy are likely to give highly diverse answers to both questions.

With regard to the former question—the impact public sentiment ought to have upon national policy—even today, the answer is far from clear. Widespread agreement exists perhaps upon two basic propositions relevant to the question. On the one hand, public sentiment cannot and does not directly "dictate" or formulate American foreign policy. On the other hand, public officials clearly cannot disregard public sentiment. As the Vietnam War experience confirmed, if they consistently do so—to the point of allowing the basis of public support to become eroded—they risk a dramatic repudiation of existing policy by the citizenry.

Influential as it may be, public opinion does not make or formulate American foreign policy. Public opinion is neither capable of playing such a role nor should national officials allow it to dictate the nation's diplomacy. The American democracy is a "representative" system of government, in which officials chosen by, and accountable to, the electorate actually formulate and carry out national policy. The American system is not—nor was it ever intended to be—a direct democracy, or a "participatory democracy," in which citizens actually formulate and administer national policy. Practically, in a nation of over 200 million people, such a course is completely infeasible.[65]

Moreover, a direct and decisive role by public opinion in the foreign policy process encounters several other fundamental problems. One of these was posed at the beginning of the chapter—and despite the advances made in the measurement and evaluation of public opinion during the last generation, it *remains* a difficult question today. What is the most authentic expression of public opinion on any given foreign policy issue? Is it merely majority sentiment on any outstanding question, as revealed by public opinion polls? (Increasingly, it has come to be recognized that such polls have serious limitations and imperfections as accurate barometers of public thinking.) Is "public opinion" to be determined by merely quantitative criteria, without reference to the level of information or interest the American people exhibit toward foreign policy issues? Conversely, does public opinion consist of those viewpoints communicated most vocally and with greatest intensity of belief by pressure groups, which usually have a vested interest in a particular diplomatic course of action? What constitute the most accurate indexes of public opinion in the United States—public opinion surveys, newspaper and media opinion, State Department and White House "mail counts," analyses of mail received by members of the House and Senate (and frequently such diverse sources yield *differing* indications of public sentiment)?

Still another problem is: *At what point* should national officials be guided by their determination of public opinion? They might, for example, be guided by the principle that they should follow public opinion blindly and automatically, even if they believe it to be ignorant and unenlightened on important diplomatic issues. Or, they could take the position that they will heed public opinion—but only after the American people have been "given the facts" or otherwise educated about a particular foreign policy issue, enabling them to form an intelligent and enlightened opinion about it. The dilemma is illustrated by experience with the Panama Canal treaties negotiated under the Carter Administration. If President Carter and his advisers had blindly followed public opinion toward the treaties initially, the agreements would almost certainly have been rejected by executive and legislative officials as unacceptable to the American people. If, however (as actually occurred), national officials, joined by private citizens' groups, undertook an educational campaign designed to inform the American people about the alternatives available to the United States in this case—and if this campaign did successfully *change* existing public attitudes—then the Carter Administration could legitimately maintain that the treaties should be ratified, since they were in conformity with the wishes of the American people.[66] In reality, nearly all modern chief executives and their advisers have subscribed to President Carter's conception of the relationship between public opinion and policy formulation in the United States.

Parameters of Public Opinion

In the concluding section of this chapter, let us make explicit certain ideas about, and characteristics of, American public opinion as it relates to the foreign policy process. We may conveniently do so by focusing upon several general principles or parameters normally governing the role and influence of public opinion in the foreign policy field.

At the outset, it must be reiterated that in the American democratic setting, public opinion is an important—and sometimes a *crucial*—force influencing the foreign policy of the United States. If executive officials did not sufficiently understand the dominant influence public opinion can exert upon external policy before the Vietnam War, during that conflict they were provided with a dramatic lesson in it. As experience during that traumatic episode demonstrated, the foreign policy of the United States must possess "legitimacy": that is, it must be perceived by the American people as compatible with their underlying ideological and ethical values, and as conducive to their welfare. If the nation's foreign policy lacks legitimacy—or if a majority of the American people is convinced that this is the case—then national leaders will find it impossible to pursue the policy successfully.

If the Vietnam War provided a particularly striking example of the impact of public opinion on the foreign policy process, the same principle governs American foreign policy in less spectacular cases. In Soviet-American relations; in the provision of economic and technical aid to needy societies; in efforts by the United States to resolve the Arab-Israeli conflict; in American diplomacy toward Latin American nations—in these and countless other policy areas, the diplomacy of the United States must have a foundation in public support or acceptance if it is to achieve worthwhile objectives.

With respect to these and other problems in the foreign policy field, a subtle but crucial distinction must be made concerning the impact of public opinion on American diplomacy. All policies of the United States abroad do not necessarily have a high and visible degree of enthusiastic *support* in American public opinion. In fact, it may safely be asserted that very few such policies receive the unambiguous and evident endorsement of American public opinion (one example during most of the post-World War II period was the

American people's consistent support for a policy of resistance toward Communist expansionism). At a minimum, however, the major policies of the United States abroad cannot encounter pervasive and durable *public opposition* if they are to be successful. This is perhaps merely another way of saying that, in most cases, the American people are clearer about what *they do not want* in the foreign policy field than about the positive goals that ought to be pursued by national leaders and the desired methods for achieving them. (Americans, for example, made it abundantly clear to the White House that they did not want a continuation of massive American military involvement in the Vietnam War —and in time, national policy was responsive to that demand. Public sentiment was much less forceful and unambiguous concerning what American foreign policy toward Asia *ought to be* in the post-Vietnam War era.)*

After acknowledging the influential role that public opinion plays in the foreign policy process, it remains true that its impact upon American diplomacy is also *highly variable,* in some ways unpredictable, and often substantially determined by the particular issue or conditions confronting American policy makers in the external environment. As all informed students of American diplomacy are aware, the influence of public opinion often differs markedly in the sphere of Soviet-American relations, or of international trade questions, or American foreign policy toward sub-Saharan Africa. Toward one particular policy question, public opinion may have a decisive impact upon the foreign policy of the United States—virtually "forcing the hand" of the President and his advisers to pursue a designated course of action. Thus, at the end of World War II American public opinion compelled the Truman Administration to adopt an increasingly "tough" position in responding to Soviet expansionist moves abroad. Similarly, in 1980 American public opinion became increasingly insistent that the Carter Administration take a firm and decisive position with the government of Iran, in efforts to gain the release of Americans held as hostages in Tehran.

By contrast, in many other recent foreign policy issues the impact of public opinion has been minimal, to the point of being undetectable. It would be difficult, for example, to identify the role of public opinion in shaping the Reagan Administration's policies toward the problem of revolutionary unheaval in Central America or toward the next stage of negotiations in the Arab-Israeli dispute.

We may generalize the point being made here by recognizing two broad categories of public responses to foreign policy questions. One pattern is exhibited toward what might be called "normal" or noncrisis conditions abroad. For the preponderance of day-to-day issues confronting the United States abroad, the reaction of the general public in the United States is usually predictable: The ordinary citizen has a very low level of interest or involvement in such questions; his knowledge about

---

*An interesting example of this phenomenon was described at length by ex-Secretary of State Henry Kissinger in connection with the Vietnam War. As public dissatisfaction with, and opposition to, the war mounted in the United States, Kissinger notes that the views of the antiwar critics were "constantly in flux"—changing frequently in response to North Vietnam's viewpoints and positions and to circumstances in Southeast Asia. As a *Washington Post* editorial concluded, the protests of antiwar groups "can give little useful or specific counsel to the President" concerning specific policies to be pursued in Vietnam. The Nixon Administration may have heard a "loud shout" of protest, but this is "not a strategy" for ending the war. The problem facing policy makers was "in the interpreting and the application of a great outpouring of protest in any practical, meaningful way. . . ." Henry Kissinger, *White House Years* (Boston: Little, Brown and Co., 1979), pp. 254–255; 292–293; the *Washington Post* editorial is cited on p. 293.

them is extremely primitive (often to the point of being nonexistent); and he is usually content to leave the formulation and administration of American policy toward these questions to the nation's chosen leaders, particularly the President and his advisers. Some recent studies of American public opinion indicate that the degree of overall citizen indifference toward foreign policy questions *has increased* in the post-Vietnam War period.[67] Implicitly perhaps, the ordinary citizen "knows that he does not know" the facts, or have the requisite information, necessary to make sound judgments in the foreign policy realm. Under these conditions, on many specific issues "public opinion" often becomes the self-serving viewpoints expressed vocally and intensely by special interest groups.

In this classical behavior pattern, executive and legislative policy makers normally have wide latitude to formulate and carry out foreign policy within very broad parameters set by public opinion. They may confidently assume that in most such cases, they will not be deterred by general public opinion in the United States, so long as their policies meet two important criteria. The American people expect that the policies of the United States government will not patently offend their most deeply cherished values or be plainly inimical to their welfare. Under these conditions, perhaps the greatest challenge confronting executive and legislative officials is accurately ascertaining what kind of foreign policy the people of the United States *actually desire* in an extraordinarily complex and unstable external environment.[68]

The second familiar behavior pattern of public opinion as it affects the foreign policy process is in many respects very different. This is the role and influence of public sentiment in responding to extraordinary or "crisis" conditions abroad, particularly those involving a perceived threat to American security. This may be illustrated by a dramatic example: the public response to the Japanese attack against American military installations at Pearl Harbor on December 7, 1941. Literally within a matter of a few hours, American public opinion underwent a dramatic transformation. With little or no dissent, Americans overwhelmingly supported the Roosevelt Administration's decision to defend the nation's diplomatic and security interests against Japanese aggression. In the process, the long-standing American attachment to isolationism and to neutrality were abandoned. After Pearl Harbor, the change in the overall direction of American foreign policy—toward an "internationalist" vis-à-vis an isolationist posture —was dramatic and perhaps inexorable.[69]

Admittedly, the case of the Japanese attack on Pearl Harbor was an exceptional event in the diplomatic history of the United States; fortunately, there has been no real counterpart to it since 1941. Yet there have been countless other episodes in American diplomacy before and after Pearl Harbor that illustrate the same basic behavior pattern by American public opinion. In responding to *any* external crisis involving the security of the United States, public opinion has exhibited certain familiar characteristics. A foreign crisis is likely to "galvanize" public opinion in the United States, causing it suddenly to become deeply involved in, and concerned about, developments overseas. On all sides, the American people are likely to demand that the President "do something" or take decisive action in responding to threats to national security or American lives.[70] During such crises, the people—including their legislative representatives on Capitol Hill—call for decisive "leadership" by the chief executive in protecting the nation's diplomatic and security interests.

Two examples may be cited to illustrate the point. In 1961, the Kennedy Administration undertook the ill-fated "Bay of Pigs" invasion of Cuba;* and in 1980, the Carter Administration employed the armed forces to rescue Americans held hostage in Iran. Both missions failed to achieve their objectives and resulted in diplomatic setbacks for the United States. Yet neither President Kennedy nor President Carter experienced a loss of public support following these failures; and both chief executives were widely applauded for "trying" to defend the nation's diplomatic interests. One student of public opinion has said that a President is "more damned if he fails to act than if he takes [decisive] action" in foreign affairs; in the American people's view, "It is better for a President to act ineptly than to fail to act at all." (Significantly, during periods of external crisis, there is customarily no discernible public demand that Congress provide the diplomatic leadership required.)[71]

In crisis situations, once the President has identified a threat to national security and has called for public support in responding to it, the American people almost invariably give the chief executive the support he requests. Members of the House and Senate are virtually compelled to cooperate with the chief executive and to display "national unity" in the face of a foreign crisis. Accordingly, the President possesses an extremely broad mandate from public opinion to respond to the crisis as he and his advisers think best, with a high degree of confidence that the American people and Congress will support their decision.

Time and again since World War II, in responding to external crises American public opinion has exhibited this general behavior pattern. Specific mention may be made of the Truman Administration's numerous efforts to counter Communist expansionism in the early postwar era (climaxed by President Truman's decision to resist the Communist threat to South Korea in 1950); repeated efforts by the United States to maintain the Western position in Berlin in the face of Soviet threats; the Eisenhower Administration's effort to preserve the independence of Lebanon from what was identified (correctly or not) as a Communist threat against it; both in 1961 and in 1962, the Kennedy Administration's attempts to deal with a Communist threat to hemispheric security posed by the actions of Castro's Cuba; beginning in the mid-1950s, efforts by successive administrations to maintain the security and independence of South Vietnam and other independent nations of Southeast Asia; the Ford Administration's effort to gain the release of American naval personnel captured by the government of Cambodia in the *Mayaguez* affair; and more recently, the Carter Administration's efforts to secure the release of American hostages held prisoner in Iran and, in the same period, to counter the massive Soviet incursion into neighboring Afghanistan.

In such cases, American public opinion has almost always exhibited the characteristics we have identified. It has shown a high degree of concern about the existing foreign policy crisis; it has demanded a response by national leaders that safeguards American diplomatic and security interests; it has given the President virtual *carte blanche* to deal with the crisis as he thinks best under the circumstances; and it has expected him to supply the vigorous leadership demanded by public sen-

*The "Bay of Pigs" episode occurred on April 17, 1961, when a force of some 1200 anti-Castro Cubans, aided and supported by the American government, invaded Cuba in an unsuccessful attempt to overthrow Castro's Communist regime. The failure of the mission was a diplomatic setback for the new Kennedy Administration, although the plan had originally been conceived under the Eisenhower Administration. For more detailed discussion, see Arthur Schlesinger, Jr., *A Thousand Days* (Boston: Houghton Mifflin Co., 1965), pp. 233–267; and Theodore C. Sorensen, *Kennedy* (New York: Harper & Row, 1965), pp. 291–310.

timent. Conversely, public opinion is likely to react negatively toward an incumbent administration that *fails to act* (or gives the appearance of inaction) in responding to an external crisis.[72]

Several other characteristics of American public opinion may be identified more briefly. One of them is highlighted by Earl Ravenal's assessment:

> Not only do the American people speak with many voices [on foreign policy issues], but they also say different things on different days of the week. On odd days, they may think they can maintain ambitious foreign policy goals; on even days, they count costs.

Referring to American viewpoints during the closing stage of the Vietnam War, the commentator referred to the "contradictory mandates" conferred by public opinion upon policy makers of the Nixon Administration. Toward that conflict, the American people wanted their leaders to win "without the necessary means; or get out and be punished. . . . In effect, they [the people] would have told [officials in Washington] to go and make bricks without straw."[73]

As these judgments indicate, American public opinion on foreign policy questions is customarily marked by the existence of *incongruities, ambiguitues, and contradictions*. Citizens want officials in Washington to take a "firm" stand against Communism; but they also support the concept of détente and they call for reductions in the defense budget. Alternatively, Americans often approve the idea that the United States should contribute to meeting the needs of less developed societies; concurrently, however, they call for a reduction in the foreign aid budget. Or, they support the idea that the United States should "cooperate" closely with other countries in the solution of common problems; but they express skepticism about America's reliance or dependence upon the United Nations and other international agencies.

One study accounts for the existence of such dichotomies or contradictions by concluding:

> These seeming contradictions come about because people hold attitudes toward the political system on several different levels. Individuals may hold attitudes simultaneously toward an institution [such as the presidency] as a symbol or an ideal, toward appraisals of particular officeholders and their performance, and toward the general policies carried out by a series of officeholders of the institution. Thus, a [citizen] may hold the office of president in high respect, dislike the current occupant, and still support the basic kinds of policies that the incumbent and his predecessors have advocated.[74]

It may be added that such dichotomies may also arise and be sustained in other instances by the existence of genuine confusion in the public mind about international issues; by the impact upon public thinking of rapidly changing events abroad; and by the precise wording of questions asked of citizens in public opinion surveys.

Another important and related characteristic of public opinion toward both domestic and foreign policy issues is *its highly eclectic and pragmatic aspect*. Traditionally (as we observed at length in Chapter 2), Americans have been a remarkably *nonideological* people, who customarily shun philosophically rigid positions and doctrinaire approaches to public policy questions. Throughout their history, Americans have shunned extremist positions on public policy questions. During the Vietnam War, for example, majority sentiment in the United States could be described as neither clearly "hawkish" nor "dovish" in its approach to the conflict. Some studies have found, for example, that the extreme "dovish," or peace at any price, point of view—often vocally (and sometimes violently) expressed by antiwar groups—in fact *alienated* a majority of the American people, perhaps impelling them to support the government's existing policies toward the war to a degree that they otherwise would not have done![75]

Reflecting the traditionally pragmatic inclinations of the American society, public sentiment toward foreign affairs remains highly eclectic and responsive to conditions at home and abroad. A recent study of American public attitudes in the post-Vietnam War period has documented many of these attitudinal traits. It found that in their approach to the Vietnam conflict and other issues,

> . . . Americans have resisted and rejected many [ideological] Movement ideas . . . . They are for some defense cuts, but will not buy major slashes [in defense spending that are] seen as irresponsible. They do not think America's sun is setting. They do not think America has been a force of malevolence overseas.

During and after Vietnam, American public opinion consistently displayed "an attitudinal accommodation by the massive majority." In their approach to foreign policy questions, "Americans chose eclectically what they thought made sense and rejected what they thought didn't." As in the past, the American people subjected a given idea or proposal in the foreign policy field to one overriding test: "Did it make common sense?" If not, it was unlikely to receive any significant support in American public opinion.[76]

Finally, we must take note of what many informed students of public opinion believe is the essentially "cyclical" nature of popular sentiment in the United States. In the heyday of isolationism before World War II, the American mood was one of "withdrawal" from, and indifference toward, global affairs and of intense preoccupation with domestic issues. The preferred isolationist position was interrupted, however, by interventionist episodes when the American people have supported—and in some instances demanded —efforts by their leaders to use the nation's power abroad for diplomatic purposes. After the interventionist impulse had run its course, the American society usually reverted once again to its cherished isolationist mentality.[77]

After World War II, the United States formally abandoned isolationism as its foreign policy credo and assumed certain enduring commitments in global affairs. Yet even after isolationism had been repudiated, American attitudes toward international relations still exhibited the kind of cyclical quality we have described. On the premise that there are varying degrees—or different kinds—of interventionism or "internationalism," the approach of the American people to external affairs has varied considerably since World War II.

The difference between the period of the Vietnam War and the post-Vietnam era illustrates the point. During the former era, for several years American opinion supported massive efforts by the United States to influence the course of political events in Southeast Asia. After the war, American opinion clearly reflected a "neo-isolationist" frame of mind that lasted until the end of the 1970s.* During this phase, avoiding "another Viet-

*The term *neo-isolationism* is employed here to describe a modified version of the old isolationist point of view that has been exhibited by various prominent individuals and groups in the United States since World War II. The neo-isolationist basically accepts the fact that the United States is a superpower, with important global and regional commitments; but he wishes to keep these obligations *limited,* to reduce some of them, and to be cautious in assuming new ones. For two species (a conservative and liberal version) of this viewpoint, see Cecil V. Crabb, Jr., *Policy-Makers and Critics: Conflicting Theories of American Foreign Policy* (New York: Praeger Publishers, 1976), pp. 214–299.

nam" sometimes appeared to be the motivating impulse of American foreign policy. By 1980, as the result of a series of greater or lesser threats to national security (in Cuba, in Iran, and in Afghanistan), the public temper again changed, exhibiting clear interventionist tendencies in responding to a number of external issues.[78] Even then, however, little public support existed for the kind of *indiscriminate interventionism* witnessed during the 1960s. As one American official said at the end of 1979, after America experienced threats to its security and diplomatic interests in the Middle East, there was public "support for a more interventionist policy—but within limits. This does not mean a blank check for the President to go to war."[79]

Yet in evaluating the cyclical nature of American public attitudes, a point needs to be remembered that was emphasized in Chapter 2. Dissimilar as they may appear, the isolationist and interventionist impulses may well have a common goal. Following the former approach, Americans have traditionally devoted themselves to their desired pursuit—domestic affairs—by ignoring the outside world, under the misconception that events abroad do not affect their well-being directly. In the latter approach, they have sought to achieve basically the same goal by a different method: massive (and usually short lived) interventionism, whereby external problems are "solved" and the overseas environment is transformed into one allowing the American society to concentrate mainly upon its own internal concerns.

As in the old isolationist era, American public opinion continues to display what one commentator calls an "abject contempt" for foreign policy issues. During the 1980s, no less than during the 1930s, citizens exhibit a "strong and pervasive skepticism" toward foreign affairs; and they "see foreign policy as a handicap for democracy." The American

people remain preoccupied with domestic concerns. This propensity, however, overlooks the paradox about the role of public opinion in contemporary American diplomacy:

> ... the more domestic [the American people] are determined to be, the more global they will have to become.... [and] the more global they are determined to be, the more domestic they will have to become.[80]

Or, as former Secretary of State Dean G. Acheson said over a generation ago about the challenging role of American public opinion in the foreign policy process:

> ... it [public involvement in foreign affairs] is a long and tough job and one for which we as a people are not particularly suited. We believe that any problem can be solved with a little ingenuity and without inconvenience to the folks at large. We have trouble-shooters to do this. And our name for problems is significant. We call them headaches. You take a powder and they are gone. These pains about which we have been talking are not like that. They are like the pain of earning a living. They will stay with us until death.[81]

NOTES

1. See the "Introduction" to Norman R. Luttbeg, ed., *Public Opinion and Public Policy: Models of Political Linkage* (Homewood, Ill.: Dorsey Press, 1974), p. 1.

2. Allen D. Monroe, *Public Opinion in America* (New York: Dodd, Mead and Co., 1975), p. 4.

3. President Wilson's views are cited in Sidney Warren, ed., *The President as World Leader* (New York: McGraw-Hill, 1967), p. 97; and Louis W. Koenig, *The Chief Executive*, rev. ed. (New York: Harcourt Brace Jovanovich, 1968), p. 184.

4. Quoted in Joseph E. Kallenbach, *The Ameri-*

can *Chief Executive: The Presidency and the Governorship* (New York: Harper & Row, 1966), p. 370.

5. Quoted in Robert E. Elder, *The Policy Machine* (Syracuse, N.Y.: Syracuse University Press, 1960), p. 137.

6. John S. Dickey, "The Secretary and the American Public," in Don K. Price, ed., *The Secretary of State* (Englewood Cliffs, N.J.: Prentice-Hall, 1960), p. 163.

7. See the discussion of the role of public opinion as it related to American policy toward the Vietnam War in Henry Kissinger, *White House Years* (Boston: Little, Brown and Co., 1979), pp. 288–303, 453–454, 510–517, 1010–1016.

8. See, for example, the assessments by members of Congress of President Carter's performance in domestic and foreign affairs, in *U.S. News and World Report,* **87** (August 13, 1979), 21–23; and the "appeal" by former White House official Theodore C. Sorensen to Carter to "regain control" over foreign policy, in *New York Times,* September 21, 1979.

9. For these and other definitions of public opinion, see Dan Nimmo and Thomas D. Ungs, *American Political Patterns* (Boston: Little, Brown and Co., 1969), pp. 171–173; Daniel Katz, et al., eds., *Public Opinion and Propaganda* (New York: Holt, Rinehart and Winston, 1954), pp. 50–51; and Kimball Young, *Social Psychology* (New York; Appleton-Century-Crofts, 1956), pp. 330–332.

10. The views of Kornhauser and other modern students of public opinion are cited in Bernard C. Hennessy, *Public Opinion* (Belmont, Calif.: Wadsworth Pub. Co., 1965), pp. 97–98.

11. James M. Burns, *Roosevelt: The Lion and the Fox* (New York: Harcourt Brace Jovanovich, 1956), p. 248.

12. See James Chace, "Is a Foreign Policy Consensus Possible?" *Foreign Affairs,* **57** (Fall, 1978), 1–17; and David W. Moore, "The Public is Uncertain," *Foreign Policy,* **35** (Summer, 1979), 68–74.

13. See the views of Thomas L. Hughes, "Liber-

als, Populists, and Foreign Policy," *Foreign Policy,* **20** (Fall, 1975), 102; and of Smith Simpson, *Anatomy of the State Department* (Boston: Houghton Mifflin, 1967), p. 194.

14. Barry B. Hughes, *The Domestic Context of American Foreign Policy* (San Francisco: W. H. Freeman, 1978), p. 199.

15. See the estimates in the study of public opinion in the Chicago area in: John E. Rielly, ed., *American Public Opinion and U.S. Foreign Policy: 1975* (Chicago: Chicago Council on Foreign Relations, 1975), p. 8; and Hughes, *The Domestic Context of American Foreign Policy,* pp. 23–24.

16. See the article by Roger Morris, in *New York Times,* January 29, 1980.

17. Ralph B. Levering, *The Public and American Foreign Policy: 1918–1978* (New York: William Morrow and Co., 1978), pp. 152–153. This is an illuminating study of public attitudes, calling attention to the change in public viewpoints from the isolationist to the interventionist period in American diplomacy.

18. For further discussion of the elite or "informed" segment of American public opinion and its impact upon the policy process, see Hughes, *The Domestic Context of American Foreign Policy,* pp. 23–24; Rielly, ed., *American Public Opinion and U.S. Foreign Policy: 1975,* p. 8; and Ronald J. Stupal, *American Foreign Policy: Assumptions, Processes, and Projections* (New York: Harper & Row, 1976), p. 81.

19. For the viewpoint of intellectuals toward American foreign policy—and the impact of the Vietnam War upon this stratum of public opinion—see Simpson, *Anatomy of the State Department,* p. 194; and Irving Kristol, "American Intellectuals and Foreign Policy," *Foreign Affairs,* **45** (July, 1967), 594–610.

20. The conviction that the American government—particularly Congress—is more susceptible to the influence of lobbies today than in the past has been expressed by a number of qualified observers. See, for example, the viewpoints of the former chairman of the Senate Foreign Relations Committee, ex-Senator J. William Fulbright, in "The Legis-

lator as Educator," *Foreign Affairs,* **57** (Spring, 1979), 719–733.

21. R. Joseph Monsen, Jr., and Mark W. Cannon, *The Makers of Public Policy: American Power Groups and Their Ideologies* (New York: McGraw-Hill, 1965), p. 1.

22. The view that American business and commercial (often joined by agricultural) interests had a decisive impact upon American diplomacy in the twentieth century is the theme of William Appleman Williams, *The Tragedy of American Diplomacy* (Cleveland, Ohio: World Publishing Co., 1959). Other informed students of American foreign relations believe that the study greatly exaggerates the impact of these pressure groups upon the nation's external policies.

23. See *Legislators and Lobbyists* (Washington, D.C.: Congressional Quarterly, 1965), p. 11.

24. Hughes, *The Domestic Context of American Foreign Policy,* p. 157.

25. Ibid., pp. 158–159.

26. The evolution of America's relations with China in the late eighteenth and early nineteenth centuries, emphasizing the role of business and commercial interests in them, is traced out in: John K. Fairbank, *The United States and China* (Cambridge, Mass.: Harvard University Press, 1958); Foster Rhea Dulles, *China and America* (Princeton, N.J.: Princeton University Press, 1946); and Thomas H. Etzold, ed., *Aspects of Sino-American Relations Since 1784* (New York: Franklin Watts, 1978).

27. For a detailed discussion of the political influence of international business corporations, see Abdul A. Said and Luiz R. Simmons, eds., *The New Sovereigns: Multinational Corporations as World Powers* (Englewood Cliffs, N.J.: Prentice-Hall, 1975). A briefer treatment is Joan E. Spero, *The Politics of International Economic Relations* (New York: St. Martin's Press, 1977), pp. 88–121. For a discussion of the role of multinational corporations in the recent political affairs of Latin America, see Richard W. Mansbach, et al., *The Web of World Politics: Nonstate Actors*

in the Global System (Englewood Cliffs, N.J.: Prentice-Hall, 1976), pp. 189–213.

28. Lobbying activities by labor organizations in foreign relations is the subject of the study by Ronald Radosh, *American Labor and United States Foreign Policy* (New York: Random House, 1969). See also the symposium on "Labor's International Role," *Foreign Policy,* **26** (Spring, 1977), 204–246.

29. Hughes, *The Domestic Context of American Foreign Policy,* p. 165.

30. Other examples of lobbying by labor organizations are cited in ibid., pp. 165–167; and in *Legislators and Lobbyists,* pp. 5–7.

31. Agricultural dimensions of post-World War II foreign policy are highlighted in: "The Question of Changing U.S. Food Export Policy," *Congressional Digest,* **53** (December, 1954), 289–314; Donald F. McHenry and Kai Bird, "Food Bungle in Bangladesh," *Foreign Policy,* **27** (Summer, 1977), 72–89; and Raymond F. Hopkins, "How to Make Food Work," ibid., 89–109.

32. Our discussion of lobbying activities by agricultural groups in the foreign policy sphere draws from Monsen and Cannon, *The Makers of Public Policy,* pp. 102–108; and from Hughes, *The Domestic Context of American Foreign Policy,* pp. 168–169.

33. President Eisenhower's views on the political influence of the Military-Industrial Complex are set forth in Dwight D. Eisenhower, *Waging Peace: 1956–1961* (Garden City, N.Y.: Doubleday and Co., 1965), pp. 614–616. Interpretive studies of the phenomenon are: George Thayer, *The War Business* (New York: Avon Books, 1969); Ralph Lapp, *The Weapons Culture* (Baltimore: Penguin Books, 1969); and *The Power of the Pentagon* (Washington, D.C.: Congressional Quarterly, 1972).

34. Current examples of efforts by groups associated with the Military-Industrial Complex to influence the national defense budget are available in the annual volumes of the *Congressional Quarterly Almanac* and in the *Congressional Quarterly Weekly Report.*

35. See Samuel Lubell, *The Future of American Politics* (New York: Harper & Row, 1952), pp. 132–148.

36. R. M. MacIver, ed., *Group Relations and Group Antagonisms* (New York: Harper & Row, 1944), p. 37. See particularly the chapter in this study by Max Ascoli dealing with the viewpoints of Italian-Americans.

37. In his efforts to protect the freedom and independence of Poland from Soviet hegemony during and after World War II, President Franklin D. Roosevelt at one point informed Soviet Premier Stalin, "... I have several million Poles in the U.S., a great many of whom are in the Army and Navy." He and other American officials repeatedly cautioned Stalin that they felt obliged to represent the viewpoints of Polish-American citizens who demanded independence for Poland after the Axis defeat. See Martin F. Herz, *Beginnings of the Cold War* (New York: McGraw-Hill, 1966), pp. 36, 47, 51–52.

38. A worthwhile study of the influence of the Irish-American minority is Carl Wittke, *The Irish in America* (Baton Rouge, La.: Louisiana State University Press, 1956), p. 105 and *passim*.

39. The viewpoints of Irish-Americans on specific diplomatic issues is treated in Thomas A. Bailey, *Woodrow Wilson and the Great Betrayal* (New York: Macmillan Co., 1945), pp. 24–27; Wittke, *The Irish in America*, pp. 163, 288–291; and Cordell Hull, *The Memoirs of Cordell Hull*, II (New York: Macmillan Co., 1948), p. 718.

40. See the analysis of efforts by individuals and groups supporting the cause of Northern Ireland to influence governmental and public viewpoints in the United States by Bernard Weinraub, in *New York Times*, September 21, 1979.

41. See the "Introduction," in George W. Shepherd, Jr., ed., *Racial Influences on American Foreign Policy* (New York: Basic Books, 1970), p. 5. For a discussion of black American opinion on United States policy toward Africa, see the symposium on "African Policy and Black Americans," *Foreign Policy,* **15** (Summer, 1974), 109–152.

42. *The Congressional Quarterly Weekly Report,* **37** (December 1, 1979), 2703.

43. The role and ultimate dismissal of Andrew Young as ambassador to the United Nations is discussed in Cecil V. Crabb, Jr., and Pat Holt, *Invitation to Struggle: Congress, the President and Foreign Policy* (Washington, D.C.: Congressional Quarterly, 1980), p. 98; and in *U.S. News and World Report,* **84** (June 19, 1978), 37–39.

44. See the discussion of Israeli-Egyptian-American peace negotiations in *Newsweek,* **93** (March 12, 1979), 24–25.

45. *The Washington Lobby* (Washington, D.C.: Congressional Quarterly, 1971), p. 29.

46. A wealth of data about foreign lobbying activities in the United States is available in the Senate Foreign Relations Committee, *Activities of Non-Diplomatic Representatives of Foreign Principals in the United States.* 88th Cong., 1st Sess., 1963. The quotation is from pp. 2–3.

47. See the discussion of the Cyprus question in ex-President Gerald R. Ford's memoirs, *A Time to Heal* (New York: Harper & Row, and The Reader's Digest Association, 1979), pp. 137–138, 199. A detailed discussion of the Cyprus crisis is provided in Laurence Stern, "How We Failed in Cyprus," *Foreign Policy,* **19** (Summer, 1975), 34–79.

48. For discussions of these and other foreign efforts to influence American diplomacy in recent years, see the discussion of "foreign pressures" and of several case studies involving lobbying by foreign interests in *The Washington Lobby* (Washington, D.C.: Congressional Quarterly, 1971), pp. 29–35, 75–93; and "Middle East Lobbying," *Congressional Quarterly Weekly Report,* **39** (April 22, 1981), 1523–1530.

49. A detailed description of lobbying by government agencies is contained in *The Washington Lobby,* 3rd ed. (Washington, D.C.: Congressional Quarterly, 1979). President Johnson's views of the importance of legislative liaison

are contained in his memoirs, *The Vantage Point: Perspectives of the Presidency, 1963–1969* (New York: Holt, Rinehart and Winston, 1971), pp. 322–324; 440–444.

50. See the analyses of the Carter Administration's relations with Congress by Steven V. Roberts, in *New York Times,* August 5, 1979; by *Washington Post* reporter Barry Sussman, in the Baton Rouge *Morning Advocate,* August 5, 1979; and by James Reston, in *New York Times,* April 25, 1980.

51. For a detailed discussion of the alliance between governmental and private groups that lobbied in behalf of the new Panama Canal treaties, see Crabb and Holt, *Invitation to Struggle: Congress, the President and Foreign Policy,* pp. 65–89.

52. For the text of this letter to President Ford, see *New York Times,* January 16, 1975. Our discussion of the nature and activities of the Zionist lobby draws heavily from: *The Middle East: U.S. Policy, Israel, Oil and the Arabs,* rev. ed. (Washington, D.C.: Congressional Quarterly, 1980), pp. 89–95; and Crabb and Holt, *Invitation to Struggle,* pp. 89–113.

53. Arab viewpoints toward the United States and other Western countries—a central theme of which is the lack of understanding in the West about Islam and modern Arab nationalism —are identified and discussed in: Charles D. Cremeans, *The Arabs and the World* (New York: Praeger Publishers, 1963), pp. 47–66; H. P. Castelberry, "Arabs' View of Postwar American Foreign Policy," *Western Political Quarterly,* **12** (March, 1959), 9–36; and Mohammed T. Mehdi, *A Nation of Lions . . . Chained: An Arab Looks at America* (San Francisco: New World Press, 1962). A recent reiteration of this idea is contained in the informative study by G. H. Jansen, *Militant Islam* (New York: Harper & Row, 1979), pp. 49–86.

54. See Zvi Ganin, *Truman, American Jewry, and Israel, 1945–1948* (New York: Holmes and Neier Publishers, 1979), especially pp. 99–109.

55. The nature and influence of the Arab lobby in the United States are described in *The Middle East: U.S. Policy, Israel, Oil and the Arabs,* pp. 96–100.

56. For evidence of changing American attitudes toward Israel, and toward the Palestine controversy, see the poll data contained in Rielly, ed., *American Public Opinion and U.S. Foreign Policy: 1975,* pp. 16–20; Daniel Yankelovich, "Farewell to 'President Knows Best,'" *Foreign Affairs,* **57** (Special Issue, 1978), 682–684; the Gallup Poll, reproduced in the Baton Rouge *Morning Advocate,* January 28, 1979; and the *New York Times/ CBS News* survey, in *New York Times,* November 8, 1979.

57. See the views of Seth T. Tillman, as quoted in *The Middle East: U.S. Policy, Israel, Oil and the Arabs,* p. 100.

58. The "new agenda" of international relations in the years ahead was emphasized by former Secretary of State Henry Kissinger. For his views, and a discussion of the implications of this new agenda, see Joseph S. Nye, Jr., "Independence and Interdependence," *Foreign Policy,* **22** (Spring, 1976), 129–162. For a more detailed analysis of emerging issues in global politics, see Dennis Pirages, *Global Ecopolitics: the New Context for International Relations* (North Scituate, Mass.: Duxbury Press, 1978).

59. For more extended discussion of internal changes in the membership and procedures of Congress, see Crabb and Holt, *Invitation to Struggle,* pp. 50–56, 191–199.

60. Elder, *The Policy Machine,* pp. 142–143, 147.

61. Dickey, "The Secretary and the American Public," pp. 140–142.

62. See the Gallup Poll findings showing public sentiment toward the Iranian crisis in: *Newsweek,* **95** (May 5, 1980), 24–26; and the Baton Rouge *Morning Advocate,* May 1, 1980.

63. See Dickey, "The Secretary and the American Public," pp. 142–147.

64. Simpson, *Anatomy of the State Department,* pp. 184–205; and Elder, *The Policy Machine,* pp. 131–146.

65. The crucial distinction (sometimes forgotton by recent critics of American foreign policy) between government directly *by* the people and government *by representatives of the people* is a major theme of an older, but still relevant, analysis of the interaction between public opinion and governmental policy. See Walter Lippmann, *The Public Philosophy* (Boston: Little, Brown and Co., 1955).

66. See the discussion of the Panama Canal treaties as a case study in recent American diplomacy, in Crabb and Holt, *Invitation to Struggle*, pp. 65–89.

67. Levering, *The Public and American Foreign Policy*, p. 161.

68. The wide latitude possessed by executive officials to formulate and administer foreign policy, without seriously offending public sentiment, is perhaps the major finding in the analysis by Bernard C. Cohen, *The Public's Impact on Foreign Policy* (Boston: Little, Brown and Co., 1973). Thus, Cohen concludes that an incumbent President finds it relatively "easy most of the time to ignore public preferences when he cannot otherwise mobilize or neutralize them." The chances that the President and other executive officials will lose political support or suffer other adverse effects because of public opposition to their foreign policies are "very slim, so slim that we cannot seriously treat it as an operative sanction" inhibiting their diplomatic moves. See especially p. 186.

69. One of America's most influential voices on foreign affairs in the post-World War II period—Senator Arthur H. Vandenberg (Republican of Michigan)—described December 7, 1941, as the day that "ended isolationism" for Americans. See his discussion of his own "conversion" to an internationalist point of view after that event, in Arthur H. Vandenberg, Jr., ed., *The Private Papers of Senator Vandenberg* (Boston: Houghton Mifflin Co., 1952), pp. 1–21.

70. See, for example, the analysis of American public sentiment toward recent wars and lesser conflicts in which the United States has been engaged, in John E. Mueller, *War, Presidents and Public Opinion* (New York: John Wiley and Sons, 1973), particularly pp. 208–213.

71. W. Lance Bennett, *Public Opinion in American Politics* (New York: Harcourt Brace Jovanovich, 1980), pp. 353–354; and see Monroe, *Public Opinion in America*, pp. 165–167, 215–226.

72. During his tenure in the White House, President Jimmy Carter confronted public dissatisfaction about his failure to act decisively in meeting internal and external challenges. For evidence of public attitudes, see "Carter: Running with the Leadership Issue," *Congressional Quarterly Weekly Report*, **37** (October 13, 1979), 2267–2274; and the views of Louis Harris, Burns Roper, and other informed students of American public opinion, in *U.S. News and World Report*, **87** (August 27, 1979), 20.

73. Earl C. Ravenal, "Nixon's Challenge to Carter," *Foreign Policy*, **29** (Winter, 1977–78), 37.

74. Monroe, *Public Opinion in America*, p. 164.

75. See the analysis of American public opinion toward the Vietnam War in ibid., pp. 199–216.

76. Ben J. Wattenberg, *The Real America: A Surprising Examination of the State of the Union* (Garden City, N.Y.: Doubleday and Co., 1974), pp. 203–213. See also Monroe, *Public Opinion in America*, pp. 200–202.

77. The cyclical nature of American public opinion as it relates to foreign affairs is the theme of F. L. Klingberg, "The Historical Alternation of Moods in American Foreign Policy," *World Politics*, **4** (January, 1952), 239–273. See also the discussion of the isolationist viewpoint, and of the impulse toward "liberal and humanitarian interventionism," in Cecil V. Crabb, Jr., *Policy-Makers and Critics: Conflicting Theories of American Foreign Policy* (New York: Praeger Publishers, 1976), pp. 1–81.

78. For the change in the mood of the American people at the end of 1979 and in early

1980—when diplomatic and national security issues once again dominated public consciousness—see Martin Tolchin in *New York Times,* January 23, 1980; and the evidence contained in public opinion surveys in *U.S. News and World Report,* **87** (December 10, 1979), 21–24.

79. See the views of an unnamed executive official, whose views are cited in *U.S. News and*

World Report, **87** (December 10, 1979), 24.

80. Thomas L. Hughes, "Liberals, Populists, and Foreign Policy," *Foreign Policy,* **20** (Fall, 1975), 102.

81. Former Secretary of State Dean Acheson's views on the role of public opinion in foreign relations are quoted in Stupak, *American Foreign Policy,* p. 53.

Chapter 9

Soviet-American Relations:
The Cold War Era

For a quarter-century after World War II, the omnipresent reality dominating the international environment was Soviet-American hostility. Then, after a brief interlude of détente between the superpowers (discussed more fully in Chapter 10), by the early 1980s, Soviet-American relations were once again characterized by rising tensions and mutual suspicions.

Labeled the "Cold War" in the late 1940s, this contest extended into virtually every quarter of the globe and affected almost all other major and minor international issues. The economic recovery and defense of Western Europe; the political development of societies in Eastern Europe; the ability of the Arabs and Israelis to settle their longstanding differences; the economic development of Africa; the provision of American, Soviet, Chinese, and European economic assistance to needy societies; the stability of Asia; the effort to reduce worldwide expenditures for armaments and the diversion of at least some of these funds for peaceful, more constructive

purposes; the success of the United Nations—all these and many more significant issues were directly affected by the condition of Soviet-American relations.

This is not to suggest of course that serious international problems would not have existed in the absence of the Cold War. By the 1980s, it was apparent that certain other global issues—like the population explosion, the world food shortage, and the concern of needy societies with national development—were tending to overshadow the Soviet-American rivalry as a source of acute international concern. Yet the Cold War was perhaps *the* principal challenge to international stability and peace after World War II. For example, under the Reagan Administration, Soviet-American military competition—and deep American concern about the diplomatic implications of growing Soviet military power—had again emerged as a paramount issue in the foreign policy of the United States.

The decade of the 1980s witnessed an intensification in the long-standing tensions between the United States and the Soviet Union, after Moscow carried out a massive military invasion of Afghanistan late in 1979. Responding to that Soviet move, President Jimmy Carter labeled the Soviet incursion into Afghanistan as the most serious threat to global peace since the end of World War II. In this and other locales (such as East Africa and Cuba), tensions continued to characterize relations between the superpowers. Those officials and citizens who imagined that the era of the Cold War had ended had been compelled by events to rethink their conclusions.

What precisely was this conflict that had come to be known as the Cold War? What were the stakes at issue between the two superpowers, the United States and the Soviet Union? How did the contest arise? What were the objectives on each side? How did one side respond to moves by the other? The dominant global problem of the contemporary era cannot be understood without an effort to answer such questions. Authoritative evidence was often unavailable to explain why the Kremlin periodically launched a war of nerves against the Western position in Berlin, or to account fully for America's implication in the campaign against Communist groups in Iran in the late 1940s. Relevant materials often remained locked in the archives of the Kremlin or the State Department. The student of international relations was compelled to depend upon official statements, journalist accounts, secondary sources, and the like; his conclusions about Washington's or Moscow's intentions frequently consisted of inferences and suppositions, and (perhaps most unsatisfactory) efforts to divine the true motives of policy makers in both countries. Even that final authority, the "historian of the future," will probably be confronted with some insoluble problems related to the Cold War, particularly those involving what might be viewed as the

"irrational" nature of Soviet behavior or deciding what President Truman really had in mind when he proclaimed the Truman Doctrine early in 1947. Even when additional source materials become available, the *motives* and *true intentions* of decision makers are likely to remain a subject of intense controversy.

The starting point of our inquiry into the origins and nature of the Cold War is a subject too often neglected by the American people (not excluding many of their officials in the executive and legislative branches). At the outset, some attention needs to be devoted to certain *traditional and historic goals and methods of Russian foreign policy* that antedate the Communist Revolution of 1917. The more Soviet behavior in global affairs since World War II is examined, the more it becomes evident that what we have chosen to call the "enduring goals" of Russian diplomacy continue to motivate Moscow's external policies and create tensions for Soviet-American relations.

Enduring Goals of Russian Foreign Policy

The Centrality of Historical Insights

Engraved upon the National Archives building in Washington are the words: "What Is Past Is Prologue." These words serve as an appropriate introduction to the subject of Russia's diplomatic behavior before 1917. Americans venerate their past; they "commemorate" outstanding events from their own history on innumerable occasions. It may be questioned, however, whether they are inclined to view the past "as prologue," at least insofar as the Cold War is concerned. To many citizens, that conflict began no earlier than the closing months of World War II, when the Red Army overran Eastern Europe; for others, perhaps, it really started when Lenin seized control of the Russian government in 1917, imposing a Communist system upon it and launching the U.S.S.R. on the path of world domination. All too willingly (if unintentionally), large numbers of Americans have accepted the Kremlin's view: that Russia under Marxism became a totally new state, whose goals and methods bore no relation to Czarist regimes or to other non-Communist systems.

Yet, as we have suggested, history shows a remarkable continuity in Russia's external behavior, irrespective of its system of government or ideology. At this stage, two examples must suffice. (Others will become apparent as our discussion proceeds.)

Is world domination believed to be the cardinal diplomatic goal of the Kremlin? "A strange superstition prevails among the Russians, that they are destined to conquer the world . . . ," said a State Department dispatch in the mid-nineteenth century.[1] And is the Kremlin thought by the West to be utterly unprincipled in its dealings with other countries, so much so that its promises are looked upon as worthless? A Russian historian once described Czarist diplomacy as follows:

> The diplomatic methods of the Muscovite boyars often threw the foreign envoys into desperation, particularly those who wanted to carry on their business forthrightly and conscientiously. . . . [I]n order not to fall into their nets it was not enough to make certain that they were lying; it was also necessary to decide what the purpose of the lie was; and what was one to do then? If someone caught them lying, they did not blush and they answered all reproaches with a laugh.[2]

At the time of the Russo-Japanese War in 1905, Theodore Roosevelt declared that "Russia is so corrupt, so treacherous and shifty . . . that I am utterly unable to say whether or not it will make peace, or break off negotiations at any moment."[3]

These examples are cited at the beginning of our study of Russian-American relations to stress the importance of setting contemporary Cold War problems within the requisite historical context. Americans are prone to think of the Cold War as a conflict between Soviet Communism and Western democracy. Ideological elements are unquestionably present. Yet such an oversimplified approach gives rise to many dangers and misapprehensions. Students of foreign policy must not jump to the conclusion that Russian diplomacy before 1917 is unrelated to present-day Soviet diplomatic behavior. They must be skeptical of the viewpoint—a cardinal article of faith in the Communist creed—that Marxist-Leninist-Stalinist ideological compulsions furnish the most useful keys to understanding Russia's activities in the international community since 1917. They must not try to arrive at a guide to Soviet diplomatic conduct merely by piecing together the utterances and writings of high-ranking Communist spokesmen.*

What is basic for understanding Soviet diplomatic goals and methods at any stage is not so much what Lenin or Stalin or lesser Communist luminaries have *said* Soviet Rus-

---

*A number of studies of Soviet foreign policy in the recent period implicitly foster such a view. One outstanding example is Nathan Leites' work, *A Study of Bolshevism* (New York: Free Press, 1953). This is a thorough and valuable compendium of Communist doctrinal statements on a variety of subjects. Leites attempts, as it were, to provide a kind of "code" to the behavior of the Kremlin in world affairs. Yet, by focusing almost entirely upon ideological influences, this study inherently suggests that motivations arising from historical, geographical, strategic factors—not to mention the Soviet Union's day-by-day response to developments in the outside world—are relatively unimportant in explaining the U.S.S.R.'s diplomacy. As we shall see in this chapter and the next, this seems at best a highly questionable assumption.

sia was doing or going to do in world affairs, but rather what Russia has in fact *done* in both the Czarist and in the Communist periods. The creation of "People's Democracies" by the bayonets of the Red Army in Eastern Europe does not differ from old-style Czarist imperialism in the same area merely because Stalin baptized his hegemony with quotations from Marx and Lenin. The Czars could invoke a variety of slogans too, such as "legitimacy" and Pan-Slavism, to justify what was in essence *Machtpolitik*.

Age-old Russian foreign policy goals and methods, blended and overlaid with Communist ideological compulsions, provide the key to the foreign policies of the Kremlin. More and more since 1917, Soviet Russia has given evidence of diplomatic atavism, a characteristic which is not, of course, peculiar with Russia. One of the most fascinating aspects of Soviet diplomacy is the degree to which Stalin and his successors have ingeniously fused the historic diplomatic ambitions of Old Russia with the Communist faith. Because Americans generally give insufficient attention to the historical elements of Russian foreign policy, we shall devote considerable space here to analyzing them.

Expansionism—The Keynote of Historic Russian Policy

A newspaper reporter during the Crimean War in the mid-1850s wrote of Russia:

> The Russian frontier has advanced: towards Berlin, Dresden and Vienna . . . towards Constantinople . . . towards Stockholm . . . towards Teheran. . . . The total acquisitions of Russia during the last 60 years are equal in extent and importance to the whole Empire she had in Europe before that time.

And in another dispatch the same reporter declared that:

> And as sure as conquest follows conquest, and annexation follows annexation, so sure would the conquest of Turkey by Russia be only the prelude for the annexation of Hungary, Prussia, Galicia, and for the ultimate realization of the Slavonic Empire. . . . The arrest of the Russian scheme of annexation is a matter of the highest moment.

So wrote a German correspondent —Karl Marx—who was to have no little influence on the future course of Russian history.[4] The word that best characterizes Russian foreign policy throughout history and furnishes the most evident and important link between Russia's past and present policies in the international community is the word *expansionism*. Beginning as an insignificant twelfth-century city in the valley of the Dnieper, by the post-World War II period Moscow was the center of an empire that embraced one-fourth of the human race and 13 million square miles.[5]

The saga of Imperial Russia was a story of almost uninterrupted territorial expansion, initially over the great Eurasian plain that stretches from Poland and European Russia to the borders of Persia, India, and China; and then, after the plain had been occupied and consolidated, of continual pressure against the natural boundaries that surround Russia, such as the Dardanelles, the Himalayas, the deserts of Central Asia, and the river systems of Manchuria.

Patiently, bit by bit, successive Czars pushed back the boundaries of Russia, and in doing so they sometimes created troublesome international problems. Peter the Great finally won the long-coveted "window on the West" when he wrested much of the Baltic region from Sweden; Catherine the Great participated in Poland's three partitions, in 1772, 1793, and 1795, and pushed Russian frontiers steadily southward to encroach upon the Turkish

Empire. Her successors continued the march southward and eastward by maintaining pressure against the frontiers of Turkey, Persia, Afghanistan, and India—generating the "Eastern Question," one of the most vexatious diplomatic issues during the nineteenth century. At Tilsit in 1807, Alexander I and Napoleon attempted to divide most of Europe between them. And after Napoleon's defeat, Alexander annexed Poland, Finland, and Bessarabia, and engaged in intrigues in virtually every country in Europe. Nicholas I and Alexander II sponsored explorations and colonization movements eastward into Central Asia and Siberia, bringing Russia ultimately into conflict with Japanese and, to a lesser extent, British and American diplomatic ambitions in the Orient.

It is instructive to recall Czarist territorial ambitions at the beginning of World War I. Had Imperial Russia been victorious, it expected to push its territory westward to incorporate what was the Poland of 1919–1939; annex East Prussia and all of the area west of the Vistula; annex Eastern Galicia; overthrow the defunct Turkish government and realize Russia's ancient ambition to control the Straits; and annex Turkish territories bordering Transcaucasia.[6]

Czarist expansionism derived from several impulses. First of all, Russia pushed inexorably across the Eurasian plain in much the same way as Americans trekked across their continent. Prince Michael Gorchakov wrote of his country's history that Russia, in common with all countries, was "forced to take the road of expansion dictated by necessity rather than by ambitions, a road on which the chief difficulty is to know where to stop."[7] The tendency to expand into territorial vacuums is not a peculiarly Soviet, nor even Czarist, trait.

Second, the expansionist tendencies of the Czarist state sprang in part from politico-strategic necessities. The vast, frontierless Eurasian plain facilitated Russian internal expansionism, but it also greatly aided foreign incursions into the interior of Russia. Historically, the response of the Czarist state was to provide for defense in depth by creating an extensive buffer zone around its vulnerable geographic heartland. Safeguarding the military approaches to the interior has been a cardinal principle of Russian diplomacy since the time of Peter the Great.

This historic propensity is closely related to a paramount goal of Soviet foreign policy that, according to George F. Kennan and other leading students of Russian diplomacy, continues to motivate the external behavior of the Soviet state. This is Russia's age-old concern about, and desire for, *security from possible foreign threats*. As we shall see, the idea that Soviet foreign policy since World War II has been actuated by a determination to promote national security is a conspicuous theme in the "re-examinist" interpretation of the Cold War. This dominant impulse in Soviet diplomacy, for example, was identified by Kennan as the primary explanation for Moscow's military incursion into Afghanistan at the end of 1979. As Kennan analyzed it, the Kremlin had recently become profoundly disturbed by certain American moves (like the improvement in NATO's defenses and the Carter Administration's decision to increase national defense spending); and Communist policy makers were perhaps also apprehensive about recent developments in the Middle East—such as a resurgence of Islam and the U.S.S.R.'s exclusion from the process of Israeli-Egyptian peace negotiations—leading the Kremlin to protect the security of its borders adjacent to the Persian Gulf area.*

---

*Following a massive Soviet military incursion into Afghanistan at the end of 1979, and the buildup of Soviet forces in the country thereafter, George F. Kennan, former State Department official and perhaps America's

Third, expansionism by the nineteenth century came to have an economic rationale. Russia, along with the other great powers, wanted a stake in foreign markets, to increase both the treasury and Russian prestige. The search for colonies led primarily to Manchuria, where Russian imperialism clashed with the territorial and economic ambitions of Japan, England, and the United States. As was true of American and British imperialism, economic concessions necessitated protection by Russian diplomats and soldiers.

Fourth, a recurrent motif in Russian expansionism was the "historic mission" of Russia to deliver lesser people from their cultural and spiritual backwardness and to usher in the earthly millennium. Since we shall examine Russian messianic thought in a later portion of the chapter, we shall merely observe here that the messianic aspirations of certain secular and religious thinkers within Russia coincided perfectly at several points

with the diplomatic ambitions of the Czarist state. The foreign policies of Alexander I (1801–1825) illustrate the point. Alexander exhibited a calculating Machiavellianism, combined with a fervent and mystic idealism. He was capable of both the Treaty of Tilsit (1807), whereby he and Napoleon divided Europe between them; and of the high-minded, if totally impractical, Holy Alliance (1815), in which Christian principles were to be made the basis of international conduct. Europeans, writes a contemporary British historian, must have wondered whether Alexander was not "just a cunning hypocrite, cultivating liberal sympathies and evangelical piety as a cloak to hide vast plans of aggressive ambitions. . . ." He was apt to "identify his own interest, or whims, with the good of humanity." Professing that all men ought to be free—at the very time he was annexing Poland, Finland, and Bessarabia—Alexander "desired all men to be free on condition they did what he wanted them to do."[8]

The Search for Warm Water Ports

Closely related to expansionism is Russia's age-old search for warm water ports. Landlocked around most of its borders, Russia has always needed accessible and usable outlets to the sea. The ports of Murmansk, Archangel, and Leningrad are icebound a considerable portion of the year. To the south, Russian traffic on the Black Sea has always been at the mercy of Turkey, which controls the Dardanelles, or Turkey's protectors, such as Great Britain and, to a lesser degree, France during the eighteenth and nineteenth centuries. Since 1947, the United States has filled the vacuum created by the decline of British power in the Straits area and throughout the Near and Middle East as a whole.

South and eastward, Russian diplomacy

---

leading Kremlinologist, believed that deep feelings of insecurity prompted Communist policy makers to take this step. In Kennan's view, a "war atmosphere" had been created between the superpowers, primarily by the United States. For many years, as Kennan assessed the matter, the Kremlin was more preoccupied "with problems that confront them" than with "plans for [America's] undoing." He believed that the Soviet hierarchy faced "very serious and growing internal problems," and that Moscow's venture into Afghanistan was mainly a "defensive" policy move; it posed no imminent or long-range threat to the Persian Gulf area or to American security—provided the United States did not overreact to it and escalate Cold War tensions. The main threat to American security in the region was not the Soviet Union, but America's own "self-created dependence on Arab oil and our involvement in a wholly unstable Israeli-Arab relationship, neither of which is susceptible of correction by purely military means, and in neither of which is the Soviet Union a factor." Kennan's views on Soviet diplomacy in Afghanistan was actively contested by officials of the Carter Administration. See *New York Times*, February 1, 1980; *U.S. News and World Report*, **88** (March 10, 1980), 33–34; and *Newsweek*, **95** (February 11, 1980), 42–43.

has sought to force a breakthrough to the sea by intermittent pressure upon Persia, Afghanistan, and India. In addition to furnishing rich prizes to incorporate into the Russian Empire, acquisition of passageways through these countries would give Russia access to the trade routes of the world. The modern American policy of containment had its origins along the Persian-Russian border and in the bleak hills of the northwest frontier in India during the nineteenth century. A dominant objective of British diplomacy during the age of *Pax Britannica* was to prevent Russian penetration of the Middle East. Throughout British colonial history, Russia was continually probing soft spots in the British defense perimeter and endeavoring to enlist other people, such as the Afghan tribesmen along the Indian frontiers, to further Russia's diplomatic ambitions.

Still further eastward, Russia advanced over Siberia and Central Asia toward the shores of the Pacific. The Czars at last acquired outlets to the sea when they obtained or leased ports in Siberia and Manchuria late in the nineteenth century. With the completion of the Trans-Siberian Railroad by 1900, these ports became useful, although they were icebound a goodly part of the year, were extremely vulnerable to foreign attack (as the Russo-Japanese War proved) and even though they were some 6000 miles from European Russia. Russia's search for eastern seaports, coupled with the necessity to assure their accessibility over the railroads of north China, inevitably drew it into the maelstrom of great-power imperialistic rivalry in the Far East.[9]

Are Soviet policy makers today still seeking outlets to the sea? The question hardly requires an answer. Soviet incorporation of the Baltic states; intermittent pressure on Turkey to give the U.S.S.R. a larger voice in safeguarding the Turkish Straits and determining policy toward them; Communist intrigue in the northern provinces of Iran in 1946; support for the Greek rebels in 1946–1947; more recent economic blandishments to Afghanistan, India, and Burma; Communist machinations in Syria, Egypt, and other Middle Eastern countries—all of these indicate that there has been little diminution in the traditional Russian urge to reach the sea. Some students of Soviet foreign policy were convinced that Moscow's penetration of, and attempt to subjugate, Afghanistan at the end of 1979 was a contemporary manifestation of this historic diplomatic impulse. As we observed in Chapter 5, one of the Kremlin's current military objectives—the creation of a large and powerful ocean-going navy—almost inescapably dictates a revival of this traditional Russian diplomatic goal.

The "Iron Curtain Complex"

When Winston Churchill stated in 1946 that an iron curtain had descended over Europe, he was coining a phrase that applied equally well to earlier stages in the history of Russia's relations with Europe. An "iron curtain complex" has been characteristic of the Russian attitude toward the outside world for centuries. When a *cordon sanitaire* or formidable geographical barriers did not effectively seal Russia off from contact with its neighbors, then a spiritual iron curtain has done so during most periods of Russian history. Estrangement and hostility took many forms: rigorous government censorship of ideas and communications from abroad; limited contacts between Russian citizens and foreigners; official coolness, amounting often to outright discrimination, toward foreign diplomats in Russia; belief in the inherent superiority of Russian customs and institutions; and unwillingness to cultivate sincere and lasting ties of friendship with other countries. With some significant exceptions, almost every period of Russian history has exhibited a deep-seated xenophobia.*

In pre-Soviet history many factors engendered suspicion and hostility toward the outside world. In some periods, like the late nineteenth and early twentieth centuries, Russia was militarily much weaker than other countries suspected. The Russo-Japanese War and World War I showed this. Furthermore, Russia was economically backward. The contrast between its rate of industrialization and standard of living and that of its advanced Western neighbors was a source of constant embarrassment and insecurity. Moreover, under both the Czars and the Communists, Russia has feared the impact of Western political ideals upon a population restive under despotism. Then, too, neither the Czarist nor Communist regime has relished having the whole apparatus of state oppression—the ubiquitous secret police, the massive bureaucracy, the Siberian prison camps, the policies of censorship and suppression of designated minorities—exposed to the gaze and ridicule of the world. Lurid accounts of these aspects of Russian life have always fostered tension between Russia and other countries. To avoid unfavorable reports in foreign countries, Russia has preferred to close the door to foreigners entirely

or to permit them to see only a few selected showplaces.

Intense suspicion and fear of the outside world has been engendered also by Russia's historical experiences under both the Czars and the Bolsheviks. The motif of cataclysm, perennial danger from abroad, and impending doom is a recurrent theme in Russian literature and political writing. In large measure it is a product of Russian geography and of history dictated by geographical conditions. The eminent British scholar Sir Bernard Pares has written: "The Great Russian people were hammered out of peaceful, silent, pacific elements by constant and cruel blows from enemies on all sides, which implanted into the least intelligent of Russians an instinct of national defense...."[10] And Mazour adds that "The motivating background of Russia's foreign policy is predominantly the need for security...." He continues:

> The Napoleonic Wars culminating with the occupation of Moscow, the Crimean War ending with the disaster at Sevastopol, the Russo-Turkish War..., World War I ending with Allied intervention, and above all World War II with its appalling devastation—these are experiences which no nation can forgive or forget.

Whether justified or not, he feels that, inevitably, Russia will seek "a *cordon sanitaire* in reverse, with its bayonets turned westward.... it is the ABC of national strategy."[11]

Fostered by countless invasions throughout history, the Russian legacy of suspicion and fear of the outside world is exemplified in the attitude of the reactionary Pobedonostsev, adviser to Alexander III (1881–1894). Pobedonostsev was convinced that "it is impossible to rely upon any of our so-called 'friends' and 'allies,' that all of them are ready to hurl themselves upon us at that

---

*While xenophobia has been characteristic of the Russian *government,* there existed a considerable interchange of cultural and political ideas between Russian citizens and the outside world under the Czars. Barghoorn, in fact, maintains that the Russian population as a whole has traditionally been highly receptive to ideas from abroad and that, even under the Communists, Soviet citizens have shown keen interest in the viewpoints of foreigners. See Frederick C. Barghoorn, *Soviet Russian Nationalism* (New York: Oxford University Press, 1956), pp. 162–164. For an illuminating treatment of the impact of American political ideas upon the Czarist state in the eighteenth and nineteenth centuries, consult Max M. Laserson, *The American Impact on Russia* (New York: Macmillan, 1950).

very minute when our weakness or errors become apparent."[12]

The "Third Rome" Idea and Russian Messianism

The Communist hope of redeeming mankind through the "world revolution" and achieving utopia is a variant of a theme that pervades historic Russian theological and philosophical thought. In a penetrating study of Russian national character, Nicolas Berdyaev states that: "Messianic consciousness is more characteristic of the Russians than of any other people except the Jews. It runs all through Russian history right down to its communist period."[13] Its earliest origins are to be found in the conception of Moscow as the "Third Rome." After the fall of Rome in the fifth century and the collapse of the Byzantine Empire in the fifteenth, the center of Orthodox Christianity shifted to Moscow. To Russian theologians this signified a profound and God-ordained change in the direction of history. Thus the monk Philotheus informed Basil III, Grand Duke of Moscow:

> The first Rome collapsed owing to its heresies, the second Rome fell victim to the Turks, but a new third Rome has sprung up in the north, illuminating the whole universe like the sun. . . . The first and second Rome have fallen, but the third will stand till the end of history, for it is the last Rome. Moscow has no successor; a fourth Rome is inconceivable.[14]

"The Mission of Russia," comments Berdyaev, "was to be the vehicle of the true Christianity. . . . There enters into the messianic consciousness the alluring temptation of imperialism."[15]

Strongly reinforcing the theological designation of Moscow as the Third Rome were the viewpoints of the Slavophiles and their nineteenth-century successors, the Pan-Slavists. Compounded of Russian nationalism, mystic ties of race, German idealism, and Hegelian philosphy, Slavophilism predicted the inevitable decay of Europe and the redemption of mankind by the Slavs. "Western Europe is on the high road to ruin," Prince Odoevsky wrote. Advancing the theme of *ex Oriente lux* that permeates Russian philosophic and religious thought, he believed that:

> We Russians, on the contrary, are young and fresh and have taken no part in the crimes of Europe. We have a great mission to fulfill. Our name is already inscribed on the tablets of victory: the victories of science, art and faith await us on the ruins of tottering Europe.[16]

And the Russian mystic Peter Chaadaev believed that "we have a vocation to solve a great many of the problems of the social order . . . to give an answer to questions of great importance with which mankind is concerned."[17] Describing man's quest for spirituality and holiness, the immortal Dostoevsky stated in 1880: "I speak only of the brotherhood of man, not of triumphs of the sword. . . . For I am convinced that the heart of Russia, more than any other nation, is dedicated to this universal union of all mankind. . . ."[18]

The Pan-Slav movement late in the nineteenth century also contained messianic elements. According to its leading spokesmen, Russian cultural-historical affinity with the Slavs gave the Russian state a special responsibility as protector and defender of their interests. The Pan-Slavs, writes Florinsky, "were in general agreement that it was the historic mission of Russia to liberate the Slavs from a foreign and religious and political yoke. . . ."[19]

Other influences evident in certain

periods of Russian thought also supported messianism and assigned to Moscow a dominant role in achieving the salvation of mankind. One of these was nihilism. Another was anarchism. Berdyaev summarizes the viewpoint of the most famous Russian anarchist, Michael Bakunin, as follows:

> What is needed is to set fire to a world-wide blaze; it is necessary to destroy the old world; upon the ashes of the old world, on its ruins, there will spring up a new and better world of its own accord. . . . Collectivism or communism will not be an affair of organization; it will spring out of the freedom which will arrive after the destruction of the old world.[20]

Also important is the attention given in Russian Orthodox theological thought to the coming of the Kingdom of God. In contrast to Roman Catholic and Protestant thought, Russian Orthodox theology has always emphasized the early apocalyptic message of the Church. The coming of the Kingdom of God will mean the "transfiguration of the world, not only the transfiguration of the individual man." Salvation is conceived of as total and corporate for society.[21]

Russian messianism, concludes Berdyaev, is perfectly compatible with the mission of Marxism-Leninism-Stalinism to redeem mankind and recreate society anew upon the ruins of the old order. "Russian communism is a distortion of the Russian messianic idea; it proclaims light from the East which is destined to enlighten the bourgeois darkness of the West."[22] Analyzing the messianic elements in contemporary Soviet policy, Barghoorn observes that the Kremlin "holds out to mankind the vision and prophecy of the earthly paradise, the harmonious society without coercion and inequality. This is the utopian aspect of Soviet Rus-

sia's message to the world. . . ."[23] The point is well exemplified by an article in *Izvestia* on February 22, 1948, which discusses Russia's contribution to humanity in World War II:

> The Soviet Army . . . stretched out a brotherly, helping hand to the peoples of Europe languishing in Fascist Slavery. The European peoples have to thank the Soviet Army for their liberation. . . . The Soviet Army saved European civilization from the Fascist barbarians, honorably and worthily performed its historic liberating mission. . . . As always, the Soviet Army stands on guard to protect the peaceful labor and tranquility of the peoples. Always, it stands on guard for peace throughout the world.[24]

The Soviet-American Confrontation

The Pattern of Relations Before World War II

One of the keys to understanding the tensions developing between the United States and the Soviet Union after World War II is to be found in the history of relations between the two countries down to the time of Nazi Germany's attack upon Russia on June 22, 1941. Lack of trust and of meaningful communication between the two were conspicuous features of the Cold War. The antipathy between Marxism and Western liberal democracy unquestionably fostered animosities. Less widely grasped, however, was the fact that the pattern of Russian-American relations before the contemporary period played a part in setting the stage for Cold War hostilities.

In general terms, relations between Russia and America throughout the nineteenth century and for some 40 years of the twentieth could be described as *fragmentary, intermittent, and not infrequently hostile.* The absence of sustained contact between the two societies was a noteworthy reality. Insofar as European affairs were concerned, the United States was dedicated to an isolationist mentality which dictated a policy of noninvolvement in the Old World's quarrels and diplomatic rivalries.

Czarist Russia did not espouse isolationism. To the contrary, even while Czarist governments experienced one internal crisis after another, they pursued an "active" foreign policy abroad, intervening repeatedly in Europe's affairs, trying to extend Russian influence into the Mediterranean and Persian Gulf, threatening Britain's position in Afghanistan and India, and extending their interests to eastern Asia. At the same time, like America, Russia was heavily occupied with domestic affairs. America's westward expansion had its counterpart in Russia's eastward expansion into Asia and Siberia, to the shores of the Pacific. As will be explained more fully in Chapter 15, when the United States championed the principle of the "Open Door" in China early in the twentieth century, Washington was as concerned about an exclusive *Russian* influence over Chinese affairs as by any other threat to its trading and commercial opportunities on the Asian mainland.*

The ideological rivalry characteristic of the Cold War in the modern period was foreshadowed by the clash between American democratic ideas and ideals and Czarist absolutism before 1917. To the American mind, Czarism stood as the epitome of Old World political reaction and despotism. Nor could a starker contrast be found than that between dynamic American capitalism and Russia's stagnant economic system, which was marked by periodic famines. At intervals, as during the suppression of Louis Kossuth's revolt in

Hungary against the Austro-Hungarian Empire (which received massive support for its antirevolutionary activities from Moscow), Americans vocally railed against autocracy and predictably supported the revolutionary cause. Kossuth received a hero's welcome when he visited the United States; Secretary of State Daniel Webster delivered a passionate endorsement of Hungarian independence. Again in 1863, Americans denounced Russian intervention to crush a Polish revolt against Czarist autocracy.[25] Ideological estrangement between the two countries was fostered late in the century by the lectures and writings of George Kennan,† who had traveled widely in Russia. To thousands of Americans, Kennan depicted life in the Czar's Siberian prison camps and other evidence of Russian political backwardness.[26]

Successive Czarist regimes reciprocated hostility toward the United States. To the Russian nobility, the youthful and "upstart" American republic had embarked upon a democratic experiment that was bound to fail. Meanwhile, however, its very existence encouraged revolts against established and "legitimate" authority in Europe. Americans could always be counted upon to believe the worst about the government of Russia; their continuing support for political revolutionaries alienated the Czar and all other politically conservative groups. American diplomats deplored the restrictions which nearly always inhibited their movements and contacts in the Czar's domain. Censorship, the activities of the Czar's secret police, and other evidences of "barbarous" Russian behavior alienated Americans. Czarist Russian did not even formally recognize the American Repub-

*The Russian threat to China's territorial integrity occasioned considerable anxiety in Washington. One diplomatic historian has said that Russian expansionism constituted "the main threat to the open door" in China. See Richard W. Leopold, *The Growth of American Foreign Policy: A History* (New York: Knopf, 1962), pp. 218–219.

†The George Kennan alluded to above was a distant relative of the contemporary American diplomat and historian, George F. Kennan, who is widely (and perhaps erroneously) regarded as the "author" of America's postwar containment policy.

lic until 1809; treaty relations between the two governments were not established until 1824.[27]

As is not uncommon in the annals of diplomacy, even in the contemporary era, ideological estrangement did not necessarily preclude harmonious Russian-American relations on other levels. Strategically and diplomatically, Moscow and Washington were sometimes drawn into collaboration against a common enemy: Great Britain. After 1815, London took the lead in checking Russian expansionist tendencies in areas like the Middle East and western Asia. For a century or more after their own revolution, Americans remained intensely suspicious of British power and intentions, despite the fact that enforcement of the Monroe Doctrine depended for many decades upon England's sea power. Ocassionally, therefore, Russia and America found themselves in agreement against Great Britain, although these episodes were usually short lived and involved little sustained cooperation.*

By 1900, a new common enemy had replaced Great Britain. This was Imperial Japan, which in time posed the severest threat

to America's Open Door principle in China. In 1904–1905, Japan administered a humiliating defeat to Czarist Russia in the Russo-Japanese War. Thanks to the mediation of President Theodore Roosevelt, however, the ensuing settlement in the Treaty of Portsmouth proved more favorable to Moscow than Russia had a right to expect on the basis of its poor military showing. Although Japan had long been regarded as America's protégé (the country had been opened to Western contact by Commodore Matthew Perry in 1853), by the early 1900s its diplomacy engendered growing apprehension in Washington, as well as in London. Seeking to create a more favorable balance of forces in the Far East, President Roosevelt used his position as "honest broker" between Russia and Japan to mitigate Tokyo's harsh demands upon Moscow.[28]

America and the Communist Revolution

The origins of the Cold War, some commentators are convinced, must be traced back to World War I, particularly to the months immediately following the seizure of power in Russia by Nikolai Lenin and his Bolshevik followers. As every student of modern history is aware, Lenin's revolution did not topple the ancient and increasingly inept Czarist political structure; that had been accomplished in the spring by the revolutionary group (in which Marxists were in a minority) which chose Alexander Kerensky as its leader. Dedicated to democracy and pledged to hold national elections, Kerensky was warmly approved in the West. At last, the hard crust of Russian political backwardness had been penetrated and democracy appeared on the verge of becoming established in the largest nation on the globe.

Lenin's seizure of power from the Kerensky regime on November 7, 1917, ap-

---

*An outstanding example of Anglophobia as a force producing Russian-American goodwill was provided in 1863, when a Russian fleet entered New York Harbor. Americans interpreted this move as Czarist support for the Union during the Civil War; the presence of the fleet apparently signified Moscow's readiness to provide tangible assistance to the Union cause. As historians discovered much later, Britain and Russia were on the verge of hostilities (Czarist forces had just crushed the Polish revolt); Moscow thus used New York harbor as a sanctuary for its inferior fleet, to escape the Royal Navy in the case of hostilities. If war erupted, the Russian fleet might have used this American base to attack British commerce. For a discussion of this episode and citation of available evidence, see Thomas A. Bailey, *A Diplomatic History of the American People,* 8th ed. (New York: Appleton-Century-Crofts, 1969), pp. 364–365.

peared a tragedy to many Western minds for several reasons. It aborted what seemed a Russian progression toward democratic government and delivered the control of Russia's affairs to a conspiratorial group employing totalitarian methods. It presaged the emergence of a new and perhaps more dangerous form of despotic rule in Russia, one possibly even more dangerous than Czarism. It brought to power a band of revolutionaries who were openly scornful of the Judeo-Christian moral code and other canons of civilized conduct. It raised innumerable questions about Russia's behavior abroad, since a fundamental tenet of the Marxist credo was promotion of "world revolution." The Bolshevik government's withdrawal from World War I also placed new burdens upon the Allies in defeating the Central Powers.

For these reasons, it would be an understatement to say that President Wilson and other Allied leaders greeted the Communist Revolution in Russia with something less than enthusiasm. For a longer period even than its European allies, the United States withheld diplomatic recognition, refused to trade with the Soviet Union, and otherwise pursued a policy of noncooperation with the Communist regime. President Wilson's preference (in Russia and elsewhere) for "orderly reform" of antiquated governmental and political systems was well known. Moreover, Lenin's government showed no disposition to pay Czarist war debts or to compensate foreigners for confiscated property. The executions and imprisonments which followed the Communist coup alienated Western opinion. Above all, perhaps, the international objectives of Bolshevism—the undisguised Marxist goal of fomenting "proletarian revolutions" in other countries—aroused deep apprehensions outside Russia.[29]

The months that followed Russia's withdrawal from World War I (formalized by the Treaty of Brest-Litovsk with Germany early in 1918) witnessed an intensification of tensions between Lenin's government and the Western Allies. Indeed, some commentators —the "re-examinists," who dispute official and "orthodox" interpretations of the Cold War—are convinced that this period was crucial in bringing Soviet-American hostilities to a new peak after World War II. In their view, the Allies tried to apply the strategy enunciated by that militant foe of Communism, Winston Churchill, who advised Western governments to strangle the Bolshevik baby in its cradle! Beginning in 1918, America, Britain, France, and Japan actively intervened in Russia's affairs. For several months thereafter (American troops withdrew early in 1920), Western governments supported the "White Invasions" that sought to overthrow Lenin's regime. Communist officials in time defeated the counterrevolutionaries—and in the process emerged with greater national strength and a more monolithic political control than they had possessed earlier. These events reenforced the view of Soviet officials that Russia was in danger of "capitalist encirclement" by its foreign enemies.[30]

Against this "re-examinist" point of view, the official and more orthodox interpretation holds that America's participation in the foreign interventions within Russia was always very limited vis-à-vis the French, British, and Japanese roles. America's *military* goal was to prevent Allied war materials from falling into German hands and to assist a military force known as the Czech Legion to escape from Russia and continue the war on the western front. Far from endeavoring to overthrow Lenin's government by outside force, America's *political* objective was to block and limit Japanese expansionism in Siberia and possibly Tokyo's annexation of Soviet territory in Asia.[31] Soviet authorities in effect acknowledged that America's role in the "White Invasions" was limited in the years that followed.[32]

This episode in Soviet-American relations, however, is a classic example of the fact that what is objectively true may be less important than what people (or governments) *believe to be true*. Unquestionably, the Allied interventions in Russia provided evidence to support the preexisting Marxist conviction that hostility and enmity surrounded the Soviet system on all sides. Believing in the concept of "capitalist encirclement," Lenin and his supporters were quickly confronted with its reality.[33] The "White Invasions" no doubt also reenforced traditional Russian fears about the security of their country and the vulnerability of many of their frontiers.

From the Revolution to the New Deal

For nearly 15 years after the Bolshevik Revolution, the policy of the United States toward Soviet Russia underwent little significant change. After it became apparent that the Soviet regime was not going to be overthrown, American policy under Wilson and successive Republican Presidents was shaped by three fundamental considerations: extreme ideological hostility between American democracy and Soviet Communism; disagreements between the two countries over Communist repudiation of Czarist war debts and confiscation of foreign-owned property; and Communist intrigue in the internal affairs of other countries through the instrumentalities of the Third International and local Communist parties directed from Moscow.

By the early 1930s certain influences growing out of internal affairs within the two countries and out of the international community were reshaping relations between them.

One of these was the desire of both countries to expand their foreign trade. By the late 1920s Russia had embarked upon the ambitious First Five-Year Plan, by which she hoped substantially to raise agricultural and, to a lesser extent, industrial output. Imports from America would greatly assist in this goal. Meantime, vocal groups throughout the United States were calling for an extension of American markets to Russia, and were bringing pressure to bear upon Congress and the White House to achieve that end.

On the international scene, the imperialistic designs of Japan, Germany, and Italy signaled the end of traditional American-Japanese friendship and drove both the United States and Russia to take steps to promote their own security. Once again, a common enemy was forcing the two nations to collaborate. The first step was the resumption of diplomatic relations. They were renewed between the two nations after the Kremlin pledged noninterference in the internal affairs of the United States through Communist groups directed from Moscow, and agreed to make a satisfactory settlement on repudiated Russian debts and confiscated foreign property.[34] For the first time since the Communist Revolution, the United States and the Soviet Union were prepared to maintain normal and friendly relations.*

---

*Neither of these conditions was fulfilled to the satisfaction of the State Department. Tension characterized relations between the two countries from 1933 to World War II over such questions as the activities of the Comintern and the harassment of State Department officials in Moscow. Department of State, *Foreign Relations of the United States. The Soviet Union: 1933–1939* (Washington, D.C.: U.S. Government Printing Office, 1952), pp. 132–134, 224–225, 446–451. The debt question dragged on for years before it was settled, with the State Department convinced that Russia had never intended to resolve the issue fairly.

The Road to War

As the Axis menace began to threaten the security of Europe and the world, events moved in a series of diplomatic crises toward their inexorable climax in World War II. Not until it was attacked by Japan at Pearl Harbor on December 7, 1941, did the United States officially abandon its policy of nonintervention in Europe's diplomatic quarrels, although private and governmental opinion in the United States nearly always was favorable to the victims of Axis aggression. America's policy of "aid short of war" to Great Britain in the months before Pearl Harbor was a crucial element in that country's heroic stand against Germany after the defeat of France. President Roosevelt's detractors also pointed to a hardening of America's attitudes toward expansionist Japan—a posture which some observers at the time and later were certain "drove" Japanese officials to attack the United States. Nevertheless, the United States in the main stood aloof from efforts inside and outside the League of Nations to stem the tide of Axis aggression against countries like China, Ethiopia, Austria, Czechoslovakia, and Poland. Receiving little besides moral support from Washington, policy makers in London and Paris resorted to a policy of "appeasement" of Axis demands, on the tragically mistaken assumption that reasonableness and conciliation would satisfy Axis territorial ambitions and avert war.

The emergence of the Cold War in the late 1940s cannot be understood intelligently without some grasp of the sequence of steps leading to World War II. In the "re-examinist" view, Soviet behavior during and after World War II is explicable only in terms of events during the 1930s. Intense Soviet suspicion of the intentions of Western governments; Moscow's wartime and postwar moves in Germany and Eastern Europe; the U.S.S.R.'s view of, and behavior in, the United Nations after 1945; the inability of the wartime Allies to agree upon postwar settlements for Germany or to preserve Allied unity after the Axis defeat—these and other Cold War controversies must be evaluated against a background of mounting diplomatic crisis during the 1930s.

While space is not available to reconstruct this sequence of events in great detail, we must at least take note of the major developments which may have contributed to later Cold War animosities. For our purposes, perhaps the central fact was the growing distrust prevailing between the Soviet Union and the West as the world moved toward the abyss of war. The existing pattern of alienation and suspicion that had characterized relations between Soviet Russia and the Western powers became greatly intensified during the interwar period. As they faced a resurgent Germany under a Nazi dictatorship, an expansionist Italy, and a Japan devoted to aggrandizement in the Pacific, Western policy makers operated upon the premise that the Communist government of Russia was as untrustworthy and unreliable as ever. In some measure (by discrediting socialist and other non-Marxist political groups in Europe), Marxists had in fact contributed to the rise of Nazism; weakened by economic dislocations and by Stalin's "purges" of some of Russia's best military leaders, Russia was in no position to contribute to League of Nations efforts designed to contain Axis expansionism. Consequently, Western leaders were unimpressed by Soviet delegate Maxim Litvinov's impassioned pleas at Geneva for collective action against the dictators. Such demands were regarded as either insincere propaganda gestures, or efforts by Soviet policy makers to embroil Western governments in a conflict with Berlin, Rome, and Tokyo, while Russia remained aloof. Confronted with their own internal political and economic problems after the Great Depression, Britain and France ignored Russian entreaties in favor of "appeasement."

From their perspective, Soviet policy makers might legitimately have concluded that the Western powers were so blinded by their antipathy toward Communism that they were unable to discern their own vital interests, much less Russia's. Soviet officials had read Hitler's *Mein Kampf,* and they had to assume that Western officials were also familiar with Hitler's avowed objectives. Foremost among these was the *Drang nach Osten,* the "drive to the East," in which the major targets were Poland and the Ukraine, Russia's agricultural heartland. In short, Hitler proposed to *dismember Russia.* Besides this, Hitler had another goal that met with widespread approval in certain Western circles: Time and again, he proclaimed his determination to *eliminate Bolshevism* as a political force disturbing international stability. Conditioned by Marxist ideology to be profoundly distrustful of the motives of capitalist states, Russia's Communist elite found their worst fears confirmed by Western behavior in dealing with Axis aggrandizement. Did the evident lack of Western interest in joining with the U.S.S.R. in a common front against the Axis mean that Washington, London, and Paris regarded Communism as a greater threat that Hitlerism? So long as the dictators expanded *eastward,* were Western officials content to let aggression go unchecked? Did conservative groups in the West actually *favor* Hitler's effort to liquidate the Communist threat forever?

Such questions even today are very difficult to answer with assurance. Lacking access to the Kremlin's archives, and even to relevant materials from Western sources, the student of the Cold War must often rely upon partial evidence; his conclusions frequently are little better than inferences based upon a "reading between the lines" of available sources, and he must often judge the behavior

of nations during the 1930s on the basis of their behavior in earlier periods. Even when such problems do not exist, judging the *real motives* of policy makers, as distinct from their apparent or declared objectives, is always risky. Yet it seems a safe enough assertion that, during the 1930s, Western diplomatic activities strongly reenforced existing Soviet conceptions of the outside world. Similarly, Western views of Communism were strengthened by Soviet behavior during this fateful era.

Munich and the Nazi-Soviet Pact

Two developments during the late 1930s brought many of the attitudes and suspicions we have described into focus and led to new tensions in Western-Soviet relations. One of these was the Munich crisis (September 29–30, 1938) and its aftermath. Earlier in the spring, Hitler had executed his *Anschluss* with Austria, whereby that country was "reunited" with the German Fatherland and its independence lost. Next on Hitler's timetable was Czechoslovakia, whose Sudetenland was inhabited largely by Germans. Harassed by an escalating German war of nerves, backed ultimately by the threat of an invasion, the government of Czechoslovakia remained prepared to fight for its freedom, provided its military allies—France and Soviet Russia—supported its independence. (Britain had a defense treaty with France, although it had none with Czechoslovakia.) If Czechoslovakia and its allies stood firm, war seemed inevitable, since Hitler gave no indication of retreating from his demands for the dismemberment of the most promising democracy in Eastern Europe. To avert this calamity, Britain's Prime Minister Neville Chamberlain and France's Premier Edouard Daladier met Hitler at his headquarters near Munich in September.

The ensuing Munich Agreement—heralded by Chamberlain as achieving "peace in our time"—was a triumph for the Axis. Hitler got the Sudetenland, and when he moved to incorporate the whole of Czechoslovakia into the Third Reich several months later, he acquired one of the most important munitions factories in Europe (the modern Skoda arms works), as well as a strategic gateway for pursuing his *Drang nach Osten*. If it had any appeal at all by this stage, the concept of "collective security" under the League of Nations had been totally undermined.

What was Moscow's behavior during the Munich crisis? Ostensibly, it was exemplary. Perhaps because it realized Czechoslovakia's strategic importance for Russia's own security, or because it was convinced that the Axis threat was ultimately aimed at Russia, or because it believed that only *collective* action could deter the dictators, for these or some other reasons the Kremlin reiterated its pledge to defend Czechoslovakia—alone, if necessary. Soviet representatives were not invited to the Munich Conference (nor, for that matter, were Czech delegates); Moscow was not consulted about what steps it was ready to take to contain aggression. For reasons we have already noted, London and Paris seriously doubted Moscow's ability to oppose the Axis powers effectively. Collective defense efforts were, therefore, rejected by the West in favor of appeasing Hitler's demands.

Whatever the truth of the matter—and even today, the diplomatic record of the 1930s (particularly of Soviet intentions and behavior) is far from clear—the Munich crisis was unquestionably a watershed in modern history. That it whetted Hitler's appetite for new conquests can hardly be doubted; within a few months he had annexed the whole of Czechoslovakia, and a year after the Munich Conference, he had launched his blitzkrieg against Poland. The Munich Conference also greatly widened the "credibility gap" between the West's professions and its behavior. Munich emerged as the acme of unprincipled disregard for the rights of small states and of calloused indifference to ethical precepts in statecraft. Most fundamentally for our purposes, the Munich Conference destroyed any prospect of Western-Soviet cooperation against Axis aggression. While they may have gained time at Munich (as defenders of the agreement frequently argue), Western governments ultimately confronted an infinitely more dangerous Axis—and, as we shall see, they now faced it *alone*.

Within a few brief weeks, Berlin and Moscow arrived at a détente, leaving Hitler free to attack the West and giving Stalin a free hand to establish Soviet hegemony in Eastern Europe, and perhaps in time in the Middle East. Frustrated in its efforts to forge an anti-Axis front, after Munich the Kremlin abandoned the effort and arrived at an understanding with Nazi Germany. To the West, the Nazi-Soviet agreement (August 31, 1939) symbolized totalitarian duplicity, proving to many minds that little choice existed between dictatorships of the political right or left. At Munich, the appeasers had sowed the wind. Now—confronted with a far stronger Axis and a neutralized Russia—they were reaping the whirlwind. Stalin was prepared, as he was many times before and after, to lay aside ideological considerations for the sake of Russian strategic and diplomatic objectives.

From this treaty, he gained time in which to build up Soviet forces for a possible showdown with Hitler; he acquired territory—the Baltic region and eastern Poland—which served as a military buffer zone and as a new frontier for Communist penetration, and a base from which to exert new pressures against Turkey and Persia. The Nazi-Soviet Pact was a disaster for the West and a masterpiece of *Realpolitik* for the Kremlin. Proof of

Soviet perfidy, to many Western minds, was the fact that Russia was negotiating with both German and Western representatives *concurrently,* when it decided to arrive at an accommodation with Berlin!

No sooner had this accord shocked the world than Hitler moved (on September 1, 1939) to attack Poland. With eastern Poland now under Russian domination, and western Poland quickly overrun by German forces, the independence of the country disappeared. After conquering Poland, having no fear of a "two-front war" with Russia, Hitler launched his attack against the Low Countries and France; the latter surrendered on June 22, 1940.

What interpretation can legitimately be placed upon Soviet Russia's conduct during this period? By the Nazi-Soviet Pact, the Kremlin had plainly turned the tables on the advocates of appeasement. The diplomatic historian Thomas A. Bailey has stated the "orthodox" interpretation. In his view, Stalin "cleverly contrived to turn Hitler against the democracies in the expectation that they would bleed one another white, while he emerged supreme."[35] Soviet gains from the understanding with Germany both advanced traditional Russian foreign policy goals and furthered the Marixist objective of world revolution—all at the expense of the West. Re-examinist commentators hold a contrary view. They interpret the Nazi-Soviet Pact as Stalin's "answer" to Western diplomacy at Munich, whose result (if not deliberate intention) was to turn Hitler's ambitions eastward at Russia's expense. If Soviet policy makers could not persuade the West to collaborate in "collective security" measures to stop Axis expansionism, then they had no alternative but to protect their interests unilaterally, by making a deal with Hitler.[36]

As though Stalin's conduct in dividing Europe with Hitler were not outrageous enough, another Soviet move evoked new Western (especially American) disapprobation. This was Russia's attack upon Finland late in 1939 and into 1940. Not unexpectedly, American opinion was overwhelmingly pro-Finnish in the David-and-Goliath contest. President Roosevelt outspokenly denounced Moscow's "wanton disregard for law" in its absorption of Finland.[37] Russia's Finnish campaign aroused worldwide indignation—so much so that the League of Nations (in a move of dubious legality) *expelled* the Soviet Union from the world organization. To the Kremlin and its apologists, this constituted still further evidence of the outside world's deep aversion to Communism. Japan, Italy, and Germany, for example, had flagrantly disregarded the League's instructions and had openly embarked upon a path of conquest; yet they had tamely been permitted to "withdraw" from the League of Nations, at their own option. Russia alone had been given eviction papers. Small wonder, re-examinists argued in the years ahead, that thereafter the Soviet Union would be loath to entrust its security or its vital diplomatic interests to another international assembly, such as the United Nations.[38]

The "Strange Alliance" During World War II

Modern history has witnessed a number of diplomatic revolutions—none perhaps more epochal than the one that took place less than two years after the Nazi-Soviet Pact. That Hitler had altogether abandoned his cherished goal of attacking Russia was dubious. Having conquered Western Europe, and momentarily expecting Britain's collapse, Berlin began to plan *Operation Barbarossa:* the long-awaited offensive against the U.S.S.R. There was no reason to think—and many Western observers shared the view with the Germans—that Russia could successfully resist the Nazi war machine any better than other victims of Nazi aggression. On June 22, 1941,

German troops crossed the Russian frontier. Overnight, official and unofficial opinion in the West reversed itself: Russia was now the underdog, and "Uncle Joe" Stalin quickly took his place with President Roosevelt and Prime Minister Churchill to form the Big Three directing Allied strategy. Churchill expressed the prevailing sentiment when he said that if the Devil himself opposed Hitlerism, then Britain would ally itself with the Devil! FDR promptly promised Moscow American assistance; and during the course of the war, American aid to Russia totaled some $11 billion.[39]

Yet even this climactic turn of events in no sense eliminated long-standing sources of discord among the wartime Allies or produced an era of wholehearted cooperation among them. Major and minor frictions characterized their relations throughout the conflict. Repeatedly, Western governments complained about Russia's lack of cooperation (such as Moscow's refusal to make airfields available to Allied planes) and the absence of Soviet "appreciation" for supplies (sent at great hardship on the dangerous "Murmansk run" through the Arctic) furnished during Russia's darkest hour. Americans stationed in Moscow during the war echoed the familiar refrain that they were subjected to numerous restrictions by Soviet authorities and often humiliated.

From the Soviet viewpoint, Western attitudes and behavior during the war often confirmed Communist suspicions. Some segments of Western opinion had long desired a confrontation between Hitlerism and Stalinism; after this mutual exhaustion, Western nations would be arbiters of the world. An advocate of this idea in the United States was Senator (later President) Harry Truman, who urged the Roosevelt Administration to assist *both* Germany and Russia in the hope that two obnoxious dictatorships would be eliminated![40] Although President Roosevelt rejected this view, many high-ranking American military leaders (including Chief of Staff General George C. Marshall) were certain that Russian defenses would soon collapse before the Nazi onslaught.[41]

If these disputes tended to be minor, military strategy and (as the end of the war approached) political issues fomented real tensions among the Allies. Remembering the Nazi-Soviet Pact, Western officials were apprehensive throughout the war about a new German-Soviet understanding at the expense of the West. Keeping Russia in the war—and doing everything possible to inhibit Moscow from making a separate peace—remained dominant Western objectives. In addition, American military leaders repeatedly urged President Roosevelt and his civilian advisers *to secure Soviet entry into the war against Japan at the earliest possible date.* Through the early months of the war (particularly while the contest with Germany hung in the balance), Moscow held to a position of neutrality toward Japan, while American and other Allied forces bore the brunt of the Pacific campaign. American commanders understandably sought Russian assistance in this theater; it was deemed vital for the final assault on the Japanese home islands, when the Allies expected very high casualties. Finally, at the Yalta Conference early in 1945, Stalin gave his pledge: Soviet forces would enter the war against Japan 90 days after the defeat of Germany (which occurred on May 7, 1945). When Russia did declare war against the Japanese Empire (on August 8)—between the dropping of the first and second atomic bombs on Japanese cities—its participation was no longer needed. As it had done many times in the past, orthodox historians and many Americans concluded, the Kremlin had calculatingly timed its moves, not to make an effective contribution to Japan's defeat but merely to share in the spoils of peace making. The re-examinist contention was that Stalin had kept his word: At America's insistent urging, Soviet troops engaged Japanese forces in Manchuria on virtually the same day Stalin had pledged at Yalta.

In the early phase of the war, Soviet leaders had their own demands—the leading one perhaps being for the West to open a "second front" in Europe to relieve German military pressure on Russia. In the Soviet view, Churchill and Roosevelt had promised to invade Europe as early as 1942; yet it was not until June 6, 1944, that the D-Day invasion actually took place. What accounted for this delay? The explanation in Washington and London was that a military operation of this magnitude took time and massive preparation; it simply could not be mounted without the most careful planning and military buildup. During the months preceding the invasion of France, Allied airpower "softened up" Germany, disrupting its supply and transportation systems, in preparation for a final Allied attack.

Soviet leaders, Moscow's protests and inquiries made clear, were unconvinced by such arguments. Did Western policy makers intentionally seek the "mutual exhaustion" of Germany and Russia, so that London and Washington could dictate a postwar settlement? Western officials rejected such ideas categorically. Re-examinist commentators during the war and afterward were convinced that Soviet Russia had legitimate grievances and causes for deep concern about Western conduct.[42]

Political Issues in World War II

Many of the political questions that were to become sources of sharp Cold War animosity in the late 1940s periodically challenged Allied cohesiveness during World War II. Particularly after the tide of battle had turned against the Axis powers, these issues came more and more to the forefront. Toward most

of them, President Roosevelt's approach was uncomplicated: He preferred to defer "political" decisions until the war had been successfully terminated. Recalling the secret agreements that had compounded the problem of peace making after World War I and that had aroused great public resentment, FDR repeatedly demanded that major political questions be deferred, lest they impair Allied unity. Far better than FDR, British Prime Minister Winston Churchill recognized the intimate and indissoluble *connection* between military and political decisions; he knew that the shape of the military frontiers at the end of the war would have a vital bearing upon political settlements made thereafter. Time and again, Churchill advocated military moves dictated wholly or in large part by *political* objectives. An outstanding example was his plan for an invasion of the "soft underbelly" of Europe, carrying Western forces into the Balkans and Eastern Europe, instead of a cross-channel invasion through western France. Churchill's avowed goal was to interpose Western troops between the Soviet Red Army and as much of Europe as possible, leaving Germany and much of Eastern Europe under Anglo-American control. President Roosevelt had little sympathy with this scheme. Even more fundamentally, American military advisers ruled it out as being militarily infeasible, possibly even disastrous: Europe's "soft underbelly" was in reality a formidable military challenge which American commanders did not care to assume. American officials thus held out for an invasion of France, a strategic plan which the British in time accepted. With hindsight, in the light of Cold War tensions developing after 1945, Churchill's idea still seems attractive to many Americans. If it had been carried out successfully, much of Europe might now be free of Communist control! Leaving aside the question of its military hazards, we need to keep in mind that all through the war a fear haunted Western policy makers: the specter of a separate Russian peace with Germany. We can of course do little more than speculate about the possible outcome of Churchill's plan. A few years earlier, however, when Moscow believed its interests were being jeopardized by Britain and France, Stalin's "answer" had been the Nazi-Soviet Pact, which virtually guaranteed Germany a free hand against the West![43]

Not even Roosevelt could successfully defer all important political questions until the war's end. On the eastern front, Soviet forces held back the German attack at Stalingrad; by early 1943, the Red Army had begun a series of offensives that would place Soviet forces in Berlin two years later. As it cleared Russian territory of the Axis invaders, the Red Army liberated Eastern Europe. Decisions about the political future and boundaries of these nations had to be made. By the second half of 1944, Western forces were moving toward the Rhine. Despite some success in its Ardennes counteroffensive at the end of the year, the German army was being defeated (Italy had already surrendered on September 8, 1943). Only in the Pacific (which was always regarded as a secondary theater of war) was the end of the war viewed as perhaps still two years away.

More than any other single issue, the problem of the postwar political order in Eastern Europe ultimately destroyed Allied unity and produced the Cold War. As it had many times in history, this region engendered intense diplomatic and political antagonisms. Even today, many commentators are convinced that the problems of Germany and Eastern Europe *remain* the principal obstacles to a Soviet-American détente. For example, the threatened invasion and occupation of Poland by Soviet forces in the early 1980s once again called the future of détente into serious question.

Even before the war was over, it became apparent that Western and Soviet conceptions of the future of Eastern Europe and Germany tended to diverge significantly. Western governments (British and French officials, more than American) were aware of traditional *Russian* ambitions in Eastern Europe and of ancient animosities such as that between the Poles and the Russians. The Czars had "partitioned" Poland three times at the end of the eighteenth century; Russian troops had crushed Poland's independence movement in 1863. In the Nazi-Soviet Pact, Stalin had successfully gained Russian dominance over half of Poland. On their part, the Poles were understandably apprehensive about Russian expansionism and often outspokenly anti-Communist. Polish forces had played a prominent role in the "White Invasions" that sought to overthrow Lenin's government. During the 1920s and 1930s, Polish-Russian relations were more often than not hostile. As for the Baltic states and Finland, these had been created out of *Russian* territory by the peace makers after World War I. The new Communist government of Russia, gripped by pressing internal problems and threatened by foreign invasions, was in no position to resist the Versailles settlement. Yet there was no reason to suppose that Russian policy makers regarded the map of Europe as it was drawn after World War I to be permanent. Several of the lesser Axis states (specifically, Hungary, Rumania, Bulgaria, and Finland) had joined Germany in attacking Russia, causing billions of dollars' worth of property damage and millions of civilian and military casualties. Western officials thus had ample grounds for concern about Soviet moves in Eastern Europe.

In 1940, the evidence subsequently indicated that Soviet forces had been responsible for the "Katyn forest massacre," in which some 8000 Polish army officers had been killed, presumably to prevent any effective resistance to ensuing Communist rule in Poland.[44] Then in August 1944, there occurred the "Warsaw Uprising," in which Polish forces resisting German domination (the "Polish underground") were virtually wiped out by the German army—while the Soviet Red Army remained some 15 to 20 miles from the Polish capital. Again, critics of Soviet behavior believed that Stalin's government had *deliberately* refrained from aiding the Polish resistance, and had allowed it to be decimated by superior German force, in order to eliminate any possible rival to a Soviet-imposed Communist regime after the war.[45]

Yalta—The Pinnacle of Unity

By the end of 1944, these and other issues eliciting disagreement among the Allies (like the nature of the proposed United Nations) demanded settlement. They became the main items of the Big Three conference at Yalta in the Crimea on February 3–11, 1945.

The military situation existing at the time of the Yalta Conference had a direct bearing upon the results achieved.[46] Russian forces were moving against Vienna, having already liberated most of Poland and East Prussia. By contrast, Anglo-American troops were just beginning to move forward again, after stopping Germany's counteroffensive in the Battle of the Bulge. In the Pacific, Western leaders looked forward with considerable anxiety to a massive and bloody "island hopping" campaign, climaxed by a fierce struggle against the Japanese home islands. (The Yalta Conference was held, it must be remembered, before the atomic bomb had been successfully tested; it was, one American official said, a "scientific question mark.") In Europe, the Red Army was moving forward, while the Western Allies had yet to cross the Rhine.

The future of Poland—called by Churchill the key issue at the conference—was an urgent and highly contentious matter. FDR and Churchill proposed that Poland's borders

as of 1941 (which followed the "Curzon line" drawn after World War I) be recognized. At length, Stalin accepted this idea, with the understanding that, to compensate for the loss of territory in the east, Poland would be given territory in the west at Germany's expense. The formal delineation of Poland's frontiers was deferred until a peace conference; but since none was ever held, this agreement became the *de facto* determination of postwar Poland's boundaries.

Confronted with the actual or impending occupation of Eastern Europe by the Soviet Red Army, Churchill and Roosevelt endeavored to secure guarantees from Stalin concerning respect for the political freedom of the countries in that region. In a "Declaration on Liberated Europe," the Big Three pledged to support "interim governmental authorities broadly representative of all democratic elements in the population"; these new regimes were expected to hold free elections responsive to the will of the people at an early date. (Here, as in the case of other wartime and postwar agreements among the Allies, semantical and ideological differences in time generated deep-seated disagreement. Churchill and Roosevelt naturally interpreted such terms as "all democratic elements" in terms consonant with the Western conception of democracy and representative government. Stalin viewed it as a synonym for pro-Communist groups and others sympathetic to the Marxist cause; and he believed it legitimately eliminated "anti-democratic," or anti-Communist, elements from participation in the new governments.)

No less crucial to the future of Anglo-American-Soviet cooperation was the problem of Germany. Hitler's defeat was now imminent. Accordingly, in the Yalta Agreement, the Allies reached a consensus upon the terms of surrender and upon the principle of the "complete disarmament, demilitarization, and dismemberment" of the Third Reich. Each of the major Allies was to have a zone of occupation in Germany, with France being given its zone out of the spheres administered by Britain and the United States. An Allied Control Commission was to serve as a unifying mechanism for occupation policy. And in what was to become another source of intense disagreement within a few months, it was agreed "as a basis for discussion" that Germany would pay $20 billion in reparations, one-half of which would go to the U.S.S.R. Aware that after World War I the United States had to take care of European nations burdened with huge reparations payments, FDR refused to accept massive Soviet reparations claims that would leave Germany impoverished. Since no formal peace treaty with Germany was ever possible, reparations claims were settled on an *ad hoc* basis.

As the war in Europe approached the closing phase, American officials were becoming increasingly preoccupied with the struggle in the Pacific. Before the atomic bomb (successfully tested in early summer) had been perfected, it was anticipated that the war against Japan might last another 18 to 24 months.* For Americans, Soviet participation in the war against Japan was deemed essen-

tial: FDR went to Yalta determined to obtain Stalin's pledge on that point. At Yalta, Stalin promised that within 60 to 90 days after the defeat of Germany, Soviet troops would strike Japan. In return, Britain and America agreed to several concessions to Russian interests in Asia: They recognized Outer Mongolia as a Soviet satellite; they agreed that gains made by Japan in the Russo-Japanese War (1904–1905), such as the southern half of Sakhalin Island and the Soviet naval base at Port Arthur, would be returned to Russia; they acknowledged Russia's preeminent position in the railway system of Manchuria and north China (the system had originally been built largely with Russian funds). Churchill and Roosevelt also persuaded Stalin to conclude a treaty with the Nationalist government of China, thereby providing *de facto* recognition of Chiang Kai-shek's government as the legitimate ruling authority vis-à-vis the Chinese Communist movement under Mao Tse-tung.

Yalta is often referred to as the "high tide of Allied unity." All the participants in the conference were ostensibly pleased with its results, even if some issues (like German reparations) had been left formally unresolved. Western leaders believed at the time—and a

---

*In the light of the development of nuclear weapons by the United States in the closing months of World War II, it is perhaps difficult today to understand the apprehensions among American military advisers concerning the prospect of a long and difficult military campaign against Japan after the defeat of the Axis powers in Europe, entailing a series of battles expected to last perhaps a year and a half or more after Germany surrendered. Robert E. Sherwood has written, in connection with the Yalta Conference early in 1945, that American officials counted heavily upon Russia's participation in this contest; in the Pacific, General Douglas MacArthur's strategy for defeating Japan was "based on the assumption that the Russians would contain *the great bulk* of Japanese forces on the Asiatic mainland as they had contained the Germans in Eastern Europe." If Moscow did so, this would mean

"the saving of countless American lives" and might make the invasion of the Japanese home islands "unnecessary." See Robert E. Sherwood, *Roosevelt and Hopkins*, 2 (New York: Bantam, 1948), p. 512, italics inserted. As events turned out, this strategy was based upon faulty Allied intelligence about Japan's military strength. In reality, the "great bulk" of Japan's forces in Asia did not exist! They had been periodically drained off to supply Japan's island defense bastions, but this fact was unknown to American military strategists, since of course it was carefully concealed by Tokyo. By early 1945, Japan was much closer to military defeat—even in the absence of the atomic bomb, much less Soviet Russia's entry into the war—than the Roosevelt Administration realized. See E. M. Zacharias, *Behind Closed Doors: The Secret History of the Cold War* (New York: Putnam's, 1950).

goodly number of commentators later agreed with them—that they had obtained several major concessions from Stalin, particularly respecting the "democratization" of European zones which were then (or were rapidly falling) under Russian military control. Moscow also pledged to enter the war against Japan, thereby lessening the prospect of high British and American casualties. Despite earlier indications to the contrary, Allied unity had been preserved; progress had been made in postwar planning; the evidence indicated that the same spirit of wartime cooperation among the Big Three would assure international stability and order after the war was over.*

*The euphoria that surrounded the Yalta Conference at the time stands in strange contrast to the furor which it generated in the years ahead. By the late 1940s and early 1950s, the Yalta Conference had become synonymous with FDR's "softness" toward Communism and his "appeasement" of Stalin. FDR's poor health (the President died on April 12) is often cited as a primary cause of the wholesale "concessions" allegedly made to the Soviet Union. As we have seen, overt concessions were made, chiefly in the Far East; as events turned out, the atomic bomb obviated the necessity for Soviet participation in the war with Japan. But at Yalta, American policy makers had no knowledge either that development of the A-bomb was imminent or that it was so powerful. Even without the A-bomb, as navy officials in the Pentagon insisted, Japan was closer to defeat than was generally realized; but this was a minority view among FDR's military advisers at the time. Curiously, the charge of American "appeasement" is usually directed at the Eastern European provisions of the Yalta Agreement. In this area, Americans had nothing to "concede": The entire region within a short time would be under Russian military domination. Apprehensive about Moscow's intentions, Churchill and Roosevelt obtained Stalin's pledge to "democratize" the political regimes established in this region and to hold "free elections" in the future. Events after Yalta made clear that, at worst, Stalin was totally disregarding this pledge or, at best, Western and Soviet interpretations of it were antithetical. Monolithic Marxist political systems soon appeared in Eastern Europe. Repeatedly, London and Washington protested this development *on the basis of the Yalta understanding.* After the Republicans won the presidency in the United States in 1952, many leading

Cold War: The "Orthodox" View

The euphoria produced by the Yalta Conference lasted only a few weeks. President Roosevelt's death in April, re-examinists are convinced, was a tragedy not only for America but for international politics as well. FDR, according to this view, was certain that Allied unity would endure into the postwar stage, introducing a new era of global stability and understanding. His death left the management of American foreign affairs in the hands of a new chief executive who was both inexperienced and, as events soon revealed, antagonistic toward the Soviet Union. President Truman's advisers were regarded as even more skeptical than he about cooperation with Moscow and prone to adopt a "tough" stance in dealing with the Kremlin.[47]

While FDR's death admittedly created new uncertainties for international politics, it must also be recognized that even before he died Roosevelt had expressed real apprehension about the future course of Soviet-American relations.[48] Had he lived several months longer, FDR would have been faced with problems like reconciling divergent interpretations of the Yalta Agreement; finding a formula that would balance Western and Soviet interests in Eastern Europe; and securing Allied agreement upon a peace treaty with Germany. As a master of the political process, Roosevelt had (or *thought* he had) a rapport with "Uncle Joe" Stalin which Truman lacked, and which would somehow preserve cooperative relations among the Allies in dealing with a range of complicated and dif-

members of the GOP urged President Eisenhower and Secretary of State John Foster Dulles to "repudiate" the unpopular Yalta Agreement. Eisenhower and Dulles in time refused, because they realized that if America did so, its legal basis for objecting to unilateral Soviet activities in the region would be impaired. See Sherman Adams, *First-Hand Report* (New York: Harper & Row, 1961), pp. 92–93.

ficult diplomatic issues. Yet something more than personal magnetism was required to impart common purposes to Great Britain, the United States, the Soviet Union, and the other wartime allies after the Axis defeat.[49]

Hardly had the heads of state left Yalta than controversies erupted among them over the meaning of the agreements reached at this conference—and, more specifically, over Soviet behavior in Eastern Europe. As always, American officials were especially concerned about Moscow's political moves in Poland. The new President, Harry Truman, said in his *Memoirs* that shortly after he entered the White House, the "full picture" of what was happening in Eastern Europe became clear:

> The plain story is this: We and the British wanted to see the establishment in Poland of a government truly representative of all the people. The tragic fact was that, though we were allies of Russia, we had not been permitted to send our observers into Poland. Russia was in full military occupation of the country at the time and had given her full support to the so-called Lublin government—a puppet regime of Russia's own making.

Even by this early date, Truman was convinced, Moscow had shown disregard for the Yalta Agreement. "Properly carried out," this understanding would have satisfied the legitimate interests of the Big Three in Poland and elsewhere in Eastern Europe. But Britain and America now faced "the failure of the Russians to live up to this agreement."[50] A short time later, American Ambassador Averell Harriman in Moscow cabled the President that the West confronted a "barbarian invasion of Europe," growing out of Russia's imposition of totalitarian regimes upon areas under its military control. A "reconsideration" of America's policies toward the Soviet Union was imperative; American policy makers had to accept the idea that Moscow

was unlikely to "act in accordance with the principles to which the rest of the world held in international affairs." Citing Stalin's indicated interest in American aid to rehabilitate Russia, Ambassador Harriman, reflecting the views in no small measure of his top assistant in the Moscow Embassy, George F. Kennan,*

---

*Regarded (not altogether correctly) as the formulator of America's policy of containment early in 1947, George F. Kennan became one of the State Department's leading Kremlinologists. Kennan was fluent in the Russian language and extremely well informed in Russian history, and had spent several years of diplomatic service in Moscow. In a still illuminating essay written in September 1944, Kennan analyzed Soviet domestic and foreign policy. Several themes are prominent in his essay, such as the basic continuity between Czarist and Stalinist goals and behavior. Stalin, Kennan wrote, "had settled firmly back into the throne of Ivan the Terrible and Peter the Great." Differing with other postwar American Kremlinologists, Kennan did *not* view Communist ideology as the driving force behind Soviet behavior at home and abroad; he saw Marxist dogma primarily as *instrumental* to the achievement of Russia's goals and as a rationalization of them. Always mindful of Russia's vulnerable position and its humiliation at the hands of foreign nations since 1917, Stalin's government relied upon its own efforts to alter this state of affairs; it had no real confidence that other nations would protect Russian interests. Even before the war had ended, the Kremlin's objective was "to increase in every way and with all possible speed the relative strength of the Soviet Union in world affairs, and to exploit to the utmost for this purpose the rivalries and differences among other powers." As Germany's defeat loomed, Moscow saw an opportunity to complete what it had begun with the Nazi-Soviet Pact of 1939: the establishment of its power in Eastern Europe. Less interested in whether governments in this area were avowedly Marxist, the Kremlin was concerned with whether they were pro-Soviet and amenable to Soviet influence. By the end of 1944, it was clear to Kennan that Moscow was committed to the goal "of becoming the dominant power of Eastern and Central Europe." In another essay written in May 1945, Kennan analyzed Soviet policy in this region in terms of two objectives: gaining Western "recognition" of Soviet control over the region, and obtaining American aid for Russian rehabilitation and economic progress. See George F. Kennan, *Memoirs (1925–1950)* (New York: Bantam, 1967), pp. 531–582.

urged the Truman Administration to adopt a hard line in dealing with the Kremlin and to insist that concessions to Russia be matched by Soviet concessions to American demands.[51]

With the passage of time also, American public opinion became increasingly disaffected with Moscow's wartime and postwar behavior. Favorable toward the Soviet ally during the war—and prepared to give the Kremlin the benefit of the doubt on a number of controversial issues—public sentiment in the United States gradually changed; and by the early postwar period, the American people were exerting considerable pressure on officials in Washington to resist Moscow's diplomatic demands. (At the same time, as we noted in Chapter 8, public opinion not infrequently espouses contradictory and incompatible ideas. While calling for "firmness" by the Truman Administration in responding to Soviet diplomatic moves, the American people also demanded the rapid demobilization of the armed forces at the end of the war—leaving the Administration very little power except a small nuclear arsenal upon which to base a policy of diplomatic "firmness" toward the Kremlin.)

By the end of 1946 or early 1947, the main lines of American diplomatic strategy toward the Soviet Union had been adopted by President Truman and his advisers. America's "containment" strategy was perhaps most eloquently and persuasively explained by George F. Kennan—and, with appropriate variations required by time and circumstances, it has served as the basis for American foreign policy until the end of the Vietnam War.[52] Throughout most of the 1970s (and this point of view was especially identified with the Carter Administration), the idea that containment had become obsolete was pervasive. But by the early 1980s—in the light of Moscow's continuing military buildup, its effort to dominate Afghanistan, and its attempt to subjugate Poland—the "revival of containment" was a prominent theme among governmental officials and commentators on contemporary American foreign policy. Although its application might differ in the 1980s from the early postwar era, the goal of containment accurately described the objectives of the Reagan Administration toward the Soviet Union. Unless and until genuine détente could be created and maintained between the superpowers, containment once again defined America's strategy in responding to Soviet threats against Western Europe, the Persian Gulf area, or Latin America. The obstacles confronting more cooperative Soviet-American relations are analyzed more fully in Chapter 10.

In what we have called the "orthodox" interpretation of the Cold War, as American officials assessed it, the responsibility for growing tensions in Soviet-American relations *rested squarely with Communist policy makers in the Kremlin*. They had seized every opportunity available to them during and after World War II to promote the Soviet Union's historic and ideological objectives, often at the expense of weaker countries, irrespective of the opinions of the Western Allies and of the consequences for global peace and security. Official American thinking on this point was perhaps most poignantly expressed by George F. Kennan's metaphor, likening Soviet power to "a fluid stream which moves constantly, wherever it is permitted to move, toward a given goal." The dominant Soviet objective is to assure that its power "has filled every nook and cranny available to it in the basin of world power." As Communist policy makers see it, "there should always be pressure, increasing pressure, toward the desired goal."[53] Faced with a Soviet effort to subjugate Afghanistan, beginning late in 1979, officials of the Carter and Reagan administrations would likely find little in Kennan's analysis with which to disagree.

On the basis of this analysis of Soviet policy motivations, early in 1947 the Truman Administration committed the United States to a strategy of "containment" for countering Soviet expansionism moves. (We shall discuss the origins and elements in this strategy more fully in Chapter 11, dealing with American policy toward Western Europe.) Here, it suffices to observe that in the years ahead the containment strategy had several concrete manifestations. The United States supplied military aid to Greece, Turkey, and the NATO allies, and other countries confronting an actual or possible Communist threat to their independence. American troops were committed to two major wars—the Korean War (officially called "a police action") and the Vietnam conflict—in efforts to prevent Communist expansionism. Another aspect of the containment idea has been the American program of massive economic and technical assistance to other countries—beginning with the European nations in the early postwar period and, in more recent years, to societies throughout the Third World. In the latter context particularly, American assistance has been viewed as an "alternative" to Communism; officials in Washington anticipated that it would enable less developed societies to develop progressive and stable political systems, capable of resisting Communist inroads.

Beginning with the Rio Treaty of hemispheric defense in 1947, followed by the North Atlantic Treaty Organization (NATO) in 1949,* the United States has also sponsored and joined a number of alliance systems designed to bolster the security of the non-Communist world. In addition, it has engaged in several less formal and *de facto* military commitments (such as repeated guarantees of Israeli security and pledges to assist Yugoslavia to maintain its independence) that were in some measure motivated by the containment idea. Beginning with the period of the Korean War, the American government has also been required to maintain a large, expensive, and modern defense establishment available to apply the containment strategy in distant parts of the world. By the 1980s—in response to criticisms that the United States was unprepared to project its power into areas like the Persian Gulf region—executive and legislative officials were agreed that a new "Rapid Deployment Force" was urgently required to strengthen the nation's defense posture.

Future chapters, dealing with American foreign policy toward particular regions and global issues, will call attention to specific manifestations of the containment idea that has guided the diplomacy of the United States toward the Soviet Union since 1947. Our interest is served here by reiterating that, according to the "orthodox" interpretation, the origins of the Cold War can be traced chiefly to Soviet diplomatic ambitions and moves during and after World War II, to which the American strategy of containment was—and remains—predominantly *a response*. It follows, to the minds of most American officials and citizens, that the decision to alleviate or end the Cold War also rests primarily with Soviet policy makers. It requires them to curb their expansionist ambitions, to cease political intervention in the affairs of other countries, to refrain from sponsoring revolutionary movements against other governments, and to

---

*The Rio Treaty and other developments in hemispheric defense policy are discussed more fully in Chapter 14; NATO and other aspects of Western defense are dealt with in Chapter 11.

desist from other actions fostering regional and global feelings of insecurity and apprehension about Moscow's intentions.

"Revisionist" Interpretations of the Cold War

As our discussion thus far has indicated, the "orthodox" or official explanation of the Cold War has been challenged by another group of commentators who have collectively offered a "revisionist" or "re-examinist" interpretation of Soviet-American tensions.[54] According to the revisionist approach, the underlying premises of American foreign policy toward the Soviet Union since World War II have been faulty—and the containment policy, based upon that assessment, has been an inappropriate and ineffectual American response to the Communist challenge. Revisionist interpreters have indicted postwar American diplomacy toward the U.S.S.R. for a long list of sins of both commission and omission.

According to this point of view, the American people and their leaders failed to understand a number of key facts and realities about Soviet diplomatic behavior. America, for example, has never sufficiently recognized the deep Soviet anxiety (it might even be called a phobia) about *national security*. As a result of its historical experiences and certain geographical realities, the Soviet state is preoccupied with the preservation of its security against actual and potential enemies. Instead of recognizing this Soviet anxiety, and endeavoring to alleviate it, America has too often deepened this Russian fear (such, for example, as in America's evident interest in the postwar political destiny of Eastern Europe, or its unwillingness to "share" information about the atomic bomb with Moscow during and after World War II).

Revisionists also believe that after World War II Americans grossly exaggerated both the *ability* of the Soviet Union to undertake expansionist moves against weaker societies and its *desire* to do so. In view of its enormous war losses, for example, and of the debilitated condition of its economic system, the U.S.S.R. was in no position to threaten the security of Western Europe. The so-called Communist threat to the security of the West was, therefore, largely an illusory danger—perhaps deliberately created by certain anti-Communist groups in the West to serve their own political purposes and ideological goals. In more recent years, the Communist threat to the security and independence of the Third World has also been magnified out of all proportion to its actual importance. To the minds of Cold War revisionists, most Third World societies are *not* "vulnerable" or receptive to Communist domination directed from Moscow. Political leaders and citizens throughout the Third World are as resistant to control by the Soviet Union as they have traditionally been to subjugation by colonial powers or other outside forces. Merely because Third World countries have no desire to be politically controlled by, or diplomatically linked with, the United States does not mean that they welcome Soviet hegemony. Their diplomatic stance is one of "nonalignment"—or independence from *any* diplomatic bloc sponsored by one of the superpowers.

A related theme in revisionist interpretations is the idea that the Cold War stems from an American failure to understand, and to come to terms with, the *idea of revolutionary change* which has gripped the international system since World War II.[55] The American people and their leaders have not grasped the fact that most societies throughout the Third World *desire* such revolutionary changes in nearly all aspects of their national life; nor have Americans realized sufficiently that throughout much of the world, revolutionary upheaval *is inevitable,* regardless of what Washington thinks of the process.

America's failure to accommodate itself to the existence of a revolutionary global environment has had several highly adverse consequences for the foreign policy of the United States. It has meant, for example, that too often Americans have forgotten—and have overlooked the international significance of—their own *revolutionary* heritage, as epitomized by the Declaration of Independence and the Bill of Rights in the Constitution. It has meant that Americans have too often been prone to attribute the impulse toward revolutionary change solely to Communist efforts—failing to realize that, if the Communist Revolution in Russia had never occurred, the desire for radical change would remain undiminished in many societies throughout the contemporary world. And it has meant that—since Washington has often interpreted the containment policy as requiring support for the political status quo in other countries—the United States has permitted Marxist groups to become the champions and instigators of radical political and economic change, thereby greatly enhancing their prestige and popular following. In regions like Latin America or black Africa, the United States has not infrequently allowed Communist elements to gain a strong position "by default," since Washington appeared to oppose *any* fundamental alteration in the status quo.

Re-examinist interpreters of the Cold War believe that, ever since the Bolshevik Revolution in Russia in 1917, America and other Western societies have exhibited a deep-seated "anti-Communist" phobia that has strongly colored and distorted their approach to diplomatic issues. The "Communist threat," for example, was often invoked by groups sympathetic to Hitlerism before and during World War II—and, in most instances, the threat was no more real then than it was after the war. In more recent years, this same anti-Communist impulse has been reflected in, and perpetuated by, influential groups in the American society (like the Military-Industrial Complex, discussed in Chapter 8) having a vested interest in maintaining a high state of Cold War tensions.

Another theme conspicuous in the viewpoints of revisionist commentators on the Cold War—and an idea especially prominent during and immediately after the Vietnam War—was the "arrogance of American power."[56] Identified with ex-Senator J. William Fulbright (Democrat of Arkansas), this idea for a time enjoyed wide circulation and support among certain students of modern American diplomacy. As Fulbright analyzed the matter, Soviet-American tensions stemmed in no small measure from America's own "imperial" urges, from the emergence of the United States as a superpower, and from the nation's desire (perhaps as much unconscious as conscious) to impose its own economic and political model upon other countries. With other revisionists, Fulbright believed that Americans had failed to understand, and to adapt their policies to, the existence of revolutionary movements throughout the world. American efforts to assist or support existing (particularly nondemocratic) governments often appeared "arrogant" to foreigners; and neither the American people nor their leaders had been sensitive enough to the desires and needs of other countries since World War II. These lacunae in American policy had undermined the nation's diplomatic efforts and often had enhanced the appeal of Communism in foreign societies.

The common theme in our brief summary of the revisionist explanation of the Cold War is the idea that in most respects it stemmed *from deliberate or indeliberate failures in American foreign policy* since the Second World War. Owing in no small measure to America's own attitudes and behavior, Soviet officials gained the impression that the United States threatened Russian security; that it opposed revolutionary changes abroad; that it favored the maintenance of conservative and reactionary political regimes in other countries; and that it was indifferent to the Soviet Union's legitimate internal and external needs. By revisionist logic, most of Moscow's moves in external affairs for a generation or more are explicable as "defensive" steps, taken in response to actual or threatened American actions.

It is not possible in limited space to resolve the continuing debate between orthodox and revisionist interpreters of the Cold War, and no attempt will be made to do so. It suffices to make a few brief observations about the controversy and the factors influencing it. In the first place, the admonition needs to be reiterated that was expressed earlier in the chapter: Even today, the student of Soviet-American relations lacks access to important documents and other materials (such as those in the Kremlin's and the State Department's archives) upon which to base authoritative judgments about Soviet and American diplomatic behavior.

In the second place, even if such materials were freely available—and a great deal of useful source material of course *is* accessible to scholars and commentators on Soviet-American relations and other diplomatic questions—judgments would still vary widely concerning the *meaning* of certain key events and developments, or upon the weight to be accorded particular factors or variables determining the foreign policy of the United States and the Soviet Union. For example, what was the influence of President Roosevelt's personality and his particular operating "style" upon foreign policy decision making within the United States during World War II? Or, how did the fact that Stalin suffered from certain deep-seated psychological disorders influence

Soviet policy toward the outside world until his death in 1953? Still another relevant question is: What impact did differing American and Soviet conceptions of "democracy" have upon their diplomacy in Eastern Europe during and after the war? Whatever the answers to such questions, they are bound to be heavily tinged with subjectivism and arbitrary judgments, thereby eliciting highly divergent judgments by qualified commentators.

In the third place, the debate between orthodox and revisionist interpreters of the Cold War must be placed in the context of historical perspective. Debates of this kind are *a unique feature of the American society*—and they have taken place with regard to every war in which the United States has been engaged! Even today, widely differing interpretations are available with regard to the "causes" of the Revolutionary War, the War of 1812, the Civil War, the Spanish-American War, World War I, World War II, the Korean War, the Vietnam War—along with a host of lesser conflicts to which the United States has been a party for the past two centuries.[57] The controversy over the origins and nature of the Cold War, for example, is remarkably similar to the debate that occurred for almost two decades over the reasons why the United States entered World War I. In that instance, the "orthodox" interpretation was that America's participation in the war could be explained chiefly by reference to one overriding fact: Imperial Germany had "provoked" the United States into entering the conflict by repeatedly attacking its citizens and property. After that conflict, a "revisionist" school of thought emerged in the American society which attributed the nation's decision to go to war to a variety of other influences. These included: successful British propaganda and diplomatic efforts designed to draw the United States into the conflict on the Allied side; propaganda activities by what were called the "munitions makers" and the "Merchants of Death" (an earlier counterpart to the Military-Industrial Complex) designed to stimulate war-related economic and commercial activities in the United States; President Woodrow Wilson's personal preference for the Allied cause; and failure by American officials and people alike to "understand" German viewpoints and goals. As in the Cold War, this revisionist school of thought maintained in effect that America's entry into World War I *was an aberration* or a fundamental mistake in the nation's foreign policy, in no way promoting its own security and diplomatic interests and dictated by self-serving groups at home and abroad.[58] It should be added, however, that (as in the case of the Cold War) this interpretation of America's involvement in the First World War remained a *minority viewpoint* among diplomatic historians. After extensive investigation by congressional committees, little reliable evidence was produced to show that "munitions makers"—or any other group except the nation's executive and legislative leaders—had been responsible for the decision of the United States to go to war in 1916.

Finally, with regard to the Cold War and other conflicts in which the United States has been involved, the revisionist point of view may be related to a characteristic of the American approach to foreign relations we discussed at length in Chapter 2: the traditional *American aversion to the concept of power* and its role in international relations. As was emphasized there, Americans have never been comfortable with the concept of power; they do not readily accept the idea that nations—least of all, their own nation—use it to achieve diplomatic goals; they still believe perhaps that "power politics" can be eliminated from global political relationships; and they are loath to admit that the United States has legitimate security and diplomatic interests which must from time to time be defended by reliance upon military force and other forms of power.

From this perspective, it follows that the nation's participation in armed conflicts, or *quasi*-military contests like the Cold War, represent aberrant behavior or deviations from an ethical norm. Such behavior, revisionists assume, must therefore have been at variance with the desires of the American people, must have been advocated by self-serving domestic and foreign interests, and must somehow have been "imposed" or foisted upon the officials of the American government (without perhaps their being aware that this had occurred). In the nature of the case, it is very difficult for revisionists to demonstrate convincingly exactly *how* the American democratic process miscarried, to produce decisions against the people's will and interests (and, in fact, revisionist studies tend to be understandably vague on this crucial point). Moreover, they almost never address themselves to a phenomenon that was highlighted by the nation's adoption of the containment policy in 1947: The Truman Administration was subjected to massive and continuing pressure *by American public opinion* to exhibit greater "firmness" in dealing with the Communist challenge abroad. In most instances, the same phenomenon could be discerned with regard to other military conflicts in which the United States has been involved—not excluding (for most of its duration) the Vietnam War.

Another American propensity related to revisionism—often remarked upon by foreign commentators—needs also to be mentioned briefly. More than any society perhaps known to world history, Americans tend to revel in exposés and revelations of wrongdoing, poor judgments, and maladministration by their elected officials. For reasons that are not altogether clear (but which are perhaps related to the reluctant emergence of the United

States as a superpower in global affairs), periodically Americans are addicted to "guilt trips" and to expressions of *mea culpa* about their international role. The re-examinist interpretation of the origins and nature of the Cold War clearly fits that tradition.

NOTES

1. Thomas A. Bailey, *America Faces Russia* (Ithaca, N.Y.: Cornell University Press, 1950), p. 62. A history of Russian-American relations, focusing on the role of public opinion.

2. Frederick C. Barghoorn, *Soviet Russian Nationalism* (New York: Oxford University Press, 1956), p. 163. An analysis of nationalism and Soviet Communism since 1917.

3. Quoted in Bailey, *America Faces Russia*, p. 198.

4. Marx' views were paralleled by those of his colleague, Friedrich Engels. See the essay by Engels, from his *The Russian Menace to Europe*, included in Robert A. Goldwin, et al., eds., *Readings in Russian Foreign Policy* (New York: Oxford University Press, 1959), pp. 74–92.

5. George B. Huszar, et al., *Soviet Power and Policy* (New York: Thomas Y. Crowell, 1955), pp. 22–23. A helpful symposium, covering various aspects of historic and more recent Soviet policy.

6. E. Carman Day, *Soviet Imperialism* (Washington, D.C.: Public Affairs Press, 1950), p. 11.

7. Michael T. Florinsky, *Russia: A History and an Interpretation*, Vol. II (New York: Macmillan, 1953), p. 982. A thorough and scholarly account that is rich in detail and short on interpretation.

8. K. W. B. Middleton, *Britain and Russia*, Vol. II (London: Hutchinson, n.d.), pp. 33–34.

9. Florinsky, *Russia: A History and an Interpretation*, Vol. II, pp. 1262, 1270–1271.

10. Anatole G. Mazour, *Russia: Past and Present* (New York: Van Nostrand, 1951), p. 114. A succinct and readable textbook on Russian history, with many illuminating insights.

11. Ibid., p. 116.

12. Melvin C. Wren, "Pobedonostsev and Russian Influence in the Balkans, 1881–1888," *Journal of Modern History,* **19** (June, 1947), 132.

13. Nicolas Berdyaev, *The Russian Idea* (New York: Macmillan, 1948), pp. 8–9. A highly original, provocative study of Russian character and viewpoints.

14. Quoted in Mazour, *Russia: Past and Present,* pp. 51–52.

15. Berdyaev, *The Russian Idea,* pp. 8–9.

16. Quoted in Mazour, *Russia: Past and Present,* p. 31.

17. Quoted in Berdyaev, *The Russian Idea,* p. 37.

18. Quoted in Mazour, *Russia: Past and Present,* p. 19.

19. Florinsky, *Russia: A History and an Interpretation,* Vol. II, p. 987.

20. Quoted in Berdyaev, *The Russian Idea,* p. 148.

21. Ibid., p. 195.

22. Ibid., pp. 249–250.

23. Ernest J. Simmons, ed., *Continuity and Change in Russian and Soviet Thought* (Cambridge, Mass.: Harvard University Press, 1955), p. 531. A symposium containing several thought-provoking essays on Russian policy.

24. Quoted in Department of State, *Communist Perspective* (Washington, D.C.: Division of Research for USSR and Eastern Europe, Office of Intelligence Research, 1955), p. 512.

25. Harold E. Blinn, "Seward and the Polish Rebellion of 1863," *American Historical Review,* **45** (July, 1940), 828–833.

26. See, for example, the reissue of George Kennan's *Siberia and the Exile System* (Chicago: University of Chicago Press, 1958).

27. American aversions to Czarism are discussed in "Russian-American Relations, 1917–1933: An Interpretation," *American Political Science Review,* **28** (June, 1934), 388. The au-

thor contends that American estrangement from Russia stems from attitudes formed in the Czarist period.

28. Winston B. Thorson, "American Public Opinion and the Portsmouth Peace Conference," *American Historical Review,* **53** (April, 1948), 439–464.

29. For official and unofficial American opinions on the Bolshevik Revolution, see George F. Kennan, *Russia Leaves the War* (Princeton, N.J.: Princeton University Press, 1956); Jules Davids, *America and the World of Our Times* (New York: Random House, 1960), pp. 115–117; Bernard S. Morris, *International Communism and American Policy* (New York: Atherton Press, 1966), pp. 125, 130; William A. Williams, *American-Russian Relations: 1781–1947* (New York: Holt, Rinehart and Winston, 1952), pp. 105–131.

30. This viewpoint has perhaps been most forcefully presented by D. F. Fleming, *The Cold War and Its Origins,* Vol. I (Garden City, N.Y.: Doubleday, 1961, two vols.), pp. 31–32; see also Williams, *American-Russian Relations,* pp. 131–157.

31. See Bailey, *America Faces Russia,* pp. 636–637; Davids, *America and the World of Our Times,* pp.115–117. Monographic studies of this still controversial episode in American diplomatic history are L. I. Strakhovsky, *The Origins of American Intervention in North Russia, 1918* (Princeton, N.J.: Princeton University Press, 1937); the same author's *Intervention at Archangel* (Princeton, N.J.: Princeton University Press, 1944); and Betty M. Unterberger, *America's Siberian Expedition, 1918–1920* (Durham, N.C.: Duke University Press, 1956).

32. See *The Memoirs of Cordell Hull,* Vol. I (New York: Macmillan, 1948), p. 299.

33. Robert P. Browder, *The Origins of Soviet-American Diplomacy* (Princeton, N.J.: Princeton University Press, 1953), p. 9.

34. Department of State, *Foreign Relations of the United States, The Soviet Union: 1933–1939* (Washington, D.C.: U.S. Government Printing Office, 1952), pp. 6–9; Williams, *American-Russian Relations,* pp. 236–237.

35. Bailey, *America Faces Russia,* p. 709.

36. Our treatment of Soviet-Western relations during the 1930s draws from a large number of sources. One of the most scholarly and dispassionate is Max Beloff, *The Foreign Policy of Soviet Russia, 1929–1941* (New York: Oxford University Press, 1949, two vols.). In general, Beloff takes a very limited view of both Russia's capabilities and its desire to cooperate with the West to halt Axis expansionism during the 1930s. A more recent analysis is by the distinguished Russian scholar, George F. Kennan, *Russia and the West Under Lenin and Stalin* (Boston: Little, Brown and Co., 1960). A detailed treatment of the Munich crisis is John Wheeler-Bennett, *Munich: Prologue to Tragedy* (New York: Duell, Sloan and Pearce, 1948). Interpretations emphasizing the essentially defensive nature of Soviet diplomatic behavior during this period are Peter G. Filene, ed., *American Views of Soviet Russia* (Homewood, Ill.: Dorsey, 1968); William A. Williams, *The Tragedy of American Diplomacy* (Cleveland: World Publishing, 1959), pp. 135–143; and the same author's *American-Russian Relations,* pp. 234–253. Perhaps the most capable assertion of the "re-examinist viewpoint" on the interwar period is Fleming, *The Cold War and Its Origins,* Vol. I, pp. 53–97. The official American view of the Nazi-Soviet Pact, highly critical of Moscow's diplomacy, is the State Department's publication, *Nazi-Soviet Relations, 1939–1941* (Washington, D.C.: U.S. Government Printing Office, 1948).

37. Bailey, *America Faces Russia,* p. 713.

38. For the re-examinist explanation of Soviet Russia's attack against Finland, see Fleming, *The Cold War and Its Origins,* Vol. I, pp. 101–104; and Williams, *American-Russian Relations,* pp. 254–255. Even American opinion normally favorable to Moscow, however, was shocked by the Finnish War; see Filene, *American Views of Soviet Russia,* pp. 137–141.

39. Bailey, *America Faces Russia,* pp. 726–727.

40. The views of Truman and others in this vein are cited in Fleming, *The Cold War and Its Origins,* Vol. I, pp. 135–137.

41. See the views of General Marshall in George C. Marshall, *Ordeal and Hope* (New York: Viking, 1965), pp. 72, 240.

42. See Williams, *American-Russian Relations,* p. 265; and Walter LaFeber, *America, Russia, and the Cold War, 1945–1966* (New York: Wiley, 1968), pp. 5–6.

43. Churchill's politico-military strategy, involving an Allied invasion through the "soft underbelly" of Europe, is discussed in Fleming, *The Cold War and Its Origins,* Vol. I, pp. 154, 159–160, 164–167; and Gaddis Smith, *American Diplomacy During the Second World War: 1941–1945* (New York: Wiley, 1966), pp. 46–47.

44. For discussions of the Katyn massacres, presenting evidence pro and con regarding Russia's involvement, see Smith, *American Diplomacy During the Second World War,* pp. 70–71; Fleming, *The Cold War and Its Origins,* Vol. I, pp. 228–230. Alexander Werth, *Russia at War, 1941–1945* (New York: Avon Books, 1964), pp. 606–612, presents a balanced analysis of this and other wartime issues involving the Soviet Union. Werth makes the significant point that at the Nuremberg war crimes trials, the evidence of German complicity in the Katyn massacres was regarded as too slender to indict Nazi officials for the crime.

45. Evidence on the controversial "Warsaw uprising" is still mixed and incomplete, particularly as regards Soviet intentions. Indictments of Moscow's behavior are Stanislaw Mikolajczyk, *Rape of Poland* (New York: Whittlesey House, 1948); and Arthur B. Lane, *I Saw Poland Betrayed* (Indianapolis: Bobbs-Merrill, 1948). Less polemical, but favorable to the Soviet view, is Fleming, *The Cold War and Its Origins,* Vol. I, pp. 233–237. Werth's account in *Russia at War,* pp. 786–801, is thorough, presenting many of the military difficulties confronting Soviet commanders as they approached Warsaw.

46. For the text of the Yalta Agreement, see the useful compendium prepared for the Senate Foreign Relations Committee, *A Decade of American Foreign Policy: Basic Documents, 1941–1949,* 81st Cong., 1st Sess., 1950, pp. 27–34. Useful commentaries are Werth, *Russia at War,* pp. 876–886; Smith, *American Diplomacy During the Second World War,* pp. 129–136; Fleming, *The Cold War and Its Origins,* Vol. I, pp. 191–218. Primary sources on the Yalta Conference are James F. Byrnes, *Speaking Frankly* (New York: Harper & Row, 1947), pp. 21–45; and Edward R. Stettinius, *Roosevelt and the Russians: The Yalta Conference* (Garden City, N.Y.: Doubleday, 1949).

47. See the views of Fleming, *The Cold War and Its Origins,* Vol. I, pp. 214–215, 266; and Williams, *The Tragedy of American Diplomacy,* pp. 163–169.

48. See Byrnes, *Speaking Frankly,* pp. 54–55; 57–59.

49. See the discussion of the last months of the Roosevelt Administration's diplomacy in Daniel Yergin, *Shattered Peace: the Origins of the Cold War and the National Security State* (Boston: Houghton Mifflin Co., 1978), pp. 1–109; and Martin F. Herz, *Beginnings of the Cold War* (New York: McGraw-Hill, 1966), pp. 3–153.

50. Harry S Truman, *Memoirs,* I (Garden City, N.Y.: Doubleday and Co., 1955, 2 volumes), pp. 14–17, 23, 25.

51. Ibid., p. 71. See also the views of George F. Kennan, whose views on Soviet wartime and postwar diplomacy were highly influential in the policies adopted by the Truman Administration, as contained in his *Memoirs (1925–1950)* (New York: Bantam Books, 1967), pp. 227–284.

52. The containment policy was perhaps most clearly and succinctly enunciated by George F. Kennan, writing under the pseudonym of "X," in "The Sources of Soviet Conduct," *Foreign Affairs,* **25** (July, 1947), 556–583. The article is also reproduced as an appendix to Kennan's *American Diplomacy: 1900–1950* (New York: New American Library, 1952), pp. 102–121.

53. Kennan, *American Diplomacy,* p. 112.

54. The list of revisionist studies of the Cold War is voluminous. The following are among the leading studies: Fleming, *The Cold War and Its Origins;* Williams, *American-Russian Relations;* Williams, *The Tragedy of American Diplomacy;* Ronald Steel, *Pax Americana,* rev. ed. (Baltimore: Penguin Books, 1980); Raymond Aron, *The Imperial Republic: The United States and the World, 1945–1973* (Cambridge, Mass.: Winthrop Publishers, 1974); Amaury de Riencourt, *The Coming Caesars* (New York: Capricorn Books, 1957); David Horowitz, *The Free World Colossus* (New York: Hill and Wang, 1971); Gabriel Kolko, *The Roots of American Foreign Policy* (Boston: Beacon Press, 1969); Richard J. Barnet, *Roots of War: The Men and Institutions Behind U.S. Foreign Policy* (Baltimore: Penguin Books, 1972); John C. Donovan, *The Cold Warriors: A Policy-Making Elite* (Lexington, Mass.: D. C. Heath, 1974); Stephen E. Ambrose, *Rise to Globalism,* rev. ed. (Baltimore: Penguin Books, 1980); Richard J. Walton, *Cold War and Counter-Revolution: the Foreign Policy of John F. Kennedy* (Baltimore: Penguin Books, 1972); N. D. Houghton, ed., *Struggle Against History: U.S. Foreign Policy in an Age of Revolution* (New York: Simon and Schuster, 1968); Michael Parenti, ed., *Trends and Tragedies in American Foreign Policy* (Boston: Little, Brown and Co., 1971).

55. For studies on American foreign policy focusing upon Washington's alleged hostility toward revolutionary movements abroad, see Richard J. Barnet, *Intervention and Revolution: America's Confrontation with Insurgent Movements Around the World* (New York: World Publishing Co., 1968); Melvin Gurtov, *The United States Against the Third World: Antinationalism and Intervention* (New York: Praeger Publishers, 1974); and J. William Fulbright, *The Arrogance of Power* (New York: Random House, 1966), pp. 67–157.

56. This theme is developed in detail in Fulbright's book, *The Arrogance of Power, passim.*

57. For an illuminating discussion of "revisionism" as a recurrent phenomenon in American diplomatic history, see Dexter Perkins, "American Wars and Critical Historians," *Yale Review,* **40** (Summer, 1951), 681–695.

58. For more detailed discussion of revisionist theories about American participation in World War I, see Wayne S. Cole, *Senator Gerald P. Nye and American Foreign Relations* (Minneapolis: University of Minnesota Press, 1962); Warren I. Cohen, *The American Revisionists: the Lessons of Intervention in World War I* (Chicago: University of Chicago Press, 1967); and John E. Wiltz, *In Search of Peace: the Senate Munitions Inquiry, 1934–1936* (Baton Rouge, La.: Louisiana State University Press, 1963).

Chapter 10

Soviet-American Relations:
The Future of Détente

In mid-June 1979, President Jimmy Carter and Soviet President Leonid Brezhnev met in Vienna for a summit conference between the superpowers. In his toast to the Soviet leader, President Carter said:

> We have come to Vienna in search of common understanding in a spirit of common sense. We have come to explore, to clarify, and to attempt to resolve all our differences. We have come to take one more step toward avoiding a nuclear conflict in which some few might survive but which no one can win. . . . Let us pledge to seek new areas of common understanding in the same spirit of common sense. Let us pledge our continuing cooperation and honesty in our discussions, enhanced security of both nations, and—above all—a peaceful world.

In his toast to President Carter, Soviet leader Brezhnev lauded the principle of "peaceful coexistence" as the dominant concept in Soviet-American relations. Brezhnev

called for "the successful development of peaceful relations between the Soviet Union and the United States" and for the achievement of "a durable world peace."[1]

By the 1970s, such episodes in Soviet-American relations had become commonplace. On both sides of the Iron Curtain, officials widely referred to the new era in Soviet-American relations that had superseded the period of active Cold War conflict. Although spokesmen for the Reagan Administration were extremely critical of specific Soviet actions in foreign affairs (such as the Russian invasion of Afghanistan late in 1979 and the buildup of Soviet power in Cuba), President Reagan and his advisers gave no indication of desiring to return to the period of unrestrained Soviet-American competition, risking the outbreak of global nuclear war.

What was meant by the concept of détente between the superpowers? How did Soviet and American interpretations of the concept differ, and how did this fact per se produce new sources of misunderstanding between

Moscow and Washington? What forces produced this new stage in Soviet-American relations (and was it, in fact, as *new* as many commentators imagined)? How durable was détente, and what forces were likely to determine its future? These are the significant questions with which this chapter is concerned. We begin our inquiry by examining two interrelated questions: the historical evolution of the concept of détente and the meaning of the concept as interpreted in Moscow and Washington.

Détente: Its Evolution and Meaning

Some Preliminary Observations

By the end of the Vietnam War (if not, as some commentators viewed it, even earlier), relations between the superpowers had evolved into the stage of détente—an era that was, in many fundamental respects, different from the Cold War that had existed for almost a generation before.

If the Cold War had witnessed tendencies by the superpowers to go to the "brink of war" (as in the Cuban Missile Crisis of 1962), détente found Washington and Moscow endeavoring to refrain from such direct confrontations and to limit the proliferation of nuclear weapons throughout the international system. Fierce and often uncompromising ideological competition had characterized Soviet-American relations during the Cold War. After both the superpowers accepted the principle of détente, they deemphasized ideological differences between them and accommodated themselves to the "erosion of ideology" (or growing lack of interest in ideological disputes) throughout the world. During the period of intense Cold War antagonisms, both the United States and the Soviet Union engaged in "active" or "interventionist" diplomacy in distant parts of the world. The

"illusion of American omnipotence" had its counterpart in Soviet confidence that the forces of history were on the side of an "inevitable" and worldwide Communist victory.* In the new era of détente, the nuclear giants were more inclined to accept the existence of a highly variegated and "pluralistic" international system, most of whose members had political and economic orders closely resembling neither the American nor the Soviet model. By the late 1950s, successive administrations in Washington became more tolerant of contemporary systems like "African democracy" and "Arab socialism." For their part, officials in the Kremlin at length were compelled to accept, and to adapt their policies to, novel species of "national Communism," entailing diverse forms of Marxism and widely varying patterns of reliance upon (or independence from) the U.S.S.R. Yet paradoxically, even when Carter and Brezhnev were exchanging toasts to the future of détente, the superpowers were engaged in efforts to achieve (or to maintain) military "superiority"; intense Cold War competition between them existed in parts of Africa and the Middle East; and within a few months of the Vienna summit meeting, the Soviet invasion of Afghanistan produced one of the most serious and far-reaching ruptures in Soviet-American relations witnessed since World War II.

At the outset, several general observations need to be made about the evolution toward détente as the governing principle of Soviet-American relations. As our preceding discussion suggests, the difference in the pattern of their relationship in the eras of Cold War and détente were often *primarily matters of degree and emphasis.* To cite but one noteworthy example: The distinction between the two stages lay in the *kinds* of conflict or ri-

*The "illusion of American omnipotence" as a dominant idea in the foreign policy of the United States is discussed more fully in Chapter 2.

valry permitted (or excluded) between the superpowers, not in the presence or absence of such conflicts.

Progress in achieving détente in Soviet-American relations also proceeded *very unevenly,* over a period of many years. If by the 1970s the two nations clearly sought to avoid overt nuclear confrontation, overall military competition between them continued unabated; and little diminution in this rivalry could be expected during the 1980s.

This is perhaps but another way of saying that, from the beginning, the scope of détente has been a contentious issue between Washington and Moscow. During the Cold War, hostility between the nuclear giants affected virtually *every aspect* of their interactions. In this respect, the Cold War resembled the concept of "total war" witnessed during World War II: No important realm of Soviet-American relations was unaffected by the antagonism and hostility existing between the belligerents. In the American view (as Washington's subsequent insistence upon the concept of "linkage" implied), this same pattern ought to govern Soviet-American relations during the era of détente. The anticipated "relaxation of tensions" should be extended to all significant dimensions of their relations. Or, to apply an idea conspicuous in American foreign policy during the early post-World War II era: Moscow should "prove by deeds, and not words" that it was dedicated to international peace and stability by its conduct across a wide range of Soviet actions.

As we shall see more fully in due course, however, this was not the Soviet conception of détente.

The Forces Producing Détente

The forces responsible for a fundamental change in Soviet-American relations—from Cold War hostilities and antagonisms to acceptance of the principle of détente are—in the main, identical to those transforming the international system from a "bipolar" to a "multipolar" order. Since we examined these forces in detail in Capter 1, we shall reiterate them only briefly here.

A crucial development was the acquisition of nuclear arsenals by both of the superpowers—leading to the existence of a "nuclear balance of terror" between them. The United States and the Soviet Union were now deterred from relying directly upon nuclear weapons for the pursuit of their national objectives.

The emergence of the Third World—and the adoption by most of its members of a foreign policy position of diplomatic "nonalignment"—also encouraged détente between the superpowers. Increasingly, the Third World has proved resistant to efforts by the United States and the Soviet Union to "dictate" its foreign policy orientation or its political systems.

Another key development fostering détente has been the growth of "polycentrism"—or what are sometimes called numerous varieties of "national Communism"—within the Communist world. Beginning with the defection of Yugoslavia from the Soviet bloc in the late 1940s, from Europe to Latin America one Marxist state after another has reduced its dependence upon the Soviet Union and allowed nationalistic factors to influence its internal and external policies. Polycentrism has presented the Kremlin with a twofold challenge: The tendency has destroyed the cohesion of a once tightly knit "Communist bloc" under Moscow's direction; and the Kremlin must now devote time, energy, and attention to preserving minimal cohesion among the members of the Communist community, and it has sometimes been hard pressed to gain recognition of its position of primacy in the international Communist movement.

Within the general tendency toward polycentrism, one particular development —the "break" between the Soviet Union and the People's Republic of China that became evident by the early 1960s—deserves special mention. The dissolution of the Sino-Soviet axis—followed by increasingly ominous and deep-seated conflicts between these two Communist power centers—had a profound impact upon the nature of the international system. By the end of the 1970s, the Sino-Soviet axis had been superseded by growing Sino-American cooperation on several fronts, raising at least the possibility that the two countries might become *de facto* military allies against the common Soviet danger. (The implications of this momentous development in American foreign policy are analyzed more fully in Chapter 15.)

Comparable developments induced the United States to accept the idea of détente. As we shall see in Chapter 11, in time the NATO alliance began to suffer from "disarray." Since the early 1960s, the Western coalition has remained in a condition of greater or lesser disunity—and has encountered a series of difficult problems disrupting its cohesion. No evidence exists that these problems will be overcome in the near future.

Finally, a more recent inducement for both the United States and the Soviet Union to endorse détente as the governing principle of their relations has been the necessity for both countries to concentrate upon *pressing domestic problems*. The Soviet Union continues to experience a number of acute economic problems—principally, in raising agricultural production and in meeting its need for "high technology" industrial goods and know-how. The level of political dissidence within the

U.S.S.R. remains high. Soviet citizens continue to demand more and better consumer goods, along with programs like improved housing, health care, and other services.

In the United States, especially since the termination of the Vietnam War, executive officials confronted comparable demands from citizens and Congress. During the 1970s, in the aftermath of the bitter Vietnam experience, the American people demanded foreign policy "retrenchment" and a reduction in the nation's overseas commitments. Expenditures for national defense (as a percentage of the nation's Gross National Product or vis-à-vis the level of Soviet defense spending) declined. Internal problems—many of which had been neglected during the Vietnam War—demanded the attention of public officials. As long as American attitudes toward international affairs were governed by what was sometimes called the "Vietnam War syndrome," the United States did not have the inclination—nor did its leaders possess the means—to compete with the Soviet Union for influence in distant parts of the world, like black Africa. These realities largely induced Americans to embrace the concept of détente.

When did détente largely supersede the Cold War as the basic pattern of Soviet-American relations? That question elicits almost as many answers as there are informed students of modern international relations, a partial explanation for which may lie in the fact that the concept of détente has no universally accepted meaning. Let us take note of three essentially different answers to the question.

The Challenge of Classical Diplomacy

One school of thought holds that the contemporary concept of détente—or the decision of the nuclear giants to avoid direct military conflict and to cooperate in many dimensions of their relations—is actually a very old idea that is intrinsic to the process of diplomacy. Proponents of the *Realpolitik* approach to international relations particularly emphasize the idea that the task of the diplomat is to resolve actual and potential global conflicts peacefully on the basis of agreements reflecting the "national interests" of the states involved in them.* Throughout history, diplomats have confronted this challenge and, while Soviet-American relations today admittedly contain certain unique elements, it remains the function of diplomacy in the contemporary international system.

Successfully meeting the challenge may be difficult, but history provides many examples indicating that it is not impossible. After the Crusades, for example, the members of Christendom and of Islam managed to "coexist" reasonably well for a period of several centuries, despite their religious and ideological differences. A formula permitting peaceful coexistence was finally found after the devastating and bloody Thirty Years' War in Europe (1618–1648), enabling Protestants and Catholics to live amicably on the European continent without a resumption of religiously inspired conflicts.

*One of the ablest and most vocal proponents of this viewpoint was Walter Lippmann, who contended that the achievement that is currently called détente had always been the task of diplomats. "The history of diplomacy," Lippmann once said, "is the history of relations among rival powers, which did not enjoy political intimacy, and did not respond to appeals to common purpose. Nevertheless, there have been settlements. Some of them did not last very long. Some of them did. For a diplomat to think that rival and unfriendly powers cannot be brought to a settlement is to forget what diplomacy is about. There would be little for diplomats to do if the world consisted of partners, enjoying political intimacy, and responding to common appeals." Lippmann's views are quoted in Daniel Yergen, *Shattered Peace: the Origins of the Cold War and the National Security State* (Boston: Houghton Mifflin Co., 1978), p. 295.

The ability of powerful nations to resolve their differences peacefully—or, in the case of America and Soviet Russia, to achieve détente—is no less a transcendent challenge of diplomacy today. Several steps are requisite for its success: (1) diplomats (and behind them, of course, national officials and public opinion) must *prefer* agreement to violent methods for resolving international disputes; (2) diplomats must at all times recognize that other countries have "national interests" (and sometimes "vital interests") which they are devoted to and are determined to promote; (3) agreements reached must, therefore, take account of these conflicting interests, leaving no party to them completely "unsatisfied" and determined to alter them by force; (4) if the diplomatic process is to operate with maximum results, national officials and citizens must be willing to understand the viewpoints and interests of other countries, and be prepared to arrive at agreements from which all parties to them benefit; and (5) the nation's leaders must be willing and able to convince the people that agreements reached on this basis are preferable to the main alternative—reliance upon nuclear and lesser forms of military power to achieve national objectives.

The informed student of international relations will be aware that the diplomatic process described above resembles what is sometimes called a "non-zero sum game," or a contest (like a trade agreement or a labor-management bargaining session) in which there is no clear "winner" or "loser." Theoretically (if diplomats do their job skillfully), all parties to the agreement may "win" or benefit; or (if the agreement fails to preserve peace among them), all may equally "lose" or suffer harm. The underlying presupposition on which this classical view of the diplomatic process is based is the twofold idea that "politics is the art of the possible"; and that it entails *a continuing effort* to resolve, ameliorate, adjust, and manage disputes arising among the members of the international system.

Proponents of this viewpoint contend that the approach is fully applicable to the specific problem of Soviet-American relations. Evidence to support this contention is available from the history of relations between the two countries since the Communist Revolution of 1917. There is the overriding fact, for example, that despite their deep ideological differences, the two nations *have never engaged in a direct military conflict with each other for a period of more than 60 years.* (Their closest armed collision was the Cuban Missile Crisis of 1962, during which it became evident that Washington and Moscow sought to avoid a direct military confrontation.)

In the postwar period, despite the omnipresent threat of nuclear devastation, both superpowers have avoided *using* their formidable nuclear arsenals; and they have also agreed to inhibit the spread of nuclear weapons throughout the international system. In innumerable instances—such as the "Berlin Blockade" in the late 1940s, the Korean and Vietnam conflicts, and a host of lesser encounters in Latin America, the Middle East, and Asia—the superpowers have sought to avoid head-on military confrontation, and thus far they have been successful in doing so. Meanwhile, since World War II Washington and Moscow have also arrived at a number of informal and implicit understandings designed to minimize tensions between them. Thus, the United States has implicitly recognized Soviet dominance in Eastern Europe and has not sought to challenge that reality. Until the early 1960s (when the Soviet Union created an increasingly influential "presence" in Cuba), the United States thought it had a comparable pledge by the Kremlin to respect the American sphere of influence in the Western Hemisphere. Spokesmen for the Reagan Ad-

ministration, for example, believed that Soviet intrusions into the hemisphere seriously jeopardize the existence of détente. Such evidence indicates that the peaceful resolution of Soviet-American differences—or, by some definitions, détente—is possible and, in fact, has occurred in several crucial areas of mutual relations.

Stages in Détente

A second school of thought about the emergence of détente as the controlling principle in Soviet-American relations is in many respects very different. It conceives of relations between the two superpowers since World War II in two rather distinct stages, each of which has certain dominant and antithetical characteristics: the period of Cold War and the period of détente. In this view, therefore, détente is envisioned as a *distinct stage* in the evolution of Soviet-American diplomacy that came after the Cold War. Several forces that we have already identified produced fundamental changes in the international system, thereby radically altering the existing pattern of Soviet-American relations.

When did this transition in Soviet-American relations occur? As we have indicated, informed students of modern international relations give highly diverse answers to this question. As some commentators see it, the death of the Soviet dictator Joseph Stalin (on March 6, 1953) was a climactic event, profoundly altering the pattern of Soviet-American relations, as it affected many other aspects of Soviet life. As Louis J. Halle has explained the impact of this development, Stalin "had raised international tensions to a point of extreme danger for the Soviet state." His successors were thus compelled to retrench diplomatically and to modify Soviet behavior throughout the international system.[2] Or, as Bell interprets this era, Stalin's successor, Soviet Premier Georgi Malenkov, immediately committed the Soviet Union to the principle of détente with the United States, in large part in order to reduce Soviet military and diplomatic vulnerability created by Stalin's internal and external policies.[3]

Within a few months, there followed the signing of the Korean War cease-fire agreement (on July 27, 1953). Then in July 1955, a summit conference headed by President Dwight D. Eisenhower and Soviet Premier Nikita Khrushchev was held in Geneva. The conference between American and Soviet officials "had been held in a cordial atmosphere, which represented a sharp departure from the vitriolic recriminations" of earlier meetings. Agreements had been reached "to study ways of increasing friendship between the peoples of the West and of the Soviet Union, and these contacts could, we thought, presage the beginning of a more open society in the U.S.S.R." Yet, not uncharacteristically after such widely publicized summit conferences, Eisenhower also alluded to the disillusionment that the meeting ultimately fostered among American officials. Subsequent Soviet behavior proved "a grievous disappointment" in the light of hopes aroused by the Geneva conference.[4]

Other commentators place the beginning of détente in the late 1950s, and believe that it was symbolized by Soviet Premier Nikita Khrushchev's visit to the United States in 1959, during which Khrushchev and President Eisenhower held another summit meeting at Camp David. After that meeting, American and Soviet officials declared that the Cold War had ended, and a feeling of "relief and euphoria" about Soviet-American relations pervaded the international system.[5] Not untypically, the "spirit of Camp David" proved as ephemeral and elusive as most spirits! Even before the Eisenhower Administration left office, American officials planned a massive military operation to displace Castro's Marxist regime in Cuba—viewed in Washington as merely a puppet of the Soviet Union. And within a few months, Castro publicly disclosed his Communist orientation and his close ties with Moscow. The stage was, therefore, set for the most serious Cold War encounter since World War II: the Cuban Missile Crisis of 1962.

Still other commentators believe that détente did not exist between the United States and the Soviet Union until the Kennedy Administration—and, more specifically, until after the successful resolution of the Cuban Missile Crisis late in 1962. Early in 1961, the new Kennedy Administration gave American military as well as other forms of support to an effort by Cuban exile groups to overthrow the Castro regime in Cuba. The Bay of Pigs operation was a military disaster—and it resulted in a massive diplomatic defeat for the United States. Perhaps emboldened by this outcome—and confident that America's new President was inexperienced and cautious after the Bay of Pigs fiasco—the Soviet government began to install offensive missiles in Cuba.

The ensuing Cuban Missile Crisis* involved a complex series of events—entailing the danger of a direct Soviet-American nuclear confrontation—which it is unnecessary to recapitulate here.[6] Our purpose is served by noting that in time this dangerous encounter *was resolved peacefully:* Moscow removed its missiles from Cuba in return for a promise by Washington not to attempt another overthrow of the Castro government. As it related to the emergence of détente, the Cuban crisis had several noteworthy consequences. It forcefully reminded leaders and citizens on both sides of the Iron Curtain that the world had

---

*The Bay of Pigs episode and the Cuban Missile Crisis are discussed in greater detail in Chapter 14.

come dangerously close to the "brink of war," risking nuclear devastation for human civilization.[7] There was of course no guarantee that, in another Soviet-American encounter, rationality and restraint would prevail in Washington and Moscow.

The Soviet-American confrontation in Cuba had another result which, as some commentators view it, was crucial in the emergence of détente: it impressed Moscow with the Soviet Union's *military inferiority* vis-à-vis the United States, and it made the Communist hierarchy determined to achieve at least military parity (some observers believe, military superiority) toward its Cold War rival. From time to time after 1962, Soviet leaders were reported as having said that Moscow would "never again" confront the United States from a militarily inferior position. (The ensuing Soviet military buildup and its implications for American foreign policy were analyzed in greater detail in Chapter 5.)

Momentum in the direction of détente was maintained by the new Johnson Administration. Shortly after taking office in 1964, President Lyndon B. Johnson announced America's commitment to a policy of "building bridges" toward Eastern Europe and the Soviet Union. His Administration sought to

> ... build bridges across the gulf which has divided us from Eastern Europe. They will be bridges of increased trade, of ideas, of visitors and of humanitarian aid.[8]

Yet progress toward détente suffered a massive setback in the years ahead. Perhaps the main roadblock was the Vietnam War—viewed in the United States as a familiar Cold War encounter between American-supported forces of freedom and democracy against Soviet-supported (and Chinese-supported) forces of Communism and tyranny. Every step America took to escalate the conflict against the Communist enemy in Southeast Asia was matched by the Soviet Union and Communist China, in supplying military, economic, and other forms of aid to the government of North Vietnam and its political organization, the Viet Cong. After several years' military effort directed at bolstering the security of South Vietnam and other countries in Southeast Asia against Communist hegemony —and in the face of steadily mounting internal opposition to America's involvement in the Vietnam conflict—American officials finally admitted that the cause was hopeless. The Vietnam War was officially ended on January 27, 1973, terminating America's prolonged and draining involvement in that traumatic encounter.

In contrast to the Cuban Missile Crisis of 1962, the Vietnam War was a dramatic diplomatic and military defeat for the United States—affecting American attitudes toward foreign affairs for a decade or so thereafter. On the basis of the outcome in Vietnam, Soviet policy makers might well have concluded that they had *achieved* the military parity with the United States which they sought; and (as the Soviet conception of détente permitted) they could support "wars of national liberation" throughout the Third World with little fear of an effective American response. One key fact about the Vietnam conflict generally escaped notice: Throughout that prolonged military encounter, the superpowers had been extremely careful *not* to engage their own forces directly or to allow the struggle to "escalate" into another Soviet-American confrontation. In that sense, there existed implicit recognition in both Washington and Moscow that détente was indispensable to global peace and security.

A number of other developments during the period of the Vietnam War were also deleterious to progress toward détente. One was the massive Soviet military invasion of Czechoslovakia in 1968—when the Red Army placed the country under direct Soviet military occupation and political control. To American minds, this Soviet act was a reversion to "Stalinist" external behavior. Another significant development was the "third round" in the Arab-Israeli conflict that engulfed the Middle East a year earlier. This renewal of Arab-Israeli hostility resulted in an overwhelming Israeli military victory. Because of its close ties with Israel, America was widely blamed by the Arab states for this result; and the influence of the United States in the Middle East declined sharply. By contrast, Moscow was provided new opportunities for Soviet influence and intervention throughout the Middle East. For several years after 1967, the growth in Soviet influence within Egypt, for example, was especially striking.

Internal developments within both the United States and the Soviet Union added momentum to détente. Within the United States, after Vietnam most Americans were disinclined to engage in new foreign adventures, and they urged policy makers to concentrate upon domestic problems. Similarly, the Soviet hierarcy confronted ongoing political dissidence, rising consumer demands, and restiveness among the peoples of Eastern Europe concerning Soviet rule. During the 1970s, Soviet leaders must have felt confident that the U.S.S.R. would ultimately "win" the arms race, which the American society engaged in with little evident enthusiasm in the post-Vietnam War period.

For these reasons, other commentators mark the emergence of détente at the end of the Vietnam War. Although a formal cease-fire agreement was not signed in that conflict until January 27, 1973, active American participation in the war had begun to wind down several months earlier (beginning in mid-1971). The anticipated end of the conflict in Southeast Asia naturally affected Soviet-American relations. In May 1972, President Richard M. Nixon visited Soviet President Leonid Brezhnev in Moscow for a new round of summit talks. On May 26, 1972, the United States and the Soviet Union signed a document declaring that thereafter their relations would be "on the basis of peaceful coexistence." Both sides believed that the Moscow meeting had resulted in a new era in Soviet-American relations, which henceforth would be governed by the principles of détente.[9] Soviet officials particularly were elated, since by signing this document the United States now subscribed to a concept—peaceful coexistence between capitalism and Communism—that had formed part of the Marxist ideology since 1917.[10] This leads us to discuss the third view of détente: the Communist doctrine of peaceful coexistence as a principle of Soviet foreign policy.

The Marxist Concept of "Peaceful Coexistence"

According to a third interpretation of détente, the concept is merely a contemporary variant of an idea that has long been prominent in Communist ideology. This is the concept of the "peaceful coexistence" between capitalism (or other non-Marxist systems) and Communism. Peaceful coexistence has been a conspicuous Communist ideological theme for more than a half-century. Time and again after 1917, Lenin and other Soviet officials called for peaceful coexistence between the Soviet Union and possible adversaries—as in the case of Nazi Germany during the late 1930s or the United States during the 1970s.

Thus in the early post-World War II period (when the United States still had a monopoly on nuclear weapons), one Soviet spokesman wrote that

Soviet foreign policy proceeds from the fact of the coexistence for a long period of the two systems—capitalism and socialism [i.e., Soviet Communism]. From this it follows that cooperation between the USSR and countries with other systems is possible, provided that the principle of reciprocity is observed and that obligations once assumed are honored. Everyone knows that the USSR has always honored the obligations it has assumed.[11]

A decade later, Soviet Premier Nikita Khrushchev gave a report to the Supreme Soviet (or Soviet parliament), in which the necessity for peaceful coexistence between capitalism and Communism was a dominant *motif*. Against the "policy of maintaining and intensifying international tension," which was the approach of American-led "imperialist reaction," the Soviet leader called for agreement upon the principle of peaceful coexistence:

> Experience shows that the only correct path in the development of international relations is a policy of peaceful coexistence, a policy of strengthening peace and friendship among peoples.

Khrushchev went on to explain that,

> In advocating a policy of peaceful coexistence of states with different social systems, we, of course, have no intention of asserting that there are no contradictions between socialism [i.e., Soviet Communism] and capitalism, that complete "harmony" can be established between them, or that a reconciliation of the communist and bourgeois ideologies is possible. . . . The ideological differences are irreconcilable; they will exist. But this does not exclude peaceful coexistence and peaceful competition between socialist and capitalist countries.*

*In dealing with the Kremlin's ideological statements, the student is urged to bear in mind a distinction that often becomes blurred in the news media and in popular usage.

By contrast, Khrushchev believed that "an imperialist attempt to unleash a world war would lead to incredible destruction and loss; the use of atomic and hydrogen weapons and ballistic rockets would bring in its wake tremendous disaster to all mankind." True Communists "work from the premise that wars are not necessary to advance socialism."[12]

The devotion of the Soviet Union to the concept of peaceful coexistence was also a central theme in the report by President Leonid Brezhnev to the 25th Congress of the Communist Party early in 1976. On that occasion, Brezhnev defined the "main purpose" of Soviet foreign policy as bringing about "a change of direction in the development of international relations," from a condition of "cold war to the peaceful coexistence of states with different social systems." This would entail a "change from tension, carrying the threat of [nuclear] explosion, to détente and normal, mutually advantageous cooperation."[13]

According to its own ideological system, the Soviet Union is referred to as a "socialist," not a "Communist" state. Its official name is the Union of Soviet *Socialist* Republics. The ultimate goal of the system, of course, is to create a Communist order, but as the Kremlin sees it the transition to Communism has not yet occurred. Alternatively, the Soviet Union is sometimes described as being in the stage of "Communist construction" or preparing the foundation for the ultimate transition from socialism to Communism. The student also needs to keep in mind that, as the Kremlin employs the term, "socialism" has a special meaning—referring only to the Soviet system and those modeled closely after it. As the Kremlin sees it, the "socialist" parties or governments of Western Europe—or the "Arab socialist" regimes of the Middle East—are deviant movements, having little in common with the Soviet system. It is helpful to recall that in the early 1900s, the Marxist movement split into two branches. One of them—the *Bolsheviks*—became the dominant group after the Communist revolution in Russia. The other branch—the *Mensheviks*—rapidly lost influence within Russia but supplied the ideas and concepts underlying many of the socialist movements that became influential in Western Europe.

Several aspects of the Communist doctrine of peaceful coexistence need to be emphasized. First, in recent years there has been a tendency for Soviet officials to use the terms *peaceful coexistence* and *détente* synonymously; in most respects, the latter is merely an updated version of the former. As one commentator has said, while there may be subtle differences between the two concepts in Marxist ideology, these "stem rather from the situation in which they are applied than from the basic substance of the idea itself."[14]

Second, it is essential to note that the idea of peaceful coexistence is one of what might be called two "antiphonal themes" in Marxist ideology relating to the Soviet Union's relations with capitalist (or other non-Marxist) states. In opposition to the concept of peaceful coexistence, Lenin, Stalin, and other Soviet leaders have also emphasized the idea that tension, hostility, conflict, and violence would characterize the Soviet Union's relations with non-Communist nations—often described by such terms as "capitalist warmongers," "rotten imperialists," and comparable phraseology. In this conception, Marxist ideologists envision the global transition to an international Communist system as involving greater or lesser political conflicts, not excluding global war.

Thus in 1919, Lenin asserted:

> . . . We are living not merely in a state but in a system of states and the existence of the Soviet Republic side by side with imperialist states for a long time is unthinkable. One or the other must triumph in the end. And before that end supervenes, a series of frightful collisions between the Soviet Republic and the bourgeois [capitalist] states will be inevitable.[15]

The following year, Lenin wrote that ". . . as long as capitalism and socialism exist, we cannot live in peace; in the end one or the other will triumph—a funeral dirge will be sung over the Soviet Republic or over world capitalism."[16]

Similarly, in 1963 (during the same period he advocated peaceful coexistence between the superpowers), Soviet Premier Khrushchev said that:

> We are wholeheartedly for the destruction of imperialism and capitalism. We not only believe in the inevitable downfall of capitalism, but we do everything to ensure this will be achieved by means of the class struggle and as quickly as possible.[17]

Third, the existence of these two contrary themes in Communist ideology raises the difficult question: Which idea—peaceful coexistence or Lenin's idea of "frightful collisions" between capitalism and Communism—is the *authentic* expression of Communist ideology? What does the Kremlin *really believe,* that conflict (perhaps including global war) between capitalism and Communism is inevitable, or that the two systems can resolve their differences without recourse to global violence? Such questions permit no easy answers.

One approach to the problem is to take note of the difference between strategy and tactics in Marxist thought. Strategy refers to the long-range, *ultimate goals* of the Soviet Union in international affairs—such as the eventual global victory of Communism or the concept of "world revolution," to which the Kremlin is still ideologically committed. Tactics refer to the short-range—often highly expediential—*methods* used by the Soviet Union to accomplish its long-range purposes. Thus, one way of resolving the dilemma created by the presence in Marxist thought of the antithetical ideas of peaceful coexistence and conflict with non-Communist states is to say that peaceful coexistence is essentially *a tactical response* during a particular period to external conditions deemed temporarily adverse for pursuing the long-range strategy of world revolution or other ultimate Marxist objectives. Lenin, for example, wrote a book entitled *Two Steps Forward, One Step Backward,* propounding the idea that in the pursuit of its goals, the Soviet regime was compelled to modify its behavior in the light of conditions confronting it at home and abroad. On occasion, Lenin used the analogy of a sailboat which "tacks" in the face of adverse winds toward its ultimate destination.[18]

While this may be a legitimate way of understanding the ideas of peaceful coexistence and of conflicts with capitalism in Marxist thought, behind that dilemma is perhaps an even more difficult question: What role does *Communist ideology itself play* in the formulation and implementation of Soviet foreign policy? Two extreme positions—together with a number of intermediate ones—are possible in responding to this always complex, but still extremely important, question. One position is that Communist ideology has *no relationship* to the external behavior of the Soviet state, whose diplomacy is predominantly determined by strategic, historic, and other factors that were identified and discussed in Chapter 9.

This point of view was typified by the observation of French President Charles de Gaulle that "ideology is merely the fig leaf of national ambition." According to this interpretation, the primary contribution of Marxism to the Soviet Union's foreign policy is to provide it with some kind of *ideological justification or legitimacy,* thereby presumably enhancing its appeal to Soviet citizens, to Marxist and crypto-Marxist groups in other countries, and to the "proletariat" throughout the world. Soviet expansionism, for example, is clearly a more palatable and acceptable phenomenon if

it is depicted by the Kremlin as an effort to "liberate" subject peoples from imperialism rather than as an effort by the Soviet Union to enhance its own national power and global influence.

Alternatively, Soviet foreign policy may be interpreted as an effort to *apply the tenets of Marxist ideology directly to the conduct of foreign affairs.* From this perspective, the diplomatic behavior of the Soviet Union is "dictated" by ideological, more than any other, considerations. Accordingly, the most reliable guide to the external behavior of the U.S.S.R. consists of the ideological pronouncements of leading Communist spokesmen, beginning with Karl Marx and extending through Lenin, Leon Trotsky, Stalin, Khrushchev, and more recent political leaders of the U.S.S.R. Such ideological statements and publications supposedly provide reliable guidance to the "operational code" of the Soviet Union in dealing with internal and external issues.[19]

Between these two extremes, many other possible interpretations of the relationship between ideology and Soviet foreign policy are available. For example, it is possible to say that the contribution of ideology to the diplomatic behavior of the Soviet Union *varies considerably,* depending upon the circumstances facing the Communist hierarchy at home and abroad, the personalities of Soviet leaders, and other salient conditions. Under Stalin—who was primarily an opportunist and a master political manipulator—ideology had relatively little influence upon the Soviet Union's international conduct, whereas under other leaders (like Lenin) it had a relatively greater weight. And even under a single leader like Stalin, ideology may influence Soviet foreign policy more heavily in one period than in another period.

Another explanation holds that since 1917, Soviet foreign policy has been *progressively less subject to ideological influences* and more heavily affected by such factors as the Communist perception of external reality, the influence of certain groups (like the Communist Party membership or the armed forces) upon Soviet decision making, opportunistic considerations affecting Moscow's diplomatic conduct, the policies pursued by the United States and its allies, and other important variables. According to this interpretation, after Stalin's death in 1953 there gradually occurred a process known as "de-ideologization." Throughout the world, ideologies—and conflicts among nations stemming from ideological differences—were rapidly losing their appeal. This global phenomenon presumably affected the Soviet approach to foreign relations no less than it affected the approach of other countries.[20]

Finally, the existence of the dilemma posed in Communist thought by the presence of the concept of peaceful coexistence and of conflict with capitalism may be in some measure explained by saying that each position is available to Soviet policy makers for use in responding to essentially different conditions abroad. The ideological principle of peaceful coexistence, for example, has periodically been invoked by the Kremlin when it faced "objective conditions" deemed unfavorable for the pursuit of revolutionary or expansionist goals. Let us take note of merely two examples.

During the 1920s, Lenin and Stalin relied upon the concept of peaceful coexistence after it became evident that external conditions were not favorable for the pursuit of revolutionary goals abroad—without serious jeopardy to the security and well-being of the newly established Soviet state. A companion doctrine associated with Stalin—the concept of "Socialism in one country" —meant that Moscow had come to terms with this reality. In effect, it modified Marxist ideology to say that a Communist regime *could* successfully exist in the U.S.S.R. for an indefinite period in the future, without becoming part of a larger regional or global Communist system. Under this doctrine, the Soviet Union served as a kind of global "custodian" for the world revolution—now deferred to an unspecified time in the future.

In more recent years—after both the United States and the Soviet Union acquired nuclear arsenals—different considerations perhaps motivated the Kremlin to proclaim its devotion to the principle of peaceful coexistence: chiefly, the nuclear balance of terror. As statements by Khrushchev and his successors repeatedly emphasized, Soviet authorities were cognizant that a nuclear conflict with the United States jeopardized the future of civilized society, not excluding Soviet society, on the earth. Again, by proclaiming the necessity for peaceful coexistence between the capitalist and Communist systems, the Kremlin was adjusting its ideology, and presumably its behavior, to reality. While military strategists in the United States and the Soviet Union might assess the particular results of global nuclear war somewhat differently—for example, Soviet spokesmen were confident that Russia would survive a nuclear exchange —on both sides ample awareness existed that the effects of a nuclear holocaust would be devastating, both for the belligerents and for most other countries as well. The Kremlin's emphasis upon the doctrine of peaceful coexistence signified agreement with officials in other capitals on that inescapable reality.

The opposite side of the coin, of course, was the idea that the Kremlin might at some future point abandon the ideal of peaceful coexistence (when this could be done safely and advantageously) and revert to its revolutionary, hard-line posture toward the United States and other non-Communist countries. Given the increasing destructiveness and accuracy of nuclear weapons—and their steady proliferation throughout the international system—it is difficult to foresee a time when a rational process of decision making in the Kremlin could lead to such a conclusion.[21]

Détente and Its Connotations

Acceptance of the contemporary concept of détente required less of an adjustment in the Soviet perspective on external affairs than it did for officials and citizens in the United States. For Moscow, the concept of peaceful coexistence had long served as a kind of functional equivalent for the recent idea of détente. For Washington, the shift from a Cold War approach to acceptance of détente proved, in some respects, a more difficult transition. As we shall see, Americans have never perhaps been fully comfortable with the notion of détente. For many years, they have been uncertain about the requirements of détente, and they have been hard pressed to decide whether the United States or the Soviet Union gains the most from a condition of détente. To no inconsiderable extent, ambiguities and uncertainties surrounding the concept of détente fostered this American reaction.

What exactly is meant by the idea of détente between the superpowers? A former high-ranking State Department official has observed that the French term *détente* has no exact meaning—even in French! Today, the term has become as "cheap and commercial," and as imprecise, as "the spirit of Christmas"! The existence of a host of related and familiar terms—like *the spirit of Camp David* or the idea of a *thaw* in Soviet-American relations or *the relaxation of international tensions*—compounds the problem of trying to define détente accurately and to gain uniformity in the usage of the term.[22]

Numerous definitions of détente are available. One authority describes it as a "new era" in Soviet-American relations, in which

> . . . each of the two countries, regardless of rhetoric, tended to accept the other as a legitimate superpower in the international system, and their interaction began to take on the features of power balancing in the classical *Realpolitik* sense. As the environment, rules, and structure of the revised global system clarified, the need for a recourse to anti-Communist or anti-capitalist notions as a guide to action receded. Indeed, personnel changes in both countries reflected this situation, for national security technocrats, who perceived the world in at least somewhat similar conceptual frameworks, increasingly replaced ideologists in key foreign policy spheres in the two states. While conflict did not disappear, it was in general of a realist-political, as opposed to ideological-political, type. Furthermore, conflict tended to be indirect, i.e., carried out through proxies and clients.[23]

In 1977, Soviet President Brezhnev defined détente more simply by saying:

> Détente means first of all overcoming the Cold War and then a transition to normal, stable relations among states. Détente means the willingness to resolve differences and disputes not by force, not by threats and sabre-rattling, but by peaceful means at the conference table. Détente means a certain trust and the ability to consider each other's legitimate interests.[24]

In 1974, Secretary of State Henry Kissinger told a congressional committee that détente was essentially "a process of managing relations with a potentially hostile country in order to preserve peace while maintaining our vital interests." President Jimmy Carter later defined détente in Soviet-American relations as "progress toward peace," involving efforts by the two superpowers to resolve their mutual problems.[25]

Détente has also been described as a process by which "both superpowers . . . control their rivalry when their interests diverge, and . . . cooperate to their mutual advantage when their interests more or less coincide. . . ."[26] America's leading Kremlinologist, George F. Kennan, has said that détente means simply the ability of the United States and the Soviet Union "to take into consideration each other's legitimate interests."[27] One student of Soviet-American relations calls attention to an interesting connotation of the Russian word *razryadka* (the Soviet term for détente). The literal translation of the term is "to discharge a weapon" or "slackening the bowstring of a crossbow." (This commentator emphasizes that *razryadka* does *not* mean destroying one's weapons or ammunition!) Still another student of contemporary international politics believes that détente means the "conscious and deliberate *reduction* of tensions" between the superpowers, in contrast to Cold War, which assumed the "conscious *maintenance* of tensions at a relatively high level."[28]

Détente is also a concept that has more than one level of meaning. As one student of Soviet-American relations conceives it, the term has at least two rather different aspects. There is what can be called "necessary détente," or the realization by the superpowers that nuclear conflict between them would be catastrophic for human civilization. This mutual recognition requires them "to evolve techniques for avoiding not only a nuclear conflict but also those international situations which might lead to one." On another level, there is what might be called discretionary, or "optional," détente between the United States and the Soviet Union. This entails active cooperation between the superpowers on important issues—such as trade, cultural relations, scientific exchange, and other activities

—"under conditions of strict reciprocity," whereby concessions by one side would be matched by comparable concessions by the other side.[29]

It will perhaps contribute to enlightenment about the essential meaning of détente if we consider it in the context of four possible kinds of relationships between the United States and the Soviet Union. At one end of the scale would be maximum conflict and hostility—perhaps resulting in *regional or global war*. Détente is obviously different from, and seeks to avoid, that frightful prospect. Another possible condition of Soviet-American relations is *Cold War,* with which all students of post-World War II American foreign policy are familiar. As the term implies, Cold War differs from the former condition primarily in that the two superpowers do not engage in *direct military hostilities* with each other. Otherwise, Cold War denotes a condition of more or less acute tension between Washington and Moscow. Theoretically, détente also differs from this state of affairs—and is regarded by Washington and Moscow alike as an improvement over the Cold War that pervaded the international system for more than 20 years after World War II.

At the opposite end of the spectrum is a possible condition of Soviet-American relations accurately described by the old diplomatic term *entente* (illustrated by the Triple Entente, or the Anglo-French-Russian alliance during World War I). Entente denotes a high level of *agreement* among the parties concerned and *cooperative efforts* to achieve common goals, particularly in protecting their mutual security interests. In the recent period, entente describes the "special relationship" that has existed between the United States and Great Britain since World War II or (in theory, if not always in practice) the relationship existing among the members of the NATO alliance system. Quite clearly, entente and the contemporary concept of détente are *not* synonymous terms. However much they may disagree about what détente means in theory and practice, both Soviet and American officials agree that it does *not* signify completely peaceful, cordial, and cooperative relations between the superpowers, comparable to modern Anglo-American relations.

On our scale, détente thus occupies a position somewhere between Cold War and entente. It entails a significant *reduction* in tensions between the United States and the Soviet Union vis-à-vis the period of the Cold War—in some dimensions of their relationships much more than others. It perhaps implies an *ongoing effort* by Washington and Moscow to discover new areas of possible agreement. And it signifies restraint by the United States and the Soviet Union in the employment of military power in the pursuit of their foreign policy objectives. At the same time, détente does not denote the appearance of genuine friendship and common purposes in Soviet-American relations.*

We may also perhaps shed light on the meaning of détente by briefly taking note of what it does *not* mean. Détente does not signify the end of ideological differences and discords between the United States and the Soviet Union. It does not imply a willingness by

Washington or Moscow to renounce reliance upon military forces to achieve its foreign policy goals. (During the era of détente, even nuclear weapons served the purpose of deterrence of one superpower by the other; and there was no indication that either side was prepared to abandon its reliance upon nuclear weapons for that purpose.) It does not mean the end of propaganda exchanges between the United States and the Soviet Union. Nor does it imply any significant diminution in economic competition and rivalry between the two superpowers. (According to his later interpretation, Khrushchev's defiant challenge to America—"We will bury you!"—meant that the Soviet Union intended to overtake and surpass the United States economically.) Nor did détente entail any significant lessening in rivalry between the superpowers for positions of strength and influence in the Third World. Paradoxically, for example, some of the most intense competition between the United States and the Soviet Union occurred in the Third World (as in certain regions of Africa) while both countries subscribed to the principle of détente!

While substantial agreement exists between Washington and Moscow concerning the meaning of détente—and its central requirement perhaps is *restraint by the superpowers in pursuing their goals by reliance upon nuclear weapons*—other aspects of the concept have elicited continuing differences of interpretation between them. What are the "ground rules" of Soviet-American relations in the era of détente? Experience has shown that widely dissimilar viewpoints exist between the Soviet and the American positions on this question.

The Soviet Conception of Détente

To the minds of Soviet officials, détente has several important connotations, and entails a

---

*A leading student of contemporary Soviet-American relations has utilized a different scale to describe détente. The figure 100 would represent global war between the superpowers; the Cold War (which of course varies in intensity) could be represented by the figure 70. Détente would then be represented by a figure of 50—signifying the existence of what some commentators have called a condition of "peaceful engagement" between the superpowers. Although détente may be variously represented on such scales, the key fact about Soviet-American relations under détente perhaps is that they involve a *mixture* of conflict and limited cooperation in dealing with major international issues. See Coral Bell, *The Diplomacy of Détente* (New York: St. Martin's Press, 1977), pp. 236–237.

number of requirements, that are fully or partially unacceptable to policy makers and public opinion in the United States. This fact has sometimes generated intense controversy between Moscow and Washington concerning whether détente really exists and the behavior needed to preserve it.

Initially, we may note that Soviet officials have repeatedly proclaimed their belief in the idea of détente and have extolled it as the principle that ought to regulate Soviet-American relations, as emphasized in an official 1977 Soviet statement:

> Who does not know that it is the Soviet Union that has always consistently and persistently favored, and continues to favor, good relations with the [United States] based on the principles of peaceful coexistence? Who does not know that it is the Soviet Union that in recent years has made more than 70 concrete proposals aimed at détente, at ensuring peace, at disarmament and at improving relations among states?[30]

In the same period, a leading Soviet authority on American foreign policy extolled the concept of détente and called specifically for closer cooperation between the superpowers in several key areas of their relationships: the limitation of armaments; trade and commerce; science and medicine; engineering and space exploration; and in the overall pattern of their political relationships (as in collaboration between Washington and Moscow to prevent the eruption of new violence in the Middle East).[31]

Moreover, Soviet officials are never in doubt concerning the origins of threats to détente. Not unexpectedly, détente is endangered by the attitudes and policies of the United States and its diplomatic supporters. The 22nd Communist Party Congress found that "Imperialism is the only source of the war

danger. The imperialist camp is making preparations for the most terrible crime against mankind—a world thermonuclear war...."[32]

An editorial in *Pravda* in 1978 accused the Carter Administration of whipping up "war hysteria"; of escalating the arms race; and of intervening in Soviet internal affairs. The transition from the Carter to the Reagan Administration did not ease Soviet anxieties about America's intentions. *Pravda,* for example, found very little significant difference between the two administrations in terms of their "intoxication" with building up America's armed forces, presumably for some future use against the Soviet Union. The national election of 1980 had not really changed the affinity of America's "ruling circles" for imperialist and militaristic conduct.[33]

In the midst of these Soviet charges, three themes were conspicuous in the Kremlin's assessment of American foreign policy as it affected the future of détente. One was the idea that the United States sought to achieve, and to maintain, military superiority over the U.S.S.R. Moscow believed that this American action was highly inimical to the future of détente and to global peace.[34] Another was that the United States had repeatedly sought to intimidate the Soviet Union—specifically, by playing the "China card," or threatening to create a new Sino-American axis directed against the Soviet Union's interests in Asia and on a global scale.[35] Still another idea prominent in the Soviet assessment was the "unpredictability" of American foreign policy as exemplified by the policies of the Carter Administration. As the Kremlin saw it, détente was expected to *stabilize* Soviet-American relations; but under President Carter, American diplomacy had become highly unpredictable, capricious, and subject to sudden and irrational changes.[36]

Communist spokesmen have also repeatedly insisted that détente represents a *perma-*

nent change in Soviet foreign policy, not merely a tactical or expediential shift in Russian policy to accommodate temporary conditions. Peaceful coexistence, one Soviet authority has insisted, "is not a tactic but a strategy of Lenin's party. . . ."[37] Repeatedly, Soviet officials have denied that détente was a temporary or merely expediential response by the Kremlin to external developments. Détente, said Soviet Premier Brezhnev in 1980, is "the result of diverse efforts and is the common achievement of peace-loving states." The "fruits of détente" were valuable to all nations; and the Kremlin believed it necessary "to go forward" in strengthening and expanding détente to new areas of superpower collaboration.[38]

Yet as the Kremlin interprets it, peaceful coexistence and détente imply no diminution in the ideological struggle between Communist and non-Communist countries. Soviet President Brezhnev said in 1976 that "Détente does not in the slightest abolish, nor can it alter, the laws of the class struggle. . . ."[39] The following year, the 25th Communist Party Congress meeting in Moscow found no relaxation of ideological tensions between capitalism and Communism. To the contrary, such struggles were "increasingly coming to the fore" in international relations.[40]

The principle that détente signified no lessening in ideological struggles had certain corollaries. It meant, for example, that the Kremlin opposed what Marxists called "revisionism": efforts to dilute and weaken Communist ideology by adapting it to conditions or traditions of particular countries (as in Third World societies). Moscow also rejected "convergence," or the idea that capitalism and Communism were evolving toward each other and the implication that in time the differences between them would disappear (or become unimportant). Nor did the Kremlin accept an idea (prevalent in the West by the 1970s) that

several species of "national Communism" had appeared, capable of maintaining varying degrees of independence in their diplomatic behavior.[41]

Détente, as the earlier statement by President Brezhnev emphasized, meant no diminution in the global class struggle.[42] Several years earlier, another Communist spokesman stated that Soviet foreign policy was still "implemented under the conditions of a fierce class struggle in the international arena, and the fight between the forces of socialism and imperialism and progress and reaction."[43] Détente, said another Communist official in 1973, "cannot represent a departure from class principles of our foreign policy."[44]

The general principle that "revolutionary struggle" continues during the era of détente leads to one of the most important—and, in the American view, objectionable—ideas associated with the concept. This is the unswerving Communist commitment to support what Marxists describe as "wars of national liberation" throughout the world. The 22nd Communist Party Congress declared in 1961 that the Soviet Union was not opposed to all wars and other forms of violence in international relations:

> The [Communist Party of the Soviet Union] and the Soviet people continue to oppose all wars of conquest, including wars between capitalist countries, and local wars aimed at strangling people's emancipation movements, and consider it their duty to support the sacred struggle of the oppressed peoples and their just anti-imperialist wars of liberation.[45]

After détente became the guiding principle of Soviet-American relations, this same idea was preserved and reiterated in Marxist thought. Détente, said a Soviet publication in 1977, "creates fresh possibilities for stepping up the struggle against imperialism.''[46] Three years later, another Soviet source said:

> Yes, we are on the side—and we make no bones about it—of the peoples that are waging a struggle for social and national liberation, and we believe that theirs is a just struggle.[47]

Consonant with its ideological conviction that no conflict exists between the idea of détente and support for "wars of national liberation," the Soviet Union has intervened actively in behalf of various political causes throughout the Third World in recent years. Thus, a *Pravda* editorial early in 1976 stated that it was Moscow's "internationalist duty" to support anticolonial forces seeking to gain independence for the Portuguese colony of Angola.[48] Soviet intervention in Angola was massive and extremely influential in determining the future political orientation of that country.[49] One informed commentator found that, more generally throughout Africa, détente had witnessed no lessening in the Soviet Union's ambitions on that continent.[50]

An overt and large-scale Soviet military incursion into Afghanistan—beginning at the end of 1979 and ultimately involving upwards of 80,000 Soviet troops—provided graphic evidence of the Communist commitment to the "liberation" of Third World societies.* American officials regarded the Soviet thrust into Afghanistan as an extremely serious threat to the peace and security of the Middle East. Other nations inside and outside the Middle East condemned Moscow's blatant reliance upon military force to achieve its political goals.

Soviet officials, however, attributed the crisis in Afghanistan to "counterrevolutionary efforts" led by the United States and to the "machinations of the CIA."[51] As a Soviet journal said early in 1980:

> Needless to say, there has not been and is no Soviet "intervention" or "aggression" [in Afghanistan]. Rather, we are helping the new Afghanistan, at the request of its government, to defend the country's national independence, freedom and honor from armed aggressive actions from outside.

American and other foreign allegations about Soviet "aggression" in Afghanistan "are being made maliciously, for the purpose of facilitating the achievement of these states' imperialist designs."[52]

As a more general phenomenon, the era of détente had witnessed no significant reduction in Soviet efforts to influence, or to establish a strong position in, the Third World. Indeed, one result of détente was that—as the superpowers were committed to achieving and maintaining stability on the level of nuclear weapons—the differences between them tended to get "transferred" to the Third World and to be expressed in local conflicts pervading that zone.[53]

Another corollary of détente conspicuous in Communist thought is that it has no necessary application *to Soviet internal policy.* As in the past, Moscow remains highly resistant to outside efforts to "interfere" in its domestic affairs—regardless of whether such moves are prompted by America's commitment to the idea of promoting international human rights, protecting the interests of Soviet Jews and other minorities within the Soviet society, fostering democracy within the U.S.S.R., or for other reasons. Efforts by the American Congress during the early 1970s directed at compelling Soviet authorities to liberalize regulations governing Jewish emi-

---

*The Soviet attempt to subordinate Afghanistan—and America's response to it—are analyzed more fully in Chapter 15.

gration, for example, encountered implacable and vocal Soviet opposition.[54] Rapoport believes that détente has produced no significant change in the traditional hostility of Russian authorities to alien political ideas.[55] Simes believes that it is a misreading of the concept of détente to expect that it will lead to a "democratization" of Soviet society.[56]

The common denominator of these rather disparate Soviet connotations of détente revolves around a concept which (as we shall see more fully below) is emphasized heavily in the American understanding of the idea. This is the concept of "linkage"—or the notion that the relaxation of tensions between the two superpowers anticipated by détente should occur in *every major area of Soviet-American relations,* from arms control and a reduction in military expenditures, to increased trade, tourism, and cultural exchange between the superpowers, to cooperation between Washington and Moscow in resolving regional disputes.

In the Soviet view, such "linkage" has never been a necessary component of détente. As Simes has observed, détente has not fundamentally changed long-standing Soviet assessments of the role of military power in achieving diplomatic goals; it has not altered the Kremlin's determination to achieve military parity with (perhaps even superiority over) the United States; time and again, Soviet officials have indicated their intention of avoiding "another Cuba," when in 1962 Moscow was forced to make concessions to Washington because of Soviet military weakness.[57] As we have seen, détente has produced no diminution in Moscow's interest or involvement in political developments in the Third World—including its readiness to rely upon force to achieve its objectives.[58]

Ulam has said that the Soviet hierarchy has always rejected the idea of "linkage" as an integral part of détente. In the Kremlin's view,

every specific global issue or dispute must be "considered on its own . . . merits."[59]

The American Conception of Détente

On the basis of our discussion thus far, it will of course come as no surprise that the American understanding of détente differs in a number of fundamental respects from the Soviet version of the idea. Sharply contrasting differences of opinion between Washington and Moscow over what détente means remind us of a comment made several years ago about acrimonious debates within the United Nations: "Everyone loves a good fight—especially about peace," or more accurately perhaps in this case, about the relaxation of global tensions. Ironically, misunderstandings between the United States and the Soviet Union over the requirements of détente have themselves become another source of fundamental disagreements between the superpowers.

Several features of the American conception of détente merit brief examination. In the first place, American officials—together with American public opinion—have repeatedly endorsed the basic idea of détente, construing the concept at this stage to mean essentially achieving an end to the Cold War, avoiding nuclear and other forms of military conflict between the superpowers, and progressing toward the resolution of specific disputes between them. As was explained in detail in Chapter 9, in the prevailing American view, the United States did not instigate the Cold War conflict with the Soviet Union during and after World War II. As illustrated by the diplomacy of the Roosevelt Administration, the United States prefers friendly and cooperative relations with the Soviet Union to maintain global peace and security. The American containment policy was adopted in 1947 *in response* to the challenge of Soviet expansionism. But implicit in that policy from the beginning was the idea that—after the United States had demonstrated its willingness and ability to contain Soviet expansionism successfully—in time a fundamental change would occur in Soviet diplomatic behavior, leading to a more stable and peaceful global environment. In George F. Kennan's phrase, a "mellowing" was expected to occur in Soviet conduct, presumably leading to an ultimate diminution in Cold War tensions—and perhaps in time in the nature of the Soviet Communist system itself.

Long before the term *détente* gained wide currency, American chief executives and other officials expressed America's desire for harmonious relations with the Soviet Union. At the end of his memoirs, President Dwight D. Eisenhower described the long-standing American objective in its relations with the Soviet Union:

> But for some decades our purposes abroad have been the establishment of universal peace with justice, free choice for all peoples, rising levels of human well-being, and the development and maintenance of frank, friendly, and mutual contacts with all nations willing to work for parallel objectives.[60]

But more than any other recent chief executive perhaps, it was President John F. Kennedy who exemplified and emphasized America's commitment to what came to be called détente with the Soviet Union. To Kennedy's mind, no problem confronting the United States transcended the challenge of preventing a nuclear holocaust. In his inaugural address in 1961, Kennedy said: "Let us never negotiate out of fear, but let us never fear to negotiate." On another occasion, he said that "The world has long since passed the time when armed conflict can be the solution to international problems." Kennedy was con-

vinced that civilization would be imperiled by a Soviet-American nuclear confrontation. If the tragedy of a nuclear exchange occurred, he anticipated "150 million fatalities in the first eighteen hours." In contrast to some of his predecessors, Kennedy did not believe that the Cold War could be "won" by either side. His aim was

> ... to dampen it down, to outlast it, to make it possible for the long-run forces of liberty and truth to work their way naturally and peacefully, to prevent the cold war from monopolizing our energies to the detriment of all other interests.

Kennedy was convinced that if Soviet-American competition could be confined to peaceful channels, in the end the cause of human freedom and liberty would prevail over Communism and tyranny.[61]

After the Vietnam War, new expressions of interest in détente came from American officials. President Richard M. Nixon's national security adviser, Dr. Henry Kissinger, believed that it was incumbent upon the United States and the Soviet Union to take the lead in creating a new and more stable global system, founded upon a recognition of their mutual interests. As a devotee of the *Realpolitik* school of international relations, Kissinger was convinced that ideological, economic, and other differences need not be an impediment to détente between the superpowers.* Under the

---

*As we noted in our earlier discussion of the concept of national power (Chapter 1), the school of thought known as *Realpolitik*—tracing its ideological orgins from the political ideas of Machiavelli, Hobbes, Metternich, and Bismarck—believes that power is the pivotal concept of international relations. All members of the international system seek to maximize and preserve their power; they are devoted above all else to the pursuit of their "national interests"; and peace and stability in the international system can be maintained by preserving the "balance of power" among the most influential members. In the post-

Nixon Administration, détente received tangible expression in the Vladivostok accord between the United States and the Soviet Union; and this agreement in turn led to the SALT I strategic arms-control agreement between them in 1972.[62]

An improvement in Soviet-American relations, as a crucial step toward promoting global peace and stability, was a high priority diplomatic goal of the Carter Administration. On June 7, 1978, President Jimmy Carter addressed the graduates of the U.S. Naval Academy, devoting his speech to the American conception of détente with the U.S.S.R. In his address, Carter emphasized the importance of Soviet-American relations in the foreign policy of the United States. Underscoring America's commitment to peace, Carter said:

> Détente between our two countries is central to world peace. It is important for the world, for the American public and for you as future leaders of the Navy to understand its complex and sensitive nature.

World War II period, the *Realpolitik* approach to American foreign policy has been prominently reflected in the thought of students like Walter Lippmann, Hans J. Morgenthau, and Henry Kissinger. Kissinger, for example, after the Vietnam War called for a "new structure" in the international system based on the balance of power principle. For more detailed elaboration of this approach, see Ira S. Cohen, *Realpolitik: Theory and Practice* (Encino, Calif.: Dickenson Pub. Co., 1975); Hans J. Morgenthau, *In Defense of the National Interest* (New York: Alfred A. Knopf, 1952), and *A New Foreign Policy for the United States* (New York: Praeger Publishers, 1969). For Kissinger's thought, see Henry A. Kissinger, *Nuclear Weapons and Foreign Policy* (New York: W. W. Norton, 1969) and David Landau, *Kissinger: The Uses of Power* (New York: Thomas Y. Crowell, 1974). A critique of *Realpolitik,* evaluating the leading ideas in this approach, is available in Cecil V. Crabb, Jr., *Policy-Makers and Critics: Conflicting Theories of American Foreign Policy* (New York: Praeger Publishers, 1976), pp. 165–214.

To Carter's mind, détente meant "the easing of tension between nations" and the discovery of "new means by which they can live with each other in peace." Carter called for "widening the scope of cooperation" between the two superpowers. Although it presaged a number of fundamental changes in American foreign policy, the election of Ronald Reagan to the presidency in 1980 signified no abandonment of Washington's interest in détente with Moscow. Thus (even while his administration was in the process of imposing new trade restrictions upon the U.S.S.R. because of Soviet intervention in Poland), Reagan declared: "The United States wants a constructive and mutually beneficial relationship with the Soviet Union. We intend to maintain a high-level dialogue." Yet Reagan cautioned the Kremlin that Soviet-American relations could evolve in one of two directions: "toward greater mutual restraint and cooperation, or further down a harsh and less rewarding path." As other chief executives before him had emphasized, Reagan believed that the outcome would ultimately be decided by *Soviet behavior* in such critical areas as Poland, the Persian Gulf region, and Latin America.[63]

As these statements make clear, the United States and the Soviet Union hold different conceptions of the meaning and major implications of détente. To the American mind, certain prerequisites are required for genuine or successful détente—and some of these ideas have been consistent elements in American foreign policy since the Truman Administration. Détente was (in the words of former Secretary of State Henry Kissinger) essentially "a mode of management of adversary power."[64] It was an effort to maintain international stability and peace—especially in the avoidance of nuclear conflicts—on the basis of certain explicit and implicit understandings between the superpowers concerning how they would (or would not) demean themselves diplomatically. Or, as a State Department publication explained détente in 1978, its "central element" was the "need to assure stability in the nuclear confrontation" between the United States and the Soviet Union. Its goal "is a stable US-Soviet relationship that will permit us to manage our competition successfully, and thereby advance US security and world peace."[65]

So defined, détente was not what many Americans thought it was or expected it to be. As the American ambassador to the Soviet Union, Malcolm Toon, said in 1978, considerable "misunderstanding" about détente existed from time to time among the American people, and this contributed to "an extreme swing of the pendulum of our relations" with the Soviet Union. The concept of détente sometimes engendered "uncritical and heedless euphoria" in the minds of Americans and perhaps other citizens. Unwarranted meanings and expectations should not be ascribed to détente. Successful détente, for example, "does not mean that a millennium of friendship or mutual trust has arrived" between the former Cold War adversaries. In Toon's view:

> At most the concept [of détente] represents a growing sense in this nuclear age of the need to cooperate on some matters, to regulate competition [between the United States and the Soviet Union] on others, and to agree on the means of diffusing tensions which could lead to dangerous confrontation. And that is all. Nothing more.[66]

More specifically, three dominant ideas or concerns have been prominent in the American approach to détente with the Soviet Union. One of these—which can be traced back to earlier American apprehensions about the Marxist doctrine of peaceful coexistence—is whether the Soviet Union really

wants peace with the United States and *desires* to maintain stability in the international system. Time and again, American officials have expressed doubts on this score.

Is Moscow's avowal of devotion to détente in the contemporary period merely a modern example of the familiar Soviet "peace offensive," conducted many times in the past when policy makers in the Kremlin judged a peaceful diplomatic line advantageous for the pursuit of their goals? As Dr. Henry Kissinger assessed it, Moscow had relied upon détente (or its doctrinal equivalent) frequently in the past—usually during periods of internal or external Soviet weakness. Yet the end of such periods—in which the Kremlin called for the "relaxation of tensions" with its adversaries —had brought "an opportunity for expanding Communism" and strengthening Soviet hegemony over weaker countries.[67]

Other students of contemporary international politics shared many of Kissinger's doubts about Moscow's motives in subscribing to détente and the benefits accruing to the United States from the concept. One school of thought, for example, attributes Moscow's interest in détente chiefly to *Soviet weakness*. In a number of key dimensions of Soviet policy—Moscow's inability to prevent and control internal political dissidence, the poor performance record of the Soviet economy (particularly in the crucial agricultural sector), the U.S.S.R.'s lack of success in establishing a dominant position in most Third World societies and in curtailing Western influence in them—the Communist hierarchy encounters obstacles to its expansionist foreign policy goals. Hence, as in the past, the Kremlin embraces the idea of détente in an attempt to prevent its adversaries from capitalizing diplomatically upon Soviet weaknesses.[68] In this view, Soviet acceptance of détente is a tacit admission by the Kremlin that it is unable to compete with the United States in the Cold

War arena.* If and when Moscow's competitive position improves—and Soviet authorities believe they can *win* in a contest with the United States—then their enthusiasm for détente will wane, to be replaced by a new era of "revolutionary struggle" against capitalism.

Deep misgivings about the sincerity of the Soviet commitment to détente affect the attitudes of many Americans on the subject. The Senate's reluctance to give its consent to the SALT II arms-control agreement in 1979–1980, for example, stemmed in no small measure from pervasive doubts in Congress about the genuineness and permanence of the Soviet commitment to détente. The Soviet invasion of Afghanistan late in 1979—followed by the steady expansion of Russian forces in that country—did not allay pervasive American misgivings about Soviet intentions. During his successful bid for the presidency in 1980, Ronald Reagan complained that America had been "out-negotiated [by the Soviet Union] for quite a long time." Moscow had "managed, in spite of all our attempts at arms limitation, to go forward with the biggest

military buildup in the history of man." Reagan opposed SALT II, but he favored a new arms accord that achieved "a reduction of ... nuclear weapons to the point that neither one of us represents a threat to the other." In the absence of such an agreement, Reagan believed the United States could and should compete successfully against the U.S.S.R. on the plane of military rivalry.[69]

A second motif in the American view of détente (almost wholly lacking in the Soviet conception) is that the concept should be viewed *broadly and dynamically*. As President Carter said in his speech at the Naval Academy, the United States seeks "to *increase* our collaboration with the Soviet Union" to encompass all major areas of tension and controversy between the superpowers.[70] Or, as Secretary of State Cyrus Vance asserted in the same period, the United States and the Soviet Union need to "consult" on "the entire range of U.S.-Soviet relations." Not only should Washington and Moscow endeavor to avert crises involving the use of conventional or nuclear military power, but they should also "seek to expand other areas of mutually beneficial cooperation."[71] Again, at the Vienna summit meeting with Soviet President Leonid Brezhnev on June 15–18, 1979, President Carter said:

> We will try to broaden our communications with the Soviets and to create new channels of understanding between our two countries....
>
> We will seek new areas where more cooperation might be forthcoming and also less competition.

Carter called upon Soviet officials to join their American counterparts in seeking "new areas of common understanding" in behalf of a peaceful world.[72]

Implicit in this American understanding

*One experienced Washington observer, writing in mid-1980, noted that both the United States and the Soviet Union were experiencing internal problems. The American society, for example, had an all-time high inflation rate concurrently with a severe economic recession. Yet in his view, "The most serious crisis is in the Communist world." He noted that "Moscow can raise armies but it cannot feed its own people. It is falling steadily behind in the new computerized industrial and scientific world, and it is counting on the West and Japan for modern technology as it is depending on the United States, Canada, Argentina and Australia for its grain. Not even the Communist parties of Western Europe or the new developing nations even consider, let alone argue, that Moscow has an acceptable economic or social model for their societies. Cuba is only the latest example of the spectacular failure of the Communist system." At a time when thousands of Cuban refugees were seeking to enter the United States, this observer commented: "There is not ... a single instance of any refugees trying to get *into* the Soviet Union or Cuba. They are all running away." James Reston, in *New York Times*, May 18, 1980.

of détente is the notion that it is *an ongoing process,* in which Soviet-American agreements in one area are extended into other areas likely to generate tensions between them. As officials in Washington envision it, the scope of détente would be gradually broadened; and the ultimate objective would be an overall resolution of Soviet-American tensions in behalf of a peaceful and stable international system. As we have seen, this expectation in the American mind has no counterpart in the Soviet interpretation of détente.

This leads us to consider the third—and in some respects, unquestionably the most important—element in the American view of détente: the idea of "linkage." Referring to the Soviet and Cuban intervention in Angola and other Third World countries, Secretary of State Kissinger said that the United States rejected the idea of "selective détente"—or the decision by Communist officials to have cooperative relations with the United States in some spheres and to engage in revolutionary struggle and other forms of conflict with it in other spheres. Under the Reagan Administration, former Secretary of State Henry Kissinger and other Republicans became vocally critical of the White House for simultaneously denouncing Soviet intervention in Poland, Afghanistan, Central America and other regions, and concurrently endeavoring to maintain détente with the Kremlin. After Washington provided credits to bankrupt Poland, for example, one commentator observed that in some respects, the Reagan Administration appeared to be even more interested in preserving détente than its Democratic predecessor. Conservatives within Reagan's own party denounced his devotion to détente and concluded that—despite its harsh anti-Communist rhetoric—his Administration "loves commerce more than it loathes Communism."[73]

To the American mind, the essential precondition for the existence of détente between the superpowers is *peaceful and cooperative Soviet behavior* as a member of the international system. If Moscow desires détente (or the Soviet variant, "peaceful coexistence"), its devotion to this goal must be reflected in its *conduct* toward Poland, Afghanistan, East Africa, Central America and other regions likely to engender international conflicts. The test of détente in American eyes is whether it leads to Soviet-American cooperation in dealing with such diverse questions as arms control, respect for human rights in Poland and other settings, and ongoing Communist revolutionary movements in the Western Hemisphere.

An alternative way of looking at the concept of "linkage" is to say that it represents a specific manifestation of another idea that has been conspicuous in America's post-World War II approach to the Soviet Union: insistence upon the principle that "peace is indivisible." In practice, this means that a particular Soviet action (like Moscow's invasion of Czechoslovakia in 1968 or its intrusion into Afghanistan in 1979) threatens the overall fabric of international peace and the future of Soviet-American relations. In the American view, verbal Soviet avowals of devotion to détente—coupled with simultaneous efforts by the U.S.S.R. to impose its hegemony upon weaker countries—make a mockery of détente and add new elements of instability and unpredictability to the international system.

The idea of "linkage" was particularly associated with the viewpoints of Dr. Henry Kissinger, who held the positions of national security adviser to the President and secretary of state under the Nixon and Ford administrations. Kissinger's support for the idea of "linkage" was always more consistent than his *practice* in negotiating with the Soviet Union;

and this same duality in American policy continued to characterize American foreign policy after he left office in 1976.* In connection with the SALT II strategic arms-limitation agreements in 1979, Kissinger (in the words of one reporter) proposed to the Senate Foreign Relations Committee that "future strategic arms negotiations with the Soviet Union be

*Our discussion of the American idea of "linkage" as an aspect of détente perhaps gives insufficient emphasis to the fact that the official and public position with regard to "linkage" has been ambivalent and inconsistent. Directly and indirectly, from the Nixon to the Reagan administrations American officials underscored the importance of "linkage" between verbal Soviet support for détente and Soviet diplomatic behavior. Yet Washington has not always followed its own principle consistently. In fact, even Dr. Henry Kissinger more than once defended the concept of détente with the Soviet Union *against* those who wanted to link it with an improvement in Moscow's behavior in areas like intervention in the Thrid World or the treatment of Soviet Jews. In 1975 (after Soviet and Cuban forces intervened massively in Angola), Kissinger continued to negotiate a strategic arms-control agreement with Soviet officials—even while he condemned Moscow's intervention in Angola. Kissinger called Soviet behavior in Angola "irresponsible" and "inconsistent" with the concept of détente; yet he also believed that American interests were served by arriving at a SALT II strategic arms agreement with Moscow. Similarly, officials of the Carter Administration usually avoided any direct reference to "linkage" in their approach to the Soviet Union (in part, perhaps, because they realized it was an idea inflammatory to the Kremlin). Yet in reality, the Carter Administration's diplomacy gave considerable emphasis to "linkage." After the Soviet incursion into Afghanistan late in 1979, for example, President Carter was outspoken in condemning Moscow's move, in emphasizing the fact that it endangered détente, and in seeking to enlist worldwide support for various kinds of sanctions against the Soviet Union. Moreover, President Carter "withdrew" the SALT II arms-control agreement from further Senate consideration because of expansionist Soviet policies in Afghanistan, in Cuba, and other settings. Bernard Gwertzman, in *New York Times,* August 2, 1979. The same division in the American mind has been evident on the issue of Soviet-American trade. See Henry Kissinger, *White House Years* (Boston: Little, Brown and Co., 1979), pp. 1271–1273.

halted if the Russians do not practice military restraint around the world." In his view, the Senate should demand that any renewal of the provisions of SALT II be contingent upon the demonstration of "restraint" by Moscow in other policy areas, such as Soviet diplomacy in Latin America or the Middle East or the arms race in weapons not covered by SALT II.[74] In brief, if the leaders of the Kremlin genuinely desire a "relaxation of tensions" with the United States and other countries, then Moscow should refrain from arousing tensions and anxieties outside its own borders stemming from fears of Soviet aggressiveness.

More concretely, American officials have applied the concept of "linkage" to several crucial areas of Soviet-American relations. As Kissinger assessed the concept, détente required "Soviet restraint in such trouble spots as the Middle East, Berlin, and Southeast Asia...."[75] Several years later, Ambassador Toon complained that, although it endorsed détente with the United States,

> ... the Soviet Union has continued to serve as protector and supporter of radical, essentially anti-Western currents in the Third World—which the Soviets have labeled "national liberation movements." Such a view of the world offers us little comfort.[76]

In 1982, the Reagan Administration directly "linked" further progress in arriving at a Soviet-American arms control agreement to Moscow's continuing intervention in Poland to suppress political dissent. The problem of arms control, one State Department official asserted, "cannot be insulated from other events." Secretary of State Haig repeatedly emphasized that Moscow's intervention in Poland was a major "setback" for détente.[77]

In the official American view, détente also precludes attempts by the Soviet Union *to achieve military superiority* over the United States. Détente requires acceptance by both superpowers of the notion of military "parity" or "equivalency" between them. Secretary of State Vance said in 1978 that "Neither we nor the Soviets should entertain the notion that military supremacy can be attained."[78]

Still another specific dimension of "linkage" deemed important by American officials was the idea of *Soviet-American collaboration* in resolving international and regional disputes likely to escalate into conflicts between the two superpowers. At the Vienna summit conference in 1979, President Carter called upon Soviet officials to join the United States in an effort to "broaden our communications ... and to create new channels of understanding" between the two governments.[79] As it prepared to take office in 1981, the Reagan Administration called for a new era of Soviet-American "cooperation," although it believed that in reality "competition" had become the rule in relations between the superpowers.[80]

Finally, in the American perception, détente has another requirement that has proven to be one of the most contentious issues in recent Soviet-American relations. This is the expectation that détente will lead to, and be tangibly expressed in, *significant changes in Soviet internal policy,* particularly as they relate to the treatment of political dissidents. At the summit conference in Helsinki in 1975, President Gerald Ford emphasized to Soviet President Brezhnev

> ... the deep devotion of the American people and their government to human rights and fundamental freedom and thus to the pledges that this conference has made regarding the freer movement of people, ideas, [and] information.

History would judge the success of the conference, "not by what we say here today but by what we do tomorrow" in respecting basic human freedoms. In Ford's view, the "message" he wished to convey to Moscow and other capitals—"that America still cared" about human freedom throughout the world—"had come through loud and clear."*

Throughout the 1970s, the "linkage" between Soviet internal policy and détente was a conspicuous concern of the United States Congress, particularly in legislative deliberations on American trade policy toward the U.S.S.R. Despite White House objections, in 1974 Congress made the granting of preferential trade concessions to Moscow—a step widely viewed as essential in an anticipated expansion of Soviet-American commerce—contingent upon the easing of the Kremlin's restrictions on Jewish emigration. This congressional move elicited a highly negative reaction from Soviet officials, who viewed it as gross American interference in the U.S.S.R.'s "internal affairs"; and they rejected more favorable American terms of trade rather than submit to such "dictation" by Washington.[81] Again in 1978, the Carter Administration placed restrictions upon the shipment of equipment and technology needed by the Soviet Union to expand its oil production. This move stemmed from deep concern by officials in the executive and legislative branches over continued Soviet suppression of individuals

---

*Ironically, the Helsinki summit conference—at which international respect for human rights was a central agenda issue—had a curious result. According to some interpretations, it was a "propaganda victory" for the Kremlin, since it seemed to "ratify," or legitimatize, Soviet hegemony over the "captive peoples" of the Baltic region and Eastern Europe. President Ford and other American officials vigorously denied that such an interpretation of the conference was justifiable. See Gerald R. Ford, *A Time to Heal* (New York: Harper & Row, and The Reader's Digest Association, 1979), pp. 305–306.

and groups dissenting from the Communist regime.[82]

This specific manifestation of "linkage" perhaps exemplified as well as any other single issue the differences between the American and Soviet understanding of détente. For Americans (especially legislative officials), détente without visible progress toward a more "open" and democratic political order behind the Iron Curtain seemed a highly dubious concept, if not indeed a diplomatic "trap," for non-Communist countries. The Soviet position on the question appeared to symbolize Moscow's overall approach to the problem of more cooperative Soviet-American relations: The Kremlin wished to exploit the advantages offered by détente, without in any fundamental way altering its internal and external behavior. For Soviet policy makers, as we have seen, this particular manifestation of the American concept of "linkage" was anathema. It was totally unacceptable to the Kremlin, as a patent American attempt to intervene in Soviet internal affairs—with the ultimate objective of undermining and perhaps destroying the Communist system of government. As such, "linkage" became merely a new American tactic for waging the Cold War.

The Postwar Quest for Arms Control

Pre–World War II Negotiations

In no sphere of Soviet-American relations perhaps have the utility and meaning of détente been more graphically tested than in efforts since World War II to limit the arms race and to arrive at durable agreements curtailing military competition among the members of the international system. In modern history, the quest for effective arms control has been long, arduous, and beset with innumerable pitfalls and failures. In the Rush-Bagot Agreement (1817), the United States and Canada reached an understanding providing for the nonfortification of their common boundary. Perhaps because it proved so exceptional, this "unguarded frontier" between the two countries was a noteworthy achievement in the effort to discourage reliance upon armed force by two neighboring states. The first international effort in modern history to limit the acquisition and use of armaments was made at the first Hague Conference in 1899; a second Hague Conference was held eight years later. Characteristically, these efforts failed to achieve overall arms limitation, although they did "codify" the rules of warfare and established mechanisms for the peaceful "arbitration" of international disputes. These early negotiations paved the way for the creation of the International Court of Justice (ICJ), established as part of the United Nations system after World War II.*

*Our discussion of post–World War II negotiations over arms control draws heavily upon the documentary materials and commentary contained in United States Arms Control Agency, *Arms Control and Disarmament Agreements: Texts and Histories of Negotiations* (Washington, D.C.: Government Printing Office, 1980). Historical perspective on the subject is provided in James T. Shotwell and Marina Salvin, *Lessons on Security and Disarmament from the History of the League of Nations* (New York: Columbia University Press, 1949). A brief but enlightening treatment of the problems hindering arms reduction may be found in Inis L. Claude, Jr., *Swords Into Plowshares: The Problems and Progress of International Organization*, 3rd ed. (New York: Random House, 1964), pp. 261–285. Among the numerous studies of post–World War II arms-control negotiations are: James E. Dougherty and J. F. Lehman, Jr., eds., *Arms Control for the Late Sixties* (Princeton, N.J.: D. Van Nostrand Co., 1967); David V. Edwards, *Arms Control in International Politics* (New York: Holt, Rinehart and Winston, 1969); Elizabeth Young, *A Farewell to Arms Control?* (Baltimore: Penguin Books, 1972); Morton A. Kaplan, ed., *SALT: Problems and Prospects* (Morristown, N.J.: General Learning Press, 1973); Robert L. Pfaltzgraff, Jr., ed., *Contrasting Approaches to Strategic Arms Control*

The post-World War I period witnessed new efforts to limit national military arsenals—usually with minimal results. Two developments during this period may be noted briefly. One was the Washington Naval Armaments Conference (1921–1922), at which the principal naval powers reached agreement limiting the number of major ships in their respective fleets. Many historians are convinced that the effect of this accord was to enhance Japan's naval position in Asian waters, thereby encouraging its military elite to embark upon a course of expansionism and hegemony. The other development occurred in 1928, when (largely at America's instigation) most nations of the world signed the Kellogg-Briand Pact to "outlaw" war as an instrument of national policy. Again, the utility of this accord in restraining future Axis expansionism seemed highly questionable, although violation of this international agreement was one indictment brought against Axis "war criminals" in the Nuremberg trials.

The Baruch Plan and Nuclear Arms Control

The effort to limit national armaments was renewed after World War II. Articles 11 and 47 of the United Nations Charter, for example, required the new international organization to promote agreements reducing the level of global armaments (although the United Nations gave this goal a somewhat lower priority than its predecessor, the League of Nations). The development of nuclear weapons—and their use in warfare against Japan—added unprecedented urgency to the quest.

By the end of 1946, the United States had proposed a new and comprehensive nuclear disarmament scheme, known as the

(Lexington, Mass.: D.C. Heath, 1974); Strobe Talbott, *Endgame: The Inside Story of SALT II* (New York: Harper & Row, 1980); and Robin Ranger, *Arms and Politics, 1958–1978* (New York: Macmillan, 1979).

"Baruch Plan," to assure that nuclear energy would henceforth be used for peaceful purposes. The Baruch Plan was a complex measure, entailing a series of "stages," at the end of which the United States would share its nuclear technology with the international community. In Washington's view, the key to the plan's success—and to nearly all other nuclear disarmament schemes proposed after World War II—was *an effective system of inspection and control* whereby national compliance with the plan's requirements could be independently verified (presumably by an agency of the United Nations). Confronted with overwhelming Soviet superiority in ground forces available to the Kremlin to pursue its expansive foreign policy goals, the United States was consistently unwilling to entrust its security to Russian pledges or mere statements of good faith.

By contrast, as we observed in Chapter 9, xenophobia and deep anxiety about national security have long colored Russian attitudes toward the outside world. In the aftermath of World War II—when the Soviet Union was physically devastated and economically debilitated—the Kremlin was more than ordinarily loath to allow a large contingent of foreign inspectors on Russian soil. Nor was the Kremlin willing to forgo acquisition of nuclear weapons because of American suspicions that it was not complying with the provisions of the Baruch Plan. In addition, some commentators are persuaded that in the years after 1946, what Moscow sought—and what in time it achieved—was *military superiority* over the United States in at least some weapons' categories. In any case, the ensuing Soviet-American deadlock over the Baruch Plan set the pattern for disagreement that was to doom subsequent proposals for achieving nuclear arms reduction after 1946. For a generation or so thereafter, Soviet-American negotiations on arms limitation were characterized by two somewhat contradictory tendencies: progress in achieving limited agreement on selected aspects of the disarmament problem, coupled with almost uninterrupted escalation in the destructive power of both the nuclear and conventional weapons available to the superpowers.

Limited Arms Control Measures

Despite the failure of the Baruch Plan to halt the nuclear arms race, the search for acceptable arms-control measures continued. Some success was achieved in securing agreement among the United States, the Soviet Union, and other countries on more limited proposals involving the limitation of national armaments in specified areas. For example, on June 23, 1961, the United States, the Soviet Union, and ultimately 20 other nations accepted the principle of the "demilitarization" of Antarctica. Thereafter, that continent was to be used solely for scientific and other peaceful purposes. Two years later, American and Soviet officials agreed to install a "Hot Line" communications system between Washington and Moscow, permitting almost instantaneous communications between high-level officials of the two countries. Designed to prevent a "war by accident" between the superpowers, the Hot Line has been used several times (as in successive crises in the Middle East) to reduce the prospect of a Soviet-American confrontation.

Another significant arms-control agreement became effective on October 10, 1963. This treaty—in time, signed by over 90 countries—banned the testing of nuclear weapons or devices in the atmosphere, under water, and in outer space (while certain carefully controlled underground explosions were permitted under its terms).

Four years later (on October 10, 1967), another international agreement banned the use of outer space for military purposes; in time almost 60 nations, including the United States and the Soviet Union, ratified this instrument. In reality, of course, the line between "military" and "peaceful" uses of outer space is indistinct at best: Many space vehicles and orbiting space satellites have (or can easily acquire) direct military application by the United States, the Soviet Union, and other countries. (As we shall see, space satellites now play a crucial role in "monitoring" compliance with later arms-limitation agreements such as SALT I.)

Another landmark in the postwar record of disarmament negotiations was the Nuclear Non-Proliferation Treaty (NPT), which entered into force on March 5, 1970. Ever since 1945, American and Soviet policy makers alike have been cognizant of—and increasingly concerned about—the risks inherent in the infinite "proliferation" of nuclear weapons throughout the international system. Statistically, the chances of a global nuclear holocaust increase directly, as one country after another seeks to join the "nuclear club." Moscow risked the dissolution of the Sino-Soviet alliance rather than share its nuclear arsenal with Communist China. Similarly, the United States has repeatedly insisted upon maintaining ultimate control over the nuclear weapons available for the defense of the NATO area—a fact that in time led France to develop its own independent nuclear *force de frappe*.

Theoretically, the principle of nuclear nonproliferation has enjoyed widespread support by the members of the international system; some 92 nations eventually ratified the NPT. Among the conspicuous exceptions was the People's Republic of China. And even among several nations that did ratify the NPT—such as France, Brazil, India, Pakistan, and Israel—the agreement posed no discernible obstacle to their actual or planned acquisition of a nuclear arsenal. The problem of nuclear proliferation might of course be even more acute today without the NPT. Yet from the beginning, perhaps, it did not lie within the power of the United States and the Soviet Union to prevent countries determined to do so from acquiring nuclear weapons.

The early 1970s witnessed other steps toward arms limitation. On May 18, 1972, for example, an international agreement prohibiting the installation of nuclear and other methods of mass destruction on the seabed became effective. In 1975, the superpowers (joined in time by more than 70 other nations) agreed not to produce or stockpile bacteriological, chemical, or comparable weapons using toxic substances. This agreement extended the precedent established during World War II, when the belligerents refrained from using poison gas (as had been done during World War I) to achieve their military goals.

Meanwhile, despite these limited agreements, on both sides of the Iron Curtain—and throughout the international system generally—weapons stockpiles and military budgets were steadily increasing. Advances in military technology made nuclear and conventional weapons alike more destructive and dangerous to human society. Against this ominous background, Soviet and American officials endeavored once again to reach agreement upon a broader scheme for limiting the nuclear arms race. That effort was centered in the Strategic Arms Limitations Talks which finally produced two arms-limitations proposals, known as SALT I and SALT II.

SALT I and "Quantitative" Arms Control

By the early 1970s, Soviet and American officials judged circumstances propitious for a renewal of negotiations aimed at curtailing the arms race in nuclear weapons. As we have already observed, by that period a condition of approximate nuclear parity or "equivalence" existed between the superpowers; and policy makers on both sides of the Iron Curtain expressed their devotion to the principle of détente as the basis of Soviet-American relations.

Negotiations directed at achieving a new Soviet-American arms-control agreement began at the end of 1969—and the discussions continued for some two and a half years thereafter. Initially, efforts were directed at obtaining agreement upon a *quantitative* arms-control measure, or one that limited the *number* of delivery vehicles (such as missiles and bombers) possessed by the superpowers. Finally, on May 26, 1972, President Richard Nixon and President Leonid Brezhnev signed two treaties known as the Strategic Arms Limitation Treaties (or SALT I); after they were ratified by both countries, these agreements became effective on October 3, 1972. One of the documents limited the deployment of antiballistic missile (ABM) systems by both countries. This understanding would "freeze" arms competition between the two nations in one extremely expensive category of modern armaments; and it would contribute to stabilizing the military balance between them. (For several years, Soviet authorities had been engaged in extensive ABM construction, causing growing concern in Washington that the U.S.S.R. might have a greater capacity to "survive" a nuclear exchange between the superpowers, thereby possibly tempting the Kremlin to precipitate a conflict with the United States.)

The other accord consisted of a five-year "interim" agreement dealing with the number of nuclear-armed missiles allowed in the Soviet and American stockpiles. (In contrast to the SALT II agreement that followed, SALT I did not attempt to calculate or restrict the overall nuclear firepower of the Soviet and American missile fleets.) In principle, SALT I attempted to preserve nuclear "symmetry" or parity between the United States and the Soviet Union by "freezing" the number of missile launchers each country was permitted to possess. Any future increase in the size of these fleets would have to be accompanied by a dismantling or destruction of outmoded launching vehicles—thereby maintaining the military balance of power. SALT I also precluded the signatories from "converting" short-range missiles into long-range ones and from taking other steps imperiling the military equilibrium established by the agreement. As long as they adhered to such restrictions, both countries were allowed to modernize and improve their missile systems—and in the years that followed the United States and the Soviet Union took full advantage of that opportunity.*

*The key point about the SALT I agreement was that it was a *quantitative* arms control measure that limited the number of strategic weapons both sides might possess without significantly restraining the firepower, destructiveness, accuracy and other characteristics of their respective weapons' systems. Without violating the provisions of the SALT I accord, therefore, the United States and the Soviet Union could—and both sides did—forge rapidly ahead in the "modernization" and qualitative improvement of their military arsenals. For example, the United States began to produce low-flying Cruise missiles capable of eluding enemy radar; it planned to produce and deploy a new family of more accurate and destructive MX missiles; and to replace the aging B-52. (Prototypes of a new "stealth" bomber, capable of eluding radar detection, were in the developmental stage.) Soviet officials of course were similarly engaged in making major qualitative improvements in their arseanl. Their efforts included the production and installation of a new family of SS-20 missiles capable of devastating Western Europe; enhancement of the firepower and accuracy of the Soviet missile fleet; and ongoing expansion of Russian naval power, including the construction of new missile-firing submarines. The SALT I accord, it needs to be remembered, in no way constrained Soviet-American competition in "conventional" (non-nuclear) weapons. When SALT I was signed in 1972, the United States possessed 1054 land-based intercontinental-ballistic missiles (ICBMs), while the Soviet Union had 1,618 (including those under construction). The provisions of SALT I did not apply to "mobile" ICBMs, such as those later planned by the United States for its new MX missile system. In submarine-launched missiles—a major component of America's defense "triad"—SALT I permitted an increase in missile levels on both sides. The American arsenal, for example, was allowed to expand from 656 to

Several brief observations may be made about the implications of SALT I and its impact upon détente between the United States and the Soviet Union. Unquestionably, SALT I was an historic agreement—the first since World War II under which the superpowers succeeded in "capping the volcano," or placing quantitative limits upon the number of nuclear-armed missiles each was permitted to possess. If (as the subsequent history of SALT II negotiations underscored) this breakthrough left many unresolved problems in the path of effective arms control, SALT I at least offered encouragement that these obstacles could ultimately be removed; and the agreement provided impetus for a new round of arms-limitation negotiations between the superpowers.

A novel feature of the SALT I accords was the fact that, for the first time, the United States and the Soviet Union agreed upon the principle of self-inspection and self-enforcement: Orbiting space satellites and other scientific devices would provide each side with evidence of compliance (or noncompliance) by the other. To date, this system appears to have operated to the reasonable satisfaction of Soviet and American officials.

Yet as every informed student of Soviet-American relations is aware, SALT I had a

710 submarine-launched missiles. The Soviet Union was permitted to increase its comparable missiles from 740 to 950—but this major increase in Soviet seapower had to be matched by an equivalent reduction in outmoded land- or sea-based Russian missiles. As Soviet officials were acutely aware, the provisions of SALT I did *not* apply to the nuclear weapons possessed independently by America's NATO allies. Soviet spokesmen, for example, asserted that if there were a significant growth in NATO's nuclear naval power, then the limitations imposed by SALT I upon its own sea-launched missile systems would no longer be binding. The SALT I agreements, along with certain ancillary understandings between the United States and the Soviet Union concerning them, are contained in United States Arms Control and Disarmament Agency, *Arms Control and Disarmament Agreements*, pp. 132–154.

number of defects; and it left unanswered perhaps the most difficult questions inherent in the quest for arms control. Since it was not a "qualitative" arms-control measure, SALT I did little or nothing to restrain military spending by the United States, the Soviet Union, or the members of the Third World. As in the past, the superpowers continued to engage in intensive competition for the production and acquisition of more advanced, accurate, and destructive weapons' systems. Nor was there any convincing evidence that SALT I significantly improved the overall climate of Soviet-American relations. A decade after SALT I, the future of détente seemed more precarious than it had been at any time since the Cuban Missile Crisis of 1962.

Perhaps the dominant conclusion to be drawn from these adverse developments was a lesson with which commentators on disarmament negotiations throughout modern history were amply familiar: National competition in armaments is fundamentally *a symptom* of underlying hostilities, suspicions, and clashing ambitions among members of the international system. Slowing the momentum of the arms race may be a desirable goal in its own right; but it does not per se eliminate these basic sources of instability and violence in international politics, nor does it necessarily produce an overall reduction in tensions between the superpowers.

SALT II and the Future of Arms Control

As anticipated by the SALT I discussions, Soviet and American officials continued their search for a more comprehensive arms-limitation accord by focusing particularly upon "qualitative" problems involved in disarmament. These discussions—extending from late 1972 until mid-1979—proved to be lengthy, intricate, and difficult. At a meeting at Vladivostok in November, 1974, President Gerald Ford and President Leonid Brezhnev

agreed upon an overall framework for the accord ultimately embodied in the SALT II treaty, which was signed by Presidents Carter and Brezhnev on June 18, 1979. As reflected in SALT II's detailed and complex provisions, the paramount goal was to establish and maintain a strategic balance between the superpowers with respect to a wide variety of weapons in their nuclear arsenals—from ICBMs and medium-range missiles to sea-based missiles to bombers to planned improvements in each nation's strategic force (like the Cruise missile being produced by the United States and the new Soviet Backfire bomber). For the first time, SALT II attempted to limit the number of MIRVed missiles the United States and the Soviet Union might possess; and it sought to restrict the overall "throw-weight" (an index of missile destructiveness) of each country's missile fleet.*

Without entering into a detailed analysis of SALT II's intricate and often highly technical terms, it is sufficient to call attention to a few of its major provisions, particularly those

---

*The text of the SALT II arms-limitation agreement, along with certain protocols and understandings accompanying it, may be found in United States Arms Control and Disarmament Agency, *Arms Control and Disarmament Agreements,* pp. 201–239. The initials MIRV stand for "Multiple Independent Reentry Vehicle"—describing a relatively new family of strategic missiles that have been "converted" from the earlier single nuclear warhead to missiles capable of carrying *several* nuclear warheads that can be independently targeted. The conversion of America's missile fleet to MIRVed vehicles means in effect that Moscow's problem of providing an adequate defense against a missile attack has been rendered infinitely more difficult. Although the United States gained an early lead in MIRVed missiles, the Soviet Union has rapidly been closing this gap. Specific qualitative limitations upon the strategic arsenals of the United States and the Soviet Union permitted by the SALT II agreement included: a ceiling of 2250 long-range missiles, bombers, and other delivery vehicles by 1981; a limit of 1320 MIRVed missiles and heavy bombers; a ban on the future construction of ICBM launchers and on any increase in

that elicited strong criticisms from opponents of SALT II in the United States. Under SALT II, Moscow would be permitted to retain 326 large ICBMs (SS-18s); after they were MIRVed, each missile could carry up to 10 accurate warheads (and in time could be modified to fire 30 or 40 smaller nuclear warheads). Critics of SALT II were convinced that—even with the planned deployment of America's new Cruise missiles, the construction of a new "stealth" bomber, and other improvements—ultimately the Soviet Union would gain a substantial military advantage in this category of weapons. Moscow's installation in the early 1980s of over 300 SS-20 missiles capable of devastating the NATO area did not reassure officials of the Reagan Administration that Soviet policy makers really desired to maintain a strategic balance with the United States. As explained more fully in Chapter 11, this escalation in the arms race revived the old controversy about the adequacy of NATO's defense capabilities—a long-standing source of contention within the Western alliance. Predictably, this Soviet move was "answered" by American countermoves, such as the installation of Cruise missiles within the NATO area

and suggestions by officials in Washington that in the event of Soviet aggression the United States might rely upon the neutron bomb, if necessary, to repel a Soviet attack. In turn, these developments engendered growing public concern at home and abroad about Soviet-American arms competition and led to mounting public demands that officials renew the quest for effective arms control.

Still another controversial aspect of SALT II was the problem of "verification" of each side's compliance with its terms. (Washington's belated discovery of a large contingent of Soviet troops in Cuba in mid-1979 created new anxieties in the American society with regard to this problem.) Throughout the post-World War II period, skeptics had been apprehensive that Moscow might—and if it had the opportunity, it almost certainly would—circumvent the terms of any arms control agreement in its determination to gain military superiority over the United States. To the American mind, the problem of an effective inspection and control system lay at the heart of any effort to curb the arms race. In the 1980s, no less than the late 1940s, the American people and their leaders continued to believe that this was the crux of the disarmament issue.*

Beyond these specific complaints about the provisions of SALT II as they related to American security, the treaty encountered

---

the number of ICBM launchers; varying limitations imposed upon the number of nuclear warheads allowed for different kinds of missiles; ceilings on the launch-weight and throw-weight of nuclear-armed missiles; a ceiling on the number of Cruise missiles the United States could add to its stockpile, along with a ban on the development of the planned Soviet SS-16 missile; and a ban on the production of new weapons that are technologically feasible (such as ship-launched long-range missiles and mobile launchers for ICBMs). For the details of these and other prohibitions contained in SALT II, see United States Arms Control and Disarmament Agency, *Arms Control: 1979* (Washington, D.C.: Government Printing Office, 1979), pp. 14–15. Useful commentary on the provisions and implications of SALT II is available in *U.S. Defense Policy: Weapons, Strategy, Commitments,* 2nd ed., (Washington, D.C.: The Congressional Quarterly, 1980), pp. 15–31.

*American attitudes on this question were forcefully illustrated by the results of a *Newsweek* poll taken early in 1982. Some 68 percent of the respondents indicated that they were frequently worried or concerned about the possibility of nuclear war; the same percentage either strongly favored or advocated a "freeze" of the existing American and Soviet nuclear arsenals. At the same time, 67 percent of those interviewed expressed genuine concern about the "verification" of any agreement reached between the United States and the Soviet Union, and said that such verification was essential for any acceptable arms control scheme. See *Newsweek,* **XCIX** (April 26, 1982), 24.

another, and perhaps even more formidable, obstacle to its ratification by the United States. By the end of the 1970s, a serious deterioration occurred in Soviet-American relations, raising real questions about the future of détente and leading some commentators to conclude that a new "Cold War atmosphere" now pervaded the international system. Americans had become deeply disturbed about several aspects of the Soviet Union's global and regional behavior. In Southeast Asia (where the Russian-supported government of North Vietnam sought to establish its hegemony); in Afghanistan and the Persian Gulf area (where Moscow was seeking to consolidate a new position of strength, possibly threatening Western access to the region's oil supplies); in Europe (where a militarily superior Warsaw Pact confronted an internally divided NATO); in the Caribbean area and Central America (where Marxist groups were fomenting revolution in several countries)—in these and other areas, Americans believed that the U.S.S.R. was deliberately exploiting its current military advantage and was seeking to "challenge" the global position and interests of the United States.*

As congressional and public skepticism toward SALT II mounted within the United States, the Carter Administration eventually concluded that prospects for its approval by the Senate were nil. Accordingly, on January 3, 1980, President Carter took the unusual step of "withdrawing" the treaty from further Senate consideration. In the months that followed, American foreign policy was marked by two contrary tendencies. On the one hand, under the Carter and Reagan administrations (as was emphasized in Chapter 5), American defense spending was substantially increased in an effort to strengthen the nation's military capability. On the other hand, the impetus toward effective arms control also remained strong. During the early 1980s, vocal groups inside and outside the United States called for an "arms freeze" between the United States and the Soviet Union; and concern about the consequences of possible nuclear war was at the forefront of public attention. The Reagan Administration, however, consistently refused to accept the idea of an "arms freeze" or a moratorium on the production of new missiles, bombers, and other weapons. Despite the popularity of this idea with some groups, the Reagan White House believed such a move would leave the United States at a serious military disadvantage vis-à-vis the U.S.S.R. and would reenforce the already prevalent viewpoint that American power had declined. Instead, President Reagan and his advisers called for renewed efforts to *reduce* the American and Soviet armaments stockpile. Designated START (for Strategic Arms Reductions Talks), this new attempt to curb the arms race would require many months, if not several years, before American and Soviet officials negotiated an acceptable proposal. In the interim, it was safe to predict, Soviet-American arms competition would continue, and the escalating arms race would remain as a major cause of tension and suspicion between the superpowers.

Détente: A Balance Sheet

Détente in Perspective

In the concluding section of this chapter, we shall endeavor to draw up a balance sheet for détente as the guiding principle of Soviet-

---

*North Vietnam's expansionist behavior after the Vietnam War is discussed more fully in Chapter 15; the Soviet Union's invasion of Afghanistan and the resulting threat to the Western position in the Persian Gulf area are analyzed in Chapter 12; the military disparity between NATO and the Warsaw Pact is evaluated in Chapter 11; and Communist-sponsored and other revolutionary activities in Latin America are described in Chapter 14.

American relations. Diplomatically, what has the Soviet Union gained from détente, and what has it lost, by its support? How has détente promoted, and how has it impaired, the foreign policy goals of the United States? What are some of the major factors likely to determine the future of détente as the basis for Soviet-American relations?

Before examining such questions, however, let us take note of two general observations offered about the concept by informed students of contemporary Soviet-American relations. Bell has cautioned us to keep in mind that the future of détente remains uncertain and perhaps precarious, since "all détentes in diplomatic history have proved perishable in due course." On the basis of experience, it is, therefore, "unreasonable to assume that this one [in Soviet-American relations] will prove immortal."[83] Americans particularly needed to be forewarned that détente was not necessarily a *permanent* condition and that a number of forces in the international system were adverse to its continuation.

Another study of détente has arrived at basically the same conclusion by a different process. In Steibel's view,

> ... the bottom line of détente is the calculus of beneficial versus harmful results [for each of the superpowers]. The current debate has produced both. They need to be weighed one against the other, especially in the major areas [of policy disagreement between the United States and the Soviet Union].... Détente, obviously, is unfinished business. It responds faithfully to changing conditions, and both aims and tactics change accordingly. There is no inevitable outcome. Either lasting peace or nuclear holocaust, or any of the permutations in between, could ensue.[84]

On the assumption that rational considerations govern the decision-making process in the United States and the Soviet Union —and that there is no "war by accident" between the superpowers—the future of détente is likely to be crucially determined by a single paramount consideration. This is the extent to which officials in Washington and Moscow determine that it serves their foreign policy interests. In *Realpolitik* terms, détente will endure as long as it promotes the "national interests" of the United States and the Soviet Union.

Soviet Gains and Losses from Détente

That détente has resulted in certain diplomatic gains for Moscow can hardly be doubted. On the basis of experience with détente, Soviet officials could discover at least five important advantages in the concept for the pursuit of Communist foreign policy goals.

In the first place—in company with the American society, and all others on the globe—the Soviet Union has benefited from the prevention of nuclear war and the stability which détente has provided in preserving the nuclear balance between the superpowers. Soviet leaders have themselves repeatedly called attention to the dangers inherent in nuclear devastation; and the evidence indicates that the Kremlin is fully cognizant of the disastrous consequences that would accompany a nuclear holocaust. Although Communist spokesmen have also boasted of the U.S.S.R.'s ability to survive a nuclear conflagration (whereas, in their view, capitalist societies would not), the Kremlin remains aware that such a conflict would exact a frightful cost from Soviet society.

In the second place, for Soviet officials détente has contributed to the achievement of one of their high priority foreign policy goals: American acceptance of the U.S.S.R. as an "equal" in the international system, expressed most tangibly perhaps in the achievement of a condition of military parity with the United

States. By the 1980s, few informed students of Soviet-American affairs doubted that—on the military level at least—the U.S.S.R. ranked as a superpower, that its military strength was formidable, and that (based upon its growing military power) Moscow could now project its influence into virtually any region of the globe. No less today than in the earlier post-World War II period, Soviet-American relations served as the axis of the international system and were the most crucial factor determining its evolution toward peace or war. The transition from a "bipolar" to a "multipolar" international system has not fundamentally altered that underlying reality.

In the third place, Moscow had unquestionably derived certain significant *economic benefits* from détente. The Reagan Administration's decision to provide substantial credits to the bankrupt Communist government of Poland provided tangible evidence of that gain. Rescuing its Eastern European satellite from financial ruin would have imposed severe strains upon an already fragile Soviet economic system. In the view of some commentators, even if détente characterizes Soviet-American relations, the Kremlin is likely to face even more critical economic problems and shortcomings in the future. A high level of military spending (from 11 to 14 percent of the U.S.S.R.'s annual GNP); perennial agricultural shortages and crop failures; declining labor productivity; pervasive morale problems among its workers; a political environment which stifles scientific and technological creativity—these and other factors dictate continuing reliance upon the West by the Soviet Union for many years to come.[85] In the absence of détente, economic stringencies behind the Iron Curtain might well generate new—and even more disruptive—political discontents with Communist rule.*

In the fourth place, détente has been a useful diplomatic tool for the Kremlin under two dissimilar conditions. Paradoxically, détente is advantageous for Moscow both during periods of Soviet *weakness* and of Soviet *strength*. When Marxists judge "objective conditions" abroad to be unfavorable for an expansionist foreign policy, for example, détente discourages the opponents of the U.S.S.R. from exploiting Soviet weakness. By contrast, when policy makers in Moscow believe that the Soviet Union has a favorable power position vis-à-vis the United States and other adversaries, it champions détente as a means of "ratifying" Soviet occupation of Afghanistan or the continuation of Soviet hegemony over Eastern Europe. In this case, by espousing détente Soviet leaders are being guided by Napoleon's aphorism: "A conqueror is always a lover of peace"!

Finally, its frequent and often enthusiastic endorsement of détente has been useful for the Kremlin on the propaganda-ideological front. It has enhanced the Soviet Union's image as a "peaceloving country" that seeks to deliver mankind from the threat of nuclear conflagration, in opposition to to the policies of "warmongers" and "the forces of global reaction." That this stance has enhanced Communism's appeal to some groups outside Moscow's orbit, for example, can hardly be doubted. To undiscriminating minds, this fact sometimes translates into the idea that the

---

*In 1980, a leader of the Polish Communist government said about Soviet authorities: "They have a sense of being

a besieged fortress. The Soviet Union is a superpower, but mainly because of its military might. In other areas—technology, productivity, labor standards—they lag far behind [the United States and other industrialized nations]. They use power when scared. You Americans fail to understand the siege mentality" of the Kremlin. Quoted by John Darnton, in *New York Times,* May 24, 1980. The views of several authorities on the Soviet Union's mounting economic and financial problems are presented by Charles J. Hanley in the Baton Rouge *Sunday Advocate,* December 13, 1981.

Soviet Union champions peace, while the United States calls for a return to the Cold War. Even American efforts to *clarify the meaning* of détente have sometimes been used by Communist propagandists to document Washington's opposition to the idea.

For the Soviet Union, the coin of détente clearly has another side. The concept also has certain diplomatic *disadvantages* in the pursuit of Russian foreign policy objectives. Several of these may be identified briefly.

Some students of Soviet-American relations are convinced that (as was true of the concept of peaceful coexistence earlier), Moscow's commitment to détente stems from an overall position of *Soviet weakness* vis-à-vis the United States. In some pivotal respects, détente may well have "institutionalized" those weaknesses, tending to perpetuate Russia's relatively inferior position to the United States and other advanced Western nations (including Japan). In the economic sphere, for example, according to several fundamental indicators, the position of the Soviet Union has deteriorated—and the evidence indicates that this process will likely continue to occur in the future. Even on the military plane, while the U.S.S.R. has succeeded in achieving a position of military "equivalence" with the United States, as a long-range matter it is doubtful that the Kremlin is able to compete successfully in an intensified arms race against the United States and its allies. On this issue, we need to be reminded about an aspect of "national power" considered in Chapter 1: with regard to military force and its underlying foundation of economic capability, a nation's *potential power* may be more crucial than its existing military strength in determining its ability to achieve foreign policy objectives.

Insofar as a Soviet expectation concerning détente may have been to "freeze" the existing balance of military power as it existed at the end of the Vietnam War—thereby perpetuating a military disparity in its favor—Mos-

cow had failed to achieve its objective. By the end of the 1970s, as we observed in Chapter 5, the American people and their leaders had become apprehensive about growing Soviet military power and were determined to redress the military balance. Under the Carter Administration, the White House and Congress alike were committed to an expansion in American defense spending; and the Reagan Administration pledged to carry the process of strengthening the nation's military establishment even further.

Economically, détente has been a mixed blessing for the Soviet society and for the Communist hierarchy. It has perpetuated Soviet *dependence* upon the West to meet many of its economic needs, rather than compelling the Kremlin to resolve the long-standing and difficult problems responsible for Russia's poor economic performance in many crucial spheres. Détente has intensified a dilemma that has existed for the Communist regime ever since 1917. How can the Soviet Union aspire and claim to be a superpower when it is increasingly unable to supply its society's most elemental need, food? Or how can it threaten to "bury" capitalism by compiling a superior economic record, when with every passing year it falls farther behind the West in "high technology" production and know-how? From a military perspective, how can it hope to maintain a position of military parity (perhaps even superiority), when it must import the advanced computers needed to produce modern armaments and war materiel? Détente has not resolved such dilemmas for the Kremlin, nor is there any indication that solutions to them will be found in the near future.

Détente has also had unexpected results for Moscow in the realm of human rights and political stability. A concrete illustration is provided by the Helsinki agreement of 1975, viewed by the Kremlin as a notable diplomatic victory because (according to some interpretations) it "legitimatized" Soviet dominance over the Baltic and Eastern Europe. Yet for Moscow the Helsinki accord proved to be a double-edged sword. Thus, early in 1982, Secretary of State Alexander Haig sharply condemned the Soviet Union for its failure to adhere to the requirements of the Helsinki agreement in its effort to suppress anti-Communist political movements in Poland. In the American view, the existence of the Helsinki accord furnished legal justification for the involvement of the United States in the Polish crisis.[86]

But the most serious disadvantages of détente for Moscow are to be found perhaps in the sphere of Sino-Soviet relations. On that front, it would be difficult to identify *any* real gain for the Soviet Union from détente. As we shall see more fully in Chapter 15, during the period of détente Sino-Soviet relations continued to deteriorate. To the minds of some commentators, by the 1970s hostility between the two countries constituted perhaps the most serious threat to international peace anywhere on the globe. The distrust and enmity existing between these two former Communist allies resulted in a number of military "incidents" between them; the Sino-Soviet frontier was an increasingly volatile zone of tension and potential armed conflict; and according to some authorities, the Soviet military buildup witnessed in recent years was aimed primarily *at China*.[87] The period of Soviet-American détente had thus resulted in the fulfillment of a "bad dream" for Russian military strategists: the possibility of a "two-front" war simultaneously with the United States and its NATO allies, and with the People's Republic of China.

Meanwhile, détente had also witnessed a fundamental change in Sino-American relations, as will be explained more fully in Chapter 15. Beginning with the Nixon Administration, the United States and China undertook a "normalization" of their relations, leading to the establishment of regular diplomatic relations between them in 1979.[88] In almost every dimension of their relationship—in diplomacy; in economic and commercial transactions; in science, technology, and cultural exchange—the United States and China drew closer, while China and the Soviet Union drifted apart.

Détente in the American Diplomatic Ledger

Détente has also had decidedly mixed consequences for the foreign policy of the United States. On the positive side of the ledger—and a gain which some might feel outweighs all its disadvantages—is the fact that détente has substantially reduced the risk of global nuclear war. Aside from the overall ethical and humanitarian aspects of that development, from an ethnocentric viewpoint, as the most advanced society on the globe, the United States perhaps benefits more directly from that achievement than any other single country. It seems highly questionable, for example, whether democracy as a system of government could survive in the ashes of a nuclear conflagration between the superpowers; and many of the other consequences of such a conflict for American society would be incalculable and catastrophic.

America's acceptance of détente as the guiding principle of relations between the superpowers accords with the nation's traditional interest in peace; with the desires of the American people (although, as we noted in Chapter 8, public opinion toward the Soviet Union since World War II has been highly variable and inconsistent); and with the desires of public opinion abroad. Détente, for example, is a popular idea throughout Western Europe—where leaders and citizens are aware that in any nuclear exchange between the superpowers they would be the first casualties. Insofar as the foreign policy of the United States should reflect "a decent respect for the opinions of mankind," these factors provide a powerful inducement for American support of détente.

Within the framework of détente, American foreign policy has also become more flexible and adaptive than was the case at the height of the Cold War. Today, American officials and public opinion routinely accept the reality that numerous and diverse species of Communism exist within the contemporary international system; and these pose varying degrees of threat to the security and ideological values of the non-Communist world. Since the late 1940s, for example, the United States has assisted the Marxist regime of Yugoslavia to strengthen its security and to solve its internal problems. At a later stage, the Johnson Administration adopted the policy of "building bridges" to Eastern Europe, in which American assistance and trade were inaugurated for other Marxist countries. Under conditions of détente, American foreign policy has become less doctrinally rigid and more eclectic in its approach to a variety of political systems throughout the Third World.

Another gain for American foreign policy has been the impact of détente upon what was once viewed in Washington as a monolithic movement known as "international Communism," dominated by the Soviet Union. If the concept of "international Communism" ever possessed the internal cohesiveness Americans ascribed to it, in the era of détente it possessed little utility. The United States, said Secretary of State Haig in 1982, must "continue to differentiate among Communist countries themselves." Washington recognized that the policies and behavior of some Communist nations (such as the U.S.S.R. and Cuba) threatened American diplomatic and security interests, while the behavior of other Marxist regimes (like

Yugoslavia and Rumania) usually did not. For their part, as a Polish official publicly recognized, an objective of the smaller nations was to "melt the ice" between the superpowers in an effort to achieve greater policy-making independence. By the early 1980s, the Kremlin was in some measure deterred from intervening massively in the Polish crisis out of fear of the impact upon the future of détente.[89]

Perhaps the most dramatic example of "national Communism," however, appeared in Europe, where the concept of "Euro-Communism" had emerged.[90] Whatever that idea meant precisely (and specific manifestations of it were likely to vary from one country to another), it clearly signified an overall weakening of the Kremlin's control over the Communist parties of Western Europe. On a number of occasions (such as the Soviet invasion of Czechoslovakia in 1968 and its military incursion into Afghanistan in 1979), condemnations of Moscow's behavior by spokesmen for Euro-Communism have been pointed and vocal.

Gains to the United States from détente have been noteworthy in three specific policy areas. One of these relates to the Vietnam War. Support for détente in Washington and Moscow permitted the Vietnam conflict to remain a "limited war": At no point during that encounter did there appear to be a serious danger of a direct Soviet-American confrontation. The existence of détente also facilitated the termination of the Vietnam War. On several occasions, Washington enlisted Soviet help in bringing that conflict to an end on terms that were at least minimally acceptable to the parties to it.

Détente has also contributed in some measure to America's limited success in resolving the Arab-Israeli conflict and promoting regional stability in the Middle East. As we shall see more fully in Chapter 12, many obstacles lie in the path of a peaceful resolution of Arab-Israeli differences. Despite the existence of an Israeli-Egyptian peace treaty, conditions in the Middle East remain highly volatile; and little progress has been made in resolving other questions (such as the future of the West Bank of Palestine), engendering hostility between Israel and its Arab neighbors. Our interest in the Middle East is confined here to emphasizing two points about the impact of détente upon recent events in that region.

The first is that difficult as the attempt to eliminate Arab-Israeli differences has been under conditions of détente, it would have been infinitely *more difficult,* if not altogether impossible, if the superpowers had converted the Middle East into an active theater of Cold War hostility. The second consequence of détente for American foreign policy in the Middle East has been *the virtual exclusion of the Soviet Union* from any effective peace-making or peace-keeping role in the area. Such progress as has been made in settling the Arab-Israeli conflict has been achieved primarily at the instigation of the United States, of Israel, and of Egypt. The Soviet Union has made little or no positive contribution to that process—except not to oppose it directly. By contrast, Moscow *has* given diplomatic, military, and economic support to several Arab states belonging to the "rejection front" that is adamant against Israeli-Egyptian-American peace-making efforts; and the Kremlin has approved, and materially supported, the Palestine Liberation Organization (PLO) in its effort to carry on the struggle against Israel. While détente has produced no overt or concerted Soviet-American collaboration in resolving Middle East tensions, it has at least largely kept the Arab-Israeli quarrel (in contrast to certain other regional conflicts) relatively insulated from direct competition between the superpowers.

The most notable gain for American diplomacy from détente, however, most likely lies in a realm we have already discussed from the Soviet perspective: Sino-American relations (dealt with more fully in Chapter 15). In terms of its impact upon the international system, this "diplomatic revolution"—the dissolution of the Sino-Soviet axis, followed by the "normalization" in relations between the People's Republic of China (PRC) and the United States—must be ranked among the most momentous developments since World War II. Its implications for Soviet foreign policy were far-reaching—and nearly all of them were detrimental. The relaxation of Sino-American tensions—accompanied, by the early 1980s, by positive cooperation between the two countries in several key policy spheres—has engendered deep concern in the Kremlin. The emergence of China as a nuclear power, with a steadily expanding missile arsenal, serves as a potent restraint upon Soviet external behavior. Moreover, as in contexts like black Africa, much Soviet diplomatic activity today must now be directed at counteracting *Chinese* influence, no less than American, in foreign settings. The existence of a powerful China no doubt has also been a restraining influence upon the external behavior of smaller Communist countries (like North Vietnam and North Korea), whose governments have preserved close ties with Moscow.

On the other side of the diplomatic ledger, détente has not been without certain costs for the United States. In several respects, the "price" of détente has been high—so high as to convince some critics of the concept that its drawbacks for America outweigh its gains. Right-wing and conservative groups within the American society, for example, have long complained that détente was a diplomatic and ideological snare for the United States, calculatingly designed by the Kremlin to promote its own foreign policy objectives under the most favorable conditions.[91]

As critics of détente assess it, America's acceptance of the concept has had a number of specific disadvantages and has contributed to American diplomatic setbacks on several fronts. By subscribing to détente, for example, Washington appears to have "accepted" Soviet domination over Eastern Europe—thereby permitting the Kremlin to gain an objective it has pursued avidly since World War II. (Conversely, there has been no corresponding inclination by Moscow to "accept" an exclusive sphere of influence by the United States in Latin America or any other region.)

Critics of the idea also believe that America's acceptance of détente contributed to the condition that emerged as one of the dominant issues of the presidential election of 1980: a position of American *military weakness* that has seriously impeded the ability of the United States to protect its diplomatic and security interests from Latin America to the Persian Gulf area. No less crucially, as supporters of Ronald Reagan emphasized repeatedly during the campaign, the global and regional *perception* of American weakness and "indecision" have become serious impediments to achieving the nation's foreign policy goals.

Conceivably, the Soviet Union's military superiority in some weapons' categories came about because the American people and their leaders misunderstood détente and entertained unrealistic expectations concerning it. For many Americans, détente was equivalent to peaceful and cooperative Soviet-American relations; it would soon produce an end to the arms race; and the international system would finally achieve the stability that had been lacking since the end of World War II. Such hopes of course have proved illusory. In some cases, Moscow has unquestionably exploited the "spirit of Camp David" and

other manifestations of détente for its own advantage; even while they extolled détente, Soviet policy makers continued to build a formidable military machine behind the Iron Curtain.

Détente, it must also be admitted, has proven to be a complex, bewildering, and difficult concept for officials in Washington to administer and for the American people to understand clearly. Even more than the condition of Cold War, détente has engendered real problems for the role of public opinion in the foreign policy process, for executive-legislative relations, and for unified decision making within the executive branch. In these three crucial policy realms, pervasive misunderstanding has existed over the meaning of détente, over permissible Soviet and American conduct under it, and over the necessity and utility of particular foreign policy programs. As our earlier discussion emphasized, the basic problem is that détente *is* inherently an ambiguous and many-faceted concept. The Soviet and American interpretations of it do differ fundamentally. Moreover, as a relatively new concept in international relations, the meaning of détente has often had to evolve from experience with its application to a range of diverse issues arising between the United States and the Soviet Union. There is no "codebook" for détente, no list of permissible and impermissible behavior which government leaders can consult for guidance in applying détente to particular cases.

Such realities present an infinitely more difficult challenge to the American democracy than they do to authoritarian regimes like the Soviet Union. To some degree, the uncertainty and "lack of consensus" characteristic of American foreign policy during the 1970s, for example, could be attributed to confusion existing in the public and official American mind about the meaning of détente and its necessary implications. During the Carter Administration, this confusion lay at the very center of the American foreign policy process. For some four years, the President's national security adviser, Zbigniew Brzezinski, championed a "hard line" view of détente, in which the idea of ongoing *conflict* between the superpowers was emphasized; until his resignation in 1980, by contrast Secretary of State Cyrus Vance believed that détente essentially denoted efforts on several fronts to *resolve* outstanding Soviet-American differences. Such dichotomies were no less present in the approach of President Ronald Reagan and his foreign policy advisers. Time and again, Reagan emphasized that the preservation of peace would be a leading goal of his Administration; at the same time, he called upon Americans to "compete" successfully against the Soviet Union; and he demanded that America's military position be significantly strengthened.[92]

Two concluding observations may be made about the future of détente as the foundation stone of Soviet-American relations. One is that détente has been—and will almost certainly remain—an *evolving* concept. Both in theory and practice, its precise meaning and implications are likely to be fundamentally influenced by changes within the United States, within the Soviet Union, and within the international system. A key factor likely to affect the meaning of détente in the years ahead, for example, is the nature of the *political leadership* existing in both countries. The anticipated struggle for power in what has come to be called the post-Brezhnev era in the Soviet Union, for example, could have a profound impact upon the Soviet conception of détente.

The United States will of course also experience future political changes, and these could no less affect the American understanding of the meaning and implications of détente. By the early 1980s, on Capitol Hill and throughout American public opinion, consid-

erable dissatisfaction existed with the results of détente, chiefly perhaps on the plane of military competition between the United States and the Soviet Union. As we observed in Chapter 8, by this period the "decline of American power" abroad occasioned deep public and congressional anxiety—a phenomenon many Americans (rightly or wrongly) attributed to acceptance of détente as the governing principle of Soviet-American relations. Such public and congressional discontents could be translated into an irresistible public demand for American policy makers to reevaluate the concept of détente and the benefits it confers upon the United States.

Implicit in the idea that détente is evolving is recognition of a second general characteristic of the concept. This is the idea that, even while they may be described under the rubric of détente, Soviet-American relations are likely to experience considerable *fluctuation* within any given period of time. Détente may—and on the basis of experience almost certainly will—experience "setbacks"; and conversely, it may, and probably will, also include periods of expanding cooperation between the superpowers. Even with regard to a single issue—such as Soviet-American relations in a region like black Africa—détente will likely include elements of both rivalry and cooperation between the nuclear giants on particular African questions. On both sides of the Iron Curtain, official and private spokesmen will in some periods predict "the end of détente"; during other periods, they are likely to refer to its "inevitability" and its promising future.

A third consideration likely to influence the future of détente was a realization on both sides of the Iron Curtain that, despite its defects and limitations, détente *was preferable to any of its attainable alternatives.* For example, in a major speech on Soviet-American relations in 1982, Secretary of State Alexander Haig predicted that rivalries and tensions between the superpowers would continue. The competition, however, had to be "constrained by another central fact of our times—nuclear weapons. Total victory by military means has become a formula for mutual catastrophe." The American approach to the U.S.S.R. was based upon a belief that "competition will proceed," but that "the use or threat of force" must be constrained. America's goal, Haig asserted, was to "make clear to the Soviet Union that there are penalties for aggression and incentives for restraint." Haig anticipated no "early, sudden or dramatic reconcilation of Soviet and American interests." The United States wanted "the competition of democracy and Communism to be conducted in peaceful and political terms, but we will provide other means if the Soviet Union insists upon violent methods of struggle."[93]

On the assumption that entente between the two superpowers is an unattainable condition for the foreseeable future—if ever—then détente is a more attractive diplomatic option than Cold War, and certainly more attractive than overt hostilities, between the nuclear giants. If détente has left many sources of tension in Soviet-American relations, the concept has a twofold advantage over alternative principles. It is based upon mutual recognition in Washington and Moscow that nuclear war would be a catastrophe for the human race. And détente envisions, and in certain limited areas has actually produced, *some progress* in resolving the issues dividing the superpowers. Those two gains provide powerful incentives for the continuance of détente as the foundation stone of Soviet-American relations.

NOTES

1. See the toasts by Presidents Jimmy Carter and Leonid Brezhnev at the Vienna Summit Conference, June 15–18, 1979, in the State Department publication, "Vienna Summit," Selected Documents No. 13 (Washington, D.C.: Department of State, Bureau of Public Affairs, 1979), pp. 2–3.

2. Louis J. Halle, *The Cold War as History* (New York: Harper & Row, 1975), pp. 314–315.

3. Coral Bell, *The Diplomacy of Détente: the Kissinger Era* (New York: St. Martin's Press, 1977), p. 9.

4. Dwight D. Eisenhower, *Mandate for Change* (Garden City, N.Y.: Doubleday and Co., 1963), pp. 503–529.

5. See Halle, *The Cold War as History,* pp. 365–367. For a discussion of the Camp David summit meeting, see Dwight D. Eisenhower, *Waging Peace* (Garden City, N.Y.: Doubleday and Co., 1965), pp. 413–449.

6. An informative study of the Cuban Missile Crisis of 1962 is Robert F. Kennedy, *Thirteen Days* (New York: New American Library, 1969).

7. Thus, in 1963, President Kennedy publicly warned that in a full-scale nuclear exchange between the superpowers lasting less than 60 minutes, upwards of 300 million people would likely be killed. Several years earlier, Soviet Premier Khrushchev had estimated the number of victims of a global nuclear war at around 500 million people. See Norman A. Graebner, "The Limits of Choice," in Norman A. Graebner, ed., *The Cold War: A Conflict of Ideology and Power,* 2nd ed. (Lexington, Mass.: D. C. Heath, 1976), p. 219.

8. President Johnson's views are cited in George Ball, *Diplomacy for a Crowded World: An American Foreign Policy* (Boston: Little, Brown and Co., 1976), p. 112.

9. See ibid., p. 89, and Dimitri K. Simes, *Détente and Conflict: Soviet Foreign Policy, 1972–1977* (Beverly Hills, Calif.: Sage Publications, 1977), pp. 11, 18. President Richard M. Nixon's visit to Moscow in 1972 is discussed and evaluated in Henry Kissinger, *White House Years* (Boston: Little, Brown and Co., 1979), pp. 1202–1258.

10. See Kissinger, *White House Years,* pp. 1241–1242.

11. See the excerpt from Andrei Zhadanov's book *The International Situation,* published in

Moscow in 1947, in Alvin Z. Rubinstein, ed., *The Foreign Policy of the Soviet Union* (New York: Random House, 1960), pp. 237–238.

12. See the excerpt from Premier Khrushchev's report to the Supreme Soviet on November 7, 1957, as contained in ibid., pp. 30–32.

13. For the text of Brezhnev's speech, see the publication by the American Association of Slavic Studies, "The Documentary Record of the 25th Congress of the Communist Party of the Soviet Union," *Current Soviet Policies, 7* (1976), 4–14.

14. Bell, *The Diplomacy of Détente,* p. 9.

15. See the quotations from Lenin's thought in Department of State, *Communist Perspective* (Washington, D.C.: Department of State, Division of Intelligence and Research, 1955), pp. 383–384.

16. Ibid., p. 384.

17. Khrushchev's views are quoted in Jerry A. Hough, "The Stalin-Trotsky Split: A Lesson for Kremlinologists," *The Reporter, 29* (December 5, 1963), 39.

18. The distinction between strategy and tactics in Marxist ideology is highlighted in Department of State, *Communist Perspective,* pp. 440–455.

19. The idea that Marxist ideology supplies the principal key to the behavior of Soviet officials is the theme of Nathan Leites, *A Study of Bolshevism* (New York: Free Press, 1953), and the same author's *The Operational Code of the Politburo* (New York: McGraw-Hill, 1951).

20. On the decline of ideology, see George Lichteim, "What is Left of Communism?" *Foreign Affairs, 46* (October, 1967), 78–95.

21. For discussions of the concept of peaceful coexistence, see Nikita S. Khrushchev, "On Peaceful Coexistence," *Foreign Affairs, 38* (October, 1959), 1–18; and Louis J. Halle, "The Struggle Called Coexistence," *New York Times Magazine* (November 15, 1959), 14, 110–118.

22. Ball, *Diplomacy for a Crowded World,* pp. 85–86.

23. Edward E. Azar, "Soviet and Chinese Roles in the Middle East," *Problems of Communism, 28* (May–June, 1979), 20.

24. Brezhnev's views are quoted in Simes, *Détente and Conflict,* p. 7.

25. Secretary of State Henry Kissinger's views on the meaning of détente are quoted by David A. Andelman, in *New York Times,* January 7, 1980. President Jimmy Carter's views are cited in Helmut Sonnenfeldt, "Russia, America, and Détente," *Foreign Affairs, 56* (January, 1978), 276.

26. Simes, *Détente and Conflict,* p. 9.

27. Kennan's views are cited in ibid., p. 8.

28. See ibid., pp. 14–15; and Bell, *The Diplomacy of Détente,* pp. 1–2. Italics are in the original.

29. See the testimony by Adam Ulam before the Senate Foreign Relations Committee, in its *Détente: Hearings . . . on United States Relations with Communist Countries,* August 1–October 8, 1974. 93rd Cong., 2nd Sess., 1975, pp. 115–116.

30. "Soviet Comment on Vance Visit," *Current Digest of the Soviet Press, 29* (May 4, 1977), 1–4.

31. See the long analysis of Soviet-American relations by G. Arbatov in *Pravda,* April 2, 1976, as reprinted in "Arbatov Reviews US-Soviet Relations," *Current Digest of the Soviet Press, 28* (April 28, 1976), 1–5.

32. See the excerpt from the report of the 22nd Communist Party Congress, in Philip Mosely, "The Meaning of Coexistence," in Graebner, ed., *The Cold War,* p. 140.

33. See "*Pravda* Rebuts Carter Policy Speech," *Current Digest of the Soviet Press, 30* (July 12, 1978), 1–4; and the summary of the *Pravda* editorial of November 2, 1980, by Anthony Austin in *New York Times,* November 3, 1980.

34. See the analysis by G. Arbatov, in "Arbatov: Soviet Goal is Nuclear Parity," *Current Digest of the Soviet Press, 29* (March 2, 1977), 1–4.

35. See "Leaders' Speeches Accent World Affairs," *Current Digest of the Soviet Press, 32* (March 19, 1980), 1–4.

36. Soviet reactions to the diplomacy of the Carter Administration are discussed in Adam

Ulam, "U.S.-Soviet Relations: Unhappy Coexistence," *Foreign Affairs*, (Special Issue, 1978), 556–559.

37. See the views of G. Shakhnazarov on the concept of peaceful coexistence, in "What is Detente?—The Soviet View," *Current Digest of the Soviet Press*, **27** (January 28, 1976), 1–5.

38. See the views of Soviet Premier Brezhnev in *Pravda*, February 5, 1980, as cited in "World Politics," *Current Digest of the Soviet Press*, **32** (March 5, 1980), 19.

39. Brezhnev's views are quoted in Bell, *The Diplomacy of Détente*, p. 4.

40. See "Détente Brings Subversion, Military Warned," *Current Digest of the Soviet Press*, **29** (March 2, 1977), 5–7.

41. Anatol Rapoport, *The Big Two: Soviet-American Perceptions of Foreign Policy* (Indianapolis, Ind.: Bobbs-Merrill, 1971), pp. 5–7.

42. Brezhnev's views are quoted in Simes, *Détente and Conflict*, p. 22.

43. See the quotation from the (unnamed) Moscow military district commander, in Ball, *Diplomacy for a Crowded World*, pp. 89–90.

44. See Nikolay V. Podgorny's views in Simes, *Détente and Conflict*, p. 20.

45. See the declaration of the 22nd Communist Party Congress, as cited in Mosely, "The Meaning of Coexistence," in Graebner, ed., *The Cold War*, p. 142.

46. "Détente Brings Subversion, Military Warned," 5–7.

47. "Zamyatin Scores Carter's 'Sabre-Rattling,'" *Current Digest of the Soviet Press*, **32** (March 26, 1980), 4–6.

48. "Angola: Reiterating the Soviet Position," *Current Digest of the Soviet Press*, **28** (February 4, 1976), 4–5.

49. Soviet and Cuban intervention in Angola is discussed in Gerald R. Ford, *A Time to Heal*, (New York: Harper & Row, and The Reader's Digest Association, 1979), pp. 345–346, 358–359.

50. Colin Legum, "The African Environment," *Problems of Communism*, **27** (January–February, 1978), 1–2.

51. "Disturbances in Kabul: the Soviet Version," *Current Digest of the Soviet Press*, **32** (March 26, 1980), 6–8.

52. "Is the US Bringing Back the Cold War?" *Current Digest of the Soviet Press*, **32** (February 13, 1980), 1–8.

53. See Robert Legvold, "The Super Rivals: Conflict in the Third World," *Foreign Affairs*, **57** (Spring, 1979), 755–779.

54. See the discussion of the Nixon Administration's efforts to ease restrictions on Jewish emigration from the U.S.S.R., in Kissinger, *White House Years*, pp. 1271–1272.

55. Rapoport, *The Big Two*, pp. 161–162.

56. Simes, *Détente and Conflict*, p. 9.

57. Ibid., pp. 39–40.

58. For numerous examples of the Soviet readiness to employ force to achieve diplomatic goals, see James M. McConnell and Bradford Kismukes, "Soviet Diplomacy of Force in the Third World," *Problems of Communism*, **28** (January-February, 1979), 14–28.

59. Ulam, "U.S.-Soviet Relations," *Foreign Affairs*, 560.

60. Eisenhower, *Waging Peace*, p. 621.

61. See the excerpts from President Kennedy's views on relations with the Soviet Union in Theodore C. Sorensen, *Kennedy* (New York: Harper & Row, 1965), pp. 509–514.

62. Soviet-American negotiations at Vladivostok on the limitation of strategic weapons are discussed in Ford, *A Time to Heal*, pp. 213–219.

63. For the text of President Jimmy Carter's speech on June 7, 1978, see *New York Times*, June 8, 1978; and see the text of President Reagan's speech on Soviet-American relations in ibid., December 30, 1981.

64. Kissinger's views on détente are quoted in Bell, *The Diplomacy of Détente*, p. 1.

65. See "US-Soviet Relations," in the publication by the Bureau of Public Affairs, Department of State, called *Gist*, (August, 1978), 1.

66. For U.S. Ambassador Malcolm Toon's views on the meaning and implications of détente, see the text of his speech on September 15, 1979, "A Close Look at the Soviet Union and U.S.-U.S.S.R. Relations," *Current Policy* (Washington, D.C.: Department of State), **38** (October, 1979), 1–5.

67. Dr. Kissinger's views on the nature and goals of Soviet "peace offensives" are cited at length in Bell, *The Diplomacy of Détente*, pp. 21–22.

68. See, for example, the eloquent article by Aleksander Solzhenitsyn, "Misconceptions about Russia Are a Threat to America," *Foreign Affairs*, **58** (Spring, 1980), 797–835; this essay highlights a number of Soviet weaknesses.

69. See the views of Ronald Reagan on Soviet-American relations in *New York Times*, October 30, 1980.

70. *New York Times*, June 7, 1978. Italics inserted.

71. See the statement made by Secretary of State Cyrus Vance to the House International Relations (now, Foreign Affairs) Committee, in *New York Times*, June 20, 1978.

72. See the State Department's publication, "Vienna Summit," pp. 1–3.

73. The views of Henry Kissinger on détente are cited in Legvold, "The Super Rivals," pp. 760–761 and *New York Times*, January 24, 1982. Other criticisms of détente may be found in Norman Podhoretz, "The Neo-Conservative Anguish Over Reagan's Foreign Policy," *New York Times Magazine*, May 2, 1982, 30–34, 86–97.

74. See the excerpts from Dr. Kissinger's testimony to the Senate Foreign Relations Committee quoted by Bernard Gwertzman, in *New York Times*, August 2, 1979.

75. See the views of various American officials on the idea of "linkage," quoted by David A. Andelman, in *New York Times*, January 7, 1980.

76. See the text of the statement by Ambassador Malcolm Toon to the Senate Foreign Relations Committee, issued by the Department of State, "SALT and U.S.-Soviet Relations," *Current Policy*, **76** (July 25, 1979), p. 3.

77. See Bernard Gwertzman's analysis of the Reagan Administration's diplomacy toward Soviet intervention in Poland in *New York Times*, January 23, 1982.

78. See the text of Vance's statement on Soviet-American relations, in *New York Times*, June 20, 1978.

79. See the text of the speech by Secretary Vance in *New York Times*, June 19, 1980.

80. See the views of President Ronald Reagan's foreign policy adviser, Richard V. Allen, in *U.S. News and World Report*, **89** (November 24, 1980), 54.

81. Congressional efforts to make the granting of favorable terms of trade to the U.S.S.R. contingent upon easing restrictions on emigration by Soviet Jews are discussed in Gerald R. Ford, *A Time to Heal*, pp. 138–139, 224–225.

82. Richard Burt, in *New York Times*, July 19, 1978.

83. Bell, *The Diplomacy of Détente*, p. 250.

84. Gerald L. Steibel, *Détente: Promises and Pitfalls* (New York: Crane, Russak and Co., 1975), pp. 12–13.

85. See Jane P. Shapiro, "The Soviet Consumer in the Brezhnev Era," *Current History*, **75** (October, 1978), 100–104, 128–131; and Robert C. Stuart, "The Soviet Economy," ibid., 109–113, 126–127.

86. See William G. Hyland, "Brezhnev and Beyond," *Foreign Affairs*, **58** (Fall, 1979), 51–67; and the address by Secretary of State Haig, "Poland and the Future of Europe," as distributed by the State Department (Current Policy No. 362), January 12, 1982, 1–5.

87. Although somewhat dated in its discussion, the analysis of growing Sino-Soviet animosity by Harrison E. Salisbury provides graphic evidence of the nations' increasingly hostile relationship. See his *War Between Russia and China* (New York: Bantam Books, 1970). And for a detailed discussion of historical background, see Harry Schwartz, *Tsars, Mandarins, and Commissars: A History of Chinese-Russian Relations*, rev. ed. (Garden City, N.Y.: Doubleday and Co., 1973).

88. See the discussion of the "normalization" in Sino-American relations in Kissinger, *White House Years*, pp. 684–788; 1049–1097.

89. See the views of Secretary of State Haig in *New York Times*, April 28, 1982; and of the Polish view of détente by John Darnton, ibid., May 24, 1980.

90. James O. Goldsborough, "Eurocommunism after Madrid," *Foreign Affairs,* **55** (July, 1977), 800–815; and Walter Z. Laqueur, "American and West European Communism," in James R. Schlesinger. ed., *Defending America: Toward a New Role in the Post-Détente World* (New York: Basic Books, 1977), pp. 49–65.

91. For an informative discussion of the prospects for détente in the early 1980s, see Strobe Talbott, "U.S.-Soviet Relations: From Bad to Worse," *Foreign Affairs,* **58** (Special Issue, 1979), 515–540.

92. For the views of President Reagan and his advisers toward relations with the Soviet Union, see *U.S. News and World Report,* **89** (November 17, 1980), 22–25, 41; David E. Rosenbaum, in *New York Times,* November 2, 1980; Richard Burt, in *New York Times,* November 13, 1980; and James M. Markham, in *New York Times,* November 18, 1980.

93. See the text of Secretary of State Haig's speech in *New York Times,* April 28, 1982.

Chapter 11

Western Europe:
Pivot of American Foreign Policy

An experienced American diplomatic official and perceptive student of the nation's foreign policy has asked: "What does it mean to have the nations of Western Europe free and allied with us?" Western Europe "is an area with a combined industrial production far superior to that of the Soviet Union . . . the source of much of the world's scientific discovery and modern technology." But even more crucially, "the most important values and purposes of Western Europeans are shared by Americans—the very elements that give meaning to our own national life. Americans still depend on the Old Continent for the good health and continued enrichment of our common civilization."[1]

Another recent student of American foreign relations has said that

> . . . the irresolute, divided, and sometimes overtly self-seeking Europeans are still the one body of humanity whose welfare and security is inextricably bound with our own. Our economic prosperity, our cultural vital-

ity . . . require a secure, prosperous, creative, and stable Europe. For all its defects, the Europe that exists is the only Europe we have, and it is time that it be made the central concern of our policy.[2]

For a number of reasons, it is appropriate that we begin our discussion of American foreign policy toward the major geographic regions by focusing upon relations between the United States and Western Europe. The fundamental transformation in American foreign policy—from the traditional stance of isolationism to the postwar approach of internationalism—was symbolized by basic changes in the nation's approach to Western Europe. The Cold War with the Soviet Union began in Europe; it was precipitated by actual or threatened Soviet intervention in Eastern Europe, in Greece, and in several other countries of Western Europe. The containment policy enunciated by the Truman Administration was directed initially against Soviet expansionism in the Mediterranean area. When it was signed in 1949, the North Atlantic Treaty signified America's formal abandonment of isolationism as its guiding diplomatic principle toward Europe. By most criteria, European-American relations remained the foundation stone of the foreign policy of the United States.

European-American Relations in Perspective

For an understanding of contemporary American foreign policy toward Western Europe, a brief historical perspective on European-American relations is necessary.

A Century of the Monroe Doctrine

From the earliest days of the Republic, the United States has conceived of itself as a new and unique nation whose appointed mission required it to stand aloof from the quarrels and vicissitudes of the Old World. Geography separated the two worlds by thousands of miles of ocean; the American Revolution signified a spiritual-ideological breach. For well over a century thereafter, Americans were concerned primarily with domestic problems and challenges, especially expansion across the continent. George Washington had sounded the keynote of the American outlook in his Farewell Address in 1796, when he declared that "Europe has a set of primary interests, which to us have none or a very remote relation." This view was also supported by Thomas Jefferson, who stated in 1813 that: "The European nations constitute a separate division of the globe; their localities make them a part of a distinct system; they have a set of interests of their own in which it is our business never to engage ourselves." America, on the other hand, "has a hemisphere to itself. It must have its separate system of interests; which must not be subordinated to those of Europe. . . ."[3]

Thus, when President Monroe delivered his classic message to Congress in 1823, he was adding very little to the position already taken by the United States in regard to European affairs since independence. The key thought expressed by the Monroe Doctrine with respect to Europe* was that: "In the wars of European powers in matters relating to themselves we have never taken any part, nor does it comport with our policy so to do. It is only when our rights are invaded or seriously menaced that we resent injuries or make preparation for our defense." Warning the Holy Alliance to stay out of American affairs, Monroe stated "that we should consider any attempt on their part to extend their system to any portion of this hemisphere as dangerous to our peace and safety. With the existing colonies or dependencies of any European power we have not interfered and shall not interfere."[4]

At the time neither the United States nor Europe was conscious that Monroe was enunciating a principle of American foreign policy that would apply for over a hundred years thereafter. The influences that prompted Monroe's speech were twofold: threatened intervention by the Holy Alliance to return the newly independent states of Latin America to Spain, and machinations of Czarist Russia in the Northwest, climaxed by the imperial ukase of 1821 which virtually proclaimed the Pacific Northwest a Russian sphere of influence. The Monroe Doctrine had been America's response to these two threats. Over the course of time it became the most famous principle of American foreign policy.

*The Monroe Doctrine had two aspects, one governing America's relations with Europe, the other, Europe's relations with the Western Hemisphere. While the first aspect remained relatively unchanged for over a century, except of course for World War I, the other was subject to numerous amendments and modifications in the years that followed 1823. The Western hemispheric applications of the Monroe Doctrine are discussed in Chapter 14.

However, the self-abnegation pledge that the United States would not interfere in European affairs was not nearly so sweeping as is sometimes supposed. Monroe pledged only noninterference in "the wars of the European powers in matters relating to themselves...." Thus, the Monroe Doctrine from its inception applied only (1) to Europe's *wars* and (2) to those wars that *were exclusively of European concern.*

The Monroe Doctrine's stipulations relating to America's relationships with Europe became the guiding principles of American foreign policy until the Truman Doctrine was proclaimed in 1947. There were, of course, a number of exceptions to the noninterference principle, notably America's participation in World Wars I and II. But even these examples can be deemed compatible with the Monroe Doctrine, since in both cases American vital interests were very much involved. German submarines forced the United States into World War I. The Japanese attack on Pearl Harbor, followed by the German declaration of war against the United States, compelled our entry into World War II. It is significant that all through World War II the United States believed that the greatest threat to its own security emanated *from Europe;* hence American policymakers consistently gave a higher priority to the European theater of war than they did to the Pacific theater.

For nearly a hundred years after 1823, American involvement in the politics of Europe was episodic and transitory. Woodrow Wilson's ill-fated attempt to reorient American foreign policy around the principle of "collective security" is too well known to require elaboration here. Senate and public opposition to the League of Nations graphically reaffirmed American isolationist attitudes toward Europe. America did not officially participate in the League's activities, although it sent unofficial "observers" to attend League deliberations, and cooperated on

a limited scale with a number of the League's social and humanitarian activities.[5] During the 1930s, isolationism made the population insensitive to the most elementary facts concerning the nation's security and the security of the North Atlantic region with which America's destiny was increasingly linked. "Aid short of war" was the most that the American people would support—and sometimes there was very little public support even for this—prior to the Japanese attack on Pearl Harbor in 1941.

Prerequisites of an Isolationist Policy

For almost a hundred years, isolationism accorded both with the desires of the American people and with existing geographic-diplomatic realities, although by the turn of the century many of these realities were beginning to change. Isolationism was finally abandoned as the policy of the United States, not willfully, but as an inescapable reaction to the facts of international life in the postwar nuclear age, and more specifically as a reaction to the inescapable challenge posed by the Soviet threat.

Three conditions made possible America's historic withdrawal from the political affairs of the Old World. These conditions have either disappeared altogether today or else they have so changed as to make an isolationist course by the United States nothing short of suicidal.

1. America was geographically isolated from the world. This fact, as much as any other, explains America's ability for over a hundred years to stay out of great-power conflicts in Europe and to a lesser degree in Asia. America could follow isolationism as a policy because the United States was separated from the storm centers of diplomatic controversy by formidable geographical barriers. Thousands of miles of ocean cut America off from Europe and Asia; the polar icecap and northern Canadian wastelands posed an impenetrable obstacle to the north; no threat could come from the weak, unstable governments that existed in Latin America. In the modern period, annihilation of distance by the fast ocean liner, the submarine, radio and telephone, and finally the jet airplane and supersonic missile has eliminated the geographical fact of isolation from the outside world. Within minutes, destruction could be rained on American cities by a potential aggressor; and, conversely, American retaliatory power could be launched speedily against an enemy. Isolationism will not suffice as a policy, therefore, because isolation is no longer a reality.

2. Europe's diplomatic troubles were America's well-being.   The United States was also fortunate that suspicion and rivalry among the great powers of Europe prevented them from uniting behind an anti-American policy. As a rule, the United States had only one thing to fear from the Old World: a new grand coalition that might arise to despoil the young nation and to jeopardize its continued independence. Occasionally this danger appeared imminent, as illustrated by the Holy Alliance's threatened intervention in Latin America in the early 1820s. In the main, however, European countries could never subordinate their differences sufficiently to collaborate against the United States. Repeated diplomatic conflicts on the Continent during the nineteenth century—occasioned by Russia's several attempts to penetrate the Near East, France's efforts to reestablish its former position of greatness, countless nationalistic rebellions against entrenched autocracies, Bismarck's determination to make Germany a great power—kept the great powers in an almost constant state of diplomatic ferment and intensified existing hostilities. Europe's infrequent incursions into Western hemispheric affairs—such as French intervention in Mexico during the Civil War—produced controversies among the European states themselves, out of fear that one country would increase its power over the others. Meantime, on the Continent age-old jealousies and antagonisms made European countries reluctant to embark upon expansionist policies in the Western Hemisphere, so long as the fear existed that the first danger to their security lay in Europe. In *Realpolitik* terms, repeated threats to the European balance of power for more than a century after the Monroe Doctrine were crucial in preserving the security of the United States.

These conditions do not obtain in the contemporary age. They were destroyed by a combination of World War I, the imperialistic ambitions of Hitler and Mussolini, World War II, the wartime and post-World War II policies of the U.S.S.R., independence movements in former colonial areas, the injection of ideological considerations into world politics on a far greater scale than in the nineteenth century—all contributing to the decline of Britain, Germany, France, and Italy as great powers on the European scene and militating against reinstitution of a balance-of-power system comparable to that prevailing earlier.

3. American security was protected by the Pax Britannica and the subsequent Anglo-American entente.   The nineteenth century was the age of *Pax Britannica*—unquestionably one of the most stable and benign eras known to the history of international relations. Britain ruled the seas. Utilizing strategic bases in its scattered colonies, it intervened repeatedly to put down threats to international peace and order, whether they came from the diplomatic intrigues of Russia in the Near East, or Germany in Persia, or the Holy Alliance in Latin America. For more than a century after independence, the American people were suspicious of Great Britain, believing firmly that Downing Street harbored territorial ambitions on the American continent and, in more general terms, that it sought to frustrate American diplomatic goals. This frame of mind persisted until around 1900.

Actually, in spite of this prevailing antagonism toward Britain, a fundamental indentity of interest lay beneath the surface of Anglo-American relations throughout most of the nineteenth century. Historians are agreed that British acceptance of the principles of the Monroe Doctrine—at least those parts relating to European activities in the Western Hemisphere—goes far toward explaining whatever success the doctrine achieved for several decades after 1823 in realizing American diplomatic objectives. Britain was perhaps even more concerned than America about the possibility of other great powers' establishing a strong position in Latin America, thereby enhancing their capacity to jeopardize British sea communications and trade routes. Britain could accept the idea, therefore, that this hemisphere was a special preserve of the United States—a country that possessed no navy worth mentioning and that harbored no expansive tendencies at British expense.

Until about 1900, Americans rarely perceived the relationship between their own security and British power. After that date, however, both countries began openly to acknowledge their mutual interests. Britain feared the growing naval might and imperialist ambitions of Germany and Japan. The age-old imperialistic objectives of Czarist Russia threatened more than ever to infringe upon British colonial and trade interests in the Far East. America, although beginning to expand its navy, had few imperialistic designs that clashed with those of Great Britain. As maritime and trading countries, both nations shared a desire to preserve freedom of the seas and unimpeded access to world markets. Ideological affinity provided another link in the chain of Anglo-American cooperation. British support of the Open Door policy in China at the turn of the century and negotia-tion of the Hay-Pauncefote Treaty in 1901, preparing the way for American construction of the Panama Canal, signified the new official harmony that characterized Anglo-American relations.

Nevertheless, it could not be said that American citizens as a whole understood the crucial role of this entente in preserving their security. Periodically, vocal citizens' groups "twisted the lion's tail" and railed against the alleged evils of the British Empire. A majority of Americans appeared to be ignorant of the part played by Anglo-American cooperation in defending the vital interests of the United States. The "inarticulate major premise" of American foreign policy after 1900 has been the assumption that Great Britain and the United States are friends and that in an overwhelming majority of cases their diplomatic objectives are complementary, rather than antagonistic. Britain's dramatic decline as a great power after World War II, a process that actually began with World War I, drove home to Americans as never before how vital for international peace and stability had been Britain's former role as protector of the balance of power in Western Europe and chief defender against Russian expansion across the frontiers of Europe, the Middle East, and Asia.

In view of the (often unacknowledged) benefits Americans derived from the age of *Pax Britannica,* it was perhaps fitting that after World War II there occurred a reversal of roles: Now it was the *Pax Americana* that safeguarded British security and various forms of assistance by the United States that contributed to the well-being of a weak and internally divided Britain.

Containment, Recovery, and Rearmament

The Origins of Containment

As our discussion in Chapter 9 emphasized, by 1947 the Monroe Doctrine as a principle of

American policy toward Europe had been superseded by the Truman Doctrine's principle of containment. Reduced to its essentials, the new policy anticipated firm and sustained American resistance to Soviet expansionist tendencies. Containment received its most persuasive justification at the hands of George F. Kennan, a high-ranking State Department official and recognized authority on Soviet Russia. In a widely circulated article on "The Sources of Soviet Conduct,"[6] Kennan enunciated the containment idea as America's response to the challenge of Soviet expansionism and hostility toward non-Communist countries. The immediate postwar period had witnessed Soviet hegemony over Eastern Europe, Communist intrigue in such countries as Iran, Turkey, Greece, Indochina, and China, as well as Soviet intransigence on such questions as disarmament and control of nuclear weapons. By 1947 it had become apparent on all sides that the wartime policy of great-power collaboration had collapsed.

It was Kennan's belief, sharply challenged by other leading students of international politics,[7] that successful implementation of the containment idea would not only prevent further Soviet incursions into the non-Communist world but would also in time bring about a "mellowing" in the Kremlin's attitudes and policies toward the outside world, possibly aiding the emergence of a less despotic regime internally, and less aggressive behavior externally, by the Soviet government.

Containment received its first application in the Greek-Turkish Aid Program of 1947. After that came the Marshall Plan, the North Atlantic Pact, the Mutual Defense Assistance Program, and the Mutual Security Program. Hand in hand with these developments went efforts by the United States to encourage greater economic, military, and political integration on the continent of Europe. All of these were manifestations of the containment idea. Whatever specific forms America's relations with Western Europe in the postwar period might take, one goal remained uppermost: to make the North Atlantic area as impregnable as possible against threats to its security emanating from behind the Iron Curtain, irrespective of whether they came from a threatened Soviet military attack or Communist intrigue in the political affairs of Western Europe.

Our analysis of post-World War II European-American relations will focus upon three major issues: American military and economic aid programs for Western Europe; the defense of the North Atlantic area; and political and economic unification movements on the European continent.

The Greek-Turkish Aid Program

In an historic foreign policy address on March 12, 1947, President Truman declared that "it must be the policy of the United States to support free people who are resisting subjection by armed minorities or outside pressures."[8] The President's statement—soon known as the Truman Doctrine—was prompted by the crisis in Greece, where Communist-led rebels were seeking to overthrow the existing government. For almost two years, British troops had supported the Greek government's effort to restore stability. But Britain was near bankruptcy. Some liquidation of British overseas commitments therefore became imperative, leaving the United States the alternative of either assuming many of these commitments or accepting further Communist intrusions into the free world. The situation in Greece took on added urgency because, at long last, Russia appeared on the verge of achieving its age-old desire to break through into the Mediterranean area.

President Truman consequently asked Congress for an appropriation of $400 million to resist Communist expansionism in Greece and to bolster the defenses of nearby Turkey, which had also experienced intermittent Soviet pressures during and since World War II. After prolonged study, Congress granted this request in May, thereby establishing the pattern of economic-military aid to countries confronted with Communist aggression. Along with Yugoslavia's later defection from the Soviet bloc, American economic and military aid proved to be of crucial importance in preserving the political independence of Greece and assuring its continued adherence to the free world alliance.

The European Recovery Program

Even before Congress had approved the Greek-Turkish Aid bill, the Truman Administration had begun studies of Western Europe's progressively critical economic plight. Wartime and early postwar relief programs like the United Nations Relief and Rehabilitation Administration (UNRRA) had done little or nothing to eliminate the underlying causes of economic instability in Europe. By mid-1947, widespread economic distress, contributing to political turbulence, existed in Europe. In a major foreign policy address on June 5, 1947, Secretary of State George C. Marshall took note of Europe's crisis and suggested that America would be prepared to extend long-range assistance for reconstruction, provided Europe itself took the lead in presenting a carefully worked-out plan for utilizing American resources to promote lasting regional recovery.

Europe was quick to respond. Even Soviet Russia and its satellites expressed an interest in participating in the Marshall Plan. By midsummer, however, Communist propaganda organs had begun to denounce the Marshall Plan as an instrument of American imperialism. Neither Russia nor its satellites

participated in the discussions that finally resulted in the presentation of a concrete program to the State Department. Lacking access to the Kremlin's archives, no Westerner can be certain of the reason behind Moscow's refusal to participate in the Marshall Plan. No bars originally existed against Russia's association with the plan, although as time passed, the program came more and more to be presented to Congress and the American public as an anti-Communist measure. Several hypotheses may be suggested. Russia was apparently unwilling to accept any "conditions" for the use of American aid, particularly any that would involve extensive American "supervision" of its administration. Moreover, in the light of an increasingly anti-Soviet attitude within the United States, and especially in Congress, Russia may have actually feared an expansion in American influence in the sensitive Eastern European satellite zone. Ideological considerations may also have colored Russia's decision. The Kremlin may have thought that long-awaited revolutionary forces could work more successfully in economically debilitated countries.

Whatever the reasons for the Kremlin's obduracy, it is apparent that Soviet refusal to join in the plan was a major blunder in Russia's postwar foreign policy. Perhaps more than any other factor, the Marshall Plan was responsible for the decline of Communist influence in Western Europe after 1948. Initially there had appeared considerable opposition within the United States to so costly a measure. This opposition was largely overcome by presenting the plan to Congress as part of the "containment" strategy, a maneuver that would hardly have been possible had Soviet Russia been a participating country.

In accordance with American demands, the nations of Western Europe formed a regional association, called the Organization for European Economic Cooperation (OEEC), to make exhaustive studies of the region's long-term needs and to draw up plans for using American assistance in the most effective way.* By mid-August, the OEEC had submitted a proposal calling for nearly $30 billion in American funds, an estimate that was eventually scaled down to $17 billion over a four-year period. By the end of the program, $12.5 billion had actually been appropriated by Congress for European recovery.[9]

The Marshall Plan officially came to an end in 1951. At the time of its expiration, there was no question but that it had largely achieved its basic purpose of rehabilitating the economic systems of the OEEC countries. By 1951, European production had either reached or exceeded prewar levels. Using American assistance as a kind of catalyst, the Europeans recovered their economic vitality and began to stabilize their internal political conditions. In the years that followed, as we shall see, Western Europe became in some respects the most economically dynamic region on the globe.

The Shift to Military Aid

The change to military aid, for reasons to be discussed later, began in 1950 with the Mutual Defense Assistance Program. In 1952, economic, military, and technical assistance for underdeveloped countries were combined into a single program, known as the Mutual Security Program. Military aid extended under the MSP resulted in a vast increase in Western

*The OEEC remained in existence until 1961, when it was superseded by a new organization, called the Organization for Economic Cooperation and Development (OECD). By the end of the 1970s, OECD had 24 members, several of which (like Australia and Japan) were outside Western Europe and the Atlantic area. With the passage of time, perhaps the most important dimension of OECD activity lay in providing foreign economic and technical assistance to less developed countries.

Europe's defense efforts. By 1957, Europe was spending $13 billion on its own defense.[10]

By the late 1950s and early 1960s, it had become apparent that Europe's military defense position was infinitely stronger than it had been ten years earlier. This did not mean that no problems beset NATO's efforts to strengthen Western security; we shall examine many of these later in the chapter. Western Europe, nevertheless, was no longer considered one of the most inviting areas for Communist expansionism. This realization underlay the reduction in American military assistance to Europe. In submitting his foreign aid budget for 1965, President Johnson could report to Congress that: "The Western European nations in the North Atlantic Treaty Organization now supply almost all the financial support for their own military forces and also provide military assistance to others."[11] From this point on, American military assistance to Europe consisted chiefly of the five infantry divisions, plus supporting ground and air forces, which the United States maintained on the European continent. These not only afforded a visible symbol of America's deep involvement in European security; they also served as an integral part of the NATO "shield" designed to safeguard Europe from attack.

As we shall see at a later stage, throughout the years that followed, the respective "contributions" made by the United States and its European allies to the common defense effort became a contentious issue in European-American relations. To the minds of American officials (especially members of Congress), the United States continued to "subsidize" NATO, long after the European partners had regained their economic vitality and capacity to assume a larger share of the defense burden.[12] For their part, Europeans believed that the United States supported NATO chiefly in its *own* interests; and, as the wealthiest member of the alliance, America could afford to make a larger contribution than its weaker and smaller NATO partners.

NATO: Soviet Challenge and Western Response

Origins of NATO

A significant landmark in American postwar foreign policy toward Europe was the creation of the NATO defense community.* Just as economic assistance to Greece and Turkey in 1947 had led to the much more comprehensive and prolonged European Recovery Program, so too was sustained economic assistance to Europe followed by efforts to bolster the military strength of the free world. Initially, these efforts took the form of a military alliance among the nations of Western Europe, which became the nucleus of the North Atlantic Treaty.

Several developments in the 1947–1949 period spurred efforts within both the United States and Europe to establish a unified defense system for the North Atlantic area. European Communist parties had agitated militantly against the Marshall Plan. During the late 1940s Communist groups in such countries as France and Italy appeared to be gaining in strength. Moscow's propaganda organs meanwhile were carrying on a virulent anti-American campaign. In China, the Nationalist government was collapsing before the Communist rebel forces. Then in the spring of 1948 came the Soviet-engineered coup in Czechoslovakia, an event that hastened favorable congressional action on the Marshall Plan. There followed the Berlin blockade of 1948–1949. Here an avowed objective of Soviet foreign policy was to drive the West—and above all, the United States—out of Germany. Had the Kremlin succeeded in this goal, Western Europe would have been left in a highly precarious military-economic position.

Increasingly, Europe's leaders were aware of the need for closer military cooperation among members of the North Atlantic area. With the active encouragement of the United States, five of them on March 17, 1948, signed the Brussels Treaty.† This pact formed a "collective defense arrangement within the framework of the United Nations Charter. . . ." Concurrently, the Senate Foreign Relations Committee, working in close conjunction with the State Department, was attempting to draft a legislative resolution paving the way for American association with a European security system. This resolution, known as the Vandenberg Resolution for its instigator, Senator Arthur H. Vandenberg, was approved by the Senate on June 11, 1948, by a vote of 64–6. It called for "association of the United States, by constitutional process, with such regional and other collective arrangements as are based on continuous and effective self-help and mutual aid, and as affect its national security."[13] The Senate, in other words, was overwhelmingly in favor of a closer military union between the United States and Western Europe. Europe had created the embryo of such a union under the

---

*The original signatories of NATO were: the United States, Canada, the United Kingdom, Belgium, Luxembourg, Norway, Iceland, the Netherlands, Denmark, France, Italy, and Portugal. Greece and Turkey joined in 1952; and the Federal Republic of Germany became a member in 1955. As a result of the dispute between Greece and Turkey over Cyprus in 1974 (in which both sides believed they failed to receive NATO support), Greece withdrew from the alliance; by 1980, negotiations were in progress aimed at its readmission to NATO.

†Original signatories of the Brussels defense pact were Belgium, France, Luxembourg, the Netherlands, and the United Kingdom. Italy and the Federal Republic of Germany joined the pact at a later stage.

Brussels Pact; it remained for the United States to join in this effort and for the pact to be extended to other countries. This was done under the North Atlantic Treaty, which the United States ratified on July 21, 1949.

The American Military Commitment Under NATO

By making explicit what had been implicit in the Greek-Turkish Aid Program, in the Marshall Plan, and in the firm resistance to Soviet pressure during the Berlin blockade earlier, the North Atlantic Treaty signified that the United States had accepted the principle that its own security was inextricably linked with the independence of its North Atlantic neighbors. The North Atlantic Treaty is a short document, containing only 14 articles. The key article, expressive of the philosophy behind this military union, is Article 5, by which: "The parties agree that an armed attack against one or more of them in Europe or North America shall be considered an attack against them all. . . ." In the event of an attack, each signatory will exercise the "right of individual or collective self-defense" and will "individually and in concert with the other Parties" take "such actions as it deems necessary, including the use of armed force, to restore and maintain international peace and security."

Several points about the obligations assumed by the United States under the North Atlantic Treaty require emphasis. An obvious, although sometimes overlooked, fact about the treaty is that it created essentially *a military alliance,* designed to protect its members from what was envisioned as the gravest threat to Western security: a Soviet military thrust westward into a highly vulnerable Europe.

To say that NATO was, and remains, essentially a military alliance is not to overlook its expanding activities in various nonmilitary spheres, like political consultation, cultural affairs, and education. Article 3 of the North Atlantic Treaty, for example, commits the members to engage in "continuous and effective self-help and mutual aid," which will "maintain and develop their individual and collective capacity to resist armed attack." In the pursuit of this goal, since 1949 NATO has engaged in a variety of ancillary and "supportive" activities directed at promoting greater cohesion among its members. President Nixon also once referred to NATO as an instrument for fostering greater economic and political unity among the Western allies. Yet these activities and conceptions of NATO should not obscure the fact that it was fundamentally a military alliance among nations facing a common danger. As such, NATO's fortunes and its degree of internal cohesion would almost certainly be functions of the *perceived danger confronting its members during any given period.*

The geographic compass of NATO, as specified in the treaty, also is noteworthy. NATO's orbit is Europe and North America, a fact that has been productive of misunderstandings on both sides of the Atlantic. From the beginning, attempts to "internationalize" NATO by extending its activities beyond the North Atlantic area have been uniformly unsuccessful. During the 1960s, for example, the United States repeatedly failed to gain NATO support for its involvement in Vietnam. Far from viewing the Vietnam conflict as an issue requiring their participation, most of America's Western allies regarded the struggle in Southeast Asia not only as peripheral to their interests but as a threat to the unity and security of the North Atlantic area. The Carter Administration experienced only slightly greater success in gaining NATO backing for its attempt to obtain the withdrawal of Soviet troops from Afghanistan. As explained more fully in Chapter 12, the United States and its European allies fundamentally disagreed on the nature of the Soviet threat and on its implications for Western security.

America's obligations under NATO, in the event of an attack against one or more of the signatories, also requires brief elaboration. Among the security agreements to which the United States is a party, the North Atlantic pact (along with the Rio Treaty of Western hemispheric defense signed in 1947) contains a unique obligation. Article 5 of the NATO treaty provides that "if such an armed attack occurs, each of them . . . *will* assist the Party or Parties so attacked by taking forthwith, individually and in concert with the other Parties, such action as it deems necessary including the use of armed force, to restore and maintain the security of the North Atlantic area." The language of the treaty thus *requires* the United States to respond to an enemy attack against the NATO area, while leaving the mode of response discretionary.

In reality, America's response to aggression against the West has not been in real doubt since World War II. The nature of modern warfare, coupled with the lessons taught by America's involvement in two global conflicts during the twentieth century, have created a *de facto* obligation upon which the NATO security system is built. Secretary of State Dean Acheson made this clear to the Senate in 1949;[14] Secretary of State John Foster Dulles admitted publicly in 1957 that, if the NATO area were attacked, American forces would almost certainly engage in battle without waiting for a declaration of war by Congress;[15] the same idea was implicit in the "warning" delivered by NATO to the Soviet Union after the crisis in Czechoslovakia in 1968.[16]

In summary, then, NATO entailed a profound change in American foreign policy by making clear the determination of the United States to fight beyond its own shores to protect the security of the Atlantic system. And it signified a *de facto,* if not *de jure,* alteration in the American constitutional system by notifying potential aggressors that the United States would retaliate instantly, without waiting for a declaration of war, if an attack occurred against its friends in the North Atlantic sphere.

Structure and Organization

NATO's organizational structure reflects the fact that it is a military alliance of independent states, not a supranational authority. In NATO's organizational hierarchy, the highest authority is the North Atlantic Council, comprising the permanent representatives (or ministers) of the member states. Meetings of the council (which the foreign ministers, defense ministers, and other high-ranking officials within the member governments may attend) are held at least twice a year. The secretary-general of NATO serves as chairman of the council. Decisions within the council are normally made on the basis of consensus (not majority vote); and the council provides guidance to the alliance on a broad range of policy questions related to NATO's mission and activities.

NATO has a number of standing committees—like the Defense Planning Committee (DPC), which discusses the alliance's military strategy; the Committee on the Challenges of Modern Society, which seeks to improve cooperation among the members and studies environmental problems; and a number of other specialized committees.

The highest military authority within NATO is the Military Committee (MC), composed of the chiefs of staff of the member nations (or their representatives). Its function is to study military problems confronting the alliance, to make recommendations to the NATO council on military questions, and to provide guidance to the NATO military command, headed by the supreme allied commander of NATO forces. At a lower level, NATO's military structure is organized into four separate commands: the European Command; the Atlantic Ocean Command; the English Channel Command; and the Canada-United States Regional Planning Group.[17]

The Evolution of NATO

Since its creation in 1949, NATO has been a dynamic organization, experiencing a number of significant changes. Following the outbreak of the Korean War early in June 1950, the Supreme Headquarters Allied Powers, Europe (SHAPE) was established, with General Dwight D. Eisenhower as the first supreme commander. By tradition, that position has always been held by an American general. In 1952, Greece and Turkey joined the Western alliance, followed by the Federal Republic of Germany in 1955. In 1966, after the election of General Charles de Gaulle as president of the Fifth Republic, France "withdrew" from participation in NATO's organizational structure and joint military planning activities—although Paris repeatedly emphasized that France *remained* a member of NATO, shared the alliance's overall objectives, and proposed to use French armed forces for the defense of Europe. (In the years that followed, French authorities engaged in *de facto* collaboration in a number of NATO activities.)

Also during the late 1960s, an important report (the "Harmel Report on the Future Tasks of the Alliance") adopted by NATO underscored the crucial importance of promoting European security and promoting Soviet-American détente. Ever since its adoption in 1967, the European allies have provided a strong impetus to Washington and Moscow to preserve and strengthen détente. A year later most of the European members of NATO (with the notable exception of France) established what came to be called the *Eurogroup,* consisting of the defense ministers of the member countries. The Eurogroup sought to achieve a higher degree of unity among the European members of NATO on military and political questions, particularly as they related to Europe's future and well-being; and it also sought to encourage the continued presence and improvement of American and Canadian armed forces in the NATO area. Throughout the years that followed, the Eurogroup experienced a limited degree of success in increasing financial support for NATO by the European members—thereby responding to a long-standing American complaint that the United States was bearing a disproportionate share of the common defense burden.

Late in 1973, the members of NATO undertook the first of a continuing series of negotiations designed to achieve the goal of "mutual and balanced force reductions" (sometimes called MBFR) between the Western alliance and the Warsaw Pact* on the European continent. The central idea of MBFR was that—rather than a steadily escalating arms race in the heart of Europe—it was desirable to reduce armed force levels on both sides of the Iron Curtain, provided it did not create a military imbalance jeopardizing the security of

*The Soviet-led counterpart to NATO—the Warsaw Pact—was established as the result of a defense agreement signed in Warsaw in May 1955. Members of the Warsaw Pact are: Bulgaria, Czechoslovakia, the German Democratic Republic (East Germany), Hungary, Poland, Rumania, and the Soviet Union. The commander in chief of Warsaw Pact forces has always been a high-ranking Soviet military commander. At the end of the 1970s, the Warsaw Pact had a total of some 3.6 million troops, of which approximately half were ground forces, with the other half almost equally divided between air force and naval units. [*The Europa Year Book: 1979* (London: Europa Publications, 1979), pp. 273–274.] More contemporary information about the Warsaw Pact is provided in subsequent volumes in this series.

the nations involved. These force reductions would be *mutual,* in the sense that both Western and Communist military strength on the European continent would be scaled down. They would be *balanced,* in the sense that neither side would gain a military advantage from any agreement reached. To date, little progress has been made in achieving the goal of MBFR. In Europe, as in other areas of actual or potential Soviet-American conflict, each side has continued to strengthen and modernize its armed forces.[18]

In 1974, a conflict between Greece and Turkey over Cyprus led to the former's partial withdrawal from the Western alliance (as well as to serious misunderstandings between the United States and Turkey), which weakened NATO's internal cohesion. The following year, after many months of preliminary negotiations, the Helsinki Agreement, reached at the conclusion of the Conference on Security and Cooperation in Europe (CSCE), was signed. Convened largely at the initiative of the European states themselves, this conference had a significant impact upon Soviet-American détente and the stability of Europe. As the months passed (and as NATO continued to face a disparity in its military forces vis-à-vis the Warsaw Pact), it was questionable how much the CSCE actually promoted stability on the European continent.

Two developments in the late 1970s were significant in the evolution of NATO. One was the adoption by the Defense Planning Committee in 1977 of a long-term strategic plan for the 1980s, designed to improve NATO's defense capabilities. The following year, a decision was made by NATO's Nuclear Planning Group to improve its theater nuclear forces, primarily by the introduction of advanced American missiles. As we observed in Chapter 10, this NATO decision became a source of intense controversy between the United States and the Soviet Union.

By this step Moscow accused Washington of jeopardizing détente; American and other Western officials defended the move, as being dictated by the continuing buildup of Warsaw Pact military forces in missile firepower, as well as in other categories of military force.

The Accomplishments of NATO

The occasion of NATO's thirtieth anniversary in 1979 witnessed numerous and fulsome tributes to the alliance's central role in promoting Western security and to its accomplishments. One student of European-American relations said: "For the first 30 years of its existence, NATO has worked remarkably well. In fact it has turned out to be the most successful alliance the world has ever known." NATO's secretary-general declared that "thanks to the existence of the North Atlantic Alliance, Europe has known thirty years of peace." A former American ambassador to NATO noted that "The alliance has been and is a highly successful creature"; its experience had been characterized by significant "innovations"; and NATO "has been and is highly credible as a deterrent to Soviet aggression, both to its members and the Soviet Union."[19]

As European-American relations entered the 1980s, NATO had three singular achievements to its credit. The first was that, after a generation of important changes in the nature of the international system, *the Western alliance still survived.* This reality was no inconsiderable accomplishment, underscoring two key facts about the alliance. One was that it was clearly *a resilient and adaptive mechanism;* its members had made a number of important changes in its structure and guiding principles since 1949. The other fact was that—despite the shift from Cold War to détente, changes in military technology, and other significant tendencies—NATO clearly remained *a relevant and useful defense mechanism.* For the most part, the disputes and disagreements existing among its members could be accurately described as "family quarrels" among nations sharing common values and a broad consensus on a range of specific international issues. In neither the United States nor Western Europe was there any noteworthy sentiment in favor of "dismantling" NATO (even the government of France cooperated with the alliance more actively than during the period of President Charles de Gaulle's administration). Viewed from a different perspective, controversies and misunderstandings among the members of NATO were often directed at the question of how to make the alliance function *more effectively,* rather than at reducing its importance or contribution to Western defense.

A second outstanding accomplishment of NATO is its role in deterring Soviet aggression against the non-Communist nations of Western Europe. Admittedly, this is a somewhat speculative and subjective aspect of NATO's contribution. The Soviet Union's ultimate intentions toward Western Europe since World War II elicit widely divergent interpretations from informed students of Soviet behavior. As some students of Soviet affairs assess the matter, the U.S.S.R. was too weak internally, and too preoccupied with its own domestic problems, to pose a direct military threat to Western security after World War II.

This point of view of course has been repeatedly challenged by other officials and commentators, such as President Harry S Truman and his advisers, who urged him to adopt the containment strategy in 1947. In their view, Western Europe's early postwar economic and military weakness "invited" Soviet aggression. As George F. Kennan explained it in his justification of the containment policy, Soviet power was inherently expansive and would move to "fill up" or threaten *any* vulnerable position accessible to Moscow. With its large population and vast industrial capacity, Western Europe made an inviting target for Soviet hegemony. As events like the Soviet invasion of Czechoslovakia in 1968 and the massive Russian military incursion into Afghanistan in 1979 made clear, not even the principle of détente dissuaded the leaders of the Kremlin from relying upon military force to achieve their objectives when they believed circumstances required it.

The question of whether the U.S.S.R. has had aggressive designs on Western Europe since World War II is a classic example of the difficulties involved in trying to divine Soviet diplomatic intentions; and doubtless it will continue to elicit varying responses. But this much seems certain: The existence of NATO has unquestionably strengthened the Western strategy of deterrence, giving policy makers in the Kremlin added cause to consider most carefully the consequences of possible aggression. The cost to the Soviet Union of a possible military invasion of Western Europe has been greatly increased by the creation and survival of NATO. Moreover, NATO's presence contributes to the actual *defense* of the North Atlantic region rather than to its "liberation" from Communist domination, as the Allies were required to undertake to free Europe from Axis control during World War II. As leaders and people of Western Europe are well aware, the region's liberation from Axis hegemony was a prolonged, highly destructive, and socially and politically disruptive process—which they have no desire to repeat in the nuclear age!

A third and related achievement of NATO has been its contribution in reducing *the fear of war* on the European continent and—in view of the central importance of Europe as an arena of Soviet-American competition—apprehensions about the likelihood of global nuclear war. Since the late 1940s, the prospect of a military confrontation between the superpowers on the European continent has steadily lessened—to the point that, by the 1980s, many groups were convinced that it had disappeared entirely. As we shall see in discussing some of NATO's continuing problems, this fact had certain negative, as well as positive, consequences for American foreign policy. Nevertheless, the lessening of anxieties on both sides of the Iron Curtain about the imminence of a Soviet-American conflict in Europe had to be reckoned a significant gain. It was, for example, an essential element in the emergence of détente between the superpowers and in their ability to cooperate in at least some areas of their mutual relations. It also played a role in the ability of the nations of Western Europe to take steps (which we shall examine more fully at a later stage) toward greater economic and political collaboration in pursuit of the larger goal of European unity.

NATO in "Disarray"—Continuing Sources of Disunity

Late in the spring of 1980, as President Jimmy Carter prepared to visit several European countries, one of America's most experienced political commentators observed that, once again, the United States and its European allies were sharply divided about how to deal with several major global problems. Among the European allies, the viewpoint was pervasive that President Carter's diplomatic leadership was confused and inept, causing serious dissension among the members of the Western alliance. Such European attitudes, it was reported, "infuriates Carter," who wants the Western Allies to "shape up, shut up, and support him." Evidence of serious disunity among the NATO partners did not disappear

with the Reagan Administration. American officials vocally complained about the lack of "support" their policies received from the European allies in dealing with the Soviet threat to Poland and the Persian Gulf area, Marxist-sponsored revolutions in Latin America, and several other key global issues. By the early 1980s, many Americans—and the sentiment was especially evident in Congress—were calling for a substantial reduction of American armed forces within the NATO area. The proposal was motivated in part by efforts to reduce defense expenditures. But it was no less prompted by a long standing American conviction that the NATO allies were not contributing their "fair share" to the common defense effort. Meanwhile, on the European continent the same complaint was heard that had been expressed since 1949: The United States consistently failed to "consult" its principal allies before it adopted important policies affecting their interests.[20]

These were merely some recent manifestations of the problem of "disarray" that has beset the Western alliance since NATO's establishment in 1949. For over a generation, NATO has experienced a multitude of major and minor problems weakening its cohesion and impairing its effectiveness. During some periods, as in the early 1980s, controversies and fundamental policy disagreements among the Western allies sometimes reached an acute stage, raising questions about NATO's future. At no time since 1949 has evidence of "disarray" been entirely lacking from NATO's experience.

Among the sources of disunity within the NATO defense system, some stemmed from transitory and relatively unimportant causes, whereas others involved more deep-seated and recurrent problems. Let us concentrate upon the latter category of problems, identifying and examining four important and recurrent issues engendering controversy among the members of the Western alliance.

1. The Problem of NATO Defense Strategy. Throughout its history, the unity of NATO has been impaired by controversies among its members concerning the strategic principles underlying its approach to European defense. For a brief period after World War II, the American nuclear monopoly served as a counterweight to Soviet supremacy in ground forces; but after 1945, the Kremlin forged ahead rapidly to acquire its own nuclear stockpile. By 1953, the Soviet Union had exploded its first hydrogen bomb; four years later, it launched the first Russian intercontinental ballistic missile and—in an event that graphically underscored ongoing Soviet technological progress—put the "Sputnik" space satellite into orbit. By around 1960, the two superpowers were on their way toward achieving a condition of "nuclear parity" or "nuclear equivalence," in which their nuclear arsenals were sufficiently potent to devastate each other—along with nearly all other countries on the globe.

As long as the United States possessed nuclear superiority over the Communist bloc, the security of the West was preserved by relying upon the doctrine of "massive retaliation," identified particularly during the Eisenhower Administration with Secretary of State John Foster Dulles. According to this doctrine, any Communist threat to the security of the NATO area would be "answered" by an American nuclear response aimed at the Soviet heartland itself. American policy makers assumed that the Kremlin was aware of this risk; and realization of the fateful consequences of Soviet aggression was, therefore, the major deterrent to Russian expansionism. Even during the 1950s, however, critics questioned whether in a crisis the United States was

prepared to unleash global nuclear weapons to protect Western Europe, if this meant almost certain Soviet retaliation against American territory. Yet for some 15 years after World War II, the concept of "massive retaliation" served as the strategic principle guiding NATO defense efforts.[21]

Even when the United States largely possessed a monopoly over nuclear weapons —and as the Soviet nuclear arsenal steadily expanded, the problem became increasingly critical—considerable doubt existed in Western Europe concerning the "credibility" of the American nuclear deterrent. Among the British, French, and other Europeans, as one commentator expressed it, a conviction existed that the United States itself is now

... vulnerable to nuclear attack and cannot be counted on to commit suicide for London or Paris. How could an American president call down the day of judgment upon American cities to avert or answer attacks on European ones?[22]

The existence of such doubts—coupled with the Soviet Union's ongoing military build-up in nearly all categories of armed force—in time dictated fundamental changes in NATO defense strategies. By the early 1960s, two new strategic principles—"forward strategy" and "flexible response"—were adopted by NATO. The concept of "forward strategy" meant that NATO would endeavor to *defend* the security of Europe *as far to the east as possible,* in an effort to prevent Warsaw Pact forces from penetrating the NATO area and occupying territory in non-Communist Europe. Any attempt to defend Western Europe on this principle dictated that NATO forces must be entrenched along the eastern military frontier; that they be maintained in a high state of military "readiness"; and that they be strong enough and adequately equipped to contest any potential attack against Europe by the Soviet Union and its satellites. It is worth reiterating that the members of NATO were unanimous in their desire to *defend* Europe from possible aggression rather than to "liberate" it after successful aggression had occurred.

The concept of "flexible response" replaced the old principle of massive retaliation. According to the strategic doctrine of "flexible response," NATO could rely upon several possible options in responding to aggression, ranging from use of "conventional" (nonnuclear) weapons, to "tactical" nuclear weapons,* to strategic nuclear weapons directed against the Soviet Union and other Communist countries. The basic idea was that NATO's response to an attack would be dictated by nature of the attack itself and by prevailing circumstances. NATO would not *automatically* respond to aggression by launching a counterattack with strategic weapons; but, it is essential to note, the employment of such weapons remained a kind of last resort option available to the Western allies if other means (including diplomacy) failed to eliminate the threat to European security. Implementation of the principle of flexible response also required NATO forces to be trained and equipped for a variety of contingencies—including the possible use of tactical nuclear weapons on the battlefield. This strategic principle also greatly reduced the possibility of triggering a global war "by accident" because of a military encounter along the NATO frontier.

Irrespective of whether the older concept of massive retaliation or the more recent principles of forward strategy and flexible response guided the NATO defense effort, for over a generation the basic question has remained: Is Washington prepared to risk the wholesale destruction of the American society in order to protect Europe from Soviet hegemony? Even by the 1980s, considerable doubt was expressed on the European continent concerning the credibility of America's nuclear deterrent. Paradoxically, by this period also, many Europeans expressed the opposite complaint: that the United States *would* use its nuclear arsenal against a Soviet military incursion into the NATO area, thereby leaving much of the continent uninhabitable. The quandary for officials in Washington, therefore, was that they were expected to "reassure" the NATO allies that the American nuclear deterrent was credible while simultaneously taking account of a significant growth in "anti-nuclear war" sentiment within Western Europe!

2. The Problem of Equitable "Sharing" of Alliance Burdens. A second perennial issue engendering disunity within the Western alliance for a generation or more has been the problem of arriving at a formula for the equitable "sharing" of the financial and military costs of regional security. The problem has been exemplified by the American military commitment to NATO and by efforts (centered particularly in Congress since the early 1960s) to reduce it.

By the early 1980s, the United States had approximately 250,000 troops stationed in the NATO area. In addition, by this period a new American Rapid Deployment Force

---

*The distinction between "strategic" and "tactical" nuclear weapons is at best imprecise. Theoretically, tactical nuclear armaments are those designed to be used *on the battlefield* against the armed forces of the enemy; they are relatively short-range weapons, such as artillery and rockets equipped with small nuclear warheads. By contrast, "strategic" nuclear arsenals are intended for use against an enemy's principal urban centers, industrial installations, and military bases. Since tactical nuclear weapons have never actually been employed in warfare, the distinction between these two categories of nuclear weapons may or may not be meaningful.

(RDF) was being formed, consisting of from 100,000 to 200,000 troops capable of projecting American power to crisis areas.*

During and after the Vietnam War —and again in the early 1980s—considerable sentiment existed within Congress and among certain elements of American public opinion for substantially reducing America's military contribution to NATO. At intervals, some advocate of this course argued that, from the available evidence, the United States often appeared to be more interested in preserving the independence of Western Europe than did the Europeans! For many years, for example, the European allies were contributing as a percentage of their national incomes half as much (or less) to the common defense effort as the United States.[23] By the 1980s, many Americans believed that the efforts made by the Carter and the Reagan administrations to strengthen the Western defensive position were not being "matched" by comparable efforts by the NATO partners. The reduction (or threatened reduction) of American force levels in Europe, some critics believed, would stimulate the allies to expand their own defense efforts proportionately. This approach was remarkably akin to the prevailing American mentality after World War I, in which millions of citizens were willing to "let Europe stew in its own juice"!

Predictably, the European perspective on this issue was quite different. As most Europeans assessed the matter, the United States was the largest, wealthiest, and most powerful member of the alliance. Accordingly, it was fitting that the United States shoulder a larger burden in assuring regional defense than its allies. Moreover, since the establishment of NATO in 1949, the Ameri-

can objective in sponsoring and supporting the alliance has remained constant: It was above all to promote *the security of the United States* by keeping the Communist threat as far to the east as possible. In the light of this prevailing mentality, periodic threats by Americans to reduce their contribution to NATO would most likely have the opposite result from that intended. If the United States substantially cut its troop commitment within the NATO area, the consequence would almost certainly be a revival of "neutralist" sentiment in Western Europe, accompanied by efforts (as in the case of West Germany) to arrive at an "accommodation" with the Soviet Union.

Europeans also believe that Americans often tend to be ignorant of, or oblivious to, certain political consequences inherent in any significant expansion of Western Europe's military establishment. The problem is exemplified by the anxieties existing in France, Belgium, and other European states concerning the possibility of an increase in the armed forces of the Federal Republic of Germany (West Germany). Since 1949, next to the United States, West Germany has made a larger contribution than any other member to the NATO defense effort. For countries where memories of Nazi military domination are still vivid, fears of German militarism remain intense. Any significant expansion in West Germany's contribution to NATO would, it is feared, give that country a more influential voice in Europe's political and financial affairs. Moreover, an expanded German military establishment would also unquestionably arouse Soviet apprehensions, thereby jeopardizing the existence of détente.

Different problems beset any proposed expansion of British or French forces in NATO. In the light of Great Britain's acute economic problems since World War II, there

*The nature of the Rapid Deployment Force and problems associated with its use to achieve American foreign policy goals are analyzed in greater detail in Chapter 12.

has been little possibility that its contribution to the Western defense effort could be increased significantly. Under President Charles de Gaulle, France withdrew from the NATO defense structure; any expansion in its armed forces would, therefore, likely occur in its *national* defense establishment—a move almost certainly propelling France even further in the direction of military and diplomatic independence. For the smaller members of NATO, no conceivable increase in their contributions would fundamentally alter the balance between American and European forces available to the Western alliance.

The problem of the equitable "sharing" of the common defense has created controversy within NATO for over a generation; and it will almost certainly continue to do so in the future.* The question of whether the contribution of a particular member of NATO is "fair" is an inherently subjective matter, the answer to which will be heavily influenced by viewpoints and factors uniquely associated with that particular country and its foreign policy goals. Moreover, the answer will also be in some measure a function of another issue fomenting dissension within the Western alliance: the relative balance between NATO and Warsaw Pact forces on the European continent.

3. The Problem of the Military Balance in Europe. In mid-1980, as the United States and its European allies sought to arrive at common policies on several regional and global issues, an informed student of contemporary international politics defined the overriding problem facing the Western alliance as the prospect that "the Soviet Union may have become the paramount power in Eurasia." As a result of Russia's continuing military buildup, the Western allies confronted a dangerous tendency. This was

> ... the "neutralization" of Europe. The Soviet Union has used its strenuous buildup of nuclear and conventional forces to dissolve the foundations of European security doctrines relying on the United States for ultimate protection. With nuclear parity between the superpowers, the American nuclear guarantee has lost much of its credibility. In the European theater, Soviet military superiority, both conventional and nuclear, has reinforced public sentiment in favor of neutrality.

After more than a decade devoted to augmenting its military forces, said an official of the Reagan Administration, "the Soviet Union threatens Europe directly through its local superiority... as well as indirectly through its ability to project force into other regions of vital interest to Europe, such as the Persian Gulf."[24]

Even before NATO's establishment in 1949, Western policy makers were concerned about the military imbalance existing between the United States and its allies and the Soviet Union and its allies. In his widely quoted speech at Fulton, Missouri, on March 5, 1946, British Prime Minister Winston Churchill alerted the world to Europe's acute military vulnerability and to the ominous prospect that Moscow might rely on superior military force to extend the Iron Curtain westward. After the establishment of NATO, the Western allies endeavored to expand and strengthen their conventional armed forces in an effort to counterbalance the strength of the Soviet Red Army and of the Eastern European satellite

---

*By the period of the Reagan Administration, American officials had become concerned about a possible retrenchment in West Germany's contribution to NATO. In the face of acute internal financial problems, German officials were considering cutting back a planned increase in their military budget. By contrast, the Reagan Administration called upon the European allies to increase their defense spending by approximately 7 percent annually. See Richard Burt, in *New York Times,* November 9, 1980.

forces. Even then, for a decade or so after NATO's creation the principal counterweight to Communist ground forces remained the American nuclear arsenal that served as the mainstay of European defense.

Although NATO's armed forces were continually being modernized and strengthened, by the end of the 1970s according to many criteria the military balance in Europe had tilted dangerously in favor of the Warsaw Pact. During the 1970s (when for most of the period détente governed Soviet-American relations), the Soviet Union increased its military forces by some 33 percent to a total of 4.8 million men, or twice as large as America's armed forces; Russian military spending increased by some 50 percent, while America was decreasing its defense outlays; Moscow acquired some 50,000 tanks, versus 11,000 for the United States; and it deployed some 750 warheads on the new Russian SS-20 missiles trained on Europe, during a period when NATO installed no new theater missiles in its arsenal. As events during late 1970s and early 1980s indicated, Moscow was prepared to use its formidable military establishment against Poland, Afghanistan, and other countries in pursuit of its foreign policy objectives. On the NATO front, an especially serious aspect of this disparity was the superiority of the Warsaw Pact in "conventional" (non-nuclear) weapons. As a high-ranking State Department official said of Warsaw Pact forces during the early 1980s: "Their 50,000 tanks are hardly necessary to defend against NATO forces whose only mission is to safeguard our own territory." Assuming that both sides avoided reliance upon nuclear weapons, the Warsaw Pact's advantage in conventional forces posed an ominous threat to Western security.[25]

In his report to Congress at the end of the 1970s on the *status* and problems of the Western defense establishment, Secretary of Defense Harold Brown emphasized the wi-

dening disparity between Western NATO and Communist armed strength in the European theater. Brown believed that an attack against the NATO area by Warsaw Pact forces was both the "most plausible" and the most "demanding" or dangerous threat confronting American security. Resisting such an attack successfully would impose heavy "pressures" upon existing NATO defense forces; the ability of the West to withstand such an assault successfully would depend in large measure upon how much "warning time" NATO was given before it confronted aggression. Noting that current Soviet military doctrine emphasized the importance of tactical surprise, sudden attack, and the rapid deployment of attacking forces, Brown informed Congress that the Soviet Union's ability to carry out a successful military thrust against the NATO area was steadily improving.[26]

Evidence of a growing military imbalance between NATO and Warsaw Pact forces was available on all sides, and it occasioned genuine concern for Western strategists. For example, at the end of the 1970s a study by the International Institute for Strategic Studies found that in only one major category of weapons (submarine-launched ballistic missiles) were NATO forces superior to their Warsaw Pact adversaries. In all other categories—such as intermediate-range missiles, nuclear-armed aircraft, tanks, and infantry—the advantage clearly lay with the Soviet Union and its allies. Other studies showed that in mainline battle tanks, NATO forces were outnumbered by a margin of 2 to 1; the Warsaw Pact's combined land and tactical troops exceeded NATO's by some 75 percent.[27] For some Western officials, the most disturbing aspect of the problem was that this disparity *appeared to be widening* with each passing year.[28] Another report found that among NATO field commanders, the belief existed that at current force levels,

NATO could successfully defend Western Europe for only two or three days—after which its defenses would either be overwhelmed or the world would be plunged into global nuclear war.[29] Such prospects underscored one of the long standing problems plaguing European defense: A substantial increase in Western conventional forces was obviously needed, but few members of the alliance were prepared to undertake it. As an example, this step would entail two highly unpopular measures by the American government: even larger increases in national defense spending; and almost certainly, the reimposition of the draft in order to obtain the military personnel needed to bolster NATO's conventional strength significantly.

Admittedly, for a number of reasons the existing military imbalance in Europe was in some respects less ominous for the West than it was sometimes depicted. In the first place, NATO's armed forces were intended for *European defense:* According to traditional military doctrine, an attacking force required substantial superiority (on the order of from a 3 to 1 to a 5 to 1 advantage) to achieve its objectives. By this standard, NATO defense forces did not appear to be at a serious military disadvantage.

Moreover, gross comparisons of armed strength between two adversaries or alliance systems often have little meaning or relevance. As was emphasized in Chapter 1, power is always *a relative concept.* Whether NATO forces were really "adequate" for the defense of Western Europe, for example, depended upon many tangible and intangible factors—such, as for example, *where* an attack would be launched against the NATO military frontier, the *nature* of the assault directed at NATO forces, the *timing* of a threat to the security of NATO, internal political conditons within the countries belonging to the alliance, the response of countries (like

the People's Republic of China) not belonging to NATO, and a host of other contingencies, many of which could not be anticipated with assurance. Along with military commanders throughout history, NATO strategists usually plan on the basis of "the worst possible contingency;" that is, they tend to overestimate the enemy's strength and to underestimate their own. In that sense, NATO forces have *always* confronted a military disparity in Europe—and most probably, they always will!

In addition, NATO possesses some strengths which the Soviet Union and its satellites cannot match. For example, collectively the members of NATO have a population of some 559 million people, while the Warsaw Pact countries have a population of 364 million. By the late 1970s, the NATO countries had an average per capita Gross National Product of over $6000 annually vis-à-vis some $2800 annually for the Communist side. Insofar as productive capacity is a vital element in military strength, the West possessed a marked superiority over its Communist adversary.[30]

The United States and its European allies have followed two somewhat contradictory courses in their response to the military imbalance existing on the continent. One of these has already been identified: the effort to achieve a *reduction* in the level of armed forces on both sides of the Iron Curtain. Formally called "mutual and balanced force reductions" (or MBFR), this attempt to reverse the tendency toward ever-increasing NATO and Warsaw Pact military strength has achieved no conspicuous success. A basic premise of MBFR is that no reduction in armaments in Europe should be "destabilizing" or prejudicial to Western security. In turn, this requirement dictates that negotiators on both sides agree upon military "equivalencies" in NATO and Warsaw Pact forces—which has proved an all but impossible undertaking. How is it possible, for example, to "equate" one NATO infantry division with one Warsaw Pact infantry division—when military units differ greatly in size, in armaments, in training, in experience, and in overall effectiveness? Yet the primary reason why negotiations to achieve MBFR have been unproductive is the same reason why Soviet-American disarmament efforts since World War II have yielded more deadlocks than agreements. As we noted in Chapters 9 and 10, even in the era of détente Cold War rivalries and suspicions exist between the superpowers; a high level of national armaments is probably more of a reflection than it is a basic cause of Soviet-American tensions and animosity. Since the Cold War originated in Europe—and since that region has remained its most crucial arena for over a generation—it is perhaps inevitable that the quest for MBFR would encounter insurmountable obstacles.

The other approach to the military disparity between NATO and Warsaw Pact forces has been to *improve the military capability* of Western defense forces, in an effort to close (or at least narrow) the existing military gap. The "modernization" of NATO forces has proceeded apace for over a generation—and it remains a continuing challenge to Western statesmen.[31] The acquisition of tactical nuclear weapons by the NATO defense command, for example, was designed to offset the Warsaw Pact's long-standing advantage in ground forces (in time, of course, Communist forces also acquired tactical nuclear armaments). By the early 1980s, three other steps contemplated by the Carter and Reagan administrations—the production of a new strategic bomber to replace the old B-52s; deployment of new missile systems in Europe and possibly other areas; and the development of the "neutron bomb"—were designed to strengthen the military position of NATO versus the Warsaw Pact.*

---

*Late in 1979, the United States and its NATO allies agreed upon a program designed to strengthen Western defenses by the installation of two new missile systems within the NATO area. One system would consist of 464 low-flying Cruise missiles, designed to elude enemy radar detection. The other was the Pershing II mobile surface-to-surface missile, under production at that time. It was anticipated that these new missile systems would not become operational for several years (possibly a decade); and during that period, Communist forces would continue to possess superiority in missile forces on the continent. The Soviet SS-20, for example, was a relatively new missile, with a range of upwards of 4000 miles and three independently targeted warheads. The new Soviet "Backfire" bomber, carrying nuclear weapons, could reach any point within the NATO defense zone. Until NATO's new missile system became operational, it was estimated that the West had 18 intermediate-range ballistic missiles in Europe versus 710 SS-20 missiles available to the Soviet Union; and Communist forces had a 2 to 1 advantage in bombers capable of carrying nuclear weapons. See Drew Middleton, in *New York Times,* October 19, 1979; and Flora Lewis, in *New York Times,* December 13, 1979.

The neutron bomb (or "low radiation bomb") was developed by the United States during the late 1970s. Its proposed deployment in the NATO area would go far toward offsetting the Warsaw Pact's superiority in armored forces—since the neutron bomb was essentially an anti-personnel weapon that would be highly effective against massed enemy armored and infantry forces. The Carter Administration decided against deployment of the bomb, after encountering strong Soviet (and some European) criticism; and Washington wanted to achieve an overall reduction in global armaments in the SALT II strategic arms-limitation agreement with Moscow. By mid-1980, Paris announced that French forces (which were not integrated into the NATO defense system) would be equipped with the neutron bomb. Military analysts believed that this step would give Western military commanders still another option (according to the doctrine of "flexible response") in responding to a possible Warsaw Pact threat to the security of the NATO area. The French decision would also likely precipitate reconsideration of the neutron bomb issue by the United States and the other NATO allies. See Drew Middleton, in *New York Times,* June 27, 1980; and Richard Holloran, in

While the future of many of these proposed new weapons systems remained in doubt, continuing Soviet aggressiveness—exemplified by Moscow's massive military incursion into Afghanistan late in 1979—supplied powerful incentives for maintaining the credibility of the NATO shield. Throughout his campaign for the presidency, Ronald Reagan repeatedly emphasized his determination to reverse the military imbalance existing between NATO and Warsaw Pact forces; and he pledged to reactivate certain defense projects (such as a new strategic bomber and expanded naval construction) that had been shelved by his predecessor, in an effort to remedy the problem of Western military weakness.[32]

Besides these concrete steps, individually and collectively the members of NATO were increasing their contribution to the joint defense effort. By 1980, for example, the members of NATO had agreed to increase their defense expenditures by an increment of from 3 to 4 percent annually for the period 1981-1986. (Even then, however, military expenditures by the Warsaw Pact would exceed those of the NATO countries.) Both the Carter and Reagan administrations sought to reassure the NATO allies concerning the firmness of the American commitment to NATO defense. Tangible evidence of America's vital involvement in European security was provided by such measures as a modest increase in the level of American armed forces stationed in the NATO area; a significant expansion in the defense budget of the United States; the creation of a new Rapid Deployment Force (RDF) which, while intended mainly for use in the Persian

Gulf area, could be deployed in Europe; and the installation of new Cruise missiles on the European continent, which would at least partially counterbalance the recent buildup of Warsaw Pact forces. In view of these steps taken by the United States to enhance Western security, officials in Washington renewed their plea that the other members of the alliance also increase their contributions to the common goal.

For a number of reasons, theoretical comparisons of the military strength of the United States and its allies versus the Soviet Union and its allies were always crude approximations. The question of whether NATO forces were "adequate" to the task assigned them depended heavily upon the circumstances under which they would be used. Despite its alleged military shortcomings, thus far NATO has been strong enough to dissuade the Warsaw Pact from "testing" Western military resolve by a Communist military thrust across the Iron Curtain. Today no less than in the past, Soviet officials are fully mindful that external aggression against the NATO area would incur incalculable risks—not excluding the possible devastation of Soviet society itself.

4. The Problems of "Consultation" and Confidence. A fourth condition engendering "disarray" within NATO consists in fact of two separate, although closely interrelated factors, which we shall consider together. Since 1949, the lack of "consultation" between the United States and its European partners has periodically strained the cohesion of the alliance. And to no inconsiderable degree, the origins of this problem can be traced to a lack of confidence which the individual members of NATO have exhibited toward the policies and political leadership of the other members.

For over a generation, the United States has routinely accused its European allies of failure to "consult" with Washington before

New York Times, June 28, 1980. For a detailed discussion of the implications and problems created by this new weapon, see Brigadier General Edwin F. Black, "The Neutron Bomb and the Defense of NATO," *Military Review,* **58** (May, 1978), 53–62.

important political and military decisions were taken; and the European capitals have directed the same basic complaint against officials in the United States. For example, two leading members of NATO—Great Britain and France—joined with Israel to mount an invasion of Egypt, thereby precipitating the "Suez Crisis" of 1956 and risking the possibility of a Soviet-American military encounter in the Middle East. In this instance, the NATO allies *deliberately* refrained from informing Washington of their planned move against Egypt, knowing that the Eisenhower Administration would (and did) oppose it. This crisis seriously impaired the unity of NATO.[33] In other instances, America's European allies have engaged in unilateral military and political actions, with little or no advance consultation with Washington. During the spring of 1980, French President Giscard d'Estaing held a "little summit" meeting with Soviet Prime Minister Leonid Brezhnev to discuss common problems. A few weeks later West German Chancellor Helmut Schmidt planned a trip to Moscow for the same purpose. Officials in Washington did not conceal their chagrin at such displays of diplomatic independence by the European allies. For their part, the NATO partners complained about America's failure to consult them prior to making diplomatic moves for which Washington expected their support. Consequently, instilling a new sense of cooperation and solidarity within NATO was listed as a high priority goal of the Reagan Administration.[34]

Yet despite their complaints about allied behavior, successive administrations in Washington have exhibited the same tendency. Repeatedly, Washington has made major and minor diplomatic decisions with no significant consultation with its NATO partners. A noteworthy example was the series of steps taken by American officials, beginning in the mid-1950s and for a 15-year period thereafter, in escalating the military involvement of

the United States in the Vietnam War. Nor was there any significant advance consultation between American and European officials during the most dangerous and serious Cold War encounter in the postwar era: the Cuban Missile Crisis of 1962.[35] In this and other cases, the major allies were given advance notice of the decision that had been made by American officials; but they played little discernible role in formulating that decision.

Again in 1980, President Jimmy Carter issued the "Carter Doctrine," committing the United States to the defense of the Persian Gulf area (following the revolution in Iran and the Soviet invasion of Afghanistan). To the degree that the United States was serious about this commitment, the doctrine obviously had profound repercussions for the security of NATO and for America's role in it. Yet the Carter Doctrine was a unilateral policy declaration by the United States, in the formulation of which the European allies played no part. As time passed, many members of NATO openly criticized the doctrine and refused to join the United States in measures (such as curtailing East-West trade and a "boycott" of the Moscow Olympic Games in 1980) designed to implement it. As the weeks passed, it became apparent that the United States and its European allies disagreed fundamentally over the proper response to make to events in the Persian Gulf area.

The lack of consultation on key diplomatic issues that has been characteristic of NATO since its inception may be symptomatic of a deeper problem we have already identified: a lack of confidence by one member of the alliance in the policies of its partners.* To

---

*As some informed commentators on European-American relations have pointed out, complaints about America's lack of "consultation" with its European allies are sometimes motivated by internal political considerations and are not always intended to be taken literally.

a succession of postwar administrations in Washington, the political leaders of Western Europe have sometimes appeared weak and indecisive; too prone to compromise with the Soviet Union and with Marxist elements within their own countries; too preoccupied with their own internal problems and pursuits—like increasing Europe's standard of living; and too inclined to "second-guess" the United States militarily and diplomatically, while concurrently failing to make their proportionate contribution to Western defense efforts. After the "third round" in the Arab-Israeli conflict in 1967—during which the oil-producing states cut off petroleum shipments to the West—the NATO allies seemed determined to pursue their separate national interests in the Middle East, even if it meant jeopardizing subsequent American attempts to resolve the Arab-Israeli controversy. Officials in Washington were convinced that such European initiatives were divisive, short-sighted, and, in the end, "counterproductive" in their implications for peace and stability in the troubled Middle East.[36]

At intervals during recent years, the European allies have expressed serious doubts about the constancy and effectiveness of American diplomatic leadership. The Watergate scandal destroyed the Nixon presidency and created deep concern abroad about America's ability to provide needed leadership in foreign affairs. During the

Carter Administration, time and again doubts were expressed in Europe and other regions about the "decisiveness" of the President and his advisers; and the "predictability" of American diplomatic behavior was widely questioned. A different lament was heard about the diplomacy of the Reagan Administration. By the 1980s, considerable skepticism existed within Europe that the Administration *had* a clear and consistent foreign policy. President Reagan and his advisers were in the process of remedying many of the military weaknesses that had inhibited American diplomacy since the end of the Vietnam War. The manner in which America's growing power would now be *used* to achieve diplomatic objectives, however, often left Europeans and other foreigners mystified. Along with many American citizens, Europeans were concerned about whether officials in Washington mistakenly believed that the possession of impressive military force was equivalent to its use in a manner that could command public support at home and collaboration by the nation's principal allies abroad.

By the early 1980s, NATO was gripped by an acute "crisis of confidence" stemming from fundamental policy differences between the United States and its allies on a number of important regional and global issues. The European members of NATO did not bother to conceal their disagreements with, and their apprehensions about, the diplomacy of the Carter Administration. A report from Great Britain found a pervasive belief that "Carter cannot lead and cannot deliver on matters of [diplomatic] consequence." Another report from Paris emphasized growing French diplomatic "independence" from the United States. As one French diplomat said, "The U.S. must recognize that Europe has its own interests and ideas, that the Europe-U.S. relationship should be one of partners, not teacher-pupil."

Thus, on the Carter Administration's initial decision to deploy the neutron bomb, Washington *did* consult West Germany about the matter; officials in Bonn endorsed the idea *privately,* but they were reluctant to do so *publicly* out of fear of seeming to be subordinate to the United States on a controversial issue in internal German politics! See Gregory F. Treverton, "Nuclear Weapons and the 'Gray Area,'" *Foreign Affairs,* **57** (Summer, 1979), 1075–1090. The author concludes that, in reality, the European allies want and expect the United States to "lead" the Western coalition diplomatically.

From Bonn, West German assessments of American diplomatic leadership were no less openly critical. In the German view, relations among the Western allies were at a "low ebb," with basic policy disagreements becoming increasingly evident among its members. German leaders expected few tangible results from a forthcoming Western "summit" conference to be held in Venice. Although it had continually urged the allies to support American policy in the Middle East, the United States had thus far produced no meaningful "energy policy," lessening America's own growing dependence upon Middle East oil supplies; nor did such a policy seem likely to emerge in the near future. As Italian officials assessed the condition of the alliance, the forthcoming Venice meeting would largely serve as an occasion "to air discontent that divides the U.S. from its allies" on several major international issues.[37]

As one student of the Western alliance assessed the matter, NATO's crisis of confidence derived from two broad tendencies: the changes that had occurred in American foreign policy after the Vietnam War, such as confusion in the public and official mind about the nation's goals and its relative military decline; and, by contrast, growing European political and economic strength, making the allies more self-confident and diplomatically independent. Still other developments produced disunity within NATO on outstanding diplomatic issues: the lack of "consensus" within the United States after the Vietnam War concerning the nation's international role; and, as we shall see more fully in the remainder of this chapter, the failure of the European allies to arrive at common policies among themselves and to make any noteworthy progress toward achieving European political unity.

As the new Reagan Administration, for example, prepared to take office, an editorial in the *New York Times* dealt with the "Allies in Trouble." It took note of certain long-standing European fears and complaints about American diplomatic leadership; and it observed that after the Republican victory, Europeans now expected the United States to "act as a leader" in evolving common approaches to international problems affecting their mutual interests. Yet, as Secretary of State Alexander Haig candidly acknowledged in 1982: "The allies must know where we are going if we expect them to go with us." Under both the Carter and Reagan administrations, genuine confusion often existed across the Atlantic concerning the goals and direction of American foreign policy in dealing with specific global issues. This fact virtually guaranteed disunity within the NATO alliance and disaffection within Europe toward American diplomacy.[38]

In seeking to determine the root causes of the "crisis of confidence" that has perhaps been present within NATO since the creation of the Western alliance, four pivotal facts about the problem need to be borne in mind. The first one—and perhaps the most important key to NATO's continuing "disarray"—is that the pact was designed to be *principally a military alliance or coalition against a widely perceived common danger:* the Soviet threat to European and American security. By the 1980s, two contrary conclusions held by officials on both sides of the Atlantic engendered disagreements about the future of NATO. On the one hand, as we have observed, the military balance on the European continent clearly favored the Communist side—so much so as perhaps to "invite" some kind of military threat against the NATO defense zone. On the other hand, despite this military imbalance, many Europeans unquestionably believed that the danger of war between the United States and the Soviet Union had diminished perceptibly. Justified or not, this prevalent conviction went far toward explaining the "crisis of NATO."

Second, many of the problems associated with disunity among the Western allies may be in large part an outgrowth of *NATO's success* in achieving its dominant objective—the preservation of European security for over a generation. As the years passed, the European allies could engage in independent diplomatic initiatives *more safely,* as a result of the reduced danger of a Communist threat to their national independence. According to some commentators, the nations of Europe may have been the primary beneficiaries of détente. As one assessment concluded:

> It is a fallacy to say the Soviets were the great beneficiaries of détente. True, they gained time to build their mighty arsenal, which they probably would have managed anyway. .... But it was the West Germans—and the East Europeans—who made the big gains, in emotional, moral, social, cultural and human terms as well as in commerce.

As we observed in Chapter 10, the European assessment of the value of détente was often more sanguine about its advantages for the West than the American evaluation. In dealing with contentious issues like East-West trade, or the Soviet invasion of Afghanistan, there was a greater inclination in Europe to believe that disputes between the United States and the Soviet Union "can be reasoned away" and to urge that every effort be made "to persuade the Russians to ease off."[39]

Third, disagreements between the United States and its NATO allies on major diplomatic and security questions might also provide evidence of a long-awaited (and perhaps inevitable) development: the diplomatic "reemergence" of Western Europe, or the exertion of European influence in international affairs proportionate to its demonstrated economic strength and productive capacity.

Fourth, the lack of unity sometimes characteristic of NATO deliberations was an inherent outgrowth of the political principle with which its members were identified: the concept of democracy. NATO is an exercise in political "pluralism" versus the model of political authoritarianism existing across the Iron Curtain. As one observer summarized the viewpoint of French President Giscard d'Estaing concerning the "disunity" evident within NATO:

> Compared to the problems of the Soviet Union and its "allies" in Eastern Europe, the problems of the West, he feels, are difficult but manageable in time; whereas the problems of the Communist system may very well be structural and [will] grow.[40]

Or, as President Jimmy Carter said on the eve of the Vienna "summit" meeting among the Western allies: "We are not the Warsaw Pact, held together by one nation's tanks. We are bound by shared ideals, shared goals and shared respect." The fact that NATO was a coalition of democratic nations was graphically illustrated in the spring of 1981, when the French electorate chose François Mitterand as president of the Fifth Republic, thereby ending the long political dominance by right-wing and centrist political forces that had governed the country since 1958. Although Mitterand was a Socialist, and had been elected with the support of the French Communist Party, he was a supporter of NATO and had been openly critical of such Soviet behavior as Moscow's invasion of Afghanistan. Yet the new French government was expected to be more independent of Washington than its predecessors (as in its policy toward the Middle East); and the challenge of arriving at joint NATO policies would likely be compounded by this reorientation in the internal French political system.[41]

European Political and Economic Unity

In 1948, a committee of the Hague Congress on European Unity observed that:

> Judged from any standpoint—political, economic or cultural—it is only by uniting herself that Europe can overcome her immediate difficulties and go forward to fulfill her mission for the future.... It is impossible to keep problems of economic collaboration and defense separate from those of general political policy.

Successful implementation of joint economic or military policies, the committee was convinced, required sooner or later "the renunciation or, to be more accurate, the joint exercise of certain sovereign powers."[42]

The dream of a politically unified Europe is as old as history. The list of illustrious personages advocating this ideal—Dante, Pope Leo X, Erasmus, Grotius, Thomas More, Sully, Fichte, Kant, Mazzini, Churchill, to list but a few—testifies to the importance and durability of the idea. Yet down to World War II, the idea of European political unification was a dream espoused chiefly by intellectuals. The same historical forces that engendered extensive economic and military collaboration among nations in the North Atlantic community—Soviet hegemony over the heartland of Eurasia; the decline of England, France, and Germany as great powers; Europe's early postwar economic debilitation and military vulnerability; the continuing challenge posed by expansive Communism—convinced Western policy makers that political unification must at least be postulated as an ultimate goal.

Such convictions have spawned a profusion of often highly varied plans, institutions, and approaches whose professed goal is political unification. In the space available, we may focus only upon the more important tendencies and developments in the recent period.

The Council of Europe

In March 1948, the French National Assembly called for the creation of a European constituent assembly to lay the basis for a European federation. Accordingly, on May 5, 1949, the Council of Europe came into existence, with its headquarters at Strasbourg. From 10 original members, the council ultimately expanded to 21, making it the largest body on the Continent concerned with political and economic integration (except for the Organization for Economic Cooperation and Development, or OECD). Unlike NATO, the Council of Europe contained several "neutrals" (e.g., Austria and Ireland), which took no formal part in Western defense activities.

From the beginning, the Council of Europe has mirrored, more than it has overcome, disunity on the European continent. It has been torn between those seeking an "organic" unification of Europe in which national sovereignty would be significantly reduced, and the "functionalists" who desire cooperation among the European nations in limited areas of activity. Created as an organ to promote the political integration of Europe, the council has drifted away from this objective toward more attainable and immediately useful goals. If it has not been successful in achieving its original purpose, it has nonetheless made several useful contributions. Its most constructive service perhaps has been as a convenient and prestigious platform from which to "keep alive" the ideal of European unity. It has sometimes played a valuable role in coordinating the activities of regional organizations within Europe; it has performed useful functions in social, cultural, and legal spheres. And—in what is surely one of the landmarks of contemporary international law —it established the European Court and the Commission of Human Rights.[43]

Economic Integration Schemes

With strong American encouragement, the Europeans took several steps in the early post-World War II period to promote economic unity, in an effort to overcome the region's traditional jealousies and rivalries. Even before the war ended, Belgium, Luxembourg, and the Netherlands formed a customs union (known as Benelux); a comparable agreement was reached between France and Italy in 1949.

Another strong impetus toward regional economic and financial collaboration in Western Europe was supplied by the Marshall Plan, or European Recovery Program, inaugurated in 1948. A leading goal of the ERP—repeatedly emphasized by officials in Washington—was to promote the reconstruction of Europe *on a regional basis*. (As we observed earlier, initially an invitation to participate in the ERP was extended to the Soviet Union and the smaller Marxist nations of Eastern Europe. But after a preliminary expression of interest in the program, Moscow refused to participate in it—a decision that was of course also binding upon its Eastern European satellites.)[44] Thereafter, progress toward achieving economic and political unification was confined largely to Western Europe.

The Organization for European Economic Cooperation (OEEC), established to administer the Marshall Plan, emphasized the necessity for a regional approach to the problem of European reconstruction. Its successor (the Organization for Economic Cooperation and Development, or OECD) was broadened to include not only European na-

tions but also the United States, Canada, and Japan. OECD sought to promote economic growth and expansion; to eliminate trade barriers; and to provide economic and technical assistance from the industrialized nations to the developing nations. Because of Europe's earlier colonial ties with the area, and its continuing economic involvement in African affairs in more recent years, in time OECD concentrated foreign aid activities heavily on the African continent. Lacking historic ties with Africa, and providing substantial foreign aid to other regions, the United States was largely content to let the members of OECD meet Africa's need for external financial and technical assistance.

In the early postwar period also, other schemes were being formulated and adopted to promote European economic cooperation —and in time, to achieve the goal of political unification. One approach to the problem was what is known as "functionalism," or limited cooperation among two or more countries in a specific area of economic enterprise. Many "functionalists" on both sides of the Atlantic believed that successful regional collaboration in a limited sphere of economic activity would have a "spillover effect," generating new momentum for European economic and political unification.

A leading example of this approach was the European Coal and Steel Community (ECSC), an outgrowth of the Schuman Plan, set up by the Benelux countries, France, Germany, and Italy on April 18, 1951. As a prominent advocate of European economic integration, Walter Hallstein, has described ECSC: "Its essential characteristics were that it was 'supranational,' that it was practical, and that it was partial [in its scope].[45] Unlike OEEC or OECD, the Coal and Steel Community possessed supranational authority to formulate regulations and directives binding upon its members in coal and steel production. Moreover, as Hallstein has emphasized, a singular characteristic of ECSC was its *evolutionary* character. From the beginning, its instigators conceived of ECSC as an undertaking that would gradually, and on the basis of experience, chart a course toward expanded supranational collaboration in other phases of European economic life.[46] As an ultimate goal (whose realization would take years and would encounter many obstacles), ECSC envisioned creating what Robert Schuman had called "the European federation which is indispensable to the maintenance of peace."[47]

ECSC was a significant step down the path of European economic unity, therefore, not alone because it represented a successful venture in supranational collaboration in one industrial activity. It was perhaps even more significant for what it foreshadowed. This was the far more ambitious European Common Market, whose goals, organizational pattern, and implications for America we shall examine below.

Another sector approach to economic collaboration among European nations was Euratom, which began operating in 1958. Its members were the Benelux nations, France, Germany, and Italy. Unlike ECSC, which it resembled in many respects, Euratom dealt with an area—the peaceful application of atomic energy—in which there was no backlog of competing national traditions to be overcome. The organization was intended to deal with one of Europe's most pressing shortages—fuel; short on coal reserves, Europe had become increasingly dependent upon importations of oil, especially from the Middle East.

A succession of crises in the Middle East—in 1956, in 1967, and in 1973—underscored Europe's extreme vulnerability to an "oil boycott" imposed by the major Middle Eastern oil-producing countries. Accordingly, the development and expansion of peace-time nuclear energy—coupled with an ongoing search for alternative sources of oil (like the North Sea)—have received higher priority in Europe than in any other region. Control over nuclear technology on a regional basis was impaired by French President Charles de Gaulle's insistence upon the possession of the *force de frappe,* or an independent French nuclear arsenal. In company with other states that did not currently belong to the "nuclear club," France did not subscribe to the principle of nuclear "nonproliferation"; in French eyes (and it was an attitude also shared in nations like Communist China and India), failure to develop and control its own *force de frappe* would relegate France permanently to the level of a second- or third-rank power.

The European Community

The movement leading to what in time came to be called the European Community was the culmination of the impulse toward economic collaboration—and ultimate political unity—among the nations of Western Europe. Economically (if not diplomatically), the European Community represents one of the most influential forces on the globe; and it is not unreasonable to expect that its diplomatic influence will increasingly reflect its economic, financial, and commercial importance.

The European Community (EC) evolved through a series of steps, a crucial one being the creation of the European Common Market in 1958, established by the Treaty of Rome. The original members of the Common Market (known as "the Six") were: France, the Federal Republic of Germany, Italy, and the Benelux nations (Belgium, the Netherlands, and Luxembourg). For a period of several years, another organization, led by Great Britain—called the European Free Trade Area (EFTA)—provided an alternative approach to regional economic collaboration.* On the European continent, three new "communities" —the European Coal and Steel Community, Euratom, and the Common Market— sought to promote regional economic collaboration in dealing with specific problems.

In 1967, these separate communities were merged into a single entity—the European Economic Community (EEC). Early in 1973, after prolonged debate on the question, Great Britain (along with Denmark and Ireland) joined the European Economic Community. Greece was scheduled to become a member in 1981; and it was expected that Spain and Portugal would also join the organization in the near future. Perhaps in recognition of the fact that, from the beginning, ultimate *political unity* has been a professed goal of the movement, in time the organization was referred to merely as the European Community.

With the passage of time, the European Community developed a complex set of institutional mechanisms to formulate and administer its policies.[48] A single *Commission* was established in 1967 (resulting from a merger of the separate commissions for the Common Market, ECSC, and Euratom). Appointed by the member governments of the EC, the Commission ensures that its activities are in accordance with the Treaty of Rome; and it prepares for consideration recommendations for changes in the organization.

The *European Council* serves as the major policy-making body. Its members are the heads of state (or heads of government) of nations belonging to the EC. The Council normally meets three times each year. An EC *Council of Ministers* coordinates the economic policies of the nations belonging to the community; and it makes the day-by-day decisions necessary to carry out the provisions of the Treaty of Rome. Each member government designates one representative on the Council of Ministers. Decisions are reached by majority vote, although (because of a system of "weighted voting") the larger members have a greater influence in the Council's deliberations.

A *European Parliament* serves as the EC's legislative body. Its members were initially chosen by the separate legislative bodies of the member nations. The Parliament supervises the operations of the EC's executive agencies; discusses the annual reports submitted by other EC agencies; and exercises limited budgetary control over the European Community. As a step toward "democratizing" the European Community, the first popular elections to fill seats in the European Parliament were held on June 7–10, 1979. Consisting of 410 members, the new popularly chosen European Parliament was expected to become a vocal champion of even greater progress toward regional political collaboration.

A *Court of Justice* (consisting of one judge from each member state) was created to insure that the Community's activities were in accordance with legal requirements and that justice is served in the EC's manifold operations. The Community also has several ancillary organizational units, like the European Investment Bank, the Economic and Social Committee, and the European Development Fund.

---

*The European Free Trade Area (EFTA) was established in 1960 to promote expanded trade among its members in industrial and agricultural goods. In contrast to the European Common Market, EFTA had much more limited aims; EFTA, for example, did *not* anticipate the ultimate political union of its members. Led by Great Britain, EFTA was considerably weakened by London's decision in 1973 to join the Common Market. Current members of EFTA are: Austria, Iceland, Norway, Portugal, Sweden, and Switzerland (Finland is an "associate member"). For additional data on EFTA, see *The Europa Year Book: 1979*, I (London: Europa Publications, 1979, 2 vols.), p. 201; subsequent volumes in this series provide up-to-date information.

Since its creation, the European Community has steadily broadened its activities and has endeavored to concert the policies of its members on a variety of fronts. A European Monetary System (EMS) was introduced early in 1979. Its purpose was to prevent wide fluctuations in the value of European currencies and to facilitate financial transactions (by use of a new European Currency Unit) among its members. Since the early 1960s, another high priority goal has been a Common Agricultural Policy (CAP) for the members of the Community. The purpose of CAP was to stabilize Europe's food prices and to promote increased agricultural productivity. Nearly three-quarters of the EC's annual budget is devoted to this aspect of its operations.

The European Community has also sought to formulate and gain its members' adherence to a common energy policy, in an effort to reduce the region's vulnerability to an oil boycott imposed by Middle East suppliers. Under EC auspices, the search for alternative energy sources—such as coal, solar energy, and peacetime nuclear power generation—has been intensified. Even so, by the early 1980s Western Europe remained heavily dependent upon the oil supplies of the Middle East to meet its energy requirements.

From the beginning, a high priority goal of the European Community was to foster and expand trade, both among its members and between the EC and the outside world. In this sphere of its activities, the European Community has been conspicuously successful. By the early 1980s, total exports by the members of the European Community equalled some $660 billion annually, making the EC the largest single force in world trade. As was explained more fully in Chapter 6, during the post-World War II era, Western Europe had become a primary importer of American goods and services.

Another significant and expanding dimension of the European Community's activities has been its economic relations with the Third World. Early in 1975, the first Lomé Convention was signed (at Lomé, Togo) between the members of the Community and some 46 countries in Africa, the Caribbean, and the Pacific area. Other Third World states adhered to the convention in the years that followed, in order to avail themselves of the favorable terms of trade and other economic and financial benefits the agreement provided its members. On October 31, 1979, a new agreement (Lomé II) was signed between the European Community and 68 Third World countries. The new accord provided for new benefits in such areas such as trade, the stabilization of export revenues, finance, and foreign economic and technical aid to the less developed societies. During its five-year lifetime, the European Development Fund, for example, was expected to disburse some $4.5 billion in development grants to the signatories of the Lomé II agreement.[49]

The Future of European Unity

With strong American encouragement and support at almost every step, the nations of Western Europe have made impressive progress toward greater regional cooperation since World War II—more progress than in any previous era of history. Tangible evidence of Europe's achievements on this front was available on all sides. There was the existence of the elaborate and successfully functioning institutional machinery of the European Community that we have already described. In the light of Europe's centuries-old history of rivalry and entrenched nationalism, this fact alone was a notable accomplishment.

In addition, as one report described it, by the end of the 1970s the European Community had become "an economic giant" rivaling the United States. By the 1980s, the European Community had emerged as the most powerful trade nexus, and the largest single market, on the globe. The EC's 270 million consumers purchased one-quarter of the world's total imports; and the members of EC supplied one-fifth of the world's total exports. In just over two decades since EC's establishment, its members had witnessed an increase from $1200 to $9000 in annual per capita income. Another notable accomplishment was the fact that the European Community (in contrast to most other regions of the world) had become self-sufficient in food production. The existence of the EC had also had a profound effect upon the trade policies of other countries such as the United States and Japan, forcing them to liberalize or eliminate tariffs and other trade restrictions. In brief, if the European allies wanted to be treated as "equals" by the United States—and if their diplomacy reflected a higher degree of independence than ever—it was because, in economic and commercial affairs at least, they *were America's equal.*[50]

Despite this record of accomplishment, some informed students of European affairs believed that, paradoxically, the quest for European unity had lost momentum and that the unity already achieved was seriously endangered. One report (analyzing the implications of the popularly elected European Parliament) found that "the goal of a united Europe is as elusive as ever"; the democratically chosen European Parliament would likely have no greater success in translating the vision into reality than its predecessors.[51] Several months later, on the eve of a Venice meeting of the members of the European Community, another commentator called attention to the existence of basic *intra-European differences,* as well as disagreements between America and its European partners. The atmosphere at the meeting was one of "defeatism," in terms of solving acute

problems like inflation and unemployment on a regional basis. Noting that the site of the meeting (Venice) was physically sinking, *The Sunday Times* of London lamented that a conference in "a sinking city will be appropriate symbolism for our prospects."[52]

For many years, a proclaimed goal of the European Community (and its predecessors) was greater "consultation" among its members on diplomatic issues, for the purpose of arriving at a common foreign policy. With rare exceptions, the EC has been unable to achieve that objective—and current prospects are that it will remain elusive.[53] The failure has numerous major and minor causes. Let us briefly identify several major obstacles to future European political and diplomatic cooperation.

First, the same process has occurred *within* European political systems that Europeans have complained vocally about within the American government. Increasingly, fundamental differences of opinion could be identified on major diplomatic issues. Thus, following an electoral victory by the Conservative Party in Britain early in May 1979, significant differences existed between high British officials over how best to approach the continental members of the European Community. Prime Minister Margaret Thatcher advocated a "hard line" strategy—emphasizing Britain's dissatisfaction with its terms of membership in the EC—while many of her subordinates favored a more conciliatory approach. Within France, comparable policy differences existed in the government of President Giscard d'Estaing: The President and his subordinates differed fundamentally over such issues as America's alleged "decline" as a superpower and over the reasons for Moscow's aggressive behavior in invading Afghanistan. Comparable disagreements over basic policy questions existed within the government of West Germany. Chancellor Helmut Schmidt advocated a more conciliatory approach, in an effort to preserve Soviet-American détente; many of his foreign policy advisers favored strengthening NATO's defenses, as an alternative approach to negotiations with the Soviet Union.[54]

Second, the internal cohesion of several Western European states has been jeopardized in recent years by the movement known as "Euro-Communism," or the resurgence of Marxist political strength in key European nations like France, Italy, and Portugal. The emergence of Euro-Communism not only imposed new strains upon intra-European relations; for several years, it also created considerable apprehension among policy makers in Washington, who were deeply concerned about its impact upon the future of NATO and overall European stability. Throughout the first half of the 1970s, for example, officials of the Nixon and Ford administrations did not hesitate to express their anxieties about the consequences of growing political strength by the Communist parties of Western Europe. As Washington assessed the phenomenon, the emergence of Euro-Communism posed a serious threat to European security and suggested the existence of a kind of "internal decay" that was occurring within European societies, despite their economic prosperity and productivity.

Insofar as Euro-Communism was an obstacle to regional cooperation or to constructive European-American relations during the 1970s, in time the problem largely solved itself. In national elections held in Spain, Italy, and France in 1977–1978, Marxist organizations suffered serious reverses. The Communist Party of Italy—a leader in advocating the concept of "national Communism," or the adaptation of Marxist ideas to the national traditions and needs of particular countries—publicly endorsed the idea of Western European political integration. The Communist

Party of Spain disavowed several basic Leninist ideas long endorsed by the Soviet Union. The French Communist Party was unable to arrive at a durable compromise with its long-time political rivals, the Socialists; the result was that the Communists lost ground in France. By the end of the 1970s, the threat posed by Euro-Communism had largely been eclipsed by reliance upon terrorism by leftist and other politically dissident groups, especially in Italy. As one commentator explained it, on the European political left terrorism had "outflanked Euro-Communism" as a source of imminent political instability.[55]

Third, the growth in the size of the membership of the European Community created new barriers to intra-European cooperation. As "the Six" expanded into "the Nine"—and, in time, would likely become "the Twelve"—the challenge of arriving at unified positions on major economic and political issues was inescapably compounded. Great Britain and its usual trading partners have become increasingly apprehensive about the impact of certain European Community policies upon their economic well-being—and under its new Conservative government, London demanded "adjustments" in EC policies and regulations more favorable to Great Britain. In turn, France was concerned about the economic implications for its own stability and prosperity of the planned admission of countries like Spain and Portugal into the European Community. As the EC already confronted problems of overproduction in commodities like butter and wine, one French official said: "We can't afford to create an olive-oil ocean to add to our butter mountain and our wine lake."[56]

Fourth, experience has shown that, during periods of economic crisis, the members of the European Community revert to old patterns of nationalistic behavior. This became evident during the conflicts that erupted between Israel and the Arab states in 1967 and again in 1973. During neither conflict (but especially in the 1967 war) were the members of the European Community able to concert their policies in response to an actual or threatened curtailment of oil shipments from the Middle East. Instead, the European states in the main made independent overtures to the Middle East oil-producing states, in an effort to assure an adequate supply for their own needs.[57]

Fifth, intra-European differences have been engendered for many years by the conflict among several available models of future economic and political development. The economic and political "unification" of Europe, for example, can take many specific forms—two of which attract a wide following on the European continent. One of these was suggested by French President Charles de Gaulle's concept of *Europe des patries* ("Europe of the fatherlands"), or a loose confederation of European states which largely retained their national sovereignty and diplomatic independence. During his tenure in office (1958–1969), de Gaulle was dedicated to restoring *la grandeur* to France; and in the Gaullist conception, little doubt existed concerning which European state was destined to be the leader of *Europe des patries*. Even after his death, the ideas of General de Gaulle enjoyed wide support within France and among his admirers throughout Europe.[58]

At the other end of the spectrum is the model of European unity (most vocally espoused by the Netherlands) involving "organic" unity, in which the members would relinquish a substantial degree of sovereignty to a supranational institution. The existing European Parliament, for example, might acquire at least some of the powers long exercised by Europe's national legislatures; and other supranational institutions would be strengthened and given the ability to reach decisions binding upon all the member states. By this process, ultimately a "United States of Europe" would come into existence.

Controversy over the precise form that future economic and political unity ought to take continues to divide the members of the European Community. On the basis of the evidence to date, it appears that the Gaullist conception is nearer to the viewpoint held by majority sentiment throughout Western Europe.

Sixth, the impulse toward European political unity was being restrained by potent *nationalist forces and aspirations* prevalent throughout contemporary Europe; in some respects, these barriers were more formidable than at any time since World War II. A number of commentators believed that the movement toward European political unity had largely reached an impasse, with little prospect of gaining new momentum in the near future. The objective announced at a 1972 European summit conference in Paris—that political unity would become a reality by 1980—had proved unattainable.[59] Within most European countries "protectionist" sentiment—threatening the emergence of new common economic policies to deal with pervasive problems, like unemployment and inflation—was gaining adherents. Competition was also growing among the European states for access to the markets of the Third World; and contention over Japan's aggressive export policies in Western markets also elicited different responses among the European states. Meanwhile, the prevailing reaction of most Europeans to the elections held to fill seats in the European Parliament in 1979 was largely one of apathy.[60]

The external behavior of the three most influential nations in Western Europe was massively influenced by nationalistic impulses. Under its new Conservative government, Great Britain was seeking, as Prime Minister Margaret Thatcher defined the goal, to "put the Great back into Britain." This involved lessening Britain's longtime "dependence" upon the United States and demanding that the other members of the European Community grant concessions which, in British eyes, made membership in the European Community more beneficial. This new British approach—popularly known as "Thatcherism"—bore many resemblances to the earlier Gaullism.[61]

As during the Gaullist era, under President Giscard d'Estaing, France remained attached to the idea of strong European initiatives in regional and global affairs, with France playing a leading role. The idea that Europe should serve as a "third force" between the two superpowers continued to enjoy widespread support; and French opposition to an expansion of the powers of the European Parliament remained strong. In sub-Saharan Africa, France continued to play an assertive, and sometimes crucial, role.[62]

Among the members of the European Community, enthusiasm for Soviet-American détente was most conspicuous in the foreign policy of West Germany. Bonn's preoccupation with preserving and extending détente was fully explicable: The German nation remained divided, and was still highly vulnerable to Soviet threats, while the United States was located some 4000 miles away. (For their part, Soviet policy makers had long endeavored to encourage German initiatives aimed at gaining Western support for détente.) Moreover, under Chancellor Helmut Schmidt West Germany had emerged as in some respects America's most outspoken critic within the European Community. In Bonn's view, Washington had achieved little success in stabilizing the value of the dollar, in successfully dealing with rapid inflation, or in reducing its own massive reliance upon foreign oil imports—problems which seriously weakened the security and cohesion of the West. To

German minds, Bonn's policy of *Ostpolitik*—a contemporary version of Prince Bismarck's advice to "Always keep a channel open to the Russians"—remained both a necessity and a continuing source of misunderstanding with America and other Western allies.[63]

Finally, many of the problems in European-American relations—and perhaps even in the relations among the nations of Western Europe themselves—become more explicable when the dilemma that lies at the heart of the Western coalition is recognized frankly. Since World War II, a kind of love-hate or attraction-repulsion dichotomy has existed on both sides of the Atlantic Ocean. Americans, for example, have wanted their European partners to be "strong" and "independent" —but not to the point of seriously contesting America's "leadership" position within the Western alliance! On the European continent, as a prominent French political analyst has observed, attitudes toward the United States have been similarly ambivalent. In his view:

> Every Western statesman experiences two contradictory feelings [toward Washington]: satisfaction that the United States exists and annoyance that the life and death of his fellow citizens depend in large measure on the decisions of a foreign and distant President. . . .[64]

With the passage of time, the nations of Western Europe have collectively become more economically and financially powerful vis-à-vis both the United States and the Soviet Union. Yet paradoxically, their "dependence" upon the United States, particularly in the sphere of regional defense, remains largely unchanged; and Europe's continued reliance upon foreign oil imports makes the region perhaps even more vulnerable than ever to developments abroad. Europeans dislike and chafe under such realities—but thus far, they have evolved no effective substitutes for them.

NOTES

1. George W. Ball, *Diplomacy for a Crowded World: An American Foreign Policy* (Boston: Little, Brown and Co., 1976), pp. 153–154.

2. Edward N. Luttwak, "European Insecurity and American Policy," in Robert Conquest, et al., *Defending America: Toward a New Role in the Post-Détente World* (New York: Basic Books, 1977), p. 186.

3. Julius W. Pratt, *A History of United States Foreign Policy* (Englewood Cliffs, N.J.: Prentice-Hall, 1955), p. 168.

4. Ibid., p. 169.

5. Ibid., pp. 527–528.

6. George F. Kennan, "The Sources of Soviet Conduct," *Foreign Affairs*, **25** (July, 1947), 556–583.

7. For a penetrating analysis of the deficiencies of the doctrine of containment, many of which were clearly illustrated in time, see Walter Lippmann, *The Cold War* (New York: Harper & Row, 1957).

8. *Congressional Record*, Vol. 93, 1980–1981.

9. See William A. Brown and Redvers Opie, *American Foreign Assistance* (Washington, D.C.: Brookings Institution, 1953), p. 175.

10. House Foreign Affairs Committee, *Hearings on the Mutual Security Act of 1957*, 88th Cong., 1st Sess., 1957, p. 24.

11. See the text of President Johnson's budget message in *New York Times*, January 22, 1964.

12. For a detailed discussion of prevailing executive and legislative attitudes toward America's contribution to NATO, see Cecil V. Crabb, Jr., and Pat Holt, *Invitation to Struggle: Congress, the President and Foreign Policy* (Washington, D.C.: Congressional Quarterly Press, 1980), pp. 120–124.

13. Department of State, *American Foreign Policy, 1950–1955* (General Foreign Policy Series, No. 117, I), pp. 819–820.

14. See ibid., pp. 822, 835.

15. Hugh Sidey, *John F. Kennedy: President* (New York: Atheneum, 1963), p. 184.

16. Following the invasion of Czechoslovakia by Warsaw Pact forces, NATO conveyed "a warning" to the Kremlin concerning future threats to European security. Secretary of State Dean Rusk declared that the security of Yugoslavia and Austria were of direct concern to the Western alliance. See *New York Times*, November 16 and 17, 1968.

17. Information on the current organizational structure of NATO may be found in *The Europa Year Book: 1979* (London: Europa Publications, 1979), pp. 236–237. This publication provides up-to-date information on NATO.

18. A succinct discussion of MBFR is provided in "Europe: Mutual and Balanced Force Reductions Talks," *Gist* (Washington, D.C.: Department of State, October, 1978), pp. 1–2.

19. For these and other tributes to NATO's accomplishments, see the publication *NATO at 30* (Washington, D.C.: The Atlantic Council of America, 1979); and Hedley Bull, "A View from Abroad: Consistency Under Pressure," *Foreign Affairs*, **57** (Special Issue, 1978), 447.

20. See James Reston, in *New York Times*, May 23, 1980; the views of Senator Charles Percy, as reported in ibid., November 20, 1980; and the views of Richard V. Allen in *U.S. News and World Report*, **89** (November 24, 1980), 55. A detailed analysis of the Reagan Administration's viewpoints toward NATO is available in the State Department publication "The Alliance at a Crossroad," *Current Policy*, **350** (December 2, 1981), 1–4.

21. For further discussion of the doctrine of "massive retaliation," see: Richard Goold-Adams, *John Foster Dulles: A Reappraisal* (New York: Appleton-Century-Crofts, 1962), pp. 100–119; Townsend Hoopes, *The Devil and John Foster Dulles* (Boston: Atlantic-Little Brown, 1973), pp. 191–202; and Morton H. Halperin, *Defense Strategies for the Seventies* (Boston: Little, Brown, and Co. 1971), pp. 38–54, 99–113.

22. See Edwin H. Fedder, *NATO: The Dynamics of Alliance in the Postwar World* (New York: Dodd, Mead and Co., 1973), pp. 41–45.

23. For data on the contributions of the members of NATO to the common defense effort, see the statistical information contained in *NATO Review,* **28** (February, 1980), 31–33; and *U.S. News and World Report,* **88** (April 28, 1980), 20–22.

24. See *New York Times,* June 17, 1980; and the views of Richard Burt in the State Department's publication, "NATO and Nuclear Deterrence," *Current Policy,* **319** (September 23, 1981), 1–5.

25. Donald Watt, "The European Initiative," *Foreign Affairs,* **57** (Special Issue, 1978), 585. A more recent analysis of the challenge confronting NATO by the buildup of Warsaw Pact forces is provided in the State Department's publication, "Preserving Western Independence and Security," *Current Policy,* **327** (October 15, 1981), 1–5.

26. See the views of Secretary of Defense Harold Brown in the Department of Defense's *Annual Report: Fiscal Year 1980* (Washington, D.C.: Government Printing Office, 1979), pp. 88–100.

27. See the data from studies by the International Institute for Strategic Study, in *New York Times,* October 21, 1979.

28. See the views of Secretary of Defense Harold Brown in the Department of Defense's *Annual Report: Fiscal Year 1980,* pp. 88–89.

29. See the report on the meeting of NATO foreign and defense ministers in *New York Times,* May 25, 1980.

30. See "NATO's Answer to the Soviet Challenge," in *U.S. News and World Report,* **84** (June 12, 1978), 26–32.

31. For more detailed discussion of specific steps taken to strengthen NATO's defensive position, see *Idem;* "Carter and NATO," ibid., **84** (April 3, 1978), 35–36; the symposium on "Balance of Forces in Central Europe," *NATO Review,* **27** (October, 1979), 1–31; and Drew Middleton, in *New York Times,* May 25, 1980.

32. For a discussion of a variety of new weapons scheduled to be produced by the United States and its allies in the years ahead, see Drew Middleton, in *New York Times,* January 7, 1980; Richard Halloran, in ibid.,

January 29, 1980; Martin Tolching, in ibid., May 22, 1980; and see the text of the Carter-Reagan debate in ibid., October 30, 1980.

33. The "Suez Crisis" of 1956 is discussed more fully in Dwight D. Eisenhower, *Waging Peace* (Garden City, N.Y.: Doubleday and Co., 1965), pp. 20–103.

34. See the summary of the major foreign policy objectives of the Reagan Administration in *New York Times,* November 9, 1980.

35. The response of the NATO allies to President Carter's new doctrine opposing Soviet intervention in Afghanistan is discussed by R. W. Apple, Jr., in *New York Times,* June 23, 1980; by Flora Lewis, in ibid., June 24, 1980; and by Bernard Gwertzman, in ibid., June 27, 1980.

36. For discussions of independent diplomatic initiatives by the NATO allies—particularly in seeking a Soviet withdrawal from Afghanistan and a solution to the Arab-Israeli conflict—see Bernard Gwertzman, in *New York Times,* May 22, 1980; James Reston, in ibid., May 23, 1980; dispatch by Flora Lewis, in ibid., June 15, 1980; and Anthony Lewis, in ibid., June 16, 1980.

37. See the reports on prevalent attitudes in Europe toward the "summit" conference to be held in Venice, in *U.S. News and World Report,* **88** (June 23, 1980), 20–22.

38. For fuller discussion of these and other factors producing a "crisis of confidence" within NATO, see the chapter on "Faltering NATO Alliance," in *America's Changing World Role* (Washington, D.C.: Editorial Research Reports, 1974), pp. 43–63; Alex A. Vardamis, "German-American Military Fissures," *Foreign Policy,* **34** (Spring, 1979), 87–107; Eugene J. McCarthy, "Look No Allies," *Foreign Policy,* **30** (Spring, 1978), 3–17; Christopher J. Makins, "Bringing in the Allies," *Foreign Policy,* **35** (Summer, 1979), 91–109; and the editorial in *New York Times,* November 20, 1980; and Secretary Haig's views on the Western alliance in ibid., April 28, 1982.

39. Flora Lewis, in *New York Times,* June 20, 1980.

40. See the report by James Reston of an inter-

view with French President Giscard d'Estaing, in *New York Times,* June 18, 1980.

41. See the excerpts from President Carter's speech in *New York Times,* June 20, 1980. For a discussion of the implications of the French national election in mid-1981, see Flora Lewis and James Black, in ibid., May 11, 1981.

42. Quoted in F. C. S. Northrop, *European Union and United States Foreign Policy* (New York: Macmillan Co., 1954), pp. 6–7.

43. *The Europa Year Book: 1979,* pp. 166–172. For up-to-date information on the Council of Europe, see subsequent publications in this series.

44. The impact of the Marshall Plan upon Europe's post-World War II recovery is emphasized in Walter Z. Laqueur, *The Rebirth of Europe* (New York: Holt, Rinehart and Winston, 1970); and in Richard Mayne, *The Recovery of Europe: From Devastation to Unity* (New York: Harper & Row, 1970).

45. Walter Hallstein, *United Europe* (Cambridge, Mass.: Harvard University Press, 1963), p. 13.

46. Ibid., p. 13.

47. Quoted in ibid., p. 17.

48. Detailed data on the organizational structure and evolution of the European Community are available in *The Europa Year Book: 1979,* I, pp. 177–182. Later volumes in this series provide current information.

49. For more extended discussion of the Lomé I and Lomé II agreements, see Peter Blackburn, "Europe Looks South," *Europe,* **215** (September-October, 1979), 26–29; and Arthur S. Banks, ed., *Political Handbook of the World: 1979* (New York: McGraw-Hill, 1979), pp. 15–16.

50. See the data on the European Community presented in *U.S. News and World Report,* **86** (June 11, 1979), 32; and the analyses of the European Community's progress and problems by John Vinocur in *New York Times,* February 11, 1981 and November 8, 1981.

51. *Idem.*

52. R. W. Apple, Jr., in *New York Times,* June 18, 1980.

53. For a discussion of efforts by the members of the European Community to arrive at a common foreign policy, see Robert S. Wood, "The Diplomacy of the Enlarged European Community," *World Affairs,* **137** (Summer, 1974), 3–23.

54. Flora Lewis, in *New York Times,* May 1, 1980.

55. For more detailed discussion of Euro-Communism and the American response to the movement, see Robert J. Lieber and Nancy I. Lieber, "Eurocommunism, Eurosocialism, and U.S. Foreign Policy," in Kenneth A. Oye, et al., eds., *Eagle Entangled: U.S. Foreign Policy in a Complex World* (New York: Longman Inc., 1979), pp. 264–289; Charles Gati, "The 'Europeanization' of Communism?" *Foreign Affairs,* **55** (April, 1977), 539–553; and Jean-François Revel, "The Myths of Eurocommunism," *Foreign Affairs,* **56** (January, 1978), 295–305.

56. R. W. Apple, Jr., in *New York Times,* June 10, 1980.

57. See John A. Cicco, "The Atlantic Alliance and the Arab Challenge: the European Perspective," *World Affairs,* **137** (Spring, 1975), 303–326.

58. For a discussion of more contemporary versions of Gaullist ideas concerning European unity, see Walter Filley, "Western Europe," in *Political Handbook of the World: 1979* (New York: McGraw-Hill, 1979), pp. 14–17.

59. See David Watt, "The European Initiative," *Foreign Affairs,* **57** (Special Issue, 1978), 572–589; and Paul Lewis, in *New York Times,* March 18, 1979.

60. See Bull, "A View from Abroad...," 447–448; and Fritz Stern, "Germany in a Semi-Gaullist Europe," *Foreign Affairs,* **58** (Spring, 1980), 874.

61. Sanford J. Ungar, "Dateline Britain: Thatcherism," *Foreign Policy,* **35** (Summer, 1979), 181–187.

62. See Watt, "The European Initiative," 578–587; and James O. Goldsborough, "Dateline Paris: Africa's Policeman,"

Foreign Policy, **33** (Winter, 1978–79), 174–190.

63. See Joseph Joffe, "All Quiet on the Eastern Front," *Foreign Policy,* **37** (Winter, 1979–80), 161–176; Stern, "Germany in a Semi-Gaullist Europe," 870; and Marion Donhoff, "Bonn and Washington: the Strained Relationship,"

Foreign Affairs, **57** (Summer, 1979), 1052–1065.

64. See the views of the French political analyst, Alfred Grosser, on the attitudes of Europeans toward the United States, in *Newsweek,* **95** (June 23, 1980), 33–34.

Chapter 12

The Middle East:
Israel and the Arabs, Oil, and the Persian Gulf Area

Among the far-reaching changes in the international community brought about by World War II, few surpass in importance the emergence of the Middle East as a maelstrom of great-power conflict. In recent years, the Middle East has exhibited many of the characteristics associated with the Balkans of the pre-World War I era.* Turmoil and ferments,

*The term "Middle East," it must be recognized at the outset, has no universally accepted definition. Depending upon the precise criteria employed for determining its boundaries, the region varies in size and extent. According to its *geographic location,* the Middle East is the area between Europe and Asia to the north and Africa to the south; the region is thus a "bridge" connecting three continents—which is one key to its cultural and ethnic diversity. (Many geographers prefer to call the region "Southwest Asia.") By a *linguistic standard*—believed by many commentators to be the most meaningful—the Middle East includes: the countries of North Africa (Morocco, Algeria, Tunisia, and Libya), sometimes called "the Maghreb"; Egypt and the northern Sudan; Saudi Arabia, North and South Yemen, Kuwait, and the smaller states of the Persian Gulf area; Jordan, Syria, Lebanon,

engendering manifold controversies and antagonisms among great and small powers, appear endemic to the region. While the United States at an early stage in its history developed a fairly well-understood body of principles that governed American diplomatic behavior toward Europe and Asia, it had no foreign policy at all for the Middle East before World War II. This fact furnishes one key to American diplomatic efforts in the Middle East in the postwar period. Foreign policy officials in the United States have been required to formulate and carry out policies and pro-

and Iraq. In these states, Arabic is the dominant (although of course not the only) language. It should be noted that according to this criterion, Turkey and Israel are not considered part of the Middle East; nor is Iran (historically called Persia), whose language is *Farsi,* which is different from Arabic. The Islamic religious faith is the dominant religion of the area, although other religious faiths—such as several denominations of Christianity and Judaism—exist there. Today, a majority of Moslems lives *outside* the Middle East (e.g. in sub-Saharan Africa, on the Indian subcontinent, and in the Soviet Union).

grams toward an area with which they have had little or no historical experience and for which lessons from their domestic history afforded minimum guidance—and to do this at a time when turbulence within the area necessitated quick and difficult judgments.

How has the United States responded to events and crises in the modern Middle East? What goals have motivated American diplomacy toward that crucial region? What difficulties and continuing problems confront American foreign policy toward the Middle East in the years ahead? We may conveniently endeavor to answer such questions by focusing attention upon three basic issues in America's relations with the Middle East: the evolution of American diplomatic interests and involvement in the region; the still volatile Arab-Israeli conflict; and the emergence of the Persian Gulf area as a critical zone affecting the security and diplomatic interests of the United States.

American Involvement in the Middle East

Before World War II, the United States really had no foreign policy toward the Middle East. For more than a century and a half after the Revolutionary War, as we noted at length in Chapter 11, the United States was devoted to an "isolationist" foreign policy, entailing little or no involvement in external political affairs and crises. Another reason why contacts between the United States and the Middle East were minimal before World War II was that, after the collapse of the Ottoman Empire at the end of World War I, nearly all the nations in the region formed part of some European colonial system—particularly those of Great Britain and France. Until the end of World War II, France controlled North Africa, Lebanon, and Syria. Britain was dominant in Egypt, the Sudan, Jordan, Palestine, and Iraq. In addition, the Persian Gulf area was a Brit-

ish "sphere of influence."* Under international law and diplomatic custom, colonies and other dependencies did not maintain diplomatic relations with foreign countries.

Religious and Educational Activities

Among the societies of the West, Americans were latecomers in establishing contact with the Middle East. In the years after Napoleon's conquest of Egypt in 1798—awakening Western interest in "Egyptology" and other aspects of Middle Eastern culture—Americans began to develop ties with the region.

The first stage in this process involved the activities undertaken by missionaries and religious organizations. American Protestant missionaries entered Lebanon in the early 1820s. Owing to the missionary enterprise, the Syrian Protestant College—later renamed the American University in Beirut (AUB) —was established in 1866. In time, AUB, became (at least in some fields) the most outstanding institution of higher learning in the Middle East. By the end of the nineteenth century, AUB was a highly influential center for the emergence and promotion of Arab nationalism—a movement which, ironically, by the post-World War II period was

*The concept of "spheres of influence" is illustrated by the history of Iran, which escaped becoming a "colony" of a European power. Yet for some two centuries before its revolution in 1979, both Russia and Great Britain endeavored to bring Iran within its sphere of influence. During some periods, Russian power was dominant in the north, while British power controlled southern Iran. While Iran was nominally independent, particularly in matters of foreign and defense policy, its behavior was massively influenced by London and Moscow. By the early 1950s, the United States had largely displaced both the Soviet Union and Great Britain as the most influential foreign power in Iran. For a discussion of Iran's "dependency" upon the United States, see Amin Saikal, *The Rise and Fall of the Shah* (Princeton, N.J.: Princeton University Press, 1980), pp. 46–71.

directed against Western influence in the area.

American missionary and philanthropic organizations also founded Robert College in Turkey (in 1863)—providing one of the first opportunities available for qualified women in the Middle East to receive a higher education. The American University in Cairo (AUC) was also established (in 1919) by American groups interested in the advancement of Egypt. Even after Egyptian authorities placed all educational institutions under governmental control, following Nasser's revolution in 1952, AUC was permitted to operate and to exercise substantial *de facto* autonomy.[1]

American Political Influence

Political ideas and principles identified with the United States have been influential in the modern Middle East. In the pre-World War II period, the thought and ideas of President Woodrow Wilson exemplified this phenomenon. The Wilsonian concept of "self-determination"—or the belief that separate nationalities should become politically independent —was especially appealing to Arabs during and after World War I. As a result of their participation on the Allied side during the war, Arabs expected that they would receive independence at the end of the war. After they realized that self-determination did not apply to the Middle East—and they discovered that most of the region was placed under either French or British colonial jurisdiction—the Arabs felt a pervasive and profound sense of "betrayal" by the West.* Yet Wilsonian ideas attracted many converts throughout the Mid-

dle East and provided a stimulus to Arab nationalism in the years ahead. Until the creation of the State of Israel (in 1948), the United States enjoyed widespread prestige and admiration in the Arab world.[2]

Similarly, during and after World War II, the idealism identified with President Franklin D. Roosevelt also found wide appeal throughout the Middle East. FDR was an outspoken opponent of colonialism; according to some commentators, he viewed it as a serious threat to postwar freedom and stability; and on numerous occasions he expressed his opposition to the reimposition of British, French, and other Western colonial control over dependent peoples at the end of the war. Both Roosevelt, and his successor, President Harry S Truman, used their influence to bring about an end to European colonial systems in the Middle East and in other areas.[3]

Emerging Strategic Interests

World War II underscored the strategic importance of the Middle East for the security of the United States and its allies. Most military historians, for example, regard the Battle of North Africa—in which initially British, and later British, American, and French forces finally defeated German General Erwin Rommel's Afrika Corps—as a major turning point of World War II. The Allied victory in North

---

*In the Hussein-McMahon correspondence and other assurances, beginning on July 14, 1915, Great Britain had promised the Arabs political independence if they would revolt against Turkey and join the Allied cause. By conducting the "Revolt in the Desert," the Arabs fulfilled their part of the understanding. A few months later, however, in the Sykes-Picot agreement between Britain and

France (a secret accord, later revealed by the new Communist government of Russia), London and Paris arrived at an understanding dividing the Middle East between them after the war. The Sykes-Picot agreement in effect determined the political future of the Middle East. As a result of its terms, and of earlier colonization efforts, the French empire in the Middle East consisted of: North Africa (Morocco, Algeria, and Tunisia); Syria; and Lebanon. Britain's empire in the Middle East encompassed: Egypt and the Sudan; the newly created Kingdom of Trans-Jordan; Iraq; and the administration of a League of Nations "Mandate" over Palestine. In addition, British power was largely dominant in the Persian Gulf area.

Africa was an essential step in establishing naval and air supremacy over the Mediterranean area; it preserved the oil fields of the Middle East for use by the Allies; and (if the German Army had become dominant in North Africa) it may have averted a serious Axis threat to the security of the sea lanes of the south Atlantic, followed by the even more ominous prospect of an invasion of the Western Hemisphere.[4]

During the war also, the United States joined Great Britain and the Soviet Union in a tripartite occupation and administration of Iran (or Persia), whose oil fields were vital to the Allied war effort. The ruler of Iran since 1925, Reza Shah, was openly pro-German in his sympathies. As a result, he was deposed by the Allied powers early in the war, and his young son (who later ruled as Reza Shah Pahlavi, until his overthrow in 1979) became the nominal ruler. From the beginning of his reign, the Shah was dependent upon foreign powers. Throughout World War II, Allied control over Iran and the Persian Gulf area generally played an essential role in assuring victory over the Axis powers.[5]

America and the Arab-Israeli Dispute

For some two decades or more before World War II, American officials and citizens also became interested and involved in the controversy between pro-Israeli and pro-Arab forces over the future of Palestine. Toward the end of the nineteenth century the Zionist Movement was established and began to work energetically for the achievement of its goal—the creation of a "national home" for Jews in the historic land of Palestine. In time, this objective was broadened into the idea of creating what was sometimes called a "Jewish Commonwealth" or the State of Israel, which came into being on May 14, 1948.

During and after World War I, this Zionist goal received enthusiastic endorse-

ment by governmental officials and private groups within the United States. President Woodrow Wilson, for example, was a vocal champion of Zionist goals, as was Supreme Court Justice Felix Frankfurter. Zionist aspirations were also endorsed by resolutions of Congress and by comparable resolutions passed by a number of state legislatures.[6] President Franklin D. Roosevelt also repeatedly and publicly expressed his approval of Zionist objectives.[7] (Yet FDR also promised Arab leaders at the end of World War II that no steps affecting the future of Palestine would be taken by the Allies that were contrary to Arab interests.)[8] After Roosevelt's death, President Harry S Truman added his voice and influence to those supporting Zionist aims in Palestine.[9]

By the late 1930s, official sentiment in Great Britain had moved to a more pro-Arab position. (Among other reasons for the change, as World War II approached, London feared the adverse effects upon Arab opinion of continued Zionist agitation for control over Palestine.) As a result, Zionist groups shifted their base of operations to the United States. During and after World War II, as we noted in our earlier analysis of public opinion (Chapter 8), pro-Israeli groups mounted an intensive and continuing campaign to influence American opinion favorably toward the Zionist cause. By the early postwar period, the United States had emerged as a potent champion of Israel's cause in the international system. American influence, for example, was crucial in the decision by the United Nations to "partition" Palestine into separate Jewish and Arab states (a plan that was nullified by the results of the "first round" of fighting between Israeli and Arab forces after British troops withdrew from Palestine).[10] For three decades or more after 1948, the United States remained Israel's benefactor and closest supporter in its continuing controversy with the Arab states.

Commercial and Economic Links

By the post-World War II period, the United States had developed extensive and important commercial ties with the Middle East, particularly in the oil industries of the region. In 1908, oil was first discovered in significant commercial quantities in Iran. In order to provide cheap fuel for the Royal Navy, Great Britain took the lead in the early exploration and development of the Persian oil fields. Within a few years, however—as substantial oil deposits were discovered in adjacent Middle Eastern countries—other foreign business interests (often supported by their home governments) became active in the nascent oil industry of the region. In the Middle East, the United States government supported the same principle—the concept of the "Open Door"—that Washington had espoused for many years in Asia: American business firms should have equal participation with those of other countries in the exploration, production, and marketing of Middle East oil.

Even before World War I (as early as 1909), American business interests had acquired "concessions" from the Ottoman Empire to prospect for, and produce, oil in Middle Eastern fields. In time, American involvement in the Middle East oil industry came to be heavily concentrated in two countries: Saudi Arabia and Kuwait. On May 29, 1933, the Standard Oil Company of California received a large concession to develop the oil reserves within Saudi Arabia. When other firms joined the venture, a new corporation—the Arabian American Oil Company (ARAMCO)—was formed.* In time, ARAMCO became the most influential foreign corporation in the Middle East oil industry, ultimately exporting as much as 10 million barrels of oil daily; and Saudi Arabia emerged as the leading oil producing state, not only in the region but in the world. From the early 1930s, Saudi Arabia's economic destiny was linked closely to America; and as time passed—when Saudi Arabia became the oil giant of the Middle East—the economic well-being of the United States was in turn vitally affected by the decisions of the government of Saudi Arabia.

Located at the head of the Persian Gulf, the tiny state of Kuwait (slightly smaller than the state of New Jersey) has also maintained close economic links with the United States. Late in 1934, Kuwait granted a concession to the Anglo-Iranian Oil Company and to the Gulf Oil Corporation to develop its oil resources. The operating affiliate of these two firms—the Kuwait Oil Company—explored and developed the vast Burgan oil field. After the Iranian Revolution of 1979, Kuwait in time became the third-largest oil producer in the region; and by the end of the 1970s Kuwait had the highest per capita income (estimated at over $15,000 annually) of any country on the globe.[11]

America and the Middle East Before World War II

While the United States had established contacts with, and acquired interests in, the Middle East before World War II, several salient facts about this background period are worth noting. In the main, America's relations with the societies of the Middle East were episodic and fragmentary. The United States had no *sustained* contact with the region prior to World War II.

Moreover, American involvement in the Middle East in the pre-World War II period came about for the most part as the result of activities by *private* citizens' groups and business organizations in the United States. This

*ARAMCO was jointly owned and operated as a consortium of four major American oil companies: Standard Oil of California, the Texas Company (Texaco), Standard Oil of New Jersey, and Socony. Following a series of negotiations, it came into existence in 1947. See Robert B. Krueger, *The United States and International Oil* (New York: Praeger Publishers, 1975), p. 52.

aspect of early American involvement in the Middle East had both a positive and negative dimension. On the positive side, it meant that (in contrast to the European colonial powers) the United States government was not engaged in colonialism in the region; and Washington was not required (as were Britain and France) to intervene militarily to impose its political authority upon Middle Eastern societies.

A negative consequence of the dominant role played by private organizations in pre-World War II American activities in the Middle East was the fact that religious organizations, business firms, and other private groups were sometimes oblivious to the long-term foreign policy implications of their activities in the region; and the United States government often exercised little or no *effective control* over their activities. Even when they did not intentionally do so, private citizens' groups perhaps inevitably became embroiled in the political life of Middle Eastern societies. And in some cases—Protestant missionary enterprises in the Sudan were an outstanding example—missionary groups on the scene, often vocally supported by their affiliated religious organizations within the United States, actively sought to influence political decisions affecting their interests. In such a setting, political tensions within the country were often aggravated and made more difficult to resolve.

In time also, in pursuing their objectives American business corporations and interests acquired a substantial degree of *de facto* freedom from control by officials in Washington. In the post-World War II period, ARAMCO became the epitome of a multinational corporation whose activities had momentous consequences for the society within which it operated. Decisions made by ARAMCO with regard to the development, production, and marketing of petroleum products had a crucial impact upon American foreign policy in the Middle East. Yet such decisions by ARAMCO, often working in close concert with the government of Saudi Arabia, were often arrived at with little or no consideration given to their diplomatic implications, to their impact upon America's overall position in the Middle East, or to their future effects for the well-being of the American society.

In addition, these nongovernmental activities in the region meant that America's relations with the Middle East were highly *fragmented and uncoordinated.* Insofar as the United States had a "foreign policy" toward the region at all down to the end of World War II, it consisted of several distinct and isolated activities that collectively lacked coherence or central direction. Almost never did officials in Washington concern themselves about the overall impact of pro-Zionist groups or American oil companies upon long-term American diplomatic interests in the Middle East.

The Arab-Israeli Conflict

The Palestinian Controversy in Perspective

Over 40 years ago, a commission appointed by the British government to investigate the causes of violence and political upheaval in Palestine reported that:

> An irrepressible conflict has arisen between two national communities within the narrow bounds of one small country [Palestine]. About 1,000,000 Arabs are in strife, open or latent, with some 400,000 Jews. There is no common ground between them. . . . The conflict was inherent in the situation from the outset. . . . [and] the conflict has grown steadily more bitter. . . . The intensification of the conflict will continue . . . it seems probable that the situation, bad as it now is, will grow worse. The conflict will go on, the gulf between the Arabs and Jews will widen.[12]

Since the end of World War II—by some criteria, since the period of World War I—the Middle East has been gripped by a conflict that tends to affect nearly every aspect of its life and to plunge the region into a new round of military hostilities, not excluding the prospect of a Soviet-American confrontation. With suitable adaptations to take account of events since 1937, the quotation cited above could accurately describe conditions in the Middle East in the early 1980s. Assuming that it began during World War I, the Arab-Israeli conflict has entered its second half century; and prospects are far from favorable that the sources of contention between the belligerents will soon be resolved.

For a number of fundamental reasons, the Arab-Israeli controversy has been—and remains—a central issue in American diplomacy. Directly or indirectly, the United States has been a party to the dispute since the late 1940s, when the state of Israel was established; its existence has been repeatedly contested by the Arab states. To the Arab mind, the United States played a decisive role in the creation of Israel; and since 1948, America has emerged as Israel's most influential supporter in the international system. Nearly every dimension of United States-Arab relations in the postwar period has been profoundly affected by this fact. To the minds of many commentators, America's long-standing identification with Israel has been the principal barrier to Arab-American friendship. The outbreak of war between Israel and the Arab states has posed the ever-present danger of a direct Soviet-American confrontation in the Middle East, with the attendant risk of global war.

By the 1970s, the United States and other industrialized nations had become extremely vulnerable to an "oil boycott" imposed by major oil-producing states of the Middle East as a weapon in their ongoing campaign against Israel and its foreign supporters. The continued existence of the Arab-Israeli conflict also aggravated existing internal tension in several Middle Eastern countries (such as Jordan and Lebanon), adding another source of political upheaval to an already volatile region. In nearly all Arab countries, political leaders had to be extremely careful about overly close identification with the United States, because of popular resentment toward Israel and its foreign supporters. Moreover, as we observed in Chapter 8, Washington's policy toward the Arab-Israeli conflict was a contentious issue in American public opinion and domestic political life. Few foreign policy questions, it is safe to say, aroused such pressure group activity—and evoked such strong public reactions—as American diplomacy toward the Arab-Israeli dispute. For these reasons, the quarrel between Israel and its Arab neighbors has preoccupied foreign policy officials in the United States for more than a generation. Until Arab-Israeli differences are resolved, the Middle East is likely to remain perhaps the most volatile region in the contemporary international system.

The Zionist Movement

Although its historic antecedents can be traced back to Old Testament times, the Zionist Movement—whose ultimate goal was the reestablishment of a Jewish state in Palestine—emerged toward the end of the nineteenth century.* This was a period of intense

---

*At this stage, the reader needs to be reminded of a point made earlier, in Chapter 8. Although the origins of the Zionist Movement go back into ancient Jewish history and religious tradition, Zionism is essentially a *political* movement, whose goal became the creation of a Jewish national state in Palestine. In America, for example, this Zionist goal was supported by many non-Jewish individuals and groups (like President Harry S Truman and several religious organizations). It has been consistently endorsed by majorities in the American Congress and by

and recurrent anti-Semitism in Europe (particularly in Eastern Europe and Czarist Russia). In this context, a Jewish journalist living in the Austro-Hungarian Empire named Theodor Herzl published an analysis of the "Jewish problem" entitled *The Jewish State* (1896). Herzl's position was that Jews would always be second-class citizens in the countries in which they lived until they had a "homeland" of their own, Israel. Under the auspices of Zionist organizations, Jewish settlers began to acquire land in Palestine and to establish agricultural settlements (the "Kibbutz" movement) even while Palestine was still governed by the Ottoman Empire.[13]

A landmark in the realization of Zionist objectives was the Balfour Declaration, issued by Great Britain on November 2, 1917. In this statement—announced by the British cabinet as part of its efforts to win Jewish support throughout Europe for the Allied war effort—London substantially accepted the Zionist goal and promised to support it. The Balfour Declaration stated:

> His Majesty's Government view with favour the establishment in Palestine of a National Home for the Jewish People, and will use their best endeavors to facilitate the achievement of this object, it being clearly understood that nothing shall be done which may prejudice the civil and religious rights of existing non-Jewish communities in Palestine, or the rights and political status enjoyed by Jews in any other country.[14]

---

state legislatures. Conversely, all Jews are not necessarily Zionists. Some believe that the "rebirth" or revival of Israel should be viewed as a theological or spiritual regeneration, not a political objective. Arabs have said time and again that they *are* anti-Zionist: They oppose the creation and policies of the state of Israel. But they are *not* anti-Jewish or anti-Semitic, in the sense that they oppose Jewish culture or the Jewish religious faith. Arabs have repeatedly pointed out that Jews found sanctuary in the Middle East during periods of persecution in the West.

Several points about this historic pronouncement are worth noting. In the declaration, Great Britain promised to support the cause of a Jewish "National Home" in Palestine after the war. Whatever that concept meant precisely, in later years British officials emphasized that it was *not* synonymous with the creation of a Jewish *national state* embracing all (or most) of Palestine, as Zionists in time demanded. The Balfour Declaration was also *a highly qualified and conditional commitment:* In it, Britain pledged not to prejudice the rights of "existing non-Jewish communities in Palestine" (principally, of course, the Arabs, who comprised over 80 percent of Palestine's population). Moreover, during and after World War I Arabs complained vocally that Great Britain had no legal right to issue the Balfour Declaration. Palestine was not a British possession or territory. In Arab eyes, this pledge also was directly contrary to other pledges—given earlier to Arabs—that the countries of the Middle East would become independent after World War I.[15]

For supporters of Zionism, the issuance of the Balfour Declaration was a significant victory and a notable step forward in the achievement of their goals. After World War I, Jewish immigration into Palestine continued apace. The movement was greatly accelerated by the emergence of Nazism in Germany; one of Hitler's avowed goals was the solution of the "Jewish problem" by the extermination of Europe's Jewish population. In the ensuing Holocaust, millions of European Jews died in Hitler's concentration camps; those who could tried to escape—and many of these sought refuge in Palestine.

Great Britain emerged from World War I with a League of Nations "Mandate" over Palestine. This meant that the country was under the legal jurisdiction of the international community; and British administration was directed at the ultimate goal of self-government. The terms of the Mandate also specified that Great Britain was to implement the provisions of the Balfour Declaration in Palestine. During the interwar period, the history of Palestine was punctuated by continuing episodes of violence and conflict between Zionists and Arabs—both of whom in time opposed British policies. Inside and outside Palestine, Arabs became alarmed about ongoing Jewish immigration and settlement in the country; Arabs blamed London for encouraging Zionist aspirations at their expense. Hitler's attempt to exterminate Europe's Jews of course reenforced Zionists in their conviction that continued access to Palestine was essential and that Jews would remain unprotected in all countries until the state of Israel came into being.

Caught in this crossfire—and increasingly alarmed about the threat of war in Europe—Great Britain sought on several occasions to find some basis of agreement between Zionists and Arabs on the Palestine issue. London's attempts repeatedly failed. At length, on May 17, 1939, London issued a "White Paper" on the Palestine problem designed to resolve the issue.[16] It called for substantial reductions in the level of Jewish immigration into Palestine, and after five years, such immigration was to cease altogether; the transfer of land to Jewish settlers in the country was also sharply curtailed. As in the past, Zionists and Arabs alike rejected this scheme. Zionists were adamant in their insistence upon unimpeded access to Palestine as one means of escaping Hitler's barbarities toward the Jewish population of Europe. After the issuance of the White Paper, as depicted in the popular novel *Exodus,* Jewish groups continued to enter Palestine despite British objections; and the conflict involving Jewish, Arab, and British forces in the country intensified.

The Palestine question was eclipsed by

World War II (but, although largely unpublicized, the conflict continued during the war). After the Axis defeat, the Palestine issue erupted once more. Zionist groups (having transferred their base of operations during the war to the United States) remained committed to achieving their goals; the Arabs of the Middle East were no less determined to oppose them. Meanwhile, as we have noted in other contexts, Great Britain emerged from the war with its power greatly impaired. Confronted with a renewal of the contest in Palestine, British policy makers decided to relinquish the Mandate over Palestine and to withdraw their forces from the country. In 1947, London informed the newly created United Nations (the successor to the League of Nations) of that momentous decision.

As Great Britain itself had done many times previously, the United Nations embarked upon a detailed "study" of the Palestine controversy in an effort to find a solution to it. Its proposed solution (considered earlier and rejected by Great Britain) was the "partition" of the country into separate Jewish and Arab states; theoretically (since both proposed states would be miniscule and neither would be economically viable), they would preserve close economic and other ties with each other. The "partition " plan for troubled Palestine was adopted by the UN General Assembly by a vote of 33 to 13 on November 29, 1947. A few months later, the planned British evacuation of Palestine was carried out.[17]

The Creation of Israel and the "First Round"

The United Nations had no more success than Great Britain in resolving the Palestine controversy. The Zionists were disappointed about the small area allocated to them in Palestine; even the proposed Jewish state would have an Arab majority. But on balance,

Zionists *accepted* the plan as better than any available alternatives to it. The Arab reaction was predictable and less equivocal: Inside and outside Palestine, Arab opinion was overwhelmingly hostile to it. Arabs vowed to oppose the division of Palestine by all means at their disposal, including the use of armed force.

In the months following the UN's adoption of the partition proposal, active warfare—sometimes called the "first round" in the postwar Arab-Israeli conflict—erupted in the area. At the moment of its birth, the new state of Israel—proclaimed by Jewish authorities in Jerusalem on May 14, 1948—faced extinction from the Arab military threat. But determined to preserve their newly gained independence, Jewish groups in Palestine—heavily supported by Zionist organizations abroad—mounted a determined and ingenious (one is tempted to call it "miraculous") defense effort against the numerically superior enemies. Following a series of brilliant military engagements, Israel won the "first round" against its adversaries. The state of Israel—greatly enlarged by the addition of new territories to it—now appeared to have been securely established and (for the time being at least) to be safe from overt Arab military threats.[18]

Yet the "first round" in the Arab-Israeli quarrel left a residue of bitter enmity and a long list of unresolved issues that kept the Middle East in a condition of actual or incipient war for over a generation thereafter. Israel's military victory in 1947–1948 did nothing to make the Arabs "accept" its existence or abandon their animosity to it. Arabs widely blamed the United States for Israel's existence and for the expansion of its borders in the "first round." The Truman Administration had been active diplomatically in gaining United Nations support for the partition of Palestine.[19] After the plan was adopted, of-

ficial and private American support for Israel (and Arabs seldom distinguished between them) was essential for its survival. Arabs viewed Israel as a new Western colonial outpost in the Middle East that had been "imposed" upon them during a period of Arab weakness and backwardness.

Another intractable issue growing out of the "first round" was the complex "Arab refugee" issue, to which no solution has yet been found. During the war, a large number (variously estimated as high as 900,000) of Palestinian Arabs became refugees. In time, most of them became wards of the United Nations, which administered the refugee camps (primarily in the Gaza Strip in Egypt, in Jordan, and in Lebanon) in which they lived. As the years passed, the refugee camps emerged as hotbeds of political agitation and anti-Israeli sentiment; groups opposing Israel (like the Palestine Liberation Organization and related movements) often recruited their members from the ranks of the Arab refugees. As on other issues, the Israeli and Arab interpretations of why the refugee problem arose—and of how it ought to be solved—differed markedly. To the Israeli mind, the refugee problem was an outgrowth of Arab determination to "drive Israel into the sea" and of violent Arab opposition to Israel's existence. Arabs contended that the Arab refugees of Palestine had been "driven from their lands" by Zionist groups, who subsequently incorporated these lands into territories controlled by Israel; some of the lands were used for the resettlement of new settlers to Israel in the years ahead. Even today, the full truth of how the Arab refugee problem came to be created is perhaps not fully known. There is perhaps some validity in both explanations of the phenomenon. What is less debatable is that the existence of the refugee camps added another source of controversy to the already inflamed Arab-Israeli dispute.[20]

The Continuing Pattern of Violence

Although victorious in the "first round" against its Arab adversaries, Israel found that Arab animosity toward it remained undiminished. The Arab states refused to make peace with Israel; they imposed an economic boycott upon commerce with Israel (and upon foreign firms doing business with it); the Suez Canal was closed to Israeli-bound traffic; and the Arab states refused to recognize Israel or have any form of diplomatic relations with it. Since the United States was identified by Arabs as Israel's mentor, several of the Arab states turned to Soviet Russia for assistance in pursuing their continuing struggle against Zionism. Moscow, which had originally voted *for* the creation of the state of Israel in the United Nations, shifted to a pro-Arab stance, which it has continued to the present day.

The Egyptian Revolution of July 23, 1952, carried out by military officers led by Colonel Gamal Abdel Nasser, was a climactic event both for Egypt and for the regional stability of the Middle East. Within a few months, President Nasser of Egypt had emerged as the most influential Arab spokesman and an aspirant to a leadership role in the emerging Third World. In company with most Arabs, Nasser was anti-Zionist and determined to continue the struggle against Israel; and he also sought to modernize one of the most backward societies on the globe—goals which were, in many respects, incompatible. A high national priority of Nasser's government was the modernization of the Egyptian armed forces. Nasser initially sought the assistance of the United States and other Western governments in achieving this objective; but his efforts were rebuffed in Washington and other Western capitals. Nasser also requested large-scale American economic assistance for the construction of the Aswan High Dam—a vast and complex engineering project that was expected to transform the Egyptian economic system (especially agriculture) by providing a new source of electric power and adding new productive land through the extension of irrigation. After the Egyptian government accepted an offer of arms aid from the Soviet Union, the Eisenhower Administration abruptly informed Nasser that American funds would not be available for the construction of the Aswan High Dam project. Washington's refusal to provide economic assistance to Egypt prompted Nasser's government to seek Soviet aid for the project. From the late 1950s until Soviet officials and aid technicians were expelled from Egypt in 1972, the U.S.S.R. served as Egypt's principal benefactor and supplier of economic and military assistance.[21]

The other momentous consequence of the Aswan Dam episode was Nassar's decision on July 26, 1956, to "nationalize" the Suez Canal (previously owned and operated by the British-controlled Suez Canal Company). Nasser's act precipitated a new armed conflict (the Suez Crisis of 1956, or the "second round" in the Arab-Israeli quarrel) in the Middle East. Chagrined at Nasser's anti-Western stance and his most recent act in nationalizing the Suez Canal, Great Britain, France, and Israel planned a joint military operation against Egypt, with the avowed purpose of overthrowing Nasser's regime. British and French paratroops landed in Egypt (with little effective Egyptian resistance); and Israeli forces occupied the country up to the east bank of the Suez Canal. Again, Israel and its allies scored a dramatic military victory over their Arab adversaries.

Anglo-French-Israeli officials, however, miscalculated badly with regard to two developments related to the Suez Crisis. One of these—the most crucial factor affecting the outcome of events—was the reaction of the United States. The Eisenhower Administration had been kept in ignorance of the impending invasion of Egypt by its Western allies and Israel. After the military strike had been successfully carried out, Washington demanded that foreign forces immediately be evacuated from Egyptian territory. (In the same period, the Soviet Union had invaded Czechoslovakia, placing that country under Moscow's direct military control. The Administration's view was that aggression could not simultaneously be *condemned* when engaged in by the Kremlin and *accepted* when carried out by America's friends and allies.) Under strong American pressure, the Anglo-French-Israeli incursion into Egypt was reversed. A United Nations "Emergency Force" (UNEF) was stationed along the Egyptian-Israeli frontier to prevent a new outbreak of violence.

The other major consequence of the Suez Crisis was that—despite his country's military defeat—President Nasser of Egypt emerged from it with his prestige and standing within the Arab world greatly enhanced. Owing largely to American diplomatic intervention (for which Washington received little credit among the Arab states), Egyptian sovereignty was preserved and the external threat to overthrow Nasser's government failed to accomplish its purpose. Paradoxically, these events *improved* Nasser's image at home and abroad, and Arab animosity toward Israel and its foreign supporters remained undiminished.[22] After the Suez Crisis, several Arab states drew even closer to the Soviet Union.

Meanwhile, Israel remained dependent upon American assistance—particularly the *private* contributions and loans provided by the Jewish community and other friends of Israel in the United States. For three decades or more, this assistance has been crucial in enabling Israel to meet its internal needs and to preserve its national security.

Jewish immigration into Israel also continued at a high level. By the mid-1950s, the nature of this movement had begun to change fundamentally, presenting Israel with a new set of social, economic, and political problems. Down to that period, the early settlers of Israel ("the pioneers") had largely come from the West. Called the *Ashkenazim* or "Western Jews," this group (from central and eastern Europe) had founded the state of Israel and largely controlled its economic and political life. The second wave of immigrants into Israel consisted of the "Oriental Jews" or the *Sephardim,* (originally from Spain and Portugal) whose homelands were the countries of the Middle East and the Mediterranean area. These immigrants were often drawn from the lower economic and social classes; not infrequently, they were illiterate, unskilled, and destitute. The "assimilation" of the Oriental Jews imposed an enormous financial burden upon the government of Israel. As time passed, this group believed that it faced discrimination by the *Ashkenazim* who continued to dominate most spheres of Israeli life. The electoral victory of the right-wing Likud Party, led by Menachem Begin, in 1977 signified the growing political influence of this segment of the Israeli population.[23]

The Six-Day War and its Aftermath

A series of events early in 1967 led to the outbreak of the "third round" in the Arab-Israeli conflict. With Arab animosity toward Israel unabated—and with Israel resorting from time to time to massive "retaliatory" attacks against its enemies—the threat of war hung ominously over the region. Late in May, President Nasser demanded the withdrawal of the UN Emergency Force from Egyptian territory; and he moved to block Israeli use of the Gulf of Aqaba (from which Israeli received its strategic oil supplies, chiefly from Iran). On June 5, 1967, the government of

Israel launched a "preemptive strike" against Egypt, Syria, and Jordan. The Russian-equipped Egyptian and Syrian air forces were almost totally destroyed on the ground, leaving Arab armored and infantry forces virtually defenseless against superior Israeli airpower. In the Sinai, Egyptian forces were decimated; and comparable defeats were inflicted upon Syrian and Jordanian troops. In brief, the "Six-Day War" was a military disaster for the Arab cause. Israeli forces occupied the Sinai up to the eastern shore of the Suez Canal; captured the Old City of Jerusalem (formerly administered by Jordan); occupied the West Bank of the Jordan River (Jordan's most productive sector); and improved its defensive positions at Syria's expense in the Golan Heights area.[24]

Besides these territorial and strategic changes, the Six-Day War had a number of significant long-term consequences for the stability of the Middle East. The enemies of Israel began to rely much more heavily upon a new tactic—guerrilla warfare and terrorism—to express their hostility. After 1967, the Palestine Liberation Organization (PLO) and other guerrilla organizations allied with it became the most active and resourceful antagonists of Israel in the Middle East.* Using

bases in Jordan (and later in Lebanon), Arab guerrilla groups mounted a continuing campaign of raids, assassinations, bombings, and other forms of violence against Israel and its supporters. Following its customary policy of "massive retaliation," Israel responded with air and ground strikes against guerrilla bases and Arab villages in Jordan, Lebanon, and other locales, in an effort to "punish" those responsible for such deeds.

For Jordan particularly, the activities of the PLO and other guerrilla groups posed an increasingly serious internal threat to the authority and stability of King Hussein's regime. With tension between the monarchy and the PLO mounting steadily, late in 1970 the long-expected internal crisis erupted. King Hussein's Bedouin-dominated military forces were "unleashed" against the Arab guerrillas. In the devastation that followed, the PLO and other guerrilla groups were defeated and expelled from Jordan; they took sanctuary in southern Lebanon.[25] As they had done in Jordan, these guerrilla organizations defied the

---

*According to some commentators, the Palestine "resistance" movement can be traced back to the period of World War I, when Arab Palestinians actively opposed both Zionism and British mandatory rule in Palestine. Yet it was not until the devastating Arab defeat in the 1967 war in the Middle East that Palestine guerrilla organizations began to play an active role in opposing Israel. Earlier victories by guerrilla movements over French forces in Algeria—along with the success of the Viet Cong against superior American military forces in Vietnam in this period—provided an inducement to Arabs to follow this course. The largest and most influential of these groups—the Palestine Liberation Organization (PLO)—had been established in 1964; it was led by Yasir Arafat, who endeavored to stay on reasonably amicable terms with most Arab governments. Among Palestine

resistance groups, the Arafat-led PLO (with its military arm, *Al Fatah*) was considered "moderate" in its political goals and methods. Other guerrilla organizations—such as the Popular Front for the Liberation of Palestine, led by Dr. George Habash—not only militantly opposed Israel but also advocated political revolutions against established Arab governments (such as Egypt and Saudi Arabia). In time, some Arab governments established and supported their own resistance movements—such as *As Saiqa* (controlled by the Ba'ath Party of Syria) and *Fatah al Islam* (controlled by Saudi Arabia). As the nominal "leader" of a coalition of Palestine resistance organizations, Yasir Arafat was increasingly challenged to impose central authority and cohesion upon the movement. For background on the emergence of these organizations, see Hisham Sharabi, *Palestine and Israel: the Lethal Dilemma* (New York: Pegasus, 1969), pp. 182–210. For more detailed discussion, see Gerard Chaliand, *The Palestinian Resistance* (Baltimore: Penguin Books, 1972); and Charles A. Joiner, *The Fedayeen and Arab World Politics* (Morristown, N.J.: General Learning Press, 1974).

authority of the feeble and internally divided government of Lebanon, and they were in time largely responsible for plunging that country into a civil war that continues to the present day.[26]

A lasting and momentous consequence of the Six-Day War also was the Arab states' discovery of "oil power" as an effective diplomatic weapon. Before 1967, the major oil-producing states of the Middle East had seldom used this vital resource to promote their diplomatic objectives; in 1967, for the first time, they employed the weapon against Israel and its Western supporters. The oil boycott caused economic distress in the United States—but it proved potentially disastrous for the industrialized European nations, which depended heavily upon the Middle East for their petroleum supplies. As described in Chapter 11, after 1967 the NATO allies began to make an intensive search for alternative energy sources. They were aware that America had partially met their needs during the Six-Day War by oil shipments from its own reserves. But with its own oil resources diminishing—and with consumption in the United States continuing to climb—America was in no position to ship oil to Western Europe in a future Middle Eastern conflict.

The 1967 war had another significant result: For the first time—largely in response to the Israeli "annexation" of the Old City of Jerusalem—Saudi Arabia and the smaller states rimming the Persian Gulf became involved in the Arab-Israeli conflict. As the center of the Wahhabi (or "Puritanical") sect of Sunni Islam, and as the nation controlling the two holy shrines of Mecca and Medina, Saudi Arabia was uniquely offended by Israel's act.

Saudi opposition to Israel after 1967 took two concrete and sometimes menacing forms. Using its vast oil wealth, Saudi Arabia provided large subsidies to the Palestine Liberation Organization and other guerrilla groups carrying on the struggle against Israel. And as the largest oil-producing state in the Middle East, Saudi Arabia's views were likely to prove crucial in determining whether the Arab states once again relied upon "oil power" to achieve their diplomatic goals.[27]

The Six-Day War removed none of the underlying causes of tension between Israel and its Arab neighbors. Having again demonstrated their military prowess, Israelis became increasingly frustrated to discover that the Arabs were unwilling to make peace and to engage in normal diplomatic relations with the state of Israel. Throughout the years that followed, the Israeli society was required to devote an inordinately high percentage of its governmental revenues to defense expenditures. As for the Arab states, they viewed the military debacle of 1967 as merely a "temporary" setback in their anti-Zionist campaign; and they were determined to reverse that outcome in the future.

The Yom Kippur War and Its Consequences

Against this background, another "round" in the ongoing Arab-Israeli conflict was perhaps inevitable. On September 28, 1970, Egyptian President Gamal Abdel Nasser died. After an internal power struggle—in which he successfully defeated both left-wing and right-wing efforts to seize power—Anwar el-Sadat emerged as the new leader of Egypt. Initially (although in time he departed from many of Nasser's internal and external policies), Sadat vowed to continue on the course Nasser had set—including an active Egyptian role in spearheading the opposition to Israel.[28] On several occasions, Sadat promised his fellow Egyptians that they would be victorious against Israel. Events were to reveal that Sadat's speeches were not merely idle boasts or propaganda exercises.

Political Changes in the Arab World

Meanwhile, the overall political environment within the Middle East was undergoing significant changes, several of which had major implications for the Arab-Israeli conflict. For example, the Ba'ath Party—another militantly anti-Israeli organization—had gained control of Syria and Iraq. While both countries had Ba'athist governments, the "right-wing Ba'ath" controlled Syria, while the "left-wing Ba'ath" led Iraq. After the dissolution of the United Arab Republic (UAR)—the ill-fated union between Syria and Egypt—in 1961, the Ba'ath Party established its political dominance in Syria. Military elements—consisting predominantly of Alawites, a Shi'ite minority centered in northwestern Syria—were the dominant group within the Ba'athist regime. In 1970, General Hafez al-Assad became president of Syria. At home, Assad embarked upon a series of sweeping reforms designed to modernize the country and to improve its economic productivity. Assad's regime encountered mounting domestic opposition—largely from the Sunni Moslem majority that was deeply suspicious of Alawite goals and motives. Abroad, Assad was determined to carry on the confrontation with Israel, to regain Israeli-occupied Syrian territories, and to make Syria an influential regional power. Relations between Syria and Iraq became progressively more hostile and suspicious.[29] After the eruption of the Iraqi-Iranian war in 1980, Syria openly supported Iran (a non-Arab country) against Iraq in this conflict!

By contrast, the "left-wing Ba'ath," which gained control of Iraq early in 1963, was a civilian-led regime in which military elements were subordinate. The Iraqi Revolution of July 14, 1958, had resulted in the overthrow of the Hashemite monarchy and the inauguration of radical changes in many aspects of national life. For a decade or more thereafter,

authorities in Baghdad were severely challenged to deal with the Kurdish rebellion in the northern provinces, to unify the country politically, and to meet the economic needs of the society. After several changes in government, a Ba'ath-led coup in 1963—followed by successful Ba'athist efforts to subdue its political rivals—gradually brought a measure of political stability to this strife-torn country.

By the mid-1970s, the dominant figure in the Iraqi political system was the "strong man" Saddam Hussein. President Hussein was an ambitious, ruthless, and determined national leader whose goals were to modernize the country internally and to make Iraq an influential regional power (particularly after the collapse of the Iranian monarchy in 1979). As the head of a Ba'athist-controlled government, Hussein was militantly anti-Zionist; and he was intent upon playing an influential role in the "Rejectionist Front" against Israel. After the collapse of the Iranian monarchy—followed by a period of prolonged internal strife that greatly weakened the authority and effectiveness of the Ayatollah Khomeini's government—in September, 1980, Iraq's armed forces invaded southern Iran. Initially, Iraqi troops scored significant military gains, seizing a substantial portion of Iranian territory and largely closing down the Iranian oil industry. These developments of course posed a new and grave challenge to an already crisis-prone government in Tehran. For a time, it appeared that Saddam Hussein's regime would achieve its goal of becoming the new arbiter of the Persian Gulf area. By the spring of 1982, however, the tide of battle in the Iraqi-Iranian war had turned. Iran (which was some two and a half times larger than its opponent) had launched a successful counteroffensive, inflicting heavy casualties upon the Iraqi invader and freeing most of Iranian territory. The Ba'athist government of Iraq appeared to have failed in its effort to seize Iran's principal oil-producing area and to topple its ideological rival, the clerically-dominated government of Iran. Indeed, by mid-1982—in view of the mounting cost of the war to Iraq and its growing casualties—the future of Saddam Hussein's regime now hung in the balance. An impending Iraqi defeat could leave Iran in the position it had achieved under the Shah: the dominant military power of the Persian Gulf region.[30]

Important political developments had also occurred elsewhere in the Arab world. On September 1, 1969, the Libyan monarchy headed by King Idris—for several years viewed as one of the most "pro-American" governments in the region—was overthrown by a military *coup*. Under the revolutionary regime, led by Colonel Muammar al-Qaddafi, fundamental changes took place in all aspects of Libyan life. Qaddafi reversed Libya's former pro-Western stance; relations between Libya and Egypt became overtly hostile; and in time Qaddafi became an outspoken adversary of Israel. (Funds from Libya's oil income were used to support the PLO and other guerrilla groups carrying on the struggle against Zionism.) Libya also became a vocal member of the Rejectionist Front opposed to a peace treaty with Israel.[31]

We have already referred to the civil war in Jordan that erupted in 1970–1971 between the forces loyal to the monarchy and Arab guerrilla organizations. Although King Hussein's Bedouin-based army won that contest, in the years that followed his regime suffered two reverses impairing its authority and prestige. One was the adverse economic effects stemming from Israel's occupation of the fertile "West Bank"—Jordan's principal agricultural sector. The other adverse force was the diplomatic defeat sustained by Jordan when, at an Arab summit conference in Morocco in October 1974, the Arab states recognized the Palestine Liberation Organiza-

tion as the "legitimate" representative of, and spokesman for, the Arabs of Palestine. Toward the Arab-Israeli dispute, the Jordanian government became increasingly skeptical about a peace settlement, particularly when it discerned no change in Israel's determination to retain the West Bank and the Old City of Jerusalem under its jurisdiction. Moreover, by the early 1980s, Jordanian officials faced two new developments directly affecting the country's foreign policy orientation: renewed efforts by Arab guerrilla organizations to use Jordanian territory for attacks against Israel; and the war between Iraq and Iran (in which Jordan became one of Iraq's most vocal supporters). Since Iraq had emerged as one of the most vocal centers of anti-Americanism in the Middle East, Jordan's behavior caused genuine apprehensions in Washington.

After Nasser's death in 1970, Anwar Sadat became the new president of Egypt. For several months, Sadat continued Nasser's policies: Cairo remained at the forefront of Arab opposition to Israel; Egyptian-American relations continued to be distant and mutually suspicious; and Egypt preserved close ties with the Soviet Union. For example, in 1971 Egypt signed a 15-year treaty of friendship with the U.S.S.R.

Then in July 1972, Sadat electrified the world by announcing that he had ordered the "expulsion" of 15,000 or more Soviet officials and aid technicians from Egyptian soil! His act was motivated by three dominant considerations. One was the fact that internal opposition (particularly among the Egyptian military) had risen steadily against this large and alien Russian presence. On numerous occasions, Russian officials had offended Egyptian dignity and had threatened its political independence. Second, Sadat feared that—in his forthcoming offensive against Israel—the Soviet Union might endeavor to *restrain* Egyptian behavior. Third, in order to achieve both his internal and external goals, Sadat concluded that an improvement in Egypt's relations with the United States was imperative. Ever since the Six-Day War in 1967, no formal relations had existed between the United States and Egypt. As a result, Egypt was denied two things that Sadat came to believe were essential to achieve his goals: American economic assistance and private investment needed to promote Egypt's internal development; and—as the only foreign country with sufficient influence to do so—the cooperation of the United States in changing Israel's external policies.

On October 6, 1973—while Israel was celebrating the Jewish holy day of Yom Kippur—the "fourth round" in the Arab-Israeli conflict erupted. In a reversal of the 1967 events, this time the Egyptian armed forces surprised Israeli defenders by crossing the Suez Canal in force and breaching the Bar Lev Line, opening the Sinai and southern Israel to Egyptian forces. Using modern Soviet-supplied equipment, the Egyptian army and air force took a heavy toll among Israeli defenders. Meanwhile, Syrian forces were attacking Israeli units stationed on the Golan Heights. The oil-producing states of the Middle East again cut off petroleum shipments to the United States and Western Europe, thereby aggravating the "energy crisis" that was beginning to grip these countries.

After sustaining initial defeats—and only after Israeli tanks and other equipment were replaced from American stocks airlifted to the area—the Israeli armed forces rallied and launched a successful counteroffensive. The Syrians were driven back; for a time, Israeli forces threatened to attack the city of Damascus. Against Egypt, Israeli infantry, tanks, and aircraft reversed the tide of battle. Until they were restrained by diplomatic pressure from Washington, Israeli forces threatened to cross the Suez Canal and oc-

cupy portions of Egyptian territory. By late October, the belligerents finally accepted a UN-sponsored cease-fire agreement strongly advocated by the United States.[32] Once the fighting had stopped, early in 1974 American Secretary of State Henry Kissinger embarked upon his "shuttle diplomacy," which, it was hoped, would finally discover a durable basis for peace in this protracted and dangerous conflict.

The United States as a Peacemaker

Since the end of World War II, the United States has endeavored to play two very different roles with regard to the Arab-Israeli conflict. On the one hand, as we have seen, since 1948 America has been—and it remains—Israel's principal source of external support. On the other hand, ever since the eruption of the "first round" of violent conflict in the Arab-Israeli controversy, the United States has also endeavored to serve as an energetic *peacemaker* in the Middle East. To the Arab mind, at least, these roles have often been contradictory and self-defeating.

From the late 1940s through the early 1980s, the United States has sought to discover a peaceful solution to the conflict between Israel and its Arab neighbors. Washington supported United Nations efforts in 1948 and afterward to establish and maintain an effective cease-fire agreement between the belligerents. The Eisenhower Administration used its influence decisively in 1956 to bring the Suez Crisis to an end. During and after the "third round" in 1967, Washington demanded that Israel show restraint in exploiting its military victory against the Arabs. In the years that followed, American officials condemned terrorist attacks by the PLO and other organizations against Israel and its supporters; and they also criticized the government of Israel for "annexing" the Old City of Jerusalem, for engaging in "massive retaliation" against Arab states, and for encouraging (or not stopping) the expansion of Jewish settlements in the disputed "West Bank" territories.

Following the 1973 war, American efforts to discover a formula for peace in the Middle East intensified. Under the Nixon and Ford administrations, Secretary of State Henry Kissinger devoted countless hours to "shuttle diplomacy," in which he and his aides met personally with the leaders of Israel and the Arab states directly involved in the Palestine question.[33] American diplomatic initiative was crucial in arranging a military disengagement between Israel and Syrian and Egyptian forces, thereby lessening the risk of new military encounters on these sensitive frontiers. A three-year renewal of the disengagement agreement was signed early in 1975. According to its terms, Israel (with great reluctance) gave up control over the strategic Mitla and Gidi passes in the Sinai; and it agreed to return the Abu Rudeis oil fields (Israel's only domestic source of oil) to Egypt.

President Sadat's government also made significant concessions: For the first time since 1948, Israeli-bound shipping was permitted transit through the Suez Canal after it had been reopened; and—in a pledge which brought Sadat into conflict with Arab leaders and masses outside Egypt—Cairo promised not to rely upon armed force to resolve outstanding differences with Israel. Some 200 American technicians were stationed along the Israeli-Egyptian cease-fire line in order to monitor compliance with the agreement. In addition, Washington agreed to increase its military and economic aid to Israel substantially. At least an implicit agreement to provide American assistance to Sadat's government was also part of the long-term cease-fire accord.[34]

Further progress toward resolving Israeli-Arab differences foundered upon an issue which had come increasingly to the forefront after the 1967 war: the formal inclusion of the Palestine Liberation Organization as the official "spokesman" for the Palestinian Arabs in the peace negotiations. At an Arab summit conference in Rabat, Morocco, in October 1974, the PLO won a recognition of this right from the Arab states. Israel's consistent view—usually supported in Washington—on the issue was unambiguous: Since the PLO was dedicated to the state of Israel's destruction, under no circumstances would Israeli negotiators meet with its representatives on matters affecting the security and future of Israel.

The issue of PLO inclusion in Arab-Israeli peace talks was a delicate and difficult question for American officials, in light of the adamant opposition of Israel and its supporters in the United States to this step. A pivotal question—What group or groups were the legitimate "representatives" of the Palestinians?—evoked widely varying responses. Another significant aspect of the problem was the question: At *what stage* should spokesmen for the Palestinians join the Arab-Israeli peace discussions? Neither the Carter nor the Reagan Administration provided unambiguous answers to such inquiries. The issue of Palestinian representation in the Arab-Israeli negotiations continued to serve as a formidable roadblock to progress in achieving stability in the Middle East.

After the 1973 war, efforts to convert the Israeli-Egyptian cease-fire agreement into an overall peace settlement of the Arab-Israeli controversy proved unsuccessful. Continuing disagreement on key issues (several of which we shall examine below) blocked the path to peace and raised anew the specter of a "fifth round" in the Middle East. At length, President Sadat of Egypt took an historic step. Beset at home with increasingly acute internal problems—and compelled to expend a disproportionate share of Egypt's budget on modern armaments—Sadat announced his willingness to visit Israel in an effort to break the diplomatic logjam. His speech to the Israeli Knesset on November 17, 1977, was an historic occasion. If they seldom agreed with the Egyptian leader's position, Israelis applauded Sadat's courage and initiative. In other Arab states, his peacemaking efforts were greeted with profound skepticism and hostility. Shortly thereafter, Prime Minister Menachem Begin returned the courtesy by visiting the Egyptian port city of Ismalia.[35]

Intensive efforts to maintain the momentum toward an Israeli-Egyptian peace treaty followed—culminating in a summit conference among Israel, Egypt, and the United States at the presidential retreat at Camp David, beginning early in September 1978. The diplomatic sessions proved long, arduous, and frustrating. But in the end, a "Framework for Peace in the Middle East" was agreed to and signed on September 17, 1978. This agreement was followed by a Treaty of Peace between Israel and Egypt on March 26, 1979. A detailed document, this agreement ended the state of war between the two countries; provided for a step-by-step withdrawal of Israeli forces from the Sinai peninsula and the return of this territory to Egyptian sovereignty; called for the establishment of diplomatic relations between them; and pledged the two belligerents to live in peace with each other. The parties to the agreement hoped that in the near future, the remaining issues inflaming Arab-Israeli relations would be resolved and that other Arab states would be induced to arrive at comparable understandings with Israel.[36]

The Carter Administration had played a crucial role in the Camp David peace accords; and the United States incurred certain obligations as a result of them. Israel demanded—and received—a renewal of an American pledge to support it, in case Egypt violated the terms of the accord. The Carter Administration also pledged some $3 billion in military assistance to Israel; and Egypt was scheduled to receive some $1.5 billion in military aid to improve its armed forces. After seeking extensive American financial aid for several years, Sadat's government was also promised $500 million in economic assistance over the next three years. Under the Reagan Administration, American officials time and again reiterated their commitment to a continuation of the search for peace in the Arab-Israeli conflict. With American encouragement, Israel and Egypt carried out the terms of the Camp David peace accord (entailing an Israeli evacuation of the Sinai and its return to Egyptian sovereignty). Egypt's new President, Hosni Mubarek, appeared determined to maintain peaceful relations with Israel and, even more than his predecessor Anwar Sadat, to concentrate upon Egypt's increasingly critical internal problems. At the same time, Mubarek could also be expected to restore Egypt's damaged relations with moderate Arab governments (such as Saudi Arabia and Jordan). Meanwhile, the behavior of the Israeli government under Menachem Begin cast a pall over the prospects for further progress in resolving the Arab-Israeli quarrel. Israel's "annexation" of the Golan Heights (taken from Syria in the 1973 war)—along with its often harsh efforts to counteract PLO influence among the West Bank Arabs—inflamed Arab opinion and reduced the prospects for a peaceful resolution of outstanding differences between the belligerents to virtually nil. Within the United States, policy makers seemed mainly preoccupied with creating a "strategic consensus" in the Middle East in behalf of efforts to preserve the security of the Persian Gulf area (a question we shall examine more fully at a later stage). Most Arab states resisted new efforts by

Washington to link them closely with the United States. Within Israel, and among many of its supporters in America, the view prevailed that the Reagan Administration's policies had "tilted" toward the Arabs, to the detriment of Israel's security and economic needs. In this context, most commentators believed that the Middle East would remain a center of ongoing political strife and instability—perhaps the most dangerous and turbulent region on the globe.[37]

Obstacles to an Arab-Israeli Settlement

While it was a milestone in the troubled history of Arab-Israeli relations, the peace treaty between Israel and Egypt left a number of major and minor issues unresolved. In the years following this historic accord, little or no discernible progress was made in eliminating these deep-seated sources of tension in the Middle East. In the remaining space, let us concentrate upon four pivotal questions that kept the region inflamed and created the possibility of a "fifth round" in this ongoing controversy.

1. *The policies of the "Rejectionist Front."* President Sadat's overtures toward Israel in the interests of peace left him increasingly "isolated" in the Arab world. The Arab "Rejectionist Front"—spearheaded by states like Syria, Iraq, and Libya, along with the Palestine Liberation Organization and other guerrilla groups—disavowed the Egyptian-Israeli peace treaty. Even the "moderate" and usually pro-Western governments in Jordan and Saudi Arabia criticized Sadat's actions and refused to join in negotiations seeking to extend the peace agreement to other countries.

Each country participating in the "Rejectionist Front" perhaps had its own reasons for doing so. Some (like Syria and Iraq) were severely divided internally; for many years,

the campaign against Zionism had unquestionably been used by established political leaders to achieve at least a modicum of national unity and to divert popular attention from domestic problems. Some members of the front also were intensely suspicious and resentful of Egypt's claim to "leadership" of the Middle East under Presidents Nasser and Sadat—a fact that was highlighted by the rejoicing among many anti-Israeli groups over Anwar Sadat's assassination by fanatical Moslem terrorists late in 1981. One report spoke of "jubilation in most of the Arab world" over Sadat's death, since the Egyptian leader was widely viewed as a "traitor" to the Arab cause. As the center of the Wahhabi sect of Islam, Saudi Arabia was particularly offended by Israel's "annexation" of the Old City of Jerusalem, containing the third holiest shrine in Islam (the Dome of the Rock mosque). Throughout the Arab world, pervasive sympathy also existed for the plight of the Palestinians, many of whom had lost their ancestral homes because of the conflict with Israel. As much perhaps as any other single issue, the existence of the Palestinian refugee question inflamed Arab animosity toward Israel and blocked the path to peace in the Middle East.[38]

2. *The role of the PLO and other Palestinian groups.* A second complex and highly controversial issue hindering the search for peace in the Middle East was the role of the Palestine Liberation Organization and other groups purporting to represent the Palestinian Arabs in the controversy. As we observed earlier, after the Six-Day War in 1967, the Arab enemies of Israel increasingly relied upon guerrilla warfare, assassinations, and acts of terrorism to achieve their objectives. This strategy had several purposes: to "dramatize" the plight of the dispossessed Palestinians and gain worldwide publicity for their cause; to keep the Israeli society in a state of

tension and anxiety, compelling it to maintain a high level of military readiness, at great expense; to provoke the government of Israel into massive "retaliatory" raids against Jordan or Lebanon, thereby incurring the censure of the outside world; and to prove that Israel would not enjoy true security until the grievances of the Palestinian Arabs had been satisfied. In the Israeli view, such terrorist activities had another purpose: They demonstrated convincingly that the PLO and other Arab guerrilla organizations were *unprepared to make peace with Israel under any circumstances*. For this reason, Israeli authorities were unwilling to accord any legitimacy to the PLO or to negotiate with it.

Confronted with Arab reliance upon guerrilla tactics against Israel, officials in the United States were in turn faced with difficult choices. Throughout most of the post-World War II period, the United States has agreed with, and supported, the Israeli position that the PLO and related organizations should not be a party to Arab-Israeli peace negotiations. Yet by the period of the Carter Administration, American officials were also mindful of a dominant reality (reminiscent of the problem arising in their own earlier and equally reluctant negotiations with the Viet Cong, the Communist guerrilla organization involved in the Vietnam War). Since 1967, the PLO had in fact emerged as an active party to the Arab-Israeli quarrel; its guerrilla and other activities were largely beyond the control of the established Arab governments; and over the years, the PLO had attracted a wide following and had gained considerable prestige in the Middle East. The reality was, therefore, that if peace were ever to be achieved in the Middle East, any agreement reached would of necessity have to include the PLO; otherwise, Israel would never gain the peace and security it sought.

Adding to the complexity of the prob-

lem, however, was the fact that as the years passed, fundamental disagreements on goals and tactics increasingly characterized the approach of Arab guerrilla organizations opposing Israel. As the designated leader of the PLO, Yasir Arafat was sorely challenged to maintain a common front and to "control" the organizations under his nominal authority. What exactly *was* the position of the PLO and other groups purporting to speak for the Palestinians on the crucial issue of Israel's right to exist and to enjoy security of its borders? For Israel, for the United States, and for other countries it was extremely difficult to get unambiguous answers to such questions.[39]

By the early 1980s, therefore, American foreign policy on the matter of the inclusion of the PLO in Arab-Israeli peace discussions was pulled into two contrary directions. Washington was highly reluctant to break with Israel, which remained adamantly opposed to this step. Conversely, American officials had become increasingly aware that, if the PLO and other representatives of the Palestinians were excluded from such diplomatic discussions, a peaceful resolution of the Arab-Israeli conflict would remain an elusive quest.[40]

3. *The Arab refugee question.* For over a generation, another problem had blocked the path to peace in the Middle East. The passage of time had done little or nothing to reduce its importance or its complexity. This was the question of the future of the Arab refugees who had been displaced from Palestine, beginning with the 1947–1948 war and in the other periods of active warfare that followed the creation of the state of Israel.*

---

*The "refugee issue" as an element in the Arab-Israeli conflict is a complex phenomenon, involving often widely varying estimates of the numbers of people involved and differing interpretations concerning its origins and its solution. It should be noted that two groups of refugees are involved—the Arabs who, since the late 1940s, have been

As we have already seen, the Arab states and Israel took diametrically opposite positions on the causes and the solution of the refugee problem. In brief, the Arab states demanded that Israel take back those Arabs who had been displaced from their lands in Palestine and that "compensation" be made to them for lands seized by the state of Israel since 1948. Israel's view was that most of the refugees had to be "resettled" in Arab lands (like Iraq, which had abundant land); that Israel might readmit a limited number of Arab refu-

gees, within the context of an overall peace settlement with its Arab neighbors; and that the Arab states owed compensation to the thousands of "Jewish refugees" who had fled Arab countries after the creation of the state of Israel. The impasse on the refugee issue has blocked the path to peace in the Middle East for over a generation.

The refugee issue is compounded by a number of almost incalculable elements in the problem. By the early 1980s, how many Arabs in fact still regarded themselves as "refugees" from Palestine and desired to return to it? In actuality, an indeterminate number had accepted *de facto* resettlement in countries like Kuwait, Saudi Arabia, and other locales (not excluding the United States). Or, what kind of "compensation" could Israel offer the Arab refugees that would be acceptable both to them and to the state of Israel? By the 1980s, how many Arabs regarding themselves as refugees (including perhaps their children) actually desired to become citizens of Israel and to live peacefully within its borders vis-à-vis those who were members or supporters of the PLO and other guerrilla organizations? Answers to such questions remained elusive and highly speculative.[41]

4. *The problem of the "West Bank" territories.* Since the 1973 war, a critical issue in Arab-Israeli peace negotiations has been the future of the "West Bank" territories— comprising largely Arab-inhabited lands under Israeli military occupation. Considered part of the state of Jordan since the 1947–1948 war, these territories were seized by the Israeli armed forces in the Six-Day War (1967); ever since, control over them has been regarded by Israeli officials as crucial to the nation's security. By extending its authority over these territories, Israel brought some 800,000 additional Arabs under its jurisdiction—and in the process has created a frustrating dilemma affecting the future of Israel.

---

displaced from Palestine; and, as Israel sees it, Jewish groups who were coerced into leaving their homelands in Arab countries after 1948. In the former category, there are in turn two rather distinct categories of Arab refugees. One group—estimated as high as some 900,000—was displaced from Palestine after the 1947–1948 war. Most of these eventually lived in refugee camps (principally in Egypt, Jordan, Syria, and Lebanon) operated by the United Nations. As time passed—with no resolution of Arab-Israeli differences—the Palestine Liberation Organization and other anti-Israeli organizations recruited their followers from Palestinians living in the refugee camps.

Then, after the 1967 war, another large group of Palestinian Arabs, estimated at more than 800,000, found themselves living under Israel's jurisdiction, either as citizens of the Old City of Jerusalem (which Israel formally "annexed") or inhabiting the Israeli-occupied "West Bank" of the Jordan River, formerly a part of the state of Jordan. By the late 1970s, the total number of displaced Palestinians was estimated as high as some 4 million people.

While the focus of world attention has usually been on the *Arab* refugees, the state of Israel has insisted for a generation or more that this problem cannot be viewed or solved in isolation. By some accounts, there are close to 1 million *Jewish* refugees from Arab states, many of whom were compelled to emigrate to Israel after 1947–1948; these refugees also have unsettled claims against Arab governments. For current data on the refugee issue, see *The Middle East: U.S. Policy, Israel, Oil and the Arabs,* 4th ed. (Washington, D.C.: Congressional Quarterly, 1979), pp. 26–33. More extended discussion of various aspects of the refugee issue may be found in Michael Curtis, et al., eds., *The Palestinians: People, History, Politics* (New Brunswick, N.J.: Transaction Books, 1975).

The position of the Arab states is that no peace with Israel is possible until it relinquishes control over the West Bank territories. For the PLO, these lands are the nucleus for a future Arab-dominated "Palestinian state"—a concept that is of course anathema to Israel. For Jordan, the loss of the West Bank was a severe blow to its economic viability and its future.

The extension of Israeli control over the lands of the West Bank has confronted the state of Israel with difficult choices. On the one hand, under the regime of Prime Minister Menachem Begin, the dominant Likud Party has repeatedly asserted Israel's "historic" rights to this territory; and it has either actively encouraged, or it has not effectively opposed, new and continuing Jewish "settlements" on lands long claimed by the Arabs. On the other hand, anti-Israeli sentiment among the Arab population of the West Bank has steadily mounted—particularly as the number of Jewish settlements in the area has increased. Almost daily in recent years, some violent "incident" has erupted in this zone. The PLO and other guerrilla organizations have gained prestige and recruits among the West Bank Arabs, as disaffection toward Israel has spread among the population. Within the Israeli society, opinion has tended to fragment on whether the government should or should not formally "annex" the West Bank.[42]

Thus far, these issues have defied successful resolution by those seeking to end the animosity between Israel and the Arab states. The prevailing Israeli attitude may be summarized by saying that—after four successful military encounters against its Arab enemies—the state of Israel *is determined to maintain its own security* at whatever cost or sacrifice required. Israel is not reassured by Arab or PLO promises; and (except for Egypt) it discerns no significant diminution in

Arab hostility toward it. Israel has already made substantial "concessions" (such as returning the Sinai oil fields) in order to achieve peace with Egypt; and it is not disposed to make further major concessions until there is a fundamental change in Arab enmity toward Israel.

As for the Arabs (other than Egypt), their attitudes toward Israel are equally uncompromising. After discovering the diplomatic utility of "oil power," Arabs believe that they possess a weapon capable of forcing Israel and its American mentor to accept their terms. Moreover, Israel's adversaries believe that "time is on their side." Upwards of 150 million Arabs oppose some 3 million (non-Arab) Israelis. In the years ahead—as many Israelis themselves were aware—this disparity will almost certainly widen. The extension of Israel's authority over the West Bank territories created new internal strains for the Israeli society and presented its officials with an excruciating dilemma. On the one hand, the government of Israel was determined that the West Bank must not become a center of anti-Zionist agitation and growing PLO influence. Under Prime Minister Begin, many Israeli officials were also sympathetic to attempts by militant Jewish groups to confiscate and settle Arab lands on the West Bank. On the other hand, enforcing its authority over the increasingly restive West Bank Arab population compelled Israel to place the area under *de facto* military occupation; to restrict Arab political freedoms; and, in the process, to violate many of its own professed democratic principles and ethical norms. The result was growing political tensions and policy disagreements within the Israeli society over how to respond to Arab demands and grievances. In addition, the government of Israel faced serious economic and financial problems. By the early 1980s, inflation exceeded 150 percent annually; Israel had the highest level of defense spending of any nation; and its dependence upon private and governmental aid from abroad (mainly from America) was as great as ever. Such realities offered little inducement for Arab opponents of Zionism to arrive at a peaceful settlement with Israel.

America and the "Arc of Crisis"

American Diplomatic Involvement in the Persian Gulf Area

By the 1970s, the diplomatic and security interests of the United States had become deeply involved in a zone frequently designated the "Arc of Crisis." This zone extended from East Africa, through the states bordering the Persian Gulf, eastward to Afghanistan.[43] Existing and future sources of tension in this unstable region caused deep concern among policy makers in Washington, who were severely challenged to formulate effective responses to them.

American officials had become deeply concerned about developments in the Arc of Crisis for three paramount reasons. First, as the United States found itself confronted with a continuing "energy crisis," the people and their leaders were reminded almost daily of the importance of continued access to the oil resources of this region and of related problems, like the latest price increases announced by OPEC.* The military security and economic prosperity of America's major allies—the members of NATO and Japan—were even more dependent upon the continued availability of Middle East oil.

Second, the Arc of Crisis is a zone of active Communist diplomatic and military interventionism. Even while it called for détente with the United States, Moscow actively sought to influence the course of political events in the area. As we shall see more fully in Chapter 13, the Soviet Union (along with its ally, Castro's Cuba) was directly and mas-

---

*The Organization of Petroleum Exporting Countries (OPEC) was established in September 1960. Original members were Iran, Iraq, Kuwait, Saudi Arabia, and Venezuela. Eight other states—the United Arab Emirates, Qatar, Libya, Algeria, Ecuador, Nigeria, Gabon, and Indonesia—subsequently joined the organization. Among the five largest oil-producing members of OPEC—Saudi Arabia, Iran, Iraq, Venezuela, and Kuwait—four were located in the Persian Gulf area. Before Iranian oil production declined substantially (after the Iranian Revolution of 1979), these four states collectively produced some 60 percent of OPEC's oil output of 30 million barrels daily. During some periods, Saudi Arabia alone produced 8 to 10 million barrels daily—or approximately one-third of OPEC's total output. Yet by the early 1980s, OPEC may well have passed its zenith as an organization that was able to dictate world oil prices and to exact major political concessions from the advanced nations. Several developments—OPEC's own pricing policies, steps in the United States and other industrialized nations to reduce oil consumption, and increased output by non-OPEC states (such as Mexico and Great Britain)—had created a substantial surplus of oil on the world market. As a result, the price of OPEC-produced oil dropped sharply; and the internal unity of the organization was severely tested by deep-seated controversies within it over the proper strategy to follow under these radically altered circumstances. By the early 1980s also, the government of Iran was gradually resuming oil production. This fact further jeopardized efforts by the members of OPEC to preserve price levels; and (as it had done under the Shah), Iran was once more selling oil to Israel. These developments prompted some commentators to foresee a steady decline in OPEC's economic and diplomatic power and to refer to OPEC as an "oil cartel on the skids." As always, OPEC's future and effectiveness were likely to be determined primarily by the policies of its most influential member—Saudi Arabia. Background information on OPEC is provided in *The Middle East*, 5th ed. (Washington, D.C.: Congressional Quarterly, 1981), pp. 82–98, and "Oil Cartel on the Skids?" *Newsweek,* **98** (August 31, 1981), 39–40. For a prediction that OPEC's monopolistic power may be ending, see S. Fred Singer and Stephen Stamas, "An End to OPEC?" *Foreign Policy,* **45** (Winter, 1981–82), 115–126.

sively involved in the political conflicts in East Africa; to the south, for many years the Soviet Union had assisted rebel groups challenging the authority of established governments in Zimbabwe (formerly Southern Rhodesia) and South Africa. On the Arabian Peninsula, the government of South Yemen was controlled by Marxist elements, massively assisted by the Kremlin. To the north, although their dependence upon Moscow had begun to lessen by the 1980s, for several years Syria and Iraq had maintained close ties with the Soviet Union. Further to the east, after the overthrow of the Shah's dynasty in 1979, Iran lapsed into a condition of incipient or actual anarchy. American officials feared that Moscow would attempt to exploit the "power vacuum" that had developed in this important Persian Gulf state.

But it was in neighboring Afghanistan that the Soviet-American confrontation took its most potentially serious form. Late in 1979 the Kremlin launched a massive military invasion of the country, in an attempt to place it under direct Soviet military and political hegemony. President Jimmy Carter called the crisis in Afghanistan "the most serious threat to peace" since World War II; and in response to the Afghanistan crisis, the United States embarked upon an intensive program to strengthen and modernize its armed forces.

Third, the Arc of Crisis is a region of indigenous political instability and turbulence. Even without the involvement of the superpowers in the area, the existence of rival political forces and ideologies keep the region in a state of actual or potential upheaval. Revolutionary political movements—like the Ba'ath Party (particularly its Iraqi wing)—sought converts among societies bordering the Persian Gulf and sponsored revolutionary activities against such "traditional" governments as those in Saudi Arabia and Kuwait. Yet the left-wing Ba'ath of Iraq was also in conflict with the right-wing Ba'ath that governed Syria. And by the early 1980's, the latter was on the verge of an armed conflict with Jordan. The Palestine Liberation Organization and other Arab guerrilla groups were also active in the Persian Gulf area. The large alien populations of Saudi Arabia and Kuwait were especially receptive to the PLO's anti-Israeli campaign. Some Arab guerrilla organizations, we need to recall, were no less dedicated to the overthrow of existing Arab governments than they were to continuing the conflict with Israel. The collapse of the Iranian monarchy in 1979 plunged that country into a long period of internal chaos; and by 1980 open warfare had erupted between Iran and Iraq, adding a new source of instability to an already volatile region.

We may conveniently bring such disparate forces and developments in the Arc of Crisis into sharper focus by examining four specific problems confronting American foreign policy in that zone.

Middle East Oil and OPEC

An experienced student of Middle Eastern affairs has said that "The energy crisis which in October [1973] threw the world into a panic, and for which no solution has as yet been found, was and is in reality the Middle East oil crisis."[44] Beginning with the Six-Day War in 1967, the United States and other industrialized nations of the world discovered painfully how dependent they had become upon access to the oil reserves of the Middle East.

Throughout most of the postwar era, America's dependence upon foreign oil was negligible. Following the 1967 war in the Middle East—when the United States had to supply its European allies from its own reserves—the nation's reliance upon external oil supplies escalated rapidly. By 1973, for example, the United States was importing some

3.3 million barrels of oil daily; by 1977, American oil imports reached 8.5 million barrels daily. After that year, foreign oil purchases by the United States declined. By 1981, for example, foreign oil purchases by the United States had dropped to just over 5 million barrels daily—a major factor in the oil glut that was eroding OPEC's financial and political power. Even so, as we noted in Chapter 6, petroleum imports constituted the largest single item in America's trade deficit, costing the United States approximately $90 billion in 1980. While the United States had significantly reduced its dependence upon overseas oil, most commentators believed that for an indefinite period in the future, the American society *would remain massively dependent upon foreign oil sources*. The "world oil surplus" that had appeared during the early 1980s, most informed commentators believed, would almost certainly prove temporary. In any case, the demand for foreign oil in the United States and other advanced nations would likely remain high for the foreseeable future.

America's massive dependence upon access to Middle East oil had a number of specific consequences for the foreign relations of the United States. It meant, for example, that the United States was "involved" in the affairs of the Middle East as never before. If Americans were not aware of it earlier, they now understood that their national security was directly affected by developments in the Arc of Crisis. To envision the worst possible scenario: A complete and prolonged denial of Western access to the oil fields of the Middle East (perhaps by a Soviet-instigated attempt to close the Persian Gulf or a renewal of an oil embargo by the members of OPEC) would be a crippling economic blow to the United States and nearly all other industrialized nations. It would most probably, for example, destroy the cohesion of the Western alli-

ance—as, one by one, its members sought to arrive at separate agreements and "understandings" with the major Middle East oil producers.

The growing dependence of the United States upon Middle Eastern oil unquestionably *had*—as the members of OPEC intended—influenced American diplomacy in the Middle East. By the 1970s, the American people and their leaders were more receptive to the Arab point of view on the Palestine controversy. While support for Israel remained strong within the American society, the United States was less prone to support Israel *uncritically and automatically* on issues related to the Arab-Israeli conflict. This "erosion" in pro-Israeli sentiment within the United States caused genuine concern to officials and private groups within Israel and their supporters abroad. Even while official relations between them remained tense, the United States also had somewhat better relations with some of the more radical and anti-Israeli Arab states. American private investment, for example, was growing in Iraq; and the government of Algeria publicly indicated a desire to improve relations with the United States (a major purchaser of Algeria's natural gas exports).[45]

Three activities by, and developments within, OPEC caused continuing apprehension among American officials. At the forefront of concern perhaps was OPEC's repeated demand for major increases in the price of its oil exports. For many years, American and other foreign consumers obtained "cheap" oil from Middle Eastern producers at a cost of $3 or less per barrel; by the early 1980s, the price had risen to over *10 times* this figure! With the United States importing almost half of its petroleum requirements, this was the largest single item in a worsening American balance of international payments.

Along with many other governments, officials in Washington were also disturbed by the *growing fragmentation and lack of cohesion* exhibited by members of OPEC in dealing with their customers. The Iraqi-Iranian war added a new element of disunity to OPEC's deliberations. This produced great uncertainty among the industrialized nations concerning the permanence of agreements reached with OPEC on oil price levels and related questions.[46]

A related concern in Washington was the relative decline of Saudi Arabia's traditional influence in OPEC's decision-making process. As a country that had long been oriented toward the United States, Saudi Arabia usually served as a voice of "moderation" in OPEC's decision making. Yet, for reasons we shall examine more fully below, by the late 1970s its influence within OPEC was being strongly challenged.

Saudi Arabia: "Oil Giant" of the Middle East

The future of the Persian Gulf area will in no small measure be determined by developments on the Arabian Peninsula, where the internal and external policies of the Kingdom of Saudi Arabia are likely to be crucial to the outcome. The present-day government of Saudi Arabia is an outgrowth of two major forces shaping its political destiny. One was the conversion of the Saudi tribe to the sect of Sunni Islam known as Wahhabism in the mid-eighteenth century.[47] Named for its leader Mohammed Abd al-Wahhab, the Wahhabis are sometimes called the "Puritans" or the "Fundamentalists" of Sunni Islam, because of their rigid insistence upon literal adherence to the provisions of the Koran in all spheres of life. Traditionally, the Wahhabis have vehemently opposed "secular" tendencies or movements aimed at the "reform" of Islam.

The other crucial historical development was the emergence of the Saudi tribe as the dominant political force on the peninsula. During the nineteenth and early twentieth centuries, the Saudis defeated their rivals—such as the Hashemites, who were driven north after World War I—and extended their control over most of the peninsula, thereby bringing the holy cities of Mecca and Medina under Wahhabi control. The Kingdom of Saudi Arabia, under its first ruler King Ibn Saud I, was proclaimed on September 24, 1932.

King Ibn Saud I was a "patriarchal" tribal leader who ruled over a remote and backward country where nomadism, primitive agriculture, and fighting had been the traditional pursuits of the Bedouin tribes. The future of Saudi Arabia was revolutionized by the discovery of oil in the late 1930s. Yet its oil industry did not become important until after World War II. Although he governed like a tribal sheikh, Ibn Saud I really began the process of modernization in Saudi Arabia. After his death in 1953, his son Ibn Saud II ruled for the next 11 years. His reign was marked by such extravagance, corruption, and indifference to the national welfare that in time the royal family deposed Ibn Saud II, sending him into forced retirement.

By contrast, the new ruler—Crown Prince Feisal—was a devout Moslem and was determined to use the country's rising income for the society's betterment. Under Feisal, a series of internal reforms—together with a preliminary national development program—was adopted. Feisal's enlightened rule was cut short when he was assassinated in 1975 by a deranged member of the royal family, who was promptly executed in accordance with Koranic provisions. Feisal's successor was Crown Prince Khalid; but because he was seriously ill, since 1975 the *de facto* ruler has been Crown Prince Fahd.[48]

Contemporary Saudi Arabia is a land of enormous contrasts, of frenzied economic activity, and of diverse political crosscurrents. Approximately the size of the United States east of the Mississippi River, Saudi Arabia has estimated its population as ranging from 6 to 9 million people (census data for the country are highly unreliable). It has a relatively homogeneous population, consisting chiefly of Sunni Moslems of the Wahhabi sect (although there is a small Shi'ite minority in the northeast). A highly significant fact about the society is that—in order to meet a chronic labor shortage—upwards of 2 million foreigners reside in it; one out of every three or four people in Saudi Arabia is a foreigner. At the end of the 1970s, the per capita income of Saudi Arabia was approximately $10,000 annually, and it is increasing rapidly.

The dominant fact about this otherwise primitive country is of course the presence of vast oil and gas resources and of the petroleum and related industries based upon them. Saudi Arabia has oil reserves estimated at 175 billion barrels (bbls.)—or one-fourth of the known oil reserves of the world. In recent years, it has produced as much as 10 million barrels of oil daily, or one-third of OPEC's total output. With its own oil reserves diminishing (and with imports from Venezuela declining), the United States has become progressively more dependent upon access to the oil supplies of Saudi Arabia (along with Kuwait). The mounting global demand for oil—coupled with the Saudi government's growing share of ARAMCO's income—has meant that the state's revenues have soared.* They reached $63 billion annually at the end

*Beginning in the early 1960s, the government of Saudi Arabia demanded an increasing share in the ownership, management, and income of ARAMCO. By 1972 Saudi Arabia owned 60 percent of ARAMCO; and by the early 1980s, ARAMCO was to be totally government-owned. Thereafter, the company would prospect for, produce, and distribute oil on the basis of contracts and consulting fees negotiated with the Saudi government.

of the 1970s; and every increase in the price of OPEC oil raised Riyadh's income substantially. Relying upon its vast oil wealth, in 1980 Saudi authorities adopted a national development plan, calling for the expenditure of $250 billion over the next five years. American firms and government agencies were playing a key role in carrying out this ambitious program.[49]

Since the 1930s, close ties have existed between the United States and Saudi Arabia. As we have noted, ARAMCO was an American oil consortium that made Saudi Arabia into the leading oil-producing state on the globe. During World War II (although the country was officially "neutral"), Saudi Arabia contributed to the Allied war effort. Down to the early 1960s, American air bases in the country contributed to the defense of the Middle East. (These bases were closed at the request of Saudi officials, who sought to improve their rapport with other, sometimes anti-Western, Arab states.)

The 1967 war in the Middle East marked a turning point in Saudi-American relations. During that conflict, Saudi Arabia joined other Arab states in imposing an oil boycott against the West; and the same tactic was employed by Middle East oil producers in the 1973 war. Yet after the latter conflict, Saudi Arabia also took the lead in getting OPEC to lift the oil embargo. In the years that followed, Saudi officials used their influence (not always successfully) to prevent OPEC from adopting exorbitant price increases. In return, Saudi Arabia unquestionably expected that Washington would exact concessions from Israel on such diplomatic issues as the future of the Old City of Jerusalem and political autonomy for the Palestinians.

The collapse of the Iranian monarchy—followed at the end of 1979 by the Soviet invasion of Afghanistan—created new uncertainties in Saudi-American relations. As we shall see, America's pledge to defend the security of the Persian Gulf area, forcefully expressed in the Carter Doctrine, created a host of new problems in Saudi-American relations.

Down to the late 1970s, the monarchy of Saudi Arabia appeared to be a synonym for political "stability" and continuity in a region characterized by political upheaval. Yet the seizure of the Great Mosque in Mecca by dissident political groups late in 1979 called attention to the existence of certain forces at home and abroad that were threatening Saudi Arabia's traditional political system. As one of the few remaining monarchies on the globe, the government of Saudi Arabia faced increasingly serious challenges to its authority. One informed student of Middle Eastern affairs has said: "It is a widespread and well based assumption that the regime of the House of Saud cannot long endure, neither in its present form nor in any improved model; and that [the Iranian Revolution in 1979] has considerably shortened its life expectancy."[50] The Iraqi-Iranian war erupting in 1980 added a new element of uncertainty to Saudi Arabia's political future.

While this may be an extreme verdict on the Saudi government's political future, it is reasonable to expect that the future will witness growing dissidence within the country, along with pressure by external forces to produce a fundamental change in the country's political system. Saudi Arabia's Shi'ite minority (which has customarily supplied a large number of workers in the oil industry) is unquestionably influenced by the emergence of the new religiously based political regime in Iran. Among Saudi Arabia's large alien population, which has little loyalty to the monarchy, some sympathy no doubt exists for foreign political ideologies and programs, such as those advocated by the Palestine Liberation Organization and the Ba'ath Party. Yet to date, the royal family of Saudi Arabia has done little to broaden its political base or to relinquish its tight control over the governmental system.

Within the Persian Gulf political environment, several species of political "radicalism" and revolutionary movements have sought to gain converts. As one study of the region has observed, in recent years the Persian Gulf states

... have been occupied with the politics of radicalism. In the context of the gulf's tribal regimes, radicalism could be one of many demands: political reform, labor unions, individual rights, popular participation in government, the right to dissent. It also obviously means rejection of the existing political status quo and the attempt to change it utilizing all available means, including violent revolution.

Several "models" of revolutionary ideologies and programs are available—from Iraq, from South Yemen, from Libya, from the PLO and other Arab guerrilla organizations.[51] Thus far, while Saudi Arabia and most other Persian Gulf states have successfully resisted such forces, it seems certain that revolutionary agitation will exist in the Persian Gulf milieu for many years to come and that it will present new threats to the Saudi family's long-dominant political position.

The Iranian Revolution of 1979 also proved traumatic for Saudi Arabia. To the surprise of most foreign observers, one of the oldest (and most ostensibly "stable") monarchies in the world was overthrown with relative ease—a fact that inevitably raised questions about the future of monarchy in other settings. A possible Iranian victory in the Iraqi-Iranian war would also give impetus to Islamic fundamentalism throughout the Persian Gulf area. Although both claimed to be Koranic-based governments, Saudi Arabia and the new revolutionary regime in Iran were intensely suspicious and hostile toward each other. Besides ideological enmity, each nation was (or sought to be) the dominant political influence in the Persian Gulf region.

Communist gains in the region—particularly in East Africa and in neighboring South Yemen—also posed threats to the security and independence of Saudi Arabia. The Soviet Union's massive military penetration of Afghanistan late in 1979 possibly signaled a new effort by Moscow to "break through" to the Persian Gulf and to extend its hegemony to other nearby states. The small Saudi army is unequal to the task of preserving national security in the face of a direct Communist threat to the independence of Saudi Arabia and the smaller Persian Gulf states. For this reason, by the late 1970s Riyadh sought to purchase large quantities of modern American aircraft and other weapons to strengthen its military position—a request that engendered deep anxiety and opposition from Israel and its supporters in the United States.[52]

The Revolution in Iran

On January 16, 1979, the ruler of Iran—Shah Mohammed Reza Pahlavi—left the country, abdicating his throne after a 37-year reign. Out of the revolutionary ferment that led to his downfall, there emerged a hitherto obscure and mystical figure—the Ayatollah Ruhollah Khomeini—who became the leader of a new regime, designated an "Islamic Democracy."* This fundamental reorientation in Iran's inter-

---

*In the Shi'ite branch of Islam dominant in Iran, the religious leaders are known as *imams, mullahs,* or *ayatollahs.* Islam has no formal "clergy" or system of religious hierarchy. The religious leaders attain their positions on the basis of their acknowledged piety, knowledge, and leadership capacity. Shi'ites believe in the existence of a "Hidden Imam," or successor to Mohammed the Prophet, who will someday reappear. Meanwhile, the ayatollahs and other religious authorities lead the Islamic community in his name.

nal and external policies had profound diplomatic and strategic implications for the United States, as well as for other countries in the Persian Gulf area.

Contemporary Iran is a country of over 636,000 square miles (approximately two and one-half times the state of Texas); most of the country consists of mountainous, plateau, and desert areas. Iran's population is some 35 million people; and (in company with several other states in the Middle East) it has a very rapid rate of population increase. Some 98 percent of the people are Moslem, with a majority belonging to the Shi'ite branch. Historically called Persia, the country differs from its Arab neighbors in its ethnic origins, its cultural traditions, and its language (Persian or Farsi). By the late 1970s, Iran had a per capita Gross National Product of over $2100 annually. Before production dropped sharply after the revolution, Iran was the second largest oil-producing state in the Middle East, producing some 5.2 million barrels daily.

The modern history of Iran began with the regime of Reza Shah, who successfully carried out a coup in 1921 and was elected hereditary Shah four years later. Basing his power upon the army, Reza Shah undertook a number of reforms and innovations (such as modernization of the armed forces, the improvement and extension of education, industrialization, and development of the oil industry) designed to improve conditions in this primitive society. Yet under Reza Shah's rule, the members of the royal family also amassed great wealth; and several critical problems in Iran—such as widespread corruption and expanding governmental bureaucracy—received little attention. Because of his avowedly pro-German sympathies, when the Allies (Britain, the United States, and Soviet Russia) took over the administration of Iran early in World War II, Reza Shah was deposed in favor of his young son.[53]

Iran played a key role in World War II. Its oil resources were vital to the Allied war effort; and it provided a southern route for the shipment of American Lend-Lease supplies into the Soviet Union. After the war, Iran experienced two crises that were to have a long-range impact upon its political development and diplomatic orientation. One of these grew out of the large and influential Soviet presence in northern Iran during and immediately after World War II. In the northwestern province of Azerbaijan particularly, Soviet officials assisted in the creation of the Tudeh Party, or Communist Party of Iran, which preserved close ties with Moscow. Relying upon its military presence, the Tudeh Party, and other methods, the Kremlin sponsored revolutionary activities and separatist movements in Azerbaijan against the authority of the central government. After Iran appealed to the newly formed United Nations against this overt Soviet intervention, Moscow finally withdrew its armed forces from the country.[54]

The other early postwar crisis involved the Iranian government's nationalization of the Anglo-Iranian Oil Company, which had largely developed the country's oil industry. By the late 1940s—following a period of political upheaval in Iran—Dr. Mohammad Mossadeq had emerged as the dominant political figure. An ardent Iranian nationalist, the unpredictable and opportunistic Dr. Mossadeq was determined to nationalize the giant Anglo-Iranian Oil Company that had long dominated the country's economic (and, critics said, its political) life.

Although it unquestionably had popular support, the Iranian government's decree of March 15, 1951, nationalizing the oil industry ultimately plunged the country into economic and political chaos. Iran was unable to market its oil abroad (and several of its Arab neighbors exploited Iran's distress by supplying its principal oil customers); as the months

passed, the country approached economic stagnation and political paralysis. The ensuing political melee encompassed a wide assortment of forces:

> Conflict in the streets of Tehran . . . involved Tudeh groups . . . pro-Shah groups . . . Mossadeghists . . . military forces supporting the Shah, police contingents backing Mossadegh, and direct American intervention on behalf of the King.[55]

In this turbulent context, officials of the Eisenhower Administration became convinced that Iran was in danger of succumbing to Communist domination. Through the activities of the Central Intelligence Agency, American military advisers, and other means, Washington used its influence to depose Dr. Mossadeq. The son of Reza Shah, Reza Shah Pahlavi, was returned from residence abroad and reinstalled as the ruler of Iran. Assured of Washington's support—and relying upon the loyalty of the American-equipped Iranian armed forces—over the years that followed the Shah became the political master of the country. Throughout most of his reign, Iranian-American relations were extremely close; and inescapably, the United States became identified with the activities and fortunes of the Shah's regime.[56]

For the next 25 years, Reza Shah Pahlavi consolidated his power within Iran, largely eliminating any organized opposition to it. Confident of the support of the steadily growing armed forces—and relying upon his efficient and ruthless secret police (SAVAK)—the Shah and his followers dominated the Iranian political system. At home, he envisioned his regime as the modern embodiment of the royal dynasties that had ruled ancient Persia. Abroad, he aspired to make Iran the "successor" to Great Britain as the arbiter of the Persian Gulf area. Eventually, the Shah believed that Iran would become a *global* power.

The Shah's reign, however, consisted of something other than political repression. In response to official American urging, the monarchy also promulgated a sweeping set of internal reform and modernization measures, collectively known as the "White Revolution." The Shah's motto was that "Westernization is our welcome ordeal." On many fronts—in agriculture (still the dominant pursuit of the country) and in land reform; in education and an extensive campaign to wipe out illiteracy; in health, sanitation, and welfare measures; in the emancipation of women; in strengthening and modernizing the armed forces—the monarchy sought to bring sweeping changes to Iran. In the words of one commentator, the Shah endeavored to transform

> ... Iran from an economically poor, socially feudal and divided, and politically bankrupt country into a prosperous, just, industrialized, self-sufficient and truly independent ... nation.[57]

A few years before his political demise, the Shah boasted that in the near future Iran would have a standard of living equal to that of Western Europe.

Although it had a number of positive accomplishments to its credit, on balance the White Revolution must be judged a failure —and this fact was a crucial element in the monarchy's collapse. The revolution failed in several critical respects. Many of the reforms promulgated by the palace were poorly administered and unevenly implemented. Dramatic progress in some sectors of Iranian life contrasted starkly with extreme backwardness (if not retrogression) in other sectors. In addition, the problem of maldistribution of income throughout Iranian society became progressively more acute. As a rule, the tangible benefits of the White Revolution accrued more heavily to the "Westernized" elite of Iranian society than they did to the masses. The wealth accumulated and displayed by the Iranian *nouveaux riche* created mounting discontent among the peasants and the slum dwellers, whose conditions showed little noteworthy improvement.

Moreover, in time nearly every segment of Iranian society objected to one or more aspects of the Shah's administration. Businessmen were disaffected by the high rate of inflation and the growth of the governmental bureaucracy. Workers were disenchanted because their wages did not keep pace with the cost of living. The Iranian peasantry found that land reform and other measures designed to uplift agriculture had brought little discernible improvement in their lives. Shi'ite religious leaders and their followers became increasingly outspoken in criticizing the "secular" nature of the Shah's program (some features of which were designed to reduce their traditional authority in several spheres of Iranian life). At home and abroad, students condemned the Shah because of the activities of SAVAK and the authoritarian nature of his regime. Nearly all groups joined in deploring the privileges and wealth enjoyed by the royal family and those in the Shah's favor.

Finally, the principal failure of the Shah's White Revolution was to be found in the political realm. Although from time to time, the Shah stated that his ultimate goal was a "democracy" compatible with the Iranian tradition, during his reign he did little to achieve it. To the end, the monarchy (for important political decisions and governmental appointments, the Shah personally) retained tight control upon the levers of political power; it did nothing of significance to broaden the political base; and down to 1979, the government continued to deal harshly with its critics. These realities meant that political opposition groups had to resort to clandestine and increasingly more violent methods for expressing their criticisms.[58]

Opposition to the Shah's rule came to be centered in the mosques, which had long served as bases for antigovernmental sentiment in Iran. Joined by Communists, students, business groups, and in time nearly all segments of Iranian society, the Shi'ite clergy emerged as the leaders of the revolutionary movement that toppled the monarchy and established a new regime, headed by the Ayatollah Khomeini. While Iran's religious leaders were by no means monolithic in their political objectives, Khomeini's goal was to create a new political order governed by Islamic principles (an "Islamic Democracy"). In practice, this meant ridding Iran of Western and secular influences which, according to Khomeini and his followers, corrupted the society and made it susceptible to foreign control. As time passed—and as the idea of a Koranic-based state came under sharp attack by left-wing critics and other groups within Iran—Khomeini's government was ruthless in dealing with its political opponents. By the early 1980s, Khomeini and his supporters appeared to dominate the Iranian political process. Critics of the regime had been eliminated, were in exile abroad, or had been effectively suppressed.[59]

Diplomatic Implications of the Iranian Revolution

In both domestic and foreign affairs, the revolution in Iran had to be ranked among the more momentous events in the postwar Middle East. The new Iranian government transformed the country's foreign relations. Because of its long-standing and intimate ties with the Shah's regime, after the revolution the United States became "the Great Satan" in the eyes of most Iranians. The storming of the United States Embassy in Tehran, followed by the seizure of American hostages on November 4, 1979, intensified ill feelings in both countries. The Carter Administration's ill-fated attempt to rescue the hostages late in April 1980—along with the repeated failure of diplomatic efforts to secure the hostages' release—provided another source of hostility and mutual suspicion.

Under the Ayatollah Khomeini's regime, Iran's relations with other countries also changed fundamentally. For the first time, Iran became an active center of anti-Israeli opposition; Khomeini and his followers publicly expressed their support for the Palestine Liberation Organization and other anti-Zionist groups. By late 1980, active warfare existed between Iran and Iraq; each government openly called for the overthrow of the other. Iran's relations with Saudi Arabia and other Persian Gulf states similarly deteriorated. Throughout the Persian Gulf region, pervasive apprehension existed about the idea of a Shi'ite-led "Islamic Democracy" and about a possible resurgence of Iranian aspirations toward regional hegemony.[60]

To say the demise of the Iranian monarchy was a serious diplomatic reversal for the United States would be to understate the matter. On several counts, the Iranian Revolution was a major and disillusioning setback for policy makers in Washington and for American public opinion. At home, the unexpected and relatively easy victory of the Iranian revolutionaries seriously undermined public confidence in the Carter Administration's diplomatic astuteness and leadership. For a decade or more, President Carter and his predecessors appeared oblivious to accumulating evidence that the Shah's political position was declining. Washington's lack of preparation for this event was widely regarded as a critical "intelligence failure" by the American government. The Iranian Revolution also resulted in a marked deterioration in the American position in the Middle East. One of the largest and most influential states in the region—long regarded as pro-Western and as a "bastion" against Communist inroads—now became a center of anti-Western sentiment and agitation.

Yet the collapse of the Iranian monarchy did not necessarily promote Moscow's long-term interests in the Middle East. While the United States suffered a major diplomatic defeat from that development, the new Iranian government was equally fearful and distrustful of Soviet intentions toward Iran and its neighbors. Internally, the Ayatollah Khomeini and his supporters frequently denounced Communism as incompatible with "Islamic Democracy"; and the government took steps to suppress Marxist-instigated threats to its authority. In foreign affairs, Tehran vehemently denounced the Soviet invasion of Afghanistan and warned Moscow against efforts to subordinate other Middle Eastern countries.[61]

In mid-1980, several months after his followers had toppled the monarchy in Iran, the Ayatollah Khomeini stated publicly that "The machinery of government is in a state of anarchy...." The aging religious leader lamented that "There is no need for hardship to be inflicted from the outside. We go for each other's throats and destroy ourselves."[62] Almost daily after coming to power, Khomeini's regime faced some new challenge to its authority and stability—from left-wing political dissidents who rejected the idea of a Koranic-based state; or from Kurds, Baluchis, or other ethnic minorities who demanded greater autonomy; or from the Iraqi invaders; or from impending economic collapse. In time, however, Khomeini and his followers defeated internal political opposition groups, turned the military tide against the Iraqi enemy, and began to restore a modicum of in-

ternal order. Gradually, Iran began to resume limited oil production (with Iran's reentry into the world oil market threatening to undermine even further OPEC's ability to maintain a stable price level). In terms of its political future, perhaps the dominant question facing Iran was whether Khomeini's "Islamic Democracy" would survive the aging leader's death. A combination of unique factors had placed him at the head of the new Iranian government—not the least of which was the veneration accorded him by the masses and other religious leaders. In his absence, powerful centrifugal forces might once again seriously weaken Iran's national cohesion.[63]

As near-anarchy appeared to exist in Iran—with economic conditions rapidly deteriorating, and with the machinery of government all but immobilized by internal rivalries and quarrels—the country confronted three grave dangers. One was that the tendency toward anarchy and internal fragmentation would continue, ultimately destroying Iran's cohesion as a nation and leaving it more vulnerable than ever to external dangers. Another was that the Soviet Union might try to exploit Iran's internal weakness for its own diplomatic purposes, thereby strengthening its position in the Persian Gulf area. The third threat to Iran's future as a nation was the conflict with Iraq, erupting in the fall of 1980.

The Iraqi-Iranian War

At the end of September 1980, the Ba'athist government of Iraq launched a massive surprise attack against Iran's southwestern provinces. Iraq's goals in this conflict apparently entailed a number of short-range and long-range objectives.* Ostensibly, Baghdad's pur-

*Our discussion of the Iraqi-Iranian war and its implications draws upon coverage provided in the *New York Times, Newsweek,* and *U.S. News and World Report* during the period of hostilities. See specifically special

pose was to achieve a "rectification" of the disputed border between the two countries, particularly as it related to control over the strategic Shatt-al-Arab waterway at the head of the Persian Gulf. After its forces invaded Iran, Baghdad announced that an agreement (made with the Shah of Iran in 1975) delimiting the border was null and void. Iraq's border claims, however, concealed other, more long-term goals. In time, it became clear that the Iraqi attack had a twofold motivation: to bring about the overthrow of the Ayatollah Khomeini's revolutionary government in Iran; and to establish the Ba'athist-controlled government of Iraq as the dominant power within the Persian Gulf area.

As we have seen, under Saddam Hussein Iraq had achieved unprecedented internal stability; and it was perhaps endeavoring to become the acknowledged "leader" of the Arab world. Iraq's military incursion into adjacent Iranian territories sought to destroy Iran's oil-producing capability (centered in the Abadan refinery complex); and Baghdad also evidently expected that the Arab minority living in the war zone would revolt against Tehran's authority.

After the initial Iraqi attack—resulting in massive destruction of Iran's oil facilities and Iraqi occupation of large salient of southwestern Iran—the conflict between the two countries deteriorated into a prolonged "war

---

dispatch from Beirut, in *New York Times,* September 18, 1980; Youseff M. Ibrahim, in ibid., October 4, 1980; Richard Burt and Youssef M. Ibrahim, in ibid., October 7, 1980; and Henry Tanner, in ibid., October 12, 1980. Analyses of the conflict are also provided in *Newsweek,* **96** (October 20, 1980), 40–44; and in *Time,* **116** (October 13, 1980), 51–59, and ibid. (October 27, 1980), 34–39. An illuminating analysis of Baghdad's goals in attacking Iran is provided in Claudia Wright, "Behind Iraq's Bold Bid," *The New York Times Magazine,* October 26, 1980, pp. 43, 109–117.

of attrition" that drained their resources and created a new threat to the stability of the Persian Gulf area. Oil exports from both countries (especially from Iran) were severely curtailed; and as the war dragged on, Baghdad and Tehran alike sought allies to support their respective causes.

As a result of the war, the oil output of both Iraq and Iran was severely curtailed. (As we have already noted, however, by the early 1980s OPEC faced a global oil surplus which substantially reduced the demand for and price of oil shipments from the Middle East.) Yet a prolonged military conflict in the Persain Gulf area—particularly if it involved other major oil-producing states, like Kuwait—could have serious economic repercussions for such industrialized regions as Western Europe and Japan.

The diplomatic and strategic consequences of the war between Iraq and Iran were no less momentous. In company with several governments within the Middle East, officials in Washington feared that the Iraqi-Iranian conflict would provide new opportunties for expanded Soviet influence in the region. In recent years, for example, Iraq had been a major recipient of Soviet military aid; and Moscow attempted to resupply Iraq's equipment needs during the course of the war. (Informed observers of political developments in the Middle East, however, also knew that the left-wing Ba'ath that ruled Iraq was militantly *anti-Communist* and opposed to Soviet hegemony in the Middle East. Baghdad, for example, had been outspokenly critical of the Soviet incursion into Afghanistan.) As some commentators assessed the matter, Moscow's interests would best be served by a prolonged and indecisive military engagement between Iraq and Iran, leaving both countries exhausted and vulnerable to Soviet influence.

For the nations of the Middle East, the

Iraqi-Iranian war created new sources of internal and intraregional tensions. Located at the head of the Persian Gulf, tiny Kuwait was understandably apprehensive about its security. The prospect of a decisive victory by *either* belligerent—leaving the winner as perhaps the arbiter of the Persian Gulf area—engendered anxieties in Kuwait, as in other smaller states on the Arabian peninsula.

Attitudes toward the conflict by the government of Saudi Arabia were equally ambivalent and apprehensive. On the one hand, Iraq was an *Arab* country, seeking to overthrow a government that had been visibly hostile toward the Wahhabi regime of Saudi Arabia. On the other hand, the left-wing Ba'ath of Iraq was also one of the most zealous sponsors of revolution throughout the Persian Gulf area—and the monarchy of Saudi Arabia was a prime target of Ba'athist revolutionaries! Egypt's response to the Iraqi-Iranian conflict was interesting. In time, Cairo aided its longtime rival, Iraq; but it also moved closer to the United States—as exemplified by Cairo's willingness to permit the newly created American Rapid Deployment Force (RDF) to carry out military exercises in the Egyptian desert. The government of Israel's response to the Iraqi-Iranian conflict was no less interesting and anomalous. Iraq was a leader of the "Rejectionist Front" against Israel. Yet the Ayatollah Khomeini's regime had also become a vocal opponent of Zionism. In time, Israeli influence was cast on the side of Iran. Israel supplied Tehran with sorely needed military equipment and spare parts, while Iran furnished Israel one of its basic requirements—Persian Gulf oil. Indirectly at least, through the "Israeli connection" American power was contributing to Iran's military resurgence and its reemergence as a dominant force in the Persian Gulf area!

The war between Iraq and Iran also created new policy dilemmas and posed difficult choices for the United States. A decisive victory by neither country was in America's diplomatic interests—nor was an indefinitely prolonged military engagement between them. As we have seen, since the collapse of the Iranian monarchy, relations between the United States and Iran had been strained. Yet officials in the United States did not look forward to Iran's internal collapse or its defeat by Iraq—developments that might well enhance Soviet power in the Middle East and fuel the Arab-Israeli conflict. Among the Arab states, the Ba'athist government of Iraq remained a center of anti-American, no less than anti-Israeli, agitation. At the same time, an indefinite prolongation of the Iraqi-Iranian conflict would keep the Persian Gulf area in a continuing state of instability and would, sooner or later, produce severe economic dislocations for America's European allies and Japan.

Consequently, officials of the Carter and Reagan administrations concluded that America's best course lay in attempting to encourage a cease-fire, and ultimately a lasting peace, in the Iraqi-Iranian conflict on terms acceptable to both parties. Given Washington's extremely limited influence with both belligerents, however, this was not an approach that promised quick or certain results. As the country possessing the military advantage, Iraq appeared determined to insist upon acceptance of its terms before agreeing to a truce; for its part, Iran remained dedicated to driving out the Iraqi invader and administering a defeat to its ideological adversary. Meanwhile, as the war dragged on toward an inconclusive result, at the request of governments like Kuwait and Saudi Arabia, the United States sent military equipment to friendly regimes in the Persian Gulf area to strengthen their military establishments against both belligerents. In addition, the United States intensified efforts begun several months earlier, in response to the Soviet invasion of Afghanistan, to bolster its military position in the volatile Persian Gulf region.

The Soviet Invasion of Afghanistan

At the end of December 1979, Soviet troops crossed the border into Afghanistan, in an effort to place that Islamic and fiercely independent country under Moscow's hegemony. Afghanistan is a landlocked, remote, and primitive state with an area of just over 250,000 square miles (slightly smaller than Texas), and a population of some 21 million people. As one study has said of it:

> No central government of that vast and mountainous country has ever had more than a tenuous grip on its more remote areas. Given long-standing Afghan racial and religious antipathies to Soviet penetration, the more a [Marxist] regime in Kabul appears to be a puppet of the Soviet Union, the stronger popular resistance is likely to become.[64]

Events throughout the months that followed were to confirm this prediction.

The Soviet effort to subordinate Afghanistan climaxed a prolonged (and generally unsuccessful) effort by the Kremlin and its Marxist supporters in the country to establish a Communist regime that could command popular support. On July 17, 1973, the monarchy under King Zahir was overthrown by Mohammed Daoud and military units loyal to him. For the next 10 years, in Lenczowski's words, Afghanistan "veered between the extremes of anarchy and despotism." Internal opposition to his regime was mounting; and late in April 1978, Daoud was ousted in a

successful coup. The new ruler was Mohammed Taraki, leader of the Marxist Khalq Party, who proclaimed Afghanistan to be a Soviet-style "Democratic Republic." Taraki moved rapidly to impose a Marxist system upon Afghanistan at home and to lean heavily upon the Soviet Union in foreign affairs. Meanwhile, among the Islamic and independent people of Afghanistan, popular opposition to the Taraki regime mounted steadily.[65]

Events in Afghanistan unfolded rapidly, as Marxist groups, supported by the Kremlin, tried to strengthen their disintegrating political base. On September 14, 1979, Taraki's regime was overthrown, and a new government—under former Prime Minister Hafizullah Amin—took office. But this change did little to win the support of the people for a Communist political system. By the end of the year, Msocow was faced with two unpalatable choices: It could acquiesce in the almost inevitable demise of the Amin government; or it could intervene directly into the country's political affairs to impose and maintain a Communist political system in Afghanistan. The Kremlin chose the latter alternative: On December 29, some 30,000 Russian troops invaded Afghanistan. Two days earlier, President Amin had been assassinated and a new government under another handpicked spokesman for the Kremlin, Babrak Karmal, was installed in Kabul. This change in regimes did nothing to reverse mounting public opposition to Communist rule.

Overt Soviet military intervention in Afghanistan shocked the international community; and it was a traumatic event for policy makers in Washington. For the first time, the Kremlin had *employed undisguised military force* to impose its will upon a Third World country. Nor did it escape global attention that this was an Islamic state. Moreover, Soviet behavior strongly implied that the "Brezhnev Doctrine" (previously invoked only in Moscow's relations with Eastern Europe) was now applicable to *any country* having a Marxist government.* The Russian incursion into Afghanistan also had profound implications for a subject dealt with extensively in Chapter 10: the future of Soviet-American détente. How was it possible, the American people and their leaders asked, for Moscow simultaneously to call for détente with the United States and engage in a ruthless campaign to subdue Afghanistan and to threaten the security of the Persian Gulf area generally?

Besides these questions, officials in Washington and other foreign capitals were mystified by Soviet motives—and by Moscow's future intentions—in its efforts to subordinate Afghanistan. What policy calculations led to this move by the Kremlin? What were Moscow's immediate goals? Even more crucial, what did the Russian effort to dominate Afghanistan portend with regard to other possible Soviet threats to the security of neighboring countries like Iran and Pakistan, and to other states bordering the Persian Gulf? Informed students of Soviet affairs provided a wide range of answers to such questions.

One explanation—advanced frequently throughout the months after Soviet troops

crossed the border into Afghanistan—was that the venture was "Russia's Vietnam." As Alexander the Great had discovered in ancient history—and as Great Britain found out at the end of the nineteenth century—the Afghan tribesmen are fierce, determined, and skillful fighters; their devotion to Islam made them prepared to engage in a *jihad* (or Moslem "holy war") against Infidel invaders. As the weeks passed, the Red Army found itself confronted with a relentless and effective guerrilla campaign against Communist rule, waged by the Afghan rebels. By day, Soviet forces controlled the cities and the highways of Afghanistan; by night, relying upon their knowledge of the terrain and their support of the people, the rebels controlled the countryside and inflicted mounting casualties upon the besieged Russian garrisons.

Military analysts believed that in time, the Kremlin would again confront a difficult choice. On the one hand, it would have to increase substantially the size of its military commitment in Afghanistan (and some commentators believed Moscow would need 400,000 or more troops) in order to establish effective Communist control over the country. Few qualified observers doubted that the Soviet Union *could* achieve its goals in Afghanistan. But the Soviet hierarchy could elect this course only by seriously weakening Russian defenses in the NATO area and along the Sino-Soviet border; and this alternative would impose a massive drain upon Soviet resources. On the other hand, Soviet officials would have to conclude that their venture in Afghanistan had failed—and (as America had done in Vietnam) accept the loss of prestige and "credibility" that this decision inevitably entailed. If the Kremlin followed this course, it would logically seek to negotiate "a way out" of its predicament in Afghanistan. Most nations of Western Europe urged Washington

---

*The "Brezhnev Doctrine" was announced by the Kremlin, following the massive military invasion of Czechoslovakia by Warsaw Pact forces on August 20, 1968. The doctrine justified this Soviet intervention in Czechoslovakia by saying that Moscow was permitted to rely upon military force to prevent a "deviation from socialism" and to avert the "restoration of a capitalist order" in states having a Marxist system. The doctrine also permitted Soviet intervention to counter "a threat to the security of the socialist [i.e., Soviet-led Communist] community as a whole." See the article from *Pravda* explaining the meaning and rationale of the doctrine in Senate Government Operations Committee, *Czechoslovakia and the Brezhnev Doctrine,* 91st Cong., 1st Sess., 1969, pp. 1–3, 15, 21.

to encourage and facilitate Moscow's adoption of the latter alternative.[66]

The Carter Doctrine

In his State of the Union address to Congress on January 23, 1980, President Jimmy Carter devoted most of his message to the Soviet Union's incursion into Afghanistan. In the process, he enunciated what came to be called the "Carter Doctrine," committing the United States to the defense of the Persian Gulf area. While in some respects the doctrine merely made explicit certain principles of American foreign policy that had long been implicit in the nation's approach to the Middle East, issuance of the Carter Doctrine had to be regarded as a highly significant development in the diplomatic history of the United States.[67]

Noting that the "1980s have been born in turmoil, strife, and change," Carter identified two crucial developments in the Middle East—the overthrow of the Iranian monarchy, followed by the seizure of American hostages; and the Soviet invasion of Afghanistan—as directly affecting American interests. He accused the new Iranian government of trying to "blackmail" the United States and warned Tehran that "a severe price will be paid" if harm came to the Americans held captive in Iran.

The bulk of Carter's message, however, was devoted to a denunciation and an analysis of the implications of Moscow's effort to subjugate Afghanistan. Identifying Soviet-American relations as "the most critical factor" affecting the peace and security of the international system, Carter emphasized that in recent years both superpowers had sought to achieve détente. He admonished Moscow: "We superpowers ... have the responsibility to exercise restraint in the use of our great military force." In the American view, "The in-

tegrity and the independence of weaker nations must not be threatened." Carter unequivocally condemned Moscow for embarking upon this "radical and ... aggressive new step" that imperiled détente; and he stated that the United States did not propose to engage in "business as usual" with the Soviet Union, as long as its effort to dominate Afghanistan continued.

President Carter described the Soviet invasion of Afghanistan as "the most serious threat to peace since the Second World War." Then the President announced his "doctrine," or the principle that would guide American foreign policy in response to it:

> Let our position be absolutely clear: An attempt by any outside force to gain control of the Persian Gulf region will be regarded as an assault on the vital interests of the United States ... and such an assault will be repelled by any means necessary, including military force.

For a number of reasons, the issuance of the Carter Doctrine was a noteworthy event. By his declaration, President Carter took his place with President James Monroe, who in 1823 established the precedent of embodying important principles of American foreign policy in what was ultimately called a diplomatic "doctrine." As explained in earlier chapters, Carter's statement could be interpreted as merely an adaptation of the Truman Doctrine (1947) committing the United States to the strategy of containment directed against Communist expansionism; and it was also in some respects a restatement of the Eisenhower Doctrine, issued in 1957, according to which the United States proposed to resist Communist encroachments in the Middle East.* The

*The Truman Doctrine was discussed at length in Chapters 9 and 11. The Eisenhower Doctrine was

Carter Doctrine officially and forcefully acknowledged a reality we have emphasized in the preceding pages: America's security and economic well-being had become increasingly dependent upon continued access to the Persian Gulf area.

What was the future of the Carter Doctrine? Would it prove to be anything more than the kind of verbal diplomatic announcement, often characteristic of America, that in the absence of concrete steps to enforce it might actually *weaken* America's position in global affairs and its influence in the Middle East? Or by contrast, would the issuance of the Carter Doctrine mark a new era of deeper American involvement in the affairs of the Persian Gulf area, as Washington supplied evidence of its determination to *defend* the region from external threats? The future of the Carter Doctrine as an instrument of American foreign policy was likely to be massively conditioned by how officials in the United States—supported by American public opinion—provided answers to four pivotal questions about it.

First, how accurately and realistically had officials in Washington assessed the *reasons* for the Soviet penetration of Afghanistan and its implications for regional security? Had Washington, in other words, identified

the challenge correctly and, on that basis, formulated a realistic response to it?

The text and tone of the President's message to Congress leave no doubt about the Carter Administration's conclusions. Denouncing the Soviet move as "an aggressive new step," the Administration believed that it reflected the Kremlin's long-standing desire to dominate weaker countries and to impose a Communist system on them. Despite its expressed devotion to détente, Moscow had flagrantly relied upon armed force to subjugate Afghanistan, thereby precipitating a new round in the Cold War. It followed that the Kremlin would similarly threaten the security of other states in the area if its hegemony over Afghanistan were unopposed. Therefore, as it had done many times in the past, the United States must "contain" this new Soviet expansionist tendency by all the means—including reliance upon military force—at its disposal. The Reagan Administration that took office in 1981 was perhaps even more suspicious of Soviet motives in the Middle East and elsewhere than its predecessor.

The Carter Administration's analysis of Soviet behavior in Afghanistan was disputed by informed students of Russian diplomacy at home and abroad. In time, a highly diverse range of explanations and theories concerning Moscow's motivations in Afghanistan—and in the Middle East generally—was available to the student of American foreign policy. These varied between what might be called "minimalist" and "maximalist" interpretations —with some explanations falling in between these extreme assessments of Soviet behavior.

In the former category was the distinguished Kremlinologist George F. Kennan, who was convinced that the Kremlin's move against Afghanistan was explicable primarily by reference to age-old Russian anxieties about the security of its borders (apprehensions that had been aggravated by such Amer-

---

promulgated after the Suez Crisis of 1956. According to this policy statement, the United States would protect the security of any Middle Eastern state whose independence was threatened by "international communism." Under the Eisenhower Doctrine, American troops were landed in Lebanon in mid-July 1957 to prevent that country from being plunged into civil war—instigated in some measure, Washington believed, by Communist forces in the Middle East. For a discussion of this episode, see Dwight D. Eisenhower, *Waging Peace* (Garden City, N.Y.: Doubleday and Co., 1965), pp. 262–291; and the commentary on the Lebanese crisis by J. C. Hurewitz, in Leonard Binder, ed., *Politics in Lebanon* (New York: John Wiley, 1966), pp. 230–238.

ican moves as the planned improvement of NATO forces). Other commentators were convinced that Moscow believed (mistakenly, as events turned out) that Soviet forces in Afghanistan could quickly eliminate internal opposition to a Communist political system. Now Soviet policy makers were trapped in a "quagmire" in Afghanistan from which the Kremlin would like to escape—if the crisis were not converted into a Cold War encounter with the United States.

Among the "maximalist" interpretations available were the idea that, by its attempt to subjugate Afghanistan, Moscow was deliberately seeking to upset the global balance of power; that it was intentionally embarking upon a course of expansionism when, under the Carter Administration, the United States appeared militarily weak and diplomatically indecisive; and that Moscow's ultimate objective was realization of the centuries-old Russian diplomatic goal of dominance in the Persian Gulf area. Some commentators also believed that the Soviet Union's own approaching "energy crisis" was a pivotal consideration in its attempt to penetrate the Persian Gulf area.[68]

Irrespective of which theory (or theories) of Soviet behavior was correct, both the Carter and the Reagan administrations took an extremely serious view of Soviet expansionism in the Persian Gulf area. As we noted in Chapter 10, for example, President Reagan and his advisers reaffirmed the key concept of "linkage" in the American view of détente with the Soviet Union: If Moscow desired cooperative relations with Washington, it would have to demonstrate *by its actions* in Afghanistan and elsewhere that it was devoted to peaceful goals.

Second, the contribution of the Carter Doctrine in achieving American diplomatic goals would also depend upon success in solving a related problem: the ability of the United

States and its NATO allies to arrive at a common position in responding to the crisis in Afghanistan. Thus far, as we observed in Chapter 11, Soviet intervention in Afghanistan had added to the "disarray" existing within NATO. With the possible exception of the Conservative government of Great Britain, most of the NATO allies disagreed with Washington's assessment of Soviet behavior in Afghanistan; and they showed little inclination to support the implementation of the Carter Doctrine. Led by West Germany, the European allies expressed deep concern about the future of détente. Officials in European capitals did *not* believe that the Soviet invasion of Afghanistan signaled a renewal of the Cold War; nor were they greatly apprehensive that, from their base in Afghanistan, Soviet forces would threaten the security of other countries bordering the Persian Gulf. As the Russian invader continued to encounter fierce resistance from the Afghan rebels, most of the European allies advocated reliance upon diplomacy—instead of armed force—to secure a Soviet evacuation of the country. In the European view, two other causes of regional instability—the ongoing Arab-Israeli conflict and the eruption of warfare between Iraq and Iran—overshadowed the crisis in Afghanistan. Toward both of these conflicts, the members of NATO were exercising independent diplomatic initiatives in behalf of a settlement.[69]

Third, the long-range utility of the Carter Doctrine would also be crucially affected by the responses of the countries bordering, or adjacent to, the Persian Gulf area. Again, the United States faced formidable obstacles in its efforts to implement the Carter Doctrine. Throughout most of the region the reaction to the doctrine emphasized two dominant themes. One was widespread, and in some cases vehement, opposition to any proposed American military buildup in the Persian Gulf area, particularly if this envisioned stationing American troops within countries close to Afghanistan. Alone among the Arab states, President Sadat's government in Egypt offered to provide airfields and other facilities to implement the Carter Doctrine; in time, Oman also made facilities available to the United States to protect the Persian Gulf. Although its security was directly jeopardized by the Soviet presence in Afghanistan, on the eastern flank of the Persian Gulf region Pakistan carefully avoided close military cooperation with the United States after the Soviet invasion of Afghanistan. While nearly all states in the area condemned, and were clearly apprehensive about, the Soviet incursion into Afghanistan, few were willing to establish close military ties with the United States. After war erupted between Iraq and Iran, most nations in the region feared the reaction of these belligerents to a significant American military buildup in the area. America's long-standing ties with Israel also dampened Arab enthusiasm for an expanded American power base in the Middle East.[70]

Finally, the value of the Carter Doctrine—and its place in the annals of American diplomacy—would be determined substantially by the steps taken by the United States to carry out its provisions. In the months preceding the Soviet incursion into Afghanistan, the United States had suffered two diplomatic reverses impairing its "credibility" and raising questions about the steadfastness of its foreign policy. One of these was Washington's belated discovery of Soviet combat forces in Cuba in 1979. Initially, the Carter Administration had described this Soviet military presence in the Western Hemisphere as "unacceptable," but in fact (after finding no effective means for gaining their removal), Americans "accepted" their presence in the Caribbean. As we have already seen, the other event undermining America's diplomatic and military credibility

was the overthrow of the Iranian monarchy early in 1979. Against this background, the Carter Doctrine, committing the United States to defend the Persian Gulf area against Soviet hegemony, appeared to many critics as another not untypical example of America's tendency to engage in an empty diplomatic "verbalization," which the United States had neither the will nor the capacity to enforce.

Coming at a time when the overall level of the American armed forces was at the lowest point since the Korean War, President Carter's pledge to protect the Persian Gulf area imposed a heavy burden upon the nation's military capabilities. In order to provide the military capacity needed to enforce the Carter Doctrine, the White House called for the creation of a new, powerful, and highly mobile Rapid Deployment Force (RDF) capable of projecting American power to the Persian Gulf region and possibly other endangered locales. Consisting of army, navy (including marine), and air force units, the RDF was envisioned as a new strike force of from 100,000 to 200,000 troops, enabling the United States to respond quickly to a new threat in the Persian Gulf area or other regions where its security interests were endangered. American officials hoped that the mere existence of this new military unit would *deter* Moscow from new expansionist moves in the region.[71] The Reagan Administration endorsed both the general goal of strengthening America's military posture and the more specific objective of augmenting the power of the United States in the Middle East, by the creation of the Rapid Deployment Force and other measures. It remained to be seen whether these ideas—adding significantly to America's defense burden—could be implemented while, simultaneously, the Republican Administration also carried out its promise to reduce tax levels and overall governmental spending.

Several months after Soviet troops crossed the border into Afghanistan, Secretary of Defense Harold Brown publicly acknowledged two pivotal facts about the Carter Doctrine. The burden of protecting the security of the Persian Gulf area would have to be borne largely *by the United States alone;* and the successful defense of the region would entail a substantial increase in American defense spending—estimated to add some $5 billion or more annually to the national defense budget. On the basis of experience with defense estimates, it could safely be predicted that, if anything, this estimate was too low![72]

As a relatively recent development in American foreign relations, the Carter Doctrine faced an uncertain future. The electoral landslide that gave the Republican Party control of the White House and the Senate beginning in 1981 presaged a number of changes in the substance and style of American diplomacy. For many of the Carter Administration's critics, the Carter Doctrine epitomized one of the major defects of its foreign policy: a tendency to rely upon rhetorical statements—unsupported by requisite military and other kinds of power—to protect the nation's external interests. Yet before it relinquished office, the Carter Administration had taken a number of steps to strengthen the American position in the Persian Gulf and adjacent areas. The Rapid Deployment Force had been created; it was undergoing training in the United States and in the Middle East; and efforts were being made to solve a number of specific problems—such as providing adequate logistical support for the RDF—that might inhibit its effectiveness.

After Ronald Reagan entered the White House in 1981, officials of his administration reiterated America's firm commitment to the security of the Persian Gulf area. In effect, the Carter Doctrine had become the Carter-Reagan Doctrine as a major guideline of American diplomacy. Even more than his Democratic predecessor, Reagan was determined to resist Soviet expansionism into this vital zone and to provide the United States with the military capability of doing so. The substantial buildup of American naval strength advocated by the Administration provided tangible evidence of this approach. Admittedly, numerous—and in some instances, very difficult—obstacles confronted effective implementation of this strategy in the Middle East. Yet, for an indefinite period in the future, the principle embodied in the Carter Doctrine—that American security was vitally affected by developments in the Persian Gulf area—would continue to guide the foreign policy of the United States.[73]

NOTES

1. Early American religious and cultural contacts with the Middle East are explained more fully in Harry N. Howard, "The United States and the Middle East," in Tareq Y. Ismael, *The Middle East in World Politics* (Syracuse, N.Y.: Syracuse University Press, 1974), pp. 115–119.
2. For the impact of Wilsonian ideas upon the Middle East, see George Lenczowski, *The Middle East in World Affairs,* 4th ed. (Ithaca, N.Y.: Cornell University Press, 1980), pp. 792–793. See also Samuel Halperin, *The Political World of American Zionism* (Detroit, Mich.: Wayne State University Press, 1961), pp. 187–188.
3. The anticolonial attitudes and policies of Presidents Roosevelt and Truman are discussed in Gaddis Smith, *American Diplomacy During the Second World War* (New York: John Wiley and Sons, 1966), pp. 81–119.
4. The strategic implications of the Middle East in World War II are analyzed in Lenczowski, *The Middle East in World Affairs,* pp. 689–694; and its more recent strategic importance is emphasized in ibid., pp. 694–735.

5. American policy in Iran and the Persian Gulf area during World War II is dealt with more fully in Amin Saikal, *The Rise and Fall of the Shah* (Princeton, N.J.: Princeton University Press, 1980), pp. 25–46.

6. The views of President Woodrow Wilson and other prominent Americans on the Zionist movement are discussed in Halperin, *The Political World of American Zionism*, pp. 187–188; and in Arthur Hertzberg, ed., *The Zionist Idea: A Historical Analysis and Reader* (Garden City, N.Y.: Doubleday, 1959), pp. 514–524.

7. President Roosevelt's views and policies respecting Zionism are discussed more fully in Zvi Ganin, *Truman, American Jewry, and Israel, 1945–1948* (New York: Holmes and Meier, 1979), pp. 1–20.

8. See the account of President Roosevelt's meeting with King Ibn Saud of Saudi Arabia early in 1945, in Walter Laqueur, *A History of Zionism* (New York: Holt, Rinehart and Winston, 1972), pp. 553–556.

9. The Truman Administration's policies toward Zionism and Israel in the early postwar period are dealt with in detail in Ganin, *Truman, American Jewry, and Israel, 1945–1948;* and in Harry S Truman, *Memoirs,* Vol. 2 (Garden City, N.Y.: Doubleday and Co., 1956), pp. 156–169.

10. The reasons and consequences of the decision of Zionist organizations to shift their base of operations to the United States are identified in Ganin, *Truman, American Jewry, and Israel, 1945–1948*, pp. 2–19. America's role in the creation of the state of Israel is described in Truman, *Memoirs,* Vol. 2, pp. 132–169; and in Dean Acheson, *Present at the Creation* (New York: W. W. Norton, 1969), pp. 169–183.

11. See Lenczowski, *The Middle East in World Affairs,* pp. 579–580; and William R. Polk, *The United States and the Arab World* (Cambridge, Mass.: Harvard University Press, 1965), pp. 236–240.

12. See the excerpt from the report submitted to the British government by a royal commission appointed to investigate the conflict in Palestine in 1937, in Polk, *The United States and the Arab World,* pp. 170–172.

13. Terrence Prittie, *Israel: Miracle in the Desert* (New York: Praeger Publishers, 1967), pp. 17–20.

14. The text of the Balfour Declaration is cited in Polk, *The United States and the Arab World,* p. 111; and see subsequent British explanations of its meaning and purpose in ibid., pp. 161–164.

15. See the discussion of British-Arab negotiations during World War I in Lenczowski, *The Middle East in World Affairs,* pp. 79–82; and in Polk, *The United States and the Arab World,* pp. 100–120.

16. The British White Paper of 1939 is discussed in Fred J. Khouri, *The Arab-Israeli Dilemma* (Syracuse, N.Y.: Syracuse University Press, 1968), pp. 25–27.

17. The events leading to the decision by the United Nations to "partition" Palestine are described in ibid., pp. 43–68.

18. The "first round" of conflict between Israel and its Arab neighbors in 1947–1948 is analyzed in ibid., pp. 68–102.

19. See Truman, *Memoirs,* Vol. 2, pp. 136–150; and Khouri, *The Arab-Israeli Dilemma,* pp. 43–67.

20. The origins and implications of the Arab refugee problems are dealt with in Khouri, *The Arab-Israeli Dilemma,* pp. 123–182; and see several chapters devoted to various aspects of the Arab refugee issue in Michael Curtis, et al., eds., *The Palestinians: People, History, Politics* (New Brunswick, N.J.: Transaction Books, 1975).

21. For discussions of Soviet policy toward Egypt beginning in the mid-1950s, see R. D. McLaurin, *The Middle East in Soviet Policy* (Lexington, Mass.: D. C. Heath, 1975), pp. 8–15; and Jaan Pennar, *The U.S.S.R. and the Arabs: the Ideological Dimension, 1917–1972* (New York: Crane, Russak and Co., 1973), pp. 62–71. America's attempt to apply the containment principle to the Middle East is discussed in Nadav Safran, *From War*

to War: The Arab-Israeli Confrontation, 1948–1967 (New York: Pegasus, 1969), pp. 100–137.

22. The origins and consequences of the "Suez Crisis" of 1956 are analyzed in Dwight D. Eisenhower, *Waging Peace* (Garden City, N.Y.: Doubleday and Co., 1965), pp. 20–58; Leonard Mosley, *Dulles: A Biography of Eleanor, Allen, and John Foster Dulles and Their Family Network* (New York: Dial Press, 1978), pp. 404–434; and Anthony Eden, *The Suez Crisis of 1956* (Boston: Beacon Press, 1960).

23. The problems posed for Israel, economically, politically, and in other spheres, by the large influx of "Oriental Jews" are discussed in Prittie, *Israel: Miracle in the Desert,* pp. 89–106; and in Peter Mansfield, *The Middle East: a Political and Economic Survey,* 4th ed. (New York: Oxford University Press, 1973), pp. 363–367; for more current information, see later volumes in this series.

24. The causes, major events, and results of the Six-Day War are dealt with in Trevor N. Dupuy, *Elusive Victory: The Arab-Israeli Wars, 1947–1974* (New York: Harper & Row, 1978), pp. 221–387. A briefer account is Khouri, *The Arab-Israeli Dilemma,* pp. 242–293.

25. The conflict between the Jordanian government and the PLO and other Arab guerrilla organizations is described in Anne Sinai and Allen Pollack, eds., *The Hashemite Kingdom of Jordan and the West Bank* (New York: American Academic Association for Peace in the Middle East, 1977), pp. 28–36.

26. The origins and consequences of the Lebanese civil war are analyzed in Norman F. Howard, "Tragedy in Lebanon," *Current History,* **72** (January, 1977), 1–6, 30–32. For current information on events in Lebanon, see *The Middle East Annual Review: 1979* (Chicago: Rand-McNally, 1980), pp. 257–264, and later volumes in this series.

27. Changes in Saudi Arabia's foreign policy after the 1967 war are discussed more fully in: Fred Halliday, *Arabia Without Sultans: A Survey of Political Instability in the Arab World* (New York: Random House, 1975), pp. 82–93; and Ramon Knauerhase, "Saudi Arabia: Our Conservative Ally," *Current History,* **78** (January, 1980), 17–22.

28. The internal power struggle in Egypt following Nasser's death, resulting in Sadat's victory over his rivals, is dealt with in R. Michael Burrell and Abbas R. Kelidar, *Egypt: The Dilemmas of a Nation—1970–1977* (Beverly Hills, Calif.: Sage Publications, 1977). For Sadat's strategy in the Yom Kippur War, see Anwar el-Sadat, *In Search of Identity* (New York: Harper & Row, 1978), pp. 232–271.

29. Background on the Syrian political system and the emergence of the right-wing Ba'ath regime under General Assad is provided in Anne Sinai and Allen Pollack, eds., *The Syrian Arab Republic* (New York: American Academic Association for Peace in the Middle East, 1976). A more recent assessment of Syria's internal and foreign policies is: Stanley Reed, "Dateline Syria: *Fin De Régime,*" *Foreign Policy,* **39** (Summer, 1980), 176–190.

30. Internal and external developments in Iraq are discussed in *Middle East Annual Review,* 1979, pp. 223–230, and in later volumes in this series. The Iraqi-Iranian war and its implications are analyzed in Richard W. Cottam, "Revolutionary Iran and the War with Iraq," *Current History,* **80** (January, 1981), 5–10, 38–39; and in Adeed I. Dawisha, "Iraq: the West's Opportunity," *Foreign Policy,* **41** (Winter, 1980–81), 134–154. Iran's counteroffensive in 1982 is described by Henry Tanner in *New York Times,* April 1, 1982, and by Drew Middleton in ibid., April 9, 1982.

31. Background on the Libyan revolution and on its goals is provided in Ruth First, *Libya: the Elusive Revolution* (Baltimore: Penguin Books, 1974). A more recent treatment, focusing upon Qaddafi's diplomacy, is John K. Cooley, "The Libyan Menace," *Foreign Policy,* **42** (Spring, 1981), 74–94.

32. The causes and major consequences of the

1973 war in the Middle East are assessed in Walter Laqueur, *Confrontation: the Middle East and World Politics* (New York: Bantam Books, 1974). Another analysis, written from an Arab perspective, is Bodri Z. Zohdy, *The Ramadan War, 1973* (New York: Hippocrene Books, 1978).

33. Secretary Kissinger's "shuttle diplomacy"—an intensive effort to find a formula for peace in the Middle East—is described and evaluated in Edward R. F. Sheehan, *The Arabs, Israelis and Kissinger: A Secret History of American Diplomacy in the Middle East* (New York: Thomas Y. Crowell, 1976). This aspect of Kissinger's diplomacy is also dealt with extensively in the second volume of his memoirs.

34. See Sadat, *In Search of Identity,* pp. 271–318.

35. Arab attitudes toward the Israeli-Egyptian peace settlement and outstanding issues in the Arab-Israeli conflict are depicted in Edward W. Said, *The Question of Palestine* (New York: Random House, 1979), pp. 182–238.

36. Stages in the search for peace in the Middle East after the Israeli-Egyptian treaty are described in *The Middle East,* 5th ed. (Washington, D.C.: Congressional Quarterly, 1981), pp. 21–29.

37. Recent developments in the Arab-Israeli conflict are described and analyzed by leading authorities in the symposium on "The Middle East," *Foreign Affairs,* **60** (Spring, 1982), 769–814. The Reagan Administration's approach to Middle Eastern issues is dealt with in Norman Podhoretz, "The Neo-Conservative Anguish Over Reagan's Foreign Policy," *The New York Times Magazine,* May 2, 1982, pp. 30–36, 94–97.

38. For discussions of the policies of individual members of the "Rejectionist Front" toward Israel after the 1973 war, see the discussion of specific countries in *Middle East Annual Review: 1979;* and in *The Middle East: U.S. Policy, Israel, Oil and the Arabs,* 4th ed. (Washington, D.C.: Congressional Quarterly,

1979). Arab reactions to President Sadat's death—and assessments of its implications for stability in the Middle East—are available in Boutros Boutros-Ghali, "The Foreign Policy of Egypt in the Post-Sadat Era," *Foreign Affairs,* **60** (Spring, 1982), 769–788; in El Hassan Bin Talal, "Jordan's Quest for Peace," ibid., 802–813; and in Stanley F. Reed, "Dateline Cairo: Shaken Pillar," *Foreign Policy,* **45** (Winter, 1981–82), 175–186.

39. See, for example, the conflicting statements attributed to the PLO and other Palestine guerrilla organizations, in *New York Times,* July 9, 1980.

40. In July 1980, for example, Secretary of State Edmund Muskie said that a successful resolution of the Arab-Israeli conflict would require inclusion of representatives of the Palestinian people. See the text of his speech in *New York Times,* July 8, 1980.

41. More detailed discussion of the Arab refugee question may be found in Hisham Sharabi, *Palestine and Israel: the Lethal Dilemma* (New York: Pegasus, 1969), pp. 165–182; Terrence Prittie, "Middle East Refugees," in Curtis, et al. *The Palestinians: People, History, Politics,* pp. 51–77.

42. Growing support for the PLO among the Arabs living in the West Bank territories is described in Michael C. Hudson, "The Palestinians: Retrospect and Prospects," *Current History,* **78** (January, 1980), 39–40. Israeli attitudes on several issues blocking a peace settlement with the Arabs are conveyed in Yitzhak Shamir, "Israel's Role in a Changing Middle East," *Foreign Affairs,* **60** (Spring, 1982), 789–801.

43. See George Lenczowski, "The Arc of Crisis: Its Central Sector," *Foreign Affairs,* **57** (Spring, 1979), 796–821.

44. Benjamin Schwadran, *Middle East Oil: Issues and Problems* (Cambridge, Mass.: Schenkman Publishing Co., 1977), p. 1.

45. The forces leading Syria and Iraq to develop closer ties with the United States are discussed in *The Middle East: U.S. Policy,*

Israel, Oil and the Arabs, pp. 129–131, 158–163. Algeria's expressed desire for more cooperative relations with the United States is analyzed by Pranay G. Gupte in *New York Times,* April 25, 1982.

46. Data on the evolution of OPEC, its growing oil revenues, and its economic and political policies are provided in ibid., pp. 70–88; in Robert S. Pindyck, 'OPEC's Threat to the West," *Foreign Policy,* **30** (Spring, 1978), 36–53; and in Alan L. Madian, "Oil Is Still Too Cheap," ibid., **35** (Summer, 1979), 170–180.

47. More detailed discussion of the Wahhabi sect of Sunni Islam may be found in R. Bayly Winder, *Saudi Arabia in the Nineteenth Century* (New York: St. Martin's Press, 1965), pp. 1–16.

48. The political history of Arabia since the nineteenth century is dealt with in *idem;* and in David E. Long, *Saudi Arabia* (Beverly Hills, Calif.: Sage Publications, 1976), pp. 18–42.

49. Economic data on Saudi Arabia are taken from Long, *Saudi Arabia,* pp. 42–57; from *The Middle East: U.S. Policy, Israel, Oil and the Arabs,* pp. 152–158; and from *The Middle East Annual Review: 1979,* pp. 315–338.

50. G. H. Jansen, *Militant Islam* (New York: Harper & Row, 1979), p. 195.

51. A more detailed discussion of radical and revolutionary political forces in the Persian Gulf area may be found in Emile A. Nakhleh, *Arab-American Relations in the Persian Gulf* (Washington, D.C.: American Enterprise Institute, 1975), pp. 30–38.

52. For analyses of forces and tendencies affecting the political future of Saudi Arabia, see Thomas Ferris, "Riding the Saudi Boom," *The New York Times Magazine,* March 25, 1979, pp. 23, 46–54; Youssef M. Ibrahim, in *New York Times,* February 25, 1980; and *U.S. News and World Report,* **86** (April 2, 1979), 23–26. An informative discussion of Saudi Arabia's foreign policy is: William B. Quandt, "Riyadh Between the Superpowers," *Foreign Policy,* **44** (Fall, 1981), 37–57.

53. The regime of Reza Shah is treated in Richard W. Cottam, *Nationalism in Iran* (Pittsburgh, Pa.: University of Pittsburgh Press, 1979), pp. 254–258; and in Lenczowski, *The Middle East in World Affairs,* pp. 170–174.

54. Saikal, *The Rise and Fall of the Shah,* p. 38.

55. James A. Bill and Robert W. Stookey, *Politics and Petroleum: The Middle East and the United States* (Brunswick, Ohio: King's Court Communications, 1975), p. 40.

56. For more detailed discussion of the Iranian oil crisis and America's involvement in the political events accompanying it, see Saikal, *The Rise and Fall of the Shah,* pp. 35–46. An official version of the American role in the Shah's restoration is provided in Dwight D. Eisenhower, *Mandate for Change* (Garden City, N.Y.: Doubleday and Co., 1963), pp. 159–166. A highly critical account of the American role is Richard J. Barnet, *Intervention and Revolution: America's Confrontation with Insurgent Movements Around the World* (Chicago: World Publishing Co., 1968), pp. 225–229.

57. Saikal, *The Rise and Fall of the Shah,* p. 82.

58. Assessments of the White Revolution—and of the monarchy's loss of popular support—may be found in Saikal, *The Rise and Fall of the Shah,* pp. 71–97; and Sepher Zabih, "Iran Today," *Current History,* **66** (February, 1974), 66–70, 87.

59. The reasons why political opposition in Iran has traditionally been centered in the mosques are explained in Jansen, *Militant Islam,* pp. 161–164. The ideology and goals of the Ayatollah Khomeini are presented more fully in *Sayings of the Ayatollah Khomeini: Political, Philosophical, Social and Religious* (New York: Bantam Books, 1980); and in Eric Rouleau, "Khomeini's Iran," *Foreign Affairs,* **59** (Fall, 1980), 1–21.

60. The deterioration in Iranian-Iraqi relations is described by John Kifner, in *New York Times,* April 12, 1980; and in Claudia Wright, "Iraq—New Power in the Middle East," *Foreign Affairs,* **58** (Winter, 1979–1980), 257–278.

61. For the new Iranian government's views on Communism at home and abroad, see the statements by the Iranian foreign minister at the Islamic Conference, as reported by Marvin Howe, in *New York Times,* May 22 and 23, 1980; and the statement by the Ayatollah Khomeini, as reported by John Kifner, in ibid., April 27, 1980.

62. The Ayatollah Khomeini's views on deteriorating conditions within Iranian society are quoted in *Newsweek,* **95** (June 23, 1980), 38.

63. Internal political developments in Iran during the early 1980s are described and evaluated by John Kifner in *New York Times,* January 18, 1982; April 13, 1982; April 21, 1982; and April 25, 1982. See also the discussions in *U.S. News and World Report,* **92** (April 12, 1982), 27; and ibid., (April 26, 1982), 21–22.

64. Leslie H. Gelb and Richard H. Ullman, "Keeping Cool at the Khyber Pass," *Foreign Policy,* **38** (Spring, 1980), 12.

65. The recent political development of Afghanistan is discussed in Lenczowski, *The Middle East in World Affairs,* pp. 253–260.

66. Events in Afghanistan following the Soviet invasion—highlighting the rising opposition to the Russian presence—are discussed by Drew Middleton, in *New York Times,* June 12, 1980; dispatch by Leslie H. Gelb, in ibid., July 9, 1980; and in *U.S. News and World Report,* **88** (March 3, 1980), 21–22, (March 10, 1980), 32–33.

67. The text of President Jimmy Carter's message to Congress on January 23, 1980, enunciating the Carter Doctrine, may be found in *Weekly Compilation of Presidential Documents,* **16** (January, 1980), 194–200.

68. For several diverse explanations of Soviet behavior and motives in Afghanistan, see the interviews with George F. Kennan and Richard F. Pipes, in *U.S. News and World Report,* **88** (March 10, 1980), 33–34; Hedrick Smith, "Russia's Power Strategy," *The New York Times Magazine,* January 27, 1980, p. 29; and Bernard Gwertzman, in *New York Times,* December 30, 1979; Craig R. Whitney, in ibid., January 3, 1980, February 16, 1980; William Safire, in ibid., March 10, 1980; and Drew Middleton, in ibid., April 6, 1980.

69. The views of the NATO allies toward the crisis in Afghanistan are described by John Vinocur and Drew Middleton, in *New York Times,* February 17, 1980; by Graham Hovey in ibid., February 22, 1980; and by Richard Burt in ibid., March 7, 1980. See the discussion of Secretary of State Vance's "mission" to Europe in *U.S. News and World Report,* **88** (March 3, 1980), 6.

70. The reaction of several states in the Middle East, in Southeast Asia, and throughout the Third World generally to the Carter Doctrine is discussed by Henry Tanner, in *New York Times,* January 15, 1980; in the letter by the U.S. ambassador to Kuwait, William A. Stoltzfus, in ibid., February 13, 1980; and by Bernard Lewis, in ibid., March 29, 1980; and by Bernard D. Nossiter, in ibid, April 19, 1980.

71. For an analysis of the creation of the Rapid Deployment Force, and of problems confronting its effective use in the Persian Gulf area, see Drew Middleton, in *New York Times,* July 14, 1979; Richard Halloran, in ibid., January 5, 1980; and Drew Middleton, in ibid., March 1, 1980; and *U.S. News and World Report,* **88** (February 25, 1980), 33.

72. See the interview with Secretary of Defense Harold Brown, in *U.S. News and World Report,* **89** (August 4, 1980), 26–28.

73. The obstacles confronting successful implementation of the Carter Doctrine are identified and analyzed in greater detail in a study by Cecil V. Crabb, Jr., *The Doctrines of American Foreign Policy: Their Meaning, Role, and Future* (Baton Rouge: Louisiana State University Press, 1982), Chapter 8.

Chapter 13

Sub–Saharan Africa:
New Nations and Ancient Problems

For the past quarter century, American foreign policy toward sub-Saharan Africa can largely be understood in terms of two somewhat contradictory impulses: attempts by the United States to "identify" with African aspirations and goals, and Washington's efforts to maintain limited political, economic, and military commitments on the African continent.*

During the summer of 1980, Vice-

*Unless otherwise indicated, the focus in this chapter will be upon what is usually referred to as sub-Saharan, or black Africa. The states of North Africa (Morocco, Algeria, Tunisia), along with Libya and Egypt, are normally grouped with the countries of the Middle East, since their populations are primarily Arab, their dominant language is Arabic, and their religion is Islam. The Sudan (territorially, the largest country on the continent) is an unusual case: The northern half of the country is predominantly Arab and Islamic; the south is ethnically linked with black Africa, and its people adhere to various indigenous religions (although there is a substantial Christian minority). It is noteworthy, however, that Egypt—often viewed as the most influential country in the Middle East—is located on the African continent; Cairo is the largest city in Africa.

President Walter Mondale visited Nigeria —one of the largest independent African nations, and one that recently sought to make a transition from authoritarian to democratic rule. In Lagos, Mondale alluded to a "fundamental change in America's relations with Africa," based upon three ideas common to Africans and to Americans. One was a commitment to the concept of justice—and on the African scene, this meant above all "an Africa free from racism and oppression." Another shared ideal was "personal dignity"; therefore, America sought "an Africa free from want and suffering." Still another mutual interest was peace, leading to "an Africa free from war and from foreign domination." Mondale pledged the United States to assist "nations in Africa to build their societies and strengthen their institutions" and "to help friendly nations strengthen themselves against outside interference" in their political affairs.[1]

Yet official expressions of American interest in African affairs and efforts by the United States to cement more cordial Afro-

American relations have been counterbalanced by a continuing reluctance in Washington to assume extensive commitments on the African continent. During the 1960s, for example, the concept of "low profile" was often employed to describe America's diplomatic posture in Africa. As late as 1975, a State Department official described sub-Saharan Africa as the "unchallenged occupant of the bottom rung of American foreign policy priorities."[2] President Jimmy Carter (who visited the continent in 1978) was the first American chief executive to pay an official state visit to independent African nations.

America's Diplomatic Stake in Africa

What considerations lie behind a rising official and public American interest in the political destiny of sub-Saharan Africa? Several considerations underlie that phenomenon. Let us examine some of these briefly.

The African Continent—An Overview

Growing American interest in the affairs of black Africa stems in part from certain basic geographic, demographic, and economic realities. For many centuries, Africa was regarded as the "dark" or the "unknown" continent. Even today, most Americans are ignorant of the region's principal characteristics and features.

By the end of the 1970s, Africa had a population of some 450 million people—twice the population of the United States. Its population is increasing at an overall rate of 2.6 percent annually, which means that Africa's population will double in approximately 25 years. In area, Africa is three times the size of the continental United States.[3]

Another distinguishing characteristic of the African continent is the fact that its people are divided into upwards of 2000 tribal and subtribal units. Over 700 separate languages and dialects are spoken throughout Africa; and this fact has posed a formidable barrier to the emergence of a genuine sense of national cohesion or national loyalty among these disparate tribal and linguistic groups. As a rule, national boundaries were drawn (usually by the European colonial powers) in Africa without regard to tribal affinities or respect for "traditional" tribal areas. After the African states received their independence, ancient tribal animosities and grievances frequently manifested themselves in violence and political upheaval.

Another salient fact about contemporary Africa is the paradox created by the existence of vast resources and potential wealth, on the one hand, versus the existence of pervasive poverty, on the other hand. Africa possesses an enormous potential for economic development. The continent has large supplies of important raw materials—like uranium, columbite, cobalt, beryllium, manganese, chrome, and gold. In addition, Africa has emerged as a leading oil-producing region: By the end of the 1970s, for example, African states (including those in North Africa) provided some 40 percent of America's total oil imports—or some 15 percent of total national consumption.[4] The principal African producers are: Algeria, Libya, and Nigeria.

Yet with all its resources and potential wealth, Africa ranks at the bottom of the major regions in terms of its standard of living, its productive output, and its near-term economic prospects. For the 54 independent nations on the African continent, the average per capita income is just over $400 annually; and if South Africa and oil-rich Libya are omitted, the average drops to $308 per capita GNP annually. With a population approximately double America's, Africa produces an overall Gross National Product of $178 billion annually—or approximately one-tenth of America's yearly output of goods and services.[5] The majority of the independent African states is classified among what one observer calls the "undeveloping" societies: They are among the poorest societies on the globe, and prospects for an early improvement in their economic conditions are unpromising. To the contrary, for the poorer African societies economic deterioration in the years ahead seems inescapable.

According to a study by the World Food Council, 26 nations throughout the world were faced with "abnormal food shortages"—17 of them located on the African continent. In the year 1980, estimates by the United Nations were that some 20 million people in Africa confronted the specter of famine. Several African states—such as Kenya, Zambia, and Zimbabwe—that had once been substantial food exporters now were unable to feed their rapidly growing populations. Overall, during the 1970s, Africa's per capita food output *declined* by 1 percent, while its net population growth rate was from 2.5 to 3 percent annually. The widely publicized food shortage that had existed for several years in the region known as the "Sahel" (or the African countries bordering the southern Sahara Desert) provided merely a graphic example of a crisis pervasive throughout the continent.[6] On another crucial front—education—Africa's needs also lagged significantly behind its resources: Only 11 percent of Africa's school-age population attended elementary or secondary schools; and only some 1.4 percent of those Africans in the 20- to 24-year age bracket were enrolled in colleges and universities.[7] Famine and other forms of economic hardship were of course a key element in another hallmark of the contemporary African scene: the region's ongoing and widespread political instability and reliance upon violence to achieve political goals.

The immediate economic prospects for most nations in sub-Saharan Africa are not favorable. In the words of one commentator, economic trends in Africa afford "few grounds for optimism." Studies by the Organization of African Unity (OAU) and by the UN Commission for Africa, for example, show a "sharp deterioration" in Africa's overall economic performance; and they anticipate an "Africa-wide crisis of development in the 1980s if steps [are] not taken immediately to reverse accelerating downward trends." At their present rate of development (or more accurately, in most cases, *non-development*) African states will fall behind other Third World societies in the years ahead. One estimate holds, for example, that on the basis of recent economic tendencies, some 75 years will be required for African societies to double their already extremely low national incomes.[8]

American interest in African affairs in recent years has been fostered by another reason. With its 54 independent states, Africa is numerically the largest of the regional groupings within the contemporary international system. The African states, for example, comprise approximately one-third of the total membership of the United Nations; and they include almost half of the nations belonging to the Third World, most of which consider themselves diplomatically "non-aligned" vis-à-vis the United States and the Soviet Union.

For a decade or more, official and public American interest in developments on the African continent has also been stimulated by the growing preoccupation with African affairs exhibited by the black community within the United States. Comprising some 24 million people, the nation's black American population has become increasingly attuned to African problems and Washington's response to them. A new organization called TransAfrica was established in 1978 to communicate the concerns of black Americans regarding developments in Africa to national policy makers. Late in 1980, the "Black Caucus" in the House of Representatives successfully defeated a move designed to loosen restrictions on American arms shipments to anti-Communist groups in Africa.[9]

Still another hallmark of contemporary Africa—and a condition engendering deep concern among policy makers in Washington —is the continent's *ongoing political instability*. Ever since they achieved their political independence, beginning in the late 1950s, most African societies have been engaged in what one commentator has called the "painful search for political stability."[10] During his visit to Africa in 1980, Vice-President Walter Mondale found a pattern of chronic political turmoil, violence, and pervasive gloom about Africa's future. One African political leader stated: "If things continue as they are, only eight or nine countries [in sub-Saharan Africa] will survive the next few years." One report found the African continent "reeling from wars, coups, racial strife and the ever present danger of face-to-face competition between the [United States and the Soviet Union]." Although most African societies lived on the margin of poverty, collectively the African nations were spending over $50 billion annually on arms purchases and national defense. Since they acquired independence from the European colonial powers, the African nations had experienced "11 wars and at least 51 coups" against established governments. Regional disputes and rivalries—such as those between Morocco and Algeria over territory in the Western Sahara (formerly the Spanish Sahara) or between Ethiopia and Somalia in the eastern horn of the continent—kept Africa in conflict and diverted its resources from the urgent challenge of national development. Such local and regional conflicts also invited external intervention by the superpowers and (as in the case of Castro's Cuba) their "client" states in African political affairs.[11] The evidence indicated convincingly that the search for political stability in Africa would continue for many years in the future; that it would likely result in many setbacks and failures; and that there were no "quick fixes" for the African continent's pattern of chronic political instability.[12]

American interest and involvement in African problems derive from two other sources. Since we shall examine them in detail at a later stage, here we may make only brief reference to them. One is the central importance of *racial issues* on the African continent. Among all the regions of the world, Africa is most directly and uniquely concerned with the achievement cf racial justice. Insofar as racial issues possess international implications, this fact provides another compelling reason why the student of American foreign policy must devote attention to contemporary Africa.

A separate (although often related) issue engendering deep American interest in African affairs is the presence of the Cold War on the African continent. Despite the desire of many African leaders to "insulate" the continent from direct Soviet-American rivalry, with the passage of time Africa has become a Cold War arena. By the end of the 1970s, in the American view at least, Soviet-American relations in Africa had become a testing ground for the concept of détente. As we observed in Chapter 10, the concept of "linkage" loomed large in the American conception of détente—and black Africa provided a crucial test of whether (or to what degree) American policy makers would be successful in gaining Soviet acceptance for the principle of linkage.

The American "Discovery" of Africa

For many years, African leaders and informed students of the continent's affairs have complained about America's "neglect" of Africa. The complaint is not without justification. Among the principal regions, Africa has been —and by many criteria, it remains—the area of *lowest* American diplomatic priority and involvement. As late as 1978, Senator Frank Church (Democrat of Idaho), chairman of the Senate Foreign Relations Committee, stated publicly that the United States had "no vital interests in Africa."[13] In the same period, another student of African affairs lamented that no officer assigned to the State Department's Office of Southern African Affairs had prior firsthand experience serving in the country or countries for which he was responsible.[14]

However unfortunate, America's lack of preparation for diplomatic interaction with contemporary Africa is understandable. Before the liquidation of the European colonial systems in Africa in the late 1950s, America's contacts with the continent were fragmentary and, for the most part, confined to nonpolitical issues. Very early, Yankee traders had participated in the lucrative slave trade. In its infancy, the American Republic had continuing quarrels with the rulers of the Barbary Coast. The United States was instrumental in establishing Liberia as an independent country in 1822. Moreover, American delegates participated in the Berlin Conference of 1884–1885, from which the European colonial "scramble" for Africa is dated. The boundaries of many African countries were agreed upon at this conference. During World War II, American military planners became acutely conscious of the strategic significance of Africa and the adjacent Arab world. One of the most decisive battles of this conflict was fought along the desert strip of North Africa. For many decades, American missionaries and educators have also been active on the African continent.[15] Beyond these develop-

ments, American contact with Africa has been minimal.

"As Africa was the last continent to be opened to the world at large," writes Rupert Emerson, "so it was the last to be discovered by the United States...."[16] Africa perhaps remained "the dark continent" more for Americans than for any other group in Western society. If official recognition of the importance of Africa had been slow, within recent years it has been almost frenziedly rapid. For many years, African affairs tended to be dealt with by officials whose primary concern was Western Europe or the Middle East. Finally, in 1958, the State Department set up a Bureau of African Affairs. Besides this new agency, other State Department and governmental agencies became heavily involved with African affairs—like the Bureau of International Organization Affairs in the State Department, which was keenly aware of the greatly enhanced role of African states in the United Nations.[17]

By the late 1950s, American officials acknowledged (Africans often said belatedly) that the era of Western colonialism was over. The civil rights movement in the United States also supplied an impetus to closer Afro-American relations. Rupert Emerson has written: "The ferment of Africa and the ferment of the Negro American could not possibly be kept separate from each other in watertight compartments."[18]

America's newly acquired interest in Africa was symbolized by the viewpoints and policies of President John F. Kennedy and his advisers. As a member of the Senate, Kennedy had long been interested in African questions and had been a vocal advocate of anticolonial and antiracial movements on the African scene. More perhaps than any post-World War II American President, Kennedy was widely admired throughout Africa and the

Third World generally. Yet the Kennedy Administration was seldom able to generate significant interest in Africa on Capitol Hill or to convince Congress that American economic assistance to African states ought to be substantially increased.[19]

For a decade or more after Kennedy's death in 1963, American interest in Africa was eclipsed by the nation's mounting and traumatic involvement in the Vietnam War. America's "neglect" of Africa, for example, was intimately related to growing disillusionment within the United States toward the United Nations—an organization that, as many Americans saw it, was increasingly "dominated" by the members of the Third World and attuned primarily to their interests. Increasingly, Americans came to regard the United Nations as a body whose deliberations were "irresponsible" and inimical to American diplomatic interests. In African eyes, American policy was often suspect because of its failure to support the cause of freedom and racial justice on the African continent; because of its undue preoccupation with the Vietnam conflict and other Cold War encounters; and because of its evident indifference to the problem of African development, as attested by the relatively low level of American economic assistance to nations in that region.

During the period of American diplomatic "retrenchment" that followed the Vietnam War, African questions continued to enjoy low priority in the diplomacy of the United States. Under the Nixon and Ford administrations—a period in which the viewpoints of Dr. Henry Kissinger massively influenced American foreign policy—Africa appeared important to the United States only as it played a part in America's "global" strategy in dealing with the Soviet Union. Africans were widely convinced, on the basis of sub-

stantial evidence, that Washington had little inherent interest in their problems per se and limited incentive to become directly involved in such challenges as promoting the development of African societies.[20] The "Angola Crisis" of 1975—during which Congress prohibited the White House from military or other forms of intervention to counter growing Soviet influence on the African continent—exemplified the American reluctance to become deeply involved with African issues. (We shall examine events in Angola in greater detail at a later stage.)

For the first three years of his tenure in the White House, President Jimmy Carter exhibited an interest in African questions seldom witnessed in American policy since World War II. The President and Secretary of State Cyrus Vance were convinced that a new "African perspective" was essential for American foreign policy. On one particular issue of paramount interest to Africans—the promotion of international human rights—the diplomacy of the Carter Administration marked a new era in postwar American foreign relations.[21] Carter's appointment of a prominent black American civil rights leader, Andrew Young, as ambassador to the United Nations evoked wide approval from Africans and other societies throughout the Third World.[22] On the basis of another criterion—the level of American economic assistance to African countries—significant changes were also made by the Carter Administration. During most of the 1970s, for example, Africa had been allocated some 7 percent of America's total foreign economic assistance budget.* Under the Carter Adminis-

*For fiscal year 1977, for example, American economic assistance to sub-Saharan African countries totaled some $219 million. The Carter Administration made an effort to increase Africa's allocation of American foreign assis-

tration, that total increased to from 12 to 18 percent of the foreign aid allocation.[23]

America's "Low Profile" in Africa

Although some changes occurred in the tone and content of American foreign policy toward Africa in the early years of the Carter presidency, it remained true that, in comparison with other regions of the world, Africa continued to have a low ranking on the American diplomatic scale of values. While the proportion of American foreign assistance allocated to Africa had risen, for example, the region was still what one observer has called the "stepchild" of the American development assistance program. To cite but one illustration: Despite the existence of endemic famine conditions on the African continent, Africa receives about one-half as much agricultural and food aid under Public Law-480 (the "Food for Peace" program) as Asia and the Middle East. In 1979, the *total* amount of developmental assistance extended by the United States to African countries was less than one-fifth of the

amount Washington provided to two countries—Israel and Egypt—alone. Similarly, military aid by the United States to African societies has remained extremely limited—equaling some 2 percent of military assistance provided by the United States to all foreign countries. Even then, American military aid to Africa was largely concentrated upon five countries: the Sudan, Kenya, Zaire, Zambia, and Cameroon.[24] In view of his relative lack of interest in international racial and human rights issues—and his Administration's determination to reduce overall governmental spending—it seemed likely that under President Ronald Reagan the African continent would continue to rank low on the scale of American diplomatic priorities.

After the Vietnam War, the United States also remained reluctant to become embroiled in most African local and regional political disputes. As we have already noted, in 1975 Congress dramatically prohibited the Ford Administration from intervening militarily in the Angolan crisis—causing the Ford-Kissinger team to conclude that legislators were totally indifferent to Communist gains on the African continent. With a few notable exceptions—and a conspicuous one was American support for the government of Morocco's claims to the phosphate-rich territory of the Spanish Sahara—executive officials remained cautious about involving the United States in political disputes on the African scene. Again in 1980, the House of Representatives rejected an effort by the outgoing Carter Administration to expand American arms aid to Angola.

Yet such continuing evidence of America's "low profile" on the African continent contrasted sharply with a significant expansion in African-American relations in another sphere: trade and commerce. Although few Americans appear to be aware of it, as time passed the independent nations of Africa

tance significantly, with the White House recommending a total of over $533 million for fiscal year 1981. Yet this gain was substantially offset by two adverse factors: the continued high rate of inflation, and the growing number of independent African states seeking increased American assistance. In terms of the overall volume of external assistance provided to African countries, in fiscal year 1981 American aid would comprise only some 8 percent of the total. Primary emphasis in American foreign assistance programs to Africa was given to improving African agricultural output. See the statement by Goler T. Butcher, before the Africa subcommittee of the House Foreign Affairs Committee on February 7, 1980, in "$787 Million Request For Economic and Security Assistance," *Department of State Bulletin*, **80** (April, 1980), 21–22. As is true of all regions, Africa's share of the American foreign assistance budget varies, depending in large part upon how "foreign aid" is defined. For example, for many years, the United States has been the largest contirbutor to several programs operated by the United Nations that have benefited African countries.

emerged as some of the nation's most important trading partners. Nigeria, for example,
had become a major supplier of American petroleum imports; and for most African countries, the United States and Western Europe
provided the primary markets for their exports.[25] By the late 1970s, overall American
trade with Africa was almost $29 billion an-
nually. (As we observed in Chapter 6, after
the normalization in Sino-American relations
by the Carter Administration, the prospect of
expanded trade between the two countries enticed many American business corporations
and pro-business groups. Yet in 1978, Sino-
American trade totaled only some $1.1 billion
annually—or some 5 percent of the volume of
American trade with Africa. In that year,
trade between the United States and five African states—Nigeria, Libya, Algeria, South
Africa, and Egypt—exceeded the level of
Sino-American trade.)[26] Exports of goods and
services from the United States to black
Africa by the end of the 1970s were approximately $1.6 billion annually; an additional
$1.3 billion in exports were purchased by the
government of South Africa. By contrast,
American purchases from black African countries were running from $8 to $10 billion annually.[27] The data presented above call attention to a condition of "interdependence" between the United States and African states
that would in all likelihood become even more
pronounced in the future.

Africa and the "Arc of Crisis"

By the beginning of the 1980s, evidence existed of still further changes in American
foreign policy toward sub-Saharan Africa. As
during the Nixon-Ford era (when the viewpoints of Dr. Henry Kissinger massively
influenced American diplomacy), officials in
Washington were assessing African questions
within a broader regional and global context.

More specifically, American diplomacy toward Africa was crucially affected by developments in the Persian Gulf–Indian Ocean area,
where the United States had become deeply
concerned about Soviet ambitions. Moreover,
in time President Carter's human rights campaign in Africa and other settings encountered
obstacles: National policy makers confronted
"the limits of American power" in terms of
their ability to change the policies and practices of other governments as these affected
the protection of human rights. In this period
also, a discernible "conservative shift" occurred in American public opinion, as indicated by public opinion polls and the results
of congressional elections. As Chapter 8
explained in greater detail, the post-Vietnam
War mood of national self-doubt and diplomatic retrenchment had been superseded by
mounting public and congressional concern
about America's relative military and diplomatic weakness and about Soviet gains on the
African continent, the Persian Gulf area, and
other settings. Moreover, experience had
demonstrated that it was difficult (if not impossible) to formulate and administer a *consistent*
human rights policy abroad, while maintaining
constructive American relations with a majority of governments throughout the Third
World. On several occasions, President Ronald Reagan and his advisers publicly stated
their conviction that, in contrast to the Carter
Administration, emphasis upon the international promotion of human rights did not rank
among the primary foreign policy goals of the
Republican Administration. As in the collapse
of Idi Amin's barbarous regime in Uganda, the
evidence suggested that the most effective
remedies for oppressive governments were
those devised by the societies most directly
concerned.[28]

Changes in the American approach to
Africa were also related to another development, examined more fully in Chapter 12: the

issuance of the Carter Doctrine designed to guarantee continued access by the United States and other advanced nations to the oil supplies of the Persian Gulf area. Under the Reagan Administration, America's commitment to this goal was likely to remain undiminished. Indeed, Republican policy makers might perhaps be more inclined than their Democratic predecessors to strengthen the military position of the United States in the "Arc of Crisis," including its East African flank. Before he left the White House, President Carter approved a new agreement with Somalia, providing for American access to military base facilities in that country.

Racial Conflicts in Sub-Saharan Africa

"Human Rights" and Recent American Diplomacy

On May 22, 1977, President Jimmy Carter said that five central principles would guide the foreign policy of his Administration. The first principle, Carter declared, was

> ... America's commitment to human rights as a fundamental tenet of our foreign policy.... we can already see dramatic worldwide advances in the protection of the individual from the arbitrary power of the state. For us to ignore this trend would be to lose influence and moral authority in the world. To lead it will be to regain the moral stature that we once had.
>
> The great democracies are not free because we are strong and prosperous. I believe we are strong and prosperous because we are free.... in free nations and in totalitarian countries as well, there is a preoccupation with the subject of human freedom, human rights. And I believe it is incumbent on us in this country to keep that discussion, that debate, that contention alive.[29]

More than any modern American chief executive, President Carter identified the United States with the cause of human rights throughout the world, making it a centerpiece of his diplomacy. And in no region of the world were the implications of this fact perhaps more crucial than in American relations with the nations of black Africa. In 1979, a State Department official informed the House Foreign Affairs Committee that "The human rights policy of the United States is, in the final analysis, critical to our moral authority and, thereby, the exercise of American influence in Africa and the world." This official believed that in recent years, America's relations with most African states had improved. In his view, "The progress made is partly attributable to our own renewed emphasis on human rights, which has identified the United States with African aspirations for justice."[30]

A few months later, another State Department official underscored the same theme in discussing American foreign policy toward perhaps the most complex and intractable human rights problem confronting the international system: the challenge of achieving racial justice in South Africa. In the official American view, South Africa's apartheid system "remains among the most persistent human rights abuses before the world community." The goal of American policy in responding to this particular challenge was stated succinctly:

> We look forward to a South Africa in which race, creed, or color form no basis for distinction and in which fundamental human rights and freedoms are guaranteed to all.[31]

Such statements reflected realization in Washington that for Africans, no single issue transcended in importance the achievement of racial justice on the African continent. In 1959, for example, President Sékou Touré of Guinea enunciated the fundamental principle that would largely govern African attitudes toward the outside world: "Yes or No—are you for the liberation of Africa?" By "liberation," Touré meant racial equality and justice for the black majority. Another African spokesman said that the concept of apartheid (or racial separateness) "is to most Africans a greater danger than the dictatorship of the proletariat."[32]

Sub-Saharan Africa's preoccupation with racial issues is of course understandable and natural in view of the continent's ethnic background and its recent history. While examples of racial discrimination may be found in every region of the world, they are a matter of unique concern to the predominantly black population of sub-Saharan Africa. Irrespective of their tribal and linguistic divisions, Africans are united by a sense of racial consciousness vis-à-vis the white elites that have long been politically dominant in African societies. Moreover, the urgency of racial questions in contemporary Africa is in part an outgrowth of the continent's colonial experience. Colonialism was frequently justified on the grounds of white racial and cultural superiority over the "primitive" societies found in black Africa. As apologists for colonialism viewed it, foreign hegemony would benefit "darkest Africa" immeasurably because of exposure to superior white culture; some defenders of the colonial impulse believed that they had a mission to bring "civilization" to this remote and backward region. To the African mind, therefore, the protracted campaign against European *colonial* domination was inextricably linked with the quest for *racial justice and equality*. For millions of Africans, achieving self-rule and freedom meant essentially two things: liquidation of the European colonial empires; and creating a new system in which—politically, economically, and socially—Africans possessed equality with whites.

While examples of racial tensions and discords may be found in nearly all the nations of sub-Saharan Africa, in the space available we shall confine our attention to two significant cases—Zimbabwe (formerly, Southern Rhodesia) and South Africa—that have presented major and especially difficult challenges for American foreign policy.*

The Case of Southern Rhodesia

For many years, a test case of Africa's ability to solve racial questions was provided by Southern Rhodesia, or, as it was officially called after 1980, Zimbabwe. Claimed late in the nineteenth century for Great Britain by the African explorer Cecil Rhodes, Southern Rhodesia became a "self-governing colony" in 1923. Its abundant raw materials, rich lands, and salutary climate attracted white settlement, although whites never comprised more than 5 percent of the total population of the country. In time, however, the white element became economically and politically dominant. The white philosophy of "parallel development" for the blacks was clearly designed to perpetuate white rule, until such a time as the black majority was "fit" for political par-

---

*While the emphasis in our discussion of African racial questions is on the conflict between black versus white groups within Africa, this fact should not be interpreted to mean that other forms of racial discrimination are absent in contemporary Africa. Efforts by white regimes in Southern Rhodesia and South Africa to maintain racially discriminatory systems have provided the most graphic and widely publicized instances of racial injustice on the African scene. Yet modern Africa has also witnessed other forms of racial injustice—such as black-instigated discrimination against Asians in East Africa, resulting in the "expulsion" of thousands of Indians from the area. Some of the tribal conflicts that have beset black Africa in recent years have also not infrequently had racial or ethnic roots. After the political "settlement" that finally brought stability to Southern Rhodesia in 1980, the country's whites were deeply concerned about whether they would in turn be subjected to racial discrimination and injustice.

ticipation, a development which lay many decades, perhaps generations, in the future. As anticolonialist agitation swept postwar Africa, white attitudes in Southern Rhodesia hardened. Defying efforts by British officials, African nationalists, and the United Nations to improve the condition of Rhodesia's black majority, on November 11, 1965, the government of Southern Rhodesia proclaimed its "independence." This act—held to be illegal by Great Britain, the United States, and African governments alike—precipitated a continuing conflict between Rhodesia and the outside world. Finding that racial discrimination in Rhodesia constituted a threat to international peace, the UN Security Council on December 16, 1966, voted to impose economic sanctions against the country; this embargo was tightened by subsequent Security Council resolutions.[33]

American diplomacy in the Rhodesian crisis paralleled Washington's position toward African colonial disputes. Time and again, American officials at the UN and outside it denounced discriminatory racial policies adopted by governments like those of Southern Rhodesia and South Africa. Beginning with the Kennedy Administration in 1962, official American criticism became sharper than ever. Washington also joined London and the majority of nations at the UN in holding that Southern Rhodesia's declaration of independence was contrary to international law and in refusing to recognize the act as valid. After it became evident that the government of Southern Rhodesia was taking little account of global opinion in its internal policies, early in 1970 the Nixon Administration moved to deny formal recognition to it by closing the American consulate in Salisbury. A few days later, Washington sharply condemned racial discrimination in Africa and pledged to bring about its elimination.[34]

In the period of diplomatic retrenchment

that followed America's massive involvement in the Vietnam War, little support existed in public sentiment, or on Capitol Hill, for a policy of "confrontation" between the United States and Southern Rhodesia. While it might be assumed that a majority of Americans favored the *principle* of racial justice in Africa and elsewhere, they were not prepared to support "interventionist" policies abroad designed to achieve this goal. Moreover, many informed citizens and officials in both the executive and legislative branches entertained genuine doubts about the *effectiveness* of boycotts and other coercive measures directed against the government of Southern Rhodesia. Evasions and circumventions of the boycott—not least, by Communist nations and even by certain states in black Africa—were commonplace. Time and again, the White House encountered deep-seated legislative opposition to the enforcement of boycott provisions against Southern Rhodesia. A strategic reality colored Congress' approach to the issue: One of America's most vital imports—chrome ore—came from Southern Rhodesia (the principal alternative source, which few legislators favored, was the Soviet Union).[35] Moreover, by the mid-1970s the government of Southern Rhodesia had joined other foreign interests in mounting a skillful and intensive lobbying campaign in the United States to gain converts for its position.[36]

Consistent with his devotion to the cause of international human rights, on June 7, 1979, President Jimmy Carter reiterated America's support for the continuation of sanctions against the government of Southern Rhodesia. As the Carter Administration assessed the matter, the country's recently held national elections—judged by some observers as perhaps the fairest in Southern Rhodesia's history—had not fundamentally altered its political system. The vast majority of blacks had been excluded from the electoral process; and the dominant political position of the white elite in Southern Rhodesia remained unchanged. At the same time, American officials acknowledged that authorities in Southern Rhodesia had made "progress" in resolving racial tensions; and they pledged to keep the matter of sanctions "under review," in the light of future developments.[37]

The election of a new Conservative government in Great Britain, led by Mrs. Margaret Thatcher, in May 1979, marked a turning point in the resolution of the Southern Rhodesian question. Mrs. Thatcher was convinced that Great Britain could—and must—take the initiative in finding a diplomatic solution for the vexing Rhodesian problem. Intensive diplomatic negotiations—involving British and American officials, the government of Southern Rhodesia, and the leaders of African rebel groups like the Patriotic Front—ensued. (In the negotiating process, it sometimes proved as difficult to gain agreement among rival rebel and guerrilla forces on a unified position as it was to find common ground between blacks and whites.)

At length, however, after arduous negotiating sessions, a formula for a new political regime in Southern Rhodesia was finally accepted by the principal parties to the controversy. On April 18, 1980—in what would qualify as one of the most anomalous spectacles in modern history—Great Britain relinquished authority over its former colony to the avowed Marxist prime minister, Robert Mugabe, with the Prince of Wales presiding over the ceremony! The leader of Zimbabwe, as the new nation now chose to be called, exemplified the prevalent desire by most Third World countries to formulate their own distinctive ideological and political models. As what one commentator described as "a taciturn . . . Roman Catholic ascetic intellectual," Robert Mugabe was also a professed Marxist. Yet after being chosen Prime Minister on the basis of a broad public mandate, Mugabe governed the country as a "consummate pragmatist," who attempted to preserve national cohesion and to place Zimbabwe's welfare above his own ideological principles. Mugabe was aware of two paramount realities. The economic future of Zimbabwe depended upon eliciting the cooperation of the white segment of the population (which continued to hold vast economic power). And Zimbabwe required aid and investment from the West for its economic development and modernization. Significantly, Mugabe avoided close economic dependence upon Moscow. Yet, as in the case of other Third World governments, Mugabe's regime might gravitate toward the Soviet Union if it found Western officials unresponsive to its needs. Officials of the Carter and Reagan administrations (along with many legislators on Capitol Hill) were unquestionably repelled by Mugabe's avowed Marxism. Thus far, American foreign aid to Zimbabwe has been only a small fraction of the country's need for external assistance. As explained more fully in Chapter 11, however, Zimbabwe's participation in the Second Lomé Convention entitled it to assistance extended by the European Economic Community and to loans by the European Investment Bank.[38]

That the successful diplomatic resolution of the Rhodesian issue was an outstanding and far-reaching development could hardly be doubted. For many years to come, its implications would be felt within the country itself, throughout black Africa, and within the international system. Predictably, Zimbabwe would experience a prolonged—and, in some respects, traumatic—"transitional" period from white to black rule, accompanied by the existence of innumerable problems affecting its internal and external affairs. In the months following the installation of the new government, for example, mounting discord charac-

terized relations among the principal black political forces belonging to the coalition Patriotic Front. Among the 200,000 or so whites
remaining in the country, anxiety about the future prompted a notable rise in the emigration
rate; and this tendency could have highly adverse economic consequences for Zimbabwe.
Until Zimbabwe's internal situation became
more stable, foreign business corporations
were reluctant to invest in the country. Behind
the political in-fighting among rival factions
there were often ancient tribal enmities and
suspicions. The planned redistribution of the
country's fertile land—to give blacks a larger
proportionate share of it—would likely trigger
new political upheavals. Even today (in common with most other African societies), Zimbabwe's agricultural output lags behind the
country's requirements.

The transition to black majority rule in
Zimbabwe would also unquestionably have
significant regional and international implications. Ostensibly, the peaceful settlement
achieved in Zimbabwe was a testimonial to
the utility of diplomacy vis-à-vis coercive
methods in resolving international and
regional disputes. Intensive diplomatic efforts
had succeeded—where reliance upon coercive measures had failed—to produce a new
political order in Southern Rhodesia. (Proponents of boycotts and other forms of sanctions
against governments practicing *apartheid*
would of course contend that the coercive
measures imposed against Southern Rhodesia
by the international community played a key
role in making the country's white elite increasingly "receptive" to a more democratic
system.) Another lesson for contemporary international relations conveyed by the Rhodesian case was that "Middle Powers," like
Great Britain, still have a vital contribution to
make in the resolution of regional conflicts and
solving other problems engendering global
tensions. America's relatively passive or sec-

ondary role in the Rhodesian crisis may, for
example, have discouraged overt Soviet involvement in the problem. For the United
States and its Western allies, the successful
transition from white to black rule in Southern
Rhodesia went a long way toward counteracting long-standing African disaffection toward the West on racial issues.

But perhaps the most immediate foreign
policy implications of the political change in
Rhodesia would be felt in and by South
Africa—where an even more intractable deadlock between blacks and whites existed. Informed students of African affairs were divided in their assessments of the consequences of the Rhodesian settlement for the
South African problem. On the one hand, as
we have indicated, the Rhodesian case could
be viewed as a vindication of the *diplomatic
method* for resolving racial and other international controversies. By extension, this same
method ought in time to yield a solution for the
even more difficult and complex South African problem.

By contrast, other qualified observers
believed that the settlement of the Rhodesian
question *created new and urgent pressures* for
fundamental changes in the government and
society of South Africa. With another black-
controlled government on its northern border—and with black "liberation" groups
throughout Africa greatly heartened by their
victory in Southern Rhodesia—white authorities in Pretoria would find it extremely difficult to "defy the world," as they had consistently done in the past. Some students of African affairs (although by no means all) believed
that the "confrontation" between black and
white forces in South Africa, and their respective foreign supporters, would now inevitably
escalate.[39] Which interpretation was correct
depended in large part upon evidence about
how developments in South Africa—and their
implications for American foreign policy—

were evaluated. It is to that subject, therefore, that we now turn for further insight into African racial problems and their meaning for the United States.

The Case of South Africa

Two informed students of contemporary Africa have expressed a viewpoint that is pervasive among Africanists. According to Ferguson and Cotter, the issue of apartheid in South Africa qualifies as "indeed the central problem of southern Africa," and the continent is unlikely to experience political stability until the problem is solved.[40] These commentators are not alone in believing that a confrontation between the defenders and enemies of the government of South Africa is "inevitable," with momentous consequences for the international community, unless fundamental changes are made at an early date in South Africa's domestic policies.[41] A State Department official has labeled South Africa's apartheid system a form of "institutionalized and legalized racism," which is "one of the cruelest forms of human rights abuse in the world today." This official added ominously that "time is running out for the prospects of peaceful change in that country." By the early 1980s, another commentator referred to the pattern of "escalation and widening of confrontation" between the government of South Africa and its critics at home and abroad. In his view, South African society was already experiencing fundamental revolutionary changes—and even more sweeping change could be expected in the future.[42]

Strategically located at the southern tip of the African peninsula, the Republic of South Africa encompasses an area of some 440,000 square miles (about fourth-fifths the size of the state of Alaska). Its population consists (as South African officials defined them) of four major ethnic groups: 22 million Afri-cans (or blacks, belonging to several different tribal groups); 2.3 million coloreds (or persons of mixed race); 800,000 Asians; and 4.3 million whites (largely divided between the Dutch and English communities).* Comprising less than one-fifth of the total population, South Africa's white minority was the "power structure" in political, economic, and nearly all other major spheres of the country's life. Economic data on South Africa are usually cited separately from those on Africa as a whole. South Africa, for example, produces some 25 percent of Africa's total output; 90 percent of its steel; 50 percent of its power; and 40 percent of its manufacturing product.[43] A pivotal fact about the country—having a crucial impact upon the attitudes and policies of other countries toward it—is that South Africa's armed forces are probably more powerful than those of all the other African states combined. Although indisputable evidence is not available, it is widely believed that South Africa is (or is on the verge of becoming) a nuclear power.

South Africa was initially colonized by Dutch settlers in 1652 who, according to South African accounts, populated an "empty" portion of the African continent. In 1814, Great Britain seized the Cape Colony; and intensive British colonization efforts followed. Conflict between Dutch and British settlers finally erupted in the Boer War

---

*Based upon recent population growth rates among the major ethnic divisions within South Africa, one study projects that by the year 2000 the country will have 36 million blacks, 3.6 million coloreds, 1 million Asians, and 5.2 million whites. It should be emphasized, however, that there is nothing "inevitable" or irreversible about this kind of population projection. Indeed, with economic conditions *worsening* for the black population of Africa, it may reasonably be doubted that population growth rates of the past will be sustained. See Robert I. Rotberg, "How Deep the Change?" *Foreign Policy,* **38** (Spring, 1980), 127.

(1899–1902), which was won by Great Britain. The Union of South Africa was created in 1910, and in time it became a member of the British Commonwealth of Nations. Under pro-British leaders like Jan Smuts, South Africa was closely linked with the West and (vis-à-vis its domestic politics after World War II), the country had relatively liberal internal policies. The era of British influence came to an abrupt end, however, with the election of the Afrikaner- (or Boer-) oriented Nationalist Party in 1948.* Lingering distrust of Britain (and of the African and Asian members of the Commonwealth) led the Afrikaner-controlled Nationalist Party in 1961 to create the Republic of South Africa, resulting in the country's withdrawal from the Commonwealth.[44]

The era of increasingly stringent and comprehensive apartheid regulations in South Africa dates from the early 1960s, when Prime Minister H. F. Verwoerd's regime embarked upon a campaign to guarantee the "separateness" of white and nonwhite societies (under Verwoerd, apartheid discriminated against coloreds and Asians, as well as blacks). As white critics of the apartheid system complained, the major and minor regulations designed to perpetuate racial separateness restricted the freedoms of *whites,* not less than other racial groups, within the country. It is neither possible nor necessary for our purpose to describe South Africa's apartheid regulations in detail. It suffices to observe that in time they comprised an elaborate code of laws and administrative regulations governing virtually every sphere of South African life—all for the purpose of assuring white supremacy in the political process, in the economic system, in cultural affairs, and in all spheres of national activity. More specifically, apartheid laws govern such disparate activities as the pattern of land distribution and settlement within the country; labor and employment laws; secondary and higher education; the provision of basic facilities —such as housing, electricity, plumbing, and health care; participation in the political system; recreational activities; internal and foreign travel; and—perhaps most fundamentally—the right to engage in oral and written criticisms of governmental policies. To cite merely a few examples of what apartheid means in practice: 87 percent of the land of South Africa is "reserved" for the country's white minority (comprising 17 percent of the population); the average income of blacks in South Africa is one-eighth the income level of whites; spending for education for white students is some 15 times higher than for the education of black students.

Summarizing the results of South Africa's apartheid system after almost 20 years since its implementation, a State Department spokesman said:

> One group controls this country. It is skilled, generally cohesive, and white. Among whites, the Afrikaners hold a virtual monopoly of political power. . . . The African, colored, and Asian South Africans, who live in con-

---

*A longtime student of African affairs has said that until the end of World War II, "the major political problem" existing in South Africa was not the conflict between black and white elements of the population, but "between English white and Afrikaner white." Considerable sentiment existed among the latter group for the Axis cause during World War II. As their numbers increased vis-à-vis the English element among the white population, by 1948 the Afrikaners (or Boers) had finally gained control of the South African government. After that, with "the franchise . . . loaded in their favour," the Afrikaners took every step available to them to perpetuate their political dominance. As Coleman has said, the Afrikaners could and did "legislate themselves into impregnability. The golden age of Afrikanerdom had come." For over a generation after 1948, the Afrikaner-controlled government of South Africa assured its future political dominance over blacks and other nonwhites, but also over rival white political groups as well. James Cameron, *The African Revolution* (New York: Random House, 1961), pp. 32–33.

centrations of urban deprivation and expanses of rural poverty, are increasingly an integral—but not integrated—part of the society and economy.... Their contributions to South Africa are essential, but still they are denied equal access to housing, education, and social services; they are subject to mass deportations...and the Constitution, backed by stern laws, gives them inferior political status.[45]

More concretely, a report on the sprawling black-populated Johannesburg suburb of Soweto—the scene of several violent eruptions between blacks and governmental authorities in recent years—conveys the contrast present in South African society. In 1976, riots in Soweto left 575 people dead and many more injured. Yet even five years later, Soweto's population of some 1.5 million blacks were found to be living "in abject poverty and filth"; the settlement was "crime ridden and crowded," with unpaved and unlighted streets; one out of every four residents of Soweto was unemployed; half the households earned $110 or less per month. A black South African journalist said that "just a small spark or a silly incident" could ignite a new violent eruption in Soweto.[46]

At the end of the 1970s—partly in response to mounting internal pressures for change—South Africa's Prime Minister P. W. Botha announced a new set of "reforms" designed to ease racial tensions. Intended specifically to eliminate or soften what were sometimes called the "petty apartheid" regulations, these reforms covered a variety of subjects—such as a proposed "confederation" of several independent African states (such as Lesotho, Swaziland, and Botswana) and the nine black "homelands" within South Africa; the legalization of black labor unions; and a promise to end what the government called "unnecessary and offensive" apartheid

regulations. Events soon indicated, however, that these reforms did not really alter the structure of South African society. They made no real impression upon what one commentator called "the cold realities of the apartheid system," comprising "hundreds of different laws, enforced in thousands of different ways." No evidence existed that these essentially minor reforms had in any significant way altered the internal balance of political power between white and non-white elements of the society. In brief, by the early 1980s the white elite continued to dominate the South African political system and showed no inclination to change that reality. In view of this fact, another report referred to the mounting "sense of frustration" felt by the blacks of South Africa and to the potential for revolutionary upheaval present within the society.[47]

A Zulu chief from South Africa once described the country's apartheid system as a "museum piece in our time, a hangover from the dark past of mankind, a relic of an age which everywhere else is dead or dying." A white South African has said: "Apartheid is a horror which can no longer be hidden or denied. The whole world condemns and execrates it."[48] For more than a generation, racial discrimination in South Africa has evoked the censure and indignation of the international community. Responding to views of its Third World majority, over the years the United Nations has become increasingly insistent that various forms of sanctions be applied to South Africa, in an effort to compel Pretoria to modify its racial policies. After the pressure of adverse global opinion failed to achieve the desired results, in 1963 the UN General Assembly called for an embargo on arms sales and shipments to South Africa. According to one study, this effort was the "high-water mark of United Nations attempts to use anything resembling coercive pressure against

South Africa.''[49] Nearly every year thereafter, international opinion inside and outside the United Nations has routinely ''condemned'' the theory and practice of apartheid in South Africa and has urged the application of various kinds of sanctions—ranging from expelling South Africa from the United Nations, to excluding its athletes from international competition, to the imposition of an economic boycott against the state—in order to communicate the international community's abhorrence of apartheid and to compel changes in South Africa's internal policies.

The United States government voluntarily imposed a boycott on arms sales to South Africa in 1962; and in 1977, the Carter Administration announced its support of UN efforts to ban all military exports to the South African government. Washington has engaged in other measures (like restrictions on the sale of commercial aircraft to South Africa) designed to convey its opposition to the continuation of apartheid. Policy makers in Washington have also restricted South Africa's access to credit facilities in the United States.[50] Moreover, within the United States vocal campaigns have been mounted by groups demanding that coercive steps be taken to change South Africa's racially unjust system. In recent years, for example, the annual stockholders' meetings of a number of leading American business corporations have witnessed organized (but usually unsuccessful) efforts to curtail American business activities within the country.*

Complicating the South African problem also is the future of Namibia (formerly South-West Africa), over which Pretoria continues to claim jurisdiction. A large territory (twice the size of California), Namibia is extremely rich in diamonds, copper, uranium, and other raw materials that have been used by South Africa to sustain a high level of industrial progress and to support its foreign trade. (Indirectly, of course, the United States and other advanced countries benefit from the raw materials exported by South Africa from Namibia.) As in South Africa itself, the white minority in Namibia enjoys a vastly superior standard of living over the country's black population.

South African control over Namibia dates from 1915; after World War I, the League of Nations designated South Africa as the ''mandatory power'' for Namibia (meaning that in time the country was expected to become independent). In 1966, the United Nations declared that Namibia was now under its jurisdiction (a claim that South Africa refused to honor). Thereafter, black nationalist groups—vocally and materially

*American business corporations, along with private colleges and universities in the United States, have been confronted from time to time with the demand that they withdraw their investments from South Africa, as a means of protesting against the concept of apartheid. Yet many informed commentators doubt the effectiveness of this proposed move, for two fundamental reasons: Pretoria has shown no sign of modifying its racial policies in response to external sanctions of *any* kind; and the level of American investments in the country is too low to make such sanctions meaningful. Thus, American business investments in South Africa are less than $2 billion—or some 1 percent of American global investments. By contrast, Great Britain—which has shown no inclination to join in such sanctions—has investments some four times the American level in South Africa. American business corporations operating in South Africa employ some 60,000 to 70,000 black workers, or less than 1 percent of the country's total black labor force. See Desaix Myers III and David M. Liff, ''The Press of Business,'' *Foreign Policy*, **38** (Spring, 1980), 143–152; and Robert I. Rotberg, ''How Deep the Change?'' *Foreign Policy*, **38** (Spring, 1980), 139. By the 1980s, the United States bought more from South Africa—including some 37 important mineral imports—than it sold to the country; for some of these minerals the Soviet Union was the only other available source. See *U.S. News and World Report*, **88** (April 28, 1980), 43.

supported by the Soviet Union and its allies—demanded independence for Namibia and relied upon armed force to achieve it. South Africa was no less determined to preserve its hold over Namibia—either in the form of direct rule, or indirectly through a new political regime in Namibia that was subject to Pretoria's directions. The Carter Administration utilized various kinds of actual or threatened sanctions to produce a change of policy by the government of South Africa. The Reagan Administration relied more upon persuasion and positive inducements to achieve the same result. Yet neither strategy produced any discernible modification in South Africa's diplomacy. By the early 1980s, the Namibian question continued to serve as a major source of political instability in the heart of Africa.

Except for certain minor changes in its internal and external policies, the government of South Africa continues to "defy the world." The position of the white-dominated government remains basically what it has been for a generation or more: Its domestic policies are an "internal" matter which are not subject to determination by foreign nations or international organizations; nor are its foreign policies decided by other African states and political movements.[51] No evidence exists that this South African attitude will change in the near future.

Policy Alternatives for the United States

Few questions in the record of post-World War II American foreign policy have posed as many difficult choices and dilemmas for officials in Washington as the issue of apartheid in South Africa. In formulating a response to that challenge, American policy makers have had several alternatives—all of them characterized by defects, inadequacies, and adverse consequences for the United States! In their approach to the problem of South Africa, American officials almost daily confront what is sometimes called the "existential dilemma"—or the realization that whatever they do is wrong and will win them nothing more than criticism from one group or another interested in the South African question.

At the risk of some oversimplification, we may say that for over a generation officials engaged in the formulation and administration of American foreign policy have basically had three alternatives in their approach to the South African question.[52] In the first place, Washington can take the position that racial disputes within the country are essentially *an internal matter* falling exclusively within the "domestic jurisdiction" of the South African government. In effect, the United States can adopt *a "hands off" strategy of noninvolvement* toward the apartheid issue in South Africa (and toward a wide range of human rights questions in other countries). This approach would perhaps rest upon a twofold premise: the idea that racial disputes in Africa are no more a proper matter for international concern and action than are racial conflicts in Miami, Watts, or Boston; and the belief that, in the last analysis, no effective and durable solution to racial problems in Africa and other settings is likely to be found and imposed by nations and groups external to the area. The relatively low level of support in American public opinion for the imposition of sanctions against South Africa—along with Congress' reluctance to approve this action—makes this course attractive for many citizens and officials within the United States.

A policy of noninvolvement in African racial disputes unquestionably has certain advantages for the United States, particularly in the post-Vietnam War era. It safeguards against the kind of "overcommitment" in foreign relations about which Congress and many Americans complained vocally during and after the Vietnam conflict. It prevents the United States from giving verbal and diplomatic support to causes and campaigns overseas—when it is really unprepared to use its power to achieve the proclaimed goal. It avoids the kind of disillusionment with the nation's diplomatic performance that results when official rhetoric (such as that accompanying President Carter's international human rights campaign) is not followed up by decisive American action. Advocates of this approach would say that after America has successfully evolved solutions to its own racial problems, *then* it can advise South Africa and other governments about how to solve racial conflicts!

Of course, a "hands off" policy toward racial disputes in Africa also has certain evident and serious drawbacks for the United States. For example, it collides with the American society's own traditions of freedom, democracy, and respect for individual rights. It would seriously weaken the claim of the United States to be the leader of the "free world" against Communism or other movements inimical to the principles of freedom and individual liberty. Most fundamentally perhaps, official American noninvolvement in the African racial question would counteract nearly every positive step the United States has taken in the post-World War II period to influence African opinion favorably and to contain Communist influence on the continent. As many African leaders have stated, the struggle for racial equality is Africa's "Cold War"; and it is the yardstick applied by governments and masses throughout Africa to measure American and Soviet interest in their problems.

A second policy option available to American officials for dealing with the South African issue is to follow an *evolutionary approach* to the goal of achieving racial justice in Africa. A tacit premise of this strategy is a belief that the indispensable precondition for

effecting changes in South Africa's domestic policies is *to preserve communication and to maintain a "dialogue" with the country's dominant white elite*. Or, as spokesmen for the Reagan Administration defined this approach, the goal of American policy toward South Africa was "constructive engagement" between the two nations. The United States, said UN Ambassador Jeane J. Kirkpatrick, believed "that the chance for influencing governments is better if we have reasonably good relations with them." This approach to racial controversies in Africa reflects awareness that, to date, a "confrontational" or revolutionary strategy toward South Africa has paid few dividends in terms of achieving the desired result. An evolutionary strategy accepts the reality that critics of South Africa either do not possess, or are unwilling to apply, the power to *compel* fundamental changes in South Africa's apartheid system. Based upon the experience of Southern Rhodesia (Zimbabwe) earlier, any lasting resolution of the racial issue in South Africa must be acceptable to the principal elements within the country—not least, its white power structure.*

*In reality, the evolutionary approach described here antedated the Reagan Administration. Despite its proclaimed commitment to the cause of international human rights, the Carter Administration also followed this strategy toward South Africa. Thus, in 1980, a high-ranking spokesman for the administration stated that America's objective was to encourage "peaceful—but rapid change" in South Africa's apartheid system. To accomplish that goal, Washington had to maintain a "dialogue" with Pretoria. See Richard M. Moose, "U.S. Policy Toward South Africa," *Department of State Bulletin,* **80** (July, 1980), 20–22. The viewpoint of President Reagan and his advisers toward South Africa is explained more fully in Hedrick Smith, "Reagan: What Kind of World Leader?" *The New York Times Magazine,* November 16, 1980, p. 174; John de St. Jorre, "South Africa: Is Change Coming?" *Foreign Affairs,* **60** (Fall, 1981), 108–122; and the assessment by Gerald J. Bender in *New York Times,* January 8, 1982.

An evolutionary, or step-by-step, approach to the South African racial question might embody a variety of specific elements—such as dependence upon diplomatic methods, upon argument and persuasion, upon "moral sanctions," upon the force of world opinion, and upon other essentially nonviolent techniques to induce fundamental changes in South Africa's internal policies. Above all, perhaps, this strategy would endeavor to convince the country's white minority that its own interests are best served in the long run by domestic policies that alleviate racial conflicts, rather than by an entrenched apartheid system that engenders revolutionary upheaval and invites foreign intervention in the country's political affairs.

This approach to the issue of racial conflicts in South Africa also of course possesses defects and disadvantages for the United States. By definition, it will fail to satisfy revolutionary political movements in Africa and their foreign supporters, who demand sweeping changes—leading to a totally new and democratic political system—in South Africa. By contrast, South Africa's entrenched white elite is likely to be alienated by any evidence of American opposition to apartheid. An evolutionary approach to the problem is quite clearly a calculated risk: There is no guarantee that in the end it will succeed in eliminating apartheid or produce a racially just order within South Africa. Indeed (as South African officials are unquestionably aware) a gradual or progressive liberalization of the apartheid system might in fact merely *accelerate* the demand for more rapid or revolutionary changes within the society. As with all "middle-of-the-road solutions," by adopting this one, the United States might achieve little more than the alienation of *both sides* in South Africa's racial conflict.

A third policy alternative is available to the United States in dealing with South Africa. This is the course advocated by a number of black and other organizations within the American society, by many countries belonging to the Third World, and by black governments and revolutionary movements on the African scene. On all sides, the United States has been urged to translate its own ideological and diplomatic professions into effective action, by leading a confrontation against South Africa designed to *compel* its white elite to abandon apartheid. This strategy would entail a comprehensive sequence of measures—from the imposition of an economic and military boycott against the country, to the breaking of diplomatic relations, to the "ostracism" of South Africa from the United Nations and other international forums, and (if these measures do not produce the desired result) to direct reliance upon military force against the recalcitrant white-dominated South African society—to achieve the ultimate objective.

To the minds of its proponents, an American-led confrontation with South Africa would pay many dividends for the United States. As much as any development in American diplomacy since World War II, it would identify the United States forcefully and unambiguously on the side of human freedom, demonstrating the nation's genuine devotion to the cause of international human rights. It would transform American-African relations, making the nations of black Africa more positively disposed toward the United States than any step Washington could take toward that end. Conversely, it would remove one of the strongest incentives black Africans have had for relying upon the Soviet Union, Cuba, and other Communist states, thereby significantly reducing Marxist influence on the continent.

Yet a strategy of coercion against South Africa—entailing the possibility of a protracted military conflict in the region—also has innumerable and extremely serious drawbacks and unforeseen consequences for the United States and for the international system. It might—and, given the implacable opposition of South Africa's white minority, almost certainly *would*—involve a prolonged and fratricidal military contest that would keep the African continent inflamed for an indefinite period. Considering that South Africa is now (or could easily become) a *nuclear* power, this contest would risk plunging the continent, and perhaps the world, into a nuclear conflagration. Even if that disaster did not occur, the United States and other countries at the forefront of a struggle against South Africa could become bogged down for many years in an engagement whose outcome was uncertain. For the nations of black Africa—whose economic prospects are already dim—their involvement in such a conflict could prove economically ruinous. Nor is there any persuasive evidence that a violent encounter with South Africa would improve the condition of the country's black majority. From America's own wartime experience, in fact, there are strong grounds for believing that, for the country's whites and blacks alike, even more stringent restrictions would be imposed by Pretoria upon internal freedoms. For the United States a protracted and massive military engagement in southern Africa would revive memories of the Vietnam War; would inevitably weaken the defenses of the NATO area; would impair America's ability to defend the Persian Gulf area from Soviet encroachments; and would, in all likelihood, prove as internally divisive as any episode in the nation's history.

In the light of the risks involved, it is not surprising that every incumbent admininstration in Washington since World War II has rejected this course of action in dealing with the South African problem. From the American perspective, perhaps the fundamental defect in this proposed approach is failure to realize that Africa has been—and, vis-à-vis regions like Western Europe and the Middle East, it remains today—a region of relatively low diplomatic priority for the United States. As such, it is not a locale in which the United States is prepared to become massively committed, at the risk of weakening its power and of jeopardizing its security interests in other areas.

Three predictions about American foreign policy toward racial conflicts in Africa (and perhaps other settings) may be made with reasonable assurance. In the first place (as explained at length in Chapter 2), the diplomacy of the United States historically has been heavily conditioned by the essentially pragmatic, eclectic, and nondoctrinaire propensities of the American people. Traditionally, Americans have preferred "common sense" and middle-of-the road solutions to internal and external problems. The postwar American diplomatic record in dealing with racial issues on the African continent provides a conspicuous example of this historic tendency. The foreign policy of the United States toward South Africa has been criticized—and no doubt will be criticized in the future—for being equivocal, inconsistent with the nation's ideological professions, and ineffectual.

In the second place, the case of South Africa illustrates an extremely interesting and recurrent phenomenon in post-World War II American foreign policy. If it is true that (particularly before and during the Vietnam War), the United States became overextended diplomatically, and that it attempted to serve as "the policeman of the world," this American behavior pattern was often *instigated and encouraged by foreign governments and political movements*. Time and again, Washington has been pressured by governments and political movements abroad, encouraged by their domestic supporters within the United States, to assume external commitments whose scope and implications could not be anticipated. One of the ironies of the South African case is that

American policy makers have been urged to spearhead a confrontation against the strongest military power on the African continent—by many of the same groups that have complained most vocally about the "arrogance of American power," about the nation's interventionist impulses abroad, and about Washington's consequent neglect of domestic problems!

Third, in the future as in the past, American foreign policy toward South Africa will not lack for critics—from left-wing groups, from right-wing sources, and from a diverse range of opinion between these extremes. If the United States, for example, intervenes massively in the political affairs of southern Africa, it will inevitably be accused of once more trying to serve as "the policeman of the world." If it fails to do so, it is likely to face the charge that it is "indifferent" to Africa's needs and problems and that it is failing to match its diplomatic rhetoric with appropriate action. As we have seen, any conceivable approach to the South African problem will involve gains and losses, accomplishments and failures, for the United States. Part of America's "loss of innocence" accompanying its emergence as a superpower after World War II consists of the realization that no diplomatic strategy in dealing with difficult and complex issues lacks defects and liabilities. Or, as President John F. Kennedy once observed, there may be no "American solution" for every major international problem.

Cold War and Détente in Africa

By the late 1970s, the African continent had become an important testing ground for the meaning and future of détente between the United States and the Soviet Union. As officials in Washington assessed the matter, the political crisis in the former Portuguese colony of Angola in 1975 raised serious ques-

tions about Moscow's devotion to détente; and in the years that followed, massive Soviet and Cuban intervention in East Africa continued to call the future of détente into question. From another perspective, as we observed in Chapter 12, the threat of Soviet expansionism in the Persian Gulf area induced the United States to become involved in East Africa as never before, to protect the security of countries located in the "Arc of Crisis."

By late 1979, a State Department spokesman informed the House Foreign Affairs Committee that some 41,000 foreign Communist military personnel served on the African continent. Of this number, some 3800 were from Eastern Europe (with about half this total from the Soviet Union and most of the remainder from East Germany); the vast majority of these forces—estimated at some 37,000—came from Castro's Cuba. The largest concentration of these Communist forces was found in Angola and in Ethiopia. Communist "technical experts" were also present in large numbers on the African scene—a total of some 37,000, serving in 23 or more African countries. The largest group was found in Angola; but substantial numbers were also present in Ethiopia, Guinea, Mali, Mozambique, Nigeria, Somalia, Tanzania, and Zambia.[53]

Moscow's "Identification" With Africa

In company with the United States, the Soviet Union was relatively late in its "discovery" of sub-Saharan Africa and its belief that the African continent offered a fertile field for the achievement of Soviet diplomatic objectives. As late as the mid-1950s, for example, a major Soviet publication was derogatory toward what it called the "bourgeois nationalist" leaders of black Africa who led the struggle for independence from European colonialism. Many of these African leaders were reviled by

Moscow as being "tools of the West"; and their attachment to revolutionary goals was seriously questioned.[54]

A major shift in Soviet policy toward the Third World generally—and toward black Africa in particular—occurred in the mid-1950s. The Afro-Asian Solidarity Conference at Bandung, Indonesia, in 1955 was a significant turning point. At this gathering, Moscow made a concerted effort to woo the Third World—as indicated by Soviet economic aid programs for countries like Afghanistan, India, and Burma. The following year, Soviet Premier Nikita Khrushchev asserted that "the awakening of the peoples of Africa has begun"; thereafter, the Kremlin sought to win the goodwill and support of the "nationalist bourgeoisie" leaders of black Africa who had earlier been castigated by Soviet spokesmen.[55] In the months that followed, Moscow promptly recognized the independence of the Sudan, Morocco, and Tunisia from European colonial rule. The independence of Ghana (Britain's former colony, the Gold Coast) early in 1957 was similarly enthusiastically applauded by the Kremlin. During the late 1950s, such prominent African leaders as President Nasser of Egypt, Emperor Haile Selassie of Ethiopia, and President Sékou Touré of Guinea visited Moscow. In the months ahead, Soviet authorities evinced unprecedented interest in African affairs. A spokesman for the Kremlin said that "Africa . . . is developing according to the logic of Marxist-Leninist theory." And in 1960, Soviet leaders modified their ideology to accomodate the existence of what was now called "national democracy" (or the newly independent governments) emerging in the Third World. The leaders and supporters of national democracy were held to be at least *potential* adherents of Marxism.[56]

Such verbal evidence of Soviet interest in Africa was translated into various forms of Soviet diplomatic support for African causes, economic and technical assistance to newly independent African governments, and military aid to anticolonial movements and to groups struggling against white rule on the African continent. Algeria, for example, received substantial Soviet military aid and encouragement during its prolonged struggle for independence from France, which Algeria received in 1962. Several years earlier, Czechoslovakia (doubtless, with Soviet concurrence) had supplied arms aid to Egypt; and in 1956, the Soviet Union offered to construct the Aswan High Dam, after the United States declined to assume that commitment. In a number of other African states—like Guinea, Mali, Ghana, Ethiopia, Somalia, and the Sudan—Moscow provided economic assistance for a variety of projects designed to promote African development. (In its foreign aid programs, it should be emphasized, the U.S.S.R. has always been more "selective" than the United States, preferring to concentrate its assistance upon a limited number of beneficiaries.)

Belated as it was, the Soviet Union's involvement in African affairs grew rapidly; and it was encouraged by a number of factors favorable to Communist influence within African societies. The leading one perhaps was the record of *Western colonialism* on the African continent. In terms of their firsthand experience at least, Africans did not view the Soviet Union as a "colonial" power or a nation that had hegemonial ambitions at their expense. To the contrary, leading Communist theoreticians (like V. I. Lenin) provided African nationalists with some of their most telling indictments of Western capitalism's colonial impulses. Even after they received their independence, many black African nations *remained* suspicious of Western motives, believing that the United States and its European allies sought to place Africa in a position of "neocolonialism" or economic bondage. For their part,

Western leaders and masses often evinced little perceptive understanding of contemporary African political thought. In several cases, it must be recalled (as in the instance of Nasser's Egypt), initial requests by African and other Third World states for American aid were *denied* by officials in Washington, after which these countries sought assistance from Moscow. As was emphasized in the early portion of this chapter, Africa's need for external assistance is vast—almost infinite. The level of American economic assistance to Africa has always been low, and it remains so to the present time. For these reasons, many African states welcomed Soviet foreign assistance for meeting their developmental needs.

Still another factor—emphasized in the preceding section of this chapter—created a favorable environment for intervention in Africa. This was the continued existence of racial tensions, particularly in Southern Rhodesia and South Africa. After World War II, Great Britain did not possess the power (and in some periods, it lacked the inclination) to bring about a new social order in its former possessions. As we have seen, while it periodically condemned apartheid, the American government was unprepared to take the initiative in leading an international movement to coerce these two strongholds of white supremacy. The Soviet Union would, and did, encourage revolutionary and guerrilla activities against governments dominated by white elites; and it provided large-scale military and financial backing to these causes. By doing so, it won the admiration of millions of Africans.

By the post-Vietnam War period, another factor encouraged Soviet authorities to believe that Africa afforded a promising opportunity for expanding Communist influence. This was the belief that *America's global power had declined significantly,* in Africa and in other settings as well. Soviet officials were convinced that the U.S.S.R. had achieved superiority over the United States in at least certain crucial military spheres; and they anticipated that within the years ahead, this disparity would widen in Moscow's favor. Moreover, throughout most of the 1970s (while America's outlook abroad was governed by the "Vietnam War syndrome" of self-doubt and uncertainty), the Kremlin might well have concluded that the United States would not *use* its still formidable power to block Soviet interventionist moves in Africa and elsewhere. As we shall see, Congress' refusal to support proposed White House intervention in Angola in 1975–1976 reenforced existing Russian doubts about America's diplomatic resolve.[57]

Deeper insight into the Communist challenge to Africa—and America's response to it—will be afforded by a more detailed examination of two significant cases: the political crisis in Angola in the mid-1970s and Communist intervention in East Africa a few years later.

The "Angola Crisis" of 1975–1976

Portugal was the last of the European colonial powers to relinquish its African empire. The Portuguese colony of Angola—with some 7 million people, and three times the size of California—in southwest Africa finally gained its independence on November 11, 1975. Even before that event, rival political movements vied for power in the country, producing an intricate and confused pattern of political relationships.[58]

Three major political organizations sought to gain power, each of which relied upon some degree of foreign support to accomplish its goals. For several years before Angola acquired independence, the United States had developed close ties with the National Front for the Liberation of Angola (FNLA), led by Holden Roberto. Another organization was the Union for the Total Independence of Angola (UNITA), headed by Jonas Savimbi, who was considered the most democratically inclined of Angola's political leaders. A third claimant to political power was the Popular Front for the Liberation of Angola (MPLA), headed by Agostinho Neto; this organization enjoyed growing support from Moscow and other Communist countries. Since 1932, Portugal had been governed by an authoritarian regime headed by Dr. António Salazar and his successors. The overthrow of this regime on April 25, 1974—followed by a resurgence of the Communist movement within Portugal—encouraged Marxist groups within Angola and their foreign supporters to intensify their revolutionary activities.

There followed an intensive campaign by the Soviet Union and its supporters to assure a political victory by the pro-Marxist MPLA faction, led by Neto. Disturbed by mounting evidence of revolutionary upheaval and foreign intervention in Angola, several African leaders endeavored to find common ground among the Angolan political factions; and a short-lived compromise among them was reached early in 1975. Yet within a few weeks, Angola entered a new phase of political turbulence. For reasons that are not now altogether clear—but, in the official American view, derived from Moscow's determination to expand its influence on the African continent—the Soviet-supported MPLA embarked upon a renewed campaign to seize power. In the months thereafter, massive Communist arms shipments and other forms of assistance were provided to the MPLA, which gradually emerged as the most influential political movement in the country.

A novel—and, in the official American assessment, a highly disturbing—element in the Angolan crisis was the overt intervention of Cuban troops in southwest Africa. In time,

the largest single contingent of foreign forces in Angola consisted of Cuban troops and military advisers (estimated by the State Department to number some 20,000 troops and 8500 advisers and technicians by the beginning of the 1980s.) The massive involvement of Premier Castro's Cuba in African affairs was a particularly galling and frustrating development for the United States. (As we shall see more fully in Chapter 14, the United States had not only failed to overthrow Castro's government and to contain its revolutionary activities in the Western Hemisphere; but now, Castro was serving as the Kremlin's principal "client" in leading revolutionary activities on the African continent!) From the Kremlin's perspective, reliance upon Cuban forces to assure a victory for the MPLA in Angola had a number of advantages. It prevented a direct Soviet-American encounter in a region that had thus far been largely insulated from Cold War conflicts. Even more crucially, perhaps, by relying upon Fidel Castro—who sought to be recognized as a spokesman for the Third World—the Kremlin avoided (or at least minimized) the accusation that its ostensible interest in Africa derived from Russian hegemonial ambitions on the continent.

Relying upon the extensive support provided by Moscow and Havana, the MPLA steadily consolidated its power—leading the neighboring states of Zambia and Zaire to ask for American assistance to protect the security of the region. In addition, the government of South Africa independently (and without consulting the United States) supplied military equipment and personnel to the MPLA's rivals. According to some interpreters, this was a key development in enhancing African receptivity to the MPLA's revolutionary program and in assuring its ultimate political victory. During the mid-1970s in Angola, the United States sought to enlist the support of the Organization for African Unity to discover a basis for political stability in the country; Washington also appealed directly to the Soviet Union, and sought the assistance of its NATO allies, in an effort to resolve the crisis.

When these measures produced no discernible result, President Gerald Ford and his advisers decided that greatly increased American assistance for Angolan political movements challenging the Communist-supported MPLA was required. Although the Ford Administration anticipated no direct American military involvement in the Angolan crisis, the White House asked Congress to provide some $25 million in arms aid for anti-Communist forces in the area. Secretary of State Henry Kissinger succinctly stated the rationale of this request to the Senate Foreign Relations Committee:

> The questions, then, come down to this: Do we really want the world to conclude that if the Soviet Union chooses to intervene in a massive way [in Angola], and if Cuban or other troops are used as an expeditionary force, the United States will not be able to muster the unity or resolve to provide even financial assistance? ... Do we want our potential adversaries to conclude that in the event of future challenges America's internal divisions are likely to deprive us of even minimal leverage over developments of global significance?[59]

Congress' answer to the Ford Administration's request was not long delayed. On December 19, 1975, by a vote of 54 to 22, the Senate prohibited executive officials from extending American aid to anti-Communist forces in Angola. A few days later, the House of Representatives concurred in the Senate's action. Named for its sponsor, Senator Dick Clark (Democrat of Iowa), the "Clark Amendment" prohibiting American military involvement in Angola was a forceful assertion of legislative influence in the American foreign policy process.[60] An attempt by the Reagan Administration during 1981 to have Congress repeal the Clark Amendment failed. Despite growing concern by executive and legislative policy makers alike about the massive Cuban presence in this key African state, Congress was still unwilling to support overt efforts by the White House to topple the MPLA-controlled government of Angola.[61]

In Angola, the MPLA continued to rely upon external Communist support in its effort to defeat its political rivals. Although political factionalism and dissidence still existed in Angola, in time most African states recognized Neto's regime as the legitimate government of the country. African sentiment remained highly adverse to any effort by the United States, South Africa, or other outside countries to topple it.

The prolonged conflict in Angola—and the policy alternatives available to the United States in responding to it—can only be intelligently understood in the context of ongoing racial strife in southern Africa. More specifically, the crisis in Angola was closely linked with black Africa's "confrontation" with the government of South Africa and with efforts to gain independence for Angola's neighbor, Namibia. For several years, opponents of South African rule in Namibia used Angola as a base for guerrilla operations; and this fact in turn prompted retaliatory strikes by South African armed forces against guerrilla sanctuaries. This pattern of escalating violence compounded the problem of preventing a regional conflict in southern Africa that risked a new Soviet-American encounter on the continent.

Restrained by the Clark Amendment, executive officials in the United States relied upon several approaches to resolve the Angolan issue and to achieve one of their leading goals—the removal of the large Cuban military presence from the African scene. Under the Carter Administration, American policy makers overtly sought to identify with African political aspirations; to emphasize the importance of human rights as a major component of American diplomacy; and to maintain at least minimally cordial relations with revolutionary regimes in Angola and other African nations. As we have seen, the Carter White House was more receptive to applying sanctions and other pressures against South Africa than Republican administrations before and after it. It cannot be said, however, that Carter's diplomacy was conspicuously successful in achieving American goals in southern Africa.

Toward Africa and other regions, significant changes were made in American diplomacy by the Reagan Administration. Less concerned with global human rights issues, and more preoccupied with what it perceived to be Soviet aggressiveness in Africa and elsewhere, the Reagan White House gave high priority to Africa's economic and strategic value for the United States. (The preservation of cordial relations with South Africa, for example, was viewed as an essential step in maintaining continued American access to the oil fields of the Persian Gulf area—an objective whose implications were discussed in Chapter 12.) The Marxist coloration of the regime in Angola—along with its continued dependence upon the Soviet Union and Cuba—also engendered deep concern in the White House. Nevertheless, the Reagan Administration was deterred from intervening directly in the Angolan crisis by two constraints. One was the fact that the Clark Amendment continued to reflect Congress' opposition to this move. The other was realization in Washington that any overt and large-scale American involvement in the

Angolan issue would encounter widespread African criticism. For example, Nigeria (from which America received substantial oil imports) would almost certainly spearhead African opposition to this course. A resolution of the Angolan question also depended upon another factor (to be discussed in greater detail in Chapter 14): Cuban-American relations. By the 1980s, relations between Washington and Havana remained tense, with little prospect that their major policy disagreements would soon be resolved.[62]

The crisis in Angola of course was but part of a larger pattern of Soviet-American rivalry on the African continent. By the late 1970s, the main arena of this contest had become East Africa, and it is to an examination of Cold War competition in that pivotal region that we now turn.

Soviet-American Rivalry in East Africa

Over a period of several months—from February to September 1974—the forces of revolutionary change gradually undermined the monarchy in Ethiopia, ruled since 1930 by Emperor Haile Selassie I.[63] This ancient dynasty traced its lineage back to the union between King Solomon of Israel and the Queen of Sheba in the ninth century B.C.

For many years, the Ethiopian government had been closely linked with the United States. American officials viewed the Emperor's regime as a reliable bastion against Communism, and as a source of political stability on the turbulent African continent. As such, Ethiopia had been the beneficiary of substantial quantities of American economic assistance; and its military establishment was largely equipped with American-supplied weapons. (Yet before his deposition, Haile Selassie had also developed cordial relations with the Soviet Union.)

A country almost twice as large as the

state of Texas, Ethiopia has a population of over 30 million people. Yet its standard of living (particularly in the rural areas) is among the lowest in Africa. For several years before the overthrow of the monarchy, the country had been gripped by acute famine conditions and other problems—to which the government had responded with ineptitude and insensitivity. The Western-oriented elite gave little indication of a willingness to meet the society's urgent needs or to carry out long overdue political reforms. Effective opposition to the political status quo in time came to be led by disaffected military officers within the Ethiopian armed forces. They were joined by religious leaders, students, and other groups demanding radical changes in this traditional system.

Piecemeal concessions by the monarchy did little to stem the revolutionary tide. By September 12, 1976, Emperor Haile Selassie had been dethroned, and a military junta (called a "Dergue," or Council) controlled the government. Under the new military-dominated regime, Ethiopia entered a period of internal strife and upheaval, engendered by two tendencies. One was the determination of the Dergue's leaders to eliminate all domestic opposition (including potential opposition) to its authority. The other was the existence of separatist movements that threatened to destroy Ethiopia's national cohesion and make it an active arena of Soviet-American competition in East Africa. Our interest is confined to the latter source of political conflict.

Even before the collapse of the monarchy, the Ethiopian government had been confronted with a rebellion in the eastern province of Eritrea, including the important port cities of Massawa and Assab, without which Ethiopia would be a landlocked and economically crippled nation. Speaking different languages (primarily Arabic and Italian), and professing a different religion

(Islam) from Ethiopia's Christian majority, the 2 million people of Eritrea had long demanded independence; and after revolutionary ferment gripped Ethiopia, the Eritrean separatist movement intensified. Groups advocating Eritrean independence received external support from a variety of sources—such as the conservative governments of Saudi Arabia and Kuwait; radical Arab regimes in Syria, Iraq, and Libya; the Palestine Liberation Organization (PLO); and the Soviet Union and Communist China. In their view, the culturally and economically more advanced Eriterans were struggling against "Ethiopian imperialism."[64]

An even more ominous threat to Ethiopia's national cohesion, however, was posed by the insurgent movement in the southeastern Ethiopian province of Ogaden.[65] Bordering Somalia, the Ogaden was inhabited by Somali tribesmen whose resistance to Ethiopian authority was abetted by the Somali Democratic Republic. The Ogaden was ceded to Ethiopia by Great Britain in 1948—an act whose legal validity has been challenged by Somalians since the country received its independence from Britain in 1960. Following a political upheaval, late in 1969 Somalia acquired a new Marxist-oriented regime that promptly developed intimate ties with the Soviet Union. Throughout the months that followed, Moscow gained access to the east African port of Berbera, causing alarm in Washington about the security of the Red Sea-Persian Gulf-Indian Ocean area. Relying upon Soviet arms aid, during the early 1970s the government of Somalia actively assisted the cause of irredentism in the Ogaden. Meanwhile, until the monarchy's overthrow, the government of Ethiopia used American-supplied military equipment against the Ogaden insurgency.

The revolution within Ethiopia in time also produced a "diplomatic revolution": The Soviet Union supplanted the United States as

Ethiopia's principal source of external assistance; concurrently, Moscow's relations with Somalia declined, and by the end of the decade the United States and Somalia had entered a new era of economic and military collaboration. Late in 1978, Addis Ababa and Moscow signed a treaty of friendship, calling for expanded political and military collaboration between them. Following that agreement, the Cuban presence in East Africa escalated rapidly. By 1979, the State Department estimated that almost 18,000 foreign Communist military personnel were stationed in Ethiopia, of whom 16,500 were Cuban forces and military advisers. A number of African leaders—like President Gaafar al-Nimeiry of the Sudan—expressed growing apprehension about this growing "Communist presence" in East Africa, fearing that in time it might pose a threat to the security and independence of neighboring countries.[66]

This large infusion of Soviet and Cuban personnel into Ethiopia appeared to doom the Ogaden insurgency movement to defeat. Ethiopian troops and their foreign allies inflicted heavy casualities and property damage upon the Ogaden rebels. Ultimately, a classical pattern of guerrilla warfare—painfully familiar to America earlier in the Vietnam conflict, and to the Soviet Union in Afghanistan—began to emerge: Ethiopian troops and their Communist allies controlled the towns and military strongholds, while the insurgents controlled the countryside. The continuous warfare—coupled with a devastating drought that had gripped East Africa for several years—provided a continual source of political instability; created a new refugee problem (estimates were that some 1.5 million refugees had fled from the Ogaden province alone); and constituted an extremely serious drain upon Africa's already scarce food and other resources.[67]

Meanwhile, after its influence in Ethiopia declined and after the government of Somalia reduced its earlier reliance upon the Soviet Union, the United States began to develop closer ties with Somalia. Washington did not recognize—and did not overtly support—the Ogaden province's claims to independence. Yet after the Soviet Union invaded Afghanistan at the end of 1979, Washington became increasingly interested in enhancing American military strength in the Persian Gulf-Indian Ocean area. The Somalian port of Berbera—already expanded and modernized by the Soviet Union—appeared to American officials as an ideal site for naval facilities on the western flank of the Persian Gulf. At the same time (in view of Congress' prohibition against American military involvement in the earlier Angolan crisis), executive officials were extremely wary about a comparable American military intervention in East Africa. For their part, having broken with the Soviet Union, Somalian officials left no doubt that they welcomed American economic and military assistance in their conflict with Ethiopia.

After balancing these diverse interests, before it left office the Carter Administration negotiated an agreement under which the United States would provide Somalia some $40 million in arms aid, plus $5 million in economic assistance, in exchange for American use of port facilities at Berbera. The Reagan Administration was perhaps even more keenly interested East Africa's strategic importance and in curtailing Communist influence in this zone. The eastern horn of Africa played a vital role in safeguarding American access to the Persian Gulf area. By the early 1980s, despite Ethiopia's close ties with Moscow and Havana, two long-range factors could well curtail Communist influence in East Africa. One of these was the fact that—even with large Soviet and Cuban troop commitments and some $2 billion in Soviet military aid—the government of Ethiopia had not been able to impose its authority within its own borders. Thus far, Soviet and Cuban intervention had won little prestige for Communism. The other force serving to reduce Ethiopia's dependence upon the Soviet Union—which even Ethiopian officials themselves acknowledged—was the enormous challenge of reconstructing the war-ravaged country. This was a task which Moscow showed no inclination to undertake. Aid for that purpose would almost certainly have to come from the United States and from Western Europe. But perhaps the most ominous threat to political stability in East Africa stemmed from the worsening food deficit and pervasive poverty. Again, if solutions could be found to these problems, African officials would almost certainly need assistance, technical aid, and investment from the West.[68]

Africa and the Superpowers in Perspective

Our somewhat detailed examination of the political crises in Angola and in Africa's eastern "horn"—together with the experiences of several other African states in the post-colonial period—provide data supporting certain overall conclusions about Soviet-American competition on the African continent. To reiterate a point made earlier: Until the late 1950s, sub-Saharan Africa was relatively insulated from Cold War rivalries between the superpowers. In the American view, at least, the African continent remains a zone of low diplomatic priority and involvement vis-à-vis American commitments in other regions, such as Western Europe or the Middle East. America's reluctance to become deeply committed on the African continent was reinforced by the atmosphere of diplomatic retrenchment that characterized official and public thinking after the Vietnam War and continues to be reflected in American attitudes and policies toward the African continent. One reason for the low level of American involvement in African problems lies in the fact that, after the liquidation of colonialism, the United States has been largely content to allow its European allies to assume the burden of providing the bulk of Africa's developmental needs and—especially in the case of long-standing French ties with West Africa—provide assistance to incumbent governments confronting insurgent movements and other threats to their authority. For African states associated with the European Community, for example, substantial foreign aid—and access to Western markets on favorable terms—are available; and these continue to play a key role in the economic development of several African nations.*

As we have already observed, the American people and their leaders have been inadequately prepared to understand, and to respond effectively to, political developments in contemporary Africa. Americans, for example, are likely to find modern African political nomenclature and concepts difficult and confusing—and, in some cases, at variance with their own conception of democracy. Throughout the African continent, widespread support exists for ideas like "African Socialism," for one-party political systems, for virtually unlimited executive authority —and for other ideas customarily associated with Marxist regimes. By contrast, cherished American concepts—like capitalism and Western democracy—are often in disrepute

*More detailed discussion of the European Community's role in African affairs, particularly in meeting its developmental needs, may be found in Chapter 11. African states, for example, are primary beneficiaries of the second Lomé Convention signed in 1979 between the European Community and some 50 developing nations. The French role in West Africa is discussed and analyzed more fully in James O. Goldsborough, "Dateline Paris: Africa's Policeman," *Foreign Policy,* **33** (Winter, 1978–1979) 174–190; and in Jack Kramer, "Our French Connection in Africa," ibid., **29** (Winter, 1977–1978), 160–166.

on the African scene. For Africans, capitalism suggests exploitation by the village money-lender or dominant political influence by foreign corporations; while the notion of Western democracy is tainted because of its association with the era of European colonialism. Ever since the period of World War I and the Communist Revolution in Russia, nationalist leaders in Africa and the Third World generally have been attracted to the Soviet indictment of capitalism's inherently "imperialistic" nature and to Moscow's vocal and material support for anticolonial movements. African governments welcomed external Communist support in behalf of campaigns to liberate Africa from white control or to defeat insurgent movements challenging the authority of the central government. Soviet (and in some cases, Communist Chinese and Cuban) support for such causes has been welcomed by African states, in the face of American passivity (or sometimes, opposition) to them. In brief, to the American mind Africa has often appeared a fertile field for Marxist influence and control over African decision making.

Despite such widely publicized examples of Soviet and Cuban intervention in Angola and East Africa, most informed students of African political systems doubt that the region offers a favorable long-term environment for pervasive or lasting Communist influence. In the years ahead, on the basis of several leading criteria Africa's orientation is likely to be more toward the Western than toward the Communist world. Although they may have an affinity for concepts like "African Socialism," one commentator has emphasized, throughout the region:

> . . . most governments and movements—military or civilian, avowedly Marxist or ideologically eclectic—are essentially middle-class establishments. They are concerned, above all, with integrating elements of the methods,

experiences, and resources of [other societies] that seem to fit parochial needs.[69]

This same observer reminds us that "Marx never analyzed African society or an Africa-like situation." Since the African states received their independence, "no African who calls himself a Marxist has yet demonstrated how the problems of a single African country could be resolved in a Marxist context."[70] Or, as another authority on modern African political systems has expressed it, despite their tendency to employ Marxist terminology and political concepts, most African nationalist leaders have concluded that the Kremlin's "collectivist model" has little to offer their societies.[71] Several years ago, one of Africa's most prestigious leaders—President Julius Nyerere of Tanzania—pointed out (especially to foreign students of African affairs) that there was a subtle, but crucial, distinction between communism and *communalism*. Soviet-style Communism and other versions of Marxism were essentially *alien,* Western-derived ideologies having no roots in African soil. By contrast, communalism—or the idea that individuals were members of a community, and they had rights and responsibilities deriving from that fact—was a traditional African idea, antedating the colonial experience.[72] Although Nyerere and his African contemporaries have often been inexplicit concerning how communalism and other indigenous African ideas translated into specific governmental practices and policies, acceptance of Nyerere's ideas was pervasive throughout the continent. As the first president of independent Guinea, Sékou Touré once said concerning Western democracy, Marxism, and other foreign ideologies: Africans did not propose to wear "borrowed clothing that does not fit."[73]

Another longtime student of African affairs has said that a transcendent fact about

the political development of the region must
be kept continually in mind:

> ...the continent comprises a growing
> number of independent states each of which
> judges the policies of the major powers by the
> degree to which they advance or harm its
> own perceived interests.

Legum notes that "the changing environment
in postindependence Africa has opened the
way for the USSR . . . to assume a new role in
the continent's affairs. . . ." Yet in the overwhelming majority of cases, close African
identification with the Soviet Union (or its
client, Cuba) has *not* "fostered the emergence
of a new alliance system" between African
countries and the U.S.S.R. Accords reached
between them have in nearly all instances
been "temporary [agreements] and intended
to achieve mostly short-term objectives."
Legum cites the example of the Sudan—
which (in the period from 1969 to 1977)
moved from close identification with the West,
to an even stronger reliance upon the Soviet
Union, and then back to a pro-Western and
pro-Arab orientation. A more recent example
is the Marxist-oriented government of
Angola, which by the 1980s was indicating an
interest in reducing its dependency upon the
Soviet Union and Cuba by developing closer
ties with the West. This general pattern—close collaboration with the U.S.S.R.,
Cuba, and other Communist states during the
stage of Africa's revolutionary struggle, followed by efforts in time to curtail Communist
influence and "normalize" relations with the
West—has been characteristic of several new
African nations in the past two decades. In
Legum's view, Africa's relationships with
most foreign powers "are largely transient,"
for two fundamental reasons. In many cases,
African governments themselves often
proved to be "short-lived"; and Africa's basic

diplomatic orientation was toward nonalignment with either of the superpowers. The old
slogan—"hands off Africa!"—still describes
the African attitude toward the United
States, the Soviet Union, and any other external power seeking hegemony in Africa.[74]

On the basis of African experience during the post-colonial era, it is possible to identify a rather typical pattern or syndrome of
relations between the Soviet Union and a
given African state. Initially, during the long
struggle against colonial domination, Moscow
provided material and diplomatic support to
anticolonial movements on the African continent. In the post-colonial period, Soviet support was often forthcoming to particular African countries in behalf of the "liberation" of
Africa from white racial control or (as in the
cases of Angola and Ethiopia) in support of a
government's efforts to defeat insurgent
movements. As was emphasized in Chapter
10, such Soviet intervention in African affairs
has been justified by the Kremlin as legitimate
support for "national liberation movements"
throughout the Third World—a practice
which, in Moscow's view, does not con-
travene the idea of détente between the superpowers. (American officials of course hold a
contrary view of the meaning and requirements of détente.) The African state in question may also have a Marxist-oriented regime
in which Soviet "advisers" are conspicuously
present. Relying upon massive infusions of
Soviet (and more recently, Cuban) military assistance, a particular African government may
attempt to eliminate political opposition
groups, to defeat insurgent movements, or to
advance territorial claims at the expense of its
neighbors. Officials in Washington become
deeply apprehensive about the regional and
global implications of this Soviet "beachhead"
on the African continent.

Then almost invariably something "happens" to impair the Soviet Union's cordial and

influential relations with this African state. In some contexts, Moscow has intruded into the internal political affairs of its African client; or personal relations between key African and Soviet officials create tensions and misunderstandings, undermining confidence between the two governments; or Moscow balks at providing the level of economic assistance requested by its client, on terms acceptable to African officials. For these or other reasons, Moscow's influence within the African country declines—sometimes dramatically and precipitously—after which the African state involved begins to "normalize" its relations with the United States and other Western nations. The African country exhibits a more balanced and objective view of what genuine nonalignment means in foreign affairs; and it enters a new diplomatic stage in which its own national interests dictate its relations with the superpowers. With suitable local variations, one African state after another—Algeria, Egypt, the Sudan, Ghana, Guinea, Somalia, Tanzania, Zimbabwe, Mozambique, and Angola—has experienced this cycle in its foreign relations.[75]

In mid-August 1980, the leader of Zimbabwe, the avowed Marxist Robert Mugabe, for example, visited the United States, where he sought to elicit greater American understanding of, and support in solving, Zimbabwe's internal problems. From the evidence available, Mugabe was dedicated to a policy of reconciliation between the black majority and white minority of Zimbabwe's population; he was committed to a policy of national development; and (in the face of criticism by the Soviet Union and revolutionary groups in East Africa) he was determined to end the revolutionary conflict that had kept the country in turmoil for many years. In contrast to the reception accorded Marxist-oriented leaders of the Third World in the past, officials of both the Carter and Reagan administrations

sought to preserve collaborative relations with Mugabe's regime and to provide at least limited assistance enabling it to solve Zimbabwe's internal problems.[76] In the same period, another African country—Mozambique—whose government once had close ties with the Kremlin was abandoning Marxist economic principles and was seeking to expand its contacts with the West.[77]

The process we have described—whereby many African states have gone through a period of close identification with the Soviet Union, followed by disillusionment with Moscow and efforts to improve their relations with the West—has its origins in certain objective factors and conditions affecting African viewpoints. Three of these seem crucial in explaining this phenomenon. The first is that—much as their colonial experience conditioned the African mind against the West—in time most Africans accepted the idea that the long era of Western colonialism on the African continent had come to an end. In the post-colonial stage, the urgent problems facing most African governments could not be solved on the basis of an emotionally dictated policy of anti-Western sentiment and automatic suspicion of Western motives in Africa.

Second, Africans experienced a transition in their assessment of Soviet motives and goals on the continent. African nationalists were grateful to the Soviet Union and other Communist countries for assistance provided them in the liberation of Africa from colonial domination. And after independence was achieved, African governments later relied upon external Communist support for a variety of other causes to which African leaders were devoted. But as America has discovered repeatedly, neither African, nor any other, governments normally formulate their internal and external policies on the basis of "gratitude" toward other countries. In time, even Marxist-oriented African leaders began to understand that Soviet interest in the welfare and future of African societies was not totally altruistic; that Moscow's African diplomacy reflected, and was coordinated with, the Soviet Union's *international* objectives; and that African leaders themselves, or their country's well-being, were often expendable once they had served their purpose in the Soviet diplomatic scheme. In brief (in light of the fact that the United States adhered fairly consistently to its policy of "low profile" on the African continent), informed Africans realized that it was primarily the Soviet Union that was converting the region into a new Cold War arena, thereby violating Africa's professed principle of diplomatic nonalignment.

Third, and most crucially perhaps in explaining the tendency of African states to "normalize" their relations with the West, African leaders have faced the implications of certain dominant economic realities. Among these are the fact that in meeting the most urgent requirement of most African societies—*raising agricultural production*—the Soviet Union has little to offer, while the United States stands at the forefront of agricultural technology and food production. As much as any other single step, the future well-being of African societies depends upon their ability to increase agricultural (especially food) output significantly; and in achieving this goal, there is simply no substitute for American, and other Western, expertise and assistance. In other economic spheres as well—such as trade and commerce, and the expansion of foreign investment in black African countries—no feasible alternative exists to African reliance upon the United States and other advanced nations (including Japan). In still another related realm—expanding the overall level of governmental economic and technical assistance for African societies—most African officials are aware that their most promising approach lies in maintaining friendly rela-

tions with the West. In contrast to Soviet aid programs, the volume of foreign aid is much larger from Western sources; and not infrequently, it is available to African countries on more advantageous terms.

Despite temporary setbacks—and dramatic instances of Soviet or Cuban intervention in African political affairs—a number of strong ties link the United States and the independent nations of Africa. In Macebuh's view, "the United States, not the Soviet Union, has a unique opportunity to achieve permanent and mutually beneficial relations with African countries." Moscow's opportunities on the African continent usually consist of "short-term" situations "tied to periods of external or internal threat." By contrast, America's opportunity "is a potentially timeless one, because its context is peacetime."[78] As African recollections of Western colonialism dim, and as its leaders become increasingly preoccupied with solving internal problems, African nations may be expected to normalize and strengthen their bonds with the West.

NOTES

1. See the text of the address by Vice-President Walter Mondale on July 22, 1980, in the State Department publication, "Africa and the U.S.: Shared Values," Current Policy No. 203, 1980, pp. 1–3.
2. See the address by Ambassador Donald F. McHenry on December 13, 1979, in "Political and Economic Interests in Africa," *Department of State Bulletin,* **80** (April, 1980), 28–30.
3. See the data on contemporary Africa presented in William R. Cotter, "The Neglected Continent," *Africa Report,* **24** (March–April, 1979), 10.
4. See Richard Deutsch, "African Oil and U.S. Foreign Policy," *Africa Report,* **24** (September–October, 1979), 47.

5. Cotter, "The Neglected Continent," 10–11.

6. See the data on Africa presented in F. S. B. Mazadi, "The Politics of U.S. Foreign Assistance," in *Newsweek,* **96** (August 25, 1980), 51; and the report on famine conditions in Africa in ibid., 48–49.

7. See Mazadi, "The Politics of U.S. Foreign Assistance," 51; David Ottaway, "Africa: U.S. Policy in Eclipse," *Foreign Affairs,* **58** (Special Issue, 1979), 653–654.

8. See the excerpts on Africa's economic future cited in Ottaway, "Africa: U.S. Policy in Eclipse," 638, 653–654.

9. See Cotter, "The Neglected Continent," 11; and Juan de Onis in *New York Times,* November 20, 1980. The influence of black American opinion on the diplomacy of the Carter and Reagan administrations is analyzed in Carol Lancaster, "United States Policy in Sub-Saharan Africa," *Current History,* **81** (March, 1982), 99–100.

10. Ottaway, "Africa: U.S. Policy in Eclipse," 638.

11. See the report on Vice-President Mondale's tour of Africa, in *U.S. News and World Report,* **89** (July 28, 1980), 47–48.

12. Helen Kitchen, "Eighteen African Guideposts," *Foreign Policy,* **37** (Winter, 1979–1980), 86.

13. See the views of Senator Frank Church, as reported by Terence Smith, in *New York Times,* June 9, 1978.

14. Kitchen, "Eighteen African Guideposts," 76.

15. Walter Goldschmidt, ed., *The United States and Africa* (New York: Praeger Publishers, 1963), p. 4.

16. Rupert Emerson, "The Character of American Interests in Africa," in ibid., p. 3.

17. The evolution of official American concern with African developments is discussed in Vernon McKay, "The African Operations of United States Government Agencies," in ibid., pp. 273–296.

18. Rupert Emerson, *Africa and United States Policy* (Englewood Cliffs, N.J.: Prentice-Hall, 1967), p. 26.

19. For a more detailed discussion of President John F. Kennedy's views and policies toward Africa, see Arthur Schlesinger, Jr., *A Thousand Days* (Boston: Houghton Mifflin Co., 1965), pp. 551–585.

20. For the viewpoints of Dr. Henry Kissinger on African issues, see the brief references dealing with African questions in Henry Kissinger, *White House Years* (Boston, Little, Brown and Co., 1979), pp. 417, 427, 1090, and 1262.

21. See several of the essays in the symposium by Donald P. Kommers and Gilburt D. Loescher, eds., *Human Rights and American Foreign Policy* (Notre Dame, Ind.: Notre Dame University Press, 1979), and the text of President Carter's address on May 22, 1977, on pp. 302–309.

22. See Ottaway, "Africa: U.S. Policy in Eclipse," 657.

23. For a detailed analysis of the American foreign assistance budget as it affects Africa, see Mazadi, "The Politics of U.S. Foreign Assistance," 50–56.

24. Ibid., 50–52; and Cotter, "The Neglected Continent," 12.

25. Jean Herskovits, "Democracy in Nigeria," *Foreign Affairs,* **58** (Winter, 1979–80), 314.

26. See the data presented in Cotter, "The Neglected Continent," 10; and in Kitchen, "Eighteen African Guideposts," 82.

27. See Cotter, "The Neglected Continent," 10.

28. An informative discussion of American public opinion, as it affected the presidential election of 1980, is provided in Steven V. Roberts, "The Year of the Hostage," *The New York Times Magazine,* November 2, 1980, pp. 26, 30, 58–74. President Ronald Reagan's views on human rights issues and other questions affecting Afro-American relations are analyzed in Hedrick Smith, "Reagan: What Kind of World Leader?" *The New York Times Magazine,* November 16, 1980, pp. 47, 172–177.

29. See the text of President Carter's address on May 22, 1977, as reproduced in Kommers and Loescher, eds., *Human Rights and American Foreign Policy,* pp. 302–308.

30. See the statement by Deputy Assistant Secre-

tary Stephen B. Cohen to the Subcommittee on International Organizations of the House Foreign Affairs Committee, on October 31, 1979, entitled "Human Rights in Africa," Department of State, Current Policy No. 119, 1979, pp. 1–4.

31. See the statement of Assistant Secretary for Human Rights and Humanitarian Affairs Patricia M. Derian, before the same subcommittee of the House Foreign Affairs Committee on May 13, 1980, entitled "Human Rights in South Africa," Department of State, Current Policy No. 181, 1980, pp. 1–4.

32. See "Sékou Touré in America," *Africa Special Report,* **4** (November, 1959), 9; and Emmet V. Mittlebeeler, "Africa and the Defense of America," *World Affairs,* **121** (Fall, 1958), 82.

33. Background discussions of the racial problems in Southern Rhodesia may be found in: John A. Davis and James K. Baker, eds., *Southern Africa in Transition* (New York: Praeger Publishers, 1966), pp. 101–157; and in James Cameron, *The African Revolution* (New York: Random House, 1961), pp. 158–181.

34. See Davis and Baker, *Southern Africa in Transition,* pp. 101–157; and *New York Times,* March 10 and 29, 1970.

35. Congressional attitudes on the question of Southern Rhodesia are discussed in Cecil V. Crabb, Jr., and Pat Holt: *Invitation to Struggle: Congress, the President and Foreign Policy* (Washington, D.C.: Congressional Quarterly, 1980), pp. 194–196, 200.

36. For a discussion of lobbying efforts by the government of Southern Rhodsia, see the article by ex-Senator Dick Clark, in *New York Times,* January 30, 1979.

37. See the statements by President Carter and Secretary of State Vance on the Southern Rhodesian question in "Zimbabwe-Rhodesia Decision Explained," Department of State, Current Policy No. 70, 1979, pp. 1–6.

38. More detailed treatment of the challenges facing Zimbabwe may be found in Xan Smiley, "Zimbabwe, Southern Africa, and the Rise of Robert Mugabe," *Foreign Affairs,* **58** (Summer, 1980), 1060–1083; Richard W. Hull, "Zimbabwe: Time Running Out," *Current History,* **80** (March, 1981), 120–123, 130–131; and Virginia C. Knight, "Report from Zimbabwe," ibid., **81** (March, 1982), 119–121, 138.

39. Diverse interpretations of the meaning and impact of the settlement in Southern Rhodesia are offered in: Smiley, "Zimbabwe, Southern Africa, and the Rise of Robert Mugabe," 1060–1083; Richard W. Hull, "The Continuing Crisis in Rhodesia," *Current History,* **78** (March, 1980), 107–110; *U.S. News and World Report,* **89** (July 21, 1980), 55–56; and *Newsweek,* **96** (July 28, 1980), 51–52.

40. Clyde Ferguson and William R. Cotter, "South Africa—What Is To Be Done?" *Foreign Affairs,* **56** (January, 1978), 264.

41. Ibid., 260–261.

42. See the views of Patricia M. Derian in "Human Rights in South Africa," p. 1; and of Patrick O'Meara, "South Africa: the Politics of Change," *Current History,* **80** (March 1981), 111–113.

43. See the data presented in Smiley, "Zimbabwe, Southern Africa, and the Rise of Robert Mugabe," 1078.

44. Background information on the modern history of South Africa may be found in: Leo Marquard, *The Peoples and Policies of South Africa,* 4th ed. (New York: Oxford University Press, 1969); and Douglas Brown, *Against the World* (Garden City, N.Y.: Doubleday and Co., 1969). A briefer treatment is available in Cameron, *The African Revolution,* pp. 25–52.

45. See the statement by Assistant Secretary of State Patricia M. Derian, in "Human Rights in South Africa," pp. 1–2.

46. See the reports on conditions in South Africa in, "Why South Africa's Racial Split Widens," *U.S. News and World Report,* **88** (June 9, 1980), 55–56.

47. See the discussion of internal changes and reforms within South Africa in Robert I. Rotberg, "How Deep the Change?" *Foreign Policy,* **38** (Spring, 1980), 126–143; John de St. Jorre, "South Africa: Is Change Coming?"

Foreign Affairs, **60** (Fall, 1981), 106–122; and the report in *Newsweek,* **96** (August 25, 1980), 43.

48. See the views of Chief Luthuli as presented in: Clark D. Moore and Ann Dunbar, eds., *Africa: Yesterday and Today* (New York: Bantam Books, 1968), p. 293; and Brian Bunting, *The Rise of the South African Reich* (Baltimore: Penguin Books, 1964), p. 322.

49. "Issues Before the 24th General Assembly," *International Conciliation,* No. 574 (September, 1969), pp. 107–108.

50. See the statement by Assistant Secretary of State Patricia Derian, in "Human Rights in South Africa," pp. 3–4.

51. One student of African affairs has said that no external sanctions, acceptable to governments and public opinion in the West, are likely to prove effective in compelling a change in South Africa's racial policies. See Rotberg, "How Deep the Change?" 138–139. Even former UN Ambassador Andrew Young, whose viewpoints were usually sympathetic to black African sentiments, doubted the effectiveness of reliance upon sanctions against South Africa. His views are cited in Richard Deutsch, "African Issues and Presidential Politics," *Africa Report,* **25** (January–February, 1980), 20. The Namibian question is examined more fully in Kenneth Grundy, "Namibia in International Politics," *Current History,* **81** (March, 1982), 101–105, 131–132.

52. A more detailed analysis of American diplomatic alternatives in dealing with South Africa is available in James R. Cobbledick, *Choice in American Foreign Policy: Options for the Future* (New York: Thomas Y. Crowell, 1973), pp. 214–239. Other evaluations of existing and proposed American policy toward the South African question may be found in: Fredrick S. Arkhurst, ed., *U.S. Policy Toward Africa* (New York: Praeger Publishers, 1975), pp. 88–153; Alan M. Jones, Jr., *U.S. Foreign Policy in a Changing World* (New York: David McKay Co., 1973), pp. 215–241; George W. Ball, *The Discipline of Power: Essentials of a Modern World Structure* (Boston: Atlantic-Little, Brown, 1968), pp. 245–259; Randall Robinson, "Investments in Tokenism," *Foreign Policy,* **38** (Spring, 1980), 164–168; Desaix Myers III and David M. Liff, "The Press of Business," *Foreign Policy,* **38** (Spring, 1980), 143–164; and Ferguson and Cotter, "South Africa—What Is To Be Done?" 253–275.

53. See the statement by Under Secretary of State David N. Newsom before the Subcommittee on Africa of the House Foreign Affairs Committee, on October 18, 1979, in the State Department publication, "Communism in Africa," Current Policy No. 99, October 18, 1979, pp. 1–6.

54. David Morison, *The U.S.S.R. and Africa: 1945–1963* (New York: Oxford University Press, 1964), pp. 1–3.

55. Ibid., pp. 7–9.

56. Ibid., pp. 9–13.

57. Recent Soviet intervention in Africa, as a response to the changing balance of Russian and American military power, is analyzed in Walter F. Hahn and Alvin J. Cottrell, *Soviet Shadow Over Africa* (Miami, Fla.: University of Miami Press, 1976), pp. 3–25.

58. Our discussion of the political crisis in Angola relies heavily upon Nathaniel Davis, "The Angola Decision of 1975: A Personal Memoir," *Foreign Affairs,* **57** (Fall, 1978), 109–124; Kenneth L. Adelman, "The Central African States," *Current History,* **76** (March, 1979), 133–134; Gerald R. Ford, *A Time to Heal* (New York: Harper & Row, and The Reader's Digest Association, 1979), pp. 345–346, 351–359; and Ottaway, "Africa: U.S. Policy in Eclipse," 649–650.

59. See Secretary of State Kissinger's testimony before the Subcommittee on African Affairs of the Senate Foreign Relations Committee on January 29, 1976, in U.S., Congress, Senate, Foreign Relations Committee, *Hearings on Angola,* 94th Cong., 2d Sess., pp. 6–23.

60. Fuller discussion of congressional efforts to limit the President's power to intervene in Angola and other settings may be found in

Crabb and Holt, *Invitation to Struggle: Congress, the President and Foreign Policy*, pp. 113–137. See also the discussion in Ford, *A Time to Heal*, p. 346.

61. See the discussion by Juan de Onis of efforts by the Reagan Administration to obtain repeal of the Clark Amendment, *New York Times*, April 28, 1981.

62. Our discussion of the Angolan question relies upon the more extended treatments in Jon Kraus, "American Foreign Policy in Africa," *Current History*, **80** (March, 1981), 97–100, 129–130; dispatch by Juan de Onis in *New York Times*, November 20, 1980; by Anthony Lewis in ibid., January 25, 1981; and by John F. Burns in ibid., January 22, 1982.

63. Our discussion of the Ethiopian revolution and its implications relies heavily upon W. A. E. Skurnik, "Revolution and Change in Ethiopia," *Current History*, **68** (May, 1975), 206–211; John G. Merriam, "Military Rule in Ethiopia," ibid., **71** (November, 1976), 170–174; and Daniel S. Papp, "The Soviet Union and Cuba in Ethiopia," ibid., **76** (March, 1979), 110–114.

64. The Eritrean insurgency is discussed more fully in Merriam, "Military Rule in Ethiopia," 171–173; and in Papp, "The Soviet Union and Cuba in Ethiopia," 111–112.

65. The conflict between Ethiopia and Somalia over the Ogaden is analyzed more fully in Merriam, "Military Rule in Ethiopia," 173, 183–184; and in Papp, "The Soviet Union and Cuba in Ethiopia," 112–114, 129–130. See also John Darnton, in *New York Times*, June 21, 1977, and Michael T. Kaufman, in ibid., August 19, 1977.

66. See the views of President Gaafar al-Nimeiry of the Sudan on the conflict between Ethiopia and Somalia, as reported in the *New York Times*, June 21, 1977.

67. See the reports on developments in East Africa in *U.S. News and World Report*, **88** (March 3, 1980), 23; and **89** (September 1, 1980), 29.

68. Recent developments in East Africa are discussed more fully in the analysis by Richard F. Sherman in *New York Times*, December 9, 1981; and by Edith M. Lederer (AP staff writer) in the Baton Rouge *Sunday Advocate*, November 22, 1981.

69. Kitchen, "Eighteen African Guideposts," 72.

70. Ibid., 86

71. Smiley, "Zimbabwe, Southern Africa, and the Rise of Robert Mugabe," 1082–1083.

72. For the views of Julius Nyerere on African attitudes toward communism and communalism, see Paul E. Sigmund, Jr., ed., *The Ideologies of the Developing Nations* (New York: Praeger Publishers, 1963), p. 197; and see Victor C. Ferkiss, *Africa's Search for Identity* (Cleveland: World Publishing Co., 1966), pp. 10–13.

73. President Touré's views on foreign political ideologies are cited in Sékou Touré "Africa's Future and the World," *Foreign Affairs*, **41** (October, 1962), 144.

74. For an illuminating discussion of Soviet-American rivalry on the African continent—emphasizing the barriers to Communist influence over African decision making—see Colin Legum, "The African Environment," *Problems of Communism*, **27** (January-February, 1978), 1–20.

75. See the discussion of the Soviet Union's relations with African countries in Stanley Macebuh, "Misreading Opportunities in Africa," *Foreign Policy*, **35** (Summer, 1979), 166–168.

76. Prime Minister Robert Mugabe's visit to the United States and his diplomatic orientation are discussed by John F. Burns, in *New York Times*, August 24, 1980; and by Clyde Haberman, in ibid., August 25, 1980.

77. Smiley, "Zimbabwe, Southern Africa, and the Rise of Robert Mugabe," 1061.

78. Macebuh, "Misreading Opportunities in Africa," 169.

Chapter 14

Latin America:
The Search for Hemispheric Community

In perhaps the best-known foreign policy declaration in American history—the Monroe Doctrine, promulgated by President James Monroe in a message to Congress on December 2, 1823—the idea that the American republics formed a unique "community" became a foundation stone of the nation's diplomacy. In his celebrated policy statement, Monroe informed the European powers that their political systems were "different" from those existing in the newly independent nations of the Western Hemisphere. Monroe notified the capitals of Europe, therefore, that the United States would "consider any attempt on their part to extend their system to any portion of this hemisphere as dangerous to our peace and safety." Monroe's forceful warning to the European powers against future colonization in the hemisphere—an admonition later broadened to include the notion of external *political intervention* in hemispheric affairs—has served as a basic principle of American foreign policy for over a century and a half.[1]

Inter-American Relations: An Overview

The Concept of an American "Community"

The idea that the United States and its Latin American neighbors comprise a distinctive and tightly knit community has been a conspicuous *motif* in American diplomacy since the early nineteenth century. "The destiny of every nation within our inter-American system remains of foremost concern to the United States," President Richard M. Nixon declared in 1972. His Administration had accepted the principle that

> . . . geography and history and U.S. interests did give our relationship with Latin America a special—and continuing—importance. We could not treat Latin America as simply another region of the developing world. The hemisphere is unique and our political ties in it are unique.[2]

Several months earlier, President Nixon observed that "For more than a century and a

484

half, our most consistent peacetime foreign relations were hemispheric relations." Nixon was convinced that "Geography and history have bound us [the American states] together and nurtured a sense of community, now formalized in the treaties and institutions of the inter-American system."[3] President Nixon and his chief White House adviser, Dr. Henry Kissinger, called for a "new partnership" and a "new dialogue" among the nations of the New World.[4]

Does a community of interest *in fact* exist between the United States and its neighbors in the Western Hemisphere? That question has evoked sharp differences of opinion among governmental officials and informed students of hemispheric relations for almost two centuries. Even when the Monroe Doctrine was promulgated in 1823, ex-President John Quincy Adams seriously questioned whether its presumed sense of community among the nations of the New World was historically accurate and justifiable.[5] More recently, a Chilean diplomat asked, "How can you have a community that includes a rich powerful country like the United States with world-wide commitments, and underdeveloped countries like ours?"[6]

Most of the specific issues dealt with in this chapter on United States relations with Latin America can be subsumed under the general question: Does a community of interests actually exist among the nations of the Western Hemisphere? If so, what are the sources of unity and cohesion among them? And what have been concrete manifestations of this sense in the post-World War II period? Conversely, if the idea of a New World "community" is illusory, what are the principal barriers to that age-old dream?

For convenience, our discussion of United States-Latin American relations has been divided into three broad topics: the search for hemispheric security and solidarity; the Communist challenge to political stability and security in the Western Hemisphere; and the problem posed for inter-American relations by the existence of right-wing, military-dominated governments throughout Latin America. Meanwhile, however, it is essential to devote brief attention to certain geographical, economic, demographic, and other factors that have influenced United States-Latin American relations in the past and that continue to do so in the contemporary period.*

Latin America—A Profile

Use of the term *Latin America* to describe the countries in the Caribbean area, in Central America, and on the South American continent is likely to convey a misleading impression. In reality, Latin America is a region of *immense diversity and extremes,* making generalizations about the area hazardous and subject to numerous exceptions. Moreover, the diversity characteristic of Latin America is becoming *more pronounced* with the passage of time. For example, within Latin America there are regional giants like Brazil—a country that is territorially larger than the United States and contains a population of almost 120 million people—and there are very small nations (sometimes called "ministates") like Belize, Guyana, and Jamaica. Similarly, Latin America has nuclear powers (or potential nuclear powers), such as Brazil and Argentina, while the armed forces of most of the other Latin American nations are relatively weak and are used mainly for the

*Throughout this book, terms like *American foreign policy* have been used to describe the diplomacy *of the United States.* Such terms are apt to cause confusion in this chapter, since adjectives like "American" can of course also be employed when discussing Central and South American countries and the other American republics. When such terms are used in this chapter, the context will make the meaning of the reference clear.

preservation of domestic order and, in many cases, for maintaining the incumbent regime in power.

Income levels and standards of living also vary widely throughout Latin America. At one end of the scale is a country like Haiti, one of the poorest on the globe, with an annual per capita income of some $260. By contrast, oil-rich Venezuela has an average per capita income 10 times greater than Haiti's. Most Latin American nations fall in between these extremes, with the income levels often varying widely between the urban and the rural sectors of their populations. Yet even the more advanced Latin American societies—like Brazil, Argentina, Venezuela, and Mexico—have annual per capita incomes between one-fourth and one-sixth the annual personal income in the United States.

The nations of Latin America also exhibit great diversity in terms of the nature and stability of their political institutions. Mexico illustrates one extreme: The country has enjoyed political stability for many years, and by many criteria the Mexican system is among the most democratic in Latin America. By contrast, Bolivia has experienced a coup or internal political upheaval nearly every year since it achieved independence in 1825! Paraguay continues to be governed by the authoritarian regime of General Alfredo Stroessner which came to power in 1953. A number of other Latin American states—like Brazil, Argentina, Panama, Chile, and Peru—are ruled by military juntas (most of which avow their intention of ultimately instituting democratic rule). Since 1959, Cuba has had an avowedly Communist regime under Fidel Castro; Nicaragua is governed by the Marxist-oriented Sandinista movement; for several years, until 1980, Jamaica had a pro-Marxist government devoted to "democratic socialism." During some periods, anarchy or semianarchy is usually also found within Latin American societies. (In the early 1980s, Gua-

temala had been reduced to a state of anarchy by the conflict between right- and left-wing political forces.) In El Salvador and several other Latin American nations, recent years have witnessed the emergence of guerrilla and revolutionary organizations that challenged the authority of established governments.

By 1980, the nations of Latin America had a total population of some 330 million people—or almost 50 percent more people than the United States. Yet their combined Gross National Product (GNP) was some $460 billion annually, versus some $2 trillion annual GNP for the United States. A pivotal reality about Latin America exemplifies what is sometimes called the "Malthusian cycle": The region has the *highest rate of population increase* of any major region on the globe.[7] Growing at an average rate of 2.8 percent annually, Latin America's population is expected to expand from around 330 million today to some 600 million people by the year 2000; and (if present population growth rates are sustained), some demographers believe that Latin America will have some 1.3 billion people by the latter part of the twenty-first century!*

---

*Such population projections, it must be emphasized, are subject to many qualifications and unforeseeable circumstances—making them, at best, only crude approximations and "guesstimates." The above projections rest upon the premise that current population growth rates in Latin America *will* be continued into the future. In reality, it is not unreasonable to expect that—as Latin American societies are subject to the "population explosion"—certain traditional "Malthusian checks," such as rampant disease and famine, will exact a high toll on the existing population and curb future population growth. Although strong religious barriers exist against birth-control programs in Latin America—and some countries have encouraged rapid population growth as a matter of state policy—by the early 1980s, some Latin American governments were beginning to express an interest in measures designed to curb rapid population expansion. Thomas Malthus was an English clergyman whose famous essay *On Population* (1824) predicted that food produc-

The "population explosion" has profound consequences for political developments throughout Latin America. Its overall impact is to foster rising popular demands upon established governments that were already hard-pressed to meet the needs of their citizens in spheres like housing, education, and, most crucially perhaps, food production. Yet it should be noted that some Latin American states, such as Argentina, have deliberately *encouraged* rapid population growth as a matter of national policy (in Argentina's case, in order to match Brazil's emergence as a regional power).

Despite the wide diversity found throughout Latin America, it is no less true that the nations of the Caribbean and South America also share certain common ideals and aspirations. Five of these seem pertinent to our discussion. One is a pervasive belief—evident since the era of Latin American independence in the early nineteenth century—in *democracy*. Although their own political and governmental behavior not infrequently is at variance with the democratic ideal, Latin Americans are devoted to the democratic principle; the constitutional systems of several Latin American states, for example, clearly reflect the influence of the Constitution of the United States.

Second, concepts like *modernization, progress,* and *national development* are also widely supported throughout Latin America. Nearly all governments in the region are committed to the goal of national development and to the modernization of what are often primitive and backward sectors of their societies. Two conspicuous examples of national devel-

opment in recent years have been Brazil and Mexico. If progress in other Latin American states has been less impressive—and if there is a general reluctance to inaugurate the internal changes and reforms required for modernization—belief in the goal, nevertheless, remains pervasive throughout Latin America.

Third, Latin Americans share *an historically engendered suspicion and fear of the United States*—frequently referred to as the "North American Colossus." As we shall see, to a significant degree Latin America's apprehension toward the United States stems from the era of the "Roosevelt Corollary" to the Monroe Doctrine and the period of "dollar diplomacy" in the early 1900s. Even today, however, this frame of mind is evident in a deep-seated concern about Washington's intentions toward its less powerful hemispheric neighbors. To cite but a single example: Efforts by the United States to reform and strengthen the Organization of American States (OAS) have encountered recurrent opposition from Latin Americans, who look upon the organization primarily as a mechanism to protect them from hegemonial behavior by the "North American Colossus."

A fourth, and somewhat contradictory, idea pervasive throughout the other American republics is the conviction that in its post-World War II foreign policy, *the United States has neglected Latin America* and has taken its southern neighbors "for granted," particularly in the allocation of foreign assistance.* This belief was particularly endemic south of the border before the Kennedy Administration sponsored the Alliance for Progress in the early 1960s as a long-range and ambitious development program for Latin

---

tion would increase by arithmetic progression (e.g., in the sequence 1, 2, 3, 4. . .), while population would grow geometrically (e.g., in the sequence 1, 2, 4, 8, 16. . .). The result would be widespread human starvation and death, as certain "Malthusian" restraints—like war, famine, and disease—curbed population size.

*In the allocation of its foreign economic assistance since World War II, the United States has allotted approximately 10 percent of the total to Latin American countries—versus, for example, over 30 percent for Asia and 25 percent for Europe.

American modernization and development. Yet even today, the belief persists that Washington remains indifferent to the needs of its hemispheric neighbors.

A fifth, and related, idea endemic throughout the Western Hemisphere today is the belief that Latin America should *exhibit greater diplomatic independence,* lessening its historic reliance upon the United States for guidance in such areas as foreign affairs and national defense. Two specific examples of this tendency may be cited at this stage (others will be provided as our discussion proceeds). A noteworthy tendency in the recent period has been the inclination of several Latin American states to identify with the Third World, in its devotion to the principle of diplomatic non-alignment between the United States and the Soviet Union. Although the question of whether Latin America is really a part of the Third World is debatable, an affinity for many of its diplomatic and economic goals has clearly been discernible in the diplomacy of several Latin American states.[8] Another example of growing diplomatic independence by Latin America is provided by the reluctance of states throughout the region to support efforts by the United States to oppose, apply economic sanctions against, or otherwise ostracize Cuba because of its Marxist regime and its close ties with the Soviet Union. Although Latin Americans generally may not approve of Cuba's internal and external policies (such as Castro's effort in the early 1960s to install Soviet missiles on the island), they have been increasingly reluctant to treat Cuba as an outcast in the inter-American system.

Hemispheric Security and Solidarity

The Monroe Doctrine

For over a century the Monroe Doctrine defined the diplomatic behavior of the United States toward the Western Hemisphere. Two developments in the third decade of the nineteenth century induced President Monroe to enunciate what came to be the most famous principle of our foreign policy. There were, first of all, Russian colonial activities in the West. Especially significant was the Czarist imperial ukase of 1821. It virtually declared the Pacific waters around these Russian colonial outposts a closed sea, a pronouncement that seemed to the United States to presage renewed Russian colonizing efforts in North America. A second danger arose from the threatened intervention of the Holy Alliance in the affairs of the former Spanish colonies in Latin America. The United States feared that the Holy Alliance would invoke the principle of "legitimacy" in an attempt to reimpose Spanish hegemony over newly independent American possessions; or failing this, that another European country might supplant Spain as a colonial power in the Western Hemisphere.[9]

Insofar as the provisions of the Monroe Doctrine governed the foreign policy of the United States toward Latin America,* we have already cited the key idea in President Monroe's proclamation. It was that the political systems of the New World were essentially different from those of the Old World; in time, therefore, the doctrine came to mean that the United States would construe any attempt by the European powers to impose their political hegemony upon the nations of the Western Hemisphere as dangerous to its peace and security.

Several points about Monroe's pro-

---

*The Monroe Doctrine, it should be emphasized, expressed two basic principles of American foreign policy —one governing American relations with Western Europe, and the other related to European intervention in the Western Hemisphere. The former principle—enunciating America's policy of isolationism toward, or noninvolvement in, European political conflicts—was analyzed in Chapter 11.

nouncement require emphasis. The first is that this was a *unilateral* declaration by the United States. The noncolonization principle, to be sure, was also supported by the British Foreign Office and in the years ahead was enforced by the Royal Navy. Yet other powerful nations were not inclined to regard the doctrine as a fixed canon of international law, much less as a precept to which they had freely given consent. Second, as originally expressed, the noncolonization principle of the Monroe Doctrine prohibited *future* colonization by European countries. It did nothing to interfere with *existing* colonies; nor did it proscribe European diplomatic or economic influence throughout the New World. Later amplifications and corollaries of the Monroe Doctrine broadened the scope of the noncolonization principle and introduced new prohibitions against European diplomatic activity in the Americas.

Third, in the years following Monroe's proclamation the United States was unprepared on a number of occasions to back up the Monroe Doctrine with military and diplomatic force. This became evident almost immediately after 1823, when Latin American diplomats asked Washington for treaties of alliance that would commit the United States to support their continued freedom from Spanish colonial rule. These requests met with an unenthusiastic reception on the part of the State Department. Moreover, when the nations of Latin America sought to cement closer hemispheric relations at the Panama Congress of 1826, the United States held aloof from the meeting.

From the time of its inception, and even after its scope had been broadened in the light of experience, the Monroe Doctrine remained essentially a unilateral response by the United States to conditions believed to threaten its security. In substance, wrote Robert Lansing in 1914, it reflected the view that "the United States considers an extension of political control by a European power over any territory in this hemisphere, not already occupied by it, to be a menace to the national safety of the United States." Compliance with the doctrine in the last analysis rested upon the "superior power of the United States to compel submission to its will. . . ."[10] That the Monroe Doctrine has been proclaimed unilaterally by the United States meant, in the words of Secretary of State Charles Evans Hughes in 1923, that

the government of the United States reserves to itself its definition, interpretation, and application. . . . Great powers have signified their acquiescence in it. But the United States has not been disposed to enter into engagements which would have the effect of submitting to any other power or to any concert of powers the determination either of the occasions upon which the principles of the Monroe Doctrine shall be invoked or of the measures that shall be taken in giving it effect.[11]

Schooled as they are in the idea that Monroe's classic foreign policy principle was ideally suited to their country's historic desires and needs, North Americans find it difficult to understand that the doctrine could arouse apprehension in their neighbors south of the border. Over the course of time, however, Latin American nations often viewed "Yankee imperialism" as a more imminent threat than reimposition of European colonial domination. Occasionally, Latin American countries were inclined to regard the doctrine as nothing more than a thinly veiled scheme whereby the United States invoked hemispheric security as a pretext to exercise a *de facto* protectorate over weaker American states and, under the guise of protecting them from European intervention, practiced intervention itself in the affairs of nations to the south.

Corollaries of the Monroe Doctrine

Today, when the student of American foreign policy studies the Monroe Doctrine, in reality he is studying an aggregate of diplomatic pronouncements and actions based upon President Monroe's message to Congress in 1823. Let us look briefly at some of the more important highlights in the evolution of this cardinal principle of American foreign policy.

The first important amplification of the Monroe Doctrine was the *Polk Corollary* in 1845–1848. President Polk declared that the noncolonization principle of the Monroe Doctrine "will apply with greatly increased force, should any European power attempt to establish *any new colony* in North America...."[12] A half century later, in the midst of the Venezuelan boundary dispute with Great Britain, Secretary of State Richard Olney informed the British that the noncolonization principle of the Monroe Doctrine had been "universally conceded" and that it had been the "controlling factor" in the "emancipation of South America" from Spanish rule. Olney, more gifted in the role of prosecuting attorney than historian or diplomat, went on to inform the British Foreign Office categorically that:

> Today the United States is practically sovereign on this continent, and its fiat is law upon the subjects to which it confines its interposition. Why?...It is because...its infinite resources combined with its isolated position render it master of the situation and practically invulnerable as against any or all other powers.[13]

The Olney letter translated the Monroe Doctrine into a pronouncement that in effect designated the Western Hemisphere as a Yankee sphere of influence, a claim which the nations of Europe and of Latin America were reluctant to accept.

Coincident with the age of "dollar diplomacy" toward Latin American and Asian affairs in the early 1900s was the *Roosevelt Corollary* to the Monroe Doctrine. Certain Latin American nations, chiefly in the Caribbean region, were notoriously lax in the management of their governmental and fiscal affairs. Outside intervention in their affairs for the purpose of collecting legitimate debts was consequently a perennial risk. President Theodore Roosevelt concluded that the United States could not prohibit foreign intervention to enforce payment of debts unless it were willing to assume responsibilities itself for preventing gross fiscal mismanagement by its southern neighbors. After several warnings to the Latin American states about the "mismanagement" of their affairs, in 1904 Theodore Roosevelt declared that any nation that "knows how to act with reasonable efficiency and decency" need not fear intervention. But:

> Chronic wrongdoing, or an impotence which results in a general loosening of the ties of civilized society, may in America, as elsewhere, ultimately require intervention by some civilized nation, and in the Western Hemisphere the adherence of the United States to the Monroe Doctrine may force the United States, however reluctantly...to the exercise of an international police power.[14]

This then was the first Roosevelt's characteristically forthright response to the threat of intervention in Latin American affairs by European countries. Either the southern neighbors of the United States would keep their own affairs in order, or else the United States would be compelled under the Monroe Doctrine to undertake necessary housecleaning duties in such countries. On repeated occasions after 1904, the United States invoked the Roosevelt Corollary to justify intervention in Latin American affairs. This fact inevitably conveyed the impression to the other American republics that the Monroe Doctrine might protect them from the diplomatic ambitions of countries outside the Western Hemisphere, but that it could also be invoked to rationalize control over them by the United States, and to their minds this was often a distinction without a difference. Not until the Administration of the second Roosevelt were all the military contingents of the United States finally withdrawn from Latin America.

Perhaps more than any other single development in the history of United States-Latin American relations, the Roosevelt Corollary to the Monroe Doctrine—and the interventions in Latin America carried out by Washington under its provisions—created enduring ill-will and tensions in inter-American affairs. Although, as we shall see, the corollary was officially repudiated a few years later by the United States, memories of "Big Stick" diplomacy by President Theodore Roosevelt and his successors in dealing with Latin America remain vivid throughout the region to the present day. As a result of the Roosevelt Corollary and other interventionist impulses exhibited by Washington in dealing with Latin America, the Monroe Doctrine (or what is often popularly called "Monroismo") usually evokes a negative response from Latin Americans.

The Good Neighbor Policy

The impact of Wilsonian idealism, along with the evident deterioration in relations between the United States and its hemispheric neighbors as a result of the Roosevelt Corollary from 1904 onward, demanded corrective measures on the part of the State Department. Recurrent outcries from the south against "Yankee imperialism" could no longer be ignored in Washington. A significant change in the foreign policy of the United States was therefore presaged by the "Clark Memorandum" of 1928, the gist of which was that the Roosevelt Corollary had been a perversion of the original intention of the Monroe Doctrine. Then with the election of Franklin D. Roosevelt came the "Good Neighbor" policy, enunciated in FDR's First Inaugural Address and reiterated in a series of messages thereafter by Roosevelt and Secretary of State Cordell Hull. The first step in establishing good neighborly relations was to reassure the Latin American countries that the Monroe Doctrine was not a pretext to conceal Yankee imperialistic ambitions toward them. Secretary Hull stated in 1933 that the people of the United States believed that the so-called right of conquest "must be banished from this hemisphere and, most of all, they shun and reject that so-called right for themselves." In the same year, FDR repeated Wilson's earlier pledge that the United States would never again seek additional territory by conquest. Paving the way for an effective inter-American system of defense and solidarity, Roosevelt observed that political turbulence and threats to hemispheric security were no longer of special concern to the United States alone, but that they were "the joint concern of a whole continent in which we are all neighbors."[15] As it related to the Monroe Doctrine, the new Good Neighbor policy came down to this: The traditional interest of the United States in Western hemispheric security must be translated into a policy shared by all the American countries.

Washington's efforts to "multilateralize" the Monroe Doctrine—to make the preservation of hemispheric peace and security a common obligation of all the American republics—has been only minimally successful. As we shall see, for example, initiatives by the United States to convert the Organization of

American States into an effective peacekeeping force in the Western Hemisphere have repeatedly been resisted by the other members of the inter-American system.

What is the importance and relevance of the Monroe Doctrine today? It must be confessed frankly that well-informed observers within the United States and outside it give widely varying answers to this question. One school of thought, for example, is convinced that the Monroe Doctrine "is dead" as a controlling axiom of American foreign policy; that it has become outmoded as a guiding principle of American diplomacy; and that by relying upon it, Washington achieves little more than arousing the suspicions and animosities of leaders and masses throughout Latin America. Before the Cuban Missile Crisis of 1962, for example, Soviet Premier Nikita Khrushchev publicly stated his belief that the Monroe Doctrine was passé; and the attempted installation of Soviet offensive missiles in Cuba testified to Moscow's conviction that the doctrine could be flaunted with impunity.[16]

Yet the decisive and forceful response of the Kennedy Administration to the buildup of Soviet missile power in Cuba provided evidence supporting the contrary point of view: The United States was no more prepared in the 1960s than in the 1820s to accept external military intervention in the Western Hemisphere by a hostile (or potentially hostile) nation. President Kennedy's successful insistence that Soviet missiles be removed from Cuba could be interpreted as persuasive evidence that the principles embodied in the Monroe Doctrine still actuate American foreign policy. Yet it was also significant that, throughout this crucial Soviet-American encounter, President John F. Kennedy and other executive officials studiously *refrained from invoking the Monroe Doctrine* directly against

the Soviet Union or from publicly justifying America's diplomatic position by reference to its terms.[17]

We shall examine more recent evidence bearing upon the Monroe Doctrine's utility at a later stage. Here, it is sufficient to make three general points about the role of the Monroe Doctrine in American diplomacy today. The first is that, as the Cuban Missile Crisis illustrated, the President and other executive officials have become reluctant to "invoke" the Monroe Doctrine overtly or to cite it as the basis for their actions in dealing with Latin America. Officials in Washington are mindful that "Monroismo" still evokes a negative reaction throughout Latin America; the White House knows (if Congress does not always) that overt reliance upon the Monroe Doctrine will impede winning Latin American cooperation in dealing with hemispheric security issues.

The second generalization about the relevance of the Monroe Doctrine today, however, is a contrary idea. In the *public and congressional mind* the doctrine still often ranks as a sacrosanct diplomatic principle, serving as the foundation stone of American foreign policy. Legislators, for example, do not exhibit the same reluctance as the White House in referring to the Monroe Doctrine publicly and in demanding that other nations comply with its provisions.

In the third place, despite reluctance by executive officials to rely upon it publicly, the Monroe Doctrine clearly *does* continue to govern American foreign policy in the sense that the United States will resist—unilaterally if necessary—an overt external threat to regional security. It is significant, for example, that when the Carter Administration confronted a buildup of Soviet ground forces in Cuba in 1979, the White House concluded that this Russian military contingent (described as "training" forces) did *not* endanger the security of the hemisphere; and Moscow took pains to emphasize that idea to Washington. As our subsequent treatment will show, by the 1980s a difficult problem faced officials in Washington (as they confronted revolutionary upheaval, for example, in Central America): determining whether an "external" threat to regional security existed, as precluded by the Monroe Doctrine.*

The Pan-American Movement

No sooner had the countries of Latin America won their independence in the early 1800s than their leaders began to think in terms of a Pan-American movement to preserve their freedom, not alone from Europe but from their northern neighbor, the United States, as well. The great South American leader Simon Bolívar early took the lead in laying the basis

*According to some interpretations, the obsolete nature of the Monroe Doctrine was illustrated by the crisis between Great Britain and Argentina that erupted over the Falkland Islands early in April, 1982. In the view of Argentina—an interpretation widely shared throughout Latin America—Britain's reliance upon armed force to maintain its possession of these islands was a clear case of external "intervention" in the Western Hemisphere in violation of the Monroe Doctrine and of the Rio Treaty of regional defense. This was not, however, Washington's position on the Falkland Islands dispute. British claims to the islands had been established in the early 1830s and had never been contested by the United States under the Monroe Doctrine. Moreover, the people of the Falkland Islands had repeatedly made clear their preference for British, over Argentine, rule (thereby largely refuting Argentina's claim that London was imposing a "colonial" administration upon an unwilling population). Moreover, officials of the Reagan Administration were convinced that in this instance, Argentina had engaged in aggression to resolve a political dispute with Great Britain. Under these conditions, Britain's defense of its jurisdiction over the islands could hardly be construed as a threat to Argentina or to hemispheric security.

for the Pan-American movement. The United States, largely for reasons of domestic politics and the desire to preserve an attitude of nonentanglement with other countries, did not participate in the first Panama Congress of 1826. Anticipating many meetings devoted to the Pan-American ideal in the years ahead, the conference in 1826 did little beyond passing resolutions usually ignored by the governments represented. The first attempt to establish a Pan-American system therefore was a failure.

Fifty years later the movement received new impetus under Secretary of State James G. Blaine, who proposed a meeting of all the American republics in Washington in 1881 for the purpose of preventing war in the Western Hemisphere and of promoting closer economic collaboration among the nations of the region. A change in political administrations within the United States delayed these plans for eight years. But finally, in 1889, the conference was held. This conference was also devoid of tangible results, except for one: establishment of the Bureau of American Republics, later renamed the Pan-American Union, which in time evolved into one of the principal organs of the Inter-American system.[18]

The pace by which the Pan-American movement grew from little more than expressions of affinity among the American republics, accompanied by occasional conferences at which actual gains were usually negligible, was leisurely between the late 1800s and the New Deal. Interventions carried out by the United States under the Roosevelt Corollary understandably made the other American republics highly suspicious of Uncle Sam's intentions. Repudiation of the Roosevelt Corollary and the inauguration of the Good Neighbor policy were therefore necessary before significant progress could be expected toward establishing more intimate relations among countries in the Western Hemisphere.

After 1932, Pan-American cooperation gradually became a reality. The threat of Axis aggression provided another stimulus, by binding the nations of the Western Hemisphere together against a common enemy and by emphasizing their economic interdependence. Beginning with the conference at Montevideo in 1933, the Inter-American system began to take shape. The United States accepted a resolution directed principally at itself, pledging all American republics to a policy of nonintervention in the affairs of their neighbors. In return, the United States received widespread support from the Latin American governments for the New Deal principle of reciprocal trade, whereby national tariffs were lowered on the basis of mutual concessions. Three years later, at the Inter-American Conference in Buenos Aires, the American republics accepted the principle of joint consultation among all the American countries in the event of a threat to the security of the hemisphere. Additional conferences were held in 1938, 1939, 1940, and 1942. An important milestone was the conference at Mexico City in 1945, at which the Act of Chapultepec was adopted, formally declaring the determination of the American republics to pursue a common policy in meeting any threat to their security from abroad.[19]

Building on these foundations, the Rio Conference of 1947 resulted in the Treaty of Reciprocal Assistance, signed on September 2. This regional defense agreement, like NATO and similar agreements, was drawn up under Article 51 of the United Nations Charter, providing for the right of individual and regional self-defense. Pending action by the Security Council of the UN, threats to the peace within the Americas were to be dealt with by the Inter-American system.[20] Then at the Ninth Inter-American Conference at Bogotá in the spring of 1948, the formal machinery necessary to make these goals a reality—the Organization of American States (OAS)—was established. Finally, the Pan-American movement had come to fruition.

OAS—Procedures and Principles

The Inter-American system rests upon three basic "charter documents" defining its scope and procedures. First, there is the Rio Treaty of mutual assistance, safeguarding the defense of the Americas from an attack originating outside or inside the hemisphere; second, there is a document specifying the scope, organs, and duties of the OAS; and third, there is a document setting forth procedures to be followed for bringing about the pacific settlement of disputes among members of the system.

Designed to promote such goals as peace, justice, solidarity, and economic and social well-being among its members, the Organization of American States has an elaborate administrative structure. The principal policy-making body is the General Assembly, usually meeting annually, in which each member of OAS has one representative. An Organ of Consultation exists to deal specifically with threats to regional peace and security and to concert the policies of the American republics under the provisions of the Rio Treaty of hemispheric defense. An Inter-American Economic and Social Council engages in a variety of activities designed to improve socioeconomic conditions throughout the hemisphere. An Inter-American Development Bank makes loans designed to promote the national development of OAS members. A relatively new organ of the OAS—the Inter-American Commission on Human Rights —was created to gain overall regional compliance with the American Convention on Human Rights adopted at a meeting of the

OAS in 1978. (To date, several influential American states, including the United States, have not ratified this Convention.)[21]

The Organization of American States has a long list of major and minor accomplishments to its credit. These range from a myriad of cultural, social, and economic activities carried on under OAS auspices, to playing a role in the solution of regional disputes among the American republics, to promoting the cause of international human rights. In 1962, the OAS took a strong (and almost unanimous) position opposing the installation of Soviet missiles in Cuba. Two years later, the OAS mediated a dispute between the United States and Panama; and the following year, an Inter-American Peace Force, created by the OAS, assumed the responsibility for preserving the stability of the Dominican Republic.* In 1969, again the OAS played a leading role

in resolving a dispute between El Salvador and Honduras. In recent years, the question of respect for human rights by governments within the Inter-American system has been at the forefront of OAS concern. It has also adopted a code of conduct governing the operations of foreign business firms within the hemisphere, with a view to promoting more uniform and ethical business practices by multinational corporations.[22] During the Carter Administration, officials in Washington were gratified when the OAS took two actions supporting the diplomacy of the United States: The members of the OAS voted unanimously to condemn the seizure of American "hostages" by the government of Iran late in 1979; and some 25 Latin American nations joined the United States in supporting an OAS resolution condemning the Soviet invasion of Afghanistan.[23]

OAS—Problems and Prospects

The Organization of American States has emerged as unquestionably the most tangible and visible expression of a sense of community binding the United States and its Latin American neighbors. It is the oldest regional defense system; and, as we have seen, it has compiled a record of significant achievement in some fields.

Yet it is fair to say that the OAS has *not* fulfilled the high expectations entertained by advocates of the Pan-American ideal or realized its full potential as a regional organization. As judged by the record of the OAS, the question of whether the United States and the other American republics in fact constitute a community cannot be answered with assurance. Nor is it clear that a closer sense of community is emerging among the members of the Inter-American system.

The Organization of American States continues to confront two old—but still intrac-

---

*Late in April 1965, a revolution (viewed by the Johnson Administration as Communist instigated) erupted in the Dominican Republic, entailing great loss of life and destruction of property throughout the country. Responding to urgent pleas from American officials on the scene, Washington ultimately concluded that the lives of Americans and other foreigners were endangered, and on April 28, President Johnson ordered United States Marines to land in the country to preserve order and to protect foreign nationals in the country. At the same time, the Johnson Administration requested the Organization of American States to assume this function, and an OAS police force was eventually sent to the Dominican Republic. A detailed discussion of the Dominican crisis may be found in Lyndon B. Johnson, *The Vantage Point: Perspectives on the Presidency, 1963–1969* (New York: Holt, Rinehart and Winston, 1971), pp. 187–205. Critics of American policy believed that the principal objective of American intervention was to prevent a possible takeover of the Dominican government by leftist forces, led by Juan Bosch. For critical accounts of American involvement in the Dominican crisis, see Melvin Gurtov, *The United States Against the Third World: Antinationalism and Intervention* (New York: Praeger Publishers, 1974), pp. 111–126; and Martin C. Needler, *The United States and the Latin American Revolutions* (Boston: Allyn and Bacon, 1972), pp. 81–92.

table—problems hindering its evolution and effective operation. By many criteria, these difficulties are more serious today than when the OAS was established. One of these is *the great disparity in power between the United States and the other American republics*. The marked power differential between the United States and its southern neighbors—a disparity which, by some criteria, is becoming wider every year—has several fundamental implications for the future of regional organization in the Western Hemisphere. From a *Realpolitik* perspective, the OAS has never been—and perhaps will never be—an organization based upon the principle of the equality of its members. As the Latin American members of OAS are amply aware, no amount of rhetoric in Washington about the principle of equality among the American republics can alter that transcendent reality.

Moreover, a corollary of this power disparity is that the United States is a superpower, with *global* interests and responsibilities; this fact intrinsically conditions Washington's approach to Latin America and its policies in (or affecting) the OAS. As a superpower, the United States perhaps inevitably appraises developments in Latin America —and the outstanding example is the problem of Communist inroads throughout the region—within the context of its international interests and responsibilities. The other members of the OAS have a different and more limited perspective on developments within the hemisphere, focusing primarily upon the achievement of their own narrowly conceived policy interests. To cite a single example: Washington may be deeply concerned about the internal and external behavior of Castro's Cuba—as illustrated by massive Cuban intervention in black Africa—while many Latin American countries are less concerned about this aspect of Cuban policy and more interested in preventing or containing in-

terventionist moves by the United States against a sister Latin American republic.

Another significant consequence of the power disparity between the United States and the other members of the OAS is one that has proved a durable obstacle to a reform and revitalization of the organization. On numerous occasions since World War II, the United States has proposed the creation of a permanent and well-equipped OAS "police force" to deal with threats to regional security—thereby obviating the necessity for unilateral intervention by the United States. To date, that idea has attracted little support among the other members of the OAS, who have been willing to go no further than creating the kind of *ad hoc* OAS police force that ultimately assumed responsibility for preserving order in the Dominican Republic in 1965. (A substantial portion of even these forces, it should be noted, came from the United States.)*

Since its establishment perhaps, the OAS has been envisioned by officials in Washington as an instrument that could (and should) relieve the United States of the necessity for *unilateral* intervention in dealing with threats to regional peace and security. As our earlier discussion emphasized, an effective OAS provided an opportunity to "multilateralize" the Monroe Doctrine. (Critics of this approach would assert that this conception of

*A noteworthy example of reluctance by a majority of OAS members to assume greater responsibility for preserving peace and security within the hemisphere was provided in the period 1978–1979, when the Carter Administration tried to persuade the OAS to preserve order and stability during a period of political upheaval in Nicaragua. As in the past, most members of the organization opposed this idea; several of the military-dominated Latin American governments feared that it would constitute a precedent for later OAS intervention in their affairs. See "Organization of American States," *Political Handbook of the World: 1980* (New York: McGraw-Hill, 1980), pp. 576–577.

the OAS in turn rested upon a premise in Washington that the organization could routinely be counted upon to support the diplomatic goals of the United States.) In Latin American eyes, however, the OAS existed primarily for a different purpose: to protect the nations of the Caribbean and South America *against interventionism by the United States*. Interventionist moves by the United States since World War II—such as the Eisenhower Administration's anti-Communist policies toward Guatemala, the ill-fated "Bay of Pigs" intervention against Castro's Cuba in 1961, and efforts by officials in Washington to overthrow the Allende regime in Chile during the early 1970s—have done little to change this long-standing Latin American conception of the dominant purpose of the OAS.

A second formidable barrier confronting efforts to revitalize the Organization of American States is the phenomenon identified in the beginning of this chapter: *the growing diversity existing among the Latin American states themselves,* particularly in their ideologies and systems of government. At the risk of some oversimplification, we may say that in its peacekeeping operations, the OAS has been in a cross-fire between two groups having contrary ideological and political orientations: Marxist, quasi-Marxist, and other leftist-oriented governments versus the military juntas and other right-wing regimes and movements found throughout Latin America. These groups have become increasingly distrustful of one another; and each fears how a "reorganization" of the OAS, in the direction of making it a more effective regional body, might promote the fortunes of its political rivals. Would, for example, a new OAS police force be employed to promote right-wing causes in Latin America, to the detriment of left-wing revolutionary movements? Might *any* internal political upheaval within a Latin American country invite intervention by the

OAS, whose deliberations were controlled by the United States and Latin American governments sharing its diplomatic goals? Alternatively, would a reinvigorated OAS become an instrument enabling influential Latin American states, like Brazil or Argentina, to pursue their regional aspirations, at the expense of their weaker neighbors?

In the contemporary period, even more perhaps than in the past, the meetings of the OAS have produced few tangible results.* In-

---

*Many of the observations made here about the evolution and utility of the Organization of American States were illustrated by its behavior during the Falkland Islands crisis in 1982. On April 2, Argentine troops invaded the islands with the avowed objective of "liberating" them from British colonial administration (established in 1833). When Great Britain responded to what it—along with the United States and many other countries—called Argentinian "aggression," active warfare erupted in the south Atlantic. Despite intensive efforts by Buenos Aires to involve the OAS actively in the crisis—in an obvious expectation that Latin American sentiment would overwhelmingly favor its view—the contributions of the OAS were limited and relatively uninfluential. The United States, which ultimately sided with Great Britain in the quarrel, was unenthusiastic about referring the issue to the OAS. Instead, Washington preferred to rely upon the UN Security Council to resolve the crisis. Among the Latin American members of the OAS, sentiment was no less divided concerning its usefulness in dealing with the controversy. Argentina, for example, did *not* receive the unified support from the OAS that Buenos Aires anticipated. A highly significant tendency was the schism that developed within the OAS between the Caribbean states and the organization's other Latin American members. Reflecting their predominantly British and French (rather than Spanish) political traditions, the "Caribbean bloc" of 10 nations clearly resented the "clubbishness" displayed by Central and South American members, whose practice was to arrive at "understandings" that would later be adopted in formal OAS deliberations. Other Latin American nations hesitated to support Argentina overtly, fearing the consequences of doing so for their economic and commercial ties with the West. More extended treatment of recent tendencies within the OAS may be found in analyses by Barbara Crossette, *New York Times,* December 20, 1981, and April 16, 1982.

creasingly, one study has found, the member states of the OAS "reflect a growing diversity of political and economic interests." Uppermost in the Latin American mind has been "how to cope with the economic and security policies of the United States." As a result, the importance of the OAS has "declined" in recent years. Insofar as the OAS represented an attempt to forge an enduring sense of "community" among the American republics, by the 1980s that quest remained a highly elusive goal.[24]

Other Regional Unity Schemes

Besides the Organization of American States, other regional organizations have been created within the Western Hemisphere in the post-World War II period. In 1961, a *Latin American Free Trade Association* (LAFTA) was established, principally by several South American states, to remove trade barriers and restrictions among its members. LAFTA's ultimate goal—toward which little discernible progress has been made—was the creation of a Latin American common market (analogous to the European Common Market). Under the auspices of LAFTA, in 1969 an *Andean Group* (consisting of Bolivia, Colombia, Ecuador, Peru, and Venezuela, with Mexico cooperating with the group) was formed to achieve economic integration among its members and to lay the basis for the creation of a common market among them. The Andean Group has given high priority to formulating regulations governing the activities of foreign corporations within its area.

Early in June 1961, five Central American countries—Costa Rica, El Salvador, Guatemala, Nicaragua, and Honduras—joined in the creation of a *Central American Common Market* (CACM). CACM's goal was the establishment of a common market for Central

America within five years. As has been true of all regional experiments in Latin America (and elsewhere), CACM's fortunes have been directly affected by political developments and conflicts. Honduras, for example, withdrew from the organization in 1969, following a conflict with El Salvador. Then in 1978, Nicaragua imposed a 30 percent tariff on imports from the other members of CACM, in violation of the organization's provisions.

Still another regional organization—the *Latin American Economic System* (LAES) —was established in Panama late in 1975. Perhaps reflecting the experience of rival hemispheric organizations, the goals of LAES were more modest than those of competing integration schemes. They were primarily to create and promote Latin American multinational business enterprises, to protect price levels (chiefly for Latin America's main exports), to develop and expand external markets for exports, and to promote the exchange of technology and scientific information among its members. In time, 26 American republics joined LAES, making it the largest regional body concerned with economic integration and progress. Yet progress in achieving LAES's limited goals has been extremely slow. In matters of commercial and trade policy, many members of LAES confront the dilemma alluded to earlier in the chapter: the "identification" many Latin American countries today feel with the Third World, versus their historic and still important trade ties with the United States.[25]

While it is not a regional economic mechanism, brief reference must also be made to another recent effort to achieve unity among the American republics with regard to a single important issue. This was the creation in 1967, by the terms of the Treaty of Tlatelolco, of the Agency for the Prohibition of Nuclear Weapons (OPANAL). This organization was formed in response to the long-standing demand that Latin America be declared a "nuclear-free zone." To date, OPANAL's experience has not been untypical of other regional mechanisms: Its goals and activities have collided with the disparate foreign policy interests of its members. Cuba and Guyana, for example, have refused to sign the treaty; Argentina has not ratified it; and Brazil (which did sign and ratify the agreement) has refused to adhere to its terms. Several foreign countries (such as Canada, Britain, and West Germany) have engaged in keen competition to provide countries like Brazil and Argentina with nuclear technology and facilities that have a potential military application. As we shall see more fully at a later stage, Brazil has not disguised its intention of becoming a member of the nuclear club—a goal that causes deep anxieties among its weaker neighbors.[26]

Communism and Revolution in the Western Hemisphere

Latin American Communism in Perspective

During some periods since World War II, the Latin American political environment has witnessed revolutionary activities and agitation conducted by as many as *four* more or less distinct Communist and other revolutionary organizations within the region. Some Latin American Marxist organizations have been directly linked with, and supported by, the Soviet Union. On a much smaller and less influential scale, Marxist organizations in Latin America have also had ties with the People's Republic of China. (The conflict between these two branches of international Communism in some Latin American countries has often been intense and bitter.) Fidel Castro's victory in Cuba in 1959

spawned still another version of Marxism, known as Castroism; Castro contended that his species of Marxism was uniquely adapted to Latin American conditions (a claim we shall examine more fully at a later stage). Finally, in most Latin American societies there exist one or more forms of indigenous or native revolutionary movements. Variously described as "nationalist" or "populist" revolutionary movements, these political organizations advocate diverse programs entailing radical change; and they maintain a wide range of contacts with Cuba, the Soviet Union, and (as in the Sandinista movement in Nicaragua) the United States.* Not infrequently, these groups regard themselves as the true custodians of Latin America's revolutionary tradition, while leftist organizations identified with the Soviet Union are viewed as "conservative" and closely identified with the status quo. Political labels in Latin America are also sometimes deceptive and provide little guidance to an organization's program or ideological orientation. For example, for a number of years before 1970 in Chile, the Radical Party was a middle-of-the-road organization, occupying a centrist position between rightist and leftist political groups.

In attempting to understand both the revolutionary political tradition in Latin America and its opposite (right-wing and counterrevolutionary political movements), it must be borne in mind that violence has, according to one authority, become "institutionalized in the organization, maintenance, and changing of governments in Latin America." It tends to be present in nearly all

---

*Examples of these indigenous revolutionary movements within Latin America are the American Popular Revolutionary Alliance (APRA) in Peru; the National Revolutionary Party (MNR) in Bolivia; the Democratic Action movement (AD) in Venezuela; and the National Liberation Movement (PLN) in Costa Rica.

Latin American states, regardless of their particular histories, size, ethnic composition, or forms of government.*

For reasons identified in the beginning of the chapter, Latin America continues to offer a promising field for revolutionary ferment and political upheaval. Since our interest is not the Latin American political context per se—but the major implications of political developments in the region for the foreign policy of the United States—we shall focus upon a limited number of cases posing problems in United States-Latin American relations.

Soviet Goals in Latin America

From the earliest days of the Communist Revolution in Russia in 1917, the Kremlin has displayed an interest in Marxist gains in Latin America. The first Latin American Communist Party was established in Argentina in 1918; and in the months that followed, Communist organizations appeared in Mexico,

---

*See the essay by William S. Stokes, "Violence as a Power Factor in Latin American Politics," in Francisco José Moreno and Barbara Mitrani, eds., *Conflict and Violence in Latin American Politics: A Book of Readings* (New York: Thomas Y. Crowell, 1971), pp. 156–182. Stokes identifies several kinds of violent phenomena in Latin American political life; and he properly cautions against a pervasive tendency to equate all forms of violent political behavior in Latin America with "revolution." The author emphasizes that reliance upon violence has been a propensity of *both* left- and right-wing political movements in Latin America. He also challenges the assumption (held by American officials, for example, during and after the Kennedy Administration) that as economic conditions improved in many Latin American societies, reliance upon violence to achieve political goals would decline. For informative discussions of the problem of violence and revolutionary upheaval, focusing upon political turbulence in Central America, see Richard E. Feinberg, "Central America: No Easy Answers," *Foreign Affairs,* **59** (Summer, 1981), 1121–1147; and Richard Millett, "Central American Paralysis," *Foreign Policy,* **39** (Summer, 1980), 99–118.

Uruguay, Chile, Brazil, and other Latin American states. Yet for many years after 1917, Latin America was not high on the scale of Moscow's diplomatic priorities. The Communist leaders of the Soviet Union were preoccupied with revolutionary tasks at home, with defending the regime from anti-Communist forces, and with the rising Axis menace. Moreover, Soviet leaders in effect conceded that "American imperialism" precluded significant Communist influence in the Western Hemisphere.[27]

For the United States, World War II highlighted the strategic importance of Latin America. In the postwar period, Washington's apprehensions about Communist intrusions into Latin America stemmed in no small measure from recollection of the Axis threat to hemispheric security. During World War II, Nazi agents were active in a number of Latin American states, particularly Argentina. The United States was compelled to divert over 100,000 troops for protection of hemispheric security. In the postwar period, according to a high Defense Department spokesman, "In enemy hands the Latin American countries could provide bases for attack which would be dangerously close to the United States"—a fact that was brought home with the utmost gravity to citizens of the United States, when aerial photographs showed Soviet guided missiles being installed by Castro's regime in Cuba. These weapons were capable of bringing the great industrial northeastern heartland of the United States within their field of fire. Similarly, a potential aggressor would find that the "bulge" of Brazil afforded a tempting foothold for any enemy seeking to penetrate the Western Hemisphere across the South Atlantic, especially if the Middle East and northern and western portions of Africa were in hostile hands. Conversely, Brazil and its neighbors offer needed bases for air power and for radar defense units to safeguard the Americas and the South Atlantic sea lanes. Latin America also supplies the United States with a number of strategic imports. One of the most important now is thorium from Brazil, used for thermonuclear technology. Although the Panama Canal is no longer owned and operated by the United States, Washington of course remains deeply interested in its defense, its availability to American and allied shipping during time of war, and in protecting adjacent countries and waters, from which threats against the Panama Canal might be launched. The agreements by which the United States acknowledged Panamanian sovereignty over the canal explicitly recognized these realities.

Given the long-standing concern of the United States about hemispheric security—as expressed forcefully in the Monroe Doctrine—officials in Washington viewed Communist inroads throughout Latin America with genuine anxiety. It was noteworthy, for example, that the most ominous direct Soviet-American confrontation—entailing the possible risk of a nuclear exchange between the superpowers—occured *in Latin America* (during the Cuban Missile Crisis of 1962). For its part—after Moscow became a nuclear power, began to excel in space technology, and (by the late 1960s) embarked upon a campaign to gain military superiority in at least some categories of weapons—the Kremlin began to devote increasing attention to the Latin American political context. A recent study has defined Soviet diplomacy in the region by saying that:

> Moscow's present objectives in Latin America are easily defined: to strengthen Soviet influence wherever possible, to defend "Socialist" Cuba, and to weaken the still predominant position of the United States. To these ends, the Soviet Union has been prepared to cooperate with democrats, dictators, and ultraradical revolutionaries, even when they are militantly anti-Communist.

At the same time, Moscow does *not* "foresee an early victory for communism in any Latin American country." While it believes that prospects for Marxist gains throughout the region "are improving," it also recognizes that (in constrast with other regions) a number of serious impediments exist to achieving its objectives in Latin America. As a generalization, Latin America is a zone in which "mature capitalism" exists and where the "objective conditions" for a successful Marxist revolution are lacking. For this reason, "premature efforts" by the Kremlin to foment revolution in most Latin American countries would adversely affect Soviet diplomatic interests. Moscow recognizes the historic and strategic importance of Latin America to the United States; it believes that Washington will not (on the basis of experience) hesitate to intervene with military force to protect regional security; and it is aware that most Latin American countries have close political, economic, military, and other ties with the United States. For these reasons, the Soviet approach to Latin America remains highly pragmatic, opportunistic, and massively conditioned by the circumstances existing within particular Latin American countries.[28]

In order to provide more specific focus to our discussion of the Communist challenge in the Western Hemisphere, we shall briefly examine four case studies illustrating the phenomenon: the crisis in Guatemala in the mid-1950s; the communization of Cuba and its implications for American foreign policy; Washington's response to the Marxist-oriented Allende regime in Chile in the early 1970s; and the emergence of the Sandinista-led government of Nicaragua at the end of the decade.

Crisis in Guatemala

The first serious encounter between the United States and Latin American Communism occurred in Guatemala in 1954. Revolutionary ferment had long marked the political scene in Guatemala, as elsewhere in Latin America, in large part because non-Communist groups had been unable to effectuate lasting socioeconomic reforms. The Guatemalan Communist party was able to pose as the champion of nationalist aspirations while promising progress in solving bedrock economic problems.[29]

The year 1944 witnessed the beginning of a new revolutionary regime under Juan José Arévalo, who overthrew the government of the military dictator Jorge Ubico. The new government received substantial support from the lower middle classes and from the intellectuals, with many of the latter believing that a Marxist approach offered the best hope of progress for Guatemala. As is customary following revolutions in Latin America, a number of prominent and less prominent political exiles returned to Guatemala. Among these were influential individuals who espoused Communism; some of these had received revolutionary training in Moscow.

As time passed, Communists infiltrated the Guatemalan labor movement and other organizations commanding wide popular support. The equivocal policies of President Arévalo, who encouraged "participation of Communists as individuals" in the government and labor movement while "discouraging the formation of an open organized Stalinist party," enabled Communist groups to gain more and more control over Guatemalan affairs.[30] As the time for the national elections of 1951 drew near, the tempo of Communist agitation and propaganda greatly increased. Election of the Communist-sponsored candidate,

Colonel Jacobo Arbenz, as president was soon followed by the open establishment of the Guatemalan Communist party (*Partido Communista de Guatemala*, PCG). At home Arbenz, supported by the PCG, embarked upon a long overdue program of land reform. As the largest landholder in the country, the United Fruit Company—with headquarters in Boston—became the principal target of Arbenz's reform measures. Guatemalan nationalism was also directed against the alleged power of the *Empresa Eléctrica,* owned by investors within the United States, which generated four-fifths of the country's electric power.[31]

In external affairs, the Arbenz government was making little effort to conceal its growing hostility toward the United States. Guatemala provided a base for Communist-inspired intrigue throughout all the neighboring Central American states. In international affairs Guatemala's position coincided with the Kremlin's with remarkable frequency.[32] On June 30, 1954, Secretary of State Dulles publicly called attention to the "evil purpose of the Kremlin to destroy the inter-American system. . . ." He noted that "For several years international communism has been probing . . . for nesting places in the Americas. It finally chose Guatemala. . . ."[33] As early as April 7, 1951, the foreign ministers of the American republics, largely at the instigation of the United States, had issued the "Declaration of Washington," calling for "prompt action . . . against the aggressive activities of international communism. . . ."[34]

But as it watched the steady accretion in the influence of Guatemalan Communism, the Eisenhower Administration was persuaded that stronger measures were demanded. Hence Secretary of State Dulles personally attended an OAS meeting in Venezuela on March 28, 1954, where he was successful in getting the "Caracas Declaration" approved by an overwhelming vote. The Caracas Declaration—condemning Communist efforts to gain control of any American republic as a threat to regional security—was ostensibly a dramatic diplomatic victory for the United States. Discriminating observers, however, noted that—as in the past—most members of the Inter-American system remained more concerned about hegemonial moves by the "North American Colossus" than about the specter of Marxism within the region.[35]

Meanwhile, tension mounted within Guatemala—as a Communist-inspired strike in Honduras supported the Marxist cause within Guatemala, and as a shipload of arms arrived from behind the Iron Curtain. The United States successfully defeated efforts by the Soviet Union to have the United Nations consider the Guatemalan crisis (in Washington's view, the Organization of American States had prior jurisdiction in the matter). Then on June 18 an anti-Communist force under Colonel Castillo Armas crossed into Guatemala from Honduras. Within a short time the pro-Communist Arbenz government collapsed. "Each one of the American States has cause for profound gratitude," said Secretary of State Dulles. All Americans could rejoice that the citizens of that country "had the courage and the will to eliminate the traitorous tools of foreign despots."

By President Eisenhower's own admission, Washington had relied upon the Central Intelligence Agency and other means for overthrowing a Marxist-oriented regime in Guatemala.[36] Insofar as the Arbenz regime was promoting Soviet interests in the New World (and authorities on Latin America were divided on this question), the United States had successfully frustrated Moscow's first major postwar effort to gain a foothold in the Western Hemisphere.

Guatemala After 1954

What were the long-term effects of overt intervention by the United States to prevent a Communist victory in Guatemala? Did the overthrow of the Arbenz regime hinder the cause of Marxism—and did it make any real contribution to the emergence of democracy—throughout the inter-American system? Almost three decades after American intervention in the country, the prospects for political stability in Guatemala under a government that was at least making progress toward democracy were not encouraging.

With a per capita income of less than $1000 annually—and with poverty endemic among the country's Indian majority—after 1954 Guatemala moved through a succession of regimes and violent political crises. The decade of the 1970s, for example, witnessed two broad tendencies making Guatemala a center of political upheaval. One of these was the existence of continuing economic dislocations that generated mounting political discontents. The other was the pattern of ongoing political extremism, in which politically "moderate" groups found their position increasingly untenable. Left-wing dissident groups relied upon terrorism to achieve their goals; and this tendency was "answered" by repressive measures against the government's critics, carried out by the Guatemalan armed forces and by paramilitary private organizations. By the early 1980s, a condition of virtual anarchy prevailed within the country. The leaders of the ruling military junta were described by one observer as "isolated, beseiged and frightened."

In this context, late in March, 1982, Guatemala experienced still another change of government. Junior-level military officers, encouraged by civilian critics of the incumbent regime, carried out a successful coup.

Characteristically for Latin American political systems, the new regime, led by General Ríos Montt, pledged to bring an end to the prolonged violence that gripped the country, to eliminate pervasive corruption, to restore economic vitality, and to respect the rights of the Guatemalan people.

The Reagan Administration's reaction to these developments in Guatemala was equivocal. On the one hand, Washington solicited the cooperation of the Guatemalan government in countering Marxist-led subversion throughout Central America (particularly in El Salvador). On the other hand (and the sentiment was especially strong within Congress), the Guatemalan government's recent record in violating the civil rights of its own citizens—along with its failure to effect fundamental reforms within the society—did not encourage Washington to become closely identified with it.

Only the future would tell whether the change of government in Guatemala signified any basic alteration in the society's political, economic, and social environment. Unstable as the political system was, one prediction could be made with confidence: Unless and until far-reaching reforms were carried out in all spheres of national life, Guatemala would remain a source of ongoing political turbulence in Latin America.[37]

The Communization of Cuba

The gravest challenge to democracy by leftist political forces in the Western Hemisphere has come from the regime of Premier Fidel Castro in Cuba. Castro and his followers not only succeeded in imposing a Marxist order upon Cuban society; after doing so, they offered *Fidélismo* as the only "correct" revolutionary path for neighboring Latin American countries and actively sponsored insurrectionary activities in Central and South America.

From 1933 to 1944, the island of Cuba was the personal enclave of a *caudillo,* former army sergeant Fulgencio Batista. Like most Latin American dictators of his ilk, Batista depended heavily upon military support; under his administration, the Cuban army was pampered with pay increases, lucrative appointments, and access to graft. After a short-lived retirement, Batista again seized power in 1952. Thereafter, internal opposition to his regime steadily mounted—symbolized in time by one man, Fidel Castro. Relying initially upon rural support in the eastern area of the island, Castro's rebellion slowly gained ground. As Castro's forces advanced on Havana, on January 1, 1959, Batista fled into exile. Within a few days, the Eisenhower Administration had extended diplomatic recognition to the new Cuban government, led by President Manuel Urrutia. Initially, Cuban-American relations seemed cordial and promising of greater collaboration in the future.[38]

Within a few weeks, relations between Havana and Washington, however, began to go sour—with each side accusing the other of bad faith and of interventionism in its political affairs. The Castro regime's repressive policies against its political opponents and suspected anti-Castro elements evoked a highly negative public and official reaction in the United States. As the months passed, Castro's determination to sponsor revolutionary activities in other Latin American societies alarmed Washington, as well as several Latin American governments. From his perspective, Fidel Castro became convinced that Washington's professed goodwill toward his revolutionary regime was false and that officials in the United States were in fact endeavoring to overthrow or "ostracize" his new government. In Moscow, Soviet Premier Nikita Khrushchev lauded the emergence of a Marxist system in the Caribbean and informed the world that the Kremlin was "raising its voice and extending a helpful hand to the people of Cuba." The close ties that were developing between the U.S.S.R. and Communist Cuba added to anxieties in Washington about the country's political development. Late in 1960, the first shipment of Soviet arms arrived in Cuba; and a few weeks later, Castro openly proclaimed that "I am a Marxist-Leninist and will be a Marxist-Leninist until the last day of my life."

In this atmosphere of growing Cuban-American estrangement, there followed one of the strangest and most ill-fated episodes in the annals of American diplomacy: the "Bay of Pigs" invasion of Cuba in the spring of 1961. Initially planned by the Eisenhower Administration, this undertaking entailed training and supplying anti-Castro Cuban groups (mainly in Florida), who planned to invade Cuba and topple Castro's Communist regime. After some initial hesitation, President Kennedy decided to proceed with the plan—which was put into execution on April 17. Landing at the "Bay of Pigs"—and denied American air and naval support—the invasion force was largely wiped out or captured by Castro's superior forces. For the new Kennedy Administration, the experience was a dramatic diplomatic fiasco. For Castro's Cuba, the abortive "Bay of Pigs" invasion provided irrefutable proof of Washington's hostility toward his government. For the Soviet Union, the episode may well have emboldened the Kremlin to take the steps leading to the most ominous Soviet-American encounter since World War II: the Cuban Missile Crisis of 1962.[39]

The Cuban Missile Crisis

Throughout the months that followed, relations between Cuba and the United States steadily deteriorated, while Moscow and Havana drew closer together. The Soviet Union —it was evident to officials in Washington —was determined to make Castro's Cuba a "model" of Communist development for Latin America; Washington also believed that Moscow's hand could be discerned in Cuban-sponsored revolutionary agitation throughout the Caribbean area.

Then on October 22, 1962, came the long-deferred showdown: In a dramatic coast-to-coast television speech, President John F. Kennedy announced that Soviet offensive missiles had been installed in Cuba (despite promises made by Soviet officials that they had no such intention). Kennedy outlined the steps he proposed to take for dealing with this flagrant and dangerous Soviet threat to hemispheric security. Kennedy bluntly warned Soviet Premier Khrushchev that the United States would retaliate against the Soviet Union itself, if any Soviet missiles were launched from Cuba. Although he did not directly refer to the Monroe Doctrine, Kennedy left no doubt that Moscow's action threatened one of the most basic principles of American foreign policy; and he emphasized that, while the United States did not seek a military encounter with the Soviet Union, "neither will we shrink from that risk at any time it must be faced." In brief, Kennedy directed Moscow to remove its offensive missile installations from Cuba or face the consequences! The Organization of American States subsequently supported Washington's firm stand against this Soviet military intrusion into the Western Hemisphere.

In this tension-ridden context, events moved rapidly. Several messages were exchanged between Washington and Moscow in an effort to resolve the crisis peacefully. Meanwhile, Soviet ships carrying new missiles and ancillary equipment were bound for

Cuba; on President Kennedy's orders, American naval units waited to intercept them. The first break in the crisis came when these Havana-bound Soviet ships finally altered course with their lethal cargoes. After that, the tension dissipated rapidly. The United States and the Soviet Union (although not Cuba) indicated their willingness to have UN Secretary General U Thant mediate the conflict. Moscow pledged to remove its offensive missiles from Cuba and to refrain from replacing them; and, after the removal of the missiles had been verified, the United States lifted its naval blockade of the island; implicitly, the United States also agreed to engage in no new effort aimed at overthrowing the Castro regime. By the end of the year, the Cuban Missile Crisis had largely been resolved.

The Kennedy Administration's handling of the Cuban Missile Crisis must surely be ranked as one of the most outstanding diplomatic victories by the United States in the postwar period. Soviet machinations in the Western Hemisphere suffered a dramatic setback. Moscow's policy reversal during this crisis played some part in two crucial developments: the subsequent removal of Soviet Premier Khrushchev from office; and the widening rift between the Soviet Union and Communist China (with authorities in Peking highly critical of what was called Russian "capitulationism"). The episode also stands as a case study in *unified and effective foreign policy formulation and execution within the executive branch*—a quality that has often been lacking in the American foreign policy process since 1962. Above all perhaps, the Cuban Missile Crisis marked a watershed in recent American diplomacy for another reason: The outcome reflected awareness—even in the Kremlin—of *the military superiority of the United States*. As the years passed, policy makers in Washington could no longer count upon that reality to assure a successful diplo-

matic result in disputes with the Soviet Union.[40]

Cuban-American Relations After 1962

The peaceful resolution of the missile crisis did not result in the elimination of tensions between the United States and Castro's Cuba. To the contrary, in the years that followed, suspicion and ill-will between the two countries intensified. The United States endeavored—with minimum success—to gain compliance by its European allies and its Latin American neighbors with its economic boycott of Cuba and its attempt to ostracize the country from the inter-American system. Partly as a result of the boycott instigated by the United States—but even more because of the failure of its own internal economic policies—Cuba was forced to lean more and more heavily upon the Soviet Union. As internal economic conditions steadily deteriorated—leading by the early 1980s to a floodtide of disaffected Cuban refugees to the United States—Russian assistance to Cuba posed an enormous and continuing drain upon Soviet resources.* A State Department official, for

*The insight of a well-informed student of Latin American affairs regarding Castro's regime in Cuba is enlightening. Ever since the early 1960s, successive Presidents in the United States have opposed the existence of "another Cuba" in the Western Hemisphere. According to Needler, this is also a goal which Moscow might be prone to support as well! The Kremlin has "never completely accepted the Castro government in Cuba as authentically Communist in their sense"; and in time, Moscow became "quite unhappy" about its close identification with Castro's regime. Havana's "economic bungling" has required huge and continuing Soviet subsidies to keep Cuba from economic collapse; and "Castroite heresies have introduced another element of discord into a Communist camp already split several ways." Soviet defense of Cuba has led to several confrontations with the United States that were perhaps not always desired by Russian officials. Overall, "it is an open question...whether the Soviet Union could afford another Cuba, either economically or

example, said that by 1979 direct and indirect Soviet aid to Cuba totaled some $3 billion annually—a sum in excess of *all* the economic assistance provided by the the United States to its Latin American neighbors.[41]

More than any other factor, however, Castro's active diplomacy evoked misgivings in the United States. Three aspects of Cuban diplomacy aroused deep American concern.[42] One was Castro's evident determination to make the benefits of his new order available to neighboring societies, by sponsoring revolutionary activities elsewhere in Latin America. In overall terms, the effort failed (two conspicuous cases of Castro's failure to build a solid revolutionary base were Bolivia and Jamaica; voters in the latter rejected Marxism in 1980). Havana, however, provided varying degrees of support to revolutionary activities in several other Latin American states. Washington believed, for example, that Castro's agents were active for many years in the Dominican Republic, Chile, Peru, and other Latin American settings.

Officials in the United States (including members of Congress) also became genuinely concerned about evidence of ever-closer military ties between Havana and Moscow. Successive American administrations have expressed anxiety about the acquisition and expansion of Soviet military facilities on the island of Cuba. For its part, ever since the Bay of Pigs invasion and the Cuban Missile Crisis of 1962, Castro's government was concerned about the possibility of another attempt by the United States to overthrow it. For Cubans,

the continued American military presence at Guantanamo Bay provided tangible evidence of American "imperialism" and hegemony.

In August 1970, American intelligence sources gathered evidence that the Cuban port of Cienfuegos was being modernized and expanded for possible use by Soviet submarines in the Gulf of Mexico and adjacent waters. As officials of the Nixon Administration assessed the matter, this development violated the spirit (if not the letter) of the agreement reached with the Soviet Union in 1962, prohibiting the installation of Russian offensive weapons in Cuba; and it represented a new threat to the Monroe Doctrine by an increasingly powerful and still expansive Soviet state. President Richard M. Nixon and his advisers were especially alarmed that the modernized base at Cienfuegos would provide facilities for Soviet nuclear submarines operating in the Western Hemisphere. Nixon's chief foreign policy adviser, Henry Kissinger, was convinced that Moscow was seeking to "test" American resolve and intentions by this new military buildup in Cuba. Moscow of course denied that it had any hostile intentions toward the United States or other American republics by availing itself of this naval base on Cuba's southern coast.

Following prolonged study of the problem by President Nixon's advisers, American officials decided to adopt a "wait and see" attitude toward Soviet use of the base at Cienfuegos. The Nixon Administration informed Soviet officials that it viewed the establishment of a Soviet submarine base in the Western Hemisphere with the "utmost gravity"; and it reiterated President Kennedy's earlier warning against Soviet military incursions in Latin America. Throughout the weeks that followed, Washington accepted Soviet assurances that Moscow would continue to honor the agreements made in 1962 and that its use of base facilities at Cienfuegos posed no offen-

politically." See Needler, *The United States and the Latin American Revolution*, p. 34. Although it is almost never cited by American officials, the fact that Cuba poses a continuing "drain" upon the Soviet Union may well be a major reason why the United States has been reluctant to resume normal relations with Cuba, even after it had recognized such former Communist adversaries as the People's Republic of China.

sive threat to hemispheric security. Thereafter, units of the Soviet navy utilized this Cuban base, while the United States continued to monitor Russian naval activity in the Caribbean area.[43]

By late summer of 1979, developments in Cuba once again came to the forefront of concern by the American people and their leaders. In mid-August, American intelligence agencies revealed the presence in Cuba of what officials in Washington initially called a Soviet "combat brigade" (estimated to number approximately 3000 troops); an additional 10,000 Russian advisers were also believed to be stationed in Cuba. Coming at a time when the Senate was debating the SALT II arms-limitation agreement recently negotiated between the United States and the Soviet Union, this revelation had a momentous impact upon public and official opinion in the United States—particularly on Capitol Hill. Once again, it appeared that Moscow was violating earlier Soviet-American understandings on Cuba and that it was "testing" American diplomatic and military credibility. Confronted with evidence of unmistakable public and congressional anxiety about this development, President Jimmy Carter declared the presence of Soviet combat forces in Cuba "unacceptable" to the United States.[44]

Yet circumstances had changed fundamentally since the Cuban Missile Crisis of 1962. Now it was the Soviet Union that possessed military parity with, and in some categories of weapons *superiority over,* the United States. Now Soviet officials showed no inclination to withdraw Russian troops from Cuba in response to Washington's ultimatum. Moscow's intransigence rapidly cooled enthusiasm in the Senate for the SALT II accords, which were subsequently withdrawn by the White House. The dominant reality facing the United States in approaching this issue was that policy makers lacked acceptable and ef-

fective means for *compelling* Moscow's military withdrawal from Cuba. Even if the Carter Administration believed it possessed the requisite power, it was highly questionable whether—in the post-Vietnam War era—Congress or the American people would have supported its use for that purpose. As a result, the Administration was ultimately forced to accept a situation it had originally described as "unacceptable"—and this fact reinforced prevailing complaints about President Carter's diplomatic "indecisiveness."

For some two decades after the missile crisis, Cuban-American relations remained tense and unproductive. Premier Castro and his advisers were convinced that successive administrations in Washington were actively promoting the overthrow of their Communist regime—or, at a minimum, seeking its economic collapse. By the early 1980s, the Reagan Administration was no less certain that Castro's Cuba—whose policies had brought the country to the verge of economic disaster—was spearheading revolution and subversion throughout Latin America. In addition, Havana showed no inclination to withdraw its large military contingent from black Africa.

Despite these realities, by the early 1980s some evidence existed of a possible "thaw" in Cuban-American relations. With economic conditions in Cuba worsening—and with doubt existing in Havana about the future of Moscow's continued assistance to the country—Castro's government indicated an interest in resolving outstanding differences with the United States. In the American view, however, two major impediments blocked this process. One of these was Cuba's still close ties with the Soviet Union, permitting Moscow to maintain a large military presence in the Caribbean area. The other was Castro's sponsorship of revolutionary causes throughout the Western Hemisphere. As officials of the Reagan Administration viewed it, significant changes were required in Cuban conduct before any improvement could be expected in Cuban-American relations.[45]

The Allende Regime in Chile

On September 4, 1970, a momentous event occurred in Chile—long regarded by officials in the United States as a democratically governed "alternative" to Marxist and other revolutionary systems in Latin America. Following a three-way national election (in which no candidate received a majority of the votes), Dr. Salvador Allende Gossens became Chile's new President.[46] Allende was the candidate of a coalition of Marxist, other leftist, and centrist groups whose program was the achievement of socialism by reliance upon democratic methods.* The Allende regime lasted almost exactly three years (Allende died on September 11, 1973, while attempting to resist a successful military-led coup against his government).

From Santiago, the American ambassador to Chile, Edward Korry, reported to the State Department:

*In the presidential election, Salvador Allende received 36.2 percent of the vote; his right-wing opponent received 34.9 percent; and the centrist Christian Democratic nominee received 27.8 percent. The popular vote for Allende was smaller than it had been in 1964. In Allende's coalition government, Marxist parties for the first time controlled the executive branch. The government proceeded to carry out its announced socialist program, such as the nationalization of the copper industry and land reform; some leftist organizations in Chile moved even more rapidly than the Allende government to expropriate lands and take other steps to reach the proclaimed goal. See J. Samuel Valenzuela and Arthuro Valenzuela, "Chile and the Breakdown of Democracy," in Howard J. Wiarda and Harvey F. Kline, eds., *Latin American Politics and Development* (Boston: Houghton Mifflin Co., 1979), p. 251.

Chile voted calmly to have a Marxist-Leninist state, the first nation in the world to make this choice knowingly. . . . It is a sad fact that Chile has taken the path of communism with only a little more than a third of the nation approving this choice. . . . *It will have the most profound effect on Latin America and beyond; we have suffered a grievous defeat. . . .*

Apprehensions in Washington about the implications of Allende's electoral victory were reinforced after he proceeded to carry out sweeping socialistic and collectivist measures. Chile, Allende said after his first year in office, had "achieved more than Cuba" during the first year of Castro's revolution![47]

Contrary to the prevailing view in Washington, most informed students of Latin American political systems did not regard Dr. Allende as a Marxist revolutionary; he was a longtime socialist, who believed in using parliamentary means for achieving his goals. At the same time, it was also true that his coalition contained Marxist elements, some of whom did not agree with his reliance upon democratic processes; nor was Allende always successful in controlling extreme left-wing groups supporting his presidency. The Allende regime, therefore, seemed a marked contrast to the kind of moderate and pro-American government, led by President Eduardo Frei, that had governed Chile from 1964 to 1970. Under Frei and earlier leaders, Chile had acquired a reputation for political stability and a commitment to democracy that was unique in Latin America.

The Nixon Administration did not confine its disapproval of events in Chile merely to verbal opposition. Evidence uncovered in subsequent congressional investigations, and by private news sources, indicates convincingly that both the United States government and private American business corporations intervened directly in Chile's political affairs during the early 1970s. The objective of such intervention was twofold: to prevent Dr. Allende and his supporters from gaining control of the government of Chile; and, after that purpose failed, to encourage opposition to his regime, in the expectation that it would soon be ousted. Facing mounting disaffection at home because of its economic policies—and the overt hostility of the United States—the Allende administration came to an end late in 1973, when a military junta seized control of the government. That the United States was implicated in the political demise and death of Dr. Allende seems undeniable. At the same time, in view of mounting internal opposition to his regime and the overall failure of Allende's economic policies, the precise *impact* of interventionism by the United States in producing Allende's downfall remains controversial.[48]

As an important episode in recent American diplomacy toward Latin America, the Allende episode has a number of regional and global consequences. Its most lasting effect perhaps was to renew the old controversy about whether the United States had really abandoned "interventionism" in dealing with the other American republics. Critics of the Nixon Administration's diplomacy also asked whether officials in Washington understood the difference between Soviet-style Communism and other varieties of left-wing ideologies and movements found in Latin America. (By the early 1970s, American officials *were* differentiating among Soviet, Chinese, Yugoslav, Polish, and other varieties of Marxism in terms of how they affected the foreign policy interests of the United States. President Nixon, for example, brought about the "opening" with Communist China that finally led to reasonably cooperative Sino-American relations, as discussed more fully in Chapter 15.) It could be contended of course—and this

idea seemed implicit in Washington's attitude toward the Allende government—that Communist or Communist-oriented regimes *in the Western Hemisphere* pose a unique threat to American security and diplomatic interests. Not unexpectedly, the Latin American reaction to Washington's complicity in the overthrow of Allende's government was highly negative. Critics noted (as in the years that followed within Chile) that the United States was much more reluctant to intervene openly against right-wing, military-dominated governments throughout Latin America.

After the demise of the Allende regime, political developments within Chile took a totally different course; and new issues arose in Chilean-American relations. Led by General Augusto Pinochet Ugarte, the military junta that ruled Chile suspended the constitution, and it moved rapidly to establish its authority and to "restore order" to a highly unstable political environment. In the process—after the mysterious "disappearance" of some of its more outspoken political opponents, and after other repressive measures were employed against its critics—the Pinochet government acquired a notorious reputation for violating human rights. In time, the Carter Administration publicly denounced its behavior and cut off military and economic aid to it.

By late 1980, the junta governing Chile felt secure enough to ask for popular approval of its rule in a plebiscite—which it won by a margin of two to one over its opponents. (As always in Latin America, critics charged that the regime had "rigged" the plebiscite to yield a predetermined result.) Backed by the armed forces and right-wing elements within the society, Pinochet's regime sought to solve Chile's chronic economic problems, by taking such steps as reinstating a free enterprise system and denationalizing government-owned industries. The evidence to date permits no clearcut verdict on the outcome of its efforts.

In some sectors, the Chilean economy had clearly improved under Pinochet's administration. In other areas—and from the perspective of correcting longterm economic and social disabilities—results were clearly less favorable. In Chile, as in many other societies governed by military elites, in time the junta was likely to discover that military rule *per se* offered no instantaneous solutions for deep-seated problems. Indeed, in some respects military rulers might have *less* expertise in dealing with such problems than their civilian counterparts. As the months passed, it became clear that a fundamental precondition for political stability and economic progress in Chile—a foundation of *legitimacy* conferred by widespread popular support for continued military rule—remained an elusive goal. At the same time—after the profoundly traumatic Allende era—no viable alternative to right-wing rule appeared to be available or offered any better prospect for winning popular support.*

---

*The case of the Pinochet regime in Chile provides a reminder of the different political standards often employed in the northern and southern regions of the Western Hemisphere. To many critics in the United States, the military junta in Chile epitomized an authorization government whose leaders violated human rights with impunity By that standard, Washington's attempts to maintain cooperative relations with it did little more than tarnish the image of the United States throughout Latin America and the world. Yet Chileans often took a different view of the ruling junta and its policies. As one Chilean observer said: "Among the bad [political systems] one has to choose the less bad." While many Chileans admitted that the junta was authoritarian, they also pointed out that (in contrast to comparable regimes elsewhere) it was "efficient and honest"; and as time passed, it appeared to be losing some of its harsher features that evoked widespread foreign criticism. See the analyses of the Pinochet regime by Edward Schumacher in the *New York Times,* September 11, 13, and 18, 1980. A fuller and more recent evaluation is Arturo Valenzuela, "Eight Years of Military Rule in Chile," *Current History,* **81** (February, 1982), 64–69, 88.

The Sandinista Victory in Nicaragua

One of the Latin American countries that was "occupied" (from 1927-1933) by the United States Marines during the era of the Roosevelt Corollary to the Monroe Doctrine was Nicaragua. During that period, Washington's hegemony was opposed by guerrilla forces that in time gave rise to the *Sandinista National Liberation Front* (FSLN), named for its leader, Augusto Cesar Sandino. By the end of the 1970s, the government of Nicaragua was in the hands of the Marxist-oriented Sandinista movement.

The Sandinista victory brought an end to the long rule in Nicaragua by the Somoza dynasty, founded by Anastasio Somoza Garcia, who came to power early in 1937; perpetuated by his relatives, the Somoza regime was finally overthrown by a Sandinista-led revolutionary movement on July 19, 1979.[49] During its tenure in office, the Somoza family had maintained close links with the United States. Officials in Washington viewed it as a bulwark against Communist inroads in the country; and American military and economic aid to the Somozan government was (by Latin American standards) generous. Members of the Somoza family and their supporters enriched themselves and established dominant positions in the economic system. Opponents of Somoza rule (led by Marxists and other rebel organizations) were usually unsuccessful against superior government forces. One problem hampering political opposition movements in Nicaragua (as in several other Latin American countries) was that anti-Somoza forces *were highly factionalized and disunified*. The Sandinista movement, for example, consisted of three separate organizations, having diverse goals and programs.† Even after

---

†The three political factions comprising the Sandinista movement were: the *Proletarian Tendency* (which called

they had ousted the Somoza regime, the Sandinista movement continued to experience internal factionalism and rivalry among its components.

One specialist on Latin American affairs
has said that the Sandinista victory in Nicaragua was an event of "seismic importance"—not only for this small Central American country but for Latin America as a whole.
Its long-range significance was that:

> For the first time since Fidel Castro's victory
> in Cuba in 1959, a small guerrilla force,
> backed by a populace, had vanquished an en-
> tire military establishment—in this case, the
> most heavily United States-trained army in
> Latin America.[50]

Confronted with the inevitable overthrow of the Somoza dynasty in Nicaragua,
the Carter Administration initially attempted
to produce a new, moderate, and non-Communist political regime in the country. Washington's efforts to enlist the Organization of
American States in this cause failed. Then
after the Sandinista victory could no longer be
ignored, within a few weeks official American
attitudes changed; Washington made a concerted effort to establish cordial relations with
the new regime. Officials in Nicaragua were
aware that they needed large-scale American
assistance in rebuilding a country that had
been recently devastated by earthquakes and
political upheaval; and the regime perhaps
wished to prove its independence from Mos-

cow and Havana. The State Department
noted in 1982, for example, that since the
Sandinista government assumed power, Nicaragua had received some $125 million in
aid from the United States, plus "several
hundred million from other Western
donors."[51]

Yet even before the Carter Administration left office, relations between the United
States and Nicaragua had begun to deteriorate. Under the Reagan Administration, they
reached a level of ill will and animosity seldom witnessed in Latin America since the era
of "Big Stick" diplomacy around 1900. To
the Sandinista-dominated Directorate that
governed Nicaragua, the diplomacy of the
Reagan Administration followed the classical
pattern of Yankee "interventionism" in Latin
American affairs. Officials in Managua were
certain that the Reagan White House intended to overthrow the Sandinista regime,
by undertaking overt military intervention
against it if other means failed. (This was the
principal justification by Sandinista officials
for Nicaragua's large-scale military buildup
under their leadership.)

From Washington's perspective, the political development of Nicaragua under the
Sandinista movement followed a familiar pattern of events in Communist-controlled societies. Depicting itself as a "democratic" political force, once in power the Sandinista movement had postponed promised national elections until 1985; it had effectively and ruth-
lessly eliminated domestic political opposition to its rule; it was creating a formidable
military establishment, whose existence
caused anxieties in neighboring states; and
under Sandinista management, the Nicaraguan economy was on the verge of collapse, with new shortages and problems appearing almost daily. For Republican policy
makers in Washington, however, the most
serious indictment of the Sandinista regime
was its massive and acknowledged support

for guerrilla warfare); the *Prolonged Popular War Group*
(which favored lengthy revolutionary struggle in the rural
areas); and the *Third World Tendency* (advocating simultaneous multiclass, rural, and urban revolutionary activities). The Third World Tendency in time became the dominant force within the Sandinista organization. The Sandinista-led rebels also made a successful effort to appeal
to moderate and conservative elements within the Nicaraguan society. See the discussion in Thomas W.
Walker, "The Sandinist Victory in Nicaragua," *Current
History,* **78** (February, 1980), 59–60.

for revolutionary causes in other Central American societies (notably El Salvador). Having conspicuously failed to solve Nicaragua's internal problems, the Sandinistas were apparently determined to export their Communist model to other Latin American societies! Even worse, as the Reagan Administration assessed the matter, under Sandinista leadership Nicaragua had become a conduit for expanded Soviet and Cuban influence throughout the region.

For a zone as politically turbulent as Central America, predictions were more than ordinarily hazardous. It was not unreasonable to think, however, that the future course of relations between the United States and Nicaragua would be crucially affected by several key factors. One of these was the passage of time. For an extended period, the leaders of the Sandinista movement would likely remain in an "ideological" frame of mind, causing them to be intensely suspicious of the United States and unwilling to "compromise" their political principles. In time—particularly as the internal problems of Nicaragua became more acute—they might well become more "pragmatic" in their domestic and foreign policies. In this latter stage, they might recall Premier Castro's earlier advice to the Sandinista leadership, which was not to repeat Cuba's mistake by totally alienating the United States! As they had done in time with the Soviet Union and with Communist China, policy makers in Washington could also be expected to moderate somewhat their opposition to the Sandinista-led government of Nicaragua. By the early 1980s, Washington was under considerable pressure from other governments (like Mexico, France, and West Germany) to do so. Two other developments—the future of Cuban-American relations, and events in neighboring countries like Guatemala and El Salvador—were also likely to influence relations between Washington and Managua. After the national elections in

1982 in El Salvador, for example (a subject we shall examine more fully at a later stage), officials in the United States could justifiably conclude that the prospects for successful Sandinista-sponsored revolution in other Latin American societies were considerably less favorable than they had once believed. This realization—along with a desire to improve its image with other Latin American states—might induce officials in Washington to find a basis for coexistence with the government of Nicaragua.

Our examination of Communist and other revolutionary movements in postwar Latin America enables to make a few brief concluding observations about the phenomenon and America's response to it. The evidence presented indicates that Latin America has had—and will likely continue to have—what can be called a considerable "revolutionary potential." More today perhaps than in the past, Communist and other left-wing political movements find Latin America a promising field for their activities; and the idea of radical social, economic, and political change remains attractive for groups and masses throughout the Western Hemisphere.

At the same time, Latin American revolutionary organizations have become increasingly fragmented and disunified—a fact that has often detracted seriously from their popular appeal and effectiveness. Several competing revolutionary models—ranging from the experiences of the Soviet Union, Communist China, Castro's Cuba, and other foreign countries, along with revolutionary programs sponsored by indigenous movements—are available to Latin American societies.

It is also noteworthy that, following the successful communization of Cuba in 1959, the Soviet Union has gained no new satellites in Latin America. Despite fears in Washington, Castroism has *not* engulfed the region or become the dominant revolutionary model for other Latin American societies. In fact, several aspects of Castro's regime—its poor record of economic performance and unpromising prospects; its massive and continued dependence upon Moscow; and its large-scale military intervention in Africa and (more recently) Afghanistan—have frequently elicited a negative reaction throughout Latin America. Insofar as Cuba was expected to serve as a "showcase" for Soviet-style Communism, on balance the Kremlin may well have *lost* more influence from the experiment than it has gained.

The evidence provided here also supports the conclusion that the United States has thus far achieved only very limited success in preventing Communist inroads in the Western Hemisphere or in containing the process of revolutionary change. Interventionist and coercive measures—such as those utilized in the cases of Guatemala, Cuba, and Chile—have not stopped the revolutionary tide in many Latin American societies or lessened the appeal of Communism and other left-wing causes throughout the region. Indeed, as a number of critics of recent American diplomacy have contended, in the long run interventionist behavior by the United States may well *enhance* the appeal of organizations advocating revolutionary change within Latin America. Under these circumstances, such groups emerge as the defenders of Latin American sovereignty against hegemonial behavior by the "North American Colossus"!

Alternatively, for a brief period under the Carter Administration, officials in Washington adopted a different approach in dealing with the Sandinista regime in Nicaragua. In effect, the United States endeavored to use its power to convert Nicaragua into a kind of Latin American Yugoslavia (a country with which Washington has had reasonably cordial relations for many years): an independent Marxist-oriented state that was not directly linked with the Soviet Union. As we have

seen, this experiment was largely abandoned after the Reagan Administration took office in 1981. Elected upon a pledge to "make America great again," President Reagan and his advisers were convinced that the Soviet Union had embarked upon a global diplomatic offensive against the United States, in Latin American and other regions. In their view, Marxist-oriented regimes like the Sandinista government of Nicaragua were consciously or deliberately promoting the interests of the Soviet Union and Cuba in the Western Hemisphere. Apparent Sandinista involvement in revolutionary upheaval in neighboring countries clearly aroused anxieties in Washington about the regime's ultimate goals.

While prospects for cooperative relations between the United States and the Sandinista-controlled government of Nicaragua did not appear overly favorable, it was not inconceivable that in time the two countries would arrive at a *modus vivendi,* dictated by two paramount considerations. From the perspective of the United States, a Marxist regime in Nicaragua *largely controlled by indigenous radical elements* might be the least unpalatable alternative confronting American policy makers in Nicaragua and certain other Latin American societies. From the Nicaraguan viewpoint, if the Sandinista regime desires needed external assistance in achieving its goals, more collaborative relations with the United States may well be seen by its leaders as essential for domestic progress and political stability.

The Problem of Military Elites in Latin America

Military Dictatorships and American Foreign Policy

In May 1911, the long-awaited revolution in Mexico erupted against the 30-year rule of the dictator Porfirio Diaz. Advocates of democracy inside and outside Mexico had high hopes that the end of authoritarian government in the country (popularly called "Diazpotism") would usher in a new era of expanding political freedom and needed reforms. After a brief interval, however, the new leader (Francisco Madero, a known advocate of democracy) was deposed, and later executed, by General Victoriano Huerta. Huerta imposed an even more despotic regime upon Mexican society; and his seizure of power opened one of the most frustrating and tragic chapters in the history of inter-American relations.

For that passionate and tireless champion of universal democracy—President Woodrow Wilson—the subversion of Mexico's democratic experiment was a traumatic event. After the Huerta regime seized power, Mexican-American relations steadily deteriorated. His goal for Mexico, Wilson asserted, was "an orderly and righteous government"; his sympathies were with the "submerged eighty-five percent of the [Mexican] people who are now struggling toward liberty." Characterizing the new regime as "a government of butchers," led by the "unspeakable Huerta," Wilson refused to extend diplomatic recognition to it. "I am going to teach the South American republics to elect good men," Wilson pledged! In April 1914, Wilson's animosity toward the Huerta dictatorship induced him even to employ armed force against it, when United States naval forces shelled the Mexican city of Vera Cruz. Open war between the United States and Mexico was averted only because of the mediatory efforts of the ABC powers (Argentina, Brazil, and Chile). With opinion in Mexico and throughout Latin America as a whole highly adverse to Wilson's diplomacy, this episode in Mexican-American relations left a lasting residue of ill-will and resentment toward the United States south of the border.[52] Paradoxically, in time Mexico evolved into one of the most stable and, by many criteria, democratic states within the Inter-American system. As its vast oil resources were being rapidly developed, Mexico was emerging as one of the most influential nations in Latin America.*

As they have confronted other right-wing dictatorships in Latin America, chief executives who followed Woodrow Wilson also periodically sought to teach the Latin Americans to "elect good men" or democratic governments—usually with as few positive results as accompanied Wilson's diplomacy. A half century or more after the Wilson Administration, it was remarkable how little the scenario had changed. Despite Washington's concern about Communist or other revolutionary gains throughout Latin America, by the 1980s the dominant pattern throughout the Caribbean, Central America, and South America was *right-wing authoritarian governments,* usually headed directly (or controlled indirectly) by the armed forces. In many cases, Latin American military elites had been trained in, and their equipment supplied by,

*Since some selectivity is required in our discussion of American foreign policy toward Latin America, contemporary Mexican-American relations receive minimum attention here. More detailed discussion of political developments in Mexico may be found in Evelyn P. Stevens, "Mexico's One-Party State: Revolutionary Myth and Authoritarian Reality," in Wiarda and Kline, eds., *Latin American Politics and Development*, pp. 399–435. For a collection of essays dealing with a broad range of issues in Mexican-American relations, see Stanley R. Ross, ed., *Views Across the Border: The United States and Mexico* (Albuqerque: University of New Mexico Press, 1978). Another study of Mexico's social, economic, and political problems is Judith A. Hellman, *Mexico in Crisis* (New York: Holmes and Meier, 1978). Recent analyses of the principal issues in American diplomacy toward Mexico may be found in Susan K. Purcell, "Mexico-U.S. Relations: Big Initiatives Can Cause Big Problems," *Foreign Affairs,* **60** (Winter, 1981–82), 379–393; and Victor L. Urquidi, "Not by Oil Alone: the Outlook for Mexico," *Current History,* **81** (February, 1982), 78–81, 90.

the United States. In mid-1980, one report found that—two decades after the Kennedy Administration had tried to lay the foundations for durable democracy under the Alliance for Progress—military elites "still dominate [governments controlling] more than half the nations" in South America. Its conclusion was that

> Massive U.S. aid had done little to nudge the region toward democratic reforms. Instead, countries into which Washington has poured billions of dollars are the very ones where democracy has the most trouble taking root.[53]

The two Latin American giants—Brazil and Argentina—were governed by military juntas; Bolivia (which recently had *four* civilian governments in just over a year) had reverted to military control; General Stroessner's long-established dictatorship in Paraguay seemed secure; in neighboring and economically stagnant Uruguay, military officers dictated the civilian government's programs and policies; as we have seen, in the post-Allende regime, Chile was governed by the armed forces; in Panama—after winning its struggle to assert national sovereignty over the Panama Canal—the regime of General Omar Torrijos Herrera effectively controlled the country.

President Wilson and other American chief executives after him utilized coercive measures to induce Latin American societies to abandon dictatorship for democratic systems of government. Presidents John F. Kennedy and Lyndon B. Johnson relied upon the Alliance for Progress and other forms of economic assistance to achieve the goal.[54] President Jimmy Carter placed an emphasis upon the observance of human rights at the forefront of his diplomacy toward Latin America and other regions. Yet none of these approaches by the United States appears to have fundamentally altered the prevailing pattern of political rule by military elements or other right-wing groups that has long been pervasive throughout Latin America. Today, as in the past, formulating and carrying out a successful policy in dealing with Latin American dictatorships poses an extremely difficult and recurrent challenge for officials in Washington. A brief discussion of the military tradition in Latin America will provide insight into the complexities and durability of the problem.

The Military Tradition in Latin America

From the early nineteenth century—when Latin American countries acquired their independence—the armed forces have often played a dominant role in the political life of that region. Under Spanish rule, the colonial tradition in Latin America often exalted military leadership; Spanish culture had nothing corresponding to the principle of civilian supremacy over military elements which is central to the constitutional system of the United States. The wars of Latin American independence were prolonged and destructive, leaving chaos and social disorganization in their wake. The new civilian governments often lacked both the legitimacy to give them popular support and the capacity to deal with national problems successfully. By contrast, military leaders—like José de San Martín and Simón Bolívar, along with many lesser-known figures—emerged with great prestige and mass appeal. For well over a century, Latin American political life involved the interplay of three potent forces: the wealthy landowners, the Roman Catholic Church, and the armed forces. More often than not, the army (frequently allied with one or both of the other groups) served as the real locus of political power.

Based perhaps on the army's decisive

role in achieving independence, Latin American military elites asserted a claim which was to be heard many times in the years ahead. This was the idea that the armed forces were the true repository of national power and welfare; they were the real "custodians" of the society's well-being; and governmental officials were ultimately accountable to them for the welfare of the nation. The logical corollary of this doctrine of course was that military elites could, and not infrequently did, depose incumbent governments. Even disgruntled civilians often turned to the military for assistance in overturning the government in power. Military-led coups thus became a recurrent feature of Latin American political life. Or, as a recent student of political behavior in the area has expressed the idea: "The *normal* business of the military in these countries is politics."[55]

The pattern of government by the *caudillo* system thus became ubiquitous throughout Latin America.* The *caudillo* system had certain common characteristics. *Caudillo* rule tended to be extremely *personal.* The acquisition and retention of political power per se—rather than concern with ideological principles or specific programs—

*In the period immediately following Latin American independence, Edwin Lieuwen has written, the new republics quickly came under the control of *caudillos,* who were "ambitious local chieftains," usually military officers. These "army-officer politicians" normally "ruled by the sword, perverted justice, and pillaged the treasury"; the *caudillo* and his followers tended to live "as parasites upon the society they were supposed to protect." Down to the recent period, the "plethora of ambitious, opportunistic military men made politics in nearly every country little more than an endless process of dissension, intrigue, and revolutionary turmoil." Opponents of the *caudillo* (often individuals and groups "left out" in the distribution of spoils) would eventually form a new conspiratorial group and, if successful, install a new *caudillo* in office. See Edwin Lieuwen, *Arms and Politics in Latin America,* rev. ed. (New York: Praeger, 1961), pp. 18, 20.

became the dominating impulse of the system. The *caudillo* demanded unquestioning loyalty and obedience from his followers. Absolutism and *caudillo* rule thus tended to become synonymous terms. Constitutional restraints upon arbitrary governmental power, laws, elections, and other safeguards (with which the constitutions of Latin America often abounded) were customarily disregarded or circumvented by the *caudillo* and his coterie. In return for virtually uninhibited political power, the *caudillo* had certain obligations—foremost among which perhaps was to enrich and enhance the welfare of the coterie which installed and maintained him in office. The *caudillo* system customarily produced fortunes for the leader and his clique, while despoiling society at large. Meanwhile, the masses in *caudillo*-ruled Latin American societies sank deeper into economic and social backwardness.

Despite the fact that the term *revolution* has been loosely applied to the frequent changes of government in Latin America since the early nineteenth century, in reality the exchange of one *caudillo* regime for another was not a revolutionary process at all. With one notable exception—the gradual diminution in the political power of the Chuch in most Latin American societies—nothing really changed when a new goverment took office. To the contrary, most *caudillos* had (or soon developed) a powerful vested interest in the status quo, including the system of landed estates and peasant peonage, the influential role of foreign corporations in economic and political affairs, and the poverty-stricken condition of the masses. Insofar as fundamental changes occurred at all, these were usually in the direction of greater economic and social *inequality* among the various strata of society and the general deterioration in conditions throughout Latin America.

In the post-World War II period, right-wing dictatorships in Latin America discovered another persuasive reason why the status quo ought to be perpetuated: They provided a formidable barrier against Communist and other revolutionary movements promoting radical change throughout the region. For the pre-Castro Batista regime in Cuba, or the Somoza dynasty in Nicaragua, or the military junta ruling Chile after Allende's overthrow, this argument often struck a responsive chord with policy makers in Washington and among privileged groups in Latin American societies.

The "New" Military Elites of Latin America

By the 1960s, informed students of Latin American affairs detected certain fundamental changes in the nature and goals of military rule throughout Latin America.[56] One commentator on the Peruvian political system referred to that country's military elite as "the reformers in brass hats."[57] Other commentators believed that military elements in Latin America had become the principal agents of "modernization" and effective reform: In many societies, the military elite appeared to be the only group possessing the *power* to carry out long overdue social and economic changes. If Latin America was displaying an affinity for the Third World, one reason perhaps was that—in common with many African, Arab, and Asian states—military rule in the Western Hemisphere was often viewed as both inevitable and as necessary to achieve political stability and ultimate change in primitive societies.

What was "new" about direct or indirect military rule in Latin America? Several features could be identified. Along with their counterparts in the Third World, some military groups in Latin America were devoted to the goals of modernization and national development—if for no other reason perhaps than to strengthen national defense. Other professed goals of Latin American military elites were industrialization, increased national productivity, and improvement in living standards. In foreign affairs, military elements often advocated a strong, well-equipped defense establishment capable of protecting the country's security and diplomatic interests; more effective "control" over national resources and economic enterprises, thereby reducing the power often exercised historically by foreign corporations in Latin America's economic and political life; greater diplomatic independence (mainly from the United States); and resistance to American-instigated human rights campaigns or efforts by the Organization of American States to intervene in the political affairs of Latin American states. Almost without exception, the "new" military regimes of Latin America were of course uncompromisingly anti-Communist and opposed to left-wing revolutionary agitation (although some did not hesitate to enter into more cordial political, or closer economic, relations with the Soviet Union). With rare exceptions also, most military-led governments throughout Latin America avowed their devotion to the democratic ideal and pledged to restore democarcy to their particular country at some unspecified future date.

In practice, the emergence of the new military in Latin America may have been a change that was more apparent than real. Although their expressed devotion to modernization may well have been genuine—and despite the fact that military-ruled governments in Latin America *have* often promulgated long-overdue reforms—their rule ultimately rested upon *the support and loyalty of the armed forces*. In one Latin American state after another, military elites did not hesitate to *use* the modern military arsenal at their disposal against real or imagined internal opposition groups. From Chile and Argentina to Ecuador and Panama, examples could be cited to document dictatorial and repressive behavior by established military elites. Military regimes in Latin America still faced the challenge of acquiring *legitimacy,* or building a strong base of popular acceptance, that was necessary for lasting political stability. In some cases, the policies and behavior of military-led Latin American governments had unquestionably strengthened the appeal of revolutionary causes throughout the region.

In order to lend specificity to our discussion of the problem of military rule in Latin America, let us focus upon three examples of that phenomenon: Panama, Argentina, and Brazil.

A New Regime for the Panama Canal

Among all the countries of Latin America, the Republic of Panama's relations with the United States have always been unique. In an effort to assure unilateral American control over the strategic isthmus of Panama, President Theodore Roosevelt encouraged and aided Panama's independence on November 3, 1903, from Colombia.[58] Ever since the Panama Canal was completed in 1914, the Canal—together with the 10-mile wide Canal Zone, which was under American jurisdiction—has dominated the country's economic, and more recently its political, life. For Panamanians, exclusive and seemingly perpetual control over the Canal by the United States increasingly became a symbol of American colonialism and subjection.* Panama's grievances found growing support among other Latin Americans and throughout the Third

World. (If Great Britain could relinquish sovereignty to the Suez Canal, Panamanian nationalists and their supporters reasoned, why could not the United States follow the same course in Central America?) Washington's friends south of the border urged it to adopt a conciliatory policy toward Panama, as a gesture of the "good neighbor" principle supposedly actuating American diplomacy within the Western Hemisphere.

With a population of approximately 2 million people, and an area of less than 30,000 square miles (about equal to the state of South Carolina), Panama has a per capita income of some $1300 annually. In common with its Latin American neighbors, its political history has been characterized by instability and ineffectual civilian rule. In 1968, military elements seized power; within a few months, General Omar Torrijos had emerged as the dominant political figure. In due course, the military junta encouraged adoption of a new constitution and the creation of new democratic institutions—but effective political power continued to rest with General Torrijos and his supporters. Torrijos typified the "new" Latin American military: He was determined to overcome the stagnation and disunity long associated with civilian rule; to improve Panama's low standard of living; and, above all, to acquire control over the country's principal asset, the Panama Canal. Torrijos also repeatedly demonstrated that his regime was capable of using its military power effectively against leftist groups and other political opponents.

By the early 1960s, officials in Washington could no longer ignore or reject Panamanian nationalistic demands.[59] In 1963, the two countries arrived at an agreement whereby the Panamanian flag could fly side by side with the American over the Canal Zone. Yet this symbolic victory only fueled Panama's nationalistic fervor, as riots and demonstrations re-

---

*Despite a prevalent misconception in the American society, the United States never possessed "sovereignty" over, or legal title to, the Panama Canal. Panama's ultimate sovereignty over it was conceded, and reiterated several times after 1903. The United States had the right to act "as if it were sovereign" in operating the Canal and in the adjacent Canal Zone.

peatedly erupted in the country. For a period of some 13 years—from 1964 to 1977—negotiations between American and Panamanian officials proceeded at what one study called "glacial speed," in an effort to reconcile the conflicting demands of both countries.[60] Finally, in 1974 Washington accepted the principle of ultimate Panamanian control over the waterway—but even then, many months were required to arrive at detailed agreements acceptable to both governments.

Diplomatic efforts to resolve the dispute ultimately bore fruit: In August 1977, officials of the Carter Administration and of the Torrijos government signed two new treaties providing for a new regime for the Panama Canal; the treaties were signed by President Jimmy Carter and General Torrijos on September 7. Subsequently, the process of "ratifying" the treaties (especially by the United States) proved almost as complex a process as their negotiation! Public and legislative sentiment within the United States were initially skeptical about these new accords—and only a skillful and intensive public relations campaign by the White House made them acceptable to the American people and to the Senate. Opponents of the treaties were particularly concerned about the vulnerability of the Canal during time of actual or possible war and about the implications of this fact for national and regional defense. Yet Panamanian nationalists feared that the United States would invoke any right to defend the Canal in order to intervene in the country's political affairs. The matter was finally resolved by an agreement between President Carter and General Torrijos acknowledging the right of both countries to defend the waterway, while the United States explicitly renounced any right of political intervention under this agreement; American ships were allowed to go "to the head of the line" and to transit the Canal "expeditiously" during periods of military emergency.

In somewhat modified form, these assurances were added to the treaties by the Senate. The treaties finally received the necessary two-thirds vote of the Senate on April 18, 1978, and were signed by President Carter.

The successful negotiation of a new regime for the Panama Canal—on terms that largely fulfilled the demands of Panamanian nationalists—was widely hailed as an outstanding act of American statesmanship and a significant gesture of goodwill toward Latin America. From a *Realpolitik* perspective, the Canal had largely become useless for much of the world's shipping and almost impossible to defend effectively (especially against anti-American guerrilla forces seeking to render it inoperable). Although Panamanians were elated over their diplomatic victory, the United States won less goodwill with them than Washington expected. As one commentator has observed, during the process of treaty ratification in the United States, "Panama and Panamanians had daily been subjected to insult, abuse and charges running from gross incompetence to communism."* Moreover, as our preceding discussion has shown, little evidence exists that the resolution of the Panama Canal issue reversed America's declining in-

---

*In August, 1981, General Omar Torrijos was killed in a plane crash. In the months following his death, in the words of one observer, "a bitter and increasingly open struggle for power" erupted among groups seeking to gain control of the country. In contrast to what many Panamanians expected, the new canal treaties had not solved the country's deep-seated economic and social problems. Unemployment, for example, continued to climb in the post-Torrijos era. For many Panamian groups, resolution of the canal issue had done little to change their attitudes toward the United States. The Panama Canal question, one commentator found, remained "vulnerable to exploitation by nationalists on the left and right who still feel Panama deserves a better deal." See Alan Riding, "Panama: Troubled Passage for a U.S. Ally," *The New York Times Magazine*, November 22, 1981, pp. 79–80, 121–128.

fluence in other Latin American settings or significantly stemmed the "revolutionary tide" that, by the early 1980s, appeared to be sweeping Central America.[61]

Argentine-American Relations in Eclipse

A recent treatment of political developments within Argentina has observed that:

> Fifteen or twenty years ago, Argentina was a land of expectation. Citizens took pride in themselves and their resources.... Argentina was a wonderful country and was bound to be great once again.
>
> Now that premise calls for skepticism. Within the last decade, Argentina has endured a holocaust, worse yet, one inflicted by Argentines upon themselves.[62]

With a population of some 27 million people—and an area of almost 1.1 million square miles (almost five times larger than Texas)—Argentina possesses great potential for national development and regional leadership. Yet for a generation or more, its national cohesion and economic welfare have been imperiled by ongoing political upheaval (sometimes bordering on anarchy). Frequent changes of government; reliance upon terroristic methods by both pro- and antigovernment forces; economic stagnation and decline—these have been the dominant realities in Argentina's recent history.

During World War II, considerable pro-Axis sentiment existed in Argentina, although the country finally joined the Allied cause. After the war, for approximately a decade Argentina's political life was largely dominated by Colonel Juan Perón, founder of the Peronist movement. While Perón's rule became increasingly dictatorial and rested upon military support, Peronism had a wide popular following, especially among the laboring classes and trade unions.[63] Yet as Argentina experienced internal decline, in 1955 Perón was forced into exile by the country's military leaders (he returned briefly to serve as president again in 1973). After Perón died on July 1, 1974, his successor (his widow, Isabel Perón) proved incapable of resolving Argentina's increasingly acute internal problems.

Beginning on March 24, 1976, the Argentine military elite seized power directly. Periodically thereafter, spokesmen for the junta pledged to restore political stability to a society that for several years had been torn by violent conflict between anti- and progovernment groups.* The junta also endeavored to achieve economic vitality and growth. By the early 1980s, however, the evidence indicated that in both its internal and external affairs, Argentina's problems remained critical—and by some criteria they had worsened under military rule. In 1982, for example, one commentator described Argentina as "a fragmented and troubled society" that had "a most uncertain political future."[64] Under the regime headed by General Leopoldo Galtieri that assumed power at the end of 1981, internal conditions were deterio-

---

*In recent years, Argentina has been subject to widespread terrorism and other forms of violence practiced by three groups: military and police units of the government; revolutionary and guerrilla organizations opposing the government; and paramilitary or private groups, like the Argentine Anti-Communist Alliance (AAA). As in most Latin American states, the revolutionary movement is fragmented, consisting of several major and minor organizations having diverse origins and ideological orientations. The largest revolutionary group is a coalition known as the *Montonera* movement, having roots in the tradition of revolt in the rural areas. A smaller force is the People's Revolutionary Army (ERP), which has a radical Marxist coloration. Most revolutionary groups are accused by the government of receiving external (e.g., Cuban and Soviet) support; and in some instances, the charge has substantial validity. It is most probably true also, however, that violent resistance to the government's authority would exist *without* external aid and encouragement.

rating rapidly. Runaway inflation, a worsening trade deficit, repeated devaluations of the Argentine peso, rising unemployment—such conditions led large numbers of Argentina's skilled and professional classes to emigrate. Politically, the junta did not hesitate to use violence against terrorists, Communists, and other groups suspected of resisting its authority. In one of the most repressive political environments in Latin America, it was estimated that several thousand critics or suspected critics of the regime had "disappeared."

Repelled by the Argentine junta's record in violating human rights, the Carter Administration was highly and publicly critical of its behavior. For their part, authorities in Buenos Aires simultaneously denied allegations of widespread use of coercion against Argentine citizens and told officials in Washington to mind their own business. Under these conditions, Argentine-American relations were characterized mainly by mutual suspicions and recriminations.

When the Reagan Administration took office in 1981, Washington made a concerted effort to improve relations between the two countries. In Argentina and other settings, spokesmen for the new administration emphasized, the human rights issue would no longer serve as a dominant standard in determining the policy of the United States toward other countries. (Republicans had long complained, for example, that under President Carter and other Democratic leaders, concern for human rights violations had influenced American diplomacy primarily toward *right-wing* governments abroad, much less frequently toward the Soviet Union, Communist China, and other left-wing regimes.) By the early 1980s Argentina emerged as one of the few Latin American nations willing to support Washington's anti-Communist campaign in Central America.[65]

This rapprochement in Argentine-American relations, however, proved short-lived—if it ever had any real future. It was shattered by the decision of the military junta in Argentina to "liberate" the Falkland Islands from British rule. When Argentine forces invaded the islands on April 2, 1982, the ensuing conflict in the south Atlantic proved traumatic for Argentina itself, for Argentine-American relations, and for the future of the inter-American system. The Argentine government's decision to undertake military operations against the Falkland Islands, many commentators were convinced, stemmed in no small measure from an effort by the junta to divert popular attention from the society's critical domestic problems. At any rate, the Argentine military elite made two extremely serious miscalculations. It underrated British power and London's determination to resist this extension of Argentine sovereignty over British citizens. Similarly, General Galtieri's regime erred in believing that it would receive the support of the Reagan Administration in this venture. After mounting a massive naval buildup off the southern coast of Argentina, Great Britain inflicted a series of military defeats upon Argentine forces. Washington's public support for the British position in the crisis reversed the course of recent Argentine-American relations and supplied a new source of misunderstanding between the two countries. Other Latin American spokesmen, however, joined those in Buenos Aires in deploring Washington's preference for its NATO ally over its hemispheric neighbor in this crisis. After the Falkland Islands imbroglio, any remaining sense of "community" among the members of the inter-American system would be severely strained.

By contrast, Soviet influence with Argentina—at least in the short run—could be expected to increase significantly. Even before the conflict in the south Atlantic, Argentina had become one of Moscow's principal trading partners. Argentina was supplying the U.S.S.R. with substantial quantities of wheat and beef (thereby largely nullifying efforts by the United States to boycott trade with the Soviet Union). Even more disturbing to the United States, the Kremlin provided Argentina with uranium—an essential element in efforts by the Argentine junta to acquire a nuclear arsenal. While Moscow's support of Argentine claims to the Falkland Islands would unquestionably win goodwill for the Kremlin in Latin America, such gains could easily prove ephemeral. In the last analysis, Moscow had really *done nothing* to save Argentina from a humiliating defeat in its encounter with Great Britain. Nor was it likely that in Argentina—or in other Latin American societies in which military elites were politically dominant—Marxist groups would gain large numbers of new converts. As many informed commentators assessed it, the most likely alternative to military rule in Argentina was a revival of Peronism. A Perónista resurgence offered little comfort either to the United States or the Soviet Union.[66]

Brazilian-American Relations in the Balance

"As Brazil goes," President Richard M. Nixon often said, "so goes Latin America." Throughout the Western Hemisphere, and on a global scale, widespread recognition exists that Brazil is the "power giant" of Latin America. It already exercises significant power and is seeking to expand its regional influence; it is at the forefront of the "developing" nations; and (after Brazil has acquired the nuclear capability its leaders are determined to possess), it may in time exercise substantial global influence. As we shall see, in microcosm recent Brazilian-American relations have exemplified many of the challenges arising out of a rapidly changing international system. The "emergence" of Brazil could well be

a crucial test case of the ability of the United States to adapt to such changes.

Just before he assumed office as president in 1979, the leader of Brazil, General João Baptista Figueiredo called upon his countrymen to support "democracy without adjectives," or his campaign known as *abertura:* the gradual liberalization of Brazil's political life. Cautioning against any reversion to the earlier conditions of political chaos and governmental paralysis—witnessed many times in Brazil's past—General Figueiredo warned that the nation's armed forces "stand well aware of their institutional mission."[67]

Ever since 1964—when a military junta ousted the civilian government headed by President Jânio da Silva Quadros—the Brazilian armed forces have been carrying out their "institutional mission" in what is popularly referred to as "the South American Colossus." Covering an area of some 3.3 million square miles (larger than the United States, exclusive of Hawaii and Alaska), and with a population of some 120 million people, modern Brazil epitomizes the concept of a "developing" nation. As a result of continuing economic growth, Brazil had become the eighth-largest market economy on the globe; it ranked tenth in the size of its Gross National Product ($200 billion annually by 1980); it was developing the largest hydroelectric complex in the world; it stood fifteenth among the nations in the value of its exports—and these were expanding rapidly; and it either had (or was on the verge of developing) a nuclear arsenal. Brazil's size, its economic power and potential, and its national ambitions were causes of concern to its Latin American neighbors. Establishing and maintaining cooperative Brazilian-American relations would likely prove a recurrent challenge for policy makers in both Washington and Brasilia.[68]

Following a common Latin American pattern, in 1964 military elements had assumed control of the government because of the alleged "failure" of civilian leadership to deal effectively with the country's manifold and progressively more critical internal problems. One commentator has referred to the "tempestuous episodes" that characterized Brazil's national life during the early 1960s—out of which emerged

> ...a widespread if tacit acknowledgement among Brazilians of an awesome conflict potential in this country, given its size, distances, the "staggering inequalities" [existing among the population]...and the less publicized episodes of enormous cruelty and bloodletting in the past.

Moreover, for some classes within the population, there was also "the spectre (whether myth or reality) of communism" in the largest country in Latin America.[69]

After its successful coup, the military junta—relying upon the pro-government party known as the National Renovation Alliance (ARENA)—has maintained control of the levers of power. Its principal challenge comes from the *Brazilian Democratic Movement* (BDM), joined by other dissident groups. From time to time, however, the Brazilian government has been denounced by internal and external critics for imposing censorship, rigging elections, suppressing dissent, and taking other steps in violation of Brazil's professed constitutional principles.

With the Brazilian economic system in dire straits—by the end of the 1970s, for example, Brazil had accumulated foreign indebtedness of some $50 billion, the largest external debt of any developing nation—the government promulgated a series of measures designed to reduce the inflation rate, improve real wages, increase productivity, promote investment, and otherwise stimulate economic growth. Its heavy dependency upon oil imports from the Middle East has made Brazil

more pro-Arab in its diplomatic orientation and has spurred an intensive search for new oil supplies within its own borders and in offshore sites—a quest in which American oil companies have played a leading role.

The United States was the first country to recognize Brazil's independence in 1822. Since that time, as a rule close ties have existed between the two countries. Brazil, for example, supplied a large military contingent to the Allied cause in World War II; and the first peacetime defense alliance joined by the United States—the Rio Treaty of hemispheric defense (1947)—was signed near the country's capital. In common with the American society, Brazil is also an ethnic "melting pot" of diverse immigrant groups who have contributed to its vibrant national life. The United States provides the largest single market for Brazilian exports, and it is the largest supplier of the country's imports. (By the late 1970s, trade between the United States and Brazil, for example, was some 300 percent greater than between the United States and Communist China.) American firms also account for nearly one-third (or close to $4 billion) of Brazil's total foreign investment—and the rate of American investment in the Brazilian economy continues to rise.[70]

Diplomatically—in recognition perhaps that Brazil is the most powerful state in Latin America and that its influence is growing—Washington has made a special effort to preserve cordial relations with successive governments in the country. Successive American presidents have paid state visits to Brazil (Eisenhower received an especially enthusiastic welcome in 1960). Despite the overthrow of civilian authority in 1964, both President Jimmy Carter and his wife also visited Brazil, in an effort to cement friendly relations between the two countries.

Two specific issues have been at the forefront of recent Brazilian-American relations. One is a familiar problem in contemporary Latin America: actual and alleged violations of human rights by Brazilian authorities. As we have already observed, President Jimmy Carter entered the White House in 1977 with a strong professed commitment to the cause of international human rights —and since 1964 the behavior of the Brazilian junta has provided numerous examples eliciting American concern. During some periods, Brazil's regime has been severely criticized by private and public spokesmen in the United States for its record in this field. Such criticism by Washington diminished under the Reagan Administration.

From their perspective, Brazilians believe that foreign critics are not infrequently misinformed about events in their country; and they have repeatedly complained about the existence of a "double standard" in Washington, whereby American officials judge the behavior of right- and left-wing regimes in Latin America. To the Brazilian mind, Washington's preoccupation with the issue is merely a contemporary manifestation of interventionism in Latin American political affairs by the United States.* Nor does any convincing evidence exist that private and official crit-

*An interesting example illustrating this phenomenon was provided in September 1980, when military authorities ousted the civilian government of Turkey, which for several years had been deadlocked and unresponsive to the country's acute internal problems. In company with their Latin American counterparts, Turkey's military leaders pledged to "restore democracy" at an early date. News reports indicated that this development was not totally unexpected or undesired by officials of the Carter Administration, who were deeply concerned about ongoing violence and economic deterioration within Turkey. Describing attitudes in Washington toward the Turkish coup, one commentator said that its leader, General Kenan Evren, was "cautious and steady" and that he was "not like the Brazilians and Argentine generals who have seized power," since "he does not want to install a military regime that will perpetuate itself." See Drew Middleton, in *New York Times*, September 13, 1980.

icism from the United States has had any significant effect upon Brazil's internal political process.[71]

Controversy has also erupted between Washington and Brasilia over Brazil's evident determination to forge ahead in the field of nuclear power and technology—giving the country at least a potential stockpile of nuclear weapons. As Brazilian officials assessed the matter, one solution to the country's energy crisis lay in the rapid development of peacetime nuclear power—a move that would inevitably enhance Brazil's military and diplomatic power as well. Brazilian authorities refused to sign the Nuclear Non-Proliferation Treaty of 1977, the effect of which would be to relegate their country *permanently* to a position of military and diplomatic inferiority by "freezing" membership in the nuclear club. In the face of strong American opposition—and using technological assistance and equipment acquired from the government of West Germany—Brazil moved ahead with its plans to expand its nuclear capability. The result of Washington's policy toward Brazil, one student of Latin American affairs observed, was the United States "alienated a friend and old ally, and we did not get (nor will we likely get) what we sought...." After witnessing this outcome, in the early 1980s Washington relaxed its restrictions against supplying the Brazilian government with uranium. Realizing that—as much for internal political reasons as for other motivations—Brazil could not be dissuaded from becoming a nuclear power, the Reagan Administration accepted that reality. If they were to have any influence over Brazil's foreign and defense policies, officials in Washington believed they would be successful only within the context of reasonably cordial Brazilian-American relations.[72]

As much as any other country in the contemporary international system, Brazil provides an example of a rapidly developing nation that is determined to assert its independence in foreign relations and to move up to a new level of regional and global influence. To date, the United States has neither been able to prevent that transition nor, alternatively, has it created the kind of "partnership" with the power giant of South America that this new reality requires.[73]

America and Latin American Dictatorships: Continuing Policy Dilemmas

What kind of diplomatic balance sheet can be drawn up for the United States in its response to the existence and behavior of military-controlled governments in Latin America? To the extent that reducing or eliminating pervasive military involvement in the Latin American political process has been a dominant goal of Washington's diplomacy, the United States has experienced minimum success in achieving it. From Chile to Guatemala, the age-old Latin American propensity to rely upon military elements to "save the country" from civilian misrule, economic deterioration, and other evils remains as strong in the contemporary era as in the past.

It is noteworthy that military elites control the governments of some of the most *advanced* societies within Latin America. Brazil's rapid economic progress, for example, has not produced greater political stability, nor has it assured efficient and responsible rule by civilian groups. The simplistic assumption that underlay the Alliance for Progress during the 1960s—that as national development was gradually achieved throughout Latin America there would be a corresponding evolution toward, and strengthening of, democratic government throughout the region—has not been supported by events. In some Latin American societies, in fact, increasingly acute

problems—like the maldistribution of income among the major population groups or the deteriorating condition of the urban slum dwellers—encourage ongoing revolutionary activities against entrenched military elites. The ensuing pattern of political strife and violence provides still another justification for a continuation of military rule!

As for the policy of the United States toward military-controlled governments in Latin America, several observations may be made. It is emphasized in Chapters 12, 13, and 15 that a decisive military role in the political system is a widespread phenomenon throughout the Third World; Washington has been hard-pressed to respond to it constructively not only in Latin America, but in black Africa, the Middle East, and Asia as well. In Latin America, as well as other regions, the United States has vocally opposed military rule in some settings; seemingly encouraged it in others; and largely ignored it in still other locales. Not untypically, American policy makers have denounced the *idea* of military control of Latin American political systems, even while they *cooperated* with particular military-led governments to achieve common goals. Even by the 1980s, President Wilson's old dream largely remains unfulfilled: Officials in Washington have still been unable to teach Latin Americans "to elect good men"—and from the beginning, it was perhaps always naive to suppose that this lay within America's capacity.

The dominant lesson that emerges from our analysis of the problem perhaps is the conclusion that—irrespective of the particular strategy decided upon in Washington—the United States has usually had *marginal influence* in determining the nature and behavior of Latin American governments. Toward the military junta in Panama, the United States took a highly conciliatory approach, ultimately resolving the long-standing Panama

Canal issue in a manner acceptable to the Torrijos government. While there were several compelling reasons for doing so, Washington's positive response to acceptance of Panamanian nationalist demands quite clearly did *not* discourage Panama or other Latin American states from relying upon military leadership to solve national problems. Instead, by its victory over the United States in this case, the regime of General Torrijos considerably enhanced its power and prestige—as well as dramatically demonstrating Panama's "independence" from American dictation.

Different approaches by the United States, however—toward Argentina, Brazil, and the post-Allende government of Chile —resulted in perhaps even fewer diplomatic gains for Washington. Vocal denunciations of military rule by the President and his advisers; condemnations because of threats to human rights in these countries; attempts to prevent Brazil and Argentina from acquiring nuclear facilities—this pattern of behavior in Washington has had little visible effect upon the nature and behavior of the established military regimes in these states. This kind of "confrontational" approach to the problem appears to have produced little more than alienation and suspicion between the United States and the Latin American states involved. In this kind of negative atmosphere, overall relations between the United States and several key Latin American states have clearly declined.

The age-old Latin American tradition that the armed forces serve as the ultimate guardian of the nation's security and welfare remains a potent influence upon political developments south of the border. This idea is of course totally at variance with the constitutional system of the United States, where the concept of "civilian supremacy" over the military establishment remains fundamental. If military-dominated governments remain

ubiquitous throughout Latin America in the contemporary era, one compelling reason may be that civilian authorities have had no conspicuous success is solving critical social and economic problems. In view of this fact, in most Latin American societies the alternatives to military rule may often appear less attractive. It is noteworthy, for example, that even Marxist-oriented regimes—like Cuba and Nicaragua—also depend heavily upon the armed forces to achieve their goals. Above all else perhaps, our analysis of military influence upon Latin American political systems underscores the fact that the influence of the United States is likely to be minimal in determining the nature of political regimes south of the border.

NOTES

1. For the text of President Monroe's message to Congress on December 2, 1823, see James D. Richardson, ed., *A Compilation of the Messages and Papers of the Presidents, 1789–1897,* 2 (Washington, D.C.: Government Printing Office, 1896), pp. 207–220.

2. See President Richard M. Nixon's report to Congress entitled, "U.S. Foreign Policy for the 1970's: the Emerging Structure of Peace" (Washington, D.C.: the White House, 1972), p. 90.

3. See President Richard M. Nixon's report to Congress entitled, "U.S. Foreign Policy for the 1970's: Building for Peace" (Washington D.C.: the White House, 1971), pp. 45–46.

4. See Dr. Henry Kissinger's views on U.S.-Latin American relations, as cited in Francis P. Kessler, "Kissinger's Legacy: A Latin American Policy," *Current History,* **72** (February, 1977), 76–78.

5. See the views of John Quincy Adams, as cited in Julius W. Pratt, *A History of United States Foreign Policy* (Englewood Cliffs, N.J.: Prentice-Hall, 1955), pp. 180–181.

6. See the views of the Chilean diplomat Enrique

Bernstein, as quoted in Kessler, "Kissinger's Legacy: A Latin American Policy," p. 87.

7. More detailed discussion of demographic tendencies in Latin America and their implications may be found in Nicolás Sánchez-Albornoz, "The Land-Population Balance in Latin America," *Current History*, **68** (June, 1975), 254–258. The political effects of overpopulation are analyzed in Kenneth F. Johnson, "Causal Factors in Latin American Political Instability," in Francisco José Moreno and Barbara Mitrani, *Conflict and Violence in Latin American Politics: A Book of Readings* (New York: Thomas Y. Crowell, 1971), pp. 300–303.

8. Latin America's growing identification with the Third World is emphasized in Federico G. Gil, *Latin American—United States Relations* (New York: Harcourt Brace Jovanovich, 1971), pp. 285–286.

9. The context of events prompting issuance of the Monroe Doctrine is analyzed in Richard W. Leopold, *The Growth of American Foreign Policy* (New York: Alfred A. Knopf, 1962), pp. 41–54.

10. James W. Gantenbein, *The Evolution of Our Latin-American Policy* (Englewood Cliffs, N.J.: Prentice-Hall, 1955), pp. 371–372.

11. Secretary of State Hughes' views on the Monroe Doctrine are cited in ibid., pp. 387–388.

12. Ibid., p. 330; italics inserted.

13. Ibid., pp. 344–348.

14. Ibid., pp. 360–364.

15. See ibid., pp. 165–166, 401–407; and Donald M. Dozer, ed., *The Monroe Doctrine: Its Modern Significance* (New York: Alfred A. Knopf, 1965), pp. 115–133.

16. For one interpretation that the Monroe Doctrine has become obsolete and no longer governs American foreign policy toward Latin America, see the Soviet view of the Monroe Doctrine, as presented in ibid., pp. 197–205.

17. The Kennedy Administration's response to the installation of Soviet offensive missiles in Cuba is discussed more fully in Robert F. Kennedy: *Thirteen Days: A Memoir of the Cuban Missile Crisis* (New York: New American Library, 1969).

18. Pratt, *A History of United States Foreign Policy*, pp. 181–183, 346.

19. Ibid., pp. 610–611, 765; and Gantenbein, *The Evolution of Our Latin-American Policy*, p. 285.

20. Pratt, *A History of United States Foreign Policy*, pp. 767–768.

21. For current information on the Organization of American States, see "Organization of American States," *Political Handbook of the World: 1980* (New York: McGraw-Hill, 1980), pp. 576–577; subsequent volumes in this series provide up-to-date information on the structure and activities of the OAS.

22. See ibid., p. 577; and the *Europa Yearbook: 1980* (London: Europa Publications, 1980), pp. 252–254.

23. John A. Bushnell, "FY 1981 Foreign Assistance Program," *Department of State Bulletin*, **80** (April, 1980), 71.

24. "Organization of American States," *Political Handbook of the World: 1980*, p. 25. Although their discussions are somewhat dated, more recent events have not essentially outmoded the insights and conclusions contained in: G. Connell-Smith, "OAS and the Dominican Crisis," *World Today*, **21** (June, 1965), 229–236; and J. Slater, "The United States, the Organization of American States, and the Dominican Republic, 1961–1963," *International Organization*, **18** (Spring, 1964), 268–291. See also the discussion of Latin American attitudes toward the United States in *U.S. News and World Report*, **89** (September 15, 1980), 37.

25. See the discussions of "Latin American Free Trade Association," of "Andean Group," of "Central American Common Market," and of "Latin American Economic System," in *Political Handbook of the World: 1980*, pp. 570–571; 538–539; 546–547; and 570, respectively.

26. See "Latin America," in ibid., p. 25.

27. James D. Theberge, *The Soviet Presence in Latin America* (New York: Crane, Russak and Co., 1974), pp. 2–4.

28. See the discussion of Soviet strategy in Latin America in ibid., pp. 5–11.

29. For the Eisenhower Administration's assess-

ment of developments in Guatemala, see Dwight D. Eisenhower, *Mandate for Change* (Garden City, N.Y.: Doubleday and Co., 1963), pp. 420–427.

30. Department of State, *Intervention of International Communism in Guatemala,* No. 5556, Inter-American Series, Vol. 48 (1954), p. 49. This document presents the State Department's "case" against the Arbenz regime in Guatemala.

31. *Survey of International Affairs: 1954* (New York: Oxford University Press, 1956), pp. 376–378.

32. *United States in World Affairs: 1954* (New York: Harper & Row, 1955), p. 372.

33. Department of State, *Intervention of International Communism in Guatemala,* p. 30.

34. Department of State, *American Foreign Policy, 1950–55,* No. 6446, General Foreign Policy Series, Vol. 117 (1957), p. 1292.

35. See the views of Latin American spokesmen on the Caracas Declaration, as cited in William Benton, *The Voice of Latin America* (New York: Harper & Row, 1961), p. 73.

36. See Eisenhower, *Mandate for Change,* pp. 424–426. For the view that American intervention in Latin America amounted to sponsoring a "counterrevolution" in Guatemala, doing little to alter the country's underlying problems, see Edwin Lieuwen, *Arms and Politics in Latin America* (New York: Praeger Publishers, 1963), p. 94.

37. An informative analysis of the Guatemalan political environment is in Alan Riding, "Guatemala: State of Siege," *The New York Times Magazine,* August 24, 1980, 16–29, 65–67. More recent developments in the country are described in *New York Times,* March 25, 1982; and in *Newsweek,* **99** (April 5, 1982), 49–50.

38. Our discussion of the Cuban revolution relies heavily upon Lieuwen, *Arms and Politics in Latin America,* pp. 97–100; and on the document prepared for the Senate Foreign Relations Committee, *Events in United States-Cuban Relations: A Chronology,* 88th Cong., 1st Sess., 1963.

39. More detailed discussion of the "Bay of Pigs" episode may be found in Theodore C. Soren-

sen, *Kennedy* (New York: Harper & Row, 1965), pp. 291–309; and Arthur Schlesinger, Jr., *A Thousand Days: John F. Kennedy in the White House* (Boston: Houghton Mifflin Co., 1965), pp. 233–267.

40. For fuller discussion and analysis of the Cuban Missile Crisis of 1962, see: Kennedy, *Thirteen Days;* Sorensen, *Kennedy,* pp. 667–718; and Schlesinger, *A Thousand Days,* pp. 794–819.

41. See the statement by Myles R. Frechette, a State Department official, to the Inter-American subcommittee of the House Foreign Affairs Committee, in "Cuban-Soviet Impact on the Western Hemisphere," *Department of State Bulletin,* **80** (July, 1980), 77–80.

42. The leading issues in Cuban-American relations after the missile crisis are identified and evaluated in Jorege I. Dominguez, "Cuban Foreign Policy," *Foreign Affairs,* **57** (Fall, 1978), 83–109; and in George Volsky, "Cuba Twenty Years Later," *Current History,* **76** (February, 1979), 54–58, 83–84.

43. Henry Kissinger, *White House Years* (Boston: Little, Brown and Co., 1979), pp. 632–653.

44. For information on the buildup of Soviet ground forces in Cuba and the Carter Administration's response to this development, see "Background on the Question of Soviet Troops in Cuba," *Current Policy No. 93,* Department of State, October 1, 1979; and the address by President Jimmy Carter on October 1, 1979, as reprinted in "Soviet Troops in Cuba," *Current Policy No. 92,* Department of State, October 1, 1979. See also Bernard Weintraub, in *New York Times,* September 10, 1979; Richard Burt, in ibid., September 14, 1979; and Hedrick Smith, in ibid., October 7, 1979.

45. More extended discussion of Cuban-American relations under the Carter and Reagan administrations may be found in the State Department's publication "Cuba's Renewed Support for Violence in Latin America," (Special Report, # 90), December 14, 1981; in *Newsweek,* **98** (December 7, 1981), p. 54; and the analyses by Flora Lewis in *New York Times,* February 18, 1982; by

Leslie H. Gelb in ibid., April 6, 1982, and April 18, 1982.

46. For more comprehensive discussion of political developments in Chile, leading up to the national election of 1970, see J. Samuel Valenzuela and Arturo Valenzuela, "Chile and the Breakdown of Democracy," in Howard J. Wiarda and Harvey F. Kline, eds., *Latin American Politics and Development* (Boston: Houghton Mifflin, 1979), pp. 233–262.

47. See the cablegram from Ambassador Korry to the State Department, as cited in Kissinger, *White House Years,* p. 653. The italics represent emphasis supplied by President Nixon after he received the message. The quotation from Allende after his first year in office is cited in Alan Angell, "Allende's First Year in Chile," *Current History,* **62** (February, 1972), 76.

48. A detailed account of interventionist moves by private and public American groups directed against the Allende regime may be found in Robert C. Johansen, *The National Interest and the Human Interest: An Analysis of U.S. Foreign Policy* (Princeton, N.J.: Princeton University Press, 1980), pp. 196–279. This commentator believes that the "CIA and Department of Defense played a substantial role in creating conditions designed to achieve a speedy overthrow of the [Allende] government." The "extremely hard vengeful policy line" displayed by officials in Washington toward Allende was crucial in his downfall. Yet the author also believes that "some responsibility" must be assumed by Dr. Allende and his supporters for rising internal disaffection toward his regime.

49. The political system of Nicaragua before the overthrow of the Somoza regime is discussed more fully in Thomas W. Walker, "Nicaragua: the Somoza Family Regime," in Wiarda and Kline, *Latin American Politics and Development,* pp. 316–332.

50. Thomas W. Walker, "The Sandinist Victory in Nicaragua," *Current History,* **78** (February, 1980), 57.

51. For more extended treatment of develop-

ments in, and American policy toward, Nicaragua, see *Time,* **118** (December 14, 1981), 48–49; the analysis by Warren Hoge in *New York Times,* January 14, 1982; the State Department's publications, "Central America: U.S. Policy," *Gist,* April, 1982, 1–2; "The U.S. and Nicaragua," ibid., April, 1982, 1–2; and Roland H. Ebel, "Political Instability in Central America," *Current History,* **81** (February, 1982), 56–59, 86.

52. More detailed treatment of the Wilson Administration's diplomacy toward the Huerta regime in Mexico may be found in Thomas A. Bailey, *Diplomatic History of the American People,* 8th ed. (New York: Appleton-Century-Crofts, 1969), pp. 554–560.

53. *U.S. News and World Report,* **89** (August 18, 1980), 51–53.

54. For a discussion of the Alliance for Progress, see Sorensen, *Kennedy,* pp. 533–540; and for commentaries on the program, see the essays contained in Richard B. Gray, ed., *Latin America and the United States in the 1970's* (Itasca, Ill.: F. E. Peacock, 1971), pp. 75–137.

55. More detailed discussion of the military tradition in Latin American and the political role of military elites may be found in: Robert J. Alexander, *Today's Latin America,* 2nd ed. (New York: Doubleday and Co., 1968), pp. 168–183; Martin C. Needler, *Political Development in Latin America: Instability, Violence, and Evolutionary Change* (New York: Random House, 1968), pp. 43–77; and Seymour M. Lipset and Aldo Solari, eds., *Elites in Latin America* (New York: Oxford University Press, 1967), pp. 146–190.

56. Changes in the nature, goals, and policies of military elements within Latin America within the past two decades or so are identified and analyzed in *The Rockefeller Report on the Americas* (Chicago: Quadrangle Books, 1969), pp. 32–33; and in Needler, *Political Development in Latin America,* pp. 59–77; and Lipset and Solari, eds., *Elites in Latin America,* pp. 146–190.

57. For a discussion of the goals and policies of a military-led regime in a single, and backward,

Latin American country, see José Yglesias, "Report From Peru: The Reformers in Brass Hats," *The New York Times Magazine,* December 14, 1969, pp. 56–58, 128–142.

58. The acquisition of the Panama Canal site and the subsequent construction of the Canal are discussed more fully in Pratt, *A History of United States Foreign Policy,* pp. 395–412.

59. Our discussion of recent political developments within Panama, and of the negotiations leading to a new regime for the Panama Canal, relies upon: E. Bradford Burns, "Panama: A Search for Independence," *Current History,* **72** (February, 1977), 65–68, 82; the same author's, "Panama: New Treaties or New Conflicts?" ibid., **74** (February, 1978), 74–76, 87–88; and in Cecil V. Crabb, Jr., and Pat Holt, *Invitation to Struggle: Congress, the President and Foreign Policy* (Washington, D.C.: Congressional Quarterly, 1980), pp. 65–89.

60. Crabb and Holt, *Invitation to Struggle,* p. 68.

61. Richard R. Fagen, "The Carter Administration and Latin America: Business As Usual?" *Foreign Affairs* (Special Issue, 1978), 654; and *U.S. News and World Report,* **89** (November 3, 1980), 57–59.

62. Peter H. Smith, "Argentina: The Uncertain Warriors," *Current History,* **78** (February, 1980), 62. Our discussion of recent developments in Argentina, and of Argentine-American relations, draws heavily from ibid., 62–65, 85–86; David C. Jordan, "Argentina's Military Commonwealth," ibid., **76** (February, 1979), 66–70, 89–90; and David Rock, "Revolt and Repression in Argentina," ibid., **74** (February, 1978), 57–61, 83.

63. Argentine-American relations, focusing upon the Peronist era, are dealt with more fully in Harold F. Peterson, *Argentina and the United States: 1810–1960* (New York: University Publishers, 1964), pp. 427–525.

64. See the assessments of recent conditions in Argentina by James Markham in *New York Times,* May 2, 1982; and Charles Maechling, Jr., "The Argentine Pariah," *Foreign Policy,* **45** (Winter, 1981–82), 69–84.

65. See Fagen, "The Carter Administration and

Latin America," 658–659. Efforts by the Reagan Administration to improve relations with Argentina and other authoritarian regimes are described in Hedrick Smith, "Reagan: What Kind of World Leader?" *The New York Times Magazine,* November 16, 1980, 47–48, 172–177; and *U.S. News and World Report,* **91** (October 26, 1981), 51–52.

66. The causes and major implications of the Falkland Islands conflict are analyzed more fully by Edward Schumacher in *New York Times,* November 12 and December 13, 1981; by Theodore Shabad in ibid., April 18, 1982; by James Markham in ibid., May 2, 1982; and by Bernard Gwertzman and Edward Schumacher in ibid., May 23, 1982. See also the discussion of Argentina's domestic economic and political development in Gary W. Wynia, "The Argentine Revolution Falters," *Current History,* **81** (February, 1982), 74–78, 87–88.

67. President Figueiredo's views are quoted in Robert M. Levine, "Brazil: Democracy without Adjectives," *Current History,* **78** (February, 1980), 49.

68. These and other data on modern Brazil may be found in the State Department's pamphlet, "The United States and Brazil," Bureau of Public Affairs, October, 1979, pp. 1–12. For more detailed discussion on the problems of Brazilian society in the recent period, see Robert M. Levine, "Brazil's Definition of Democracy," *Current History,* **76** (February, 1979), 70–72; and Robert L. Anderson, "Brazil's Military Regime Under Fire," ibid., **74** (February, 1978), 61–65, 87.

69. See the views of James W. Rowe on the Brazilian political system, in the symposium by Robert D. Tomasek, ed., *Latin American Politics: Studies of the Contemporary Scene* (Garden City, N.Y.: Doubleday and Co., 1970), pp. 496–497. Two other essays in this collection provide insight into recent developments in Brazil. See John J. Johnson, "The Brazilian Military," pp. 516–532; and James W. Rowe, "The 1964 Overthrow of President Goulart," pp. 532–539.

70. See the State Department's publication, "The

United States and Brazil," pp. 2–11.

71. For more detailed examination of the implications of the human rights issue in Brazil, see Roger W. Fontaine, "The End of a Beautiful Relationship," *Foreign Policy*, **28** (Fall, 1977), 166–175.

72. Recent internal developments within Brazil are evaluated in Robert M. Levine, "Brazil: The Dimensions of Democratization," *Current History*, **81** (February, 1982), 60–64, 86–87. Analyses of the nuclear energy question as an issue in Brazilian-American relations may be found in Fontaine, "The End of a Beautiful Friendship," 166–175; and George H. Quester, "Nuclear Proliferation in Latin America," *Current History*, **81** (February, 1982), 52–56.

73. A comprehensive analysis of recent Brazilian foreign relations is provided in Wayne A. Selcher, *Brazil's Multilateral Relations: Between First and Third Worlds* (Boulder, Colo.: Westview Press, 1978).

Chapter 15

Asia:
The United States as a Pacific Power

Asian-American Relations in Perspective

Asian Ties After Vietnam

While the Vietnam War was still in progress, a longtime student of Asian affairs observed that "No other continent in the last half-century has experienced more dramatic and substantial changes in power and politics than has Asia." The United States "has had to marshal a succession of responses to these rapid and often bewildering upheavals." Yet despite a record of often conflicting diplomatic statements and actions, "The United States has never abandoned its posture of diplomatic or strategic involvement in the major diplomatic issues of Asia...."[1]

In the same vein, one of America's most experienced diplomats and observers of Asian developments has called attention to the nation's historic involvement in that region by saying:

> ...it was to East Asia that the greatest outpouring of American altruism [in the form of

missionary and educational enterprises] flowed. It was also the area in which Americans fought four major wars—more than anywhere else overseas. The Spanish-American, Pacific [conflict in World War II], Korean and Indochinese wars were conducted in eight East Asian countries.... The United States also intervened militarily in Korea, in China, and in the Russian Far East during the Russian Revolution.

In the light of this background, the United States has been a longtime participant in Asian affairs—a role not likely to be changed fundamentally by the Vietnam War.[2]

At the beginning of the 1980s, another perceptive student of Asian affairs, United States Ambassador to Japan Mike Mansfield, pointed out that when George Washington was President 13 American ships were anchored in the harbor of Canton, China; and for America, the "push since then has been ever westward to the Orient." Mansfield was convinced that

We're out here [in Asia] to stay because it is in our own national interest. We are beginning to see that our country's future lies in the Pacific and East Asia.... Asia as a whole is the biggest and fastest growing market we have.... What we must recognize is that out here—in the Pacific and East Asia—is where it all is, what it is all about, and it is out here where our future lies.[3]

These comments underscored a pivotal reality about American foreign policy that had not fundamentally changed in the post-Vietnam War era. The United States has been involved in the affairs of Asia for some two centuries; and despite the fact that significant changes were made in American diplomacy toward this and other regions after the Vietnam experience, the United States was still —and would almost certainly continue to be—an influential actor on the Asian scene.

America's Historic Ties with Asia

In 1784 the American ship *Empress of China* sailed from New York City to Canton. In the years that followed, the United States developed commercial, cultural, and other ties with Asia. Three episodes in American diplomatic history were especially important in shaping official and public attitudes in the United States toward this region. One of these was Commodore Matthew Perry's "opening" of Japan to the outside world in the 1850s. Perry's visit to Japan climaxed a period of westward continental expansion at home: By 1848, the United States had acquired a 1200-mile Pacific coastline, thereby whetting its interest in the affairs of Asia. The appearance of an American naval expedition in Japanese waters in 1853–1854 at last forced the hermitlike kingdom of Japan to open its doors to Western influence and, more specifically, to trade with the outside world.[4] In the years fol-

lowing Perry's visit, Japan became America's protégé in the Orient.

The second historic landmark in American policy toward Asia was the proclamation of the Open Door policy toward China at the end of the nineteenth century. Preservation of the Open Door remained a professed goal of American foreign policy until World War II. Even after the victory of Communism in China in 1949–1950, part of America's resentment toward the Communist government derived from the fact that Soviet Russia enjoyed a preferential position in Chinese affairs. Peking had abandoned the Open Door policy. Just what was this policy? What were its implications for later American-Asian relations?

Strict accuracy should make us hesitate to call the Open Door a policy at all. In a brilliant diplomatic coup, on March 20, 1900, Secretary of State John Hay announced that he had been able to secure British, German, Japanese, and American concurrence to a pledge which, in the words of a British diplomat, assured that these countries would "maintain free and equal commercial relations for all time in the Orient."[5] More concretely, Hay professed he had secured agreement to the general principle that future economic concessions granted to one of these governments by China must be granted on the same basis to the other governments. The gist of the threefold pledge was that: Each party agreed not to interfere with commercial spheres of influence currently maintained by other powers in China; Chinese tariffs would apply equally to the goods imported from these countries; and harbor dues, railroad charges, and the like, within any power's sphere of influence would be the same for other powers using these facilities.

Actually, Hay had not secured the agreement of the powers to these terms, but after his public announcement the countries involved hesitated to deny their acceptance of what appeared to be a fair, almost idealistic, agreement respecting diplomatic rivalry in China.

Historical scholarship has shown convincingly that the Open Door policy grew out of competing diplomatic ambitions in China, not the least of which were those deriving from America's desire to preserve its access to the China trade. Along with other countries, America was specifically concerned about the ambitions of Czarist Russia, whose advances in the Orient caused widespread alarm among other imperialistic countries, not so much out of abstract concern for the territorial integrity of China as out of fear that Russia's seemingly insatiable diplomatic appetite might eventually close China, Manchuria, and Korea to Western influence.[6] Says Werner Levi of the Open Door: "...every nation sought its own advantage in the policy, not the least its official originator...."[7] In the light of these facts, it may seem strange that over the course of time the Open Door policy came to be widely regarded by the American people as the quintessence of a moral, unselfish foreign policy whose dominant purpose was preservation of Chinese territorial integrity against powerful imperialist forces.

Yet the Open Door policy did nothing whatever to interfere with *existing* foreign concessions in China; nor did it prevent future ones, so long as the countries enumerated above were treated *equally* by China. The Open Door policy said nothing about the *political* inviolability of China. That China itself greeted the Open Door with something less than unrestrained enthusiasm was indicated by the fact that it did not formally adhere to the principle until 1921.[8]

As was also true of the Monroe Doctrine earlier, a key fact about the Open Door policy

was that neither at the time nor later was the United States prepared to take steps to enforce compliance with its provisions. As the years passed after 1900, American foreign policy in the Far East sometimes appeared deliberately designed to undermine the Open Door, perhaps not so much by commission as by omission. The United States was either unwilling or unable to halt progressive Japanese encroachments against the Open Door principle; and willfully or through ignorance, American policies sometimes actually facilitated Japanese expansionism at the expense of the Open Door.[9]

Nevertheless, the Open Door policy was one of the most profound influences which shaped popular attitudes toward China and, more broadly, toward Asia as a whole. Its most lasting consequence was to inculcate the view that in China's relations with the outside world, the United States occupied a preferential position. This idea had a number of important corollaries: that China was a kind of "ward" of the United States and that it looked to Washington for guidance in its internal and external affairs; that China's leaders were highly amenable to American suggestions and leadership in all fields; that China was pro-American in its attitudes and could be counted on to remain America's firm ally in Asia; that China was moving slowly but perceptibly down the path of political democracy and economic stability; that China owed a great "debt of gratitude" to the United States for moral and material help extended to it after 1900, and that this debt would weigh heavily in shaping China's attitudes toward domestic and foreign issues.

In whatever degree Americans were prone to interpret the Open Door policy as evidence of the nation's idealistic impulses, to Chinese minds the key fact about the policy perhaps was that it was formulated and promulgated *during an era of Chinese weakness.* Internally, during most of the period of the Open Door policy China was engaged in domestic political strife greatly weakening the central government's authority. In foreign affairs, it confronted the twofold threat of ongoing European colonialism and (by the 1930s) Japanese encroachments at its expense. The Open Door policy made little effective contribution to the solution of either problem; and (since the United States was unwilling to enforce the policy) it may have in fact *encouraged* Japanese expansionism against China. Many years were required before the American people and their leaders were able to adjust their thinking to the existence of a politically unified and increasingly powerful China that determined to play an influential role in regional and global affairs.

The third landmark in American Far Eastern policy before World War II was the acquisition of the Philippines in 1899. This development climaxed the acquisition of other Pacific islands such as Midway and Hawaii, obtained in 1867 and 1898, respectively. Its new strategic island bases for the first time made the United States a "Pacific power" in the military sense.[10] This fact drew America deeper and deeper into the vortex of great-power rivalry there, ordaining that sooner or later conflict would arise between the United States and the rising Japanese empire, whose diplomatic ambitions led it eventually to challenge the United States and Great Britain for mastery over the eastern Pacific area.

With other territories in Asia—India, Burma, Southeast Asia, Indonesia—the United States had no significant and direct relations at all before World War II. Washington recognized British primacy in India and Burma, French in Indochina, and Dutch in Indonesia. During and after World War II, the United States used its influence to achieve the liquidation of the European colonial systems existing in Asia, as in other regions. According to some commentators, President Franklin D. Roosevelt, for example, viewed the existence of colonialism as a greater threat to international peace and stability than he did the prospect of Soviet expansionism.[11]

In discussing a region as vast and diverse as Asia, some selectivity is necessary. Our analysis, therefore, devotes detailed attention to three important topics: America's relations with the People's Republic of China; United States policy toward Southeast Asia and the Indian subcontinent; and American diplomacy toward the eastern Pacific zone, primarily the Philippines, South Korea, and Japan.

The United States and the People's Republic of China

America and the Chinese Civil War

On October 1, 1949, a new chapter opened in the political history of one of the oldest civilizations on the globe, when the People's Republic of China (PRC) was proclaimed in Peking. For more than 30 years, China had been torn by civil war and factionalism between two rival political movements: the Kuomintang party led by Chiang Kai-shek, and the Chinese Communist party led by Mao Tse-tung. (During that same period, China had been subjected to strife and depredations from two other forces: local "warlords" who often successfully challenged the authority of the central government; and Japan's attempt to subjugate China.) By the 1930s, Chiang Kai-shek became the ostensible ruler of what was often called Nationalist China. Yet the civil war between the followers of Chiang Kai-shek and of Mao Tse-tung continued throughout the 1930s and during the period of World

War II. Both factions sometimes devoted as much time and energy to fighting against each other as they did to opposing the Japanese invader.[12]

Even before the United States was attacked at Pearl Harbor on December 7, 1941, the United States supported the government of China in its efforts to repel Japanese aggression. After Pearl Harbor, relations between the United States and its Chinese ally became even closer. During World War II, the United States supplied large quantities of military and economic assistance to Nationalist China. Owing to President Franklin D. Roosevelt's influence, China was recognized as one of the "Big Five" (along with the Soviet Union, Great Britain, France, and the United States) that had permanent representation on the UN Security Council. Roosevelt also succeeded in getting Stalin's government in Russia to recognize and deal with Chiang Kai-shek's regime as the legitimate government of China.[13]

At the end of World War II, the Chinese civil war erupted anew. The United States made a number of unsuccessful efforts to "mediate" this political conflict; and it sought to persuade Chiang's regime to introduce needed reforms, thereby hopefully reducing the appeal of Communism for the Chinese masses. In some contradiction to this approach, Washington also provided large-scale military and economic aid to Nationalist China, in an effort to assure Chiang's victory against his Communist opponents. These measures, however, failed to avert the political demise of Chiang Kai-shek's regime—which became steadily weakened because of pervasive inefficiency and internal corruption, a series of military defeats at the hands of Mao Tse-tung's guerrilla forces, and an overall deterioration in its base of popular support. In time, Chiang Kai-shek's position on the Chinese mainland became hopeless. After his defeat, Chiang and

his followers evacuated China and took refuge on the island of Formosa (Taiwan), where they established a new regime, called the Republic of China.[14]

For a number of years after 1949, the United States and Taiwan maintained close relations. Many Americans—whose views were forcefully expressed by a powerful and well-financed pressure group known as "the China lobby"—anticipated the collapse of the Communist regime and the "return" of Chiang Kai-shek to the Chinese mainland.[15] A security pact was negotiated between the United States and Taiwan on December 2, 1954; and American naval forces were used to protect Taiwan (and the islands of Quemoy and Matsu) from the hegemony of Mao Tse-tung's Communist regime on the mainland.

A Generation of Sino-American Hostility

To assert that the communization of China was a major diplomatic defeat for the United States would be to engage in understatement. As official and public opinion in the United States viewed it, Mao Tse-tung's victory in the Chinese civil war greatly enhanced the strength of, and danger posed to, the United States by, "international Communism." The ensuing defense treaty (February 14, 1950) between the Soviet Union and the People's Republic of China—signifying the formation of the Sino-Soviet axis—confirmed American fears that Communism had gained a new power base in Asia, to the detriment of the security of non-Communist nations in the region. For a decade or more after 1949, Mao Tse-tung's government engaged in a bitter "Hate America!" campaign, whose main purpose appeared to be unifying the Chinese people against a foreign enemy. Officials in Washington replied in the same vein: The United States refused to recognize the People's Republic of China, and it sought (with relatively little success) to gain the support of its friends and allies for an economic boycott against the Communist regime.

The apex of Sino-American enmity was reached during the Korean War, which erupted on June 25, 1950. Despite repeated warnings from his superiors in Washington, General Douglas MacArthur persisted in leading an advance by American and South Korean troops toward China's border on the Yalu River. Then late in November, Communist Chinese forces launched a massive counterattack, which for several months threatened to drive American and South Korean forces off the peninsula. In time, the military situation became more or less stabilized along the 38th Parallel (the border between North and South Korea); and on July 27, 1953, a cease-fire agreement in the Korean conflict was reached. The fact that American and Chinese military forces fought directly against each other during this contest provided another source of animosity between the two countries.

By the early 1960s, the United States was also becoming increasingly involved in what proved to be one of the most costly and frustrating military encounters in American history—the Vietnam War. Whatever Washington's goals were in this encounter (and they tended to vary from one period to another), one of them was to contain Communism in Southeast Asia. Without substantial support by Moscow and Peking, American officials were convinced, the Communist threat to Southeast Asia would pose no significant danger to regional security. The Chinese threat to India's northern provinces in 1962 provided additional evidence of Chinese expansionism and hostility toward its non-Communist neighbors.

Americans were disturbed by another development: China's growing involvement in the Third World. In other Asian countries (such as Indonesia), and in regions like sub-Saharan Africa, Peking was providing military, economic, and moral support to revolutionary causes. Mao Tse-tung and his followers were persuaded (and this came to be a major source of disagreement between them and Soviet officials) that China's revolutionary model was ideally adapted to the needs of other Third World societies; and for several years, Mao's regime engaged in active efforts to gain converts in other backward societies.[16]

Meanwhile, during most of his tenure as president of the People's Republic of China, the venerable leader, Mao Tse-tung, maintained a highly authoritarian regime under rigid Communist control. Actual or potential opposition to Mao's authority was systematically eliminated; and on a wide variety of subjects, "the thoughts of Mao Tse-tung" served as an infallible guide for the Chinese society in constructing a modern Communist system.

Down to the late 1950s, the official American view was that the Sino-Soviet axis was durable and that its policies were highly unified. A State Department memorandum of 1958 held that "the two partners in the Sino-Soviet alliance clearly realize their mutual dependence and attach great importance to bloc unity vis-à-vis the free world." The memorandum detected "no evidence" for believing "it would be possible to exert leverage on the Peiping regime which might ultimately be successful in weakening or even breaking the bond with Moscow."[17]

For over a decade after the Maoist victory in China, the U.S.S.R. and the PRC maintained close ideological relations, with Peking largely acknowledging Moscow's doctrinal supremacy. Similarly, during this period, the Soviet Union provided economic assistance to its Chinese ally (if never on a scale the

Chinese believed justified). Diplomatically, the United States confronted what appeared to be a monolithic Sino-Soviet axis.

The Split Between Moscow and Peking

Such outward signs of Sino-Soviet solidarity did not, however, conceal a growing rift between the two giants of the Communist world. In retrospect, it is clear now (if it was not apparent at the time) that the death of Stalin in 1953 marked a watershed in Sino-Soviet relations. The period of the mid-1950s served to bring to the surface a number of underlying differences between the two nations which, over the course of time, shattered the cohesiveness of the international Communist movement. A detailed analysis of the deterioration in Sino-Soviet relations—leading in time to the complete dissolution of the alliance between these countries—is beyond our scope. We may allude briefly to a number of long-range and short-run influences that produced this result.

In the first place, Western observers had perhaps always been prone to attribute greater cohesiveness to the Sino-Soviet axis than the facts warranted. As far back as the 1920s, and continuing through the period of World War II, Stalin's government in Russia had exhibited little confidence in Mao Tse-tung and his Communist followers. Mao's forces had achieved their victory on the Chinese mainland *in spite of* impediments and the lack of support given to them by the Kremlin.[18] After Stalin's death in 1953, Mao Tse-tung became the "senior" spokesman for the international Communist movement. If he had been disposed to defer to Stalin's judgment earlier, Mao showed no such inclination in dealing with the Soviet dictator's successors.

Growing ideological differences also fueled the Sino-Soviet dispute. With the passage of time, Peking became increasingly active in challenging Moscow's claim to leadership of the international Communist movement. In diplomatic affairs, for example, Peking accused the Kremlin of losing its revolutionary ardor and of capitulating in the face of superior American power (as in the Cuban Missile Crisis of 1962, discussed more fully in Chapter 14). Toward the Third World, China's rulers believed that their unique peasant-based Maoist system was better adapted to the needs of primitive societies —where agriculture was the dominant economic pursuit—than was the Soviet version of Marxism.[19] For a period of several years also, China's leaders spoke openly of the possibility of global nuclear war and implied that such a development would advance the cause of international Communism. During this same period, Moscow was urging caution in the employment of nuclear weapons and was emphasizing the dangers—for Russian society, no less than for all nations—of a nuclear holocaust.[20]

Behind these and other concrete manifestations of mounting tensions between the two Communist giants lay what may have been the most fundamental cause of antagonism between them. This is what one commentator called "the respective dynamism of the two great Communist states."[21] By the 1960s, an ancient theme had come prominently to the fore in Asia: the rivalry between the Russian and the Chinese empires, each of which sought to expand its influence, sometimes at the expense of the other. As much as any other influence, it was the threat of *Russian* hegemony over China, for example, that prompted the United States to issue the Open Door policy at the turn of the century. As time passed, Chinese officials repeatedly condemned Russian imperialism at their country's expense. Chinese officials have produced old maps showing portions of what they viewed as Chinese territory under Russian control. By contrast, Russians remembered the era of the Mongul Empire in their own history; they were not reassured by Communist China's ruthless annexation of Tibet; and they were mindful of Chinese expansionist moves against India. According to some commentators, Soviet fear of possible Chinese expansionism remains a dominant impulse in Russian foreign policy.[22]

Under his leadership, Mao Tse-tung said on one occasion, "China has stood up!" Among its other connotations, this meant that China intended to change its image of a weak and politically disunified country vulnerable to foreign influence and control. Both regionally and globally, the People's Republic of China intended to become an influential member of the international system whose viewpoints were listened to and respected—by the Soviet Union, no less than by other nations. Their mutual support of North Vietnam during the Vietnam War did not fundamentally reverse the steady deterioration in Sino-Soviet relations. Once that conflict had been resolved, the breach between the two Communist giants perceptibly widened and became seemingly irreparable. In 1977 Communist China openly used military force against the Soviet Union's protégé, North Vietnam; Peking intended to teach the latter a lesson designed to curb its expansionist impulses in Southeast Asia.[23] Almost daily, official sources in Peking denounced Moscow's "hegemonial" tendencies and cautioned weaker societies against Russian influence. By the 1970s, Communist China was also expressing public support for NATO, the European Community, and other movements designed to strengthen the security and cohesion of Western Europe. After the Soviet invasion of Afghanistan late in 1979, Peking joined other countries in denouncing this latest example of Soviet expansionism against a weaker neighbor.

The "Normalization" in Sino-American Relations

Before any fundamental change in the course of Sino-American relations was possible, three preconditions had to be met. One was that a prolonged period of time had to elapse, enabling both countries to outgrow the attitudes of mutual suspicion and antagonism that accompanied the Communist victory in China. Another prerequisite was that China had to break out of the Soviet orbit and pursue its own independent foreign policy goals. Finally, the prolonged and costly war in Vietnam had to be brought to an end. By the early 1970s, all of these requirements had substantially been fulfilled. (If the Vietnam conflict had not officially ended, its outcome was evident, and initial steps had been taken in arriving at a cease-fire agreement.)

Ironically, it was the Republican Administration of President Richard M. Nixon —whose supporters had long condemned earlier Democratic administrations for having "lost China" to Communism—that began the process of normalizing relations between the United States and the People's Republic of China. Early in 1970, Nixon's national security adviser, Henry Kissinger, responded to an overture from Chinese officials in Warsaw presaging a new era in Sino-American relations. As Kissinger later assessed the matter, "For twenty years, US policymakers considered China as a brooding, chaotic, fanatical, and alien realm difficult to comprehend and impossible to sway." Long-standing mutual suspicions between the two countries had made their relations sterile and unproductive. But by the early 1970s, officials in both countries "dimly perceived [the emergence of a] community of interest between the United States and China." For the first time since 1949, Kissinger believed, the leaders of both countries had begun "to regard each other in geopolitical rather than ideological terms."[24]

After a complex series of preliminary meetings and negotiations—including a secret visit to Peking by Kissinger early in July 1971—President Nixon electrified the world by announcing that he intended to visit the People's Republic of China. This move accorded with the Nixon-Kissinger strategy of designing a "new structure of peace" in the post-Vietnam War era, built upon close cooperation among what Nixon called the five great economic superpowers, the United States, Western Europe, Japan, the Soviet Union, and China."* On February 17, 1972, Nixon left Washington for a state visit to mainland China. During this historic visit (the first by an American President to China), discussions between officials of the two countries ranged over a wide variety of major and minor issues—from American and Chinese assessments of Soviet intentions, to "ping-pong diplomacy" and other forms of cultural contact between the two countries, to expanded Sino-American economic and commercial relations.[25]

Several fundamental questions of mutual interest were at the forefront of Sino-American concern. A dominant one was Chinese and American assessments of Soviet diplomatic behavior and the proper response to it. Confronted with ongoing hostility from Moscow, and with a formidable Soviet military machine along its more than 4500-mile border, China looked to American power to counterbalance the superior might of its principal adversary. If Peking did not propose, or even realistically expect, that the United

States was prepared to become a formal military *ally* of China against the Soviet Union, it hoped that a normalization of Sino-American relations would serve as a potent deterrent to Russian expansionist and other moves at China's expense.

Despite their desire to improve relations with China, officials in Washington were mindful of two paramount realities. As we observed in Chapter 10, much more than Peking, Washington was also committed to preserving and strengthening détente between the superpowers. After the traumatic Vietnam War experience, few Americans were disposed to assume new and costly foreign policy commitments—least of all, one that might commit them to a new conflict in some remote part of Asia as an ally of China against the Soviet Union.

Another significant question confronting Chinese and American officials—and historically, a source of deep anxiety in the Chinese mind—was Japan's emergence as a financial giant and the possibility that it would embark once again upon an aggressive military path. We shall examine the question of Japan's growing military power at a later stage. It suffices to emphasize here that, as Peking became increasingly concerned about Moscow's intentions, Chinese officials supported close Japanese-American military relations.

A related question in Sino-American discussions was America's future involvement in Asian affairs after the Vietnam War. Despite their earlier opposition to American intervention in Southeast Asia, Chinese officials left little doubt that they counted upon an active and influential role by the United States in Asian affairs in the post-Vietnam War era. In opposition to some critics of America's involvement in the war, Peking did *not* call for or seek an American withdrawal from this region.

For over two decades, the most difficult and controversial issue confronting the United

*It is an interesting commentary that, although Americans and others sometimes believed modern China ranked as a powerful nation, Chinese officials disclaimed that idea. Chinese Foreign Minister Chou En-lai, for example, rejected the assertion that his country had become a powerful voice in international affairs. Some American officials believed that it was mainly China's *weakness* that prompted Peking to seek a rapprochement with the United States. See Henry Kissinger, *White House Years* (Boston: Little, Brown and Co., 1979), p. 749.

States and Communist China was the future of Taiwan and of America's close military and diplomatic ties with it; and the question had lost none of its complexity with the passage of time. In the Chinese view, Taiwan was—and always had been—an integral part of China, subject to the authority of the government on the mainland. During President Nixon's visit, this traditional Chinese position was reiterated to American officials. Chinese spokesmen left no doubt that their determination to "liberate" Taiwan from the regime of Chiang Kai-shek and his followers remained undiminished. Successive American chief executives had also reiterated the position of the United States on the Taiwan question. Washington viewed the Republic of China on Formosa as an independent, non-Communist government, with which it maintained cordial ties, formal diplomatic relations, and firm military links (expressed in the American-Taiwan defense treaty of 1955). As in the past, American officials opposed any attempt by Communist China to liberate Taiwan by force, and for many years, the American Navy had been prepared to enforce this policy. During President Nixon's visit, officials of the two countries thoroughly reviewed the Taiwan question; reiterated their respective positions; and in effect "agreed to disagree" about their viewpoints toward it. In brief, the troublesome Taiwan issue was left officially unresolved. Yet Chinese and American officials arrived at a kind of tacit understanding about the question: While not abandoning its ultimate goal, Peking would not attempt to impose its authority upon Taiwan by force; while Washington would gradually loosen its ties with the Republic of China in the interests of a rapprochement with Communist China.* As a

presidential candidate, Ronald Reagan was outspokenly critical of America's "abandonment" of its old ally, Nationalist China. Yet no evidence existed that the Reagan Administration was prepared to reverse the pattern of normalization in Sino-American relations because of this issue.

In Kissinger's words, the Nixon visit to China signified nothing less than a "revolution" in Sino-American relations. As a result of it, there evolved "a relationship in which America and China reinforced each other while almost never coordinating [their diplomatic and military] tactics explicitly."[26] Yet (as our discussion of America's relations with Israel in Chapter 12 emphasized), a *de facto* entente or alliance of this kind can often be stronger than one that is expressed in a formal defense treaty or friendship pact between nations.

The Nixon-Kissinger team had laid the foundations for a formal resumption of Sino-American relations, and that process was consummated by the Carter Administration. During the 1970s, the United States and the

---

*In effect, this approach to the Taiwan question embodied what was sometimes called a "Japanese solution" to it. In 1972, Japan created a new organization, called the Interchange Association, to represent its interests in Taiwan, after Tokyo recognized the People's Republic of China. In its essence, the Japanese formula involved ending formal *diplomatic* ties with Taiwan, while maintaining commercial and other kinds of relations with the Republic of China. Experience with this Japanese approach over several years' time indicated that it had worked to the reasonable satisfaction of the parties to it. Peking apparently accommodated itself to this ingenious solution to the problem and, during the same period, improved its own relations with Japan. See Henry Scott-Stokes, in *New York Times,* December 20, 1978. At the same time, the Chinese government remained extremely sensitive about the Taiwan question, as the Reagan Administration discovered early in 1982 when Washington announced the sale of military equipment to the Republic of China. Officials in Peking objected vocally and strenuously to this sale, cautioning Washington that it might affect the future of Sino-American relations. Spokesmen for the PRC were especially forthright in emphasizing that, in their view, Taiwan was *not* an independent nation; nor had mainland China's claims to title over the island in any way been abandoned. See the analysis by Christopher S. Wren in *New York Times,* April 17, 1982.

People's Republic of China drew closer in nearly all spheres, such as cultural and scientific exchange, expanding trade relations, and diplomatic cooperation. On January 1, 1979, both capitals announced that formal diplomatic relations would be resumed between the two governments, thereby ending some 30 years of American "nonrecognition" of the Communist victory in the Chinese civil war. Concurrently, the Carter Administration announced that the American defense pact with Taiwan would be allowed to lapse. Despite some opposition in the Senate (and unsuccessful attempts to have the federal courts declare the President's actions unconstitutional), President Carter's decision was accepted by Congress and by the American people.[27]

The Value of the "China Card"

For Presidents Richard M. Nixon, who began the process, and Jimmy Carter, who consummated it, the "normalization" of Sino-American relations was viewed as a notable accomplishment of their respective administrations. This development was unquestionably one of the most momentous changes affecting the distribution of global power since World War II. More specifically, Washington's acquisition of a "China card" had major implications for several dimensions of American diplomacy. If no formal alliance existed between the United States and the People's Republic of China, growing collaboration in a variety of spheres characterized their relationships. The rapprochement between the two nations was an evident diplomatic setback for the Soviet Union, signifying the triumph of "national Communism" over Moscow's long-standing contention that it was the sole depository and interpreter of Marxist ideology. On a wide front—from common opposition to new expansionist moves by North Vietnam in Southeast Asia, to resistance to Soviet hege-

mony in the Persian Gulf area, to bolstering the NATO defense system against the Warsaw Pact—the United States and the PRC had common objectives. After 1979, intensive efforts were made by officials of both countries to "consult" on questions of mutual concern and to coordinate their diplomatic activities on a range of outstanding issues.[28] In August 1979, Vice-President Walter Mondale called attention to the emergence of close political and diplomatic ties between the two countries. Mondale asserted that "any nation which seeks to weaken or isolate [China] in world affairs assumes a stance counter to American interests."[29]

A second vital dimension of Sino-American relations was strategic-military affairs. As Washington was careful to emphasize to Moscow, the Sino-American rapprochement had *not* resulted in a military alliance between the two countries; nor was the United States interested in intensifying the conflict between these two Communist power centers. Policy makers in Washington were fully cognizant that a condition of open warfare between the Soviet Union and China would threaten the peace and security of Asia—and in time it might involve the United States in a destructive global conflict with the Soviet Union. American officials were equally aware, however, of certain strategic-military advantages from cultivating closer relations with the People's Republic of China; and these incentives were influential in changing the course of Sino-American relations.

In general terms, we may summarize these inducements by saying that the normalization of Sino-American relations created at least a possibility that had long caused deep anxieties for Soviet military planners: the risk that in any future military conflict, the Soviet Union would be required to fight a "two-front war" against NATO in Europe and against Chinese, American, and perhaps other forces in Asia. The strategic realities underlying closer Sino-American relations were high-lighted by the findings of a report by the Rand Corporation late in 1979. This study, entitled "Asian Security in the 1980s," concluded that Soviet power was growing in the region and that in the years ahead the security of several Asian states would be increasingly jeopard-ized by the U.S.S.R. and its clients (like North Vietnam). The ongoing Soviet naval buildup also posed a threat to the security of Asia's sea lanes. In several countries—notably, South Korea, Taiwan, the Philippines, and Thailand—existing or potential "leadership crises" would offer tempting opportunities for direct or indirect Soviet intervention. On the basis of this projection, the study urged that the United States and the People's Republic of China engage in even closer strategic-mili-tary cooperation in the future.[30]

Statements by officials in Peking left no doubt that Chinese authorities shared these apprehensions about Soviet policy in Asia and other regions. Chinese spokesmen had little faith in the future of Soviet-American détente or in the ability of the United States to induce more moderate Russian behavior by supplying Moscow with grain, computers, or other items badly needed by the Soviet state. Chinese of-ficials also doubted that a change in the Soviet political leadership would bring about a les-sening of Russia's inherently expansionist im-pulses. By the early 1980s, the Sino-Soviet frontier remained one of the most volatile regions on the globe.[31]

Strengthening China's military position to counter the growing Soviet threat would be no easy undertaking. China's principal mili-tary asset was its army of some 3.6 million troops—augmented by a vast military man-power pool drawn from its population of 1 billion or more people (four times the size of the Soviet population). That China's armed forces were capable of mounting an effective military campaign had been convincingly dem-

onstrated during the Korean War. (Yet it should also be noted that in that contest, American-led United Nations forces operated under certain "restraints" against their Com-munist enemy—such as Washington's prohi-bition of the use of nuclear weapons, and re-strictions against air attacks directly upon Chinese bases—that would almost certainly *not* impede Soviet forces in any military clash with Chinese troops. In their attempt to teach North Vietnam "a lesson" in 1977, China's armed forces also had only limited success.)

Despite its enormous manpower pool, China's military needs were also vast. Com-pared with the Soviet and American military arsenals, the Chinese defense establishment was deficient in almost all categories of mod-ern weapons—from rockets and missiles to vehicles capable of transporting large numbers of troops to vulnerable border areas. Peking had a small stockpile of nuclear weapons (including a limited number of short- and inter-mediate-range missiles), with which to oppose hundreds of modern missiles and other forms of nuclear armaments possessed by Russian forces along the Sino-Soviet border. China had the third-largest navy in the world, but it was designed primarily for use in coastal waters, and it lacked any significant nuclear capabili-ty. There was almost no possibility, therefore, that the Chinese navy could successfully con-test modern Soviet seapower in the Pacific region. Perhaps the most serious deficiency of the Chinese military machine lay in the realm of airpower. Although China had over 4500 combat and transport aircraft, Peking's air force consisted mainly of outmoded planes, many of which had been acquired from the U.S.S.R. during the period of the Sino-Soviet alliance.[32] In nearly all categories, Chinese military forces were inferior to their Soviet counterparts.

Chinese military weakness vis-à-vis the U.S.S.R. meant that officials in Peking were keenly interested in playing the "American card" to augment their military strength.* Early in September 1980, for example, the Chinese government reiterated its desire to acquire advanced American weapons—a move which Washington has thus far opposed. Fearing the implications for détente (as well as its repercussions for American public opinion), officials in Washington remained reluctant to inaugurate an extensive program of arms aid for China. By 1980, however, the Carter Administration had agreed to supply China with certain ancillary (or "nonlethal") military requirements. Despite his earlier misgivings about the normalization of Sino-American relations, President Ronald Reagan was likely to continue this process. Reagan was preoccupied with the military imbalance between the United States and the Soviet Union; and he was determined to "restore the margin of safety" to the United States in its position as a superpower. In response to what he perceived as a threatening pattern of Soviet behavior in Asia and other regions, in the words of one commentator, Reagan came to visualize China "as a potential partner in a three-cornered strategic poker game with the Soviet Union."[33]

After the death of Mao Tse-tung in 1976, his successors embarked upon "the four modernizations"—an explicit acknowledgment by the regime that China was still one of the most backward societies on the globe.† Despite its impressive progress since 1949 in spheres like land reform and an overall improvement in agricultural productivity, health and sanitation programs, and education, China's population of around 1 billion people (one-quarter of the human race) produced an annual Gross National Product of approximately $400 billion annually, yielding a per capita yearly income of around $400. (China thus had an annual per capita GNP of approximately one-tenth of that existing in the Soviet Union, one-twentieth of America's, and less than half of South Korea's.) Some 75 percent of the Chinese population is still engaged in agriculture (versus 5 percent in the United States)—yet the Chinese society has become increasingly dependent upon the outside world to supply needed food imports. With the Chinese population expected to reach 1.5 billion by the year 2000, if most of its modernization plans succeed (and that outcome is not of course assured), China will attain a Gross National Product approximately equal

*Early in 1980, officials at NATO headquarters in Brussels became convinced that China's relative military position vis-à-vis the Soviet Union was deteriorating. China faced the prospect of "military encirclement" by superior Soviet forces—as indicated by evidence of Moscow's ability to provide vast quantities of military aid to North Vietnam; by the ongoing buildup of modern Russian forces along the Sino-Soviet border; and by Soviet air superiority over its Chinese rival. In addition, Soviet naval forces in the Pacific were being steadily expanded and modernized; and new port facilities had been obtained in Indochina and in the southern Kurile Islands. Accordingly, one report found, Moscow's widening lead *in conventional weapons alone* might reduce the necessity for the Kremlin to rely upon nuclear armaments in the event of a war with China. See Drew Middleton, in *New York Times*, May 22, 1980.

†The announced goal for the "four modernizations" was to overcome Chinese backwardness in agriculture, industry, science and technology, and in the military sphere. Chinese officials emphasized that military modernization enjoyed the lowest priority among these four goals. This policy decision had two major implications: It meant that China would remain militarily inferior to the Soviet Union for many years; and it signified that China would largely be dependent upon foreign countries to supply it with modern weapons and ancillary military equipment. In support of its modernization drive, the Chinese government proposed to allocate the equivalent of some $600 billion between 1978 and 1985. See *U.S. News and World Report*, **86** (January 8, 1979), 15–18

to 15 percent of America's in the year 1985.[34] Even Chinese officials, therefore, conceded that the country's quest for modernization was likely to be long and difficult, with no guarantee of success.[35]

To the minds of Chinese officials, the United States had a key role to play in promoting its economic development. As one Chinese spokesman explained in the early 1980s, American technological assistance, trade, and investment were needed in three vital areas of the Chinese economic system: in the "technological renovation" of some 400,000 business enterprises; in developing China's vast oil, coal, and other energy resources; and to raise productivity in medium and small manufacturing establishments, in order to improve China's export earnings. Chinese officials urged Washington to translate declarations of friendship for China into prompt and generous assistance required to achieve national development and modernization.[36]

Officials in Washington were responsive to China's needs. The Carter Administration, for example, entered into new commercial agreements with the PRC, and the Export-Import Bank provided Peking with a $2 billion credit to purchase needed imports. Trade between the United States and China (which began in 1972) was growing; late in 1980, for example, the two countries signed an agreement calling for Chinese purchases of from 6 to 8 million tons of American wheat annually.[37] Enticed by the prospect of "one billion new customers," many American business firms sought opportunities to expand their sales in the Chinese market for products like farm machinery, food processing equipment, oil drilling and refining equipment, and many other items. Yet even with assistance provided by the United States, other countries, and international lending institutions, Peking's ability to pay for a rising volume of imports is likely to remain extremely limited.*

On balance, there could hardly be any question that America's possession of a "China card" greatly strengthened its diplomatic hand in Asia and on a global basis. Yet in the euphoric atmosphere engendered by the normalization in Sino-American relations, experienced students of Chinese behavior cautioned against unrestrained optimism about this development. Too often in earlier eras, Americans had been prone to romanticize the nature and durability of their historic ties with China—especially China's receptivity to American diplomatic guidance. One of America's leading students of Chinese history, John K. Fairbank, for example, cautioned that the "new China" was likely to follow America's precedent down to World War II: *Domestic problems* would be the dominant concern of the Chinese society for many years to come. Moreover, Americans needed to be mindful that the government of China was induced to normalize relations with the United States *primarily to serve its own internal and external interests,* such as strengthening its position vis-à-vis the Soviet Union and achieving other foreign policy objectives. The image of the "China card" held by American policy makers—available to be played when the interests of the United States so dictated —tends to obscure that fact. Even after normalization, some aspects of Chinese and American policy were not fully congruent;

---

*During the period of the Sino-American grain purchase agreement referred to above, the United States was already selling China approximately $2 billion more in goods and services than it was buying from China. This fact highlighted one of the main impediments to expanded Sino-American trade, discussed more fully in Chapter 6: the Chinese society's limited purchasing power to buy foreign-produced goods. See Bernard Gwertzman, in *New York Times,* October 10, 1980.

and what might be called the "world view" of both societies still differed fundamentally in a number of crucial respects.*

The Vietnam War and Its Aftermath

The Vietnam War

For some 30 years—from the period of World War II until the early 1970s—Indochina was

*Thus one informed student of Chinese affairs has elaborated these caveats about the normalization of Sino-American relations by emphasizing several facts about the internal and external policies of the country. If, for example, contemporary China has gravitated away from a "totalitarian" regime, it clearly remains an "authoritarian" one, in which the Communist rulers use the power of the state forcefully, and with little effective restraint, to achieve their objectives. Chinese viewpoints remain marked by such tendencies as "hyper-nationalism," "military-mindedness," and "heavy-handed self-righteousness" in dealing with external questions. In their meetings with American officials, Chinese leaders evinced little interest in concepts like "peace"; they tended to emphasize the continuance of conflict among nations and the necessity for strong national defense. Statements by Chinese officials reflected belief "in the verities of nationalism and the acceptability of using force in resolving foreign policy issues." As in the traditional Chinese distinction between themselves and the "barbarians" living in other countries, "the overall gap between China and 'non-China' is still vast" in the outlook of modern China. See Ross Terrill, "China Enters the 1980s," *Foreign Affairs,* **58** (Spring, 1980), 920–935; and John K. Fairbank, "The New China and the American Connection," *Foreign Affairs,* **51** (October, 1972), 31–44. Similarly, in 1982 another informed commentator on Sino-American relations cautioned about several "myths" prevalent in American attitudes toward China. One of these was the idea that mainland China was becoming a "modern" and powerful nation. Prospects for this development remained extremely remote. Another myth was the assumption that the United States could depend upon the PRC as a reliable friend. In their desire to improve relations with the United States, Chinese officials "are merely applying a united-front strategy [against the common Soviet antagonist], which they could change at any time." See the views of Ramon H. Myers, *New York Times,* January 22, 1982.

gripped by violent political upheaval and warfare involving foreign powers.† The first stage in this cycle of conflicts was a long-standing contest between the government of France and Indochinese nationalist groups—whose leader in time was the Marxist Ho Chi Minh. At the end of World War II, France endeavored to reimpose its colonial authority over Indochina. From their base in North Vietnam, Ho Chi Minh's forces successfully resisted the reestablishment of French colonialism; and after the decisive battle at Dien Bien Phu in May 1954, the French government abandoned its effort to maintain its colonial system in Southeast Asia.

Beginning with the Eisenhower Administration in the mid-1950s, the United States assumed a commitment to assist officials in Saigon in protecting the security of South Vietnam against Communist-led efforts to unify Indochina under North Vietnam's auspices. Although President Eisenhower and later chief executives repeatedly stated that the government and people of South Vietnam must take primary responsibility for maintaining their security, in time the United States found itself drawn deeper and deeper into the

†France succeeded in imposing a unified colonial rule over Vietnam in 1887. French rule continued over the country until 1940, when Vietnam was conquered by Japan. At the end of World War II (as occurred also in Korea), Vietnam became another divided country, when the 17th Parallel became the boundary between North and South Vietnam. This line was expected to be "temporary," and all parties to the conflicts that gripped Indochina in the years that followed agreed that Vietnam ought to be united under a single governmental administration. Ho Chi Minh and his Communist followers insisted that, after they defeated the French in 1954, he was the "recognized" leader of the Vietnamese people. South Vietnam, and its principal ally, the United States, demanded that a new government of Indochina be chosen by free elections, conducted without hindrance in both South and North Vietnam.

conflict in Southeast Asia. The American military presence in Vietnam was expanded under the Kennedy Administration; and under the Johnson Administration well over 500,000 American troops were engaged in the Vietnam War (with another 300,000 stationed in other parts of Asia).[38]

It is unnecessary for our purpose to review in detail the steps by which the United States became trapped in what was often called the "Vietnam quagmire"—by many criteria, the most frustrating and traumatic military encounter in the history of the American Republic. By a process of what one observer has called "incrementalism" (or taking a series of discrete and isolated steps over time), by the mid-1960s the United States found itself with an escalating military obligation; ultimately Washington assumed the primary responsibility for the security of Southeast Asia.[39] As the nation's military commitment in Vietnam mounted, so did internal opposition to the Vietnam War within the United States; and only a handful of foreign countries was prepared to approve (much less support) America's effort to prevent a Communist victory in Southeast Asia. Within South Vietnam, a succession of political regimes was unable to eliminate corruption and to retain the loyalty of the people—essential steps in achieving victory over the Communist adversary.

By the end of the Johnson Administration, it had become evident to impartial observers at home and abroad that a victory by North Vietnam and its foreign supporters was inevitable; no course that was politically acceptable to the United States (such as the employment of nuclear weapons against North Vietnam) was likely to change the outcome. After a number of false starts and prolonged negotiating sessions among the parties to the conflict, the Vietnam War was officially terminated on January 27, 1973, al-though hostilities continued in Indochina for several months after that date.[40] Despite intensive military and diplomatic efforts by the United States to prevent it, the war resulted in a victory for Communist forces in Southeast Asia, under the leadership of North Vietnam. As we shall see, in the years that followed, Hanoi's efforts to impose its hegemony upon Laos and Cambodia could be viewed as the next stage in the prolonged Vietnam conflict.

Inside and outside the United States, the outcome of the war in Southeast Asia was widely perceived as a graphic American diplomatic defeat. As a result of the Vietnam experience, President Richard M. Nixon publicly wondered whether the United States was becoming a "pitiful, helpless giant" in global affairs. Outspoken critics of America's role in the war, like Senator J. William Fulbright (Democrat of Arkansas), were certain that America was "a crippled giant" whose foreign policies were actuated primarily by "the arrogance of power." Other commentators likened America's position to the fate of Gulliver in Jonathan Swift's classical allegory: Uncle Sam had apparently been rendered impotent by North Vietnam, Cuba, and the other "Lilliputians" of the international system.[41] Meanwhile, during and after the Vietnam War (as was emphasized in Chapter 5), Soviet power and influence were rising. This fact reinforced assertions that American power was in eclipse; and it led to dire predictions about the diplomatic consequences of the military imbalance between the superpowers.

The "Post-Vietnam Syndrome" in American Policy

The agonizing Vietnam War episode had a profound impact upon public and official American attitudes toward the outside world. For a period of several years, "the lessons of Vietnam" were at the forefront of the national consciousness. For the American people and their leaders, avoiding "another Vietnam" became a kind of national obsession, as the United States faced new challenges in Asia, the Middle East, Africa, and other settings. Neo-isolationist currents powerfully affected American thinking. As in the old pre-World War II isolationist frame of mind, Americans turned inward, to concentrate upon domestic problems, on the premise that the solution of problems at home should take priority over massive involvement in external problems.[42] After the agony of Vietnam, some Americans doubted that the nation could achieve *any* worthwhile purpose in foreign affairs.

The "post-Vietnam syndrome" had manifold implications for American diplomacy, many of which were analyzed in our earlier discussion of public opinion (Chapter 8). Here, it is possible only to allude to some of its more significant and lasting consequences. In the sphere of internal policy making, for example, the war led to a continuing internal debate over the respective roles of executive and legislative leaders in the formulation of external policy—symbolized perhaps by the concept of the "imperial presidency." For many Americans, the dominant lesson of the Vietnam encounter was the growth of "uncontrolled" presidential power in foreign affairs and the need to restrain it, primarily by giving Congress a more effective foreign policy role. Consequently, the 1970s witnessed an intense struggle between the White House and Congress over control of the foreign policy process.[43] For perhaps a majority of legislators, a primary lesson of Vietnam was that Congress should function as a full partner with the executive branch in the formulation and administration of American foreign policy. (We have already assessed that tendency, along with the major obstacles to achieving the goal, in Chapter 7.) If the tide of congressional activism and independence had begun

to wane by the early 1980s, after Vietnam Congress would be unlikely to play the "passive" role in foreign affairs that had preceded that contest.[44]

The other realm in which the "post-Vietnam syndrome" was evident was in American public opinion, as it related to the nation's overseas responsibilities. As many commentators have observed, the Vietnam experience shattered the "anti-Communist consensus" that had undergirded American foreign policy since the end of World War II. A decade after the end of that struggle, a new consensus on the principles that ought to guide the United States in world affairs had not emerged—and some commentators doubted that substantial public agreement upon the nation's diplomatic role would be achieved in the near future. In Southeast Asia, American military power, ingenuity, and know-how had dramatically failed to achieve the nation's foreign policy objectives. Inevitably, this fact had a shattering effect upon American attitudes, morale, and self-confidence in the foreign policy field.

For an extended period after Vietnam, therefore, the American outlook toward foreign affairs generally—and toward Asian questions particularly—was characterized by confusion, self-doubt, uncertainty, and soul-searching. Had the most powerful nation in history now entered into a period of "decline" on the stage of world history? Should the nation abandon the idea of serving as "the policeman of the world" or even selected regions of it? After Vietnam, what principles should now guide the application of American power in other regions?

Some commentators were convinced that in the post-Vietnam War period, the Soviet Union had embarked upon a direct "challenge" to the American position in Asia. From Afghanistan eastward, through the Indian Ocean, to the Sea of Japan, Moscow appeared to be engaged in a formidable military buildup.

In Asia, said a spokesman for the Association of Southeast Asian Nations, confidence in American power and leadership was steadily being eroded. To the minds of many Asians, "The American government appears to be inert to the extent of surrendering political leadership and initiative to the Soviet Union." Throughout Asia, the "margin of confidence" in American power and influence had declined significantly. An official of the government of Singapore similarly informed Americans that the global contest between the United States and the Soviet Union would likely be decided in Asia. In this arena in the years ahead, "the decisive battles for world leadership would be waged." Americans must respond effectively to the Soviet challenge, or else "a Pax Sovietica is a high probability in the [1980s]." Asians might be compelled to "settle for" a Soviet hegemony, if fundamental changes were not made in American policy toward the region.[45]

We have already examined one crucial dimension of the challenge—recent Sino-American relations. In the remainder of the chapter, let us focus upon other important aspects of the problem.

Southeast Asia in the Post-Vietnam Period

Once the Vietnam War had ended, for a brief period some American officials and students of Asian affairs anticipated a rapid "normalization" in relations between the United States and North Vietnam, such as had occurred between the United States and its principal enemies, Germany and Japan, after World War II. On several occasions during the Carter and Reagan administrations, officials in Hanoi clearly indicated their interest in better relations with the United States. Internally, Vietnam faced critical economic problems and shortages—induced by a combination of wartime devastation, large-scale emigration of skilled workers and professional groups, Com-

munist mismanagement, and an extremely high level of military spending. In company with other Third World societies, Communist Vietnam was experiencing a severe food shortage (in the solution of which its Soviet mentor could provide minimal assistance). Hanoi was also finding its close ties with the Soviet Union financially disadvantageous, as well as politically questionable. Having defeated French and American efforts to control the political destiny of Southeast Asia, the intensely nationalistic leaders of Vietnam did not relish the idea that their country had now become a dependency of the Soviet Union.

Yet two constraints hindered a "normalization" of Vietnamese-American relations after the war in Southeast Asia. One of these was the fact that Washington clearly gave priority to improving relations with the People's Republic of China, whose government was deeply concerned about the growing Soviet presence in Vietnam. The other obstacle to better Vietnamese-American relations was Hanoi's expansive foreign policy at the expense of its neighbors, Laos and Cambodia. As Vietnam extended its hegemony over these countries—plunging Southeast Asia once more into a bloody conflict—thousands of refugees left the region. An untold number of these "boat people" died at sea; many thousands of others had to be given sanctuary in the United States and other countries, while the Communist regime in Hanoi appeared to be indifferent to their plight. In the post-Vietnam War era, the United States played no direct role in containing Vietnam's expansionism. After the normalization in Sino-American relations, Washington was largely content to let its Chinese friends assume that burden (and the provision of American military equipment to China was designed in part to serve that end). For their part, a decade or more after the end of the Vietnam conflict, the Communist rulers of Vietnam continued to misread American sentiment. Few Americans showed any inclination to become massively "involved" again in the affairs of Southeast Asia; nor were they prepared to cooperate with a Marxist regime that maintained a ruthless regime at home and that threatened the security of its weaker neighbors.[46]

The continued upheaval in Southeast Asia created a serious security problem for one of America's longtime Asian allies: Thailand. Traditionally, in foreign affairs successive Thai governments have followed what might be called a "bamboo strategy"—of bending in the face of adverse winds—in their relations with neighboring countries. Both before and after the Vietnam conflict, Bangkok demonstrated a remarkable facility for adapting its policies to the existing realities confronting it abroad; and by doing so, it has thus far managed to maintain Thailand's independence.[47] If, in the assessment of Thai officials, the prevailing reality in the years ahead is dominant North Vietnamese power in Southeast Asia, on the basis of experience we may anticipate that Thailand will again adjust its policies to that state of affairs.

The Indian Subcontinent

Conditioning Factors in American Policy

The Indian subcontinent contains three of the most populous countries on the globe: the Republic of India (with an estimated population of 700 million people); the Islamic Republic of Pakistan (with a population of some 80 million people); and, the newest state to be created in the region, the People's Republic of Bangladesh (containing around 90 million people). Collectively, these countries contain approximately one-fifth of the human race.*

At the same time, India, Pakistan, and Bangladesh epitomize the concept of "less developed countries," where traditionally poverty has been endemic. In these societies, a multitude of entrenched problems—religious beliefs inhibiting progress, attachment to traditional ways of life, the lack of key raw materials and other resources, low levels of agricultural production, and above all perhaps the population explosion—impedes modernization and produces ongoing political ferment. Each country is of course different. Although Pakistan has the highest per capita Gross National Product (some $200 annually, versus $140 annually for India and $85 annually for Bangladesh), by many criteria India has the best long-range prospects for economic development. By contrast, Bangladesh—whose potential for development is severely limited—is sometimes described as an economic "basket case."

Since the mid-eighteenth century, the Indian subcontinent formed part of the British Empire. Viewed in London as "the Star of the Empire," India was considered the most important British possession; and after India gained its independence (on July 18, 1947), the country became an influential member of the British-sponsored Commonwealth of Nations. The process of decolonization on the Indian subcontinent was prolonged, often bitter, and left a reservoir of ill-will and suspicion that would likely affect the political destiny of the region for generations to come. After initially refusing to do so, at length the British government accepted the demands of India's Moslem community that the subcontinent be "partitioned" into Moslem-controlled Pakistan and Hindu-controlled India. The hope was (and events revealed it to be vain) that this act

---

*The new nation of Bangladesh will receive minimum attention in this chapter. For more extended discussion of its emergence and problems, see M. Rashiduzzaman, "The Political Evolution of Bangladesh," *Current History,* **76** (April, 1979), 164–168. American foreign aid efforts in the country are assessed (very negatively) in Donald F. McHenry and Kai Bird, "Food Bungle in Bangladesh," *Foreign Policy,* **27** (Summer, 1977), 72–89.

would bring an end to the religiously based "communal" strife that had frequently engulfed the Indian society in the past.[48]

As a result of the division of India, enmity and suspicion—interspersed with periods of armed conflict—have existed between India and Pakistan. Rival claims to the former princely state of Kashmir (formally annexed by India) have served as an ongoing incendiary issue between them. New Delhi's massive support of the secessionist movement in East Pakistan in 1971 (creating the new state of Bangladesh) added fuel to existing animosities between them.

During the period of British colonialism, the United States had no official relations with India, although for many years before 1947 official and public American opinion was sympathetic to the cause of Indian independence. As we have seen in other contexts, during World War II President Franklin D. Roosevelt brought pressure to bear upon the European colonial powers to relinquish their dependencies. The anticolonial position of the United States government contributed in some measure to the achievement of independence by India and Pakistan.[49]

The United States and India in the Postwar Era

After independence, India possessed two characteristics inducing American policy makers to maintain friendly relations with it. The Republic of India ranked next to China as the second most populous nation on the globe. Even more significantly, under Mahatma Gandhi and his successor, Jawaharlal Nehru, India emerged as the world's largest democracy. To policy makers in the United States, India provided a democratic model for other Third World countries vis-à-vis Communist China and other authoritarian or totalitarian systems.[50] As time passed—with one Third World country after another adopting some

kind of authoritarian government—India's commitment to the democratic ideal was exceptional.

Largely for these reasons, India became one of the largest recipients of American foreign assistance. In Washington's view, India served as a source of stability in Asia and a voice of "moderation" in the deliberations of Third World.[51] For their part, Indian leaders like Prime Minister Nehru frequently expressed their admiration of, and indebtedness to, the American democratic tradition; and their criticisms of American foreign policy were often directed at trying to get policy makers in Washington to be guided by it in their relations with other countries.

Despite such sources of affinity between the two countries, by the mid-1960s Indian-American relations began to deteriorate. From New Delhi's perspective, several aspects of American policy elicited deep concern. At the top of the list was India's long-standing apprehension about America's ties with, and support of, Pakistan. Unlike India—whose conception of diplomatic non-alignment precluded participation in alliance systems sponsored by the superpowers —Pakistan was a formal military ally of the United States through its membership in the Southeast Asia Treaty Organization (SEATO). Despite Washington's avowals of friendship with India—and repeated assurances by the United States that the alliance with Pakistan was not directed against New Delhi's interests—in recent years official and public opinion within India has become increasingly anti-American in tone. In the military encounter between the two countries in 1971, Pakistan *used* American-supplied weapons against Indian forces—indicating to Indians that despite its reassurances, the United States has little effective control over the weapons furnished to Pakistan and other countries.

The normalization of relations between the United States and China that began in the early 1970s also created anxieties within India. Once again, the United States appeared to be "tilting" toward one of India's traditional rivals in its Asian diplomacy. Indian apprehensions about American goals in the Persian Gulf-Indian Ocean area were revived after the Soviet invasion of Afghanistan late in 1979. As usual, criticisms of Soviet hegemonial behavior from New Delhi were restrained. Prime Minister Indira Gandhi stated publicly that an even more ominous threat to Indian security was posed by "the greater involvement of all powers in the Indian Ocean." By the early 1980s, officials in Washington feared that India would draw closer to the Soviet Union in the years ahead.[52]

Other issues have also produced disaffection in India with American foreign policy. With many Third World nations, India has been chagrined by the declining volume of American foreign assistance (discussed in greater detail in Chapter 6). Viewing their country as "another Brazil"—as a nation that has vast potential for economic development —Indian officials are aware of the necessity for large-scale external aid and investment. By the early 1980s, although they were deeply concerned about Washington's close relations with Pakistan, Indian policy makers were seeking to improve relations with the United States and other Western nations. Soviet assistance to India, New Delhi had concluded, was inadequate for the country's developmental needs. Another source of Indian-American misunderstanding revolved around what the Indians believed was political intervention in their affairs by intelligence agencies of the United States government. The American military buildup in the Indian Ocean area—which accelerated rapidly after the Soviet invasion of Afghanistan in 1979—served as another contentious issue

between Washington and New Delhi. In the Indian view, the crisis in Afghanistan should be resolved primarily by reliance upon diplomacy.[53]

In turn, several aspects of India's internal and external policies elicited growing concern from official and public opinion within the United States. Sympathetic as he was toward the needs of the Third World, for example, even President John F. Kennedy believed that India would become increasingly preoccupied with progressively more serious internal problems; and Kennedy was not sanguine about the Indian government's willingness or ability to institute the reforms needed to solve them. In the years that followed, other American officials expressed genuine misgivings about the direction of India's internal and external policies. Why should a country that ranked near the bottom among all the nations on the globe in per capita income devote several billion dollars to obtaining a nuclear arsenal and developing a space program? Or why should the Indian government—which was reluctant to impose stricter tax enforcement against its own citizens—complain about the volume of American aid to India? Despite its professed devotion to peaceful methods of resolving regional and international conflicts, the government of India had shown little disposition to solve its quarrel with Pakistan over Kashmir peaceably. Although considerable criticism was heard from New Delhi about American "intervention" in Southeast Asia and the Indian Ocean area, Indian officials seemed strangely reluctant to condemn Soviet intervention in Afghanistan or attempts by North Vietnam to dominate Southeast Asia.[54] Even Indian spokesmen conceded that, from time to time, anti-Americanism in India was motivated by internal political considerations. As in other Third World settings, taking "cheap potshots at America" was an established political tactic.

At the same time, this spokesman also noted that the United States should be careful not to "invite such tactics" and should endeavor to cultivate goodwill within a society in which attachment to democracy remained strong.[55]

The United States and Pakistan

America's relations with Pakistan since 1947 have in most respects been the obverse of its relations with India. Attempts by the United States to cultivate and maintain close relations with Pakistan—especially in the realm of military collaboration—have elicited vocal objections from Indian opinion, just as efforts to preserve cordial relations with India have encountered deep suspicion in Pakistan. By the mid-1950s, officials of the Eisenhower Administration concluded that Pakistan was one of America's staunchest anti-Communist allies in Asia. Pakistan's willingness to join Middle Eastern and Asian defense pacts provided tangible evidence of its pro-American orientation.* As a military ally of the United States, Pakistan was the recipient of large-scale military assistance, as well as economic aid to promote the nation's internal development.[56]

Secessionist sentiment had long been smoldering among the people of East Pakistan, and full-scale rebellion erupted against the government of Pakistan in 1971. With massive Indian support, the people of East Pakistan asserted their independence, creating the new state of Bangladesh. Even with their

---

*In 1955, Pakistan joined the Baghdad Pact, established to promote the security of the Middle East. This alliance system changed its name to the Central Treaty Organization (CENTO) in 1959. In 1954, Pakistan also adhered to the Southeast Asia Treaty Organization (SEATO), relied upon heavily by American officials to provide legal justification for their defense of Southeast Asia from Communist hegemony. Pakistan withdrew from CENTO in 1959; and in the post-Vietnam War era, SEATO fell into disuse as an instrument of American policy in Asia.

American-supplied equipment, Pakistan's armed forces proved no match against Indian forces. Just as India had long blamed the United States for "tilting" toward Pakistan, now the latter became disaffected because of Washington's failure to support Pakistan's position during this conflict. The resulting "dismemberment" of Pakistan greatly weakened the country and was responsible in some measure for its subsequent economic and political instability. Thereafter, relations between the United States and Pakistan became perceptibly cooler—if not sometimes overtly strained.[57]

Internal political developments within Pakistan have also provided new sources of tension and misunderstanding between the two countries. Ever since 1958—when military elements under General Ayub Khan carried out a successful coup—officials in Washington have been concerned about the regime's reliance upon coercive methods to impose its authority. Domestic political upheaval and unrest within Pakistan evoked progressively harsher measures by the ruling junta, leading to repeated indictments of the Pakistan government for violating the human rights of its citizens. Under the regime of General Zia ul-Haq, who came to power in mid-1977, the subsequent execution of former President Ali Bhutto shocked American opinion and appeared to presage an even more authoritarian rule in Pakistan than had been witnessed in the past. General Zia and his followers were dedicated to creating a new Islamic-based political system in Pakistan. Under his leadership, Pakistan emerged as a vocal critic of Israel and of America's long-standing ties with it.

By the early 1980s, Pakistani-American relations tended to revolve around a new, and far-reaching, issue: the implications of the Soviet military occupation of Afghanistan. As was pointed out in Chapter 12, Moscow's precise goals in its effort to subjugate Afghanistan remained unclear; numerous explanations were advanced concerning whether the Kremlin sought to dominate the Persian Gulf area or possibly move next against the Indian subcontinent. Under the Czars, it needs to be remembered, Russia repeatedly engaged in expansionist policies toward the Indian subcontinent. Pakistan's availability as a base area, from which the Afghan rebels waged their campaign against the Russian intruder, increased the country's vulnerability in the face of the Soviet threat. Accordingly, Pakistani officials repeatedly emphasized their country's "nonaligned" position in foreign affairs and their unwillingness to become militarily identified with the United States.[58]

After spurning a $400 million military aid offer by the Carter Administration as "peanuts," by mid-1981 the government of Pakistan indicated a readiness to participate in a new American economic and military assistance agreement that did not compromise its nonaligned position or increase its military vulnerability. This new attitude was engendered in part by a significant increase in Soviet arms aid to India, which Pakistani officials obviously hoped Washington would match. As part of its strategy of building a "strategic consensus" among vulnerable nations in the Persian Gulf-Indian Ocean area, the Reagan Administration concluded that Pakistan played a pivotal role. Accordingly, the Administration proposed to allocate over $3 billion in American economic and military aid to General Zia's government. Predictably, America's overt "tilt" toward Pakistan evoked complaints from India and from critics of General Zia's regime inside and outside Pakistan. Thus far, the military-dominated government of Pakistan had failed to acquire the legitimacy needed to give it long-term stability; and it continued to employ repression in dealing with its internal critics. Expanded American assistance to Pakistan no doubt enhanced the Zia regime's prestige and

would in some measure strengthen the country's defense against external aggression. Yet on the basis of experience, it could seriously be questioned whether a substantial Pakistani military buildup—almost certain to be "matched" by an expansion of India's armed forces—would produce stability and security in the Indian subcontinent. Experience in Pakistan and other Third World countries also raised the question of whether this substantial allocation of American aid would in fact be used for purposes that were consonant with the diplomatic objectives of the United States.[59]

The United States and the East Asian Rimland

According to one school of thought, a lasting result of the Vietnam War was the realization that the United States was not really an "Asian power" but a "Pacific power."[60] Whatever this distinction meant precisely (and commentators differed widely upon its meaning), it was perhaps intended to underscore three basic facts about American diplomacy in the region.

One of these was the idea that the United States did possess important strategic and diplomatic interests in the Far East. In the post-Vietnam War period, although American forces were withdrawn from Southeast Asia (and the United States took no direct part in the subsequent conflict that gripped the peninsula of Indochina), Washington reiterated —and in some respects, *strengthened*—its ties with other Asian countries.

Second—as General Douglas MacArthur stated repeatedly before and after the Korean conflict—the United States should not become embroiled in a "land war" on the Asian continent. MacArthur's thinking reflected the earlier strategic principles identified with Captain Alfred A. Mahan and his disciples (like President Theodore Roosevelt) around 1900. This school of thought advocated primary reliance upon *seapower* —and by the period of World War II, upon airpower—rather than ground forces to protect America's strategic interests in Asia and other regions. According to this interpretation, the United States had been defeated in the Vietnam War because policy makers ignored this maxim. A logical extension of this doctrine in the post-Vietnam War era was the concept that hereafter the main component of American military strength in Asia and its periphery should consist of naval and air units —a requirement that put a new premium upon American relations with Pacific countries like Japan and the Philippines. Another corollary was the idea that other (chiefly Asian) countries would supply the bulk of the ground forces needed for regional defense.

Third, while the post-Vietnam War retrenchment in American power anticipated no wholesale withdrawal by the United States from Asian affairs, it did perhaps contemplate a change in emphasis or priority in American foreign policy. After Vietnam, American power in Asia would be anchored in the Pacific region. Accordingly, in the remainder of this chapter, we shall focus upon recent American relations with the Republic of the Philippines, with the Republic of Korea (South Korea), and with Japan.

America and the Philippines

At the end of the Spanish-American War in 1898—and only after President William McKinley had "walked the floor of the White House night after night until midnight" and agonized in prayer over the decision—the United States annexed Spain's former colony, the Philippine Islands. American officials were not alone in their reluctance about bringing the Philippines under the jurisdiction of the United States. For two years thereafter, Washington confronted the "Huk Rebellion"

led by Emilo Aguinaldo and his followers—a revolt finally suppressed only after some 70,000 American troops were committed to the campaign.[61]

As some diplomatic historians and commentators have interpreted this development, America's acquisition of the Philippines was the "great aberration" in the Asian diplomacy of the United States. Without quite realizing what it had done, the United States government now had acquired jurisdiction over, and responsibility for, a backward and culturally dissimilar society on the Asian rimland. As events subsequently proved, the Philippines occupied a key strategic position in the Pacific—a fact that the military leaders of Japan understood fully and that in time brought the United States and the Japanese Empire into diplomatic and military conflict. Yet it was not until after Japan had openly embarked upon its expansionist course during the 1930s—and finally attacked America's principal Pacific naval base at Pearl Harbor, Hawaii, on December 7, 1941—that Americans fully appreciated the strategic significance of this Pacific possession.

The McKinley Administration's reluctance to annex the Philippines was no doubt genuine, reflecting the long-standing aversion of the American people to colonialism. The Philippines passed under American jurisdiction only because of a conviction in Washington that Imperial Germany was ready to annex the archipelago if the United States did not. From the inception, therefore, in accordance with the Wilsonian doctrine of "self-determination," the United States envisioned that the Filipino society would ultimately achieve independence after it had been adequately prepared for self-rule. Americans naturally expected that in time the Philippines would emerge from this period of tutelage with a strong commitment to democracy. As we shall see, when the nascent Philippine democracy foundered, this fact was particularly disillusioning for Americans and produced ongoing tensions in Filipino-American relations.

On December 8, 1941, following the collapse of the fortresses at Bataan and Corregidor, the Philippines were incorporated into the Japanese Empire. Some four years later, the country was finally liberated from Japanese control, and a new government under Filipino leadership took office early in 1945. True to its pledge, the United States soon granted independence to the country; on July 4, 1946, Manuel A. Roxas y Acuna became the first president of the Republic of the Philippines.

One commentator on Philippine-American relations during the colonial period has said:

> ... many Filipinos ... probably look back on the period as a time of modernization, development, and national consolidation, and a minority may even regard it almost as the "golden age" of the Philippines.... Philippine nationalism mounted steadily in the period between the two world wars, but ... the element of xenophobia was largely missing.... No nationalist leader of the time seriously suggested that the Philippines should sever its cultural and emotional ties with the former colonial master.

In contrast to the experience of other Asian countries (owing in part to the brutality of the Japanese occupation), at the end of the war, "Americans returned to the Philippines more as liberators than conquerors."[62] Against this background, disputes and misunderstandings between the two countries in the years that followed had all of the earmarks of a "family quarrel."

Recurring Issues in Filipino-American Relations

The Republic of the Philippines covers an area of some 116,000 square miles (about equal to three-fourths the size of California). A majority of its population of 50 million people lives at the poverty level, earning around $500 annually; and the country's rapid rate of population increase means that the standard of living is not likely to improve significantly in the near future. Agriculture, along with trade and commerce, are the dominant economic pursuits; and the United States and Japan are the country's principal trading partners.

In common with the Latin Americans, for many years the leaders and people of the Philippines have maintained a kind of love-hate relationship with the United States. Traditionally, in three important spheres—national defense, trade, and cultural affairs—the society has preserved close ties with its American mentor. World War II underscored the strategic importance of the Philippines: The archipelago was crucial in blocking the southward expansion of Japan; and the "liberation" of the islands was an essential step in an ultimate Allied victory in the Pacific theater. For the United States, the country was no less strategically vital in the postwar era. By agreement with Manila, the United States continued to have access to key military bases in the country (the Philippines, for example, served as a vital base area for America's military efforts in the Vietnam War). On August 30, 1951, Manila and Washington signed a mutual defense treaty aimed specifically at the danger of Communist expansionism in Asia. For almost a generation, the Philippine government has been the recipient of large quantities of American military and economic aid. In 1964, Secretary of State Dean Rusk said that "if there is an attack on the Philippines from any quarter, that is an attack on the United States."[63]

After World War II, the United States and the Philippines continued to preserve close commercial ties. American-made goods of all kinds are desired by the people of the Philippines, while the United States remains the largest market for the country's exports. Since independence, cultural relations between the two countries have also been close: Several thousand Filipinos emigrate to the United States every year, and an American education is considered an essential requirement for entry into the professions and other prestigious careers within Filipino society.

Yet by the 1970s, a number of discordant notes characterized America's relations with the Philippines. Periodically since 1898, vocal anti-American sentiment has erupted within the Filipino society, many of whose members resent their economic and military "dependence" upon the United States. From the American perspective, ongoing corruption and repressive government within the Philippines has evoked deep misgivings and recurrent criticisms.

The election of President Ferdinand E. Marcos as president of the Philippine Republic in 1965 led to a period of strained relations between the two countries. In 1972, Marcos suspended the Philippine constitution. Thereafter, his rule became progressively despotic and self-serving. Since the Marcos government depended upon the American-equipped armed forces to impose its rule, many Filipinos (joined by critics inside and outside the United States) charged that the United States was "supporting dictatorships" in this and other countries. Frequent protests from Washington to Manila about the Marcos government's violations of human rights had little discernible impact in reversing the trend toward authoritarian rule.*

*Thus one study of American policy toward the Philippines (as well as other governments relying upon repression against political opposition groups) believes that the large volume of American aid to these countries has been a major factor in enabling antidemocratic regimes to maintain themselves in power. See Lauri S. Wiseberg and Harry M. Scoble, "Monitoring Human Rights Violations: the Role of Nongovernmental Organizations," in Donald P. Kommers and Gilburt D. Loescher, eds., *Human*

By the early 1980s, developments within the Philippines confronted American policy makers with extremely difficult choices. In national elections in mid-1981 (boycotted by most political opposition groups), President Marcos won what he interpreted as a new "mandate" for a continuation of his authoritarian rule. Yet within the Philippine society, conditions were deteriorating. Real wages were declining; unemployment (estimated to have reached some 25 percent of the work force) was growing; economic growth had slowed significantly; and the country's trade deficit was widening. Within this context, organized opposition to the Marcos regime was growing, with some commentators convinced that the prospects for a successful revolution against it were becoming more favorable with each passing month. At the same time, political opposition groups within the Philippines were highly factionalized and disunified concerning both their goals and their methods. Little assurance existed that, even if the authoritarian Marcos regime was ousted, its replacement would be any more dedicated to democratic values or any more capable of solving the society's internal problems.[64]

Although officials in Washington were not unmindful of the Marcos government's record in violating human rights, they were no less cognizant of other realities, as well. As we have already emphasized, one of these was the traditional role the Philippines have played in American defense policy in the eastern Pacific; and that policy incentive had lost none of its urgency in the post-Vietnam War era. If the United States expected to remain a "Pacific power" after that conflict —if it, for example, sought to meet the challenge of growing Soviet seapower in the area—it was difficult to see how this goal

Rights and American Foreign Policy (Notre Dame, Ind.: University of Notre Dame Press, 1979), p. 182.

could be accomplished without maintaining a strong American defensive position in the Philippines and adjacent waters. (In countering any future threat to the Indian subcontinent, for example, the United States and its allies would almost certainly utilize the Philippines heavily as essential bases.)

The other reality influencing American policy toward the Philippines by the early 1980s was awareness that the Carter Administration's overt emphasis upon respect for human rights had actually done little to improve relations between the two countries, nor had it resulted in any notable increase in American influence upon Manila's domestic and foreign policies. In the Reagan Administration's view, reliance upon "quiet diplomacy" offered a better prospect for achieving American diplomatic goals than the "confrontational" tactics relied upon by its predecessor. In the Philippines, as in most other Third World societies, progress in achieving democracy was likely to be a long and arduous process, marked by many setbacks. If such an evolution occurred, it would take place largely as a result of decisions made by the people and leaders of the society themselves.

The United States and South Korea

At the end of World War II, the nation formerly known as Korea found itself divided into two separate, and increasingly antagonistic, states: the American-oriented Republic of Korea (South Korea) and the Communist-ruled Democratic People's Republic of Korea (North Korea). The division of the Korean Peninsula was one of those "accidents" of, or by-products of, war that can have profound political repercussions. It resulted from an agreement between the United States and the Soviet Union, according to which the 38th Parallel would serve as a demarcation line for the purpose of receiving the surrender of Japanese forces. As relations between the super-

powers deteriorated, this "temporary" surrender line became the boundary between North and South Korea.

Since the end of World War II, relations between the United States and South Korea have largely revolved around a single dominant issue: the continuing suspicion and hostility between North and South Korea and the desire of each to reunify the peninsula under its own auspices. The Korean War—which began on June 25, 1950, and ended with an armistice agreement on July 27, 1953—was one of the two massive military encounters in Asia involving the United States since 1945. North Korea's undisguised aggression against its southern neighbor immediately prompted the Truman Administration to oppose Communist expansionism. Although Washington succeeded in having the defense of South Korea brought under the jurisdiction of the United Nations, in reality the major contribution to the defense of South Korea was made by South Korea itself, by the United States, and by some 15 other countries that participated in that cause.

It is not necessary for our purpose to review the course of the Korean War.[65] Our interest is confined to making several brief observations about that conflict, particularly its impact upon subsequent developments in Asia and upon the course of American diplomacy. As an exercise in the application of America's containment policy, the Korean War did demonstrate that the United States and its allies were prepared to use military force to limit Communist expansionism. In that sense, the United States achieved its original goal in Korea: The independence of South Korea *was* successfully preserved against an ominous Communist threat. By other criteria—such as unifying Korea under a democratic government, or "teaching a lesson" to Communist states by deterring them from future aggressive moves—the results of the Korean War were more ambiguous and debatable. As a case study in limited war, the Korean War was a traumatic engagement for the American people and their leaders. Among American citizens, it left a residue of discontent and skepticism about the outcome that may in some respects influence public attitudes toward foreign policy issues to this day. For example, the Korean encounter precipitated a heated domestic controversy: the Korean conflict (sometimes called "Mr. Truman's war") was a crucial stage in the emergence of the "imperial presidency," or virtually unchecked executive power in the foreign policy field. In large part as a result of its own choice, Congress played a negligible role in decision making during the Korean conflict, leaving the conduct of the war and the truce negotiations to the White House. (Yet several presidential decisions were subjected to outspoken congressional criticism.)

The Korean conflict also of course had far-reaching consequences for America's relations with the Soviet Union and with Communist China. Correctly or not, the Truman Administration concluded that the Stalinist government of Russia had instigated the invasion of South Korea by its client, North Korea—thereby providing incontestable proof of the Soviet Union's expansionist ambitions.[66] (To this day, Moscow's precise role in precipitating the Korean conflict remains controversial.) Then, as American and South Korean troops appeared on the verge of defeating North Korea, Communist Chinese forces entered the conflict—and the military tide turned in favor of the Communist side. American and Chinese troops thus fought each other directly in the Korean encounter; and this fact compounded the hostility and illwill existing between the two countries for many years thereafter.

Perhaps the most lasting result of the Korean War was that it left the underlying suspicion and animosity between North and South Korea unresolved. The stage of active military hostilities was finally followed by an armistice agreement, creating a "demilitarized zone" (DMZ) between the two countries. Interminable diplomatic negotiations produced no peace treaty ending the Korean War; and to this day, the DMZ remains one of the most volatile frontiers on the globe. Almost daily, some incident along the DMZ reminds the world of the continued instability of the Korean Peninsula.

Officials in Seoul and Washington, for example, are aware that the aging leader of North Korea, Kim Il Sung, has stated repeatedly that he intends to unify Korea under a Communist system during his lifetime. One commentator has depicted Kim Il Sung as an

> ... unstable, irrational dictator who might be tempted to invade the South by any shift in the military balance or hint of a reduced U.S. commitment to South Korean defense.[67]

Or, as Zagoria has phrased it, Kim Il Sung (still an admirer of the Soviet dictator Joseph Stalin) believes in "the stupefying cult of personality" and "may well be emboldened to try to take over the South once and for all before he dies."[68]

Yet in recent years, North Korea's relations with both the Soviet Union and Communist China have deteriorated—leading Kim Il Sung's regime to express interest in a possible resolution of the Korean question. Thus far, these overtures have elicited little positive response from Seoul and Washington.[69] The normalization that occurred in relations between the United States and Communist China during the 1970s significantly lessened the risk of some new aggressive move by North Korea across the demilitarized zone. This development did not, however, altogether eliminate the possibility that North Korea might act unilaterally against what Pyongyang perceived to be a weaker and internally divided South Korea. The defense treaty negotiated between the United States and South Korea late in 1953 remains in force and serves as a visible reminder of America's continuing commitment to South Korean independence. Conversely, the idea that—perhaps as part of the retrenchment of American power in Asia following the Vietnam War—America's own forces in South Korea ought to be reduced significantly has been repeatedly rejected by executive and legislative policy makers. During the late 1970s, for example, sentiment on Capitol Hill was decisively *against* any major American force reductions on the Korean Peninsula.* Since, as a presidential candidate, Ronald Reagan had deplored the global decline of American power and influence, it seemed doubtful that his Administration would contemplate a significant reduction in American power on the Korean Peninsula. During some periods the risk of a new military encounter on the Korean Peninsula also derived from another factor: the possibility that the government of South Korea (which in recent years has encountered acute internal problems) might be tempted to rely upon armed force to "settle accounts" with its Communist rival across the 38th Parallel. The continued presence of American troops within South Korea served as a deter-

rent to provocative moves by both sides in the quarrel.[70]

The Republic of Korea is a small nation of only some 38,000 square miles (slightly smaller than the state of Ohio); it has a population of some 40 million people (giving it twice as many people as its northern rival). Lacking most raw materials, the Korean society has traditionally depended upon agriculture for its livelihood. Since the end of the Korean War the society has achieved one of the most impressive economic growth rates within the Third World. Emulating their Japanese neighbors, the South Koreans embarked upon a successful program of industrialization and manufacturing; in time, the contrast between economic conditions in North and South Korea served as another source of suspicion and enmity between them.

Yet, as in a number of other Third World settings, rapid economic progress in South Korea did *not* translate into greater political stability or evolution toward democracy. To the contrary, repression by governmental authorities and internal political upheaval increasingly characterized the Korean society. The United States has had minimal success in its efforts to keep South Korea on a democratic course. As a result of elections held under American auspices in 1948, a new Korean government led by President Syngman Rhee assumed office. Syngman Rhee was an authoritarian leader (reminiscent of Chiang Kai-shek earlier in China) who was increasingly unresponsive to the needs of the country and unable to retain the loyalty of the Korean people. Faced with mounting internal disaffection, Rhee resigned in 1960. Then in 1961, General Park Chung-hee led a successful military coup. As we have already noted, under the Park regime South Korea experienced phenomenal economic growth; and some 50,000 Korean troops joined the effort to prevent a Communist victory in Indochina.

*During the early 1970s, for example, vocal sentiment was expressed in Congress and by a number of public groups favoring a substantial reduction of American armed forces in Korea. President Jimmy Carter entered the White House in 1977 with a verbal commitment to that goal. Yet after extensive investigation of the problem of South Korean security by both executive and legislative officials—as a result of which South Korea's continued vulnerability became evident—only a modest reduction of American troops (from 41,000 to 38,000) was effected by the Carter Administration. President Carter and his advisers did, however, reiterate the long-standing expectation that ultimately South Korea could meet its own security needs. More detailed examination of the question is contained in Cecil V. Crabb, Jr., and Pat Holt, *Invitation to Struggle: Congress, the President and Foreign Policy* (Washington, D.C.: Congressional Quarterly Press, 1980), pp. 113–120.

In 1975, General Park suspended the constitution and ruled thereafter by "emergency decree." As the months passed, his regime became more and more repressive in dealing with real or suspected political opposition groups. Meanwhile, agents of General Park's government within the United States were dispensing lavish sums in an effort to gain economic concessions for South Korea from American policy makers. As explained more fully in Chapter 8, the resulting "Koreagate" scandal provided a graphic example of lobbying by a foreign country to influence the American foreign policy process.[71]

On numerous occasions, officials in Washington condemned political excesses by the government of South Korea and called upon Seoul to observe the constitutional rights of the Korean people. Washington's protests, however, had no observable effect upon the behavior of Korean officials. Because South Korea is a close military ally of the United States and a major recipient of American foreign aid, Washington became identified with, and was held responsible for, the political repressions carried out by authorities in Seoul. To the degree that this occurred, America's commitment to the cause of international human rights was, therefore, seriously compromised.

Although they were repelled by political developments within South Korea, American officials were disinclined to rely upon coercive measures in their approach to the problem. A number of steps often recommended by critics of American policy—such as suspension of diplomatic relations with Seoul, or terminating United States assistance to South Korea, or withdrawal of American troops from the Korean Peninsula—were rejected by successive administrations in Washington as making little useful contribution to improvement of conditions in South Korea. No evidence existed that they would loosen the grip of the

Korean military upon the political process or otherwise enhance the prospects for the emergence of Korean democracy. Indeed—to the extent that coercive measures precipitated economic dislocations within South Korea, or made the country *more vulnerable* to renewed aggression by North Korea—the results were likely to be exactly the opposite. In the 1980s, no less than the early postwar period, American officials viewed the continued independence of South Korea as *vital to the security of the United States and its allies* (like Japan). As long as that belief continues to govern American policy in Asia, it is difficult to see how promoting *insecurity* in South Korea would promote the regional or global diplomatic interests of the United States.

In October, 1979, General Park was assassinated by another member of the Korean armed forces. The new government—led by President Chun Doo Hwan—was still dominated by the armed forces. The Hwan regime pledged to "purify" the Korean society politically before returning the country to civilian rule. (In practice, such "purification" meant that the regime applied stern measures in dealing with political opposition groups.) The new government also promised to give greater attention to South Korea's social and economic problems. As was true of its predecessors, the Hwan regime remained preoccupied with the threat to national security posed by the Communist government of North Korea—an apprehension that was shared by officials of the Reagan Administration. Neither in Seoul nor in Washington was there an inclination to reduce the American defense commitment to South Korea. Under the Reagan Administration the preservation of Korean security continued to be a high priority goal of American policy in Asia. As in the Philippines, the nature of the Korean political system was a subordinate consideration to maintaining the independence of South

Korea and to preventing a new Communist threat in East Asia.[72]

Japan and the United States—the Road to War

For approximately a half century after Commodore Perry "opened" Japan to contact with the West in 1853, relations between the United States and Japan were friendly. As one student of Japanese-American relations has said about the period that followed Perry's visit:

> The doors of Japan had been pushed wide open. America had assumed her role as Japan's Occidental neighbor and as the spearhead of Western penetration. We had established ourselves as the first and foremost Occidental friend of Japan.[73]

Yet exposure to the West had some unanticipated effects upon Japan's internal and external policies. It quickly undermined the authority of Japan's feudalistic governmental system and brought into power a group of revolutionaries whose goal, as Reischauer has described it, "was to undertake reforms, designed to regain . . . the ground lost to the West over a period of two hundred-odd years."[74] The new rulers of Japan were determined, for example, to expand and modernize the nation's armed forces—particularly its naval arm—making Japan the dominant military power in the Orient.

Japan's emergence as a powerful nation in the global arena was highlighted by its decisive defeat of Czarist Russia in the Russo-Japanese War (1904–1905), as a result of which the Russian navy was largely eliminated for a half century or so as a potent military force. Although Americans had no admiration for the despotic Czarist regime in Russia, President Theodore Roosevelt used his influence to limit Tokyo's demands upon its defeated enemies. In Roosevelt's words, he wanted to prevent Japan from "driving Russia completely out of East Asia," thereby impairing the balance of power to America's future disadvantage.[75]

After 1900, other American chief executives became increasingly apprehensive about Japanese ambitions in East Asia. During World War I, for example, Tokyo took advantage of the preoccupation of the Western powers with the European conflict to express its "Twenty-One Demands" on China; in effect, these anticipated the dismemberment of China by requiring the cession of large portions of its territory to Japan. Tokyo's diplomacy was forcefully opposed by President Woodrow Wilson, who succeeded in getting this overt challenge to the Open Door policy, and to China's territorial integrity, withdrawn.[76] Then during the 1920s, as a result of international agreements limiting naval armaments, Japan was left with preponderant naval power in Pacific waters—an advantage it was to utilize skillfully after it embarked upon the course of political and military expansionism.

According to some historians of the modern period, World War II—and the rapid deterioration in Japanese-American relations leading to the attack on Pearl Harbor on December 7, 1941—began with the Japanese incursion into Manchuria, launched on September 19, 1931. Japan's aggression against this valuable Chinese province evoked the condemnation of the civilized world. Although it did not belong to the League of Nations, the United States joined with the members of that organization in denouncing Japanese expansionism. During the Manchurian crisis, the United States issued what came to be called the Stimson Doctrine, according to which Washington refused to "recognize" the Japanese puppet state of "Manchuko" established in Manchuria and other territorial changes made by reliance upon military force. These protests had no discernible impact in diverting Japanese militarists from their aggressive course. In fact, measures like the Stimson Doctrine quite possibly had the *opposite effect:* Verbal American protests, unsupported by coercive measures designed to curb Japanese ambitions, may have convinced the warlords of Tokyo that they would encounter no effective opposition in relying upon military force to achieve their goals at the expense of China and other weaker Asian countries![77]

The Japanese Empire continued to expand at the expense of China, Korea, Southeast Asia, and the island countries of the Pacific—toward what many commentators were convinced was Tokyo's ultimate objective: the conquest of Australia. To gain that prize, however, the Japanese militarists had to remove the main obstacle in their path—the American Pacific fleet. They came very close to achieving this goal, when Japanese airpower virtually eliminated the American fleet and naval base by its attack on Pearl Harbor.

The United States declared war on Japan on December 8, 1941. Gradually, the tide of battle turned against Japan in the Pacific. In time, superior Allied power pushed Japanese forces northward, cut Tokyo's supply lines, and (by early 1945) was imposing a tight naval blockade against the Japanese home islands. After the surrender of Germany (May 7, 1945), the Allied war effort was concentrated upon achieving the unconditional surrender of Japan. That event was hastened by the development of the atomic bomb, perfected during the summer. Two nuclear bombs were used against Japan—the first against Hiroshima on August 6, and the second against Nagasaki on August 9—leading to Tokyo's capitulation and its formal surrender on September 2. Meanwhile, before this historic event, another significant development occurred: Between the first and second atomic

bombs, on August 8, the Soviet Union finally entered the war against the Japanese Empire. As we have seen, this fact gave Moscow a strong position in Manchuria and enabled it subsequently to support Communist regimes in North Korea and North Vietnam.

The Occupation and Japanese Demilitarization

After demanding Japan's unconditional surrender, the Allies (meaning principally the United States) imposed a military occupation upon the country, under General Douglas MacArthur. The Occupation (as it was widely described) produced sweeping changes in Japanese domestic and foreign affairs. As a result of the trial of major and minor Japanese "war criminals," the Occupation authorities purged the Japanese government of military influence. A new constitution was promulgated for Japan in 1947; and throughout the months that followed the Occupation authorities relinquished many of their responsibilities to Japanese officials. A new parliamentary-type government was installed in Japan; and in the years ahead, the Japanese evolved one of the most ostensibly stable and successful democratic political systems on the globe. Also, under the Occupation the large industrial combines (called the *Zaibatsu*), which had collaborated closely with military elements to promote an aggressive Japanese foreign policy, were broken up to prevent a possible resurgence of Tokyo's expansionist tendencies.

Few changes effected by the Occupation were as far-reaching as Japan's "demilitarization." Mindful of Asian apprehensions about Japanese militarism, the United States insisted upon this constitutional safeguard against a resurgence of Japanese imperialism. Accordingly, Article 9 of the new Japanese constitution that took effect on May 3, 1947, prohibits the country from maintaining a military establishment, although it may possess police and military units required to preserve internal law and order and external self-defense. After 1945, therefore, the responsibility for safeguarding Japanese security devolved primarily upon the United States.

The American Occupation came to an end on April 28, 1952, when sovereignty was restored to Japan. Thereafter Japan joined the United Nations; in the years that followed, the United States reduced its armed forces within the country from some 240,000 to 48,000 troops. On January 19, 1960, a defense treaty between the United States and Japan bound them to cooperate against external (meaning primarily Communist) threats to Japanese independence.[78]

Persistent Issues in Japanese-American Relations

In his analysis of American diplomacy in Asia after the Vietnam War, Edwin O. Reischauer predicted that the debate over Japan's links with the United States "will continue to bubble and boil" in the years ahead, but the outcome of the debate was clear. "We and the Japanese are as natural partners as the United States and Western Europe." The architect of America's postwar containment policy, George F. Kennan, concluded concerning Japanese-American relations:

> Japan is the natural ally of the United States in East Asia. The United States has a vital interest in assuring that the immense industrial potential of the Japanese archipelago does not become associated . . . with the vast manpower of mainland China or the formidable military potential of the Soviet Union. The fact that this is also a vital interest of Japan herself is what provides the basis of an effective Japanese-American alliance.[79]

Since the restoration of sovereignty to Japan, officials in Tokyo and Washington have recognized their mutual dependency. The overall framework and atmosphere of Japanese-American relations has remained friendly and cooperative. Within that setting of underlying mutual interests, however, several issues have engendered controversy and misunderstanding between the two countries. Four of these have been especially important and deserve brief examination.

Since World War II, Japan's economic advancement has been phenomenal. After its defeat in the war, the Japanese society lost little time in reconstructing and modernizing its war-ravaged industrial base and converting it into one of the most productive centers on the globe. The Japanese society's traditional ingenuity and technological ability—applied within a domestic environment of political stability, harmonious labor-management relations, and national freedom from the obligation to bear a heavy defense burden—made modern Japan an industrial giant. With an area slightly smaller than the state of California, by the early 1980s Japan had achieved a Gross National Product of over $1 trillion annually (still less than half of America's, but twice as large as West Germany's). Prospects were that, in many aspects of economic activity, Japan would continue to strengthen its position as one of the world's economic power centers.

A key element in Japanese economic activity since World War II has been the aggressive and successful promotion of Japanese exports; and the American market has been attractive for Japanese firms. Accordingly, trade questions have emerged as a contentious issue in Japanese-American relations. In the United States and other countries, pervasive apprehensions exist about the commercial policies and practices followed by what is sometimes called "Japan, Inc." From the Western Hemisphere to East Asia, Japanese firms established a commanding position in the world market for a wide variety of exports. As the sale of Japanese products within the United States increased steadily—producing a $9 billion trade deficit in America's foreign exchange accounts with Japan by the 1980s—the Carter and Reagan administrations faced a rising chorus of protectionist sentiment from business and labor groups complaining about "unfair" Japanese competition. Acknowledging this rising tide of protectionist sentiment in America, by late 1980 Japanese officials indicated their willingness to reduce automobile exports to the United States, in order to avoid stringent trade restrictions against Japanese competition in the American market.[80]

Several significant aspects of the problem of rising Japanese imports were often incompletely understood in the United States. One of these was the crucial fact that Japan had also become *one of America's best customers* in international trade. In 1979, for example, total trade between the United States and Japan amounted to almost $94 billion; and the prospects are that this volume will continue to rise. Japan is the largest single market for American agricultural exports —equaling over $5 billion in 1979—and it is a major purchaser of other commodities, like wood products. When they confronted demands for "protection" against Japanese competition, therefore, officials in Washington faced a difficult choice. Should some (perhaps less efficient) sectors of the American economy be protected against Japanese competition, at the expense of other (more productive) sectors that were able to maintain their competitive position in the international market? If restraints were placed upon certain Japanese industrial exports to the United States, in time the sale of agricultural products to Japan, and the prosperity of the agricultural community within the United States, would inevitably decline. No more today than in the past were American officials able to resolve the riddle of how to maintain high sales *to* Japan and other countries, while curtailing sales *by* Japan

and other foreign competitors in the American market.

Moreover, as officials in Tokyo repeatedly contended, the "unfairness" of Japanese competition was often a misplaced criticism. Admittedly, the Japanese government cooperated with and encouraged business enterprises in their efforts to expand foreign sales, sometimes to the point of directly or indirectly subsidizing Japanese firms. (But American business enterprises were also the recipient of various kinds of governmental assistance and subsidies.) In the Japanese view, if American business enterprises had difficulty meeting foreign competition, the basic fault lay in *declining American productivity*. Business corporations and labor unions within the United States were too often prone to blame Japan for the fact that the competitive position of the United States in world trade had deteriorated—a phenomenon caused primarily by the American society's own failure to improve its economic efficiency and to modernize its productive facilities. To cite merely one manifestation of this tendency: As the Japanese analyzed it, for too many years the American society had been a profligate consumer of energy, despite ample warnings about the approaching "energy crisis." As the demand for energy outpaced available supplies—and as the price of imported oil products escalated sharply in the world market—this fact impaired the ability of American firms to compete successfully against foreign competition. (By contrast, Japan—which was almost totally dependent upon imports to meet its petroleum needs—had not allowed this fact to erode its competitive position.) The Reagan Administration pledged intensified efforts to improve American productivity vis-à-vis Japan and other competitors.

Time and again in recent years, American officials and business groups have complained about the "double standard" implicit in Tokyo's commercial policies: The Japanese government energetically seeks to promote foreign sales, although it has imposed numerous and serious obstacles to efforts by other countries to sell products in the Japanese home market. Yet even if such restrictions are eased, the problem of America's competitive position in the world market will remain. A significant improvement in America's productive level will still be required for the United States to compete successfully against other countries seeking access to the Japanese market.*

In the years ahead, George Ball has said, "new centers of leadership can emerge [in Asia] that should . . . make it possible for us to share responsibilities with the key nations of the area, of which Japan should certainly be in the forefront." In the post-Vietnam War stage of American foreign policy, Ball said of Japan:

> Of all the great powers of the area I would expect the Japanese to achieve the greatest power and leverage, not only in Southeast Asia but in the whole Asian theater.[81]

A second source of controversy in Japanese-American relations has been a belief in the United States that Japan was not "pulling its weight" in the solution of regional and global diplomatic problems. If Japan had become a financial giant, it was still a diplomatic "pygmy"—and many Japanese appeared to favor its continued diplomatic passivity.

Toward several specific problems—such as providing foreign aid and investment capital to needy societies, and exerting greater initiative in promoting regional cooperation in Asia—Tokyo has gradually assumed a more active active role of diplomatic leadership.† Yet, as with the question of Japanese rearmament, such initiatives by Japan still aroused apprehensions among its weaker Asian neighbors.

A third, and related, issue in contemporary Japanese-American relations has been Japan's future role in promoting Asian security. As early as the period of the Korean War, Japanese bases were vital to the United States and its allies in the defense of South Korea; and several years later, Japan again played a key role in America's unsuccessful effort to defeat Communist forces in Southeast Asia. To the minds of some Americans, after the withdrawal of United States forces from Southeast Asia, Japan was the logical candidate to fill the vacuum created by the retrenchment of American power in Asia.

Yet for many years, any contemplated expansion of Japanese military power has faced several difficult obstacles. As we have seen, Article 9 of the Japanese constitution —inserted into the document largely at the instigation of the United States itself —prohibits Japan from maintaining a military establishment (although it may possess internal police and "self-defense" forces).

*One recent study of the problem concluded that "while the United States strives with some success to open the trade doors to Japan, other countries' products enter the opening door." James C. Abegglen and Thomas M. Hout, "Facing Up to the Trade Gap with Japan," *Foreign Affairs*, **57** (Fall, 1978), 154. See also the discussion of factors influencing America's trade position in *U.S. Foreign Policy: Future Directions* (Washington, D.C.: Congressional Quarterly, 1979), pp. 61–85.

†An example of more vigorous Japanese leadership in recent years is provided by Tokyo's role in the Association of Southeast Asian Nations (ASEAN), consisting of Indonesia, Malaysia, the Philippines, Singapore, and Thailand. After some initial opposition, the Japanese government has cooperated with ASEAN, by encouraging its activities and by making large-scale credits and investment capital available to its members. The encouragement of regionalism generally, and of ASEAN in particular, has been a goal of American foreign policy in Asia. See Bernard K. Gordon, "Japan, the United States, and Southeast Asia," *Foreign Affairs*, **56** (April, 1978), 579–601.

Moreover, even today the prospect of Japanese rearmament encounters pervasive apprehension among Asian countries that were subject to Japanese hegemony in the recent past. If Peking, for example, urged the United States to maintain a strong military presence in Asia after the Vietnam War, one reason was the Chinese expectation that American power would restrain any new expansionist impulse by Japan. Even the new Japanese prime minister, Zenko Suzuki, acknowledged in 1980 that a substantial increase in Japanese armed forces would arouse anxieties throughout Asia.[82] Throughout most of the postwar period, therefore, formidable obstacles have impeded a more dynamic Japanese role in the preservation of Asian security. Not the least of these barriers has been Japanese public opinion—which remains basically unsympathetic to this idea.*

*By the early 1980s, Japan had built up a "self-defense force" of some 240,000 troops. During the decade of the 1970s, Tokyo had increased its defense spending by some 8 percent annually (while the United States was *reducing* its defense appropriations by 2 percent annually during the same period). Tokyo was currently spending some $10 billion annually on national defense—giving Japan the eighth-largest military budget in the world. One development prompting a renewed Japanese concern about defense questions was the ongoing buildup of Soviet forces—coupled with a number of ominous Russian moves affecting Japanese interests—in Asia. The Soviet Union, for example, had some 350,000 troops in East Asia alone; and, utilizing naval bases in Vietnam, Moscow was continuing to expand its Pacific fleet. Meanwhile, because of crises in the Persian Gulf area, American naval strength had been weakened in the Pacific region. The Soviet invasion of Afghanistan in 1979 added to Japanese apprehensions about Moscow's intentions in Asia. Despite such developments, however, public opinion within Japan still appeared to oppose an active role by Japan in Asian defense or a significant expansion in the country's military establishment. See: Sadako Ogata, "Some Japanese Views on United States-Japanese Relations in the 1980s," *Asian Survey,* **20** (July, 1980), 694–707; the interview with Ambassador Mike Mansfield in *U.S. News and World Report,* **89** (October

Yet, by the opening of the 1980s, several forces combined to produce a reappraisal of Japan's long-standing policies on national and regional defense. In part as a result of American insistence, Tokyo agreed to increase its defense contribution. For example, Japanese forces would assume responsibility for defending the sealanes within 1,000 miles of their homeland. Prime Minister Suzuki's government also agreed to a 7.8 percent increase in the 1982 defense budget (at a time when most other budget categories were being reduced). Officials in Washington, no less than in Tokyo, were aware that any substantial or sudden Japanese military buildup might trigger serious political unrest within Japan and cause instability throughout East Asia. For over a generation, one issue—the presence of nuclear weapons in or around Japan—elicited strong and emotional Japanese opposition. Yet by the early 1980s, evidence existed for believing that Japanese sensitivity on this question was declining and that—in light of the ongoing Soviet military buildup in Asia—the Japanese were more willing than in the past to rely upon American nuclear might in the Pacific to preserve regional security. Even so, officials of the Reagan Administration continued to put pressure upon Japan to expand its defense efforts—to the point, said Secretary of Defense Caspar Weinberger in 1982, of assuming the *entire* responsibility for the defense of Japan by 1990. In addition, Weinberger reminded Tokyo that—as much as any country in the modern world—the security of Japan depended upon continued access to the oil fields of the Persian Gulf area, and he urged Japanese officials to support American strategy for defending that region.[83]

The rapprochement in Sino-American

27, 1980), 43–44; and dispatches by Henry S. Stokes and Drew Middleton, in *New York Times,* July 4, 1980.

relations described earlier in the chapter also had significant implications for Japanese diplomacy and defense policies. For the first time in recent memory, Chinese officials have called for the strengthening of the Japanese military establishment; and Peking expressed keen interest in relying upon Japan (along with the United States) as a major source of modern weapons and advanced military technology. Chinese authorities, in the words of one commentator, were "obviously most interested in recruiting a new partner to their united anti-Soviet front." Accordingly, Peking has urged the Japanese to "defend themselves against the threat of the Soviet 'polar bear' and has even urged greater Japanese military cooperation with the United States."

Recent Soviet behavior in East Asia has also aroused growing Japanese anxieties and has led to reconsideration of the principles guiding Tokyo's defense policies. A number of Russian moves affecting Japan—such as Moscow's "tough" position regarding a dispute over fishing rights, the increase in Soviet intelligence-gathering activities in adjacent waters, the expansion of Russian military power on Sakhalin Island (seized by Russia from Japan at the end of World War II) and the overall buildup of Soviet naval power in the Pacific region—have induced officials in Tokyo to rethink Japanese defense strategies and programs. At the end of 1980, official Soviet sources were mounting a sharp propaganda attack against the government of Japan, accusing it of becoming a member of a new "tripartite alliance" (or a Sino-American-Japanese axis) directed against Russian interests in Asia.[84]

The volatility of the Persian Gulf area—highlighted by the war that erupted between Iraq and Iran in the fall of 1980—provided a new incentive for changes in Japanese defense policies. Japan imports nearly all of its total petroleum requirements, with most of these oil shipments coming from Middle East suppliers. To a greater degree perhaps than any industrial nation, Japan is dependent for its continued prosperity upon access to Middle East oil. Yet among the more than 60 warships that had assembled late in 1980 to assure continued access by the United States and other non-Communist countries to the Persian Gulf area, Japan (whose small navy was designed only for defense of the home islands) was unable to make a contribution to this joint defense effort.[85]

For several years, a fourth cause of misunderstanding between Washington and Tokyo has been Japanese complaints that their viewpoints have been "ignored" by policy makers in the United States on regional and global questions. To the Japanese mind, this tendency in Washington illustrates the existence of a fundamental inconsistency in American foreign policy. On the one hand, officials in the United States have urged Japan to exert more dynamic diplomatic leadership and to shoulder a larger share of the burden involved in Asian defense. On the other hand, even as they addressed such entreaties to Japanese authorities, American policy makers have consistently neglected to ascertain Tokyo's viewpoints *in the stage of policy formulation* on issues affecting Japanese interests.

This dichotomy in the American mind was brought into sharp relief by the diplomatic behavior of the Nixon Administration. During the early 1970s, for example, Nixon called attention to the "profound goodwill and mutual respect" that was the foundation of Japanese-American relations. And Nixon asserted:

> Japan is our most important ally in Asia. It is our second greatest trading partner. It is an essential participant, if a stable world peace is to be built. Our security, our prosperity, and our global policies are therefore intimately and inextricably linked to the U.S.-Japanese relationship.[86]

Yet throughout the process of one of the most profound changes in American foreign policy since World War II—the normalization in Sino-American relations that occurred under the Nixon Administration—no evidence exists that the Japanese were consulted in advance about this development or that their viewpoints were considered in the formulation of American policy. Even President Nixon acknowledged that this reorientation in American policy had been a traumatic development for Japan.[87]

Another example of this same tendency was provided by President Jimmy Carter's issuance of the Carter Doctrine early in 1980, committing the United States to preserve the security of the Persian Gulf area. (The Carter Doctrine was analyzed more fully in Chapter 12.) Although Japan is not a Middle Eastern power, this new undertaking by the United States nonetheless clearly affected Tokyo's foreign and defense policies. Any prolonged denial of access to the oil fields of the Persian Gulf area would be economically ruinous for Japan. Moreover, in its efforts to implement the Carter Doctrine, the United States was required to weaken its military position in East Asia—and this development directly impinged upon Japanese security and upon future Russo-Japanese relations.

These were merely two examples illustrating problems implicit in the Japanese-American "partnership" that had emerged since World War II. As the Japanese interpreted it, too often in the past Washington's conception of the partnership was a relationship in which Japan quiescently *supported* American diplomatic decisions and adjusted its external policies in the light of American policy changes. If, as officials in the United States continued to insist, Japan should begin to play a diplomatic and military role consonant with its enormous economic power, then the Japanese government was entitled to be

treated as a valued ally whose viewpoints and interests were considered *before* Washington arrived at major policy decisions.

NOTES

1. See the views of Fred Greene, *U.S. Policy and the Security of Asia* (New York: McGraw-Hill, 1968), pp. 20, 24, 35.
2. John Paton Davies, "America and East Asia," *Foreign Affairs*, **55** (January, 1977), 368.
3. See the interview with Ambassador Mike Mansfield in *U.S. News and World Report*, **89** (October 27, 1980), 43–44.
4. Julius W. Pratt, *A History of United States Foreign Policy* (Englewood Cliffs, N.J.: Prentice-Hall, 1955), pp. 270–278.
5. Foster R. Dulles, *China and America* (Princeton, N.J.: Princeton University Press, 1946), p. 107.
6. Ibid., p. 107.
7. Werner Levi, *Modern China's Foreign Policy* (Minneapolis: University of Minnesota Press, 1953), p. 52.
8. Ibid., p. 55.
9. Ibid., pp. 287–297.
10. Pratt, *A History of United States Foreign Policy,* pp. 387–392.
11. According to one student of Roosevelt's diplomacy, he believed that the world must be rid "of imperialism in all its forms" if peace were to be preserved after World War II. See Willard Range, "FDR—A Reflection of American Idealism," in Warren F. Kimball, ed., *Franklin D. Roosevelt and the World Crisis, 1937—1945* (Lexington, Mass.: D. C. Heath, 1973), pp. 240–241.
12. American diplomacy toward the Chinese civil war is described and evaluated in John K. Fairbank, *The United States and China* (New York: Viking Press, 1962), pp. 246–278; and Warren I. Cohen, *America's Response to China* (New York: John Wiley and Sons, 1971), pp. 100–211.
13. America's relations with China during World War II are discussed in greater detail in Thomas H. Etzold, ed., *Aspects of Sino-*

American Relations Since 1784 (New York: Franklin Watts, 1978), pp. 127–163. For a personal memoir, highlighting misunderstandings between the two countries during World War II, see Theodore H. White, ed., *The Stilwell Papers* (New York: Macfadden Books, 1962).

14. The Truman Administration's position —emphasizing America's efforts to assist Nationalist China during and after World War II—has been set forth comprehensively in the State Department's publication, *United States Relations with China* (Washington, D.C.: Publication No. 3573, 1949). An informative interpretation of American diplomacy toward China is Herbert Feis, *The China Tangle* (Princeton, N.J.: Princeton University Press, 1953).

15. See Ross Y. Koen, *The China Lobby in American Politics* (New York: Harper & Row, 1974).

16. China's revolutionary diplomacy during the Maoist period is discussed in Devere E. Pentony, ed., *China: The Emerging Red Giant* (San Francisco: Chandler Publishing Co., 1962), pp. 140–200.

17. Howard L. Boorman et al., *Moscow-Peking Axis* (New York: Harper & Row, 1957), pp. 42–43.

18. For discussions of long-standing sources of controversy and tension between the Soviet Union and China, see George F. Kennan, *Russia and the West Under Lenin and Stalin* (Boston: Atlantic-Little, Brown, 1961). Other helpful studies in understanding the rupture between Russia and China are Conrad Brandt, *Stalin's Failure in China* (New York: W. W. Norton, 1966); and David Floyd, *Mao Against Khrushchev* (New York: Praeger Publishers, 1963).

19. See Levi, *Modern China's Foreign Policy,* p. 329.

20. Royal Institute of International Affairs, *Collective Defense in South East Asia* (London: Oxford University Press, 1956), pp. 58–59.

21. See the *Christian Science Monitor,* February 5, 1959.

22. By the end of the 1960s, one experienced reporter who had visited the Sino-Soviet frontier was convinced that armed conflict between the two countries was imminent. See Harrison E. Salisbury, *War Between Russia and China* (New York: Bantam Books, 1970).

23. For an analysis of the causes and implications of the war between China and North Vietnam in 1977, see Thomas J. Bellows, "Proxy War in Indochina," *Asian Affairs,* **7** (September–October, 1979), 13–30.

24. Henry Kissinger, *White House Years* (Boston: Little, Brown and Co., 1979), p. 685.

25. President Richard M. Nixon's historic visit to China is authoritatively discussed in ibid., pp. 1049–1096.

26. Ibid., p. 1089.

27. See the discussion of President Carter's decision to recognize the People's Republic of China, in Cecil V. Crabb, Jr., and Pat Holt, *Invitation to Struggle: Congress, the President and Foreign Policy* (Washington, D.C.: Congressional Quarterly, 1980), pp. 200–201. The State Department asserted that public opinion polls showed overwhelming public endorsement of America's move to normalize relations with Communist China. See the State Department publication, "China and the U.S.: Into the 1980s," Current Policy No. 187, June 4, 1980, p. 1.

28. These efforts are described more specifically in "China and the U.S.: Into the 1980s," pp. 1–2. The impact of the Sino-American rapprochement upon the international system is analyzed in Ross Terrill, "China and the World: Self-Reliance or Interdependence?" *Foreign Affairs,* **55** (January, 1977), 295–306. For a Chinese perspective, see Huan Xiang, "On Sino-U.S. Relations," *Foreign Affairs,* **60** (Fall, 1981), 35–54.

29. See the text of Vice-President Walter Mondale's speech in Peking on August 27, 1979, in the *New York Times,* August 28, 1979.

30. See the excerpts from the study by the Rand Corporation in the Baton Rouge *Morning Advocate,* December 28, 1979.

31. See the interview with Deputy Chinese Foreign Minister Wang Shu, in *Newsweek,* **31** (September 25, 1978), 60.

32. An informative discussion of defense problems facing China in the post-Mao era is William T. Tow, "Chinese Strategic Thought: Evolution Toward Reality," *Asian Affairs,* **7** (March–April, 1980), 248–270. See also Leo Yueh-yun Liu, "The Modernization of the Chinese Military, " *Current History,* **79** (September, 1980), 9–14.

33. See the *New York Times,* September 9 and 11, 1980. For the views of a leading American authority on modern China's military capabilities and of their implications for American foreign policy, see A. Doak Barnett, "Military-Security Relations Between China and the United States," *Foreign Affairs,* **55** (April, 1977), 584–598; and Hedrick Smith, "Reagan: What Kind of World Leader?" *The New York Times Magazine,* November 16, 1980, pp. 47–48, 172–177.

34. More detailed data on economic conditions and prospects in China are provided by Fox Butterfield, in *New York Times,* February 4, 1979; and in several articles in the symposium on "The People's Republic of China, 1980," *Current History,* **79** (September, 1980).

35. Fox Butterfield, in *New York Times,* April 24, 1979. According to one commentator, the "four modernizations" program was an implicit admission that Maoist economic policies had failed. See Liu Hsien-tung, "De-Maoization: How Far Will It Go?" *Asian Affairs,* **7** (September–October, 1979), 31–45.

36. See the views of Huan Xiang, Vice President of the Chinese Academy of Social Sciences, in the *New York Times,* September 18, 1981; and the interview with A. Doak Barnett in *U.S. News and World Report,* **86** (January 22, 1979), 43–44.

37. See the data on Sino-American trade contained in the summaries released by the Bureau of Public Affairs of the State Department, "US–PRC Economic Relations," November, 1979, pp. 1–2; and "US–China Trade Agreement," January, 1980, pp. 1–2. Forces inducing changes in many of China's traditional trade principles and policies are identified in Alexander Eckstein, "China's Trade Policy and Sino-American Relations,"

Foreign Affairs, **54** (October, 1975), 134–155.

38. America's growing military commitment to the security of South Vietnam is discussed more fully in Dwight D. Eisenhower, *Mandate for Change* (Garden City, N.Y.: Doubleday and Co., 1963), pp. 332–376; and in Arthur Schlesinger, Jr., *A Thousand Days* (Boston: Houghton Mifflin Co., 1965), pp. 320–343, 532–551.

39. The concept of "incrementalism" by which the United States gradually assumed the main responsibility for South Vietnam's defense is explained more fully in Roger Hilsman, *To Move a Nation: the Politics of Foreign Policy in the Administration of John F. Kennedy* (Garden City, N.Y.: Doubleday and Co., 1967).

40. For a detailed discussion of the steps leading to a truce in the Vietnam conflict, see Kissinger, *White House Years,* pp. 226–312, 433–522, 968–1471.

41. Senator Fulbright's thoughts on recent American diplomacy in Vietnam and other regions are contained in J. William Fulbright, *Old Myths and New Realities* (New York: Random House, 1964); *The Arrogance of Power* (New York: Random House, 1966); and *The Crippled Giant* (New York: Random House, 1972). See also Stanley Hoffmann, *Gulliver's Troubles, or the Setting of American Foreign Policy* (New York: McGraw-Hill, 1968).

42. Contemporary versions of neo-isolationist thought are identified and analyzed in Cecil V. Crabb, Jr., *Policy-Makers and Critics: Conflicting Theories of American Foreign Policy* (New York: Praeger Publishers, 1976), pp. 214–299. For a discussion of classical isolationist thinking (in which there were a number of parallels with recent neo-isolationist attitudes), see pp. 1–34.

43. The rivalry between the President and Congress for control over the foreign policy process, focusing upon the post-Vietnam War era, is the major theme of Crabb and Holt, *Invitation to Struggle.*

44. See J. William Fulbright, "The Legislator as Educator," *Foreign Affairs,* **57** (Spring, 1979), 719–733.

45. The impact of the Vietnam War upon American public opinion is analyzed in James Chace, "Is a Foreign Policy Consensus Possible?" *Foreign Affairs,* **57** (Fall, 1978), 1–17; Daniel Yankelovich, "Farewell to 'President Knows Best,'" ibid. (Special Issue, 1978), 670–693; and John E. Rielly, "The American Mood: A Foreign Policy of Self-Interest," *Foreign Policy,* **34** (Spring, 1979), 74–87. For Asian complaints about the lack of American leadership in the region after the war, see the views of S. Rajaratnam, an official of Singapore, in the *New York Times,* November 16, 1980; and the views of Wee Cho Yaw, an official of the Association of Southeast Asian Nations, as quoted in the Baton Rouge *Morning Advocate,* November 27, 1980.

46. Developments in Southeast Asia in the post-Vietnam War era are treated more fully in Bellows, "Proxy War in Indochina," 13–30; in G. W. Choudhury, "China's Policy Toward South Asia," *Current History,* **76** (April, 1979), 155–159; in Barry Wain, "The Indochina Refugee Crisis," *Foreign Affairs,* **58** (Fall, 1979), 160–181; and in the analysis by Bernard Weinraub, *New York Times,* December 28, 1981.

47. The forces influencing Thailand's diplomatic behavior are identified in Daniel Wit, *Thailand: Another Vietnam* (New York: Charles Scribner's Sons, 1968).

48. Events leading to the "partition" of India, and the emergence of India and Pakistan as independent nations, are described in: Beatrice P. Lamb, *India: A World in Transition* (New York: Praeger Publishers, 1963), pp. 73–97; and Ronald Segal, *The Anguish of India* (New York: New American Library, 1965), pp. 211–255.

49. Background discussion on American diplomacy toward this region down to the early post-World War II period is provided in W. Norman Brown, *The United States and India and Pakistan* (Cambridge, Mass.: Harvard University Press, 1953).

50. See, for example, the viewpoints of the Eisenhower Administration, as contained in President Dwight D. Eisenhower's memoirs, *Waging Peace* (Garden City, N.Y.: Doubleday and Co., 1965), pp. 485–513. President John F. Kennedy's viewpoints toward India, emphasizing its role as "the key area" of Asia, are examined in Schlesinger, *A Thousand Days,* pp. 522–531.

51. The rationale for large-scale American and other forms of Western aid to India is explained in Barbara Ward, *India and the West: Pattern for a Common Policy,* rev. ed. (New York: W. W. Norton, 1964), pp. 268–292; and in Norman D. Palmer, *South Asia and United States Policy* (Boston: Houghton Mifflin Co., 1966), pp. 133–161.

52. See the views of Prime Minister Indira Gandhi on the crisis in Afghanistan and its implications in the *New York Times,* October 22, 1980; and the interpretation of India's reaction to this crisis in Leslie H. Gelb and Richard H. Ullman, "Keeping Cool at the Khyber Pass," *Foreign Policy,* **38** (Spring, 1980), 14.

53. Recent issues in U.S.-Indian relations are dealt with more fully in: M. G. Bayne, "The Indian Ocean Naval Balance," *Asian Affairs,* **7** (November–December, 1979), 84–95; John M. Newman, "Soviet Strategy in Asia, 1977–79," ibid., **7** (May–June, 1980), 305–335; *U.S. News and World Report,* **91** (December 21, 1981), 34–35; ibid., **92** (February 15, 1982), 25; and Robert L. Hardgrave, Jr., "India Enter the 1980s," *Current History,* **81** (May, 1982), 197–202, 225.

54. India's acquisition of nuclear weapons is treated more fully in Lewis A. Dunn, "Half Past India's Bang," *Foreign Policy,* **36** (Fall, 1979), 71–89. The strategic importance of the Indian Ocean area to the United States, especially after the Soviet incursion into Afghanistan, is discussed in Zalmay Khalilzad, "The Strategic Significance of South Asia," *Current History,* **81** (May, 1982), 193–197, 228–229.

55. See the views of the Indian journalist Rahul Singh in the *New York Times,* October 21, 1981.

56. For background on Pakistani-American relations during the first two decades of Pakistan's independence, see Brown, *The United States and India and Pakistan;* and Palmer, *South Asia and United States Policy,* pp. 161–317.

57. Washington's diplomacy during the 1971 war between India and Pakistan is dealt with in Kissinger, *White House Years,* pp. 842–919.

58. The implications for Pakistan, and for Pakistani-American relations, of the Soviet invasion of Afghanistan are assessed in Gelb and Ullman, "Keeping Cool at the Khyber Pass," 12–14; and see *U.S. News and World Report,* **88** (June 30, 1980), 31–32. For a detailed analysis of the internal and external policies of General Zia's regime, see Christopher Van Hollen, "Leaning on Pakistan," *Foreign Policy,* **38** (Spring, 1980), 35–51; and the interview with General Zia in *Time,* **116** (October 13, 1980), 59.

59. Recent developments in Pakistani-American relations are analyzed more fully in William L. Richter, "Pakistan Under Zia," *Current History,* **76** (April, 1979), 168–172; and the same author's "Pakistan: A New 'Front-Line' State?" in ibid., **81** (May, 1982), 202–207, 225. See also the assessments by Michael T. Kaufman, *New York Times,* September 17, 1981; by Selig S. Harrison in ibid., December 11, 1981; and by Barnett R. Rubin in ibid., February 19, 1982.

60. See the analysis of the impact of the Vietnam War on American foreign policy in Alistair Buchan, "The Indochina War and World Politics," *Foreign Affairs,* **53** (July, 1975), 638–651. See also the views of Takenhiko Yoshihashi, "The Far East," in Abdul A. Said, ed., *America's World Role in the 70s* (Englewood Cliffs, N.J.: Prentice-Hall, 1970), pp. 105–117.

61. The quotation is from President William McKinley's own words, as cited in Thomas A. Bailey, *A Diplomatic History of the American People,* 8th ed. (New York: Appleton-Century-Crofts, 1969), pp. 473–476.

62. Robert O. Tilman, "Malaysia, Singapore and the Philippines," in Wayne Wilcox, et al., eds., *Asia and the International System* (Cambridge, Mass.: Winthrop Publishers, 1973), pp. 218–219.

63. Secretary of State Rusk's views are cited in Greene, *U.S. Policy and the Security of Asia,* p. 100.

64. Recent economic and political conditions in the Philippines are analyzed in Richard J. Kessler, "The Philippines: the Next Iran?" *Asian Affaris,* **7** (January–February, 1980), 148–161; in Belinda A. Aquino, "The Philippines Under Marcos," *Current History,* **81** (April, 1982), 160–164, 182; by William Branigin, in the Baton Rouge *Sunday Advocate,* December 20, 1981; and by Carl H. Landé, "Philippines Prospects After Martial Law," *Foreign Affairs,* **59** (Summer, 1981), 1147–1169.

65. More detailed discussion of the Korean War may be found in John W. Spanier, *The Truman-MacArthur Controversy and the Korean War* (Cambridge, Mass.: Belknap Press of Harvard University, 1959); and in Matthew B. Ridgway, *The Korean War* (New York: Popular Library, 1967).

66. Thus, in his memoirs, President Harry Truman observed that the Korean Peninsula was "one of the places where the Soviet-controlled Communist world might choose to attack." After North Korea attacked South Korea, Truman likened developments to the 1930s, when "each time that the democracies failed to act it had encouraged the aggressors to keep going ahead. Communism was acting in Korea just as Hitler, Mussolini, and the Japanese had acted. . . ." Failure to resist this Communist intrusion would "mean a third world war. . . ." See Harry S Truman, *Memoirs,* Vol. 2 (Garden City, N.Y.: Doubleday and Co., 1956), pp. 331, 333.

67. Gareth Porter, "Time to Talk With North Korea," *Foreign Policy,* **34** (Spring, 1979), 56.

68. See the views of Donald S. Zagoria, as quoted in *idem.*

69. Conditions within North Korea, and the government's changing viewpoints on a negotiated settlement of the Korean question, are analyzed in ibid., pp. 57–67.

70. See the discussion of the possibility of a South Korean move against North Korea, in ibid, pp. 60–61.

71. Recent developments within South Korea are discussed in: Kim Yong-Hwan, "Korea

Adapts to the New Economic Order," *Asian Affairs,* **7** (September–October, 1979), 8–12; Fuji Kamiya, "The Korean Peninsula After Park Chung Hee," *Asian Survey,* **20** (July, 1980), 744–753; and see the discussion of South Korea's economic conditions and problems in E. S. Browning, "East Asia in Search of a Second Economic Miracle," *Foreign Affairs,* **60** (Fall, 1981), 123–147.

72. Korean-American relations under the new regime in Seoul are discussed by James P. Sterba, in *New York Times,* June 15 and 23, 1980; and in *U.S. News and World Report,* **89** (September 8, 1980), 32. See also William R. Feeney, "U.S. Strategic Interests in the Pacific," *Current History,* **81** (April, 1982), 145–150, 183–185.

73. Edwin O. Reischauer, *The United States and Japan,* rev. ed. (New York: Viking Press, 1957), p. 10.

74. *Idem.*

75. President Theodore Roosevelt's views on the Russo-Japanese War are quoted in Richard W. Leopold, *The Growth of American Foreign Policy* (New York: Alfred A. Knopf, 1962), p. 269; and see P. J. Treat, *Diplomatic Relations Between The United States and Japan* (Stanford: Stanford University Press, 1938).

76. For a fuller discussion of Japan's "Twenty-One Demands" on China during World War I, and of President Woodrow Wilson's reactions to them, see Pratt, *A History of United States Foreign Policy,* pp. 540–541.

77. America's response to Japanese expansionism in Manchuria during the early 1930s is analyzed in Robert H. Ferrell, *American Diplomacy in the Great Depression: Hoover-Stimson Foreign Policy, 1929–1933* (New York: W. W. Norton, 1957); and the deterioration in Japanese-American relations thereafter is discussed in Herbert Feis, *The Road to Pearl Harbor* (New York: Atheneum, 1963).

78. The impact of the American military occupation upon Japanese society is discussed in detail in Reischauer, *The United States and Japan,* pp. 205–291.

79. Edwin O. Reischauer, *Beyond Vietnam: the United States and Asia* (New York: Random House, 1967), p. 135; and George F. Kennan, "After the Cold War: American Foreign Policy in the 1970s," *Foreign Affairs,* **51** (October, 1972), 222.

80. An illuminating treatment of Japanese-American trade questions is provided in James C. Abegglen and Thomas M. Hout, "Facing Up to the Trade Gap with Japan," *Foreign Affairs,* **57** (Fall, 1978), 146–168. For Japanese views on trade controversies with the United States, see Sadako Ogata, "Some Japanese Views on United States-Japan Relations in the 1980s," *Asian Survey,* **20** (July, 1980), 694–707. See also the views of Japanese Prime Minister Suzuki, in the Baton Rouge *Morning Advocate,* October 19, 1980.

81. George W. Ball, *The Discipline of Power: Essentials of a Modern World Structure* (Boston: Atlantic-Little, Brown, 1968), p. 196; and the same author's *Diplomacy for a Crowded World* (Boston: Atlantic-Little, Brown, 1976), p. 188.

82. See the views of Japanese Prime Minister Zenko Suzuki, as reported in the *New York Times,* August 19, 1980.

83. Michael Pillsbury, "A Japanese Card?" *Foreign Policy,* **33** (Winter, 1978–79), 3–31. Our discussion of the forces producing a reexamination of Japanese defense policy relies heavily upon this illuminating analysis. More recent analyses of the issue may be found in Gerald Benjamin, "Japan in the World of the 1980s," *Current History,* **81** (April, 1982), 168–173; 179–180; the assessment of Japanese-American relations by Assistant Secretary of State John H. Holdridge, "Japan and the United States: A Cooperative Relationship," as distributed by the State Department (Current Policy #374), March 1, 1982, pp. 1–6; and Gerald L. Curtis, "Japanese Security Policies and the United States," *Foreign Affairs,* **59** (Spring, 1981), 852–875.

84. Ibid., p. 16; and R. W. Apple, Jr., in *New York Times,* November 19, 1980.

85. See Drew Middleton, in *New York Times,* October 17, 1980.

86. See President Richard M. Nixon's report to Congress, *U.S. Foreign Policy for the 1970s:*

Building for Peace (Washington, D.C.: the White House, 1971), pp. 102–105; and his report for the following year, *U.S. Foreign Policy for the 1970's: the Emerging Structure of Peace* (Washington, D.C.: the White House, 1972), pp. 52–59.

87. See Richard M. Nixon, *The Memoirs of Richard Nixon,* Vol. 2 (New York: Warner Books, 1978), pp. 20–21; and *U.S. Foreign Policy for the 1970s: the Emerging Structure of Peace,* pp. 52–53. An informative discussion of the transition in Sino-Japanese relations is provided in Hong N. Kim, "Sino-Japanese Relations in the Post-Mao Era," *Asian Affairs,* 7 (January–February, 1980), 161–182.

Bibliography

Chapter 1. Foundations of American Foreign Policy

Alexander, Yonah. *Terrorism: Theory and Practice* (Boulder, Colo.: Westview Press, 1980).

Art, Robert J., and Kenneth N. Waltz. *The Use of Force: International Politics and Foreign Policy,* 2nd ed. (Washington, D.C.: University Press of America, 1981).

Barnet, Richard J. *Real Security: Restoring American Power in a Dangerous Decade* (New York: Simon and Schuster, 1981).

Bartlett, C. C. *The Rise and Fall of the Pax Americana: United States Foreign Policy in the Twentieth Century* (New York: St. Martin's Press, 1975).

Belfiglio, Valentine J. *American Foreign Policy* (Washington, D.C.: University Press of America, 1979).

Beres, Louis Rene, *Apocalypse: Nuclear Catastrophe in World Politics* (Chicago, Ill.: University of Chicago Press, 1980).

Bull, Hedley. *The Anarchical Society: A Study of Order in World Politics* (New York: Columbia University Press, 1977).

Bundy, William P., ed. *America and the World, 1980* (New York: Pergamon Press, 1981).

Cline, Ray S. *World Power Trends and U.S. Foreign Policy for the 1980s* (Boulder, Colo.: Westview Press, 1980).

Cohen, Raymond. *Threat Perception in International Crisis* (Madison, Wisc.: University of Wisconsin Press, 1979).

Conquest, Robert. *Present Danger: Towards a Foreign Policy* (Stanford, Calif.: Hoover Institution Press, 1979).

Doob, Leonard W. *The Pursuit of Peace* (Westport, Conn.: Greenwood Press, 1981).

Duignan, Peter, and Alvin Rabushka, eds. *The United States in the 1980s* (Stanford, Calif.: Hoover Institution Press, 1980).

East, Maurice A., Stephen A. Salmore, and Charles F. Hermann, eds. *Why Nations Act: Theoretical Perspectives for Comparative Foreign Policy Studies* (Beverly Hills, Calif.: Sage Publications, 1978).

Eckes, Alfred E., Jr. *The United States and the Global Struggle for Minerals* (Austin, Texas: The University of Texas Press, 1979).

Findling, John E. *Dictionary of American Diplomatic History (Westport, Conn.: Greenwood Press, 1980).

Haines, Gerald K., and J. Samuel Walker, eds. *American Foreign Relations: A Historiographical Review* (Westport, Conn.: Greenwood Press, 1981).

Holsti, Ole R., Randolph M. Siverson, and Alexander L. George, eds. *Change in the International System* (Boulder, Colo.: Westview Press, 1980).

Isaak, Robert A. *American Democracy and World Power* (New York: St. Martin's Press, 1977).

Jones, Roy E. *Principles of Foreign Policy: The Civil State in its World Setting* (New York: St. Martin's Press, 1979).

Joynt, Cary B., and Percy E. Corbett. *Theory and Reality in World Politics* (Pittsburgh, Pa.: University of Pittsburgh Press, 1978).

Kegley, Charles W., Jr., and Pat McGowan, eds. *Challenges to America: United States Foreign Policy in the 1980s* (Beverly Hills, Calif.: Sage Publications, 1979).

Lauren, Paul Gordon, ed. *Diplomacy: New Approaches in History, Theory, and Policy* (New York: Free Press, 1979).

Lockhart, Charles. *Bargaining in International Conflicts* (New York: Columbia University Press, 1979).

Luttwak, Edward N. *Strategy and Politics: Collected Essays* (New Brunswick, N.J.: Transaction Book, 1980).

Mandelbaum, Michael. *The Nuclear Revolution: International Politics Before and After Hiroshima* (New York: Cambridge University Press, 1981).

Mansbach, Richard W., and John A. Vasquez. *In Search of Theory: A New Paradigm for Global Politics* (New York: Columbia University Press, 1980).

Micholus, Edward F. *Transnational Terrorism: A Chronology of Events, 1968–1979* (Westport, Conn.: Greenwood Press, 1980).

O'Neill, Bard E., William R. Heaton, and Donald J. Alberts, eds. *Insurgency in the Modern World* (Boulder, Colo.: Westview Press, 1980).

Chapter 2. The American Ethos and Foreign Affairs

Baron, Dona, ed. *The National Purpose Reconsidered* (New York: Columbia University Press, 1978).

Belfiglio, Valentine J. *American Foreign Policy* (Washington D.C.: University Press of America, 1979).

Brown, Peter G., and Douglas MacLean, eds. *Human Rights and U.S. Foreign Policy* (Lexington, Mass.: D. C. Heath, 1979).

Bundy, William P., ed. *Two Hundred Years of American Foreign Policy* (New York: New York University Press, 1977).

Etheridge, Lloyd D. *A World of Men: the Private Sources of American Foreign Policy* (Cambridge, Mass.: MIT Press, 1978).

Farer, Tom J. *Toward a Humanitarian Diplomacy: A Primer for Policy* (New York: Columbia University Press, 1980).

Fromkin, David. *The Independence of Nations* (New York: Praeger Publishers, 1981).

Herz, Martin F., ed. *Decline of the West? George Kennan and His Critics* (Washington, D.C.: Ethics and Public Policy Center, Georgetown University, 1978).

Johansen, Robert C. *The National Interest and the Human Interest: An Analysis of U.S. Foreign Policy* (Princeton, N.J.: Princeton University Press, 1980).

Liska, George. *Quest for Equilibrium: America and the Balance of Power on Land and Sea* (Baltimore, Md.: Johns Hopkins University Press, 1977).

Newberg, Paula R., ed. *The Politics of Human Rights* (New York: Columbia University Press, 1980).

Poole, Peter A. *Profiles in American Foreign Policy: Stimson, Kennan, Acheson, Dulles, Rusk, Kissinger, and Vance* (Washington, D.C.: University Press of America, 1981).

Rubin, Barry M., and Elizabeth P. Spiro, eds. *Human Rights and U.S. Foreign Policy* (Boulder, Colo.: Westview Press, 1979).

Spanier, John, and Eric M. Uslaner. *Foreign Policy*

and the Democratic Dilemmas (New York: Holt, Rinehart, and Winston, 1981).

Stoessinger, John G. Crusaders and Pragmatists: Movers of Modern American Foreign Policy (New York: W. W. Norton, 1979).

Thompson, Kenneth W. Morality and Foreign Policy (Baton Rouge: Louisiana State University Press, 1980).

Tucker, Robert W., "The Purposes of American Power," Foreign Affairs, **59** (Winter 1980/81), 241–274.

U.S. Foreign Policy: Future Directions (Washington, D.C.: Congressional Quarterly, 1979).

Wank, Solomon, ed. Doves and Diplomats (Westport, Conn.: Greenwood Press, 1978).

Williams, William Appleman. America Confronts a Revolutionary World: 1776–1976 (New York: Morrow, 1976).

Chapter 3. The Presidency: Focal Point of the Policy Process

Alexander, L. George. Presidential Decision-Making in Foreign Policy: The Effective Use of Information and Advice (Boulder, Colo.: Westview Press, 1980).

Bessette, Joseph M., and Jeffrey Tulis, eds. The Presidency in the Constitutional Order (Baton Rouge: Louisiana State University Press, 1981).

Cronin, Thomas E. The State of the Presidency (Boston, Mass.: Little, Brown and Co., 1980).

Dallek, Robert. Franklin D. Roosevelt and American Foreign Policy, 1932–1945 (New York: Oxford University Press, 1979).

Davis, Vincent, ed. The Post-Imperial Presidency (New Brunswick, N.J.: Transaction Books, 1980).

Donovan, Robert J. Conflict and Crisis: The Presidency of Harry S Truman, 1945–1948 (New York: W. W. Norton, 1977).

Edwards, George C., III. Presidential Influence in Congress (San Francisco, Calif.: W. H. Freeman, 1980).

Falkowski, Lawrence, S. Presidents, Secretaries of State, and Crises in U.S. Foreign Relations: A Model and Predictive Analysis (Boulder, Colo.: Westview Press, 1978).

Franck, Thomas M. The Tethered Presidency (New York: Columbia University Press, 1981).

Golden, William T., ed. Science Advice to the President (New York: Pergamon Press, 1980).

Grossman, Michael B., and Martha J. Kumar. Portraying the President: the White House and the News Media (Baltimore: Johns Hopkins University Press, 1981).

Head, Richard G., Frisco W. Short, and Robert C. McFarlane. Crisis Resolution: Presidential Decision-Making in the Mayaguez and Korean Confrontations (Boulder, Colo: Westview Press, 1979).

Hoffman, Nicholas von. Make-Believe Presidents: Illusions of Power from McKinley to Carter (New York: Pantheon Books, 1978).

Meltsner, Arnold J., ed. Politics and the Oval Office (San Francisco, Calif.: Institute for Contemporary Studies, 1981).

Mollenhoff, Clark R. The President Who Failed: Carter Out of Control (New York: Macmillan, 1980).

Neumann, Robert G. "Leadership: Franklin Roosevelt, Truman, Eisenhower, and Today" Presidential Studies Quarterly, **10** (Winter, 1980), 10–18.

Neustadt, Richard E. Presidential Power: The Politics of Leadership from FDR to Carter, 3rd ed. (New York: John Wiley & Sons, 1980).

Nuechterlein, Donald E. National Interests and Presidential Leadership: The Setting of Priorities (Boulder, Colo.: Westview Press, 1978).

Orman, John M. Presidential Secrecy and Deception: Beyond the Power to Persuade (Westport, Conn.: Greenwood Press, 1980).

Pious, Richard M. The American Presidency (New York: Basic Books, 1979).

Polsby, Nelson W., ed. The Modern Presidency (Berkeley, Calif.: University of California Press, 1981).

Porter, Roger. Presidential Decision Making: The

Economic Policy Board (New York: Cambridge University Press, 1980).

Sapin, Burton M. "Isn't It Time for a Modest Presidency in Foreign Affairs? Reflections on the Carter Performance," *Presidential Studies Quarterly,* **10** (Winter, 1980), 19–27.

Schandler, Herbert Y. *The Unmaking of a President: Lyndon Johnson and Vietnam* (Princeton, N.J.: Princeton University Press, 1977).

Theoharris, Athan, ed. *The Truman Presidency: The Origins of The Imperial Presidency and the National Security State* (Pine Plains, N.Y.: Coleman, 1979).

Thompson, Kenneth W. *The Presidency and the Public Philosophy* (Baton Rouge: Louisiana State University Press, 1981).

Chapter 4. The State Department and Other Executive Agencies

Adelman, Kenneth L. "Speaking of America, Public Diplomacy in Our Time," *Foreign Affairs,* **59** (Spring, 1981), 913–937.

Beaulac, Willard L. "Our Musical Chairs Diplomacy," *Foreign Service Journal,* **55** (July, 1978), 14–15, 38–39.

Brown, Peter G., and Douglas MacLean, eds. *Human Rights and U.S. Foreign Policy: Principles and Applications* (Lexington, Mass.: D. C. Heath, 1979).

Brown, Seyom. *The Crises of Power: An Interpretation of United States Foreign Policy During the Kissinger Years* (New York: Columbia University Press, 1979).

Cabot, John M. *First Line Defense: Forty Years' Experiences of a Career Diplomat* (Washington, D.C.: Foreign Service School, Georgetown University, 1979).

Darling, F. C. "Political Functions of the United States Embassy in Thailand," *Asian Survey,* **18** (November, 1978), 1191–1207.

Emerson, John K. *The Japanese Thread: A Life in the U.S. Foreign Service* (New York: Holt, Rinehart, and Winston, 1978).

Finger, Seymour M. *Your Man at the U.N.: People,* *Politics, and Bureaucracy in the Making of Foreign Policy* (New York: Columbia University Press, 1980).

Fraenkel, Richard M., et al., eds. *The Role of U.S. Agriculture in Foreign Policy.* (New York: Praeger Publishers, 1979).

Herz, Martin F. "Maxwell Gluck and All That," *Foreign Service Journal,* **55** (May, 1978), 19–23.

Kertesz, Stephen D. "Achievements and Pitfalls of American Diplomacy," *Political Science Quarterly,* **94** (Fall, 1979), 391–405.

Lenderking, William R., Jr. "USICA and the Triumph of Bureaucratic Inertia," *Foreign Service Journal,* **56** (November, 1979), 18–19, 38–40.

Nikolayev, Y. "U.S. Diplomatic Service As Others See Us," *Foreign Service Journal,* **55** (January, 1978), 6–12.

Nuechterlein, D. E. "Concept of National Interest: a Time for New Approaches," *Orbis,* **23** (Spring, 1979), 73–92.

Perry, Jack. "On Being a Deputy Chief of Mission," *Foreign Service Journal,* **55** (August, 1978), 16–19, 38.

Poole, Peter A. "John Foster Dulles: Hard-Liner or Tightrope-Walker?" *Foreign Service Journal,* **56** (October, 1979), 30–33, 41.

Silberman, Laurence H. "Toward Presidential Control of the State Department," *Foreign Affairs,* **57** (Spring, 1979), 872-893.

Simpson, Smith. *The Crisis in American Diplomacy: Shots Across the Bow of the State Department* (North Quincy, Mass.: The Christopher Publishing House, 1980).

Thurston, Raymond L. "The Ambassador and the CIA," *Foreign Service Journal,* **56** (January, 1979), 22–24.

Valeriani, Richard. *Travels with Henry* (Boston: Houghton Mifflin Co., 1979).

Vogelgesang, S. "Diplomacy of Human Rights," *International Studies Quarterly,* **23** (June, 1979), 16–45.

Warshawsky, Howard. "The Department of State and Human Rights: a Case Study of the

Human Rights Bureau," *World Affairs,* **142** (Winter, 1980), 188–215.

Wimmel, Kenneth. "What is Public Diplomacy?" *Foreign Service Journal,* **55** (October, 1978), 31–34, 42–44.

Chapter 5. National Security Policy

Adler, Emanuel. "Executive Command and Control in Foreign Policy: the CIA's Covert Activities," *Orbis,* **23** (Fall, 1979), 671–696.

Blechman, Barry M., and Stephen S. Kaplan. *Force Without War: U.S. Armed Forces as a Political Instrument* (Washington, D.C.: The Brookings Institution, 1978).

Chester, Edward W. *The United States and Six Atlantic Outposts: The Military and Economic Consequences* (Port Washington, NY.: Kennikat Press, 1979).

Cleave, William R. Van, and S. T. Cohen. *Tactical Nuclear Weapons: An Examination of the Issues* (New York: Crane, Russak, 1978).

Collins, John M. *U.S.-Soviet Military Balance: Concepts and Capabilities* (New York: McGraw-Hill, 1980).

Cordier, Sherwood S. *Calculus of Power: The Current Soviet-American Conventional Military Balance in Central Europe,* 3rd ed. (Washington, D.C.: University Press of America, 1980).

Ebinger, Charles K. *The Critical Link: Energy and National Security* (Cambridge, Mass.: Ballinger Publishing Co., 1981).

Eysenck, H.J., and Leon Kamin. *The Intelligence Controversy* (New York: John Wiley and Sons, 1981).

Fallows, James. *National Defense* (New York: Random House, 1981).

Gabriel, Richard A. *The New Red Legions* (Westport, Conn.: Greenwood Press, 1980).

Gansler, Jacques S. *The Defense Industry* (Cambridge, Mass.: MIT Press, 1980).

Godson, Roy, ed. *Intelligence Requirements for the 1980s: Analysis and Estimates* (Washington, D.C.: National Strategy Information Center, 1980).

Graham, Daniel O. *Shall America Be Defended? SALT II and Beyond* (New Rochelle, N.Y.: Arlington House, 1979).

Hanreider, Wolfram F., ed. *Arms Control and Security: Current History* (Boulder, Colo.: Westview Press, 1979).

Harhavy, Robert, and Edward A. Kolodziej, eds. *American Security Policy and Policy-Making* (Lexington, Mass.: D. C. Heath, 1980).

Heuer, Richard J., ed. *Quantitative Approaches to Political Intelligence: The CIA Experience* (Boulder, Colo.: Westview Press, 1978).

Jordan, Amos, and William J. Taylor, Jr. *American National Security: Policy and Process* (Baltimore, Md.: Johns Hopkins University Press, 1981).

Karsten, Peter, ed. *The Military in America* (New York: Free Press, 1980).

Kinnard, Douglas. *The Secretary of Defense* (Lexington, Kent.: University of Kentucky Press, 1980).

Knorr, Klaus, and Frank N. Trager, eds. *Economic Issues and National Security* (Lawrence, Kan.: The Regents Press of Kansas, 1978).

Long, Franklin A., and Judith Reppy, eds. *The Genesis of New Weapons: Decision-Making for Military R & D* (New York: Pergamon Press, 1980).

Margiotta, Franklin D., ed. *Evolving Strategic Realities: Implications for U.S. Policy-Makers* (Washington, D.C.: National Defense University Press, 1980).

Martin, Laurence, ed. *Strategic Thought in the Nuclear Age* (Baltimore, Md.: Johns Hopkins University Press, 1980).

Morgan, Patrick M. *Deterrence: A Conceptual Analysis* (Beverly Hills, Calif.: Sage Publications, 1977).

Nelson, Keith L., and Spencer C. Olin. *Why War? Ideology, Theory and History* (Berkeley, Calif.: University of California Press, 1979).

Nitze, Paul H., Leonard Sullivan, Jr., et al. *Secur-*

ing the Seas: The Soviet Naval Challenge and Western Alliance Options (Boulder, Colo.: Westview Press, 1979).

Osgood, Robert E. *Limited War Revisited* (Boulder, Colo.: Westview Press, 1979).

Payne, Samuel B., Jr. *The Soviet Union and SALT* (Cambridge, Mass.: MIT Press, 1980).

Powers, Thomas. *The Man Who Kept the Secrets: Richard Helms and the CIA* (New York: Alfred A. Knopf, 1979).

Pranger, Robert J., and Roger P. Labrie, eds. *Nuclear Strategy and National Security Points of View* (Washington, D.C.: American Enterprise Institute for Public Policy Research, 1977).

Rose, John P. *The Evolution of U.S. Army Nuclear Doctrine, 1945–1980* (Boulder, Colo.: Westview Press, 1981).

Scott, Harriet Fast, and William F. Scott. *The Armed Forces of the USSR* (Boulder, Colo.: Westview Press, 1979).

Slack, Walter H. *The Grim Science: The Struggle for Power* (Port Washington, N.Y.: Kennikat Press, 1981).

Small, Melvin. *Was War Necessary? National Security and U.S. Entry Into War* (Beverly Hills, Calif.: Sage Publications, 1980).

Smith, Gerard. *Doubletalk: The Story of SALT I* (New York: Doubleday and Co., 1980).

Speed, Roger D. *Strategic Deterrence in the 1980s* (Stanford, Calif.: Hoover Institution Press, 1979).

Stockholm International Peace Research Institute (SIPRI). *Strategic Disarmament, Verification, and National Security* (New York: Crane, Russak & Co., 1978).

Talbott, Strobe. *Endgame: The Inside Story of SALT II* (New York: Harper & Row, 1979).

Thompson, W. Scott, ed. *National Security in the 1980s: From Weakness to Strength* (San Francisco, Calif.: Institute for Contemporary Studies, 1980).

U.S. Defense Policy: Weapons, Strategy, and Commitments, 2nd ed. (Washington, D.C.: Congressional Quarterly Press, 1980).

Wolfe, Thomas W. *The SALT Experience* (Cambridge, Mass.: Ballinger, 1979).

Wong-Fraser, Agatha S. Y. *Symmetry and Selectivity in U.S. Defense Policy: A Grand Design or a Major Mistake?* (Washington, D.C.: University Press of America, 1980).

Chapter 6. Propaganda and Economic Policy Instruments

Anell, Lars, and Birgitta Nygren. *The Developing Countries and the World Economic Order* (New York: St. Martin's Press, 1980).

Arnove, Robert F. *Philanthropy and Diplomacy: the Foundations at Home and Abroad* (Boston: G. K. Hall, 1980).

Cline, William R., Noboru Kawanabe, T. O. M. Kronjö, and Thomas Williams. *Trade Negotiations in the Tokyo Round: A Quantitative Assessment* (Washington, D.C.: The Brookings Institution, 1978).

Cohen, Stephen D. *The Making of United States International Economic Policy: Principles, Problems, and Proposals for Reform* (New York: Praeger Publishers, 1977).

Cooling, Benjamin Franklin, ed. *War, Business and World Military-Industrial Complexes* (Port Washington, N.Y.: Kennikat Press, 1981).

Denoon, David B. H., ed. *The New International Economic Order: A U.S. Response* (New York: Columbia University Press, 1979).

DePauw, John W. *Soviet-American Trade Negotiations* (New York: Praeger Publishers, 1979).

Destler, I. M. *Making Foreign Economic Policy* (Washington, D.C.: The Brookings Institution, 1980).

Feld, Werner J. *Multinational Corporations and U.N. Politics: The Quest for Codes of Conduct* (New York: Pergamon Press, 1980).

Green, Robert T., and James M. Lutz. *The United States and World Trade: Changing Patterns and Dimensions* (New York: Praeger Publishers, 1978).

Grossack, Irvin Millman. *The International Economy and the National Interest* (Bloomington, Ind.: Indiana University Press, 1980).

Hellawell, Robert, ed. *United States Taxation and Developing Countries* (New York: Columbia University Press, 1980).

Hirschman, Albert O. *National Power and the Structure of Foreign Trade* (Berkeley, Calif.: University of California Press, 1980).

Hopkins, Raymond F., and Donald J. Puchala. *Global Food Interdependence: Challenge to American Foreign Policy* (New York: Columbia University Press, 1980).

Hymer, Stephen Herbert. *The Multinational Corporation: A Radical Approach* (New York: Cambridge University Press, 1979).

Kahn, Herman. *World Economic Development: Projections from 1979 to the Year 2000* (New York: William Morrow, 1979).

Kahn, Herman, William Brown, and Leon Martel. *The Next 200 Years: A Scenario for America and the World* (New York: William Morrow, 1976).

Katzenstein, Peter J., ed. *Between Power and Plenty: Foreign Economic Policies of Advanced Industrial States* (Madison, Wisc.: University of Wisconsin Press, 1978).

Kumar, Khrishna, ed. *Transnational Enterprises: Their Impact on Third World Societies and Cultures* (Boulder, Colo.: Westview Press, 1980).

Laszlo, Ervin, and Joel Kurtzman, eds. *The Structure of the World Economy and Prospects for a New International Economic Order* (New York: Pergamon Press, 1980).

Lindblom, Charles E. *Politics and Markets: The World's Political-Economic Systems* (New York: Basic Books, 1977).

Mickelwait, Donald R., Charles F. Sweet, and Elliott R. Morss. *New Directions in Development: A Study of U.S. AID* (Boulder, Colo.: Westview Press, 1979).

Olson, Robert K. *U.S. Foreign Policy and the New International Economic Order* (Boulder, Colo.: Westview Press, 1980).

Paarlberg, Robert L. "Lessons of the Grain Embargo," *Foreign Affairs,* **59** (Fall, 1980), 144–162.

Reubens, Edwin P., ed. *The Challenge of the New International Economic Order* (Boulder, Colo.: Westview Press, 1981).

Sauvant, Karl, ed. *Changing Priorities on the International Agenda: The New International Economic Order* (New York: Pergamon Press, 1980).

Scammell, W. M. *The International Economy Since 1945* (New York: St. Martin's Press, 1980).

Turner, Louis. *Oil Companies in the International System,* 2nd ed. (Winchester, Mass.: Allen & Unwin, 1980).

Villamil, Jose D., ed. *Transnational Capitalism and National Development: New Perspectives on Dependence* (Atlantic Highlands, N.J.: Humanities Press, 1979).

Whitman, Marina V. N. *Reflections on Interdependence: Issues for Economic Theory and U.S. Policy* (Pittsburgh, Pa.: University of Pittsburgh Press, 1979).

Zurawicki, Leon. *Multinational Enterprises in the West and East* (Alphen aan den Rijn, Netherlands: Sijthoff, 1979).

Chapter 7. Congress and the Foreign Policy Process

Abshire, David M., and Ralph D. Nurnberger, eds. *The Growing Power of Congress* (Beverly Hills, Calif.: Sage Publications, 1981).

Arnold, R. Douglas. *Congress and the Bureaucracy: A Theory of Influence* (New Haven, Conn.: Yale University Press, 1979).

Cotton, Norris. *In the Senate: Amidst the Conflict and the Turmoil* (New York: Dodd, Mead, and Co., 1978).

Crabb, Cecil V., Jr., and Pat M. Holt. *Invitation to Struggle: Congress, The President and Foreign Policy* (Washington, D.C.: Congressional Quarterly Press, 1980).

Davidson, Roger H., and Walter J. Oleszek. *Congress and Its Members* (Washington, D.C.: Congressional Quarterly Press, 1981).

Dodd, Lawrence C., and Bruce I. Oppenheimer. *Congress Reconsidered,* 2nd ed. (Washington, D.C.: Congressional Quarterly Press, 1981).

Feuerwerger, Marvin C. *Congress and Israel: Foreign Aid Decision-Making in the House of Representatives, 1969—1976* (Westport, Conn.: Greenwood Press, 1979).

Franck, Thomas F., and Edward Weisband. *Foreign Policy by Congress* (New York: Oxford University Press, 1979).

Jones, Rochelle, and Peter Woll. *The Private World of Congress* (New York: Free Press, 1979).

Kanter, Arnold. *Defense Politics: A Budetary Perspective* (Chicago, Ill.: University of Chicago Press, 1979).

Malbin, Michael J. *Unelected Representatives: Congressional Staff and the Future of Representative Government* (New York: Basic Books, 1980).

Muravchik, Joshua. *The Senate and National Security: A New Mood* (Beverly Hills, Calif.: Sage Publications, 1980).

Oleszek, Walter J. *Congressional Procedures and the Policy Process* (Washington, D.C.: Congressional Quarterly Press, 1978).

Pastor, Robert A. *Congress and the Politics of U.S. Foreign Economic Policy, 1929–1976* (Berkeley, Calif.: University of California Press, 1980).

Pfiffner, James P. *The President, the Budget, and Congress: Impoundment and the 1974 Budget Act* (Boulder, Colo.: Westview Press, 1979).

Platt, Alan, and Lawrence D. Weiler, eds. *Congress and Arms Control* (Boulder, Colo.: Westview Press, 1978).

Spanier, John, and Joseph L. Nogee, eds. *Congress, the Presidency, and American Foreign Policy* (New York: Pergamon Press, 1981).

Stern, Paula. *Water's Edge: Domestic Politics and the Making of American Foreign Policy* (Westport, Conn.: Greenwood Press, 1979).

Chapter 8. The Public Context of Foreign Policy

Barnes, Samuel H., Max Kaase, et al. *Political Action: Mass Participation in Five Western Democracies* (Beverly Hills, Calif.: Sage Publications, 1979).

Graber, Doris A. *Mass Media and American Politics* (Washington, D.C.: Congressional Quarterly Press, 1980).

Halle, Louis J., ed. *Foreign Policy and the Democratic Process: the Geneva Papers* (Washington, D.C.: University Press of America, 1978).

Hanna, Mary T. *Catholics and American Politics* (Cambridge, Mass: Harvard University Press, 1979).

Holloway, Harry, and John George. *Public Opinion: Coalitions, Elites and Masses* (New York: St. Martin's Press, 1980).

Inglehart, Ronald. *The Silent Revolution: Changing Values and Political Styles Among Western Publics* (Princeton, N.J.: Princeton University Press, 1977).

Levering, Ralph B. *The Public and American Foreign Policy, 1918–1978* (New York: William Morrow, 1978).

Locander, Robert. "Carter and the Press: The First Two Years," *Presidential Studies Quarterly,* **10** (Winter, 1980), 106–119.

Mathias, Charles M., Jr. "Ethnic Groups and Foreign Policy," *Foreign Affairs,* **59** (Summer, 1981), 975–999.

Miller, Jake C. *The Black Presence in American Foreign Affairs* (Washington, D.C.: University Press of America, 1978).

Moore, David W. "SALT and Beyond: The Public Is Uncertain," *Foreign Policy,* **35** (Summer, 1979), 68–73.

Orbach, William W. *The American Movement to*

Aid Soviet Jews (Amherst, Mass.: University of Massachusetts Press, 1979).

Russett, Bruce M., and Elizabeth C. Hanson. *Interest and Ideology: The Foreign Policy Beliefs of American Businessmen* (San Francisco, Calif.: W. H. Freeman, 1975).

Said, Abdul Aziz, ed. *Ethnicity and U.S. Foreign Policy* (New York: Praeger Publishers, 1978).

Smith, Anthony. *The Geopolitics of Information: How Western Culture Dominates the World* (New York: Oxford University Press, 1980).

Yankelovich, Daniel. *New Rules: Searching for Self-Fulfillment in a World Turned Upside Down* (New York: Random House, 1981).

Chapter 9. Soviet-American Relations: The Cold War Era

Benningsen, Alexandre A., and S. Enders Wimbush. *Muslim National Communism in the Soviet Union: A Revolutionary Strategy for the Colonial World* (Chicago, Ill.: University of Chicago Press, 1979).

Betts, Richard K. *Soldiers, Statesmen, and Cold War Crises* (Cambridge, Mass.: Harvard University Press, 1977).

Bialer, Seweryn, ed. *The Domestic Context of Soviet Foreign Policy* (Boulder, Colo.: Westview Press, 1981).

Colton, Timothy J. *Commissars, Commanders, and Civilian Authority: The Structure of Soviet Military Politics* (Cambridge, Mass.: Harvard University Press, 1979).

Crozier, Brian. *Strategy of Survival* (New Rochelle, N.Y.: Arlington House Publishers, 1978).

DeSantis, Hugh. *The Diplomacy of Silence: the American Foreign Service, the Soviet Union, and the Cold War* (Chicago: University of Chicago Press, 1981).

Divine, Robert A. *Eisenhower and the Cold War* (New York: Oxford University Press, 1980).

Donaldson, Robert H., ed. *The Soviet Union in the Third World: Successes and Failures* (Boulder, Colo.: Westview Press, 1981).

Grayson, Benson Lee, ed. *The American Image of Russia, 1917–1977* (New York: Frederick Ungar Publishing Co., 1978).

Herz, Martin F. *How the Cold War is Taught* (Washington, D.C.: Ethics and Public Policy Center, Georgetown University, 1978).

Holbraad, Carsten. *Superpowers and International Conflict* (New York: St. Martin's Press, 1979).

Jacobsen, C. G. *Soviet Strategic Initiatives: Challenge and Response* (New York: Praeger Publishers, 1979).

Jönsson, Christer. *Soviet Bargaining Behavior: The Nuclear Test Ban Case* (New York: Columbia University Press, 1979).

Kirk, Grayson, and Nils H. Wessell, eds. *The Soviet Threat: Myths and Realities* (New York: Praeger Publishers, 1978).

Kratochwil, Friedrich V. *International Order and Foreign Policy: A Theoretical Sketch of Post-War International Politics* (Boulder, Colo.: Westview Press, 1978).

Kuniholm, Bruce R. *The Origins of the Cold War in the Near East: Great Power Conflict and Diplomacy in Iran, Turkey, and Greece* (Princeton, N.J.: Princeton University Press, 1980).

Liska, George. *Russia and World Order: Strategic Choices and the Laws of Power in History* (Baltimore, Md.: Johns Hopkins University Press, 1980).

Mastny, Vojtech. *Russia's Road to the Cold War: Diplomacy, Warfare, and the Politics of Communism, 1941–1945* (New York: Columbia University Press, 1979).

McCagg, William O., and Brian D. Silver, eds. *Soviet Asian Ethnic Frontiers* (New York: Pergamon Press, 1979).

Nogee, Joseph L., and Robert H. Donaldson. *Soviet Foreign Policy Since World War II* (New York: Pergamon Press, 1981).

Raymond, Ellsworth. *The Soviet State,* 2nd ed.

(New York: New York University Press, 1977).

Rubinstein, Alvin Z. *Soviet Foreign Policy Since World War II: Imperial and Global* (Cambridge, Mass: Winthrop Publishers, 1981).

Schwartz, Morton. *Soviet Perceptions of the United States* (Berkeley, Calif.: University of California Press, 1978).

Siracusa, Joseph M., and Glen S. Barclay, eds. *The Impact of the Cold War: Reconsiderations* (Port Washington, N.Y.: Kennikat Press, 1977).

Spechler, Dina Rome. *Domestic Influences on Soviet Foreign Policy* (Washington, D.C.: University Press of America, 1978).

Thompson, Kenneth W. *Interpreters and Critics of the Cold War* (Washington, D.C.: University Press of America, 1978).

Uldricks, Teddy J. *Diplomacy and Ideology: The Origins of Soviet Foreign Relations 1917–1930* (Beverly Hills, Calif.: Sage Publications, 1979).

Valenta, Jiri. *Soviet Intervention in Czechoslovakia, 1968* (Baltimore, Md.: Johns Hopkins University Press, 1979).

Wolfe, Alan. *The Rise and Fall of the "Soviet Threat": Domestic Sources of the Cold War Consensus* (Washington, D.C.: Institute for Policy Studies, 1980).

Chapter 10. Soviet-American Relations: The Future of Détente

Aspaturian, Vernon V., Jiri Valenta, and David P. Burke, eds. *Eurocommunism Between East and West* (Bloomington, Ind.: Indiana University Press, 1980).

Beam, Jacob D. *Multiple Exposure: An American Ambassador's Unique Perspective on East-West Issues* (New York: W. W. Norton, 1978).

Bell, Coral. *The Diplomacy of Détente: The Kissinger Era* (New York: St. Martin's Press, 1977).

Bertram, Christoph, ed. *Prospects of Soviet Power in the 1980s* (Hamden, Conn.: Archon Books, 1980).

Bialer, Seweryn. *Stalin's Successors* (New York: Cambridge University Press, 1980).

Bialer, Seweryn, ed. *The Domestic Context of Soviet Foreign Policy* (Boulder, Colo.: Westview Press, 1981).

Blazynski, George. *Flashpoint: Poland* (New York: Pergamon Press, 1980).

Burnstein, Morris, Zvi Gitelman, and William Zimmerman, eds. *East-West Relations and the Future of Eastern Europe: Politics and Economics* (Winchester, Mass.: Allen & Unwin, 1981).

Cohen, Stephen F., Alexander Rabinowitch, and Robert Sharlet, eds. *The Soviet Union Since Stalin* (Bloomington, Ind.: Indiana University Press, 1980).

Congressional Research Service for the House Committee on Foreign Affairs. *Soviet Diplomacy and Negotiating Behavior: Emerging New Context for U.S. Diplomacy* (Washington, D.C.: Government Printing Office, 1979).

Dismukes, Bradford, and James M. McConnell, eds. *Soviet Naval Diplomacy* (New York: Pergamon Press, 1979).

Donaldson, Robert H., ed. *The Soviet Union in the Third World: Successes and Failures* (Boulder, Colo.: Westview Press, 1981).

Duncan, W. Raymond, ed. *Soviet Policy in the Third World* (New York: Pergamon Press, 1980).

Fischer-Galati, Stephen, ed. *Eastern Europe in the 1980s* (Boulder, Colo.: Westview Press, 1981).

Gabriel, Richard A. *The New Red Legions: An Attitudinal Portrait of the Soviet Soldier* (Westport, Conn.: Greenwood Press, 1980).

Gelb, Leslie H., and Richard Ullman. "Keeping Cool at the Khyber Pass," *Foreign Policy,* **38** (Spring, 1980), 3–18.

Goldman, Marshall L. *The Enigma of Soviet Petroleum: Half-Empty or Half-Full?* (Winchester, Mass.: Allen & Unwin, 1980).

Hanson, Philip. *Trade and Technology in Soviet-Western Relations* (New York: Columbia University Press, 1981).

Hoffmann, Erik P., and Frederick J. Fleron. *The Conduct of Soviet Foreign Policy,* 2nd ed. (Hawthorne, N.Y.: Aldine Publishing Co., 1980).

Hoffmann, Erik P., and Robbin F. Laird. *"The Scientific-Technological Revolution" and Soviet Foreign Policy* (New York: Pergamon Press, 1982).

Hough, Jerry F. *Soviet Leadership in Transition* (Washington, D.C.: The Brookings Institution, 1980).

Hyland, William G. "Brezhnev and Beyond," *Foreign Affairs,* **58** (Fall, 1979), 51–66.

Kaplan, Stephen S. *Diplomacy of Power: Soviet Armed Forces as a Political Instrument* (Washington, D.C.: The Brookings Institution, 1981).

Kelley, Donald R., ed. *Soviet Politics in the Brezhnev Era* (New York: Praeger Publishers, 1980).

Legvold, Robert. "Containment Without Confrontation," *Foreign Policy,* **40** (Fall, 1980), 74–98.

Lehman, John, and Seymour Weiss. *Beyond the SALT II Failure* (New York: Praeger Publishers, 1981).

London, Kurt, ed. *The Soviet Union in World Politics* (Boulder, Colo.: Westview Press, 1980).

Neal, Fred Warner, ed. *Détente or Debacle: Common Sense in U.S.-Soviet Relations* (New York: W. W. Norton, 1979).

Neuberger, Egon, and Laura D'Andrea Tyson, eds. *The Impact of International Economic Disturbances on the Soviet Union and Eastern Europe* (New York: Pergamon Press, 1980).

Nogee, Joseph L., and Robert H. Donaldson. *Soviet Foreign Policy Since World War II* (New York: Pergamon Press, 1981).

Pipes, Richard. *U.S.-Soviet Relations in the Era of Détente* (Boulder, Colo.: Westview Press, 1981).

Rosenfielde, Steven, ed. *World Communism at the Crossroads: Military Ascendancy, Political Economy, and Human Welfare* (Boston: Nijhoff, 1980).

Schwab, George, ed. *Eurocommunism: The Ideological and Political-Theoretical Foundations* (Westport, Conn.: Greenwood Press, 1981).

Schwartz, Morton. *Soviet Perceptions of the United States* (Berkeley, Calif.: University of California Press, 1978).

Sheldon, Della W. *Dimensions of Détente* (New York: Praeger Publishers, 1978).

Sivachev, Nikolai V., and Nikolai N. Yakovlev. *Russia and the United States: U.S.-Soviet Relations from the Soviet Point of View* (Chicago: University of Chicago Press, 1979).

Solzhenitsyn, Aleksandr I. *The Mortal Danger: How Misconceptions About Russia Imperil America* (New York: Harper & Row, 1980).

Todd, Emmanuel. *The Final Fall: An Essay on the Decomposition of the Soviet Sphere* (New York: Karz Publishers, 1979).

Tökés, Rudolf, ed. *Eurocommunism and Détente.* (New York: New York University Press, 1979).

Von Geusau, Frans A. M. Alting, ed. *Uncertain Detente* (Alphen aan den Rijn, Netherlands: Sijthoff, 1979).

Wandycz, Piotr S. *The United States and Poland* (Cambridge, Mass.: Harvard University Press, 1980).

Wesson, Robert. *The Aging of Communism.* (New York: Praeger Publishers, 1980).

Wesson, Robert, ed. *The Soviet Union: Looking to the 1980s* (Stanford, Calif.: Hoover Institution Press, 1980).

Wettig, Gerhard. *Broadcasting and Détente: Eastern Policies and Their Implications for East-West Relations* (New York: St. Martin's Press, 1977).

Zagoria, Donald, Robert Legvold, and Richard J. Barnet. "America and Russia: The Rules of the Game," *Foreign Affairs,* **57** (Spring, 1979), 733–795.

Chapter 11. Western Europe: Pivot of American Foreign Policy

Agnelli, Giovanni. "East-West Trade: A European View," *Foreign Affairs,* **58** (Summer, 1980), 1016–1033.

Boggs, Carl. *The Impasse of European Communism* (Boulder, Colo.: Westview Press, 1981).

Burrows, Bernard, Geoffrey Denton, and Geoffrey Edwards. *Federal Solutions to European Issues* (New York: St. Martin's Press, 1978).

Cerny, Philip G. *The Politics of Grandeur: Ideological Aspects of de Gaulle's Foreign Policy* (New York: Cambridge University Press, 1980).

Childs, David, ed. *The Changing Face of Western Communism* (New York: St. Martin's Press, 1980).

Close, Gen. Robert. *Europe Without Defense?* (New York: Pergamon Press, 1979).

DePorte, A. W. *Europe Between the Super-Powers: The Enduring Balance* (New Haven, Conn.: Yale University Press, 1979).

Douglass, Gordon K., ed. *The New Interdependence: The European Community and the United States* (Lexington, Mass.: D. C. Heath, 1979).

Drath, Viola Herms, ed. *Germany in World Politics* (New York: Cycro Press, 1979).

Duroselle, Jean-Baptiste, and Derek Coltman, trans. *France and the United States: From the Beginnings to the Present Day* (Chicago: University of Chicago Press, 1978).

Elliott, Charles F., and Carl A. Linden, eds. *Marxism in the Contemporary West* (Boulder, Colo.: Westview Press, 1980).

Fedder, Edwin J., ed. *Defense Politics of the Atlantic Alliance* (New York: Praeger Publishers, 1980).

Feld, Werner, ed. *Western Europe's Global Reach: Regional Cooperation and Worldwide Aspiration* (New York: Pergamon Press, 1980).

Gatzke, Hans W. *Germany and the United States: "A Special Relationship?"* (Cambridge, Mass.: Harvard University Press, 1980).

Ginsburgs, George, and Alvin Z. Rubinstein, eds. *Soviet Foreign Policy toward Western Europe* (New York: Praeger Publishers, 1978).

Griffith, William E. *The Ostpolitik of the Federal Republic of West Germany* (Cambridge, Mass.: MIT Press, 1978).

Grosser, Alfred. *The Western Alliance: European-American Relations Since 1945* (New York: Continuum, 1980).

Hahn, Walter F., and Robert L. Pfaltzgraff, eds. *Atlantic Community in Crisis: A Redefinition of the Transatlantic Relationship.* (New York: Pergamon Press, 1979).

Hanrieder, Wolfram E. and Graeme P. Auton. *Foreign Policy of West Germany, France and Britain* (Englewood Cliffs, N.J.: Prentice-Hall, 1979).

Hanrieder, Wolfram F., ed. *West German Foreign Policy, 1949–1979* (Boulder, Colo.: Westview Press, 1980).

Harrison, Michael M. *The Reluctant Ally: France and Atlantic Security* (Baltimore, Md.: Johns Hopkins University Press, 1981).

Hill-Norton, Sir Peter. *No Soft Options: The Politico-Military Realities of NATO* (Montreal: McGill-Queen's University Press, 1978).

Holland, Stuart. *Uncommon Market* (New York: St. Martin's Press, 1980).

Hurewitz, Leon, ed. *Contemporary Perspectives on European Integration: Attitudes, Nongovernmental Behavior, and Collective Decision Making* (Westport, Conn.: Greenwood Press, 1980).

Ionescu, G., ed. *The European Alternatives: An Inquiry into the Policies of the European Community* (Alphen aan den Rijn, Netherlands: Sijthoff, 1979).

Ireland, Timothy P. *Creating the Entangling Alliance: The Origins of the North Atlantic Treaty Organization* (Westport, Conn.: Greenwood Press, 1981).

Jordan, Robert S. *Political Leadership in NATO: A Study in Multinational Diplomacy* (Boulder, Colo.: Westview Press, 1979).

Kaiser, Karl, and Hans-Peter Schwartz, eds. *America and Western Europe: Problems and Prospects* (Lexington, Mass.: D. C. Heath, 1979).

Kaplan, Lawrence S., and Robert W. Clawson, eds. *NATO After Thirty Years* (Wilmington, Del.: Scholarly Resources, Inc., 1981).

Katz, Samuel I., ed. *U.S.-European Monetary Relations* (Washington, D.C.: American Enterprise Institute for Public Policy Research, 1979).

Kennedy, Gavin. *Burden Sharing in NATO* (New York: Holmes & Meier, 1979).

Kennedy, Paul M. *The Realities Behind Diplomacy: Background Influences on British External Policy 1865–1980* (Winchester, Mass.: Allen & Unwin, 1980).

Kohl, Wilfrid L., and Giorgio Basevi, eds. *West Germany: A European and Global Power* (Lexington, Mass.: D. C. Heath, 1980).

Krippendorff, Ekkehart, and Volker Rittberger, eds. *The Foreign Policy of West Germany: Formation and Contents* (Beverly Hills, Calif.: Sage Publications, 1980).

Laqueur, Walter. *A Continent Astray: Europe, 1970–1978* (New York: Oxford University Press, 1979).

Leebaert, Derek, ed. *European Security: Prospects for the 1980s* (Lexington, Mass.: D. C. Heath, 1979).

Link, Werner, and Werner J. Feld, eds. *The New Nationalism: Implications for Transatlantic Relations* (New York: Pergamon Press, 1979).

Ménil, Lois Pattison de. *Who Speaks for Europe? The Vision of Charles de Gaulle* (New York: St. Martin's Press, 1978).

Myers, Kenneth A., ed. *NATO: The Next Thirty Years.* (Boulder, Colo.: Westview Press, 1980).

Nitze, Paul H., Leonard Sullivan, Jr., et al. *Securing the Seas: The Soviet Naval Challenge and Western Alliance Options* (Boulder, Colo.: Westview Press, 1979).

Schoenbaum, David. "Dateline Bonn: Uneasy Super-Ally," *Foreign Policy,* 37 (Winter 1979–80), 176–190.

Serfaty, Simon. *Fading Partnership: America and Europe After 30 Years* (New York: Praeger Publishers, 1979).

Serfaty, Simon, ed. *The Foreign Policies of the French Left* (Boulder, Colo.: Westview Press, 1979).

Shlaim, Avi, and G. N. Yannopoulos, eds. *The EEC and Eastern Europe* (New York: Cambridge University Press, 1979).

Sundelius, Bengt. *Foreign Policies of Northern Europe* (Boulder, Colo.: Westview Press, 1981).

Taylor, Phillip. *When Europe Speaks with One Voice: The External Relations of the European Community* (Westport, Conn.: Greenwood Press, 1979).

Tökés, Rudolf L., ed. *Eurocommunism and Détente* (New York: Columbia University Press, 1981).

Treverton, Gregory D. *The "Dollar Drain" and American Forces in Germany.* (Athens, Ohio: Ohio University Press, 1978).

Tsoukalis, Loukas. *The European Community and Its Mediterranean Enlargement* (Winchester, Mass.: Allen & Unwin, 1981).

Udis, Bernard. *From Guns to Butter: Technology Organizations and Reduced Military Spending in Western Europe* (Cambridge, Mass.: Ballinger, 1978).

Chapter 12. The Middle East: Israel and the Arabs, Oil, and the Persian Gulf Area

Abu-Jaber, Faiz S. *American-Arab Relations from Wilson to Nixon* (Washington, D.C.: University Press of America, 1979).

Ajami, Fouad. *The Arab Predicament: Arab Political Thought and Practice Since 1967* (New York: Cambridge University Press, 1981).

Ajami, Riad A. *Arab Response to the Multinationals* (New York: Praeger Publishers, 1979).

Akhavi, Shahrough. *Religion and Politics in Con-*

temporary Iran (Albany, N.Y.: State University of New York Press, 1980).

Alexander, Yonah, and Allan Nanes, eds. *The United States and Iran: A Documentary History* (Washington, D.C.: University Publications of America, 1980).

Amirsadeghi, Hossein, and R. W. Ferrier, eds. *Twentieth Century Iran* (New York: Holmes & Meier, 1977).

Amos, John W., II. *Arab-Israeli Military/Political Relations: Arab Perceptions and the Politics of Escalation* (New York: Pergamon Press, 1979).

Amos, John W., II. *Palestinian Resistance: Organization of a Nationalist Movement* (New York: Pergamon Press, 1981).

Aronson, Shlomo. *Conflict and Bargaining in the Middle East: An Israeli Perspective* (Baltimore, Md.: Johns Hopkins University Press, 1979).

Ayoob, Mohammed. *The Politics of Islamic Reassertion* (New York: St. Martin's Press, 1981).

Barker, Raymond William. *Egypt's Uncertain Revolution Under Nasser and Sadat* (Cambridge, Mass.: Harvard University Press, 1978).

Beling, Willard A., ed. *King Faisal and the Modernization of Saudi Arabia* (Boulder, Colo.: Westview Press, 1980).

Bezboruah, Monoranjan. *U.S. Strategy in the Indian Ocean: The International Response* (New York: Praeger Publishers, 1977).

Bill, James A., and Carl Leiden. *Politics in the Middle East* (Boston: Little, Brown and Co., 1979).

Binder, Leonard. *In a Moment of Enthusiasm: Political Power and the Second Stratum in Egypt* (Chicago: University of Chicago Press, 1978).

Borthwick, Bruce M. *Comparative Politics of the Middle East* (Englewood Cliffs, N.J.: Prentice-Hall, 1980).

Brown, William R. *The Last Crusade: A Negotiator's Middle East Handbook* (Chicago, Ill.: Nelson-Hall, 1980).

Cottrell, Alvin J., ed. *The Persian Gulf States* (Baltimore, Md.: Johns Hopkins University Press, 1979).

Cottrell, Alvin J., et al. *Seapower and Strategy in the Indian Ocean* (Beverly Hills, Calif.: Sage Publications, 1981).

Crane, Robert D. *Planning the Future of Saudi Arabia: A Model for Achieving National Priorities* (New York: Praeger Publishers, 1978).

Curtis, Michael, ed. *Religion and Politics in the Middle East* (Boulder, Colo.: Westview Press, 1981).

Dam, Nikolaos Van. *The Struggle for Power in Syria* (New York: St. Martin's Press, 1979).

Dawisha, Adeed I. "Iraq: The West's Opportunity," *Foreign Policy,* **41** (Winter 1980–81), 134–153.

Dawisha, Karen. *Soviet Foreign Policy Towards Egypt* (New York: St. Martin's Press, 1979).

Dupuy, Trevor N. *Elusive Victory: The Arab-Israeli Wars: 1947–1974* (New York: Harper & Row, 1979).

Fisch, Harold. *The Zionist Revolution: A New Perspective* (New York: St. Martin's Press, 1978).

Fischer, Michael M. J. *Iran: from Religious Dispute to Revolution* (Cambridge, Mass.: Harvard University Press, 1980).

Flapan, Simha. *Zionism and the Palestinians* (New York: Barnes & Noble, 1979).

Forbis, William H. *Fall of the Peacock Throne* (New York: Harper & Row, 1980).

Freedman, Robert O., ed. *World Politics and the Arab-Israeli Conflict* (New York: Pergamon Press, 1979).

Graham, Helga. *Arabian Time Machine: Self-Portrait of an Oil State* (New York: Holmes & Meier, 1978).

Graham, Robert. *Iran: The Illusion of Power* (New York: St. Martin's Press, 1979).

Griffiths, John C. *Afghanistan: Key to a Continent* (Boulder, Colo.: Westview Press, 1981).

Groisser, Philip. *The United States and the Middle East* (Baltimore, Md.: State University of New York Press, 1981).

Haley, P. Edward and Lewis W. Snider, eds. *Lebanon in Crisis: Participants and Issues* (Syracuse, N.Y.: Syracuse University Press, 1979).

Hallwood, C. Paul, and Stuart W. Sinclair. *Oil, Debt and Development: OPEC in the Third World* (Winchester, Mass.: Allen & Unwin, 1981).

Heikal, Mohamed. *The Sphinx and the Commissar: The Rise and Fall of Soviet Influence in the Arab World* (New York: Harper & Row, 1979).

Helms, Christine Moss. *The Cohesion of Saudi Arabia: Evolution of Political Identity.* (Baltimore, Md.: Johns Hopkins University Press, 1980).

Heradstveit, Daniel. *The Arab-Israeli Conflict: Psychological Obstacles to Peace* (New York: Columbia University Press, 1979).

Hobday, Peter. *Saudi Arabia Today: An Introduction to the Richest Oil Power* (New York: St. Martin's Press, 1978).

Hourani, Albert. *Europe and the Middle East* (Berkeley, Calif.: University of California Press, 1980).

Hudson, Michael C. *Arab Politics: The Search For Legitimacy* (New Haven, Conn.: Yale University Press, 1977).

Jansen, G. H. *Militant Islam* (New York: Harper & Row, 1980).

Jureidini, Paul A., and R. D. McLaurin *Beyond Camp David: Emerging Alignments and Leaders in the Middle East.* (Syracuse, N.Y.: Syracuse University Press, 1981).

Kass, Ilana. *Soviet Involvement in the Middle East: Policy Formulation, 1966–1973* (Boulder, Colo.: Westview Press, 1978).

Kelly, J. B. *Arabia, The Gulf, and The West* (New York: Basic Books, 1980).

Khalid, Walid. *Conflict and Violence in Lebanon: Confrontation in the Middle East* (Cambridge, Mass.: Harvard Center for International Affairs, 1980).

Khalifa, Ali Mohammed. *The United Arab Emirates: Unity in Fragmentation* (Boulder, Colo.: Westview Press, 1979).

Leitenberg, Milton, and Gabriel Sheffer, eds. *Great Power Intervention in the Middle East* (New York: Pergamon Press, 1979).

Levy, Walter J. "Oil: An Agenda for the 1980s," *Foreign Affairs* **59** (Summer, 1981), 1079–1102.

Levy, Walter J. "Oil and the Decline of the West," *Foreign Affairs,* **58** (Summer, 1980), 999–1015.

Long, David E., and Bernard Reich, eds. *The Government and Politics of the Middle East and North Africa* (Boulder, Colo.: Westview Press, 1980).

Maghroori, Ray, and Stephen M. Gorman. *The Yom Kippur War: A Case Study in Crisis Decision-Making in American Foreign Policy* (Washington, D.C.: University Press of America, 1981).

Mangold, Peter. *Superpower Intervention in the Middle East* (New York: St. Martin's Press, 1977).

McLaurin, R. D., Mohammed Mughisuddin, and Abraham R. Wagner. *Foreign Policy Making in the Middle East: Domestic Influences on Policy in Egypt, Iraq, and Syria* (New York: Praeger Publishers, 1977).

Migdal, Joel S. *Palestinian Society and Politics* (Princeton, N.J.: Princeton University Press, 1980).

Mroz, John Edwin. *Beyond Security: Private Perceptions Among Arabs and Israelis* (New York: Pergamon Press, 1981).

Naff, Thomas, ed. *The Middle East Challenge: 1980–1985* (Carbondale, Ill.: Southern Illinois University Press, 1981).

Niblock, Tim, ed. *Social and Economic Development in the Arab Gulf* (New York: St. Martin's Press, 1980).

Novik, Nimrod, and Joyce Starr, eds. *Challenges in the Middle East: Regional Dynamics and Western Security* (New York: Praeger Publishers, 1981).

Noyes, James H. *The Clouded Lens: Persian Gulf Security and U.S. Policy* (Stanford, Calif.: Hoover Institution Press, 1979).

O'Neill, Bard E. *Armed Struggle in Palestine: A*

Political-Military Analysis (Boulder, Colo.: Westview Press, 1979).

Polk, William R. *The Elusive Peace: The Middle East in the Twentieth Century* (New York: St. Martin's Press, 1980).

Ramazani, R. K. *The Persian Gulf and the Strait of Hormuz* (Alphen aan den Rijn, Netherlands: Sijthoff, 1979).

Ramazani, R. K. "Security in the Persian Gulf," *Foreign Affairs,* **57** (Spring, 1979), 821–835.

Record, Jeffrey. *The Rapid Deployment Force and U.S. Military Intervention in the Persian Gulf* (Cambridge, Mass.: Institute for Foreign Policy Analysis, 1981).

Reed, Stanley III. "Dateline Syria: Fin De Régime?" *Foreign Policy,* **39** (Summer, 1980), 176–190.

Reich, Bernard. *Quest for Peace: United States-Israel Relations and the Arab-Israeli Conflict* (New Brunswick, N.J.: Transaction Books, 1977).

Ro'i, Yaacov, ed. *The Limits of Power: Soviet Policy in the Middle East* (New York: St. Martin's Press, 1979).

Rouleau, Eric. "Khomeini's Iran," *Foreign Affairs,* **59** (Fall, 1980), 1–20.

Rubin, Barry. *Paved With Good Intentions: The American Experience and Iran* (New York: Oxford University Press, 1980).

Rubin, Jeffrey Z. *Dynamics of Third Party Intervention: Kissinger in the Middle East* (New York: Praeger Publishers, 1981).

Sayigh, Rosemary. *Palestinians: From Peasants to Revolutionaries* (New York: Monthly Review Press, 1979).

Seymour, Ian. *OPEC: Instrument of Change* (New York: St. Martin's Press, 1981).

Shaked, Haim, and Itamar Rabinovich, eds. *The Middle East and the United States* (New Brunswick, N.J.: Transaction Books, 1980).

Smooha, Sammy. *Israel: Pluralism and Conflict* (Berkeley, Calif.: University of California Press, 1978).

Vatikiotis, P. J. *The History of Egypt: From Muhammad Ali to Sadat* (Baltimore, Md.: Johns Hopkins University Press, 1979).

Zabih, Sepehr. *Iran's Revolutionary Upheaval: An Interpretive Essay* (San Francisco, Calif.: Alchemy Books, 1979).

Zartman, I. William, ed. *Elites in the Middle East* (New York: Praeger Publishers, 1980).

Chapter 13. Sub-Saharan Africa: New Nations and Ancient Problems

Adam, Heribert, and Hermann Giliomee. *Ethnic Power Mobilized: Can South Africa Change?* (New Haven, Conn.: Yale University Press, 1979).

Albright, David E., ed. *Communism in Africa* (Bloomington, Ind.: Indiana University Press, 1980).

Anglin, Douglas G., and Timothy M. Shaw. *Zambia's Foreign Policy: Studies in Diplomacy and Dependence* (Boulder, Colo.: Westview Press, 1979).

Austin, Dennis. *Politics in Africa* (Hanover, N.H.: University Press of New England, 1978).

Bissell, Richard E., and Chester A. Crocker, eds. *South Africa into the 1980's* (Boulder, Colo.: Westview Press, 1979).

Carter, Gwendolen M. *Which Way Is South Africa Going?* (Bloomington, Ind.: Indiana University Press, 1980).

Carter, Gwendolen M., and Patrick O'Meara, eds. *Southern Africa: The Continuing Crisis* (Bloomington, Ind.: Indiana University Press, 1979).

Charles, Milene. *The Soviet Union and Africa: The History of the Involvement* (Washington, D.C.: University Press of America, 1980).

Chibwe, E. C. *Afro-Arab Relations in the New World Order* (New York: St. Martin's Press, 1978).

Clifford-Vaughan, F. McA., ed. *International Pressures and Political Change in South Africa* (New York: Oxford University Press, 1978).

Cotter, William R. "How AID Fails to Aid Africa," *Foreign Policy,* **34** (Spring, 1979), 107–120.

Crocker, Chester, A. "South Africa: Strategy for

Change," *Foreign Affairs,* **59** (Winter 1980/81), 323–351.

DeLancey, Mark W. *African International Relations: An Annotated Bibliography* (Boulder, Colo.: Westview Press, 1980).

de St. Jorre, John. *A House Divided: South Africa's Uncertain Future* (New York: Carnegie Endowment for International Peace, 1977).

Farer, Tom J. *War Clouds on the Horn of Africa: The Widening Storm* (New York: Carnegie Endowment for International Peace, 1979).

Gann, L. H., and Peter Duignan. *South Africa: War, Revolution, or Peace?* (Stanford, Calif.: Hoover Institution Press, 1978).

Heldman, Dan C. *The USSR and Africa: Foreign Policy Under Khrushchev* (New York: Praeger Publishers, 1981).

Henderson, Lawrence W. *Angola: Five Centuries of Conflict* (Ithaca, N.Y.: Cornell University Press, 1979).

Herskovits, Jean "Democracy in Nigeria," *Foreign Affairs,* **58** (Winter 1979/80), 314–335.

Ibingira, Grace Stuart. *African Upheavals Since Independence* (Boulder, Colo.: Westview Press, 1980).

Legum, Colin, and Bill Lee. *The Horn of Africa in Continuing Crisis* (New York: Holmes and Meier, 1979).

Legum, Colin, I. William Zartman, Steven Langdon, and Lynn K. Mytelka. *Africa in the 1980's: A Continent in Crisis* (New York: McGraw-Hill, 1979).

Lemarchand, Rene, ed. *American Policy in Southern Africa: The Stakes and the Stance,* 2d ed. (Washington, D.C.: University Press of America, 1981).

LeoGrande, William M. *Cuba's Policy in Africa, 1959–1980* (Berkeley, Calif.: University of California Press, 1980).

Marcum, John A. *The Angolan Revolution: Exile Politics and Guerrilla Warfare (1962–1976)* (Cambridge, Mass.: MIT Press, 1978).

Mazrui, Ali A. *Africa's International Relations: The Diplomacy of Dependency and Change* (Boulder, Colo.: Westview Press, 1979).

Myers, Desaix III, et al. *U.S. Business in South Africa: The Economic, Political, and Moral Issues* (Bloomington, Ind.: Indiana University Press, 1980).

Ottaway, David, and Marina Ottaway. *Afrocommunism* (New York: Africana, 1981).

Oyediran, Oyeleye, ed. *Nigerian Government and Politics Under Military Rule, 1966–79* (New York: St. Martin's Press, 1979).

Potholm, Christian P. *The Theory and Practice of African Politics* (Englewood Cliffs, N.J.: Prentice-Hall, 1978).

Potholm, Christian P., and Richard A. Friedland, eds. *Integration and Disintegration in East Africa* (Washington, D.C.: University Press of America, 1980).

Robertson, Ian, and Phillip Whitten, eds. *Race and Politics in South Africa* (New Brunswick, N.J.: Transaction Books, 1978).

Rotberg, Robert I. *Suffer the Future: Policy Changes in Southern Africa* (Cambridge, Mass.: Harvard University Press, 1980).

Rotberg, Robert I., and John Barratt, eds. *Conflict and Compromise in South Africa* (Lexington, Mass.: D. C. Heath, 1980).

Rothenberg, Morris. *The USSR and Africa: New Dimensions of Soviet Global Power* (Washington, D.C.: Advanced International Studies Institute, 1980).

Samuels, Michael A., ed. *Africa and the West* (Boulder, Colo.: Westview Press, 1980).

Shaw, Timothy M., ed. *Alternative Futures for Africa* (Boulder, Colo.: Westview Press, 1981).

Shaw, Timothy M., and Kenneth A. Heard, eds. *The Politics of Africa: Dependence and Development* (New York: Holmes & Meier, 1979).

Stremlau, John J. *The International Politics of the Nigerian Civil War, 1967–1970* (Princeton, N.J.: Princeton University Press, 1977).

Toko, Gad W. *Intervention in Uganda: The Power Struggle and Soviet Involvement* (Pittsburgh, Pa.: University of Pittsburgh Press, 1979).

Wasserman, Gary. "Rhodesia Is Not Kenya," *Foreign Policy,* **33** (Winter, 1978–79), 31–44.

Whitaker, Jennifer Seymour, ed. *Africa and the United States: Vital Interests* (New York: New York University Press, 1978).

Wilkins, Gregory L. *African Influence in the United Nations, 1967–1975: The Politics and Techniques of Gaining Compliance to U.N. Principles and Resolutions* (Washington, D.C.: University Press of America, 1981).

Witherell, Julian W., comp. *The United States and Africa: 1785–1975.* (Washington, D.C.: Library of Congress, 1978).

Chapter 14. Latin America: The Search for Hemispheric Community

Alexander, Robert J. *The Tragedy of Chile* (Westport, Conn.: Greenwood Press, 1978).

Axline, W. Andrew. *Caribbean Integration: the Politics of Regionalism* (New York: Nichols Press, 1979).

Ball, M. Margaret. *The OAS in Transition* (New York: Alfred A. Knopf, 1978).

Beaulac, Willard L. *The Fractured Continent: Latin America in Close-Up* (Stanford, Calif.: Hoover Institution Press, 1980).

Bizzaro, Salvatore. "Mexico's Oil Boom," *Current History,* **80** (February, 1981), 49–52.

Black, Jan Knippers. *United States Penetration of Brazil* (Philadelphia: University of Pennsylvania Press, 1977).

Blaiser, Cole. *The Hovering Giant: U.S. Responses to Revolutionary Change in Latin America* (Pittsburgh, Pa.: University of Pittsburgh Press, 1976).

Blaiser, Cole, and Carmelo Mesa-Lago, eds. *Cuba in the World* (Pittsburgh, Pa.: University of Pittsburgh Press, 1979).

Carlisle, Douglas H. *Venezuelan Foreign Policy: Its Organization and Beginning* (Washington, D.C.: University Press of America, 1978).

Child, John. *Unequal Alliance: The Inter-American Military System* (Boulder, Colo.: Westview Press, 1980).

Collier, David, ed. *The New Authoritarianism in Latin America* (Princeton, N.J.: Princeton University Press, 1980).

Di Bacco, Thomas V., ed. *Presidential Power in Latin American Politics* (New York: Praeger Publishers, 1978).

Duncan, W. Raymond. *Latin American Politics: A Developmental Approach* (New York: Praeger Publishers, 1976).

Fagen, Richard R., ed. *Capitalism and the State in U.S.-Latin American Relations* (Stanford, Calif.: Stanford University Press, 1979).

Fagen, Richard R. "Dateline Nicaragua: The End of the Affair," *Foreign Policy,* **36** (Fall 1979), 178–191.

Farer, Tom J., ed. *The Future of the Inter-American System* (New York: Praeger Publishers, 1979).

Gleijeses, Piero. *The Dominican Crisis: The 1965 Constitutional Revolt and American Intervention* (Baltimore, Md.: Johns Hopkins University Press, 1979).

Grayson, George W. *The Politics of Mexican Oil* (Pittsburgh, Pa.: University of Pittsburgh Press, 1981).

Halperin, Maurice. *The Taming of Fidel Castro* (Berkeley, Calif.: University of California Press, 1981).

Handelman, Howard, and Thomas G. Sanders, eds. *Military Government and the Movement Toward Democracy in South America* (Bloomington, Ind.: Indiana University Press, 1981).

Ince, Basil A. *Contemporary International Relations of the Caribbean* (Trinidad: University of the West Indies, 1979).

Knight, Thomas J. *Latin America Comes of Age* (Metuchen, N.J.: Scarecrow Press, 1979).

Langguth, A. J. *Hidden Terrors: The Truth About U.S. Police Operations in Latin America* (New York: Pantheon Books, 1978).

Lévesque, Jacques. *The USSR and the Cuban Revolution: Soviet Ideological and Strategical Perspectives, 1959–77* (New York: Praeger Publishers, 1978).

Loveman, Brian, and Thomas M. Davies, Jr., eds.

The Politics of Antipolitics: The Military in Latin America (Lincoln, Neb.: University of Nebraska Press, 1978).

Martz, John D., and Lars Schoultz, eds. *Latin America, the United States and the Inter-American System* (Boulder, Colo.: Westview Press, 1980).

Millett, Richard. "Central American Paralysis," *Foreign Policy,* **39** (Summer, 1980), 99–117.

Millett, Richard. "The Politics of Violence: Guatemala and El Salvador," *Current History,* **80** (February, 1981), 70–74.

Millett, Richard, and W. Marvin Will, eds. *The Restless Caribbean: Changing Patterns of International Relations* (New York: Praeger Publishers, 1979).

Mitchell, Christopher. "The New Authoritarianism in Bolivia," *Current History,* **80** (February, 1981), 75–78.

Mytelka, Lynn K. *Regional Development in a Global Economy: The Multinational Corporation, Technology, and Andean Integration* (New Haven, Conn.: Yale University Press, 1979).

Orfila, Alejandro. *The Americas in the 1980s: An Agenda for the Decade Ahead* (Washington, D.C.: University Press of America, 1980).

Overholt, William H., ed. *The Future of Brazil* (Boulder, Colo.: Westview Press, 1979).

Palmer, Ransford W. *Caribbean Dependence on the United States Economy* (New York: Praeger Publishers, 1979).

Payne, A. J. *The Politics of the Caribbean Community, 1961–1979* (New York: St. Martin's Press, 1980).

Poulson, Barry W., and T. Noel Osborn, eds. *U.S.-Mexico Economic Relations* (Boulder, Colo.: Westview Press, 1979).

Roca, Sergio. "Revolutionary Cuba," *Current History,* **80** (February, 1981), 53–56.

Shaw, Royce Q. *Central America: Regional Integration and National Political Development* (Boulder, Colo.: Westview Press, 1979).

Sigmund, Paul E. *Multinationals in Latin America:*

The Politics of Nationalization (Madison, Wisc.: University of Wisconsin Press, 1980).

Sigmund, Paul E. *The Overthrow of Allende and the Politics of Chile, 1946–1976* (Pittsburgh, Pa.: University of Pittsburgh Press, 1977).

Theberge, James D. *The Soviet Presence in Latin America* (New York: Crane, Russak, 1974).

Véliz, Claudio. *The Centralist Tradition of Latin America* (Princeton, N.J.: Princeton University Press, 1980).

Walker, Thomas W. "Nicaragua Consolidates Its Revolution," *Current History,* **80** (February, 1981), 79–82.

Weinstein, Martin, ed. *Revolutionary Cuba in the World Arena* (Philadelphia: Institute for the Study of Human Issues, 1979).

Wiarda, Howard J. *The Continuing Struggle for Democracy in Latin America* (Boulder, Colo.: Westview Press, 1980).

Wynia, Gary W. *Argentina in the Postwar Era: Politics and Economic Policy Making in a Divided Society* (Albuquerque, N.M.: University of New Mexico Press, 1978).

Wynia, Gary W. "Illusion and Reality in Argentina," *Current History,* **80** (February, 1981), 62–65.

Wynia, Gary W. *The Politics of Latin American Development.* (New York: Cambridge University Press, 1978).

Chapter 15. Asia: The United States as a Pacific Power

Anderson, David L. "China Policy and Presidential Politics, 1952," *Presidential Studies Quarterly,* **10** (Winter, 1980), 79–89.

Armstrong, J. D. *Revolutionary Diplomacy: Chinese Foreign Policy and The United Front Doctrine* (Berkeley, Calif.: University of California Press, 1977).

Banerjee, Jyotirmoy. *India in Soviet Global Strategy: A Conceptual Study* (Columbia, Mo.: South Asia Books, 1977).

Barnds, William J., ed. *China and America: The*

Search for a New Relationship (New York: New York University Press, 1977).

Barnds, William J., ed. *Japan and the United States: Challenges and Opportunities* (New York: New York University Press, 1979).

Bobrow, Davis B., Steve Chan, and John A. Kringen. *Understanding Foreign Policy Decisions: The China Case* (New York: The Free Press, 1979).

Booker, Malcolm. *Last Quarter: The Next Twenty-Five Years in Asia and the Pacific* (Melbourne: Melbourne University Press, 1978).

Brugger, Bill. *China Since the "Gang of Four"* (New York: St. Martin's Press, 1980).

Bundy, McGeorge. "Vietnam and Presidential Powers," *Foreign Affairs,* **58** (Winter 1979/80), 397–407.

Charlton, Michael, and Anthony Moncrieff. *Many Reasons Why: The American Involvement in Vietnam* (New York: Hill & Wang, 1979).

Chawla, Sudershan, and D. R. Sardesai, eds. *Changing Patterns of Security and Stability in Asia* (New York: Praeger Publishers, 1980).

Cheng, Peter P. *China: U.S. Policy Since 1945* (Washington, D.C.: Congressional Quarterly Press, 1980).

Cheng, Peter P., et al. *Emerging Roles of Asian Nations in the Decade of the 1980s: A New Equilibrium* (Lincoln, Neb.: University of Nebraska Press, 1979).

Chiu, Hungdah, ed. *China and the Taiwan Issue* (New York: Praeger Publishers, 1979).

Choudhury, Golam W. *Chinese Perception of the World* (Washington, D.C.: University Press of America, 1977).

Clough, Ralph N. *Island China* (Cambridge, Mass.: Harvard University Press, 1978).

Clough, Ralph N., and William Watts. *The United States and Korea: American Perceptions and Policies* (Washington, D.C.: Potomac Associates, 1978).

Copper, John Franklin. *China's Global Role* (Stanford, Calif.: Hoover Institution Press, 1980).

Dorrance, John C. *Oceania and the United States* (Washington, D.C.: National Defense University, 1980).

Dunn, Lewis A. "Half Past India's Bang," *Foreign Policy,* **36** (Fall, 1979), 71–88.

Fifield, Russell H. *National and Regional Interests in ASEAN* (Singapore: Institute of Southeast Asian Studies, 1979).

Foster, Richard B., James E. Dornan, Jr., and William M. Carpenter, eds. *Strategy and Security in Northeast Asia* (New York: Crane, Russak & Co., 1979).

Frankel, Francine R. "India's Promise," *Foreign Policy,* **38** (Spring, 1980), 51–66.

Franklin, David. "The Great Game in Asia," *Foreign Affairs,* **58** (Spring, 1980), 936–951.

Gale, Roger W. *The Americanization of Micronesia: A Study of the Consolidation of U.S. Rule in the Pacific* (Washington D.C.: University Press of America, 1979).

Garrett, Stephen A. *Ideals and Reality: An Analysis of the Debate Over Vietnam* (Washington, D.C.: University Press of America, 1978).

Gelb, Leslie H., with Ricard K. Betts. *The Irony of Vietnam: The System Worked* (Washington, D.C.: The Brookings Institution, 1979).

Gelber, Harry G. *Technology, Defense, and External Relations in China, 1975–1978* (Boulder, Colo.: Westview Press, 1979).

Gilbert, Stephen P. *Northeast Asia in U.S. Foreign Policy* (Beverly Hills, Calif.: Sage Publications, 1979).

Gladue, E. Ted, Jr. *China's Perceptions of Global Issues* (Port Washington, N.Y.: Kennikat Press, 1981).

Gurtov, Melvin and Byong-Moo Hwang. *China Under Threat: The Politics of Strategy and Diplomacy* (Baltimore, Md.: Johns Hopkins University Press, 1980).

Herring, George C. *America's Longest War: The United States and Vietnam, 1950–1975* (New York: John Wiley & Sons, 1979).

Hollerman, Leon, ed. *Japan and the United States: Economic and Political Adversaries* (Boulder, Colo.: Westview Press, 1980).

Hsiung, James C., and Samuel S. Kim. *China in the*

Global Community (New York: Praeger Publishers, 1980).

Johnson, Stuart E., with Joseph A. Yager. *The Military Equation in Northeast Asia* (Washington, D.C.: The Brookings Institution, 1979).

Jones, Rodney W. *Nuclear Proliferation: Islam, the Bomb, and South Asia* (Beverly Hills, Calif.: Sage Publications, 1981).

Kahn, Herman, and Thomas Pepper. *The Japanese Challenge: The Success and Failure of Economic Success* (New York: William Morrow, 1980).

Kattenburg, Paul M. *The Vietnam Trauma in American Foreign Policy* (New Brunswick, N.J.: Transaction Books, 1980).

Kim, Samuel S. *China, The United Nations, and World Order* (Princeton, N.J.: Princeton University Press, 1979).

Kim, Young C., and Halpern, Abraham M., eds. *The Future of the Korean Peninsula* (New York: Praeger Publishers, 1977).

Lewy, Guenter. *America in Vietnam* (New York: Oxford University Press, 1978).

Marwah, Onkar, and Jonathan D. Pollack, eds. *Military Power and Policy in Asian States: China, India, Japan* (Boulder, Colo.: Westview Press, 1980).

Mellor, John W., ed. *India: A Rising Middle Power* (Boulder, Colo.: Westview Press, 1979).

Middleton, Drew. *The Duel of the Giants: China and Russia in Asia* (New York: Charles Scribner's, 1978).

Morrison, Charles E., and Astri Suhrke. *Strategies of Survival: The Foreign Policy Dilemmas of Smaller Asian States* (New York: St. Martin's Press, 1979).

Myers, Ramon H., ed. *Two Chinese States: U.S. Foreign Policy and Interests* (Stanford, Calif.: Hoover Institution Press, 1978).

Nelsen, Harvey. *The Chinese Military System: An Organizational Study of the Chinese People's Liberation Army* (Boulder, Colo.: Westview Press, 1981).

Oksenberg, Michel. "China Policy for the 1980s," *Foreign Affairs,* **59** (Winter 1980/81), 304–322.

O'Leary, Greg. *The Shaping of Chinese Foreign Policy* (New York: St. Martin's Press, 1980).

Overholt, William H., ed. *Asia's Nuclear Future* (Boulder, Colo.: Westview Press, 1978).

Palmer, Dave Richard. *Summons of the Trumpet: U.S.-Vietnam in Perspective* (San Rafael, Calif.: Presidio Press, 1978).

Pandey, B. N. *South and South-East Asia, 1945–1979: Problems and Policies* (New York: St. Martin's Press, 1980).

Papp, Daniel S. *Vietnam: The View from Moscow, Peking, Washington* (Jefferson, N.C.: McFarland & Co., 1981).

Passin, Herbert, and Akira Iriye, eds. *Encounter at Shimoda: Search for a New Pacific Partnership* (Boulder, Colo.: Westview Press, 1979).

Patti, Archimedes L. A. *Why Viet Nam: Prelude to America's Albatross* (Berkeley, Calif.: University of California Press, 1980).

Pillsbury, Michael. "A Japanese Card?" *Foreign Policy,* **33** (Winter, 1978–79), 3–30.

Porter, Gareth. "Time to Talk with North Korea," *Foreign Policy,* **34** (Spring, 1979), 52–73.

Pringle, Robert. *Indonesia and the Philippines: American Interests in Island Southeast Asia* (New York: Columbia University Press, 1980).

Scalapino, Robert A. *The United States and Korea: Looking Ahead* (Beverly Hills, Calif.: Sage Publications, 1979).

Schaller, Michael. *The United States and China in the Twentieth Century* (New York: Oxford University Press, 1979).

Shiels, Frederick L. *Tokyo and Washington: Dilemmas of a Mature Alliance* (Lexington, Mass.: D. C. Heath, 1980).

Singh, K. R. *Indian Ocean: Big Power Presence and Local Response* (Columbia, Mo.: South Asia Books, 1978).

Singh, Lalita Prasad. *Power Politics and Southeast Asia* (Atlantic Highlands, N.J.: Humanities Press, 1980).

Solomon, Richard H., ed. *Asian Security in the 1980s: Problems and Policies for a Time of Transition* (Santa Monica, Calif.: Rand Corporation, 1979).

Starr, John B. *The Future of U.S.-China Relations* (New York: Columbia University Press, 1981).

Stuart, Douglas T., and William T. Tow, eds. *China, The Soviet Union, and the West: Strategic and Political Dimensions for the 1980s* (Boulder, Colo.: Westview Press, 1981).

Sunoo, Harold Hakwon. *America's Dilemma in Asia: The Case of South Korea* (Chicago, Ill.: Nelson-Hall, 1979).

Swearingen, Rodger. *The Soviet Union and Postwar Japan: Escalating Challenge and Response* (Stanford, Calif.: Hoover Institution Press, 1979).

Tasca, Diane, ed. *U.S.-Japanese Economic Relations: Cooperation, Competition, and Confrontation* (New York: Pergamon Press, 1980).

Taylor, David, and Malcolm Yapp, eds. *Political Identity in South Asia* (Atlantic Highlands, N.J.: Humanities Press, 1979).

Terrill, Ross. "China in the 1980s," *Foreign Affairs*, **58** (Spring, 1980), 920–935.

Thies, Wallace J. *When Governments Collide: Coercion and Diplomacy in the Vietnam Conflict, 1964–1968* (Berkeley: University of California Press, 1980).

Tierney, John, Jr., ed. *About Face: The China Decision and Its Consequences* (New Rochelle, N.Y.: Arlington House, 1979).

Van Hollen, Christopher. "Leaning on Pakistan," *Foreign Policy*, **38** (Spring, 1980), 35–50.

Van Hollen, Christopher. "The Tilt Policy Revisited: Nixon-Kissinger Geopolitics and South Asia," *Asian Survey*, **20** (April, 1980), 339–361.

Vasey, Lloyd., ed. *Pacific Asia and U.S. Policies: A Political-Economic-Strategic Assessment* (Honolulu: The University Press of Hawaii, 1978).

Vogel, Ezra F. *Japan as Number One* (Cambridge, Mass.: Harvard University Press, 1979).

Watts, William, George R. Packard, Ralph N. Clough, and Robert B. Oxham. *Japan, Korea, and China: American Perceptions and Policies* (Lexington, Mass: D. C. Heath, 1979).

Weinstein, Franklin B. *U.S.-Japan Relations and the Security of East Asia: The Next Decade* (Boulder, Colo.: Westview Press, 1978).

Weinstein, Franklin B., and Fuji Kamiya. *The Security of Korea: U.S. and Japanese Perspectives on the 1980s* (Boulder, Colo.: Westview Press, 1980).

White, Nathan N. *U.S. Policy Toward Korea: Analysis, Alternatives, and Recommendations* (Boulder, Colo.: Westview Press, 1979).

Wich, Richard. *Sino-Soviet Crisis Politics* (Cambridge, Mass.: Harvard University Press, 1980).

Yahuda, Michael B. *China's Role in World Affairs* (New York: St. Martin's Press, 1978).

Yung-hwan Jo, and Ying-hsien Pi. *Russia Versus China and What Next?* (Washington, D.C.: University Press of America, 1980).

Ziring, Lawrence, ed. *The Subcontinent in World Politics: India, Its Neighbors and the Great Powers* (New York: Praeger Publishers, 1978).

Index